Cases and Materials in
Company Law

Cases and Materials in Company Law

Eighth edition

Len Sealy

S J Berwin Professor Emeritus of Corporate Law
University of Cambridge
Barrister and Solicitor (New Zealand)

Sarah Worthington

Professor of Law
London School of Economics and Political Science
Barrister, 3/4 South Square, Gray's Inn

OXFORD
UNIVERSITY PRESS

OXFORD
UNIVERSITY PRESS

Great Clarendon Street, Oxford OX2 6DP

Oxford University Press is a department of the University of Oxford.
It furthers the University's objective of excellence in research, scholarship,
and education by publishing worldwide in

Oxford New York

Auckland Cape Town Dar es Salaam Hong Kong Karachi
Kuala Lumpur Madrid Melbourne Mexico City Nairobi
New Delhi Shanghai Taipei Toronto

With offices in

Argentina Austria Brazil Chile Czech Republic France Greece
Guatemala Hungary Italy Japan Poland Portugal Singapore
South Korea Switzerland Thailand Turkey Ukraine Vietnam

Oxford is a registered trade mark of Oxford University Press
in the UK and in certain other countries

Published in the United States
by Oxford University Press Inc., New York

British Library Cataloguing in Publication Data

Data available

Library of Congress Cataloging in Publication Data

Data available

Typeset by Newgen Imaging Systems (P) Ltd, Chennai, India
Printed in Great Britain
on acid-free paper by
Ashford Colour Press Ltd, Gosport, Hampshire

ISBN 978–0–19–929842–6

10 9 8 7 6 5 4 3 2 1

Preface

The Companies Act 2006 received the Royal Assent on 8 November 2006. With 1,300 sections and 16 schedules, it is quite the largest piece of legislation ever to have passed through the parliamentary process. It is the product of the most extensive revision of company law in this country since limited liability was introduced in the 1850s. In normal circumstances, an eighth edition of this work would have been due well before now, but necessarily it has had to be delayed until the content of the new Act was finalised.

Although the Act is being brought into force in stages and will not become fully operative until October 2008, it is this law that students will be required to know when the time comes for them to apply their learning, and in recognition of this most Faculties are now planning to teach the new law. Accordingly, the law in this edition is stated as it will be after that date.

The 2006 Act follows a consultation exercise carried out over seven years by the Company Law Review, which was set up by the Department of Trade and Industry in March 1998 and involved a very large number of people. The Review published eight substantial consultative papers and a final report, examining the subject in great detail, including the very foundations established by our forebears in the mid-nineteenth century. It might well be assumed that the Act which has resulted from these labours would be a complete and comprehensive code, leaving little need for a book of cases and non-statutory materials. But this is not so. The Act does not seek to make a fresh start and sweep away all the past learning. Rather, it builds on what we already have. The topic of directors' duties (for instance) has, for the first time, been codified, but this has been done in terms which preserve the relevance of the established case law. Even where parts of the new law are designed to make a break with the past—eg the introduction of the statutory derivative action to replace the ancient rule in *Foss v Harbottle* (1843)—an understanding of the earlier law is needed in order to see how the new regime will fit into the general picture of shareholders' remedies.

But a case book serves a much wider purpose. Companies are not abstractions run by robots, even with the aid of computers. Everything done by a company and everything done within a company is done by human beings, and every case that comes to court involves real people. It is this that brings the subject alive, fills it with events and characters and makes it fun to study and to teach. The new Act may have introduced some new concepts and changed some of the rules, but its role will only be, as before, to serve the same needs of commerce and the people who engage in it: the same problems and questions will arise, and there will be no better way for students to understand the new law and to test how it will work in practice than by examining how it would apply to the facts of known cases.

Among the major changes made by the Act and other legislative reforms which are reflected in this new edition we may note the following: abolition of the traditional memorandum of association, and with it the need for an objects clause in the company's constitution; the new statutory formulation of directors' duties; tighter rules on the ratification of directors' wrongful acts and condonation of breaches of duty; introduction of the statutory derivative action; changes in the law governing takeovers following the implementation of the EC Directive, which has given statutory standing to the Takeover Panel and its Code; and the reform of insolvency procedures to encourage the rescue and rehabilitation of failing businesses.

In addition, case law has continued to develop since our last edition. Extracts from the judgments in over fifty older cases have had to be discarded and replaced, particularly in the areas of directors' duties, shareholder remedies and company charges (the ruling of the House of Lords in *Re Spectrum Plus Ltd* (2005) being perhaps the most dramatic). The topic of derivative loss is examined in several recent decisions. And, apart from statute and the cases, other major influences on corporate law and practice continue to grow in importance and must be included in order to give a balanced view: the regulation of the financial services industry, the rules of the Stock Exchange, self-regulatory measures such as the Combined Code on Corporate Governance, new rulings of the European Court, and directives and reform proposals from the EC Commission.

There has been some restructuring of the text and re-grouping of topics in this edition: an expanded introductory section in Chapter 1 will, it is hoped, give a better background and stimulate interest in the more general aspects of the subject in preparation for more detailed study in the later chapters.

We would like to thank the following students for timely research assistance at various stages in the preparation of the manuscript: Katherine Llorca, Ina Mitchkovska, Nick Piska and Page Wilson.

After several editions under the imprint of Butterworths, publication of the work has now passed to the Oxford University Press. We are very grateful to the Press and its expert staff for the help which we have had at all stages of production. We have endeavoured to state the law as it was available to us at 30 April 2007.

Len Sealy
Sarah Worthington
May, 2007

Len Sealy adds:
The revision of the book for this edition has been undertaken by Sarah Worthington, with only minimal input from me. There is no-one whom I would rather have had to join me as co-editor. She brings unparalleled knowledge and experience and an invigorating fresh approach to the task and, despite a heavy workload and many other commitments, has completed the work against a very tight schedule. I am most grateful for all that she has done.

Acknowledgements

We are grateful to the following for permission to reproduce copyright material and commercial documents:

3i Group plc for specimen forms: Prospectus, Annual Report and Accounts, and Notice of AGM.

Canada Law Book, a Division of The Cartwright Group Ltd (1–800–263–3269, www.canadalawbook.ca) for extracts from *Dominion Law Reports* (DLR).

Companies House for specimen forms: Certificate of Incorporation.

Ernst & Young for specimen forms: Prospectus, and Auditor's Report.

The Incorporated Council Law Reporting for extracts from *Appeal Cases* (AC), *Chancery Reports* (Ch), *King's Bench Reports* (KB), *Queen's Bench Reports* (QB), and *Weekly Law Reports* (WLR)

©Law Book Co, part of Thomson Legal and Regulatory Ltd, http://thomson.co.au for extracts from *Commonwealth Law Reports* (CLR).

LexisNexis Pty Ltd for extracts from *Australian Company Law Reports* (ACLR)

New Zealand Council of Law Reporting for extract from *New Zealand Law Reports* (NZLR).

Reed Elsevier (UK) Ltd trading as LexisNexis Butterworths for extracts from *All England Law Reports* (All ER) and *Butterworths Company Law Cases* (BCLC).

Sweet & Maxwell Ltd for extracts from *Common Market Law Reports* (CMLR) and from *British Company Cases* (BCC).

Varsity Publications for specimen form: Certificate of Incorporation.

Extracts from Statutes, Rules of the Supreme Court, the Report of the Jenkins Committee on Company Law, the Report of the Cork Committee on Insolvency, and statistical tables, are Crown Copyright material, and are reproduced under Class Licence Number C2006010631 with the permission of the Controller of OPSI and the Queen's Printer.

Every effort has been made to trace and contact copyright holders but this has not been possible in all cases. If notified, the publisher will undertake to rectify any errors or omissions at the earliest opportunity.

Contents

List of abbreviations

Abbreviation	Detail
CA 1985	Companies Act 1985
CA 1989	Companies Act 1989
CA 2006	Companies Act 2006
CDDA 1986	Company Directors Disqualification Act 1986
CLR	The collective publications of the DTI's Company Law Review
DTI	Department of Trade and Industry[0]
EA 2002	Enterprise Act 2002
FSA	Financial Services Authority
FSA 1986	Financial Services Act 1986
FSMA 2000	Financial Services and Markets Act 2000
IA 1985	Insolvency Act 1985
IA 1986	Insolvency Act 1986
IA 2000	Insolvency Act 2000

[0] The DTI is referred to throughout this text. However, following changes introduced by the government in early 2007, the DTI no longer exists. There is now a new Department for Business, Enterprise and Regulatory Reform (BERR). See http://www.berr.gov.uk/

Note: References throughout the text to CA 2006 Model Articles for Private Companies and Model Articles for Public Companies are to the *Draft* versions of these documents, both of which were still undergoing changes as this book went to press. Some of the provisions referred to in the text may not be included in the final version of these Models, or may be included in amended form or with different numbering. Appropriate caution is therefore necessary.

Table of primary legislation

References in *italics* indicate material in the Appendix

Table of secondary legislation

Table of cases

Those cases that are extracted in this book are indicated by a reference in square brackets in **bold**, with the relevant page number in *italics*.

Table of origins and destinations

Selective table of CA 2006 destinations and CA 1985 origins

Provision	CA 2006	CA 1985
Limited and unlimited companies	s 3	s 1
Private and public companies	s 4	s 1
Method of forming a company	s 7	s 1 (changed)
Memorandum of association	s 8	new
Company's constitution	s 17	new
Articles of association	s 18	s 7 (changed)
Default application of model articles	s 20	s 8 (changed)
Amendment of articles	s 21	s 9
Entrenched provisions of articles	s 22	new
Existing companies (memorandum, etc)	s 28	new
Statement of company's objects	s 31	new
Effect of company's constitution	s 33	s 14 (changed)
Company's capacity	s 39	s 35 (changed)
Power of directors to bind company	s 40	ss 35A and 35B
Constitutional limitations and transactions involving directors	s 41	s 322A
Company contracts	s 43	s 36
Execution of documents	s 44	s 36A
Companies required to have directors	s 154	s 282 (changed)
One director to be a natural person	s 155	new
Minimum age for appointment as a director	s 157	new
Validity of acts of directors	s 161	s 285 (changed)
Resolution to remove director	s 168	s 303
General duties of directors	ss 170–177	new
Directors to have regard to interests of employees	s 172(1)	s 309
Civil consequences of breach of general duties	s 178	new
Consent, approval or authorisation by members	s 180	new
Directors' declaration of interest in existing transaction	s 182	s 317 (changed)
Directors' long-term service contracts	s 188	s 319 (changed)
Substantial property transactions	s 190	s 320 (changed)

Provision	CA 2006	CA 1985
Property transactions: civil consequences of contravention	s 195	s 322 (changed)
Loans of directors	s 197ff	s 330 (changed)
Loans, etc: civil consequences of contravention	s 213	s 341
Payments for loss of office	s 215ff	s 312ff (changed)
Directors' service contracts	s 227ff	s 318 (changed)
Contract with sole member who is director	s 231	s 322B (changed)
Provisions protecting directors from liability	s 232–238	s 309A-309C
Ratification of acts of directors	s 239	new
Directors' residential addresses	s 240ff	new
Provisions for employees on cessation or transfer of business	s 247	s 719 (changed)
"Director"	s 250	s 741
"Shadow director"	s 251	s 741
Persons connected with a director	s 252	s 346
Derivative claims	s 260ff	new
Private company not required to have a secretary	s 270	new
Qualifications of company secretaries	s 273	s 286 (changed)
Resolutions	s 281	new
Ordinary resolutions	s 282	new
Special resolutions	s 283	s 278 (changed)
Written resolutions of private companies	s 288	s 381A (changed)
Authorisation required for political donations or expenditure	s 362ff	s 347A-C (changed)
Companies subject to the small companies regime	s 381ff	s 247ff (changed)
Special provisions for small companies	ss 411ff, 444	s 246
Special provisions for medium-sized companies	ss 417, 445	s 246A (changed)
Directors' report	s 415ff	s 234ff (changed)
Auditors' report	ss 475, 495ff	s 235
Functions of auditors	s 495ff	s 235ff, 389Aff
Duties of auditors	s 498	s 237
Provisions protecting auditors from liability	s 532	s 310 (changed)

Provision	CA 2006	CA 1985
Shares not to be allotted at a discount	s 580	s 100
Public company: valuation of non-cash consideration	s 593	s 103
Application of share premiums	s 610	s 130
Alteration of share capital	s 617	s 121 (changed)
Classes of shares	s 629	s 128 (changed)
Variation of class rights	s 630ff	s 125ff (changed)
Reduction of share capital	s 641ff	s 135ff (changed)
General rule against a company acquiring its own shares	s 658	s 143
Exceptions to general rule	s 659	s 143
Financial assistance for purchase of shares	s 677ff	s 151ff (changed)
Redeemable shares	s 684ff	s 159ff (changed)
Power to purchase own shares	s 690ff	s 160ff
Redemption of shares out of capital	s 709ff	s 171ff
Treasury shares	s 724ff	s 162ff
"Debenture"	s 738	s 744
Priorities where debentures secured by a floating charge	s 754	s 196
Prohibition of public offers by private companies	s 755ff	ss 81, 742A (changed)
Public company: minimum share capital	s 761	s 117 (changed)
Directors' register of interests	s 809	s 325
Distributions only out of available profits	s 829ff	s 263ff
Consequences of unlawful distribution	s 847	s 277
Registration of charges	s 860	s 395
Charges void unless registered	s 889	s 410
Arrangements and reconstructions	s 895ff	425ff
Mergers and divisions	s 902ff	s 427A, Sch 15B
Takeovers	s 942ff	new
"Squeeze out" and "sell out"	s 974ff	s 428ff (changed)
Fraudulent trading	s 993	s 458
Unfair prejudice	s 994ff	s 459ff
Registrar of Companies	s 1060ff	s 704ff (changed)
Power of court to grant relief	s 1157	s 727

Selective table of CA 1985 origins and CA 2006 destinations

Provision	CA 1985	CA 2006
Limited and unlimited companies	s 1	s 3
Private and public companies	s 1	s 4
Method of forming a company	s 1 (changed)	s 7
Articles of association	s 7 (changed)	s 18
Default application of model articles	s 8 (changed)	s 20
Amendment of articles	s 9	s 21
Effect of company's constitution	s 14 (changed)	s 33
Company's capacity	s 35 (changed)	s 39
Power of directors to bind company	ss 35A and 35B	s 40
Company contracts	s 36	s 43
Execution of documents	s 36A	s 44
Prohibition of public offers by private companies	ss 81, 742A (changed)	s 755ff
Shares not to be allotted at a discount	s 100	s 580
Public company: valuation of non-cash consideration	s 103	s 593
Public company: minimum share capital	s 117 (changed)	s 761
Alteration of share capital	s 121 (changed)	s 617
Variation of class rights	s 125ff (changed)	s 630ff
Classes of shares	s 128 (changed)	s 629
Application of share premiums	s 130	s 610
Reduction of share capital	s 135ff (changed)	s 641ff
General rule against a company acquiring its own shares	s 143	s 658
Exceptions to general rule	s 143	s 659
Financial assistance for purchase of shares	s 151ff (changed)	s 677ff
Redeemable shares	s 159ff (changed)	s 684ff
Power to purchase own shares	s 160ff	s 690ff
Treasury shares	s 162ff	s 724ff
Redemption of shares out of capital	s 171ff	s 709ff
Priorities where debentures secured by a floating charge	s 196	s 754
Directors' report	s 234ff (changed)	s 415ff
Auditors' report	s 235	ss 475, 495ff
Functions of auditors	s 235ff, 389Aff	s 495ff
Duties of auditors	s 237	s 498
Special provisions for small companies	s 246	ss 411ff, 444
Special provisions for medium-sized companies	s 246A (changed)	ss 417, 445

Provision	CA 1985	CA 2006
Companies subject to the small companies regime	s 247ff (changed)	s 381ff
Distributions only out of available profits	s 263ff	s 829ff
Consequences of unlawful distribution	s 277	s 847
Special resolutions	s 278 (changed)	s 283
Companies required to have directors	s 282 (changed)	s 154
Validity of acts of directors	s 285 (changed)	s 161
Qualifications of company secretaries	s 286 (changed)	s 273
Resolution to remove director	s 303	s 168
Directors to have regard to interests of employees	s 309	s 172(1)
Provisions protecting directors from liability	s 309A-309C	s 232–238
Provisions protecting auditors from liability	s 310 (changed)	s 532
Payments for loss of office	s 312ff (changed)	s 215ff
Directors' declaration of interest in existing transaction	s 317 (changed)	s 182
Directors' service contracts	s 318 (changed)	s 227ff
Directors' long-term service contracts	s 319 (changed)	s 188
Substantial property transactions	s 320 (changed)	s 190
Property transactions: civil consequences of contravention	s 322 (changed)	s 195
Constitutional limitations and transactions involving directors	s 322A	s 41
Contract with sole member who is director	s 322B (changed)	s 231
Directors' register of interests	s 325	s 809
Loans of directors	s 330 (changed)	s 197ff
Loans, etc: civil consequences of contravention	s 341	s 213
Persons connected with a director	s 346	s 252
Authorisation required for political donations or expenditure	s 347A-C (changed)	s 362ff
Written resolutions of private companies	s 381A (changed)	s 288
Registration of charges	s 395	s 860
Charges void unless registered	s 410	s 889
Arrangements and reconstructions	425ff	s 895ff
Mergers and divisions	s 427A, Sch 15B	s 902ff
"Squeeze out" and "sell out"	s 428ff (changed)	s 974ff
Fraudulent trading	s 458	s 993
Unfair prejudice	s 459ff	s 994ff

Provision	CA 1985	CA 2006
Registrar of Companies	s 704ff (changed)	s 1060ff
Provisions for employees on cessation or transfer of business	s 719 (changed)	s 247
Power of court to grant relief	s 727	s 1157
"Director"	s 741	s 250
"Shadow director"	s 741	s 251
"Debenture"	s 744	s 738
Memorandum of association	new	s 8
Company's constitution	new	s 17
Entrenched provisions of articles	new	s 22
Existing companies (memorandum, etc)	new	s 28
Statement of company's objects	new	s 31
One director to be a natural person	new	s 155
Minimum age for appointment as a director	new	s 157
General duties of directors	new	ss 170–177
Civil consequences of breach of general duties	new	s 178
Consent, approval or authorisation by members	new	s 180
Ratification of acts of directors	new	s 239
Directors' residential addresses	new	s 240ff
Derivative claims	new	s 260ff
Private company not required to have a secretary	new	s 270
Resolutions	new	s 281
Ordinary resolutions	new	s 282
Takeovers	new	s 942ff

1

THE COMPANY AND ITS INCORPORATION

Introduction

A company is very easily defined.[1] It is the kind of legal entity or corporate body which is brought into being by the registration procedures laid down by the Companies Act 2006 (CA 2006) and its predecessors.[2] Its creation is evidenced by the issue of a certificate of incorporation by the Registrar of Companies. Except in a few rare cases the last word of its name will be 'Ltd' (Limited) or, in the case of a public company, the unpronounceable abbreviation 'plc' (public limited company).[3] In the United States, the word corresponding to company is 'corporation', and the corporation's name normally terminates in that word (Corpn) or 'Incorporated' (Inc), although 'Limited' is sometimes used there, too.

Companies are encountered everywhere. They provide most of the goods and services we use every day. They own large and small stores; run transport, telephone and communication systems; supply water and power; and run schools and hospitals. When thinking of companies, we usually think of large organisations, although 'one-man companies' are perfectly possible.

What makes companies remarkable is that they are 'legal persons' in their own right, not simply groups of individuals working together in a common enterprise. In the study of company law, therefore, it is not only necessary to address the types of rules that enable groups of people to work together in an organisation, but also to address the rules that enable a non-human 'person' to perform a wide variety of acts for itself.

Companies in action: special attributes and key parties

Company law is about the interactions between a *company* (as a legal person in its own right), the company's *members* (and since most companies are limited by shares, these are generally it *shareholders*[4]), its *directors*, and its *creditors* (both *secured* and *unsecured*).

---

[1] Of course, the word 'company' has other meanings in everyday speech; and note in particular the abbreviation 'Co' (and especially '& Co'), which is commonly used as part of the name of an unincorporated partnership that is not a 'company' in any strict legal sense, and is also occasionally used by an individual trader.

[2] A company may also be created by Royal Charter or by special Act of Parliament. Most of these companies are a century or more old. Few such companies still exist, and the rules of 'company law' as derived from the Companies Acts and common law may not always apply to them, eg neither the *ultra vires* doctrine nor the winding-up procedure has traditionally applied to chartered companies (though there are now some exceptions). Beyond this, these types of company are mainly of interest in helping to explain some of the more arcane rules of the subject which evolved long ago and have been allowed to survive into modern times.

[3] CA 2006 ss 58–60. Exceptions are unlimited companies, charitable companies, and companies granted a dispensation under ss 60 and 61. There are Welsh equivalents for 'Limited' and 'plc'. The word 'limited' is also used by co-operatives and similar bodies registered under the Industrial and Provident Societies Act 1965, and by limited liability partnerships ('LLP'), under the Limited Liability Partnerships Act 2000.

[4] Companies may also be limited by guarantee. In a company limited by guarantee, the members do not usually pay any money to the company at the outset, but they promise (they 'guarantee') that if the company becomes insolvent,

The relevant law must provide rules to deal with the creation of companies; the ways companies deal with outsiders (eg how companies contract with their suppliers and customers, how they commit torts and crimes, and how they sue and are sued, etc); how people come to be directors and shareholders; the powers and duties of directors and shareholders in their various relationships with the company, the creditors, and each other; the regulation of disputes *within* these groups (eg how directors make decisions, how battles between majority and minority shareholders are resolved, how priorities between secured and unsecured creditors are determined); and, finally, how companies 'die', or cease to exist.

The key players in all of this are the directors and the members. The task of the directors is to manage the company (although what this means in practice is determined by the constitution of the company, which in turn is governed by the members). The directors generally act collectively, via a *board of directors*. The boards of directors in medium-sized and larger companies will typically comprise both *executive directors*, who are employed by the company and intimately involved in the day-to-day management of the company, and *non-executive directors* (NEDs), who are not so employed or intimately involved in day-to-day issues.

The members are not often closely involved in the day-to-day management of the company (unless they are also its directors), but they do exercise ultimate control over the company. They too act collectively, via the *general meeting*, usually (but not always) by majority vote. The members have the power to dismiss the directors and, often, the power to appoint them. The rights of members are essentially a matter of contract between the members and the company (agreed in the company's constitutional documents, supplemented by any subsequent agreements).

If the company has shares, the members of the company are its shareholders. These shareholders provide '*equity funding*' to the company by way of paying for their shares (and can be contrasted with the *debt funding* provided by bank loans, etc). The rights that the shareholders receive in return are set out in the terms of the share issue. Generally there are rights to *vote*, to receive *dividends* out of the company's profits while the company is a going concern (*if* the directors recommend dividends), and to share in any surplus assets of the company (ie assets remaining after all of the company's creditors have been paid in full) when the company is *wound up*. There may be more than one *class* of shareholder, with different classes having different rights to vote or to receive particular financial benefits. All these matters are settled by agreement between the company and its shareholders.

Companies are used as vehicles for all sorts of activities. Typically, they are used for conducting business, from the small corner grocery store to the large multinational corporation. Companies are also used for running many non-profit ventures. Despite the varied size and function of companies, there are certain core features that are common to most companies. Two are of central significance: the *separate legal personality* of companies (ie a company is a separate legal person, distinct from its directors and its members), and the *limited liability* of its members.[5] Both of these features are dealt with in detail in the next chapter, but deserve a word of explanation here.

The fact that a company is a legal person in its own right is fundamental to the whole structure of company law. And yet there is no fanfare about this in the Act itself: all that CA 2006 s 7 says is that 'A company is formed under this Act by . . . [and then describes how a company is formed].' But the separate legal personality of the company ensures that *it* owns property, *it* contracts with third parties, *it* is owed duties by its directors, *it* makes constitutional

they will pay the amount specified in their guarantee to the company, for the company's use in paying off its creditors. In a company limited by shares, by contrast, the shareholders promise to provide funds to the company by way of the price paid for the share, usually paid in full at the time the share is purchased. That sum is the limit of the shareholders' obligation to contribute to the capital of the company, so if the company becomes insolvent, all the shareholder is required to pay to support the company is the amount (if any) still unpaid on the shares. See IA 1986 s 74.

[5] Unless the company is an unlimited company, see below, p 19.

commitments to its members, and so on. Crucially, this independence enables the company's business assets and liabilities (and attendant risks) to be segregated from the personal assets and liabilities of the company's members and directors. This partitioning of assets is crucial to the attractiveness of companies as commercial vehicles.

The limited liability of a company's members is related to the company's separate personality, but does not follow automatically from it (after all, it is possible to have companies whose members have *unlimited* liability (CA 2006 s 3(4)[6]). Where liability of members is limited, it is either limited 'by shares' to the price of the shares or 'by guarantee' to the commitment embodied in the guarantee.[7] What this means is that the company's liabilities to third parties can *only* be met out of the *company's* assets (including, of course, the company's receipts of the full share price and the benefit of the guarantees provided by members). The company's creditors cannot seek satisfaction from the company members personally, even if the company has insufficient funds to pay its own liabilities in full. Notice that although we typically use the shorthand expression that a company is a 'limited liability company', the *company's* liability is not in fact limited at all; only its members' liability is.[8]

Sources of company law

Registered companies can only be created because legislation permits it. That same legislation is also the primary source of the rules that govern the operation of companies. Most of the relevant provisions are now to be found within the 1,300 provisions and 16 Schedules of CA 2006. That Act received Royal Assent on 8 November 2006, but there is a staggered introduction of its provisions, from January 2007 to a final date in October 2008, when every provision will be in force and the Act will be fully operational. In the transition phase, the relevant provisions from the predecessor Companies Acts 1985 and 1989 (CA 1985 and CA 1989) will continue to govern.

In this edition, the law is stated as it appears in CA 2006, on the assumption that by the time students come to apply their learning, the Act will be fully operational and will state the law that students will be required to apply.[9]

In addition to UK legislation in the form of the Companies Acts, companies are regulated by other statutes,[10] common law rules, European law (especially harmonisation directives), and certain other special rules (eg the Listing Rules of the London Stock Exchange).

UK Companies Acts

The Companies Act 2006 (especially Parts 1 to 39) either restates or amends almost all of the provisions of CA 1985 and CA 1989, as well as the Companies (Audit, Investigations and Community Enterprise) Act 2004 (C(AICE) Act 2004). The Act also codifies certain aspects of the case law, especially that relating to directors' duties. Note that CA 2006 s 2 defines 'the

---

[6] Some risky corporate ventures (eg historically, mining ventures) are set up this way to persuade outside funders of the confidence of the members in the likely success of the planned venture. But it is more usual now, in these types of cases, to set up a company limited by shares and require the shareholders (and directors) to provide unlimited personal guarantees of the company's debts. The two structures are functionally equivalent.

[7] See footnote 4 above.

[8] For further reading, see PL Davies, *Introduction to Company Law* (OUP, 2002); and RR Kraakman et al, *The Anatomy of Corporate Law* (OUP, 2004).

[9] The implementation timetable is available on the DTI website.

[10] Especially the Insolvency Act 1986 (IA 1986) and the Financial Services and Markets Act 2000 (FSMA 2000), but also by statutes that apply generally to 'legal persons', such as the Sale of Goods Act 1979 and various property law acts.

Companies Acts' (note the plural) to mean CA 2006 itself (but only the Parts specified in s 2(2)), and parts of other specified acts that remain in force (s 2(1)(b) and (c)).

CA 2006 is the product of the most extensive revision of company law since 1856. It arises from a consultation carried out over seven years, from 1998 to 2005, by the Company Law Review (CLR), which was set up by the Department of Trade and Industry (DTI). That consultation was itself preceded by substantial work and two reports delivered by the Law Commissions on directors' duties and shareholder remedies.[11]

The CLR produced eight substantial consultation documents, followed by a two-volume final report in 2001.[12] In response to this, in July 2002, the government published a two-volume White Paper, *Modernising Company Law* (Cm 5553), and then in March 2005, after another three years' work, a second and substantially revised White Paper, *Company Law Reform* (Cm 6456). The Company Law Reform Bill, which resulted from all this work, was introduced into the House of Lords in November 2005 and received Royal assent a year later in November 2006. It is reputedly the longest Bill ever considered by Parliament.

Regulatory amendments to CA 2006

The process of major company law reform is considered below. But many provisions in CA 2006 give the Secretary of State the power to make any necessary regulations by statutory instrument. This is done, as specified, by either the '*affirmative resolution procedure*' (s 1290) or the '*negative resolution procedure*' (s 1289).

The affirmative procedure requires the proposed statutory instrument to be laid before Parliament and approved by both Houses; the negative procedure does not require this, but the regulations may be annulled by resolution of either House. The latter procedure is reserved for regulations that do not increase the burdens on the affected parties (eg regulations introducing exemptions from audit requirements), the former for cases where Parliament needs to retain greater control over the delegated amendment process.

The Company Law Review

In March 1998, the DTI commissioned a fundamental review of company law. An independent Steering Group led the CLR. Its terms of reference required it to consider how core company law could be modernised in order to provide a simple, efficient and cost effective framework for British business in the twenty-first century.

The CLR presented its Final Report to the Secretary of State for Trade and Industry on 26 July 2001. This report contained a range of recommendations for substantive changes to many areas of company law, and a set of principles to guide the development of the law more generally. Most notably it proposed that the law should be as simple and as accessible as possible for smaller firms and their advisers and should avoid imposing unnecessary burdens on the ways companies operate (ie 'think small first'). See below, p 18. Many, but not all, of the provisions of CA 2006 implement CLR recommendations.

The most important documents produced as a result of the CLR law reform process are:

(a) White Paper, Company Law Reform (March 2005) Cm 6456;

(b) White Paper, Modernising Company Law (July 2002) Cm 5553-1 and Cm 5553-II;

(c) DTI, Modern Company Law for a Competitive Economy Final Report (2001) (URN 01/942 and 01/943).

---

[11] Law Commission, Company Directors: Regulating Conflicts of Interest and Formulating a Statement of Duties (Law Com No 261, 1999) (available on: http://www.lawcom.gov.uk/docs/lc261(1).pdf). This was preceded by a Consultation Paper (LCCP 153, September 1998) which is available on: http://www.lawcom.gov.uk/docs/cp153.pdf and which usefully sets out the Commission's understanding of the current law. Also Law Commission, Shareholder Remedies (Law Com No 246, 1997) available at http://www.lawcom.gov.uk/docs/lc246.pdf, and the preceding consultation paper (LCCP 142, 1996), available at http://www.lawcom.gov.uk/docs/cp142.pdf.

[12] All of these documents may be downloaded from the DTI website.

These, and all the other consultation papers,[13] are available on the DTI website.

History of legislative reform

The first Companies Act was passed in 1844. It was not concerned with the creation of companies *per se*: 'joint stock companies' already existed in considerable numbers, and had done so for over a century. This Act provided for the registration of the 'deed of settlement' of such companies (ie registration of their principal constitutional document). In return for registration, they were accorded corporate status (ie recognised by the law as entities in their own right). 'Joint stock' companies formed on the basis of a deed of settlement were different from the chartered corporations like the Hudson's Bay Company and the Bank of England, and different again from the statutory companies which sprang up in great numbers early in the nineteenth century to build the nation's railways and canals and docks.[14] They were outsized, unincorporated partnerships, running sometimes into hundreds of members, carefully set up by the skills of clever equity draftsmen so that large-scale ventures could be organised on the basis of a common fund or 'joint stock' pooled by the participants, and run by directors and managers for the benefit of all concerned. By 1844, they were too important to be ignored or outlawed and too unwieldy to fit at all easily into normal legal procedures such as litigation. The 1844 Act was the first step in giving these companies legal recognition.

A decade later, in 1855, a further Act was passed which allowed the shareholders who invested in a company to limit their liability; and a year after that a revised statute, the Joint Stock Companies Act 1856, established the framework for the modern-style company, incorporated by the process of registration and enjoying limited liability. The old 'deed of settlement' gave way to the 'memorandum and articles of association', which in the 2006 Act gave way to a simple one-document constitution, the 'articles'.

There have not been any paradigm shifts in either the institution of 'the company' or in the legislation dealing with it from 1856 to the present day. That also includes the 2006 Act: for all its welcome changes, it does not fundamentally alter the structure of the subject. Of course, Parliament has been busy in company affairs from time to time, passing amending and consolidating Acts, each bigger than the last one. Until the recent review (noted above), the last fundamental reassessment of the subject took place at the time of the Crimean War.

CA 1985 and CA 1989 are the immediate predecessors of CA 2006. Parts of these Acts will remain in force during the transition to full operation of CA 2006; indeed, some minor parts which were not re-enacted in CA 2006 will continue thereafter.[15] The efforts leading to these 1985 and 1989 statutes date from 1985, when Parliament made a fresh start by consolidating all the company related statutory provisions that were then operative into one major Act, the Companies Act 1985, and three minor ones, the Company Securities (Insider Dealing) Act 1985,[16] the Company Directors Disqualification Act 1986 (CDDA 1986) and the Companies Consolidation (Consequential Provisions) Act 1985.

---

[13] The DTI's Review (Modern Company Law for a Competitive Economy): published Consultation Documents:
No 1 (February 1999): The Strategic Framework URN 99/654
No 2 (October 1999): Company General Meetings and Shareholder Communication URN 99/1144
No 3 (October 1999): Company Formation and Capital Maintenance URN 99/1145
No 4 (October 1999): Reforming the Law Concerning Overseas Companies URN 99/1146
No 5 (March 2000): Developing the Framework URN 00/656
No 6 (June 2000): Capital Maintenance – Other Issues URN 00/880
No 7 (October 2000): Registration of Company Charges URN 00/1213
No 8 (November 2000): Completing the Structure URN 00/1335.
[14] The Companies Clauses Consolidation Act 1845, which is still in force, applies to these 'statutory' companies. This Act contains standard provisions which may be incorporated by reference into the particular Act, so making the procedure shorter and cheaper.
[15] Eg, on company investigations, see below, Chapter 12.
[16] Since repealed and replaced by the Criminal Justice Act 1993, Pt V.

But this tidying up exercise achieved very little. CA 1985 did not survive intact for long. It was a 'jumbo' enactment of 747 sections and 25 Schedules, but, in the same year it was enacted, the Insolvency Act 1985 (now almost entirely repealed and replaced by the Insolvency Act 1986) superseded nearly a third of it with sweeping new provisions. Further changes were made by the Financial Services Act 1986 (itself now superseded by the Financial Services and Markets Act 2000), and by the Companies Act 1989 (again, a substantial piece of legislation containing 216 sections and 24 Schedules).

It is an unhappy fact that the volume of companies legislation almost quadrupled in the course of the 1980s. And the process continues. Even in the lead up to the reforms embodied in CA 2006, there was a steady flow of new measures. These included some reforms of considerable importance, such as the provisions which authorise the formation of single-member companies (below, p 21) and those which have introduced a new regime to regulate the issue of prospectuses inviting the public to invest in a company's shares (below, p 591).

Case law

In all these years of reform, no Companies Act has ever been a complete code. Much of company law goes back to the days of the deed of settlement companies and the chartered and statutory corporations which flourished in earlier centuries. A great deal of the essence and spirit of the present company law is derived from this old case law rather than from anything in the Companies Acts themselves. Indeed, these Acts always assumed the existence of companies, and took for granted matters of everyday practice in company affairs, and the body of judicial precedent that has grown up over the years. The influence of these background factors has been remarkably persistent, even, sometimes, on matters where business circumstances today are quite different.

In addition to the principles of common law and equity that have evolved independently of statute (eg on directors' duties, although that has now been codified in CA 2006), there are of course many other rulings of the courts based on the Companies Acts themselves. These are sometimes on the literal wording of particular sections and sometimes on the broader interpretations of the general institutional framework that is established by the Acts (eg the 'maintenance of capital' rules (below, pp 415 ff)). In addition, there are decisions concerned with the interpretation of documents such as the company's constitutional documents or shareholders' resolutions of individual companies. Many of these are of a common or standard type (eg provisions in articles defining the functions of the board of directors, or the terms on which preference shares are issued) and so have significance for company law generally as well as for the parties in the case in question.

In some areas, practice is almost as important as the law itself. A student of English company law who did not know something of 'the City' and those bodies which have traditionally been self-regulating, such as the Stock Exchange, would gain only an imperfect impression of such matters as public issues of shares and take-over bids. It is true that the Financial Services legislation of 1986 and its successors have slowly put much of this regulation on a full statutory basis, but the older rules and practices of these various bodies remain instructive.

European law

There are many ways in which the United Kingdom's membership of the EU influences its company law. The objectives of the Treaty of Rome include the facilitating of trade and the removal of barriers to people's freedom to establish their businesses and invest their capital on a basis of equality throughout the Community. To this end, a programme for the 'harmonisation' of the domestic company laws of the member states was instituted. It seeks to remove the differences of detail between those local laws which might act as impediments to such equality. The Treaty expressly authorises and empowers its organs—the Council and the Commission—to issue '*directives*' for this purpose.

Directives

In principle, a directive is binding only on the member state, which must implement it by its own legislation; it does not immediately or directly affect individual companies or citizens as a 'source' of law. However, a number of rulings given by both the European Court and English courts have made inroads into this principle. In the first place, if a directive has been implemented by domestic legislation, recourse may be had to the text of the directive as an aid to resolve questions of statutory interpretation in relation to that legislation. This will normally require the court to give a 'purposive' rather than a restrictive construction to the statute or regulations in question, in keeping with the usual approach of the European Court *(Litster v Forth Dry Dock and Engineering Co Ltd* [1990] 1 AC 546, HL).

Even where the local legislation does not itself implement a directive, but merely covers similar ground, the European Court has ruled that it must be interpreted in the light of the wording and purpose of the directive *(Marleasing SA v La Comercial Internacional de Alimentación SA* [**1.01**]), although not where this would distort the natural meaning of the legislation *(Duke v GEC Reliance Ltd* [1988] AC 618, HL).

And if a member state has implemented a directive, or has failed to do so within the time limit fixed for implementation, the terms of the directive may be relied on as against the member state itself or a government agency or public body. Thus, in *Karella v Ministry of Industry, Energy and Technology* [**1.02**], it was held that an individual could invoke the Second EC Company Law Directive for the purpose of having legislation of the Greek Parliament declared unlawful.

By and large, the object of a directive is to set *minimum* standards: there is ordinarily nothing to stop a member state from enacting legislation which goes further than the directive prescribes. Thus, most of the provisions of the Second Company Law Directive are made to apply only to public companies, but under the United Kingdom legislation many of them were made to apply to private companies as well. And in *Siemens AG v Nold* [1997] 1 BCLC 291, the European Court of Justice held that it was in order for German law to give shareholders greater protection than was required by the directive when a company makes an issue of new shares. Even when a directive or proposed directive is only in a draft stage, it may be important to know about it, since it may indicate the lines along which tomorrow's law is likely to develop.

Regulations

Community law may also be made by regulations. A regulation, in contrast to a directive, has direct effect as part of the domestic law of each member state, although local legislation may be necessary to supplement a regulation by, for instance, providing administrative facilities (see below at p 14 for a list of regulations).

A directive does not have direct effect so as to impose obligations on an individual. Domestic legislation of a member state must be interpreted so far as possible in the light of the wording and purpose of any relevant directive.

[1.01] Marleasing SA v La Comercial Internacional de Alimentación SA [1992] 1 CMLR 305 (Court of Justice of the European Communities)

Marleasing sued a number of companies, including La Comercial. It alleged, *inter alia*, that the formation of La Comercial was void because it had been formed for the purpose of defrauding the creditors of one of its founding shareholders. The court ruled that even though this might have been a ground for declaring that a company's incorporation was a nullity under Spanish domestic law, it was not consistent with art 11 of the First EC Company Law Directive, so that the defence could not be relied on.

The Court delivered the following judgment:

> . . . It is apparent from the grounds set out in the order for reference that Marleasing's primary claim, based on, ss 1261 and 1275 of the Spanish Civil Code, according to which contracts without cause or whose cause is unlawful have no legal effect, is for a declaration that the founders' contract establishing La Comercial is void on the ground that the establishment of the company lacked cause, was a sham transaction and was carried out in order to defraud the creditors of Barviesa SA, a co-founder of the defendant company. La Comercial contended that the action should be dismissed in its entirety on the ground, in particular, that Article 11 of Directive 68/151, which lists exhaustively the cases in which the nullity of a company may be ordered, does not include lack of cause amongst them.

> The national court observed that in accordance with Article 395 of the Act concerning the Conditions of Accession of Spain and the Portuguese Republic to the European Communities, the Kingdom of Spain was under an obligation to bring the directive into effect as from the date of accession, but that that had still not been done at the date of the order for reference. Taking the view, therefore, that the dispute raised a problem concerning the interpretation of Community law, the national court referred the following question to the Court:

>> Is Article 11 of Council Directive 68/151, which has not been implemented in national law, directly applicable so as to preclude a declaration of nullity of a public limited company on a ground other than those set out in the said Article? . . .

> With regard to the question whether an individual may rely on the directive against a national law, it should be observed that, as the Court has consistently held, a directive may not of itself impose obligations on an individual and, consequently, a provision of a directive may not be relied upon as such against such a person: Case 152/84, *Marshall v Southampton and South-West Hampshire Area Health Authority*.[17]

> However, it is apparent from the documents before the Court that the national court seeks in substance to ascertain whether a national court hearing a case which falls within the scope of Directive 68/151 is required to interpret its national law in the light of the wording and the purpose of that directive in order to preclude a declaration of nullity of a public limited company on a ground other than those listed in Article 11 of the directive.

> In order to reply to that question, it should be observed that, as the Court pointed out in Case 14/83, *Von Colson and Kamann v Land Nordrhein-Westfalen*,[18] the member states' obligation arising from a directive to achieve the result envisaged by the directive and their duty under Article 5 EEC to take all appropriate measures, whether general or particular, to ensure the fulfilment of that obligation, is binding on all the authorities of member states including, for matters within their jurisdiction, the courts. It follows that, in applying national law, whether the provisions in question were adopted before or after the directive, the national court called upon to interpret it is required to do so, so far as possible, in the light of the wording and the purpose of the directive in order to achieve the result pursued by the latter and thereby comply with the third paragraph of Article 189 EEC.

> It follows that the requirement that national law must be interpreted in conformity with Article 11 of Directive 68/151 precludes the interpretation of provisions of national law relating to public limited companies in such a manner that the nullity of a public limited company may be ordered on grounds other than those exhaustively listed in Article 11 of the directive in question.

---

17 [1986] ECR 723, [1986] 1 CMLR 688.
18 [1984] ECR 1891, [1986] 2 CMLR 430 at para [26].

With regard to the interpretation to be given to Article 11 of the directive, in particular Article 11(2)(b), it should be observed that that provision prohibits the laws of the member states from providing for a judicial declaration of nullity on grounds other than those exhaustively listed in the directive, amongst which is the ground that the objects of the company are unlawful or contrary to public policy.

According to the Commission, the expression 'objects of the company' must be interpreted as referring exclusively to the objects of the company as described in the instrument of incorporation or the articles of association. It follows, in the Commission's view, that a declaration of nullity of a company cannot be made on the basis of the activity actually pursued by it, for instance defrauding the founder's creditors.

That argument must be upheld. As is clear from the preamble to Directive 68/151, its purpose was to limit the cases in which nullity can arise and the retroactive effect of a declaration of nullity in order to ensure 'certainty in the law as regards relations between the company and third parties, and also between members' (sixth recital). Furthermore, the protection of third parties 'must be ensured by provisions which restrict to the greatest possible extent the grounds on which obligations entered into in the name of the company are not valid'. It follows, therefore, that each ground of nullity provided for in Article 11 of the directive must be interpreted strictly. In those circumstances the words 'objects of the company' must be understood as referring to the objects of the company as described in the instrument of incorporation or the articles of association.

The answer to the question submitted must therefore be that a national court hearing a case which falls within the scope of Directive 68/151 is required to interpret its national law in the light of the wording and the purpose of that directive in order to preclude a declaration of nullity of a public limited company on a ground other than those listed in Article 11 of the directive.

➤ Note

It will be seen that art 11 of the Directive allows a judicial declaration of nullity to be made on the ground that a company's objects are unlawful or contrary to public policy. When the UK implemented this directive by domestic legislation, no steps were taken to include any provision based on art 11, for the reasons given below, p 28, Note 1. But, as the case of *R v Registrar of Companies, ex p A-G* [1.08] shows, such a declaration is not unknown in this country.

A directive may be invoked by an individual directly against a member state or government agency.

[1.02] Karella v Ministry of Industry, Energy and Technology
[1991] ECR I-2691, [1993] 2 CMLR 865, [1994] 1 BCLC 774 (Court of Justice of the European Communities)

Legislation enacted by the Greek Parliament (Law No 1386/1983) empowered a governmental authority called the Business Reconstruction Organisation (OAE) to take over control of a company and to increase the capital of such a company by administrative decision. The OAE took control of a company called Klostiria Velka AE and decided to increase its capital from Dr 220m to Dr 400m. Two shareholders successfully argued that this was contrary to the Second EC Company Law Directive, art 25(1), which requires an increase of capital, except in limited circumstances, to be effected by a resolution of the shareholders.

The Court delivered the following judgment:

The national court's questions essentially raise two issues. The first is concerned with art 25(1) of the Second Directive. The national court wishes to establish whether, having regard to art 41(1) of the Second Directive, art 25(1) may be relied upon against the administration by individuals in the national courts. It then asks whether art 25(1), in conjunction with art 21(1), is applicable with regard to public rules, such as those provided for in Law No 1386/1983, which govern the completely exceptional cases of undertakings which are of particular economic and social importance for society and are undergoing serious financial difficulties.

The second issue is concerned with art 42 of the Second Directive. The national court asks whether that provision may be relied upon by individuals and whether it has to be interpreted as precluding national rules of the type referred to above. . . .

The direct effect of art 25(1) of the Second Directive

As the court has consistently held, wherever the provisions of a directive appear, as far as their subject matter is concerned, to be unconditional and sufficiently precise, individuals are entitled to invoke them against the state (see, in particular, the judgment in *Becker v Finanzamt Münster-Innenstadt* Case 8/81 [1982] ECR 53).

Consequently, it should be examined whether art 25(1) of the Second Directive, which provides that any increase in capital must be decided upon by the general meeting, satisfied those conditions.

It must be held in that connection that that provision is clearly and precisely worded and lays down, unconditionally, a rule enshrining the general principle that the general meeting has the power to decide upon increases in capital.

The unconditional nature of that provision is not affected by the derogation provided for in art 25(2) of the Second Directive to the effect that the company's instrument of incorporation or the general meeting may authorise an increase in the subscribed capital up to a maximum amount which is to be fixed with due regard for any maximum amount provided for by law. That individual, clearly defined derogation does not leave member states any possibility of making the principle of the power of the general meeting subject to any exceptions other than that for which express provision is made.

The same applies to art 41(1) of the Second Directive, under which member states may derogate from art 25(1) and art 9(1) and the first sentence of art 19(1)(a) and (b) to the extent that such derogations are necessary to encourage the participation of employees or other groups of persons defined by national law in the capital of undertakings. That derogation, too, is strictly confined to the case provided for.

Moreover, the fact that the Community legislature provided for precise, concrete derogations confirms the unconditional character of the principle set forth in art 25(1) of the Second Directive.

It is appropriate therefore to answer the national court by stating that art 25(1) of the Second Directive may be relied upon by individuals against the public authorities before national courts.

Scope of art 25(1) of the Second Directive

As for the scope of art 25(1) of the Second Directive with respect to a law, such as Law No 1386/1983, it should be examined in the first place whether such a law falls within the field of application of the directive, since that legislation does not set out the basic rules on increases of capital and merely seeks to deal with exceptional situations. If that legislation falls within the field of application of the Second Directive, it should then be considered whether it can qualify for the benefit of the derogation provided for in art 41(1) of that directive.

As far as the field of application of the Second Directive is concerned, it should be stated first of all that, in accordance with art 54(3)(g) of the Treaty, it seeks to coordinate the safeguards which, for the protection of the interests of members and others, are required by member states of companies and firms within the meaning of the second paragraph of art 58 of the Treaty with a view to making such safeguards equivalent. Consequently, the aim of the Second Directive is to provide a minimum level of protection for shareholders in all the member states.

That objective would be seriously frustrated if the member states were entitled to derogate from the provisions of the directive by maintaining in force rules—even rules categorised as special or exceptional—under which it is possible to decide by administrative measure, outside any decision by the general meeting of shareholders, to effect an increase in the company's capital which would have the effect either of obliging the original shareholders to increase their contributions to the capital or of imposing on them the addition of new shareholders, thus reducing their involvement in the decision-taking power of the company.

However, that observation does not signify that Community law prevents member states from derogating from those provisions in any circumstances. The Community legislature has made specific provision for well-defined derogations and for procedures which may result in such derogations with the aim of safeguarding certain vital interests of the member states which are liable to be affected in exceptional situations. Instances of this are arts 19(2) and (3), art 40(2), art 41(2) and art 43(2) of the Directive.

In this connection, it must be held that no derogating provision which would allow the member states to derogate from art 25(1) of the Directive in crisis situations is provided for either in the EEC Treaty or in the Second Directive itself. . . .

It follows that, in the absence of a derogation provided for by Community law, art 25(1) of the Second Directive must be interpreted as precluding the member states from maintaining in force rules incompatible with the principle set forth in that article, even if those rules cover only exceptional situations . . . .

➤ Note

Despite the extensive programme for the harmonisation of companies legislation within the EU, some quite fundamental differences remain—and in many cases are likely to continue. What is more, these are often differences in the commercial practice or 'culture' as between one country and another, which are likely to survive any kind of legislative reform. For instance, in some jurisdictions such as the UK, a relatively high proportion of the shares in the larger companies are held by members of the public and institutional investors (such as pension funds) and are actively traded on the stock exchange; in others, there is extensive use of shares in 'bearer' form which can be transferred from one owner to another by simply handing over the relevant share certificate; and in yet others, major shareholdings in the leading companies are held by banks, either in their own right or as nominees for the real owners. It is very difficult to frame a single set of rules which will take account of these variations in practice. For example, it is only in a jurisdiction like the UK where there is an extensive market for shares that a 'take-over bid' can be made to work effectively; in other countries, the different patterns of shareholding (and differences in accounting practice, etc) create 'barriers' to take-overs which are every bit as insurmountable as a prohibition imposed by statute would be.

But there are also rules having a legal basis which in a particular jurisdiction may be regarded as inviolate. One such rule divides the EU member states into two groups: those which take the country of incorporation as the state whose law is, for most purposes, the governing law, and those which consider that this should be determined by the country where the company's main establishment or 'seat' (*Sitz* or *siège réel*) is located. The UK and Ireland are typical of the former; France and Germany of the latter, and it can fairly be said that 'never the twain shall meet'. So, a company cannot be incorporated in France if its main business is to be based in another country, and if a French-registered company were to move its main activities abroad then under French law it would have to be wound up. But a company incorporated in the UK can have its centre of business anywhere.

This dichotomy seems to be far too firmly entrenched to make radical change at all likely. Even so, the following case shows that there may be rather more freedom of choice than might have been expected.

The country of incorporation.

[1.03] Centros Ltd v Erhvervs-og Selskabsstryrelsen [1999] 2 CMLR 551 (Court of Justice of the European Communities)

Danish law requires that all companies should be formed with a prescribed minimum capital and that a substantial sum should be paid up on that capital prior to incorporation. Mr and Mrs Bryde, Danish citizens, formed a company in England with a nominal capital of £100 on which nothing was ever paid up. It never traded in the UK. They then sought to register a branch of this company in Denmark but the Danish authority (referred to in the report as 'the Board') refused, on the ground that this was a way of avoiding the Danish rules as to capital. The court held that the authority's refusal to register the branch was an obstacle to the freedom of establishment conferred by arts 52 and 58 of the Treaty of Rome.

The court delivered the following judgment: . . .

As a preliminary point, it should be made clear that the Board does not in any way deny that a joint stock or private limited company with its registered office in another Member State may carry on business in Denmark through a branch. It therefore agrees, as a general rule, to register in Denmark a branch of a company formed in accordance with the law of another Member State. In particular, it has added that, if Centros had conducted any business in England and Wales, the Board would have agreed to register its branch in Denmark.

According to the Danish Government, Article 52 is not applicable in the case in the main proceedings, since the situation is purely internal to Denmark. Mr and Mrs Bryde, Danish nationals, have formed a company in the United Kingdom which does not carry on any actual business there, with the sole purpose of carrying on business in Denmark through a branch and thus of avoiding application of Danish legislation on the formation of private limited companies. It considers that in such circumstances the formation by nationals of one Member State of a company in another Member State does not amount to a relevant external element in the light of Community law and, in particular, freedom of establishment.

In this respect, it should be noted that a situation in which a company formed in accordance with the law of a Member State in which it has its registered office desires to set up a branch in another Member State falls within the scope of Community law. In that regard, it is immaterial that the company was formed in the first Member State only for the purpose of establishing itself in the second, where its main, or indeed entire, business is to be conducted.

That Mr and Mrs Bryde formed the company Centros in the United Kingdom for the purpose of avoiding Danish legislation requiring that a minimum amount of share capital be paid up has not been denied either in the written observations or at the hearing. That does not, however, mean that the formation by the British company of a branch in Denmark is not covered by freedom of establishment for the purposes of Articles 52 and 58. The question of the application of those articles of the Treaty is different from the question whether or not a Member State may adopt measures in order to prevent attempts by certain of its nationals to evade domestic legislation by having recourse to the possibilities offered by the Treaty.

As to the question whether, as Mr and Mrs Bryde claim, the refusal to register in Denmark a branch of their company formed in accordance with the law of another Member State in which it has its registered office constitutes an obstacle to freedom of establishment, it must be borne in mind that that freedom, conferred by Article 52 on Community nationals, includes the right for them to take up and pursue activities as self-employed persons and to set up and manage undertakings under the same conditions as are laid down by the law of the Member State of establishment for its own nationals. Furthermore, under Article 58 companies or firms formed in accordance with the law of a Member State and having their registered office, central administration or principal place of business within the Community are to be treated in the same way as natural persons who are nationals of Member States.

The immediate consequence of this is that those companies are entitled to carry on their business in another Member State through an agency, branch or subsidiary. The location of their registered office, central administration or principal place of business serves as the connecting factor with the legal system of a particular State in the same way as does nationality in the case of a natural person.

Where it is the practice of a Member State, in certain circumstances, to refuse to register a branch of a company having its registered office in another Member State, the result is that companies formed in accordance with the law of that other Member State are prevented from exercising the freedom of establishment conferred on them by Articles 52 and 58.

Consequently, that practice constitutes an obstacle to the exercise of the freedoms guaranteed by those provisions.

According to the Danish authorities, however, Mr and Mrs Bryde cannot rely on those provisions, since the sole purpose of the company formation which they have in mind is to circumvent the application of the national law governing formation of private limited companies and therefore constitutes abuse of the freedom of establishment. In their submission, the Kingdom of Denmark is therefore entitled to take steps to prevent such abuse by refusing to register the branch.

It is true that according to the case law of the Court a Member State is entitled to take measures designed to prevent certain of its nationals from attempting, under cover of the rights created by the Treaty, improperly to circumvent their national legislation or to prevent individuals from improperly or fraudulently taking advantage of provisions of Community law.

However, although, in such circumstances, the national courts may, case by case, take account—on the basis of objective evidence—of abuse or fraudulent conduct on the part of the persons concerned in order, where appropriate, to deny them the benefit of the provisions of Community law on which they seek to rely, they must nevertheless assess such conduct in the light of the objectives pursued by those provisions.

In the present case, the provisions of national law, application of which the parties concerned have sought to avoid, are rules governing the formation of companies and not rules concerning the carrying on of certain trades, professions or businesses. The provisions of the Treaty on freedom of establishment are intended specifically to enable companies formed in accordance with the law of a Member State and having their registered office, central administration or principal place of business within the Community to pursue activities in other Member States through an agency, branch or subsidiary.

That being so, the fact that a national of a Member State who wishes to set up a company chooses to form it in the Member State whose rules of company law seem to him the least restrictive and to set up branches in other Member States cannot, in itself, constitute an abuse of the right of establishment. The right to form a company in accordance with the law of a Member State and to set up branches in other Member States is inherent in the exercise, in a single market, of the freedom of establishment guaranteed by the Treaty . . .

European directives and regulations relating to company law

The directives that have already been implemented by Parliament are listed below, along with other Community measures on company law (and closely related subjects) which have been adopted by the Council and are awaiting implementation, or are at various stages of proposal, discussion or draft.

List of EC directives and regulations which have been implemented by UK legislation or are under discussion

Directives

- *Directive 2006/46/EC* amending Directives 78/660/EC and 83/349/EC on annual accounts and consolidated accounts

- *Directive 2006/68/EC* amending Council Directive 77/91/EEC (Second Company Law Directive) as regards the formation of public limited liability companies and the maintenance and alteration of their capital

- *Directive 2005/56/EC on cross-border mergers of limited liability companies*
- *Directive 2004/109/EC (Transparency Directive)*
- *Directive 2004/39/EC (Markets in Financial Instruments Directive)*
- *Directive 2004/25/EC (Takeovers Directive)*
- *Directive 2003/58/EC amending Council Directive 68/151/EEC, as regards disclosure requirements in respect of certain types of companies; also see Directive 2003/124/EC*
- *Directive 2003/71/EC (Prospectus Directive), implemented by FSMA 2000 Part VI*
- *Directive 2003/6/EC (Market Abuse Directive) implemented by FSMA 2000 Pt VIII; also see Directive 2004/72/EC*
- *Directive 2001/86/EC supplementing the Statute for a European company with regard to the involvement of employees*
- *Directive 2001/34/EC (Consolidated Admissions and Reporting Directive)*
- *Directive 93/22/EEC (Investment Services Directive)*
- *Twelfth Company Law Directive 89/667/EEC on single-member private limited-liability companies*
- *Eleventh Company Law Directive 89/666/EEC on disclosure requirements in respect of branches of foreign companies*
- *Eighth Company Law Directive 84/253/EEC on qualification of auditors, as amended*
- *Seventh Company Law Directive 83/349/EEC on consolidated accounts*
- *Sixth Company Law Directive 82/891/EEC on demergers of public limited liability companies*
- *Fourth Company Law Directive 78/660/EEC on annual accounts of certain types of companies, most recently amended by Directive 2003/38/EC; implemented by SI 2004/16*
- *Third Company Law Directive 78/855/EEC on mergers of public limited liability companies*
- *Second Company Law Directive 77/91/EEC on capital requirements (formation of public limited liability companies and the maintenance and alteration of their capital)*
- *First Company Law Directive 68/151/EEC of 9 March 1968 on corporate powers and representation*

Regulations
- *Regulation (EC) 809/2004 on the contents of a prospectus*
- *Regulation (EC) 2273/2003 on share buy-backs*
- *Regulation (EC) 1606/2002 (IAS Regulation); also see Regulation (EC) 1725/2003*
- *Regulation (EC) 2001/2157 on the Statute for a European company (SE) (supplemented by Directive 2001/86/EC on the involvement of employees)*
- *Regulation (EC) 1346/2000 on cross-border insolvencies*
- *Council Regulation (EEC) 2137/85 on the European Economic Interest Grouping (EEIG)*

Recommendations
- Recommendations by the Company Law Slim Working Group on the simplification of the first and second Company Law Directives
- Commission Recommendation (2001/256/EC) on quality assurance for the statutory audit in the European Union: minimum requirements
- Commission Recommendation (2001/453/EC) on the recognition, measurement and disclosure of environmental issues in the annual accounts and annual reports of companies
- Commission Recommendation (2002/590/EC) on 'Statutory Auditors' Independence in the EU : A Set of Fundamental Principles'

Some proposed directives are missing from this list. A *Fifth Directive* reached the draft stage and was revised more than once but has never been adopted, largely because of opposition from the UK. It would have required all companies with a workforce above a certain size to institute a system of employee participation in management decisions, and would have included provisions governing directors' duties and the function of auditors.

A draft *Ninth Directive* would have introduced rules governing the conduct of corporate groups, including intra-group liabilities on insolvency. Like so many other directives, it was based on a German model, but this has not worked well even in Germany itself, and so the directive has now been formally withdrawn.

The *Fourth* and *Seventh Directives* have been amended several times by later directives, partly to make concessions for 'small and medium-sized enterprises' (SMEs) and partly to adjust the financial thresholds and ceilings which fix disclosure requirements for companies of different sizes.

There are noticeably fewer Regulations. Of those listed above, comment is warranted on two that allow for different formal company structures. EC Regulation No 2137/85 permits the establishment of *European Economic Interest Groupings* (EEIGs),[19] intended to be used for non-profit-making cross-border ventures for purposes such as joint research and development.

Regulation (EC) 2001/2157 (supplemented by Directive 2001/86/EC on the involvement of employees) provides a Statute for a European Company that enables the formation of supra-national companies governed in important respects by EC rather than local law. This proposal was stalled for over 30 years, partly because some of its provisions (eg as regards worker participation) were met by the same objections that had stood in the way of the adoption of the Fifth and Tenth Directives (above). Eventually political agreement on an amended text was reached. A company operating in more than one EU country can now incorporate as a '*European Company*' (SE or '*Societas Europaea*') rather than a company formed under the law of an individual member state, so avoiding the need to establish subsidiaries under all the different national laws. Many details, however, from the mechanics of registration to the rules of insolvency, are delegated to the law of the member state where the company has its main base, rather than administered from Brussels and governed by provisions of Community law. In that sense, the Regulation is less ambitious than originally intended. And the vexed question of the involvement of employees is dealt with in a separate directive.

In the area of insolvency law, Regulation 1346/2000 establishes common rules to deal with cross-border insolvency proceedings.

European law harmonisation

The EC company law harmonisation programme has attracted criticism because many of its measures have been seen as too prescriptive and regulatory in their approach, and too detailed in form, leading to widespread proliferation of rules and increases in compliance costs. This may have been true, but recent moves aim to reduce the burden, particularly for SMEs, by (for instance) relaxing the accounting requirements and, for some, removing altogether the obligation to have accounts audited.

Of course, what for one person may be an additional constraint may for another be a positive benefit: the standardisation of accounting formats may seem tiresome for those who have to comply but makes the reading easier for those relying on the accounts; and the general tightening up of the rules governing entry to the financial services markets has led not only to a 'level playing field', but more importantly to the opening up of these markets to users based anywhere in the Community—a development from which UK firms probably have stood to gain more than those of any other country.

---

[19] Supplemented by the EEIG Regulations (SI 1989/638), which set out in Sch 1 the full text of the EC Regulation.

Human Rights legislation

The UK has been a signatory to the European Convention on Human Rights from as long ago as 1950, but the principles of the Convention were not incorporated into its domestic law until the enactment of the Human Rights Act 1998. Until this Act came into force, very few cases which had implications for company law were taken to the European Court of Human Rights in Strasbourg—one notable exception being *Saunders v UK* (1996) 23 EHCR 313.

However, there is now a far greater awareness of these principles and their effect. See, for example, amendments made to the law which now restrict the use of self-incriminating statements made under compulsion in a later prosecution, and changes to the City Code on Takeovers.

Self-regulation

Finally, mention should be made of various initiatives taken independently of government which have led to reforms of a self-regulatory nature, some of them of considerable significance. The City Code on Takeovers used to be the most notable of these, although now much of this work has been put on a statutory basis. Before these recent changes, however, the Code, and the City Panel which administered it, which had been set up by the Bank of England and representatives of various professional and financial bodies without the backing of legislation, had discharged the important public function of regulating the conduct of takeovers for several decades.

Now the most important self-regulatory regime is found in the 'Combined Code'. This is a statement of principles of good governance and a code of best practice, appended to the listing rules of the Stock Exchange. It must be adhered to by all listed companies on a 'comply or explain' basis (below, Chapter 5). The Combined Code was prepared by the Committee on Corporate Governance chaired by Sir Ronald Hampel. It was published in June 1998, and built on earlier work of committees such as the Cadbury Committee. Again, this Code operates without legislative backing.

The Bank of England sponsors an independent body, the Financial Markets Law Committee, whose role is to identify issues of legal uncertainty or misunderstanding, both present and future, in the framework of the wholesale financial markets which might give rise to material risks, and to consider how such isues should be addressed. The Committee also acts as a bridge to the judiciary to help UK courts remain up to date with developments in financial markets practice.

In relation to the preparation of company accounts, the accountancy profession has its own standards-setting body, the Accounting Standards Board. This is no longer fully self-regulatory (as was its predecessor, the Accounting Standards Committee) because its role is recognised by statute (CA 2006 s 464), but it continues to be run essentially by the profession itself and has taken on increasing responsibilities with the greater focus on transparency in reporting.

The process of company law reform

Company law, perhaps more so than any other branch of commercial law, is not a field where finality is ever to be expected. There is always pressure for it to be modernised so as to take account of new developments in business practice, or for it to be reformed for some other reason (eg because the drafting of an earlier statute has proved to be defective, or because a ruling of the courts is thought to have left the law in an unsatisfactory state). The substantive aspects of the various statutory changes were summarised above, at pp 3 ff. Here we are more interested in the *process* of company law reform.

In the past, a practice developed of establishing a committee, appointed by the government every 20 years or so, with a general brief to look at the subject as a whole and make recommendations for reform. This would be followed shortly after by an amending Act, which in turn was very soon consolidated with the previous Act so that it was all brought together. The last of such committees was the Jenkins Committee, which reported in 1962. But at that point the pattern was broken. No amending legislation was introduced to implement the committee's proposed reforms (apart from an abortive Bill in the late 1970s, and some piece-meal measures in the ensuing decade), and the practice of setting up such committees was abandoned.

Besides these committees with a general brief, there were others appointed from time to time to look at a particular topic, such as the Bodkin Committee on sharepushing (1937). These reports (many never followed by legislation) contain some material of great interest, although they are now rather dated. They do, however, serve as a pointed reminder that some problems have been in need of a solution for decades.[20]

From the 1980s onwards, all the initiative for reform came from within government, and legislation was usually put in place after the publication of a consultative document inviting comments from members of the public and interested bodies. The driving force behind many statutory changes was the need to implement numerous EC directives. Time constraints meant that amendments to the primary legislation were often made by statutory instrument, frequently by enacting additional 'layers' of law which left the existing legislation in place and supplemented or qualified it with further rules.

In the course of the 1990s, the Department of Trade and Industry (DTI) set up a succession of working groups to examine possible reforms of particular topics, and also published a number of discussion documents inviting comments and suggestions from the public at large. In a few cases amending legislation followed, usually where this could be done by statutory instrument. But other reforms were simply left in abeyance until time could be found in the parliamentary schedule for a Bill. Significantly, the DTI also adopted an occasional practice of referring certain specific areas of company law to the Law Commissions. They were in a position to examine the subjects in depth, consult widely, and publish reports containing recommendations for reform. Unhappily, these recommendations, too, were put on hold until an opportunity arose to enact primary legislation.[21]

It was widely accepted that, as a result of this piecemeal approach to reform, the UK companies legislation had become very untidy, complex and difficult to understand. A thorough overhaul was thought to be essential. This was eventually initiated in 1998 with the creation of the Company Law Review (see above, p 4).

What we are interested in here is the *process* adopted for this review, although its scope was material in defining that. Mrs Margaret Beckett, then Secretary of State for Trade and Industry, announced the launch of this fundamental review of company law, and published a consult-

---

[20] These reports include: Loreburn Committee, reported 1906, leading to Companies Acts of 1907–8; Wrenbury Committee, reported 1918; Greene Committee, reported 1926, leading to Companies Acts of 1928–29; Bodkin Committee, reported 1937 (sharepushing), leading to Prevention of Fraud (Investments) Act 1939; Anderson Committee, reported 1936 (unit trusts); Cohen Committee, reported 1945, leading to Companies Acts of 1947–48; Gedge Committee, reported 1954 (no par value shares); Jenkins Committee, reported 1962; Bullock Committee, reported 1977 (employee representation); Wilson Committee, reported 1980 (financial institutions); Cork Committee, reported 1982 (insolvency), leading to Insolvency Acts of 1985 and 1986; Gower, *Review of Investor Protection*, reported 1984, leading to Financial Services Act 1986; Prentice, *Reform of the Ultra Vires Rule*, reported 1986, leading to reforms in CA 1989; Dearing, *The Making of Accounting Standards*, reported 1988; Diamond, *A Review of Security Interests in Property*, reported 1989 (company charges).

[21] See especially the consultations on directors' duties and the remedies available to minority shareholders.

ation paper with the challenging title *Modern Company Law for a Competitive Economy*. The focus of the exercise was to be on the framework of 'core' company law,[22] reviewing every aspect of the subject, including the very foundations which were put in place by the Victorians in the mid-nineteenth century. The emphasis was declared to be on clarity, simplification, consistency, predictability and transparency, with the aim of promoting competitiveness in the modern commercial and technological environment.

The project has involved very large numbers of people, many of them serving on 'working groups', each of which was charged with the examination of a separate area of the law. At the head of all these bodies was a 'Steering Group' whose members included representatives of commerce, the professions and the judiciary, academics and the DTI itself. There was, in addition, a Consultative Committee of some 40 members, and, beyond this, others assisted by undertaking research or providing information from overseas jurisdictions. All in all, the Review was the most thorough and comprehensive undertaking since the introduction of limited liability and the other reforms of the 1850s.

Now that the result of all this work has emerged in legislation, there are sure to be assessments of the extent to which it has achieved its initial ambitions.

One further matter deserves comment. That is the process of converting these reports and proposals for reform into legislation. From the 1970s, many of the suggested amendments to the law were effected by statutory instrument, under provisions such as the European Communities Act 1972 and the Deregulation and Contracting Out Act 1994, which, exceptionally, authorise the amendment of primary legislation by subordinate 'regulations' that by-pass the usual full parliamentary procedure (see above, p 4). This has certain advantages—for instance, it enables the United Kingdom government to honour its obligations to implement EC directives promptly without taking up precious parliamentary time—but it also has its drawbacks. Not only is there not the same opportunity for scrutiny and debate that a normal Bill would receive, but the amendments are necessarily restricted to doing no more than the empowering Act permits: the statutory instrument cannot effect related changes to other parts of company law, however logical or desirable such further measures might be. The consequence is that, before the enactment of CA 2006, the legislation overall had become progressively more and more diffuse and untidy.

Enactment of reforms in the future will have to pursue these familiar routes. The CLR recommended that there should be a permanent Company Law Reporting Commission to keep company law and governance under review and submit an annual report to the Secretary of State. In turn, the Secretary of State would be under a duty to consult the Commission on proposed secondary legislation (*Final Report*, Vol 1, paras 5.21–5.37). The government rejected this suggestion, saying it preferred a flexible approach, and had already shown its commitment to reform and consultation by setting up the CLR itself (White Paper, 2002, Cm 5553-I, part II, paras 5.25–5.27).

In its 2005 White Paper, the government countered with its own proposal (Cm 6456, para 6.1). It suggested that after the Companies Act 2006 was enacted, future reform and restatement of company law should be made by a special form of secondary legislation, using a procedure like that for regulatory reform orders under the Regulatory Reform Act 2001. This would have involved consultation by the Secretary of State, examination by committees of both Houses, and final approval by a resolution of each House. However, despite widespread earlier support, this proposal was defeated as an inappropriate process for large and potentially controversial reforms.

---

[22] 'Core' company law was taken to include the essential principles of company law that are common to all companies, or at least to large categories of companies such as public companies or private companies. The intention was that new legislation would exclude provisions that only applied to companies that fell into a special class for reasons unrelated to company law (such as charitable companies), or that were better treated in other statutes, eg the rules governing the offering of shares to the public, which are now dealt with as part of the securities regulation.

> Question

Are these processes satisfactory to ensure that the UK has a 'modern company law for a competitive economy'? What issues need to be considered in any revised practices?

The purpose of company law: enabling or regulatory?

Legal scholars, economists and social scientists have between them established an extensive body of literature that focuses on variants of the question: what is company law *for?*—or, perhaps, what *should* it be for? At the one extreme, there are those who advocate that its role should be primarily that of *enabling* those engaged in commerce to order their affairs in whatever way suits their purpose best, with minimal interference from the state. A strong belief in the principle of freedom of contract and in the power of market forces characterises this philosophy. At the other extreme, it is contended that the potential for abuse inherent in the concept of limited liability and in the massive economic power wielded by the largest corporations requires the imposition of strong *regulatory* measures by the lawmakers—or, alternatively, that rules of a similar prescriptive nature can be used to make the company a powerful instrument of social engineering, supplementing the law in other areas such as employment law, environmental law and so on.[23]

To some extent linked with these debates is a well-established classification of the rules of company law into those which are permissive ('may'), those which are presumptive ('may waive') and those which are mandatory ('must' or 'must not'). This analysis was pioneered by the doyen of American company law scholars, Professor Eisenberg, in an article in (1989) 89 Colum L Rev 1461.

The corporation laws of the United States jurisdictions are generally regarded as the most liberal and permissive, and those of Germany as among the most prescriptive. So far as English law is concerned, it is fair to say that while much of the nineteenth-century legislation was enabling, the innovations of the twentieth century have been increasingly more regulatory in nature. Typically, the more recent reform packages have been introduced with the avowed intention of striking a balance between interfering with business as little as possible, on the one hand, and ensuring that adequate measures are in place to curb abuse and sharp practice, on the other. But invariably caution seems to have dictated that the scales should be tipped heavily in the latter direction. CA 2006 has clearly followed this pattern in some respects, but reversed it in others. Where the overall balance now lies is not so clear.

Classification of companies

The Companies Acts recognise a number of types and classifications of company, as described below.

Limited and unlimited companies: CA 2006 s 3

CA 2006 s 3 defines a 'limited company' and an 'unlimited company'. A company may be limited by shares or by guarantee by an appropriate limiting provision in the company's constitution.

---

[23] The CLR terms this topic the 'scope' issue, putting the question: 'For what purpose and in whose interests should companies be operated and controlled?'. It is more commonly referred to as the 'stakeholder' debate, and in this book is discussed under the heading of directors' duties, below, at Chapter 6.

Where there is no such limiting provision on the liability of the company's members, a company is an 'unlimited company'.

An *unlimited company* has no limit on the liability of its members. In other words, members can be called upon to satisfy personally the whole of its liabilities to its creditors. In a *limited company*, this liability is restricted by law to an amount fixed by the terms of issue of the shares or by the company's constitutional documents. Unlimited companies are exempt from the statutory obligation to publish their accounts and reports (s 448).

Companies limited by shares and companies limited by guarantee

There are two types of limited company. In a company *limited by shares* a member is not liable for the company's debts beyond the amount remaining unpaid on his or her shares. This is, of course, in addition to what he or she (or a previous owner of the shares) has already paid on those shares. Thus, if a company allots to Smith a share of nominal value £1 'at par' (ie for a price of £1), and 60p is paid to the company by Smith on the issue of that share to him, the maximum potential liability of Smith or any later holder of that share to meet the company's debts is the outstanding balance of 40p.

In a company *limited by guarantee* a member is only liable to make a contribution to the assets of the company in the event of its being wound up, and the amount of this contribution (very commonly a nominal sum such as £5) is fixed at the outset by the company's constitution.

Companies limited by guarantee are used mainly for non-profit-making purposes, ranging all the way from some of the major charities to the local golf club. Since they must be formed without any share capital, they have to look elsewhere for their funding, for example, to subscriptions or fees.

Public and private companies: CA 2006 s 4

CA 2006 s 4 defines 'private' and 'public' companies in the following terms: a 'private company' is any company that is not a public company; and a 'public company' is a company with a certificate of incorporation that states it is a public company, and that has complied with all the necessary provisions of the Act (or former Companies Acts) as regards registration or re-registration as a public company. There is a minimum share capital requirement (the 'authorised minimum'), currently £50,000 (CA 2006 ss 761 and 763). This authorised minimum may be satisfied in sterling or the euro equivalent of the prescribed sterling amount (s 763).

Only a company limited by shares may be a public company. Public companies have the advantage of being able to offer their shares by advertisement to the public for investment (CA 2006 s 755); but they are subject to a greater degree of regulation by the law.

A *private company* is any company that is not a public company. The legislation makes a number of concessions for private companies—eg a private company may have only one director while a public company must have at least two (s 154), and a public company is subject to minimum capital requirements (ss 761ff). Only private companies may take advantage of the written resolutions procedure for decision-making (ss 288ff).

The name of a public company ends with the designation 'plc', and that of a private company with the word 'Limited' (ss 58ff).

English company law, unlike that of most other European countries, deals with both public and private companies in the same Act. From time to time there have been suggestions that the law should be re-framed so that each category has its own statute, or that the law should go even further to accommodate the special needs of the smallest businesses by having a separate, simplified, legislative regime especially designed for them (as has been done by the

Close Corporations Act in South Africa). However, neither the CLR nor the Law Commissions considered that there was any great support for such a proposal in this country, and it is unlikely to be advanced further.

Change of company status

CA 2006 ss 89ff permits a company to alter its status (eg from limited to unlimited, or from private to public) by re-registration.

In each case various conditions have to be met. These relate to: (i) the agreement of the company's members to the change of status (eg sometimes it is necessary to have the unanimous support of members, sometimes the support of a special resolution (ie 75% vote) of the members agreeing to the change); (ii) satisfying the conditions necessary for the new status; and (iii) ensuring there are no historical circumstances that militate against the change.

Charitable and community interest companies

A company of the types already mentioned may also be a charity (if it meets the legal requirements to attract that classification) or a community interest company (if it meets the requirements of Part 2 of the Companies (Audit, Investigations and Community Enterprise) Act 2004 (C(AICE)A 2004)).

A limited company wishing to register as a community interest company (CIC) must be approved by the Regulator of Community Interest Companies, who must be satisfied that the company meets the 'community interest' test and is not an excluded company. A company meets the community interest test if a reasonable person might consider that its activities are being carried out for the benefit of the community (C(AICE)A 2004 s 35(2)). Excluded companies are companies devoted to political campaigning. CICs are subject to limitations on the dividends they may pay to their members.

European public limited-liability companies (SE)

It is possible to register a European public limited-liability company (*societas europaea* or SE) in any EU State under Regulation (EC) 2157/2001. There are strict pre-conditions to be met, so that in effect the formation of an SE requires collaboration between at least two companies registered in different member states. Together they may then register as an SE. The SE must register as an SE in the member state in which it has its registered office, and it then will be treated in every state as if it were a public limited-liability company formed in accordance with the law of the member state in which it has a registered office.

Classifications based on size

The above categories are classifications of companies formally set out by CA 2006—companies are *registered* within these categories. In addition, a division of private companies and groups is made on the basis of *size* by CA 2006 ss 444ff, and 465ff, which give dispensations from certain of the accounting requirements to 'small' and 'medium-sized' companies and groups, and by CA 2006 ss 475ff, which exempt 'very small' companies from the obligation to have their accounts audited.

Since 1992, it has been possible for private companies to have a single member. (The minimum number was formerly two.) These companies are subject to some special rules under the Act (eg CA 2006 s 357, which requires decisions taken by the single member to be recorded in writing). Thus single-member companies may be regarded as a further sub-species of company for classification purposes.

Companies and partnerships

There are many types of organisation which have structures that are to a greater or lesser degree similar to those of companies, but which are governed by separate legislation. Some of these are regarded in law as being 'persons' in their own right, distinct from their members: eg building societies, friendly societies, and industrial and provident societies (ie the co-operatives). Others are not, the most familiar example being trade unions. Partnerships generally have no separate personality (although they do in Scotland, and see below).

The most important business alternatives to adopting a corporate structure are sole traders and partnerships. Neither typically has limited liability, although there are some exceptions with partnerships. Partnerships may be divided into three categories: 'ordinary' partnerships, in which every member has unlimited liability for the debts and obligations of the firm; *limited partnerships*, in which the active partners have unlimited liability but the 'sleeping' partners' liability is limited; and *limited liability partnerships*, formed and registered under the Limited Liability Partnerships Act 2000, which do have separate personality and whose members enjoy limited liability.

Incorporation, registration and the role of the registrar

Incorporation

To incorporate a company under CA 2006 s 7ff, it is necessary to draw up two basic documents, the *memorandum of association* and the company's constitution or *articles of association* (to the extent that this is not supplied by default application of the model articles, see s 20). (Note that the memorandum here is not part of the company's constitution; it is not at all the same type of document as the memorandum under the previous Companies Acts legislation.)

The memorandum must be signed or authenticated by the first member or members ('subscribers') and delivered by them or their agent[24] to the Registrar of Companies, together with the prescribed fee and certain supporting documents (see s 9ff). These include statements of the company's proposed name, registered office, whether members' liability is to be limited, proposed company directors (and secretary, if there is one[25]) and their consents to act, initial share capital (if it is a company with shares), proposed articles of association (or, by default, the model articles will apply), and, finally, a statement of compliance (s 13).

Since the documents have to include the company's name, it is prudent to check in advance that a proposed name is likely to be available. See the rules on names in CA 2006 s 53ff.

If the registrar is satisfied that the requirements of the Act as to registration are met, he will register the documents (s 14), and issue a certificate of incorporation, signed by the registrar and authenticated by his seal (s 15). Note that a company may not be formed for an unlawful purpose, so this can be grounds for refusing registration (see CA 2006 s 7(2)).

The certificate of incorporation is conclusive evidence that the requirements of the Act have been complied with and that the company is duly registered (s 15(4)).[26] The effects of

---

[24] Incorporation documents may be filed electronically.

[25] This is only compulsory for public companies: CA 2006 s 12.

[26] And can therefore only be questioned by the Attorney-General, because the Act does not bind the Crown (per Lord Parker of Waddington in *Bowman v Secular Society Ltd* [1.06] at 438–40, and *Cotman v Brougham* [1918] AC 514 at 519). For an example of a request for reversal of a decision to register a company, see *R v Registrar of Companies, ex p Attorney-General* [1.08].

incorporation are set out in s 16, including that the body corporate is capable of exercising all the functions of an incorporated company (s 16(3)).

Memorandum of association

CA 2006 s 8 deals with the memorandum of association, replacing s 3(1) of the 1985 Act. Under the new legislation the memorandum serves a more limited, but nonetheless important, purpose: it evidences the intention of the subscribers to the memorandum to form a company and become members of that company on formation. In the case of a company that is to be limited by shares, the memorandum also provides evidence of the members' agreement to take at least one share each in the company. It is not possible, or necessary, to amend or update the memorandum; if the members want to change the company's constitution, they do that by changing the articles (below, p 24 and Chapter 4).

All of the companies formed under the old Acts (such as CA 1985) will have been formed with an 'old-style memorandum' and articles. The memorandum was the primary public constitutional document of the company, setting out the company's fixed financial information, and its objects (or powers). This document was supplemented by the articles of association, which generally dealt with the internal management of the company. CA 2006 s 28 provides that any provisions in the memoranda of existing companies that are not of the type described in CA 2006 s 8 will be treated as if they were provisions in the company's articles. This includes both substantive provisions and also any provisions for their entrenchment. Existing companies will, therefore, not be required to amend their articles to reflect these statutory changes in CA 2006, but they may do so if they wish.

Constitutional documents: Articles of association and the company's objects

The articles of association (as amended from time to time) provide the company with its constitution (s 17). Every company must have articles. These will be either articles registered by the company itself on its incorporation (s 9(5)(b)), or the model articles for limited companies that are deemed by CA 2006 s 20 to apply if no articles are registered, or, if articles are registered, to the extent that the model articles are not specifically excluded or modified.

Under previous legislation (CA 1985 and its predecessors), all companies were required to have *objects*, and these objects had to be specified in the ('old-style') memorandum. So, for example, a company's objects might be the running of schools, the building of canals, or the pursuit of research into medical diseases. The 'objects' were the activities that the company had been formed to pursue. Their statement was intended to provide comfort to members and creditors, who could rest secure in the knowledge of the ventures the company would pursue. It was also intended to constrain the directors, preventing them exercising their powers for unauthorised ends. But the courts soon came to the view that purported activities outside the company's objects were void, being *ultra vires*, or outside the company's capacity to act. This had a significant and detrimental effect on both the company and those it had dealings with: contracts entered into in good faith were rendered void, with all that followed from that. This was commercially unacceptable, and statutory provisions were enacted to protect third parties while still restraining directors.

The public role played by a statement of the company's objects was recognised as inessential, and CA 2006 s 31(1) now provides that a company will have unrestricted objects unless the objects are specifically restricted by the articles. This means that unless a company makes a deliberate choice to restrict its objects, the objects will have no bearing on what a company can do. If a statement restricting the objects is made, it must be made as part of the company articles of association (CA 2006 s 31(2)).

CA 2006 s 33 provides that the company's constitution binds the company and its members to the same extent as if there were covenants on the part of the company and of each member to observe the provisions. This has significant ramifications: see below, Chapter 4.

History

Prior to the Joint Stock Companies Act 1856, companies were formed on the basis of a *deed of settlement*—an elaborate form of partnership deed. The Act of 1844 provided for the registration of the deed of settlement and the grant of corporate status in return. The 1856 Act introduced a new constitutional framework based on two documents—the *memorandum of association* and the *articles of association*—and this pattern continued under successive Companies Acts. The memorandum was the more fundamental document: the articles could not modify the memorandum, and if there was any inconsistency, the terms of the memorandum prevailed (*Guinness v Land Corpn of Ireland* (1822) 22 Ch D 349, CA). In addition, statutory provisions such as CA 1985 s 125 (CA 2006 s 22) made it possible to 'entrench' rights by writing them into the memorandum with a prohibition or restriction on their alteration.

Under CA 2006, this question of primacy as between the company's two constitutional documents, its memorandum and its articles, does not arise, as all the company's constitutional provisions are contained in the articles; the memorandum is nothing more than a statement by the first members that they intend to form a legal entity.

The question of alterability was, originally, perhaps the most important distinction between the two documents: apart from changing its name (in very limited circumstances) and increasing its capital, a company could do nothing under the Act of 1856 to alter any of the terms of the memorandum, while the articles could be changed simply by a special resolution of the members. With time it became possible to alter virtually all the provisions of the memorandum by one procedure or another, and so this distinction was of subsidiary importance. Broadly speaking, however, we can say that by its memorandum a company proclaimed to the world the *external* aspects of its constitution, such as its name, domicile, objects, status (as limited or unlimited, public or private, etc) and capital structure, while the articles were concerned with matters of *internal* organisation, which are primarily of interest to its own members and officers, eg the procedures for paying the subscription price for shares and for transferring shares, the convening and conduct of members' and directors' meetings, the appointment, removal and remuneration of directors and the payment of dividends.

Under CA 2006 s 21(1), as in CA 1985, the general rule is that provisions of a company's articles of association (its constitution) may be altered by special resolution. Through entrenchment provisions, however, more restrictive procedures can be introduced: CA 2006 s 22(2) indicates that provisions for entrenchment may only be made (a) in the company's articles on formation, or (b) by an amendment of the company's articles agreed to by all the members of the company.

Company names

The new Act introduces a system of company name adjudication to deal with problems of confusingly similar names. An application to the Companies Name Adjudicator stating the objection must be made. Two possible grounds for an application are specified in CA 2006 s 69: (a) it is the same as a name associated with the applicant in which he has goodwill; or (b) it is sufficiently similar to such a name that its use in the United Kingdom would be likely to mislead by suggesting a connection between the company and the applicant. An objection will be upheld if either of these grounds is satisfied, unless the defendant company can establish one of the defences listed in s 69(4).

The Registrar's decision to register

The registrar cannot refuse registration if the objects of the company are lawful and the documents are in order.

[1.04] R v Registrar of Companies, ex p Bowen [1914] 3 KB 1161 (King's Bench Divisional Court)

Application was made to register a proposed company named The United Dental Service Ltd. The subscribers to the memorandum were seven unregistered dental practitioners. The registrar refused to register the company unless either the memorandum was altered so as to provide that the work of the company should be undertaken only by registered dentists, or the name of the company was amended so as not to include the word 'dental' or 'dentist'. The applicants sought a writ of mandamus to compel the registrar to register the company. It was held that the registrar's refusal was unjustified, and mandamus was granted.

> LORD READING CJ: In my opinion the question turns in the main . . . upon whether the use of these words, 'The United Dental Service', would amount to an offence under the Dentists Act 1878 . . . I think these words, 'United Dental Service', imply a description of the acts to be performed, and do not imply that the persons who will perform them are persons specially qualified under the statute of 1878. The Registrar of Companies would be entitled, if the use of the proposed name would be an offence under the statute (either under this or any other statute), to refuse to register the company with that name; but, having arrived at the conclusion that that would not be the effect of the use of the words 'United Dental Service', I hold that the registrar was wrong in refusing registration upon that ground. . . .
>
> AVORY J delivered a concurring judgment.
>
> BANKES J concurred.

> ➤ Note

The registrar's powers in relation to company names have varied under successive Companies Acts. For the present law, see CA 2006 s 53ff. The use of the word 'Dental' is now restricted by regulations made under the previous CA 1985, s 29 (now see CA 2006 ss 55 and 56) and requires the consent of the General Dental Council.

The registrar may refuse to register a company whose objects are unlawful.

[1.05] R v Registrar of Joint Stock Companies, ex p More [1931] 2 KB 197 (Court of Appeal)

The registrar refused to register a company formed to sell tickets in an Irish lottery. The Court of Appeal held that the lottery was illegal in England and that his refusal was right.

> SCRUTTON LJ: This is a short point involving the construction of, s 41 of the Lotteries Act 1823. Two gentlemen proposed to sell tickets in England in connection with an Irish lottery. For some reason they did not propose to do this themselves; they proposed to form a private company to do it. It is merely conjecture on my part that this may be due to the fact that the provisions in the Act of 1823 making offenders liable to be punished as rogues and vagabonds do not apply to a company, and so the two gentlemen intending to form this company wished in this way to avoid the risk of being prosecuted under the Act. They accordingly lodged the memorandum and articles of association of the proposed company with the Registrar of Companies, who, when he saw that the object of the

company was to sell tickets in a lottery known as the Irish Free State Hospitals Sweepstake, refused to register the company. Whereupon an application was made to the court for a writ of mandamus directing the registrar to register the company. To succeed in that application the applicant must show that it is legal to sell in England tickets for the Irish Free State Hospital Sweepstake authorised by an Act of the Irish Free State. The only Act which can be supposed to authorise the selling in England is an Irish Act, but the Irish Parliament has no jurisdiction in England, and that being so, the Irish Parliament cannot authorise lottery tickets to be sold in England. The authority to sell in any place must be given by the Parliament having jurisdiction in that place, and the Imperial Parliament has given no authority to sell lottery tickets in England. . . . The appeal must be dismissed.

GREER and SLESSER LJJ delivered concurring judgments.

Registration does not establish conclusively that the objects of a company are lawful, but after the issue of a certificate of incorporation the regularity of the incorporation cannot be challenged on the grounds of illegality except in proceedings specially brought in the name of the Crown to have the registration cancelled.

[1.06] Bowman v Secular Society Ltd [1917] AC 406 (House of Lords)

The main object of the society, which was registered as a company limited by guarantee, was 'to promote . . . the principle that human conduct should be based upon natural knowledge, and not upon super-natural belief, and that human welfare in this world is the proper end of all thought and action . . . '. It was alleged that this object, involving a denial of Christianity, was against public policy, so that a bequest to the society was invalid. The House of Lords upheld the view of the courts below that this object was not unlawful. This extract from the speech of Lord Parker of Waddington is concerned with the incidental point of the conclusiveness of the certificate of incorporation. His views were supported by Lords Dunedin and Buckmaster.

LORD PARKER OF WADDINGTON: My Lords, in the present case . . . the testator has given his residuary estate through the medium of trustees for sale and conversion to the Secular Society Limited, and the question is as to the validity of this gift. There is no doubt as to the certainty of the subject-matter, or as to the testator's disposing power, or as to the validity of his will. So far as the conditions essential to the validity of the gift are concerned, the only doubt is as to the capacity of the donee.

The Secular Society Limited was incorporated as a company limited by guarantee under the Companies Acts 1862 to 1893, and a company so incorporated is by, s [18] of the Act of 1862 [CA 2006, s 16((3)] capable of exercising all the functions of an incorporated company. Prima facie, therefore, the society is a corporate body created by virtue of a statute of the realm, with statutory power to acquire property by gift, whether inter vivos or by will. The appellants endeavour to displace this prima facie effect of the Companies Acts in the following manner. If, they say, you look at the objects for which the society was incorporated, as expressed in its memorandum of association, you will find that they are either actually illegal or, at any rate, in conflict with the policy of the law. This being so, the society was not an association capable of incorporation under the Acts. It was and is an illegal association, and as such incapable of acquiring property by gift. I do not think this argument is open to the appellants, even if their major premise be correct. By the first section of the Companies Act 1900 [CA 2006, s 15(4)] the society's certificate of registration is made conclusive evidence that the society was an association authorised to be registered—that is, an association of not less than seven persons associated together for a lawful purpose. The section does not mean that all or any of the objects specified in the memorandum, if otherwise illegal, would be rendered legal by the certificate. On the contrary, if the directors of the society applied its funds for an illegal object, they would be guilty of misfeasance and liable to replace the money, even if the object for which the money had been applied were expressly authorised by the memorandum. In like manner a contract entered into by the company for an unlawful object, whether authorised by the memorandum or otherwise, could not be enforced either in law or in equity. The section does, however, preclude all His Majesty's lieges from going behind the certificate or from alleging that the society is not a corporate body with the status and capacity conferred by the Acts. Even if all the objects specified in the memorandum were illegal, it does not follow that the company cannot on that account apply its funds or enter into a contract for a lawful purpose. Every company has power to wind up voluntarily, and moneys paid or contracts entered into with that object are in every respect lawfully paid or entered into. Further, the disposition provided by the company's memorandum for its surplus assets in case of a winding up may be lawful though all the objects as a going concern are unlawful. If there be no lawful manner of applying such surplus assets they would on the dissolution of the company belong to the Crown as bona vacantia: *Cunnack v Edwards*.[27]

My Lords, some stress was laid on the public danger, or at any rate the anomaly, of the courts recognising the corporate existence of a company all of whose objects, as specified in its memorandum of association, are transparently illegal. Such a case is not likely to occur, for the registrar fulfils a quasi-judicial function,[28] and his duty is to determine whether an association applying for registration is authorised to be registered under the Acts. Only by misconduct or great carelessness on the part of the registrar could a company with objects wholly illegal obtain registration. If such a case did occur it would be open to the court to stay its hand until an opportunity had been given for taking the appropriate steps for the cancellation of the certificate of registration. It should be observed that neither, s 1 of the Companies Act 1900, nor the corresponding section of the Companies (Consolidation) Act 1908, is so expressed as to bind the Crown, and the Attorney-General, on behalf of the Crown, could institute proceedings by way of certiorari to cancel a registration which the registrar in affected discharge of his quasi-judicial duties had improperly or erroneously allowed. But . . . I do not think that the present is a case requiring such action on the part of your Lordships' House.

My Lords, it follows from what I have already said that the capacity of the Secular Society Limited to acquire property by gift must be taken as established, and, all the conditions essential to the validity of the gift being thus fulfilled, the donee is entitled to receive and dispose of the subject-matter thereof . . .

LORDS DUNEDIN, SUMNER and BUCKMASTER delivered concurring opinions.

LORD FINLAY LC dissented.

[1.07] HA Stephenson & Son Ltd v Gillanders, Arbuthnot & Co (1931) 45 CLR 476 (High Court of Australia)

EVATT J: [The] effect of formal incorporation is not regarded by the legislature as empowering the registrar to ignore compliance with the Act; but the legislature wishes to ensure that after the new legal entity has been brought into existence by the formal act of a state functionary, it will not be necessary for persons dealing with the company to ascertain at their peril whether the various statutory requirements have been complied with . . . It is not so much a power given to the registrar by the legislature, as a protection given to the public who may be dealing with the company because of the assumption that the registrar will be careful in the matter . . .

---

27 [1896] 2 Ch 679.

28 [The use of the term 'quasi-judicial' is misleading. This function of the registrar can only be described as 'ministerial': as we have seen above, in the matter of registration, he exercises no discretionary powers, still less is he concerned to adjudicate any dispute.]

[See also Salomon v Salomon & Co Ltd [2.01] and Scott v Frank F Scott (London) Ltd [4.01].]

➤ Notes

1. CA 2006 s 15(7) appears to make it unnecessary for English company law students to con-sider the topics of defective incorporation and declaration of nullity which have traditionally occupied a substantial amount of space in the textbooks in other European countries and in parts of the United States. It was not considered necessary for the UK to take any steps to implement arts 11 and 12 of the First EC Directive on Company Law, which deal with these questions. However, this may have been a misjudgement, in the light of *R v Registrar of Companies, ex p A-G* [1.08]: see R R Drury (1985) 48 MLR 644.

2. The Companies Act and many textbooks encourage the belief that companies are formed by a genuine 'association' of people with a real business that they wish to incorporate, who have constitutional documents drawn up for that specific purpose, subscribe to them and send them off to the registrar for registration. But this is to turn a blind eye to the facts. In the case of about 60% of the companies formed in the United Kingdom today, the incorporation procedure is a charade: it is purely a paper exercise carried out by people who have no inten-tion of using the company themselves for any business whatsoever. These incorporations are undertaken to meet the very considerable demand for 'ready-made' or 'shelf' companies; and (as a glance at the advertisements in any solicitors' professional journal will show) many firms exist which specialise in supplying such companies to buyers, and hold extensive stockpiles of dormant companies of every type and kind ready to be 'delivered' to customer's order. The ini-tial subscribers and officers will be clerks in the firm's employment, and the company's name a figment of someone's imagination.

3. There is one statutory exception to the principle that incorporation is freely available: the Trade Union and Labour Relations (Consolidation) Act 1992, s 10(3) states that a trade union shall not be registered as a company under CA 1985, and that any such registration is void.

4. Until quite recently, there was no recorded case in which the Attorney-General had brought proceedings to have a company's registration cancelled in the manner suggested in *Bowman v Secular Society Ltd* [1.06]. This gap has now been filled by the case next cited.

The registrar's decision to incorporate a company is subject to judicial review at the suit of the Crown.

[1.08] R v Registrar of Companies, ex p A-G (1980) [1991] BCLC 476 (Queen's Bench Divisional Court)

[The facts appear from the judgment.]

ACKNER LJ: This application has many of the indicia that one might expect to find in a students' end of term moot. It appears indirectly to have been stimulated by the action of the Policy Division of the Inland Revenue.

The Attorney-General applies to quash the incorporation and registration by the Registrar of Companies nearly a year ago, that is on 18 December 1979, of Lindi St Claire (Personal Services) Ltd as a limited company under the provisions of the Companies Act 1948 to 1976.

The grounds of the application, to state them quite briefly, are these. In certifying the incorpora-tion of a company and in registering the same the Registrar of Companies acted ultra vires or mis-directed himself or otherwise erred in law, in particular as to the proper construction and application of, s 1(1) of the Companies Act 1948 in that the company was not formed for any lawful purpose but, on the contrary, was formed expressly with the primary object of carrying on the business of prostitution, such being an unlawful purpose involving the commission of acts which are immoral and contrary to public policy.

The first point to consider is the validity of the procedure which has been adopted in this case, that is by way of application for judicial review, such application being made by the Attorney-General.

[His Lordship referred to *Bowman v Secular Society Ltd* **[1.06]** and continued:] So clearly the Attorney-General is entitled to bring these proceedings.

Now as to the facts, these come within a very short compass and they amount to the following. A firm of certified accountants, Gilson Clipp & Co, on 16 August 1979 wrote to the Registrar of Companies at Companies House, Crown Way, Maindy, Cardiff pointing out that they had received a letter from the Inland Revenue Policy Division, who stated that they considered prostitution to be a trade which is fully taxable, and that they, the certified accountants, saw no reason why their client should not be able to organise her business by way of a limited company. They asked whether the name 'Prostitute Ltd' was available for registration as a limited company, pointing out the main object of the company would be that of organising the services of a prostitute.

The registrar did not like that name and did not accept it, nor did he accept another name 'Hookers Ltd' which was offered. But subsequently two further names were offered, 'Lindi St Claire (Personal Services) Ltd' and 'Lindi St Claire (French Lessons) Ltd', and it was the former which he registered.

The memorandum of association said in terms that the first of the objects of the company was 'To carry on the business of prostitution'.

The only director of the company is Lindi St Claire, Miss St Claire describing herself specifically as 'Prostitute'. The other person who owns also one share is a Miss Duggan, who is referred to as 'the cashier'.

Leave having been obtained to apply for judicial review, Miss St Claire wrote in these terms:

I would like to say that prostitution is not at all unlawful, as you have stated, and I feel it is most unfair of you to take this view, especially when I am paying income tax on my earnings from prostitution to the government Inland Revenue.

Furthermore, I feel it is most unfair of you to imply that I have acted wrongly, as I was most explicit to all concerned about the sole trade of the company to be that of prostitution and nothing more. If my company should not be deemed valid, then it should have not been granted in the first place by the Board of Trade. It is most unfair of the government to allow me to go ahead with my company one moment, then quash it the next. . . .

It is well settled that a contract which is made upon a sexually immoral consideration or for a sexually immoral purpose is against public policy and is illegal and unenforceable. The fact that it does not involve or may not involve the commission of a criminal offence in no way prevents the contract being illegal, being against public policy and therefore being unenforceable. Here, as the documents clearly indicate, the association is for the purpose of carrying on a trade which involves illegal contracts because the purpose is a sexually immoral purpose and as such against public policy.

Mr Simon Brown submits that if that is the position, as indeed it clearly is on the authorities, then the association of the two or more persons cannot be for 'any lawful purpose'.

To my mind this must follow. It is implicit in the speeches in the *Bowman* case to which I have just made reference. In my judgment, the contention of the Attorney-General is a valid one and I would order that the registration be therefore quashed.

SKINNER J concurred.

➤ Questions

1. Tom, Dick and Harry wish to incorporate the plumbing business which they have carried on in partnership for some years. What would you say might be (i) the advantages and (ii) the

disadvantages for them in buying a ready-made company rather than having one incorporated by their own solicitor?

2. If they do decide to use a ready-made company, what steps will have to be taken in order to transfer the company to them and to make it fit for their needs?

3. What might be the consequences of the court's order in Miss St Claire's case, above [1.08], so far as concerns acts done in the year that the company was on the register?

2

CORPORATE PERSONALITY AND LIMITED LIABILITY

Introduction

We saw in the previous chapter that the separate legal personality of a company and the limited liability of its members are two key consequences of incorporation of limited companies. Both of these ideas are examined in more detail here.[1]

First, consider the idea of a company's separate legal personality, or the idea that it is a legal person in its own right, separate from the legal persons that are its members (or shareholders) and its directors. In ordinary speech, we use the word 'person' to refer to an individual human being. But in law the word has a more technical meaning: 'a subject of rights and duties'.[2] In this sense it is possible to speak of a corporation as a 'person' and recognise its separate 'personality'.

---

[1] There is a considerable body of writing on the theory, or theories, of corporate personality. No attempt has been made to select material representing the various schools of thought for inclusion in this book. For the interested reader, the following are amongst the best-known writings in English on the subject: FW Maitland, *Introduction to Gierke's Political Theories of the Middle Age* (London, 1900); F Hallis, *Corporate Personality* (London, 1930); Nekam, *The Personal Conception of the Legal Entity* (Harvard, 1938); LC Webb (ed), *Legal Personality and Political Pluralism* (Melbourne, 1958); S J Stoljar, *Groups and Entities* (Canberra, 1973); WM Geldart, 'Legal Personality'(1911) 27 LQR 90; HJ Laski, 'The Personality of Associations' (1916) 29 Harv LR 404; M Radin, 'The Endless Problem of Corporate Personality' (1932) 32 Col LR 643, and 'A Restatement of Hohfeld' (1938) 51 Harv LR 1141; M Wolff, 'On the Nature of Legal Persons' (1938) 54 LQR 494, HLA Hart, 'Definition and Theory in Jurisprudence' (1954) 70 LQR 37, 45ff, M Stokes, 'Company Law and Legal Theory' in W Twining (ed) *Legal Theory and Common Law* (1986). There is also a discussion of the topic in some general textbooks of jurisprudence.

A quite different theoretical basis for the study of companies, and of company law, is associated with the law-and-economics movement originating in the United States more than half a century ago. Economists usually speak of 'the firm', rather than the company as such, because their concern is primarily with the organisation of the different actors in the process of production of goods and services and not with the legal form which that organisation takes; however, they also see the company as a subject of study in its own right as one of the paradigm forms of business structure. There is an immense amount of literature in this area. Students could begin by reading RH Coase, 'The Nature of the Firm'(1937) 4 Economica NS 386; FH Easterbrook and DR Fischel, 'The Corporate Contract' (1989) 89 Colum L Rev 1416 and the various articles by Hart, Butler and others also collected in that number of the *Columbia Law Review*. The leading work dealing with the position in England is BR Cheffins, *Company Law: Theory, Structure and Operation* (1997). Reference may be made also to DD Prentice, 'The Theory of the Firm: Minority Shareholder Oppression: Sections 459–461 of the Companies Act 1985' (1988) 8 OJLS 55; CA Riley, 'Contracting Out of Company Law: Section 459 of the Companies Act 1985' (1992) 55 MLR 782.

[2] In this sense 'person' can, for instance, include such inanimate entities as a fund (*Arab Monetary Fund v Hashim (No 3)* [1991] 2 AC 114, [1991] BCLC 180, HL), or a Hindu temple (*Bumper Development Corpn Ltd v Metropolitan Police Comr* [1991] 1 WLR 1362, CA). Note that neither a fund nor a temple is regarded as a corporation under English law, where typically corporate personality is recognised only in a group, a municipality or an office (such as the Crown). In the two cases referred to above, the court was applying the accepted rule of the conflict of laws which states that the question whether or not a group or entity should be accorded corporate status is to be decided by the law of the jurisdiction in which it is situated or domiciled.

A company is a legal person separate and distinct from its members.

[2.01] Salomon v A Salomon & Co Ltd [1897] AC 22 (House of Lords)[3]

[The facts and arguments appear from the speech of Lord Macnaghten. Some extracts from the judgments of the trial judge and the Court of Appeal are given below [2.02].]

LORD MACNAGHTEN: Mr Salomon, who is now suing as a pauper, was a wealthy man in July 1892. He was a boot and shoe manufacturer trading on his own sole account under the firm of 'A Salomon & Co', in High Street, Whitechapel, where he had extensive warehouses and a large establishment. He had been in the trade over thirty years. He had lived in the same neighbourhood all along, and for many years past he had occupied the same premises. So far things had gone very well with him. Beginning with little or no capital, he had gradually built up a thriving business, and he was undoubtedly in good credit and repute.

It is impossible to say exactly what the value of the business was. But there was a substantial surplus of assets over liabilities. And it seems to me to be pretty clear that if Mr Salomon had been minded to dispose of his business in the market as a going concern he might fairly have counted upon retiring with at least £10,000 in his pocket.

Mr Salomon, however, did not want to part with the business. He had a wife and a family consisting of five sons and a daughter. Four of the sons were working with their father. . . . But the sons were not partners: they were only servants. Not unnaturally, perhaps, they were dissatisfied with their position. They kept pressing their father to give them a share in the concern. 'They troubled me,' says Mr Salomon, 'all the while.' So at length Mr Salomon did what hundreds of others have done under similar circumstances. He turned his business into a limited company. He wanted, he says, to extend the business and make provision for his family. In those words, I think, he fairly describes the principal motives which influenced his action.

All the usual formalities were gone through; all the requirements of the Companies Act 1862 were duly observed. There was a contract with a trustee in the usual form for the sale of the business to a company about to be formed. There was a memorandum of association duly signed and registered, stating that the company was formed to carry that contract into effect, and fixing the capital of £40,000 in 40,000 shares of £1 each. There were articles of association providing the usual machinery for conducting the business. The first directors were to be nominated by the majority of the subscribers to the memorandum of association. The directors, when appointed, were authorised to exercise all such powers of the company as were not by statute or by the articles required to be exercised in general meeting; and there was express power to borrow on debentures, with the limitation that the borrowing was not to exceed £10,000 without the sanction of a general meeting.

The company was intended from the first to be a private company;[4] it remained a private company to the end. No prospectus was issued; no invitation to take shares was ever addressed to the public.

The subscribers to the memorandum were Mr Salomon, his wife, and five of his children who were grown up. The subscribers met and appointed Mr Salomon and his two elder sons directors. The directors then proceeded to carry out the proposed transfer. By an agreement dated 2 August 1892 the company adopted the preliminary contract, and in accordance with it the business was taken over by the company as from 1 June 1892. The price fixed by the contract was duly paid. The price on paper was extravagant. It amounted to over £39,000—a sum which represented the sanguine expectations of a fond owner rather than anything that can be called a businesslike or reasonable estimate of value. That, no doubt, is a circumstance which at first sight calls for observation;

---

[3] The centenary of *Salomon*'s case was marked by a number of conferences and publications. See eg CEF Rickett and RB Grantham (eds), *Corporate Personality in the Twentieth Century* (1998), and a series of articles in (1998) 16 C & SLJ.
[4] [This expression is used descriptively. The 'private company' was first made the subject of separate statutory provision in CA 1907.]

but when the facts of the case and the position of the parties are considered, it is difficult to see what bearing it has on the question before your Lordships. The purchase-money was paid in this way: as money came in, sums amounting in all to [£20,000][5] were paid to Mr Salomon, and then immediately returned to the company in exchange for fully paid shares. The sum of £10,000 was paid in debentures[6] for the like amount. The balance, with the exception of about £1,000 which Mr Salomon seems to have received and retained, went in discharge of the debts and liabilities of the business at the time of the transfer, which were thus entirely wiped off. In the result, therefore, Mr Salomon received for his business about £1,000 in cash, £10,000 in debentures, and half the nominal capital of the company in fully paid shares for what they were worth. No other shares were issued except the seven shares taken by the subscribers to the memorandum, who, of course, knew all the circumstances, and had therefore no ground for complaint on the score of overvaluation.

The company had a brief career: it fell upon evil days. Shortly after it started there seems to have come a period of great depression in the boot and shoe trade. There were strikes of workmen too; and in view of that danger contracts with public bodies, which were the principal source of Mr Salomon's profit, were split up and divided between different firms. The attempts made to push the business on behalf of the new company crammed its warehouses with unsaleable stock. Mr Salomon seems to have done what he could: both he and his wife lent the company money; and then he got his debentures cancelled and reissued to a Mr Broderip, who advanced him £5,000, which he immediately handed over to the company on loan. The temporary relief only hastened ruin. Mr Broderip's interest was not paid when it became due. He took proceedings at once and got a receiver appointed. Then, of course, came liquidation and a forced sale of the company's assets. They realised enough to pay Mr Broderip, but not enough to pay the debentures in full: and the unsecured creditors were consequently left out in the cold.

In this state of things the liquidator met Mr Broderip's claim by a counter-claim, to which he made Mr Salomon a defendant. He disputed the validity of the debentures on the ground of fraud. On the same ground he claimed rescission of the agreement for the transfer of the business, cancellation of the debentures, and repayment by Mr Salomon of the balance of the purchase-money. In the alternative, he claimed payment of £20,000 on Mr Salomon's shares, alleging that nothing had been paid on them.

When the trial came on before Vaughan Williams J,[7] the validity of Mr Broderip's claim was admitted, and it was not disputed that the 20,000 shares were fully paid up. The case presented by the liquidator broke down completely; but the learned judge suggested that the company had a right of indemnity against Mr Salomon. The signatories of the memorandum of association were, he said, mere nominees of Mr Salomon—mere dummies. The company was Mr Salomon in another form. He used the name of the company as an alias. He employed the company as his agent; so the company, he thought, was entitled to indemnity against its principal. The counter-claim was accordingly amended to raise this point; and on the amendment being made the learned judge pronounced an order in accordance with the view he had expressed.

The order of the learned judge appears to me to be founded on a misconception of the scope and effect of the Companies Act 1862. In order to form a company limited by shares, the Act requires that a memorandum of association should be signed by seven persons, who are each to take one share at least. If those conditions are complied with, what can it matter whether the signatories are relations or strangers? There is nothing in the Act requiring that the subscribers to the memorandum should be independent or unconnected, or that they or any one of them should take a substantial interest in the undertaking, or that they should have a mind and will of their own, as one of the

---

[5] [The report reads '£30,000', but this is plainly an error. The figure of £20,000 appears in other reports of the case, eg 66 LJ Ch 35 at 49.]

[6] [This means that the sum of £10,000 was advanced by Salomon to the company as a loan, secured by a charge over the assets of the company.]

[7] *Broderip v Salomon* [1895] 2 Ch 323 [Part of the judgment of Vaughan Williams J is cited below, **[2.02]**.]

learned Lords Justices seems to think, or that there should be anything like a balance of power in the constitution of the company. In almost every company that is formed the statutory number is eked out by clerks or friends, who sign their names at the request of the promoter or promoters without intending to take any further part or interest in the matter.

When the memorandum is duly signed and registered, though there be only seven shares taken, the subscribers are a body corporate 'capable forthwith', to use the words of the enactment, 'of exercising all the functions of an incorporated company'. Those are strong words. The company attains maturity on its birth. There is no period of minority—no interval of incapacity. I cannot understand how a body corporate thus made 'capable' by statute can lose its individuality by issuing the bulk of its capital to one person, whether he be a subscriber to the memorandum or not. The company is at law a different person altogether from the subscribers to the memorandum; and, though it may be that after incorporation the business is precisely the same as it was before, and the same persons are managers, and the same hands receive the profits, the company is not in law the agent of the subscribers or trustee for them. Nor are the subscribers as members liable, in any shape or form, except to the extent and in the manner provided by the Act. That is, I think, the declared intention of the enactment. If the view of the learned judge were sound, it would follow that no common law partnership could register as a company limited by shares without remaining subject to unlimited liability.

Mr Salomon appealed; but his appeal was dismissed with costs, though the appellate court did not entirely accept the view of the court below.[8] . . .

Among the principal reasons which induce persons to form private companies, as stated very clearly by Mr Palmer in his treatise on the subject, are the desire to avoid the risk of bankruptcy, and the increased facility afforded for borrowing money. By means of a private company, as Mr Palmer observes, a trade can be carried on with limited liability, and without exposing the persons interested in it in the event of failure to the harsh provisions of the bankruptcy law. A company, too, can raise money on debentures, which an ordinary trader cannot do. Any member of a company, acting in good faith, is as much entitled to take and hold the company's debentures as any outside creditor. Every creditor is entitled to get and to hold the best security the law allows him to take.

If, however, the declaration of the Court of Appeal means that Mr Salomon acted fraudulently or dishonestly, I must say I can find nothing in the evidence to support such an imputation. The purpose for which Mr Salomon and the other subscribers to the memorandum were associated was 'lawful'. The fact that Mr Salomon raised £5,000 for the company on debentures that belonged to him seems to me strong evidence of his good faith and of his confidence in the company. The unsecured creditors of A Salomon and Co Ltd may be entitled to sympathy, but they have only themselves to blame for their misfortunes. They trusted the company, I suppose, because they had long dealt with Mr Salomon, and he had always paid his way; but they had full notice that they were no longer dealing with an individual . . .

It has become the fashion to call companies of this class 'one man companies'. That is a taking nickname, but it does not help one much in the way of argument. If it is intended to convey the meaning that a company which is under the absolute control of one person is not a company legally incorporated, although the requirements of the Act of 1862 may have been complied with, it is inaccurate and misleading: if it merely means that there is a predominant partner possessing an overwhelming influence and entitled practically to the whole of the profits, there is nothing in that that I can see contrary to the true intention of the Act of 1862, or against public policy, or detrimental to the interests of creditors. If the shares are fully paid up, it cannot matter whether they are in the hands of one or many. If the shares are not fully paid, it is as easy to gauge the solvency of an individual as to estimate the financial ability of a crowd.

One argument was addressed to your Lordships which ought perhaps to be noticed, although it was not the ground of decision in either of the courts below. It was argued that the agreement for

---

[8] *Broderip v Salomon* [1895] 2 Ch 323 at p 333. [Parts of the judgments given in the Court of Appeal are cited below, **[2.02]**.]

the transfer of the business to the company ought to be set aside, because there was no independent board of directors, and the property was transferred at an overvalue. There are, it seems to me, two answers to that argument. In the first place, the directors did just what they were authorised to do by the memorandum of association. There was no fraud or misrepresentation, and there was nobody deceived. In the second place, the company have put it out of their power to restore the property which was transferred to them . . .

LORD HALSBURY LC: My Lords, the important question in this case, I am not certain it is not the only question, is whether the respondent company was a company at all—whether in truth that artificial creation of the legislature had been validly constituted in this instance; and in order to determine that question it is necessary to look at what the statute itself has determined in that respect. I have no right to add to the requirements of the statute, or to take from the requirements thus enacted. The sole guide must be the statute itself.

Now, that there were seven actual living persons who held shares in the company has not been doubted. As to the proportionate amounts held by each I will deal presently; but it is important to observe that this first condition of the statute is satisfied, and it follows as a consequence that it would not be competent to any one—and certainly not to these persons themselves—to deny that they were shareholders.

I must pause here to point out that the statute enacts nothing as to the extent or degree of interest which may be held by each of the seven, or as to the proportion of interest or influence possessed by one or the majority of the shareholders over the others. One share is enough. Still less is it possible to contend that the motive of becoming shareholders or of making them shareholders is a field of inquiry which the statute itself recognises as legitimate. If they are shareholders, they are shareholders for all purposes; and even if the statute was silent as to the recognition of trusts, I should be prepared to hold that if six of them were [trustees for] the seventh, whatever might be their rights inter se, the statute would have made them shareholders to all intents and purposes with their respective rights and liabilities, and, dealing with them in their relation to the company, the only relations which I believe the law would sanction would be that they were corporators of the corporate body.

I am simply here dealing with the provisions of the statute, and it seems to me to be essential to the artificial creation that the law should recognise only that artificial existence—quite apart from the motives or conduct of individual corporators. In saying this, I do not at all mean to suggest that if it could be established that this provision of the statute to which I am adverting had not been complied with, you could not go behind the certificate of incorporation to show that a fraud had been committed upon the officer entrusted with the duty of giving the certificate, and that by some proceeding in the nature of scire facias you could not prove the fact that the company had no real legal existence. But short of such proof it seems to me impossible to dispute that once the company is legally incorporated it must be treated like any other independent person with its rights and liabilities appropriate to itself, and that the motives of those who took part in the promotion of the company are absolutely irrelevant in discussing what those rights and liabilities are.

I will for the sake of argument assume the proposition that the Court of Appeal lays down—that the formation of the company was a mere scheme to enable Aron Salomon to carry on business in the name of the company. I am wholly unable to follow the proposition that this was contrary to the true intent and meaning of the Companies Act. I can only find the true intent and meaning of the Act from the Act itself; and the Act appears to me to give a company a legal existence with, as I have said, rights and liabilities of its own, whatever may have been the ideas or schemes of those who brought it into existence.

I observe that the learned judge (Vaughan Williams J) held that the business was Mr Salomon's business, and no one else's, and that he chose to employ as agent a limited company; and he proceeded to argue that he was employing that limited company as agent, and that he was bound to indemnify that agent (the company). I confess it seems to me that that very learned judge becomes involved by this argument in a very singular contradiction. Either the limited company was a legal entity or it was not. If it was, the business belonged to it and not to Mr Salomon. If it was not, there was no person and no thing to be an agent at all; and it is impossible to say at the same time that there is a company and there is not.

Lindley LJ, on the other hand, affirms that there were seven members of the company; but he says it is manifest that six of them were members simply in order to enable the seventh himself to carry on business with limited liability. The object of the whole arrangement is to do the very thing which the legislature intended not to be done.[9]

It is obvious to inquire where that intention of the legislature manifested in the statute is. Even if we were at liberty to insert words to manifest that intention, I should have great difficulty in ascertaining what the exact intention thus imputed to the legislature is, or was. In this particular case it is the members of one family that represent all the shares; but if the supposed intention is not limited to so narrow a proposition as this, that the seven shareholders must not be members of one family, to what extent may influence or authority or intentional purchase of a majority among the shareholders be carried so as to bring it within the supposed prohibition? It is, of course, easy to say that it was contrary to the intention of the legislature—a proposition which, by reason of its generality, it is difficult to bring to the test; but when one seeks to put as an affirmative proposition what the thing is which the legislature has prohibited, there is, as it appears to me, an insuperable difficulty in the way of those who seek to insert by construction such a prohibition into the statute.

As one mode of testing the proposition, it would be pertinent to ask whether two or three, or indeed all seven, may constitute the whole of the shareholders? Whether they must be all independent of each other in the sense of each having an independent beneficial interest? And this is a question that cannot be answered by the reply that it is a matter of degree. If the legislature intended to prohibit something, you ought to know what that something is. All it has said is that one share is sufficient to constitute a shareholder, though the shares may be 100,000 in number. Where am I to get from the statute itself a limitation of that provision that that shareholder must be an independent and beneficially interested person? . . .

My Lords, the learned judges appear to me not to have been absolutely certain in their own minds whether to treat the company as a real thing or not. If it was a real thing; if it had a legal existence, and if consequently the law attributed to it certain rights and liabilities in its constitution as a company, it appears to me to follow as a consequence that it is impossible to deny the validity of the transactions into which it has entered . . .

LORDS WATSON and DAVEY delivered concurring opinions. LORD MORRIS concurred.

➤ Questions

1. To what do you think Lord Macnaghten was alluding when he said that the unsecured creditors of the company 'had full notice that they were no longer dealing with an individual'? Was it fair to say that 'they have only themselves to blame for their misfortunes'?

2. *Salomon*'s case has been described as a 'calamitous decision' (O Kahn-Freund (1944) 7 MLR 54). Would you agree?

3. Was there a 'very singular contradiction' in the reasoning of Vaughan Williams J, as Lord Halsbury said? (Compare *Re FG Films Ltd* [2.14], in which the company *was* held to be carrying on business as the agent of its principal shareholder.)

➤ Note

It makes no difference to the rule in *Salomon* that one member owns all or substantially all of the shares. Until 1992, when the Twelfth EC Directive on Single-Member Companies was

---

[9] In *Re Baglan Hall Colliery Co* (1870) LR 5 Ch App 346, Giffard LJ states that it 'is the policy of the Companies Act to enable business people to incorporate their businesses and so avoid incurring further personal liability.'

implemented in this country, it was necessary for a company to have at least two members. (The number in 1844 was originally set at 25, but this number was reduced to 7 by CA 1862— the Act under which Mr Salomon's company was registered—and later to 2.) However, even under the former law it was possible for one person to own all the shares in a company *beneficially* and at the same time comply with the legislation by the simple expedient of vesting one or more shares in nominees who held the shares on his behalf and acted at his direction. In many other jurisdictions, the one-person company has been recognised for a long time.

The judgments in the lower courts in *Salomon*'s case (reported as *Broderip v Salomon* **[2.02]**) deserve study in their own right as examples of 'lifting the veil'. (For this topic, see below, p 51.)

[2.02] Broderip v Salomon [1895] 2 Ch 323 (Chancery Division and Court of Appeal)

VAUGHAN WILLIAMS J: No charge of fraud . . . is involved in the amended claim; but to allow a man who carries on business under another name to set up a debenture in priority to the claims of the creditors of the company would have the effect of defeating and delaying his creditors. There must be an implied agreement by him to indemnify the company. Under the Companies Act of 1862 a man may become what is called a private company so as to obtain the benefits of limited liability. I have already held, in a case where the founder of such a company had become bankrupt and the company claimed his assets, that the company was a mere fraud, and the Court of Appeal supported that decision. In this case I propose to hold the same thing—that this business was Mr Salomon's business and no one else's; that he chose to employ as agent a limited company; that he is bound to indemnify that agent, the company; and that his agent, the company, has a lien on the assets which overrides his claims. The creditors of the company could, in my opinion, have sued Mr Salomon. Their right to do so would depend on the circumstances of the case, whether the company was a mere alias of the founder or not. In this case it is clear that the relationship of principal and agent existed between Mr Salomon and the company . . .

[His Lordship accordingly ordered that Salomon was bound to indemnify the company for the debts which, as his agent, it had incurred.

Salomon appealed to the Court of Appeal, which affirmed this decision on different grounds:]

LINDLEY LJ: The incorporation of the company cannot be disputed. (See s 18 of the Companies Act 1862 [CA 2006, ss 15 and 16].) Whether by any proceedings in the nature of a scire facias the court could set aside the certificate of incorporation is a question which has never been considered, and on which I express no opinion;[10] but, be that as it may, in such an action as this the validity of the certificate cannot be impeached. The company must, therefore, be regarded as a corporation, but as a corporation created for an illegitimate purpose. Moreover, there having always been seven members, although six of them hold only one £1 share each, Mr Aron Salomon cannot be reached under s 48 [CA 2006, ss 437 and 438] to which I have already alluded. As the company must be recognised as a corporation, I feel a difficulty in saying that the company did not carry on business as a principal, and that the debts and liabilities contracted in its name are not enforceable against it in its corporate capacity. But it does not follow that the order made by Vaughan Williams J is wrong. A person may carry on business as a principal and incur debts and liabilities as such, and yet be entitled to be indemnified against those debts and liabilities by the person for whose benefit he carries on the business. The company in this case has been regarded by Vaughan Williams J as the agent of Aron Salomon. I should rather liken the company to a trustee for him—a trustee improperly brought into existence by him to enable him to do what the statute prohibits. It is manifest that the

---

[10] [See now *R v Registrar of Companies, ex p A-G* **[1.08]**.]

other members of the company have practically no interest in it, and their names have merely been used by Mr Aron Salomon to enable him to form a company, and to use its name in order to screen himself from liability . . . In a strict legal sense the business may have to be regarded as the business of the company; but if any jury were asked, Whose business was it? they would say Aron Salomon's, and they would be right, if they meant that the beneficial interest in the business was his. I do not go so far as to say that the creditors of the company could sue him. In my opinion, they can only reach him through the company. Moreover, Mr Aron Salomon's liability to indemnify the company in this case is, in my view, the legal consequence of the formation of the company in order to attain a result not permitted by law. The liability does not arise simply from the fact that he holds nearly all the shares in the company. A man may do that and yet be under no such liability as Mr Aron Salomon has come under. His liability rests on the purpose for which he formed the company, on the way he formed it, and on the use which he made of it. There are many small companies which will be quite unaffected by this decision. But there may possibly be some which, like this, are mere devices to enable a man to carry on trade with limited liability, to incur debts in the name of a registered company, and to sweep off the company's assets by means of debentures which he has caused to be issued to himself in order to defeat the claims of those who have been incautious enough to trade with the company without perceiving the trap which he has laid for them . . .

LOPES LJ: It would be lamentable if a scheme like this could not be defeated. If we were to permit it to succeed, we should be authorising a perversion of the Joint Stock Companies Acts. We should be giving vitality to that which is a myth and a fiction. The transaction is a device to apply the machinery of the Joint Stock Companies Act to a state of things never contemplated by that Act— an ingenious device to obtain the protection of that Act in a way and for objects not authorised by that Act, and in my judgment in a way inconsistent with and opposed to its policy and provisions. It never was intended that the company to be constituted should consist of one substantial person and six mere dummies, the nominees of that person, without any real interest in the company. The Act contemplated the incorporation of seven independent bona fide members, who had a mind and a will of their own, and were not the mere puppets of an individual who, adopting the machinery of the Act, carried on his old business in the same way as before, when he was a sole trader. To legalise such a transaction would be a scandal.

But to what relief is the liquidator entitled? In the circumstances of this case it is, in my opinion, competent for the court to set aside the sale as being a sale from Aron Salomon to himself—a sale which had none of the incidents of a sale, was a fiction, and therefore invalid; or to declare the company to be a trustee for Aron Salomon, whom Aron Salomon, the cestui que trust, was bound to indemnify; or to declare the formation of the company, the agreement of August 1892, and the issue of the debentures to Aron Salomon pursuant to such agreement, to be merely devices to enable him to carry on business in the name of the company with limited liability, contrary to the true intent and meaning of the Companies Act 1862, and further, to enable him to obtain a preference over other creditors of the company by obtaining a first charge on the assets of the company by means of such debentures . . .

KAY LJ delivered a concurring judgment.

The company as a separate legal person

The property of a company belongs to it and not to its members. Neither a member nor a creditor of a company (unless a secured creditor) has an insurable interest in the assets of the company.

[2.03] Macaura v Northern Assurance Co [1925] AC 619 (House of Lords)

Macaura, the owner of the Killymoon estate in county Tyrone, sold the whole of the timber on the estate to a company, Irish Canadian Sawmills Ltd, in consideration of the allotment to him of 42,000 fully paid £1 shares. All the company's shares were held by Macaura and his nominees, and he was also an unsecured creditor of the company for an amount of £19,000. Following the sale, he effected insurance policies in his own name with the respondent insurance company and others, covering the timber against fire. Two weeks later, almost all of the timber was destroyed in a fire. A claim brought by Macaura on the policies was disallowed on the ground that he had no insurable interest in the timber.

> LORD SUMNER: My Lords, this appeal relates to an insurance on goods against loss by fire. It is clear that the appellant had no insurable interest in the timber described. It was not his. It belonged to the Irish Canadian Sawmills Ltd, of Skibbereen, co Cork. He had no lien or security over it and, though it lay on his land by his permission, he had no responsibility to its owner for its safety, nor was it there under any contract that enabled him to hold it for his debt. He owned almost all the shares in the company, and the company owed him a good deal of money, but, neither as creditor nor as shareholder, could he insure the company's assets. The debt was not exposed to fire nor were the shares, and the fact that he was virtually the company's only creditor, while the timber was its only asset, seems to me to make no difference. He stood in no 'legal or equitable relation to' the timber at all. He had no 'concern in' the subject insured. His relation was to the company, not to its goods, and after the fire he was directly prejudiced by the paucity of the company's assets, not by the fire . . .
>
> My Lords, I think this appeal fails.
>
> LORDS BUCKMASTER and WRENBURY delivered concurring opinions.
>
> LORDS ATKINSON and PHILLIMORE concurred.

➤ Note

Similarly in *JJ Harrison (Properties) Ltd v Harrison* [2001] EWCA Civ 1467, [2002] 1 BCLC 162, the court stated that there is no rule of company law which constitutes a company the trustee of its property and its members or shareholders as beneficiaries of that trust.

A company may make a valid and effective contract with one of its members. It is possible for a person to be at the same time wholly in control of a company (as its principal shareholder or member and its sole director) and an employee of that company.

[2.04] Lee v Lee's Air Farming Ltd [1961] AC 12 (Privy Council)

Lee, the appellant's late husband, had formed the respondent company to carry on his business of spreading fertilisers on farmland ('top-dressing') from the air. He held 2,999 of its 3,000 shares, and was by its articles of association appointed sole governing director and (also pursuant to the articles) employed at a salary as its chief pilot. He was killed in an aircraft crash while flying for the company. If he was a 'worker' (defined as 'any person who has entered into or works under a contract of service . . . with an employer . . . whether remunerated by wages, salary, or otherwise') then his widow was entitled to be paid compensation by his employer under the Workers' Compensation Act 1922 (NZ). The company, as required by statute, was insured against liability to pay its workers such compensation. Mrs Lee appealed successfully against the ruling of the Court of Appeal of New Zealand that Lee could not be a 'worker' when he was in effect also the employer.

The opinion of their Lordships was delivered by LORD MORRIS OF BORTH-Y-GEST:
The Court of Appeal recognised that a director of a company may properly enter into a service agreement with his company, but they considered that, in the present case, inasmuch as the deceased was the governing director in whom was vested the full government and control of the company he could not also be a servant of the company. After referring in his judgment to the delegation to the deceased of substantially all the powers of the company, North J said:[11]

'These powers were moreover delegated to him for life and there remained with the company no power of management whatsoever. One of his first acts was to appoint himself the only pilot of the company, for, although art 33 foreshadowed this appointment, yet a contract could only spring into existence after the company had been incorporated. Therefore, he became in effect both employer and worker. True, the contract of employment was between himself and the company . . . but on him lay the duty both of giving orders and obeying them. In our view, the two offices are clearly incompatible. There would exist no power of control and therefore the relationship of master-servant was not created.'

The substantial question which arises is, as their Lordships think, whether the deceased was a 'worker' within the meaning of the Workers' Compensation Act 1922 and its amendments. Was he a person who had entered into or worked under a contract of service with an employer? The Court of Appeal thought that his special position as governing director precluded him from being a servant of the company. On this view it is difficult to know what his status and position was when he was performing the arduous and skilful duties of piloting an aeroplane which belonged to the company and when he was carrying out the operation of top-dressing farm lands from the air. He was paid wages for so doing. The company kept a wages book in which these were recorded. The work that was being done was being done at the request of farmers whose contractual rights and obligations were with the company alone. It cannot be suggested that when engaged in the activities above referred to the deceased was discharging his duties as governing director. Their Lordships find it impossible to resist the conclusion that the active aerial operations were performed because the deceased was in some contractual relationship with the company. That relationship came about because the deceased as one legal person was willing to work for and to make a contract with the company which was another legal entity. A contractual relationship could only exist on the basis that there was consensus between two contracting parties. It was never suggested (nor in their Lordships' view could it reasonably have been suggested) that the company was a sham or a mere simulacrum. It is well established that the mere fact that someone is a director of a company is no impediment to his entering into a contract to serve the company. If, then, it be accepted that the respondent company was a legal entity their Lordships see no reason to challenge the validity of any contractual obligations which were created between the company and the deceased . . .

Nor in their Lordships' view were any contractual obligations invalidated by the circumstance that the deceased was sole governing director in whom was vested the full government and control of the company. Always assuming that the company was not a sham then the capacity of the company to make a contract with the deceased could not be impugned merely because the deceased was the agent of the company in its negotiation. The deceased might have made a firm contract to serve the company for a fixed period of years. If within such period he had retired from the office of governing director and other directors had been appointed his contract would not have been affected. The circumstance that in his capacity as a shareholder he could control the course of events would not in itself affect the validity of his contractual relationship with the company. When,

---

[11] [1959] NZLR 393 at 399.

therefore, it is said that 'one of his first acts was to appoint himself the only pilot of the company', it must be recognised that the appointment was made by the company, and that it was none the less a valid appointment because it was the deceased himself who acted as the agent of the company in arranging it. In their Lordships' view it is a logical consequence of the decision in *Salomon*'s case **[2.01]** that one person may function in dual capacities. There is no reason, therefore, to deny the possibility of a contractual relationship being created as between the deceased and the company. If this stage is reached then their Lordships see no reason why the range of possible contractual relationships should not include a contract for services, and if the deceased as agent for the company could negotiate a contract for services as between the company and himself there is no reason why a contract of service could not also be negotiated. It is said that therein lies the difficulty, because it is said that the deceased could not both be under the duty of giving orders and also be under the duty of obeying them. But this approach does not give effect to the circumstance that it would be the company and not the deceased that would be giving the orders. Control would remain with the company whoever might be the agent of the company to exercise it. The fact that so long as the deceased continued to be governing director, with amplitude of powers, it would be for him to act as the agent of the company to give the orders does not alter the fact that the company and the deceased were two separate and distinct legal persons. If the deceased had a contract of service with the company then the company had a right of control. The manner of its exercise would not affect or diminish the right to its exercise. But the existence of a right to control cannot be denied if once the reality of the legal existence of the company is recognised. Just as the company and the deceased were separate legal entities so as to permit of contractual relations being established between them, so also were they separate legal entities so as to enable the company to give an order to the deceased . . .

Ex facie there was a contract of service. Their Lordships conclude, therefore, that the real issue in the case is whether the position of the deceased as sole governing director made it impossible for him to be the servant of the company in the capacity of chief pilot of the company. In their Lordships' view, for the reasons which have been indicated, there was no such impossibility. There appears to be no greater difficulty in holding that a man acting in one capacity can give orders to himself in another capacity than there is in holding that a man acting in one capacity can make a contract with himself in another capacity. The company and the deceased were separate legal entities. The company had the right to decide what contracts for aerial top-dressing it would enter into. The deceased was the agent of the company in making the necessary decisions. Any profits earned would belong to the company and not to the deceased. If the company entered into a contract with a farmer, then it lay within its right and power to direct its chief pilot to perform certain operations. The right to control existed even though it would be for the deceased in his capacity as agent for the company to decide what orders to give. The right to control existed in the company, and an application of the principles of *Salomon*'s case demonstrates that the company was distinct from the deceased. As pointed out above, there might have come a time when the deceased would remain bound contractually to serve the company as chief pilot though he had retired from the office of sole governing director. Their Lordships consider, therefore, that the deceased was a worker and that the question posed in the case stated should be answered in the affirmative . . .

➤ Note

Although *Lee*'s case is undoubtedly correct as a ruling in company law, and in particular as authority for the propositions stated in the headnote above, the question whether a person should be regarded as an 'employee' of a company which he can control as a director or major shareholder may not always be so clear-cut. For instance, in the context of the legislation relating to redundancy payments, the court may consider that such a person is not to be treated as an 'employee' entitled to compensation for unfair or wrongful dismissal: *Buchan v Secretary of State for Trade and Industry* [1997] IRLR 80. See this issue discussed in *Secretary of State for Trade and Industry v Bottrill* [1999] ICR 592, CA.

The fact that one person holds all, or substantially all, of the shares in a company does not, without more, make the company's business that person's business in the eyes of the law.

[2.05] Gramophone and Typewriter Co Ltd v Stanley [1908] 2 KB 89 (Court of Appeal)

All the shares in a German company (Deutsche Grammophon Aktiengesellschaft) were held by the appellant company, which was resident for tax purposes in England. The appellant was assessed for income tax not only upon the profits of the German company actually remitted to it in England, but also on a sum of £15,000 retained by the German company and transferred by it to a depreciation fund. The unremitted profits were taxable in England only if (as the Commissioners of Inland Revenue had held) they were the profits or gains of a business 'carried on' by the *English* company. The Court of Appeal rejected this view.

BUCKLEY LJ: The question is, I think, one of fact . . . The question of fact is whether the business in Germany is carried on by the appellant company. If it is, the [appellants] do not dispute that the Attorney-General is right. If, on the contrary, the German business is not carried on by the English company, then equally the Attorney-General cannot dispute but that the English company is assessable only upon the dividends which it may receive upon its shares in the German company.

In order to succeed the Attorney-General must, I think, make out either, first, that the German company is a fiction, a sham, a simulacrum, and that in reality the English company, and not the German company, is carrying on the business; or, secondly, that the German company, if it is a real thing, is the agent of the English company. As regards the former of these, there are no facts at all to show that the German company is a pretence. It was formed in January 1900 by the union of three other companies, each of which brought in substantial properties, and of two individuals. It is duly constituted and governed according to German law, and there is no ground whatever for saying that it is other than a real German corporation carrying on business in Germany under circumstances in which the company and its officers are amenable to German law and with a view to the acquisition of profit. The only remaining question, therefore, is whether the German company is agent of the English company, whether the English company is really carrying on the business and is employing the German company to do so on its behalf. Upon this point the Attorney-General relies principally upon the fact that, as stated in para 17 of the case, the appellant company now holds all the shares of the German company. In my opinion this fact does not establish the relation of principal and agent between the English company and the German company. It is so familiar that it would be a waste of time to dwell upon the difference between the corporation and the aggregate of all the corporators. But I may point out the following considerations as bearing upon the question whether the possession of all the shares is evidence of agency. Suppose that during the year whose accounts are under review the appellant company had held no shares at all in the first six months and had held all the shares in the last six months, or suppose that, having held all the shares but ten today, it became the holder of all tomorrow and again parted with ten the next day, it cannot seriously be suggested that each time one person becomes the holder of all the shares an agency comes into existence which dies again when he parts with some of them.

Further it is urged that the English company, as owning all the shares, can control the German company in the sense that the German company must do all that the English company directs. In my opinion this again is a misapprehension. This court decided not long since, in *Automatic Self-Cleansing Filter Syndicate Co Ltd v Cuninghame* [4.05] that even a resolution of a numerical majority at a general meeting of the company cannot impose its will upon the directors when the articles have confided to them the control of the company's affairs. The directors are not servants to obey directions given by the shareholders as individuals; they are not agents appointed by and bound to serve the shareholders as their principals. They are persons who may by the regulations be entrusted with the control of the business, and if so entrusted they can be dispossessed from that control only by the statutory majority which can alter the articles. Directors are not, I think, bound to comply with the directions even of all the corporators acting as individuals. Of course the corporators have it in their power by proper resolutions, which would generally be special resolutions,[12] to remove directors who do not act as they desire, but this in no way answers the question here to be considered, which is whether the corporators are engaged in carrying on the business of the corporation. In my opinion they are not. To say that they are involves a complete confusion of ideas . . .

COZENS-HARDY MR and FLETCHER MOULTON LJ delivered concurring judgments.

[2.06] Lonrho Ltd v Shell Petroleum Co Ltd [1980] QB 358 (Court of Appeal); affd [1980] 1 WLR 627 (House of Lords)

Lonrho sought an order for discovery [disclosure] of certain documents which it claimed were in the 'power' of two multinational oil companies, Shell and BP. These documents were held in Rhodesia (now Zimbabwe) and South Africa by local subsidiaries of Shell and BP, the subsidiaries being in each case wholly owned and controlled by those companies between them. The application was refused.

SHAW LJ: This appeal poses as its principal issue a compact question as to the application and scope of RSC, Ord 24. When is a document in the power (as distinct from the possession or control) of a party to litigation so as to require him to disclose it if it relates to matters in question in that litigation?

The question seems elementary, but it poses for me at any rate a difficult philosophical problem as to what constitutes power, and I must confess to some vacillation as the arguments on either side proceeded. In the end I have come to the view that a document can be said to be in the power of a party for the purpose of disclosure only if, at the time and in the situation which obtains at the date of discovery, that party is, on the factual realities of the case virtually in possession (as with a one-man company in relation to documents of the company) or otherwise has a present indefeasible legal right to demand possession from the person in whose possession or control it is at that time.

In the present case no such sure or direct route to acquiring possession existed or exists. The relationship between Shell and BP, on the one hand, and, on the other hand, the various subsidiaries, including those which are wholly owned by the two parent companies, may afford an ultimate but not an immediate or certain prospect of acquiring possession of documents which belong to and are in the possession and control for the time being of a subsidiary. The realisation of that prospect might involve the alteration of the articles of an unwilling or recalcitrant subsidiary followed by the removal of its then directors and their substitution by others more compliant. This would involve a radical transformation of the local scene within the subsidiary company. It would involve not merely raising the corporate veil, but committing an affront on the persona of the company itself. Even then, the directors who are substituted for the recalcitrant ones may find that there exists a conflict of duty so that they have no right to comply with the requirement. It would follow that the outcome of such a procedure would be at the best dubious . . .

There are no doubt situations, such as existed in B v B (Matrimonial Proceedings: Discovery)[13] where on the established facts a company is so utterly subservient or subordinated to the will and the wishes of some other person (whether an individual or a parent company) that compliance with that other person's demands can be regarded as assured. Each case must depend upon its own facts and also upon the nature, degree and context of the control . . .

LORD DENNING MR and BRANDON LJ delivered concurring judgments.

[An appeal to the House of Lords was dismissed: [1980] 1 WLR 627.]

---

12 [An ordinary resolution is now sufficient in all cases: CA 2006 s 168.]
13 [1978] Fam 181, [1979] 1 All ER 801.

[2.07] Tunstall v Steigmann [1962] 2 QB 593, [1962] 2 All ER 417
(Court of Appeal)

Mrs Tunstall ('the tenant') carried on business as a wardrobe dealer in shop premises leased from Mrs Steigmann ('the landlord'). Mrs Steigmann also owned the next-door shop, where she carried on the business of a pork-butcher. In April 1961 the landlord gave the tenant six months' notice to quit, and resisted the latter's application for a new tenancy, made under the Landlord and Tenant Act 1954, on ground (g) of s 30(1) of that Act, which reads as follows: ' . . . that on the termination of the current tenancy the landlord intends to occupy the hold-ing for the purposes, or partly for the purposes, of a business to be carried on by him therein'. Before the matter came on for hearing, Mrs Steigmann had formed a company, in which she held all but two of the shares (and held the two also through nominees), to take over her business. The county court judge held that she might still intend to carry on the business notwithstanding that it was owned by the company, and he refused to grant the tenant a new lease. The tenant's appeal was allowed by the Court of Appeal.

WILLMER LJ: The judge decided that the landlord was entitled to succeed. He took the view that in common sense where an individual is in such complete control of the company it can truthfully be said that the intention is to occupy for the purposes of his or her business, such business being the running of the company.

Mr Bramall, in an attractive and forceful argument, has sought to support the judge's view on a number of grounds. First, he says that construing the language of the subsection in accordance with the ordinary meaning of the words used, the landlord here did intend to occupy the holding for the purposes of a business to be carried on by her. The business was in substance her business, the company being a mere piece of mechanism to enable the landlord's business to be carried on. This, it is said, was the reality; and we were invited to look at the reality and substance of the proposed occupation rather than at its form . . .

I have certainly felt the force of the argument on behalf of the landlord; but in the end I am satis-fied that it cannot prevail. There is no escape from the fact that a company is a legal entity entirely separate from its corporators—see Salomon v A Salomon & Co Ltd **[2.01]**. Here the landlord and her company are entirely separate entities. This is no matter of form; it is a matter of substance and real-ity. Each can sue and be sued in its own right; indeed, there is nothing to prevent the one from suing the other. Even the holder of 100 per cent of the shares in a company does not by such holding become so identified with the company that he or she can be said to carry on the business of the company. This clearly appears from Gramophone and Typewriter Co Ltd v Stanley **[2.05]**, a decision of this court which seems to me, on due consideration, to be destructive of the argument for the landlord. As was pointed out by Fletcher Moulton LJ, control of a company by a corporator is wholly different in fact and law from carrying on the business himself. 'The individual corporator does not carry on the business of the corporation.' This being so, I do not see how it is possible for the land-lord in the present case to assert that she intends to occupy the holding for the purpose of a busi-ness to be carried on by her. Her intention, as has been made plain, is that the company which she controls shall carry on its business on the holding. But that, unfortunately for her, is something for which the Act makes no provision . . . She cannot, therefore, successfully oppose the grant of a new tenancy.

I have reached this conclusion with some reluctance, for it seems to me that the construction of s 30(1)(g), which I have felt compelled to adopt, may well lead to some very bizarre results. Thus it will be possible for an absentee landlord, living in idleness away from the holding, to resist the grant of a new tenancy upon proof of an intention to occupy, through his agent or manager, for the pur-pose of carrying on his business through such agent or manager. On the other hand, a hard-work-ing landlord, who has transferred his business to a company of which he retains complete control, and who genuinely needs to obtain possession of the holding so that his company's business may be carried on there with the aid of his own labour, will nevertheless apparently be without any right to oppose an application for a new tenancy by a tenant however undeserving. It seems, however, impossible to escape the conclusion that this is the effect of what Parliament has enacted. If the results are thought undesirable, only Parliament can put that right . . .

ORMEROD and DANCKWERTS LJJ delivered concurring judgments.

➤ Note

The legislation has since been amended. It is now provided by s 30(3) of the Landlord and Tenant Act 1954 (inserted by s 6 of the Law of Property Act 1969) that where a landlord has a controlling interest in a company, any business to be carried on by the company shall be treated for the purpose of the Act as a business to be carried on by him.

There is a presumption that the word 'person' be construed as including a company, although the final analysis depends on the context.

[2.08] Pharmaceutical Society v London and Provincial Supply Association Ltd (1880) 5 App Cas 857 (House of Lords)

The Pharmacy Act 1868 prohibited 'any person' from selling or keeping an open shop for retailing poisons unless such person was qualified and registered as a pharmaceutical chemist. The respondent company was prosecuted for an infringement of the Act. The sale of chemicals by the company was superintended by a registered chemist, who was a salaried employee and also a minority shareholder in the company. The House of Lords held that the company had not infringed the statute.

LORD BLACKBURN: I own I have no great doubt myself . . . that the word 'person' may very well include both a natural person, a human being, and an artificial person, a corporation. I think that in an Act of Parliament, unless there be something to the contrary, probably (but that I should not like to pledge myself to) it ought to be held to include both. I have equally no doubt that in common talk, the language of men not speaking technically, a 'person' does not include an artificial person, that is to say, a corporation. Nobody in common talk if he were asked, Who is the richest person in London, would answer, The London and North-Western Railway Co. The thing is absurd. It is plain that in common conversation and ordinary speech, 'a person' would mean a natural person: in technical language it may mean the artificial person: in which way it is used in any particular Act, must depend upon the context and the subject-matter. I do not think that the presumption that it does include an artificial person, a corporation, if that is the presumption, is at all a strong one. Circumstances, and indeed circumstances of a slight nature in the context, might shew in which way the word is to be construed in an Act of Parliament, whether it is to have the one meaning or the other. . . .

But, my Lords, my conclusion, looking at this Act, is that it is clear to my mind that the word 'person' here is so used to show that it does not include a corporation, and that there is no object or intention of the statute which shows that it is requisite to extend the word to a sense which probably those who used it in legislation, were not thinking of at all. I do not think that the legislature was thinking of bodies corporate at all. Beginning with the preamble the Act says, 'Whereas it is expedient for the safety of the public that persons keeping open shop for the retailing, dispensing, or compounding of poisons, and persons known as chemists and druggists, should possess a competent practical knowledge of their business'. Stopping there it is quite plain that those who used that language were not thinking of corporations. A corporation may in one sense, for all substantial purposes of protecting the public, possess a competent knowledge of its business, if it employs competent directors, managers, and so forth. But it cannot possibly have a competent knowledge in itself.

The metaphysical entity, the legal 'person', the corporation, cannot possibly have a competent knowledge. Nor, I think, can a corporation be supposed to be a 'person known as a chemist and druggist' . . . A body corporate may keep an open shop, and no mischief is done, if . . . qualified persons perform or superintend the sale . . .

> Notes

1. This case concerned the interpretation of a statute; but the views of Lord Blackburn have also served as a guide in the construction of other documents, eg in *Re Jeffcock's Trust* (1882) 51 LJ Ch 507, where a limited company was held to be a 'person' within the terms of a power to lease conferred by will. The courts have gone so far as to hold that a company is a 'person of full age' within the meaning of the Law of Property Act 1925 (*Re Earl of Carnarvon's Chesterfield Settled Estates* [1927] 1 Ch 138)[14] but have stopped short of holding that a company is capable of 'exercising itself in the duties of piety and true religion' (*Rolloswin Investments Ltd v Chromolit Portugal Cutelarias e Produtos Metálicos SARL* [1970] 1 WLR 912), or of being deemed a rogue and a vagabond (*A-G v Walkergate Press Ltd* (1930) 142 LT 408: compare *R v Registrar of Joint Stock Companies, ex p More* **[1.05]**). In *Winkworth v Edward Baron Development Co Ltd* **[6.05]**, Lord Templeman found no difficulty in ascribing to a limited company a 'conscience'. The Scottish courts have ruled that a company is incapable of shame, and so cannot be guilty of 'shameless conduct': *Dean v John Menzies (Holdings) Ltd* 1981 SLT 50. But it has been held that a company has a reputation and so can sue in defamation: *D and L Caterers Ltd and Jackson v D'Ajou* [1945] KB 364, CA (allegation that company had procured supplies on the black market). It is entitled to protection from invasion of its privacy (*R v Broadcasting Standards Commission, ex p BBC* [2001] 1 BCLC 244, CA (secret filming of transactions in Dixons' shops), but not to compensation for wrongful conviction on a criminal charge (*R v Secretary of State for the Home Department, ex p Atlantic Commercial (UK) Ltd* [1997] BCLC 692).

2. The Interpretation Act 1978, s 5 and Sch 1, confirms the ruling in the *Pharmaceutical Society* case by providing that in any Act, unless the contrary intention appears, 'person' includes a body of persons corporate or unincorporate; and those who draft legislation regularly make distinction between the term 'person' (which includes a corporate body) and 'individual' (which does not). The use of these terms in (respectively) the Company Directors Disqualification Act 1986 and the Criminal Justice Act 1993, Pt V, means that a company can be the subject of a disqualification order prohibiting it from acting as a director, but not convicted of insider dealing.

A company's nationality is determined by the place of its registration, and it retains that nationality throughout its existence.

[2.09] Kuenigl v Donnersmarck [1955] 1 QB 515 (Queen's Bench Division)

[The facts are immaterial.]

[MCNAIR J referred to *Daimler Co Ltd v Continental Tyre & Rubber Co Ltd* **[2.12]** and continued:] Neither of these passages in Lord Simon's or Lord Wright's speeches is dealing with the question which I have to deal with, namely, whether an English company found to have enemy character by reason of enemy control ceases to be in the eye of the English law an English company and subject

---

[14] See also *Re Lindsay Bowman Ltd* [1969] 1 WLR 1443 at 1448, where Megarry J, referring to s 353(6) of the Act of 1948, said: 'In obedience to Parliament, I must assume that the artificial and impersonal entity that we know as a limited company has been endowed with the capacity not merely of having feelings but also of feeling aggrieved even though it has ceased to exist.'

to the prohibition which English law imposes on persons subject to that law. On this question there is, so far as I know, no direct authority, but such authority as there is in my judgment strongly suggests a negative answer. [His Lordship discussed the cases and continued:] Enemy character is not substituted for the original character, but is something added to it. An English company which has acquired enemy character continues to owe its very existence to English law (under which it was incorporated) and remains subject to all its obligations towards the Crown under the Companies Acts as an English company. It would, in my judgment, be absurd that the acquisition of enemy character should release it from the obligations attaching to an English company and enable it to do lawfully things which an English company not possessing enemy character was lawfully unable to do . . .

I think that it is . . . clear that, in so far as nationality can by analogy be applied to a juristic person, its nationality is determined in an inalienable manner by the laws of the country from which it derives its personality . . .

A company is capable of having a domicile. Its domicile is the place of its registration, and it retains the domicile throughout its existence.[15]

[2.10] Gasque v IRC [1940] 2 KB 80 (King's Bench Division)

A taxpayer cannot avoid income tax liability by transferring property so that income otherwise receivable by him becomes payable to a person 'resident or domiciled out of the United Kingdom': the income is deemed to remain that of the taxpayer (Finance Act 1936 s 18, now replaced by Income and Corporation Taxes Act 1988 s 739). Mrs Gasque had transferred property to MD Company Ltd, a company incorporated in Guernsey but doing some business in England. She claimed that it was domiciled in the United Kingdom, so that the statute did not apply, but the Commissioners of Inland Revenue ruled that it was domiciled in Guernsey, and assessed her to tax accordingly. The court upheld the view of the Commissioners.

MACNAGHTEN J: The only question at issue on this appeal is whether the MD Company Ltd is a 'person resident or domiciled out of the United Kingdom' within the meaning of that section.

It was suggested by Mr Needham on behalf of the appellant that by the law of England a body corporate has no domicil. It is quite true that a body corporate cannot have a domicil in the same sense as an individual any more than it can have a residence in the same sense as an individual. But by analogy with a natural person the attributes of residence, domicil and nationality can be given, and are, I think, given by the law of England to a body corporate. It is not disputed that a company formed under the Companies Acts has British nationality, though, unlike a natural person, it cannot change its nationality. So, too, I think, such a company has a domicil—an English domicil if registered in England, and a Scottish domicil if registered in Scotland. The domicil of origin, or the domicil of birth, using with respect to a company a familiar metaphor, clings to it throughout its existence . . .

➤ Note

An SE (*Societas Europea*)[16] is able to move freely within the EU changing its domicile at will. The Commission's plan for a 14th Company Law Directive would enable all EU companies to move within the Union in the same manner.

---

[15] This is the rule in English law and most other legal systems, but in others domicile may be determined by reference to some other factor such as the company's principal place of business. In some jurisdictions a corporate body is not recognised as having a domicile at all. Under the rules of private international law, the law of the domicile regulates questions relating to the validity of the company's incorporation, its dissolution, the effect of a merger, its capacity and the rights and liabilities of its members (including limited liability). It is not possible under our law for a company to transfer its incorporation and domicile to another jurisdiction, as is the case in many other countries.

[16] Regulation (EC) No 2157/2001 allows registration by the companies registrar of any member state of a European public limited-liability company. The Regulation is also known as the Statute for a European Company.

A company may have an enemy or neutral character in time of war. This is determined not by any formal test but by reference to the character of the natural person or persons really in control.

See [2.12] Daimler Co Ltd v Continental Tyre and Rubber Co Ltd

A company's residence[17] *is where it 'really keeps house and does its real business'; its 'real business' is carried on where the central management and control actually abides.*[18]

[2.11] De Beers Consolidated Mines Ltd v Howe [1906] AC 455
(House of Lords)

[The facts appear from the judgment.]

LORD LOREBURN LC: Now, it is easy to ascertain where an individual resides, but when the inquiry relates to a company, which in a natural sense does not reside anywhere, some artificial test must be applied.

Mr Cohen propounded a test which had the merits of simplicity and certitude. He maintained that a company resides where it is registered, and nowhere else. If that be so, the appellant company must succeed, for it is registered in South Africa.

I cannot adopt Mr Cohen's contention. In applying the conception of residence to a company, we ought, I think, to proceed as nearly as we can upon the analogy of an individual. A company cannot eat or sleep,[19] but it can keep house and do business. We ought, therefore, to see where it really keeps house and does business. An individual may be of foreign nationality, and yet reside in the United Kingdom. So may a company. Otherwise it might have its chief seat of management and its centre of trading in England under the protection of English law, and yet escape the appropriate taxation by the simple expedient of being registered abroad and distributing its dividends abroad. The decision of Kelly CB and Huddleston B in the *Calcutta Jute Mills Co Ltd v Nicholson*[20] and the *Cesena Sulphur Co v Nicholson*,[21] now thirty years ago, involved the principle that a company resides for purposes of income tax where its real business is carried on. Those decisions have been acted upon ever since. I regard that as the true rule, and the real business is carried on where the central management and control actually abides.

It remains to he considered whether the present case fails within that rule. This is a pure question of fact to be determined, not according to the construction of this or that regulation or by-law, but upon a scrutiny of the course of business and trading.

The case stated by the commissioners gives an elaborate explanation of the way in which this company carried on its business. The head office is formally at Kimberley, and the general meetings have always been held there. Also the profits have been made out of diamonds raised in South Africa and sold under annual contracts to a syndicate for delivery in South Africa upon terms of division of profits realised on resale between the company and the syndicate. And the annual contracts contain provisions for regulating the market in order to realise the best profits on resale. Further,

[17] The concept of a company's 'residence' is primarily of importance in revenue law, but it may also be relevant in other contexts, eg in regard to the place where documents may be served on it. A company which is resident in the United Kingdom may not change its residence without the consent of the Treasury (Income and Corporation Taxes Act 1988 s 765(1)). This provision has been held not to be incompatible with the 'freedom of establishment' principle contained in art 43 of the Treaty of Rome: *R v HM Treasury, ex p Daily Mail and General Trust plc* [1989] QB 446, [1989] 1 All ER 328, ECJ.

[18] Other cases show that the 'central management and control' of a company may in fact be divided, so that its residence is in more than one country: see eg *Union Corpn Ltd v IRC* [1952] 1 All ER 646, CA; (affd on other grounds [1953] AC 482, HL).

[19] ['Neither can it be a television entertainer or author'; per Viscount Dilhorne in *Newstead v Frost* [1980] 1 All ER 363 at 368, [1980] 1 WLR 135 at 139, HL. Nor a lorry driver: *Richmond upon Thames London Borough Council v Pinn & Wheeler Ltd* [1989] RTR 354.]

[20] (1876) 1 Ex D 428.

[21] Ibid.

some of the directors and life governors live in South Africa, and there are directors' meetings at Kimberley as well as in London. But it is clearly established that the majority of directors and life governors live in England, that the directors' meetings in London are the meetings where the real control is always exercised in practically all the important business of the company except the mining operations. London has always controlled the negotiation of the contracts with the diamond syndicates, has determined policy in the disposal of diamonds and other assets, the working and development of mines, the application of profits, and the appointment of directors. London has also always controlled matters that require to be determined by the majority of all the directors, which include all questions of expenditure except wages, materials, and such-like at the mines, and a limited sum which may he spent by the directors at Kimberley.

The commissioners, after sifting the evidence, arrived at the two following conclusions, viz: (1) That the trade or business of the appellant company constituted one trade or business, and was carried on and exercised by the appellant company within the United Kingdom at their London office. (2) That the head and seat and directing power of the affairs of the appellant company were at the office in London, from whence the chief operations of the company, both in the United Kingdom and elsewhere, were in fact controlled, managed and directed.

These conclusions of fact cannot be impugned, and it follows that this company was resident within the United Kingdom for purposes of income tax, and must be assessed on that footing. I think, therefore, that this appeal fails . . .

LORD JAMES OF HEREFORD delivered a concurring opinion.

LORDS MACNAGHTEN, ROBERTSON and ATKINSON concurred.

➤ Notes

1. The above cases show that, in English law, a company may be incorporated under the law of one jurisdiction but have its residence (its 'head and seat and directing power', to quote Lord Loreburn) in another. This is true also of the other countries which have derived their company law from England, and of the US state jurisdictions and the Netherlands. But in the rest of continental Europe there is a strict rule that a company may be incorporated only in the jurisdiction where it is to have its principal place of business (*siège réel*, or *Sitz*, usually translated 'seat'), and that if it moves its seat out of that jurisdiction it must be wound up. This difference of approach has been a source of considerable political difficulty and disagreement in EU negotiations in matters of company law. There is a belief that if the 'English' approach were to be adopted throughout the Community, many companies would seek to be incorporated in jurisdictions with the least strict legal regimes, whilst carrying on their business elsewhere in the EU. The consequence, it is feared, would be that member states would compete with each other by enacting very liberal companies legislation with minimal regulatory requirements in order to attract incorporations, and the revenues which they would bring, and that commercial standards would fall to unacceptable levels. For this reason, EU member states such as Germany, which have very prescriptive companies legislation, have striven to ensure that the rule of the 'seat' is maintained—for instance, in the EC Statute for a European Company (see above, p 21). In the US, there has for much of the past century been keen competition between the various state jurisdictions to attract incorporations from companies whose operations are based elsewhere. Delaware (one of the smallest states) has emerged as the outright winner. This phenomenon has been condemned by some commentators as a 'race to the bottom' or 'race of laxity', but others consider that the 'market' for incorporations, within which businessmen may shop around, brings with it all the merits of free competition especially in administrative simplicity, efficiency and responsiveness. Such empirical studies as have been undertaken do not demonstrate that commercial standards are any less high in Delaware than elsewhere. Indeed, it is argued that, because so much company

law expertise has come to be concentrated in the one area, Delaware has become uniquely placed to give a lead in this respect. These notions of 'place of incorporation' and 'seat' must be distinguished from the notion of 'centre of main business' (COMI), which can be crucial in cross-border insolvencies, and on which there is a substantial body of case law.

2. Many countries have a constitution or charter by which certain fundamental rights and freedoms are guaranteed, such as freedom of speech and religion, freedom to trade and do business, the privilege against self-incrimination and the right not to have property expropriated without compensation. The question whether a company should enjoy such constitutional guarantees is often one of great difficulty, and it is not surprising that courts in different jurisdictions have given conflicting rulings on what would appear to be much the same issue. The most obvious reason for such a discrepancy is likely to be the language of the relevant legislation: a charter of *human* rights, for example, is less likely to be construed so as to embrace corporate bodies than is a statement of *constitutional* freedoms. Differences in cultural or historical background may also play a part. But even where it is accepted that the freedoms and rights are to be accorded only to human beings, that is not necessarily the end of the matter. A court may be persuaded in some circumstances to 'lift the veil' (holding, for example, that interference with the right of a company to publish a newspaper is an infringement of the right to freedom of expression of the individuals concerned). Alternatively, it may accord standing to a company to challenge legislation as unconstitutional even though the company itself is not directly affected by it: thus, in *R v Big M Drug Mart Ltd* (1985) 18 DLR (4th) 321, the Supreme Court of Canada allowed such a challenge by a company, on the ground that the statute in question infringed the guarantee of freedom of religion and conscience in s 2(a) of the Canadian Charter of Rights and Freedoms, irrespective of any question whether a corporation can enjoy or exercise freedom of religion.

3. The enactment of the Human Rights Act 1998 (HRA 1998), which incorporated the European Convention on Human Rights into UK domestic law, stimulated interest in issues of this kind in this country. Although the title of the Convention refers to 'human' rights, some of its articles expressly confer rights and freedoms on 'legal' (as distinct from 'natural') persons—eg the right to property, the right to a fair trial in the determination of civil rights and the right to peaceful enjoyment of possessions. The European Court of Human Rights (ECHR) has held in a number of cases that a body corporate has *standing* to institute proceedings complaining of a violation of the Convention. As a result of the principle of separate corporate personality, if a company's Convention rights are infringed, no individual member of the entity is a victim of that breach. This means that no member has standing to apply to the ECHR or bring proceedings under the HRA 1998. The ECHR has however held that a form of derivative claim on behalf of the company would be available where it is not possible for those responsible for the company's litigation to make the application (*Credit and Industrial Bank v Czech Republic* (2003) ECHR 2003-XI).

4. While it is plain that some parts of the Convention cannot apply to companies (eg the right to life, the prohibition of torture and the right to marry), others can quite readily do so (the right to a fair trial,[22] no retrospective punishment for crimes, the right to freedom of expression[23]). One feature of the decisions of the ECHR which is rather at odds with the current attitude of our domestic courts is a much greater willingness to lift the corporate veil—eg treating shareholders as the 'victims' of an act aimed at their company.

---

[22] Article 6 of the Convention was invoked in *R (Alconbury Developments Ltd) v Secretary of State for the Environment, Transport and the Regions* [2001] UKHL 23, [2003] 2 AC 295.
[23] *R (North Cyprus Tourism Centre Ltd) v Transport for London* [2005] EWHC 1698, [2005] UKHRR 1231.

Limited liability of members and 'lifting the corporate veil'

Recall the general rule that if (as is usual) the liability of a company's members is limited 'by shares' or 'by guarantee', then the company's creditors cannot seek satisfaction from the members, even if the company has insufficient funds to pay its own liabilities in full: see above, p 20. Many of the cases cited above can be used to illustrate this. Notice in particular that members are not made liable to outsiders simply because (as members or shareholders) they controlled the company's activities and thus caused liability to be incurred (see, eg, *Salomon,* **[2.01]** and *Lee's Air Farming,* **[2.04]**).

Are there exceptions to this general rule? Are there times where the company's members *can* be called upon, by outsiders, to meet the company's unpaid liabilities? It is not difficult to imagine situations where outsiders might wish to do this. If a profitable holding company has an under-funded subsidiary that cannot meet tort liabilities to hundreds of victims of the subsidiary's negligence, then the victims may want payment from the parent company (ie from the subsidiary's shareholder—see, eg, *Adams v Cape Industries* **[2.19]**). Can they successfully seek this? The general rule says no, but are there ever any exceptions? Similarly, if a 'one-man company' is completely under-resourced and unable to meet its trading debts, but its 'one-man owner' is personally wealthy, can the company's creditors ever claim against the owner-shareholder? *Salomon* **[2.01]** was just such a case, so the general answer is clearly no, but, again, are there exceptions?

This section looks at the exceptions, and at the arguments that have been advanced both successfully and unsuccessfully by outsiders (or third parties) wishing to pursue such claims.

The meaning of 'lifting the corporate veil'

One final clarification may be helpful. 'Lifting the corporate veil' refers to the possibility of looking behind the company-framework (or behind the company's separate personality) to make the *members* liable, as an exception to the rule that they are normally shielded by the corporate shell (ie they are normally not liable to outsiders at all, and are only normally liable to pay the *company* what they agreed to pay by way of share purchase price or guarantee). Various arguments can be run: for example, the members are liable because, exceptionally, their acts are such as to constitute them 'principals' (and the company is merely an agent), or 'beneficiaries' (and the company is merely the trustee of the corporate assets for their benefit), or constructive trustees or 'knowing assistants' in a wrong committed by the company (see below, pp 58 ff). These are the possibilities examined below.

This is not to be confused with the possibility of making a company's *directors* liable. It is equally difficult for outsiders to sue the company's *directors* to make them carry liability for the company's unfulfilled obligations. Third parties must generally sue the company, not its directors. They can sue directors only when one of the agency or trust arguments aired above can be advanced (but this time in the context of the directors, not the members). *But* the directors' liability is by no means limited. The *company* can sue the directors for any wrongs they have committed to the company. These recoveries will accrue to the company, and so increase the chance that third parties will be paid. The directors' liability is not strict liability for losses (ie directors do not guarantee that the company will be a success), but liability for wrongs committed against the company, such as negligence and other breaches of duty to the company (see Chapter 6).

The process of 'lifting the corporate veil'

As already noted, the principle of separate corporate personality as confirmed[24] by *Salomon's* case and reasserted in later cases, some of which are cited above, forms the corner-stone of company law. The authority of these cases is unshakeable; and yet exceptionally in some instances the law *is* prepared to disregard or look behind the corporate personality and (it is claimed) have regard to the 'realities'[25] of the situation. To do so may involve, on the one hand, 'treating the rights or liabilities or activities of a company as the rights or activities or liabilities of its shareholders'—eg treating the business of a company as that of its principal shareholder—or, on the other hand, '[having] regard to the shareholding of the company for some legal purpose'[26]—eg looking to the nationality of the shareholders to determine whether a company is under enemy control in wartime (see the *Daimler* case **[2.12]**). This approach, known as 'lifting the veil' of incorporation, is sometimes expressly authorised by statute and sometimes adopted by the court of its own accord.

It would, perhaps, give a better perspective to the discussion if *Salomon's* case and the other cases quoted above were regarded not simply as restatements of an elementary and obvious principle, but as instances when a plea that the veil should be lifted, though perhaps initially successful, ultimately failed. (It is particularly instructive to re-examine, as examples of 'lifting the veil', the judgments of the lower courts in *Salomon's* case itself **[2.02]**, bearing in mind that the judges concerned were outstanding company lawyers of considerable experience. The judgments and speeches in this case may be contrasted with those in the *Daimler* case **[2.12]**, where a greatly enlarged Court of Appeal was almost unanimous in adhering to the orthodox line, which the Lords this time rejected.)

Some examples of 'lifting the veil' follow. But the topic cannot really be considered on its own as a phenomenon separable from the rest of company law. Again and again in the succeeding chapters we will encounter situations in which the issue before the court—or the problem faced by the legislature—has been, in essence, whether the separate personality of the company is to be respected or disregarded.

Many of the *statutory* directions to 'lift the veil' occur in revenue law (see above, p 47); Landlord and Tenant Act 1954 s 30(3) (see above, p 44), or the Trading with the Enemy Act 1939 s 2 (see above, p 46 and below, pp 54 ff). Provisions with similar effect in other statutes will occasionally be noticed. The Companies Act 2006 focuses instead on making *directors* liable for company wrongs, rather than allowing the 'veil' to be penetrated to make members liable (see below, Chapter 6).

In *Dimbleby & Sons Ltd v National Union of Journalists* [1984] 1 WLR 427 at 435, HL, Lord Diplock, whilst not wholly excluding the possibility that a contrary construction might sometimes be justified, said:

> The 'corporate veil' in the case of companies incorporated under the Companies Acts is drawn by statute and it can be pierced by some other statute if such other statute so provides; but, in view of its raison d'être and its constant recognition by the courts since *Salomon v A Salomon & Co Ltd* **[2.01]**, one would expect that any parliamentary intention to pierce the corporate veil would be expressed in clear and unequivocal language.

[24] Of course, the doctrine was recognised much earlier—see, for instance, *Edmunds v Brown and Tillard* (1668) 1 Lev 237, where members were held not liable on the bond of a corporation after its dissolution, and *Foss v Harbottle* **[11.01]**. The true significance of *Salomon's* case in its more immediate context is that it confirmed the legitimacy of the 'private' (very small) company and paved the way for its recognition by statute in 1907.

[25] It is noteworthy that an appeal to the 'realities' of the situation is often made both in the argument *for* lifting the veil and in the argument *against* it (see eg *Tunstall v Steigmann* **[2.07]**).

[26] The quoted phrases are taken from the judgment of Staughton LJ in *Atlas Maritime Co SA v Avalon Maritime Ltd* [1991] 4 All ER 769 at 779.

Judicial inroads into the principle of separate personality are numerous, and quite often made unconsciously. Commentators[27] have on the whole discerned no set pattern in the decided cases—indeed, in many instances they seem to contradict each other in the most baffling way. The plea is sometimes heard for 'some principles to be injected into this area of the law' from which 'litigants can predict when the courts will, and will not, lift the veil of the corporate entity'.[28] Perhaps there is something to be said for retaining some flexibility, especially where it enables the court to counter fraud, oppression or sharp practice[29] or to condone informality in the affairs of small companies.[30] In *Conway v Ratiu* [2006] 1 All ER 571, Auld LJ speaks of the 'readiness of the courts, regardless of the precise issue involved, to draw back the corporate veil to do justice when common sense and reality demand it.' His Lordship went on, 'there is . . . a powerful argument of principle . . . for lifting the corporate veil where the facts require it'. Laws LJ expressed 'emphatic agreement' with these statements.

On the other hand, in matters of property and contract, the courts should surely be most hesitant to lift the veil in response to superficial considerations of 'common sense' or 'reality' or 'fairness'. Those who adopt the corporate form should surely be expected to take the rough with the smooth. This was emphasised by Browne-Wilkinson V-C in *Tate Access Floors Inc v Boswell* [1991] Ch 512 at 531, where he said:

> If people choose to conduct their affairs through the medium of corporations, they are taking advantage of the fact that in law those corporations are separate legal entities, whose property and actions are in law not the property or actions of their incorporators or controlling shareholders. In my judgment controlling shareholders cannot, for all purposes beneficial to them, insist on the separate identity of such corporations but then be heard to say the contrary when discovery is sought against such corporations.[31]

A note of caution

At this point, it is perhaps appropriate to introduce a note of caution. The topic of 'lifting the veil' persists in company law textbooks (as in this one), yet all the signs are that, after a brief flurry of interest some decades ago, there is now little potential for it to develop into a doctrine of any substance. The first writers to discuss the topic appear to have been Kahn-Freund in (1944) 7 MLR 54 and Gower in the first edition of his *Modern Company Law*, published in 1954. (The cases which are cited below broadly follow Gower's analysis.) In the 1960s and early 1970s, the subject attracted a good deal of judicial attention (and, in the case of Lord Denning, positive enthusiasm). In the *DHN* case **[2.18]** the readiness of judges to use their interventionist powers and disregard the *Salomon* principle probably reached its peak. Since then, however, the trend has been almost entirely towards reasserting the orthodoxy of the

---

[27] For further reading, see PL Davies, *Gower's Principles of Modern Company Law* (7th edn, 2003), chapter 8; WG Friedmann, *Legal Theory* (5th edn, 1967), pp 556–572; O Kahn-Freund, 'Some Reflections on Company Law Reform' (1944) 7 MLR 54; AKR Kiralfy, 'Some Unforeseen Consequences of Private Incorporation' (1944) 65 LQR 231; A Samuels, 'Lifting the Veil' [1964] JBL 107; MA Pickering, 'The Company as a Separate Legal Entity' (1968) 31 MLR 481; CM Schmitthoff, '*Salomon* in the Shadow' [1976] JBL 305; M Whincup, 'Inequitable Incorporation' (1981) 2 Co Law 158; A Beck, 'The Two Sides of the Corporate Veil' in JH Farrar (ed), *Contemporary Issues in Company Law* (1987); FG Rixon, 'Lifting the Veil Between Holding and Subsidiary Companies' (1986) 102 LQR 415; S Ottolenghi 'From Peeping behind the Corporate Veil to Ignoring it Completely' (1990) 53 MLR 338; S Griffin, 'Holding Companies and Subsidiaries—the Corporate Veil' (1991) 12 Co Law 16; Lord Cooke of Thorndon, 'A Real Thing', in *Turning Points of the Common Law* (the 1996 Hamlyn lectures, 1997), and 'Corporate Identity' (1998) 16 C & SLJ 160.

[28] See the notes by Lord Wedderburn [1958] CLJ 152 at 155, (1960) 23 MLR 663 at 666.

[29] See eg *Re Darby* **[2.16]**; *Re Bugle Press Ltd* **[13.11]**; *Gilford Motor Co Ltd v Horne* **[2.17]**. There is of course, an element of question-begging in determining whether there *has* been such misuse of the privilege of incorporation, as is revealed in the attitudes of the different courts in *Salomon's* case itself.

[30] See below, p 58, and compare the cases in which a small company has been treated as a quasi-partnership for the purpose of winding up (below, p 658).

[31] But note, *Conway v Ratiu* [2006] 1 All ER 571 where it was held that conducting a transaction with a 'metaphorical corporate veil' is irrelevant to the question of fact; *Diamantides v J.P. Morgan Chase Bank* [2005] EWCA Civ 1612.

Salomon principle—not only in this country (most notably in *Adams v Cape Industries plc* [2.19]), but also in Australia, Canada, New Zealand and South Africa. To take just one example, in *Creasey v Breachwood Motors Ltd* [1993] BCLC 480, where assets had been removed from company A to company B leaving a former employee with a worthless judgment against company A, the judge thought it in the interests of justice and also found good practical reasons to lift the veil by substituting company B as defendant. But any hopes that this might be the first sign of a revival of judicial willingness to lift the veil were soon dashed: in *Ord v Belhaven Pubs Ltd* [1998] 2 BCLC 447, CA, *Creasey* was peremptorily overruled.

Statutory lifting of the corporate veil

CA 2006 seems to ignore the possibility of lifting the corporate veil to make members of a company liable for the company's wrongs. Instead, attention is given to making *directors* and other officers liable for corporate wrongs in specified circumstances. These provisions emerge in the chapters that follow; there is little value in listing them all here.

In addition, the insolvency legislation contains a number of sections providing for directors (and others) to be personally liable for the debts of a limited company, or to make a contribution to its assets in a liquidation, eg where there has been fraudulent or wrongful trading (IA 1986 ss 213–215) or the improper re-use of an insolvent company's name (ss 216–217). Finally, the Company Directors Disqualification Act 1986 (CDDA) s 15 similarly penalises a person who acts as a director in breach of a disqualification order.

None of these examples involve *ignoring* the company's separate personality; they simply impose on defaulting directors (and perhaps other individuals) a liability *additional to* that of the company.

The court may go behind the veil of incorporation in order to determine whether a company is to be characterised as an 'enemy' in time of war.

[2.12] Daimler Co Ltd v Continental Tyre and Rubber Co (Great Britain) Ltd [1916] 2 AC 307 (House of Lords)

The Continental Tyre company was incorporated in England, but all except one of its shares were held by persons resident in Germany, and all the directors resided in Germany. The secretary, who held the remaining share, resided in England and was a British subject. The issue was whether the company had standing in an English court to sue and recover a debt when a state of war existed between England and Germany. The company was allowed by the Master to sign summary judgment without proceeding to trial. His decision was affirmed by Scrutton J in chambers and by a greatly enlarged Court of Appeal (Buckley LJ dissenting). [Extracts from the judgments delivered in the Court of Appeal appear below, [2.13].] The House of Lords unanimously reversed the order of the Court of Appeal, and directed that the action be struck out as irregular, on the ground that the secretary was not authorised to commence the action; and it held further (by a majority, Lords Shaw of Dunfermline and Parmoor dissenting) that the company, though incorporated in England, was capable of acquiring an enemy character, so that leave to sign summary judgment should not have been given.

LORD PARKER OF WADDINGTON: No one can question that a corporation is a legal person distinct from its corporators; that the relation of a shareholder to a company, which is limited by shares, is not in itself the relation of principal and agent or the reverse; that the assets of the company belong to it and the acts of its servants and agents are its acts, while its shareholders, as such, have no property in the assets and no personal responsibility for those acts. The law on the subject is clearly laid down in . . . *Salomon v A Salomon & Co Ltd* [2.01] . . . I do not think, however, that it is a necessary corollary of this reasoning to say that the character of its corporators must be irrelevant to the character of the company; and this is crucial, for the rule against trading with the enemy depends upon enemy character.

A natural person, though an English-born subject of His Majesty, may bear an enemy character and be under liability and disability as such by adhering to His Majesty's enemies. If he gives them active aid, he is a traitor; but he may fall far short of that and still be invested with enemy character. If he has what is known in prize law as a commercial domicil among the King's enemies, his merchandise is good prize at sea, just as if it belonged to a subject of the enemy power. Not only actively, but passively, he may bring himself under the same disability. Voluntary residence among the enemy, however passive or pacific he may be, identifies an English subject with His Majesty's foes. I do not think it necessary to cite authority for these well-known propositions, nor do I doubt that, if they had seemed material to the Court of Appeal, they would have been accepted.

How are such rules to be applied to an artificial person, incorporated by forms of law? As far as active adherence to the enemy goes, there can be no difference, except such as arises from the fact that a company's acts are those of its servants and agents acting within the scope of their authority . . .

In the case of an artificial person what is the analogue to voluntary residence among the King's enemies? Its impersonality can hardly put it in a better position than a natural person and lead to its being unaffected by anything equivalent to residence. It is only by a figure of speech that a company can be said to have a nationality or residence at all. If the place of its incorporation under municipal law fixes its residence, then its residence cannot be changed, which is almost a contradiction in terms, and in the case of a company residence must correspond to the birthplace and country of natural allegiance in the case of a living person, and not to residence or commercial domicil. Nevertheless, enemy character depends on these last. It would seem, therefore, logically to follow that, in transferring the application of the rule against trading with the enemy from natural to artificial persons, something more than the mere place or country of registration or incorporation must be looked at.

My Lords, I think that the analogy is to be found in control, an idea which, if not very familiar in law, is of capital importance and is very well understood in commerce and finance. The acts of a company's organs, its directors, managers, secretary, and so forth, functioning within the scope of their authority, are the company's acts and may invest it definitively with enemy character. It seems to me that similarly the character of those who can make and unmake those officers, dictate their conduct mediately or immediately, prescribe their duties and call them to account, may also be material in a question of the enemy character of the company. If not definite and conclusive, it must at least be prima facie relevant, as raising a presumption that those who are purporting to act in the name of the company are, in fact, under the control of those whom it is their interest to satisfy. Certainly I have found no authority to the contrary. Such a view reconciles the positions of natural and artificial persons in this regard, and the opposite view leads to the paradoxical result that the King's enemies, who chance during war to constitute the entire body of corporators in a company registered in England, thereby pass out of the range of legal vision, and, instead, the corporation, which in itself is incapable of loyalty, or enmity, or residence, or of anything but bare existence in contemplation of law and registration under some system of law, takes their place for almost the most important of all purposes, that of being classed among the King's friends or among his foes in time of war.

What is involved in the decision of the Court of Appeal is that, for all purposes to which the character and not merely the rights and powers of an artificial person are material, the personalities of the natural persons, who are its corporators, are to be ignored. An impassable line is drawn between the one person and the others. When the law is concerned with the artificial person, it is to know nothing of the natural persons who constitute and control it. In questions of property and capacity, of acts done and rights acquired or liabilities assumed thereby, this may be always true. Certainly it is so for the most part. But the character in which property is held, and the character in which the capacity to act is enjoyed and acts are done, are not in pari materia. The latter character is a quality of the company itself, and conditions its capacities and its acts. It is not a mere part of its energies or acquisitions, and if that character must be derivable not from the circumstances of its incorporation, which arises once for all, but from qualities of enmity and amity, which are dependent on the chances of peace or war and are attributable only to human beings, I know not from what human beings that character should be derived, in cases where the active conduct of the company's officers has not already decided the matter, if resort is not to be had to the predominant character of its shareholders and corporators . . .

THE EARL OF HALSBURY LC and LORD ATKINSON delivered concurring opinions.

VISCOUNT MERSEY and LORDS KINNEAR and SUMNER concurred.

LORDS SHAW OF DUNFERMLINE and PARMOOR delivered opinions concurring in the result, but dissenting on this point.

[Part of the majority judgment in the Court of Appeal is set out below. The arguments in favour of recognising or disregarding the corporate entity could hardly be contrasted more sharply. No doubt the factor which most influenced the House of Lords was the paramountcy of the public interest in wartime.]

[2.13] Continental Tyre and Rubber Co (Great Britain) Ltd v Daimler Co Ltd [1915] 1 KB 893 (Court of Appeal)

LORD READING CJ read the judgment of the majority of the court (LORD READING CJ, LORD COZENS-HARDY MR, KENNEDY, PHILLIMORE and PICKFORD LJJ):

It cannot be disputed that the plaintiff company is an entity created by statute. It is a company incorporated under the Companies Acts and therefore is a thing brought into existence by virtue of statutory enactment. At the outbreak of war it was carrying on business in the United Kingdom; it had contracted to supply goods, it delivered them, and until the outbreak of the war it was admittedly entitled to receive payment at the due dates. Has the character of the company changed because on the outbreak of war all the shareholders and directors resided in an enemy country and therefore became alien enemies? Admittedly it was an English company before the war. An English company cannot by reason of these facts cease to be an English company. It remains an English company regardless of the residence of its shareholders or directors either before or after the declaration of war. Indeed it was not argued by Mr Gore-Browne that the company ceased to be an entity created under English law, but it was argued that the law in time of war and in reference to trading with the enemy should sweep aside this 'technicality' as the entity was described and should treat the company not as an English company but as a German company and therefore as an alien enemy. If the creation and existence of the company could be treated as a mere technicality, there would be considerable force in this argument. It is undoubtedly the policy of the law as administered in our courts of justice to regard substance and to disregard form. Justice should not be hindered by mere technicality, but substance must not be treated as form or swept aside as technicality because that course might appear convenient in a particular case. The fallacy of the appellants' contention lies in the suggestion that the entity created by statute is or can be treated during the war as a mere form or technicality by reason of the enemy character of its shareholders and directors. A company formed and registered under the Companies Acts has a real existence with rights and liabilities as a separate legal entity. It is a different person altogether from the subscribers to the memorandum or the shareholders on the register (per Lord Macnaghten in *Salomon v A Salomon & Co Ltd* [2.01]). It cannot be technically an English company and substantially a German company except by the use of inaccurate and misleading language. Once it is validly constituted as an English company it is an artificial creation of the legislature and it retains its existence for all intents and purposes. It is a living thing with a separate existence which cannot be swept aside as a technicality. It is not a mere name or mask or cloak or device to conceal the identity of persons and it is not suggested that the company was formed for any dishonest or fraudulent purpose. It is a legal body clothed with the form prescribed by the legislature. . . .

For the appellants' contention to succeed, payment to the company must be treated as payment to the shareholders of the company, but a debt due to a company is not a debt due to all or any of its shareholders: *Salomon v Salomon & Co.* The company and the company alone is the creditor entitled to enforce payment of the debt and empowered to give to the debtor a good and valid discharge. Once this conclusion is reached it follows that payment to the plaintiff company is not payment to the alien enemy shareholders or for their benefit . . .

BUCKLEY LJ delivered a dissenting judgment.

➤ Notes

1. The view of the majority of the Court of Appeal was rejected by the House of Lords, as we have seen **[2.12]**. The Trading with the Enemy Act 1939 adopts the view of the House of Lords in the *Daimler* case:

Trading with the Enemy Act 1939

2 Definition of enemy
(1) Subject to the provisions of this section, the expression 'enemy' for the purposes of this Act means—
   (a) any state, or sovereign of a state, at war with His Majesty,
   (b) any individual resident in enemy territory,
   (c) any body of persons (whether corporate or unincorporated) carrying on business in any place, if and so long as the body is controlled by a person who, under this section, is an enemy or
   (d) any body of persons constituted or incorporated in, or under the laws of, a state at war with His Majesty;
but does not include any person by reason only that he is an enemy subject.

2. There are many contexts in company law in which the question of 'control' arises, but there is no single definition which meets all cases. In *Bermuda Cablevision Ltd v Colica Trust Co Ltd* [1998] 1 BCLC 1 at 9, PC Lord Steyn said: 'Expressions such as "control" and "controlling interest" take their colour from the context in which they appear. There is no general rule as to what the word "controlled" means. . . . The expression must be given the meaning which the context requires.' The elaborate definitions of 'subsidiary' and 'holding company' in CA 2006 s 1159, and the equally elaborate, but different, definitions of 'parent undertaking' and 'subsidiary undertaking' in s 1162 show the legislative draftsman wrestling with the problem. For other illustrations, see *Lonrho Ltd v Shell Petroleum Ltd* **[2.06]**, and the discussion of the 'fraud on the minority' exception to the 'rule in *Foss v Harbottle*', below, pp 517 ff.

3. Under the Merchant Shipping Act 1988 and regulations made thereunder only fishing vessels registered as 'British' were eligible to fish under the quota for the UK fixed by the EC. Vessels owned by a company could be so registered only if 75% of their shareholders fulfilled requirements as to British nationality, residence and domicile. The European Court of Justice in *R v Secretary of State for Transport, ex p Factortame Ltd (No 3)* [1992] QB 680 held that such a restriction was contrary to art 52 of the EC treaty, which guarantees freedom of establishment to the nationals of all member states.

➤ Question

Could a landlord be guilty of an offence under the Race Relations Act 1976 if he refused to lease premises to a company incorporated in England which was owned and controlled by three Russian businessmen?

An agency relationship between a company and its shareholders or controllers may,
exceptionally, be found to exist as a matter of fact.

[2.14] Re FG (Films) Ltd [1953] 1 WLR 483 (Chancery Division)

The applicant company sought to have the film 'Monsoon' registered as a British film under the Cinematograph Films Acts 1938–1948. The Board of Trade refused the application on the ground that the film had in reality been made by a large American company, Film Group Incorporated. By the terms of an agreement between the two companies, the American company had undertaken to provide finance and all the facilities required by the applicant to make the film. The applicant company sought a declaration that it was the 'maker' within the meaning of the Act.

VAISEY J: The applicants have a capital of £100, divided into 100 shares of £1 each, 90 of which are held by the American director and the remaining 10 by a British one. The third director has no shareholding. I now understand that they have no place of business apart from their registered office, and they did not employ any staff. It seems to me to be contrary, not only to all sense and reason, but to the proved and admitted facts of the case, to say or to believe that this insignificant company undertook in any real sense of that word the arrangements for the making of this film. I think that their participation in any such undertaking was so small as to be practically negligible, and that they acted, in so far as they acted at all in the matter, merely as the nominee of and agent for an American company called Film Group Incorporated, which seems (among other things) to have financed the making of the film to the extent of at least £80,000 under the auspices and direction of the said American director, who happened to be its president. The suggestion that this American company and that director were merely agents for the applicants is, to my mind, inconsistent with and contradicted by the evidence, and a mere travesty of the facts, as I understand and hold them to be.

The applicants' intervention in the matter was purely colourable. They were brought into existence for the sole purpose of being put forward as having undertaken the very elaborate arrangements necessary for the making of this film and of enabling it thereby to qualify as a British film. The attempt has failed, and the respondent's decision not to register 'Monsoon' as a British film was, in my judgment, plainly right.

➤ Question

Can you identify any special feature of this case which might make it distinguishable from *Gramophone & Typewriter Co Ltd v Stanley* [2.05]?

➤ Notes

1. In this case a finding of agency allowed the court to 'lift the veil'. It is to be observed that a similar finding of agency by the trial judge in *Salomon*'s case [2.01] was rejected by the House of Lords. On this point, Kerr LJ in *J H Rayner (Mincing Lane) Ltd v Department of Trade and Industry* [1989] Ch 72 at 189 observed:

The crucial point on which the House of Lords overruled the Court of Appeal in that landmark case was precisely the rejection of the doctrine that agency between a corporation and its members in relation to the corporation's contracts can be inferred from the control exercisable by the members over the corporation or from the fact that the sole objective of the corporation's contracts was to benefit the members. That rejection of the doctrine of agency to impugn the non-liability of the members for the acts of the corporation is the foundation of our modern company law.

2. We must therefore conclude that an actual agency must be shown on the evidence to exist and may not be inferred merely from control of a company or ownership of its shares. Of course,

there is nothing in principle to prevent a company from being an agent of its controlling shareholders, just as it can be an agent of anyone else. Such an agency can be created by express agreement, as in fact happened in the well-known *Rylands v Fletcher* case of *Rainham Chemical Works Ltd v Belvedere Fish Guano Co Ltd* [1921] 2 AC 465, HL. There, the company whose factory blew up had agreed to occupy the land owned by its two shareholders as their agent. The existence of an agency does not violate the *Salomon* principle; on the contrary, it affirms that the company, being capable of acting as an agent, is a separate person. But if a judge were free to *infer* an agency from the mere fact of control, more or less at will, then the result would be that the veil could be lifted as often as he chose, and the law would be unpredictable.

3. One instance of this is, perhaps, *Smith, Stone & Knight Ltd v Birmingham Corpn* [1939] 4 All ER 116, where Atkinson J, on facts very similar to those of *DHN Food Distributors Ltd v Tower Hamlets London Borough Council* [2.18], allowed a holding company to claim compensation as if it were an owner-occupier, on the ground that its subsidiary (which occupied the land in question) was merely its agent for the purpose of carrying on its business. This decision of Atkinson J, which is in marked contrast to *Gramophone and Typewriter Co Ltd v Stanley* [2.05], has been the subject of some criticism, eg by Pickering, (1968) 31 MLR 481 at 494, and by Toulson J in *Yukong Lines Ltd of Korea v Rendsburg Investments Corpn of Liberia (No 2)* (see below, p 69 Note 1).

4. There was also a finding of agency in the tax case of *Firestone Tyre and Rubber Co Ltd v Lewellin* [1957] 1 WLR 464, HL, where it was held that an English company which manufactured tyres in this country, and used them to fulfil orders for its American holding company, did so as the agent of the latter. But nothing in this decision was made to turn on the fact that the holding company had control of the English company.

A trust relationship, with the company as trustee and the members as beneficiaries, may, exceptionally, be found to exist as a matter of fact.

The other argument which found support in the lower courts in *Salomon's case*, based on a *trust* rather than an agency, will similarly fall to the ground unless a trust can be affirmatively proved. The evidence of such a trust in the case next cited was, to say the least, tenuous; but the court was plainly moved to find that it existed by the close analogy with an unincorporated members' club.

[2.15] Trebanog Working Men's Club and Institute Ltd v MacDonald [1940] 1 KB 576 (King's Bench Divisional Court)

The club was incorporated under the Industrial and Provident Societies Acts 1893–1913.[32] It bought liquor in its own name, paid for it by cheque drawn on its bank account, and served it to members in exchange for a money payment. The society was charged with selling liquor by retail without a licence, and was convicted. It appealed successfully to the Divisional Court.

LORD HEWART CJ read the judgment of the court (LORD HEWART CJ, HUMPHREYS and HILBERY JJ): The first general Act dealing with unlawful sales by retail of intoxicating liquor without a justices' licence was the Licensing Act 1872, which in s 3 created the offence now contained in s 65 of the Licensing (Consolidation) Act 1910 in almost identical terms. Ever since that date it has been a

---

[32] A second appeal concerned a charge based upon similar facts against the Monkwearmouth Conservative Club Ltd, which was incorporated under the Companies Acts. The cases were treated as indistinguishable and disposed of together.

matter of general agreement that the transaction which takes place in a members' club, in which the property in the liquor is in all the members equally, when a member orders and pays for intoxicating liquor, is not a sale at all in the sense in which that word is used in s 3, but is rather to be deemed the transfer of a special property in the goods from all the other members of the club to the consumer in consideration of the price paid. The aspect of the matter is fully explained in the judgments of Field J and Huddleston B in *Graff v Evans*.[33] The club in that case was a bona fide members' club, but, by rule 7 of the club rules 'all property acquired by the club shall be vested in the trustees'—no doubt, as Field J observed in his judgment, for the purpose of enabling them to sue or take other legal proceedings with respect to injuries to the possession of the goods belonging to the club. Field J, in holding that no sale by retail of intoxicating liquor took place when a member ordered and paid for a drink, put the matter in this way: 'I think the true construction of the rules is that the members were the joint owners of the general property in all the goods of the club, and that the trustees were their agents with respect to the general property in the goods.' Huddleston B, in concurring, says: 'It seems to me clear that [the member] had a property or at least an interest in the goods which were transferred to him.' The correctness of that decision has never, so far as we are aware, been doubted . . .

In our opinion, the decision in *Graff v Evans* applies to and governs the present case. Once it is conceded that a members' club does not necessarily require a licence to serve its members with intoxicating liquor, because the legal property in the liquor is not in the members themselves, it is difficult to draw any legal distinction between the various legal entities that may be entrusted with the duty of holding the property on behalf of the members, be it an individual, or a body of trustees, or a company formed for the purpose, so long as the real interest in the liquors remains, as in this case it clearly does, in the members of the club. There is no magic in this connection in the expressions 'trustee' or 'agent'. What is essential is that the holding of the property by the agent or trustee must be a holding for and on behalf of, and not a holding antagonistic to, the members of the club. We are dealing here with a quasi-criminal case, where the court seeks to deal with the substance of a transaction rather than the legal form in which it may be clothed . . .

➤ Notes

1. Three years earlier, Lord Hewart CJ had been one of the members of the Divisional Court which heard *Wurzel v Houghton Main Home Delivery Service Ltd* [1937] 1 KB 380, DC. In this case, miners had formed two co-operative associations to run lorries for the delivery of coal to their homes, for which a payment based on mileage was made. The one association was unincorporated, and the court ruled that the lorry was being used by its co-owners, the members, to haul their own coal, and so there was no 'carriage of goods for hire or reward' in breach of the licensing laws. But the other association had been formed as a company, and it was convicted because it (as the owner of the lorry) was an entity separate from its members (who owned the coal). No argument based upon the existence of a trust was addressed to the court.

2. In *Abbey Malvern Wells Ltd v Ministry of Local Government and Planning* [1951] Ch 728, Danckwerts J held that, where all the shares in a company were held on educational trusts and the management of the company was in the hands of the trustees, the court could lift the veil of incorporation so as to impress the *company's* property with the terms of the trusts. This decision overlooks the possibility that the trustees might (quite properly) have decided to sell the shares, or some of them, and effectively have nullified the court's ruling.

3. In *Re Schuppan (a bankrupt) (No 2)* [1997] 1 BCLC 256, a matrimonial property case in which it was said, *obiter dicta*, that if the married partners had acquired property in circumstances which would have given rise to a finding that one of them, who held the

---

[33] (1882) 8 QBD 373.

legal estate, did so on a constructive trust for the other, the fact that the property was held by a company controlled by the former would not stand in the way of the court making a similar finding.

> ➤ Question

If the Trebanog Working Men's Club Ltd owned a vehicle which it used to deliver supplies of liquor to its members' homes for consumption there, would it need: (a) a retail liquor licence; (b) a licence to carry goods for hire or reward? Would it matter how payments for the supplies were reckoned?

The corporate veil may be disregarded if the company is used as a means to perpetrate a fraud.[34]

[2.16] Re Darby, ex p Brougham [1911] 1 KB 95 (King's Bench Division)

Darby and Gyde (both undischarged bankrupts, with a number of convictions for fraud) registered in Guernsey a company called City of London Investment Corporation Ltd. It had only seven shareholders and had issued a mere £11 of its nominal capital of £100,000. Darby and Gyde were its only directors and entitled to all of its profits. The corporation so formed then purported to register and float in England a £30,000 company under the name of Welsh Slate Quarries Ltd, and to sell to it a quarrying licence and plant, bought for £3,500, at a price of £18,000. The prospectus inviting the public to take debentures in the Welsh company disclosed the role of the corporation as vendor and promoter, but did not mention the names of Darby and Gyde or the fact that it was they who were to receive the profit on the sale. The Welsh company failed and went into liquidation. The liquidator claimed in the bankruptcy of Darby for the secret profit which it was alleged that he, as a promoter, had made. It was objected on Darby's behalf that it was not he but the corporation who had been promoter; but this argument found no favour with the court.

PHILLIMORE J: Now this case certainly does seem to me to be an advance upon the previous decisions. Darby and Gyde (who are two fraudulent persons, both of whom have been convicted of fraud in the present case, and of several previous crimes) registered in Guernsey a company called the City of London Investment Corporation, of which they were the proprietors. It was merely an alias for themselves just as much as if they had announced in the *Gazette* that they were in future going to call themselves 'Rothschild & Co'. It was merely a name under which they carried on business, and I am quite clear in my own mind that that was their object, and that, whenever they represented that some business was being done by or through the corporation and concealed the fact that it was being done by or through Darby and Gyde, they were by that mere fact probably perpetrating a fraud. I say this because their names and their persons were so well known generally that the chance of detection and the chances of repudiation were great in connection with any commercial transactions in which they engaged. The fraud here is that what they did through the corporation they did themselves and represented it to have been done by a corporation of some standing and position, or at any rate a corporation which was more than and different from themselves. Having registered that corporation, and being minded to perpetrate a very great fraud, they, as such corporation, agreed to buy a trivial interest in a Welsh slate quarry for a small sum in cash and a consideration in shares, and then as such corporation purported to sell this interest to the Welsh Slate Quarries Limited and thereby they made a very large profit. It is said that they concealed that profit and also that they concealed from the Welsh Slate Quarries Limited the fact that they were themselves the real vendors and promoters, and therefore it is contended that the liquidator is entitled to

[34] This principle was applied to penetrate an elaborate network of some 80 interlocking trusts and companies in *Re a Company* [1985] BCLC 333, CA and strikingly illustrated by diagrams which are reproduced in the report of the case.

recover the profit from them . . . Now they made that profit either directly or through the agency of the corporation, it does not matter which, and they may hold it if they disclosed it at the proper time . . . [His Lordship then ruled that there had been no effective disclosure, and that Gyde and Darby were bound to account for the profit which the corporation had made.]

> ## Notes

1. See also *Aveling Barford Ltd v Perion Ltd* **[8.14]**, where the veil of incorporation was disregarded in order to defeat the claims of an asset-stripper who had defrauded his company.

2. In certain circumstances, the court will exercise a power to order the 'freezing' of a person's assets, in order to prevent them from being moved out of the jurisdiction or otherwise spirited away. Such a freezing order (formerly referred to as a *Mareva* injunction) is commonly made when the owner of the assets in question is likely to have judgment entered against him in a current or pending action and the court is satisfied that there is a risk that there will be no assets available to meet this liability. The court has power, also, to make a 'restraint order' under the Criminal Justice Act 1988 s 77, preventing a person from dealing with assets which are liable to be confiscated as the proceeds of crime. It has been held in a number of cases (eg *International Credit and Investment Co (Overseas) Ltd v Adham* [1998] BCLC 134; *Re H (restraint order: realisable property)* [1996] 2 BCLC 500) that an order in such cases can extend to cover assets which are not owned by the person concerned but by a company that is controlled by him.

The veil of incorporation may be lifted to prevent the deliberate evasion of a contractual obligation.

[2.17] Gilford Motor Co Ltd v Horne [1933] Ch 935 (Court of Appeal)

The first defendant, EB Horne, had formerly been employed as managing director of the plaintiff company. He had covenanted in a written agreement not to solicit customers of the company after leaving its employment. When this employment was terminated, he began to set up his own business, undercutting the plaintiff's prices; but after taking legal advice, caused instead the formation of a company, J M Horne & Co Ltd (the second defendant) in which his wife and an employee were sole shareholders and directors. This company took over Horne's business and solicited the plaintiff's customers. Farwell J held that the covenant had been broken, but because in his view it was too wide and therefore against public policy, declined to enforce it against the defendants. The plaintiff appealed successfully against this latter ruling, and was granted an injunction against both defendants.

LORD HANWORTH MR: Farwell J heard the evidence about that company . . . He says this:

The defendant company is a company which, on the evidence before me, is obviously carried on wholly by the defendant Horne. Mrs Horne, one of the directors, is not, so far as any evidence I have had before me, taking any part in the business or the management of the business. The son, whose initials are 'JM', is engaged in a subordinate position in that company, and the other director, Howard, is an employee of the company. As one of the witnesses said in the witness-box, in all dealings which he had had with the defendant company the 'boss' or the 'guvnor', whichever term is the appropriate one, was the defendant Horne, and I have not any doubt on the evidence I have had before me that the defendant company was the channel through which the defendant Horne was carrying on his business. Of course, in law the defendant company is a separate entity from the defendant Horne, but I cannot help feeling quite convinced that at any rate one of the reasons for the creation of that company was the fear of Mr Horne that he might commit breaches of the covenant in carrying on the business, as for instance, in sending out circulars as he was doing, and that he might possibly avoid that liability if he did it through the defendant company. There is no doubt that the defendant company has sent out circulars to persons who were at the crucial time customers of the plaintiff company.

Now I have recalled that portion of the judgment of Farwell J, and I wish in clear terms to say that I agree with every word of it. I am quite satisfied that this company was formed as a device, a stratagem, in order to mask the effective carrying on of a business of Mr E B Horne. The purpose of it was to try to enable him, under what is a cloak or sham, to engage in business which, on consideration of the agreement which had been sent to him just about seven days before the company was incorporated, was a business in respect of which he had a fear that the plaintiffs might intervene and object.

Now this action is brought by the plaintiffs, the Gilford Motor Company Ltd, to enforce the terms of clause 9 of the agreement of 30 May 1929, on the ground that the defendant Horne, and the company, as his agent and under his direction, have committed breaches of the covenant which I have read. [His Lordship held that the breaches were substantiated by the evidence, and rejected the defence that the covenant was too wide to be supportable in law. He accordingly granted an injunction, which he ruled should go against the company as well as Horne.]

LAWRENCE and ROMER LJJ delivered concurring judgments.

➤ Notes

1. This decision was followed in *Jones v Lipman* [1962] 1 WLR 832, where the defendant, who had contracted to sell land to the plaintiff, later endeavoured to put the land beyond the reach of an order for specific performance by conveying it to a company which he had formed for this express purpose, and which he himself effectively owned and controlled. Ignoring the corporate veil, Russell J ordered specific performance against both the defendant and his company.

2. Lord Cooke, in his Hamlyn lecture (see above, p 53, footnote 27) says of *Jones v Lipman*, at p 17:

> Since the company was in the vendor's control, there was no difficulty in granting a decree of specific performance against him. Describing the company as a creation of the vendor, a device, sham and mask, the judge also decreed specific performance directly against it. Those epithets, however, do not appear to have been needed to justify the remedy. No particular difficulty should arise in holding that a company or any other purchaser acquiring property with actual notice that the transaction is a fraud on a prior purchaser takes subject to the latter's equity.

3. In both *Gilford Motor Co Ltd v Horne* and *Jones v Lipman*, the company whose separate existence was disregarded had been set up deliberately in an attempt to evade an *existing* obligation. This was a point emphasised in *Adams v Cape Industries plc* [2.19], where it was made clear that the law does not look with similar disfavour on the formation of a limited liability company in order to confine the *future* or *contingent* liabilities of an enterprise within specific limits.

It is common to refer to the company in cases such as these as a 'sham' or 'façade', used to mask the underlying situation. In *Adams v Cape Industries plc* the court expressed the view that 'where a façade is alleged, the motive of the perpetrator may be highly material'.

4. Note also *Gencor ACP Ltd v Dalby* [2000] 2 BCLC 734, where Dalby, the director of a public company, had dishonestly diverted assets and business opportunities from this company to a Virgin Islands company owned and controlled by Dalby himself. An order that the benefits so obtained should be disgorged was made against the offshore company as well as against Dalby personally.

This judgment was followed in *Trustor AB v Smallbone (No 2)* [2001] 1 WLR 1177, where Sir Andrew Morritt V-C held that although it is not appropriate for a court to pierce the corporate veil merely because a company is involved in some impropriety, it is entitled to do so when the latter is used 'as a device or façade to conceal the true facts and the liability of the responsible individuals'.

5. In *Acatos & Hutcheson plc v Watson* [1995] BCLC 446, A Ltd owned nearly 30 per cent of the shares in A & H plc but had no other assets. It would have been unlawful for A & H plc to acquire these shares because the 'rule in *Trevor v Whitworth*' forbids a company to own shares in itself (the rule is not the same now, see below, p 399). But Lightman J said that it was permissible for it to purchase all the shares in A Ltd, which of course meant that for all practical purposes it did, indirectly, own 30% of its own shares. He added, however, that he might have thought it appropriate to lift the veil and declare the transaction unlawful if A Ltd had been *deliberately* set up by A & H plc to acquire the shares as the first of two stages in a single scheme to evade the rule. (For a further example of a 'façade', see *Re Bugle Press Ltd* **[13.11]**.)

The veil of incorporation may sometimes be lifted to allow a group of associated companies to be treated as one.

[2.18] DHN Food Distributors Ltd v Tower Hamlets London Borough Council [1976] 1 WLR 852 (Court of Appeal)

DHN ran a wholesale cash-and-carry grocery business from premises owned by its wholly owned subsidiary company ('Bronze'). Bronze had the same directors as DHN, but it carried on no business. Its only asset was the freehold properties which DHN occupied as its licensee. A second wholly owned subsidiary owned vehicles used by DHN in its business, but it, too, carried on no operations of its own. The Council in 1970 compulsorily acquired the premises, and as a result DHN had to close down its business. Substantial compensation for disturbance (over and above the value of the land itself, which had already been paid to Bronze) could be claimed by DHN only if it had an interest in the land greater than that of a bare licensee. The Court of Appeal, reversing a ruling of the Lands Tribunal, held that the group of companies should be treated as a single economic entity, and that in consequence compensation for disturbance should be paid. In effect, DHN was treated as if it had owned the land itself.

SHAW LJ: [There] is the further argument[35] advanced on behalf of the claimants that there was so complete an identity of the different companies comprised in the so-called group that they ought to be regarded for this purpose as a single entity. The completeness of that identity manifested itself in various ways. The directors of DHN were the same as the directors of Bronze; the shareholders of Bronze were the same as in DHN, the parent company, and they had a common interest in maintaining on the property concerned the business of the group.

If each member of the group is regarded as a company in isolation, nobody at all could have claimed compensation in a case which plainly calls for it. Bronze would have had the land but no business to disturb; DHN would have had the business but no interest in the land.

In this utter identity and community of interest between DHN and Bronze there was no flaw at all. As Bronze did not trade and carried on no business, it had no actual or potential creditors other than its own parent, DHN. The directors of that company could at any time they chose have procured the transfer of the legal title from Bronze to itself. Mr Eyre again conceded that if they had gone through that formal operation the day before the notice to treat was served on 12 October 1970, they would have had a secure claim for compensation for disturbance. Accordingly, they could

---

[35] [An alternative ground for the decision of the court was that DHN did have a sufficient interest in the land, on the basis of either an irrevocable licence or a resulting trust, to claim compensation for disturbance in its own right.]

in law have sought and obtained whatever advantages were derived up to that date from a separation of title and interest between the two companies and still quite legitimately have re-disposed matters right up till October 1970 so as to qualify for compensation. They could not have been criticised, still less prevented, if they had chosen to do so. Yet if the decision of the Lands Tribunal be right, it made all the difference that they had not. Thus no abuse is precluded by disregarding the bonds which bundled DHN and Bronze together in a close and, so far as Bronze was concerned, indissoluble relationship.

Why then should this relationship be ignored in a situation in which to do so does not prevent abuse but would on the contrary result in what appears to be a denial of justice? If the strict legal differentiation between the two entities of parent and subsidiary must, even on the special facts of this case, be observed, the common factors in their identities must at the lowest demonstrate that the occupation of DHN would and could never be determined without the consent of DHN itself. If it was a licence at will, it was at the will of the licensee, DHN, that the licence subsisted. Accordingly it could have gone on for an indeterminate time; that is to say, as long as the relationship of parent and subsidiary continued, which means for practical purposes for as long as DHN wished to remain in the property for the purposes of its business.

The President of the Lands Tribunal took a strict legalistic view of the respective positions of the companies concerned. It appears to me that it was too strict in its application to the facts of this case, which are, as I have said, of a very special character, for it ignored the realities of the respective roles which the companies filled. I would allow the appeal.

LORD DENNING MR and GOFF LJ delivered concurring judgments.

➤ Question

Can this decision be reconciled with the reasoning of Browne-Wilkinson V-C in *Tate Access Floors Inc v Boswell* (cited above, p 53)?

➤ Note

Lord Denning began his judgment: 'This case might be called the "Three in one". Three companies in one. Alternatively, the "One in three". One group of three companies.' 'Group enterprise' is a common feature of modern commercial life, whether we think of domestic businesses within the United Kingdom or the great multinationals. We have already seen a number of examples in the cases: eg in *Gramophone and Typewriter Co Ltd v Stanley* [2.05]; *Re FG (Films) Ltd* [2.14]; *Lonrho Ltd v Shell Petroleum Co Ltd* [2.06]; *Smith, Stone & Knight Ltd v Birmingham Corpn* (above, p 59, Note 3); and *Firestone Tyre and Rubber Co Ltd v Lewellin* (above, p 59, Note 4); and there will be many more in the pages to come.

A 'group' of companies may consist of a holding company and one or more subsidiaries and sub-subsidiaries, or of a number of companies which have substantially the same shareholders and directors; but it is obviously possible to have an infinite variety of other arrangements connecting either closely or loosely a number of companies which carry on associated businesses or different parts of the same business.

There are some statutory provisions governing groups: for instance, those requiring the publication of consolidated accounts (CA 2006 s 399ff); and the tax laws have many rules dealing with such matters as the transfer of assets between member companies of a group (see, eg ICTA 1988 s 402ff). Employment legislation, eg in regard to redundancy payments, sometimes treats as continuous employment a succession of jobs with a number of associated companies, and also the similar position where one employer company succeeds another following a takeover or reorganisation. In all these cases, the concepts of 'group' and 'associated company' will be formally defined for the purpose of the provision in question.

The case law gives a much more confused picture. The question whether the veil of incorporation should be lifted, so as to destroy the distinct identity of the separate companies within a group and treat the 'enterprise' as being in reality one concern, is one that has come before the courts on many occasions; but no clear principle emerges. The willingness of the Court of Appeal in the *DHN* case to treat all the companies as one contrasts sharply with its insistence on applying the *Salomon* principle in *Lonrho* **[2.06]**. Indeed, in *Woolfson v Strathclyde Regional Council* 1978 SLT 159, 38 P & CR 521[36] the House of Lords upheld a decision of the Scottish courts delivered shortly after the *DHN* case in which the Scottish judges had pointedly declined to follow the English case, although the facts were quite similar.

In later parts of this book, we shall meet cases in which one company in a group has guaranteed the obligations of another (*Charterbridge Corpn Ltd v Lloyds Bank Ltd* **[3.06]**; *Rolled Steel Products (Holdings) Ltd v British Steel Corpn* **[3.07/3.17]**), paid its debts (*Armour Hick Northern Ltd v Armour Trust Ltd* [1980] 1 WLR 1520, or looked after the pay and pensions of its employees (*Re W & M Roith Ltd* (below, p 149); *Walker v Wimborne* (below, p 114, Note)). The attitude of the courts has varied at times from an indulgent blurring of the differentiation between the member companies to a strict insistence that the differentiation be respected. However, all the indications are that the *DHN* case is increasingly to be seen as a decision that is out of line with current trends. In *The Albazero* [1977] AC 774 at 807, [1975] 3 All ER 21 at 28, CA,[37] Roskill LJ described it as a fundamental principle of English law 'long established and now unchallengeable by judicial decision . . . that each company in a group of companies (a relatively modern concept) is a separate legal entity possessed of separate legal rights and liabilities so that the rights of one company in a group cannot be exercised by another company in that group even though the ultimate benefit of the exercise of those rights would enure beneficially to the same person or corporate body'.

The modern approach is well summed up in the remarks of Robert Goff LJ in *Bank of Tokyo Ltd v Karoon* [1987] AC 45n at 64:

> Counsel suggested beguilingly that it would be technical for us to distinguish between parent company and subsidiary in this context; economically, he said, they were one. But we are concerned not with economics but with law. The distinction between the two is, in law, fundamental and cannot here be abridged.

In Canada, industrial action has been held not to be 'secondary' picketing when directed by employees towards an associated company which belonged to the same group as their employer (*Canada Safeway Ltd v Local 373, Canadian Food and Allied Workers* (1974) 46 DLR (3d) 113), but the House of Lords showed no willingness to accede to a similar argument in *Dimbleby & Sons Ltd v National Union of Journalists* [1984] 1 All ER 751, [1984] 1 WLR 427, HL.[38]

The most significant of the more recent cases is *Adams v Cape Industries plc*.

[2.19] Adams v Cape Industries plc [1990] Ch 433 (Court of Appeal)

Cape, an English company, headed a group which included many wholly owned subsidiaries. Some of these mined asbestos in South Africa and others marketed the asbestos in various countries, including the US. Several hundred plaintiffs had been awarded damages by a Texas court

---

[36] This was not strictly a 'group enterprise' case. The occupier of the shop premises which were compulsorily acquired was a company of which W held 999 shares and his wife the remaining one. Part of the land was owned by W personally and the rest by a second company in which, again, W and his wife held all the shares. The judgments leave little doubt, however, that *DHN* would not have been followed even if the facts had been identical.

[37] The case went to the House of Lords on grounds which did not involve this point: [1977] AC 774, [1976] 3 All ER 129.

[38] See also *The Maritime Trader* [1981] 2 Lloyd's Rep 153, [1981] Com LR 27, in which the court refused to order the arrest of a ship owned by the defendant company's subsidiary.

for personal injuries suffered as a result of exposure to asbestos dust. The defendants included one of Cape's subsidiaries, NAAC, which was based in Illinois. The Court of Appeal held that the judgment could not be enforced against the English parent, Cape, rejecting arguments: (i) that Cape and the relevant subsidiaries should be treated as a single economic unit, following *DHN* **[2.18]**; (ii) that the subsidiaries were used as a 'façade' concealing the true facts; and (iii) that an agency relationship existed between Cape and NAAC.

The judgment of the court (SLADE, MUSTILL and RALPH GIBSON LJJ) was given by SLADE LJ: . . .

The 'single economic unit' argument

There is no general principle that all companies in a group of companies are to be regarded as one. On the contrary, the fundamental principle is that 'each company in a group of companies (a relatively modern concept) is a separate legal entity possessed of separate legal rights and liabilities:' *The Albazero*,[39] per Roskill LJ.

It is thus indisputable that each of Cape, Capasco, NAAC and CPC were in law separate legal entities. Mr Morison did not go so far as to submit that the very fact of the parent-subsidiary relationship existing between Cape and NAAC rendered Cape or Capasco present in Illinois. Nevertheless, he submitted that the court will, in appropriate circumstances, ignore the distinction in law between members of a group of companies treating them as one, and that broadly speaking, it will do so whenever it considers that justice so demands. In support of this submission, he referred us to a number of authorities.

[His Lordship referred to a number of cases, including *Harold Holdsworth & Co (Wakefield) Ltd v Caddies* **[3.12]**; *Scottish Co-operative Wholesale Society Ltd v Meyer* **[11.19]**; *DHN Food Distributors Ltd v Tower Hamlets London Borough Council* **[2.18]**. He continued:] Principally, in reliance on those authorities, Mr Morison submitted that in deciding whether a company had rendered itself subject to the jurisdiction of a foreign court it is entirely reasonable to approach the question by reference to 'commercial reality'. The risk of litigation in a foreign court, in his submission, is part of the price which those who conduct extensive business activities within the territorial jurisdiction of that court properly have to pay. . . .

We have some sympathy with Mr Morison's submissions in this context. To the layman at least the distinction between the case where a company itself trades in a foreign country and the case where it trades in a foreign country through a subsidiary, whose activities it has full power to control, may seem a slender one. . . .

It is not surprising that in many cases such as *Holdsworth, Scottish Cooperative, Revlon*[40] and *Commercial Solvents*,[41] the wording of a particular statute or contract has been held to justify the treatment of parent and subsidiary as one unit, at least for some purposes. The relevant parts of the judgments in the *DHN* case must, we think, likewise be regarded as decisions on the relevant statutory provisions for compensation, even though these parts were somewhat broadly expressed, and the correctness of the decision was doubted by the House of Lords in *Woolfson v Strathclyde Regional Council*.[42]

Mr Morison described the theme of all these cases as being that where legal technicalities would produce injustice in cases involving members of a group of companies, such technicalities should not be allowed to prevail. We do not think that the cases relied on go nearly so far as this. As Sir Godfray [counsel for Cape] submitted, save in cases which turn on the wording of particular statutes or contracts, the court is not free to disregard the principle of *Salomon v A Salomon & Co Ltd* **[2.01]** merely because it considers that justice so requires. Our law, for better or worse, recognises the creation of subsidiary companies, which though in one sense the

---

[39] [1977] AC 774 at 807.
[40] *Revlon Inc v Cripps and Lee Ltd* [1980] FSR 85.
[41] *Istituto Chemioterapico Italiano SpA and Commercial Solvents Corpn v EC Commission*: 6 and 7/73 [1974] ECR 223.
[42] 1978 SLT 159.

creatures of their parent companies, will nevertheless under the general law fall to be treated as separate legal entities with all the rights and liabilities which would normally attach to separate legal entities.

In deciding whether a company is present in a foreign country by a subsidiary, which is itself present in that country, the court is entitled, indeed bound, to investigate the relationship between the parent and the subsidiary. In particular, that relationship may be relevant in determining whether the subsidiary was acting as the parent's agent and, if so, on what terms. However, there is no presumption of any such agency. There is no presumption that the subsidiary is the parent company's alter ego. In the court below the judge refused an invitation to infer that there existed an agency agreement between Cape and NAAC comparable to that which had previously existed between Cape and Capasco and that refusal is not challenged on this appeal. If a company chooses to arrange the affairs of its group in such a way that the business carried on in a particular foreign country is the business of its subsidiary and not its own, it is, in our judgment, entitled to do so. Neither in this class of case nor in any other class of case is it open to this court to disregard the principle of *Salomon v A Salomon & Co Ltd* **[2.01]** merely because it considers it just so to do.

[His Lordship reviewed the evidence, and concluded that, although Cape was in a position to exercise overall control over the general policy of NAAC, this control did not extend to the subsidiary's day-to-day running. The contention that the group was a 'single economic unit' was accordingly rejected.]

The 'corporate veil' point

Quite apart from cases where statute or contract permits a broad interpretation to be given to references to members of a group of companies, there is one well-recognised exception to the rule prohibiting the piercing of 'the corporate veil'. Lord Keith of Kinkel referred to this principle in *Woolfson v Strathclyde Regional Council*. With reference to the *DHN* decision, he said:

I have some doubts whether in this respect the Court of Appeal properly applied the principle that it is appropriate to pierce the corporate veil only where special circumstances exist indicating that it is a mere façade concealing the true facts. . . .

Mr Morison submitted that the court will lift the corporate veil where a defendant by the device of a corporate structure attempts to evade (i) limitations imposed on his conduct by law; (ii) such rights of relief against him as third parties already possess; and (iii) such rights of relief as third parties may in the future acquire. Assuming that the first and second of these three conditions will suffice in law to justify such a course, neither of them apply in the present case. It is not suggested that the arrangements involved any actual or potential illegality or were intended to deprive anyone of their existing rights. Whether or not such a course deserves moral approval, there was nothing illegal as such in Cape arranging its affairs (whether by the use of subsidiaries or otherwise) so as to attract the minimum publicity to its involvement in the sale of Cape asbestos in the United States of America. As to condition (iii), we do not accept as a matter of law that the court is entitled to lift the corporate veil as against a defendant company which is the member of a corporate group merely because the corporate structure has been used so as to ensure that the legal liability (if any) in respect of particular future activities of the group (and correspondingly the risk of enforcement of that liability) will fall on another member of the group rather than the defendant company. Whether or not this is desirable, the right to use a corporate structure in this manner is inherent in our corporate law. Mr Morison urged on us that the purpose of the operation was in substance that Cape would have the practical benefit of the group's asbestos trade in the United States of America without the risks of tortious liability. This may be so. However, in our judgment, Cape was in law entitled to organise the group's affairs in that manner and . . . to expect that the court would apply the principle of *Salomon v A Salomon & Co Ltd* in the ordinary way. . . .

We reject the 'corporate veil' argument.

The 'agency argument'

We now proceed to consider the agency argument in relation to NAAC on the footing, which we consider to be the correct one, that NAAC must for all relevant purposes be regarded as a legal entity separate from Cape.

[His Lordship reviewed the evidence and concluded:] Having regard to the legal principles stated earlier in this judgment, and looking at the facts of the case overall, our conclusion is that the judge was right to hold that the business carried on by NAAC was exclusively its own business, not the business of Cape . . . We see no sufficient grounds for disturbing this finding of fact.

➤ Notes

1. In *Yukong Lines Ltd of Korea v Rendsburg Investments Corpn of Liberia* [1998] 1 WLR 294, Toulson J adopted a very similar line of reasoning where the question was whether the *Salomon* principle should be disregarded so as to make Mr Ramvrias, the sole shareholder of the defendant company (Rendsburg), personally liable for damages for breach of a contract to charter a ship which had ostensibly been entered into by that company. He rejected an argument that the charterparty had in reality been entered into by Rendsburg as Ramvrias's agent (in fact, the document had been signed by Ramvrias as Rendsburg's agent), and also further arguments that the company was a 'sham' or, alternatively, that the corporate veil should be lifted in the interests of justice. (The real complaint was that Ramvrias had caused Rendsburg to transfer most of its funds to another of his companies so that it would not be in a position to meet any award of damages that might be made against it. It is plain (as the judge observed) that there were other ways in which these funds might be recouped—eg in an action by Rendsburg's liquidator for breach of Ramvrias's duty as a director: see below, pp 663 ff; but *Salomon* stood in the way of giving the plaintiff any direct remedy against Ramvrias.)

2. Reference may also be made to *Re Polly Peck International plc* [1996] 2 All ER 433, where PPI, a holding company at the head of a large group, set up a specially incorporated overseas subsidiary, PPIF, in order to raise funds by a bond issue. All the funds received were on-loaned to PPI, and PPI guaranteed the subsidiary's repayment obligations. PPIF had no separate management or bank account. The court refused to lift the veil on 'group trading', 'agency' or 'sham' grounds so as to treat PPI as being in reality the borrower of the funds.

3. These and similar cases decided since *Adams v Cape Industries* [2.19] indicate that it is now very unlikely indeed that a plea that the corporate veil should be lifted in a group context will be successful. There is much interest—though perhaps more in other parts of the world than there is in this country—in the question whether a holding company should be made liable for the debts of an insolvent subsidiary, or the 'enterprise' as a whole for the obligations of one of its members.

The problem is well summarised in the following extract from the judgment of Templeman LJ in *Re Southard & Co Ltd* [1979] 3 All ER 556 at 565, [1979] 1 WLR 1198 at 1208, CA:

English company law possesses some curious features, which may generate curious results. A parent company may spawn a number of subsidiary companies, all controlled directly or indirectly by the shareholders of the parent company. If one of the subsidiary companies, to change the metaphor, turns out to be the runt of the litter and declines into insolvency to the dismay of its creditors, the parent company and the other subsidiary companies may prosper to the joy of the shareholders without any liability for the debts of the insolvent subsidiary. It is not surprising that, when a subsidiary company collapses, the unsecured creditors wish the finances of the company and its relationship with other members of the group to be narrowly examined, to ensure that no assets of the subsidiary company have leaked away, that no liabilities of the subsidiary company ought to be laid at the door of other members of the group, and that no indemnity from or right of action against any other company, or against any individual, is by some mischance overlooked.

> The anxiety of the creditors will be increased where, as in the present case, all the assets of the subsidiary company are claimed by another member of the group in right of a debenture.

Generally speaking, English case-law has adhered to the *Salomon* principle in situations such as this and, as the *Multinational Gas* case **[6.25]** illustrates, has not developed principles[43] which would allow a court to lift the veil of incorporation. This contrasts with attitudes abroad, where factors such as 'domination' and 'under-capitalisation' (or 'thin incorporation') have been relied on to build up a body of rules under which other companies in a group have been held liable to back the obligations of the 'runt of the litter'. In New Zealand and Ireland, the Companies Acts have been amended so as to give the court a discretion to order that one company in a group should make a contribution to the assets of another which is in insolvent liquidation, or to order that the liquidations of two associated companies should proceed jointly, so that their assets and liabilities are pooled.[44] The Cork Committee on Insolvency in its report (Cmnd 8558, 1982) did not suggest that this precedent should be followed in the United Kingdom, but did urge that the question be studied further. The CLR might have taken the opportunity to do so in its *Review*, but without going into detail has stated that it does not propose any reforms of the law in this area.

In the EC, there are signs that the veil of incorporation may not be considered sacrosanct in a group situation. ICI was made to pay fines, even before the United Kingdom was a member of the Community, for the breach of the EC competition laws by an overseas subsidiary.[45] And the Commission has put forward a Draft Ninth Directive on the Conduct of Groups of Companies, which would in certain circumstances make a dominant company in a group liable for losses incurred by a dependent company. But it is most unlikely that this proposal will be taken further.[46]

➤ Questions

1. If, in *FG (Films) Ltd* **[2.14]**, FG (Films) Ltd had incurred debts of £80,000 in making the film 'Monsoon' and had gone into liquidation leaving its creditors unpaid, should Film Group Inc have been held liable to the creditors?

2. The plaintiffs in *Adams* were tort victims. Some commentators argue that there is a stronger case for lifting the veil in favour of such persons. This is because, unlike those creditors whose claims are based in contract, they have not at any time been in negotiation with the company in question and able to take the risk of the company's potential insolvency into account in

---

[43] Of course, in an appropriate case a parent may be held liable on the basis of a contractual promise or a representation that it would support its subsidiary: a plea which failed in *Kleinwort Benson Ltd v Malaysia Mining Corpn Bhd* [1989] 1 All ER 785, [1989] 1 WLR 379, CA where the 'comfort letter' given by the parent company was construed as excluding an intention to create legal relations. If the subsidiary has gone into insolvent liquidation, the parent may be liable as a party to fraudulent trading under IA 1986 s 213, or (as a 'shadow director') liable for 'wrongful trading' under IA 1986, s 214. See below, pp 663 ff.

[44] At present, this can be done in England only with the approval of the prescribed statutory majorities of the creditors concerned, by a scheme of arrangement under CA 2006 ss 895ff, or, in special circumstances, under the 'power to compromise' conferred on liquidators and the court by IA 1986 s 167(1) and Sch 4. For an example of the latter, see *Re Bank of Credit and Commerce International SA (No 3)* [1993] BCLC 1490.

[45] *ICI v EC Commission* (the *Dyestuffs* case): 48, 49, 51–57/69 [1972] ECR 619, where the ECJ held that anti-competitive behaviour of a subsidiary company within the community, acting on the instructions of its parent company outside the community, was attributable to the parent so as to successfully enforce EC competition rules. In *Provimi Ltd v Roche Products Ltd* [2003] EWHC 961 (Comm), [2003] 2 All ER 683 it was held that because a group does not have legal personality, the Commission must select a specific company within the latter as an addressee of its decision, and be responsible for payment of the penalty.

[46] For further reading on this topic, see T Hadden, *The Control of Corporate Groups* (1983); DD Prentice, 'Groups of Companies: the English Experience', in KJ Hopt (ed) *Groups of Companies in European Laws* (1982), p 99; CM Schmitthoff and F Wooldridge (eds), *Groups of Companies* (1991); K Hofstetter, 'Parent Responsibility for Subsidising Corporations: European Trends' (1990) 30 ICLQ 576; IM Ramsay, 'Holding Company Liable for the Debts of an Insolvent Subsidiary: a Law and Economics Perspective' (1994) 17 UNSW Law J 520.

settling the terms of their bargain. However, it is observed by others that all tort victims face the risk that their tortfeasor may be impecunious. What are your views on this issue?

Limits to the idea of a company as a 'person'?

The cases above confirm that it is a central feature of company law (and of the law of corporations generally), whether seen from a theoretical or a practical viewpoint, that incorporation creates a new and separate legal entity, a 'being' capable of enjoying rights, exercising powers, and incurring duties and obligations. It is traditional to describe any subject of rights and duties as a legal 'person'. But it is one thing to attribute *legal* capacities to a company, and quite another to treat it as having *human* characteristics and qualities.[47] It is unnecessary and, indeed, illogical to suppose that the latter step follows from the former. And yet, after a markedly hesitant adoption of the finding that companies were separate persons, the courts have now pursued the analogy with a physical person almost as far as it is possible to go, ascribing to a company human attributes such as a reputation or an intention to defraud which at an earlier stage were regarded as unthinkable. The conclusions reached in all of the cases above are not necessarily obvious *or* necessary: it can be instructive to ask whether as a matter of policy they are desirable.

➤ Question

A company is sometimes described as:

   (i)   a 'real person';
   (ii) an 'artificial person';
   (iii) a 'fictitious person'.

Consider the appropriateness of these expressions.

Blackstone, 'Commentaries on the Laws of England' (1768)
Volume 1, p 476

[Footnotes in the original are omitted.]

'Of Corporations'

There are also certain privileges and disabilities that attend an aggregate corporation, and are not applicable to such as are sole; the reason of them ceasing and of course the law. It must always appear by attorney; for it cannot appear in person, being, as Sir Edward Coke says, invisible, and existing only in intendment and consideration of law. It can neither maintain, or be made defendant to, an action of battery or such like personal injuries; for a corporation can neither beat, nor be beaten, in it's body politic. A corporation cannot commit treason, or felony, or other crime, in it's corporate capacity: though it's members may, in their distinct individual capacities. Neither is it capable of suffering a traitor's or felon's punishment, for it is not liable to corporal penalties, nor to attainder, forfeiture, or corruption of blood. It cannot be executor or administrator, or perform any personal duties; for it cannot take an oath for the due execution of the office. It cannot be seised of lands to the use of another; for such kind of confidence is foreign to the end of it's institution. Neither can it be

---

[47] *Collins Steward Ltd v Financial Times Ltd* [2005] EWHC 262 (QB) for instance held that a corporation cannot have hurt feelings.

committed to prison;[48] for it's existence being ideal, no man can apprehend or arrest it. And there-fore also it cannot be outlawed; for outlawry always supposes a precedent right of arresting, which has been defeated by the parties absconding, and that also a corporation cannot do: for which reasons the proceedings to compel a corporation to appear to any suit by attorney are always by distress on their lands and goods. Neither can a corporation be excommunicated; for it has no soul, as is gravely observed by Sir Edward Coke: and therefore also it is not liable to be summoned into the ecclesiastical courts upon any account; for those courts act only *pro salute animae*, and their sentences can only be enforced by spiritual censures: a consideration, which, carried to it's full extent, would alone demonstrate the impropriety of these courts interfering in any temporal rights whatsoever.

➤ Notes

1. Where corporate personality is ascribed to a *group* of persons, such as a limited liability company, a chartered body such as a university, or a municipality such as a city or borough, it is referred to as a 'corporation aggregate'. Where the law personifies an *office* occupied by a single person (eg the Crown, the Bishop of Ely), it is customarily called a 'corporation sole'. The single-member company seems to be an anomalous institution which does not fit the criteria for either of these traditional classifications.

2. Blackstone's remarks (which, as he acknowledges, are based on views expressed by Coke more than a century and a half earlier) are best understood if we think of a local body such as the City of Birmingham or an institution such as the University of Cambridge as a typical 'corporation'—as Coke or Blackstone themselves would have done. At the time when they were writing, the modern company was, of course, unknown, and such commercial corporations as did exist—for example, the Hudson's Bay Company—usually had wide governmental powers as well as trading privileges.

Particular illustrations of a company's separate personality

Since the separate personality of companies is fundamental to the structure of company law, there are a wide variety of illustrations of the impact of the doctrine. The cases above are primarily directed at detecting exceptions to the rule, and identifying cases where the company's members may be liable for the company's failings. But it is important not to leave this area without appreciating that the normal rule is that the company is its own person, and this feature has a fundamental impact on engagements between the company and third parties.

Here, by way of illustration, we consider the company and its engagements with its auditors (and, in particular, the conclusion that the auditor owes duties to the *company*, not to the company's individual *members*). The same sort of analysis will also emerge when we come to look at directors' duties: directors owe their duties to the *company*, and not to individual *members* (or not unless there are special circumstances giving rise to separate duties): see pp 275 ff. Similarly, when the *company* acts, the procedures it must adopt so that the actions of human agents (directors, members, employees, etc) count as the actions of the company are determined by the company's constitution (assisted by certain statutory and common law rules designed to protect third parties in their dealings with the company): see pp 96 ff.

---

48 [*See* Companies Act 1967 s 68(5) (now, alas, repealed): 'An insurance company which contravenes sub-s (1) or (2) above shall be guilty of an offence and liable on conviction on indictment to imprisonment for a term not exceeding two years'.]

The second illustration used is that of promoters and their dealings with the company. Promoters are fiduciaries in relation to the company, and there are strong parallels with directors in this regard. (See below, pp 80 ff.)

The third illustration considered here is that of 'pre-incorporation contracts' ie contracts negotiated, and sometimes concluded, while the company is in contemplation, but before it is formally created by registration. Although the human actors may be the same as those who would be entitled to act for the company once it is formally constituted, can their acts count in that capacity before the event? (See below, pp 86 ff.)

Auditors and their relationship with the company

Until recently, it was a statutory requirement that every company should appoint an auditor or auditors. However, three exceptions are now made (see CA 2006 s 475): for 'small' companies (s 477), for 'dormant companies' (s 480) and for non-profit-making companies subject to public sector audit (s 482). These exemptions are not available to banking, insurance and certain other categories of company. And an audit must be held if members holding 10% or more of the share capital require one (s 476). There are conditions attached to all these provisions, so the Act needs to be read carefully.

CA 2006 also lays down rules for the appointment of auditors (ss 485–494), their functions and duties (ss 495–509), their removal and resignation (ss 525), and their liability (ss 532–538).

Note that after years of lobbying by auditors for changes to the law, new provisions have been introduced in CA 2006 ss 534ff that allow companies to agree to cap auditors' liability. The agreement cannot apply to more than one year's audit; it must be authorised by members (s 536 specifies the requirements); and it cannot limit liability to a sum that is less than what is 'fair and reasonable' (although the provisions of the Unfair Contract Terms Act 1977 ss 2(2) and 3(2)(a) do not apply). In the absence of such a power to contractually limit liability, and in the face of provisions such as CA 2006 s 532 making other arrangements void, the auditors had few options open to them to protect themselves against the risk of enormous claims (see below, p 77).

The standard of care to be exercised by auditors is illustrated by the cases beginning with *Re London & General Bank (No 2)* [2.20] which are cited below. But these cases (some of which are a century old) give only half of the picture, for today it is the accountancy profession itself (through the Accounting Standards Board) which is largely responsible for prescribing norms (through its *Financial Reporting Standards* ('FRSs')), for the preparation of company accounts and the duties of auditors in relation to them. Broadly speaking, an auditor is unlikely to be held to have acted negligently if he has conformed to currently accepted professional practices, but if he has departed from them, this will be regarded as strong evidence of a breach of duty (*Lloyd Cheyham & Co Ltd v Littlejohn & Co* [1987] BCLC 303). There can be little doubt that the standard of care required from auditors has progressively risen throughout the past century through the influence of the profession itself. CA 2006 also introduces criminal liability for auditors for knowingly or recklessly causing an auditors' report to include any matter that is misleading, false or deceptive in a material particular: s 507.

A rather more difficult question has been: to whom is the auditor's duty of care owed, for the purposes of civil liability? This has been largely resolved by the decision of the House of Lords in *Caparo Industries plc v Dickman* [2.23], although some aspects of it may still require clarification.

The reason why auditor's duty of care is owed to the company, and not its individual members, appears from the case of *Equitable Life Assurance Society v Ernst and Young* [2003] EWCA Civ 1114: since the contract under which the work of a company's auditors is performed is with the company as a separate person, the auditors owe an implied *contractual duty of care* to the company in and about the manner in which they perform their services. Auditors *also* have general liability in tort for negligent misstatement under which individual members may be able to claim. The scope of that duty was defined in *Johnson v Gore Wood and Co* [2003] EWCA Civ 1728. It includes anything and everything which the company in general meeting could be expected to do on the strength of that auditors' report.

Auditors must exercise reasonable care and skill, and must certify to the members or shareholders only what they believe to be true.

[2.20] Re London and General Bank (No 2) [1895] 2 Ch 673
(Court of Appeal)

This was an appeal by Theobald, one of the bank's auditors, from a judgment in which Vaughan Williams J had held him liable to reimburse the company, now in liquidation, for the amount of certain dividends which had been paid out of capital after the shareholders had been presented with a balance-sheet which Theobald had certified as correct. The appeal failed, except for a variation in the sum for which he was held liable. The main respect in which the accounts were defective was the entry of certain loans at their face value when it was known that most of the amounts were not realisable. It was held that none of the following matters absolved Theobald from liability: (1) that he had included in his report the words 'The value of the assets as shown on the balance-sheet is dependent upon realisation'; (2) that he had submitted a full report to the *directors* in which the gravity of the company's position was shown in detail; (3) that the report (to the *directors*) had initially expressed the view that no dividend should be paid, but the chairman later persuaded the auditors to delete the sentence; and (4) that the chairman had undertaken to explain the true position verbally to the shareholders in general meeting. (In fact, he had done so only in ambiguous terms.)

LINDLEY LJ: It is no part of an auditor's duty to give advice, either to directors or shareholders, as to what they ought to do. An auditor has nothing to do with the prudence or imprudence of making loans with or without security. It is nothing to him whether the business of a company is being conducted prudently or imprudently, profitably or unprofitably. It is nothing to him whether dividends are properly or improperly declared, provided he discharges his own duty to the shareholders. His business is to ascertain and state the true financial position of the company at the time of the audit, and his duty is confined to that. But then comes the question, How is he to ascertain that position? The answer is, By examining the books of the company. But he does not discharge his duty by doing this without inquiry and without taking any trouble to see that the books themselves show the company's true position. He must take reasonable care to ascertain that they do so. Unless he does this his audit would be worse than an idle farce. Assuming the books to be so kept as to show the true position of a company, the auditor has to certify that the balance-sheet presented is correct in that sense. But his first duty is to examine the books, not merely for the purpose of ascertaining what they do show, but also for the purpose of satisfying himself that they show the true financial position of the company . . . An auditor, however, is not bound to do more than exercise reasonable care and skill in making inquiries and investigations. He is not an insurer; he does not guarantee that the books do correctly show the true position of the company's affairs; he does not even guarantee that his balance-sheet is accurate according to the books of the company. If he did, he would be responsible for error on his part, even if he were himself deceived without any want of reasonable care on his part, say, by the fraudulent concealment of a book from him. His obligation is not so onerous as this. Such I take to be the duty of the auditor: he must be honest—ie must not certify what he does not believe to be true, and he must take reasonable care and skill before he believes that what he certifies is true. What is reasonable care in any particular case must depend upon the circumstances of that case. Where there is nothing to excite suspicion very little inquiry will be reasonably sufficient, and in practice I believe businessmen select a few cases at haphazard, see that they are right, and assume that others like them are correct also. Where suspicion is aroused more care is obviously necessary; but, still, an auditor is not bound to exercise more than reasonable care and skill, even in a case of suspicion, and he is perfectly justified in acting on the opinion of an expert where special knowledge is required. Mr Theobald's evidence satisfies me that he took the same view as myself of his duty in investigating the company's books and preparing his balance-sheet. He checked the cash, examined vouchers for payments, saw that the bills and securities entered in the books were held by the bank, took reasonable care to ascertain their value, and in one case obtained a solicitor's opinion on the validity of an equitable charge. I see no trace whatever of any failure by him in the performance of this part of his duty. It is satisfactory to find that the legal standard of duty is not too high for business purposes and is recognised as correct by businessmen. The balance-sheet and certificate of February 1892 (ie for the year 1891) was accompanied by a report to the directors of the bank. Taking the balance-sheet, the certificate and report together, Mr Theobald stated to the directors the true financial position of the bank, and if this report had been laid before the shareholders Mr Theobald would have completely discharged his duty to them. Unfortunately, however, this report was not laid before the shareholders . . .

In this case I have no hesitation in saying that Mr Theobald did fail to discharge his duty to the shareholders in certifying and laying before them the balance-sheet of February 1892 without any reference to the report which he laid before the directors and with no other warning than is conveyed by the words 'The value of the assets as shown on the balance-sheet is dependent upon realisation'. [His Lordship referred to the details of the balance-sheet, and to the report made to the directors, including the warning that no dividend should be paid, and continued:] A dividend of 7% was, nevertheless, recommended by the directors, and was resolved upon by the shareholders at a meeting furnished with the balance-sheet and profit and loss account certified by the auditors, and at which meeting the auditors were present, but silent. Not a word was said to inform the shareholders of the true state of affairs. It is idle to say that these accounts are so remotely connected with the payment of the dividend as to render the auditors legally irresponsible for such payment. The balance-sheet and account certified by the auditors, and showing a profit available for dividend, were, in my judgment, not the remote but the real operating cause of the resolution for the payment of the dividend which the directors improperly recommended. The auditors' account and certificate gave weight to this recommendation, and rendered it acceptable to the meeting . . .

RIGBY LJ delivered a concurring judgment.

LOPES LJ concurred.

It is not part of the duty of auditors to take stock: in the absence of suspicion, they may rely on the certificate of a manager or other apparently responsible employee.

[2.21] Re Kingston Cotton Mill Co (No 2) [1896] 2 Ch 279 (Court of Appeal)

[The facts appear from the judgment.]

LOPES LJ: [In] determining whether any misfeasance or breach of duty has been committed, it is essential to consider what the duties of an auditor are. They are very fully described in *Re London and General Bank* **[2.20]**, to which judgment I was a party. Shortly they may be stated thus: It is the duty of an auditor to bring to bear on the work he has to perform that skill, care and caution which a reasonably competent, careful and cautious auditor would use. What is reasonable skill, care and caution must depend on the particular circumstances of each case. An auditor is not bound to be a detective, or, as was said, to approach his work with suspicion or with a foregone conclusion that there is something wrong. He is a watch-dog, but not a bloodhound. He is justified in believing tried servants of the company in whom confidence is placed by the company. He is entitled to assume that they are honest, and to rely upon their representations, provided he takes reasonable care. If there is anything calculated to excite suspicion he should probe it to the bottom; but in the absence of anything of that kind he is only bound to be reasonably cautious and careful.

In the present case the accounts of the company had been for years falsified by the managing director, Jackson . . . Jackson deliberately overstated the quantities and values of the cotton and yarn in the company's mills. He did this for many years. It was proved that there is a great wastage in converting yarn into cotton, and the fluctuations of the market in the prices of cotton and yarn are exceptionally great. Jackson had been so successful in falsifying the accounts that what he had done was never detected or even suspected by the directors. The auditors adopted the entries of Jackson and inserted them in the balance-sheet as 'per manager's certificate'. It is not suggested but that the auditors acted honestly and honestly believed in the accuracy and reliability of Jackson. But it is said that they ought not to have trusted the figures of Jackson, but should have further investigated the matter. Jackson was a trusted officer of the company in whom the directors had every confidence; there was nothing on the face of the accounts to excite suspicion, and I cannot see how in the circumstances of the case it can be successfully contended that the auditors are wanting in skill, care or caution in not testing Jackson's figures.

It is not the duty of an auditor to take stock; he is not a stock expert, there are many matters in respect of which he must rely on the honesty and accuracy of others. He does not guarantee the discovery of all fraud. I think the auditors were justified in this case in relying on the honesty and accuracy of Jackson, and were not called upon to make further investigation . . .

LINDLEY and KAY LJJ delivered concurring judgments.

An auditor who has been, or ought to have been, put on inquiry is under a duty to make an exhaustive investigation.

[2.22] Re Gerrard & Son Ltd [1968] Ch 455 (Chancery Division)

The company's managing director, Croston, had caused the company's books to be falsified in three ways: (1) by altering the half-yearly stock-taking figures so as to include non-existent stock; (2) by altering invoices relating to purchases of stock so that the amounts payable were made to appear just *after*, instead of just *before*, the half-yearly 'cut off' date; and (3) (the converse of (2)) by advancing *into* the half-yearly period sums due in respect of goods sold which were in fact invoiced *after* the 'cut-off' date. The auditors ('Kevans') had accepted the explanations given by Croston and his brother-in-law Heyes (now deceased) regarding the altered invoices. The court held that Kevans had been negligent in relation to (2) and (without any finding in relation to (1) and (3)) held them liable to the company's liquidator in respect of dividends which the company had wrongly paid on the strength of the false accounts.

[PENNYCUICK J referred to *Re Kingston Cotton Mill Co (No 2)* **[2.21]** and continued:] This case appears, at any rate at first sight, to be conclusive in favour of Kevans as regards the falsification of the stock taken in isolation. Mr Walton, for the liquidator, pointed out that before 1900 there was no statutory provision corresponding to section 162 of the Companies Act 1948 [CA 2006 s 498]. That is so, but I am not clear that the quality of the auditor's duty has changed in any relevant respect since 1896. Basically that duty has always been to audit the company's accounts with reasonable care and skill. The real ground on which *Re Kingston Cotton Mill Co (No 2)* is, I think, capable of being distinguished is that the standards of reasonable care and skill are, upon the expert evidence, more exacting today than those which prevailed in 1896. I see considerable force in this contention. It must, I think, be open, even in this court, to make a finding that in all the particular circumstances the auditors have been in breach of their duty in relation to stock. On the other hand, if this breach of duty stood alone and the facts were more or less the same as those in *Re Kingston Cotton Mill Co (No 2)*, this court would, I think, be very chary indeed of reaching a conclusion different from that reached by the Court of Appeal in *Re Kingston Cotton Mill Co (No 2)* . . .

I find it impossible to acquit Kevans of negligence as regards purchases of stock before the end of each current period of account and the attribution of the price to the succeeding period of account. I will assume in their favour that Mr Nightingale [a partner in Kevans] was entitled to rely on the assurances of Mr Heyes and Mr Croston until he first came upon the altered invoices, but once these were discovered he was clearly put upon inquiry and I do not think he was then entitled to rest content with the assurances of Mr Croston and Mr Heyes, however implicitly he may have trusted Mr Croston. I find the conclusion inescapable alike on the expert evidence and as a matter of business common sense that at this stage he ought to have taken steps on the lines indicated by Mr Macnamara [an expert witness], that is to say, he should have examined the suppliers' statements and where necessary have communicated with the suppliers. Having ascertained the precise facts so far as it was possible for him to do so, he should then have informed the board. It may be that the board would then have taken some action. But whatever the board did he should in each subsequent audit have made such checks and inquiries as would have ensured that any misattribution in the cut-off procedure was detected. He did not take any of these steps. I am bound to conclude that he failed in his duty.

[His Lordship accordingly held the auditors liable for the amount of the dividends wrongly paid.]

The auditors of a company owe no duty of care either to members of the public who rely on the accounts in deciding whether to invest in the company's shares, or to existing members of the company who may also rely on the accounts for the purpose of decisions in relation to present or future investment in the company.

[2.23] Caparo Industries plc v Dickman [1990] 2 AC 605 (House of Lords)

Touche Ross & Co had audited the 1983–84 accounts of Fidelity plc, a listed company, which showed a pre-tax profit of £1.3m. Both before and after the publication of these accounts, Caparo bought Fidelity shares in the market, and subsequently it made a take-over bid, as a result of which it acquired all the shares. In these proceedings Caparo alleged that it had paid too much for the shares because the trading figures should have shown a loss of £0.4m instead of a profit, and claimed damages from the auditors on the ground that they had been negligent in certifying that the accounts showed a true and fair view of Fidelity's financial position. The House of Lords, reversing in part the judgment of the Court of Appeal, held that the auditors owed Caparo no duty of care.

[LORD BRIDGE OF HARWICH referred to a number of well-known cases, including *Hedley Byrne & Co Ltd v Heller & Partners* [1964] AC 465, HL, and continued:]

The salient feature of all these cases is that the defendant giving advice or information was fully aware of the nature of the transaction which the plaintiff had in contemplation, knew that the advice or information would be communicated to him directly or indirectly and knew that it was very likely that the plaintiff would rely on that advice or information in deciding whether or not to engage in the transaction in contemplation. In these circumstances the defendant could clearly be expected, subject always to the effect of any disclaimer of responsibility, specifically to anticipate that the plaintiff would rely on the advice or information given by the defendant for the very purpose for which he did in the event rely on it. So also the plaintiff, subject again to the effect of any disclaimer, would in that situation reasonably suppose that he was entitled to rely on the advice or information communicated to him for the very purpose for which he required it. The situation is entirely different where a statement is put into more or less general circulation and may foreseeably be relied on by strangers to the maker of the statement for any one of a variety of different purposes which the maker of the statement has no specific reason to anticipate. To hold the maker of the statement to be under a duty of care in respect of the accuracy of the statement to all and sundry for any purpose for which they may choose to rely on it is not only to subject him, in the classic words of Cardozo CJ to 'liability in an indeterminate amount for an indeterminate time to an indeterminate class': see *Ultramares Corpn v Touche*;[49] it is also to confer on the world at large a quite unwarranted entitlement to appropriate for their own purposes the benefit of the expert knowledge or professional expertise attributed to the maker of the statement. Hence, looking only at the circumstances of these decided cases where a duty of care in respect of negligent statements has been held to exist, I should expect to find that the 'limit or control mechanism . . . imposed upon the liability of a wrongdoer towards those who have suffered economic damage in consequence of his negligence'[50] rested in the necessity to prove, in this category of the tort of negligence, as an essential ingredient of the 'proximity' between the plaintiff and the defendant, that the defendant knew that his statement would be communicated to the plaintiff, either as an individual or as a member of an identifiable class, specifically in connection with a particular transaction or transactions of a particular kind (eg in a prospectus inviting investment) and that the plaintiff would be very likely to rely on it for the purpose of deciding whether or not to enter upon that transaction or upon a transaction of that kind . . .

These considerations amply justify the conclusion that auditors of a public company's accounts owe no duty of care to members of the public at large who rely upon the accounts in deciding to buy shares in the company. If a duty of care were owed so widely, it is difficult to see any reason why it should not equally extend to all who rely on the accounts in relating to other dealings with a company as lenders or merchants extending credit to the company. A claim that such a duty was owed by auditors to a bank lending to a company was emphatically and convincingly rejected by Millett J in *Al Saudi Banque v Clark Pixley*[51] . . .

The main submissions for Caparo are that the necessary nexus of proximity between it and the appellants giving rise to a duty of care stems (1) from the pleaded circumstances indicating the vulnerability of Fidelity to a take-over bid and from the consequent probability that another company, such as Caparo, would rely on the audited accounts in deciding to launch a take-over bid, or (2) from the circumstance that Caparo was already a shareholder in Fidelity when it decided to launch its take-over bid in reliance on the accounts . . .

I should . . . be extremely reluctant to hold that the question whether or not an auditor owes a duty of care to an investor buying shares in a public company depends on the degree of probability that the shares will prove attractive either en bloc to a take-over bidder or piecemeal to individual investors. It would be equally wrong, in my opinion, to hold an auditor under a duty of care to anyone who might lend money to a company by reason only that it was foreseeable as highly probable that the company would borrow money at some time in the year following publication of its audited accounts and that lenders might rely on those accounts in deciding to lend. I am content to assume the high probability of a take-over bid in reliance on the accounts which the proposed amendment of the statement of claim would assert but I do not think it assists Caparo's case . . .

[Lord Bridge referred to the statutory provisions dealing with the auditor's report (CA 1985, s 253ff), and continued:] No doubt these provisions establish a relationship between the auditors and the shareholders of a company on which the shareholder is entitled to rely for the protection of his interest. But the crucial question concerns the extent of the shareholder's interest which the auditor has a duty to protect. The shareholders of a company have a collective interest in the company's proper management and in so far as a negligent failure of the auditor to report accurately on the state of the company's finances deprives the shareholders of the opportunity to exercise their powers in general meeting to call the directors to book and to ensure that errors in management are corrected, the shareholders ought to be entitled to a remedy. But in practice no problem arises in this regard since the interest of the shareholders in the proper management of the company's affairs is

[49] 174 NE 441 (1931) at 444.
[50] *Candlewood Navigation Corpn Ltd v Mitsui OSK Lines Ltd* [1986] AC 1 at 25, PC.
[51] [1990] Ch 313.

indistinguishable from the interest of the company itself and any loss suffered by the shareholder, eg by the negligent failure of the auditor to discover and expose a misappropriation of funds by a director of the company, will be recouped by a claim against the auditors in the name of the company, not by individual shareholders.

I find it difficult to visualise a situation arising in the real world in which the individual shareholder could claim to have sustained a loss in respect of his existing shareholding referable to the negligence of the auditor which could not be recouped by the company. But on this part of the case your Lordships were much impressed with the argument that such a loss might occur by a negligent undervaluation of the company's assets in the auditor's report relied on by the individual shareholder in deciding to sell his shares at an undervalue. The argument then runs thus. The shareholder, qua shareholder, is entitled to rely on the auditor's report as the basis of his investment decision to sell his existing shareholding. There can be no distinction in law between the shareholder's investment decision to sell the shares he has or to buy additional shares. It follows, therefore, that the scope of the duty of care owed to him by the auditor extends to cover any loss sustained consequent on the purchase of additional shares in reliance on the auditor's negligent report.

I believe this argument to be fallacious. Assuming without deciding that a claim by a shareholder to recover a loss suffered by selling his shares at an undervalue attributable to an undervaluation of the company's assets in the auditor's report could be sustained at all, it would not be by reason of any reliance by the shareholder on the auditor's report in deciding to sell; the loss would be referable to the depreciatory effect of the report on the market value of the shares before ever the decision of the shareholder to sell was taken. A claim to recoup a loss alleged to flow from the purchase of overvalued shares, on the other hand, can only be sustained on the basis of the purchaser's reliance on the report. The specious equation of 'investment decisions' to sell or to buy as giving rise to parallel claims thus appears to me to be untenable.

LORDS ROSKILL, OLIVER OF AYLMERTON and JAUNCEY OF TULLICHETTLE delivered concurring opinions.

LORD ACKNER concurred.

➤ Notes

1. In *Galoo Ltd v Bright Grahame Murray* [1994] 1 WLR 1360, CA it was held that, before a claim in the tort of negligence can be maintained by a third party against an auditor, a 'special relationship' must be shown to have existed between them and, in particular, an intention (actual or inferred) on the part of the auditor that the third party should rely on the audit, together with actual reliance by the third party.

2. In the same vein, in *Al Saudi Banque v Clark Pixley* [1990] Ch 313, [1989] 3 All ER 361, it was held that a company's auditors owed no duty of care to existing or future creditors who might foreseeably lend money to the company or continue its existing credit on the faith of its audited accounts.

3. *Caparo Industries plc v Dickman* may, however, be contrasted with *Morgan Crucible Co plc v Hill Samuel & Co Ltd* [1991] Ch 295, CA, where the court declined to rule, as a preliminary point of law, that the directors and financial advisers, including the auditors, of the target company in a contested take-over bid owed no duty of care towards the bidder (whose identity was publicly known) in making representations as to the target's position, as a result of which the bidder had allegedly been induced to offer more for the shares than they were worth. This was, of course, only a preliminary ruling. There are several other cases in which a court has declined to strike out in advance an action brought by a party other than the company itself against its auditors—holding, in effect, that the elements going to establish a 'special relationship' could only be ascertained by hearing the evidence at the trial. Not too much can be read into such decisions: it is perhaps significant that there is no report of further proceedings in any of these cases.

4. And there are cases which seem to go much further. In *Barings plc v Coopers & Lybrand (a firm)* [1997] 1 BCLC 427, CA it was held that the auditors of a subsidiary owed a duty of care not only to the subsidiary, but also to its parent company. An argument (based primarily on *Prudential Assurance Co Ltd v Newman Industries Ltd (No 2)* **[11.13]**) that any damage caused by the breach of the auditors' duty would be suffered by the subsidiary, and only indirectly by the parent in its capacity as shareholder, was unsuccessful. (Is this finding affected by the recent cases on 'reflective loss' (see below, pp 543 ff)?) In *Bank of Credit and Commerce International (Overseas) Ltd v Price Waterhouse* [1998] BCLC 617, CA the position was more defensible: the question was whether the parent company's auditors might owe a duty of care to the parent in respect of the affairs of a subsidiary which had been audited separately by another firm. Because the business of all the companies in the group was so close that they were in effect interdependent, the court held that there would need to have been a constant interchange of information between the two firms of auditors, and that in the circumstances such a duty might arise.

5. In recent years, there have been increasing obligations placed on company auditors both by legislation and by extra-statutory measures. Thus, for example, an auditor is required to state whether the directors' report (required by CA 2006 s 415) is consistent with the accounts (s 496); the Listing Rules stipulate that the auditor must review the company's statement of compliance with the Combined Code. The potential exposure of firms of auditors to liability for very large sums has caused concern in accountancy circles and has been the subject of debate in many countries. One suggestion advanced for some years is that auditors should be allowed to limit their liability by contract: this is now permitted by CA 2006 ss 534ff, subject to certain conditions (see above, p 73). The alternatives were unacceptably limited. Auditors could, at least to some extent, cover their position by insurance, but this drives up the cost of the audit. Another solution is offered by the Limited Liability Partnerships Act 2000, which allows the members of auditing firms to limit their liability for losses caused by the negligence of *other* members of the firm. Another possibility suggested during this debate was to amend the law of joint liability in tort, so that (at least in this context) a tortfeasor should not be jointly and severally liable with the others who were at fault for all the loss sustained by the claimant, but only for a proportionate part of the loss corresponding to his share of the liability. In a number of cases decided in Commonwealth countries, auditors have successfully pleaded that their liability should be reduced because of the contributory negligence of the company itself (the acts of the company's directors being attributed to the company for this purpose). Examples include *Daniels v Anderson* (1995) 16 ACSR 607 and *Dairy Containers Ltd v NZI Bank Ltd* [1995] 2 NZLR 30.

6. The Combined Code (below, p 242) requires that, as a matter of good practice, the board of a listed company should establish an *audit committee* of at least three directors, all non-executive (and having a majority of 'independent' NEDs), whose duties should include keeping under review the scope and results of the audit and its cost-effectiveness, and the independence and objectivity of its auditors.

Promoters and their dealings with the company

The term 'promoter' is not defined in the Companies Act, and such attempts at definition as have been made by the courts (mainly in the nineteenth century) seem to have been concerned only to ensure that enough flexibility was retained to catch the next ingenious rogue which the pre-incorporation period might produce. The best known of these is the description given by Cockburn CJ in *Twycross v Grant* (1877) 2 CPD 469 at 541: 'one who undertakes to form a company with reference to a given project, and to set it going, and who takes the necessary steps to accomplish that purpose'.

There is an enormous body of old case law concerned with the obligations of promoters towards the companies which they form and the investing public whose capital they seek to attract. But to all intents and purposes this law has become obsolete. This is due partly to changes in the practice of marketing securities: it is unusual for a newly formed company to make an initial public issue, and not normally possible to obtain a market listing, without an established trading record. It is also due to the stringent control of such activities now imposed by statute and by the listing rules (which must be complied with in order to gain access to the Stock Exchange)[52] and the professional codes of issuing houses and others whose services are nowadays essential. There is thus little need to include extracts from these cases, insofar as they relate to promoters' duties, as these cases are now mainly historical interest.

We are simply interested in illustrations of the promoters' relationships and dealings with the company as a separate legal person. The next two cases have strong parallels with the approach taken to the relationship and dealings between a company and its directors.

Promoters are fiduciaries. A contract between the promoter and the company is voidable at the company's option unless the promoter has disclosed all material facts relating to that contract to an independent board, and the company has freely agreed to the terms.

[2.24] Erlanger v New Sombrero Phosphate Co (1878) 3 App Cas 1218 (House of Lords)

A syndicate headed by Erlanger, a Paris banker, acquired for £55,000 the lease of an island in the West Indies with the right to work its phosphate deposits. The syndicate, through Erlanger, then formed the respondent company and named its first directors. Of these, one, the Lord Mayor of London, was independent of the syndicate; two were abroad, and the remainder were mere puppets of Erlanger. The lease was then sold through a nominee to the company for £110,000, the purchase being 'ratified' without inquiry at a meeting of directors eight days after the incorporation of the company. Many members of the public subscribed for shares, but the real circumstances of the sale and purchase were not disclosed to them and were not discovered until eight months later, after the first phosphate shipments had proved a failure. The members then removed the original directors and elected a new board, which brought these proceedings to have the sale rescinded.

LORD CAIRNS LC: In the whole of this proceeding . . . the syndicate, or the house of Erlanger as representing the syndicate, were the promoters of the company, and it is now necessary that I should state to your Lordships in what position I understand the promoters to be placed with reference to the company which they proposed to form. They stand, in my opinion, undoubtedly in a fiduciary position. They have in their hands the creation and moulding of the company; they have the power of defining how, and when, and in what shape, and under what supervision, it shall start into existence and begin to act as a trading corporation. If they are doing all this in order that the company may, as soon as it starts into life, become, through its managing directors, the purchaser of the property of themselves, the promoters, it is, in my opinion, incumbent upon the promoters to take care that in forming the company they provide it with an executive, that is to say, with a board of directors, who shall both be aware that the property which they are asked to buy is the property of the promoters, and who shall be competent and impartial judges as to whether the purchase ought or ought not to be made. I do not say that the owner of the property may not promote and form a joint stock company, and then sell his property to it, but I do say that if he does he is bound to take care

[52] See below, Chapter 12.

that he sells it to the company through the medium of a board of directors who can and do exercise an independent and intelligent judgment on the transaction, and who are not left under the belief that the property belongs, not to the promoter, but to some other person . . .

LORD O'HAGAN: The original purchase of the island of Sombrero was perfectly legitimate—and it was not less so because the object of the purchasers was to sell it again, and to sell it by forming a company which might afford them a profit on the transaction. The law permitted them to take that course, and provided the machinery by which the transfer of their interest might be equitably and beneficially effected for themselves and those with whom they meant to deal. But the privilege given them for promoting such a company for such an object, involved obligations of a very serious kind. It required, in its exercise, the utmost good faith, the completest truthfulness, and a careful regard to the protection of the future shareholders. The power to nominate a directorate is manifestly capable of great abuse, and may involve, in the misuse of it, very evil consequences to multitudes of people who have little capacity to guard themselves. Such a power may or may not have been wisely permitted to exist. I venture to have doubts upon the point. It tempts too much to fraudulent contrivance and mischievous deception; and, at least, it should be watched with jealousy and restrained from employment in such a way as to mislead the ignorant and the unwary. In all such cases the directorate nominated by the promoters should stand between them and the public, with such independence and intelligence, that they may be expected to deal fairly, impartially and with adequate knowledge in the affairs submitted to their control. If they have not those qualities, they are unworthy of trust. They are the betrayers and not the guardians of the company they govern, and their acts should not receive the sanction of a court of justice.

Now, my Lords, for reasons repeatedly given by my noble and learned friends, which I shall not detail again, I think that the promoters in this case failed to remember the exigencies of their fiduciary position, when they appointed directors who were in no way independent of themselves, and who did not sustain the interests of the company with ordinary care and intelligence . . .

Apparently, there was no inquiry as to the enormous advance in the price . . . , no consideration of the state of the property—and no intelligent estimate of its capabilities and prospects. If the directors had been nominated merely to ratify any terms the promoters might dictate, they discharged their function; if it was their duty, as it certainly was, to protect the shareholders, they never seem to have thought of doing it. Their conduct was precisely that which might have been anticipated from the character of their selection, and taking that conduct and character together, I concur in, I believe, the unanimous opinion of your Lordships that such a transaction ought not to be allowed to stand.

The promoters, who so forgot their duty to the company they formed, as to give it a directorate without independence of position or vigilance and caution in caring for its interests, must take the consequences. And this without the necessary imputation of evil purpose or conscious fraud. The fiduciary obligation may be violated though there may be no intention to do injustice. If the protection, proper and needful for a person standing at disadvantage in relation to his guardian or his solicitor, or to the promoters of a company, be withheld, the guardian, the solicitor or the promoters cannot sustain a contract equitably invalidated by the want of it, merely because it may be impossible to prove that he is impeachable with indirect or improper motives . . .

LORDS PENZANCE, HATHERLEY, SELBORNE, BLACKBURN and GORDON delivered concurring opinions.

➤ Notes

1. The principles of fiduciary obligation are rules applied by the courts of equity to impose high standards of selfless conduct upon trustees and others, such as agents and solicitors, who undertake responsibility to look after the interests or handle the property of others. Company promoters and company directors (see below, Chapter 6) are subject to these rules.

2. It has been accepted at least since *Salomon v A Salomon & Co Ltd* **[2.01]** that, if there is no independent board of directors, the company may be bound by the consent of all the original *members*, provided that a full disclosure is made to them of all material facts. But, as is shown by *Gluckstein v Barnes* **[2.25]** even this will not protect a promoter if the original members themselves are not independent and the scheme as a whole is designed to attract and deceive the investing public at large.

Promoters, as fiduciaries, may not make a secret profit while acting in that capacity. Any profits so received must be accounted for to the company.

[2.25] Gluckstein v Barnes [1900] AC 240 (House of Lords)

Gluckstein and three others bought the Olympia exhibition premises in liquidation proceedings for £140,000 and then promoted a company, Olympia Ltd, to which they sold the property for £180,000. There were no independent directors. In a prospectus inviting applications for shares and debentures the £40,000 profit was disclosed, but not a further profit of some £20,000 which they had made by buying securities on the property at a discount and then enforcing them at their face value (though there was a vague reference to 'interim investments'). The company went into liquidation within four years, and the liquidator claimed in this action £6,341, part of the £20,000 received by Gluckstein.

EARL OF HALSBURY LC: My Lords, I am wholly unable to understand any claim that these directors, vendors, syndicate, associates, have to retain this money. I entirely agree with the Master of the Rolls that the essence of this scheme was to form a company. It was essential that this should be done, and that they should be directors of it, who would purchase. The company should have been informed of what was being done and consulted whether they would have allowed this profit. I think the Master of the Rolls is absolutely right in saying that the duty to disclose is imposed by the plainest dictates of common honesty as well as by well-settled principles of common law.

Of the facts there cannot be the least doubt; they are proved by the agreement, now that we know the subject-matter with which that agreement is intended to deal, although the agreement would not disclose what the nature of the transaction was to those who were not acquainted with the ingenious arrangements which were prepared for entrapping the intended victim of these arrangements.

In order to protect themselves, as they supposed, they inserted in the prospectus, qualifying the statement that they had bought the property for £140,000, payable in cash, that they did not sell · to the company, and did not intend to sell, any other profits made by the syndicate from interim investments.

Then it is said there is the alternative suggested upon the agreement that the syndicate might sell to a company or to some other purchaser. In the first place, I do not believe they ever intended to sell to anybody else other than a company. An individual purchaser might ask inconvenient questions, and if they or any one of them had stated as an inducement to an individual purchaser that £140,000 was given for the property, when in fact £20,000 less had been given, it is a great error to suppose that the law is not strong enough to reach such a statement; but as I say, I do not believe it was ever intended to get an individual purchaser, even if such an intention would have had any operation. When they did afterwards sell to a company, they took very good care there should be no one who could ask questions. They were to be sellers to themselves as buyers, and it was a necessary provision to the plan that they were to be both sellers and buyers, and as buyers to get the money to pay for the purchase from the pockets of deluded shareholders.

My Lords, I decline to discuss the question of disclosure to the company. It is too absurd to suggest that a disclosure to the parties to this transaction is a disclosure to the company of which these directors were the proper guardians and trustees. They were there by the terms of the agreement to do the work of the syndicate, that is to say, to cheat the shareholders; and this, forsooth, is to be treated as a disclosure to the company, when they were really there to hoodwink the shareholders, and so far from protecting them, were to obtain from them the money, the produce of their nefarious plans.

I do not discuss either the sum sued for, or why Gluckstein alone is sued.

The whole sum has been obtained by a very gross fraud, and all who were parties to it are responsible to make good what they have obtained and withheld from the shareholders.

I move your Lordships that the appeal be dismissed with costs.

LORD MACNAGHTEN: My Lords, Mr Swinfen Eady argued this appeal with his usual ability, but the case is far too clear for argument . . . For my part, I cannot see any ingenuity or any novelty in the trick which Mr Gluckstein and his associates practised on the persons whom they invited to take shares in Olympia Limited. It is the old story. It has been done over and over again.

These gentlemen set about forming a company to pay them a handsome sum for taking off their hands a property which they had contracted to buy with that end in view. They bring the company into existence by means of the usual machinery. They appoint themselves sole guardians and protectors of this creature of theirs, half-fledged and just struggling into life, bound hand and foot while yet unborn by contracts tending to their private advantage, and so fashioned by its makers that it could only act by their hands and only see through their eyes. They issue a prospectus representing that they had agreed to purchase the property for a sum largely in excess of the amount which they had, in fact, to pay. On the faith of this prospectus they collect subscriptions from a confiding and credulous public. And then comes the last act. Secretly, and therefore dishonestly, they put into their own pockets the difference between the real and the pretended price. After a brief career the company is ordered to be wound up. In the course of the liquidation the trick is discovered. Mr Gluckstein is called upon to make good a portion of the sum which he and his associates had misappropriated. Why Mr Gluckstein alone was selected for attack I do not know any more than I know why he was only asked to pay back a fraction of the money improperly withdrawn from the coffers of the company.

However that may be, Mr Gluckstein defends his conduct or, rather I should say, resists the demand, on four grounds, which have been gravely argued at the bar. In the first place, he says that he was not in a fiduciary position towards Olympia Limited, before the company was formed. Well, for some purposes he was not. For others he was. A good deal might be said on the point. But to my mind the point is immaterial, for it is not necessary to go back beyond the formation of the company.

In the second place, he says that if he was in a fiduciary position he did in fact make a proper disclosure. With all deference to the learned counsel for the appellant, that seems to me to be absurd. 'Disclosure' is not the most appropriate word to use when a person who plays many parts announces to himself in one character what he has done and is doing in another. To talk of disclosure to the thing called the company, when as yet there were no shareholders, is a mere farce. To the intended shareholders there was no disclosure at all. On them was practised an elaborate system of deception.

The third ground of defence was that the only remedy was rescission. That defence, in the circumstances of the present case, seems to me to be as contrary to common sense as it is to authority. The point was settled more than sixty years ago by the decision in *Hichens v Congreve*[53] and so far as I know, that case has never been questioned.

The last defence of all was that, however much the shareholders may have been wronged, they have bound themselves by a special bargain, sacred under the provisions of the Companies Act

---

[53] (1831) 4 Sim 420.

1862,[54] to bear their wrongs in silence. In other words, Mr Gluckstein boldly asserts that he is entitled to use the provisions of an Act of Parliament, which are directed to a very different purpose, as a shield and shelter against the just consequences of his fraud . . .

There are two things in this case which puzzle me much, and I do not suppose that I shall ever understand them. I mention them merely because I should be very sorry if it were thought that in those two matters the House unanimously approved of what has been done. I do not understand why Mr Gluckstein and his associates were not called upon to refund the whole of the money which they misappropriated. What they did with it, whether they put it in their own pockets or distributed it among their confederates, or spent it in charity, seems to me absolutely immaterial. In the next place, I do not understand why Mr Gluckstein was only charged with interest at the rate of 3%. I should have thought it was a case for penal interest.

In these two matters Mr Gluckstein has been in my opinion extremely fortunate. But he complains that he may have a difficulty in recovering from his co-directors their share of the spoil, and he asks that the official liquidator may proceed against his associates before calling upon him to make good the whole amount with which he has been charged. My Lords, there may be occasions in which that would be a proper course to take. But I cannot think that this is a case in which any indulgence ought to be shown to Mr Gluckstein. He may or may not be able to recover a contribution from those who joined with him in defrauding the company. He can bring an action at law if he likes. If he hesitates to take that course or takes it and fails, then his only remedy lies in an appeal to that sense of honour which is popularly supposed to exist among robbers of a humbler type. I agree that the appeal must be dismissed with costs.

LORD ROBERTSON delivered a concurring opinion.

[See also *Re Darby* [**2.16**].]

> ## Notes

1. There is a wide choice of remedies available against a promoter who has acted in breach of his fiduciary obligations. The company may bring proceedings for the restitution of a benefit which the promoter has received, either in equity on the basis of a constructive trust, or at law as a claim for money had and received. The parties to a secret bargain may also be sued in an action of deceit. Where a promoter has been promised, but has not received, a profit, bribe or other benefit, the company may itself enforce his claim for payment against the promisor, on the ground that he holds the claim as trustee for it: *Whaley Bridge Calico Printing Co v Green* (1879) 5 QBD 109.

2. There is some authority which suggests that a company may also have a remedy in *damages* against its promoter for breach of his fiduciary duty: see, eg, *Re Leeds and Hanley Theatres of Varieties Ltd* [1902] 2 Ch 809, CA; *Jacobus Marler Estates Ltd v Marler* (1913) 85 LJPC 167n, PC. It would be unusual to award damages for the breach of a purely equitable obligation: Meagher, Heydon and Leeming in *Meagher, Gummow & Lehane's Equity* (4th edn, 2002) at [5–170], say that the *Leeds* decision is 'at least questionable'.[55] (The *Marler* case may, however, be explained on the basis that the defendants were directors as well as promoters, and were held liable for their negligence in that capacity.)

---

[54] [Lord Macnaghten is referring to the fact that the contract to purchase the premises was expressly mentioned in the company's memorandum and articles; the 'bargain' was the 'statutory contract' created by the equivalent of CA 2006 s 33 (below, p 230).]

[55] See, however, IE Davidson, 'The Equitable Remedy of Compensation' (1982) 13 Melb ULR 349 and WMC Gummow, 'Compensation for Breach of Fiduciary Duty' in TG Youdan (ed), *Equity Fiduciaries and Trusts* (Toronto, 1989), ch 2, who demonstrate that compensation (not, strictly speaking, damages) was commonly awarded in an earlier period for at least some breaches of fiduciary obligation. Although it appears that this jurisdiction to award equitable compensation was lost sight of for many decades, it has now been re-established by the case law in Australia, New Zealand and Canada, and is coming to be recognised (albeit slowly) in England: see, for instance, *Target Holdings Ltd v Redferns* [1996] AC 421, HL and *Knight v Frost* [1999] 1 BCLC 364 at 373.

3. Where a promoter has sold to his company property which he did not acquire as a promoter or did not acquire with a view to launching the promotion—eg property which he inherited some years before—the remedy of rescission of the contract of sale is, of course, available to the company if he did not make a proper disclosure of his interest at the time of the sale. However, if rescission is no longer possible (eg because of supervening third-party rights), or if the company elects to affirm the contract, an alternative remedy by way of an account of profits does not lie: *Re Cape Breton Co* (1885) 29 Ch D 795, CA; *Ladywell Mining Co v Brookes* (1887) 35 Ch D 400, CA. This seemingly anomalous rule is commonly explained by saying that the promoter's alleged 'profit' is unquantifiable, and that by giving such a remedy the court would in effect be fixing a new price for the parties.

4. These old rulings on the liability of promoters are significant because there is a close parallel between the fiduciary obligations of promoters and the fiduciary obligations of directors (see below, Chapter 6), and decisions like *Re Cape Breton Co* may be relevant in the latter context. Compare the rules as they apply to directors, especially where there has been statutory intervention: see below, p 132 (in the context of CA 2006 s 41), and below, pp 276 ff (in the context of directors' statutory duties).

5. A promoter may also be liable to pay compensation to persons who subscribe for shares or other securities on the faith of listing particulars or a prospectus for which he is responsible: see below, pp 592 ff.

➤ Question

Suppose that the company on facts similar to *Re Cape Breton Co* were to bring an action for equitable compensation[56] against the promoter-vendor, and it is accepted that there is jurisdiction to award such compensation. What issues in regard to (a) causation and (b) the measure of compensation would arise, and how do you think that they should be resolved?

Pre-incorporation contracts

It is quite common for negotiations about a contract to take place, and for a contract (or what purports to be a contract) to be made, when one of the parties to this 'contract' is a company which has not yet been formed. Sometimes, the fact that the company has not been incorporated may be known to all concerned and may even be stated in the contract; on the other hand, there may have been some misunderstanding or even a misrepresentation about its existence. Such situations can give rise to all sorts of legal problems at common law, as the next few cases show, for a 'non-entity' cannot have legal rights or duties ascribed to it. Article 7 of the First EC Company Law Directive, cited below, required the member states to take steps which would have eliminated many of these problems, but the United Kingdom's response (CA 2006 s 51, cited below) has tackled only some of the issues.

➤ Questions

1. What business reasons might cause people to wish to make a pre-incorporation contract, rather than form the company first and then conclude the deal?

2. How far would it help solve the problems to use a ready-made company (above, p 28)?

---

[56] See Note 3 above.

A company has no legal existence before it is incorporated. It is incapable of entering into a contract itself, and equally incapable of acting through an agent. A person who purports to make a contract on behalf of a proposed company may be personally liable at common law.[57]

[2.26] Kelner v Baxter (1866) LR 2 CP 174 (Court of Common Pleas)

Kelner agreed with the promoters of a yet to be formed company to sell wine in the terms of the following letter:

January 27th, 1866.

> To John Dacier Baxter, Nathan Jacob Calisher, and John Dales, on behalf of the proposed Gravesend Royal Alexandra Hotel Company, Limited.
> Gentlemen,—I hereby propose to sell the extra stock now at the Assembly Rooms, Gravesend, as per schedule hereto, for the sum of £900, payable on the 28th of February, 1866.
> (Signed) John Kelner.

Then followed a schedule of the stock of wines, etc to be purchased, and at the end was written as follows:

> To Mr John Kelner.
> Sir,—We have received your offer to sell the extra stock as above, and hereby agree to and accept the terms proposed.
> (Signed) JD Baxter, NJ Calisher, J Dales, On behalf of the Gravesend Royal Alexandra Hotel Company, Limited.

The hotel business was already being carried on, and the wine was delivered and in due course consumed. On 1 February 1866 the proposed directors held a meeting at which they purported to ratify the purchase. The incorporation of the company was completed on 20 February 1866. The company failed before Kelner had been paid and so he brought this action against the promoters personally. They were held liable on the contract.

ERLE CJ: I agree that if the Gravesend Royal Alexandra Hotel Company had been an existing company at this time, the persons who signed the agreement would have signed as agents of the company. But, as there was no company in existence at the time, the agreement would be wholly inoperative unless it were held to be binding on the defendants personally. The cases referred to in the course of the argument fully bear out the proposition that, where a contract is signed by one who professes to be signing 'as agent', but who has no principal existing at the time, and the contract would be altogether inoperative unless binding upon the person who signed it, he is bound thereby: and a stranger cannot by a subsequent ratification relieve him from that responsibility. When the company came afterwards into existence it was a totally new creature, having rights and obligations from that time, but no rights or obligations by reason of anything which might have been done before. It was once, indeed, thought that an inchoate liability might be incurred on behalf of a proposed company, which would become binding on it when subsequently formed: but that notion was manifestly contrary to the principles upon which the law of contract is founded. There must be two parties to a contract; and the rights and obligations which it creates cannot be transferred by one of them to a third person who was not in a condition to be bound by it at the time it was made. The history of this company makes this construction to my mind perfectly clear. It was no doubt the notion of all the parties that success was certain: but the plaintiff parted with his stock upon the faith of the defendants' engagement that the price agreed on should be paid on the day named. It cannot be supposed that he for a moment contemplated that the payment was to be contingent on the formation of the company by 28 February. . . . I come, therefore, to the conclusion that the defendants, having no

---

[57] Now see CA 2006 s 51(1).

principal who was bound originally, or who could become so by a subsequent ratification, were themselves bound, and that the oral evidence offered is not admissible to contradict the written contract.

WILLES, BYLES and KEATING JJ delivered concurring judgments.

> ▶ Note

In the Australian case of *Summergreene v Parker* (1950) 80 CLR 304 at 323, Fullagar J said:

. . . Where A, purporting to act as agent for a non-existent principal, purports to make a binding contract with B, and the circumstances are such that B would suppose that a binding contract had been made, there must be a strong presumption that A has meant to bind himself personally. Where, as in Kelner v Baxter, the consideration on B's part has been fully executed in reliance on the existence of a contract binding on somebody, the presumption could, I should imagine, only be rebutted in very exceptional circumstances. But the fundamental question in every case must be what the parties intended or must be fairly understood to have intended.

To be liable under, or entitled to sue on, the purported contract of a yet to be formed company at common law, a person must have held himself out either as agent or as principal.

[2.27] Newborne v Sensolid (Great Britain) Ltd [1954] 1 QB 45 (Court of Appeal)

The contract in this case was for the sale to Sensolid of 200 cases of tinned ham. It was written on a printed form headed 'Leopold Newborne (London) Ltd', which ended with the typewritten words: 'Yours faithfully, Leopold Newborne (London) Ltd', followed by 'a hieroglyphic', which is interpreted in type as being Leopold Newborne.[58] The market fell, and Sensolid refused to take delivery. When sued on the contract, Sensolid pleaded that on the date when the contract was made Leopold Newborne (London) Ltd had not been incorporated, and that neither the company nor Newborne personally could enforce it. The Court of Appeal, affirming Parker J, upheld this plea.

LORD GODDARD CJ: Mr Diplock, who has argued the case for the plaintiff, bringing to our attention every point which could possibly be taken, has contended that it is governed by the well-known series of cases of which *Kelner v Baxter* **[2.26]** is one of the earliest and perhaps the best known. That was a case in which one Kelner sold wine intending to sell it to a company which was to be formed. The contract showed that it was agreed to be sold to certain men who were the proposed directors of a company which was coming into existence. They agreed to buy. The potential directors intended to buy the wine on behalf of the company, but the company was not in existence at the time the contract was made or at the time when the goods were delivered. They took delivery of the goods and, therefore, it was held that as they had contracted on behalf of a principal who did not exist they must, having received the wine, pay for it. That decision seems to me to stop far short of holding that every time an alleged company purports to contract—when there is no company in existence—everybody who is signing for the company is making himself personally liable.

Mr Diplock has also relied strongly on *Schmaltz Avery*,[59] which lays down a principle, which has been acted on in other cases, notably in *Harper & Co v Vigers Bros*[60] that where a person purports to contract as agent he may nevertheless disclose himself as being in truth a principal. If he entered into a contract as agent he can bring an action in his own name and show that he was in fact the principal. All those cases are well established and we are not departing in any way from those

---

[58] Per Lord Goddard CJ, as reported in [1953] 1 All ER 708 at 709.
[59] (1851) 16 QB 655.
[60] [1909] 2 KB 549.

decisions any more than did Parker J. What we cannot find in this case is that Mr Newborne ever purported to contract to sell as agent or as principal. The contract was one which he was making for the company, and although Mr Diplock has argued that in signing as he did Mr Newborne must have signed as agent, since the company could only contract through agents, that was not really the true position.

The company makes the contract. No doubt the company must do its physical acts, and so forth, through the directors, but it is not the ordinary case of principal and agent. It is a case in which the company is contracting and the company's contract is authenticated by the signature of one of the directors. This contract purports to be a contract by the company; it does not purport to be a contract by Mr Newborne. He does not purport to be selling his goods but to be selling the company's goods. The only person who had any contract here was the company, and Mr Newborne's signature merely confirmed the company's signature. The document is signed 'Yours faithfully, Leopold Newborne (London) Ltd', and then the signature underneath is the signature of the person authorised to sign on behalf of the company.

In my opinion, unfortunate though it may be, as the company was not in existence when the contract was signed there never was a contract, and Mr Newborne cannot come forward and say: 'Well, it was my contract.' The fact is, he made a contract for a company which did not exist. It seems to me, therefore, that the defendants can avail themselves of the defence which they pleaded and the appeal must be dismissed.

MORRIS LJ delivered a concurring judgment.

ROMER LJ concurred.

[Also see below, Judge LJ's judgment in *Braymist Ltd v Wise Finance Co Ltd*, [2.29].]

➤ Note

In *Kelner v Baxter* [2.26] the defendants were held liable *on the contract*, that is, as parties to it. In *Newborne*'s case [2.27] the question was, similarly, whether Newborne personally was a party to the contract, and it was held that he was not. These cases do not decide the alternative question whether an agent who has not contracted personally might be liable to the opposite party in damages for breach of warranty of authority on the principle of *Collen v Wright*.[61]

Parker J at first instance in *Newborne*'s case[62] appears to have doubted this 'because the principal is not in existence', but this begs the question: there are strong *obiter dicta* to the contrary in the Australian case of *Black v Smallwood*;[63] and the well-known case of *McRae v Commonwealth Disposals Commission*[64] plainly establishes that a person may impliedly warrant that what is non-existent exists.

The contrasting conclusions reached in *Kelner v Baxter* and *Newborne*'s case led to some fine distinctions being made by commentators, and to arguments whether the issue was one of form or of substance. Fortunately, we can now consider this debate settled, for all practical purposes, by the interpretation put on s 36C of CA 1985 (CA 2006 s 51) by the Court of Appeal in *Phonogram Ltd v Lane* [2.28]. Section 36C was first introduced (as s 9(2) of the European Communities Act 1972) to implement art 7 of the First EC Directive on Company Law and is substantially re-enacted in CA 2006 s 51.

[61] (1857) 8 E & B 647.
[62] [1954] 1 QB 45 at 47.
[63] [1966] ALR 744.
[64] (1950) 84 CLR 377.

Companies Act 2006

Section 51: Pre-incorporation contracts, deeds and obligations

A contract that purports to be made by or on behalf of a company at a time when the company has not been formed has effect, subject to any agreement to the contrary, as one made with the person purporting to act for the company or as agent for it, and he is personally liable on the contract accordingly.

. . .

[2.28] Phonogram Ltd v Lane [1982] QB 938 (Court of Appeal)

[The facts appear from the judgment of Lord Denning.]

LORD DENNING MR: In 1973 there was a group of 'pop' artists. They included two gentlemen called Brian Chatton and John McBurnie. The suggestion was that they should perform under the name 'Cheap Mean and Nasty'. A company was going to be formed to run the group. It was to be called 'Fragile Management Ltd'.

Before the company was formed, negotiations took place for the financing of the group . . . It was eventually arranged that money should be provided by Phonogram Ltd. The agreed amount was £12,000, and the first instalment was to be £6,000. The first instalment of £6,000 was paid.

But the new company was never formed. The group never performed under it. And the £6,000 was due to be repaid. But it was never repaid. Phonogram Ltd then tried to discover who was liable to repay the money. Mr Roland Rennie was the man who had negotiated on behalf of Phonogram. Mr Brian Lane was the man who had negotiated on behalf of the new company which was to be formed. I will read the letter from Mr Rennie to Mr Lane of 4 July 1973. It is the subject matter of this action. [Lord Denning read the letter, which contained an undertaking to repay the £6,000 if the deal was not completed. The undertaking was signed by Mr Lane, 'for and on behalf of Fragile Management Ltd'. He continued:]

. . . Phonogram Ltd say that the law of England has been much altered by s 9(2) of the European Communities Act 1972 [CA 2006 s 51]. [His Lordship read the section and continued:] That seems to me to cover this very case. The contract purports to be made on behalf of Fragile Management Ltd, at a time when the company had not been formed. It purports to be made by Mr Lane on behalf of the company. So he is to be personally liable for it.

Mr Thompson, on behalf of Mr Lane, argued very skilfully that s 9(2) did not apply. First, he said: 'Look at the directive under the European Community law which led to this section being introduced.' It is Council Directive of 9 March 1968 (68/151/EEC). In 1968 English was not one of the official languages of the European Community. So Mr Thompson referred us to the French text of art 7 of the Directive:

Si des actes ont été accomplis au nom d'une société en formation, avant l'acquisition par celle-ci de la personnalité morale, et si la société ne reprend pas les engagements résultant de ces actes, les personnes qui les ont accomplis en sont solidairement et indéfiniment responsables, sauf convention contraire.

Mr Thompson says that, according to the French text, that Directive is limited to companies which are 'en formation', that is, companies which have already started to be formed.

Mr Thompson's submission is reinforced by passages from a French textbook—Ripert *Traité Elémentaire de Droit Commercial* (7th edn, 1972). As I read the passage at pp 601 and 604 of that treatise—interpreting the French as best I can—in the case of a French company or société there may be, recognised by law, a period of time while a company is in the course of formation when people have put their signatures to what I may call 'the articles of association'. That period is called the period when the société is 'en formation'. At p 604 a parallel is drawn with a baby at the time of gestation—between the time of conception and the time of birth—and a company when it is 'en formation'.

I reject Mr Thompson's submission. I do not think we should go by the French text of the Directive. It was drafted with regard to a different system of company law from that in this country. We should go by s 9(2) of our own statute, the European Communities Act 1972 . . .

That brings me to the second point. What does 'purports' mean in this context? Mr Thompson suggests that there must be a representation that the company is already in existence. I do not agree. A contract can purport to be made on behalf of a company, or by a company, even though that company is known by both parties not to be formed and that it is only about to be formed.

[Lord Denning dealt with another point and continued:]

But I would not leave the matter there. This is the first time the section has come before us. It will have much impact on the common law. I am afraid that before 1972 the common law had adopted some fine distinctions. As I understand *Kelner v Baxter* **[2.26]** it decided that if a person contracted on behalf of a company which was nonexistent, he himself would be liable on the contract. Just as, if a man signs a contract for and on behalf 'of his horses', he is personally liable. But, since that case was decided, a number of distinctions have been introduced by *Hollman v Pullin*,[65] *Newborne v Sensolid (Great Britain)Ltd* **[2.27]** and *Black v Smallwood*[66] in the High Court of Australia. Those three cases seem to suggest that there is a distinction to be drawn according to the way in which an agent signs a contract. If he signs it as 'agent for "X" company'—or 'for and on behalf of "X" company'—and there is no such body as 'X' company, then he himself can be sued upon it. On the other hand, if he signs it as 'X' company per pro himself the managing director, then the position may be different: because he is not contracting personally as an agent. It is the company which is contracting.

That distinction was disliked by Windeyer J in *Black v Smallwood*. It has been criticised by Professor Treitel in *The Law of Contract* (5th edn, 1979), p 559. In my opinion, the distinction has been obliterated by s 9(2) of the European Communities Act 1972. We now have the clear words, 'Where a contract purports to be made by a company, or by a person as agent for a company, at a time when the company has not been formed . . . ' That applies whatever formula is adopted. The person who purports to contract for the company is personally liable.

There is one further point on s 9(2) which I must mention. In the latest edition of *Cheshire and Fifoot's Law of Contract* (9th edn, 1976), after reciting s 9(2), it says, at p 462:

How far it in fact does so will depend on the meaning given to the words 'subject to any agreement to the contrary' since it could be argued that words showing that A signs as agent express an agreement that he is not to be personally liable. If this were correct *Newborne v Sensolid (Great Britain) Ltd* would still be decided the same way. But it may be suspected that the courts will try to give more content to the subsection.

We certainly will. The words 'subject to any agreement to the contrary' mean—as Shaw LJ suggested in the course of the argument—'unless otherwise agreed'. If there was an express agreement that the man who was signing was not to be liable, the section would not apply. But, unless there is a clear exclusion of personal liability, s 9(2) should be given its full effect. It means that in all cases such as the present, where a person purports to contract on behalf of a company not yet formed, then however he expresses his signature he himself is personally liable on the contract.

SHAW and OLIVER LJJ delivered concurring judgments.

---

[65] (1884) Cab & El 254.
[66] [1966] ALR 744.

➤ Note

Section 36C (which is re-enacted in CA 2006 s 51) has been criticised because it focuses largely on the liability of the 'agent' and is, at best, ambiguous on the question whether any, and if so what, *rights* are conferred on this person. However, these doubts have been largely resolved by the decision in *Braymist Ltd v Wise Finance Co Ltd* [2.29].

[2.29] Braymist Ltd v Wise Finance Co Ltd [2002] EWCA Civ 127, [2002] Ch 273 (Court of Appeal)

A firm of solicitors (WS) had signed ('as solicitors and agents') a contract by which Braymist purported to sell land to Wise Finance. In fact, Braymist had not been incorporated at that time and the land was then held by an associated company. When Wise Finance failed to complete the purchase, the vendors claimed that they had a right to enforce the contract. The Court of Appeal held that s 36C was to be interpreted as conferring not merely liabilities on WS but also rights of enforcement.

JUDGE LJ: The critical question for decision is whether section 36C(1) of the Companies Act 1985 [CA 2006 s 51] not only provides a remedy for a person, A, who has purported to enter into a contract with a company when it was unformed (the narrow view) but also imposes obligations enforceable against A's wishes by the person purporting to act for or as agent of the unformed company, B. I describe this as the broad view. The answer to this question is not straightforward, and for some time I was persuaded by Mr Blackett-Ord that the narrow view was right. I should therefore explain why I have reached the same conclusion as Arden and Latham LJJ. There is no difficulty when A chooses to proceed with the contract. He cannot cherry-pick the parts which are convenient or favourable to him. If the contract takes effect, it takes full effect, according to its terms, and the contractual obligations as well as contractual benefits and remedies created by the purported contract, continue in accordance with the agreed terms. But what if B wishes to enforce the contract against A? Is he entitled to do so, against A's wishes, and when A has done nothing to affirm the contract or to indicate that he wishes to proceed with it?

Section 36C (1) provides: "A contract which purports to be made by or on behalf of a company at a time when the company has not been formed has effect . . . as one made with the person purporting to act for the company or as agent for it, and he is personally liable on the contract accordingly."

At common law, if "the company was not in existence when the contract was signed there never was a contract" (per Lord Goddard CJ in Newborne v Sensolid (Great Britain) Ltd [2.27], 51: see also, the judgment of Morris LJ, and the judgment of Parker J upheld by the Court of Appeal). Section 36C(1) in effect abrogates this principle. There is deemed to be a contract. The purported contract, otherwise a nullity, "has effect", not as one made with the unformed company but as one made with the purported agent, who is "personally liable" to A on the contract.

My difficulty is created by the concluding words of the subsection, "and he is personally liable on the contract accordingly". If the contract "has effect" as one made with the purported agent of the company, B would become personally liable on the contract without the concluding words of the subsection. The contract "has effect". The language of section 36C(1) reflects the broad thrust of the First Council Directive (68/151/EEC), first implemented domestically in its predecessor, section 9(2) of the European Communities Act 1972. The recital twice refers to "protecting" third parties. In section II of the Directive, which concerns the validity of obligations entered into by a company, article 7 provides:

"If, before a company being formed has acquired legal personality, action has been carried out in its name and the company does not assume the obligations arising from such action, the persons who acted shall, without limit, be jointly and severally liable therefore, unless otherwise agreed."

If the broad view is correct, the statute has gone much further than the creation of new protection for A. Plainly, as a matter of statutory construction, section 36C(1) may have extended beyond simple compliance with the Directive. Nevertheless the concluding words add something: if surplusage, they would not be there. Their presence provides a clear indication that the highlight of section 36C(1) is protection for A."

A company cannot, by adoption or ratification, obtain the benefit of a contract purportedly made on its behalf before it came into existence. A new contract must be made after its incorporation in the same terms as the old one.

[2.30] Natal Land Co & Colonization Ltd v Pauline Colliery and Development Syndicate Ltd [1904] AC 120 (Privy Council)

The respondent company claimed specific performance of an agreement to lease certain coal-mining rights, initially made on 9 December 1897 by the appellants' agent, Rycroft, with a Mrs de Carrey. It was understood by Rycroft that Mrs de Carrey was acting on behalf of a syndicate (then still not incorporated) which was incorporated as the respondent company on 22 January 1898. On 31 January, Rycroft's authority to deal further with the land in question was stopped by a telegram from the appellant company's head office in London, and he communicated this fact to the syndicate's solicitors. In September 1898, the respondent company, which had been prospecting the land in pursuance of other terms of the agreement, discovered a seam of coal and claimed its right to the lease. The Privy Council, reversing the court below, held that there was no contract to which the respondent company was a party, and refused to decree specific performance.

The opinion of the Judicial Committee was delivered by LORD DAVEY: The court, consisting of Finnemore J and Mr Acting Justice Beaumont, decided in favour of the respondents . . . and by their judgment of 29 May 1902 decreed specific performance of the agreement with costs. On the question of privity of contract, they seem to have held that a new contract on the terms of the old one had been made between the appellants and the respondent. The acts of part performance which were relied on by the learned judges as evidence of such new contract were the occupation and working of the land in question by the respondents, the expenditure of money on the faith of the agreement, and the acceptance by the appellants of the payment of £100 as a guarantee for prospecting operations. This sum, however (as already stated), was in fact paid before the incorporation of the respondents.

Their Lordships do not think it necessary to say whether the agreement was or was not voidable on the grounds alleged, or on other grounds appearing in the correspondence, because they are clearly of opinion that there was no contract between the appellants and the respondents. The contract was made with Mrs de Carrey, and even if she can be treated as having made it on behalf either of the unincorporated syndicate, who were the promoters of the respondent company, or on behalf of the company itself when incorporated, it is clear that a company cannot by adoption or ratification obtain the benefit of a contract purporting to have been made on its behalf before the company came into existence. It is unnecessary to cite all the cases in which this has been decided from *Kelner v Baxter* **[2.26]** downwards. But the facts may show that a new contract was made with the company after its incorporation on the terms of the old contract. The circumstances relied on for that purpose in the present case are not, in the opinion of their Lordships, necessarily referable to, and do not necessarily imply, a new contract with the respondents. But a conclusive reason which negatives any new contract is that Rycroft, by whose agency the new contract must be supposed to have been made, had no power or authority after 31 January 1898 to make such a contract on behalf of the appellants, and his want of authority was known to the solicitors acting for the respondents. He was not either the actual or the ostensible agent for that purpose of the appellants.

> ## Notes

1. CA 2006 repeats this rule, in that the contract must be novated. Novation may be express or implied.

2. The Jenkins Committee in its Report (Cmnd 1749, 1962, paras 44, 54(b)) considered the law unsatisfactory and anomalous, and recommended that 'a company should be enabled unilaterally to adopt contracts which purport to be made on its behalf or in its name prior to incorporation, and thereby become a party thereto to the same extent as if the contract had been made after incorporation . . .'. Many Commonwealth countries have enacted provisions which follow the lines of this recommendation, and a similar reform was projected for the United Kingdom in the abortive Companies Bill of 1973, but this proposal was not revived when the First EC Directive was implemented; and so the *Natal Land* case is still good law.

3. The traditional doctrine of privity of contract (which states that a contract cannot confer benefits or impose obligations upon someone who is not a party) could be seen as a further obstacle to allowing a company to enforce a pre-incorporation contract. The doctrine has now, in part, been abrogated by the Contracts (Rights of Third Parties) Act 1999, following a recommendation of the Law Commission (Law Com No 242, 1996). This Act allows a person who is not a party to a contract to enforce a term, in certain circumstances, provided that that person is sufficiently identified; and s 1(3) expressly states that the person need not be in existence when the contract is entered into. The Law Commission in its report (paras 8.9–8.16) acknowledged that any change made to the privity doctrine might have some impact on pre-incorporation contracts, but took the view that any considered reform of the latter topic should be dealt with separately as a matter of company law. Of course, since the 1999 Act is concerned only with the enforcement of *rights* by a third party, and not with the imposing of obligations, there is no way in which that Act could be invoked in order to make a company a party in the full sense to a pre-incorporation contract. However, there is scope for its application in a more limited sense—ie where such a contract includes a term which expressly or purportedly confers a benefit on the unformed company. This could extend to the parties agreeing (for a consideration) that the company, when formed, should have the option of entering into a contract on predetermined terms.

4. As has been mentioned above, it is very common for those wishing to incorporate a business to acquire a ready-made company for the purpose, possibly changing its name if the existing name is not thought suitable. In *Oshkosh B'Gosh Inc v Dan Marbell Inc Ltd* [1989] BCLC 507, CA, Mr Craze bought a company named E Ltd 'off the shelf' and later changed its name to DM Ltd. Before the change of name was registered the company, acting through Craze, bought goods from the plaintiff. In an action to make Craze personally liable it was held that s 9(2) of the European Communities Act 1972 [CA 2006 s 51] could not be applied because the company had been formed (albeit under another name) at the time when the contract was made: the issue of an amended certificate of incorporation under CA 1985 s 28(6) did not imply that the company had been re-formed or re-incorporated. Again, in *Badgerhill Properties Ltd v Cottrell* [1991] BCLC 805, CA 1985 s 36C was held to be inapplicable where the company was in existence but had been described by an incorrect name. In contrast, in *Cotronic (UK) Ltd v Dezonie* [1991] BCLC 721, CA, a defendant escaped personal liability under CA 1985 s 36C for a different reason. He made a contract in 1986 in the name of W Ltd in ignorance of the fact that W Ltd had been struck off the register under CA 1985 s 652 in 1981 and had ceased to exist. A new company, also named W Ltd, was incorporated in 1989 to continue the business. The court held that he could not be made liable under s 36C because he had purported to make the contract on behalf of the old company and not the new one, which no one had thought about forming in 1986.

➤ Questions

1. Could any or all of the difficulties revealed by the *Natal Land* case have been met by Mrs de Carrey *assigning* her right to the lease to the company after it had been formed?

2. It is possible to create a valid trust for the benefit of an unborn child. Could the problems revealed by the *Natal Land* case have been surmounted by having someone enter into an agreement as trustee, rather than as agent, for the yet to be formed company?

3. If the facts of *Newborne v Sensolid* **[2.27]** recurred today, could Mr Newborne enforce the contract in the light of CA 2006 s 51? What remedy could the court give?

4. Suppose that in *Phonogram Ltd v Lane* **[2.28]** there was a second pre-incorporation contract concluded by Mr Lane with Phonogram for the making of a recording and that Phonogram, in breach of this contract, refused to make the recording. What remedy, if any, would (i) the company, and (ii) Mr Lane, have?

5. Was Lord Denning in *Phonogram Ltd v Lane* right to disregard the French text? (Contrast *International Sales and Agencies Ltd v Marcus* [1982] 3 All ER 551, and *Official Custodian for Charities v Parway Estates Ltd* **[3.18]**; and see also the *Marleasing* case **[1.01]**.)

3

CORPORATE ACTIVITY AND LEGAL LIABILITY

Introduction

The previous chapter considered what it means to say that a company is a legal person. This chapter looks at how the company *acts* as a legal person: in particular, how it enters into binding contracts, commits torts and crimes, makes gifts, sues and is sued.

Rules of attribution: how does a company act?

A company must act through human agents. The principal issue to be addressed in every problem in this area is: *which acts of which people will count as acts of the company*, so that we can say that the *company* has entered into a binding contract, or the *company* has committed a tort or a crime?

Once we have established what the *company* has done, or knows, or intends, then we are usually in a good position simply to apply the normal rules of contract, torts or crime to assess whether rights have been created or infringed.

The most significant contribution to answering the question, *'Who acts for the company?'*, comes from the next case. The fundamental principles that it set out are extracted here, but a longer extract, in context, appears later in this chapter (see **[3.29]**).

[3.01] Meridian Global Funds Management Asia Ltd v Securities Commission [1995] 2 AC 500 (Privy Council)

[The facts are immaterial at this stage, but see **[3.29]** for more detail.]

> The opinion of their Lordships was delivered by LORD HOFFMANN: . . . Any proposition about a company necessarily involves a reference to a set of rules. A company exists because there is a rule (usually in a statute) which says that a persona ficta shall be deemed to exist and to have certain of the powers, rights and duties of a natural person. But there would be little sense in deeming such a persona ficta to exist unless there were also rules to tell one what acts were to count as acts of the company. It is therefore a necessary part of corporate personality that there should be rules by which acts are attributed to the company. These may be called 'the rules of attribution'.
>
> The company's primary rules of attribution will generally be found in its constitution, typically the articles of association, and will say things such as 'for the purpose of appointing members of the board, a majority vote of the shareholders shall be a decision of the company' or 'the decisions of the board in managing the company's business shall be the decisions of the company'. There are also primary rules of attribution which are not expressly stated in the articles but implied by

company law, such as 'the unanimous decision of all the shareholders in a solvent company about anything which the company under its memorandum of association has power to do shall be the decision of the company': see *Multinational Gas and Petrochemical Co v Multinational Gas and Petrochemical Services Ltd* **[6.25]**.

These primary rules of attribution are obviously not enough to enable a company to go out into the world and do business. Not every act on behalf of the company could be expected to be the subject of a resolution of the board or a unanimous decision of the shareholders. The company therefore builds upon the primary rules of attribution by using general rules of attribution which are equally available to natural persons, namely, the principles of agency. It will appoint servants and agents . . .

The company's primary rules of attribution together with the general principles of agency, vicarious liability and so forth are usually sufficient to enable one to determine its rights and obligations. In exceptional cases, however, they will not provide an answer. . . . For example, a rule may be stated in language primarily applicable to a natural person and require some act or state of mind on the part of that person 'himself', as opposed to his servants or agents. . . . In such a case, the court must fashion a special rule of attribution for the particular substantive rule. This is always a matter of interpretation: given that it was intended to apply to a company, how was it intended to apply? Whose act (or knowledge, or state of mind) was *for this purpose* intended to count as the act etc of the company? One finds the answer to this question by applying the usual canons of interpretation, taking into account the language of the rule (if it is a statute) and its content and policy. . . .

Contractual liability: general issues

The issue to be addressed here is whether a contract between the company and an outsider is binding. The company and the outsider will only be able to enforce the contract (or be sued on it) if the contract is binding. A company is a legal person, and the principles which determine the validity of contracts between legal persons are already familiar. A contract is valid and binding only if the:

(i)   contracting parties have the *capacity* to contract (or are deemed or presumed to have that capacity); and

(ii)   agents effecting the transaction on behalf of the parties have the *authority (real or apparent)* to do so (or are deemed or presumed to have that authority).

Notice that the first question relates to the *company*, and the second to its *directors* (or other agents). The first question now creates few problems (although it used to create enormous ones); the second is often critical.

Corporate capacity

A company's capacity is often constrained in its articles. For example, a charitable company may expressly limit its activities (its '*objects*') to particular types of charitable activities in a nominated field. Commercial companies can do the same, although they have less reason to be so restrictive. These legal limitations in the company's constitutional documents limit the company's *capacity*.

Historically, purported acts outside these nominated objects were void. Neither party could enforce the contract, and any benefits transferred were subject to restitutionary claims aimed at restoring the parties to their pre-contractual positions. This created great disincentives for outsiders dealing with the company, and could wreak unfair and unexpected consequences on transacting parties. Its advantage, if there was one, was for the members: they could be sure (if the directors acted properly) that their investments were confined to selected types of ventures.

In the end, the commercial disadvantages and unfairness to outsiders were seen as a price too high to pay for members' security, and the legislature stepped in with statutory provisions protecting third parties. These provisions do not go so far as to deem a company to *have* the capacity to do anything, but they prevent the validity of any act to be called into question on the grounds of lack of capacity arising from anything in the company's constitution (CA 2006 s 39(1)). This is just as beneficial for outsiders, and preserves the right of insiders (particularly the company and the members) to sue their directors (or other agents) for breaches of the company's constitution (ie for acting outside the powers given to the directors: CA 2006 s 171, below, pp 230 ff) and for causing loss to the company (eg arising from the prohibited transaction). This is why the 'capacity issue' is no longer a problem for outsiders.

These issues are explored in more detail below, pp 120 ff.

Authority of the company's agents

Even if the company does have the capacity to enter into a particular type of contract, this does not mean that anyone and everyone can decide that the company *will* commit itself. For example, a national petroleum company certainly has the capacity to sell to customers, but not everyone (not even every company employee) can decide that the company *will* sell to a particular customer or enter into a transaction above certain value limits. Only those employees (or company *agents*) with *authority* to make a sale can commit the company in this way.

The issue of authority raises its own problems. The actual authority of an agent cannot extend to the doing of anything that is not permitted by the company's constitution (eg a company that may only perform charitable works, or only publish English monographs, cannot give *actual* authority to its agents to transact other types of business). So all the analytical work that went into interpreting a company's constitutional documents for the purpose of determining a *company's* capacity, could possibly go into the same task for the purpose of determining the limits of an *agent's* actual authority.

In practice, the end result might then have been a 'vicious circle': having removed the impediment to outsiders arising from the objects and their impact on corporate capacity, they reappear in another guise, with the same effect, because of their impact on agents' authority. Again, the legislature intervened, and, in favour of third parties 'dealing with a company in good faith, the power of the directors to bind the company, or authorise others to do so, is deemed to be free of any limitation under the company's constitution' (CA 2006 s 40(1)). Note the good faith limitation.

This is not all. A company's objects are not the only constraint on actual authority. Even where the proposed dealing *is* within the company's objects, only certain people will be given actual authority to transact the particular business on behalf of the company. So, in the example above, some employees will have *actual authority* to sell bulk supplies of petroleum to wholesalers or large retailers, perhaps within certain value limits depending on seniority, others only to sell petrol to the public at domestic outlets. Employees in the latter group are unlikely to have actual authority to transact the former types of business for the company. But appearances are sometimes misleading. An employee at head office may appear to outsiders to have the necessary authority to sell supplies to wholesalers, but the company's own internal rules and organisational structure may provide otherwise. Once again, the legal rules protect the outsider in these types of cases. They do that by common law mechanisms, not statutory ones. These are the legal rules on *ostensible or apparent authority* and the '*indoor management rule*'.

Clearly all these protective rules in favour of third parties are based on an underlying policy assumption that it is only reasonable, in the circumstances, for the outsider to believe, and rely on the fact, that the company's agent has the necessary authority to transact the business in issue. Where such assumptions are *not* reasonable, the protective provision falls away.

In particular, in relation to the statutory assumptions, CA 2006 s 41 specifically provides that directors and connected persons cannot rely on s 40 to assert the validity of a transaction (although the company can, at its option, affirm the transaction).[1] This section also imposes remedies that go beyond those available at common law: the contract is voidable (subject to certain exceptions); and the parties to the transaction *and* any directors of the company who authorised the transaction are liable to account to the company for any gain made, and compensate for any losses caused.

Binding contracts between the company and third parties

When these various rules are put together, it can be seen that a contract between the company and an outsider will be binding if:

(i) the company has the capacity to enter into the contract, *or* that capacity can be assumed (using s 39(1)); *and*

(ii) the director (or other agent transacting the deal) has *either* actual authority to transact the deal (or can be deemed to have that authority using s 40), *or* has *ostensible authority*. And, in cases of either actual or ostensible authority, if the impediment to successfully demonstrating the particular form of authority is an issue of internal company procedure, then the *indoor management rule* allows the third party to assume that the internal procedures are regular.[2]

Each of these elements is examined in the sections that follow.

Capacity: what is a company legally entitled to do?

The modern relevance of a company's capacity to act was summarised above, p 96. The rather odd conclusion seems to be that a company is legally *able* to do, and accept obligations to do, certain things that are beyond its capacity. But in this section we focus on defining a company's capacity as it was intended to be settled by its members.

The decision of the House of Lords in *Ashbury Railway Carriage and Iron Co Ltd v Riche* [3.02] put paid to any suggestion that a company might have all the powers of a natural person, or even be presumed to have such powers except to the extent that they were taken away by the law or the company's constitution. It is true that very shortly afterwards in *A-G v Great Eastern Rly Co* (1880) 5 App Cas 473, HL it was conceded that a company should be regarded as having power to do anything reasonably incidental to the objects stated in the memorandum, but the confusion between objects and powers has persisted ever since, and has not been dispelled by the legislative amendments of 1989 and 2006. While CA 2006 s 39(1) states that the *validity* of a corporate *act* shall not be called into question on the ground of lack of

---

[1] See s 41(4)(d). Since, by definition, the contract is in breach of the company's constitution, it might be thought that the affirmation procedure can only proceed if the *company* has the *capacity* to affirm (s 39 is immaterial in this context). Sometimes the constitutional provision that has been breached will not touch *company* capacity (eg provisions determining which directors are to make certain decisions), but others will (eg provisions determining the type of business to be pursued by the company). In the latter case, presumably the articles will have to be altered first. In the other cases, the company has the capacity to affirm, and provided the appropriate organ makes the decision, it will be effective by *ordinary* resolution, even though a decision to amend the relevant constitutional provision generally, for the future, would have required a special resolution: see the cases below, at pp 310 ff, on ratification of past breaches committed by the directors (as this affirmation is, also by definition).

[2] More accurately, this rule allowed outsiders to presume (in the absence of facts putting the outsider on inquiry) that there has been compliance with all matters of internal (non-public) management and procedure required by the articles (or other internal rules) for the proper exercise of any power.

capacity it does not say (as have many reforming statutes overseas) that a company shall be deemed by law to *have* the full capacity of a natural person.

Cases such as *Charterbridge Corpn Ltd v Lloyds Bank Ltd* **[3.06]**, *Re Horsley & Weight Ltd* **[3.05]** and the *Rolled Steel* case **[3.07]**, which discuss the question of *corporate* powers, will therefore remain relevant, notwithstanding the protections in CA 2006 ss 39 and 40, whenever there is a question as to whether an act of the *directors* which is in excess of their powers (ie authority) requires ratification by an ordinary or a special resolution.[3]

However, if we read carefully the judgments in some cases, and particularly that of Browne-Wilkinson LJ in *Rolled Steel*, we find references to acts which are an *abuse* of the company's powers, and not just in excess of those powers. This may be a different concept. It is certainly one which can be distinguished from acts which are an abuse of the *directors'* powers under the articles, in the sense that the directors are usurping some function which is constitution-ally the responsibility of the members or shareholders (*Hogg v Cramphorn Ltd* **[6.08]**). The implications of this distinction, particularly in regard to the question of ratification, have not been fully explored. Where the directors abuse their own powers, as in *Hogg v Cramphorn Ltd*, it is well settled that the members can ratify the relevant act or decision by ordinary resolution (*Bamford v Bamford* **[11.03]**). Where they *exceed* the company's powers (ie act beyond its capacity), their act was historically not capable of ratification at common law, although it may now be ratifiable. But where they *abuse* its powers (eg directors using the company's money to pay a member's debt, as in *International Sales and Agencies Ltd v Marcus* [1982] 3 All ER 551), it would surely be just as much an abuse for the members to purport to ratify the act as for the directors to commit it in the first place. Browne-Wilkinson LJ in *Rolled Steel*, however, thought that such an act might be ratified by the *unanimous* vote of the members. This suggestion (unless he was thinking of a unanimous *informal* resolution) would be a novelty having no counterpart elsewhere in company law and is, it is submitted, misplaced. Such unanimity might mean that the act could not be challenged in a derivative suit (below, pp 535 ff) because no member would be able to come to the court 'with clean hands'; but it would surely not bind a liquidator (or possibly a new board, following a change of control). It would surely be better to say that the shareholders, even if they act unanimously, are no more competent to act in abuse of the company's powers than the directors. The ruling of the Australian court in *Kinsela v Russell Kinsela Pty Ltd* **[6.04]** could be cited in support of this view; but the reasoning in this and similar cases is coloured by the fact that the company was on the verge of insolvent liquid-ation at the material time. We will have to await further cases before we can say how far this notion of abuse of the company's powers is recognised as a separate concept in law and, if so, what the position is regarding ratification when the abuse is perpetrated by the directors.

The company's statement of objects

Current position

Before CA 2006, an old-style memorandum of a company was required to state the company's objects. CA 2006, by contrast, drops the requirement for a memorandum in this form, and makes a statement of the objects optional for companies registering after the Act comes into force (s 31(1)).[4] In other words, if a statement of objects is made it will be contained in the articles; if none is made then the company's objects are unrestricted.[5] Much of the discussion

---

[3] See fn 1.

[4] Note that EC Directive 77/91/EEC Art 2(b) requires *public* companies to state their objects in their constitution. Whether s 31(1) (which provides that a company's objects are 'unrestricted') in the absence of a 'statement' meets this requirement is not clear.

[5] Section 31(2) provides that where a company changes its articles to add, remove or alter a statement of the com-pany's objects, it must give notice to the registrar. The registrar is to register that notice, and the alteration does not take effect until it has been so registered. Section 31(3) ensures that such an amendment to the company's articles will not affect any rights or obligations of the company or render defective any legal proceedings by or against it.

below is irrelevant to companies with unrestricted objects. These companies avoid all the risks of having their actions classified as *ultra vires* (to the extent that there are such risks, given CA 2006 ss 39 and 40).

History of the development of objects clauses

The reasoning behind objects clauses was that those who invest in a company are entitled to know what type of enterprise it is. An equity investor in a gold-mining company, it has been said, would not wish to see his savings 'frittered away' in a fish and chip business; equally, those who give credit to a company may reasonably expect some indication of the scope of the activities of the enterprise with which they are dealing. But the objects clause did not survive long merely as a statement for the information of investors and creditors. It soon became the basis for the development of the '*ultra vires*' doctrine, which dominated the thinking in important areas of company law for over a century. The reforms made over the past 20 years (now reflected in CA 2006 ss 39 and 40) have deprived the doctrine of its central role, but it has not disappeared altogether.

The *ultra vires* doctrine was a rule concerned with the *capacity* of the company. It imposed artificial limitations on the acts and things which a company was regarded, in law, as capable of doing. Of course, as we saw in an earlier chapter, there are some acts which in the nature of things a company, or any other kind of corporation, simply cannot perform (eg marry or commit the crime of rape). But the *ultra vires* doctrine declared that, in addition to these natural limitations on a company's capacity, it was also to be regarded as incapable of doing anything which was not within the scope of its objects clause, or reasonably incidental thereto. The doctrine, in other words, restricted the powers of the company to matters covered by its stated objects, and any act which was outside those objects was not simply beyond the authority of the directors as a corporate organ, but beyond the capacity of the company itself—and, in the eyes of the law, a nullity having no effect whatever. It followed that not even the unanimous decision of the members could authorise or ratify such an act, as the House of Lords established in the leading case of *Ashbury Railway Carriage & Iron Co Ltd v Riche* **[3.02]** in 1875.[6]

Although the doctrine was concerned to confine the activities of a company within its stated *objects*, it necessarily had the effect also of restricting the company's *powers*. The line between objects and powers is a difficult—perhaps an impossible—one to draw. The courts did make the concession that a company should be deemed to have implied powers to do anything reasonably incidental to its declared objects (*A-G v Great Eastern Rly Co* (1880) 5 App Cas 473, HL) so that, for instance, a trading company could borrow money for the purposes of its trading business, but even then the position was not always clear. Could a company with surplus funds invest them in the shares of another company? Was this something which it had power to do, incidentally to its main business, or did it need to state in its memorandum that investing in shares was one of its objects?

---

[6] The doctrine had been applied rather earlier to 'statutory' companies incorporated by special Act of Parliament, where it had an important role to play, for these companies commonly had powers to acquire land compulsorily for the purposes of constructing the railways, canals, etc for which they were formed, and it was vital that the courts could keep the exercise of such powers under strict control. It did not apply to the 'deed of settlement' companies which were the forerunners of the modern company, since such companies, being in essence partnerships, were always free to change their constitution by agreement among the members. The *Ashbury Rly Carriage* case had the double effect of confirming that the doctrine applied to companies incorporated by registration under the Companies Acts, and also that an *ultra vires* act of a company could not be validated even by a unanimous ratification.

The doctrine of *ultra vires* has never been applied to companies incorporated by royal charter (except in regard to powers conferred upon them by statute: *Hazell v Hammersmith and Fulham London Borough Council* [1992] 2 AC 1, HL). A chartered corporation which ventured into activities not authorised by its charter ran the (largely theoretical) risk that the charter might be forfeited on the initiative of the Crown, but the transactions which it entered into were not invalidated. However, it is possible that the judges, when laying down the *ultra vires* doctrine, did recall the scandals associated with the 'trafficking' in obsolete charters which went back to the days before the Bubble Act of 1720, and wanted to ensure that similar abuses did not arise with registered and statutory companies.

The draftsmen of company memoranda, confronted with such uncertainties, chose to minimise the risk that outsiders might attack the company's actions for lack of capacity. They tried to put the matter beyond doubt by enlarging the objects clause and specifically including the making of investments as one of the objects of the company. Naturally, objects clauses become longer and longer. The judges saw it as their role to fight a rearguard action against these attempts to undermine the *ultra vires* doctrine. They protested frequently at the length and prolixity of the drafting—a futile gesture, and a rather unbecoming attitude for them to take, since most of them must, as counsel, have spent much professional time earlier on in their careers in drafting and settling the very terms which they now sought to condemn!

By contrast, the insiders consistently aimed to ensure that the capacity of their companies should be as nearly unfettered as possible. Besides enumerating objects at great length, draftsmen have adopted other devices, such as (i) specifying what are essentially powers as *objects* of the company (*Re Introductions Ltd* [3.04], the *Rolled Steel* case [3.07]), (ii) including clauses designed to ensure that no listed object should be construed restrictively by being read as merely ancillary to some other object (an all objects are 'main objects' clause: see *Cotman v Brougham* [3.03]), and (iii) authorising the company, or its directors, to determine any extensions to the company's objects as may seem warranted (a 'subjective objects' clause: see *Bell Houses Ltd v City Wall Properties Ltd* (below, p 109).

These drafting devices were received by the courts with unfavourable comment but, on the whole, grudging support, and went a considerable way to mitigate the harshness of the *ultra vires* rule by minimising the occasions when it could be invoked.

The judges for their part sought with equal persistence to cling to what was left of the doctrine, perhaps partly out of a misplaced sense of rectitude, but more justifiably because it was, after all, the strongest weapon they had to cope with cases of blatant corporate wrongdoing.

Calls for reform

As a result of the approaches described above, the *ultra vires* doctrine struck most infrequently, but then with such random effect, that it was a hazard for the very people it was supposed to protect. These were the company's own members or shareholders and its unsuspecting creditors, who might naturally enough assume that a company with a properly drafted objects clause would have the power to do anything at all. Accordingly, the case for abolishing the doctrine altogether has for decades been an unanswerable one.

This was suggested by the Cohen Committee (Cmd 6659 (1945), para 12), which recommended that every company 'should, notwithstanding anything omitted from its memorandum of association, have as regards third parties the same powers as an individual. Existing provisions in memoranda as regards the powers of companies . . . should operate solely as a contract between a company and its shareholders as to the powers exercisable by the directors'. This recommendation was not implemented because the government at the time recognised that to abrogate the *ultra vires* principle without at the same time modifying the rule that all those dealing with a company were deemed to have constructive notice of its memorandum (below, p 141) would be pointless. The outsider would simply be deemed to know that the *directors* had no *authority* to contract on a matter not covered by the objects clause (rather than that the *company* had no *capacity*). The constructive notice rule was thought too important to jettison without further consideration, so the *ultra vires* doctrine was left in place.

The Jenkins Committee (Cmnd 1749 (1962), para 42) recommended a different reform, which would have replaced the constructive notice doctrine with an elaborate set of statutory rules, but rather oddly did not urge the abolition of the *ultra vires* doctrine itself. Nothing came of that recommendation, either.

Meantime, countries all around the Commonwealth were taking steps to discard both doctrines by one technique or another, such as enacting comprehensive lists of statutory objects applicable to all companies, declaring companies to have the full legal capacity of a natural person, allowing 'unlimited objects' clauses, making the objects clause optional, and even (in the case of the Isle of Man) banning the registration of objects clauses altogether.

When the United Kingdom acceded to the Treaty of Rome in 1972, it was finally necessary to make modifications to the doctrines of *ultra vires* and constructive notice in order to comply with art 9 of the First EC Company Law Directive (below). Article 9 was concerned (*inter alia*) to ensure that a third party dealing with a company should not be disadvantaged by the possibility that the company was acting beyond its capacity. In the UK, this was effected by s 9(1) of the European Communities Act 1972 (later consolidated as CA 1985 s 35, in its original form, then CA 1985 ss 35, 35A and 35B, and now CA 2006 ss 39 and 40). The drafting of the very first of these provisions was defective in a number of respects. There were suggestions it did not even meet the demands of the Directive. The result was most unsatisfactory: the harshest effects of the *ultra vires* doctrine were undoubtedly avoided in part, but the doctrine itself was allowed to survive.

Further reform came in 1989, following recommendations made by Professor Prentice in his Report, published in 1986. These recommendations also dealt with the doctrine of constructive notice (below, pp 141 ff) and the apparent authority of corporate representatives (below, pp 143 ff). Section 35 of CA 1985 was recast, so as to prevent the validity of any act done by a company from being called into question on the ground of lack of capacity (see below, p 118). But, once again, the *ultra vires* doctrine has not been abolished.

CA 2006 is in many respects the same. The *ultra vires* doctrine therefore survives for some internal purposes; has been used as a justification for imposing a disqualification order on a director (*Re Samuel Sherman plc* [1991] 1 WLR 1070); and continues to apply to charitable companies (s 35(4)) and to bodies not governed by the Companies Acts. On the 'internal purposes', the abolition of the traditional connection between a company's objects clause and its capacity does not mean that those acting on behalf of the company now have *carte blanche* to do what they like in the company's name. A member has always had a right to seek an injunction to prevent the company from entering into what would have been an *ultra vires* transaction. And directors must observe any limitations on their powers flowing from the company's consitution (s 171), and will be liable to the company for any breaches.

The problem now is to decide just how much of the massive body of case law which the doctrine generated in its heyday it remains important to know. It will still be necessary at times to construe a company's objects clause, particularly in the context of directors' duties, so knowledge of some, at least, of the old cases will be required for this purpose. Of the cases which follow, *Ashbury Railway Carriage and Iron Co Ltd v Riche* **[3.02]** is included primarily for historical interest; the other cases remain potentially relevant. The *Rolled Steel* case **[3.07]** is crucial.

Interpreting objects clauses and defining corporate capacity

Historically (but not now[7]), a company incorporated under the Companies Acts had power at common law to do only those things authorised by the memorandum. Anything not authorised, expressly or implicitly, was ultra vires the company and void, and could not be ratified or made effective even by the unanimous agreement of the members.

[3.02] Ashbury Railway Carriage and Iron Co Ltd v Riche
(1875) LR 7 HL 653 (House of Lords)

The company was incorporated under the Act of 1862. Clause 3 of the memorandum provided as follows: 'The objects for which the company is established are to make and sell, or lend on

---

[7] See the Note following this extract.

hire, railway-carriages and waggons, and all kinds of railway plant, fittings, machinery, and rolling-stock; to carry on the business of mechanical engineers and general contractors; to purchase and sell, as merchants, timber, coal, metals, or other materials; and to buy and sell any such materials on commission, or as agents.' Clause 4 of the articles was in these terms: 'An extension of the company's business beyond or for other than the objects or purposes expressed or implied in the memorandum of association shall take place only in pursuance of a special resolution.' The company agreed to provide Riche and his brother with finance for the construction of a railway in Belgium. It later repudiated the agreement and, when sued for damages, pleaded that it was *ultra vires* the company to enter into such a contract. In the lower courts the argument turned principally on the question whether the contract, though unauthorised, had been approved by the members under article 4; but in the House of Lords it was ruled that the contract was void and that ratification, even if it had taken place, would have been wholly ineffective.

LORD CAIRNS LC: My Lords, I agree . . . that a contract of this kind was not within the words of the memorandum of association. In point of fact it was not a contract in which, as the memorandum of association implies, the limited company were to be the employed, they were the employers. They purchased the concession of a railway—an object not at all within the memorandum of association; and having purchased that, they employed, or they contracted to pay, as persons employing, the plaintiffs in the present action, as the persons who were to construct it. That was reversing entirely the whole hypothesis of the memorandum of association, and was the making of a contract not included within, but foreign to, the words of the memorandum of association.

Those being the results of the documents to which I have referred, I will ask your Lordships now to consider the effect of the Act of Parliament—the Companies Act of 1862—on this state of things . . . Your Lordships are well aware that this is the Act which put upon its present permanent footing the regulation of joint stock companies, and more especially of those joint stock companies which were to be authorised to trade with a limit to their liability.

The provisions under which that system of limiting liability was inaugurated, were provisions not merely, perhaps I might say not mainly, for the benefit of the shareholders for the time being in the company, but were enactments intended also to provide for the interests of two other very important bodies; in the first place, those who might become shareholders in succession to the persons who were shareholders for the time being; and secondly, the outside public, and more particularly those who might be creditors of companies of this kind. And I will ask your Lordships to observe, as I refer to some of the clauses, the marked and entire difference there is between the two documents which form the title deeds of companies of this description—I mean the memorandum of association on the one hand, and the articles of association on the other hand. With regard to the memorandum of association, your Lordships will find, as has often already been pointed out, although it appears somewhat to have been overlooked in the present case, that that is, as it were, the charter, and defines the limitation of the powers of a company to be established under the Act. With regard to the articles of association, those articles play a part subsidiary to the memorandum of association. They accept the memorandum of association as the charter of incorporation of the company, and so accepting it, the articles proceed to define the duties, the rights and the powers of the governing body as between themselves and the company at large, and the mode and form in which the business of the company is to be carried on, and the mode and form in which changes in the internal regulations of the company may from time to time be made. With regard, therefore, to the memorandum of association, if you find anything which goes beyond that memorandum, or is not warranted by it, the question will arise whether that which is so done is ultra vires, not only of the directors of the company, but of the company itself. With regard to the articles of association, if you find anything which, still keeping within the memorandum of association, is a violation of the articles of association, or in excess of them, the question will arise whether that is anything more than an act extra vires the directors, but intra vires the company.

The clauses of the statute to which it is necessary to refer are four: in the first place, the sixth clause [CA 2006, s 7(1)]. That provides that 'Any seven or more persons associated for any lawful purpose may, by subscribing their names to a memorandum of association, and otherwise complying with the requisitions of this Act in respect of registration, form an incorporated company, with or without limited liability.' My Lords, this is the first section which speaks of the incorporation of the company [now single member companies are allowed]; but your Lordships will observe that it does not speak of that incorporation as the creation of a corporation with inherent common law rights, such rights as are by common law possessed by every corporation, and without any other limit than would by common law be assigned to them, but it speaks of the company being incorporated with reference to a memorandum of association; and you are referred thereby to the provisions which subsequently are to be found upon the subject of that memorandum of association.

The next clause which is material is the eighth [CA 2006 s 9(2)]: 'Where a company is formed on the principle of having the liability of its members limited to the amount unpaid on their shares, hereinafter referred to as a company limited by shares, the Memorandum of Association shall contain the following things' (I pass over the first and second, and I come to the third item which is to be specified): 'The objects for which the proposed company is to be established.' That is, therefore, the memorandum which the persons are to sign as a preliminary to the incorporation of the company. They are to state 'the objects for which the proposed company is to be established'; and the existence, the coming into existence, of the company is to be an existence and to be a coming into existence for those objects and for those objects alone.

Then, my Lords, the eleventh section [CA 2006 s 33] provides: 'The memorandum of association . . . shall, when registered, bind the company and the members thereof to the same extent as if each member had subscribed his name and affixed his seal thereto, and there were in the memorandum contained, on the part of himself, his heirs, executors, and administrators, a covenant to observe all the conditions of such memorandum, subject to the provisions of this Act.' Your Lordships will observe, therefore, that it is to be a covenant in which every member of the company is to covenant that he will observe the conditions of the memorandum, one of which is that the objects for which the company is established are the objects mentioned in the memorandum, and that he not only will observe that, but will observe it subject to the provisions of this Act. Well, but the very next provision of the Act contained in the twelfth section[8] is this: 'Any company limited by shares may so far modify the conditions contained in its memorandum of association, if authorised to do so by its regulations as originally framed, or as altered by special resolution in manner hereinafter mentioned, as to increase its capital by the issue of new shares of such amount as it thinks expedient, or to consolidate and divide its capital into shares of larger amount than its existing shares, or to convert its paid-up shares into stock, but, save as aforesaid, and save as is hereinafter provided in the case of a change of name, no alteration shall be made by any company in the conditions contained in its memorandum of association.' The covenant, therefore, is not merely that every member will observe the conditions upon which the company is established, but that no change shall be made in those conditions; and if there is a covenant that no change shall be made in the objects for which the company is established, I apprehend that that includes within it the engagement that no object shall be pursued by the company, or attempted to be attained by the company in practice, except an object which is mentioned in the memorandum of association.

Now, my Lords, if that is so—if that is the condition upon which the corporation is established—if that is the purpose for which the corporation is established—it is a mode of incorporation which contains in it both that which is affirmative and that which is negative. It states affirmatively the ambit and extent of vitality and power which by law are given to the corporation, and it states, if it is necessary so to state, negatively, that nothing shall be done beyond that ambit, and that no attempt shall be made to use the corporate life for any other purpose than that which is so specified.

---

[8] [Equivalent to CA 2006 s 617, although now the articles (there is no memorandum equivalent) may now be altered in all respects.]

Now, my Lords, with regard to the articles of association, observe how completely different the character of the legislation is. [His Lordship referred to provisions in the statute corresponding to CA 1985 s 9 and continued:] Of the internal regulations of the company the members of it are absolute masters, and, provided they pursue the course marked out in the Act, that is to say, holding a general meeting and obtaining the consent of the shareholders, they may alter those regulations from time to time; but all must be done in the way of alteration subject to the conditions contained in the memorandum of association. That is to override and overrule any provisions of the articles which may be at variance with it. The memorandum of association is, as it were, the area beyond which the action of the company cannot go; inside that area the shareholders may make such regulations for their own government as they think fit.

My Lords, that reference to the Act will enable me to dispose of a provision in the articles of association in the present case which was hardly dwelt upon in argument, but which I refer to in order that it may not be supposed to have been overlooked. It appears that there has come into the articles of association of this company one which is in these words: 'An extension of the company's business beyond or for other than the objects or purposes expressed or implied in the memorandum of association shall take place only in pursuance of a special resolution.' In point of fact, no resolution for the extension of the business of the company was in this case come to; but even if it had been come to, it would have been entirely inept and inefficacious. There was, in this fourth article, an attempt to do the very thing which, by the Act of Parliament, was prohibited to be done—to claim and arrogate to the company a power under the guise of internal regulation to go beyond the objects or purposes expressed or implied in the memorandum.

Now, my Lords, bearing in mind the difference which I have just taken the liberty of pointing out to your Lordships between the memorandum and the articles, we arrive at once at all which appears to me to be necessary for the purpose of deciding this case . . . I assume the contract in itself to be perfectly legal, to have nothing in it obnoxious to the doctrine involved in the expressions which I have used. The question is not as to the legality of the contract; the question is as to the competency and power of the company to make the contract. Now, I am clearly of the opinion that this contract was entirely, as I have said, beyond the objects in the memorandum of association. If so, it was thereby placed beyond the powers of the company to make the contract. If so, my Lords, it is not a question whether the contract ever was ratified or was not ratified. If it was a contract void at its beginning, it was void because the company could not make the contract. If every shareholder of the company had been in the room, and every shareholder of the company had said, 'That is a contract which we desire to make, which we authorise the directors to make, to which we sanction the placing the seal of the company', the case would not have stood in any different position from that in which it stands now. The shareholders would thereby, by unanimous consent, have been attempting to do the very thing which, by the Act of Parliament, they were prohibited from doing . . .

LORDS CHELMSFORD, HATHERLEY, O'HAGAN and SELBORNE delivered concurring opinions.

➤ Note

This case is no longer good law. Unless provisions in the articles are entrenched, the articles can be changed by special resolution (ss 21 and 22, and see below, p 204); and special resolutions can, it seems, be passed informally (see ss 29, 281, 283, and below, p 193). Also see the Model Articles for Private Companies, regs 5 and 6.

A declaration in the memorandum that each part of the objects clause is to be construed as a substantive clause and not deemed auxiliary or subsidiary to the object primarily specified is effective to prevent a restrictive construction of the objects clause.[9]

[3.03] Cotman v Brougham [1918] AC 514 (House of Lords)

[The facts appear from the opinion of Lord Finlay.]

LORD FINLAY LC: My Lords, the Essequibo Rubber and Tobacco Estates Limited is a company which was registered on 6 April 1910. The memorandum of association is one of a type which unfortunately has become common. The Companies (Consolidation) Act 1908 requires that the memorandum of association should set out, inter alia, 'the objects of the company' (s 3) [there is no longer a CA 2006 equivalent: see ss 8, 9ff, 18]. The memorandum of this company in clause 3 set out a vast variety of objects, and wound up with the following extraordinary provision: 'The objects set forth in any sub-clause of this clause shall not, except when the context expressly so requires, be in any wise limited or restricted by reference to or inference from the terms of any other sub-clause, or by the name of the company. None of such sub-clauses or the objects therein specified or the powers thereby conferred shall be deemed subsidiary or auxiliary merely to the objects mentioned in the first sub-clause, but the company shall have full power to exercise all or any of the powers conferred by any part of this clause in any part of the world, and notwithstanding that the business, undertaking, property or acts proposed to be transacted, acquired, dealt with or performed do not fall within the objects of the first sub-clause of this clause.'

Warrington LJ expressed some doubt in his judgment in this case whether a memorandum setting out such a profusion of objects was a compliance with the Act, and it is possible that in some future case the question may arise on application for a mandamus if the registrar should refuse registration, taking the ground that the Act requires that the memorandum should be in such a form that the real objects of the company are made intelligible to the public.

In the present case no such question arises. The registrar accepted the memorandum of association and gave a certificate of incorporation, and that certificate is conclusive. The seventeenth section of the Act [CA 2006 s 15(4)] enacts that 'A certificate of incorporation given by the registrar in respect of any association shall be conclusive evidence that all the requirements of this Act in respect of registration and of matters precedent and incidental thereto have been complied with, and that the association is a company authorised to be registered and duly registered under this Act.' All that the courts can do is to construe the memorandum as it stands.

In the present case the question is whether it was intra vires of the Essequibo Rubber Company to [underwrite an issue of shares in] another company, the Anglo-Cuban Oil Bitumen and Asphalt Company Limited . . .

The question depends upon the interpretation to be put upon the third clause of the memorandum of association. This clause has thirty heads dealing with a multitude of objects and of powers. It is only necessary to refer to the eighth and twelfth heads of that clause, in addition to the general provision at the end of the clause which I have already quoted . . . [His Lordship read sub-clauses (8) and (12), both of which specifically authorised dealings in shares, and continued:] I agree with both courts below in thinking that it is impossible to say that the acquisition of these powers was ultra vires of the Essequibo Company.

It is well worthy of consideration whether, if it should appear that the law as it stands is not sufficient to cope with such abuses as are exemplified in the memorandum now in consideration, the

---

[9] The *ratio decidendi* of this case is confined to the *ultra vires* rule. As appears from the speech of Lord Parker of Waddington, the court must sometimes also construe the objects clause of the memorandum when proceedings are brought to have the company wound up under IA 1986 s 122(1)(g) (the 'just and equitable' ground) (see below, p 653). The relevant question then is whether the 'main object' or 'substratum' of the company has failed. For this purpose a clause such as that considered in *Cotman v Brougham* is ineffective, and will not prevent the court from determining the 'main object' of the company as a matter of substance.

Companies Act should not be amended so as to bring the practice into conformity with what must have been the intention of the framers of the Act. But the only question before us now is the construction of the memorandum as it stands, and in my opinion this appeal must be dismissed with costs.

LORD PARKER OF WADDINGTON: My Lords, Mr Whinney in his able argument suggested that, in considering whether a particular transaction was or was not ultra vires a company, regard ought to be had to the question whether at the date of the transaction the company could have been wound up on the ground that its substratum had failed. Upon consideration I cannot accept this suggestion. The question whether or not a company can be wound up for failure of substratum is a question of equity between a company and its shareholders. The question whether or not a transaction is ultra vires is a question of law between the company and a third party. The truth is that the statement of a company's objects in its memorandum is intended to serve a double purpose. In the first place it gives protection to subscribers, who learn from it the purposes to which their money can be applied. In the second place it gives protection to persons who deal with the company, and who can infer from it the extent of the company's powers. The narrower the objects expressed in the memorandum the less is the subscriber's risk, but the wider such objects the greater is the security of those who transact business with the company. Moreover, experience soon showed that persons who transact business with companies do not like having to depend on inference when the validity of a proposed transaction is in question. Even a power to borrow money could not always be safely inferred, much less such a power as that of underwriting shares in another company. Thus arose the practice of specifying powers as objects, a practice rendered possible by the fact that there is no statutory limit on the number of objects which may be specified. But even thus, a person proposing to deal with a company could not be absolutely safe, for powers specified as objects might be read as ancillary to and exercisable only for the purpose of attaining what might be held to the company's main or paramount object, and on this construction no one could be quite certain whether the court would not hold any proposed transaction to be ultra vires. At any rate, all the surrounding circumstances would require investigation. Fresh clauses were framed to meet this difficulty, and the result is the modern memorandum of association with its multifarious list of objects and powers specified as objects and its clauses designed to prevent any specified object being read as ancillary to some other object. For the purpose of determining whether a company's substratum be gone, it may be necessary to distinguish between power and object and to determine what is the main or paramount object of the company, but I do not think this is necessary where a transaction is impeached as ultra vires. A person who deals with a company is entitled to assume that a company can do everything which it is expressly authorised to do by its memorandum of association, and need not investigate the equities between the company and its shareholders.

The only other point which I need mention is the company's name. In construing a memorandum of association the name of the company, being part of the memorandum, can, of course, be considered. But where the operative part of the memorandum is clear and unambiguous, I do not think its obvious meaning ought to be cut down or enlarged by reference to the name of the company. It should be remembered that the name is susceptible of alteration, and it would be impossible to hold that such alteration could diminish or enlarge a company's powers. On the other hand, the name may be very material if it be necessary to consider what is the company's main or paramount object in order to see whether its substratum is gone.

I think the appeal should be dismissed with costs.

LORD WRENBURY delivered a concurring opinion.

LORD ATKINSON concurred.

➤ Question

Was it right for Lord Parker to say: 'The narrower the objects expressed in the memorandum the less is the subscribers' risk, but the wider such objects the greater is the security of those who transact business with the company'? If the protection of these interests was the justification of the *ultra vires* rule, where did the doctrine go wrong?

➤ Note

There are other approaches that help to widen the scope of a company's objects clauses. In particular:

(i) Even at common law, in addition to the powers specifically conferred by the memorandum, a company has power to do whatever could fairly be regarded as incidental to its express objects: *A-G v Great Eastern Rly Co* (1880) 5 App Cas 473, HL.

(ii) The objects of the company may be formulated so as to leave the company itself, or the directors, the power to define activities into which the company may extend its business: *H A Stephenson & Son Ltd v Gillanders Arbuthnot & Co* (1931) 45 CLR 476 (High Court of Australia). This can be achieved via a 'Bell Houses' clause (*Bell Houses Ltd v City Wall Properties Ltd* [1966] 2 QB 656, CA): ie 'To carry on any other trade or business whatsoever which can, in the opinion of the board of directors, be advantageously carried on by the company in connection with or as ancillary to . . . the general business of the company.'

Some powers—such as the power to borrow—may be construed by the court as incidental powers, even though declared by the memorandum to be objects.

[3.04] Re Introductions Ltd [1970] Ch 199 (Court of Appeal)

[The facts appear from the judgment.]

HARMAN LJ: The company started its career in 1951 in connection with the Festival of Britain and facilities to be afforded to visitors from abroad in connection with that event. It had an issued capital of £400. Subsequently for some years after 1953 it carried on a business connected with deck chairs at a seaside resort. From 1958 to 1960 it carried on no business, but in the latter year there was a transfer of shares and a new board was elected which decided to make use of the company for a venture connected with pigs. It has always been the ambition apparently of the commercial community to stretch the objects clause of a memorandum of association, thus obtaining the advantage of limited liability with as little fetter on the activities of the company as possible. But still you cannot have an object to do every mortal thing you want, because that is to have no object at all. There was one thing that the plaintiff company could not do and that was to breed pigs. The venture of pig breeding is the type of adventure which has always drawn money from the pockets of the British public, who apparently much prefer to regard themselves as owners of an apple or an apple tree or a pig rather than a mere share in a company. Anyhow, this venture, like other similar ventures, has been a disastrous failure, and the company was ordered to be wound up in 1965.

In 1960 the then new directors approached the defendant bank with a view to opening an account. This became in due course of time heavily overdrawn, and the bank, requiring security, was offered two debentures secured on the company's assets. It is common ground that before the security was given the bank was furnished with a copy of the memorandum and articles of association and also became aware, and expressly aware, that the company was carrying on as its sole business the business of pig breeding, which it has now acknowledged was ultra vires the company's powers in its memorandum. The bank has, however, relied on the fact that there is in the objects clause of the memorandum a sub-clause (N) empowering the company in general terms to borrow, in particular by the issue of debentures, and to secure the loan by charge. There is also in this memorandum a form of words which is common enough, and has been for many years; the words at the end of the objects clause are these: 'It is hereby expressly declared that each of the proceeding sub-clauses shall be construed independently of and shall be in no way limited by reference to any other sub-clause and that the objects set out in each sub-clause are independent objects of the company.' Of course, the original idea of that form of words was to avoid the old difficulty, which was that there was a main objects clause and all the others were ancillary to the main objects; and many questions of ultra vires arose out of that.

It was argued, therefore, that the only obligation of the bank was to satisfy itself that there was an express power to borrow money, and that this power was converted into an object by the concluding words of the objects clause which I have read. It was said that, if this was so, not only need the bank inquire no further but also that it was unaffected by the knowledge which it had that the activity on which the money was to be spent was one beyond the company's powers.

The judge rejected this view, and I agree with him. He based his judgment, I think, on the view that a power or an object conferred on a company to borrow cannot mean something in the air: borrowing is not an end in itself and must be for some purpose of the company; and since this borrowing was for an ultra vires purpose, that is an end of the matter.

Mr Walton, I think, agreed that if sub-clause (N) must in truth be construed as a power, such a power must be for a purpose within the company's memorandum. He says that it is 'elevated into an object' (to use his own phrase) by the concluding words of the objects clause in the memorandum, and this object, being an independent object of the company, will protect the lender and that that is its purpose. I answer that by saying that you cannot convert a power into an object merely by saying so . . .

I agree with the judge that it is a necessarily implied addition to a power to borrow, whether express or implied, that you should add 'for the purposes of the company'. This borrowing was not for a legitimate purpose of the company: the bank knew it, and, therefore, cannot rely on its debentures. I would dismiss the appeal.

RUSSELL LJ . . . If the borrowing sub-clause had expressly stated that it did not include borrowing for use in an undertaking ultra vires the company, it would have been plainly unarguable that the bank's security was valid, the bank being fully aware that the borrowing was only for use in the pig breeding business and being at least deemed to be aware that such business was wholly ultra vires the company. But in every borrowing sub-clause, that which I have stated as having been expressly stated is implicit, whether or not the objects clause contains the proviso that is contained here. Putting the matter round the other way, supposing the borrowing clause had purported expressly to include borrowing for use in a business ultra vires the company, no lender could conceivably rely upon such a provision, which would have to be ignored as mere nonsense.

KARMINSKI LJ concurred.

➤ Notes

1. In *Rolled Steel Products (Holdings) Ltd v British Steel Corpn* [3.07], Vinelott J at first instance said ([1982] Ch 478 at 497:

> The question whether a stated 'object' is truly an independent object or purpose is always a question of construction. Even borrowing and lending moneys are activities capable of being pursued as independent objects—for instance, in the case of a bank or finance company; but commonly, where a sub-clause of the memorandum of association of a company states that one of the objects of the company is 'to lend or advance' or 'to borrow and raise' money it is artificial to construe the sub-clause as anything other than a power conferred for the furtherance of what are in truth its 'substantive objects' or purposes.

2. The approach of *Re Introductions Ltd* to the construction of objects clauses, including the 'demotion' in appropriate cases of 'objects' to 'incidental powers', has been endorsed in later cases, including *Rolled Steel Products* [3.07]. However, the judgments delivered in the Court of Appeal in that case make the distinction between objects and powers for most purposes

unimportant, and declare that the decision itself in *Introductions* should be seen as having rested not on *ultra vires* grounds but on the basis that the directors had abused their powers or exceeded their authority. See the discussion below, p 117, especially Note 4.

3. One type of corporate 'object' which may call for particular attention in this connection is that of making gifts and paying pensions and gratuities, as the case next cited illustrates.

> Question

Would the bank in this case have fared better if it had asked fewer questions?

The making of gratuitous payments may be a substantive object of a company.

[3.05] Re Horsley & Weight Ltd [1982] Ch 442 (Court of Appeal)

The company's memorandum included among its objects, by clause 3(o): 'to grant pensions to employees and ex-employees and directors and ex-directors . . . ' and further provided that all the objects should be read and construed as separate and distinct objects. The respondent Mr Stephen Horsley had served the company as a director and worked for it as an estimator for many years. The other directors were Mr Campbell-Dick and Mr Frank Horsley (who were the only two members of the company at the material time) and their two wives. Just before the respondent was due to retire from active work at the age of 65, Mr Campbell-Dick and Mr Frank Horsley, purporting to act on behalf of the company, took out a retirement pension policy for his benefit at a cost of over £10,000. The company went into liquidation a year later and in these proceedings the liquidator attacked the validity of the pension payment. The Court of Appeal, affirming Oliver J, held that it had not been *ultra vires* the company to take out the pension.

[For another part of the decision, see below, **[4.31]**.]

BUCKLEY LJ:. . . It has now long been a common practice to set out in memoranda of association a great number and variety of 'objects', so called, some of which (for example, to borrow money, to promote the company's interests by advertising its products or services, or to do acts or things conducive or incidental to the company's objects) are by their very nature incapable of standing as independent objects which can be pursued in isolation as the sole activity of the company. Such 'objects' must, by reason of their very nature, be interpreted merely as powers incidental to the true objects of the company and must be so treated notwithstanding the presence of a separate objects clause: *Introductions Ltd v National Provincial Bank Ltd* **[3.04]**. Where there is no separate objects clause, some of the express 'objects' may upon construction fall to be treated as no more than powers which are ancillary to the dominant or main objects of the company.

Ex hypothesi an implied power can only legitimately be used in a way which is ancillary or incidental to the pursuit of an authorised object of the company, for it is the practical need to imply the power in order to enable the company effectively to pursue its authorised objects which justifies the implication of the power. So an exercise of an implied power can only be intra vires the company if it is ancillary or incidental to the pursuit of an authorised object. So also, in the case of express 'objects' which upon construction of the memorandum or by their very nature, are ancillary to the dominant or main objects of the company, an exercise of any such powers can only be intra vires if it is in fact ancillary or incidental to the pursuit of some such dominant or main object.

On the other hand, the doing of an act which is expressed to be, and is capable of being, an independent object of the company cannot be ultra vires, for it is by definition something which the company is formed to do and so must be intra vires. I shall use the term 'substantive object' to describe such an object of a company.

The question, therefore, is whether para (o) of clause 3 of the company's memorandum of association in the present case contains a substantive object or merely an ancillary power. Having regard to the presence of the separate objects clause, the former of these alternatives must be the case unless the subject matter of para (o) is of its nature incapable of constituting a substantive object . . .

Mr Evans-Lombe [counsel for the liquidator] . . . submits that, properly construed, para (o) should be read as conferring merely an ancillary power . . . Mr Evans-Lombe . . . submits that . . . a capacity to grant pensions to employees or ex-employees, or to directors or ex-directors, is of its nature a power enabling the company to act as a good employer in the course of carrying on its business, and as such is an incidental power which must be treated as though it were expressly subject to a limitation that it can only be exercised in circumstances in which a grant of a pension will benefit the company's business. I do not feel able to accept that contention. Paragraph (o) must be read as a whole. It includes not only pensions and other disbursements which will benefit directors, employees and their dependants, but also making grants for charitable, benevolent or public purposes or objects. The objects of a company do not need to be commercial; they can be charitable or philanthropic; indeed, they can be whatever the original incorporators wish, provided that they are legal. Nor is there any reason why a company should not part with its funds gratuitously or for noncommercial reasons if to do so is within its declared objects.

Mr Evans-Lombe relies upon the finding of Oliver J that there is no evidence that the company did or could derive any benefit or that the question was considered by anyone connected with the transaction. He says that the provision of the pension must accordingly be accepted as having been purely gratuitous, that is to say, a gift which could and did confer no consequent benefit upon the company. Accepting this to have been the case, the transaction nonetheless falls, in my view, precisely within the scope of para (o) and, in my judgment, the purposes referred to in that paragraph are such as to be capable of subsisting as substantive objects of the company and, having regard to the separate objects clause, must be so construed. For these reasons the liquidator fails, in my view, on the ultra vires point . . .

CUMMING-BRUCE and TEMPLEMAN LJJ delivered concurring judgments.

➤ Question

'Borrowing is not an end in itself and must be for some purpose of the company.' Compare this statement from the judgment of Harman LJ, in *Re Introductions* [3.04] with that of Vinelott J in the *Rolled Steel* case [3.07]: 'Even borrowing and lending moneys are activities capable of being pursued as independent objects, for instance, in the case of a bank.' Is the distinction a valid one? For what purpose or purposes does a bank borrow money?

➤ Notes

1. The transaction in *Re Horsley & Weight Ltd* might now be open to attack under IA 1986, s 238, as being 'at an undervalue'.

2. In the Court of Appeal in *Brady v Brady* [8.08], Nourse LJ expressed views which suggest that the *ratio decidendi* of *Re Horsley & Weight Ltd* may have a restricted application. He said:

In its broadest terms the principle is that a company cannot give away its assets. So stated, it is subject to the qualification that in the realm of theory a memorandum of association may authorise a company to give away all its assets to whomsoever it pleases, including its shareholders. But in the real world of trading companies, charitable or political donations, pensions to widows of ex-employees and the like apart, it is obvious that such a power would never be taken. The principle is only a facet of the wider rule, the corollary of limited liability, that the integrity of a company's assets, except to the extent allowed by its constitution, must be preserved for the benefit of all those who are interested in them, most pertinently its creditors.

The House of Lords reversed the decision of the Court of Appeal in this case without commenting on these remarks.

The state of mind of those acting on behalf of a company, eg its directors, is irrelevant to the question of capacity.

[3.06] Charterbridge Corpn Ltd v Lloyds Bank Ltd [1970] Ch 62 (Chancery Division)

The plaintiff company asked the court to declare that a legal charge, given by a company referred to as 'Castleford' to the defendant bank as security for the due performance of its obligations under a guarantee, was void, being *ultra vires* Castleford. The guarantee was itself security for the indebtedness to the bank of another company ('Pomeroy') and other companies in the same group as Castleford, all of which were controlled and run by Mr Pomeroy. It was alleged that the guarantee and charge were *ultra vires* because at the time when they were given, Mr Pomeroy had not *bona fide* intended to further the interests of Castleford. The court held that this was irrelevant.

PENNYCUICK J: Pomeroy, in causing Castleford to enter into the guarantee, and, later on, the legal charge, was looking to the interests of the group as a whole. He considered it in the interest of the group as a whole that Castleford should enter into these transactions and that the other companies in the group should enter into comparable transactions. He did not, at the time of the transaction, take into consideration the interest of Castleford separately from that of the group. Mr Watkins and Mr Barber [officers of the defendant bank] likewise looked to the group as a whole. They believed the transactions to be proper ones. They likewise did not at the time of the transactions take into consideration the interest of Castleford separately from that of the group.

To avoid any possible misunderstanding, these findings do not, of course, imply that either Mr Pomeroy or the bank officers believed that the transactions were prejudicial to Castleford. They simply did not give separate consideration to the interest of Castleford . . .

It will be borne in mind that the present action is based exclusively upon the contention that it was ultra vires Castleford, ie outside its corporate powers, to give the guarantee and legal charge. On this footing the guarantee and legal charge were a nullity.

Apart from authority, I should feel little doubt that where a company is carrying out the purposes expressed in its memorandum, and does an act within the scope of a power expressed in its memorandum, that act is an act within the powers of the company. The memorandum of a company sets out its objectives and proclaims them to persons dealing with the company and it would be contrary to the whole function of a memorandum that objects unequivocally set out in it should be subject to some implied limitation by reference to the state of mind of the parties concerned.

Where directors misapply the assets of their company, that may give rise to a claim based on breach of duty. Again, a claim may arise against the other party to the transaction, if he has notice that the transaction was effected in breach of duty. Further, in a proper case, the company concerned may be entitled to have the transaction set aside. But all that results from the ordinary law of agency and has not of itself anything to do with the corporate powers of the company.

[His Lordship discussed the earlier cases and continued:] I conclude upon this view of the authorities that they contain nothing which makes it necessary for me to accept the second head advanced by Mr Goulding. In my judgment, the state of mind of the directors of Castleford and of the bank's officers is irrelevant upon this issue of ultra vires.

That is sufficient to dispose of the action; but in case I am wrong on my view of the law, I must proceed to express a conclusion upon the contention that in creating the guarantee and legal charge, the directors were not acting with a view to the benefit of Castleford. That is a question of fact, and the burden of proof lies on the plaintiff company. As I have already found, the directors of Castleford looked to the benefit of the group as a whole and did not give separate consideration to the benefit of Castleford. Mr Goulding contended that in the absence of separate consideration, they must, ipso facto, be treated as not having acted with a view to the benefit of Castleford. That is, I think, an unduly stringent test and would lead to really absurd results, ie unless the directors of a company addressed their minds specifically to the interest of the company in connection with each particular transaction, that transaction would be ultra vires and void, notwithstanding that the transaction might be beneficial to the company. Mr Bagnall for the bank contended that it is suffi-cient that the directors of Castleford looked to the benefit of the group as a whole. Equally I reject that contention. Each company in the group is a separate legal entity and the directors of a particu-lar company are not entitled to sacrifice the interest of that company. This becomes apparent when one considers the case where the particular company has separate creditors. The proper test, I think, in the absence of actual separate consideration, must be whether an intelligent and honest man in the position of a director of the company concerned, could, in the whole of the existing circumstances, have reasonably believed that the transactions were for the benefit of the company. If that is the proper test, I am satisfied that the answer here is in the affirmative . . .

➤ Note

The *Charterbridge* case may be contrasted with the Australian High Court's decision in *Walker v Wimborne* (1976) 137 CLR 1. In this case, directors were held liable on a misfeasance sum-mons for moving funds among companies in the same group, and for using funds of some of the companies for the payment of wages and salaries of persons who were not *bona fide* employees of those companies, but worked elsewhere in the group. (Exceptionally, it was held to be in order for one of the companies to pay a pension to a retiring director, although his services seem to have been rendered to the group as a whole.) In the course of his judgment, Mason J said:

> The word 'group' is generally applied to a number of companies which are associated by common or interlocking shareholdings, allied to unified control or capacity to control. In such a case the pay-ment of money by company A to company B to enable company B to carry on its business may have derivative benefits for company A as a shareholder in company B if that company is enabled to trade profitably or realise its assets to advantage. Even so, the transaction is one which must be viewed from the standpoint of company A and judged according to the criterion of the interest of that com-pany . . .
>
> [The] emphasis given by the primary judge to the circumstance that the group derived a benefit from the transaction tended to obscure the fundamental principles that each of the companies was a separate and independent legal entity, and that it was the duty of the directors of Asiatic to consult its interests and its interests alone in deciding whether payments should be made to other companies. In this respect it should be emphasised that the directors of a company in discharging their duty to the company must take account of the interest of its shareholders and its creditors. Any failure by the directors to take into account the interests of creditors will have adverse conse-quences for the company as well as for them. The creditor of a company, whether it be a member of a 'group' of companies in the accepted sense of that term or not, must look to that company for payment. His interests may be prejudiced by the movement of funds between companies in the event that the companies become insolvent.

However, it should be emphasised that *Walker v Wimborne* was not concerned with corporate capacity, but with directors' duties. In *Charterbridge* itself, Pennycuick J made it clear that these were distinct issues, as the case next cited confirms.

An act which comes within the scope of a power conferred expressly or impliedly by the company's constitution is not beyond the company's capacity by reason of the fact that the directors entered into it for some improper purpose.

[3.07] Rolled Steel Products (Holdings) Ltd v British Steel Corpn [1986] Ch 246 (Court of Appeal)

Clause 3 (κ) of the memorandum of RSP empowered it to give guarantees. It guaranteed the obligation of SSS, an associated company, to BSC and gave security over its property in transactions which were in no way for its own advantage but did benefit one of its own directors, Shenkman. All the shareholders of RSP were aware of the irregularity of these transactions, and so also was BSC. Vinelott J at first instance [1982] Ch 478 held that the knowledge of BSC that the transactions did not further the objects of RSP made them *ultra vires* and void, and incapable of validation by the members' consent. The Court of Appeal, though ruling that the transactions were unenforceable on other grounds [3.17], held that they were not *ultra vires*, and declared that the line of cases on which the judge had relied (including *Re Introductions Ltd* [3.04]), should not be understood as establishing that an improper purpose could affect the question of a company's capacity.

BROWNE-WILKINSON LJ: In my judgment, much of the confusion that has crept into the law flows from the use of the phrase 'ultra vires' in different senses in different contexts. The reconciliation of the authorities can only be achieved if one first defines the sense in which one is using the words 'ultra vires'. Because the literal translation of the words is 'beyond the powers', there are many cases in which the words have been applied to transactions, which, although within the capacity of the company, are carried out otherwise than through the correct exercise of the powers of the company by its officers: indeed, that is the sense in which the judge seems to have used the words in this case. For reasons which will appear, in my judgment, the use of the phrase 'ultra vires' should be restricted to those cases where the transaction is beyond the capacity of the company and therefore wholly void.

A company, being an artificial person, has no capacity to do anything outside the objects specified in its memorandum of association. If the transaction is outside the objects, in law it is wholly void. But the objects of a company and the powers conferred on a company to carry out those objects are two different things: see *Cotman v Brougham* [3.03]. If the concept that a company cannot do anything which is not authorised by law had been pursued with ruthless logic, the result might have been reached that a company could not (ie, had no capacity) to do anything otherwise than in *due* exercise of its powers. But such ruthless logic has not been pursued and it is clear that a transaction falling within the objects of the company is capable of conferring rights on third parties even though the transaction was an abuse of the powers of the company: see, for example, *Re David Payne & Co Ltd*.[10] It is therefore established that a company has capacity to carry out a transaction which falls within its objects even though carried out by the wrongful exercise of its powers.

In my judgment, for this purpose the position of a company is analogous to that of a human being who has fiduciary powers. If two trustees convey trust property in breach of trust, the conveyance is not void. As human beings they have the capacity to transfer the legal estate: their capacity to transfer flows from their status as human beings, not from the powers conferred on them as trustees. Even if their powers under the trust instrument did not authorise the conveyance, the legal estate will vest in the transferee. Beneficiaries under the trust would be entitled, if they learnt in time, to restrain the execution of such conveyance in excess of the powers of the trustees. If the beneficiaries only discovered the position after the conveyance, the transferee, if he took with notice, would be personally liable as a constructive trustee and the property conveyed could be recovered: but the conveyance would not be a nullity. So in the case of a limited company, if a

10 [1904] 2 Ch 608, CA.

transaction falls within the objects of the company (and is therefore within its capacity) it is effective to vest rights in a third party even if the transaction was carried out in excess or abuse of the powers of the company. If the members of the company learn of what is proposed in time, they will be able to restrain such transaction: if they only discover the facts later, their remedy lies against those who have wrongly caused the company to act in excess or abuse of the company's powers. If a third party has received the company's property with notice of the excess or abuse of powers, such third party will be personally liable as a constructive trustee and the company will be able to recover the property: see *Belmont Finance Corpn Ltd v Williams Furniture Ltd (No 2)* **[8.10]**.

However, the analogy between companies and trustees is not complete. As an artificial person, a company can only act by duly authorised agents. Apart from questions of ostensible authority, directors like any other agents can only bind the company by acts done in accordance with the formal requirements of their agency, eg by resolution of the board at a properly constituted meeting. Acts done otherwise than in accordance with these formal requirements will not be the acts of the company. However, the principles of ostensible authority apply to the acts of directors acting as agents of the company and the rule in *Turquand*'s case **[3.15]** establishes that a third party dealing in good faith with directors is entitled to assume that the internal steps requisite for the formal validity of the directors' acts have been duly carried through. If, however, the third party has actual or constructive notice that such steps had not been taken, he will not be able to rely on any ostensible authority of the directors and their acts, being in excess of their actual authority, will not be the acts of the company.

The critical distinction is, therefore, between acts done in excess of the capacity of the company on the one hand and acts done in excess or abuse of the powers of the company on the other. If the transaction is beyond the capacity of the company it is in any event a nullity and wholly void: whether or not the third party had notice of the invalidity, property transferred or money paid under such a transaction will be recoverable from the third party. If, on the other hand, the transaction (although in excess or abuse of powers) is within the capacity of the company, the position of the third party depends upon whether or not he had notice that the transaction was in excess or abuse of the powers of the company. As between the shareholders and the directors, for most purposes it makes no practical difference whether the transaction is beyond the capacity of the company or merely in excess or abuse of its power: in either event the shareholders will be able to restrain the carrying out of the transaction or hold liable those who have carried it out. Only if the question of ratification by all the shareholders arises will it be material to consider whether the transaction is beyond the capacity of the company since it is established that, although all the shareholders can ratify a transaction within the company's capacity, they cannot ratify a transaction falling outside its objects.

In this judgment I therefore use the words 'ultra vires' as covering only those transactions which the company has no capacity to carry out: ie those things the company cannot do at all as opposed to those things it cannot do properly.

The two badges of a transaction which is ultra vires in that sense are (1) that the transaction is wholly void and (consequentially) (2) that it is irrelevant whether or not the third party had notice. It is therefore in this sense that the transactions in *Re David Payne & Co Ltd* and *Charterbridge Corpn Ltd v Lloyds Bank Ltd* **[3.06]** were held not to be ultra vires. The distinction between the capacity of the company and the abuse of powers was also drawn by Oliver J in *Re Halt Garage (1964) Ltd* **[5.04]** . . .

For these reasons, in considering a claim based on ultra vires, the first step must be to determine what are the objects (as opposed to the powers) of a company. Not all activities mentioned in the objects clause are necessarily objects in the strict sense: some of them may only be capable of existing as, or on their true construction are, ancillary powers: *Cotman v Brougham* and *Re Introductions Ltd.* And this may be the position even if the memorandum of association contains the usual 'separate objects' clause: such a clause is not capable of elevating into an object of the company that which is in essence a power: see *Re Introductions Ltd* **[3.04]**.

If, on construction of the objects clause, the transactions fall within the objects (as opposed to the powers), it will not be ultra vires since the company has the capacity to enter into the transaction. If the objects clause contains provisions (whether objects or powers) which show that a transaction of the kind in question is within the capacity of the company, that transaction will not be ultra vires . . .

The main difficulty in reconciling the authorities is *Re Introductions Ltd*. In my judgment, however, the decision in that case accords with the views I have expressed. The bank seeking to enforce the debenture had actual knowledge that the company was going to use the borrowed moneys for a purpose (pig breeding) which was wholly outside its main objects. The provision relating to borrowing in the memorandum of association was construed as being an ancillary power to borrow for the purposes of the company's business. Accordingly, the lender had actual notice of all the facts necessary to appreciate that the borrowing was in excess of the powers, ie, an abuse of powers. It is to be noted that in the Court of Appeal judgments the transaction is nowhere categorised as ultra vires and void. Indeed, . . . the Court of Appeal held that the liability of the bank depended on the fact that it had notice. Buckley J at first instance described the borrowing as being ultra vires: but, in my judgment, this was merely an unguarded use of language since he also regarded the bank's knowledge of the facts as being a crucial element rendering the debenture unenforceable . . . In my judgment, the *Introductions* case is not a decision relating to ultra vires in the strict sense: it is an example of a case in which a third party has entered into a transaction with a company with actual notice that the transaction was an abuse of power and accordingly could not enforce the transaction against the company . . .

Applying those principles to the present case, in my judgment, no question of ultra vires arises.

SLADE and LAWTON LJJ delivered concurring judgments.

➤ Notes

1. Whether they acknowledged it or not, the members of the Court of Appeal in this case were making a break with the past and laying down a new rule. Their reasoning is undoubtedly more logical, but their treatment of earlier—indeed, binding—Court of Appeal decisions such as *Re Introductions Ltd* [3.04] is controversial. Do you think Rolled Steel *can* be reconciled with earlier decisions, including the well-known case of *Sinclair v Brougham* [1914] AC 398, HL? (This last case was overruled by the House of Lords in *Westdeutsche Landesbank Girozentrale v Islington London Borough Council* [1996] AC 669, but not on the issue of whether the transaction in issue *was* void.)

2. The events in *Rolled Steel Products* occurred before the European Communities Act 1972 came into force—ie before there was any provision in the law corresponding to CA 1985 ss 35–35A and, now, CA 2006 s 39. But this would not have saved BSC, since the court held that it had not been 'acting in good faith'.

3. The judgments in *Rolled Steel Products* refer throughout to ratification by the *unanimous* consent of all the shareholders. It is not clear whether the members of the court had in mind precedents such as *Multinational Gas* [6.25] and *Re Horsley & Weight Ltd* [3.05/4.31], where the consent had to be unanimous because it was given informally (see below, p 193), or whether they were intending to lay down a new rule. On previous authority, a resolution validly passed by majority vote at a general meeting would be effective to ratify: *see North-West Transportation Co Ltd v Beatty* [4.34] and *Bamford v Bamford* [4.33]. On this point, see further below, pp 221 ff, and note the changes made to these approval and ratification rules by CA 2006 ss 180 and 239.

4. The distinction made in cases such as *Re Introductions Ltd* [3.04] between a substantive object and a 'mere' power loses a lot of point in the light of the decision in *Rolled Steel*, but it may remain of some relevance to the question of whether the directors have exceeded or

abused their corporate powers (see below, p 285). Would a ruling by the court that a particular act is within the objects of the company, rather than its powers (as in *Re Horsley & Weight Ltd* [3.05]), be conclusive, or merely strengthen the directors' case?

Protecting third parties (outsiders) against the consequences of limitations on corporate capacity

The judgments in the *Rolled Steel* case [3.07] draw a distinction between the company's power or *capacity* to do an act (absence of which renders the contract *void*), and the directors' exercise of that power for improper ends (which renders the contract *voidable*, but *only* against third parties who are not *bona fide* purchasers for value without notice of the company's interest). This distinction will save many transactions with third parties that had previously been regarded as beyond capacity, when it was thought that the company's powers could not (at law) be exercised for improper ends.

In addition to this protection, the legislature has intervened in ways described earlier, allowing all third parties to make certain assumptions about the company's capacity, and allowing all third parties acting in good faith (with the exception of directors and connected parties) to make certain assumptions about the directors' authority. See above, pp 96 ff. The provisions are extracted below for ease of access. The good faith exception is considered in more detail below, at pp 132 ff.

Companies Act 2006 ss 39 and 40

39 A company's capacity

(1) The validity of an act done by a company shall not be called into question on the ground of lack of capacity by reason of anything in the company's constitution.

(2) This section has effect subject to section 42 (companies that are charities).

40 Power of directors to bind the company

(1) In favour of a person dealing with a company in good faith, the power of the directors to bind the company, or authorise others to do so, is deemed to be free of any limitation under the company's constitution.

(2) For this purpose—

    (a) a person "deals with" a company if he is a party to any transaction or other act to which the company is a party,

    (b) a person dealing with a company—

        (i)   is not bound to enquire as to any limitation on the powers of the directors to bind the company or authorise others to do so,

        (ii) is presumed to have acted in good faith unless the contrary is proved, and

        (iii) is not to be regarded as acting in bad faith by reason only of his knowing that an act is beyond the powers of the directors under the company's constitution.

(3) The references above to limitations on the directors' powers under the company's constitution include limitations deriving—

    (a) from a resolution of the company or of any class of shareholders, or

    (b) from any agreement between the members of the company or of any class of shareholders.

(4) This section does not affect any right of a member of the company to bring proceedings to restrain the doing of an action that is beyond the powers of the directors.

But no such proceedings lie in respect of an act to be done in fulfilment of a legal obligation arising from a previous act of the company.

(5) This section does not affect any liability incurred by the directors, or any other person, by reason of the directors' exceeding their powers.

(6) This section has effect subject to—

section 41 (transactions with directors or their associates), and

section 42 (companies that are charities).

[Note: CA 2006 s 41 is an important qualification to these general rules. It alters dramatically the presumptions where the transaction is with directors or their associates.]

Companies Act 1985 (as amended by CA 1989, s 108, following the Prentice Report)

35 A company's capacity not limited by its memorandum

(1) The validity of an act done by a company shall not be called into question on the ground of lack of capacity by reason of anything in the company's memorandum.

(2) A member of a company may bring proceedings to restrain the doing of an act which but for subsection (1) would be beyond the company's capacity; but no such proceedings shall lie in respect of an act to be done in fulfilment of a legal obligation arising from a previous act of the company.

(3) It remains the duty of the directors to observe any limitations on their powers flowing from the company's memorandum; and action by the directors which but for subsection (1) would be beyond the company's capacity may only be ratified by the company by special resolution.

A resolution ratifying such action shall not affect any liability incurred by the directors or any other person; relief from any such liability must be agreed to separately by special resolution.

First EC Directive No 68/151/EEC

Article 9

1. Acts done by the organs of the company shall be binding upon it even if those acts are not within the objects of the company, unless such acts exceed the powers that the law confers or allows to be conferred on those organs.

However, Member States may provide that the company shall not be bound where such acts are outside the objects of the company, if it proves that the third party knew that the act was outside those objects or could not in view of the circumstances have been unaware of it; disclosure of the statutes[11] shall not of itself be sufficient proof thereof.

2. The limits on the powers of the organs of the company, arising under the statutes or from a decision of the competent organs, may never be relied on as against third parties, even if they have been disclosed.

3. If the national law provides that authority to represent a company may, in derogation from the legal rules governing the subject, be conferred by the statutes on a single person or on several persons acting jointly, that law may provide that such a provision in the statutes may be relied on as against third parties on condition that it relates to the general power of representation; the question whether such a provision in the statutes can be relied on as against third parties shall be governed by Article 3.[12]

---

11 [ie the memorandum and articles.]

12 [Article 3 refers to the registration of documents in a central register to be maintained by each member state, and the publication of particulars thereof in the national Gazette. This is provided for in the case of the United Kingdom by CA 2006 Part 35, see below, pp 582 ff.]

Agency and authority in corporate contracting

Re-read pp 97–99 above, which summarise the issues that need to be considered in deciding whether an agent acting for the company has successfully bound the company in contract to the third party.

Actual and ostensible or apparent authority of corporate agents

The cases below illustrate the courts' approach. There is a summary of the relevant principles below, at pp 143–144. The judgment of Diplock LJ in *Freeman and Lockyer* **[3.08]** is the *locus classicus*.

Explaining the principles of agency

[3.08] Freeman and Lockyer v Buckhurst Park Properties (Mangal) Ltd [1964] 2 QB 480 (Court of Appeal)

Two men had formed the defendant company to buy and resell a large estate. Kapoor was a property developer; Hoon had contributed half of the capital but played no active part in the company's business. Kapoor, Hoon and a nominee of each were appointed the four directors of the company, and under the articles all four were needed to constitute a quorum. Hoon spent much time abroad, leaving all the day-to-day management of the company's affairs to Kapoor. After an initial plan for the immediate resale of the land had fallen through, Kapoor decided to develop the estate and engaged the plaintiffs, a firm of architects and surveyors, to apply for planning permission. The company later refused to pay the plaintiffs' fees on the ground that Kapoor had had no authority to engage them. The county court judge held that the company was bound. The Court of Appeal affirmed his decision.

DIPLOCK LJ: The county court judge made the following findings of fact: (1) that the plaintiffs intended to contract with Kapoor as agent for the company, and not on his own account; (2) that the board of the company intended that Kapoor should do what he could to obtain the best possible price for the estate; (3) that Kapoor, although never appointed as managing director, had throughout been acting as such in employing agents and taking other steps to find a purchaser; (4) that Kapoor was so acting was well known to the board . . .

The county court judge did not hold (although he might have done) that actual authority had been conferred upon Kapoor by the board to employ agents. He proceeded on the basis of apparent authority, that is, that the defendant company had so acted as to be estopped from denying Kapoor's authority. This rendered it unnecessary for the judge to inquire whether actual authority to employ agents had been conferred upon Kapoor by the board to whom the management of the company's business was confided by the articles of association.

I accept that such actual authority could have been conferred by the board without a formal resolution recorded in the minutes, although this would have rendered them liable to a default fine under s 145(4) of the Companies Act 1948 [CA 2006 s 183]. But to confer actual authority would have required not merely the silent acquiescence of the individual members of the board, but the communication by words or conduct of their respective consents to one another and to Kapoor. [His Lordship discussed the evidence and continued:] I myself do not feel that there is adequate material to justify the court in reaching the conclusion of fact (which the county court judge refrained from making) that actual authority to employ agents had been conferred by the board on Kapoor.

This makes it necessary to inquire into the state of the law as to the ostensible authority of officers and servants to enter into contracts on behalf of a corporation. It is a topic on which there are confusing and, it may be, conflicting judgments of the Court of Appeal . . . We are concerned in the present case with the authority of an agent to create contractual rights and liabilities between his principal and a third party whom I will call 'the contractor'. This branch of the law has developed pragmatically rather than logically owing to the early history of the action of assumpsit and the consequent absence of a general jus quaesitum tertii [sic] in English law. But it is possible (and for the determination of this appeal I think it is desirable) to restate it upon a rational basis.

It is necessary at the outset to distinguish between an 'actual' authority of an agent on the one hand, and an 'apparent' or 'ostensible' authority on the other. Actual authority and apparent authority are quite independent of one another. Generally they co-exist and coincide, but either may exist without the other and their respective scopes may be different. As I shall endeavour to show, it is upon the apparent authority of the agent that the contractor normally relies in the ordinary course of business when entering into contracts.

An 'actual' authority is a legal relationship between principal and agent created by a consensual agreement to which they alone are parties. Its scope is to be ascertained by applying ordinary principles of construction of contracts, including any proper implications from the express words used, the usages of the trade, or the course of business between the parties. To this agreement the contractor is a stranger; he may be totally ignorant of the existence of any authority on the part of the agent. Nevertheless, if the agent does enter into a contract pursuant to the 'actual' authority, it does create contractual rights and liabilities between the principal and the contractor . . .

An 'apparent' or 'ostensible' authority, on the other hand, is a legal relationship between the principal and the contractor created by a representation, made by the principal to the contractor, intended to be and in fact acted upon by the contractor of a kind within the scope of the 'apparent' authority, so as to render the principal liable to perform any obligations imposed upon him by such contract. To the relationship so created the agent is a stranger. He need not be (although he generally is) aware of the existence of the representation but he must not purport to make the agreement as principal himself. The representation, when acted upon by the contractor by entering into a contract with the agent, operates as an estoppel, preventing the principal from asserting that he is not bound by the contract. It is irrelevant whether the agent had actual authority to enter into the contract.

In ordinary business dealings the contractor at the time of entering into the contract can in the nature of things hardly ever rely on the 'actual' authority of the agent. His information as to the authority must be derived either from the principal or from the agent or from both, for they alone know what the agent's actual authority is. All that the contractor can know is what they tell him, which may or may not be true. In the ultimate analysis he relies either upon the representation of the principal, that is, apparent authority, or upon the representation of the agent, that is, warranty of authority.

The representation which creates 'apparent' authority may take a variety of forms of which the commonest is representation by conduct, that is, by permitting the agent to act in some way in the conduct of the principal's business with other persons. By so doing the principal represents to anyone who becomes aware that the agent is so acting that the agent has authority to enter on behalf of the principal into contracts with other persons of the kind which an agent so acting in the conduct of his principal's business has usually 'actual' authority to enter into.

In applying the law as I have endeavoured to summarise it to the case where the principal is not a natural person, but a fictitious person, namely, a corporation, two further factors arising from the legal characteristics of a corporation have to be borne in mind. The first is that the capacity of a corporation is limited by its constitution, that is, in the case of a company incorporated under the Companies Act, by its memorandum and articles of association; the second is that a corporation cannot do any act, and that includes making a representation, except through its agent. [Lord Diplock discussed aspects of the ultra vires and constructive notice doctrines (now, of course, repealed), and continued:]

The second characteristic of a corporation, namely, that unlike a natural person it can only make a representation through an agent, has the consequence that in order to create an estoppel between the corporation and the contractor, the representation as to the authority of the agent which creates his 'apparent' authority must be made by some person or persons who have 'actual' authority from the corporation to make the representation. Such 'actual' authority may be conferred by the constitution of the corporation itself, as, for example, in the case of a company, upon the board of directors, or it may be conferred by those who under its constitution have powers of management upon some other person to whom the constitution permits them to delegate authority to make representations of this kind. If follows that where the agent upon whose 'apparent' authority the contractor relies has no 'actual' authority from the corporation to enter into a particular kind of contract with the contractor on behalf of the corporation, the contracor cannot rely upon the agent's own representation as to his actual authority. He can rely only upon a representation by a person or persons who have actual authority to manage or conduct that part of the business of the corporation to which the contract relates.

The commonest form of representation by a principal creating an 'apparent' authority of an agent is by conduct, namely, by permitting the agent to act in the management or conduct of the principal's business. Thus, if in the case of a company the board of directors who have 'actual' authority under the memorandum and articles of association to manage the company's business permit the agent to act in the management or conduct of the company's business, they thereby represent to all persons dealing with such agent that he has authority to enter on behalf of the corporation into contracts of a kind which an agent authorised to do acts of the kind which he is in fact permitted to do usually enters into in the ordinary course of such business. The making of such a representation is itself an act of management of the company's business. Prima facie it falls within the 'actual' authority of the board of directors, and unless the memorandum or articles of the company either make such a contract ultra vires the company or prohibit the delegation of such authority to the agent,[13] the company is estopped from denying to anyone who has entered into a contract with the agent in reliance upon such 'apparent' authority that the agent had authority to contract on behalf of the company.

If the foregoing analysis of the relevant law is correct, it can be summarised by stating four conditions which must be fulfilled to entitle a contractor to enforce against a company a contract entered into on behalf of the company by an agent who had no actual authority to do so. It must be shown:

(1) that a representation that the agent had authority to enter on behalf of the company into a contract of the kind sought to be enforced was made to the contractor.

(2) that such representation was made by a person or persons who had 'actual' authority to manage the business of the company either generally or in respect of those matters to which the contract relates;

(3) that he (the contractor) was induced by such representation to enter into the contract, that is, that he in fact relied upon it; and

(4) that under its memorandum or articles of association the company was not deprived of the capacity either to enter into a contract of the kind sought or be enforced or to delegate authority to enter into a contract of that kind to the agent.[14]

The confusion which, I venture to think, has sometimes crept into the cases is in my view due to a failure to distinguish between these four separate conditions, and in particular to keep steadfastly in mind (a) that the only 'actual' authority which is relevant is that of the persons making the representation relied upon, and (b) that the memorandum and articles of association of the company are always relevant (whether they are in fact known to the contractor or not) to the questions (i) whether condition (2) is fulfilled, and (ii) whether condition (4) is fulfilled and (but only if they are

---

[13] [These remarks must now be read in the light of CA 2006 s 40.]

[14] [This fourth requirement will not now be relevant, in the light of the reforms mentioned in the preceding footnote, except in the case where the 'contractor' cannot bring himself within CA 2006 s 40, eg because he was not dealing in good faith.]

in fact known to the contractor) may be relevant (iii) as part of the representation on which the contractor relied.

In each of the relevant cases the representation relied upon as creating the 'apparent' authority of the agent was by conduct in permitting the agent to act in the management and conduct of part of the business of the company. Except in *Mahony v East Holford Mining Co Ltd* **[3.16]**, it was the conduct of the board of directors in so permitting the agent to act that was relied upon. As they had, in each case, by the articles of association of the company full 'actual' authority to manage its business, they had 'actual' authority to make representations in connection with the management of its business, including representations as to who were agents authorised to enter into contracts on the company's behalf. The agent himself had no 'actual' authority to enter into the contract because the formalities prescribed by the articles for conferring it upon him had not been complied with. In *British Thomson-Houston Co v Federated European Bank Ltd* [[1932] 2 KB 176, CA], where a guarantee was executed by a single director, it was contended that a provision in the articles, requiring a guarantee to be executed by two directors, deprived the company of capacity to delegate to a single director authority to execute a guarantee on behalf of the company, that is, that condition (4) above was not fulfilled; but it was held that other provisions in the articles empowered the board to delegate the power of executing guarantees to one of their number, and this defence accordingly failed. In *Mahony*'s case no board of directors or secretary had in fact been appointed, and it was the conduct of those who, under the constitution of the company, were entitled to appoint them which was relied upon as a representation that certain persons were directors and secretary. Since they had 'actual' authority to appoint these officers, they had 'actual' authority to make representations as to who the officers were. In both these cases the constitution of the company, whether it had been seen by the contractor or not, was relevant in order to determine whether the persons whose representations by conduct were relied upon as creating the 'apparent' authority of the agent had 'actual' authority to make the representations on behalf of the company. In *Mahony*'s case, if the persons in question were not persons who would normally be supposed to have such authority by someone who did not know the constitution of the company, it may well be that he contractor would not succeed in proving condition (3), namely, that he relied upon the representations made by those persons, unless he proved that he did in fact know the constitution of the company . . .

The cases where the contractor's claim failed, namely *Houghton & Co v Nothard, Lowe & Wills Ltd* [[1927] 1 KB 246, CA], *Kreditbank Cassel GmbH v Schenkers Ltd* [[1927] 1 KB 826] and the *Rama Corpn* case,[15] were all cases where the contract sought to be enforced was not one which a person occupying the position in relation to the company's business which the contractor knew that the agent occupied, would normally be authorised to enter into on behalf of the company. The conduct of the board of directors in permitting the agent to occupy that position, upon the which the contractor relied, thus did not of itself amount to a representation that the agent had authority to enter into the contract sought to be enforced, that is, condition (1) was not fulfilled. The contractor, however, in each of these three cases sought to rely upon a provision of the articles giving to the board power to delegate wide authority to the agent as entitling him to treat the conduct of the board as a representation that the agent had had delegated to him wider powers than those usually exercised by persons occupying the position in relation to the company's business which the agent was in fact permitted by the board to occupy. Since this would involve proving that the representation on which he in fact relied as inducing him to enter into the contract comprised the articles of association of the company as well as the conduct of the board, it would be necessary for him to establish first that he knew the contents of the articles (that is, that condition (3) was fulfilled in respect of any representation contained in the articles) and secondly that the conduct of the board in the light of that knowledge would be understood by a reasonable man as a representation that

---

15 [*Rama Corpn Ltd v Proved Tin and General Investments Ltd* [1952] 2 QB 147, [1952] 1 All ER 554, concerning a contract negotiated by a single non-executive director.]

the agent had authority to enter into the contract sought to be enforced, that is that condition (1) was fulfilled. The need to establish both these things was pointed out by Sargant LJ in *Houghton*'s case in a judgment which was concurred in by Atkin LJ; but his observations, as I read them, are directed only to a case where the contract sought to be enforced is not a contract of a kind which a person occupying the position which the agent was permitted by the board to occupy would normally be authorised to enter into on behalf of the company . . .

In the present case the findings of fact by the county court judge are sufficient to satisfy the four conditions, and thus to establish that Kapoor had 'apparent' authority to enter into contracts on behalf of the company for their services in connection with the sale of the company's property, including the obtaining of development permission with respect to its use. The judge found that the board knew that Kapoor had throughout been acting as managing director in employing agents and taking other steps to find a purchaser. They permitted him to do so, and by such conduct represented that he had authority to enter into contracts of a kind which a managing director or an executive director responsible for finding a purchaser would in the normal course be authorised to enter into on behalf of the company. Condition (1) was thus fulfilled. The articles of association conferred full powers of management on the board. Condition (2) was thus fulfilled. The plaintiffs, finding Kapoor acting in relation to the company's property as he was authorised by the board to act, were induced to believe that he was authorised by the company to enter into contracts on behalf of the company for their services in connection with the sale of the company's property, including the obtaining of development permission with respect to its use. Condition (3) was thus fulfilled. The articles of association, which contained powers for the board to delegate any of the functions of management to a managing director or to a single director, did not deprive the company of capacity to delegate authority to Kapoor, a director, to enter into contracts of that kind on behalf of the company. Condition (4) was thus fulfilled.

I think the judgment was right, and would dismiss the appeal.

WILLMER and PEARSON LJJ delivered concurring judgments.

➤ Question

In *Hopkins v TL Dallas Group Ltd* [2004] EWHC 1379, Ch, Lightman J suggested that directors' actual authority is limited to acting in the interests of the company and in accordance with their fiduciary duty. He said:

. . . Before I look at the facts I should say a word on the relevant law. The authority of an agent is "actual (express or implied) where it results from a manifestation of consent that he should represent or act for the principal expressly or impliedly made by the principal to the agent himself": Bowstead & Reynolds on Agency 17th ed ("Bowstead") Article 22(1). This authority extends to doing "whatever is necessary for, or ordinarily incidental to, the effective execution of his actual authority": Bowstead Article 27. The authority may in appropriate circumstances extend to raising funds and giving security for borrowings for the purpose of fulfilling the functions and duties assigned to him. Where a board of directors appoint one of the members to an executive position "they impliedly authorise him to do all such things as fall within the usual scope of that office" *Hely-Hutchinson v Brayhead Ltd* **[3.09]**, at 583).

The grant of actual authority to an agent will not normally include authority to act for the agent's benefit rather than that of his principal and therefore, without agreement, the scope of actual authority will not include this. The grant of actual authority should be implied as being subject to a condition that it is to be exercised honestly and on behalf of the principal: *Lysaght Bros & Co Ltd v. Falk* (1905) 2 CLR 421. It follows that, if an act is carried out by an agent which is not in the interests of his principal, for example signing onerous unconditional undertakings, then the act will not be within the scope of the express or implied grant of actual authority. As a result there cannot be actual authority: "the agent is simply not authorised to act contrary to his principal's interests: and hence that an act contrary to those interests is outside his actual authority. The transaction is therefore void unless the third party can rely on the doctrine of apparent authority" (Bowstead para 8–218).

Does this ignore completely the decision of the Court to Appeal in *Rolled Steel* **[3.07]**?

[3.09] Hely-Hutchinson v Brayhead Ltd [1968] 1 QB 549, [1967] 3 All ER 98 (Chancery Division and Court of Appeal)

Richards was chairman of directors of the defendant company and its chief executive or '*de facto* managing director', who often committed the company to contracts on his own initiative and only disclosed the matter to the board subsequently. The board acquiesced in this practice. The plaintiff (referred to in the judgment as Lord Suirdale) was chairman and managing director of another company, 'Perdio', which it was planned should eventually be merged with the defendant. As part of an agreement to put more money into Perdio, the plaintiff (who had been made a director of the defendant company) was given certain letters (referred to as C 23 and C 26) signed by Richards, by which the defendant agreed to guarantee the repayment of money owed to the plaintiff and to indemnify him against certain losses. When sued on these undertakings, the defendant alleged that Richards had had no authority to make the contract in question. Roskill J held that Richards had *apparent* authority to bind his company; the Court of Appeal affirmed his decision, but on the grounds that he had *actual* authority.

ROSKILL J: The set-up in Brayhead is easy to envisage. It was an industrial holding company with a large number of subsidiaries. Its directors were in the main working directors, each in charge of a section of the holding company's subsidiaries. One would look after electronics, another engineering, and so on. They would all come back to Mr Richards for advice and—which is more important—decisions from time to time on matters concerning their own particular group. The final decision—and the final decision most especially on any matter concerning finance—was Mr Richards' and nobody else's. Sometimes, I dare say, the directors persuaded him to take or to refrain from taking a particular step; no doubt, like any wise chief executive, he sought and obtained advice before he made up his mind; but in all these cases the final decision, I am quite satisfied, rested with him and with nobody else.

If one goes through the minutes and documents which have been put before me, one can see repeated examples of Mr Richards acting in this way. Sometimes, of course, the matter would come back to the board for formal ratification after he had committed Brayhead perhaps technically without express authority. On other occasions, of which there are a number of examples in the minutes, he plainly committed Brayhead and then, as it were, reported the matter afterwards . . . I have no doubt that the board knew that he was doing this sort of thing all the time, and that whenever he thought it was necessary he assumed, or purported to assume, authority to bind Brayhead and that the board allowed him to do it and acquiesced in his doing it. That is not to say, to use Mr Finer's phrase yesterday, that all the directors were 'Yes men'; I am sure they were nothing of the kind. Mr Richards knew they were nothing of the kind. Mr Richards was a forceful personality; he knew his own mind. I think he quite clearly was allowed by Brayhead to hold himself out as having ostensible or apparent authority to enter into commitments of the kind which he entered into or purported to enter into, when he signed C23 and C26 . . .

[The Court of Appeal affirmed the decision of ROSKILL J, but on the grounds that Richards had *actual* authority.]

LORD DENNING MR: I need not consider at length the law on the authority of an agent, actual, apparent or ostensible. That has been done in the judgments of this court in *Freeman and Lockyer v Buckhurst Park Properties (Mangal) Ltd* **[3.08]**. It is there shown that actual authority may be expressed or implied. It is *express* when it is give by express words, such as when a board of directors pass a resolution which authorises two of their number to sign cheques. It is *implied* when it is inferred from the conduct of the parties and the circumstances of the case, such as when the board of directors appoint one of their number to be a managing director. They thereby impliedly authorise him to do all such things as fall within the usual scope of that office. Actual authority, express or implied, is binding as between the company and the agent, and also as between the company and others, whether they are within the company or outside it.

Ostensible or apparent authority is the authority of an agent as it *appears* to others. It often coincides with actual authority. Thus, when the board appoint one of their number to be managing director, they invest him not only with implied authority, but also with ostensible authority to do all such things as fall within the usual scope of that office. Other people who see him acting as managing director are entitled to assume that he has the usual authority of a managing director. But sometimes ostensible authority exceeds actual authority. For instance, when the board appoint the managing director, they may expressly limit his authority by saying he is not to order goods worth more than £500 without the sanction of the board. In that case his *actual* authority is subject to the £500 limitation, but his *ostensible* authority includes all the usual authority of a managing director. The company is bound by his ostensible authority in his dealings with those who do not know of the limitation . . .

Apply these principles here. It is plain that Mr Richards had no express authority to enter into these two contracts on behalf of the company: nor had he any such authority implied from the nature of his office. He had been duly appointed chairman of the company but that office in itself did not carry with it authority to enter into these contracts without the sanction of the board . . . The judge held that Mr Richards had ostensible or apparent authority to make the contract, but I think his findings carry with it the necessary inference that he had also actual authority, such authority being implied from the circumstance that the board by their conduct over many months had acquiesced in his acting as their chief executive and committing Brayhead Ltd to contracts without the necessity of sanction from the board.

LORDS WILBERFORCE and PEARSON delivered concurring judgments.

➤ Notes

1. *Guinness plc v Saunders* **[5.02]** provides a dramatic illustration of how easy it is to purport to contract with parties who lack actual authority to bind the company (here, it was a sub-committee of the board that lacked actual authority to negotiate remuneration issues), and the dire consequences that can ensue.

2. In *British Bank of the Middle East v Sun Life Assurance Co of Canada (UK) Ltd* [1983] BCLC 78, HL, it was held that a branch manager of a multinational insurance company had no 'usual' authority to represent to a bank that a subordinate employee had actual authority to execute undertakings to pay moneys to the bank. The evidence was that all such undertakings were in practice executed by insurance companies at their head office.

3. This decision may be contrasted with *First Energy (UK) Ltd v Hungarian International Bank Ltd* [1993] BCLC 1409, CA. The senior manager in charge of the Manchester office of the defendant bank (as the plaintiff company's representative knew) had no actual authority to sanction a credit facility for the plaintiff. However, he had signed a letter to the plaintiff offering to provide it with finance. He had no actual authority to sign this letter, either; but he was held to have had ostensible authority, by virtue of his position, to communicate such an offer on behalf of the bank—ie to inform the plaintiff that head office approval had been given for the offer to be made—and so the bank was bound. (Note: it is not possible to rely upon the ostensible authority of an individual if the person transacting with the company knew that the act was beyond the actual authority of the acting official: *Criterion Properties plc v Stratford UK Properties llc* **[3.10]**.)

4. Remember that acts that are beyond the actual authority of directors or other agents of a company can be ratified: see below, pp 347 ff.

➤ Questions

1. Is it right to think in terms of the 'usual' authority of a managing director? Is it not likely that the terms of appointment of managing directors will vary from case to case? (See *Harold Holdsworth & Co (Wakefield) Ltd v Caddies* **[3.12]**).

2. If Richards had implied actual authority to make the contract in *Hely-Hutchinson v Brayhead Ltd*, should not the trial judge in *Freeman and Lockyer* **[3.08]** have made a similar finding about Kapoor? (Also see the summary below at pp 143–144.)

[3.10] Criterion Properties plc v Stratford UK Properties LLC [2004] UKHL 28, [2004] BCLC 570, [2004] 1 WLR 1846 (House of Lords)

[More detailed facts appear in Lord Scott's opinion.] This was an appeal against a decision of the Court of Appeal ([2003] BCLC 50) that a 'poison pill' arrangement was binding on the claimant company and should not be set aside. The 'poison pill' was intended to thwart a hostile takeover of Criterion. The issue needed to be considered whether it was open to the board of directors of a public company to authorise the signing on the company's behalf of a 'poison pill' agreement intended to deter outsiders from making offers to members to purchase their shares. In particular was the further issue whether it was open to a board to authorise the signing of a 'poison pill' agreement where, as here, the deterrence consisted of a contingent divesting of the company's assets. These were issues to which s 35A of the Companies Act 1985 [CA 2006 s 40] was relevant. The House of Lords dismissed the appeal.

LORD NICHOLLS OF BIRKENHEAD:

4 . . . If a company ('A') enters into an agreement with B under which B acquires benefits from A, A's ability to recover these benefits from B depends essentially on whether the agreement is binding on A. If the directors of A were acting for an improper purpose when they entered into the agreement, A's ability to have the agreement set aside depends upon the application of familiar principles of agency and company law. If, applying these principles, the agreement is found to be valid and is therefore not set aside, questions of 'knowing receipt' by B do not arise. So far as B is concerned there can be no question of A's assets having been misapplied. B acquired the assets from A, the legal and beneficial owner of the assets, under a valid agreement made between him and A. If, however, the agreement is set aside, B will be accountable for any benefits he may have received from A under the agreement. A will have a proprietary claim, if B still has the assets. Additionally, and irrespective of whether B still has the assets in question, A will have a personal claim against B for unjust enrichment, subject always to a defence of change of position. B's personal accountability will not be dependent upon proof of fault or 'unconscionable' conduct on his part. B's accountability, in this regard, will be 'strict'.

LORD SCOTT OF FOSCOTE:

Introduction

6 This appeal arises out of an application for summary judgment made in an action in which the appellant, Criterion Properties plc ('Criterion'), is seeking to establish that an agreement into which it had apparently entered is not binding upon it and should be set aside. The respondent, Stratford UK Properties LLC (which I will refer to as 'Oaktree' for reasons I will later explain) contends, on the contrary, that there is nothing the matter with the agreement and has counterclaimed for specific performance.

Criterion's case

28 This is a case in which Criterion appears to have entered into a contract with Oaktree granting Oaktree the put option that I have described. The SSA was signed by Mr Glaser and Mr Palmer,

purporting to do so on Criterion's behalf. Did they have actual authority to do so? That is the first question. But there are sub-questions. It is accepted that Criterion in general meeting did not authorise or subsequently ratify the SSA. But did the board of Criterion do so? If the board did do so, did it have the power to do so? The effect of s 35A of the Companies Act 1985, may have to be taken into account. If the answer to these sub-questions is 'No', then it would seem to follow that Mr Glaser and Mr Palmer had no actual authority to sign the SSA.

29 If Mr Glaser and Mr Palmer had no actual authority to sign the SSA, did they have apparent, or ostensible, authority to do so? The answer to this question depends on a number of considerations as to which there is at present no clear evidence and at least one of which raises an issue of considerable public importance. The issue I have in mind is whether it is open to a board of directors of a public company to authorise the signing on the company's behalf of a 'poison pill' agreement intended to deter outsiders from making offers to shareholders to purchase their shares. And, in particular, is it open to a board to authorise the signing of a 'poison pill' agreement where, as here, the deterrence consists of a contingent divesting of company assets? The issue of the apparent authority of the board, or of Mr Glaser and Mr Palmer, must also take into account the features of the SSA that went beyond simply including provisions to deter an unwanted predator but would have deterred also the most desirable of predators, would have entrenched the chairman's and the managing director's continuance in their then current offices, and would have put them in a position in which their voluntary decision to relinquish office would potentially attract a heavy financial penalty for their company. Could it be said that they, or any of them, had apparent authority to conclude such an agreement? Here, too, s 35A of the Companies Act 1985, may be relevant.

30 This case turns, in my opinion, on the 'authority' issue. If Mr Glaser and Mr Palmer either had actual authority to conclude the SSA, given by a person or body with power to confer that authority (see British *Bank of the Middle East v Sun Life Assurance Co of Canada (UK) Ltd* [1983] 2 Ll Rep 9 and especially Lord Brandon of Oakbrook at p 17), or, if they did not have actual authority, had apparent authority to do so, then I can see no reason why the SSA should not be held enforceable against Criterion. If, on the other hand, Mr Glaser and Mr Palmer had neither actual nor apparent authority to conclude the SSA, then the SSA could not be held enforceable against Criterion. Mr Glaser and Mr Palmer might be liable to Oaktree for breach of warranty of authority, but the SSA would not be Criterion's contract. The conscionability or unconscionability of Oaktree's behaviour in seeking to hold Criterion to the SSA would in either case be irrelevant.

31 Both Hart J and the Court of Appeal thought that the SSA was clearly contrary to the commercial interests of Criterion. Hart J thought that Oaktree must have known, or be taken to have known, that that was so. I do not wish to be taken to be saying that knowledge of this sort on the part of Oaktree, or knowledge by Oaktree that Mr Glaser and Mr Palmer were, in signing the SSA, in breach of the duty they owed to Criterion, would be irrelevant to the authority issue. If a person dealing with an agent knows that the agent does not have actual authority to conclude the contract or transaction in question, the person cannot rely on apparent authority. Apparent authority can only be relied on by someone who does not know that the agent has no actual authority. And if a person dealing with an agent knows or has reason to believe that the contract or transaction is contrary to the commercial interests of the agent's principal, it is likely to be very difficult for the person to assert with any credibility that he believed the agent did have actual authority. Lack of such a belief would be fatal to a claim that the agent had apparent authority.

32 In my opinion, the authority issue cannot be resolved by your Lordships on this appeal. The authority issue was not addressed in the courts below, as in my opinion it should have been, and as a result your Lordships have not had the assistance of the courts below in identifying the principles which should be applied in determining the issue. Nor have counsel had much opportunity, in the period between the opening of the appeal when my noble and learned friend Lord Nicholls of Birkenhead raised the point and the conclusion of the hearing on the following day, to research the point. Moreover there are, as I have endeavoured to indicate, a number of factual matters that may be relevant to the issue that have not yet been placed in evidence. In these circumstances it seems

to me, to my regret, that your Lordships cannot finally resolve the issue here and now but must leave the issue either to be resolved at trial or, perhaps, if Criterion are so advised, on a further Civil Procedure Rules, Pt 20 application.

33 I would for these reasons dismiss the appeal.

LORDS RODGER OF EARLSFERRY, WALKER OF GESTINGTHORPE, and CARSWELL agreed.

➤ Question

The validity of the contract in this case was seen a question of the directors' authority to commit the company to the arrangement. Given the judgments in *Rolled Steel*, and the law on 'improper purposes' (see directors' duties, below, p 285), is this the most appropriate approach? Is it the only approach that protects third parties dealing with defaulting directors?

➤ Notes

1. In *AMB Generali Holding AG v Manches* [2005] EWCA Civ 1237, the court held that although a company that has endowed one of its members with ostensible authority (eg by virtue of an appointment to a given position) may withdraw that authority by sacking the 'agent,' third parties may continue to rely upon the initial representation unless and until the withdrawal of authority is communicated to them specifically.

2. A third party only has an obligation to inquire whether the transaction is outside the agent's authority if the circumstances of the transaction are somehow abnormal or suspicious: *Hopkins v TL Dallas Group Ltd* [2004] EWHC 1379, Ch.

'Usual authority' and its uses

See the Summary below at pp 143–144.

[3.11] Biggerstaff v Rowatt's Wharf Ltd [1896] 2 Ch 93 (Court of Appeal)

In consideration of cash advances made to the defendant company, Davy (the defendant's managing director) signed letters hypothecating various debts to Harvey, Brand & Co. By the articles the directors (who had power to hypothecate debts) were authorised to appoint a managing director and to delegate to him such of their powers as they thought fit. There was neither a minute showing what powers had been delegated to Davy nor, indeed, even of his appointment as managing director, although he had acted as such. The Court of Appeal (reversing North J) held that the hypothecations were valid.

[Another part of the decision is cited below, [10.11].]

LOPES LJ: The question as to the hypothecation of debts is quite distinct. It is said that the managing director had no power to hypothecate them. There is no doubt that Mr Davy was the managing director and acted as such, and according to the articles the directors could have given him the power which he purported to exercise. There is an absence of evidence that they had done so, but is that enough to make his acts void? In *Lindley on Companies*, 5th edn, p 159, the law is thus laid down: 'Upon principle, therefore, where persons are in fact employed by directors to transact business for a company the authority of those persons to bind a company within the scope of their employment cannot be denied by the company, unless—(1) their employment was altogether beyond the powers of the directors; or unless—(2) the persons employed have been appointed irregularly, and those who dealt with them had notice of the irregularity. Where the power to appoint an agent for a given purpose exists, irregularity in its exercise is immaterial to a person dealing with the agent bona fide and without notice of the irregularity in his appointment' . . .

Every word of that applies here. It cannot be said but that Mr Davy was acting within the limits of his apparent authority, or that Harvey, Brand & Co were not acting bona fide, or that they had not a right to assume the Mr Davy was duly appointed.

LINDLEY and KAY LJJ delivered concurring judgments.

➤ Note

This case seems to have been argued and decided primarily on the basis of the indoor management rule (ie the directors' *could have* delegated the necessary authority pursuant to a provision in the articles—and see below, at p 135, for the need for the third party to know of the relevant article) rather than on the basis of agency principles (ie the usual powers of a managing director would include this power, and by implication the board of directors has vested the power in the agent by appointing him to the position (actual authority) or has represented to the third party that the agent is a managing director, impliedly with this authority (ostensible authority)).

The functions of a managing director are not fixed by law, but depend on the particular terms of his appointment.

[3.12] Harold Holdsworth & Co (Wakefield) Ltd v Caddies
[1955] 1 WLR 352 (House of Lords)

[The facts appear from the opinion of Earl Jowitt.]

EARL JOWITT: My Lords, the appellants are a limited company carrying on business as worsted yarn spinners at Balne Mills, Wakefield, Yorkshire. In 1947 the appellant company had purchased from the respondent the entire share capital of a company known as the British Textile Manufacturing Co Ltd, whom I refer to as the Textile Company. The business of the Textile Company, which was carried on at Irvine, Ayrshire, was the manufacture of knitted articles of wool clothing. The appellant company thus became, and remained at all material times, the beneficial owners of all the shares in the Textile Company. They were also beneficial owners of all the shares in two other limited companies . . .

By an agreement between the appellant company and the respondent dated April 1, 1949, which was to operate as from October 1, 1948, the respondent was appointed managing director of the appellant company . . . Clause 1 of that agreement was in the following terms:

> [The respondent] shall be and he is hereby appointed a managing director of the [appellant] company and as such managing director he shall perform the duties and exercise the powers in relation to the business of the company and the business (howsoever carried on) of its existing subsidiary companies at the date hereof which may from time to time be assigned to or vested in him by the board of directors of the company.

Other clauses in that agreement provided that the respondent was to hold the said office for five years; that he was to devote his whole time and attention to his duties under the agreement and in all respects to conform to, and comply with, the directions and regulations of the board; and that he was to receive a salary of £2,500 per annum together with a commission on profits . . . Differences of opinion arose between the respondent and his fellow directors of the appellant company, and culminated in the passing of a resolution by the appellant company's board in the following terms:

Management at Balne Mills: The board decided that the managing director confine his attentions to British Textile Manufacturing Co Ltd only. Permanent arrangements for management at Balne Mills will be made later. Meanwhile the board requested Mr R P Pitcher to assume responsibility for local supervision. The managing director wished it recorded that as a director he did not agree with the decision.

The respondent regarded this resolution as a repudiation of the agreement and, by letter of 19 June 1950, intimated to the appellant company that, as they had so repudiated the agreement, he regarded himself as no longer bound to give, and intimidated that he would not give, his services to the appellant company.

My Lords . . . I am clearly of the opinion that the resolution did not constitute any breach of the agreement. I think that, on the true construction of cl 1 of the agreement of 1949, the respondent was to perform such duties and exercise such powers in relation to the business of the appellant company, and to perform such duties and exercise such powers in relation to the business of the Textile Company and the other subsidiaries, as might from time to time be vested in him by the appellant company's board. In directing the respondent on 10 May 1950, to confine his attention to the Textile Company, the board of the appellant company were, in my opinion, merely exercising the right given to them by the agreement.

The Lord President (Lord Cooper) took a different view, because he considered that the appointing of managing director was

> a well recognised title in company administration, carrying responsibilities of a familiar nature and involving sundry obligations and liabilities under the Companies Act. The [respondent] was not appointed to perform such duties, if any, as the board might assign to him.

The Lord President, having formed this view, no doubt considered that the resolution which called on the respondent to devote his whole time to the affairs of the Textile Company prevented him from carrying out those responsibilities, obligations and liabilities which, on this view, he had the right to perform for the appellant company, by virtue of his office as their managing director. My Lords, with the greatest respect for the Lord President, I do not think that the respondent, by the mere fact that he was appointed managing director of the appellant company, had any responsibilities, obligations or liabilities which would prevent the appellant company ordering him to devote his full time to a subsidiary, and I am of the opinion that the appellant company had, by cl 1 of the agreement, expressly preserved their right to call on the respondent to devote his time to the affairs of the Textile Company if they judged this course desirable.

Being of the opinion that there was no relevant breach of contract averred, I think the action should have been dismissed without proof, and, accordingly, I would allow the appeal.

VISCOUNT KILMUIR LC and LORDS MORTON OF HENRYTON and REID delivered concurring opinions. LORD KEITH OF AVONHOLM dissented.

➤ Question

Are the decisions in *Biggerstaff v Rowatt's Wharf Ltd* **[3.11]**, *Freeman & Lockyer v Buckhurst Park Properties (Mangal) Ltd* **[3.08]** and *Hely-Hutchinson v Brayhead Ltd* **[3.09]** consistent with the ruling in this case?

The secretary of a company has usual authority to bind the company in matters concerned with administration.

[3.13] Panorama Developments (Guildford) Ltd v Fidelis Furnishing Fabrics Ltd [1971] 2 QB 711 (Court of Appeal)

The secretary of the defendant company, Bayne, hired cars from the plaintiff, ostensibly for the company's business; but in fact he fraudulently used them for his own purposes. The company was held bound by the contracts to pay the hire charges.

LORD DENNING MR: [Counsel] says that the company is not bound by the letters which were signed by Mr Bayne as 'Company Secretary'. He says that, on the authorities, a company secretary fulfils a very humble role: and that he has no authority to make any contracts or representations on behalf of the company. He refers to *Barnett v South London Tramways Co*[16] where Lord Esher MR said: 'A secretary is a mere servant; his position is that he is to do what he is told, and no person can assume that he has any authority to represent anything at all . . .' Those words were approved by Lord Macnaghten in *George Whitechurch Ltd v Cavanagh*.[17] They are supported by the decision in *Ruben v Great Fingall Consolidated* **[9.12]**. They are referred to in some of the textbooks as authoritative.

But times have changed. A company secretary is a much more important person nowadays than he was in 1887. He is an officer of the company with extensive duties and responsibilities. This appears not only in the modern Companies Act, but also by the role which he plays in the day-to-day business of companies. He is no longer a mere clerk. He regularly makes representations on behalf of the company and enters into contracts on its behalf which come within the day-to-day running of the company's business. So much so that he may be regarded as held out as having the authority to do such things on behalf of the company. He is certainly entitled to sign contracts connected with the administrative side of a company's affairs, such as employing staff and ordering cars, and so forth. All such matters now come within the ostensible authority of a company's secretary.

Accordingly I agree with the judge that Mr R L Bayne, as company secretary, had ostensible authority to enter into contracts for the hire of these cars, and therefore, the company must pay for them. Mr Bayne was a fraud. But it was the company which put him in the position in which he, as company secretary, was able to commit the frauds. So the defendants are liable. I would dismiss the appeal, accordingly.

SALMON LJ: I think there can be no doubt that the secretary is the chief administrative officer of the company. As regards matters concerned with administration, in my judgment, the secretary has ostensible authority to sign contracts on behalf of the company. If a company is ordering cars so that its servants may go and meet foreign customers at airports, nothing, to my mind, is more natural than that the company should hire those cars through its secretary. The hiring is part of his administrative functions. Whether the secretary would have any authority to sign a contract relating to the commercial management of the company, for example, a contract for the sale or purchase of goods in which the company deals, does not arise for decision in the present case and I do not propose to express any concluded opinion upon the point; but contracts such as the present fall within the ambit of administration and I entertain no doubt that the secretary has ostensible power to sign on behalf of the company . . .

MEGAW LJ concurred.

Statutory deeming provisions to avoid constitutional limitations on directors' authority

The relevant provision is extracted above, at pp 118–119. The provision must be read carefully. It allows third parties 'dealing with' the company (defined in s 40(2)) in 'good faith' (with provisions on this in s 40(2)(b)) to deem the power of the 'directors'[18] (not other agents) to bind the company to be free of any 'limitation under the company's constitution' (defined more widely than limitations in the articles (see s 40(3)).

Note CA 2006 s 41. It excludes the presumptions permitted by CA 2006 s 40 where the dealing is with the directors of the company or its holding company, or any persons connected with these directors. Effectively, these 'insiders' are irrebuttably presumed to know the true

---

[16] (1887) 18 QBD 815, CA.

[17] [1902] AC 117.

[18] The predecessor provision in CA 1985 s 35A referred to the 'board of directors', which gave it limited application in practice. Presumably this change is intended to widen the application of the provision.

state of affairs. The remedies available to the company are wider than those available at common law, and are set out in s 41 (see below, p 135).

Meaning of good faith in CA 2006 s 40.

[3.14] TCB Ltd v Gray [1986] Ch 621 (Chancery Division); affd on other grounds [1987] Ch 458n (Court of Appeal)

Gray was sued on a guarantee which he had given to the plaintiff TCB to secure the indebtedness of a company called Link, of which Gray was a director. The debenture evidencing Link's debt had been signed by one Rowan purporting to act as Gray's attorney, but Link's articles required a director to sign personally. The court ruled that TCB, which had acted on the debenture in good faith, was protected by s 9(1) of the European Communities Act 1972 [CA 2006 s 40].

BROWNE-WILKINSON V-C: The debenture was not signed by any director of Link, but by an attorney for a director. There is no power in the articles of Link for a director to act by an attorney. Therefore, says Mr Brodie, on the principle delegatus non potest delegare the seal was not affixed in accordance with the requirements of the articles; accordingly the debenture is not the act of Link.

Apart from s 9(1) of the European Communities Act 1972, there would be much force in these submissions. But in my judgment that section provides a complete answer. Under the old law, a person dealing with a corporation was required to look at the company's memorandum and articles to satisfy himself that the transaction was within the corporate capacity of the company and was to be carried through in accordance with the requirements of its articles. The rigour of those requirements was only tempered to the extent that the rule in *Royal British Bank v Turquand* **[3.15]** allowed third parties to assume that acts of internal management had been properly carried out. It has been generally assumed that the old law has to a large extent been swept away by s 9(1) of the Act of 1972 . . . Section 9(1) was passed to bring the law of England into line with article 9 of Council Directive 68/151/EEC. In approaching the construction of the section, it is in my judgment relevant to note that the manifest purpose of both the directive and the section is to enable people to deal with a company in good faith without being adversely affected by any limits on the company's capacity or its rules for internal management. Given good faith, a third party is able to deal with a company through its 'organs' (as the directive describes them) or directors. Section 9(1) achieves this in two ways: first it 'deems' all transactions to be authorised; second, it deems that the directors can bind the company without limitations. The second part of the subsection reinforces this by expressly abolishing the old doctrine of constructive notice of the contents of a company's memorandum and articles. It being the obvious purpose of the subsection to obviate the commercial inconvenience and frequent injustice caused by the old law, I approach the construction of the subsection with a great reluctance to construe it in such a way as to reintroduce, through the back door, any requirement that a third party acting in good faith must still investigate the regulating documents of a company.

Mr Brodie, whilst accepting that TCB had no actual or imputed knowledge of any irregularity in the execution of the debenture, at first submitted that TCB did not act 'in good faith' within the meaning of the section since TCB was put on inquiry by the unusual manner in which the debenture had been executed. He said that TCB should have looked at the articles and would then have discovered the irregularity. Accordingly, he submitted, they were not acting 'in good faith'. On further consideration Mr Brodie abandoned this argument, to my mind rightly. The last words of the second part of s 9(1) expressly provide that good faith is to be presumed: the second part further provides the person dealing with the company is *not* bound to inquire as to limitations on the powers of directors. In my judgment, it is impossible to establish lack of 'good faith' within the meaning of the subsection solely by alleging that inquiries ought to have been made which the second part of the subsection says need not be made.

Mr Brodie's next submission was that, in order for s 9(1) to apply at all, the first requirement is that there must be a transaction by the company. Since Link never sealed the debenture in the only way authorised by the articles, there was here no transaction by Link at all; the debenture was not the act of Link. If this argument is right, it drives a coach and horses through the section. In every dealing with the company the third party would have to look at its articles to ensure that the company was binding itself in an authorised manner. In my judgment the section does not have the effect. The section is dealing with purported actions by a company which, having regard to its internal documents, may be a nullity, eg acts outside its corporate capacity. In such a case under the old law the purported act of the company would not be the act of the company at all. Yet the first part of s 9(1) deems it so to be. Similarly a document under seal by the company executed otherwise than in accordance with its articles was not, under the old law, the act of the company: but s 9(1) deems it so to be since the powers of the directors are deemed to be free from limitations, ie as to the manner of affixing the company's seal. In my judgment, s 9(1) of the Act applies to transactions which a company purports to enter into and deems them to be validly entered into . . .

Accordingly the necessary basis for s 9(1) of the Act of 1972 to apply, as between Link and TCB, exists. It follows that the debenture was valid, and Mr Gray's second line of defence also fails.

➤ Notes

1. In *Barclays Bank Ltd v TOSG Trust Fund Ltd* [1984] BCLC 1 at 17, Nourse J made the following observations on the meaning of the phrase 'in good faith':

[Counsel for the defendants] said that even if the assignment agreement was ultra vires the trust fund nevertheless, in favour of the agency, it is deemed, by virtue of s 9(1) of the European Communities Act 1972 to have been intra vires, on the ground that at all material times the agency acted in 'good faith', that is to say that it genuinely and honestly believed that it was within the trust fund's corporate powers to enter into the assignment agreement. Counsel for the plaintiffs, on the other hand, says that before s 9(1) can apply the agency must have acted not only genuinely and honestly, but in circumstances where it neither knew nor ought to have known the lack of vires. That means, he says, that the agency must have acted not only genuinely and honestly, but reasonably as well . . .

My view of that question is this. In the case of a transaction decided on by the directors s 9(1) has abolished the rule that a person who deals with a company is automatically affected with constructive notice of its objects clause. But, by retaining the requirement of good faith, it nevertheless ensures that a defence based on absence of notice shall not be available to someone who had not acted genuinely and honestly in his dealings with the company. Notice and good faith, although two separate beings, are often inseparable. There is a most valuable account of their liaison in the speech of Lord Wilberforce in the recent case of *Midland Bank Trust Co v Green*.[19] What it comes to is that a person who deals with a company in circumstances where he ought anyway to know that the company has no power to enter into the transaction will not necessarily act in good faith. Sometimes, perhaps often, he will not. And a fortiori where he actually knows. Next, a person who acts in good faith will sometimes, perhaps often, act in a manner which can also be described as being reasonable. But I emphatically refute the suggestion, if such it is, that reasonableness is a necessary ingredient of good faith. That would require the introduction of an objective standard into a subjective concept and it would be contrary to everything which the law has always understood of that concept. In my judgment a person acts in good faith if he acts genuinely and honestly in the circumstances of the case. Beyond that it is neither possible nor desirable to attempt an examination of the circumstances in which s 9(1) may or may not apply.

[19] [1981] AC 513 at 528 and 529, HL.

[The decision of Nourse J was reversed on another point: [1984] 1 All ER 628, CA; affd [1984] AC 626, HL; but no comment was made about this passage in any of the judgments on appeal.]

2. In *Wrexham Association Football Club Ltd v Crucialmove Ltd* [2006] EWCA Civ 237, CA, the court held that CA 1985 s 35A [CA 2006 s 40] does not protect a person who failed to inquire about matters in circumstances in which he should have done so (eg, where the third party does not deal with the entire board of directors, but needs to establish whether the board has authorised the dealing—note that this was in the context of CA 1985 s 35A, which protects dealings with the 'board of directors', not simply the 'directors' as in CA 2006 s 40).

3. In *Smith v Henniker-Major and Co* [2002] EWCA Civ 762, [2003] Ch 182, CA, the court discussed whether there is an 'irreducible minimum' that has to be established before a person can rely on CA1985 s 35A (CA 2006 s 40). For example, can the provision be relied upon where the person dealing on behalf of the company is not a director at all? No conclusion emerges from the judgments (see Robert Walker LJ at [41] and contrast with Carnwath LJ at [103]-[108]). Given the policy of the Directive that is being implemented, is a restrictive or expansive approach preferable? What are the risks of either extreme in these approaches?

Transactions involving directors or their associates: CA 2006 s 41

As noted earlier, CA 2006 s 40 cannot be relied upon by directors or their associates. CA 2006 s 41 ensures this, and provides a variety of remedies for the company (see above, pp 132–133). The terms of CA 2006 s 41 raise several questions.

➤ Questions

1. In *Smith v Henniker-Major and Co* [2002] EWCA Civ 762, [2003] Ch 182, CA, the court refused to allow a director to rely on CA 1985 s 35A. Does CA 2006 s 41 provide an effective answer to this case?

2. If the facts of *Guinness v Saunders* **[5.02]** were to recur, would CA 2006 s 41 be applicable?

3. If the directors have no *actual* authority to bind the company, and directors and their associates cannot rely on presumptions in s 40 (or, presumably, on common law assumptions of ostensible authority), then the resulting transaction is *void* under the ordinary rules of agency. What, if anything, is achieved by declaring that it is voidable (as s 41 does)? Given the common law rule, what is the impact of the saving provision in s 41(1) that preserves the operation of other rules of law that may call into question the validity of the transaction?

The 'indoor management rule'

The 'indoor management' or 'internal management' rule, also known as the rule in *Royal British Bank v Turquand* **[3.15]**, allows a person dealing with a company to assume, in the absence of circumstances putting him or her on inquiry, that all matters of internal management and procedure have been duly complied with (*Omnia praesumuntur rite et solemniter esse acta*). So, although under the doctrine of constructive notice (see below, at p 141) such a person was taken to be aware of the provisions of the company's memorandum and articles, and thus of any restrictions contained in those documents, he was not bound to inquire further. He could take it for granted that its officers had been duly appointed, that meetings had been properly summoned and conducted and that resolutions had been passed by requisite majorities.

The development of the rule, and of various limitations on its application, can be seen in the cases below.

The question must now be asked, however: what is the standing of the rule, and the scope for its application, now that the doctrine of constructive notice has been abolished (see CA 2006 s 40(2)(b))? If the rule was itself only a qualification to the doctrine, will it not have been swept away also? For various reasons, it is probably wrong to take that view.

In the first place, although it is true that the rule did operate to mitigate the effects of the doctrine of constructive notice, that was never its only function. It is a rule of wider scope. A person dealing with a company is, and always has been, subject to uncertainty as to whether its officers have been properly appointed, its resolutions duly passed, etc, whether or not the question arises in connection with a provision in the company's constitution. He simply has to take it for granted that the internal affairs *have* been regularly conducted (and, for that matter, must accept that the company's internal affairs are none of his business). The issues which arose in *Mahony v East Holyford Mining Co* [3.16], for instance, did not depend upon the bank having had knowledge or notice of any particular provision in the company's constitutional documents, and the same issues could still arise today after the doctrine of constructive notice has been abolished.

Secondly, although the indoor management rule is commonly regarded as operating only in favour of a person dealing with a company in good faith (see eg *Rolled Steel Products (Holdings) Ltd v British Steel Corpn* [3.07], the presumption of regularity in fact applies in a much wider range of situations. It may be necessary to fall back on the common law rule for the protection of someone who is not 'dealing with' a company (s 40), as in the Australian case *Australian Capital Television Pty Ltd v Minister of Transport and Communications* (1989) 7 ACLC 525, where the *Turquand* rule was applied in the context of an application to a government minister for a broadcasting licence.

However, it is plain that the occasions on which the indoor management rule will be pleaded are likely to be rare in the future, for a number of reasons:

(i)   There will no longer be any need to raise it, as so often in the past, by way of rejoinder to a contention that the person was affected by the constructive notice doctrine.

(ii)   In any case, since the important decision in *Freeman & Lockyer v Buckhurst Park Properties (Mangal) Ltd* [3.08] it has become very common to use arguments based on the law of agency rather than the internal management rule to resolve questions in this area.

(iii)   Furthermore, there are now a considerable number of statutory provisions designed to protect third parties against possible internal irregularities in a company's decision-making. See, eg, CA 2006 ss 40, 41, 44, 775. The more such specific provisions there are, and the more widely they are drafted, the less will be the need to fall back on the common law.

Along with the *Turquand* rule itself, the present scope of the 'exceptions' to the rule must similarly be clarified. It is plain from the *Rolled Steel* case [3.07/3.17] that a person who knows or has notice of the irregularity in question or has been put on inquiry will continue to be barred from relying on the rule. But the former 'exception' which denied protection to a person who could have discovered the irregularity by inspecting the company's registered documents (*Irvine v Union Bank of Australia* (1877) 2 App Cas 366, PC) has plainly been abolished along with the constructive notice rule.

A person dealing with a company is entitled to assume, in the absence of circumstances putting him on inquiry, that there has been due compliance with all matters of internal management and procedure required by the articles.

[3.15] Royal British Bank v Turquand (1856) 6 E & B 327 (Exchequer Chamber)

Turquand was sued, as the official manager of a coal mining and railway company incorporated under the Act of 1844, on a bond for £2,000 which had been given by the company to the plaintiff bank to secure its drawings on current account. The bond was given under the seal of the company and signed by two directors and the secretary, but the company alleged that under the terms of its registered deed of settlement the directors had power to borrow only such sums as had been authorised by a general resolution of the company, and in this case no sufficiently specific resolution had been passed. The Court of Exchequer Chamber, affirming the judgment of the Court of Queen's Bench, held that even so the company was bound by the bond.

JERVIS CJ: I am of opinion that the judgment of the Court of Queen's Bench ought to be affirmed. I incline to think that the question which has been principally argued both here and in that court does not necessarily arise, and need not be determined. My impression is (though I will not state it as a fixed opinion) that the resolution set forth in the replication goes far enough to satisfy the requisites of the deed of settlement. The deed allows the directors to borrow on bond such sum or sums of money as shall from time to time, by a resolution passed at a general meeting of the company, be authorised to be borrowed: and the replication shows a resolution, passed at a general meeting, authorising the directors to borrow on bond such sums for such periods and at such rates of interest as they might deem expedient, in accordance with the deed of settlement and the Act of Parliament; but the resolution does not otherwise define the amount to be borrowed. That seems to me enough. If that be so, the other question does not arise. But whether it be so or not we need not decide; for it seems to us that the plea, whether we consider it as a confession and avoidance or a special non est factum, does not raise any objection to this advance as against the company. We may now take for granted that the dealings with these companies are not like dealings with other partnerships, and that the parties dealing with them are bound to read the statute and the deed of settlement. But they are not bound to do more. And the party here, on reading the deed of settlement, would find, not a prohibition from borrowing, but a permission to do so on certain conditions. Finding that the authority might be made complete by a resolution, he would have a right to infer the fact of a resolution authorising that which on the face of the document appeared to be legitimately done.

POLLOCK CB, ALDERSON and BRAMWELL BB, and CRESSWELL and CROWDER JJ concurred.

[3.16] Mahony v East Holyford Mining Co (1875) LR 7 HL 869 (House of Lords)

The liquidator of the respondent company sued Mahony as public officer of the National Bank, Dublin, alleging that the bank had paid moneys from the company's account without due authorisation. The bank had acted upon a letter signed by one Wall as secretary of the company, enclosing a copy of a 'resolution' of the board of directors. This 'resolution' named three directors, and instructed the bank to pay cheques signed by any two of them and countersigned by the secretary. Specimen signatures were attached. The instruction was entirely in accordance with the company's memorandum and articles, and would have been in order, except that there had never been any proper appointment of directors or a secretary by the company, such roles having been simply assumed by those who had formed the company. The House of Lords held that the company was bound by cheques which the bank had honoured in accordance with the instructions contained in the letter.

LORD HATHERLEY: My Lords, it appears to me . . . that the judgment in this case should be entered for the defendant.

It is a point of very great importance that those who are concerned in joint stock companies and those who deal with them should be aware of what is essential to the due performance of their duties, both as customers or dealers with the company, and as persons forming the company, and dealing with the outside world respectively. On the one hand, it is settled by a series of decisions, of which *Ernest v Nicholls*[20] is one and *Royal British Bank v Turquand* **[3.15]** a later one, that those

[20]   (1857) 6 HL Cas 401, HL.

who deal with joint stock companies are bound to take notice of that which I may call the external position of the company. Every joint stock company has its memorandum and articles of association; every joint stock company, or nearly every one, I imagine (unless it adopts the form provided by the statute, and that comes to the same thing) has its partnership deed under which it acts.[21] Those articles of association and that partnership deed are open to all who are minded to have any dealings whatsoever with the company, and those who so deal with them must be affected with notice of all that is contained in those two documents.

After that, the company entering upon its business and dealing with persons external to it, is supposed on its part to have all those powers and authorities which, by its articles of association and by its deed, it appears to possess; and all that the directors do with reference to what I may call the indoor management of their own concern, is a thing known to them and known to them only; subject to this observation, that no person dealing with them has a right to suppose that anything has been or can be done that is not permitted by the articles of association or by the deed . . .

This being the case, a banker dealing with a company must be taken to be acquainted with the manner in which, under the articles of association, the moneys of the company may be drawn out of his bank for the purposes of the company. My noble and learned friend on the woolsack has read those articles by which, in this case, the bankers were informed that cheques might be drawn upon the bank by three directors of the company. And the bankers must also be taken to have had knowledge, from the articles, of the duties of the directors, and the mode in which the directors were to be appointed. But, after that, when there are persons conducting the affairs of the company in a manner which appears to be perfectly consonant with the articles of association, then those so dealing with them, externally, are not to be affected by any irregularities which may take place in the internal management of the company. They are entitled to presume that that of which only they can have knowledge, namely, the external acts, are rightly done, when those external acts purport to be performed in the mode in which they ought to be performed. For instance, when a cheque is signed by three directors, they are entitled to assume that those directors are persons properly appointed for the purpose of performing that function, and have properly performed the function for which they have been appointed . . .

LORD CAIRNS LC and LORDS CHELMSFORD and PENZANCE delivered concurring opinions.

The presumption of regularity cannot be relied on by a person who has notice of an irregularity or has been put on inquiry.

[3.17] Rolled Steel Products (Holdings) Ltd v British Steel Corpn [1986] Ch 246 (Court of Appeal)

[For the facts and another part of the decision, see above, [3.07].]

SLADE LJ: Mr Shenkman unquestionably had a personal interest in the proposed guarantee and debenture which fell for consideration at the board meeting of the plaintiff on 22 January 1969. Under article 17 of the plaintiff's articles of association he was entitled to vote as a director in regard to these transactions and to be counted in the quorum of two directors required by article 18(a), notwithstanding his personal interest, if, but only if he declared his interest 'in manner provided by s 199 of the Companies Act 1948' [CA 2006, s 177]. . . . The judge, as I have said, accepted the evidence of Mr Shenkman that there had been no meeting of the board of the plaintiff before 22 January 1969 at which the desirability of the plaintiff giving a guarantee had been considered;

---

[21] [Lord Hatherley's reference to the company's 'partnership deed' is obscure. Companies incorporated before the Act of 1856 registered a deed of settlement instead of a memorandum and articles of association, and this could properly be referred to as a 'partnership deed'; but the allusion to a 'form provided by the statute' can only be to what is now Table A. It seems best to assume that by 'articles' His Lordship means [old style] 'memorandum' and by 'deed of partnership', 'articles'.]

and that he had made no declaration of his personal interest at the board meeting of 22 January 1969. I can see no grounds for challenging either of these findings of fact. Mr Shenkman and Mr Ilya Shenkman were the only two directors present and voting at the last-mentioned board meeting . . .

[His Lordship accordingly ruled that the directors were acting in breach of the articles in purporting to authorise and in executing the guarantee and debenture. He continued:]

The only remaining questions in this context are whether the judge was right by his judgment to give leave to amend the defence so as to plead that Colvilles[22] was entitled to rely on the resolution as a resolution passed at a properly constituted board of directors at which, Mr Shenkman and Mr Ilya Shenkman having been the only directors present, a proper disclosure of Mr Shenkman's interest had been made . . .

The possible relevance of the rule in *Royal British Bank v Turquand* **[3.15]** in the present context is obvious.

However . . . persons dealing with a company registered under the Companies Acts must be taken not only to have read the memorandum and articles of a company, but to have understood them according to their proper meaning: see *Palmer's Company Law*, 23rd edn (1982), vol 1, para 28-02 and the cases there cited.

Colvilles and BSC, therefore, must be taken to have known that, under the articles of the plaintiff, a quorum of two was required for the transaction of the business of its directors, and of the provisions of those articles relating to the declaration of a personal interest. They were well aware of the personal interest of Mr Shenkman in the transactions proposed on 22 January 1969.

The signed minutes of the board meeting of that day, a copy of which was subsequently supplied to Colvilles' solicitors (and indeed had been drafted by them) made no mention whatever of any declaration of a personal interest by Mr Shenkman. Since Colvilles and its legal advisers must be taken to have had knowledge of the relevant provisions of the plaintiff's articles, they must also be taken to have known that the resolution could not have been validly passed *unless Mr Shenkman had duly declared his personal interest at that board meeting or a previous board meeting.*

If, therefore, the defendants are to be allowed both to take and succeed on the *Turquand*'s case point, this must mean that, in the circumstances subsisting in late January 1969, they were *as a matter of law* entitled to assume (contrary to the fact and without further inquiry) that Mr Shenkman had duly declared his personal interest either at the board meeting of 22 January 1969 or a previous board meeting of the plaintiff.

This contention might well have been unanswerable if the rule in *Turquand*'s case were an absolute and unqualified rule of law, applicable in all circumstances. But, as the statement of the rule quoted above indicates, it is not. It is a rule which only applies in favour of persons dealing with the company in good faith. If such persons have notice of the relevant irregularity, they cannot rely on the rule . . .

[His Lordship held that, in any event, the judge had been wrong to allow the amendment to the pleadings.]

LAWTON and BROWNE-WILKINSON LJJ delivered concurring judgments.

> Notes

1. The presumption of regularity cannot be relied on by 'insiders', ie persons who by virtue of their position in the company are in a position to know whether or not the internal regulations have been observed: *Howard v Patent Ivory Manufacturing Co* (1888) 38 Ch D 156 (Chancery Division); *Morris v Kanssen* [1946] AC 459. By contrast, the court was the remarkably indulgent to the plaintiff in allowing that a person who, though a director of a company, was not acting as such, could be treated as an 'outsider' for the purpose of the rule: *Hely-Hutchinson v Brayhead Ltd* **[3.09]**.

22 [Colvilles was a steel company which was later taken over by BSC.]

2. The presumption of regularity does not apply in the case of forgery: *Ruben v Great Fingall Consolidated* [1906] AC 439 (House of Lords).

The interaction between the indoor management rule and agency rules

The 'indoor management' rule, or rule in *Royal British Bank v Turquand*, appears in its simplest form in relation to such questions as the due execution of documents, the passing of authorising resolutions and the regularity of elections and appointments. In all these cases, if nothing has occurred which is evidently contrary to the provisions of the company's constitution, the outsider may assume the regularity of all matters internal to the company and its organisation.

Where, however, the issue is whether a single person has, or is deemed to have, authority to represent the company as its representative or agent, these questions of indoor management may become confused with other questions arising from the ordinary laws of agency. The position may be illustrated by various examples. If a person has been appointed to the office of secretary or managing director and acts as such, but there was some technical defect in the procedure by which he or she was appointed, the indoor management rule will apply so as to protect an outsider dealing with the agent. On the other hand, when a person has been appointed as the company's agent either specially, to act in a particular transaction, or generally (eg, to manage a branch office), the questions whether he has exceeded the authority conferred upon him and, if so, whether the company as principal is nevertheless bound vis-à-vis a third party, are matters which ought to be determined by the ordinary rules of agency (see the cases and commentary above).

A more complex problem arises when a person holding *some* office in the company (commonly a director) purports to act on behalf of the company in a matter which is not within the scope of such an officer's usual activities, but *would* be within the normal functions of another office to which he might have been appointed—eg a managing director. Such a person may, depending on the evidence, be regarded as either (1) a managing director defectively appointed, (2) a person held out by the company[23] as a managing director although never appointed as such, or (3) an officer of limited powers who has without authority simply exceeded those powers. On the first view, the matter is one governed by the indoor management rule;[24] on the second, by the rules of agency;[25] and in either case the third party with whom he deals will be protected. On the third view, the company will not be bound whichever set of rules is applied. It is perhaps not surprising that the cases sometimes fail to keep the *Turquand* and the agency principles distinct.

Many of the older cases seem to have been argued and decided primarily on the basis of the indoor management rule (eg, see *Biggerstaff v Rowatt's Wharf Ltd* [3.11], above), but they should all now be reconsidered in the light of the judgments in *Freeman & Lockyer v Buckhurst Park Properties (Mangal) Ltd* [3.08], where the problems raised in cases of this nature were reformulated as issues of agency.

[23] The agent may be 'held out' by the company's documents, or by the board or other duly constituted authority, or there may be circumstances which estop the board or other organ of the company from denying that he is a managing director.

[24] It has been held that, in order to succeed under this head, the third party must have actual knowledge of the article conferring the power to delegate: see *Houghton & Co v Northard Lowe & Wills Ltd* [1927] 1 KB 246, CA.

[25] In this case, knowledge of the existence of a power to delegate is unnecessary.

Constructive notice and its abolition

In *Ernest v Nicholls* (1857) 6 HL Cas 401, the House of Lords ruled that a person dealing with a company should be deemed to have notice of that company's registered constitutional documents.

It did not necessarily follow that, because the law gave everyone the *opportunity* to find out about a company's registered documents, there was a corresponding *duty* to do so; and perhaps only an English chancery judge, to whom the notion of constructive notice would have been so familiar, would so readily have run the two ideas together, and disregarded the obvious *non sequitur*. Commercial law generally regards the concept of constructive notice with disfavour; and there is much to be said for the view that, since company transactions (especially as regards outsiders) are mostly of a commercial nature, a rule which deems the world at large to have constructive notice of the registered documents should not have been allowed to gain a footing, still less to have become a central feature of the law.

On the other hand, at the time the doctrine was established, most companies (including the one concerned in *Ernest v Nicholls*) did not have limited liability, so there was some reason to a rule of law that called on those dealing with a company to make investigations. But once limited liability became the norm, and especially after it became the usual practice for shares to be paid up in full, the real trading risk shifted from the shareholders to the creditors, and the constructive notice doctrine ceased to have any proper justification. Businessmen need to make decisions promptly, and for them access to the relevant documents held by the registrar could only be had at too great a cost in time and trouble.

Most jurisdictions have now abolished the constructive notice rule. In England, the argument for reform was first raised by the Jenkins Committee in 1962 as a necessary corollary to that committee's proposal for the reform of the *ultra vires* doctrine. But, as we have seen (above, pp 117 ff), no step was taken until our entry to the EC required modifications to domestic company law to comply with the First Directive.

After years of relatively unsatisfactory statutory amendments to comply with this directive, we have now reached the stage where CA 2006 s 40(2)(b) provides that 'a person dealing with a company is not bound to enquire as to any limitation on the powers of the directors to bind the company or to authorise others to do so . . .'. In addition, the presumptions in s 40 apply to all those dealing with the company in good faith, and a person 'is not to be regarded as acting in bad faith by reason only of his knowing that an act is beyond the powers of the directors under the company's constitution'. This effectively abolishes the doctrine of constructive notice of the contents of the company's registered documents, and imposes no penalty for failure to take the time to search.

The doctrine of constructive notice might have been challenged much earlier in its history but for the fact that its harshest effects were mitigated by the development, almost contemporaneously with the doctrine itself, of the 'indoor management' or 'internal management' rule, also known as the rule in *Royal British Bank v Turquand* [3.15] (see above, pp 135 ff).

Third parties do not have constructive notice of events published in the Gazette

The UK has in place an additional disclosure regime of 'official notification': as against third parties, companies may not rely on their implementation of certain specified constitutional changes and other events unless they have been properly notified to the registrar and published by him in the *Gazette* (see below, pp 582 ff for details). This provision is designed for the protection of third parties (no matter how rarely they might read the Gazette!). Given the protective aim, third parties are not punished by being fixed with constructive notice of the contents of events once they are published in the Gazette. This emerges from the next case.

[3.18] Official Custodian for Charities v Parway Estates Ltd [1985] Ch 151, [1984] 3 All ER 679 (Court of Appeal)

The question was whether the plaintiffs, as landlords of a large property in Shepherd's Bush, had waived their right to forfeit a lease in the event of the liquidation of the defendant company, their tenant. An order for the compulsory liquidation of the company had been made on 26 February 1979 and official notification of this event was gazetted on 8 March. The appointment of a liquidator was gazetted the following August. But the landlords were unaware of these matters and went on accepting rent until mid-1981. It was held that the landlords should not be deemed to have notice of the events gazetted and so they had not waived their right to forfeit.

DILLON LJ: It is common ground that . . . receipt by the plaintiffs of rent after the defendant had gone into liquidation cannot have operated as a waiver of the right to forfeit the lease if at the time that the rent was received the plaintiffs had had no notice that the defendant had gone into liquidation.

It is also common ground that before s 9 of the European Communities Act 1972 [CA 2006, s 1079] came into force, the registration in the Companies Registry and subsequent promulgation in the London Gazette of the fact that a company was in liquidation or of the appointment of a liquidator did not operate as notice to all the world, and more particularly did not operate as notice to the company's landlord, that the company was in liquidation. This was decided in *Ewart v Fryer*.[26] The effect of s 9 of the 1972 Act is therefore crucial to the argument.

Section 9 was enacted in anticipation of the entry of this country into the European Economic Community, in order to comply with [EC Council Directive 68/151] which was adopted on 9 March 1968. Section 9 deals with a number of different aspects of company law covered by the Directive. The provisions directly relevant to the present case are those of sub-ss (3) and (4) but sub-s (1) [CA 2006 s 40] is also of importance . . .

Mr Nugee QC [Counsel for the tenant] submits that on the true construction of s 9 official notification of an event is to be treated as giving notice of that event to all the world. In this submission he has the support of *Palmer's Company Law*, . . . [His Lordship read a passage from the 23rd edition of that textbook and continued:]

It is to be noted that the statement in *Palmer*:

The object of this measure is to give persons in the United Kingdom and the other member states of the EEC official notification that an important change in the constitution of the company has occurred,

does not wholly accord with the wording of the Directive. A version of the Directive in the English language and apparently taken from the Official Journal of the European Communities has been put before us. In this the provisions which have led to s 9(3) and (4) appear in a section headed 'Disclosure', and the relevant recital states:

Whereas the basic documents of the company should be disclosed in order that third parties may be able to ascertain their contents and other information concerning the company, especially particulars of the persons who are authorised to bind the company.

Even without reference to the Directive, I have no doubt, on the wording of s 9, that that section was primarily intended for the protection of persons dealing with a company rather than for the protection of the company. This is apparent not least from the opening words of s 9(1) 'in favour of a person dealing with a company in good faith' and from the opening words of s 9(4) 'A company shall not be entitled to rely against other persons on the happening of any of the following events . . .'.

---

[26] [1901] 1 Ch 499, CA: aff'd sub nom *Fryer v Ewart* [1902] AC 187, HL. [In fact, the only report which mentions this point is that of the ruling of the trial judge in (1900) 82 LT 415.]

This question whether official notification of a relevant event constitutes notice of that event to all the world, is an important question. If indeed the notification does constitute notice to all, the very many landlords who are not in the habit of studying the London Gazette regularly or effecting regular searches of the files of their company tenants in the Companies Registry will be at risk of inadvertently waiving the forfeiture of leases by accepting rent after the company tenant has gone into liquidation.

The deputy judge, after considering the wording of s 9(4) and the views expressed in *Palmer's Company Law* . . . , concluded that sub-s (4) did not impute knowledge to anyone and did not impute notice to anyone. It was essentially negative in its impact. It provided that a company cannot rely upon a relevant event if it is not in the Gazette but it did not make the positive counter proposition that a company can rely upon that event—it can rely on everyone having notice of that event—merely because it is in the Gazette. I agree with the deputy judge's analysis of the subsection and with his conclusion . . .

KERR and STEPHENSON LJJ concurred.

> ➤ Question

What is the effect of CA 2006 s 1079 on a resolution such as that held to have been passed in *Cane v Jones* **[4.18]**?

Summary of agency principles

These are three-party problems. The goal is to bind the *principal* (the company) in contract to the *third party* using the efforts of the *agent* (who is probably a company director or company employee).

The *actual authority* of the agent is determined by looking solely at the principal-agent relationship: what authority has the *principal* actually given the *agent*? The third party is irrelevant to this determination. If the board of directors, or someone authorised by the board, effects the transaction for the company, there are few problems. The articles typically give the board (not an individual director) the authority to manage the business of the company. This includes the authority to enter into contracts on behalf of the company, *and* to delegate that authority to others. If the agent obtains his or her authority in this way, then the agent will have actual authority *from the company* to transact on behalf of the company (but must observe any limitations in the grant of authority, eg authority only for specific tasks, or only within specific financial limits, etc).

Problems arise if it is not so clear who purported to act *for the company* in granting actual authority to the agent. The agent cannot obtain actual authority if the person delegating it did not have actual authority to so delegate (see the way this delegation from the board of directors was found in *Hely-Hutchinson* **[3.09]**).

Delegation of actual authority by the company to the agent can be implied. The agent will then have *implied actual authority*. Delegation of authority may be implied by appointing a person to a particular role in the company; then the assumption is that the individual has implied actual authority to do all the things necessary to fulfil that role. The cases sometimes say that the agent has '*usual*' authority to do what the job requires (but see below for the potential confusion).

Ostensible authority, on the other hand, arises from the relationship between the *principal* and the *third party*. The agent is irrelevant to the analysis. The agent's ostensible authority is the authority he is represented by the principal to the third party as having. This may be more or less extensive than the agent's actual authority. Again, some care is needed, because the representation to the third party must be by the *company* (the principal), since the goal is to bind the principal in contract to the third party. The person acting for the company in making the representation must have the necessary (actual) authority to make it (it is not possible to 'build ostensible authority on ostensible authority').

Again, a representation can be implied. Appointment of a person to a particular role can constitute a representation to outsiders that the person has all the authority that usually goes with that role. A managing director can usually do certain things, as can a marketing director or the company's secretary. So 'usual' authority rears its head again. But notice this time that the appointment serves as a representation *to the third party*. The ostensible authority it will support is only the authority carried by the representation, which must be made by the company to the third party. Care must therefore be taken with the idea of 'usual authority'—it can be employed in two quite different situations.

The third party's *bona fides* are not relevant when the agent has actual authority to transact for the company.[27] But they are relevant when the third party wishes to rely on ostensible authority: then the third party must be able to assert that there was reliance, and that it was reasonable.

Two further points need to be made for completeness. First, no authority of any sort is generated by mere assertion by the *agent* to the third party that the agent is authorised, no matter how credible the assertion. Second, the deeming provisions permitted by CA 2006 s 40 (relating to corporate capacity constraints) and the indoor management rule (relating to internal procedural matters) can be relied upon to expand the assertion by the third party of the agent's actual or ostensible authority.

An amendment of the company's articles will not excuse a breach of contract

A company cannot, by altering its articles, justify a breach of contract.

[3.19] Baily v British Equitable Assurance Co [1904] 1 Ch 374 (Court of Appeal)

The plaintiff, who was not a member, had taken out a life policy with the company, whose by-laws (made under the authority of the original deed of settlement) provided that profits from such policies should be distributed to policyholders without deduction. In 1903 it was proposed to register the company under the Companies Act, with articles of association altering the by-laws so as to authorise the transfer of a percentage of such profits to a reserve fund. The plaintiff claimed a declaration that his policy was not affected by the altered articles. Kekewich J and the Court of Appeal granted the declaration.[28]

> The judgment of the Court of Appeal (VAUGHAN WILLIAMS, STIRLING and COZENS-HARDY LJJ) was ready by COZENS-HARDY LJ: It is . . . contended that, as the company was registered under s 209 of the Companies Act 1862,[29] it thereby acquired power by special resolution to alter . . . all or any of the by-laws, and that the plaintiff is seeking to restrain the company from altering by-law no 4 in exercise of this statutory power. And it is said that, apart from the statute, the deed of settlement itself contained a power to alter the by-law, of which power the plaintiff had notice. We cannot

---

[27] Although, of course, the normal contract rules apply if the third party has induced the company, via its agent, to enter into the contract because of the third party's fraud or misrepresentation, etc.

[28] This decision was reversed by the House of Lords (*British Equitable Assurance Co Ltd v Baily*, below) on the basis of a different construction of the policy. But the validity of the passage cited was not disputed by the House of Lords; and indeed, Lord Macnaghten expressly approved it.

[29] [This section directed the compulsory re-registration of certain companies under the 1862 Act.]

assent to this argument. As between the members of a company and the company, no doubt this proposition is to some extent true. The rights of a shareholder in respect of his shares, except so far as may be protected by the memorandum of association, are by statute made liable to be altered by special resolution: see *Allen v Gold Reefs of West Africa Ltd* **[4.23]**.

But the case of a contract between an outsider and the company is entirely different, and even a shareholder must be regarded as an outsider in so far as he contracts with the company otherwise than in respect of his shares. It would be dangerous to hold that in a contract of loan or a contract of service or a contract of insurance validly entered into by a company there is any greater power of variation of the rights and liabilities of the parties than would exist if, instead of the company, the contracting party had been an individual. A company cannot, by altering its articles, justify a breach of contract . . .

In the present case there was a contract for value between the plaintiff and the company, relating to the future profits of a particular branch of the company's business, and the company ought not to be allowed, by special resolution or otherwise, to break that contract. The appeal must be dismissed.

➤ Note

A contract may, of course, be construed as incorporating the terms of the articles whatever they may be, and however they may be varied from time to time, just as a person joining a club is taken to agree that he will abide by the club's rules as they may be formulated at any given time. An alteration of the articles would then not be a breach of contract by the company at all (unless it were held to violate an implied term that the company would not alter its articles mala fide or unreasonably). *Baily*'s case went to the House of Lords, where the decision of the Court of Appeal was reversed on the basis of such a construction.[30]

[3.20] British Equitable Assurance Co Ltd v Baily [1906] AC 35 (House of Lords)

LORD LINDLEY: My Lords, this appeal turns entirely on the contracts entered into between the insurance company and its participating policy-holders, represented by Mr Baily . . . These contracts are to be found in the policies themselves. By each policy the company agree to pay the executors of the assured a fixed sum out of the funds of the company, 'and all such other sums, if any, as the said company by their directors may have ordered to be added to such amount by way of bonus or otherwise, according to their practice for the time being. Provided always, that this policy is made subject to the conditions and regulations hereon indorsed.' That is the contract between the parties; but the indorsed conditions and regulations are part of it, and the fifth is important. The company was formed as long ago as 1854, and the object of the fifth regulation is to limit the liability of the members of the company. But the regulation throws light on the position of the policy-holders and on what they can claim under their policies. The fifth indorsed condition or regulation in effect provides that the funds of the company, 'after satisfying prior claims and charges according to the provisions of the deed of settlement and by-laws of the company for the time being, shall alone be liable for the payment of the moneys payable under the policy . . .'.[31] The reference to the deed of settlement and by-laws for the time being is all-important; for the by-laws determine how the profits of the company are to be disposed of, and those by-laws are subject to alteration from time to time

---

[30] Also see *Shuttleworth v Cox Bros & Co (Maidenhead) Ltd* **[5.09]**. A similar distinction was made in *Equitable Life Assurance Soc v Hyman* **[4.03]**: should the contract containing the 'guarantee' be read as subject to the discretionary power conferred by the article in question, or would an exercise of the discretion that was inconsistent with the guarantee be a breach of contract?

[31] [Note this early example of an attempt to limit the liability of members by contract before this was made possible by statute.]

by an extraordinary meeting of the shareholders of the company . . . The policy-holders are not shareholders, and have no voice in making or altering by-laws; but the sum payable under any policy, in addition to the fixed sum mentioned in it, is made by the policy itself to depend upon what the directors may have ordered to be added to such sum, and that depends upon their practice for the time being. The practice of the directors in its turn depends on how the profits are to be ascertained and divided in accordance with the by-laws, which may be altered from time to time, as above pointed out.

My Lords, I am quite unable to adopt the view taken by the courts below as to the inability of the company to alter their by-laws as they have done, and, inter alia, to make a sinking fund without the consent of the policy-holders . . .

Of course, the powers of altering by-laws, like other powers, must be exercised bona fide, and having regard to the purposes for which they are created, and to the rights of persons affected by them. A by-law to the effect that no creditor or policy-holder should be paid what was due to him would, in my opinion, be clearly void as an illegal excess of power. But in this case it is conceded that the alteration contemplated, and sought to be restrained, is fair, honest and business-like, and will, in the opinion of the directors and shareholders of the company, be beneficial as well to the policy-holders as to the shareholders. The sole question is whether such an alteration infringes the rights of the policy-holders. In my opinion it clearly does not.

I am of opinion that the appeal should be allowed . . .

LORDS MACNAGHTEN and ROBERTSON delivered concurring opinions.

Contracts and the execution of documents

The general rule at common law was that a contract was not binding upon, or enforceable by, a corporation unless it was executed under the company's common seal. But this general rule was subject to exceptions, particularly in relation to routine contracts of relatively minor importance, and it was widely relaxed in favour of trading corporations.

The present position for companies incorporated under the Companies Acts is set out in CA 2006 ss 43–52. The use of a seal is now optional (s 43(1)), and a company may make a contract with no more formality than is required in the case of an individual (s 43(2)). Moreover, a 'purchaser' taking under a document in good faith and for valuable consideration is given very wide statutory protection by s 44(5), wide enough, it would appear, to include a document which is an outright forgery. Section 44(2)(b) also proposes a new option of signature by one director in the presence of a witness who attests that signature. It also removes from private companies the option of signature by a director and a secretary: the government has recognized that this is unnecessarily restrictive for a private company with a single director.

Corporate gifts

Problems of some complexity may arise when a company makes a gift, such as a donation to a charity or a political party, or when it enters into a transaction which, although perhaps not strictly gratuitous, has an altruistic character—such as guaranteeing someone else's bank overdraft. Agreements to pay remuneration to a company's staff or officers may also be open to challenge (or, at least, arouse suspicion) on the ground that the sums may not have been genuinely earned; and, *a fortiori*, the payment of bonuses and pensions in recognition of past services may also be called into question as being unauthorised or unmerited.

The cases show that the courts have, over the years, viewed such payments with no great enthusiasm, and sometimes with outright hostility. The reasons for this are varied. Creditors, of course, stand to be prejudiced if corporate assets are given away, but they are given only limited protection by the rules of company law and virtually no direct access to the courts to have these rules enforced while the company is a going concern. Naturally enough, therefore, the courts will be about to the potential need to intervene indirectly on their behalf (eg in a suit brought by a liquidator) and to seek to upset such transactions, especially in cases where the company has become insolvent not long after the gifts were made.

Perhaps the strongest factor influencing the judges, more especially in the Victorian period, has been the difficulty of reconciling notions of altruism with the capitalist ethos. It seems to have been accepted practically without question until only a decade or two ago that the sole purpose of any company was to make the greatest possible profits for its members. Even today, this approach is by no means dead, and most people would assume that this was at least a company's predominant purpose. A corporate gift which diminishes profits violates this philosophy, unless it can be justified on the ground that it is likely to bring a greater benefit in the longer term.

Nowadays, opinion has changed, and there is greater support for the view that 'responsible' companies ought not to neglect 'wider' interests such as those of their employees, clients and customers, the community, the environment and so on. However, the 'members' money' attitude can still influence questions such as the propriety of corporate gifts to charity or donations to political parties: why, it is asked, should company directors, or even majority members, decide where this benevolence is to be bestowed, when there are likely to be other members who would choose to do something quite different with their share of the money if it were paid out to them?

Of course, the 'members' money' approach rests on the basic assumption that companies *are* formed with the paramount aim of earning profits, and that the investors contribute their capital on that understanding, and that the members' views on all this should prevail. This may be apt in the vast majority of instances; but we should not forget that the Companies Act does allow the corporate form to be used for all sorts of purposes, and there is nothing to say that business and profits must come first. The corporate form is adopted by many charitable organisations, and could clearly be used by an enterprise that allowed its investors a limited return, after which its excess profits were to go to philanthropy or to some other object. Many co-operatives are registered companies, established to run businesses that make *no* profit. And there is no reason why a 'one-man' company should not have as its objects *both* the carrying on of its founder's business *and* the support of his family—especially after his death—and any other objects of his benevolence.

The decision in *Re Horsley & Weight Ltd* [3.05] confirms that, even at common law, the making of gratuitous payments can be construed as a corporate object if the company's memorandum is framed in sufficiently explicit terms. But prior to this decision, it was the *ultra vires* doctrine which was relied on by the judges to strike down many such transactions. Unhappily, in their zeal to keep corporate generosity within what they saw as proper bounds, they allowed a degree of confusion to creep into their reasoning, failing (for instance) to distinguish between corporate capacity and the directors' authority, in some cases, and between a company's express powers and its implied powers in others.

It was not until the Court of Appeal re-stated the law in the *Rolled Steel* case [3.07] that some logic was restored to the subject. But the result was that the *ultra vires* ground could be invoked only rarely to upset these gratuitous transactions. Now the rule cannot be invoked at all. The courts must have recourse instead to the rules on directors' authority and abuse of their powers, to the 'maintenance of capital' rules (below, pp 390 ff), the statutory 'wrongful trading' provision, and perhaps to other newer concepts, in order to counter the misapplication of corporate assets by transactions of this kind.

Some of the older cases are still worth noting, even if they are now mainly of historical interest:

(i) *Hutton v West Cork Rly Co* (1883) 23 Ch D 654, CA: it was held that a power to make payments to employees could not be implied after the company had ceased to be a going concern. Powers could be implied only as incidental to the company's business, and not when it had no business. Some passages from the celebrated judgment of Bowen LJ are still of interest. He said:

> The money which is going to be spent is not the money of the majority. That is clear. It is the money of the company, and the majority want to spend it. What would be the natural limit of their power to do so? They can only spend money which is not theirs but the company's, if they are spending it for the purposes which are reasonably incidental to the carrying on of the business of the company. That is the general doctrine. Bona fides cannot be the sole test, otherwise you might have a lunatic conducting the affairs of the company, and paying away its money with both hands in a manner perfectly bona fide yet perfectly irrational. The test must be what is reasonably incidental to, and within the reasonable scope of carrying on the business of the company . . .
>
> Most businesses require liberal dealings . . . Take this sort of instance. A railway company, or the directors of the company, might send down all the porters at a railway station to have tea in the country at the expense of the company. Why should they not? It is for the directors to judge, provided it is a matter which is reasonably incidental to the carrying on of the business of the company; and a company which always treated its employees with Draconian severity, and never allowed them a single inch more than the strict letter of the bond, would soon find itself deserted—at all events, unless labour was very much more easy to obtain in the market than it often is. The law does not say that there are to be no cakes and ale, but there are to be no cakes and ale except such as are required for the benefit of the company.
>
> Now that I think is the principle to be found in the case of *Hampson v Price's Patent Candle Co*.[32] The Master of the Rolls there held that the company might lawfully expend a week's wages as gratuities for their servants; because that sort of liberal dealing with servants eases the friction between masters and servants, and is, in the end, a benefit to the company. It is not charity sitting at the board of directors, because as it seems to me charity has no business to sit at boards of directors qua charity. There is, however, a kind of charitable dealing which is for the interest of those who practise it, and to that extent and in that garb (I admit not a very philanthropic garb) charity may sit at the board, but for no other purpose . . .

(ii) *Hutton*'s case was followed in the twentieth century by Plowman J in *Parke v Daily News Ltd* [1962] Ch 927, where the company was again moribund, and it was proposed to devote the whole of the purchase-moneys received from the sale of its newspaper business to the benefit of employees displaced by the transaction. (This was before the days of statutory redundancy payments.)

[**Note**: *Hutton*'s and *Parke*'s cases are no longer good law, because of the provisions of CA 2006 s 247 and IA 1986 s 187, which specifically reverse them.]

(iii) *Evans v Brunner, Mond & Co Ltd* [1921] 1 Ch 359. Eve J held that it was reasonably incidental to the objects of a large chemical company to make substantial donations to universities and other institutions for general scientific research. The learned judge brushed aside arguments that it was the community at large, rather than the company or anyone connected with it, who would be benefited; that the company's trade rivals would derive an equal advantage from the expenditure; and that such indirect gain as the company might secure was out of all proportion to the cost.

(iv) *Re Lee, Behrens & Co* [1932] 2 Ch 46. The directors had voted an annuity to the widow of the company's former managing director. The company had express power to make such

---

[32] (1876) 45 LJ Ch 437.

provision, but Eve J, in a judgment which was for many years thought to be a ruling on *ultra vires*, struck the payment down as being not 'reasonably incidental to the carrying on of the company's business' and not 'for the benefit of and to promote the prosperity of the company'. This reasoning, if it was intended to relate to the company's *capacity*, was plainly inappropriate where there was an express power, and it has been rejected in many modern cases. If the decision is defensible at all, it must be on the ground that the directors had acted in breach of duty: see the *Rolled Steel* case **[3.07]**.

(v)   A similar criticism applies to *Re W & M Roith Ltd* [1967] 1 WLR 432, where the company had altered its memorandum specifically in order to take power to pay a widow's pension, and had entered into a service agreement with her husband some two months before his death which included a provision for payment of the pension. He had in fact worked for the company and a sister-company for more than 20 years previously. Plowman J followed *Re Lee, Behrens & Co* uncritically. The case must now be regarded as of dubious authority.

Note that CA 2006 s 366 prohibits companies from making donations or incurring political expenditure unless the transaction or the expenditure is authorised by the members of the company. Certain exemptions are specified, with various conditions and ceiling amounts specified.

Tort liability

There are two routes to finding a company liable in tort. The company may be *primarily* liable for committing the tort, just as any natural person might be, and the usual consequences will follow. To establish such primary liability, however, it is essential to identify the person whose acts will count as the acts of the company (as in the *Meridian Global* case **[3.29]**, using Lord Hoffmann's attribution rules), and then to establish that those acts are sufficient to attract liability in tort.

The second route to fixing a company with liability in tort is to find the company *vicariously liable* for the tort. In this case, it is essential to find some individual who is primarily liable for the tort (and who might be sued personally by the claimant). Once that is done, it is then necessary to explain why the company is vicariously liable for that person's acts or omissions. Employers and principals are typically held to be vicariously liable for the acts of their employees or agents in the conduct of their employment or agency (but not for their acts outside this context, of course). Vicarious liability has been described as 'a loss distribution device based on the grounds of social and economic policy'.[33] Liability attaches to the company not because it is regarded as having committed the tort, but because it has created the risk that the tort would be committed.[34] It follows that the company's capacity to commit the tort is irrelevant.[35] Where vicarious liability is established, the individual and the company are jointly liable to the victim for the tort.[36]

One of the problems in this area is whether the individual who 'acts for the company' and whose acts attract *primary* liability in tort on the company, should also be primarily liable *personally* for the same tort (since the facts will usually enable that to be established—eg employee negligence cases). If this is always the case, then the corporate form is not quite the

---

[33] Lord Millett in *Dubai Aluminium Company Ltd v Salaam* [2002] UKHL 48, [2003] 2 AC 366, [107].

[34] *Ibid*, Lord Nicholls, at [21].

[35] For example, a company may be vicariously liable for an employee's defamatory libel, even though the company itself could not have acted with the necessary malice: *Citizens' Life Assurance Co Ltd v Brown* [1904] AC 423.

[36] *Lister v Romford Ice & Cold Storage Co Ltd* [1957] AC 555, HL.

insulating device in tort that it is in contract (where an agent acting for the company can fasten liability on the company while avoiding any personal obligations under the contract that is negotiated). For a potential resolution of the issues, see *Williams v Natural Life Health Foods* [**3.22**].

The cases below illustrate the operation of these rules.

A company may be liable in tort.

[3.21] Campbell v Paddington Corpn [1911] 1 KB 869
(King's Bench Divisional Court)

The plaintiff occupied premises in Edgware Road of which the balcony and front rooms could be let to persons wishing to view public processions. She had agreed to let a balcony to Mr Albert Ginger to watch the funeral procession of King Edward VII, but had to release him from the contract when the defendant corporation unlawfully erected a stand in the street outside, which blocked the view. In the county court, she was awarded £90 damages. The Corporation's appeal to the Divisional Court was dismissed.

AVORY J: Three objections are taken to this verdict. First, it is said that the defendants, the mayor, aldermen and councillors of the metropolitan borough of Paddington, being a corporation, are not liable because the borough council had no legal right to do what they did, and therefore the corporation cannot be sued. This stand was erected in pursuance of a formal resolution of the borough council. To say that, because the borough council has no legal right to erect it, therefore the corporation cannot be sued, is to say that no corporation can ever be sued for any tort or wrong. The only way in which this corporation can act is by its council, and the resolution of the council is the authentic act of the corporation. If the view of the defendants were correct no company could ever be sued if the directors of the company after resolution did an act which the company by its memorandum of association had no power to do. That would be absurd. The first objection therefore fails, and the defendants are liable to be sued . . .

[The second and third objections are not material.]

LUSH J delivered a concurring judgment, dismissing the appeal.[37]

➤ Notes

1. Also see *Director General of Fair Trading v Pioneer Concrete (UK) Ltd* [1995] 1 AC 456, referred to in *Meridian Global* [**3.29**], below.

2. The principle established by *Campbell's* case extends to acts which are unlawful as well as to acts which prior to the coming into force of CA 1989 would have been beyond a company's capacity under the *ultra vires* doctrine (above, p 97). It therefore remains relevant despite the abolition of that doctrine. It is, of course, also relevant in relation to bodies to which the doctrine still applies. *Poulton's* case could still be authoritative in relation to an act of an employee which was outside the scope of his company's objects clause, since the scope of his employment would necessarily be restricted by any limitations in its memorandum. However, if the victim of the tort had been 'dealing with' the company (eg in a case of deceit or negligent misrepresentation), he could invoke CA 2006 s 40.

---

[37] Part of the judgment of Lush J is cited below.

Avoiding findings of personal liability in tort against both the company and the person whose acts count as those of the company.

[3.22] Williams v Natural Life Health Foods Ltd [1998] 2 All ER 577, [1998] 1 WLR 830 (House of Lords)

Williams and his partner approached the defendant company with a view to obtaining a franchise from it to run a health food shop in Rugby. They were given a brochure and, later, detailed financial projections for the scheme. Encouraged by these, they entered into a franchise agreement. The project was a failure. The advice they had been given was negligent, and although the company would have been held liable for their loss, it had been dissolved. The plaintiffs therefore sought to have the company's managing director and principal shareholder, Mistlin, held personally liable. Mistlin's expertise had been highlighted in the brochure, and he had played a prominent part in producing the projections, but he had played no part in negotiation of the franchise agreement with them. They succeeded at first instance, and by a majority in the Court of Appeal, but this ruling was reversed by the House of Lords.

LORD STEYN: . . . A company is a separate entity, distinct from its directors, servants or other agents. The trader who incorporates a company to which he transfers his business creates a legal person on whose behalf he may afterwards act as director. For present purposes, his position is the same as if he had sold his business to another individual and agreed to act on his behalf. Thus the issue in this case is not peculiar to companies. Whether the principal is a company or a natural person, someone acting on his behalf may incur personal liability in tort as well as imposing vicarious or attributed liability upon his principal. But in order to establish personal liability under the principle of *Hedley Byrne* [[1964] AC 465, HL], which requires the existence of a special relationship between plaintiff and tortfeasor, it is not sufficient that there should have been a special relationship with the principal. There must have been an assumption of responsibility such as to create a special relationship with the director or employee himself. . . .

The touchstone of liability is not the state of mind of the defendant. An objective test means that the primary focus must be on things said or done by the defendant or on his behalf in dealings with the plaintiff. Obviously, the impact of what a defendant says or does must be judged in the light of the relevant contextual scene. Subject to this qualification, the primary focus must be on exchanges (in which term I include statements and conduct) which cross the line between the defendant and the plaintiff. Sometimes such an issue arises in a simple bilateral relationship. In the present case a triangular position is under consideration: the prospective franchisees, the franchisor company, and the director. In such a case where the personal liability of the director is in question, the internal arrangements between a director and his company cannot be the foundation of a director's personal liability in tort. The inquiry must be whether the director, or anybody on his behalf, conveyed directly or indirectly to the prospective franchisees that the director assumed personal responsibility towards the prospective franchisees. . . .

It is important to make clear that a director of a contracting company may only be held liable where it is established by evidence that he assumed personal liability and that there was the necessary reliance. . . .

Mr Mistlin owned and controlled the company. The company held itself out as having the expertise to provide reliable advice to franchisees. The brochure made clear that this expertise derived from Mr Mistlin's experience in the operation of the Salisbury shop. In my view these circumstances were insufficient to make Mr Mistlin personally liable to the plaintiffs. Stripped to essentials, the reasons of Langley J [the trial judge], the reasons of the majority in the Court of Appeal and the arguments of counsel for the plaintiffs can be considered under two headings. First, it is said that the terms of the brochure, and in particular its description of the role of Mr Mistlin, are sufficient to amount to an assumption of responsibility by Mr Mistlin. In his dissenting judgment [in the Court of Appeal] Sir Patrick Russell rightly pointed out that in a small one-man company 'the managing director will almost inevitably be the one possessed of qualities essential to the functioning of the company'. By itself this factor does not convey that the managing director is willing to be personally answerable to the customers of the company. Secondly, great emphasis was placed on the fact that it was made clear to the franchisees that Mr Mistlin's expertise derived from his experience in running the Salisbury shop for his own account. Hirst LJ summarised the point by saying that 'the relevant knowledge and experience was entirely his qua Mr Mistlin, and not his qua director'. The point will simply not bear the weight put on it. Postulate a food expert who over ten years gains experience in advising customers on his own account. Then he incorporates his business as a company and he so advises his customers. Surely, it cannot be right to say that in the new situation his earlier experience on his own account is indicative of an assumption of personal responsibility towards his customers. In the present case there were no personal dealings between Mr Mistlin and the plaintiffs. There were no exchanges or conduct crossing the line which could have conveyed to the plaintiffs that Mr Mistlin was willing to assume personal responsibility to them. Contrary to the submissions of counsel for the plaintiffs, I am also satisfied that there was not even evidence that the plaintiffs believed that Mr Mistlin was undertaking personal responsibility to them. Certainly, there was nothing in the circumstances to show that the plaintiffs could reasonably have looked to Mr Mistlin for indemnification of any loss. For these reasons I would reject the principal argument of counsel for the plaintiffs. . . .

LORDS GOFF OF CHIEVELEY, HOFFMANN, CLYDE and HUTTON concurred.

➤ Question

What are the advantages and disadvantages of this decision for those dealing with companies (especially small companies) and those involved in managing such companies? Is the decision consistent with the rules that apply in respect of contractual liability (see above) and criminal liability (see below)? Is it defensible on policy grounds? And on doctrinal grounds?

Criminal liability

Some crimes have a mental element. To find the company liable for those, it is necessary to attribute the relevant mental element of one person (or corporate organ) within the company to the company itself. This is most usually done by identifying the 'directing mind and will of the company' (Lord Reid in *Tesco Supermarkets Ltd v Natrass* [3.27]). This rule, however, suffers from the defect that finding such a personal representative is only likely in very small companies, not in large ones. The rather unfair consequence is that it is much easier to find small companies liable in crime than large ones. Sometimes the problem can be overcome by using Lord Hoffmann's 'attribution rules' to find the person whose mental element *for these purposes* (ie for the purposes of the act constituting *this* crime) is to count as the mental element of the company (*Meridian Global* case [3.29]). It is not possible to make the company *vicariously liable* for crimes with a mental element: this would, in effect, be making the company criminally liable for all the criminal intents of anyone associated with the company.

On the other hand, where there is no mental element to the crime (ie so that the commission or omission of the act automatically attracts liability), then vicarious liability is possible. This is the usual rule in relation to offences relating to health and safety or environmental protection, for example. The *Tesco Supermarkets* case [3.27] is a case in point.

Finally, there is the problem of corporate killing. This issue has been given some prominence in the press over the past decade, with a series of public disasters making it clear that it is difficult to find a large company liable for manslaughter, even when the business has been operated with inadequate regard to the health and safety of the public. Again, the problem is that it is often impossible to find one individual with the necessary criminal failings who can be identified with the company, and courts have rejected the use of aggregation to find the company liable by aggregating the failings of a series of individuals that, in total, add up to a corporate failing that might attract criminal liability (as is done in establishing vicarious liability in tort). See *Attorney-General's Reference (No 2 of 1999)* [2000] QB 796[38] and *R v Stanley* (19 October 1990 unreported, on the Herald of Free Enterprise disaster).

The Law Commission has reported on the problem (*Legislating for the Criminal Code: Involuntary Manslaughter* Law Com No 237, 1996), there was a Home Office consultation paper in 2000, and a draft bill was published in the White Paper, *Corporate Manslaughter: The Government's Draft Bill for Reform* (Cm 6498, 2005). In July 2007, the Corporate Manslaughter and Corporate Homicide Act become law. It establishes a new offence of corporate manslaughter that is committed by a company if the way in which its activities are managed or organised by its senior executives causes the death of a person *and* amounts to a gross breach of the relevant duty of care the company owed to the person. The company if guilty will be subject to a fine and perhaps other appropriate orders.

The cases extracted below illustrate the process the courts were required to adopt prior to this new Act.

Mental state, *mens rea* and criminal liability

The mental state of a person who is 'the directing mind and will' of a company may be attributed to the company itself.

[3.23] Lennard's Carrying Co Ltd v Asiatic Petroleum Co Ltd [1915] AC 705 (House of Lords)

The appellant company Lennard's Carrying Co Ltd owned a ship, the *Edward Dawson*, which (together with her cargo which belonged to the respondents) was destroyed at sea as a result of a fire caused by the defective condition of her boilers. The appellant company as owner would have been exonerated from liability by the terms of the Merchant Shipping Act 1894 s 502 (now repealed), if it could show that the loss happened without its 'actual fault or privity'. The House of Lords held that the concepts of fault and privity were capable in law of being attributed to a corporate body, but that on the facts the appellant had failed to show that it came within the exception.

VISCOUNT HALDANE LC: The appellants are a limited company and the ship was managed by another limited company, Messrs J M Lennard & Sons, and Mr J M Lennard, who seems to be the active director in J M Lennard & Sons, was also a director of the appellant company, Lennard's Carrying Company Limited. My Lords, in that state of things what is the question of law which arises? I think that it is impossible in the face of the findings of the learned judge, and of the evidence, to contend successfully that Mr J M Lennard has shown that he did not know or can excuse himself for not having known of the defects which manifested themselves in the condition of the ship, amounting to unseaworthiness. Mr Lennard is the person who is registered in the ship's register and is designated as the person to whom the management of the vessel was entrusted. He appears to have been the active spirit in the joint stock company which managed this ship for the appellants; and under the circumstances the question is whether the company can invoke the protection of s 502

[38] The case arose out of the Southall train disaster, when two trains collided at high speed and seven people were killed, but the charges of manslaughter resulted in acquittals on the direction of the judge, for want of evidence to bring home either an *actus reus* or a *mens rea* to a 'directing mind and will'. The Court of Appeal confirmed that this was the correct approach in law.

of the Merchant Shipping Act to relieve it from the liability which the respondents seek to impose on it . . .

Now, my Lords, did what happened take place without the actual fault or privity of the owners of the ship who were the appellants? My Lords, a corporation is an abstraction. It has no mind of its own any more than it has a body of its own; its active and directing will must consequently be sought in the person of somebody who for some purposes may be called an agent, but who is really the directing mind and will of the corporation, the very ego and centre of the personality of the corporation. That person may be under the direction of the shareholders in general meeting; that person may be the board of directors itself, or it may be, and in some companies it is so, that that person has an authority co-ordinate with the board of directors given to him under the articles of association, and is appointed by the general meeting of the company, and can only be removed by the general meeting of the company. My Lords, whatever is not known about Mr Lennard's position, this is known for certain, Mr Lennard took the active part in the management of this ship on behalf of the owners, and Mr Lennard, as I have said, was registered as the person designated for this purpose in the ship's register. Mr Lennard therefore was the natural person to come on behalf of the owners and give full evidence not only about the events of which I have spoken, and which related to the seaworthiness of the ship, but about his own position and as to whether or not he was the life and soul of the company. For if Mr Lennard was the directing mind of the company, then his action must, unless a corporation is not to be liable at all, have been an action which was the action of the company itself within the meaning of s 502. It has not been contended at the Bar, and it could not have been successfully contended, that s 502 is so worded as to exempt a corporation altogether which happens to be the owner of a ship, merely because it happens to be a corporation. It must be upon the true construction of that section in such a case as the present one that the fault or privity is the fault or privity of somebody who is not merely a servant or agent for whom the company is liable upon the footing respondeat superior, but somebody for whom the company is liable because his action is the very action of the company itself. It is not enough that the fault should be the fault of a servant in order to exonerate the owner, the fault must also be one which is not the fault of the owner, or a fault to which the owner is privy; and I take the view that when anybody sets up that section to excuse himself from the normal consequences of the maxim respondeat superior the burden lies upon him to do so.

Well, my Lords, in that state of the law it is obvious to me that Mr Lennard ought to have gone into the box and relieved the company of the presumption which arises against it that his action was the company's action. But Mr Lennard did not go into the box to rebut the presumption of liability and we have no satisfactory evidence as to what the constitution of the company was or as to what Mr Lennard's position was . . . Under the circumstances I think that the company and Mr Lennard have not discharged the burden of proof which was upon them, and that it must be taken that the unseaworthiness, which I hold to have been established as existing at the commencement of the voyage from Novorossick, was an unseaworthiness which did not exist without the actual fault or privity of the owning company.

LORD DUNEDIN delivered a concurring opinion.

LORDS ATKINSON, PARKER OF WADDINGTON and PARMOOR concurred.

➤ Questions

1. Was Mr Lennard 'the directing mind and will' of JM Lennard & Sons, or of Lennard's Carrying Co Ltd, or of both? Was this question important?

2. How far do you think that the decision in Lennard's case depended upon the fact that the onus of proof under the statute was on the appellants, who were required to prove a negative? Who would have won the case if the onus of proof had been on the respondents?

[3.24] H L Bolton (Engineering) Ltd v T J Graham & Sons Ltd
[1957] 1 QB 159 (Court of Appeal)

In this case a corporate landlord was held capable of 'intending' (through its managing directors) to occupy premises for its own use.

DENNING LJ: [The] question is whether the landlords have proved the necessary intention to occupy the holding for their own purpose. This point arises because the landlords are a limited company. Mr Albery says that there was no meeting of any board of directors to express the landlords' intention, and that therefore the landlords—the company—cannot say that it has the necessary intention.

[His Lordship stated the material facts on this part of the case and continued:]

[The] judge has found that this company, through its managers, intend to occupy the premises for their own purposes. Mr Albery contests this finding, and he has referred us to cases decided in the last century; but I must say that the law on this matter and the approach to it have developed very considerably since then. A company may in many ways be likened to a human body. It has a brain and nerve centre which controls what it does. It also has hands which hold the tools and act in accordance with directions from the centre. Some of the people in the company are mere servants and agents who are nothing more than hands to do the work and cannot be said to represent the mind or will. Others are directors and managers who represent the directing mind and will of the company, and control what it does. The state of mind of these managers is the state of mind of the company and is treated by the law as such. So you will find that in cases where the law requires personal fault as a condition of liability in tort, the fault of the manager will be the personal fault of the company. [His Lordship referred to *Lennard's Carrying Co Ltd v Asiatic Petroleum Co Ltd* **[3.23]** and *R v ICR Haulage Ltd* **[3.26]** and continued:] So here, the intention of the company can be derived from the intention of its officers and agents. Whether their intention is the company's intention depends on the nature of the matter under consideration, the relative position of the officer or agent and the other relevant facts and circumstances of the case. Approaching the matter in that way, I think that although there was no board meeting, nevertheless, having regard to the standing of these directors in control of the business of the company, having regard to the other facts and circumstances which we know, whereby plans had been prepared and much work done, the judge was entitled to infer that the intention of the company was to occupy the holding for their own purposes. I am of opinion, therefore, that the judge's decision on this point was right . . .

HODSON and MORRIS LJJ concurred.

➤ Note

Although the 'directing mind and will' is the most common criterion for attribution, there have been cases in which a person who was not part of the directing mind and will of a company was identified with it. To hold otherwise, would allow those persons who are the actual directing mind of the company to insulate the latter from liability by delegating their functions. See: *Director General of Fair Trading v Pioneer Concrete (UK) Ltd* [1995] 1 AC 456; and *Re Bank of Credit and Commerce International SA (No. 15)* [2005] EWCA Civ 693, [2005] 2 BCLC 328.

A company is capable of having an intent to deceive.

[3.25] DPP v Kent and Sussex Contractors Ltd [1944] KB 146 (King's Bench Divisional Court)

The company was charged with offences under the petrol rationing regulations involving (a) making use of a false document with intent to deceive, and (b) making a statement which was known to be false in a material particular. The justices held that the company could not in law be guilty of these offences since there was implicit in them an act of will or state of mind which could not be imputed to a body corporate, and dismissed the informations. The prosecutor appealed by way of case stated to the Divisional Court, which ruled that a company was capable of committing the offences in question, it being sufficient that the particular officer responsible (in this case the transport manager) had the required intention or knowledge.

VISCOUNT CALDECOTE CJ: This special case raises the question whether a limited company, being a body corporate, can in law be guilty of the offences charged against the respondents, or whether a company is incapable of any act of will or state of mind such as that laid in the information. Mr Carey Evans submits that a company can only be held to be responsible in respect of the intention or knowledge of its agents, the officers of the company, to the same extent as a private individual is responsible for the acts of his agent, and, therefore, that the respondent company cannot be held to form the intention or to have the knowledge necessary to constitute the offences charged. He has not disputed the abstract proposition that a company can have knowledge and can form an intention to do an act. A company cannot be found guilty of certain criminal offences, such as treason or other offences for which it is provided that death or imprisonment is the only punishment, but there are a number of criminal offences of which a company can be convicted . . .

In the present case the first charge against the company was of doing something with intent to deceive, and the second was that of making a statement which the company knew to be false in a material particular. Once the ingredients of the offences are stated in that way it is unnecessary, in my view, to inquire whether it is proved that the company's officers acted on its behalf. The officers are the company for this purpose. Mr Carey Evans stoutly maintained the position that a company cannot have a mens rea, and that a mens rea cannot be imputed to it even if and when its agents have been known to have one, but the question of mens rea seems to me to be quite irrelevant in the present case. The offences created by the regulation are those of doing something with intent to deceive or of making a statement known to be false in a material particular. There was ample evidence, on the facts as stated in the special case, that the company, by the only people who could act or speak or think for it had done both these things, and I can see nothing in any of the authorities to which we have been referred which requires us to say that a company is incapable of being found guilty of the offences with which the respondent company was charged. The case must go back to the justices with an intimation of our opinion to this effect, and for their determination on the facts.

HALLETT and MACNAGHTEN JJ delivered concurring judgments.

> ➤ Question

Was it true to say that 'the question of *mens rea* seems to be quite irrelevant in the present case'? If it had been thought relevant, would the decision have been the same?

A company can be indicted for a common law conspiracy to defraud.

[3.26] R v ICR Haulage Ltd [1944] KB 551 (Court of Criminal Appeal)

The company was convicted with others at Maidstone Assizes on an indictment charging a common law conspiracy to defraud. The conviction was upheld on appeal.

The judgment of the Court of Criminal Appeal (HUMPHREYS, CROOM-JOHNSON and STABLE JJ) was read by STABLE J: The question before us is whether a limited company can be indicted for a conspiracy to defraud . . .

It was conceded by counsel for the company that a limited company can be indicted for some criminal offences, and it was conceded by counsel for the Crown that there were some criminal offences for which a limited company cannot be indicted. The controversy centred round the question where and on what principle the line must be drawn and on which side of the line an indictment such as the present one falls. Counsel for the company contended that the true principle was that an indictment against a limited company for any offence involving as an essential ingredient 'mens rea' in the restricted sense of a dishonest or criminal mind, must be bad for the reason that a company, not being a natural person, cannot have a mind honest or otherwise, and that, consequently, though in certain circumstances it is civilly liable for the fraud of its officers, agents or servants, it is immune from criminal process. Counsel for the Crown contended that a limited company, like any other entity recognised by the law, can as a general rule be indicted for its criminal acts which from the very necessity of the case must be performed by human agency and which in given circumstances become the acts of the company, and that for this purpose there was no distinction between an intention or other function of the mind and any other form of activity.

The offences for which a limited company cannot be indicted are, it was argued, exceptions to the general rule arising from the limitations which must inevitably attach to an artificial entity, such as a company. Included in these exceptions are the cases in which, from its very nature, the offence cannot be committed by a corporation, as, for example, perjury, an offence which cannot be vicariously committed, or bigamy, an offence which a limited company, not being a natural person, cannot commit vicariously or otherwise. A further exception, but for a different reason, comprises offences of which murder is an example, where the only punishment the court can impose is corporal, the basis on which this exception rests being that the court will not stultify itself by embarking on a trial in which, if a verdict of Guilty is returned, no effective order by way of sentence can be made. In our judgment these contentions of the Crown are substantially sound, and the existence of these exceptions, and it may be that there are others, is by no means inconsistent with the general rule . . .

[His Lordship referred to the authorities, including *DPP v Kent and Sussex Contractors Ltd* **[3.25]** and *Pharmaceutical Society v London and Provincial Supply Association* **[2.08]**, and continued:] In our judgment, both on principle and in accordance with the balance of authority, the present indictment was properly laid against the company, and the learned commissioner rightly refused to quash. We are not deciding that in every case where an agent of a limited company acting in its business commits a crime the company is automatically to be held criminally responsible. Our decision only goes to the invalidity of the indictment on the face of it, an objection which is taken before any evidence is led and irrespective of the facts of the particular case. [Whether] in any particular case there is evidence to go to a jury that the criminal act of an agent, including his state of mind, intention, knowledge or belief is the act of the company, and, in cases where the presiding judge so rules, whether the jury are satisfied that it has been proved, must depend on the nature of the charge, the relative position of the officer or agent, and the other relevant facts and circumstances of the case.[39] It was because we were satisfied on the hearing of this appeal that the facts proved were amply sufficient to justify a finding that the acts of the managing director were the acts of the company and the fraud of that person was the fraud of the company, that we upheld the conviction against the company, and, indeed, on the appeal to this court no argument was advanced that the facts proved would not warrant a conviction of the company assuming that the conviction of the managing director was upheld and that the indictment was good in law.

➤ Questions

1. Contrast the reasoning in these cases with the categorical statement of Blackstone (above, p 71): 'A corporation cannot commit treason, or felony, or other crime, in it's corporate capacity . . .' Is it possible to account for the change? Why do you think that it was not until as late as 1944 that the breakthrough in making companies liable for crimes involving *mens rea* was made?

---

[39] [This sentence was criticised as being too widely stated by Lord Reid in *Tesco Supermarkets Ltd v Natrass* **[3.27]**.]

2. What indications are there in the judgments that the decisions of the court in *Kent and Sussex Contractors* and *ICR Haulage* were based on *policy* considerations?

➤ Notes

1. The two cases last cited, and *Moore v I Bresler Ltd* [1944] 2 All ER 515, which was decided in the same year, established that a company may be guilty of a criminal offence, including an offence involving *mens rea*. (The doctrine of *ultra vires* might have been seen as an obstacle to imposing liability, but it does not seem to have been raised in any of the key cases—presumably because it had long been regarded as irrelevant to the corresponding question in tort: *Campbell v Paddington Corpn* **[3.21]**.)

2. In later cases, there has been some uncertainty as to which officers, agents or servants of a company may be identified with the company itself for the purpose of ascribing to it a criminal or similar intention. In *Moore v I Bresler Ltd* (above), the secretary of the company and a branch sales manager were so regarded; in *DPP v Kent and Sussex Contractors Ltd* **[3.25]** and in *The Lady Gwendolen* [1965] P 294, CA, the only officer concerned was the transport manager; and in *National Coal Board v Gamble* [1959] 1 QB 11, [1958] 3 All ER 203 it appears to have been assumed that a weighbridgeman's knowledge and intention were to be attributed to the Coal Board, although the contrary view was taken on the same point in *John Henshall (Quarries) Ltd v Harvey* [1965] 2 QB 233, [1965] 1 All ER 725. It is perhaps significant that the *Lennard's Carrying* case (and the 'directing mind and will' test of identification) was not mentioned in the judgments (nor even, apparently, by counsel) in any of the criminal law cases referred to above—although the link between the two was soon made by contemporary textbooks. In the case next cited, the House of Lords had the opportunity to review the question. As will be seen, the *Lennard*'s test of identification is central to their Lordships' reasoning. However, their decision appears to assume the existence of a stratification of managerial functions which in the case of many companies may be far from obvious. It may well be begging the question to describe a transport manager as a 'superior officer' and the manager of a large retail shop as a 'subordinate'. In other contexts, the courts have not been so willing to see a significant difference between running a company's affairs and running part only of those affairs: see *Harold Holdsworth & Co (Wakefield) Ltd v Caddies* **[3.12]**.

3. It is now becoming apparent that the ruling in *Tesco Supermarkets* (below), notwithstanding its claims to be authoritative, is not to be the last word on the subject. The signs of a retreat from a strict insistence on a 'directing mind and will' test of identification in a criminal context are clear. The catalyst has, no doubt, been the decision in the *Pioneer Concrete* case (above, p 155), where the issue was whether the companies concerned could be held to be in contempt of court through the acts of employees who were of no more than middle-management status. The leading statement of the law is now to be found in the Privy Council's opinion, delivered by Lord Hoffmann, in *Meridian Global Funds Management Asia Ltd v Securities Commission* **[3.29]**. On the basis of this latter ruling, we can now say that there is no single test of identification but rather a range of 'rules of attribution' which vary from case to case; and *Tesco Supermarkets* may be seen as a decision reached in the special context of the Trade Descriptions Act 1968 rather than a pronouncement of general application to criminal law cases across the board.

The mental state of one who occupies a subordinate position in the company will not be ascribed to the company itself.[40]

[3.27] Tesco Supermarkets Ltd v Nattrass [1972] AC 153 (House of Lords)

Tesco, an incorporated company owning a chain of several hundred supermarkets, was charged with an offence under the Trade Descriptions Act 1968, in selling a packet of washing powder for 3s 11d (19½ p), when it had been advertised at 2s 11d (14½ p). An assistant at the company's Northwich branch, Miss Rogers, had restocked the shelves with normally priced packets after supplies of 'special offer' packets bearing a lower price had temporarily run out. She had not informed the branch manager, Mr Clements, of this, while he for his part had failed to detect the discrepancy between the 'special offer' posters and the price of the powder on the shelves. Mr Clements was in complete charge of this store and its 60 employees.

Under s 24 (1) of the Trade Descriptions Act, it is a defence for the accused to prove that the commission of the offence was due to the act or default of another person, and that the accused has taken all reasonable precautions and exercised all due diligence to avoid the commission of the offence. In quashing the conviction of Tesco, which had been upheld by the Divisional Court, the House of Lords ruled that for the purpose of the company's criminal liability, the branch manager did not represent its 'directing mind and will', but was merely a subordinate. It followed that the company could plead that the manager's acts were those of 'another person' within the terms of the statutory defence; and that it had discharged the burden of proving that it had taken all reasonable precautions and exercised all due diligence by showing that its managers had been issued with proper instructions.

LORD REID: Where a limited company is the employer difficult questions do arise in a wide variety of circumstances in deciding which of its officers or servants is to be identified with the company so that his guilt is the guilt of the company.

I must start by considering the nature of the personality which by a fiction the law attributes to a corporation. A living person has a mind which can have knowledge or intention or be negligent and he has hands to carry out his intentions. A corporation has none of these: it must act through living persons, though not always one or the same person. Then the person who acts is not speaking or acting for the company. He is acting as the company and his mind which directs his acts is the mind of the company. There is no question of the company being vicariously liable. He is not acting as a servant, representative, agent or delegate. He is an embodiment of the company or, one could say, he hears and speaks through the persona of the company, within his appropriate sphere, and his mind is the mind of the company. If it is a guilty mind then that guilt is the guilt of the company. It must be a question of law whether, once the facts have been ascertained, a person in doing particular things is to be regarded as the company or merely as the company's servant or agent. In that case any liability of the company can only be a statutory or vicarious liability.

In *Lennard's Carrying Co Ltd v Asiatic Petroleum Co Ltd* [3.23] the question was whether damage had occurred without the 'actual fault or privity' of the owner of a ship. The owners were a company. The fault was that of the registered managing owner who managed the ship on behalf of the owners and it was held that the company could not dissociate itself from him so as to say that there was no actual fault or privity on the part of the company . . .

Reference is frequently made to the judgment of Denning LJ in *HL Bolton (Engineering) Co Ltd v TJ Graham & Sons* [3.24]. [His Lordship quoted part of the judgment, which is cited above, [3.24], and continued:] In that case the directors of the company only met once a year: they left the

---

[40] See, however, *Meridian Global Funds Management Asia Ltd v Securities Commission* [3.29]. In this case, Lord Hoffmann stated that it would be a mistake to seize upon the phrase 'directing mind and will' and use that as the sole criterion for determining whose thoughts and/or actions will be attributed to a company. The question should be 'whose act was . . . intended to count as the act of the company?'

management of the business to others, and it was the intention of those managers which was imputed to the company. I think that was right. There have been attempts to apply Lord Denning's words to all servants of a company whose work is brain work, or who exercise some managerial discretion under the direction of superior officers of the company. I do not think that Lord Denning intended to refer to them. He only referred to those who 'represent the directing mind and will of the company, and control what it does'.

I think that is right for this reason. Normally the board of directors, the managing director and perhaps other superior officers of a company carry out the functions of management and speak and act as the company. Their subordinates do not. They carry out orders from above and it can make no difference that they are given some measure of discretion. But the board of directors may delegate some part of their functions of management, giving to their delegate full discretion to act independently of instructions from them. I see no difficulty in holding that they have thereby put such a delegate in their place so that within the scope of the delegation he can act as the company. It may not always be easy to draw the line but there are cases in which the line must be drawn. *Lennard's* case was one of them.

In some cases the phrase alter ego has been used. I think it is misleading. When dealing with a company the word alter is I think misleading. The person who speaks and acts as the company is not alter. He is identified with the company. And when dealing with an individual no other individual can be his alter ego. The other individual can be a servant, agent, delegate or representative but I know of neither principle nor authority which warrants the confusion (in the literal or original sense) of two separate individuals . . .

In the next two cases a company was accused and it was held liable for the fault of a superior officer. In *DPP v Kent and Sussex Contractors Ltd* **[3.25]** he was the transport manager. In *R v ICR Haulage Ltd* **[3.26]** it was held that a company can be guilty of common law conspiracy. The act of the managing director was held to be the act of the company. I think that a passage in the judgment is too widely stated:

> [Whether] in any particular case there is evidence to go to a jury that the criminal act of an agent, including his state of mind, intention, knowledge or belief is the act of the company, and, in cases where the presiding judge so rules, whether the jury are satisfied that it has been proved, must depend on the nature of the charge, the relative position of the officer or agent, and the other relevant facts and circumstances of the case.

. . . I think that the true view is that the judge must direct the jury that if they find certain facts proved then as a matter of law they must find that the criminal act of the officer, servant or agent including his state of mind, intention, knowledge or belief is the act of the company. I have already dealt with the considerations to be applied in deciding when such a person can and when he cannot be identified with the company. I do not see how the nature of the charge can make any difference. If the guilty man was in law identifiable with the company then whether his offence was serious or venial his act was the act of the company but if he was not so identifiable then no act of his, serious or otherwise, was the act of the company itself . . .

[His Lordship discussed a number of other cases and concluded:] The Divisional Court decided this case on a theory of delegation. In that they were following some earlier authorities. But they gave far too wide a meaning to delegation. I have said that a board of directors can delegate part of their functions of management so as to make their delegate an embodiment of the company within the sphere of the delegation. But here the board never delegated any part of their functions. They set up a chain of command through regional and district supervisors, but they remained in control. The shop managers had to obey their general directions and also take orders from their superiors. The acts or omissions of shop managers were not acts of the company itself.

In my judgment the appellants established the statutory defence. I would therefore allow this appeal.

LORD MORRIS OF BORTH-Y-GEST, VISCOUNT DILHORNE and LORDS PEARSON and DIPLOCK delivered concurring opinions.

➤ Note

As noted above, some of the observations and assumptions in the above cases should be reconsidered in the light of the Privy Council's ruling in *Meridian Global Funds Management Asia Ltd v Securities Commission* [**3.29**]. In that case Lord Hoffmann, giving the opinion of the Judicial Committee, said that when the question arises of attributing the act or state of mind of an individual to a company, different rules should be invoked in different circumstances, depending upon the rule of law which is being applied. It would follow that the cases on the Merchant Shipping Acts, such as *Lennard's Carrying Co Ltd v Asiatic Petroleum Co Ltd* [**3.23**] and *The Lady Gwendolen* [1965] P 294, CA, should not be considered under the same rubric as those involving the question of *mens rea*, and possibly also that the criteria for imputing a mental state in intentional crimes such as conspiracy to defraud and in crimes not involving intention, such as manslaughter, may not be the same (although Lord Reid in the *Tesco Supermarkets* case (above, p 160: 'I do not see how the nature of the charge can make any difference') seems not to support this view).

➤ Questions

1. Lord Diplock in *Tesco Supermarkets Ltd v Nattrass* said ([1972] AC 153 at 199–200):

> My Lords, a corporation incorporated under the Companies Act 1948 owes its corporate personality and its powers to its constitution, the memorandum and articles of association. The obvious and the only place to look to discover by what natural persons its powers are exercisable, is in its constitution. The articles of association, if they follow Table A, provide that the business of the company shall be managed by the directors and that they may 'exercise all such powers of the company' as are not required by the Act to be exercised in general meeting. Table A also vests in the directors the right to entrust and confer upon a managing director any of the powers of the company which are exercisable by them. So it may also be necessary to ascertain whether the directors have taken any action under this provision or any other similar provision providing for the coordinate exercise of the powers of the company by executive directors or by committees of directors and other persons, such as are frequently included in the articles of association of companies in which the regulations contained in Table A are modified or excluded in whole or in part.
>
> In my view, therefore, the question: what natural persons are to be treated in law as being the company for the purpose of acts done in the course of its business, including the taking of precautions and the exercise of due diligence to avoid the commission of a criminal offence, is to be found by identifying those natural persons who by the memorandum and articles of association or as a result of action taken by the directors, or by the company in general meeting pursuant to the articles, are entrusted with the exercise of the powers of the company.

Is this the same test as Lord Reid's? What do you consider that Lord Diplock meant by 'the powers of the company'? Who in the Tesco organisation was 'entrusted' with the exercise of the relevant power, and what was this power?

2. Could the state of mind of the secretary of a company ever be attributed to the company? (See the *Panorama* case [**3.13**], and consider what might be said of the role in a company's articles.)

3. Does Lord Reid's analysis allow for the possibility that a company could have more than one individual, acting independently, 'speaking and acting as the company' at the same time? Should it?

4. If a corporate body is to be convicted on the basis of a confession, whose confession is necessary?

A company cannot commit conspiracy with the one person who is solely responsible for its acts.

[3.28] R v McDonnell [1966] 1 QB 233 (Bristol Assizes)

The defendant was charged on an indictment containing, *inter alia*, two counts of conspiring with a company to defraud. Each of the companies was wholly under his direction and control. It was held that the charges could not be sustained.

> NIELD J: [It] is essential to note that both counsel agree the facts necessary for the determination of these points, and in particular, without any doubt or equivocation, that the defendant was at all material times the sole person in either of the companies I have named responsible for any of the acts of the company and that no one else had any authority to act for the company or any responsibility for the acts of the company.
>
> Four principal points arise. [Points 1–3 are omitted] . . . The fourth, and the principal point in my opinion, is the submission that the conspiracy charges cannot stand since in the particular circumstances here the defendant and the company were, in effect, one and the same person with one and the same mind, and that a conspiracy in law requires the agreement of at least two persons and two minds . . .
>
> I am told that there is no English authority upon this particular point, and so one comes freshly to it, although assisted by some authority not directly in point and by persuasive authorities from overseas, to which I would attach great weight. It is important at the outset to emphasise two things. It is not a company which is here being proceeded against, it is an individual defendant; and further, this is a criminal trial and one of gravity so that problems of difficulty must at all times be resolved favourably to an accused person . . .
>
> I have . . . considered all the cases which have been cited to me by counsel, and at the end one is presented with a new situation in that there is no English authority upon the point. I have reached the conclusion that . . . these charges of conspiracy cannot be sustained, upon the footing that in the particular circumstances here, where the sole responsible person in the company is the defendant himself, it would not be right to say that there were two persons or two minds. If it were otherwise, I feel that it would offend against the basic concept of a conspiracy, namely, an agreement of two or more to do an unlawful act, and I think it would be artificial to take the view that the company, although it is clearly a separate legal entity, can be regarded here as a separate person or a separate mind, in view of the admitted fact that this defendant acts alone so far as these companies are concerned . . .

➤ Questions

1. Half of the shares in Black & White Ltd are owned by Black and half by White, and they are its only directors. Can Black, White and the company be indicted for a conspiracy on the basis of acts of Black and White? Can Black and the company be indicted for a conspiracy on the basis of acts of Black at a time when White was away on holiday?

2. It has been held that a person in total control of his one-man company is capable of stealing the property of the company *(Re A-G's Reference (No 2 of 1982)* [1984] QB 624, CA): see below, p 164. Is this decision consistent with *R v McDonnell?*

> **Note**

The *policy* of making corporate bodies liable to criminal prosecution in addition to or instead of those officers or agents who are personally at fault has been questioned by writers.[41] If both are proceeded against, and the officers are substantial members, they are doubly punished; if the company only is prosecuted and the wrongdoers have no stake in it, the fine will, in effect, be levied wholly on innocent members or customers, while if it is barely solvent, its creditors will suffer. Commentators have suggested that sanctions other than fines might be imposed, ranging all the way from 'naming and shaming' the company to ordering its dissolution.

What does a company know?

The question whether and in what circumstances knowledge should be imputed to a company or other corporate body is one of considerable complexity. Clearly, information which has been given to a corporate organ acting within its sphere of responsibility (eg a document laid before the directors at a board meeting or the members at a general meeting) has been brought home to the company.

This would also be true of information communicated to a person who is the company's 'directing mind and will' if there is an individual whose relationship to the company can be so described. Thus, in *El Ajou v Dollar Land Holdings Ltd* [1994] 1 BCLC 464, CA the question was whether DLH had received money with knowledge that it was the proceeds of fraud. The knowledge of its chairman, Ferdman, was attributed to DLH because it was held that for all purposes relevant to the transaction he was its directing mind and will.

In any area of activity where the members or the directors are competent to act by informal unanimous agreement, knowledge of a matter communicated to all those concerned could readily be attributed to the corporate body.

It is where the knowledge is that of one or more individuals only, whether officers, agents or employees of the company, who do not come into one of the above categories, that the question becomes more difficult. In *Regina Fur Co Ltd v Bossom* [1957] 2 Lloyd's Rep 466 at 468, Pearson J said:

> The general effect of the authorities is, in my opinion, that in deciding whether in a particular case the knowledge of the agent is to be imputed to the company, or other principal, one should consider, mainly at any rate, (1) the position of the agent in relation to the principal and whether the agent had a wide or narrow sphere of operations, and (2) the position of the agent in relation to the relevant transaction and whether he represented the principal in respect of that transaction.

From this it would follow that information communicated to a company secretary, as the officer charged with general authority in the administrative affairs of the company (see the *Panorama* case **[3.13]**) will almost invariably be deemed to be known to the company.

---

[41] The arguments are well summarised in Glanville Williams, *Criminal Law* (2nd edn, 1961) § 283. For further reading, see LH Leigh, *The Criminal Liability of Corporations in English Law* (1969). CRN Winn, 'The Criminal Responsibility of Corporations' (1929) 3 CLJ 398; RS Welsh, 'The Criminal Liability of Corporations' (1946) 62 LQR 345; Sir R Burrows, 'The Responsibility of Corporations under Criminal Law' (1948) 1 Journal of Crim Sci 1; LH Leigh, 'The Criminal Liability of Corporations and other Groups' (1977) 9 Ottawa L Rev 247; LH Leigh, 'A Comparative View' (1982) 80 Mich L Rev 1508; C Wells, *Corporations and Criminal Responsibility* (1993); GR Sullivan, 'The Attribution of Calpability to Limited Companies' [1996] CLJ 515; CMV Clarkson, 'Kicking Corporate Bodies and Damning Their Souls' (1996) 59 MLR 557.

In *J C Houghton & Co v Nothard, Lowe & Wills* [1927] 1 KB, CA, the court was concerned with the question whether the knowledge of a single director should be imputed to the company. Viscount Sumner in the House of Lords was of the view that:

> where knowledge may lead to a modification of the company's rights according as it is or is not followed by action, the knowledge which is relevant is that of the directors themselves, since it is their board that deals with the company's rights. . . . What a director knows or ought in the course of his duty to know may be the knowledge of the company, for it may be deemed to have been duly used so as to lead to action which a fully informed corporation would proceed to take on the strength of it.

Two exceptions are recognised to this rule relating to the knowledge of an agent.

The first is where the knowledge is received by him in a private capacity, in circumstances where he is under no obligation to communicate it to his principal—in Viscount Sumner's words, not 'in the course of his duty'. In *Re David Payne & Co Ltd* [1904] 2 Ch 608, CA money was lent by a company which the borrower intended to use for an improper purpose. One of the lending company's directors was aware of this fact, but because he had received the information privately his knowledge was not ascribed to the company.

The second exception is made where the 'agent' is himself a wrongdoer, as was the case in *Houghton*'s case itself. Viscount Sumner went on to say:

> It has long been recognised that it would be contrary to justice and common sense to treat the knowledge of such persons as that of the company, as if one were to assume that they would make a clean breast of their delinquency.

The reasoning on this point was applied in *Belmont Finance Corpn Ltd v Williams Furniture Ltd* **[8.10]** and in *Heron International Ltd v Grade* **[6.03]**. It was also part of the basis of the decision in *Re A-G's Reference (No 2 of 1982)* [1984] QB 624, CA.[42] The question there was whether a person in total control of a one-man company could in law steal its property. The court held that where the controller had acted dishonestly in relation to the company, his own knowledge was not to be attributed to the company, and it followed that a jury was not bound to conclude that the company must be taken to have consented to the controller's acts. The question of dishonesty was a separate issue, which should also be put to the jury—ie the question whether the defendant had established that he had an honest belief, based on the company's 'true' consent, that he was entitled to appropriate the company's funds.

Again, in *R v Roziek* [1996] 1 BCLC 380, the accused had been charged with obtaining property from certain finance companies by deception. If the branch managers with whom he had dealt were aware of the facts, to the extent that they were parties to his dishonesty, it could not be argued that the companies had been deceived as a result of their knowledge: in that event it was necessary to show that some other employees, who had had the authority to issue the cheques in question to the accused, had been deceived. Since the jury had not been directed along these lines, Roziek's convictions were quashed.

In *El Ajou* it was stressed that the 'directing mind and will' approach and the 'agency' question were separate issues. Indeed, in that case the knowledge of Ferdman was attributed to the company on the first but not the second of these grounds because, *qua* agent, it was not his duty to communicate the information to his principal.

In contrast, in the case next cited, the position was the reverse: the knowledge was deemed to be that of the company on agency principles without regard to the question whether the particular individual was the company's directing mind and will.

The next case is crucial in this area.

---

[42] See GJ Virgo, 'Stealing from the Small Family Business' [1991] CLJ 464; DW Elliot, 'Directors' Thefts and Dishonesty' [1991] Crim LR 732.

[3.29] Meridian Global Funds Management Asia Ltd v Securities Commission [1995] 2 AC 500 (Privy Council)

Under the Securities Amendment Act 1988 (NZ), a person who became a 'substantial security holder' in a 'public issuer' (ie a company whose shares were listed for trading on the Stock Exchange) was required to give notice to the authorities 'as soon as the person knows, or ought to know' that he had become such a holder. Two senior investment managers of Meridian, Koo and Ng, acting within their authority but for improper purposes of their own, bought in its name shares in a listed company, ENC, which made Meridian a 'substantial security holder' in ENC. The knowledge of Koo, as the agent primarily involved in the transaction, was attributed to Meridian (so bringing it under an obligation to give the statutory notice) because, on construction of the statutory provision, this was the appropriate test of attribution rather than whether he was the company's directing mind and will.

The opinion of their Lordships was delivered by LORD HOFFMANN: . . . The phrase 'directing mind and will' comes of course from the celebrated speech of Viscount Haldane LC in *Lennard's Carrying Co Ltd v Asiatic Petroleum Co Ltd* **[3.23]**. But their Lordships think that there has been some misunderstanding of the true principle upon which that case was decided. It may be helpful to start by stating the nature of the problem in a case like this and then come back to *Lennard's* case later.

Any proposition about a company necessarily involves a reference to a set of rules. A company exists because there is a rule (usually in a statute) which says that a persona ficta shall be deemed to exist and to have certain of the powers, rights and duties of a natural person. But there would be little sense in deeming such a persona ficta to exist unless there were also rules to tell one what acts were to count as acts of the company. It is therefore a necessary part of corporate personality that there should be rules by which acts are attributed to the company. These may be called 'the rules of attribution'.

The company's primary rules of attribution will generally be found in its constitution, typically the articles of association, and will say things such as 'for the purpose of appointing members of the board, a majority vote of the shareholders shall be a decision of the company' or 'the decisions of the board in managing the company's business shall be the decisions of the company'. There are also primary rules of attribution which are not expressly stated in the articles but implied by company law, such as 'the unanimous decision of all the shareholders in a solvent company about anything which the company under its memorandum of association has power to do shall be the decision of the company': see *Multinational Gas and Petrochemical Co v Multinational Gas and Petrochemical Services Ltd* **[6.25]**.

These primary rules of attribution are obviously not enough to enable a company to go out into the world and do business. Not every act on behalf of the company could be expected to be the subject of a resolution of the board or a unanimous decision of the shareholders. The company therefore builds upon the primary rules of attribution by using general rules of attribution which are equally available to natural persons, namely, the principles of agency. It will appoint servants and agents whose acts, by a combination of the general principles of agency and the company's primary rules of attribution, count as the acts of the company. And having done so, it will also make itself subject to the general rules by which liability for the acts of others can be attributed to natural persons, such as estoppel or ostensible authority in contract and vicarious liability in tort.

It is worth pausing at this stage to make what may seem an obvious point. Any statement about what a company has or has not done, or can or cannot do, is necessarily a reference to the rules of attribution (primary and general) as they apply to that company. Judges sometimes say that a company 'as such' cannot do anything; it must act by servants or agents. This may see an unexceptionable, even banal remark. And of course the meaning is usually perfectly clear. But a reference to a company 'as such' might suggest that there is something out there called the company of which one can meaningfully say that it can or cannot do something. There is in fact no such thing as the company as such, no Ding an sich, only the applicable rules. To say that a company cannot do something means only that there is no one whose doing of that act would, under the applicable rules of attribution, count as an act of the company.

The company's primary rules of attribution together with the general principles of agency, vicarious liability and so forth are usually sufficient to enable one to determine its rights and obligations. In exceptional cases, however, they will not provide an answer. This will be the case when a rule of law, either expressly or by implication, excludes attribution on the basis of the general principles of agency or vicarious liability. For example, a rule may be stated in language primarily applicable to a natural person and require some act or state of mind on the part of that person 'himself', as opposed to his servants or agents. This is generally true of rules of the criminal law, which ordinarily impose liability only for the actus reus and mens rea of the defendant himself. How is such a rule to be applied to a company?

One possibility is that the court may come to the conclusion that the rule was not intended to apply to companies at all; for example, a law which created an offence for which the only penalty was community service. Another possibility is that the court might interpret the law as meaning that it could apply to a company only on the basis of its primary rules of attribution, ie if the act giving rise to liability was specifically authorised by a resolution of the board or a unanimous agreement of the shareholders. But there will be many cases in which neither of these solutions is satisfactory; in which the court considers that the law was intended to apply to companies and that, although it excludes ordinary vicarious liability, insistence on the primary rules of attribution would in practice defeat that intention. In such a case, the court must fashion a special rule of attribution for the particular substantive rule. This is always a matter of interpretation: given that it was intended to apply to a company, how was it intended to apply? Whose act (or knowledge, or state of mind) was *for this purpose* intended to count as the act etc of the company? One finds the answer to this question by applying the usual canons of interpretation, taking into account the language of the rule (if it is a statute) and its content and policy.

The fact that the rule of attribution is a matter of interpretation or construction of the relevant substantive rule is shown by the contrast between two decisions of the House of Lords, *Tesco Supermarkets Ltd v Nattrass* **[3.27]** and *Director General of Fair Trading v Pioneer Concrete (UK) Ltd*.[43] In the *Tesco* case the question involved the construction of [s 24(1) of] the Trade Descriptions Act 1968.

[His Lordship summarised the facts and issues in that case, and continued:] The House of Lords held that the precautions taken by the board were sufficient for the purposes of section 24(1) to count as precautions taken by the company and that the manager's negligence was not attributable to the company. It did so by examining the purpose of section 24(1) in providing a defence to what would otherwise have been an absolute offence: it was intended to give effect to 'a policy of consumer protection which does have a rational and moral justification'. This led to the conclusion that the acts and defaults of the manager were not intended to be attributed to the company. . . .

On the other hand, in *Director General of Fair Trading v Pioneer Concrete (UK) Ltd*, a restrictive arrangement in breach of an undertaking by a company to the Restrictive Practices Court was made by executives of the company acting within the scope of their employment. The board knew nothing of the arrangement; it had in fact given instructions to the company's employees that they were not to make such arrangements. But the House of Lords held that for the purposes of deciding whether the company was in contempt, the act and state of mind of an employee who entered into an arrangement in the course of his employment should be attributed to the company. This attribution rule was derived from a construction of the undertaking against the background of the Restrictive Trade Practices Act 1976: such undertakings by corporations would be worth little if the

---

[43] [1995] 1 AC 456, [1995] 1 All ER 135, HL.

company could avoid liability for what its employees had actually done on the ground that the board did not know about it. . . .

Against this background of general principle, their Lordships can return to Viscount Haldane LC. In *Lennard's Carrying Co Ltd v Asiatic Petroleum Co Ltd* **[3.23]** the substantive provision for which an attribution rule had to be devised was section 502 of the Merchant Shipping Act 1894, which provided a shipowner with a defence to a claim for the loss of cargo put on board his ship if he could show that the casualty happened 'without his actual fault or privity'. The cargo had been destroyed by a fire caused by the unseaworthy condition of the ship's boilers. The language of section 502 excludes vicarious liability; it is clear that in the case of an individual owner, only his own fault or privity can defeat the statutory protection. How is this rule to be applied to a company? Viscount Haldane LC rejected the possibility that it did not apply to companies at all or (which would have come to the same thing) that it required fault or privity attributable under the company's primary rules. Instead, guided by the language and purpose of the section, he looked for the person whose functions in the company, in relation to the cause of the casualty, were the same as those to be expected of the individual shipowner to whom the language primarily applied. Who in the company was responsible for monitoring the condition of the ship, receiving the reports of the master and ship's agents, authorising repairs etc.? This person was Mr Lennard, whom Viscount Haldane LC described as the 'directing mind and will' of the company. It was therefore his fault or privity which section 502 attributed to the company. . . .

Once it is appreciated that the question is one of construction rather than metaphysics, the answer in this case seems to their Lordships to be . . . straightforward. The policy of section 20 of the Securities Amendment Act 1988 is to compel, in fast-moving markets, the immediate disclosure of the identity of persons who become substantial security holders in public issuers. Notice must be given as soon as that person knows that he has become a substantial security holder. In the case of a corporate security holder, what rule should be implied as to the person whose knowledge for this purpose is to count as the knowledge of the company? Surely the person who, with the authority of the company, acquired the relevant interest. Otherwise the policy of the Act would be defeated. Companies would be able to allow employees to acquire interests on their behalf which made them substantial security holders but would not have to report them until the board or someone else in senior management got to know about it. This could put a premium on the board paying as little attention as possible to what its investment managers were doing. Their Lordships would therefore hold that upon the true construction of section 20(4)(e), the company knows that it has become a substantial security holder when that is known to the person who had authority to do the deal. It is then obliged to give notice under section 20(3). The fact that Koo did the deal for a corrupt purpose and did not give such notice because he did not want his employers to find out cannot in their Lordships' view affect the attribution of knowledge and the consequent duty to notify.

It was therefore not necessary in this case to inquire into whether Koo could have been described in some more general sense as the 'directing mind and will' of the company. But their Lordships would wish to guard themselves against being understood to mean that whenever a servant of a company has authority to do an act on its behalf, knowledge of that act will for all purposes be attributed to the company. It is a question of construction in each case as to whether the particular rule requires that the knowledge that an act has been done, or the state of mind with which it was done, should be attributed to the company. Sometimes, as in *Director General of Fair Trading v Pioneer Concrete (UK) Ltd* and this case, it will be appropriate. Likewise in a case in which a company was required to make a return for revenue purposes and the statute made it an offence to make a false return with intent to deceive, the Divisional Court held that the mens rea of the servant authorised to discharge the duty to make the return should be attributed to the company: see *Moore v I Bresler Ltd.*[44] On the other hand, the fact that a company's employee is authorised to drive a lorry does not in itself lead to the conclusion that if he kills someone by reckless driving, the

[44] [1944] 2 All ER 515, DC.

company will be guilty of manslaughter. There is no inconsistency. Each is an example of an attribution rule for a particular purpose, tailored as it always must be to the terms and policies of the substantive rule.

➤ Note

In *Deutsche Genossenschaftsbank v Burnhope* [1995] 1 WLR 1580, HL the question arose, in construing an insurance policy, whether there had been a theft of certain valuable documents by 'a person present on the premises' of the bank. The crime was attributed to a company, the necessary *mens rea* being found in the intention of its principal executive director. But the only individual who had at any time been physically present on the premises was a junior employee who had been sent to collect the documents. The House of Lords declined to identify this employee with the company so as to hold that it was a 'person present' within the term of the policy.

➤ Question

Can a corporation forget? How (if at all) might this come about?

Litigation: procedural issues

Conduct of litigation

Blackstone (above, p 71) quoted Sir Edward Coke as authority for the view that a company must always appear in court by attorney, 'for it cannot appear in person, being invisible, and existing only in intendment and consideration of the law'. The courts have for many centuries strenuously insisted on this rule, both in civil and in criminal cases, and it has only been by statute that inroads have been made into it—and then mainly in relation to lower courts such as the magistrates' courts. So we have the paradox that the law is happy to identify a company with the individual who is its 'directing mind and will' for the purpose of making it criminally liable, while at the same time it will refuse to allow the company to appear before it in the person of the same individual. This remains the basic rule: in *RH Tomlinssons (Trowbridge) Ltd v Secretary of State for the Environment* [1999] 2 BCLC 760, CA it was solemnly affirmed by the Court of Appeal. However, the Civil Procedure Rules, which came into effect on 26 April 1999, allow a company (with the leave of the court) to appear by an *employee* and, by implication, to appear 'in person' in other ways, so that the rule has now been superseded for civil cases in the county courts and the High Court.

Service of documents

CA 2006 s 1139: Service of documents on company

A document may be served on a company registered under this Act by leaving it at, or sending it by post to, the company's registered office.

4

SHAREHOLDERS AS AN ORGAN
OF THE COMPANY

General issues

In Chapter 2 we saw how the law recognises a company as a person in its own right, capable of having rights, owning property, making contracts, accepting or incurring obligations, committing wrongs and conducting litigation. Chapter 3 then addressed the practical matter of the way in which this artificial legal person functions: how its corporate will is manifested, its decisions taken and its acts performed. Plainly, a company cannot do anything except through human beings who are its members and officers and, vicariously, through its employees and agents.

In neither of these earlier chapters was much attention given to the role of the shareholders, or, more generally, the members of the company.[1] Yet both CA 2006 and individual companies' constitutions assume a limited, but nonetheless significant, role for the company's members. The Act gives members certain rights and reserves to them certain important decisions, to the exclusion of the company's directors. This is usually done when there is a substantial risk associated with leaving power in the hands of the directors. So members, not directors, must approve certain types of contracts between the company and its directors.[2] In addition, members have the right to decide upon changes to the constitution of their company[3] and to the rights attached to their shares.[4] Some of these statutory rules are mandatory; others can be strengthened or relaxed by the company's own articles. In addition, the members have the right to remove directors,[5] and, when wrongs have been committed against the company but the directors (perhaps through self-interest) are not inclined to purse the claims, the members can sometimes pursue these claims and obtain a remedy for the company.[6]

Beyond this, the members' additional rights are derived from the company's constitution itself. This is the agreement that divides a company's power between the directors and the members. As noted earlier, the principal constitutional document (and the one on which this chapter focuses) is the company's *articles*: see CA 2006 ss 17 and 18. This sets the constitutional framework for the company. If the 2006 Model Articles for Private Companies is taken as typical for small companies, we see it contains details about meetings of members, appointment and termination of directors and their duties and proceedings, delegation of power, issues of shares and payment of dividends, and the use of the company's seal. The overriding assumption is that the directors, not the members, will manage the business of the company (but see below, pp 180 ff).

---

[1] Indeed, this chapter might have been better entitled 'Members as an Organ of the Company', since not every company is limited by shares: see CA 2006 s 112.

[2] CA 2006 ss 182–231, see below, pp 221 ff.

[3] CA 2006 s 21, see below, pp 204 ff.

[4] CA 2006 ss 626–640, see below, pp 443 ff.

[5] CA 2006 s 168, see below, pp 256 ff.

[6] CA 2006 ss 260–264, see below, pp 535 ff.

Despite this rather unequal power split, the members and the directors constitute the two 'organs' of the company. The term signifies their constitutional authority to act *as* the company rather than merely to represent the company as its agent under an authority derived from some superior corporate source.

These two organs share between them the most important corporate functions, and (except in the case of the single-member company, the wholly-owned subsidiary or the company with only one director) each organ normally acts by decisions (resolutions) taken at meetings. The organ constituted by the members is called '*the general meeting*' and by the directors '*the board of directors*' or 'the board'. This recognises that a *meeting* is the focus of corporate decision-making by these organs.

Historically, members' meetings were often well attended, with vigorous debate and meaningful voting. Nowadays, the 'meetings' of very small companies are perfunctory affairs, if held at all. And attendance at the meetings of large companies is commonly unrepresentative and the 'business' a routine rubber-stamping of the directors' proposals. But old concepts die hard: both the courts and the legislative reformers have striven to preserve some vestiges of the democratic ideal in their attitude to corporate governance, even when it seems to be plain on all sides that the struggle is a hopeless one.

This chapter considers the members' rights and duties under the CA 2006 and the company's constitution, but first a little more needs to be said about the division of power effected by the statute and the articles.

Division of power within companies

The introduction above, however brief, shows clearly that the constitutions of modern companies, with the backing of the law, have put the power to run the company's business in the hands of the directors, and have left the members a very minor role. Typically this extends to the declaration of a dividend, the election or re-election of directors and the appointment of auditors—and even in these matters there may be little for them to do except rubber-stamp the recommendations of the directors.

In other words, the role of the member has become more and more that of a passive investor (no doubt partly from choice, but also from apathy and a sense of impotence), while power has progressively come to be concentrated in the hands of the directors, especially the executive directors. The larger and more widely dispersed the membership or shareholding of the company, the more marked this difference between 'ownership' and 'control' usually is. (This trend has in part been reversed by the growth of the institutional members such as the pension funds, unit trusts and insurance companies and, more recently, buy-out funds.[7])

Reformers, motivated both by idealistic notions of 'shareholder democracy' as an end in itself, and also by a sense that directors do have too much power over 'other people's money', which is at times abused ('the unacceptable face of capitalism'), have lobbied for new legislation that consciously seeks to put a larger share of real control into the hands of the members. During the term of the 1948 Act, and with increasing vigour since then, member approval has been required for certain decisions (see above, p 169, for illustrations). The procedures for these member-authorisations are sometimes quite rigidly prescribed, and the consequences of failing to observe the formalities very severe. The costs of compliance, both in money and in time, can prove a heavy price to pay for the theoretical gain. By contrast, in many North American jurisdictions reformers have accepted the case for a reduction in member-consents in the interests of business efficiency.

---

[7] See below, p 184.

In some European companies codes, most notably that of Germany, the problems associated with the concentration of power in the hands of the board of directors have been tackled in another way. In these systems, there is provision for a '*two-tier*' management structure, consisting of a managerial (or executive) board and a supervisory board, the former having charge of matters of day-to-day management and the latter being responsible for the control of the executive board and, in particular, having the power of appointment and removal of its personnel. These supervisory boards in Germany also play an important role in ensuring worker-participation in management, or '*co-determination*'. In most German public companies, one third of the members of the supervisory board must be elected by the company's employees, while the other two-thirds are elected by the members.

The Draft Fifth EC Directive on Company Law, in its original form (9 October 1972), contained proposals for the adoption of this model for public companies by all the member states of the EU. Such a change, if implemented in the UK, would have introduced a further 'organ' into our hierarchy of corporate management, and would have called for a basic reconsideration of the principles laid down in the cases on which we currently rely. However, the move was resisted by various governments, and a compromise in relation to SEs allowing the British to retain their own system, was eventually reached.[8]

Otherwise, concern for employees' interests has been limited to some very modest provisions in the Companies Acts, such as CA 2006 s 172 (directors to have regard to interests of employees in their duty to promote the success of the company), and CA 2006 s 247 and IA 1986 s 187 (power to make over assets to employees on a cessation of business or in a liquidation). The directors' annual report must give certain information about its employment policies and employee involvement, and there are inducements in the tax legislation to establish employee share-ownership schemes—and these have now become relatively common.

All of this only serves to show that in the *constitutional* split of power, the directors reign supreme. This chapter looks at what few, but sometimes crucial, collective and personal rights the members do have under the constitution, and how they must exercise those rights. There is little by way of general control over the directors here. That is left to mechanisms discussed in Chapters 5 and 6.

Articles and their interpretation

If the articles, as the company's primary constitutional document, define the division of powers between the members and the directors, then it is important to know how their terms are interpreted. Orthodox rules of contractual interpretation generally apply, since the articles constitute a contract between the company and its members,[9] but the cases below illustrate particular problems and limitations. It emerges that the articles constitute a rather unusual type of contract. (This is even more apparent when the personal rights arising under this contract are considered: see below, pp 230 ff.)

---

[8] By this compromise, the Statute for a European Company allows an SE to adopt either a one-tier or a two-tier board structure (Regulation (EC) No 2157/2001, arts 38–51). The former is the equivalent of the British company system and the board in this case is called the administrative organ. In the two-tier system there is a management and a supervisory organ. The functions of each of these organs have been prescribed in the Act. Under Directive 2001/86/EC, the form of employee involvement in an SE is to be determined by negotiation between the management or administrative organs of the existing companies and representatives of their companies' employees.

[9] CA 2006 s 33, see below, pp 230 ff.

The court has no jurisdiction to rectify the memorandum or articles of association.

[4.01] Scott v Frank F Scott (London) Ltd [1940] Ch 794 (Court of Appeal)

[The facts appear from the judgment.[10]]

The judgment of the Court of Appeal (SCOTT, CLAUSON and LUXMOORE LJJ) was delivered by LUX-
MOORE LJ: The . . . question which falls to be considered is whether the defendants are entitled to
have the articles of association rectified in the manner claimed by them. Bennett J [at first instance]
said he was prepared to hold that the articles of association as registered were not in accordance
with the intention of the three brothers who were the only signatories of the memorandum and articles of association, and down to the date of Frank Stanley Scott's death the only shareholders
therein. Bennett J, however, held that the court has no jurisdiction to rectify articles of association
of a company, although they do not accord with what is proven to have been the concurrent intention of all the signatories therein at the moment of signature. We are in complete agreement with
this decision. It seems to us that there is no room in the case of a company incorporated under the
appropriate statute or statutes for the application to either the memorandum or articles of association of the principles upon which a court of equity permits rectification of documents whether inter
partes or not . . .

The articles cannot be supplemented by additional terms implied from extrinsic circumstances.

[4.02] Bratton Seymour Service Co Ltd v Oxborough [1992] BCLC 693 (Court of Appeal)

The company was set up to manage the commercial aspects of a development consisting of a
number of flats, the shares being held by the flat-owners. The question for the court was
whether it was possible to imply into the company's articles a term that the members should
make contributions for the upkeep of the garden, swimming pool and other communal
amenity areas of the development. The Court of Appeal held that no such term could be
implied.

STEYN LJ: . . . Section 14(1) of the Companies Act 1985 [now see CA 2006 s 33] provides that 'the
memorandum and articles, when registered, bind the company and its members to the same
extent as if they respectively had been signed and sealed by each member'. By virtue of s 14 the
articles of association become, upon registration, a contract between a company and members. It
is, however, a statutory contract of a special nature with its own distinctive features. It derives its
binding force not from a bargain struck between parties but from the terms of the statute. It is binding only insofar as it affects the rights and obligations between the company and the members acting in their capacity as members. If it contains provisions conferring rights and obligations on outsiders, then those provisions do not bite as part of the contract between the company and the
members, even if the outsider is coincidentally a member. Similarly, if the provisions are not truly
referable to the rights and obligations of members as such it does not operate as a contract.
Moreover, the contract can be altered by a special resolution without the consent of all the contracting parties. It is also, unlike an ordinary contract, not defeasible on the grounds of misrepresentation, common law mistake, mistake in equity, undue influence or duress. Moreover, . . . it cannot be
rectified on the grounds of mistake.

---

[10] Recall that CA 2006 abolishes the company's memorandum, in this form, and s 28 provides that the provisions of
any existing company memorandum which are not required to be in the new-style memorandum will be treated as provisions of the articles, amendable by special resolution. The 'new-style memorandum of association' (s 8) is a statement
of intent in prescribed form authenticated by the subscribers to the new company.

Turning now to the present case, the question is whether the implied term of requiring members to contribute to maintenance of the amenities can be implied not on the basis of any language to be found in the articles, but on the basis of extrinsic circumstances. The question is, is it notionally ever possible to imply a term in such circumstances? I will readily accept that the law should not adopt a black-letter approach. It is possible to imply a term purely from the language of the document itself: a purely constructional implication is not precluded. But it is quite another matter to seek to imply a term into articles of association from extrinsic circumstances.

Here, the company puts forward an implication to be derived not from the language of the articles of association but purely from extrinsic circumstances. That, in my judgment, is a type of implication which, as a matter of law, can never succeed in the case of articles of association. After all, if it were permitted, it would involve the position that the different implications would notionally be possible between the company and different subscribers. Just as the company or an individual member cannot seek to defeat the statutory contract by reason of special circumstances such as misrepresentation, mistake, undue influence and duress and is furthermore not permitted to seek a rectification, neither the company nor any member can seek to add to or to subtract from the terms of the articles by way of implying a term derived from extrinsic surrounding circumstances. If it were permitted in this case, it would be equally permissible over the spectrum of company law cases. The consequence would be prejudicial to third parties, namely potential shareholders who are entitled to look to and rely on the articles of association as registered. Despite Mr Asprey's lucid and incisive argument, I take the view that on this ground alone the implication cannot succeed.

DILLON LJ and SIR CHRISTOPHER SLADE delivered concurring judgments.

When determining the meaning of an amendment of the articles of association, the courts will not consider the effect which the alteration was intended to have, or circumstances in which the alteration was made, but the court will however add words to avoid absurdity, or imply a term which is strictly necessary proceeding from the express words of the articles viewed objectively in their commercial setting. The next case is an illustration.

'Implied terms' in the articles

[4.03] Equitable Life Assurance Society v Hyman [2002] 1 AC 408 (House of Lords)

The relevant article (art 65) gave the directors a wide discretionary power to pay bonuses on its members' life assurance policies, and in exercise of this power the directors had paid some policyholders a larger bonus than others. This was contrary to 'guarantees' which had been given when certain of the members took out their policies. Lord Steyn said that the articles should be read as containing an implied term that the directors would not exercise their discretion 'in a manner which deprived the guarantees of any substantial value'.

LORD STEYN: It is necessary to distinguish between the processes of interpretation and implication. The purpose of interpretation is to assign to the language of the text the most appropriate meaning which the words can legitimately bear. The language of article 65(1) contains no relevant express restriction on the powers of the directors. It is impossible to assign to the language of article 65(1) by construction a restriction precluding the directors from overriding GARs ['guaranteed annuity rate' policies]. To this extent I would uphold the submissions made on behalf of the Society. The critical question is whether a relevant restriction may be implied into article 65(1). It is certainly not a case in which a term can be implied by law in the sense of incidents impliedly annexed to particular forms of contracts. Such standardised implied terms operate as general default rules: see *Scally v Southern Health and Social Services Board* [1992] 1 AC 294. If a term is to be implied, it could only be a term implied from the language of article 65 read in its particular commercial setting. Such implied terms operate as ad hoc gap fillers. In *Luxor (Eastbourne) Ltd v Cooper* [1941] AC 108, 137 Lord Wright explained this distinction as follows:

> "The expression 'implied term' is used in different senses. Sometimes it denotes some term which does not depend on the actual intention of the parties but on a rule of law, such as the terms, warranties or conditions which, if not expressly excluded, the law imports, as for instance under the Sale of Goods Act and the Marine Insurance Act . . . But a case like the present is different because what it is sought to imply is based on an intention imputed to the parties from their actual circumstances."

It is only an individualised term of the second kind which can arguably arise in the present case. Such a term may be imputed to parties: it is not critically dependent on proof of an actual intention of the parties. The process "is one of construction of the agreement as a whole in its commercial setting": *Banque Bruxelles Lambert SA v Eagle Star Insurance Co Ltd* [1997] AC 191, 212e, per Lord Hoffmann. This principle is sparingly and cautiously used and may never be employed to imply a term in conflict with the express terms of the text. The legal test for the implication of such a term is a standard of strict necessity. This is how I must approach the question whether a term is to be implied into article 65(1) which precludes the directors from adopting a principle which has the effect of overriding or undermining the GARs.

The inquiry is entirely constructional in nature: proceeding from the express terms of article 65, viewed against its objective setting, the question is whether the implication is strictly necessary. My Lords, as counsel for the GAR policyholders observed, final bonuses are not bounty. They are a significant part of the consideration for the premiums paid. And the directors' discretions as to the amount and distribution of bonuses are conferred for the benefit of policyholders. In this context the self-evident commercial object of the inclusion of guaranteed rates in the policy is to protect the policyholder against a fall in market annuity rates by ensuring that if the fall occurs he will be better off than he would have been with market rates. The choice is given to the GAR policyholder and not to the Society. It cannot be seriously doubted that the provision for guaranteed annuity rates was a good selling point in the marketing by the Society of the GAR policies. It is also obvious that it would have been a significant attraction for purchasers of GAR policies. The Society points out that no special charge was made for the inclusion in the policy of GAR provisions. So be it. This factor does not alter the reasonable expectations of the parties. The supposition of the parties must be presumed to have been that the directors would not exercise their discretion in conflict with contractual rights. These are the circumstances in which the directors of the Society resolved upon a differential policy which was designed to deprive the relevant guarantees of any substantial value. In my judgment an implication precluding the use of the directors' discretion in this way is strictly necessary. The implication is essential to give effect to the reasonable expectations of the parties. The stringent test applicable to the implication of terms is satisfied.

➤ Questions

1. Why did this case need to be decided as a matter of contractual interpretation of the articles, rather than a matter of (improper) exercise of discretion by the directors?

2. Lord Steyn clearly had in mind the distinction between 'constructional' implied terms and ones derived from extrinsic circumstances which he had put forward in *Bratton Seymour* (to which he did not refer). Is it clear from these two cases how the line is to be drawn?

➤ Notes

1. If the understanding between the founding members as to the basis on which a company is to be incorporated differs from the constitutional arrangements of the company when formed, this may be a reason for winding up the company on the 'just and equitable' ground (IA 1986 s 122, see below, pp 653 ff). And a member whose 'legitimate expectations' are

disappointed, even though they are not formally recorded as constitutional provisions or terms, may also be granted discretionary relief under CA 2006 s 994, on the ground of 'unfairly prejudicial' conduct: see below, pp 552 ff.

2. In Australia, on facts similar to *Scott v Frank F Scott (London) Ltd* **[4.01]**, the court has refused rectification but indicated that if new proceedings were brought it would be willing to give a remedy in the nature of specific performance ordering the defendant members to vote in favour of a special resolution to remedy the defect: *Simon v HPM Industries Pty Ltd* (1989) 15 ACLR 427, SC (NSW); *Re Freehouse Pty Ltd* (1997) 26 ACSR 662, SC (Vic).

Division of powers between the general meeting and the board

The division of powers between the members in general meeting and the board of directors is determined by the company's articles. The relevant Model articles for private companies from the 1985 and 2006 Acts are set out below. The cases that follow explain the ramifications of such provisions.

2006 Model Articles for Private Companies

3 Limits on Directors' Functions

(1) The shareholders may, by special resolution:

   (a) alter the scope of the directors' functions; or

   (b) require the directors to act in a specified manner.

(2) No special resolution passed under paragraph (1) shall have retrospective effect.

Companies (Tables A to F) Regulations 1985

Table A

70 Subject to the provisions of the Act, the memorandum and the articles and to any directions given by special resolution, the business of the company shall be managed by the directors who may exercise all the powers of the company. No alteration of the memorandum or articles and no such direction shall invalidate any prior act of the directors which would have been valid if that alteration had not been made or that direction had not been given. The powers given by this regulation shall not be limited by any special power given to the directors by the articles and a meeting of directors at which a quorum is present may exercise all powers exercisable by the directors.

Where the articles limit the powers of the company in general meeting, such articles cannot be disregarded even by a majority sufficiently large to alter the articles. A formal alteration must be made and then acted upon.

[4.04] Imperial Hydropathic Hotel Co, Blackpool v Hampson (1882) 23 Ch D 1 (Court of Appeal)

The articles provided that the directors were to hold office for a period of three years and to retire by rotation. At a general meeting specially summoned for this and other purposes, resolutions were carried for the removal of two directors (who were not due for retirement under the articles) and the election of others in their place. The company in this action claimed a declaration that the directors had been validly removed. It was held that the articles could not be disregarded in this way.[11]

> COTTON LJ: There is nothing in the Act or in the articles which directly enables a general meeting to remove directors; but the way it is put is this—that there is power in these articles, as there is power in the Act, by a meeting duly called to pass a resolution altering the articles; and it is said that here there was a resolution which would have been effectual to alter the articles that these directors whom the articles did not authorise to be removed should be removed. Now in my opinion it is an entire fallacy to say that because there is power to alter the regulations, you can by a resolution which might alter the regulations, do that which is contrary to the regulations as they stand in a particular and individual case. It is in no way altering the regulations. The alteration of the regulations would be by introducing a provision, not that some particular director be discharged from being a director, but that directors be capable of being removed by the vote of a general meeting. It is a very different thing to pass a general rule applicable to every one who comes within it, and to pass a resolution against a particular individual, which would be a *privilegium* and not a law. Now here there was no attempt to pass any resolution at this meeting which would affect any director, except those who are aimed at by the resolution, no alteration of the regulations was to bind the company to those regulations as altered; and assuming, as I do for the present purpose, as the second meeting seems to have been regular according to the notice, that everything was regularly done, what was done cannot be treated in my opinion as an alteration first of the regulations, and then under that altered regulation as a removal of the directors . . .
>
> JESSEL MR and BOWEN LJ delivered concurring judgments.

[Also see *Boschoek Pty Co Ltd v Fuke* [**4.32**].]

Where the general management of the company is vested in the directors, the members have no power by ordinary resolution to give directions to the board or to overrule its business decisions.

[4.05] Automatic Self-Cleansing Filter Syndicate Co Ltd v Cuninghame [1906] 2 Ch 34 (Court of Appeal)

Article 96 of the company's articles of association vested in the directors 'the management of the business and the control of the company' in terms similar to the 1985 Table A, article 70; and article 91(1) specifically empowered them to sell any property of the company on such terms and conditions as they might think fit. At a general meeting a resolution was passed directing the board to sell the company's undertaking to a new company formed for the purpose, but the directors disapproved of the proposed terms and declined to carry out the sale. It was held that the shareholders had no say in the matter, which was for the board alone to decide.

> COLLINS MR: This is an appeal from a decision of Warrington J, who has been asked by the plaintiffs, Mr McDiarmid and the company, for a declaration that the defendants, as directors of the company, are bound to carry into effect a resolution passed at a meeting of the shareholders in the company on 16 January. . . .
>
> The point arises in this way. At a meeting of the company a resolution was passed by a majority—I was going to say a bare majority, but it was a majority—in favour of a sale to a purchaser, and the directors, honestly believing, as Warrington J thought, that it was most undesirable in the interests

---

[11] But now see CA 2006 s 168, which gives the general meeting power to remove the directors by ordinary resolution notwithstanding the terms of the articles: see below, p 256.

of the company that that agreement should be carried into effect, refused to affix the seal of the company to it, or to assist in carrying out a resolution which they disapproved of; and the question is whether under the memorandum and articles of association here the directors are bound to accept, in substitution of their own view, the view contained in the resolution of the company. Warrington J held that the majority could not impose that obligation upon the directors, and that on the true construction of the articles the directors were the persons authorised by the articles to effect this sale, and that unless the other powers given by the memorandum were invoked by a special resolution, it was impossible for a mere majority at a meeting to override the views of the directors. That depends, as Warrington J put it, upon the construction of the articles. [His Lordship read the relevant articles and continued:] Therefore in the matters referred to in article 97(1) the view of the directors as to the fitness of the matter is made the standard; and furthermore, by article 96 they are given in express terms the full powers which the company has, except so far as they 'are not hereby or by statute expressly directed or required to be exercised or done by the company', so that the directors have absolute power to do all things other than those that are expressly required to be done by the company; and then comes the limitation on their general authority—'subject to such regulations as may from time to time be made by extraordinary resolution'. Therefore, if it is desired to alter the powers of the directors, that must be done not by a resolution carried by a majority at an ordinary meeting of the company, but by an extraordinary resolution. In these circumstances it seems to me that it is not competent for the majority of the shareholders at an ordinary meeting to affect or alter the mandate originally given to the directors, by the articles of association. It has been suggested that this is a mere question of principal and agent, and that it would be an absurd thing if a principal in appointing an agent should in effect appoint a dictator who is to manage him instead of his managing the agent. I think that that analogy does not strictly apply to this case. No doubt for some purposes directors are agents. For whom are they agents? You have, no doubt, in theory and law one entity, the company, which might be a principal, but you have to go behind that when you look to the particular position of directors. It is by the consensus of all the individuals in the company that these directors become agents and hold their rights as agents. It is not fair to say that a majority at a meeting is for the purposes of this case the principal so as to alter the mandate of the agent. The minority also must be taken into account. There are provisions by which the minority may be overborne, but that can only done by special machinery in the shape of special resolutions. Short of that the mandate which must be obeyed is not that of the majority—it is that of the whole entity made up of all the shareholders. If the mandate of the directors is to be altered, it can only be under the machinery of the memorandum and articles themselves. I do not think I need to say more . . .

COZENS-HARDY LJ delivered a concurring judgment.

➤ Notes

1. The decision in *Cuninghame*'s case marked the beginning of a departure from the traditional nineteenth-century view which regarded the members in general meeting as constituting 'the company' and the directors as their delegates or agents. This older view is well illustrated by the wording of s 90 of the Companies Clauses Consolidation Act 1845,[12] and the remarks of Cotton LJ in *Isle of Wight Rly Co v Tahourdin* (1883) 25 Ch D 320, CA, deciding a case under this section (which gave the directors general management power, but 'subject . . . to the control and regulation of any general meeting especially convened for the purpose'. The directors had succeeded at first instance in securing an injunction to restrain the holding of a general meeting which had been requisitioned by a number of shareholders. He said (at 329):

We are of opinion that this injunction ought not to have been granted. It is a very strong thing indeed to prevent shareholders from holding a meeting of the company, when such a meeting is

[12] An Act containing special provisions for regulating companies incorporated by a special Act of Parliament.

the only way in which they can interfere, if the majority of them think that the course taken by the directors, in a matter which is intra vires of the directors, is not for the benefit of the company . . .

Directors have great powers, and the court refuses to interfere with their management of the company's affairs if they keep within their powers, and if a shareholder complains of the conduct of the directors while they keep within their powers, the court says to him, 'If you want to alter the management of the affairs of the company go to a general meeting, and if they agree with you they will pass a resolution obliging the directors to alter their course of proceeding.'

2. Three further points may be made about *Cuninghame*'s case:
   (i) It is not the *law* that has changed between 1883 (the date of *Tahourdin*'s case) and today, so much as commercial practice. All that the courts have done is to recognise that practice. There is nothing in the law which would prevent a company from having a provision in its articles which gave supervisory powers in the widest terms to its members, or allowed them to override the director's decisions—indeed, Art 70 (1985 Table A) itself has such a provision (but a special resolution is needed).
   (ii) Art 70 (1985 Table A) uses the words 'the business of the company shall be managed by the directors . . . '. The ruling in *Cuninghame*'s case does not apply to decisions outside the company's business and its management. In *Re Emmadart Ltd* [1979] Ch 540, [1979] 1 All ER 599, it was held that directors had no power under such an article to resolve to put their company into liquidation.
   (iii) Until the revision of Table A in 1985, the wording of the article corresponding to art 70 was ambiguous: there was a power reserved to the company in general meeting to prescribe 'regulations' binding on the directors (see eg CA 1948, Table A art 80). But what was meant by 'regulations' in this context was never settled; and some commentators (eg Goldberg, (1970) 33 MLR 177; Sullivan, (1977) 93 LQR 569) argued that if due weight were given to this provision art 80 ought to be construed as giving the members power to override the autonomy apparently conferred on the directors by *Cuninghame*'s case. Their view was supported by the first-instance decision of Neville J in *Marshall's Valve Gear Co Ltd v Manning, Wardle & Co Ltd* [1909] 1 Ch 267. The problem is still very much a live one, for there are many thousands of companies that have articles in this old form. But all the indications are that a modern court would not go out of its way to restore the nineteenth-century position in the face of the shift in business practice over the last hundred years; and in *Breckland Group Holdings Ltd v London & Suffolk Properties Ltd* **[11.07]**, Harman J expressed the view that *Marshall*'s case could not stand against the overwhelming weight of authority to the contrary.

3. Following *Cuninghame*'s case, the Court of Appeal in *Gramophone and Typewriter Co Ltd v Stanley* **[2.05]** declined to 'lift the veil' so as to identify a subsidiary with its holding company, partly on the ground that the control of the affairs of the subsidiary was assigned to its *directors*. The same approach was adopted in the cases which follow.

[4.06] Quin & Axtens Ltd v Salmon [1909] AC 442 (House of Lords)

The company's two managing directors, Salmon and Axtens, held between them the bulk of the company's ordinary shares. Article 75 of the articles provided that the business of the company should be managed by the directors, who might exercise all the powers of the company 'subject to such regulations (being not inconsistent with the provisions of the articles) as may be prescribed by the company in general meeting'. Article 80 stated that no resolution of a meeting of the directors having for its object (*inter alia*) the acquisition or letting of certain premises should be valid if either Salmon or Axtens dissented. The directors resolved to acquire and to let various properties, but Salmon dissented. An extraordinary general meeting was then held at which the members by a majority passed similar resolutions. The House of Lords, upholding the decision of the Court of Appeal, held that the members' resolutions were inconsistent with the articles and granted an injunction restraining the company from acting on them.

LORD LOREBURN LJ: My Lords, I do not see any solid ground for complaint against the judgment of the Court of Appeal.

The bargain made between the shareholders is contained in articles 75 and 80 of the articles of association, and it amounts for the purpose in hand to this, that the directors should manage the business; and the company, therefore, are not to manage the business unless there is provision to that effect. Further the directors cannot manage it in a particular way—that is to say, they cannot do certain things if Mr Salmon or Mr Axtens objects. Now I cannot agree with Mr Upjohn in his contention that the failure of the directors upon the objection of Mr Salmon to grant these leases of itself remitted the matter to the discretion of the company in general meeting. They could still manage the business, but not altogether in the way they desired . . .

LORDS MACNAGHTEN, JAMES OF HEREFORD and SHAW OF DUNFERMLINE concurred.

[4.07] John Shaw & Sons (Salford) Ltd v Shaw [1935] 2 KB 113 (Court of Appeal)

As part of the settlement of a dispute concerning sums owing to the plaintiff company by Peter, John and Percy Shaw (three brothers who were shareholders in, and directors of, the plaintiff company), the articles were altered so as to hand over all control of the financial affairs of the company and the management of its business to three independent persons known as 'permanent directors'. Two of the brothers, however, later failed to accept certain other provisions of the settlement, and as a result it was resolved at a meeting of the permanent directors that the present action should be instituted against them. But before the hearing of the suit the shareholders held an extraordinary meeting, at which a resolution was passed directing the board to discontinue the action forthwith. Du Parcq J disregarded the shareholders' resolution and gave judgment for the plaintiff company. The defendants appealed.

GREER LJ: [This] cause of action, whether likely to succeed or not, was one in respect of which the permanent directors were, in my opinion, empowered to commence and carry on.

I am therefore of opinion that the learned judge was right in refusing to dismiss the action on the plea that it was commenced without the authority of the plaintiff company. I think the judge was also right in refusing to give effect to the resolution of the meeting of the shareholders requiring the chairman to instruct the company's solicitors not to proceed further with the action. A company is an entity distinct alike from its shareholders and its directors. Some of its powers may, according to its articles, be exercised by directors, certain other powers may be reserved for the shareholders in general meeting. If powers of management are vested in the directors, they and they alone can exercise these powers. The only way in which the general body of the shareholders can control the exercise of powers vested by the articles in the directors is by altering their articles, or if opportunity arises under the articles, by refusing to re-elect the directors of whose actions they disapprove.[13] They cannot themselves usurp the powers which by the articles are vested in the directors any more than the directors can usurp the powers vested by the articles in the general body of shareholders . . .

[ROCHE LJ agreed, for other reasons, that the action had been competently brought, while SLESSER LJ, again for other reasons, thought that it had not. But he agreed, or 'inclined to the view', that the shareholders could not interfere with a power conferred by the articles on the permanent

---

13 [The members can now also remove the directors by ordinary resolution, by provisions first introduced into CA 1948: now see CA 2006 s 168.]

directors, except by altering the articles. The court unanimously held, however, that the defendants were entitled to succeed on the substantive issue of the case, and allowed the appeal.]

➤ Note

The above cases may be taken to have established that, where the directors in pursuance of a power conferred upon them have instituted litigation in the company's name, the members in general meeting may not interfere and direct that the proceedings be discontinued. But in the converse case, where the majority of members have instituted or consented to the institution of proceedings in the company's name, and the *directors* object to their being continued, the law is less clear. Certainly if the directors are themselves defendants or if the allegation is that they are party to a wrong against the company, the rule in *Foss v Harbottle* **[11.01]** appears to allow the majority members the ultimate say and even, where the directors are themselves majority members, to permit a minority member to bring a derivative action.

The company in general meeting may act if there is no board competent or able (eg because of deadlock) to exercise the powers conferred upon it.

[4.08] Barron v Potter [1914] 1 Ch 895 (Chancery Division)

The two directors of the company were not on speaking terms, so that effective board meetings could not be held. The plaintiff, Canon Barron, had requisitioned a members' meeting at which additional directors had purportedly been appointed. The defendant objected that the power to make such appointments was vested by the company's articles in the directors. It was held that, in view of the deadlock, the power in question reverted to the general meeting, and so the appointments were valid.

WARRINGTON LJ: [Having held that no proper board meeting had been held, continued:] The question then arises, Was the resolution passed at the general meeting of the company a valid appointment? The argument against the validity of the appointment is that the articles of association of the company gave to the board of directors the power of appointing additional directors, that the company has accordingly surrendered the power, and that the directors alone can exercise it. It is true that the general point was so decided by Eve J in *Blair Open Hearth Furnace Co v Reigart*[14] and I am not concerned to say that in ordinary cases where there is a board ready and willing to act it would be competent for the company to override the power conferred on the directors by the articles except by way of special resolution for the purpose of altering the articles. But the case which I have to deal with is a different one. For practical purposes there is no board of directors at all. The only directors are two persons, one of whom refuses to act with the other, and the question is, What is to be done under these circumstances? On this point I think that I can usefully refer to the judgment of the Court of Appeal in *Isle of Wight Rly Co v Tahourdin* [above, p 177], not for the sake of the decision, which depended on the fact that it was a case under the Companies Clauses Consolidation Act 1845, but for the sake of the observations of Cotton and Fry LJJ upon the effect of a deadlock such as arose in the present case. Cotton LJ says: 'Then it is said that there is no power in the meeting of shareholders to elect new directors, for that under the 89th section the power[15] would be in the remaining directors. The remaining directors would no doubt have that power if there was a quorum left. But suppose the meeting were to remove so many directors that a quorum was not left, what then follows? It has been argued that in that case, there being no board which could act, there would be no power of filling up the board so as to enable it to work. In my opinion that is utterly

---

[14]   (1913) 108 LT 665.
[15]   [Section 89 of the Act enabled the remaining directors to fill up interim vacancies on the board: compare the 2006 Model Articles.]

wrong. A power is given by the 89th section to the remaining directors "if they think proper so to do" to elect persons to fill up the vacancies. I do not see how it is possible for a non-existent body to think proper to fill up vacancies. In such a case a general meeting duly summoned for the purpose must have power to elect a new board so as not to let the business of the company be at a dead-lock . . .'. Those observations express a principle which seems to me to be as applicable to the case of a limited company incorporated under the Companies (Consolidation) Act 1908 as to a case falling under the Companies Clauses Consolidation Act 1845, and moreover to be a principle founded on plain common sense. If directors having certain powers are unable or unwilling to exercise them—are in fact a non-existent body for the purpose—there must be some power in the company to do itself that which under other circumstances would be otherwise done. The directors in the present case being unwilling to appoint additional directors under the power conferred on them by the articles, in my opinion, the company in general meeting has power to make the appointment . . .

➤ Note

A similar decision was reached in *Foster v Foster* [1916] 1 Ch 532, where there was a dispute over which of two directors should be appointed managing director, there being three directors in all. Although the power to appoint was conferred by the company's articles upon the directors, another article forbade a director from voting in respect of any contract in which he was interested. It was therefore not possible to carry any motion, in view of the disqualification of one director and the opposition of another. Peterson J held that in these circumstances competence to deal with the matter reverted from the board to the general meeting.

➤ Questions

1. Warrington J's reasoning is based largely on the decision in *Tahourdin*'s case which, as he points out, depended on the Companies Clauses Consolidation Act 1845 (above, p 177). Was he right to treat the case of a company registered under the Companies Acts as indistinguishable?

2. Suppose a situation the reverse of that in *Barron v Potter* [**4.08**], where the members cannot act but there is a board of directors capable of functioning. Could the directors exercise powers reserved by the articles to the general meeting? If not, what could be done to resolve matters?

Procedures for general meetings

Various practical issues are important in the mechanics of the exercise of power by the general meeting. How are decisions taken? What counts as a majority? How is this assessed if not all members attend the meeting? What exactly are 'meetings'? Are meetings always necessary? Is a meeting needed if everyone agrees? Are ordinary and special resolutions managed differently in these respects? Many of the answers can be found in the Act; some are provided in a company's articles. The cases below illustrate some of the issues, although by no means all.

General issues

At common law, a corporate body may act by a majority vote given at a meeting of members duly summoned.

[4.09] A-G v Davy (1741) 2 Atk 212 (Lord Chancellor)

[The facts as given in the report were as follows:]

> King Edward VI by charter incorporated twelve persons, by name, to elect a chaplain for the church of Kirton, in Lincolnshire. By another clause three of the twelve were to choose a chaplain to officiate in the church of Sandford, within the parish of Kirton, but with the consent and approbation of the major part of the inhabitants of Sandford.
>
> Upon a late vacancy, two of the three chose a chaplain, with the consent of the major part of the inhabitants of Sandford; the third dissented. The question was whether this was a good choice.

> LORD HARDWICKE LC: It cannot be disputed that wherever a certain number are incorporated, a major part of them may do any corporate act; so if all are summoned, and part appear, a major part of those that appear may do a corporate act, though nothing be mentioned in the charter of the major part.
>
> This is the common construction of charters, and I am of opinion that the three are a corporation for the purpose they are appointed, and the choice too was confirmed, and consequently not necessary that all the three should join; . . . it is not necessary that every corporate act should be under the seal of the corporation, nor did this need the corporation seal.

To constitute a meeting, there must prima facie be more than one person present.

[Although see Note 2 below indicating exceptions for single-member companies.]

[4.10] Sharp v Dawes (1876) 2 QBD 26 (Court of Appeal)

A meeting of a company governed by the Stannaries Acts[16] was summoned for the purpose, *inter alia*, of making a call (ie a demand from the company that members pay further unpaid amounts on their shares). It was attended by only one member, Silversides, and the secretary (who was not a member); and the following proceedings took place, as recounted in a notice sent to all members:

> At a general meeting of the shareholders, held at 2, Gresham Buildings, Basinghall Street, London, EC, on Wednesday, the 30th day of December, 1874, pursuant to notice, R H Silversides, Esq, in the chair,
>
> The notice convening the meeting having been read,
>
> The minutes of the last meeting were confirmed.
>
> The financial statement, ending the 28th of November, showing a balance of £83 11s 5d against the shareholders, having been read, it was
>
> Resolved—'That the same be received and passed.'
>
> Captain William Taylor's report having been read, it was
>
> Resolved—'That the same be received and passed, and, together with the financial statement, be printed and circulated among the shareholders.'
>
> Resolved—'That a call of 4s 6d per share be now and is hereby made payable to the secretary, and that a discount of 5% be allowed if paid by the 20th of January, 1875.'

---

[16] These tin-mining companies were unincorporated and governed by special statutes.

Resolved—'In consequence of the death of Lieut-Col ET Nicolls, and until the appointment
of a shareholder to act in his stead, that all cheques be signed by Mr RH Silversides and
Mr Granville Sharp jointly.'
(Signed) RH Silversides, Chairman.
Resolved—'That a vote of thanks be given to the chairman.'
(Signed) Granville Sharp, Secretary.

[The call was in due course made on a member, Dawes, who refused to pay it. It was held that
the meeting was a nullity and the call was invalid.]

LORD COLERIDGE CJ: This is an attempt to enforce against the defendant a call purporting to have
been made under s 10 of the Stannaries Act 1869. Of course it cannot be enforced unless it was
duly made within the Act. Now, the Act says that a call may be made at a meeting of a company
with special notice, and we must ascertain what within the meaning of the Act is a meeting, and
whether one person alone can constitute such a meeting. It is said that the requirements of the Act
are satisfied by a single shareholder going to the place appointed and professing to pass resolutions . . . [The] word 'meeting' prima facie means a coming together of more than one person. It
is, of course, possible to show that the word 'meeting' has a meaning different from the ordinary
meaning, but there is nothing here to show this to be the case. It appears therefore to me that this
call was not made at a meeting of the company within the meaning of the Act.

MELLISH LJ: In this case, no doubt, a meeting was duly summoned, but only one shareholder
attended. It is clear that, according to the ordinary use of English language, a meeting could no more
be constituted by one person than a meeting could have been constituted if no shareholder at all
had attended. No business could be done at such a meeting, and the call is invalid.

BRETT and AMPHLETT JJA concurred.

➤ Notes

1. CA 2006 s 318(1) now provides that in the case of a company limited by shares or guarantee
and having only one member, one qualifying person present at a meeting is a quorum. In any
other case, two qualifying people must be present (provided they do not both represent the
same member). To be a qualifying person under this section, one must be a member in person, a corporate representative or appointed by proxy (s 318(3)). Section 324 extends the right
to appoint proxies to members of all companies.

2. The single-member company having a one-person 'meeting' presents evidentiary problems, which CA 2006 s 357 attempts to meet by requiring the decision to take the form of a
written resolution, or the single member to provide the company with a written record of the
decision. Failure to comply with this requirement is punishable by a fine, but non-compliance
does not affect the validity of the decision itself.

3. Some amusement can occasionally be found in all this procedural detail. *Neptune (Vehicle
Washing Equipment) Ltd v Fitzgerald* [1995] BCLC 352 shows that a literal approach to statutory provisions can lead to absurdity bordering on farce. The case concerned the rule laid
down by CA 1985 s 317 (now CA 2006 s 177), which imposed on directors a duty to declare
any personal interests in contracts or proposed contracts with the company 'at a meeting of
the directors of the company'. The company in question had only one director. Lightman J
said (at pp 818–819, 359–360):

. . . a sole director cannot evade compliance with s 317 by considering or committing the company
to a contract in which he is interested otherwise than at a director's meeting or by delegating the
decision-making to others.

In the context of legislation which specifically authorises sole directorships and where Table A
provides for a committee of one, the legislature cannot have intended by use of the word 'meeting' in s 317 to exclude from its ambit and the achievement of the statutory object sole directors,

and I so hold. This conclusion is reinforced by the consideration that the concept of the holding of a director's meeting in case of a sole directorship is familiar to company lawyers.

Two different situations may arise. The sole director may hold a meeting attended by himself alone or he may hold a meeting attended by someone else, normally the company secretary. When holding the meeting on his own, he must still make the declaration to himself and have the statutory pause for thought, though it may be that the declaration does not have to be out loud, and he must record that he made the declaration in the minutes. The court may well find it difficult to accept that the declaration has been made if it is not so recorded. If the meeting is attended by anyone else, the declaration must be made out loud and in the hearing of those attending, and again should be recorded. In this case, if it is proved that the declaration was made, the fact that the minutes do not record the making of the declaration will not preclude proof of its making. In either situation the language of the section must be given full effect: there must be a declaration of the interest.

CA 2006 s 177 now replaces CA 1986 s 317, but fails to solve this problem, it seems. There is a specific rule (a writing requirement) where a sole director makes a declaration at a directors' meeting if the company is required to have more than one director; and s 177 itself provides that a declaration need not be made 'to the extent that the other directors are already aware of the interest'. The CLR had proposed that sole directors be required to make a declaration to the company's *members* prior to entering into a transaction in which they had a personal interest. (Professor Sealy's comment, 'A classicist's reaction might be: *O spem vanissimam!*' may have been taken to heart: there is no such requirement in CA 2006.)

'Voice' in the general meeting

Difficulties faced by members.

[4.11] Re Dorman Long & Co Ltd [1934] Ch 635 (Chancery Division)

[These remarks were made in reference to a scheme of arrangement under CA 1985 ss 425–427, but they are applicable generally to meetings of large companies.]

MAUGHAM J: It may be observed that when the Joint Stock Companies Arrangement Act 1870 was passed, in the majority of cases all the persons concerned with an arrangement could go to the meeting, listen to what was said and vote for or against the arrangement according to the views which they were persuaded to take. In these days, in many of the cases that come before me, only a fraction of the persons who are concerned can get into the room where the meeting is proposed to be held, and in the great majority of cases, the proxies given to the directors before the meeting begins have in effect settled the question of the voting once for all. It is perhaps not unfair to say that in nearly every big case not more than 5 per cent of the interests involved[17] are present in person at the meeting. It is for that reason that the court takes the view that it is essential to see that the explanatory circulars sent out by the board of the company are perfectly fair and, as far as possible, give all the information reasonably necessary to enable the recipients to determine how to vote. I am assuming, of course, that following the usual procedure, explanatory circulars are sent out, because, I may observe, there is nothing in the Act to render them essential. In a sense, in all these cases, the dice are loaded in favour of the views of the directors: the notices and circulars are sent out at the cost of the company, the board have had plenty of time to prepare the circulars and all the facts of the case are known the them, proxy forms are made out in favour of certain named directors and, although it is true that the word 'for' or 'against' may be inserted in the modern proxy

---

17 [The CLR suggests that the figure today is probably nearer to 1%.]

form, the recipients of the circulars very often are in doubt as to whether the persons named as proxies are bound to put in votes by proxy with which they are not in agreement. If we contrast with that position the position of a class of objectors, it is to be observed that a member of the class who receives a notice of the meeting and a circular from the directors is generally alone: he has no funds with which to fight the case and he has no information, except, sometimes, that information which has been contained in reports and balance sheets which have probably long ago been relegated to the waste paper basket. In any case, he has a minimum of information, his personal interest in the matter may be exceedingly small, probably he knows few persons in the same position as himself and, if he manages to get in touch with them, they together have to raise funds for the purposes of an opposition, which is often an expensive matter. They have then to get the names and addresses of the members of the class who are concerned, and to frame and send out a circular representing their views. Very often there is scarcely sufficient time for those purposes between the moment when the notice of the meeting reaches objectors by post and the date of the meeting. Proxies sent out by the directors can easily be lodged forty-eight hours before the meeting. It is quite plain that opponents may find it most difficult, after they have come together and have raised the necessary funds and have agreed on a circular and have sent out their notices, to lodge such proxies as they may have been able to obtain forty-eight hours before the meeting.

In my opinion the court ought to bear in mind these considerations when it has before it, as it often has, a case where the whole matter is really determined by the proxies that have been given before the meeting is held . . .

➤ Notes

1. In an attempt to redress the imbalance to which Maugham J refers, the Act now gives members holding together at least 5% of a company's shares (or minimum of 100 members with an average stake of at least £100 paid up) the right to have a statement circulated to members: see CA 2006 s 314. But the requisitionists must be prepared to face the burden (which may be quite considerable) of paying the expenses incurred, unless the company resolves otherwise (see ss 316, 338, 340). The cost of distributing one such circular to the shareholders of the Burmah Oil company in 1978 was put at £16,592—a figure which would have multiplied dramatically at today's prices.[18] For quoted companies, also see s 527. And members of private companies holding together at least 5% of the company's shares can, similarly, requisition the circulation of written resolutions (see below, pp 192–193): see ss 292–295.

2. Note also that CA 2006 s 303 empowers members holding at least 10% of the voting rights to require the directors to call an extraordinary general meeting of the company or, if the directors fail to do so, to convene it themselves. But the directors are not obliged to act on such a requisition if its object is something that the general meeting is not competent to do, eg to give directions to the board on a matter of business policy (see above, p 170): *Rose v McGivern* [1998] 2 BCLC 593.

3. The articles of most companies allow a member to be represented at meetings and to vote through an agent called a *proxy*, and this right is recognised and confirmed by CA 2006 s 324. The word 'proxy' is also used to refer to the document signed by the member to give the representative the member's authority to act. Advocates of greater 'shareholder democracy' regard the proxy system as an important weapon in their cause, since it ensures that account is taken of the views of any members who are unable to attend a meeting personally. But even so, as Maugham J explained in the extract above, the directors still have the advantage in many respects. A member may ordinarily revoke a proxy by exercising his right to vote in person: *Cousins v International Brick Co Ltd* [1931] 2 Ch 90, CA.

[18] JML Stone [1980] New LJ 152.

4. One remarkable phenomenon which has been largely overlooked by the law is the rise in the number of shares—and particularly shares in listed public companies—that are held by 'institutional' shareholders, such as the pension funds, insurance companies, unit trusts and mutual funds.[19] The percentage of their holdings overall has grown from about a quarter in the 1960s to about two-thirds in more recent years, and in some companies may be as high as 80% or more. These bodies hold the long-term savings of millions of citizens, and are managed by specialist professionals who, on the one hand, are in competition with each other but, on the other, are bound by the very nature of their function not to take unwarranted risks with the funds for which they are responsible. Views differ on the extent to which these institutions and their professionals should be expected, or even required, to monitor the performance of those charged with the management of the companies held in their portfolios. Plainly, these large members are in a position to wield considerable influence both in the affairs of a particular company (most notably in a takeover situation) and in the development of general standards of corporate governance.

The Combined Code (see below, pp 242 ff) states that they 'have a responsibility to make considered use of their votes', and that they 'should be ready, where practicable, to enter into a dialogue with companies based on the mutual understanding of objectives'. The CLR also drew attention to the risk of conflicts of interest inherent in the position of a fund manager: suppose, for instance, that the same institution is both an investor in a company and trustee of its pension fund, or similarly involved with both bidder and target in a takeover bid.

Reform of the law relating to general meetings

Both the CLR and a separate, earlier, DTI consultation document raised issues relating to the general meeting (especially the annual general meeting (AGM)) and members' resolutions. These were accompanied in some (but not all) cases by recommendations for reform. It is perhaps best simply to list the most important of the questions upon which comments have were invited, so that the perceived concerns are apparent:

(i)   Many shares are now held by nominees, and with the growing use of CREST (see below, p 441), the proportion is bound to increase: what steps can, or should, be taken to see that the beneficial (ie the 'real') owners of the shares receive information from the company, and possibly also be permitted to attend meetings, to vote, etc?

(ii)   Should the law be changed so as to oblige companies to circulate members' resolutions without charge?

(iii)   AGMs of public companies are usually attended by a very small percentage of members, and those who do attend are often quite unrepresentative. The bulk of the shares are likely to be held by institutional shareholders, and this fact and the likelihood that proxy votes will be cast in favour of management proposals mean that everything may well have been settled in advance. It is widely accepted that the AGM no longer serves its original democratic function as an occasion for general debate and decision-making on matters of company policy: indeed, the discussion is likely to be hijacked by 'campaigners' who have bought a few shares in order to gain publicity for their own separate agendas. Should the traditional AGM be abolished? Is there a better replacement? Should some restriction be put on the right of 'campaigning' shareholders to speak?

(iv)   In what ways could the law be changed so as to facilitate the use of modern (and developing) technology, in regard to communication with members, meetings held at several locations, electronic voting, etc?

[19] See J Farrar and M Russell, 'The Impact of Institutional Investment on Company Law' (1984) 5 Co Law 107; PL Davies, 'Institutional Investors in the United Kingdom' in T Baums et al (eds), *Institutional Investors and Corporate Governance* (1994); and John C Coffee Jr, 'Institutional Investors as Corporate Monitors: Are Takeovers Obsolete?' in JH Farrar (ed), *Takeovers, Institutional Investors and the Modernization of Corporate Laws* (1993).

The essentials of a 'meeting'

In Canada, it has been held that two persons cannot hold a 'meeting' by telephone: *Re Associated Color Laboratories Ltd* (1970) 12 DLR (3d) 388. This decision surely misses the point, for the essence of a meeting is not physical presence, but the ability of all the members to participate simultaneously, and instantaneously, in the proceedings—a need which modern communications technology is well fitted to meet, even where there are multiple participants. It also fails to meet an obvious commercial need. It is therefore not surprising that the ruling has been reversed, as regards to directors' meetings, by the Canada Business Corporations Act s 114(9), and that some more recent Commonwealth cases accept the possibility that a meeting may be held by conference telephone or video link—see eg *Re GIGA Investments Pty Ltd* (1995) 17 ACSR 472.[20]

The CLR recorded general support for the view that the requirements for meetings should be capable of being met 'by a dispersed meeting, held at more than one location, with two-way real-time communication between participants', and it proposed that if necessary the law should be clarified to permit this.

In *Byng v London Life Association Ltd* [1990] Ch 170, CA, **[4.12]** more members turned up to attend a meeting than could be accommodated in the cinema which had been notified as the venue. Overflow rooms with audio-visual links had been arranged, but these facilities did not work; and, in any case, some people could not get in and had to stay outside in the foyer. The Court of Appeal held, *inter alia*, that: (i) the assembly in the cinema was a 'meeting' which was capable of being adjourned to another place, even though (since many members who wished to attend were excluded) it was not capable of proceeding to business; and (ii) that it was not essential to a meeting that all members should be present in one room or face to face, provided that proper audio-visual links were in place which would enable everyone present to see and hear what was going on and participate in the proceedings. Browne-Wilkinson V-C said, at p 565:

> The rationale behind the requirement for meetings in the Companies Act 1985 is that the members shall be able to attend in person so as to debate and vote on matters affecting the company. Until recently this could only be achieved by everyone being physically present in the same room face to face. Given modern technological advances, the same result can now be achieved without all the members coming face to face: without being physically in the same room they can be electronically in each other's presence so as to hear and be heard and to see and be seen. The fact that such a meeting could not have been foreseen at the time the first statutory requirements for meetings were laid down, does not require us to hold that such a meeting is not within the meaning of the word 'meeting' in the Act of 1985. . . .
>
> I have no doubt therefore that in cases where the original venue proves inadequate to accommo-date all those wishing to attend, valid general meetings of a company can be properly held using overflow rooms provided, first, that all due steps are taken to direct to the overflow rooms those unable to get into the main meeting and, second, that there are adequate audio-visual links to enable those in all the rooms to see and hear what is going on in the other rooms. Were the law otherwise, with the present tendency towards companies with very large numbers of shareholders and corresponding uncertainty as to how many shareholders will attend meetings, the organisation of such meetings might prove to be impossible.

➤ Questions

1. Do you think that it is essential for a valid meeting to be held by electronic link-up that the participants should be able to: (i) *see* as well as to hear each other? or (ii) intervene or partici-pate, verbally, in any discussion taking place at meeting?

[20] Even so, it may be hard to convince a court that a resolution was passed in the course of such an informal commu-nication, especially where this is required by statute: the court might need to see the specific wording that was agreed upon.

2. CA 2006 reserves to the government the power to require institutional investors to disclose how they have voted certain types of shares they own or in which they have an interest. The government has stated that it will only use this power if a voluntary regime fails to improve disclosure, and after full consultation. What is the reasoning behind the moves to compel disclosure, and the methods of enforcing it?

Formalities

CA 2006 s 311 requires the notice of a general meeting to state the time and date of the meeting, as well as the place where it is to take place. Subject to any provisions in the company's articles, the notice must also state the general nature of the business to be dealt with. In the case of a listed company, an explanatory circular must also be sent out if any business other than ordinary business is to be discussed or decided at a general meeting (LR r 13.8.8R(1)). What constitutes ordinary business is to be decided by each company.

If the notice convening a meeting is not sufficiently full and specific to enable the members receiving it to decide whether or not they ought in their own interest to attend, then any resolutions passed at such meetings may be held invalid: *Tiessen v Henderson* [1899] 1 Ch 861.

CA 2006 adopts a policy of enfranchising indirect investors, and now allows members to appoint more than one proxy for a meeting, and allows proxies to vote and speak at meetings notwithstanding anything in the company's articles (see CA 2006 ss 324ff).

Role of the Chairman

It is the chairman's function at a general meeting to preserve order, see that proceedings are properly conducted and ensure that the sense of the meeting is properly ascertained. The chairman has no power to take into his or her own hands decisions that the meeting itself is competent to make: *National Dwelling Society v Sykes* [1894] 3 Ch 159. If the meeting is not competent to act, the next case indicates what the Chairman is to do.

A chairman may adjourn a meeting on his or her own initiative where the meeting itself is unable to consider the question, but only subject to a duty when doing so to take care to ensure that the adjourned meeting will be properly representative of the membership.

[4.12] Byng v London Life Association Ltd [1990] Ch 170, [1989] 1 All ER 560 (Court of Appeal)

An extraordinary general meeting of the company had been summoned for 12 noon at Cinema 1, The Barbican Centre, London. Because of an unexpectedly large turnout of some 800 members, this venue was too small. At 12.45 pm Dawson, the chairman, acting on his own initiative and without following the procedure prescribed by article 18 of the company's articles, announced that he was adjourning the meeting to 2.30 pm at the Café Royal, about one mile away. Only 600 people could attend this adjourned meeting, at which certain resolutions were passed. Byng and others sought declarations that these resolutions were invalid. The Court of Appeal upheld their contentions, ruling that although the chairman had a common law power to adjourn the meeting in circumstances such as these where the views of the members could not be ascertained, and despite the fact that he had acted throughout on advice and in good faith, he had failed in his duty to take into account all relevant considerations, such as the fact that members who were unable to attend the afternoon meeting could not arrange proxies in the time available, with the consequence that the adjourned meeting would not be representative.

BROWNE-WILKINSON V-C: In my judgment, were it not for article 18, Mr Dawson would at common law have had power to adjourn the meeting at the cinema since the inadequacy of the space available rendered it impossible for all those entitled to attend to take part in the debate and to vote. A motion for adjournment could not be put to the meeting as many who would be entitled to vote on the motion were excluded. Therefore, at common law it would have been the chairman's duty to regulate the proceedings so as to give all persons entitled a reasonable opportunity of debating and voting. This would have required him either to abandon the meeting or to adjourn it to a time and place where the members could have a reasonable opportunity to debate or vote. I see no reason to hold that in all circumstances the meeting must be abandoned: in my judgment the chairman can, in a suitable case, merely adjourn such meeting.

What then is the effect of article 18 which expressly confers on the chairman power to adjourn but only with the consent of a quorate meeting? Mr Potts submits that the chairman's power to adjourn having been expressly laid down and expressly circumscribed, there is no room for the chairman to have any implied power at common law . . .

Like the judge, I reject this submission. In my judgment article 18 regulates the chairman's powers of adjournment to the extent that its machinery is effective to cover the contingencies which occur. Therefore if the circumstances are such that it is possible to discover whether or not the meeting agrees to an adjournment, article 18 lays down a comprehensive code. But if the circumstances are such that the wishes of the meeting cannot be validly ascertained, why should article 18 be read as impairing the fundamental common law duty of the chairman to regulate proceedings so as to enable those entitled to be present and to vote to be heard and to vote? . . . Say that there was a disturbance in a meeting which precluded the taking of any vote on a motion to adjourn. Would this mean that the meeting had to be abandoned even though a short adjournment would have enabled peace to be restored and the meeting resumed? Again, say that in the present case the adjoining Barbican theatre had been available . . . so that a short adjournment to the theatre would have enabled an effective meeting of all members wishing to attend to be held that morning. Can it really be the law that because a valid resolution for such an adjournment could not be passed in the cinema (many members entitled to vote being excluded from the cinema) no such adjournment could take place?

I do not find that any principle of construction requires me to hold that an express provision regulating adjournment when the views of the meeting can be ascertained necessarily precludes the existence of implied powers when consent of the meeting cannot be obtained . . . Accordingly, I reach the conclusion that in any circumstances where there is a meeting at which the views of the majority cannot be validly ascertained, the chairman has a residual common law power to adjourn 'so as to give all persons entitled a reasonable opportunity of voting' and, I would add, speaking at the meeting . . .

Since such power is only exercisable for the purpose of giving the members a proper opportunity to debate and vote on the resolution, there must in my judgment be very special circumstances to justify a decision to adjourn the meeting to a time and place where, to the knowledge of the chairman, it could not be attended by a number of the members who had taken the trouble to attend the original meeting and could not even lodge a proxy vote. To overlook this factor is to leave out of account a matter of central importance. True it is that those who were available for the afternoon meeting would have been inconvenienced by an adjournment to another date or the convening of a wholly new meeting since they would either have to have attended at the fresh meeting or to have lodged proxies. But in my judgment this could not outweigh the central point that the form of the adjournment was such as undoubtedly to preclude certain members from taking any part in the meeting either by way of debate or by way of vote . . .

Accordingly, although Mr Dawson acted in complete good faith, his decision to adjourn to the Café Royal on the same date was not one which, in my judgment, he could reasonably have reached if he had properly apprehended the restricted nature and purposes of his powers. Therefore in my judgment his decision was invalid . . .

MUSTILL and WOOLF LJJ delivered concurring judgments.

➤ Note

These cases are concerned with the role of the chairman at a meeting of members (or, indeed, any other meeting, such as a meeting of a class of members or a meeting of creditors). Depending upon the terms of the company's articles, this person will often be the chairman of the board of directors. Does this make any legal or practical difference to proceedings?

Power of the court to order meetings: CA 2006 s 306

Where it is 'impracticable' to call a general meeting of the company in the ordinary way, the court may direct that a meeting may be called or conducted in any way that it thinks fit (CA 2006 s 306). In particular, it may direct that one person shall be deemed to constitute a quorum at a meeting—a power which is commonly invoked where the number of members had fallen to one.

In *Re British Union for the Abolition of Vivisection* [1995] 2 BCLC 1, the court held that the section could be applied where previous attempts at holding a general meeting had been frustrated by a disruptive minority, leading to breaches of the peace and intervention by the police. It was ordered that the meeting should be held with only an executive committee attending in person, the bulk of the membership voting by postal ballot.

However, the s 306 machinery may not be used to override class rights, or rights entrenched in a shareholders' agreement: see *Harman v BML Group Ltd* [1994] 2 BCLC 674, [1994] 1 WLR 893, CA; or to resolve a deadlock where the company's own constitution contains no provision to cope with such a situation: *Ross v Telford* [1998] 1 BCLC 82, CA (both cases dealing with the predecessor, CA 1985 s 371). But *Union Music Ltd v Watson* **[4.13]**, below, explains the limits of these restrictions and the potential usefulness of the court's power.

[4.13] Union Music Ltd v Watson [2003] EWCA Civ 180, [2003] 1 BCLC 453 (Court of Appeal)

This case concerned Russell Watson (W), the internationally famous opera singer. U applied under CA 1985 s 371 for an order for a general meeting of Arias (A), a company of which U was the majority shareholder (51%) and one of its directors. W was the only other shareholder and director. A shareholders' agreement provided that shareholders should exercise their voting rights so that A could not hold any meeting or transact any business at a meeting unless all shareholders or their representatives were present. A disagreement arose between W and U. W threatened not to attend any meetings. This created a deadlock. No business could be transacted, and no new directors could be appointed to deal with business without a shareholders' meeting. The trial judge refused the application. The Court of Appeal allowed the appeal, agreeing that s 371 did not allow the court to override entrenched or class rights, or to break the deadlock between two equal shareholders, but the instant case involved no such rights and the shareholdings were not equal.

PETER GIBSON LJ: I venture to make a few preliminary observations about s 371. It is a procedural section plainly intended to enable company business which needs to be conducted at a general meeting of the company to be so conducted. No doubt the thinking behind it is that a company should be allowed to get on with managing its affairs, and that should not be frustrated by the impracticability of calling or conducting a general meeting in the manner prescribed by the articles and the Act. . . .

But the power confers on the court a discretion and, like all discretions, it must be exercised properly having regard to the relevant circumstances. The authorities provide examples of cases where the power has been exercised and where it has not. The fact that there are quorum provisions in Table A requiring two members' attendance will not in itself be sufficient to prevent the court making an order under s 371, where the applicant is seeking a proper order such as the appointment of a director, something which a majority shareholder would have the right to procure in ordinary circumstances. . . .

I can see no sufficient reason why the order should not be made so that the deadlock in the board can be broken. Of course, I acknowledge that that means that the majority shareholder will have his way by the appointment of a director of its choice, save where the parties have agreed to complete equality. One side or the other has to prevail, and I cannot see that the contractual provisions in the agreement provide a sufficient reason why the power should not be exercised. Companies should have effective boards able to take decisions. I would therefore be prepared to make an order for the calling of a meeting to consider the question of the appointment of a further director and to allow the voting on that, even though only one member is present at that meeting. . . .

Harman v BML Group Ltd [1994] 2 BCLC 674, [1994] 1 WLR 893 turned on the fact that there was a class right attached to a class of shares, which the convening of a general meeting was designed to override. That, this court held, could not be done. I add the comment that that is hardly surprising in view of the elaborate provisions in Ch II of Pt V of the Act prescribing the procedures and conditions for varying any class rights [CA 2006, ss 629–640]. The company in question had a share capital consisting of 290,000 A shares and 210,000 B shares. There were four A shareholders but only one B shareholder, a Mr Blumenthal. A shareholders' agreement provided that Mr Blumenthal should be entitled to remain in office as director so long as he, or any family company of his, should be the owner of the B shares, and that a general meeting should be inquorate unless the B shareholder, or his proxy or representative, attended.

Dillon LJ, giving a judgment with which Leggatt and Henry LJJ agreed, said that the provision requiring the B shareholder to be present was essential to entrench Mr Blumenthal's right to remain a director and was a special provision to secure his directorship. Dillon LJ also said ([1994] 2 BCLC 674 at 680, [1994] 1 WLR 893 at 898):

> 'Class rights have to be respected and I regard the right of Mr Blumenthal, as the holder of the B shares, to be present in the quorum as a class right for his protection which is not to be overridden by this [the s 371] machinery.'

He made it clear that it was not for the court to make a new shareholders' agreement and impose it on the parties.

The present case is not one with entrenched or any class rights, as it seems to me. There is nothing in the agreement or in the memorandum and articles of Arias which confers any right on Mr Watson as shareholder which is not also conferred on Union as shareholder. There are simply no classes of shares: there is but a single class. I would add at this point that we were taken by Mr Freedman to *Cumbrian Newspapers Group Ltd v Cumberland & Westmorland Herald Newspaper & Printing Co Ltd* **[9.05]** for the proposition that a class right could exist even though there was only one type of share in issue and the rights of the shareholders were the same. In my judgment, nothing that was said by Scott J in the *Cumbrian* case supports so broad, and indeed astonishing, a proposition. There is, in my view, no assistance from the Cumbrian case towards resolving the dispute in the present case.

The *Ross* case [*Ross v Telford* [1998] 1 BCLC 82, CA] was a case where a husband and wife were the only two directors of each of two companies. They were equal shareholders of one of the companies. The shareholders of the second company were the husband and the first company. In an acrimonious divorce the district judge had directed that the net proceeds arising out of the liquidation or sale of either company should be divided equally. An action had been brought by the second company against a bank, alleging that the wife had forged the husband's signature on cheques. The husband wanted a meeting to be called under s 371 to ratify the second company's action, with a nominee chosen by him representing the first company shareholder. Thus, the deadlock would have been broken if the order had been made. . . . [In allowing the appeal against the order] this court accepted submissions from the wife that the court cannot make an order under the section so as to permit a 50 per cent shareholder to override the wishes of the other 50 per cent shareholder, that s 371 was a procedural section not designed to affect substantive voting rights or to shift the balance of power between shareholders in a case where they had agreed that a power should be shared equally, and where the potential deadlock is something which must be taken to have been agreed for the protection of each shareholder.

In the present case the shareholdings were not equal. The agreement was not designed to ensure that power should be shared equally. Initially, as I have noted, Mr and Mrs Watson, who might be expected to have been in one camp, were the majority on the board, with the majority shareholder left as the minority on the board. The deadlock happens to have been caused by Mrs Watson ceasing to be a director. Union, as the majority shareholder, could be expected to be able to remove or appoint a director. I do not agree with the judge's suggestion that the parties had contracted for a situation of deadlock. What the parties had contracted for, I accept, was that if Mr Watson chose not to attend or be represented at a general meeting, then there could be no general meeting.

Clause 6.1.18 [of the shareholders' agreement], however, seems to me more in the nature of a quorum provision than a provision for a class right, which it plainly was not, or a substantive right. . . .

There is no doubt that if, as one would expect, Union exercises its voting rights at a meeting not attended by Mr Watson or his proxy, it would be doing so in contravention of cl 6.1.18. For the reasons which I have already given, I do not see that as being an insuperable obstacle in the way of the court making an order under s 371. The court should consider whether the company is in a position to manage its affairs properly. It ought also to take into account the ordinary right of a majority shareholder to remove or appoint a director in exercise of his majority voting power. A meeting would be limited to the single act of enabling the appointment of a new director to be considered and voted on. Taking the view that I do that cl 6.1.18 is in the nature of a quorum provision rather than a provision confirming a substantive right, it seems to me that the judge was wrong to rely on that provision to refuse to order the meeting.

I would add that I also disagree with the judge's view that Union had chosen the wrong means in view of the possibilities of a derivative action or a s 459 petition [CA 2006, s 994]. I see no reason why a shareholder in the position of Union should not utilise the simple means afforded by s 371 rather than incur the greater difficulties and expense of the other possibilities. . . .

[He therefore proposed to make an order for the calling of a meeting to consider the question of the appointment of a further director and to allow the voting on that, even though only one member would be present at that meeting.]

BUXTON LJ delivered a concurring judgment.

MORLAND J concurred with both.

Decisions without general meetings

Written resolutions

Under s 288 of CA 2006, private companies are no longer required to hold general meetings. Instead, their normal mode of decision-making will be by *written resolution*. Section 288(2) indicates two exceptions to this practice: a resolution to remove either a director or an auditor before the expiration of his term of office may not be passed as a written resolution. These are the only two exceptions, and the section applies to private companies only.

The required majority for a written resolution is the same as if the resolution had been proposed at a meeting, ie generally a simple majority (over 50%) (s 288). Proposed resolutions must be sent to members (hard copy, electronic form, or via a website: ss 293 and 298). Alternatively, if it will not cause undue delay, a single document can be passed from one member to another (s 293). The proposed written resolution must be circulated to all eligible members (defined in s 289 as the person entitled to vote at the time the first copy of the resolution is sent or submitted to a member for agreement).

The procedure for indicating agreement to a circulated resolution is set out in s 296, which also provides that once a member has agreed, that agreement cannot be withdrawn.

The resolution must be passed within 28 days of the circulation date, or such other period as is specified in the company's articles (s 297).

In *Wright v Atlas Wright (Europe) Ltd* [1999] 2 BCLC 301, CA, there is an *obiter* discussion of the relationship between this written resolution procedure and the more informal *Duomatic* principle (discussed next): see Note below, p 196.

Informal resolutions and the 'Duomatic principle'

The written resolution procedure outlined above is restricted to private companies (and is inappropriate for public companies). The informal procedures described below are, in principle, of general application, but in practice will also be restricted to private companies.

A company is bound in a matter intra vires by the unanimous but informal agreement of its members.

[4.14] Re Express Engineering Works Ltd [1920] 1 Ch 466 (Court of Appeal)

Five persons, who were the only directors and members of the company, resolved at a directors' meeting to purchase certain property from a syndicate in which they were themselves interested. The company's articles disqualified a director from voting as a director in relation to any contract in which he was interested. The liquidator sought to have the transaction set aside; but the court held that the unanimous, though informal, agreement of the five as *members* bound the company.

LORD STERNDALE MR: It was contended on the one hand that the issue of the debentures was invalid for this reason, that all the directors being interested parties were precluded by article 9 from voting, and that though the five persons acting together as corporators undoubtedly could make the contract they could only do so in a properly constituted general meeting. On the other hand it was argued that the contract could not be called invalid if every shareholder knew of and sanctioned it; and further, that whatever the draftsman of the minutes may have styled the meeting, it was in fact a meeting of all the corporators, and they were able, whatever they might call themselves, to waive technicalities and meet together and make any contract they chose. As authority for that the appellant relied upon what was said by Lindley LJ in delivering the judgment of the court in *Re George Newman & Co*:[21]

> It may be true, and probably is true, that a meeting, if held, would have done anything which Mr George Newman desired; but this is pure speculation, and the liquidator, as representing the company in its corporate capacity, is entitled to insist upon and to have the benefit of the fact that even if a general meeting could have sanctioned what was done, such sanction was never obtained. Individual assents given separately may preclude those who give them from complaining of what they have sanctioned; but for the purpose of binding a company in its corporate capacity individual assents given separately are not equivalent to the assent of a meeting.

There were, however, two differences between that case and the present one. First, the transaction there was ultra vires,[22] and, secondly, in that case there never was a meeting of the corporators.

---

[21] [1895] 1 Ch 674 at 686.
[22] [The company had made Newman, a director, a gift of £3,500 to spend on his house.]

In the present case these five persons were all the corporators of the company and they did all meet, and did all agree that these debentures should be issued. Therefore it seems that the case came within the meaning of what was said by Lord Davey in *Salomon v Salomon & Co* **[2.01]**. 'I think it is an inevitable inference from the circumstances of the case that every member of the company assented to the purchase, and the company is bound in a matter intra vires by the unanimous agreement of its members.' It is true that a different question was there under discussion, but I am of opinion that this case falls within what Lord Davey said. It was said here that the meeting was a directors' meeting, but it might well be considered a general meeting of the company, for although it was referred to in the minutes as a board meeting yet if the five persons present had said, 'We will now constitute this a general meeting,' it would have been within their powers to do so, and it appears to me that that was in fact what they did. The Appeal must therefore be dismissed.

WARRINGTON and YOUNGER LJJ delivered concurring judgments.

A general meeting is unnecessary if all the members in fact assent to the transaction.

[4.15] Parker & Cooper Ltd v Reading [1926] Ch 975 (Chancery Division)

The company had issued a debenture to Reading as security for a loan; it was sealed and signed by two directors as prescribed by the articles but the seal had not been affixed in their presence as the articles required. It was also alleged that the two directors had not been validly appointed. The transaction had been discussed between all the four members from time to time, and they had all individually assented, but no general meeting had been held. The liquidator disputed the validity of the debenture, but it was held to be enforceable.

ASTBURY J [after stating facts and holding that everything had been done with the utmost bona fides and solely for the benefit of the company]: For the purposes of my judgment, I will assume that the defendants Reading and Botterill were not validly or formally appointed directors. But they believed that they were, and they continued during the remaining history of the company to act as such. I will assume again that the sealing of the debenture was quite irregular. The company had the benefit of the money. The debenture was issued with the assent of every shareholder, and the question is whether the plaintiffs, or rather the liquidator, ought to succeed in obtaining a declaration that the debenture and the resolution authorising it were inoperative and invalid, so that the creditors may get the advantage of the defendant Reading's £1,750 and deprive him of the security on which he made that advance.

Unless I am bound by authority to give this relief I certainly do not propose to do so. It is, however, suggested that I am so bound, because the shareholders' assent to the irregular transactions was not given at any actual meeting. [His Lordship discussed *Re George Newman & Co* (referred to above, p 193) and *Re Express Engineering Works Ltd* **[4.14]** and continued:] All three judges [in *Re Express Engineering Words Ltd*] no doubt refer to the fact that there had been a meeting. But I cannot think that they came to their decision because the five shareholders happened to meet together in one room or one place, as distinct from agreeing to the transaction inter se in such manner as they thought fit . . .

Now the view I take of both these decisions is that where the transaction is intra vires and honest, and especially if it is for the benefit of the company, it cannot be upset if the assent of all the corporators is given to it. I do not think it matters in the least whether that assent is given at different times or simultaneously . . .

[See also *Re Halt Garage (1964) Ltd* **[5.04]**; *Re Horsley & Weight Ltd* **[3.05]**; *Rolled Steel Products (Holdings) Ltd v British Steel Corpn* **[3.07/3.17]**; *Multinational Gas and Petrochemical Co v Multinational Gas and Petrochemical Services Ltd* **[6.25]**.]

> ➤ Note

In *Re Duomatic Ltd* [1969] 2 Ch 365, it was held that a company would normally be bound by the informal agreement of all its *voting* members (but that even so, non-voting members were entitled to receive the disclosure stipulated for by CA 1985 s 312, now CA 2006 s 217). Curiously, this case has since received greater recognition than it probably deserves, in that practising lawyers now commonly refer to the rule established by *Express Engineering* and later cases as '*the Duomatic principle*' overlooking the fact that the principle had been established many decades earlier.

[4.16] EIC Services Ltd v Phipps [2003] EWHC 1507, [2003] 1 WLR 2360 (Court of Appeal)

[NEUBERGER J provided *his* view of the rationale of for the *Duomatic* principle:[23]]

. . . the essence of the *Duomatic* principle . . . is that, where the articles of a company require a course to be approved by a group of shareholders at a general meeting, that requirement can be avoided if all members of the group, being aware of the relevant facts, either give their approval to that course or so conduct themselves as to make it inequitable for them to deny that they have given their approval. Whether the approval is given in advance or after the event, whether it is characterized as agreement, ratification, waiver or estoppel and whether the member of the group give their consent in different ways at different times, does not matter.

 [Because the members were not aware of the crucial fact that their consent was required to the directors' actions, their unanimous approval did not count.]

[4.17] Euro Brokers Holdings Ltd v Monecor (London) Ltd [2003] EWCA Civ 105, [2003] 1 BCLC 506 (Court of Appeal)

[The facts are immaterial.]

MUMMERY LJ [He described the varied circumstances in which the principle applies:]
 . . . I see nothing in the circumstances of the present case to exclude the Duomatic principle. It is a sound and sensible principle of company law allowing the members of the company to reach an agreement without the need for strict compliance with formal procedures, where they exist only for the benefit of those who have agreed not comply with them. What matters is the unanimous assent of those who ultimately exercise power over the affairs of the company through their right to attend and vote at a general meeting. It does not matter whether the formal procedures in question are stipulated for in the articles of association, in the Companies Acts or in a separate contract between the members of the company concerned. What matters is that all the members have reached an agreement. If they have, they cannot be heard to say that they are not bound by it because the formal procedure was not followed. The position is treated in the same way as if the agreed formal procedure had been followed. The particular context for the application of the principle in this case is that cl 11(2) of the shareholders' agreement requires the notice to be issued by the board. That is a formal corporate procedure. It is irrelevant that the requirement is in a separate agreement entered into by the shareholders in EBFL, rather than in the articles. The shareholders entered into that agreement for the very same purpose as the contract between them constituted

---

[23] Upheld on appeal: [2004] EWCA Civ 1069, [2005] 1 WLR 1377.

by the articles, namely to regulate the relationship between the shareholders in the governance of EBFL. As Neuberger J said in *Re Torvale Group Ltd* [1999] 2 BCLC 605 at 617:

> The articles constitute a contract, and if the parties to that contract, or if the parties for whom the benefit of a particular term has been included in that contract, are happy unanimously to waive or vary the prescribed procedure for a particular purpose, then . . . it seems to me that there is no good reason why it should not be capable of applying.

I fail to see why the agreement of the only two shareholders in EBFL to meet a call for capital without the need for a notice issued by the board of EBFL should not be as binding on them as if the call were made pursuant to a notice issued by the board, which would have happened had there been communication between the directors appointed by the members at a formal meeting and resolution of a properly constituted board. When the members of EBFL decided to respond to the capital call it did not matter to them that it had been communicated by Mr Pask rather than by the board.

➤ Notes

Some glosses may be added to this line of cases.

1. The *Duomatic* principle was extended in *Deakin v Faulding* and *Shahar v Tsitsekkos* [2004] EWHC 2659, so that the agreement of the beneficial owner of the shares is effective where the trustee can be compelled to vote in accordance with the beneficial owner's wishes.

2. The principle has been applied to special and extraordinary resolutions: see *Cane v Jones* **[4.18]** and to decisions taken by a group or class of shareholders: *Re Torvale Group Ltd* [1999] 2 BCLC 605.

3. In contrast with the rule for informal written resolutions introduced by s 288 (see above, p 192), the informal consent of the members must be unanimous. See *Re d'Jan* **[6.14]**, where the principal shareholder held 99% of the shares and his wife 1%. He could not argue that there had been a unanimous informal members' resolution (ratifying his negligence), because, although his wife was likely to have supported him, the issue was never in fact raised.

4. Further, in *Re New Cedos Engineering Co Ltd* [1994] 1 BCLC 797 it was emphasised that the principle of *Parker & Cooper Ltd v Reading* **[4.15]** cannot be invoked in order to enable something to be done informally which those concerned would not be competent to do, formally, at a general meeting. In *New Cedos* the number of registered members had been reduced to one, so that no 'meeting' complying with the company's articles could effectively be held. It was ruled that nothing done informally by this sole member was equivalent to a decision of the members reached at a meeting.

5. At least where the question is one of acquiescence in a corporate irregularity, it may not be necessary to show that a particular member positively assented to the proposal, if he stood by, knowing that he had power to stop it, while the other members gave it support. This appears from *Re Bailey, Hay & Co Ltd* [1971] 1 WLR 1357.

6. After earlier uncertainty, it is now established that there is a similar rule applying to directors' resolutions (see below, p 255).

7. The relationship between the common law principle and the statutory 'written resolution' procedure was discussed by the Court of Appeal in *Wright v Atlas Wright (Europe) Ltd* [1999] 2 BCLC 301, CA (although the discussion is *obiter dicta* since the events in question occurred before the written resolution procedure was first introduced by CA 1989). A service contract had been entered into between the company and Wright (the former managing director of the company) appointing him a consultant for life at an annual fee. The formalities prescribed by CA 1985 s 319 (the holding of a meeting at which certain documentation must be produced)

[now see CA 2006 s 188, which is different] had not been followed, but the company's sole member was fully informed of the arrangement and had signed an agreement recording it. The court held that, since the purpose of s 319 was the protection of the company's members, they could override any formal (including statutory) requirements regarding the passing of resolutions at general meetings. (The court was not deterred from taking this view by the very peremptory terms in which s 319, and especially subsections (5) and (6), is expressed.) However, it went on to express the view that where there was some other underlying intention of a statutory provision, such as the protection of creditors or, perhaps, future members, this would not be so; and so it was possible to distinguish the earlier decision in *Re RW Peak (Kings Lynn) Ltd* [1998] 1 BCLC 193, in which Lindsay J had held that unanimous members' consent, given informally, was not sufficient to bypass the statutory procedure for a repurchase of shares prescribed by CA 1985 s 164.

An informal, unanimous agreement between members may be effective as an extraordinary or special resolution.

[4.18] Cane v Jones [1980] 1 WLR 1451, [1981] 1 All ER 533 (Chancery Division)

In 1946, two brothers, Percy and Harold Jones, formed a company to run the family business. Each was a director and the shareholding was divided equally between members of Percy's family and members of Harold's family. The articles gave the chairman a casting vote at both directors' and shareholders' meetings; but Harold's daughter Gillian (the plaintiff, Mrs Cane) claimed that an agreement had been made between all the shareholders in 1967 which provided (*inter alia*) that the chairman should cease to be entitled to use his casting vote, so that Percy (who was currently chairman) did not have a decisive vote in the company's affairs. The court held that this was so, and that the informal agreement had had the same effect as a special resolution altering the articles. It was immaterial that the statutory obligation to register such resolutions had not been complied with.

MICHAEL WHEELER QC (sitting as a deputy judge of the High Court): . . . Now as to the arguments about the effect of the 1967 agreement. Mr Weaver contends that it operated as an alteration of the articles on what was conveniently called in argument 'the *Duomatic* principle' based on *Re Duomatic Ltd*[24] and the principle is, I think, conveniently summarised in a short passage in the judgment in that case of Buckley J where he says, [1969] 2 Ch 365 at 373:

> . . . I proceed upon the basis that where it can be shown that all shareholders who have a right to attend and vote at a general meeting of the company assent to some matter which a general meeting of the company could carry into effect, that assent is as binding as a resolution in general meeting would be.

Applying that principle to the present case, Mr Weaver says that the agreement of all the shareholders embodied in the 1967 agreement had the effect, so far as requisite, of overriding the articles. In other words, it operated to deprive the chairman for the time being of the right to use his casting vote . . .

For the first and third defendant, Mr Potts . . . answers . . . that on its true interpretation in relation to a special or extraordinary resolution the *Duomatic* principle only applies if there has been (i) a resolution, and (ii) a meeting; and that here he says, with some truth, there was neither a resolution nor a meeting of the four shareholders . . .

---

[24] [1969] 2 Ch 365.

[Michael Whealer QC referred to CA 1948 ss 10 and 141 [CA 2006 ss 21 and 283], and to a number of decided cases, and continued:] The first of Mr Potts' two arguments—namely that there must be a 'resolution' and a 'meeting'—does not appear to have been raised in any of the . . . reported cases which were convened with special or extraordinary resolutions. But it is not an argument to which I would readily accede because in my judgment it would create a wholly artificial and unnecessary distinction between those powers which can, and those which cannot, be validly exercised by all the corporators acting together.

For my part I venture to differ from Mr Potts on the first limb of his argument, namely that articles can *only* be altered by special resolution. In my judgment, s 10 of the Act is merely laying down a procedure whereby *some only* of the shareholders can validly alter the articles: and if, as I believe to be the case, it is a basic principle of company law that all the corporators, acting together, can do anything which is intra vires the company, then I see nothing in s 10 to undermine this principle . . .

Some light is also, I think, thrown on the problem by s 143(4) of the Act of 1948 [CA 2006 s 29(1)]. Section 143 deals with the forwarding to the Registrar of Companies of copies of every resolution or agreement to which the section applies; and sub-s (4) reads:

> This section shall apply to—(a) special resolutions; (b) extraordinary resolutions; (c) resolutions which have been agreed to by all the members of a company, but which, if not so agreed to, would not have been effective for their purpose unless, as the case may be, they had been passed as special resolutions or as extraordinary resolutions . . .

Paragraph (c) thus appears to recognise that you can have a resolution, at least, which has been agreed to by all the members and is as effective as a special or extraordinary resolution would have been . . .

I should add in passing that a copy of the 1967 agreement was never, as far as I am aware, sent to the Registrar of Companies for registration. It may be that there is a gap in the registration requirements of s 143. But be that as it may, the fact that the 1967 agreement was drafted as an agreement and not as a resolution, and that the four signatories did not sign in each other's presence does not in my view prevent that agreement overriding pro tanto—and so far as necessary—the articles of the company; in my judgment Mr Potts' first argument fails and . . . the chairman of the company has no casting vote at board or general meetings . . .

➤ Notes

1. The contention of counsel that the agreement of 1967 had the effect 'so far as requisite' of 'overriding' the articles exposes the central weakness of the ruling in this case. There can be little doubt that the 1967 agreement was, essentially, nothing more than a shareholders' agreement which (because of the doctrine of privity) could be enforced only by the immediate parties. The plaintiff was not such a party, having inherited her shares at a later date. It is difficult to reconcile the lax view taken of the importance of formalities in this case with the stricter approach of *Scott v Frank F Scott (London) Ltd* **[4.01]** and the *Bratton Seymour* case **[4.02]**.

2. This case was followed in *Re Home Treat Ltd* [1991] BCLC 705, in what was clearly a very indulgent ruling. The company, which was in administration, had carried on the business of a nursing home for many years without having power to do so under its objects clause. The administrator wished to continue to run the business with a view to selling it as a going concern. Harman J held that, since the company's only members had agreed to the change of activity, it must be deemed to have changed its memorandum under CA 1985 s 4. It is inconceivable that such a view would have prevailed a generation ago. (See eg the ruling of the judge's father in *Re Introductions Ltd* **[3.04]**.)

3. Now see CA 2006, which predictably provides that the articles may be amended by special resolution (s 21), but then includes in s 29(1), in terms that may well accommodate these

cases, the resolutions and agreements that must be sent to the registrar (s 30). The implication is that these arrangements will serve to amend the articles.

> Questions

1. Did the judge in *Cane v Jones* rule that the agreement *was* a special resolution, or only that it was as good as one?

2. Suppose that Thomas, a stranger, bought out all Percy's family's shares and was appointed chairman, without any knowledge of the events of 1967. Would he have a casting vote? Could he rely on the equivalent of CA 2006 s 33 to enforce the 'articles'?

Limitations on the exercise of members' voting rights

General issues

The general meeting operates by majority rule. Sometimes decisions are taken by ordinary resolution; in more serious cases (such as changing the company's constitution), they are taken by special resolution. In either case, the dissenting minority will have changes forced upon them to which they have not agreed. This would not happen under normal contract rules. On the other hand, members know, when they take up shares, that their rights are subject to 'majority rule'. In these circumstances, what protections does the law offer to dissenting members against having their rights overridden by the majority? There are very few routes for redress, but the members may be able to complain that, in the circumstances:

(i)   the impugned resolution is ineffective, as an objectionable exercise of power by the members. This ground of complaint relies on equitable control over the exercise by members of their voting rights. These controls, to the extent that they exist, appear to be enforced with more vigour in some circumstances (such as alteration of the articles and class rights) than in others, and to impose weak constraints in any event. (See below, pp 230 ff.)

(ii)   the company should be wound up on the 'just and equitable' ground: IA 1986 s 122(1)(g). (See below, pp 653 ff.)

(iii)   the court should order a remedy (such as compulsory buy-out of the complainant's shares) to combat the unfair prejudice inflicted by the majority (CA 2006 s 994). (See below, pp 552 ff.)

Only the first is dealt with in this chapter. The principles emerge from the cases.

A member's vote is a property right which, prima facie, may be exercised in the member's own interest and as he or she thinks fit. A member voting as such is under no fiduciary duty to the company, and this is true also of a director when voting as a member.

[4.19] Northern Counties Securities Ltd v Jackson & Steeple Ltd
[1974] 1 WLR 1133, [1974] 2 All ER 625 (Chancery Division)

The defendant company had given an undertaking to the court to use its best endeavours to obtain a stock exchange quotation for its shares, and to allot a certain number of these shares to the plaintiffs. It was necessary, under stock exchange rules, for the consent of the defendant company in general meeting to be obtained to the issue of shares. After the company had for more than a year failed to take any steps to comply with its undertaking, the plaintiffs moved for orders against the company and its directors: (a) that they should summon the required meeting; (b) that they should send a circular to members calculated to induce them to vote in favour of the resolution, and warning them that the defeat of the resolution would amount to a contempt of court; and (c) restraining the directors, as members, from voting against the resolution. The court granted orders that the meeting be summoned and that a circular be sent inviting the members to support the resolution, but ruled that neither the members generally nor the directors voting as members would be in contempt of court if they opposed the resolution.

WALTON LJ: Mr Price [counsel for the plaintiffs] argued that, in effect, there are two separate sets of persons in whom authority to activate the company itself resides. Quoting the well known passages from Viscount Haldane LC in *Lennard's Carrying Co Ltd v Asiatic Petroleum Co Ltd* **[3.23]** he submitted that the company as such was only a juristic figment of the imagination, lacking both a body to be kicked and a soul to be damned. From this it followed that there must be some one or more human persons who did, as matter of fact, act on behalf of the company, and whose acts therefore must, for all practical purposes, be the acts of the company itself. The first of such bodies was clearly the board of directors, to whom under most forms of articles . . . the management of the business of the company is expressly delegated. Therefore, their acts are the defendant company's acts; and if they do not, in the present instance, cause the defendant company to comply with the undertakings given by it to the court, they are themselves liable for contempt of court. And this, he says, is well recognised: see RSC, Ord 45, r 5(1), whereunder disobedience by a corporation to an injunction may result directly in the issue of a writ of sequestration against any director thereof. It is of course clear that for this purpose there is no distinction between an undertaking and an injunction: see note 45/5/3 in *The Supreme Court Practice* (1973).

This is, indeed, all well established law, with which Mr Instone [counsel for the directors] did not quarrel, and which indeed his first proposition asserted. But, continues Mr Price, this is only half of the story. There are some matters in relation to which the directors are not competent to act on behalf of the company, the relevant authority being 'the company in general meeting', that is to say, a meeting of the members. Thus in respect of all matters within the competence—at any rate those within the exclusive competence—of a meeting of the members, the acts of the members are the acts of the company, in precisely the same way as the acts of the directors are the acts of the company. Ergo, for any shareholder to vote against a resolution to issue the shares here in question to the plaintiffs would be a contempt of court, as it would be a step taken by him knowingly which would prevent the defendant company from fulfilling its undertaking to the court. Mr Price admitted that he could find no authority which directly assisted his argument, but equally confidently asserted that there was no authority which precluded it.

Mr Instone indicted Mr Price's argument as being based upon 'a nominalistic fallacy'. His precise proposition was formulated as follows: 'Whilst directors have special responsibilities as executive agents of the defendant company to ensure that the company does not commit a contempt of court, a shareholder, when the position has been put before the shareholders generally, who chooses to vote against such approval will not himself be in contempt of court.' . . .

In my judgment, these submissions of Mr Instone are correct. I think that in a nutshell, the distinction is this: when a director votes as a director for or against any particular resolution in a directors' meeting, he is voting as a person under a fiduciary duty to the company for the proposition that the company should take a certain course of action. When a shareholder is voting for or against a particular resolution he is voting as a person owing no fiduciary duty to the company and who is exercising his own right of property, to vote as he thinks fit. The fact that the result of the voting at the meeting (or at a subsequent poll) will bind the company cannot affect the position that, in voting, he is voting simply in exercise of his own property rights.

Perhaps another (and simpler) way of putting the matter is that a director is an agent, who casts his vote to decide in what manner his principal shall act through the collective agency of the board of directors; a shareholder who casts his vote in general meeting is not casting it as an agent of the company in any shape or form. His act therefore, in voting as he pleases, cannot in any way be regarded as an act of the company . . .

I now come to paragraph 4 of the notice of motion, which seeks an order restraining the individual respondents [ie the directors] and each of them from voting against the resolution. Mr Price says that, as the executive agents of the defendant company, they are bound to recommend to its shareholders that they vote in favour of the resolution to issue the shares, and hence, at the least, they cannot themselves vote against it, for they would thereby be assisting the defendant company to do that which it is their duty to secure does not happen. If, as executive officers of the defendant company, they are bound to procure a certain result if at all possible, how can they, as individuals, seek to frustrate that result?

I regret, however, that I am unable to accede to Mr Price's arguments in this respect . . . . I think that a director who has fulfilled his duty as a director of a company, by causing it to comply with an undertaking binding upon it is nevertheless free, as an individual shareholder, to enjoy the same unfettered and unrestricted right of voting at general meeting of the members of the company as he would have if he were not also a director . . .

[See also *Pender v Lushington* [**11.15**]; *North-West Transportation Co Ltd v Beatty* [**4.34**]; *Burland v Earle* [**11.10**]; and *Peter's American Delicacy Co Ltd v Heath* [**4.26**].]

➤ Notes

1. *Halton International Inc (Holdings) Sarl v Guernroy Ltd* [2005] EWHC 1968, Ch reinforces this finding. The defendant, a member of the company, was given the power to exercise the votes of all other members for the purpose of raising fresh capital in any way he saw fit. The defendant member passed a resolution suspending the pre-emption rights of the other members which were inserted in the company articles, thereby increasing his voting rights in the selection of investors. The court held that the voting agreement did not give rise to any fiduciary duties on the part of the acting member. His actions were authorised by the agreement and were therefore upheld.

2. The rule that a member owes no duties to the company and can exercise his rights entirely as he pleases, without regard to the effect of doing so upon the company, is not confined to the right to vote. In *Stothers v William Steward (Holdings) Ltd* [1994] 2 BCLC 266 it was applied to the right of a member (subject, of course, to any provision in the articles) to transfer his shares to a person of his choice.

3. Quite exceptionally, the courts have on rare occasions been prepared to order that a member's votes should be cast, or at least not cast, in a certain way—in effect, to restrain him from acting perversely. In *Standard Chartered Bank Ltd v Walker* [1992] 1 WLR 561, [1992] BCLC 603 a member with a minority holding of shares was ordered not to vote against a restructuring agreement where the consequence of his doing so would have been that the company would collapse and his shares (which had been charged to the company's banks) would become worthless. Similarly, in *Theseus Exploration NL v Mining & Associated Industries Ltd* [1973] Qd R 81 an injunction was granted against majority members restraining them from voting to remove the existing directors and replace them with a board intent on a policy of destructive asset-stripping.

➤ Question

How, if at all, can these cases be seen as consistent with cases that seem to impose restrictions on members when voting to alter the articles, or members when voting to alter class rights (see below, pp 204 ff and 221 ff)?

A contract by a member to vote in a particular way, or as directed by another person, is binding and may be enforced by a mandatory injunction.[25]

[4.20] Puddephatt v Leith [1916] 1 Ch 200 (Chancery Division)

The plaintiff had mortgaged shares in the company to the defendant and transferred them into his name. By a contemporaneous letter, the defendant had undertaken to vote the shares as directed by the plaintiff. The court ordered him to comply with the undertaking.

SARGENT J [after stating the facts and holding that the undertaking to vote in accordance with the plaintiff's wishes contained in the letter constituted a collateral agreement binding on the defendant, continued]: In my opinion, therefore, the right of the plaintiff is clear, and the only remaining question is whether she is entitled to a mandatory injunction to enforce her right. It is not disputed that she is entitled to a prohibitive injunction, and in my opinion she is also entitled to a mandatory injunction. Prima facie this court is bound . . . to give effect to a clear right by way of a mandatory injunction. There are no doubt certain exceptions from this rule, as in the case of a contract of service, because in such cases, it is impossible for the court to make its order effective, but . . . in the present case, in as much as there is one definite thing to be done, about the mode of doing which there can be no possible doubt, I am of opinion that I ought to grant not only the prohibitive but also the mandatory injunction claimed by the plaintiff, and I make an order accordingly.

➤ Notes

1. The specific undertaking given in this case displaced the normal rule that a mortgagee of shares may exercise the voting rights in respect of those shares free of any dictation from the mortgagor: *Siemens Bros & Co Ltd v Burns* [1918] 2 Ch 324, CA. Similarly, an *unpaid* vendor of shares who remains on the share register retains the voting rights free from dictation by the purchaser (*Musselwhite v CH Musselwhite & Son Ltd* [1962] Ch 964), although (at least where the contract is specifically enforceable) these rights may be inhibited by a fiduciary obligation to have regard to the purchaser's interests (*Michaels v Harley House (Marylebone) Ltd* [2000] Ch 104, CA). And once the purchaser has paid the full price, the vendor holds the shares as a bare trustee (*Hawks v McArthur* **[9.16]**), and must vote the shares as directed by the purchaser (*Re Piccadilly Radio plc* [1989] BCLC 683).

2. This case concerned a single shareholder. A contract between several shareholders, agreeing to co-ordinate their votes, or delegating to one the power to cast votes for all—commonly known as 'voting trust'—is lawful. It is more widely used in the United States than in this country, and can be a powerful tool either to concentrate control behind the management, or to use as a countervailing force against it.[26]

A decision carried by the votes of majority members may be set aside if it is 'oppressive' of the minority.

[4.21] Clemens v Clemens Bros Ltd [1976] 2 All ER 268 (Chancery Division)

The plaintiff held 45% and her aunt ('Miss Clemens') 55% of the shares in the defendant company. The company's articles gave existing members a pre-emptive right if another member wished to transfer his shares. The plaintiff therefore had an expectation of total control of the company after her aunt's death, and 'negative control' (ie the power to block a special

---

[25] Contrast the position as regards directors, see below, p 241.

[26] Of course, such a contract between shareholders may regulate other matters besides voting. See the discussion of shareholder agreements, below pp 229 ff.

resolution) in the aunt's lifetime. The aunt and four non-shareholders were the directors. The directors proposed that the company's capital should be increased by issuing 200 ordinary shares to each of these four directors, and 850 ordinary shares to an employees' trust; and resolutions to this effect were passed by the aunt's votes at a general meeting. Although it was claimed that the object of the resolutions was in the company's interests (namely, to give the directors and employees a stake in the company) the court took the view that the real object was to deprive the plaintiff of her degree of control, and the resolutions were set aside.

FOSTER J: For the plaintiff it was submitted that the proposed resolutions were oppressive, since they resulted in her losing her right to veto a special or extraordinary resolution and greatly watered down her existing right to purchase Miss Clemens' shares under article 6. For the defendants it was submitted that if the two shareholders both honestly hold differing opinions, the view of the majority must prevail and that the shareholders in general meeting are entitled to consider their own interests and vote in any way they honestly believe proper in the interests of the company.

There are many cases which have discussed a director's position. A director must not only act within his powers but must also exercise them bona fide in what he believes to be the interests of the company. The directors have a fiduciary duty, but is there any similar, restraint on shareholders exercising their powers as members at general meetings? [His Lordship read extracts from the judgments in a number of cases, including *Greenhalgh v Arderne Cinemas* **[4.27]**,[27] and continued:]

I think that one thing which emerges from the cases to which I have referred is that in such a case as the present Miss Clemens is not entitled to exercise her majority vote in whatever way she pleases. The difficulty is in finding a principle, and obviously expressions such as 'bona fide for the benefit of the company as a whole', fraud on a 'minority' and 'oppressive' do not assist in formulating a principle.

I have come to the conclusion that it would be unwise to try to produce a principle, since the circumstances of each case are infinitely varied. It would not, I think, assist to say more than that in my judgment Miss Clemens is not entitled as of right to exercise her votes as an ordinary shareholder in any way she pleases. To use the phrase of Lord Wilberforce,[28] that right is 'subject . . . to equitable considerations . . . which may make it unjust . . . to exercise [it] in a particular way'. Are there then any such considerations in this case?

I do not doubt that Miss Clemens is in favour of the resolutions and knows and understands their purport and effect; nor do I doubt that she genuinely would like to see the other directors have shares in the company and to see a trust set up for long service employees. But I cannot escape the conclusion that the resolutions have been framed so as to the put into the hands of Miss Clemens and her fellow directors complete control of the company and to deprive the plaintiff of her existing rights as a shareholder with more than 25% of the votes and greatly reduce her [pre-emptive] rights . . . They are specifically and carefully designed to ensure not only that the plaintiff can never get control of the company but to deprive her of what has been called her negative control. Whether I say that these proposals are oppressive to the plaintiff or that no one could honestly believe they are for her benefit matters not. A court of equity will in my judgment regard these considerations as sufficient to prevent the consequences arising from Miss Clemens using her legal right to vote in the way that she has and it would be right for a court of equity to prevent such consequences taking effect.

➤ Note

This case may have reached a just result on the merits (although even that is doubtful, for there was a long history of non-co-operation by the niece), but it is very difficult to defend the judge's use of the authorities. The citation of *Greenhalgh* **[4.27]** draws on a line of decisions concerned with special resolutions for the alteration of articles, which had never before been

---

[27] [See the Note at the conclusion of this extract.]
[28] *Ebrahimi v Westbourne Galleries Ltd* **[14.14]**.

applied to other types of resolution. Further, it is surely misunderstood, for having read the passage from *Greenhalgh's* case in which Evershed MR suggested the test of the 'individual hypothetical shareholder', Foster J commented: 'If that is right, the question in the instant case must be posed thus: did Miss Clemens, when voting for the resolutions, honestly believe that those resolutions, when passed, would be for the benefit of the plaintiff?' With respect, it must be observed that the plaintiff was no more a hypothetical shareholder than Miss Clemens herself; and if the test had been understood in this sense in *Greenhalgh's* case itself, the decision must surely have gone in Greenhalgh's favour. These cases show how unhelpful the 'hypothetical shareholder' test is, especially in regard to small companies.

Again, in quoting Lord Wilberforce, the judge is borrowing from the winding-up cases, contrary to the ruling in *Bentley-Stevens v Jones* [1974] 1 WLR 639.

➤ Questions

1. Did Foster J consider that a member in the position of Miss Clemens was under a duty to (i) the company, or (ii) her fellow-shareholder? If so, what was the nature of this duty? If not, what was the rule or principle which he was applying?

2. If the aunt did owe such a duty, did the niece owe the company, or her fellow-shareholder, any corresponding duty?

3. Can the *Clemens* and *Greenhalgh* [4.27] cases be reconciled?

Alteration of the articles

CA 2006 s 21: Alteration of articles

There is no power to alter the new-style memorandum (the s 8 'memorandum of association'), but then it does not contain elements that members would need or want to change. Under art 28(1), the provisions of existing companies contained in old-style memoranda which are not of the kind mentioned in s 8 of the new Act, will automatically be treated as provisions of the company's articles of association.

Provisions in the company's articles will be able to be amended by special resolution (s 21), unless they have been entrenched under s 22. Section 22 allows the articles to contain a '*provision for entrenchment*' nominating specified provisions of the articles that can be amended or deleted only if conditions or procedures more stringent than a special resolution are met. A provision for entrenchment can be inserted in the articles only on formation of the company or by an amendment of the company's articles which is agreed upon by *all* its members (s 22(2)).

If such a provision for entrenchment was contained in the company's old-style memorandum, it will automatically be treated as part of the company's articles under the new legislation (s 28(2)), so the entrenchment will be preserved. Notice of the existence, amendment, or deletion of provisions of entrenchment must be given to the Companies House (s 23, and s 13 for the 'form of compliance').

CA 2006 s 25 retains the principle that a member of a company is not bound by any alteration made to the articles after he or she becomes a member if the alteration has the effect of increasing liability to the company or imposing a requirement to take more shares in the company. A member may however give written consent to such an alteration and, in that case, will be bound by it.

Earlier case law thus remains relevant.

Predecessor provisions

Until CA 2006 came into force, companies were required to have both a *memorandum and articles* (see above, p 99). There were different statutory rules for altering each of them.

Indeed, when the memorandum of association was first introduced as the basic constitutional document of a company by the Joint Stock Companies Act 1856, none of its provisions could be altered (apart from the capital clause pursuant to an increase of capital). Over time, the position was reached under CA 1985 where it was possible to alter any of the clauses of the memorandum, except that fixing the company's domicile, by the use of the appropriate procedure. The company's name could be changed under CA 1985 s 28, the objects clause under s 4, the company's status as limited or unlimited, public or private, and so on, by the various procedures set out in Pt II of the Act, and the capital provisions under ss 121, 125 and 135.

The alteration of a company's objects (see above, p 99), contained in the memorandum, required a special resolution, and the court become involved only if the holders of 15 per cent or more of the issued share capital of any class made an objection by applying to the court within 21 days. The court then had an absolute discretion to confirm or disallow the alteration. It is perhaps significant that the only reported cases on the exercise of the court's discretion, under both the 1985 Act and previous procedures, seem to have been concerned with non-commercial organisations. See *Re Cyclists' Touring Club* [1907] 1 Ch 269 and *Re Hampstead Garden Suburb Trust Ltd* [1962] Ch 806.

By contrast, the Acts had always allowed the articles to be altered by special resolution, with no statutory constraints except for the protection given by s 125 in relation to variation of 'class rights'.[29] (See below, pp 221 ff.)

With these bald requirements set by statute, judges have been left with the task of formulating more specific rules controlling the power of majority members to alter articles. Unfortunately the principles that have emerged are anything but clear. As a rule, the courts have been content to fall back on such broad general phrases as '*bona fide* for the benefit of the company as a whole', apparently without appreciating that these expressions mask rather than explain the decisions they are making. The difficulty posed by the juxtaposition of the 'benefit of the company' test with the basic concept of the member's vote as a property right is all too rarely faced in the judgments (with the notable exception of *Peter's American Delicacy Co Ltd v Heath* **[4.26]**). If it had been, the cases that follow might have yielded more intelligible principles.

A contract by a company not to alter its articles will not be enforced by injunction.

[4.22] Punt v Symons & Co Ltd [1903] 2 Ch 506 (Chancery Division)

By articles 95 and 97 of the defendant company's articles GG Symons, as governing director, was given the power to appoint and remove directors, and after his death the same power was exercisable by his executors. The company had also agreed in a separate contract, relating to the purchase of Symons' business, that it would not alter these articles. After the death of Symons, friction arose between his executors and the directors, which led to a proposal from the directors to rescind the articles in question by special resolution. The executors moved for an injunction.[30]

BYRNE J: The first point taken is that passing the resolution would be a breach of the contract which was entered into with the testator; and that the plaintiffs as executors are entitled to enforce the terms of the agreement by restraining any alteration of the articles. I think the answer to this argument is—that the company cannot contract itself out of the right to alter its articles, though it cannot, by altering its articles, commit[31] a breach of contract. It is well established as between a

---

[29] Note also CA 1985 s 16, which renders ineffective any alteration which increases the liability of a member or obliges him to take more shares-unless he agrees in writing to be bound by the alteration.

[30] They succeeded on another ground, viz that the directors had improperly issued new shares to 'pack' the shareholders' meeting: see below **[4.23]**.

[31] [For 'commit', we should here read 'justify': see the fn 33 below, p 208.]

company and a shareholder, the right not depending upon a special contract outside the articles, that this is the case. It has not been, so far as I know, the precise subject of reported decision as between a contractor and a company where the contract is independent of and outside the articles . . . [His Lordship referred to *Allen v Gold Reefs of West Africa* **[4.23]**; and to an unreported decision *Re Ladies' Dress Association Ltd*, in which a contract not to alter any article was not enforced. He continued:] That appears, so far as I can judge, to be a decision upon the point now before me. Whether that be so or not, I am prepared to hold that in the circumstances of the present case the contract could not operate to prevent the article being altered under the provisions of s 50 of the Companies Act 1862 [CA 2006 s 21], whatever the result of that alteration may be.

[See also *Baily v British Equitable Assurance Co* **[3.19]** and *Southern Foundries (1926) Ltd v Shirlaw* **[5.07]**.]

➤ Notes

1. The opinion expressed in this case is supported by the emphatic *obiter dictum* of Lord Porter in *Southern Foundries (1926) Ltd v Shirlaw* **[5.07]**. It is therefore to be preferred, it is submitted, to the contrary view of Sargant J in *British Murac Syndicate Ltd v Alperton Rubber Ltd* [1915] 2 Ch 186, which was based on the mistaken view that *Punt's* case had been overruled by *Baily v British Equitable Assurance Co* **[3.19]**.

2. However, it does not follow that a contractual undertaking by a company that its articles will not be altered might not be enforced in other ways. Lord Porter clearly thought that, if a company *acted upon* its altered articles in a way which was in breach of an existing contract, a remedy in damages would lie. In principle, this must be correct; and further, in principle also, an injunction might in such circumstances be granted, in the discretion of the court, restraining the company from acting upon its altered articles.

3. As Byrne J notes, it was already a well-established rule that a company could not restrict the right to alter its articles by a provision in the articles themselves. This was decided by Jessel MR in *Walker v London Tramways Co* (1879) 12 Ch D 705, where he held that a provision in the company's articles declaring that certain articles were 'essential' and unalterable was ineffective.

4. This ruling is but one illustration of a more general principle that a company cannot bargain away its right to exercise the powers conferred upon it by statute. The extent to which there is such a rule, and (assuming that there is) whether there ought to be such a rule, was matter of considerable debate, following the decision in *Russell v Northern Bank Development Corpn Ltd* **[8.01]**. There is clear authority establishing that a company cannot contract not to alter its articles (*Punt's* case, above) nor contract not to alter its capital (*Russell*). This principle would surely also extend to such matters as contracting not to go into liquidation or to petition for a winding-up order. But it is easy to demonstrate that there may be good commercial reasons why a company might wish to bind itself not to do at least some of these things— for instance, a bank lending money to a company may make it a condition of the loan that the company will not reduce its capital—and, indeed, this has been done in practice for many years. So, following the ruling in *Russell*, there has been pressure for Parliament to change the law so as to make contractual undertakings given in such circumstances binding. The case for retaining a general principle of this kind is greatly weakened by the fact that there are many alternative ways of doing indirectly what cannot at present be achieved directly—for example, by a shareholders' agreement (below p 229), by attaching 'class rights' to certain shares (see the *Cumbrian Newspapers* case **[9.05]** by entrenching the rights which it is sought to protect in the memorandum (see CA 1985 s 17(2)(b)), or by the use of 'weighted' voting rights (see *Bushell v Faith* **[5.05]**). And, in the example of the bank loan, the bank could stipulate that the

money would become immediately repayable if the company should summon a general meeting to consider a proposed resolution to reduce capital.

➤ Question

In *Walker v London Tramways* Co (above), Jessel MR did not give a reasoned judgment but simply asserted that no company could contract itself out of CA 1962 s 50 (the equivalent of CA 2006 s 21). What reasoning do you think that he might have used; and would you agree?

The power to alter a company's articles must be exercised 'bona fide for the benefit of the company as a whole'. An alteration so made is valid and binding on the members and may affect their existing rights as members. It may, however, amount to a breach of an independent contract.

[4.23] Allen v Gold Reefs of West Africa Ltd [1900] 1 Ch 656 (Court of Appeal)

Article 29 of the company's articles of association gave it 'a first and paramount lien' for debts owing by a member to the company 'upon all shares (not being fully paid) held by such members'. The company altered this article by deleting the words 'not being fully paid'. Only one shareholder, Zuccani (who had died insolvent), was affected by this alteration: he had had fully paid shares allotted to him when the company was formed, and had later acquired other shares, that were not fully paid, on which calls were overdue. His executors challenged the company's right to claim a lien on his fully paid shares pursuant to the altered article. Kekewich J held that the company could not enforce its lien. The Court of Appeal reversed this decision, and upheld the alteration.

LINDLEY MR: The articles of a company prescribe the regulations binding on its members: Companies Act 1862, s 14 [CA 2006 s 21]. They have the effect of a contract (see s 16 [CA 2006 s 33]); but the exact nature of this contract is even now very difficult to define. Be its nature what it may, the company is empowered by the statute to alter the regulations contained in its articles from time to time by special resolutions (ss 50 and 51 [CA 2006 ss 21, 283]); and any regulation or article purporting to deprive the company of this power is invalid on the ground that it is contrary to the statute: *Walker v London Tramways Co.*[32]

   The power thus conferred on companies to alter the regulations contained in their articles is limited only by the provisions contained in the statute and the conditions contained in the company's memorandum of association. Wide, however, as the language of s 50 is, the power conferred by it must, like all other powers, be exercised subject to those general principles of law and equity which are applicable to all powers conferred on majorities and enabling them to bind minorities. It must be exercised, not only in the manner required by law, but also bona fide for the benefit of the company as a whole, and it must not be exceeded. These conditions are always implied, and are seldom, if ever, expressed. But if they are complied with I can discover no ground for judicially putting any other restrictions on the power conferred by the section than those contained in it. How shares shall be transferred, and whether the company shall have any lien on them, are clearly matters of regulation properly prescribed by a company's articles of association. This is shown by Table A in the Schedule to the Companies Act . . . Speaking, therefore, generally, and without reference to any particular case, the section clearly authorises a limited company, formulated with articles which confer no lien on fully paid-up shares, and which allow them to be transferred without any fetter, to alter those articles by special resolution, and to impose a lien and restrictions on the registry of transfers of those shares by members indebted to the company.

[32] (1879) 12 Ch D 705. [See also *Punt v Symons & Co Ltd* [4.22].]

But then comes the question whether this can be done so as to impose a lien or restriction in respect of a debt contracted before and existing at the time when the articles are altered. Again, speaking generally, I am of opinion that the articles can be so altered, and that, if they are altered bona fide for the benefit of the company, they will be valid and binding as altered on the existing holders of paid-up shares, whether such holders are indebted or not indebted to the company when the alteration is made. But, as it will be seen presently, it does not by any means follow that the altered article may not be inapplicable to some particular fully paid-up shareholder. He may have special rights against the company, which do not invalidate the resolution to alter the articles, but which may exempt him from the operation of the articles as altered.

But, although the regulations contained in a company's articles of association are revocable by special resolution, a special contract may be made with the company in the terms of or embodying one or more of the articles, and the question will then arise whether an alteration of the articles so embodied is consistent or inconsistent with the real bargain between the parties. A company cannot break its contracts by altering is articles,[33] but, when dealing with contracts referring to revocable articles, and especially with contracts between a member of the company and the company respecting his shares, care must be taken not to assume that the contract involves as one of its terms an article which is not to be altered.

It is easy to imagine cases in which even a member of a company may acquire by contract or otherwise special rights against the company, which exclude him from the operation of a subsequently altered article. Such a case arose in *Swabey v Port Darwin Gold Mining* **[5.06]** where it was held that directors, who had earned fees payable under a company's articles, could not be deprived of them by a subsequent alteration of the articles, which reduced the fees payable to directors.

I take it to be clear that an application for an allotment of shares on the terms of the company's articles does not exclude the power to alter them nor the application of them, when altered, to the shares so applied for and allotted. To exclude that power or the application of an altered article to particular shares, some clear and distinct agreement for that exclusion must be shown, or some circumstances must be proved conferring a legal or equitable right on the shareholders to be treated by the company differently from the other shareholders.

This brings me to the last question which has to be considered, namely, whether there is in this case any contract or other circumstance which excludes the application of the altered article to Zuccani's fully paid-up vendor's shares. [His Lordship ruled that there was no such special circumstance, and continued:]

The fact that Zuccani's executors were the only persons practically affected at the time by the alterations made in the articles excites suspicion as to the bona fides of the company. But, although the executors were the only persons who were actually affected at the time, that was because Zuccani was the only holder of paid-up shares who at the time was in arrear of calls. The altered articles applied to all holders of fully paid shares, and made no distinction between them. The directors cannot be charged with bad faith.

After carefully considering the whole case, and endeavouring in vain to discover grounds for holding that there was some special bargain differentiating Zuccani's shares from others, I have come to the conclusion that the appeal from the decision of the learned judge, so far as it relates to the lien created by the altered articles, must be allowed . . .

ROMER LJ delivered a concurring judgment.

VAUGHAN WILLIAMS LJ dissented.

---

[33] [Later cases (eg **[4.24]** and **[4.25]**) make it plain that this sentence should be understood to mean 'a company *cannot justify* a breach of contract by pleading the valid alteration of its articles', and not 'a company *cannot alter* its articles if to do so would break an existing contract'.]

[4.24] Sidebottom v Kershaw, Leese & Co Ltd [1920] 1 Ch 154 (Court of Appeal)

The defendant company had altered its articles by introducing a provision which gave the directors power to buy out, at a fair price, the shareholding of any member who competed with the company's business. The plaintiffs, who were minority shareholders and who carried on a competing business, unsuccessfully challenged the validity of the alteration.

LORD STERNDALE MR: There are two objections to this alteration: one is a very broad one indeed. It is that whatever alterations a company may be empowered to make in its articles varying the terms upon which its members may hold their shares, it cannot alter its articles so as to provide a means of what was called 'expelling', as in this case, by buying out a particular member and making him cease to be a member. I cannot find that such an exception as that is anywhere stated in any of the authorities as existing . . . but there is no doubt—in fact I think it is established by *Phillips v Manufacturers' Securities Ltd*[34]—that a power such as this is a perfectly valid power in the case of original articles, and it seems to me that prima facie if it could be in the original articles, it could be introduced into the altered articles provided only it is done bona fide for the benefit of the company as a whole. Therefore, in my opinion, it comes back to the same thing. The introduction into an altered article of a power of buying a person out or expelling him can only be held invalid if the alteration is not made bona fide for the benefit of the company . . .

A second argument was addressed to us, which was this: I think Mr Jenkins rather deprecated it being put in this form, but in my opinion this is what it came to: An alteration cannot be for the benefit of the company as a whole if in fact it is a detriment to one of the members of the company, because the company as a whole means the whole body of corporators and every individual corporator, and if one of them has detriment occasioned to him by the alteration, it cannot be for the benefit of the company as a whole. I must say that I find it very difficult to follow that argument, but it seems to me to be exactly met by *Allen v Gold Reefs of West Africa* **[4.23]**, because undoubtedly the alteration that was made there was not for the benefit of the shareholder, of whom the plaintiff, Mr Allen, was the executor, because it made his fully paid-up shares subject to a lien to which they were not subject before, and thereby, as I have pointed out, made it possible to get rid of Mr Allen, or Mr Allen's testator, altogether by compulsorily buying up his shares if the debt were not satisfied.

In my opinion, the whole of this case comes down to rather a narrow question of fact, which is this: When the directors of this company introduced this alteration giving power to buy up the shares of members who were in competing businesses did they do it bona fide for the benefit of the company or not? It seems to me quite clear that it may be very much to the benefit of the company to get rid of members who are in competing business . . . I think there can be no doubt that a member of a competing business or an owner of a competing business who is a member of the company has a much better chance of knowing what is going on in the business of the company, and of thereby helping his own competition with it, than if he were a non-member; and looking at it broadly, I cannot have any doubt that in a small private company like this the exclusion of members who are carrying on a competing business may very well be of great benefit to the company. That seems to me to be precisely a point which ought to be decided by the voices of the business men who understand the business and understand the nature of competition, and whether such a position is or is not for the benefit of the company. I think, looking at the alteration broadly, that it is for the benefit of the company that they should not be obliged to have amongst them as members persons who are competing with them in business, and who may get knowledge from their membership which would enable them to compete better.

[34] (1917) 116 LT 290, CA.

That brings me to the last point. It is said that that might be so were it not for the fact that the directors and the secretary have said, 'This is directed against Mr Bodden', and therefore it is not done bona fide for the benefit of the company, but it is done to get rid of Mr Bodden.[35] If it were directed against Mr Bodden for any malicious motive I should agree with that—the thing would cease to be bona fide at once; but these alterations are not as a rule made without some circumstances having arisen to bring the necessity of the alteration to the minds of the directors. I do not read this as meaning anything more than this: 'It was the position of Mr Bodden that made us appreciate the detriment that there might be to the company in having members competing with them in their business, and we passed this, and our intention was, if it became necessary, to use it in the case of Mr Bodden; that is what we had in our minds at the time; but we also had in our minds that Mr Bodden is not the only person who might compete, and therefore we passed this general article in order to enable us to apply it in any case where it was for the good of the company that it should be applied.' It is a question of fact. I come to the conclusion of fact to which I think the Vice-Chancellor came, that the directors were acting perfectly bona fide, that they were passing the resolution for the benefit of the company; but that no doubt the occasion of their passing it was because they realised in the person of Mr Bodden that it was a bad thing to have members who were competing with them . . .

For these reasons I think this is a valid article. I think the alteration was within the competence of the company, and therefore this appeal must be allowed with costs here and below.

WARRINGTON LJ and EVE J delivered concurring judgments.

➤ Notes

1. The CLR took the view that the principle that a decision to change a company's articles must be taken *bona fide* for the benefit of the company as a whole was well established and should be retained. This position was accepted in the recent case of *Constable v Executive Connections Ltd* [2005] EWHC 3 (Ch), which concerned the addition of a power to expel a member of the company via a compulsory purchase of shares. Mr Christopher Nugee QC applied the above case, but added:

> I do not regard the law in this area as clear or easy to apply. There are no recent English cases and the older ones are . . . difficult. Indeed, the more one looks at the decided cases, the harder it is to know precisely where the line is to be drawn between those cases where the introduction of a compulsory transfer provision will be upheld and those where it will not.

2. It is rather curious that in both this case and *Allen*'s case (above) there are references to the good faith of the *directors*, when it is plain from the rest of the judgments that it is the *bona fides* of the majority members who pass the special resolution that is crucial. Of course, it would be easy to imagine a situation where the directors have an improper motive in introducing the proposal for change, and simply carry the opinion of the majority along with them. This may be what is being alluded to in the two cases. In fact, the directors in *Sidebottom*'s case held over half of the company's issued shares, and the majority in favour of the resolution was overwhelming.

3. In the case next cited, Peterson J favoured an objective test of what was 'for the benefit of the company'. This view was disapproved in *Shuttleworth v Cox Bros & Co Ltd* [5.09], but it has, in the view of some writers, been to some extent revived by the reformulated test suggested in *Greenhalgh v Arderne Cinemas Ltd* [4.27].

---

[35] [Bodden was not, in fact, a plaintiff.]

[4.25] Dafen Tinplate Co Ltd v Llanelly Steel Co (1907) Ltd
[1920] 2 Ch 124 (Chancery Division)

The defendant company altered its articles so as to introduce a power enabling the majority of the shareholders to require any member (with one named exception) to transfer his shares at a fair value to an approved transferee. The plaintiff company, had transferred its custom as a purchaser of steel from the defendants to a rival company. It held shares in the defendant company and opposed the alteration. Peterson J upheld its objection, because *in his own view* the alteration was wider than necessary.

PETERSON J: In *Sidebottom*'s case **[4.24]** the Court of Appeal sanctioned an alteration of the articles of association which enabled the directors to require a shareholder who carried on a competing business, or was a director of a company carrying on a competing business, to transfer his shares, and it did so on the ground that the alteration was for the benefit of the company as a whole. It has been suggested that the only question in such a case as this is whether the shareholders bona fide or honestly believed that that alteration was for the benefit of the company. But this is not, in my view, the true meaning of the words of Lindley MR or of the judgment in *Sidebottom*'s case. The question is whether in fact the alteration is genuinely for the benefit of the company . . .

The question of fact then which I have to consider is whether the alteration of the articles which enables the majority of the shareholders to compel any shareholder to transfer his shares, can properly be said to be for the benefit of the company. It may be for the benefit of the majority of the shareholders to acquire the shares of the minority, but how can it be said to be for the benefit of the company that any shareholder, against whom no charge of acting to the detriment of the company can be urged, and who is in every respect a desirable member of the company, and for whose expropriation there is no reason except the will of the majority, should be forced to transfer his shares to the majority or to anyone else? Such a provision might in some circumstances be very prejudicial to the company's interest. For instance, on an issue of new capital, the knowledge that he might be expropriated as soon as his capital was on the point of producing profitable results might well exercise a deterrent influence on a man who was invited to take shares in the company . . . In my view it cannot be said that a power on the part of the majority to expropriate any shareholder they may think proper at their will and pleasure is for the benefit of the company as a whole. To say that such an unrestricted and unlimited power of expropriation is for the benefit of the company appears to me to be confusing the interests of the majority with the benefit of the company as a whole. In my opinion the power which, in this case, has been conferred upon the majority of the shareholders by the alteration of the articles of association in this case is too wide and is not such a power as can be assumed by the majority. The power of compulsory acquisition by the majority of shares which the owner does not desire to sell is not lightly to be assumed whenever it pleases the majority to do so. The shareholder is entitled to say non haec in foedera veni; and while on the authorities as they stand at present it is possible to alter the articles in such a way as to confer this power, if it can be shown that the power is for the benefit of the company as a whole, I am of opinion that such a power cannot be supported if it is not established that the power is bona fide or genuinely for the company's benefit . . .

[4.26] Peter's American Delicacy Co Ltd v Heath (1939) 61 CLR 457
(High Court of Australia)

As a result of an oversight by the draftsman, the company's articles of association contained inconsistent provisions governing the distribution of profits. Profits distributed as *dividends* were payable in proportion to the amounts paid up on shares, but distributions of *capitalised* profits ('bonus shares') were to be in proportion to the nominal value of shares held. The issued capital consisted of 511,000 fully paid and 169,000 partly paid shares.

At a general meeting the articles were altered by special resolution so that the distribution of capitalised profits was to be made on the same basis as cash dividends, ie in proportion to the amounts paid up on shares. Some holders of partly paid shares objected, and their objection was upheld at first instance; but on appeal the High Court ruled that the alteration was valid.[36]

RICH J: Company law confers a power of alteration on a general meeting of shareholders requiring for any positive alteration a three-fourths majority. There is no other body to whom the question can be submitted. No rights given by articles of association can prevail against a three-fourths majority and it is well understood that all are subject to it. It is true that the power of alteration must be exercised bona fide with a view to the advancement of the company considered as a whole and not with a view to the advancement of the interests of a majority of voters or of a section of the company only . . . But in deciding what is for the interest of the company and what is bona fide, the constitution of the company, the condition and effect of the various articles of association and the extent to which rights are conferred upon different classes of shareholders are relevant and important . . . Where the very problem which arises contains as inherent in itself all the elements of a conflict of interests between classes of shareholders these authorities do not mean that the power of alteration is paralysed, they mean only that the purpose of bringing forward the resolution must not be simply the enrichment of the majority at the expense of the minority. The resolution in the present case was brought forward to solve a difficulty and make possible a capitalisation. It can hardly be supposed that the only solution of such a difficulty which can be lawfully adopted is that which gives the minority an advantage at the expense of the majority. In my opinion the case presents nothing but an ordinary example of an honest attempt on the part of the directors to clear up a difficulty by securing an alteration of the articles not unjust to any class of shareholders, but at the same time conserving the interests of the shareholders who form the great majority of the company . . .

In my opinion the appeal should be allowed.

DIXON J: Primarily a share in a company is a piece of property conferring rights in relation to distribution of income and of capital. In many respects the proprietary rights are defined by the articles of association, and it is easy to see that a power of alteration might be used for the aggrandisement of a majority at the expense of a minority. For example, if there were no check upon the use of the power, it is conceivable that a three-fourths majority might adopt an article by which the shares which they alone held would participate, to the exclusion of other shares, in the surplus assets in winding up or even in distributions of profit by way of dividend. Again, authority might be obtained under an alteration so as to convert the assets or operations of a company into a source of profit not of the company but of persons forming part of or favoured by the majority. It has seemed incredible that alterations of such a nature could be made by the exercise of the power. But reliance upon the general doctrine that powers shall be exercised bona fide and for no bye or sinister purpose brings its own difficulties. The power of alteration is not fiduciary. The shareholders are not trustees for one another, and, unlike directors, they occupy no fiduciary position and are under no fiduciary duties. They vote in respect of their shares, which are property, and the right to vote is attached to the share itself as an incident of property to be enjoyed and exercised for the owner's personal advantage. No doubt the exercise of the right affects the interests of others too, and it may be that an analogy may be found in other powers which though given to protect the donee's own interests affect the property rights of others, as, for instance, does a mortgagee's power of sale. Some such analogy probably gave rise to the suggestion made in Buckley on *The Companies Acts* that the limitation on the power is that the alteration must not be such as to sacrifice the interests of the minority to those of a majority without any reasonable prospect of advantage to the company as a whole . . .

---

[36] See the Note following this case.

Apart altogether from altering articles of association, the voting strength of a majority of share-holders may be used in matters of management and administration to obtain for themselves advantages which otherwise would enure for the benefit of all the members of the company, and in some circumstances such an attempt on the part of the majority to secure advantages to the prejudice of the minority conflicts with ordinary notions of fair dealing and honesty. Often when this is done the thing attempted will be found by its nature to fall outside the power of the members in general meeting and even outside the corporate powers of the company. But this is not necessarily the case, and a thing not of its own nature ultra vires may be invalidated by the effect which it produces or is intended to produce in benefiting some shareholders at the expense of others or individuals at the expense of the company . . .

An example of a misuse of power on the part of shareholders constituting a majority in the administration of a company's affairs is the unjustifiable refusal to allow an action to be maintained in the name of the company to redress a wrong to it by one of themselves[37] . . .

In these formulations of general principle there is an assumption that vested in the company or in the minority of shareholders, as the case may be, is an independent title to property, to rights or to remedies, and the ground of the court's intervention is that by the course adopted by the majority, the company or the minority will be deprived of the enjoyment of that to which they are so entitled. The conduct of the majority is then given some dyslogistic description such as 'fraudulent', 'abuse of powers' or 'oppression'. A chief purpose of articles of association is to regulate the rights of shareholders inter se, and their relations to the profits and surplus assets of the company are governed by the provisions of the articles. A power to alter articles of association is necessarily a power to alter the rights of shareholders inter se, including their mutual rights in respect of profits and surplus assets. It is therefore evident that some difficulty must arise in applying to resolutions for the alteration of articles a statement of principle which assumes the independent existence of rights which should not be impaired or destroyed. Prima facie rights altogether dependent upon articles of association are not enduring and indefeasible but are liable to modification or destruction; that is, if and when it is resolved by a three-fourths majority that the articles should be altered. To attempt to distinguish between alterations which deserve the epithet fraudulent or oppressive or unjust and those deserving no moral censure without explaining the considerations upon which the distinction depends, is to leave the whole question to general notions of fairness and propriety . . . To base the application of these descriptions to a particular resolution upon the fact that it involves a modification or defeasance of rights of a valuable or important nature, is in effect to go back to the discarded distinction between articles affecting the constitution and those affecting the administration of the company or to a distinction very like it. To base the application of the epithets upon the circumstance that the majority obtain a benefit by the change seems to involve some departure from the principle that the vote attached to a share is an incident of property which may be used as the share-holder's interests may dictate . . .

The chief reason for denying an unlimited effect to widely expressed powers such as that of altering a company's articles is the fear or knowledge that an apparently regular exercise of the power may in truth be but a means of securing some personal or particular gain, whether pecuniary or otherwise, which does not fairly arise out of the subjects dealt with by the power and is outside and even inconsistent with the contemplated objects of the power. It is to exclude the purpose of securing such ulterior special and particular advantages that Lord Lindley used the phrase 'bona fide for the benefit of the company as a whole'. The reference to 'benefit as a whole' is but a very general expression negativing purposes foreign to the company's operations, affairs and organisations. But unfortunately, as appears from the foregoing discussion, the use of the phrase has tended to cause misapprehension. If the challenged alteration relates to an article which does or may affect an individual, as, for instance, a director appointed for life or a shareholder whom it is desired to expropriate, or to an article affecting the mutual rights and liabilities inter se of shareholders or

---

37 [See below, pp 517 ff.]

different classes or descriptions of shareholders, the very subject-matter involves a conflict of interests and advantages. To say that the shareholders forming the majority must consider the advantage of the company as a whole in relation to such a question seems inappropriate, if not meaningless, and at all events starts an impossible inquiry. The 'company as a whole' is a corporate entity consisting of all the shareholders. If the proposal put forward is for a revision of any of the articles regulating the rights inter se of shareholders or classes of shareholders, the primary question must be how conflicting interests are to be adjusted, and the adjustment is left by law to the determination of those whose interests conflict, subject, however, to the condition that the existing provision can be altered only by a three-fourths majority. Whether the matter be voting rights, the basis of distributing profits, the basis of dividing surplus assets on a winding-up, preferential rights in relation to profits or to surplus assets, or any other question affecting mutual interests, it is apparent that though the subject-matter is among the most conspicuous of those governed by articles and therefore of those to which the statutory power is directed, yet it involves little if anything more than the redetermination of the rights and interests of those to whom the power is committed. No one supposes that in voting each shareholder is to assume an inhuman altruism and consider only the intangible notion of the benefit of the vague abstraction called by Lord Robertson in *Baily's* case **[3.19]** 'the company as an institution'. An investigation of the thoughts and motives of each shareholder voting with the majority would be an impossible proceeding . . . [When] the very question to be determined is a conflict of interests, unless the subject-matter is held outside the power, the purpose of the resolution, as distinguished from the motives of the individuals, often must be to resolve the conflict in favour of one and against the other interest.

In my opinion it was within the scope and purpose of the power of alteration for a three-fourths majority to decide the basis of distributing shares issued for the purpose of capitalising accumulated profits or profits arising from the sale of goodwill, and in voting for the resolution shareholders were not bound to disregard their own interests. I am far from saying that the resolution for the alteration of the articles would have been bad if the existing articles had been uniform and clear in requiring that, however the 'capitalisation' was effected, the basis of distribution should be the number of shares respectively subscribed for by members. But the facts of the case were that by one method, the older indirect method, a capitalisation might have been effected which would mean a distribution according to capital paid up. Doubts were felt about the propriety of adopting this course, and doubts were agitated as to the meaning of the article providing for the direct method. If there were no capitalisation, the accumulated profits would not be distributed in proportion with capital subscribed. In these circumstances the holders of partly paid shares had no 'right' to receive the profits in proportion with capital paid up. As the articles stood they were entitled only to receive shares in that proportion if and when issued by way of direct capitalisation. That event would never be likely to occur; for the holders of fully paid shares were perfectly entitled to prevent it and would no doubt do so. In these circumstances it appears to me that the resolution involved no oppression, no appropriation of an unjust or reprehensible nature and did not imply any purpose outside the scope of the power . . .

LATHAM CJ delivered a concurring judgment.

MCTIERNAN J concurred.

➤ Note

Ironically, this powerfully reasoned case may no longer carry weight in its native Australia. In *Gambotto v WPC Ltd* (1995) 182 CLR 432, (1995) 127 ALR 417, the High Court ruled that the '*bona fide* for the benefit of the company as a whole' test should be replaced by a test which asks whether the alteration or proposed alteration is 'beyond any purpose contemplated by the articles or oppressive as that expression is understood in the law relating to corporations' ((1995) 127 ALR 417 at 425). The case itself was concerned with an alteration of the articles which gave the company rights to buy out minority shareholders compulsorily, and it would be tempting to treat the judgment as limited to the special case of alterations conferring expulsion rights; but the court went out of its way to disown the English line of authority in general terms.

This new test is clearly one which is almost entirely, if not wholly, objective; and one which will allow the court to play a much more interventionist role. A test based on 'proper purposes' has already gone some way towards displacing one based on '*bona fides*' for the purpose of reviewing directors' discretionary decisions: see below, pp 285 ff. However, it is doubtful whether *Gambotto* would be followed in this country (and see also the most recent Privy Council confirmation of this in the *Citco* case [**4.29**], below).

The CLR drew attention to the fact that the alteration of articles was undoubtedly of bene-fit to the company as a whole (it stood to gain tax advantages), and the minority were to be fully compensated. It considered that there is no case for displacing the '*bona fide* in the best interests of the company as a whole' test with some other concept to deal specially with expropriation cases.

➤ Question

Is it consistent to say that the power to alter articles 'shall be exercised *bona fide* and for no bye or sinister purpose' and (in the next sentence) 'the power of alteration is not fiduciary'?

[4.27] Greenhalgh v Arderne Cinemas Ltd[38] [1951] Ch 286 (Court of Appeal)

The articles of the defendant (a private company) provided that existing members should have pre-emptive rights if a member wished to sell his shares. Mallard, the managing director, had negotiated with an outsider, Sol Sheckman, for the sale to Sheckman of a controlling interest in the company at 6s [30p] per share. Mallard had procured the passing of a special resolution to give effect to this agreement. In effect this negated the pre-emptive rights of the existing members. One of the latter, Greenhalgh, claimed a declaration that the resolutions were invalid as a fraud on the minority.[39] The Court of Appeal, affirming Roxburgh J, refused a declaration.

EVERSHED MR: The burden of that case is that the resolution was not passed bona fide and in the inter-ests of the company as a whole, and there are, as Mr Jennings has urged, two distinct approaches.

The first line of attack is this, and it is one to which, he complains, Roxburgh J paid no regard: this is a special resolution, and, on authority, Mr Jennings says, the validity of a special resolution depends upon the fact that those who passed it did so in good faith and for the benefit of the com-pany as a whole. The cases to which Mr Jennings referred are *Sidebottom v Kershaw, Leese & Co Ltd* [**4.24**], Peterson J's decision in *Dafen Tinplate Co Ltd v Llanelly Steel Co (1907) Ltd* [**4.25**] and, finally, *Shuttleworth v Cox Bros & Co (Maidenhead) Ltd* [**5.09**]. Certain principles, I think, can be safely stated as emerging from those authorities. In the first place, I think it is now plain that 'bona fide for the benefit of the company as a whole' means not two things but one thing. It means that the shareholder must proceed upon what, in his honest opinion, is for the benefit of the company as a whole. The second thing is that the phrase 'the company as a whole' does not (at any rate in such a case as the present) mean the company as a commercial entity, distinct from the corporators: it means the corporators as a general body. That is to say, the case may be taken of an individual

---

[38] This was the last of many actions between the parties. The parties were involved in seven actions, five of which went to the Court of Appeal; Greenhalgh lost all but the first (Gower, *Modern Company Law* (4th edn, 1979), pp 624–626). See further below, [**9.08**].

[39] For the meaning of this phrase, see below, pp 517 ff.

hypothetical member and it may be asked whether what is proposed is, in the honest opinion of those voted in its favour, for that person's benefit.

I think that the matter can, in practice, be more accurately and precisely stated by looking at the converse and by saying that a special resolution of this kind would be liable to be impeached if the effect of it were to discriminate between the majority shareholders and the minority shareholders, so as to give to the former an advantage of which the latter were deprived. When the cases are examined in which the resolution has been successfully attacked, it is on that ground. It is therefore not necessary to require that persons voting for a special resolution should, so to speak, dissociate themselves altogether from their own prospects and consider whether [the proposal is] for the benefit of the company as a going concern. If, as commonly happens, an outside person makes an offer to buy all the shares, prima facie, if the corporators think it a fair offer and vote in favour of the resolution, it is no ground for impeaching the resolution that they are considering their own position as individuals.

Accepting that, as I think he did, Mr Jennings said, in effect, that there are still grounds for impeaching this resolution: first, because it goes further than was necessary to give effect to the particular sale of the shares; and, secondly, because it prejudiced the plaintiff and minority share-holders in that it deprived them of the right which, under the subsisting articles, they would have of buying the shares of the majority if the latter desired to dispose of them.

What Mr Jennings objects to in the resolution is that if a resolution is passed altering the articles merely for the purpose of giving effect to a particular transaction, then it is quite sufficient (and it is usually done) to limit it to that transaction. But this resolution provides that anybody who wants at any time to sell his shares can now go direct to an outsider, provided that there is an ordinary reso-lution of the company approving the proposed transferee. Accordingly, if it is one of the majority who is selling, he will get the necessary resolution. This change in the articles, so to speak, franks the shares for holders of majority interests but makes it more difficult for a minority shareholder, because the majority will probably look with disfavour upon his choice. But, after all, this is merely a relaxation of the very stringent restrictions on transfer in the existing article, and it is to be borne in mind that the directors, as the articles stood, could always refuse to register a transfer. A minority shareholder, therefore, who produced an outsider was always liable to be met by the directors (who presumably act according to the majority view) saying, 'We are sorry, but we will not have this man in.' . . .

As to the second point, I felt at one time sympathy for the plaintiff's argument, because, after all, as the articles stood he could have said: 'Before you go selling to the purchaser you have to offer your shares to the existing shareholders, and that will enable me, if I feel so disposed, to buy, in effect, the whole of the shareholding of the Arderne company.' I think that the answer is that when a man comes into a company, he is not entitled to assume that the articles will always remain in a particular form; and that, so long as the proposed alteration does not unfairly discriminate in the way which I have indicated, it is not an objection, provided that the resolution is passed bona fide, that the right to tender for the majority holding of shares would be lost by the lifting of the restriction. I do not think that it can be said that this is such a discrimination as falls within the scope of the prin-ciple which I have stated . . .

ASQUITH and JENKINS LJJ concurred.

➤ Notes

1. See also *Clemens v Clemens Bros Ltd* [4.21], where the issue before the court was similar, although no alteration of the articles was involved; the court, although purporting to apply the same principles, reached the opposite conclusion.

2. We should bear in mind that all[40] the events complained of in the sorry history of Mr Greenhalgh and his company took place before there was any statutory provision allowing

---

[40] In the case of the last in the round of the many resolutions, just *one day* before CA 1948 s 210 came into force! Did the controllers of Arderne Cinemas Ltd have 'the foresight of a Hebrew prophet'?

the court to grant relief to a minority shareholder on the ground of 'oppression' (CA 1948 s 210) or 'unfairly prejudicial' conduct (CA 1985 s 459, CA 2006 s 994): see below, p 552. Given the long history of the 'salami tactics' by which Mr Greenhalgh's stake in the company was systematically eroded, he might well have succeeded in an application for relief under these provisions—although there is a possibility that they will be construed more restrictively following the ruling of the House of Lords in *O'Neill v Phillips* [11.24].

3. *Greenhalgh v Arderne Cinemas Ltd* is a very difficult judgment. We can put some of the problems which it raises in the form of questions, but it is not possible to give any confident answer to most of them.

> ## Questions

1. The first test posed by Lord Evershed seems to be a subjective one: the shareholders' *bona fide* opinion is determinative. In the next paragraph, with talk of discrimination, the test is apparently an objective one. Are the two passages consistent with each other, or is the court having the best of both worlds?

2. Is it possible to reconcile 'the corporators as a general body' (distinct from 'the company as a commercial entity') and 'the company as a going concern'? What weight do you think should be given to the phrase 'at any rate in such a case as the present'? Are Lord Evershed's remarks intended to be confined to special resolutions, or to special resolutions altering articles, or to apply generally to all resolutions?

3. A claimant does not go to court unless he has a grievance. Would it not be true to say that in all the *unsuccessful* cases in which an alteration has been challenged, as well as the successful ones, the minority were complaining of discrimination?

4. Whom should the court identify as 'the individual hypothetical member' in a case such as *Clemens v Clemens Bros Ltd* [4.21], where the only two actual shareholders have fallen out?

[4.28] Rights and Issues Investment Trust Ltd v Stylo Shoes Ltd [1965] Ch 250 (Chancery Division)

The defendant company passed special resolutions increasing the issued share capital and doubling the voting rights of the management shares. The purpose was to preserve the voting strength of the existing 'management shares' notwithstanding the new issue. The resolutions were carried by a large majority at a general meeting of the company and approved by a class meeting of the ordinary shareholders;[41] the holders of management shares did not vote on either occasion. The court ruled that the resolution altering the voting rights was valid.

PENNYCUICK J: I am not persuaded that there has been here any discrimination against or oppression of the holders of the ordinary shares. What has happened is that the members of this company, other than the holders of the management shares, have come to the conclusion that it is for the benefit of this company that the present basis of control through the management shares should continue to subsist notwithstanding that the management shares will henceforward represent a smaller proportion of the issued capital than heretofore. That, it seems to me, is a decision on a matter of business policy to which they could properly come and it does not seem to me a matter in which the court can interfere. So far as I am aware there is no principle under which the members of a company acting in accordance with the Companies Act and the constitution of the particular

---

[41] On 'class meetings', see below, pp 433 ff.

company and subject to any necessary consent on the part of a class affected, cannot, if they are so minded, alter the relative voting powers attached to various classes of shares. Of course, any resolution for the alteration of voting rights must be passed in good faith for the benefit of the company as a whole, but, where it is so, I know of no ground on which such an alteration would be objectionable and no authority has been cited to that effect. So here this alteration in voting powers has been resolved upon by a great majority of those members of the company who have themselves nothing to gain by it so far as their personal interest is concerned and who, so far as one knows, are actuated only by consideration of what is for the benefit of the company as a whole. I cannot see any ground on which that can be said to be oppressive . . .

> Notes

1. It is apparent from such cases as *North-West Transportation Co Ltd v Beatty* **[4.34]** and *Northern Counties Securities Ltd v Jackson & Steeple Ltd* **[4.01]** that the holders of the management shares were under no legal obligation to abstain from voting. Their self-denying act was, however, a very effective piece of window-dressing. In contrast with the rule which normally governs the acts of *directors*, there is no common law rule that a vote by an interested shareholder renders a decision invalid, or even raises a presumption of *mala fides*. The only situation in which it is clearly improper to exercise the voting rights attached to shares (fraud apart) is where the validity of the shares concerned is at stake, when to allow the vote would be to beg the very question in issue: see *Hogg v Cramphorn Ltd* **[6.08]** and *Bamford v Bamford* **[11.03]**.

2. It has from time to time been suggested that it would be a desirable change in the law to allow some issues to be resolved by submitting them to the votes of 'independent' members only. But this would be very difficult to enforce (consider eg relatives, nominees, trustees and friends of 'interested' members), and it would deprive those with most at stake from a meaningful say in their company's affairs.

3. Denying 'interested' members a vote is easier, and there are, indeed, one or two special situations where the holders of 'interested' shares are disfranchised by statute (CA 2006 s 239 is the most obvious one, but also ss 695, 717), and by the Listing Rules in regard to transactions between a listed company and a 'related party', such as a substantial shareholder or director.

4. In *Smith v Croft (No 2)* **[11.14]**, Knox J held that it was proper for the court, in deciding whether to allow a minority shareholder's action to be brought as an exception to the Rule in *Foss v Harbottle* (below, pp 531 ff), to have regard to the views of 'independent' shareholders, ie those who were not involved in the proposed litigation as defendants or as persons closely connected with them. The judgment (and that of the Court of Appeal in *Prudential Assurance Co Ltd v Newman Industries Ltd (No 2)* **[11.16]** on which it is based) comes very close to suggesting that this issue is to be resolved by summoning a general meeting, perhaps under the direction of the court, at which the defendants and those in their camp should be disenfranchised. This was something that the Court of Appeal said that it had no power to do in *Mason v Harris* (1879) 11 Ch D 97, but it appears to have become an accepted part of modern thinking—and, indeed, has now been adopted as a statutory rule in many contexts (eg the ratification of breaches of directors' duties: below, pp 221 ff and pp 348 ff).

Confirmation of orthodoxy.

[4.29] Citco Banking Corporation NV v Pusser's Limited [2007] BCC 205, [2007] UKPC 13 (Privy Council)

Before the events in issue in this appeal, the company had share capital of $4.4m divided into 4.4m class A shares of $1 each, of which 1,673,217 shares and warrants for another 248,000 had been issued. Each class A share or warrant carried one vote. At an extraordinary general meeting, the company by special resolution amended its articles of association to create 200,000 class B shares, each carrying 50 votes. It also resolved that 200,000 of the class A shares held by the chairman of the company, Mr Charles S Tobias, be converted into class B shares. The resolutions were carried by 1,125,665 votes to 183,000, the dissenting shares all being held by Citco. Citco alleged that the resolutions were invalid because they were passed in the interests of Mr Tobias, to give him indisputable control, and not *bona fide* in the interests of the company. The trial judge agreed; the Court of Appeal reversed his decision and held the resolutions valid. The Privy Council upheld this finding.

LORD HOFFMANN delivered the judgment of the Privy Council:

12 Section 89 of the Act [broadly equivalent to CA 2006 s 21] contains no qualification of the power of a 75% majority to amend the articles of association. But the courts have always treated the power as subject to implied limitations. The problem has been to say where the line should be drawn. [He then examined the authorities, including *Allen v Gold Reefs of West Africa Ltd* **[4.23]**, *Dafen Tinplate Company Ltd v Llanelly Steel Company (1907) Ltd* **[4.25]**, *Shuttleworth v Cox Bros and Co (Maidenhead) Ltd* **[5.09]**, and continued:]

17 These were cases in which the amendment operated to the particular disadvantage of a minority of shareholders: Mr Zuccani's estate in Allen's case and the director whose removal was proposed in Shuttleworth's case. But the same principle must apply when an amendment which the shareholders bona fide consider to be for the benefit of the company as a whole also operates to the particular advantage of some shareholders. This is illustrated by *Rights & Issues Investment Trust Ltd v Stylo Shoes Ltd* **[4.28]**, . . .

18 These principles, together with the proposition that the burden of proof is upon the person who challenges the validity of the amendment (see *Peters' American Delicacy Company Ltd v Heath* (1939) 61 CLR 457, per Latham CJ at p 482) appear to their Lordships to be clearly settled and sufficient for the purpose of deciding this case. It must however be acknowledged that the test of "bona fide for the benefit of the company as a whole" will not enable one to decide all cases in which amendments of the articles operate to the disadvantage of some shareholder or group of shareholders. Such amendments are sometimes only for the purpose of regulating the rights of shareholders in matters in which the company as a corporate entity has no interest, such as the distribution of dividends or capital or the power to dispose of shares. In the Australian case of *Peters' American Delicacy Company*, to which reference has been made, the amendment provided that shareholders should thenceforth receive dividends rateably according to the amounts paid up on their shares rather than, as previously, according to the number of shares (fully or partly paid) which they held. It was, as Dixon J pointed out (at p 512), "inappropriate, if not meaningless" to ask whether the shareholders had considered the amendment to be in the interests of the company as a whole. Some other test of validity is required. In *Greenhalgh v Arderen Cinemas Ltd* **[4.27]**, where the amendment was to remove a pre-emption clause to facilitate a sale of control to a third party, Sir Raymond Evershed MR tried to preserve the application of the traditional test by saying that in such cases "the company as a whole" did not mean the company as a corporate entity but "the corporators as a general body" and that it was necessary to ask whether the amendment was, in the honest opinion of those who voted in favour, for the benefit of a hypothetical member. Some commentators have not found this approach entirely illuminating but for the purposes of this appeal it is not necessary to discuss such cases any further. In this case, as in the *Stylo Shoes* case, it would have been perfectly rational to ask whether the vesting of voting control in Mr Tobias was in the interests of the company as a whole.

19 Their Lordships also note that in *Gambotto v WCP Limited* (1995) 182 CLR 432 the High Court of Australia created a new rule for amendments which they characterised as conferring powers of "expropriation" of the shares of a minority. Such an amendment could be justified only if it was reasonably apprehended that the continued shareholding of the minority was detrimental to the company, its undertaking or the conduct of its affairs and expropriation was a reasonable means of eliminating or mitigating that detriment. It was not enough in such a case that the amendment was

considered by the majority shareholders to be in the interests of the company as a corporate entity or even that it actually was for the company's benefit. In a joint judgment, Mason CJ, Brennan, Deane and Dawson JJ said at p 446:

> "Notwithstanding that a shareholder's membership of a company is subject to alterations of the articles which may affect the rights attaching to the shareholder's shares and the value of those shares, we do not consider that, in the case of an alteration to the articles authorizing the expropriation of shares, it is a sufficient justification of an expropriation that the expropriation, being fair, will advance the interests of the company as a legal and commercial entity or those of the majority, albeit the great majority, of corporators. This approach does not attach sufficient weight to the proprietary nature of a share and, to the extent that English authority might appear to support such an approach, we do not agree with it."

20 The *Gambotto* rule appears to have come as something of a surprise to the profession in Australia (see the full discussion in *Heydon v NRMA Ltd* (2000) 51 NSWLR 1) but their Lordships need not consider it further because this was clearly not a case of expropriation which would have attracted its application. It is sufficient to say that, as the High Court observed, it has no support in English authority.

21 Their Lordships therefore return to the present appeal. . . .

24 The Court of Appeal, reversing the judge, said (at paragraph 16) that where he went wrong in principle was "when he attempted to step into the commercial arena". Their Lordships take this to mean that the judge fell into the same error as Peterson J in *Dafen Tinplate Company Ltd v Lianelly Steel Company (1907) Ltd* **[4.25]**, namely that he took it upon himself to decide whether the amendment was for the benefit of the company. The Court of Appeal said that he should instead have applied the test laid down in *Shuttleworth's* case, namely, whether reasonable shareholders could have considered that the amendment was for the benefit of the company. The Court of Appeal considered that it would have been reasonable for shareholders to have accepted in good faith the arguments put forward by Mr Tobias as to why the amendment would be in the interests of the company. The only shareholder who gave evidence at the trial was Mr de Vos, who said that he had thought the amendments were in the best interests of the company as a whole. It was not necessary for Mr Tobias and the company to prove to the judge that the arguments were justified by the facts.

25 Their Lordships consider that this reasoning is correct. Mr Todd QC, who appeared for Citco, said that in a case in which one shareholder gained a personal advantage by the amendment, as Mr Tobias did in this case, it was necessary to show that even without his votes, the amendment would have been passed. In *Rights & Issues Investment Trust Ltd v Stylo Shoes Ltd* **[4.28]**, Pennycuick J laid some stress upon the fact that the resolution had been passed at a separate meeting of ordinary shareholders at which the holders of management shares did not vote. In this case there was, prior to the amendment, only one class of shares, but Mr Todd said that it was necessary to show that the resolution would have passed even without the votes controlled by Mr Tobias.

26 Their Lordships do not think that the *Stylo Shoes* case decided that in a case like this, shareholders who particularly stand to gain from the amendment should not vote. As Evershed MR said in *Greenhalgh v Arderen Cinemas Ltd* **[4.27]**, 291:

> "It is . . . not necessary to require that persons voting for a special resolution should, so to speak, dissociate themselves altogether from their own prospects . . . "

27 If Mr Tobias bona fide considered that the amendment was in the interests of the company as a whole, and there has been no attack on his bona fides, their Lordships do not see why he should not vote. This is only one aspect of the general principle that shareholders are free to exercise their votes in their own interests. As Lord Davey said in *Burland v Earle* **[11.10]**, 94:

> "Unless otherwise provided by the regulations of the company, a shareholder is not debarred from voting or using his voting power to carry a resolution by the circumstance of his having a particular interest in the subject-matter of the vote."

28 In any case, it appears to their Lordships that even the test proposed by Mr Todd was satisfied. The only evidence as to the number of shares controlled by Mr Tobias was that of Mr de Vos, who said that it amounted to 28% of the issued share capital. He was cross-examined on this point, with counsel for Citco seeking to establish that Mr Tobias actually controlled very few shares, but stuck to 28%. He did also say that Mr Tobias was indirectly able to exercise the votes of 51% of the share capital, but this was consistent with the additional votes being simply those of supporters who had decided to entrust Mr Tobias with their proxies. Of the 28%, Mr Tobias did not vote the 62,439 shares registered in his own name. If he had not voted the 460,245 shares registered in the names of his wife and Piccadilly Properties Ltd, which made up the rest of the 28%, the votes cast in favour of the resolution would have been 665,420 out of a total of 848,420. This would still have been 78%.

29 Their Lordships will therefore humbly advise Her Majesty that the appeal should be dismissed with costs.

Variation of class rights

See pp 443 ff, and the cases extracted there.

Members' consent, authorisation or ratification of directors' breaches

Breaches of duty by directors are not always inimical to the company's interests. Consider *Regal Hastings v Gulliver* **[6.16]** or *Brady v Brady* **[8.08]**. If the company's directors propose to engage in an activity that is beyond their powers, or in breach of their duties to the company, but is nevertheless an activity that the majority of the members wish the company to pursue, the members may:[42]

(i)   take the decision themselves to commit the company to the activity (but see above, pp 180 ff, on the members' limited power to manage the company's business in this way);

(ii) authorise the directors to engage in the activity (again, the members need to have the necessary power to authorise the directors to proceed).

More commonly, the members will only discover the directors' breach after the event. If they nevertheless support the directors' activity, they may:

(i)   ratify (or, more accurately, affirm) the impugned transaction, if that is necessary for its validity;

(ii) ratify (waive or forgive) the breach, so that the directors are secure in the commitment that the company will not sue them at a later date for the wrongdoing: this might be especially important if the company is taken over and a new board is put in place, or the company becomes insolvent and a liquidator is appointed, so that the members now expressing support for the directors are no longer in a position to deliver their promises.

Each of these options seems to have slightly different requirements attached to it. The cases that follow expose some of the rules. In addition, CA 2006 enacts new requirements.

These authorisation and ratification decisions warrant such detailed scrutiny because of the acknowledged risk that defaulting directors, in their role as members, often have the power to obtain or at least influence company decisions that may permit them to get away with unacceptable wrongdoing.

CA 2006 s 180: Consent, approval or authorisation by members

This is a general section covering each of: *authorisation* by the directors, according to the terms of the Act, of what would otherwise be a conflict of interest for one of their board

---

[42] See S Worthington, 'Corporate Governance: Remedying and Ratifying Directors' Breaches' (2000) 116 LQR 638.

members; *approval* by the members of transactions required by statute to have such approval; and, finally, preservation of the general law on *authorisation by the company* of anything that would otherwise be a breach of duty by the directors. This last option is the one under review in this section.

CA 2006 s 239: Ratification of acts of directors

CA 2006 s 239 preserves the current law on ratification of acts of directors, but with one significant change. Any decision by a company to ratify conduct by a director amounting to negligence, default, breach of duty or breach of trust in relation to the company must be taken by the members, and without reliance on the votes in favour by the director (as members) or any connected person. Section 252 defines what is meant by a person being connected with a director. For the purposes of this section it may also include fellow directors (s 252(5)(d)).

If the ratification decision is taken at a meeting, those members whose votes are to be disregarded may still attend the meeting, take part in the meeting and count towards the quorum for the meeting (if their membership gives them the right to do so) (s 239(4)).

The company in general meeting may by ordinary resolution ratify an act of the directors which is within the powers of the company but beyond the authority or competence of the directors.

[4.30] Grant v United Kingdom Switchback Railways Co (1888) 40 Ch D 135 (Court of Appeal)

Article 100 of the articles of association of Thompson's Patent Gravity Switchback Railways Co (the second defendant) disqualified any director from voting at a board meeting in relation to any contract in which he was interested. The directors of this company agreed to sell the company's undertaking to the United Kingdom Co (the first defendant) despite the fact that they were the promoters of the purchasing company. [The remaining facts appear from the judgment.]

COTTON LJ: This is an appeal from a decision of Mr Justice Chitty refusing an injunction to restrain Thompson's Company and the United Kingdom Company from carrying into effect a contract for the sale of part of the undertaking of the former company to the latter. The ground of the application was that the directors of Thompson's Company had no authority to enter into the contract, as the articles prohibited a director from voting upon a contract in which he was interested, and here all the directors but one were interested. An application for an injunction was made in the Long Vacation, and ordered to stand over till the Michaelmas Sittings, the companies undertaking not to act upon the agreement in the meantime, but being left at liberty to call meetings of their shareholders with reference to the agreement. A general meeting of the shareholders of Thompson's Company was accordingly held, and passed a resolution approving and adopting the agreement, and authorising the directors to carry it into effect. Mr Justice Chitty under these circumstances refused an injunction, and the plaintiff has appealed.

It was argued for the appellant that the directors could not, being interested, make a contract which would bind their company, and that a general meeting could not, by a mere ordinary resolution, affirm that contract, for this would be an alteration of the articles, which could only be effected by a special resolution. This is a mistake. The ratifying of a particular contract which had been entered into by the directors without authority, and so making it an act of the company, is quite a different thing from altering the articles. To give the directors power to do things in future which articles did not authorise them to do would be an alteration of the articles, but it is no alteration of the articles to ratify a contract which has been made with authority.

It was urged that the contract was a nullity, and could not be ratified. That is not the case. There was a contract entered into on behalf of the company, though it was one which could not be enforced against the company. Article 100 prevented the directors from binding the company by the contract, but there was nothing in it to prevent the company from entering into such a contract. Two passages in *Irvine v Union Bank of Australia*[43] were referred to. Being in the same judgment, they must be taken together, and they appear to me to express what I have said—that power to do future acts cannot be given to directors without altering the articles, but that a ratification of an unauthorised act of the directors only requires the sanction of an ordinary resolution of a general meeting, if the act is within the powers of the company.

LINDLEY and BOWEN LJJ delivered concurring judgments.

[4.31] Re Horsley & Weight Ltd [1982] Ch 442, [1982] 3 All ER 1045 (Court of Appeal)

[For the facts and another part of the decision, see [3.05].]

BUCKLEY LJ: I now turn to the second head of Mr Evans-Lombe's argument, viz that the purchase of the pension was effected by Mr Campbell-Dick and Mr Frank Horsley without the authority of the board of directors or of the company in general meeting, and was an act of misfeasance which was not validated as against the company's creditors by virtue of the fact that Mr Campbell-Dick and Mr Frank Horsley were the only shareholders. Ignoring for the moment that Mr Campbell-Dick and Mr Frank Horsley were the only shareholders, the transaction in question was indeed carried out by them without the sanction of any board resolution, whether antecedent, contemporary or by way of subsequent ratification. It was an unauthorised act which they were, as two only of the company's five directors, incompetent to carry out on the company's behalf. It therefore cannot stand unless it has in some way been ratified. The question is whether the fact that Mr Campbell-Dick and Mr Frank Horsley were the only shareholders of the company has the effect of validating the transaction.

Mr Evans-Lombe has submitted that there is a general duty incumbent on directors of a company, whether properly described as owed to creditors or not, to preserve the company's capital fund (which he identifies as those assets which are not distributable by way of dividends) and not to dispose of it otherwise than for the benefit or intended benefit of the company. He submits that creditors dealing with the company are entitled to assume that directors will observe that duty; and that creditors although they are not entitled to interfere in the day-to-day management of a company which is not in liquidation, are entitled through a liquidator to seek redress in respect of a breach of the duty. Consequently, Mr Evans-Lombe submits, the members of the company cannot, even unanimously, deprive the creditors of any remedy so available to them.

On this part of the case Mr Evans-Lombe mainly relies upon *Re Exchange Banking Co, Flitcroft's Case* [8.13] . . . The facts of that case were very different from those of the present case and the principles applicable were, in my opinion, also different. A company cannot legally repay contributed capital to the contributors otherwise than by way of an authorised reduction of capital. Nothing of that kind occurred in the present case. There is nothing in the statute or in the general law which prevents a company or its directors expending contributed capital in doing anything which is an authorised object of the company. In the present case the cost of effecting the pension policy was, in my view, incurred in the course of carrying out an express object of the company.

It is a misapprehension to suppose that the directors of a company owe a duty to the company's creditors to keep the contributed capital of the company intact. The company's creditors are entitled to assume that the company will not in any way repay any paid-up share capital to the shareholders

43   (1877) 2 App Cas 366, PC.

except by means of a duly authorised reduction of capital. They are entitled to assume that the company's directors will conduct its affairs in such a manner that no such unauthorised repayment will take place. It may be somewhat loosely said that the directors owe an indirect duty to the creditors not to permit any unlawful reduction of capital to occur, but I would regard it as more accurate to say that the directors owe a duty to the company in this respect and that, if the company is put into liquidation when paid-up capital has been improperly repaid, the liquidator owes a duty to the creditors to enforce any right to repayment which is available to the company. On the other hand, a company and its directors acting on its behalf, can quite properly expend contributed capital for any purpose which is intra vires the company. As I have already indicated, the purchase of the pension policy was, in my view, intra vires the company. It was not, however, within the powers of Mr Campbell-Dick and Mr Frank Horsley acting not as members of the board of directors but as individual directors. Unless the act was effectually ratified it cannot bind the company. They were, however, the only two shareholders. A company is bound in a matter which is intra vires the company by the unanimous agreement of its members (per Lord Davey in *Salomon v A Salomon & Co Ltd* **[2.01]**; and see *Re Express Engineering Works Ltd* **[4.14]** even where that agreement is given informally: *Parker & Cooper Ltd v Reading* **[4.15]**. That both Mr Campbell-Dick and Mr Frank Horsley assented to the transaction in question in the present case is beyond dispute. They both initialled the proposal form and they both signed the cheques for the premiums. Their good faith has not been impugned, nor, in my view, does the evidence support any suggestion that in effecting the policy they did not honestly apply their minds to the question whether it was a fair and proper thing for the company to do in the light of the company's financial state as known to them at the time. In my judgment, their assent made the transaction binding on the company and unassailable by the liquidator . . .

CUMMING-BRUCE and TEMPLEMAN LJJ delivered concurring judgments, in the course of which they made the following comments:

CUMMING-BRUCE LJ: On these facts it is unnecessary to decide whether, had misfeasance by the directors been proved, it was open to them in their capacity as shareholders to ratify their own negligence and so to prejudice the claims of creditors. It would surprise me to find that the law is to be so understood.

TEMPLEMAN LJ: If, however, there had been evidence and a finding of misfeasance and it appeared that the payment of £10,000 in the event reduced the fund available for creditors by that sum, or by a substantial proportion of that sum, I am not satisfied that the directors convicted of such misfeasance, albeit with no fraudulent intent or action, could excuse themselves because two of them held all the issued shares in the company and as shareholders ratified their own gross negligence as directors which inflicted loss on creditors. I should be sorry to find the scope of s 333 [IA 1986, s 212] so restricted and need not do so on this occasion.

An ordinary resolution of members which purports to ratify an irregular act of the directors is ineffective if it itself contravenes the articles.

[4.32] Boschoek Pty Ltd v Fuke [1906] 1 Ch 148 (Chancery Division)

The directors had purported to appoint Fuke managing director at a remuneration of £700 per annum notwithstanding that he did not hold 'in his own right' the number of qualification shares prescribed by the articles and that the maximum remuneration of the whole board was fixed by the articles at £500. The company later confirmed the appointment by resolutions passed unanimously at a general meeting; but the court ruled that the resolutions were invalid.

SWINFEN EADY J: The . . . ground on which the plaintiff company has objected to the validity of the . . . resolutions passed at this meeting is that they could only have been properly passed after the articles had been altered by special resolution. The company in general meeting could not appoint, and could not ratify, as from December 1901, the appointment of Fuke as managing director at £700 per annum as he had not the necessary qualification, and the maximum remuneration of the whole board was fixed by the articles at £500. The articles, until altered, bound the shareholders in general meeting as much as the board. The present case is unlike that of *Irvine v Union Bank of Australia*,[44] to which reference was made, as in that case the limitation of the power of borrowing and mortgaging was merely a limitation of the authority of the directors, and not a limitation of the general powers of the company. It was argued that the acts of the directors in excess of their authority might be ratified by the company and rendered binding, and that contention succeeded. Articles must first be altered by special resolution before the altered articles can be acted upon: *Imperial Hydropathic Hotel Co, Blackpool v Hampson* **[4.04]**.

A general meeting may also ratify an act of the directors which is voidable as an irregular exercise of their powers.

[4.33] Bamford v Bamford [1970] Ch 212 (Court of Appeal)

The directors of Bamfords Ltd (referred to in the judgment as the 'the company') issued 500,000 shares at par to FH Burgess Ltd, one of the principal distributors of the company's products. They did so in exercise of a power vested in them by the articles, but (so the plaintiffs alleged) improperly, being primarily for the purpose of forestalling a take-over bid by JC Bamford (Excavators) Ltd. When the validity of the allotment was challenged by the issue of a writ, the directors convened a members' meeting at which the allotment was ratified and approved. (The newly issued shares were not voted.[45]) The Court of Appeal held as a preliminary point of law, on the assumption that the facts alleged were true, that such a ratification would be effective.

HARMAN LJ:. . . [This] is a tolerably plain case. It is trite law, I had thought, that if directors do acts, as they do every day, especially in private companies, which, perhaps because there is no quorum, or because their appointment was defective, or because sometimes there are no directors properly appointed at all, or because they are actuated by improper motives, they go on doing for years, carrying on the business of the company in the way in which, if properly constituted, they should carry it on, and then they find that everything has been so to speak wrongly done because it was not done by a proper board, such directors can, by making a full and frank disclosure and calling together the general body of the shareholders, obtain absolution and forgiveness of their sins; and provided the acts are not ultra vires the company as a whole everything will go on as if it had been done all right from the beginning. I cannot believe that this is not a commonplace of company law. It is done every day. Of course, the majority of the general meeting will not forgive and approve, the directors must pay for it.

[His Lordship referred to *Regal (Hastings) Ltd v Gulliver* **[6.16]** and continued:] So it seems to me here that these directors, on the assumptions which we have to make, made this allotment in breach of their duty—mala fide, as it is said. They made it with an eye primarily on the exigencies of the takeover war and not with a single eye to the benefit of the company, and, therefore, it is a bad allotment. But it *is* an allotment. There is no doubt that the directors had power to allot these shares. There is no doubt that they did allot them. There is no doubt that the allottees are on the register and are for all purposes members of the company. The only question is whether the allotment, having been made, as one must assume, in bad faith, is voidable and can be avoided at the instance of the company—at their instance only and of no one else, because the wrong, if wrong it be, is a wrong done to the company. If that be right, the company, which had the right to recall the allotment,

---

[44] (1877) 2 App Cas 366, PC.
[45] Compare *Hogg v Cramphorn* **[6.08]**, and see the reference to that case in the Note above, p 218,

has also the right to approve of it and forgive it; and I see no difficulty at all in supposing that the ratification by the decision of December 15 in the general meeting of the company was a perfectly good 'whitewash' of that which up to that time was a voidable transaction. And that is the end of the matter . . .

RUSELL LJ delivered a concurring judgment.

KARMINSKI LJ concurred.

[For another part of the decision, see [11.03].]

[4.34] North-West Transportation Co Ltd v Beatty
(1887) 12 App Cas 589 (Privy Council)

[The facts appear from the judgment.]

The opinion of their Lordships was delivered by SIR RICHARD BAGGALLAY: The plaintiff, Henry Beatty, is a shareholder in the North-West Transportation Company Limited, and he sues on behalf of himself and all other shareholders in the company, except those who are defendants. The defendants are the company and five shareholders, who, at the commencement of the action, were the directors of the company. The claim in the action is to set aside a sale made to the company by James Hughes Beatty, one of the directors, of a steamer called the *United Empire*, of which, previously to such sale, he was sole owner.

The general principles applicable to cases of this kind are well established. Unless some provision to the contrary is to be found in the charter or other instrument by which the company is incorporated, the resolution of a majority of the shareholders, duly convened, upon any question with which the company is legally competent to deal, is binding upon the minority, and consequently upon the company, and every shareholder has a perfect right to vote upon any such question, although he may have a personal interest in the subject-matter opposed to, or different from, the general or particular interests of the company.

On the other hand, a director of a company is precluded from dealing, on behalf of the company, with himself, and from entering into engagements in which he has a personal interest conflicting, or which possibly may conflict, with the interests of those whom he is bound by fiduciary duty to protect; and this rule is as applicable to the case of one of several directors as to a managing or sole director. Any such dealing or engagement may, however, be affirmed or adopted by the company, provided such affirmance or adoption is not brought about by unfair or improper means, and is not illegal or fraudulent or oppressive towards those shareholders who oppose it.

The material facts of the case are not now in dispute . . .

It is proved by uncontradicted evidence, and is indeed now substantially admitted, that at the date of the purchase the acquisition of another steamer to supply the place of the *Asia* was essential to the efficient conduct of the company's business; that the *United Empire* was well adapted for that purpose; that it was not within the power of the company to acquire any other steamer equally well adapted for its business; and that the price agreed to be paid for the steamer was not excessive or unreasonable . . .

It is clear upon the authorities that the contract entered into by the directors on 10 February could not have been enforced against the company at the instance of the defendant JH Beatty, but it is equally clear that it was within the competency of the shareholders at the meeting of the 16th to adopt or reject it. In form and in terms they adopted it by a majority of votes, and the vote of the majority must prevail, unless the adoption was brought about by unfair or improper means.

The only unfairness or impropriety which, consistently with the admitted and established facts, could be suggested, arises out of the fact that the defendant JH Beatty possessed a voting power as a shareholder which enabled him, and those who thought with him, to adopt the bye-law, 12 and thereby either to ratify and adopt a voidable contract, into which he, as a director, and his co-directors had entered, or to make a similar contract, which latter seems to have been what was intended to be done by the resolution passed on 7 February.

It may be quite right that, in such a case, the opposing minority should be able, in a suit like this, to challenge the transaction, and to show that it is an improper one, and to be freed from the objection that a suit with such an object can only be maintained by the company itself.

But the constitution of the company enabled the defendant JH Beatty to acquire this voting power; there was no limit upon the number of shares which a shareholder might hold, and for every share so held he was entitled to a vote; the charter itself recognised the defendant as a holder of 200 shares, one-third of the aggregate number; he had a perfect right to acquire further shares, and to exercise his voting power in such a manner as to secure the election of directors whose views upon policy agreed with his own, and to support those views at any shareholders' meeting; the acquisition of the *United Empire* was a pure question of policy, as to which it might be expected that there would be differences of opinion, and upon which the voice of the majority ought to prevail; to reject the votes of the defendant upon the question of the adoption of the bye-law would be to give effect to the views of the minority, and to disregard those of the majority.

[See also *Burland v Earle* **[11.10]**.]

➤ Questions

This case has been understood for well over a century as one of the leading authorities for the principle set out in the headnote, on the basis that the *directors* had entered into a contract which was voidable because of Beatty's undisclosed personal interest, but was rescued from invalidity because the contract was *ratified* by the members' resolution—a resolution on which, it was held, Beatty was not debarred from voting. A number of Sir Richard Baggallay's remarks are consistent with this view of the matter (eg his reference to a 'contract entered into by the directors on 10 February'). Later commentators have gone further, interpreting the case as one where there was a breach of duty by Beatty which he was able to whitewash by the use of his own votes. The CLR adopts this approach, taking *North-West Transportation v Beatty* as illustrating the case of a *wrongdoing* director voting in his capacity as a shareholder to ratify the transaction. It proposes by way of an amendment to the law that the member in question should be disenfranchised and the resolution should only be capable of being carried by a majority of disinterested shareholders (as is now the case: CA 2006 s 239). A close examination of the facts, and of the arguments of counsel, however, suggest that the whole point of the proposed 'by-law' was to put the proposal that the company should buy the ship *before the members* for them to decide. Is there any material difference between the constraints that operate on the exercise of powers by members to affirm a voidable transaction, to waive a breach of duty, or to take a corporate decision *ab initio*? If there is a difference, how can an observer decide what the members are trying to vote on?

[See also *Burland v Earle* **[11.10]** and the *Multinational Gas* case **[6.25]**.]

➤ Notes

1. The principle established by these cases is subject to the limitation recognised in such cases as *Cook v Deeks* **[6.15]** and *Menier v Hooper's Telegraph Works* **[11.11]**: the power to ratify cannot validate acts of fraud or expropriation, or, perhaps more specifically, that directors guilty of such acts cannot, in their capacity as members, ratify or condone their own wrongdoing. This rigorous approach has been extended to ratification of directors' negligence where that negligence also leads to personal benefit (*Daniels v Daniels* [1978] Ch 406, see below, p 348).

2. But even that simple statement has its difficulties. On one measure, a company's claim against its defaulting directors is a 'corporate asset'. Accordingly, for the members to agree to waive the right, or give it away, amounts to much the same thing as 'giving away' a corporate opportunity as in *Cook v Deeks* **[6.15]**. That is something the members in general meeting could not do, at least where the resolution was carried by the votes of the wrongdoers. Yet examples abound of just this sort of ratification, where directors control the general meeting and are permitted to vote in favour of resolutions that allow them to keep the benefits of contracts with the company (*North-West Transportation Co Ltd v Beatty* **[4.34]**), or escape claims for compensation for negligence (*Pavlides v Jensen* [1956] Ch 565).

3. Two further points are material. First, there must be a members' decision to ratify: as *Re D'Jan of London Ltd* **[6.14]** shows, it is not enough that the decision of the general meeting would certainly have gone in favour of the errant director (here, the director owned 99% of the shares and his wife 1%). Secondly, as a company approaches insolvency, the shareholders lose their right to vote to distribute corporate assets to particular individuals to the detriment of the claims of the company's creditors (*Kinsela v Russell Kinsela Pty Ltd* **[6.04]**).

Summary of limitations on members' voting

These cases appear to establish a general rule that members are free to use the votes attached to their shares as they think fit and that they may, if they so wish, use them to advance their own interests. This proposition is certainly true of most business and policy decisions, such as whether to make a purchase or whom to appoint a director. However, there are a number of particular limitations on members' freedom to vote as they choose, some of which are well recognised and others of more questionable standing. It is not easy to unite these exceptions by any common theme, although it is probably significant that they belong mostly in the area of intra-corporate disputes, where one group of members is complaining that the others have used their more powerful voting strength to gain an unfair advantage.

Some of these special situations are:

(i)   Majority members may not use their votes to appropriate to themselves property which belongs to the company or to condone their own fraud (*Cook v Deeks* **[6.15]**; *Menier v Hooper's Telegraph Works* **[11.11]**).

(ii)   Where there is a resolution on an issue which affects the rights of members *inter se*, such as an alteration of the articles or a variation of class rights, the majority must act '*bona fide* in the interests of the company (or class) as a whole' (*Allen v Gold Reefs of West Africa Ltd* **[4.23]**; *British America Nickel Corpn Ltd v O'Brien* **[9.06]**).

(iii) Where it is sought to bring an action against persons who have allegedly committed wrongs against the company—or at least those wrongs coming within the elusive 'fraud on the minority' category—the alleged wrongdoers may not use their votes to stop the action being brought (an exception to the rule in *Foss v Harbottle* **[11.01]**: see below, pp 522 ff).

(iv)   There are certain *statutory* remedies which may be sought by members who are disadvantaged as a result of some act of the majority, even though what is complained of is within the legal power of the majority. The most popular of these statutory remedies are relief against 'unfairly prejudicial' conduct (on predecessor provisions, see the influential *Scottish Co-operative Wholesale Society Ltd v Meyer* **[11.19]**, and, more generally, see below pp 552 ff), and winding up on the 'just and equitable' ground (*Ebrahimi v Westbourne Galleries Ltd* **[14.14]**).

(v)   *Clemens v Clemens Bros Ltd* **[4.21]** and *Re Halt Garage (1964) Ltd* **[5.04]** appear to impose vaguer limitations on the members' voting powers: first, that votes must be not used 'oppressively', and secondly, that they must be used for 'genuine' purposes. Neither limitation is supported by weighty authority; and nor is either strong enough to make any significant inroad into the line of cases which lay down the general rule.

It would be wrong to deduce from any of the exceptional situations listed above that a member is thereby placed under a *duty* to vote against his own interests, in the altruistic way disowned by Dixon J in the *Peter's American Delicacy* case **[4.26]**, although this is a trap which judges occasionally do fall into (*Re Holders Investment Trust Ltd* **[8.05]**). The realistic choice faced by controlling members wishing to avoid having their role in the general meeting decision questioned may well be between abandoning or modifying the proposal on the one hand and, on the other, taking a calculated risk and pressing ahead in the knowledge that the burden of proof on any minority members seeking to challenge a decision has traditionally been a difficult one to discharge. However, the body of case law under CA 1985 s 459 (the 'unfair prejudice' section, now CA 2006 s 994: see below, pp 552 ff), and cases such as *Clemens v Clemens Bros Ltd* **[4.21]**, suggest that the balance may be tipping towards minority members.

> **Question**

Should members exercising their majority power be constrained to vote both *bona fide* and for proper purposes?[46]

Shareholders' agreements

The company's constitution may be supplemented by a *shareholders' agreement*—a contract, usually of a quite formal kind, entered into by the shareholders either at the time of the company's formation or at some subsequent time (eg when a family company, in need of extra capital to finance an expansion of its business, invites an outsider to join the company as an additional shareholder).[47]

To be fully effective, it is necessary that all of the members for the time being should be made parties to the agreement, and so the use of a shareholders' agreement is practicable only if the membership is not too large. The company itself is sometimes also joined as a party, but there are dangers in doing so if there is any risk that it will be held to have fettered its statutory powers (see *Russell v Northern Bank Development Corpn Ltd* **[8.01]**).[48]

The shareholders' agreement is used, almost as a matter of routine, to supplement the constitutional documents of smaller companies in Canada and the US, and its importance has been recognised by legislation in those jurisdictions. Here in the UK, we have been slower to recognise its potential as a drafting and planning aid, but its use is now standard practice for some purposes, eg joint ventures, management buy-outs, and in loan related securities required by lenders.

A shareholders' agreement might typically contain provisions that each of the shareholders should be entitled to appoint a director, that no shareholder should vote in support of an alteration of the company's articles or its capital unless all the members agreed to it, and that

---

[46] See S Worthington, 'Corporate Governance: Remedying and Ratifying Directors' Breaches' (2000) 116 LQR 638.
[47] See PD Finn, 'Shareholder Agreements' (1978) 6 ABL Rev 97.
[48] Even if the company is not a party to the agreement, it may be able to rely on it as a defence: in *Snelling v John G Snelling Ltd* [1973] QB 87, the shareholders had lent money to the company and had agreed with each other that none of them would require the company to repay their loans while certain other funding arrangements were in place. The court refused to allow one of the shareholders to sue for repayment in breach of this agreement. (Is this defensible?)

except in specified circumstances a shareholder would not require the repayment of money which he or she had lent to the company.

The main advantage of a shareholders' agreement is that its terms cannot be altered by a majority vote or special resolution, unlike the articles of association or the company's capital structure (see above pp 204 ff). Further, contractual obligations are in principle enforceable as of right, and, where appropriate, by injunction. By contrast, most company law remedies are discretionary, and a member who has only a minority shareholding may have no standing to take a complaint to the court.

On the other hand, there are disadvantages, the main one being that under the rules of privity of contract a shareholder agreement is binding only on its immediate parties and not on anyone who later takes a transfer of shares or joins the company as a new member. (The Contracts (Rights of Third Parties) Act 1999 is unlikely to be relevant in this context, since it is concerned only with rights and not obligations.)

Judges have been known to *imply* a shareholders' agreement and give effect to it (eg in *Pennell Securities Ltd v Venida Investments Ltd* (25 July 1974, noted Burridge (1981) 44 MLR 40)), and the terms of a shareholders' agreement will carry much weight in proceedings brought by a minority shareholder for relief against 'unfairly prejudicial' conduct (below, pp 552 ff) or for a winding-up order on the 'just and equitable' ground (below, pp 653 ff). For examples of the use of a shareholders' agreement, see *Russell v Northern Bank Development Corpn Ltd* [8.01].

Members' personal rights under the constitution

It might seem strange to be looking at members' personal rights in a chapter devoted to the collective rights of members as an organ of the company. But the role of the members as such an organ is defined in the articles, and the members may need to enforce the rights granted there in order to exercise the constitutional powers they see as theirs. Of course, members also seek to make claims under the articles to obtain purely personal remedies for wrongs allegedly done to them in breach of specific provisions in the articles. These latter claims generally have nothing to do with the exercise of members' constitutional rights. Whether the same approach is warranted in both types of cases is a moot point.

The articles constitute a contract binding on the company and each of the company's members (CA 2006, s 33). It might seem to follow that the shareholders, as members, have personal rights under this contract and can sue the company, or other members, to enforce those rights. Two impediments lie in the face of such claims:

(i)   The courts have imposed an enormously restrictive interpretation on the types of rights that are protected under the contract, reading into the statutory provision limitations that, *prima facie*, are nowhere suggested. So, a member must sue 'as member',[49] and 'mere irregularities' cannot be remedied.[50]

(ii) In addition, where the same facts give rise to a potential claim by the *company* against the wrongdoers, the member's claim may be disallowed because his or her losses are merely '*reflected losses*' that will be remedied once the company recovers its losses. This rule is applied as a substantive rule, not merely a procedural rule that (very properly) denies double recovery.[51]

---

[49] See the *Hickman* [4.37] and *Eley* [4.36] cases.
[50] See *Pender v Lushington* [11.15] and *MacDougall v Gardiner* [11.04], and below pp 502 ff.
[51] See *Johnson v Gore, Wood & Co* [11.17] and *Giles v Rhind* [11.18], and below at pp 543 ff.

Contractual effect of the company's constitution

CA 2006 s 33: Effect of company's constitution

(1) The provisions of a company's constitution bind the company and its members to the same extent as if there were covenants on the part of the company and of each member to observe those provisions. . . .

CA 1985 s 14: Effect of memorandum and articles

(1) Subject to the provisions of this Act, the memorandum and articles, when registered, bind the company and its members to the same extent as if they respectively had been signed and sealed by each member, and contained covenants on the part of each member to observe all the provisions of the memorandum and of the articles. . . .

Despite the seemingly clear words, this provision has been an endless source of varying interpretations and conflicting analyses. The least of the problems with the 1985 Act was whether the company was a party to the contract. CA 2006 makes it clear that it is. But, beyond that, the words in the new provision largely duplicate its predecessor, so the same uncertainties seem destined to plague this area. The extracts below are all likely to remain relevant.

Any member has the right[52] to enforce observance of the terms of the constitution, by virtue of the contractual effect given to the constitution by CA 2006 s 33.

[4.35] Wood v Odessa Waterworks Co (1889) 42 Ch D 636 (Chancery Division)

The articles empowered the directors, with the sanction of a general meeting of members, to declare a dividend 'to be paid' to the shareholders. The company passed an ordinary resolution proposing to pay no dividend but instead to give the shareholders debenture-bonds (in effect, obliging them to lend back to the company the money which could have been paid as dividends, for anything up to thirty years). Wood, a shareholder, sought an injunction to restrain the company from acting on the resolution. It was held that the proposal was inconsistent with the articles, and the injunction was accordingly granted.

STIRLING J: It was not disputed that profits available for the payment of a dividend by the company had been actually earned . . . Neither was it disputed that the company had power to create a charge on the assets of the company, or to raise money by means of such a charge, or to apply the money so raised in payment of a dividend. The question, simply, is whether it is within the power of a majority of the shareholders to insist against the will of a minority that the profits which have been actually earned shall be divided, not by the payment of cash, but by the issue of debenture-bonds of the company bearing interest at £5 per cent and repayable at par by an annual drawing extending over thirty years. It is to be inferred from the terms in which the bonds are offered for subscription that the company cannot issue them in the open market except at a discount of at least £10 per cent. Now the rights of the shareholders in respect of a division of the profits of the

---

[52] See the Notes below, pp 233 and 236.

company are governed by the provisions in the articles of association. By s 16 of the Companies Act 1862 [CA 2006 s 33] the articles of association 'bind the company and the members thereof to the same extent as if each member had subscribed his name and affixed his seal thereto, and there were in such articles contained a covenant on the part of himself, his heirs, executors, and administrators, to conform to all the regulations contained in such articles, subject to the provisions of this Act'. Section 50 of the Act [CA 2006 s 21] provides the means for altering the regulations of the company contained in the articles of association by passing a special resolution, but no such resolution has in this case been passed or attempted to be passed; and the question is, whether this is a matter as to which the majority of the shareholders can bind those shareholders who dissent. The articles of association constitute a contract not merely between the shareholders and the company, but between each individual shareholder and every other; and the question which I have just stated must in my opinion be answered in the negative if there be in the articles a contract between the shareholders as to a division of profits, and the provisions of that contract have not been followed . . . That then brings me to consider whether that which is proposed to be done in the present case is in accordance with the articles of association of the company. Those articles provide . . . that the directors may, with the sanction of a general meeting, declare a dividend to be paid to the shareholders. Prima facie that means to be paid in cash. The debenture-bonds proposed to be issued are not payments in cash; they are merely agreements or promises to pay: and if the contention of the company prevails a shareholder will be compelled to accept in lieu of cash a debt of the company payable at some uncertain future period. In my opinion that contention ought not to prevail . . .

Where the rights of an individual member have been infringed, personal action to recover individual loss is possible, even though the conduct complained of may also constitute a wrong to the company itself.

See *Pender v Lushington* [11.15]. These claims will face the '*reflective loss*' arguments discussed below, pp 543 ff.

The articles do not constitute a contract between the company and someone who is not a member.

[4.36] Eley v Positive Government Security Life Assurance Co Ltd (1876) 1 Ex D 88 (Court of Appeal)

Article 118 of the company's articles provided: 'Mr William Eley, of No 27, New Broad Street, in the City of London, shall be the solicitor to the company, and shall transact all the legal business of the company, including parliamentary business, for the usual and accustomed fees and charges, and shall not be removed from his office except for misconduct.' Eley, the plaintiff, who had himself drafted the company's documents for registration, and who became a member several months after its incorporation, sued the company for breach of contract in not employing him as its solicitor. In the Exchequer Division, it was held that the articles did not create any contract between Eley and the company. Eley appealed, but the Court of Appeal affirmed the decision.

LORD CAIRNS LC: This case was first rested on the 118th article. Articles of association, as is well known, follow the memorandum, which states the objects of the company, while the articles state the arrangement between the members. They are an agreement inter socios, and in that view, if the introductory words are applied to article 118, it becomes a covenant between the parties to it that they will employ the plaintiff. Now, so far as that is concerned, it is res inter alios acta, the plaintiff is no party to it. No doubt he thought that by inserting it he was making his employment safe as against the company; but his relying on that view of the law does not alter the legal effect of the articles. This article is either a stipulation which would bind the members, or else a mandate to the directors. In either case it is a matter between the directors and shareholders, and not between them and the plaintiff . . .

LORD COLERIDGE CJ and MELLISH LJ concurred.

➤ Notes

1. The judgments do not deal with the question whether it was relevant that Eley did take shares in the company at a later stage and so would then have become entitled to enforce whatever rights his membership conferred on him.

2. This case is commonly cited as authority for the proposition that the articles could confer rights on Eley only in his capacity as a member and not as the company's solicitor. But this reasoning forms no part of the *ratio decidendi*, and was first put forward in *Hickman*'s case [4.37].

3. The Contracts (Rights of Third Parties) Act 1999 abrogates in part the traditional doctrine of privity of contract, by providing that a term in a contract which purports to confer a benefit on a person who is not a party to it may in stated circumstances be enforced by that person. Theoretically, this provision might now have enabled a person in the position of Mr Eley to enforce a term such as art 118, but s 6(2) of the 1999 Act expressly excludes the s 33 contract from its scope.

The effect of s 33 is to bind the company itself, as well as the members, by the terms of the articles. But the contract which s 33 creates affects the members only in their capacity as members, and not in any special or personal capacity (eg as director).

[4.37] Hickman v Kent or Romney Marsh Sheep-Breeders' Association [1915] 1 Ch 881 (Chancery Division)

The defendant association was incorporated as a non-profit-making company. Article 49 of its articles of association provided that disputes between the association and any of its members should be referred to arbitration. Hickman, a member, brought this action complaining of various irregularities in the affairs of the association, including the refusal to register his sheep in its published flock book, and a threat to expel him from membership. The association was granted a stay of proceedings on the ground that the statutory provision corresponding to the present s 33 made article 49 an agreement to arbitrate, enforceable as between the association and a member.

ASTBURY J: This is a summons by the defendants to stay proceedings in the action pursuant to s 4 of the Arbitration Act 1889 [now Arbitration Act 1996 s 9]. The action is against the defendant association and their secretary Chapman, and the plaintiff, who became a member in 1905, claims certain injunctions and a declaration and other relief in respect of matters arising out of and relating solely to the affairs of the association. In substance he claims to enforce his rights under the association's articles . . . [After stating the objects of the association and reading article 49 as to arbitration, his Lordship continued:] This is a common form of article in private companies, and the objects of this association being what they are, it and its members might be seriously prejudiced by a public trial of their disputes, and if this summons fails, as the plaintiff contends that it should, these arbitration clauses in articles are of very little, if any, value.

It is clear on the authorities that if there is a submission to arbitration within the meaning of the Arbitration Act 1889, there is a prima facie duty cast upon the court to act upon such an agreement . . .

In the present case the defendants contend, first, that article 49, dealing as it does with the members of the association, in their capacity of members only, constitutes a submission within the meaning of the Arbitration Act, or, secondly, that the contract contained in the plaintiff's application for membership and the association's acceptance of it amounts to such a submission. The plaintiff contests both these propositions, and independently of the particular dispute in this case, the arguments, especially upon the first of these contentions, have raised questions of far-reaching importance.

I will first deal with the question as to the effect of article 49. [His Lordship read s 14(1) of the 1908 Act (equivalent to the present CA 2006 s 33), and referred to the long-standing dispute among leading textbook writers as to its precise effect. He continued:]

The principal authorities in support of the view that the articles do not constitute a contract between the company and its members are *Pritchard's Case*,[53] *Melhado v Porto Alegre Rly Co*,[54] *Eley v Positive Life Assurance Co* **[4.36]** and *Browne v La Trinidad*.[55]

In *Pritchard's* case the articles of association of a mining company provided that the company should immediately after incorporation enter into an agreement with De Thierry the vendor for the purchase of the mine for £2,000 and 3,200 fully paid shares. The articles were signed by the vendor and six other persons, and the directors allotted the 3,200 shares to the vendor or his nominees, but no further agreement was made with him. It was held, affirming the decision of Wickens V-C, that the articles of association did not constitute a contract in writing between the vendor and the company within s 25 of the Companies Act 1867, and that the shares could not therefore be considered as fully paid.[56] Mellish LJ in giving judgment said: 'I am of opinion that the articles of association cannot be considered as a contract in writing between De Thierry and the company for the sale of the mine to them. It may, no doubt, be the case, if no other contract was entered into, and if De Thierry signed these articles and they were acted upon, that a court of equity would hold that as between him and the company—from their acting upon it—there was a binding contract; but in themselves the articles of association are simply a contract as between the shareholders inter se in respect of their rights as shareholders. They are the deeds of partnership by which the shareholders agree inter se.'

[The discussion of *Melhado v Porto Alegre Rly Co* and *Eley v Positive Life Assurance Co* is omitted.]

In *Browne v La Trinidad* before the formation of the company an agreement was entered into between B and a person as trustee for the intended company, by which it was stipulated (inter alia) that B should be a director and should not be removable till after 1888. The sixth clause of the articles provided that the directors should adopt and carry into effect the agreement with or without modification, and that subject to such modification (if any) the provisions of the agreement should be construed as part of the articles. The agreement was acted upon, but no contract adopting it was entered into between the plaintiff and the company. It was held that treating the agreement as embodied in the articles, still there was no contract between B and the company that he should not be removed from being a director, the articles being only a contract between the members inter se, and not between the company and B . . . Lindley LJ said: 'Having regard to the construction put upon [s 33] in the case of *Eley v Positive Live Assurance Co* and subsequent cases, it must be taken as settled that the contract upon which he relies is not a contract upon which he can maintain any action, either on the common law side or the equity side. There might have been some difficulty in arriving at that conclusion if it had not been for the authorities, because it happens that this gentleman has had shares allotted to him, and is therefore a member of the company. Having regard to the terms of [s 33], there would be some force, or at all events some plausibility, in the argument that, being a member, the contract which is referred to in the articles has become binding between

---

[53] (1873) 8 Ch App 956.
[54] (1874) LR 9 CP 503.
[55] (1887) 37 Ch D 1, CA.
[56] [This section required the registration in advance of all contracts for the issue of shares for a consideration other than cash.]

the company and him. Of course that argument is open to this difficulty that there could be no contract between him and the company until the shares were allotted to him, and it would be remarkable that, upon the shares being allotted to him, a contract between him and the company, as to a matter not connected with the holding of shares, should arise.'

Now in these four cases the article relied upon purported to give specific contractual rights to persons in some capacity other than that of shareholder, and in none of them were members seeking to enforce or protect rights given to them as members, in common with the other corporators. The actual decisions amount to this. An outsider to whom rights purport to be given by the articles in his capacity as such outsider, whether he is or subsequently becomes a member, cannot sue on those articles treating them as contracts between himself and the company to enforce those rights. Those rights are not part of the general regulations of the company applicable alike to all shareholders and can only exist by virtue of some contract between such person and the company, and the subsequent allotment of shares to an outsider in whose favour such an article is inserted does not enable him to sue the company on such an article to enforce rights which are res inter alios acta and not part of the general rights of the corporators as such . . .

The wording of [s 33] is difficult to construe or understand. A company cannot in the ordinary course be bound otherwise than by statute or contract and it is in this section that its obligation must be found. As far as the members are concerned, the section does not say with whom they are to be deemed to have covenanted, but the section cannot mean that the company is not to be bound when it says it is to be bound, as if, etc, nor can the section mean that the members are to be under no obligation to the company under the articles in which their rights and duties as corporators are to be found. Much of the difficulty is removed if the company be regarded, as the framers of the section may very well have so regarded it, as being treated in law as a party to its own memorandum and articles.

It seems clear from other authorities that a company is entitled as against its members to enforce and restrain breaches of its regulations. See, for example, *MacDougall v Gardiner* **[11.04]**, *Pender v Lushington* **[11.15]** and *Imperial Hydropathic Hotel Co, Blackpool v Hampson* **[4.04]**. In the last case Bowen LJ said: 'The articles of association, by [s 33], are to bind all the company and all the shareholders as much as if they had put their seals to them.'

It is also clear from many authorities that shareholders as against their company can enforce and restrain breaches of its regulations, and in many of these cases judicial expressions of opinion appear, which, in my judgment, it is impossible to disregard.

[His Lordship referred to a number of other cases, including *Wood v Odessa Waterworks Co* **[4.35]** and *Salmon v Quin & Axtens Ltd*.[57] He continued:]

In all these last mentioned cases the respective articles sought to be enforced related to the rights and obligations of the members generally as such and not to rights of the character dealt with in the four authorities first above referred to.

It is difficult to reconcile these two classes of decisions and the judicial opinions therein expressed, but I think this much is clear, first, that no article can constitute a contract between the company and a third person; secondly, that no right merely purporting to be given by an article to a person, whether a member or not, in a capacity other than that of a member, as, for instance, as solicitor, promoter, director, can be enforced against the company; and, thirdly, that articles regulating the rights and obligations of the members generally as such do create rights and obligations between them and the company respectively . . .

In the present case, the plaintiff's action is, in substance, to enforce his rights as a member under the articles against the association. Article 49 is a general article applying to all the members as such, and, apart from technicalities, it would seem reasonable that the plaintiff ought not to be allowed in the absence of any evidence filed by him to proceed with an action to enforce his rights under the articles, seeing that the action is a breach of his obligation under article 49 to submit his disputes with the association to arbitration . . .

[57] [1909] 1 Ch 311, CA, affd [4.06].

➤ Notes

1. It is apparent that for a considerable period before *Hickman*'s case there had been uncertainty about the scope and effect of the statutory provision which is now CA 2006 s 33. The controversy centred on three related questions:

   (a) who were the parties to the 'statutory contract'—the members and the company, or just the members?

   (b) were the members deemed to have covenanted with each other, or with the company, or both?

   (c) could one member sue another directly on the contract, or could he enforce the statutory rights only through the company?

2. It is now settled that the company should be treated as a party to the contract contained in its own memorandum and articles: see *Hickman*'s case **[4.37]**. Indeed, this question has been conclusively resolved in the 2006 Act, which makes explicit mention of both the company and its members and provides that the contract may contain rights which are directly enforceable by one member against another. Also see *Rayfield v Hands* **[4.38]**, although on the question of one member enforcing rights against another, much may depend on what it is exactly that the right purports to confer.

3. But in his attempts to reconcile the decisions—or at least the results reached—in the earlier cases, it has to be conceded that Astbury J paid little regard to the actual *ratio decidendi* of some of them, and added a gloss to CA 1908 s 14(1) which appears to contradict its express wording ('*all* the provisions of the memorandum and articles of association').[58] It is really quite remarkable that so shaky a first-instance decision was tacitly accepted for the greater part of a century in relation to CA 1908 s 14(1) and CA 1985 s 14, and endorsed without any discussion by the Court of Appeal in *Beattie v E & F Beattie Ltd* [1938] Ch 708. In that case the defendant, a director, also sought to invoke an arbitration clause contained in the articles, when he was sued by his company for the return of certain sums which it was alleged had been improperly paid to him. The court ruled that since he was being sued in his capacity as a *director* and not that as a *member*, he could not rely on the 'statutory contract'.

4. *Hickman*'s case may have laid some earlier controversies to rest, but it has generated several new ones of its own.

5. First, there are a number of cases which it is not easy to reconcile with the '*qua* member' rule: eg *Pulbrook v Richmond Consolidated Mining Co* **[5.01]**, *Imperial Hydropathic Hotel Co, Blackpool v Hampson* **[4.04]**, *Quin & Axtens Ltd v Salmon* **[4.06]**. In each of these, rights more in the nature of management-rights than member-rights were enforced.

6. Second, there is an inherent conflict in the two propositions which may be deduced from the cases, viz: (a) that any member has a right to have the provisions of the corporate constitution duly observed; and (b) that s 33 cannot be relied on to enforce the rights of a non-member, or the 'outsider-rights' of one who is a member (but also a director, solicitor, etc), which the articles purportedly confer.

7. Some commentators (eg Lord Wedderburn, [1957] CLJ 194 at 212) have sought to resolve the problem by saying that a member can sue under s 33 to enforce his right to have all the provisions of the corporate constitution observed, even where this would have the consequence of indirectly enforcing 'outsider-rights', so long as he *sues* in his capacity as a member. So, for instance, a disinterested member of the Positive Life company could have sued for an injunction to restrain the company from employing any solicitor other than the constitutionally

---

[58] R Gregory (1981) 44 MLR 526 argues that for these reasons the decision in *Hickman*'s case is insupportable, and that it should be reconsidered despite its long acceptance.

appointed Mr Eley, and by the same argument Mr Eley himself, suing *qua* member, could have obtained similar relief.

8. Others would argue that a solution to the conflict lies in a narrowing of proposition (a) above, to say that it is not *every* provision of the memorandum and articles that can be enforced by a member, but only those which are of a 'constitutional' character. (This requires us to beg the question, eg by saying that the stipulation that Mr Eley should be solicitor was not part of the corporate constitution but peripheral to it.) More specifically, GD Goldberg (1972) 35 MLR 362,[59] would confine the members' statutory contractual right to that of having the company's affairs conducted by the particular *organ* of the company which is specified as the appropriate body in the Act or in the memorandum or articles of association. GN Prentice (1980) 1 Co Law 179, considers that it is necessary to go further, and ask whether the provision in question affects the power of the company to *function*: only then can a member sue to enforce a non-member right.

9. None of these arguments is really convincing, however far they may go towards reconciling the inconsistent decisions. Each of them involves writing even more by way of gloss into CA 1985 s 14 (now CA 2006 s 33) than Astbury J did, and reading more into some of the judgments than the judges themselves said. Section 14 (and now s 33) was enacted to cover a gap which was thought to have been created when the memorandum and articles replaced the deed of settlement in 1856, and in particular to ensure that a company could enforce a member's liability to pay calls. Its relevance in today's conditions may be regarded as questionable, for it perpetuates the notion that the only 'constituents' of a company are its members (ignoring the claims of employees, management and other 'stakeholders' whose interests in the company and its constituents are arguably quite as significant), and it also puts the relationship between members and company into a contractual straitjacket—a characteristically nineteenth-century approach to many difficult legal questions—which is far from appropriate. (It is also evident that the 'contract' created by s 33 departs radically in a number of respects from the contract of classic tradition: see Note 11 below.)

10. A similar gloss was put by the courts on CA 1948 s 210, the early precursor of CA 2006 s 994 (the 'unfair prejudice' provision, see below, pp 552 ff): a member bringing a complaint to the court under that section had to show that the conduct in question affected him *qua* member. Section 994, and CA 1985s 459 before it, has been re-worded so as to meet many of the criticisms which were levelled at s 210, but no attempt was made to deal with this point. The judges have accordingly been obliged to construe the new section in the same way; but (at least in cases where the company is a 'quasi-partnership') some flexibility has been achieved by giving a fairly broad meaning to the concept of a 'membership' interest. In *Ebrahimi v Westbourne Galleries Ltd* [14.14], the House of Lords did not feel constrained to put the same restriction on the statutory provision which allows a member to petition to have the company wound up.

11. Third, it is not possible to say that every 'right' which the memorandum or articles purport to confer on a member is enforceable in an absolute sense.[60] The statutory contract which these documents are deemed to create is very different from the classical stereotype, such as a contract for the sale of goods. It is a 'relational' contract,[61] intended to establish a framework for an ongoing set of relationships, rather than one containing a discrete set of obligations which, once performed, will come to an end. Relational contracts necessarily embody an underlying element of 'give-and-take', rather than outright right and wrong. Moreover, many constitutional irregularities are curable by a majority resolution of the

[59] Reaffirmed in (1985) 48 MLR 158.

[60] See RR Drury, 'The Relative Nature of the Shareholder's Right to Enforce the Company Contract' [1986] CLJ 219.

[61] On relational contracts, see IA Macneil, 'Contracts: Adjustment of Long-Term Economic Relations under Classical, Neo-Classical and Relational Contract Law' (1978) 72 North Western UL Rev 854.

members, or even capable of being condoned by acquiescence or inertia. In *MacDougall v Gardiner* **[11.04]**, for instance, a member's undoubted right to call for a poll was denied him, but the court declined to come to his aid because the matter could be put right (if anyone wanted to) by the company's own internal mechanisms. Even irregularities which the majority have no power to condone may be defeated by the procedural rule known as *Foss v Harbottle* **[11.01]**, under which the member may find that he has no access to the court unless he can carry the majority along with him **[11.14]**. Any claim that s 33 gives a member a 'right' to have the terms of the constitution observed is defective unless it acknowledges that the right is qualified in these senses.

One member may sue another on the contract created by the articles without joining the company as a party.

[4.38] Rayfield v Hands [1960] Ch 1 (Chancery Division)

Article 11 of the articles of association of Field-Davis Ltd provided: 'Every member who intends to transfer shares shall inform the directors who will take the said shares equally between them at a fair value . . . ' Rayfield, a member, sought to compel the defendants, the three directors of the company, to purchase his shares in accordance with this provision. The court declared that they were bound to do so.

VAISEY J dealt first with a question of construction, and continued:

The next and most difficult point taken by the defendants, as to which it would appear that there is no very clear judicial authority, is that article 11, as part of the company's articles of association, does not do what it looks like doing, that is, to create a contractual relationship between the plaintiff as shareholder and vendor and the defendants as directors and purchasers. This depends on s 20(1) of the Companies Act 1948 [CA 2006 s 33]. [His Lordship read the section and passages from various textbooks. He continued:]

Now the question arises at the outset whether the terms of article 11 relate to the rights of members inter se (that being the expression found in so many of the cases), or whether the relationship is between a member as such and directors as such. I may dispose of this point very briefly by saying that, in my judgment, the relationship here is between the plaintiff as a member and the defendants not as directors but as members.

In *Re Leicester Club and County Racecourse Co*,[62] Pearson J, referring to the directors of a company, said that they 'continue members of the company, and I prefer to call them working members of the company,' and on the same page he also said: 'directors cannot divest themselves of their character of members of the company. From first to last . . . they are doing their work in the capacity of members, and working members of the company . . . ' I am of opinion, therefore, that this is in words a contract or quasi-contract between members, and not between members and directors.

I have now to deal with the point for which there is considerable support in the cases, that the notional signing and sealing of the articles creates a contractual relation between the company on the one hand and the corporators (members) on the other, so that no relief can be obtained in the absence of company as a party to the suit. The defendants' case in so far as it is based on this point seems to be met by two recent decisions of the Court of Appeal. I refer first to *Smith and Snipes Hall Farm Ltd v River Douglas Catchment Board*,[63] and to the judgment of Denning LJ in that case, which was a case of a covenant made, not by or with but for the benefit of the plaintiffs, and thereby enabling them to sue without the intervention of the covenantee. Section 56 of the Law of Property Act 1925 was referred to in terms which it is not necessary for me to repeat here. This same

---

[62] (1885) 30 Ch D 629 at 633.
[63] [1949] 2 KB 500, CA.

principle is further exemplified by the case of *Drive Yourself Hire Co (London) Ltd v Strutt*,[64] see especially the judgment of Denning LJ as there reported.[65] The case of the plaintiff may also be said to rest upon the well-known decision of *Carlill v Carbolic Smoke Ball Co*,[66] to which I need not refer except to say that it seems to me to be relevant here. To the like effect is *Clarke v Earl of Dunraven*,[67] upon which the plaintiff here also relied . . .

[His Lordship discussed a number of other cases, including *Hickman*'s case **[4.37]** and continued:]

The conclusion to which I have come may not be of so general an application as to extend to the articles of association of every company, for it is, I think, material to remember that this private company is one of that class of companies which bears a close analogy to a partnership; see the well-known passages in *Re Yenidje Tobacco Co* **[14.13]**.

Nobody, I suppose, would doubt that a partnership deed might validly and properly provide for the acquisition of the share of one partner by another partner on terms identical with those of article 11 in the present case. I do not intend to decide more in the present case than is necessary to support my conclusion, though it may be that the principles upon which my conclusion is founded are of more general application than might be supposed from some of the authorities on the point.

I will make an appropriate declaration of the plaintiff's rights, or will order the defendants to give effect to them, and if necessary there must be an inquiry to ascertain the fair value of the shares . . .

➤ Notes

1. The judge in this case circumvented the difficulty raised by *Hickman*'s case **[4.37]** and *Beattie v E & F Beattie Ltd* (above, Note 3, p 236) by the blunt assertion that the article affected the directors 'not as directors but as members'. In the case before him, the directors did happen to be members, and were, in fact, required by the company's articles to hold shares. But in many companies this is not so. The judgment as a whole rather too readily assumes that directors are bound to be members—something that was more likely to be true a century ago when the *Leicester Racecourse* case was decided than it is today.

2. In *Newtherapeutics Ltd v Katz* [1991] Ch 226, Knox J held that the appointment of a person to the office of director did not of itself establish a contractual relationship between him and the company. He might, and commonly would, also enter into a contract (eg of employment) with the company; but merely as officeholder such rights and duties as he had were not based on any contract, express or implied. Vaisey J's reference to *Carlill v Carbolic Smoke Ball Co* and *Clarke v Earl of Dunraven* would not appear to be compatible with this ruling.

Potential for improvement?

CA 2006 s 33 substantially re-enacts its predecessor, CA 1985 s 14. This is despite the fact that both the Law Commissions (*Shareholder Remedies*, L Com No 246, 1997) and the CLR considered possible amendments to CA 1985 s 14, particularly with a view to defining by statute which rights are 'membership' rights (as distinct from rights which are better seen as vested in the company itself), and are accordingly rights which a member can enforce in his personal capacity. Both bodies initially toyed with, but eventually rejected, the idea of setting out in the legislation a non-exhaustive list of such 'personal' rights (eg to attend and vote at meetings

---

[64] [1954] 1 QB 250, CA.
[65] [Lord Denning's dicta in these cases were disapproved in *Beswick v Beswick* [1968] AC 58, HL. But it is arguable that the decision in *Beswick*'s case as a whole gives some support to the reasoning of Vaisey J here.]
[66] [1893] 1 QB 256, CA.
[67] [1897] AC 59, HL.

and to receive dividends). The CLR also considered whether it would be preferable to declare *all* obligations imposed by the constitution to be enforceable by individual members (subject to an exception where the complaint is trivial or where to pursue it would be pointless), unless the contrary is provided in the constitution. What are the advantages and disadvantages of each approach?

5

THE BOARD OF DIRECTORS AS AN ORGAN OF THE COMPANY

General issues

The company is an artificial legal person, and can only act through its human representatives. We saw in the last chapter that a company's constitution typically divides management power between the board of directors and the general meeting. Members cannot instruct the directors on how to exercise the powers assigned to the directors (see above, pp 175 ff). Indeed, many members of medium to large companies (but not small ones) are attracted to the corporate form precisely because it provides investment opportunities without management responsibilities (the famous 'separation of ownership and control'). Instead, management is conducted by the directors.

The 'agency problems' associated with this are obvious: the directors may use their extensive powers for their own benefit rather than for the benefit of the passive member investors. What mechanisms are typically put in place to manage this problem? As it turns out, there are relatively few imposed by law, and the detailed construction and implementation of risk management and reward strategies is left largely to individual companies to work out for themselves. Some of the external regulatory controls include:

(i) *Controls over the appointment and dismissal of directors*: CA 2006 gives members certain guaranteed rights, by far the most important being the absolute right to dismiss directors by ordinary resolution (CA 2006 s 168), although even this can be rendered ineffective by defensive voting arrangements. CA 2006 does little to impose eligibility criteria on potential directors.

(ii) *Controls over the particular division of powers between the board of directors and the members*: see above, pp 170 ff for the general issues, including the rule that changes to the constitution are reserved to the members (s 21), and below at pp 380 ff and 433 ff for particular examples in the context of capital reductions and class rights.

(iii) *Legal duties imposing minimum standards on directors' performance of their management functions*: see the next chapter, on directors' duties.

(iv) *Controls over the structure and composition of the board of directors and its sub-committees*: CA 2006 imposes few requirements, but public listed companies are subject to the 'comply or explain' regulations in the Combined Code.

(v) *Public disclosure of information about the company's directors and their activities*: eg CA 2006 provides for public registers of directors, annual accounts, directors' reports, etc, subject to certain exemptions for smaller companies.

(vi) *Service contracts and remuneration packages*: CA 2006 provides for disclosure to, and members' approval of, most of these arrangements.

(vii) *Disqualification of unfit directors, with criminal sanctions and banning for defined periods*: see Company Directors Disqualification Act 1986 (CDDA 1986), below, pp 264 ff.

Corporate governance and the Combined Code for listed companies

The relatively few legal rules relating to the appointment, tenure and remuneration of directors allow those who control a company considerable scope to look after their own interests, generally without any serious risk of being successfully challenged by the minority.[1] Even where the directors do not hold the majority of voting shares, the passive attitude of most members towards company general meetings and corporate decisions means that directors can often ensure they are re-elected when their terms expire, that their service contracts contain advantageous provisions, and that directors' fees, salaries and perks are set at an attractive level. Of these, the level of directors' remuneration came in for obvious attack and unfavourable comment.

This issue of directors' remuneration was one of the issues considered by the 'Cadbury Committee', set up in 1991 jointly by the Stock Exchange, the Financial Reporting Council and the accountancy profession under the chairmanship of Sir Adrian Cadbury to consider the subject of 'corporate governance', and particularly its financial aspects. Its report, published in December 1992, did not propose changes in the law, but the adoption on a voluntary basis by larger (listed) companies of a Code of best practice, which addressed many of these matters of public concern, including the question of directors' remuneration.

Although the Cadbury Code had no statutory backing, in practice it became virtually obligatory for listed companies to adhere to it in most respects, because the Stock Exchange made it a requirement that every company should provide a statement with its accounts indicating whether it had complied with the Code and, where it had not, to give reasons for its non-compliance.

The Cadbury Committee spawned various successor committees seeking to improve upon its work. The most important are the Greenbury (1995), Hampel (1998), and Higgs and Smith (2003) Reports. The Hampel committee, established under the chairmanship of Sir Ronald Hampel to review the working of the Cadbury Code, also undertook a consolidation exercise. Its final report, published in 1998, produced a new Code (referred to as the 'Combined Code')[2] which dealt more generally with matters of corporate governance, incorporating rules of best practice from both the Cadbury and Greenbury committees' recommendations. This Code is appended to the Listing Rules, and every listed company must include in its annual report a statement of whether it has applied the principles of the Code, how it has applied them, and, to the extent that it has not applied them, the reasons why it has not. This justifies the 'comply or explain' description of the regulatory regime.

Note that Combined Code is different from legislation in two ways. First, it is not the product of a Parliamentary process, but of a series of committees representing business and financial interests that have elaborated the Code in recent years. Secondly, the Combined Code is binding only on listed companies (by virtue of a provision in the Listing Rules) but, even then, only on a 'comply or explain' basis (see above): Listing Rule 9.8.6(5) and (6).[3]

---

[1] It is important to be aware of the differences between executive and non-executive directors (see below, p 244); appointed, *de facto* and shadow directors, see below pp 356 ff, alternate directors and nominee directors. These different categories are not mutually exclusive.

[2] This is available in its current form on http://www.frc.org.uk/corporate/combinedcode.cfm.

[3] Available on: http://fsahandbook.info/FSA/html/handbook/LR.

Regulation of listed companies by the Combined Code

The Combined Code addresses various aspects of board structure and internal management, and indicates *best practice* for improved standards of corporate governance for listed companies.[4]

Qualities of board members

For listed companies, the London Stock Exchange Listing Rules, r 3.8, requires directors collectively to have 'appropriate expertise and experience for the management of its business'. It also requires companies generally to ensure that each director is free of potential conflicts, and, where these exist, to ensure that appropriate arrangements are in place to avoid detriment to the company's interests. Rule 3.9 requires the company to consult with the Exchange at an early stage if there are potential conflicts of interest issues for any of the company's directors.

The Combined Code does not suggest (even on a 'comply or explain' basis) that directors of listed companies ought to have particular qualifications. It does, however, suggest in Supporting Principle A.3 that '[t]he board should be of sufficient size that the balance of skills and experience is appropriate for the requirements of the business and that changes to the board's composition can be managed without undue disruption.' Principle A.3.2 also suggests that smaller companies[5] have at least two independent non-executive directors, and that all other companies have at least half the board, excluding the chairman, comprising non-executive directors determined by the board to be independent. Principle A.3.1 defines 'independent'.

The Combined Code recommends the use of Nomination Committees to make recommendations to the board on all new board appointments. This committee should be chaired by the chairman of the board or by a non-executive director, and should have a majority of non-executive directors as members. The composition of the committee should be identified in the company's annual report.

The Combined Code also states that every director should receive training on the first occasion that he or she is appointed to the board of a listed company, and subsequently as necessary. The extent of training and by whom it should be given is left open.

Separation of the roles of chairman and managing director

The Combined Code takes the view that the posts of chief executive officer (CEO) or managing director (where the chief executive officer is also a director) and chairman of the board should not normally be held by the same person, and that there should be a clear and written division of responsibilities that will ensure a balance of power and authority with no one individual having unfettered powers of discretion. If the company nevertheless decides that one person should hold both posts, this should be publicly justified. In addition, a third person should be identified, a 'senior independent director' (by implication a non-executive director ('NED')), to whom the concerns of the NEDs can be conveyed.

Although the Higgs Report recommended a blanket prohibition on the CEO (or managing director) of a company subsequently being appointed chairman, the 2003 Combined Code takes a more lenient line and permits a former managing director to become chairman after consultation with the company's members.

Although it is only listed companies that are under any formal obligations concerning the Combined Code, the failure to have safeguards in place in a relatively small company drew unfavourable comments from Arden J in *Re Macro (Ipswich) Ltd* **[11.22]**.

---

[4] See P Davies, 'Post-Enron Developments in the United Kingdom' in Ferrarini et al (eds), *Reforming Company and Takeover Law in Europe*, 2004, p 183.

[5] A smaller company is one that is not included in the FTSE 350 throughout the year immediately prior to the reporting year.

Balance of executive and non-executive directors

There is a substantial practical difference between the office of a director remunerated, if at all, by the payment of directors' fees (*a non-executive director*) and that of a person who, in addition to serving as a director, holds a management or executive position within the company, whether on a full-time or part-time basis, and is paid a salary in respect of this employment (*an executive director*).

The law generally treats both categories of director similarly as a matter of principle, but the difference between an executive director and a NED can be very important in practice. For instance, an executive director is likely to have greater authority to represent the company in its dealings with third parties; to be more difficult to remove because of entitlements to substantial compensation for loss of office; to be subjected to higher standards of skill and care in the discharge of his or her duties; and, as a working 'insider', to have better access to market sensitive and other information and much greater knowledge of the company's affairs than a NED.

New significance has been accorded to the role of the NED in the Combined Code, following the recommendations of each of the contributing committees to that Code. The 2003 Combined Code now prescribes that half the number of board members should be independent NEDs in the case of FTSE 350 companies; that board committees should be dominated by independent NEDs (with the exception of the remuneration committee, which should be constituted exclusively by NEDs), and that these committees should take on more responsibilities; that NEDs should be appointed from a wider range of possible candidates; and that NED's tenure on the board can in theory run longer than nine years, subject to both a re-election process every three years and a thorough review of any decision to re-elect an NED beyond the six year mark. According to the 2003 Combined Code, NEDs will no longer qualify as 'independent' if they have held their position for longer than nine years.

Directors' remuneration

The Combined Code makes various recommendations related to remuneration of directors. It suggests that companies should have a formal and transparent policy on executive remuneration, as well as a remuneration committee consisting wholly of non-executive directors charged with responsibility for fixing the remuneration packages of individual directors. No director should be involved in deciding his or her own remuneration. Decisions on the remuneration of executive directors should be taken by a remuneration committee made up exclusively of non-executive directors (paras B.2.1 and B.2.2). The remuneration of NEDs should be set by the board itself unless the articles require this remuneration to be determined by the members (para B.2.3).

Every company's annual report should contain a statement of its remuneration policy, and details of the remuneration of each individual director. The Turnbull (1999) and Higgs (2003) reports were especially influential in strengthening the role of NEDs in the management of the company.

Despite these developments, directors' salary and benefits packages continue to attract unfavourable attention: awards that are thought to be excessive (especially if they are out of step with the performance of the company or individual in question) draw weighty criticism from the media and in Parliament. Further efforts in recent years have focused on increasing the transparency of decisions concerning director's remuneration. These requirements are reinforced by CA 2006.

Nominations Committees

The Combined Code, Main Principle A.4, states that '[t]here should be a formal, rigorous and transparent procedure for the appointment of new directors to the board'. A listed company's board should establish a nomination committee to make recommendations to the board on all new appointments (para A.4.1). A majority of the members of the nomination committee should be independent NEDs, and the chair should be either the chair of the board or an independent NED.

Combined Code provision A.7.1 requires all directors of listed companies to submit themselves for the re-election at least every three years, and sufficient biographical detail should be supplied on a person submitted for election so as to enable members to take an informed decision on the election. The rules make specific reference to the need to refresh the board and maintain the independence of non-executive directors.

> **Questions**

In *Equitable Life Assurance Society v Bowley* [2003] EWHC 2263, at [41], Langley J suggested that 'a company may reasonably, at the least, look to non-executive directors for independence of judgment *and supervision of the executive management*' [emphasis added]. Companies do not appoint NEDs without good reason; they are usually chosen for their specific expertise, experience or business connections. NEDs who provide these services can expect to be paid reasonably well for their contributions, but of course this means that they may become financially dependent on the company to a greater or less extent. Is it realistic to expect NEDs to be 'independent', and to supervise executive management? Equally, is it realistic to expect companies to appoint and pay fees to individuals who have little to offer apart from independence and a policing role?

Appointment of directors

Apart from providing that a public company must have at least two directors and a private company at least one (CA 2006 s 154), and stipulating that vacancies on the board of a public company shall not normally be filled by a single resolution appointing a number of candidates en bloc (CA 2006 s 160), the Act has little to say about the appointment of directors; and so the matter is left to the articles of the particular company.

On eligibility, in a departure from preceding law, CA 2006 allows persons over the age of seventy to act as directors of public companies without members' approval, and establishes a new *minimum* age qualification for all directors of sixteen (s 157). In addition, CA 2006 stipulates that at least one natural person must act as director of a company (s 155(1)).

A company's articles typically provide that the first directors will be appointed by the subscribers to the memorandum and that thereafter directors will be elected by the members in general meeting[6] and that a proportion, such as one-third, should retire every year but being eligible for re-election. Casual vacancies are usually filled by co-option by the remaining directors. In small companies, by contrast, the directors will very likely be appointed on a permanent basis by the articles themselves, as in *Lee's Air Farming Ltd* **[2.04]**.

In the absence of any provision in the articles, the general meeting has inherent power to appoint directors by ordinary resolution.[7] If the articles give exclusive power of appointment to a specific person or group (eg the board of directors or the vendor of a business), then the power of appointment of the general meeting is displaced, although the general meeting does have the power to change the articles.

---

[6] CA 2006 Model Articles for Private Companies, reg 17, provides for appointment by *either* the general meeting or the board of directors. There is the same provision for public companies (Model Articles, reg 19), but if the appointment is made by the directors it is subject to confirmation by the members (reg 20).

[7] *Worcester Corsetry Ltd v Witting* [1936] Ch 640.

The power of the majority to appoint directors must 'be exercised for the benefit of the company as a whole and not to secure some ulterior advantage' (see *Re HR Harmer Ltd*, below, p 555). This seems to require the general meeting to act for proper purposes.[8] Also see above, pp 204 ff.

A company's articles may legitimately confer the right to appoint the directors (or one or more of them) on a third party, such as a majority member, or the sole trader whose business was incorporated. This power may be given directly, or attached to a special class of shares (on classes of shares, see below, pp 426 ff).

If the articles do not provide for such a right in third parties, then its creation by contract may be difficult. When the members alone have the right to appoint, then the directors cannot by agreement with a stranger give the latter a power to appoint a director. Where both groups have power to appoint directors, then one group (or a subset of that group) cannot by contract usurp the powers of the other. In any event, the members have the ultimate right to dismiss any directors of whom they disapprove by ordinary resolution, and without cause (CA 2006 s 168, see below, p 256).

The appointment of a person as a director of a company does not take effect unless the person properly agrees to the appointment. If someone has been appointed, but is wrongly prevented from acting, there is authority suggesting that the director (or any member) may bring an action to enforce the right to act: *Pulbrook v Richmond Consolidated Mining Co* [5.01]). Where someone who has not been properly appointed is acting as a director, a member may sue to restrain him from continuing to act.

The appointment of *managing directors* and other *executive directors* is usually a question for the board.[9] Of course, to be eligible the appointee must be a director, appointed by the customary constitutional process; and if removed as a director for any reason, the appointee will automatically lose his management or executive office as well (see below, pp 256 ff).

[5.01] Pulbrook v Richmond Consolidated Mining Co
(1878) 9 Ch D 610 (Chancery Division)

A director was required by the company's articles, by way of qualification for the post, to hold 'as registered member in his own right' shares to the nominal amount of £500. Pulbrook had mortgaged his qualification shares, and delivered to the mortgagee an unregistered transfer. The directors, on learning of this, refused to allow him to sit on the board. Jessel MR held: (1) that he still held the shares 'in his own right'; and (2) that he had suffered an individual wrong for redress of which he could sue in his own name.[10]

JESSEL MR: In this case a man is necessarily a shareholder in order to be a director, and as a director he is entitled to fees and remuneration for his services, and it might be a question whether he would be entitled to the fees if he did not attend meetings of the board. He has been excluded. Now, it appears to me that this is an individual wrong, or a wrong that has been done to an individual. It is a deprivation of his legal rights for which the directors are personally and individually liable. He has a right by the constitution of the company to take a part in its management, to be present, and to vote at the meetings of the board of directors. He has a perfect right to know what is going on at these meetings. It may affect his individual interest as a shareholder as well as his liability as a director, because it has been sometimes held that even a director who does not attend board meetings is bound to know what is done in his absence.

---

[8] In *Theseus Exploration NL v Mining and Associated Industries Ltd* [1973] QdR 81, the court issued an interim injunction to prevent members of the company electing certain persons as directors, because there was sufficient evidence that those persons intended to use the company's assets solely for the benefit of the majority member.

[9] Recall that the functions of a managing director are not set by law: *Harold Holdsworth & Co (Wakefield) Ltd v Caddies* [3.12].

[10] See the discussion on members' personal rights, above, pp 230 ff.

Besides that, he is in the position of a shareholder, or a managing partner in the affairs of the company, and he has a right to remain managing partner, and to receive remuneration for his service. It appears to me that for the injury or wrong done to him by preventing him from attending board meetings by force, he has a right to sue. He has what is commonly called a right of action, and those decisions which say that, where a wrong is done to the company by the exclusion of a director from board meetings, the company may sue and must sue for that wrong, do not apply to the case of wrong done simply to an individual. There may be cases where, by preventing a director from exercising his functions in addition to its being a wrong done to the individual, a wrong is also done to the company, and there the company have a right to complain. But in a case of an individual wrong, another shareholder cannot on behalf of himself and others, not being the individuals to whom the wrong is done, maintain an action for that wrong. That being so, in my opinion, the plaintiff in this case has a right of action.

[His Lordship then ruled that he still held the qualification shares 'in his own right', and so had been properly elected a director. He accordingly granted an injunction.]

> Note

It is probably impossible to square all the remarks in this judgment either with the *ratio decidendi* of *Hickman's* case **[4.37]** or with the view (commonly associated with Lord Wedderburn: see his article in [1957] CLJ 194, 212) that every member of a company has a right to have the provisions of the corporate constitution observed. (On these questions, see further above, pp 230 ff and below, pp 498 ff.) The difficulties can be highlighted by supposing that in the case above the company's articles did not require a director to hold shares, and that the excluded director held none.

Eligibility for appointment as a director

The age restrictions imposed by CA 2006 have been mentioned (see above, p 245). The general law also prevents bankrupts and certain classes of individuals from acting as directors, and a company's own articles can impose further restrictions.

But, in addition, a significant aspect of the control of companies in the general public interest lies in the prohibition of certain people (as a class, or specifically) from acting as company directors. The courts may declare certain individuals disqualified from directing or managing companies by making disqualification orders or accepting disqualification undertakings under the Company Directors Disqualification Act 1986 (see below, pp 264 ff).

Further restrictions (subject to some limited exceptions) have been imposed by the Insolvency Act 1986 s 216 to prevent the '*phoenix syndrome*'. The goal is to prevent directors (including shadow directors, see below, pp 359 ff) of companies that have gone into insolvent liquidation from being directors (or in any way promoting, managing or being involved in a company or unincorporated business, whether or not as directors) that uses the same or substantially the same registered business or trading name as that used by the insolvent company during the 12 months preceding insolvency. Breach of this restriction is an offence punishable by fine or imprisonment (IA 1986 s 216). In addition, the individual may be personally liable for the debts and liabilities incurred by the company during the period that he or she is involved in its management (IA 1986 s 217). Liability is strict and ignorance is no defence.

Defective appointments and the validity of acts of directors: CA 2006 s 161

Despite all the preceding rules on appointment of directors, the acts undertaken by those acting as directors are generally valid even if the appointment is flawed. This means that third parties dealing with the company are generally protected, and the company's remedy is to take action, if appropriate, against those responsible for the appointments and those acting improperly as directors.

CA 2006 s 161 replaces the more limited provision in CA 1985 s 285, which was typically supplemented in the articles by wider terms such as those now appearing in CA 2006 s 161 (see, eg, CA 1985, Table A art 92). This rule supplements the protective provisions discussed earlier in the context of corporate contracting (see above, pp 118 ff). Third parties could only rely on CA 1985 s 285 if they had acted in good faith. The material words in the new section are identical, so presumably the same limitation will apply, even though the provision itself is silent on the issue.

Despite the breadth of the wording in CA 2006 s 161, the limitations read into its predecessor may continue to apply. In particular, defective appointment cases used to require that there must, at some stage, have been a *purported* appointment of the person to the role of director. As Lord Simonds put it in *Morris v Kanssen*:[11]

> There is, as it appears to me, a vital distinction between (a) an appointment in which there is a defect or, in other words, a defective appointment, and (b) no appointment at all. In the first case it is implied that some act is done which purports to be an appointment but is by reason of some defect inadequate for the purpose; in the second case, there is not a defect, there is no act at all. The section does not say that the acts of a person acting as director shall be valid notwithstanding that it is afterwards discovered that he was not appointed a director.

Publicity and the appointment of directors: CA 2006 ss 162 and 167

Under CA 2006, the company must: (i) register particulars about its directors with the registrar at Companies House (s 167); (ii) keep its own register of directors (ss 162–164); and (iii) keep its own register of directors' residential addresses (s 165). (Public companies must also keep a register of secretaries: ss 275, 277–279.)

It is not clear why companies still need to maintain their own registers of directors, open for inspection by members for no fee and to others for a fee, when most people searching the records prefer the anonymity of Companies House.

The separate register of residential addresses (not open for inspection) is a 2006 change, introduced because directors' addresses need no longer be filed at Companies House. Indeed, CA 2006 now contains several provisions protecting the privacy of directors' residential addresses (see ss 240–246). The change reflects a growing concern for the safety of directors and their families, especially after some of the tactics used by campaigners, particularly against directors of companies involved in the use of animals in biomedical research.

The company and its defaulting officers (including shadow directors, see below pp 359 ff) are liable to fines on conviction for any failure to comply with these provisions.

---

[11] [1946] AC 459.

Additional publicity is required about directors of public companies, especially details of salary, qualifications and experience, that appear in annual reports for the company.

Directors' service contracts

In practical terms, directors could be made virtually irremovable by negotiating for service contracts with very long terms, so that companies could then only get rid of the directors by paying prohibitive sums as compensation. A board of directors acting in collusion could see to it that every member of the board was protected in this way.

To avoid this risk, the legislation now provides that no service contract may be made to run for more than two years without the prior authorisation of the members (ss 188–189).[12] Without this approval, the relevant terms are void and a term is deemed to be included in the contract allowing the company terminate the contract at any time on reasonable notice. The rule applies to both contracts of service and contracts for services (CA 2006 s 227), and also to engagements with shadow directors (CA 2006 s 223(1)(a)).

In addition, all directors' service contracts must be open for inspection by the members (ss 227–230), and every company must give, in a note to its annual accounts, information about aggregate directors' remuneration (CA 2006 s 412). (A small company can omit this information from the accounts it files at Companies House.) All unquoted/unlisted companies must give statistical information, but are not required to identify payments to each director by name.

Remuneration of directors

Directors have no *prima facie* entitlement to remuneration.[13] Provision for payment is therefore usually made in the articles, and the appropriate decision-making process is as determined there. CA 2006 ss 188 and 189 (noted above) limit the company's power to determine its own procedures, and ss 227–30 impose disclosure obligations. Beyond these restrictions, the company is free to determine its own practices.

It is crucial for directors that there *is* clear constitutional authority for any agreements that are made, and that the proper procedures have been followed. Without these, the purported arrangements are void (see *Guinness plc v Saunders* **[5.02]**) and directors are not entitled as of right to any remuneration, whether upon a *quantum meruit*, 'equitable allowance', or otherwise. Indeed, if a person is not a director, he or she will fare better in obtaining payment for any services rendered (see *Craven-Ellis v Canons Ltd* **[5.03]**).

The power to pay directors' remuneration must be strictly observed.

[5.02] Guinness plc v Saunders [1990] 2 AC 663 (House of Lords)

In January 1986, the board of Guinness appointed a committee of three directors, Saunders, Roux and Ward, to handle the day-to-day decisions in connection with a takeover bid which Guinness had made for another company, Distillers. The bid was ultimately successful. Ward

---

[12] For companies with a stock exchange listing, the Combined Code sets a standard of terms of one year or less.
[13] *Hutton v West Cork Railway Co* (1883) 23 ChD 654, 672; *Guinness plc v Saunders* **[5.02]**.

had been paid a fee of £5.2m for his part in the bid, which he said had been agreed by the committee. The company's articles empowered the board of Guinness to fix the remuneration of individual directors, and contained several provisions allowing it to delegate various of its functions. The House of Lords declined to construe the articles in a way that invested the committee with power to pay remuneration to one of its own members, and ordered Ward to repay the £5.2m.

LORD TEMPLEMAN: . . . Mr Ward admits receipt of £5.2m from Guinness and pleads an agreement by Guinness that he should be paid this sum for his advice and services in connection with the bid. Mr Ward admits that payment was not authorised by the board of directors of Guinness.

The articles of association of Guinness provide:

Remuneration of directors.

90. The board shall fix the annual remuneration of the directors provided that without the consent of the company in general meeting such remuneration (excluding any special remuneration payable under article 91 and article 92) shall not exceed the sum of £100,000 per annum . . .

91. The board may, in addition to the remuneration authorised in article 90, grant special remuneration to any director who serves on any committee or who devotes special attention to the business of the company or who otherwise performs services which in the opinion of the board are outside the scope of the ordinary duties of a director. Such special remuneration may be made payable to such director in addition to or in substitution for his ordinary remuneration as a director, and may be made payable by a lump sum or by way of salary, or commission or participation in profits, or by any or all of those modes or otherwise as the board may determine.

Articles 90 and 91 of the articles of association of Guinness depart from the Table A articles recommended by statute, which reserve to a company in general meeting the right to determine the remuneration of the directors of the company.[14] But by article 90 the annual remuneration which the directors may award themselves is limited and by article 91 special remuneration for an individual director can only be authorised by the board. A committee, which may consist of only two or, as in the present case, three members, however honest and conscientious, cannot assess impartially the value of its work or the value of the contribution of its individual members. A director may, as a condition of accepting appointment to a committee, or after he has accepted appointment, seek the agreement of the board to authorise payment for special work envisaged or carried out. The shareholders of Guinness run the risk that the board may be too generous to an individual director at the expense of the shareholders but the shareholders have, by article 91, chosen to run this risk and can protect themselves by the number, quality and impartiality of the members of the board who will consider whether an individual director deserves special reward. Under article 91 the shareholders of Guinness do not run the risk that a committee may value its own work and the contribution of its own members. Article 91 authorises the board, and only the board, to grant special remuneration to a director who serves on a committee.

It was submitted that article 2 alters the plain meaning of article 91. In article 2 there are a number of definitions each of which is expressed to apply 'if not inconsistent with the subject or context'. The expression 'the board' is defined as 'The directors of the company for the time being (or a quorum of such directors assembled at a meeting of directors duly convened) or any committee authorised by the board to act on its behalf.'

The result of applying the article 2 definition to article 91, it is said, is that a committee may grant special remuneration to any director who serves on a committee or devotes special attention to the

---

[14] [The 2006 Model Articles for private and public companies now reserve this decision to the directors, subject to the requirements of the Act, and any other terms in the articles.]

business of the company or who otherwise performs services which in the opinion of the committee are outside the scope of the ordinary duties of a director. In my opinion the subject and context of article 91 are inconsistent with the expression 'the board' in article 91 meaning anything except the board. Article 91 draws a contrast between the board and a committee of the board. The board is expressly authorised to grant special remuneration to *any* director who serves on *any* committee. It cannot have been intended that any committee should be able to grant special remuneration to any director, whether a member of the committee or not. The board must compare the work of an individual dir-ector with the ordinary duties of a director. The board must decide whether special remuneration shall be paid in addition to or in substitution for the annual remuneration determined by the board under article 90. These decisions could only be made by the board surveying the work and remuneration of each and every director. Article 91 also provides for the board to decide whether special remuneration should take the form of participation in profits; the article could not intend that a committee should be able to determine whether profits should accrue to the shareholders' fund or be paid out to an individual director. The remuneration of directors concerns all the members of the board and all the shareholders of Guinness. Article 2 does not operate to produce a result which is inconsistent with the language, the subject and the context of article 91. Only the board possessed power to award £5.2m to Mr Ward . . .

[Lord Templeman ruled further that (i) none of Guinness's other articles conferred a power on the committee to pay Ward remuneration; (ii) Ward was not entitled to sue Guinness for professional services rendered as a solicitor; (iii) Saunders, as chairman, had no actual or ostensible authority to agree that Ward should be paid the sum; and (iv) that since the articles made express provision for the way in which directors should be remunerated, Ward had no claim by way of quantum meruit.]

LORD GOFF OF CHIEVELEY delivered a concurring opinion.

LORDS KEITH OF KINKEL, BRANDON OF OAKBROOK and GRIFFITHS concurred.

If the director's appointment is void, remuneration on a quantum merit basis may be possible.

[5.03] Craven-Ellis v Canons Ltd [1936] 2 KB 403 (Court of Appeal)

[The facts appear from the judgment.]

GREER LJ: The signatories to the memorandum and articles, being entitled to elect the first direct-ors, nominated Mr Phillip du Cros, the plaintiff, and Mr A W Wheeler as the first directors on 15 August 1928, and on 23 August the directors co-opted Sir Arthur de Cros as a director. Under the articles these directors could act without qualification for two months, but after that time they became incapable of acting as directors as none of them had acquired the necessary qualification. The only issued shares of the company were in the two signatories to the memorandum, but there is little room for doubt that these gentlemen were nominees of the du Cros'. Be this as it may it is clear that on the expiration of the two months, the directors having no qualification ceased to be directors, and were unable to bind the company except as de facto directors by agreements with outsiders or with shareholders . . . On 14 April 1931 an agreement was executed under the seal of the company, purporting to be between the company and the plaintiff, stating the terms on which he was to act by resolution of the unqualified directors. The plaintiff in this action sought to recover from the defendant company the remuneration set out in the agreement, and as an alternative, sought to recover for his services on a quantum meruit. Until the company purported to put an end to his engagement he continued to perform all the services mentioned in the agreement.

The company, having had the full benefit of these activities, decline to pay either under the agreement or on the basis of a quantum meruit. Their defence to the action is a purely technical defence, and if it succeeds the Messrs du Cros as the principal shareholders in the company, and the company, would be in the position of having accepted valuable services and refusing, for purely technical reasons, to pay for them.

As regards the services rendered between 31 December 1930 and 14 April 1931, there is, in my judgment, no defence to the claim. These services were rendered by the plaintiff not as managing director or as a director, but as an estate agent, and there was no contract in existence which could present any obstacle to a claim based on a quantum meruit for services rendered and accepted.

As regards the plaintiff's services after the date of the contract, I think the plaintiff is also entitled to succeed. The contract, having been made by directors who had no authority to make it with one of themselves who had notice of their want of authority, was not binding on either party. It was, in fact, a nullity, and presents no obstacle to the implied promise to pay on a quantum meruit basis which arises from the performance of the services and the implied acceptance of the same by the company . . .

I accordingly think that the defendants must pay on the basis of a quantum meruit not only for the services rendered after 31 December 1930, and before the date of the invalid agreement, but also for the services after that date. I think the appeal should be allowed, and judgment given for such a sum as shall be found to be due on the basis of a quantum meruit in respect of all services rendered by the plaintiff to the company until he was dismissed . . .

GREENE LJ delivered a concurring judgment.

TALBOT J concurred.

➤ Questions

1. On the purported contract with the company the plaintiff, as an 'insider', was deemed to have constructive notice both of the supposed directors' want of competence and of his own ineligibility for appointment as the managing director, because he was not a director. In the light of *Hely-Hutchinson v Brayhead Ltd* **[3.09]**, would he now be considered an 'insider'? In any event, would the protections available to third parties contracting with the company (see above, pp 118 ff and CA 2006 s 161) provide any assistance where the company has no board of directors?

2. On the *quantum meruit* claim, the judgment rests in part upon the assumption that 'the company' accepted the plaintiff's services. Which organ or agent of the company could in the circumstances be deemed to have done so? (There were some outside members.)

3. Why was this reasoning not acceptable in the context of a validly appointed director in *Guinness plc v Saunders*?

4. In *Re Richmond Gate Property Co Ltd* [1965] 1 WLR 335, Plowman J held that a managing director was not entitled to remuneration on a *quantum meruit* basis, because the articles of the company provided that a managing director was to receive 'such remuneration . . . as the directors may determine', and the company had gone into liquidation without any consideration of the matter by the directors. The existence of an express arrangement about remuneration, the judge held, ruled out any possibility of an alternative claim based on a *quantum meruit*. The case depends in part on a misunderstanding of *Craven Ellis v Canons Ltd*, and may be open to criticism on other grounds also, so that its authority is questionable. After *Guinness plc v Saunders*, how would a court decide this case?

Setting the amount to be received by a director by way of remuneration

It is permissible to pay directors remuneration when the company has made no profits, and even when the company is not solvent (subject to any other misfeasance this may involve). The amount of remuneration is for the members (or other authorised body) to fix, and need not necessarily be determined by the market value of those services. But an award of remuneration must be 'genuine' and not a 'disguised gift' or an unlawful return of capital to a member.

[5.04] Re Halt Garage (1964) Ltd [1982] 3 All ER 1016 (Chancery Division)

Mr and Mrs Charlesworth were the only directors and members of the company, and initially they had both worked in the business, drawing sums as directors' remuneration under express powers in the memorandum and articles. In 1967 Mrs Charlesworth became ill and ceased to take an active part in the business, but she remained a director and continued to draw remuneration at a reduced rate. From 1968 onwards, the company became unprofitable, and in 1971 it went into insolvent liquidation. The liquidator claimed that Mrs Charlesworth had no right to be paid after she had given up work, and also that Mr Charlesworth had been paid more than the market value of his services, and sought restitution of the sums allegedly overpaid. The payments to Mr Charlesworth were upheld, even those made after the company had ceased to be profitable. But Mrs Charlesworth was obliged to refund that part of the money paid to her which the judge held was not a 'genuine award of remuneration' but a 'disguised gift out of capital'.

OLIVER J: Now there is no presumption that directors' remuneration is payable only out of divisible profits . . .

Counsel for the liquidator does not go to the extent, in fact, of suggesting that when a company has fallen on bad times the directors must either close the business down immediately or go on trying to pull it round for nothing . . . What I think counsel's submission comes to is this, that while the company has divisible profits remuneration may be paid on any scale which the shareholders are prepared to sanction within the limits of available profits, but that, as soon as there cease to be divisible profits, it can only lawfully be paid on a scale which the court, applying some objective standard of benefit to the company, considers to be reasonable. But assuming that the sum is bona fide voted to be paid as remuneration, it seems to me that the amount, whether it be mean or generous, must be a matter of management for the company to determine in accordance with its constitution which expressly authorises payment for directors' services. Shareholders are required to be honest but, as counsel for the respondent suggests, there is no requirement that they must be wise and it is not for the court to manage the company.

Counsel for the liquidator submits, however, that if this is right it leads to the bizarre result that a meeting of stupid or deranged but perfectly honest shareholders can, like Bowen LJ's lunatic director,[15] vote to themselves, qua directors, some perfectly outlandish sum by way of remuneration and that in a subsequent winding up the liquidator can do nothing to recover it. It seems to me that the answer to this lies in the objective test which the court necessarily applies. It assumes human beings to be rational and to apply ordinary standards. In the postulated circumstances of a wholly unreasonable payment, that might, no doubt, be prima facie evidence of fraud, but it might also be evidence that what purported to be remuneration was not remuneration at all but a dressed-up gift to a shareholder out of capital . . .

This, as it seems to me, is the real question in a case such as the present. The real test must, I think, be whether the transaction in question was a genuine exercise of the power. The motive is more important than the label. Those who deal with a limited company do so on the basis that its affairs will be conducted in accordance with its constitution, one of the express incidents of which is that the directors may be paid remuneration. Subject to that, they are entitled to have the capital kept intact. They have to accept the shareholders' assessment of the scale of the remuneration, but they are entitled to assume that, whether liberal or illiberal, what is paid is genuinely remuneration and that the power is not used as a cloak for making payments out of capital to the sharholders as such . . .

[His Lordship referred to Mrs Charlesworth's illness, and continued:] The fact is that, however valuable and exacting may have been the services which Mrs Charlesworth had rendered in the

15   [In *Hutton v West Cork Rly Co* above, p 148.]

past, her continued directorship contributed nothing to the company's future, beyond the fact that she was and remained responsible as a director and was able to make up the necessary quorum for directors' meetings (of which remarkably few took place if the minutes are any accurate guide).

On the other hand, it is said that the Companies Act 1948 imposes on every company incorporated under its provisions an obligation to have a director and it contemplates that those who assume the responsibilities of office, whether they carry them out well or ill, may be paid for that service in such way and in such measure as the company's regulations prescribe or permit. Here the company's constitution conferred on it in express terms a power to award to a director a reward or remuneration for the bare fact of holding office, and that power the company purported to exercise. If it be legitimate for the company to award some remuneration, however nominal, to Mrs Charlesworth for acting as a director and taking on herself, for good or ill, the responsibilities which that office entails, at what point, counsel for the respondents asks, does it become beyond the company's power to do that which its constitution permits it to do and how can the court take on itself the discretion as to quantum which is vested in the shareholders, there being, ex concessis, no mala fides? I have not found the point an easy one, but on the view that I take of the law the argument of counsel for the respondents is very difficult to meet if the payments made really were within the express power conferred by the company's constitution.

But of course what the company's articles authorise is the fixing of 'remuneration', which I take to mean a reward for services rendered or to be rendered; and, whatever the terms of the resolutions passed and however described in the accounts of the company's books, the real question seems to me to be whether the payments really were 'directors' remuneration' or whether they were gratuitous distributions to a shraholder out of capital dressed up as remuneration.

I do not think that it can be said that a director of a company cannot be rewarded as such merely because he is not active in the company's business. The mere holding of office involves responsibility even in the absence of any substantial activity, and it is indeed in part to the mere holding of office that Mrs Charlesworth owes her position as a respondent in these proceedings. I can see nothing as a matter of construction of the article to disentitle the company, if the shareholders so resolve, from paying a reward attributable to the mere holding of the office of director, for being, as it were, a name on the notepaper and attending such meetings or signing such documents as are from time to time required. The director assumes the responsibility on the footing that he will receive whatever recompense the company in general meeting may think appropriate. In this case, however, counsel for the liquidator is entitled to submit that the sums paid to Mrs Charlesworth were so out of proportion to any possible value attributable to her holding of office that the court is entitled to treat them as not being genuine payments of remuneration at all but as dressed-up dividends out of capital . . .

[His Lordship considered the evidence, and ruled that only £10 out of the £30 per week which had been paid to Mrs Charlesworth while she was ill was genuinely 'remuneration'. He ordered her to repay the balance.]

➤ Questions

1. Mrs Charlesworth was a member. Could Oliver J have reached the same conclusion if she had not held shares?

2. Earlier in his judgment, Oliver J said:

It is commonplace in private family companies, where there are substantial profits available for distribution by way of dividend, for the shareholder directors to distribute those profits by way of directors' remuneration rather than by way of dividend, because the latter course has certain fiscal disadvantages. But such a distribution may, and frequently does, bear very little relation to the true market value of the services rendered by the directors . . . Yet it is very difficult to see why the payment of directors' remuneration, on whatever scale the company in general meeting chooses, out of funds which could perfectly well be distributed by way of dividend, should be open to attack merely because the shareholders, in their own interests, choose to attach to it the label of directors' remuneration . . .

Does this mean that different rules apply if a company has undistributed profits?

3. Could Mrs Charlesworth have kept the payments if:

   (a) the company had been solvent at the time they were made;

   (b) the members had believed that the company was solvent, when in fact it was not?

4. Could a failure to ensure that the board fixes salaries that are affordable by the company show a director's unfitness and be a ground for a disqualification order under the CDDA 1986?

5. Could a directors' (or majority members') decision to award 'excessive' remuneration be open to challenge as a 'fraud on the minority' (see below, pp 653 ff) or 'unfair prejudice' (see below, pp 552 ff)?

> Notes

1. In *Barclays Bank plc v British & Commonwealth Holdings plc* [1996] 1 BCLC at 9 Harman J said that he found the decision in *Halt Garage* difficult to accept because, in his view, it is not possible for a resolution to be held valid in part and unlawful as to the rest: the irregularity should have led to a finding that it was void *in toto*. (The Court of Appeal ([1996] 1 BCLC 1 at 26ff) did not refer to this point.) What would this have meant for the liquidator's claim?

2. The payments to Mrs Charlesworth might now be caught by IA 1986 s 238 (as a 'transaction at an undervalue', subject to the time limits fixed by that section). In an appropriate case, IA 1986 s 423 might also be applicable (this has no time limits but requires proof of an intention to put assets beyond the reach of the company's creditors). See below, pp 663 ff.

3. The reasoning of Oliver J was followed by Hoffmann J in *Aveling Barford Ltd v Perion Ltd* **[8.14]** to strike down as not 'genuine' and as an unauthorised return of capital a sale of land made at an undervalue by a company to another company controlled by its principal member. Can these cases be seen as part of an emerging a new doctrine which may be invoked where corporate assets are wrongfully depleted for the benefit of insiders?

Acting as a board of directors: meetings and decisions

Normally the board is expected to act by majority resolution on decisions taken at board meetings. After some early doubts, it is now established that the informal and *unanimous* agreement of the directors is, for all ordinary purposes, equivalent to a resolution passed at a duly convened meeting: see *Runciman v Walter Runciman plc* [1992] BCLC 1084 at 1092; *Base Metal Trading Ltd v Shamurin* [2004] EWCA Civ 1316, CA. (Recall that the same rule applies to members, see above, p 197.)

In practice, most companies have articles containing specific provisions for various forms of decision-making, so overriding the general law on meetings and unanimous assent. The articles may allow directors to record their consent to a decision in writing: see eg Model Articles for Public Companies, regs 16 and 17. The Model Articles for Private Companies go further, and allow for either majority or unanimous decisions (regs 7 and 8), with no discussion needed for unanimous decisions, and no meeting needed for majority decisions, and generally the votes of interested directors will not count towards the necessary majority (reg 14).

As with members' 'meetings', it is now also becoming generally accepted that directors' 'meetings' may be conducted by telephone or other electronic link: see above, p 192.

If the articles do not make the necessary provisions, the general law rule that unanimous informal decisions of the directors are binding may need to be relied upon. However, in *Guinness plc v Saunders* **[5.02]**[16] the Court of Appeal declined to accept that a *statutory* requirement of disclosure to a 'meeting of directors' (CA 1985 s 317(1) here; now see CA 2006 s 177) could be deemed to have been complied with simply because every individual member of the board knew of the matter. Fox LJ said ([1988] 1 WLR 863 at 868) that disclosure to 'a meeting of the directors of the company' is 'a wholly different thing from knowledge of individuals and involves the opportunity for positive consideration of the matter by the board as a body'. (For further discussion, see below, pp 298 ff.)

Removal of directors

Both the CA 2006 and a company's articles provide mechanisms for the termination of appointments of directors. The trigger may be dissatisfaction with the director's performance; but, equally, it may simply be part of the company's process of management renewal, as with directors' retirement by rotation. In addition, a director may simply resign.

Removal by the members

CA 2006 ss 168–169 provide wide powers for the removal of directors, by ordinary resolution, before the expiration of the director's period of office and notwithstanding anything in the company's articles or in any agreement between the company and the director (s 168(1)). Special formalities must be observed and a director is guaranteed certain protections (such as the right to protest his or her removal).

CA 2006 s 168 does not derogate from any other powers that might exist apart from this section (s 169(5)(b)). This means that all articles, including those that provide for dismissal of directors without the special protections inherent in s 168, remain valid (eg see below, on dismissal by the board). Nor does the section deprive the director of any compensation or damages payable in respect of the termination of the appointment as director or of any appointment terminating with that as director (s 168(5)(a)).

The intended impact of CA 2006 s 168 can sometimes be neutered, however. It is possible, although only in private companies, to put in place weighted voting rights that can make it impossible for the ordinary members to use the powers in s 168: see *Bushell v Faith* **[5.05]**. Such weighted voting is inappropriate in public companies, and impossible in listed companies (the London Stock Exchange would refuse listing).

Special voting rights may protect directors against removal under CA 2006 s 168.

[5.05] Bushell v Faith [1970] AC 1099 (House of Lords)

Bush Court (Southgate) Ltd had capital of £300 in £1 shares, with 100 shares held by Faith and each of his sisters, Mrs Bushell and Dr Bayne. Article 9 of the articles of association provided: 'In the event of a resolution being proposed at any general meeting of the company for the removal from office of any director, any shares held by that director shall on a poll in respect of such resolution carry the right to three votes per share . . .' Faith was thus able to record 300 votes and outvote his sisters, who recorded 200 votes between them, by demanding a poll on a motion to remove him from office. Ungoed-Thomas J held that art 9 was invalid because it

---

[16] The House of Lords affirmed the decision of the Court of Appeal on grounds that did not raise this question.

infringed CA 1948 s 184 (the equivalent of CA 2006 s 168), but his decision was reversed on appeal. The House of Lords (Lord Morris of Borth-y-Gest dissenting) upheld the effectiveness of the article.

LORD DONOVAN: My Lords, the issue here is the true construction of s 184 of the Companies Act 1948 [CA 2006 s 168] and I approach it with no conception of what the legislature wanted to achieve by the section other than such as can reasonably be deducted from its language.

Clearly it was intended to alter the method by which a director of a company could be removed while still in office. It enacts that this can be done by the company by ordinary resolution. Furthermore, it may be achieved notwithstanding anything in the company's articles, or in any agreement between the company and the director.

Accordingly any case (and one knows there were many) where the articles prescribed that a director should be removable during his period of office only by a special resolution or an extraordinary resolution, each of which necessitated inter alia a three to one majority of those present and voting at the meeting, is overridden by s 184. A simple majority of the votes will now suffice; an ordinary resolution being, in my opinion, a resolution capable of being carried by such a majority. Similarly any agreement, whether evidenced by the articles or otherwise, that a director shall be a director for life or for some fixed period is now also overreached.

The field over which s 184 operates it thus extensive for it includes, admittedly, all companies with a quotation on the Stock Exchange.

It is now contended, however, that it does something more; namely that it provides in effect that when the ordinary resolution proposing the removal of the director is put to the meeting each shareholder present shall have one vote per share and no more: and that any provision in the articles providing that any shareholder shall, in relation to *this* resolution, have 'weighted' votes attached to his shares, is also nullified by s 184. A provision for such 'weighting' of votes which applies generally, that is, as part of the normal pattern of voting, is accepted by the appellant as unobjectionable: but an article such as the one here under consideration which is special to a resolution seeking the removal of a director falls foul of s 184 and is overridden by it.

Why should this be? The section does not say so, as it easily could. And those who drafted it and enacted it certainly would have included among their numbers many who were familiar with the phenomenon of articles of association carrying 'weighted votes'. It must therefore have been plain at the outset that unless special provision were made, the mere direction that an ordinary resolution would do in order to remove a director would leave the section at risk of being made inoperative in the way that has been done here. Yet no such provision was made, and in this Parliament followed its practice of leaving to companies and their shareholders liberty to allocate voting rights as they pleased . . .

LORDS REID and UPJOHN delivered concurring opinions.

LORD GUEST concurred.

LORD MORRIS OF BORTH-Y-GEST (dissenting): Some shares may . . . carry a greater voting power than others. On a resolution to remove a director shares will therefore carry the voting power that they possess. But this does not, in my view, warrant a device such as article 9 introduces. Its unconcealed effect is to make a director irremovable. If the question is posed whether the shares of the respondent possess any added voting weight the answer must be that they possess none whatsoever beyond, if valid, an ad hoc weight for the special purpose of circumventing s 184. If article 9 were writ large it would set out that a director is not to be removed against his will and that in order to achieve this and to thwart the express provisions of s 184 the voting power of any director threatened with removal is to be deemed to be greater than it actually is. The learned judge thought that to sanction this would be to make a mockery of the law. I think so also.

► Notes

1. As Lord Donovan observes, companies with a listing on the Stock Exchange may not circumvent CA 2006 s 168 by provisions in their articles, for this is forbidden by the Listing Rules. *De facto*, therefore, we have one regime for listed companies and another for all other companies.

2. One important consequence of CA 2006 s 168 is that a member or group of members together holding more than half of the shares in a company may remove the board and replace it with directors of their own choice. For this reason, a take-over bid is usually made conditional upon acceptances being received which will take the bidder's holding to at least 51% of the voting shares.

3. 'Weighted voting' is not the only technique by which a director may be made irremovable, or virtually so. The draftsman of the company's articles in *Bushell v Faith* could have achieved much the same position if its shares had been divided into three classes (eg 100 'A' shares, 100 'B' shares and 100 'C' shares) and it was provided that each class of share should carry the exclusive right to appoint one director. Each member would then have had the protection of the rules relating to class rights (see below, p 433). Alternatively, the three members could have entered into a shareholders' agreement which guaranteed each of them a permanent seat on the board: see *Russell v Northern Development Corporation Ltd* **[8.01]**, in which the precedent of *Bushell v Faith* was of considerable weight.

Dismissal by the board

Articles often provide that the office of director is to be vacated if all the other members of the Board make a written request for the director's resignation. An early suggestion (since dropped) for Model Articles for Private Companies gave power to the directors only if:

> the directors decide that that person, having repeatedly and without reasonable excuse failed to participate in processes by which majority decisions may be taken, should cease to be a director.

Like all powers held by directors, exercise of this power is subject to the directors' duties to act for proper purposes, in good faith to promote the success of the company, and in a way that does not involve unacceptable conflicts of interest (see Chapter 6).

Directors acting after their office is vacated

If directors continue to act after their office is vacated, for whatever reason, their acts will generally continue to bind the company: see CA 2006 s 161(1)(c) and s 161 generally. Also see above, pp 120 ff, on a company's dealings with third parties.

Rights of directors on termination of appointment

Compensation claims for loss of office

Recall that directors have no entitlement to remuneration and generally no claim to any kind of tenure unless specifically provided for by contract. Even then, they cannot specifically enforce their rights to remain in office; they can only claim damages for breach.[17]

---

[17] The removal of a director may sometimes justify the making of a winding-up order on the 'just and equitable' ground, at least in a small company (see below, pp 653 ff), or, alternatively, amount to 'unfairly prejudicial' conduct within CA 2006 s 994 (see below, pp 552 ff).

If there is a contract between the director and the company, then dismissal from office under CA 2006 s 168 may be a breach of contract. This will be the case if the contract is for a fixed period which has not expired, or if the director is entitled to a period of notice. Alternatively (or in addition), dismissal of a person from the office of director may breach a second contract between the director and the company if the director can perform the second contract only by being a director. For example, a contract between the managing director and his company may depend upon the person continuing to be a director of the company.

The company will then be liable in damages,[18] and the damages payments may be large. This is why provision is made to ensure that members can discover the terms of their directors' contracts of service (CA 2006 ss 228–229), and why long-term contracts are subject to approval by the members (CA 2006 s 188). The cases extracted below all concern arguments that termination of a directorship was *not* a breach of contract between the company and the director.

A contract that incorporates the provisions of a company's articles is subject to the articles being altered in the usual way, although an alteration cannot have retrospective effect.

[5.06] Swabey v Port Darwin Gold Mining Co (1889) 1 Meg 385 (Court of Appeal)

The articles provided that the directors were to be remunerated at the rate of £200 per annum. In July 1888 the company passed a special resolution altering the articles so that directors were thereafter to receive £5 per month. Swabey, a director, thereupon resigned office and claimed three months' accrued fees at the old rate. Stephen J rejected his claim, but he was successful in the Court of Appeal.

> LORD ESHER MR: The articles do not themselves form a contract, but from them you get the terms upon which the directors are serving. It would be absurd to hold that one of the parties to a contract could alter it as to service already performed under it. The company has power to alter the articles, but the directors would be entitled to their salary at the rate originally stated in the articles up to the time the articles were altered.
>
> LORD HALSBURY LC delivered a concurring judgment.
>
> LINDLEY LJ concurred.

It may be a breach of contract for a company to alter its articles or to act, personally or vicariously, upon a power created by altering its articles.

[5.07] Southern Foundries (1926) Ltd v Shirlaw [1940] AC 701 (House of Lords)

In 1933, the respondent was by a written agreement appointed managing director of the appellant company ('Southern') for ten years. In 1936, after Southern had been taken over by Federated Foundries Ltd ('Federated'), Southern altered its articles so as to include, *inter alia*, a new article 8 which empowered Federated by a written instrument to remove any director of Southern. In 1937 Federated exercised this power and removed the respondent from his directorship. He sued Southern for breach of contact and Federated for wrongly procuring the breach of contract. He was awarded £12,000 damages against both defendants (a substantial

---

[18] CA 2006 s 168 does not deprive the director of any compensation or damages payable in respect of termination of the appointment as director or of any appointment terminating with that as director (s 168(5)(a)).

sum at the time, hence the appeals), and the award was upheld by the Court of Appeal (Sir Wilfrid Greene MR dissenting), and by the House of Lords (Viscount Maugham and Lord Romer dissenting).

LORD ATKIN: My Lords, the question in this case is whether the appellant company have broken their contract with the respondent made in December 1933 that he should hold the office of managing director for ten years. The breach alleged is that under the articles adopted by the company, after the agreement, the respondent was removed from the position of director of the company by the Federated Foundries Ltd. There can be no doubt that the office of managing director could only be held by a director, and that upon the holder of the office of managing director ceasing for any cause to be a director the office would be ipso facto vacated. Under the articles in existence at the date of the agreement, by article 89 the office of a director could be vacated on the happening of six various events, bankruptcy, lunacy, etc, including the giving by the director of one month's notice to resign; while by article 105 the company by extraordinary resolution could remove him from his office. I feel no doubt that the true construction of the agreement is that the company agreed to employ the respondent and the respondent agreed to serve the company as managing director for the period of ten years. It was by the constitution of the company a condition of holding such office that the holder should continue to be a director: and such continuance depended upon the terms of the articles regulating the office of director. It was not disputed, and I take it to be clear law, that the company's articles so regulating the office of director could be altered from time to time: and therefore the continuance in office of the managing director under the agreement depended upon the provisions of the articles from time to time. Thus the contract of employment for the term of ten years was dependent upon the managing director continuing to be a director. This continuance of the directorship was a concurrent condition. The arrangement between the parties appears to me to be exactly described by the words of Cockburn CJ in *Stirling v Maitland*:[19] 'If a party enters into an arrangement which can only take effect by the continuance of an existing state of circumstances'; and in such a state of things the Lord Chief Justice said: 'I look on the law to be that . . . there is an implied engagement on his part that he shall do nothing of his own motion to put an end to that state of circumstances under which alone the arrangement can be operative.' That proposition in my opinion is well-established law. Personally I should not so much base the law on an implied term, as on a positive rule of the law of contract that conduct of either promiser or promisee which can be said to amount to himself 'of his own motion' bringing about the impossibility of performance is in itself a breach. If A promises to marry B and before performance of that contract marries C, A is not sued for breach of an implied contract not to marry anyone else, but for breach of his contract to marry B. I think it follows that if either the company of its own motion removed the respondent from the office of director under article 105, or if the respondent caused his office of director to be vacated by giving one month's notice of resignation under article 89, either of them would have committed a breach of the agreement in question . . .

The question that remains is whether if the removal by the company would have been a breach by the company, the removal under the altered articles by the Federated Foundries Ltd was a breach by the company. In this matter the Master of the Rolls agreed with the other members of the Court of Appeal; but all the members of this House are not agreed. My Lords, it is obvious that the question is not as simple as in the case just considered of the removal being by the Southern Foundries Ltd; but I venture respectfully to think that the result must be the same. The office of director involves contractual arrangements between the director and the company. If the company removes the director it puts an end to the contract: and indeed the contract relations cannot be determined unless by events stipulated for in the contract, by operation of law, or by the will of the two parties. The altered article 8 which gives power to the Federated Foundries Ltd to remove from office any director of the company is, when analysed, a power to the Federated to terminate a

[19] (1864) 5 B & S 840 at 852.

contract between the Southern and its director. It is an act which binds the Southern as against its promisee; and if a wrong to the respondent if done by the Southern it surely must be a wrong to the respondent if done by the Federated who derive their power to do the act from the Southern only. If a landlord gives power to a tenant to discharge the landlord's servants, gardener or gamekeeper, it is the master, the landlord, who is bound by the consequences of that discharge whether rightful, or whether wrongful, and so involving the payment of damages . . . The action of the Federated was, I think I may say avowedly, taken for the sole purpose of bringing the managing director's agreement to an end. I do not think that it could be said that the Southern committed any breach by adopting the new articles. But when the Federated acted upon the power conferred upon them in the new articles they bound the Southern if they acted in such a way that action by the Southern on the same articles would be a breach. It is not a question of agency but of acting under powers conferred by contract to interfere with a contract between the party granting the power and a third person . . .

LORD PORTER: The general principle therefore may, I think, be thus stated. A company cannot be precluded from altering its articles thereby giving itself power to act upon the provisions of the altered articles—but so to act may nevertheless be a breach of the contract if it is contrary to a stipulation in a contract validly made before the alteration.

Nor can an injunction be granted to prevent the adoption of the new articles and in that sense they are binding on all and sundry, but for the company to act upon them will none the less render it liable in damages if such action is contrary to the previous engagements of the company. If, therefore, the altered articles had provided for the dismissal without notice of a managing director previously appointed, the dismissal would be intra vires the company but would nevertheless expose the company to an action for damages if the appointment had been for a term of (say) ten years and he were dismissed in less . . .

LORD WRIGHT delivered a concurring opinion.

VISCOUNT MAUGHAM and LORD ROMER dissented.

➤ Notes

1. A *managing director* is often both the chief executive officer (CEO) of a company and a director who works full-time for the company for a salary. The functions of a managing director are not fixed by law, but depend upon the particular terms of the appointment: *Harold Holdsworth & Co (Wakefield) Ltd v Caddies* [3.12]. As noted above, under the articles of most companies, a managing director will automatically lose office on ceasing for any reason to be a director: see eg Table A, art 84. In larger companies, there may be more than one managing, or executive, director, but there will only be one *chief* executive officer (CEO).

2. The *Shirlaw* case was followed by Diplock J in *Shindler v Northern Raincoat Co Ltd* [1960] 1 WLR 1038, where the managing director had a written service agreement appointing him for ten years. By contrast, in the case next cited, the appointment was an informal one, and the only source from which the terms of the contract could be determined was the articles themselves. There was therefore no breach of contract when the company exercised a power of removal which was expressly contained in the articles.

[5.08] Read v Astoria Garage (Streatham) Ltd [1952] Ch 637 (Court of Appeal)

The defendant company's articles included article 68 of Table A of the 1929 Act, which provided that the directors might appoint a managing director for such term and at such remuneration as they might think fit; ' . . . but his appointment shall be subject to determination *ipso facto* if he ceases from any cause to be a director, or if the company in general meeting resolve that his tenure of the office of managing director . . . be determined'. Read was appointed managing director at a salary of £7 per week by a resolution of the board. Seventeen years later the board, with the approval of the company in general meeting, gave him notice terminating his employment. It was held that he had no claim for wrongful dismissal.

JENKINS LJ: There is no record anywhere of any terms on which the plaintiff was appointed managing director beyond the minute of resolution no 4 which was passed at the first meeting of the directors by which the plaintiff was appointed managing director at a salary of £7 a week from 1 February 1932, and the articles of association of the company. The company's articles adopted Table A, with certain modifications. Amongst the articles of Table A adopted was article no 68. [His Lordship read the article.]

It is argued by Mr Harold Brown for the plaintiff that, notwithstanding the provisions of article 68, there was a contract between the plaintiff and the defendant company in the nature of a contract of general hiring—a plain contract of employment, one of the terms of which was the plaintiff's employment should not be determined by the defendant company except by reasonable notice. The judge came to the conclusion that the terms of the plaintiff's appointment were not such as to entitle him to any notice in the event of the company choosing under article 68 to resolve in general meeting that his tenure of office as managing director be determined, and, in my judgment, the judge was clearly right . . .

The directors purported by a resolution of the board to appoint him managing director. In my view, it is really clear beyond argument that the directors must be taken to have been making that appointment with reference to the provisions of article 68 of Table A—it was only under that article that they could make the appointment. Accordingly, in my view, the resolution, containing as it did no other special terms beyond the fixing of the remuneration of £7 a week, and containing nothing whatever amplifying, or inconsistent with, the provisions of article 68, must be taken to have been an appointment of the plaintiff as managing director on the terms of article 68, and accordingly it was an appointment upon terms, inter alia, that it should be subject to termination if the company in general meeting resolved that the plaintiff's tenure of the office of managing director be determined . . .

We were referred to various authorities on this topic which, in one form or another, has been fairly often before the courts. The first was the well-known case of *Nelson v James Nelson & Sons Ltd*[20] . . .

It is to be observed that this was a case in which there was an actual agreement with the plaintiff that he should be managing director for a period which was inconsistent with the unfettered exercise by the directors of their power under the articles to revoke the appointment of a managing director; and it seems to me that this is a vital distinction from the present case, in which there is no vestige of any contract beyond the minute of the resolution making the appointment and the article by reference to which, in my view, the appointment was made . . .

In my view, on the facts of this case, the position was simply that the plaintiff was appointed to be managing director in accordance with article 68 of the 1929 Table A with such tenure of office as was provided for by that article, and had no special right to receive any particular notice of the termination of his employment in the event of the company deciding to determine it and doing so by a resolution in general meeting. Accordingly, in my view, the learned judge came to a right conclusion on the plaintiff's second claim; and in the result the appeal fails on both points, and should be dismissed.

MORRIS LJ concurred.

► Note

In *Nelson v James & Sons Ltd* [1914] 2 KB 770, CA, Nelson had been appointed managing director of the company by a written agreement 'for so long as he shall remain a director of the company and retain his qualification and shall efficiently perform the duties of the said office'.

[20] [1914] 2 KB 770. [See the Note following.]

The board revoked his appointment. It did not allege any breach of the terms of the agreement but purported to rely upon a provision in the articles authorising them to do so. The company argued that in any agreement entered into by the directors for the appointment of a managing director a term must be implied giving them the right to revoke such appointment. It was held, however, that no term could be incorporated by implication from the articles into this contract so as to override its express terms, and that Nelson's dismissal was unjustified. He was awarded £15,000 damages. Is this finding consistent with the cases cited above?

Complaint that alteration of the articles is invalid as an objectionable exercise of power by the members.

[5.09] Shuttleworth v Cox Bros & Co (Maidenhead) Ltd
[1927] 2 KB 9 (Court of Appeal)

The plaintiff had been removed from the position of 'permanent' director, to which he had been appointed by the articles, in the circumstances described by Atkin LJ in his judgment. This followed the discovery of irregularities in the accounts between him and the company. He claimed his dismissal was wrongful. The Court of Appeal, affirming Avory J, upheld the validity of the company's action.

ATKIN LJ: The plaintiff was a director of the defendant company from May 1921, when the company was incorporated, until 1926. Up to 1924 he was a director on the terms of article 18, which provided that he and others should be the first directors of the company, that they should be permanent directors, and that each of them should be entitled to hold office so long as he should live, unless he should become disqualified from any of the causes specified in article 22. At that time article 22 provided that the office of director should be vacated in any of the events specified in the six clauses of the article. In 1924 the company passed an altered article by a special resolution . . . adding to the six clauses of article 22 a seventh clause: 'If he shall be requested in writing by all the other directors to resign his office.' Some ten or eleven months after article 22 was altered he was requested in writing to resign his office. He claims in this action that the clause added to the article is invalid, and that he still remains a director . . .

[The] contract that they shall be permanent directors at a salary is contained in the articles only . . . In these circumstances the proper inference appears to be that there was a contract that the plaintiff should be a permanent director, but a contract . . . which could be altered by a special resolution of the company in accordance with the provisions of the Companies Act; and inasmuch as the contract contemplated the permanent office being vacated in one of six contingencies, it is not inconsistent with the contract that the article should be altered so as to add a seventh contingency. In other words, it is a contract made upon the terms of an alterable article, and therefore neither of the contracting parties can complain if the article is altered. Consequently I cannot find that there has been any breach of contract in making the alteration.

The only other question is whether the article is upon general principles objectionable as being not honestly made within the powers of the company. Here the limits to the power of the company to alter its articles have to be considered. Certain limits there are, and they have been laid down in several cases, notably by Lindley MR in *Allen v Gold Reefs of West Africa Ltd* **[4.23]** . . . There in a reasoned and lucid judgment the Master of the Rolls uses the phrase 'bona fide for the benefit of the company'. But neither this court nor any court should consider itself fettered by the form of words, as if it were a phrase in an Act of Parliament which must be accepted and construed as it stands. We must study what its real meaning is by the light of the principles which were being laid down by the Master of the Rolls when he used the phrase . . . The only question is whether or not the shareholders, in considering whether they shall alter articles, honestly intend to exercise their powers for the benefit of the company. If they do then, subject to one or two reservations which have been explained, the alteration must stand. It is not a matter of law for the court whether or not a particular alteration is for the benefit of the company; nor is it the business of a judge to review the decision of every company in the country on these questions. And even if the question were not for the shareholders themselves, but for some other body, it must be a question of fact. In this case there is a finding of fact by the jury that the alteration was for the benefit of the company; but I do not decide the case on that ground. In my view the question is solely for the shareholders acting in good faith. The circumstances may be such as to lead to one conclusion only, that the majority of the shareholders are acting so oppressively that they cannot be acting in good faith; or, to put it in another way, it may be that their decision must be one which could [not] be taken by persons acting in good faith with a view to the benefit of the company. But these are matters outside and apart from the question, does this or that tribunal consider, in the light of events which have happened, that the alteration was or was not for the benefit of the company? With great respect to a very learned judge I cannot agree with the judgment of Peterson J to the contrary on this point.[21] In my view the passage which has been cited from the judgment of Lord Sterndale MR in *Sidebottom*'s case **[4.24]** makes it clear that in his view the ultimate decision is to be the decision of the majority of the shareholders . . .

   BANKES and SCRUTTON LJJ delivered concurring judgments.

➤ Question

In what circumstances might it be possible for directors to advance this sort of argument successfully? (See above, pp 256 ff.)

Other payments for loss of office

By contrast, any *voluntary or non-contractual* termination payment must be approved by the members (CA 2006 ss 215–222). CA 2006 s 222 specifies the remedies for breach of this requirement subject to limited exceptions. The remedies are: any such payment to the director is held on trust for the company; and, any director who authorised such payment is jointly and severally liable to indemnify the company for any loss resulting from the payment. For the avoidance of doubt, these rules do not apply to any *bona fide* payment by way of damages for breach of contract, or by way of pension in respect of past services, or any payment required to by made by virtue of the terms of the director's contract.

Directors disqualification orders

Acting in the public interest, the Secretary of State for Trade and Industry may apply to the courts to have certain individuals disqualified from acting as directors.[22] The courts have wide statutory powers to order that directors of companies that have gone into insolvent liquidation, or people who have committed serious or persistent breaches of company law, shall be banned from being directors of a company or being concerned (directly or indirectly) in their management, except with the leave of the court. The legislation on disqualification orders is consolidated in the Company Directors Disqualification Act 1986 (CDDA 1986).[23] Under this Act, the court may make an order against a person who has:

   (i)   been convicted of an indictable offence in connection with the formation or management of a company (s 2);

[21] In *Dafen Tinplate Co Ltd v Llanelly Steel Co (1907) Ltd* **[4.25]**.
[22] Or may direct the Official Receiver to make the application, if it comes under CDDA 1986 s 6.
[23] See A Walters, 'Directors' Duties: Impact of the CDDA' (2000) 21 Co Lawyer 110.

(ii)   been persistently in breach of his or her obligations under the Companies Act, eg to file returns (ss 3, 5);

(iii)   been guilty of fraud or fraudulent trading revealed in a winding up (s 4);

(iv)   been a director of a company that has become insolvent and who is found 'unfit' to be concerned in the management of a company (s 6); or similarly been found 'unfit' after a statutory investigation into the affairs of a company (s 8);

(v)   been guilty of fraudulent or wrongful trading as defined in IA 1986 ss 213–214 (s 10).

A *disqualification order* may ban the person from being a director or being concerned in the management of a company for up to fifteen years in the more serious cases (such as fraudulent trading) and up to five years in other cases (such as persistent failure to file returns with the registrar).

Of these provisions, CDDA 1986 ss 6 and 8 are of particular interest because of the statutory concept of 'unfitness', which is elaborated in CDDA 1986, Sch 1. These provisions amplify the directors' traditional common law duties of care and skill; indeed, this is a 'growth area' in which new standards of conduct are being set and a greater awareness of the responsibilities of directors is being fostered.[24]

An enormous number of cases are heard and reported in this area. Those cited below provide an illustration. Two are particularly significant. In the early decision of *Re Sevenoaks Stationers (Retail) Ltd* **[5.11]**, the Court of Appeal laid down guidelines for the exercise of this jurisdiction. And *Re Barings plc (No 5)* **[5.12]** is probably the best example of the significant role that disqualification cases are now playing in the development of the law on directors' duties of care, skill and diligence.

The DTI Insolvency Service has a special unit charged with the task of enforcing this branch of the law. Whenever a company goes into receivership, administration or insolvent liquidation, a report on the conduct of every director has to be made to the Department by the insolvency practitioner concerned (see below, p 679). Disqualifications are currently being made at the rate of about 1,200 per annum. The Registrar maintains a register of the names of those against whom disqualification orders have been made (CDDA 1986 s 18).

When the Act was introduced, it made no provision for directors to admit that their conduct justified a finding of 'unfitness' and, in effect, plead guilty to the charge brought against them. As a result, every case carried the burden and expense of a contested trial, and the resulting workloads inevitably led to delays.[25] Now disqualification can be imposed without any court hearing at all. The CDDA 1986 was amended in 2000 to allow the Secretary of State to accept *disqualification undertakings* from directors that for specified periods they will not to do any of the things normally prohibited by a disqualification order. Such undertakings have consequences identical in all material respects to disqualification orders (see CDDA 1986 ss 1A, 7(2A) and 8(2A)). In the past few years, about 77% of all disqualifications are a result of undertakings rather than court orders.

Human rights issues have arisen. In *Saunders v UK* (below, p 602), the court decided it was an infringement of human rights for statements obtained under compulsion (in company investigations) to be used as evidence in criminal prosecutions of the individual in question. Such usage is no longer allowed. Nevertheless, these statements are regularly relied on in disqualification proceedings, and both the European Court of Human Rights and UK courts have ruled that, since the nature of these proceedings is essentially civil and regulatory, not

---

[24] Especially when the possible liability of directors for wrongful trading (below, p 671) is also taken into account.

[25] This difficulty was initially overcome by judicial ingenuity: under what was known as the '*Carecraft*' procedure (named after *Re Carecraft Construction Co Ltd* [1993] 4 All ER 499), if a director was willing to concede that a finding of unfitness was appropriate, and also agree that a period of disqualification within a certain range (say, four to six years) was merited, the court could proceed on the basis of an agreed statement of facts and dispose of the case without a full hearing. This procedure remains available, but in practice it has been overtaken by the improved statutory provisions.

criminal, no violation of human rights is involved: see *DC, HS and AD v UK* [2000] BCLC 710 and *Re Westminster Property Management Ltd* [2000] 2 BCLC 396, CA.

CDDA 1986 ss 6 and 8 compared.

[5.10] Re JA Chapman and Co Ltd [2003] EWHC 532, [2003] 2 BCLC 206 (Chancery Division)

PETER SMITH J: The application is made under section 8 CDDA 86 following a report from inspectors following an investigation under section 447 of the Companies Act 1985. In the case of an application under section 8 CDDA 86 the Court has a discretionary power of disqualification against a person where it is satisfied that his conduct in relation to the company makes him unfit to be concerned in the management of a company.

This contrasts with the applications that are normally made under section 6 CDDA 86, where the Court is under an obligation to make a disqualification order against a person where such unfitness is satisfied.

There are a number of differences between the two sections. First, as I have said under the power of disqualification under section 8 the Court retains a discretionary power not to disqualify even if the Defendant's conduct is unfit. That must be read in the light of the observations of Lloyd J in *re Atlantic Computers Plc* [unreported 15 June 1998] where he observed that it would be unusual for the Court to use its discretion in this way. Second, under section 8 there is no minimum period of disqualification whereas under section 6 there is a minimum of 2 years. Third there is no limitation period for proceedings under section 8. Fourth, there is no requirement for the company to become insolvent for an application under section 8. Fifth, the application under section 8 must be made by the Secretary of State. The Official Receiver cannot apply and finally, the County Court has no jurisdiction under section 8.

Nevertheless, there are a number of similarities. I have already observed the test is the same as to unfitness. Second, it is established that the disqualification periods (if any) set out under section 6 in *re Sevenoaks Stationers (Retail) Ltd* **[5.11]** are to be applied to the period of disqualification under section 8 see *re Samuel Sherman Plc* [1991] 1 WLR 1070.

Guidelines for exercise of the jurisdiction.

[5.11] Re Sevenoaks Stationers (Retail) Ltd [1991] Ch 164 (Court of Appeal)

Cruddas, a chartered accountant, was a director of five companies which had become insolvent with a total net deficiency of £600,000. The defaults proved against him in respect of one or more of the companies included: failing to keep proper accounting records; failing to ensure that annual returns were filed and that annual accounts were prepared and audited; causing the companies to incur debts when he ought to have known that they were in severe financial difficulties; causing them to trade while insolvent; and failing to pay Crown debts in respect of PAYE and NIC contributions and VAT. The Court of Appeal upheld the judge's finding that he was 'unfit to be concerned in the management of a company' (CDDA 1986 s 6). A disqualification order for five years was imposed.

DILLON LJ: . . . [This] appeal has an importance beyond its own facts, since it is the first appeal against a disqualification order which has come to this court . . .

I would for my part endorse the division of the potential 15 year disqualification period into three brackets, which was put forward by Mr Keenan for the official receiver to Harman J in the present case and has been put forward by Mr Charles for the official receiver in other cases, viz: (i) the top bracket of disqualification for periods over 10 years should be reserved for particularly serious cases. These may include cases where a director who has already had one period of disqualification imposed on him falls to be disqualified yet again. (ii) The minimum bracket of two to five years' disqualification should be applied where, though disqualification is mandatory, the case is, relatively, not very serious. (iii) The middle bracket of disqualification for from six to 10 years should apply for serious cases which do not merit the top bracket.

I will come back to the appropriate bracket and period of disqualification when I have considered the facts and other issues.

[His Lordship discussed the facts, and continued:]

It is beyond dispute that the purpose of s 6 is to protect the public, and in particular potential creditors of companies, from losing money through companies becoming insolvent when the directors of those companies are people unfit to be concerned in the management of a company. The test laid down in s 6—apart from the requirement that the person concerned is or has been a director of a company which has become insolvent—is whether the person's conduct as a director of the company or companies in question 'makes him unfit to be concerned in the management of a company'. These are ordinary words of the English language and they should be simple to apply in most cases. It is important to hold to those words in each case.

The judges of the Chancery Division have, understandably, attempted in certain cases to give guidance to what does or does not make a person unfit to be concerned in the management of a company. Thus in *Re Lo-Line Electric Motors Ltd*,[26] Sir Nicholas Browne-Wilkinson V-C said:

Ordinary commercial misjudgment is in itself not sufficient to justify disqualification. In the normal case, the conduct complained of must display a lack of commercial probity, although I have no doubt in an extreme case of gross negligence or total incompetence disqualification could be appropriate.

Then he said that the director in question

has been shown to have behaved in a commercially culpable manner in trading through limited companies when he knew them to be insolvent and in using the unpaid Crown debts to finance such trading.

Such statements may be helpful in identifying particular circumstances in which a person would clearly be unfit. .

This is not a case in which it was alleged that Mr Cruddas had, in the colloquial phrase, 'ripped off' the public and pocketed the proceeds. On the contrary, and as the judge found, he had lost a lot of his own money . . . There was evidence that Mr Cruddas had remortgaged his home to raise money to pay creditors of the companies, and he claimed to have lost from £200,000 to £250,000 of his own money.

I turn next to the question of Crown debts. As to this the judge said:[27]

In the circumstances I am faced with admitted deficiencies of a most serious character, including in particular Crown debts in total of an order of £120,000 which were left outstanding . . . It is, in my judgment, a badge of commercial immorality to cause moneys which have been taken under force of law from third parties (PAYE deductions, after all, are taken under compulsion of law from wages which are owed to employees; VAT is taken under compulsion of law from members of the public who purchase goods as an addition to the price of the goods) to be not paid over to the Crown.

There have been differing views expressed by Chancery judges about the significance of Crown debts on a disqualification application and the phrase has tended to become something of a ritual

---

[26] [1988] Ch 477 at 486.
[27] [1990] BCLC 668 at 671.

incantation. In some earlier cases, Harman J regarded such Crown debts as 'quasi-trust moneys'. That view has not however been followed by other judges, and the official receiver does not seek to resurrect it. A different view was expressed by Hoffmann J in *Re Dawson Print Group Ltd*,[28] where he said, in a passage with which I entirely agree:

> but the fact is that, no doubt for good reasons, the Exchequer and the Commissioners of Customs and Excise have chosen to appoint traders to be tax collectors on their behalf with the attendant risk. That risk is, to some extent, compensated by the preference which they have on insolvency. There is, as yet, no obligation on traders to keep such moneys in a separate account, as there might be if they were really trust moneys. They are simply a debt owed by the company to the revenue or the Commissioner of Customs and Excise. I cannot accept that failure to pay these debts is regarded in the commercial world generally as such a breach of commercial morality that it requires in itself a conclusion that the directors concerned are unfit to be involved in the management of the company.

The official receiver cannot, in my judgment, automatically treat non-payment of any Crown debt as evidence of unfitness of the directors. It is necessary to look more closely in each case to see what the significance, if any, of the non-payment of the Crown debt is.

Mr Cruddas made a deliberate decision to pay only those creditors who pressed for payment. The obvious result was that the . . . companies traded, when in fact insolvent and known to be in difficulties, at the expense of those creditors who, like the Crown, happened not be pressing for payment. Such conduct on the part of a director can well, in my judgment, be relied on as a ground for saying that he is unfit to be concerned in the management of a company. But what is relevant in the Crown's position is not that the debt was a debt which arose from a compulsory deduction from employees' wages or a compulsory payment of VAT, but that the Crown was not pressing for payment, and the director was taking unfair advantage of that forbearance on the part of the Crown, and, instead of providing adequate working capital, was trading at the Crown's expense while the companies were in jeopardy. It would be equally unfair to trade in that way and in such circumstances at the expense of creditors other than the Crown . . .

[His Lordship reviewed the various defaults which had been established against the respondent, and fixed a disqualification period of five years.]

BUTLER-SLOSS and STAUGHTON LJJ concurred.

[5.12] Re Barings plc (No 5) [1999] 1 BCLC 433, [2000] 1 BCLC 523 (Chancery Division and Court of Appeal)

The Barings Group, a long-established banking organisation of unquestionable standing, collapsed in 1995 owing to unauthorised trading activities carried out by a single trader, Leeson, in Singapore, which resulted in massive losses. In these proceedings disqualification orders were sought against three of its former directors who were based in London. Their honesty and integrity were not challenged, but it was alleged that they had been guilty of serious failures of management in relation to Leeson's activities, thereby demonstrating such a high degree of incompetence as to justify their disqualification. More specifically: they had left Leeson in sole control of both the dealing and settlement offices in Singapore, ignoring an internal audit recommendation that the roles be separated; they had met Leeson's requests for funding on a huge scale without proper inquiry; and they had not instituted appropriate internal management controls. Jonathan Parker J, at first instance, held that the case for disqualification had been made, and his ruling was upheld on appeal.

JONATHAN PARKER J: '[E]ach individual director owes duties to the company to inform himself about its affairs and to join with his co-directors in supervising and controlling them' (see *Re Westmid*

---

[28] [1987] BCLC 601.

Packing Services Ltd [1998] 2 BCLC 646 at 653, [1998] 2 All ER 124 at 130 per Lord Woolf MR, giving the judgment of the Court of Appeal). Later in the judgment Lord Woolf MR said:

It is of the greatest importance that any individual who undertakes the statutory and fiduciary obligations of being a company director should realise that these are inescapable personal responsibilities.

This does not mean, of course, that directors cannot delegate. Subject to the articles of association of the company, a board of directors may delegate specific tasks and functions. Indeed, some degree of delegation is almost always essential if the company's business is to be carried on efficiently: to that extent there is a clear public interest in delegation by those charged with the responsibility for the management of a business . . .

But just as the duty of an individual director as formulated by the Court of Appeal in *Re Westmid Packing Services Ltd* does not mean that he may not delegate, neither does it mean that, having delegated a particular function, he is no longer under any duty in relation to the discharge of that function, notwithstanding that the person to whom the function has been delegated may appear both trustworthy and capable of discharging the function . . .

It is not in dispute in the instant case that where delegation has taken place the board (and the individual directors) will remain responsible for the delegated function or functions and will retain a residual duty of supervision and control . . . The precise extent of the ritual duty will depend on the facts of each particular case, as will the question whether it has been breached. These are matters which are in dispute in the instant case. It is the Secretary of State's case (denied by the respondents) that each of the respondents was incompetent in failing to discharge his individual duties as a director . . .

Where there is an issue as to the extent of a director's duties and responsibilities in any particular case, the level of reward which he is entitled to receive or which he may reasonably have expected to receive from the company may be a relevant factor in resolving that issue. It is not that the fitness or otherwise of a respondent depends on how much he is paid. The point is that the higher the level of reward, the greater the responsibilities which may reasonably be expected (prima facie, at least) to go with it. As Sir Richard Scott V-C said when making a disqualification order in respect of Mr Maclean (see *Re Barings plc, Secretary of State for Trade and Industry v Baker* [1998] BCLC 583 at 586):

[Counsel for the respondent] made the point that if an efficient system is in place, or if the individual in question has good reason for believing there to be an efficient system in place, the delegation within the system of functions to be discharged in accordance with the system by others cannot be the subject of serious criticism if, in the event, the persons to whom responsibilities are delegated fail properly to discharge their duties. That may be so up to a point in theory, but the higher the office within an organisation that is held by an individual, the greater the responsibilities that fall upon him. It is right that that should be so, because status within an organisation carries with it commensurate rewards. These rewards are matched by the weight of responsibilities that the office carries with it, and those responsibilities require diligent attention from time to time to the question whether the system that has been put in place and over which the individual is presiding is operating efficiently, and whether individuals to whom duties, in accordance with the system, have been delegated are discharging those duties efficiently.

In summary, the following general propositions can, in my judgment, be derived from the authorities to which I was referred in relation to the duties of directors:

(i)   Directors have, both collectively and individually, a continuing duty to acquire and maintain a sufficient knowledge and understanding of the company's business to enable them properly to discharge their duties as directors.

(ii) Whilst directors are entitled (subject to the articles of association of the company) to delegate particular functions to those below them in the management chain, and to trust their competence and integrity to a reasonable extent, the exercise of the power of delegation does not absolve a director from the duty to supervise the discharge of the delegated functions.

(iii) No rule of universal application can be formulated as to the duty referred to in (ii) above. The extent of the duty, and the question whether it has been discharged, must depend on the facts of each particular case, including the director's role in the management of the company.

[An appeal by one of the directors was dismissed: [2000] 1 BCLC 523.]

[5.13] Re Landhurst Leasing plc [1999] 1 BCLC 286 (Chancery Division)

The company, which was in the leasing finance business, had had a meteoric rise followed by a calamitous collapse. Its principal directors, Ball and Ashworth, had been sentenced to terms of imprisonment for offences of corruption and dishonesty. The present disqualification proceedings were brought against three minor players, formerly employees of the company, who had been made directors at a relatively late stage in the company's history. Despite the fact that control of the business remained very much in the hands of Ball and Ashworth and that their roles in the company's affairs continued, as before, to be essentially that of employees, it was held that they could not accept office as directors without assuming corresponding responsibilities, and that it was no answer to a charge of misconduct that they had left to others matters for which the board as a whole had to accept responsibility. Disqualification orders were made against two of the three respondents.

HART J: . . . [T]he Court of Appeal in *Re Westmid Packing Services Ltd, Secretary of State for Trade and Industry v Griffiths* [1998] 2 BCLC 646 at 653, [1998] 2 All ER 124 at 130 accepted as correct the following propositions:

> . . . the collegiate or collective responsibility of the board of directors of a company is of fundamental importance to corporate governance under English company law. That collegiate or collective responsibility must however be based on individual responsibility. Each individual director owes duties to the company to inform himself about its affairs and to join with his co-directors in supervising and controlling them. A proper degree of delegation and division of responsibility is of course permissible, and often necessary, but total abrogating of responsibility is not. A board of directors must not permit one individual to dominate them and use them, as Mr Griffiths plainly did in this case. Mr Davis commented that the appellants' contention (in their affidavits) that Mr Griffiths was the person who must carry the whole blame was itself a depressing failure, even then, to acknowledge the nature of a director's responsibility. There is a good deal of force in that point.

Closely allied to the difficulty of distinguishing the responsibilities and conduct of the individual directors from that of the board as a whole is the question of the extent to which an individual director may trust his or her colleagues. The judgment of Romer J in *Re City Equitable Fire Insurance Co Ltd* **[11.20]** is usually taken as authority for the general proposition that director may rely on his co-directors to the extent that (a) the matter in question lies with their sphere of responsibility given the way in which the particular business is organised and (b) that there exist no grounds for suspicion that that reliance may be misplaced. But even where there are no reasons to think the reliance is misplaced, a director may still be in breach of duty if he leaves to others matters for which the board as a whole must take responsibility . . .

[Dealing with the case against one of the respondents, his Lordship continued:] A director in the position of Mr Illidge from September 1991 onwards was necessarily in a difficult position, arriving in the post as he did at a time when it must have been already known to the chairman and the managing directors that the company was about to face possibly terminal difficulties and that knowledge was not being fully shared with him. In setting a standard against which his conduct must be judged for the purposes of the 1986 Act a balance must be struck between the need on the one hand not to deter honest and competent employees (as it is accepted he was) from accepting board appointment in such circumstances and the desirability on the other of reinforcing the hands of those accepting such office by emphasising that their duties require them to act with independence and courage. I have not found striking that balance easy in Mr Illidge's case. I have borne in mind the comparatively short time during which he was a director. I have also borne in mind that, where I have found him to be open to criticism, it is very doubtful whether had he acted differently the course which events ultimately took would have been significantly altered. What has caused me difficulty is deciding whether or not the cumulative effect of the omissions for which I have criticised him compel a conclusion that his conduct did not meet the standards which today are expected of a company director. That conduct appears to me to reveal a pattern . . . of acquiescence in Mr Ball's suppression of information to the auditors and to the board. I do not accept the case he now seeks to make that he was in fact at all times reassured by what Mr Ball told him. I think he well appreciated that a potentially parlous situation had developed, and was conscious that Mr Ball was not sharing that information with the non-executive directors. I consider that this situation obtained for a sufficiently long period during his directorship for it to have been a serious failure on his part not at some stage to take steps to see that the matter was raised at board level. While I have considerable sympathy for him in the position in which he found himself, I have regretfully come to the conclusion that the conduct was such as to require me to disqualify him. My regret is due to the fact that I have little doubt that in any normal context he is a man who is perfectly fit to be concerned in the management of a company.

[His Lordship made a similar finding against a second respondent, Dyer, but held that the case against a third respondent had not been made out.]

[5.14] Secretary of State for Trade and Industry v Carr [2006] EWHC 2110, [2006] All ER (D) 59

C, a director of a public listed company, settled a substantial compensation claim by F against that company for $US18 million. Then, according to the Secretary of State, C participated in false accounting processes which were intended to hide the company's real financial position from creditors, members and possible investors, making possible a more positive financial outlook than was warranted. Although C had already been acquitted of criminal charges relating to some of the conduct which the subject of the application under CDDA 1986 s 8, he was nevertheless disqualified for 9½ years.

DAVID RICHARDS J:

Disqualification

The allegations which I have held to be established amount to deliberate and dishonest conduct on the part of Mr Carr in the performance of his duties as a director of a listed company. They were not isolated acts but amounted to a sustained attempt over an extended period to conceal and misrepresent the true position as regards the claim by Ford and its settlement by the company. Both were highly material in the context of the group. It involved concealing information which, as I find, he knew should be disclosed to the board, the auditors, the Stock Exchange, and others and should be disclosed in the accounts. It further involved the use of false accounting treatments, leading to the approval and publication of accounts which he knew to be false, achieved only by misleading the auditors as to the true position. Similarly improper conduct is shown by the treatment of the Rover payment.

These are, in my judgment, very serious matters, which make a substantial period of disqualification inevitable. The top bracket of disqualification for 10 to 15 years is invoked in particularly serious cases, of which in my view this is one. My starting point is that the period of disqualification in this case should be in that bracket, subject to any counter-balancing circumstances.

Submissions were made to me on behalf of Mr Carr as to matters which I should take into account in fixing the period of disqualification. There are some to which I attach no weight. First, I attach no weight to the fact that Mr Carr lost the value of his shareholding, which over a period had cost him approximately £2 million, exceeding, as was submitted, the total value of his remuneration over his period of employment. All other shareholders also lost the value of their shares, but they were deprived by Mr Carr's conduct of the timely provision of highly material information to which they were entitled. If the group had been able to survive, the concealment of the Ford claim and settlement might well have benefited him in terms of the value of his shareholding. Mr Carr's personal financial loss does not lessen the seriousness of his conduct or the need to protect the public. At most, it can be said that he did not make money from his misconduct.

Secondly, attention was drawn on Mr Carr's behalf to the periods of disqualification for those former directors who had given undertakings at the date of the hearing. I do not regard these periods, which range from 3 to 6 1/2 years, as providing any useful guidance. Their misconduct, as summarised in the schedules to their undertakings, is not comparable in terms of the duration, scope or, save in some instances, seriousness of the case against Mr Carr. I have not seen Mr Jeffrey's undertaking or the schedule of allegations to which he has admitted. Mr Carr was not only himself closely involved in the matters which I have established against him, but he was also, as chief executive, senior to Mr Jeffrey.

There are other factors which, to a greater or lesser extent, I do take into account. First, while not agreeing to give an undertaking, his decision not to defend the application has saved time and expense for the court, the Secretary of State and witnesses. I should however note that this is not motivated by any apparent recognition of wrongdoing on Mr Carr's part, and it is in the circumstances a factor of only very slight significance. Secondly, there is no evidence or suggestion of other misconduct and he had previously enjoyed a successful career. Thirdly, and significantly, following his resignation from the company and its collapse in December 1999, both of which were well-publicised, he has had no significant management responsibilities. The disqualification proceedings did not commence until August 2004, following delivery of the Inspectors' report in January 2003. I should also take account of the period since the hearing of this application. Fourthly, before the issue of the disqualification proceedings, the Secretary of State was prepared to accept an undertaking for a period of 9 years.

In all the circumstances, I consider that a period of disqualification for 91/2 years is appropriate.

➤ Note

Other recent cases provide further illustration of the types of factors the court will consider in the context of directors' disqualification orders. It was held in *Secretary of State for Trade and Industry v Reynard* [2002] EWCA Civ 497 that a former director's conduct during the disqualification proceedings themselves could properly be taken into account by the court for sentencing purposes. Also, in *Ghassemian v Secretary of State for Trade and Industry* [2006] EWHC 1715, Lewison J held that a director's lack of cooperation with regulators (in this case, the Official Receiver and the FSA) could constitute a ground of unfitness for being a company director. Exceptionally, in *Secretary of State for Trade and Industry v Jonkler* [2006] EWHC 135, S, a former director who had previously agreed to a disqualification undertaking of five years under CDDA 1986, was released from this undertaking when the Secretary of State discontinued disqualification proceedings against her ex husband, O, on the basis that the Secretary no longer believed it was in the public interest to subject O to a disqualification order.

6

DIRECTORS' DUTIES

General issues

Directors normally have exclusive power to manage the business of the company. The advantage of a board of directors is both concentrated expertise, relative independence from the company's various stakeholders (such as members or shareholders, and executive management), and the efficiency of centralised decision-making. The disadvantage, however, is that the directors may manage the company in their own interests rather than in the interests of those they are supposed to serve. There are several ways of addressing this risk.

One option is to give more power to the members. Clearly it would not help to have the members make all the company's decisions. However, in earlier chapters we saw that certain crucial decisions are reserved to the members and that they have the power to remove the directors by ordinary resolution, with all the benefits that this implies by way of implicit or explicit threat to underperforming directors. Another option is to insist on certain governance arrangements within the board of directors and certain procedures in the decision-making process itself. Again, in the last chapter we saw that the Combined Code for public listed companies sets out rules of best practice for the composition of the board and its various sub-committees. In addition, adequate disclosure to those likely to be most affected by the activities of the directors is always helpful. That, too, is required by CA 2006, Part 15 (requirements for accounts and directors' reports, including the forward-looking '*business review*')[1] and, for larger companies, Part 16 (requirement for audited accounts).

All of these regimes are directed at creating incentives (or threats) to improve directors' performance. But the third option for dealing with the various agency problems arising from centralised decision-making is the one most familiar to lawyers: legal duties are imposed on directors which set limits within which they must exercise their powers. These legal duties are the subject of this chapter.

Historically, these duties were developed by the courts of equity, largely by analogy with the rules applying to trustees (the roles have fundamental similarities, but also certain important differences[2]). One of the most significant changes introduced by CA 2006, Part 10 is to codify these common law and equitable duties applying to directors.

Codification was recommended by the Law Commissions,[3] and the CLR published a draft code in its Final Report,[4] along with extensive commentary.[5] The primary reason for recommending

---

[1] There are few if any cases on the directors' obligations to make disclosure in this way, but reformers have certainly seen the importance of disclosure, and CA 2006 makes specific provisions which bear concentrated attention: see CA 2006, Part 15 on accounts and reports, and especially ss 415ff on the content of the directors' report, including the 'business review' provisions (s 417).

[2] Trustees must conserve property, while directors must take business risks. Trustees must act unanimously, or seek the court's guidance; but directors may act by a quorum, and must accept the principle of majority rule. See further LS Sealy, 'The Director as Trustee' [1967] CLJ 83.

[3] *Company Directors: Regulating Conflicts of Interest and Formulating a Statement of Duties* (Law Com No 261, Cm 4436, 1999), Part 4.

[4] *Modern Company Law for a Competitive Economy: Final Report*, Vol 1, Annex C.

[5] See S Worthington, 'Reforming Directors' Duties' (2001) 64 MLR 439, published before the CLR produced its final report.

codification was to make the relevant rules clear and accessible—for both directors and those affected by their decisions. CA 2006 s 170 sets out the scope and nature of the codified general duties, and these then follow in successive sections:

(i) Duty to act within powers (s 171): see below, pp 284 ff.

(ii) Duty to promote the success of the company (s 172): see below, pp 293 ff

(iii) Duty to exercise independent judgment (s 173): see below, pp 298 ff

(iv) Duty to exercise reasonable care, skill and diligence (s 174): see below, pp 300 ff

(v) Duty to avoid conflicts of interest (s 175): see below, pp 308 ff

(vi) Duty not to access benefits from third parties (s 176): see below, pp 330 ff

(vii) Duty to declare interest in a proposed or existing transaction or arrangement (s 177 and s 182): see below, pp 331.

This codification supersedes the older case law. But those cases will remain relevant to the interpretation of the new statutory provisions, since the codified duties are generally formulated in a way that quite faithfully reflects the older case law. Indeed, the rules set out in the Act are deliberately expressed at a sufficiently high level of generality so as to be capable of judicial development within their terms. Commentators have noted that all the rules are now formulated as 'duties', although it is not clear what, if any, practical significance attaches to this (although clearly Vinelott J's distinction in *Movitex v Bulfield*[6] between a 'duty' and a 'disability' will no longer be recognised).

The remedies for breach have not been codified. The common law and equitable rules are simply imported into the Act (s 178): see below, pp 334 ff. But the protective rules that allow certain activities, that might otherwise constitute breaches, to be authorised (before the event) or ratified (afterwards) have been codified. Additionally, a new ban on implicated directors voting as shareholders in ratifying resolutions (ss 180 and 239) has been included: see below, pp 347 ff. This means that many older authorities will be relegated to oblivion,[7] and others reappraised, particularly those involving small companies where the quest for 'independent' shareholders may well be a meaningless exercise.

Additional rules

In working through this chapter, do not forget that directors are subject to various other rules and regulations. CA 2006 itself imposes substantial disclosure obligations, noted above, and there are various rules that apply when directors seek funding for the company (see below, Chapters 7, 9 and 10), or make use of the company's capital and profits (see below, chapter 8). Breach of these rules may attract criminal sanctions, as well as civil ones.

The IA 1986 also empowers the court to review directors' conduct in the period leading up to insolvency, and to penalise directors who have failed to operate according to the statutory standards (see below, Chapter 14).

In addition, if a company goes into insolvent liquidation or administration, or an administrative receiver is appointed, a director whose conduct makes him 'unfit to be concerned in the management of a company' may have a disqualification order made against him (see above, pp 264 ff).

For the purpose of applying these various sanctions, the courts are free (and, in some cases, expressly directed) to assess the conduct of a director by objective standards. The context of insolvency also removes many (but not all) of the problems associated with proving causation and quantifying loss.

<hr>

[6] [1988] BCLC 104.
[7] Eg *Re Cape Breton Co* (1885) 29 Ch D 795, CA, affd sub nom *Cavendish Bentinck v Fenn* (1887) 12 App Cas 652, HL; and *North-West Transportation Co Ltd v Beatty* [4.34].

As a result of these differences, the developing law on directors' duties has in the past few decades been driven to a much greater extent by rulings under the statutory provisions just mentioned (including, to some extent, by proceedings under CA 1985 s 459 (now CA 2006 s 994, relief for 'unfairly prejudicial conduct': see below, pp 552 ff)) than by traditional case law dealing with the general duties of directors.

For example, the judgment in *Re Barings plc (No 5)* **[5.12]** (a disqualification case) contains leading statements on the duty of senior directors to ensure that proper management systems within the company are maintained. It is doubtful whether any claim against these directors would have succeeded (or even been brought) at common law (or under the new codified provisions in CA 2006), because of the difficulty in establishing that the directors' failure to discharge this duty was the cause in law of the company's loss.

Directors' duties are owed to the company

The statement that directors' duties 'are owed by a director of a company to the company' (s 170(1)) may seem unnecessary. But the notion reflects a debate that has raged for well over two decades, and maybe for most of the last century in one form or another. Indeed, historically, the argument centred on the meaning in this context of the term 'the company' (or 'the company as a whole', as it is sometimes put), so the debate may well continue, despite s 170, unless s 172 (the duty to promote the success of the company) has put matters to rest.

What lies at the heart of these debates? In relation to shareholders' or members' decisions, where similar expressions are used requiring shareholders to act in the interests of 'the company', there are *obiter dicta* equating the phrase with 'the shareholders, collectively' or 'the shareholders, present and future' (see above, pp 204 ff). This interpretation may be justifiable simply because, in most of these cases, the decision is one that primarily, if not exclusively, affects the shareholders' or members' rights and interests *inter se*. The question is more difficult with directors' decisions.

Until fairly recently, it would not have occurred to anyone to doubt that in this context, too, 'the company' meant 'the shareholders collectively' or 'the shareholders present and future', for no other interest group was recognised as having any stake in the corporate enterprise. So, for example, in cases like *Hutton v West Cork Rly Co* and *Parke v Daily News Ltd* (above, pp 148 ff), generosity to employees was held to be lawful only if it could be justified by reference to the long-term interests of the shareholders.

But in the last decade or two this view has been under attack as being increasingly out of keeping with contemporary values. It is now widely accepted that the claims of other interest groups—commonly referred to as 'stakeholders'—such as the company's workforce and its customers and suppliers, may deserve recognition as much as those of the passive investors in the enterprise. Then there are those who would go even further, and require the 'responsible company' (and its directors) to have regard to wider considerations, such as the community, the environment, charitable and other good causes and even the national interest.

The law does, of course, meet some of these demands by specific legislation: employment laws, insolvency laws, environmental laws, and so on. But company law has responded reluctantly and tentatively to the pressure for change. The few statutory provisions added to the 1985 Act were open to criticism as being merely symbolic (CA 1985 s 309—duty to have regard to the interests of employees, but giving employees no right of action), or permissive rather than obligatory (CA 1985 s 719—power to provide for company employees on cessation or transfer of the company's business); and a favourite ploy was simply to require publicity to be given to the company's policy or practice in a particular matter (eg employment of the disabled) by a statement in the directors' annual report to the shareholders (CA 1985 Sch 7). The judges, too, have largely been content to utter moralising or hortatory *obiter dicta* without making any serious attempt to frame new rules of law. On the other hand, it is probably true that there are limits to what company law, as such, can or ought to do in this difficult area. For instance, if directors were expected to have regard to the (often conflicting) claims of many different stakeholders their decisions would, in effect, be un-reviewable by any judicial or other process.[8]

The terms of reference for the CLR's work included an instruction to consider how company law could be framed so as to 'protect, through regulation where necessary, the interests of those involved with the enterprise, including shareholders, creditors and employees'. This question (referred to as the 'scope' issue) was considered at some length, primarily in the context of directors' duties. The issue pitted wide-ranging *pro-stakeholder* approaches against narrower *pro-shareholder* approaches. The *'pluralists'*, in the former camp, contended that a statement of directors' duties should oblige directors to have regard to the interests of all 'stakeholders' in the enterprise (and even, where appropriate, prioritise the interests of some stakeholders ahead of those of the shareholders). The other camp favoured retention of a shareholder-oriented approach, but conceded that this might be framed in an 'inclusive' way, so that, in assessing what might be likely to promote success of the company for the members' benefit, directors should take into account the interests of stakeholders (and wider interests, such as the environment) in so far as they believed, in good faith, that these factors were relevant. (The CLR called this approach *'enlightened shareholder value'*.) The conclusion of the CLR was that the 'inclusive' pro-shareholder approach is to be preferred, not least because the 'pluralist' alternative would pose difficulties in formulation of principles and their enforcement.[9]

CA 2006 s 172, imposing on directors a duty to promote the success of the company, adopts the enlightened shareholder value approach.

Directors' duties are rarely owed to individuals within or associated with the company

The corollary of what has just been said, is that directors do *not* generally owe their duties to anyone other than the company.[10] Nevertheless, that has not prevented shareholders, employees, creditors and other third parties from attempting to sue directors, claiming remedies for the wrongs allegedly committed by directors against them personally.[11] These claimants would

---

[8] See LS Sealy, 'Directors' "Wider" Responsibilities—Problems Conceptual, Practical and Procedural' (1987) 13 Mon ULR 164; also the well-known debate between AA Berle, Jr and E Merrick Dodd in (1931) 44 Harv LR 1049, (1932) 45 Harv LR 1145, 1365 and (1942) 9 U Chic LR 538, and JL Weiner, 'The Berle-Dodd Dialogue on the Nature of Corporations' (1964) 64 Col LR 1458; and, for a detailed exploration of the 'stakeholder', JE Parkinson, *Corporate Power and Responsibility* (1993). On the stakeholder debate generally, see Easterbrook and Fischel, *Economic Structure of Corporate Law* (Harvard, 1991), ch 1; G Kelly and J Parkinson, 'The Conceptual Foundations of the Company: A Pluralist Approach' [1998] CfiLR 174; A Alcock, 'The Case against the Concept of Stakeholders' (1996) 17 *Company Lawyer* 177.

[9] The then Secretary of State for Trade and Industry, Patricia Hewitt, in introducing the *Draft Regulations on the Operating and Financial Review and Directors' Report: A Consultative Document (London: DTI 2004)*, expressed her view of the functions and responsibilities of the modern companies, affirming the conclusion reached by the Steering Group: " . . . What are companies for? The primary goal is to make a profit for their shareholders . . . [but] we [also] expect companies to generate the wealth that provides good public services and a decent standard of living for everyone . . . Good working conditions, good products and services and successful relationships with a wide range of other stakeholders are important assets, crucial to stable, long-term performance and shareholder value . . ."

[10] See the very limited exception below, pp 278 ff.

[11] Note, however, that shareholders can sometimes pursue 'derivative claims' to enforce wrongs done *to the company*, not to the shareholders personally. And shareholders also have distinctive personal rights, and avenues for pursuing them. See below, Chapter 11.

often (but not always) have no trouble establishing a legitimate claim against the company, but if the company is insolvent, then directors with deep pockets become attractive targets.

Directors do not normally owe fiduciary duties to individual members or shareholders.

[6.01] Percival v Wright [1902] 2 Ch 421 (Chancery Division)

The plaintiffs offered to sell their shares, and the defendants (the chairman and two other directors) agreed to buy them at £12.50 per share. After completion of the transfers, the plaintiffs discovered that at the time the board had been negotiating with an outsider for the sale to him of the company's whole undertaking at a price which represented well over £12.50 per share, but this information had not been disclosed to the plaintiffs. In fact, the takeover negotiations ultimately proved abortive. The plaintiffs claimed that the directors stood in a fiduciary relationship towards them as shareholders, and sought to avoid the transfers on the grounds of non-disclosure; but the court held that there was no fiduciary relationship between directors and the shareholders individually.

SWINFEN EADY J: The position of the directors of a company has often been considered and explained by many eminent equity judges. [His Lordship discussed a number of cases dealing with directors' duties to their company, and continued:]

The plaintiff's contention in the present case goes far beyond this. It is urged that the directors hold a fiduciary position as trustees for the individual shareholders, and that, where negotiations for sale of the undertaking are on foot, they are in the position of trustees for sale. The plaintiffs admitted that this fiduciary position did not stand in the way of any dealing between a director and a shareholder before the question of sale of the undertaking had arisen, but contended that as soon as that question arose the position was altered. No authority was cited for that proposition, and I am unable to adopt the view that any line should be drawn at that point. It is contended that a shareholder knows that the directors are managing the business of the company in the ordinary course of management, and impliedly releases them from any obligation to disclose any information so acquired. That is to say, a director purchasing shares need not disclose a large casual profit, the discovery of a new vein, or the prospect of a good dividend in the immediate future, and similarly a director selling shares need not disclose losses, these being merely incidents in the ordinary course of management. But it is urged that, as soon as negotiations for the sale of the undertaking are on foot, the position is altered. Why? The true rule is that a shareholder is fixed with knowledge of all the directors' powers, and has no more reason to assume that they are not negotiating a sale of the undertaking than to assume that they are not exercising any other power. It was strenuously urged that, though incorporation affected the relations of the shareholders to the external world, the company thereby becoming a distinct entity, the position of the shareholders inter se was not affected, and was the same as that of partners or shareholders in an unincorporated company. I am unable to adopt that view. I am therefore of opinion that the purchasing directors were under no obligation to disclose to their vendor shareholders the negotiations which ultimately proved abortive. The contrary view would place directors in a most invidious position, as they could not buy or sell shares without disclosing negotiations, a premature disclosure of which might well be against the best interests of the company. I am of opinion that directors are not in that position.

There is no question of unfair dealing in this case. The directors did not approach the shareholders with the view of obtaining their shares. The shareholders approached the directors, and named the price at which they were desirous of selling. The plaintiffs' case wholly fails, and must be dismissed with costs.

[Also see *Peskin v Anderson* [2001] 1 BCLC 372, CA.]

➤ Note

Directors are subject to 'insider dealing' rules, see below, p 594. As the rules then stood, this transaction would not have been caught, since the shareholders made the offer to sell at a nominated price and the directors merely accepted. Would modern 'insider dealing' rules change the outcome? Should they?

Exceptionally, directors may owe fiduciary duties to individual members or shareholders, eg when they undertake to act as the members' or shareholders' agents.

[6.02] Coleman v Myers [1977] 2 NZLR 225 (New Zealand Court of Appeal)

The defendants were directors of a family company. The first defendant made a take-over offer to all the other shareholders and ultimately succeeded in acquiring total control of the company. The plaintiffs were minority shareholders who had reluctantly agreed to sell when the first defendant invoked statutory powers of compulsory purchase under a section equivalent to CA 2006, s 979. They then brought an action against the defendants alleging, *inter alia*, breaches of fiduciary duty owed by the defendants as directors to the plaintiffs as shareholders. Mahon J at first instance considered that *Percival v Wright* [6.01] had been wrongly decided, although he found in favour of the defendants on other grounds. On appeal, the New Zealand Court of Appeal did not regard *Percival v Wright* as having been wrong on its own particular facts, but did hold that a fiduciary relationship had existed between the directors and the shareholders in the special circumstances of *Coleman*'s case: the company was a private company with shares held largely by members of the one family; the other members of the family had habitually looked to the defendants for business advice; and information affecting the true value of the shares had been withheld from the other family shareholders by the defendants. The defendants were accordingly held liable to compensate the plaintiffs.

> In the course of his judgment, WOODHOUSE J, referring to *Percival v Wright*, said: In my opinion it is not the law that anybody holding the office of director of a limited liability company is for that reason alone to be released from what otherwise would be regarded as a fiduciary responsibility owed to those in the position of shareholders of the same company. Certainly their status as directors did not protect the defendants in a Canadian case which finally made its way to the Privy Council: see *Allen v Hyatt*.[12] The decision in that case turned upon the point that the directors of the company had put themselves in a fiduciary relationship with some of their shareholders because they had undertaken to sell shares of the shareholders in an agency capacity. But there is nothing in the decision to suggest that in the case of a director the fiduciary relationship can arise only in an agency situation. On the other hand, the mere status of company director should not produce that sort of responsibility to a shareholder and in my opinion it does not do so. The existence of such a relationship must depend, in my opinion, upon all the facts of the particular case . . .
>
> As I have indicated it is my opinion that the standard of conduct required from a director in relation to dealings with a shareholder will differ depending upon all the surrounding circumstances and the nature of the responsibility which in a real and practical sense the director has assumed towards the shareholders. In the one case there may be a need to provide an explicit warning and a great deal of information concerning the proposed transaction. In another there may be no need to speak at all. There will be intermediate situations. It is, however, an area of the law where the courts can and should find some practical means of giving effect to sensible and fair principles of commercial morality in the cases that come before them; and while it may not be possible to lay down any general test as to when the fiduciary duty will arise for a company director or to prescribe the exact conduct which will always discharge it when it does, there are nevertheless some factors that will

[12] (1914) 30 TLR 444, PC.

usually have an influence upon a decision one way or the other. They include, I think, dependence upon information and advice, the existence of a relationship of confidence, the significance of some particular transaction for the parties and, of course, the extent of any positive action taken by or on behalf of the director or directors to promote it. In the present case each one of those matters had more than ordinary significance and when they are taken together they leave me in no doubt that each of the two directors did owe a fiduciary duty to the individual shareholders.

➤ Note

A similar approach was adopted in *Re Chez Nico (Restaurants) Ltd* [1992] BCLC 192 and *Platt v Platt* [1999] 2 BCLC 745.

Directors whose company is the 'target' in a take-over bid may owe duties to their company's members or shareholders.

[6.03] Heron International Ltd v Lord Grade [1983] BCLC 244, [1982] Com LR 108 (Court of Appeal)

Associated Communications Corp. plc (ACC) was the subject of rival take-over bids from companies referred to in the judgment as 'Bell' and 'Heron'. The capital of ACC consisted of 150,000 voting shares and over 54 million non-voting shares. Article 29(A) of the company's articles provided that the transfer of any voting share could only be made to a person nominated by the directors and with the approval of the Independent Broadcasting Authority (IBA).

The judgment of the court (LAWTON, TEMPLEMAN and BRIGHTMAN LJJ) was read by LAWTON LJ: Under article 29(A) if a shareholder desires to sell his shares, it is for the directors and not the IBA to decide who shall be the purchaser and transferee . . . Thus, [if] the directors are purporting to operate under article 29(A) . . . , they must consider whether a transfer should be allowed to take place to an intended transferee. In the present case, for example, the directors as a whole were under a duty to decide whether to sanction a sale by any director of voting shares to Bell. This duty to determine which person shall acquire and be registered as the holder of voting shares in ACC is a fiduciary power which the directors must exercise in the interests of the company and in the interests of the shareholders of the company. The fact that the directors as individuals held between them a majority of the voting shares did not authorise them to reflect their individual inclinations. The directors as directors had a duty to consider whether, in the exercise of the fiduciary power vested in them by article 29, they should agree to voting shares being transferred to Bell. In the declaration which the directors signed on 11 February 1982 they appear to be unaware of the fiduciary duties imposed upon them by article 29 because they assert that they will accept the Bell offer irrespective of what advice they may be obliged to give other shareholders. They could not advise shareholders to refuse Bell's offer and, at the same time, as directors allow their own voting shares to be transferred to Bell. Either it is in the interests of ACC and of all their shareholders, voting and non-voting, that Bell should take over ACC or it is in the interests of them all that Heron should take over ACC; and it is in the interests of all shareholders that they should not be deprived of an opportunity to sell their shares to the highest bidder . . .

Where directors have decided that it is in the interests of the company that the company should be taken over, and where there are two or more bidders, the only duty of the directors, who have powers such as those contained in article 29, is to obtain the best price. The directors should not commit themselves to transfer their own voting shares to a bidder unless they are satisfied that he is offering the best price reasonably obtainable. Where the directors must only decide between rival bidders, the interest of the company must be the interests of the current shareholders. The future of the company will lie with the successful bidder. The directors owe no duty to the successful bidder or to the company after it has passed under the control of the successful bidder. The successful bidder can look after himself, and the shareholders who reject the bid and remain as shareholders do so with their eyes open, having rejected that price which the directors consider to be the best price reasonably obtainable. Thus, as a result of article 29, the directors owed a duty to the general body of shareholders who were shareholders on 13 January 1982 to obtain for the shareholders the opportunity to accept or reject the best bid reasonably obtainable.

The directors of ACC could not consistently with their duty decide to sell and transfer their individual voting shares to Bell at 66p and, at the same time, advise other shareholders to reject the Bell bid on the grounds that the price was lower than the price obtainable from Heron.

This does not mean that the directors were bound to refuse to commit themselves or to commit the company to Bell on 13 January 1982. What it does mean is that, when the directors considered the ultimatum presented by Mr Holmes à Court [a director of Bell] on 13 January 1982, they should have asked themselves whether there was a reasonable possibility of obtaining a higher bid either from Heron or a third party or from Bell, or whether it was vitally necessary, in the interests of the company and of the existing shareholders, that the Bell offer should be immediately embraced.

[His Lordship examined the evidence, and concluded that (notwithstanding the above remarks) the directors had not acted unreasonably or in breach of duty in deciding that the bid from Bell should be accepted.]

> Question

Which 'duty' was in issue here?

> Notes

1. For further cases dealing with the duties of directors in a takeover, see *Re a Company* **[13.12]** and *Dawson International plc v Coats Patons plc* **[13.13]**. These cases show that the directors' duty to the shareholders in *Heron International Ltd v Lord Grade* depended upon the special power contained in the company's article 29(A).

2. Also see *Mills v Mills* **[6.10]**, in which it was recognised that in matters affecting the relative rights of different categories of members or shareholders, where no considerations of the paramount interest of the company as a corporate body arise, the directors owe a duty to act fairly as between the different classes of shareholders.

Directors' 'duties' to creditors

There are *obiter dicta* in a number of cases to the effect that directors owe a duty to have regard to the interests of *creditors* of their company. Sometimes this is put more loosely as a duty *owed to* the creditors.[13] But in many other cases the suggestion that directors owe a duty to creditors is emphatically rejected: see eg *Re Halt Garage (1964) Ltd* **[5.04]**; *Re Horsley & Weight Ltd* **[3.05]**; the *Multinational Gas* case **[6.25]**; and *Kuwait Asia Bank EC v National Mutual Life Nominees Ltd* **[6.31]**.

---

[13] There is an extensive literature on this topic. See eg LS Sealy, 'Directors' "Wider" Responsibilities—Problems Conceptual, Practical and Procedural' (1987) 13 Monash L Rev 164; S Worthington, 'Directors' Duties, Creditors' Rights and Shareholder Intervention' (1991) 18 Melbourne University Law Review 121; R Grantham, 'The Judicial Extension of Directors' Duties to Creditors' [1991] JBL 1; A Keay, 'The Duty of Diectors to Take Account of Creditors' Interests: Has It any Role to Play?' [2002] JBL 379; Hirt, 'The Wrongful Trading Remedy in UK Law: Classification, Application and Practical Significance' (2004) 1 *European Company and Financial Law Review* 71; Davies, 'Directors' Creditor-Regarding Duties' (2006) 7 *European Business Organization Law Review* 301.

Each of these statements must be taken in its context. It would be contrary to all reason to burden directors with any duty towards creditors when the company is solvent: their function is to make judgements about business risks, and to take those risks—and usually, when negotiating with outside parties, to drive as hard a bargain as they can. Similarly, creditors cannot expect their business with a solvent company to be preferred over other stakeholders—or, in the limit, to be risk free. Those who give credit to limited liability companies are taken to be aware of this. The dicta in the four cases cited above confirm this. Moreover, the law gives no standing to the creditors, individually or collectively, to sue to redress a breach of any such supposed duty: *Yukong Line Ltd of Korea v Rendsburg Investments Corpn of Liberia* [1998] 2 BCLC 485.

The picture is different when a company is insolvent, or nearly so. It is in keeping with trends in the law of insolvency (eg in relation to 'wrongful trading': see below, p 671) for a judge to say that the directors of an ailing company must have regard to the interests of the company's creditors—not because any duty directly owed to the creditors has come into being,[14] but because it is the creditors' position in the company's liquidation which will be affected by the directors' acts. Even so, the only duty of the directors that the law is able to recognise continues to be that owed to the company as confirmed by the *Yukong* case (above). Further, it is only indirectly, through a liquidator acting on behalf of the company (or an administrator or, perhaps, a receiver), that the creditors' interests are represented.

Judicial statements that directors are obliged to have regard to the interests of their company's creditors will be found invariably to have been made in the context just described. See the cases below.

[6.04] Kinsela v Russell Kinsela Pty Ltd (1986) 10 ACLR 395 (NSW CA)

STREET CJ: The learned judge at first instance held, as I have noted, that he was bound by authority to hold that the approval by all the shareholders validated an action which would otherwise be beyond the powers of the directors provided that there had been a full and frank disclosure to the shareholders of all the circumstances relevant to the proposed transaction . . .

The authorities to which His Honour submitted, notwithstanding the generality of their enunciations of principle, were not intended to, and do not, apply in a situation in which the interests of the company as a whole involve the rights of creditors as distinct from the rights of shareholders. In a solvent company the proprietary interests of the shareholders entitle them as a general body to be regarded as the company when questions of the duty of directors arise. If, as a general body, they authorise or ratify a particular action of the directors, there can be no challenge to the validity of what the directors have done. But where a company is insolvent the interests of the creditors intrude. They become prospectively entitled, through the mechanism of liquidation, to displace the power of the shareholders and directors to deal with the company's assets. It is in a practical sense their assets and not the shareholders' assets that, through the medium of the company, are under the management of the directors pending their liquidation, return to solvency, or the imposition of some alternative administration . . .

It is, to my mind, legally and logically acceptable to recognise that, where directors are involved in a breach of their duty to the company affecting the interests of shareholders, then shareholders can either authorise that breach in prospect or ratify it in retrospect. Where, however, the interests at risk are those of creditors I see no reason in law or in logic to recognise that the shareholders can authorise the breach. Once it is accepted, as in my view it must be, that the directors' duty to a company as a whole extends in an insolvency context to not prejudicing the interests of creditors . . . the shareholders do not have the power or authority to absolve the directors from that breach.

---

[14] *Dicta* to this effect in *Nicholson v Permakraft (NZ) Ltd* [1985] 1 NZLR 242 at 249, per Cooke J are, it is submitted, too wide.

➤ **Note**

This case clearly has relevance for issues of ratification, discussed below, pp 348 ff.

[6.05] Winkworth v Edward Baron Development Co Ltd
[1986] 1 WLR 1512 (House of Lords)

LORD TEMPLEMAN: [A] company owes a duty to its creditors, present and future. The company is not bound to pay off every debt as soon as it is incurred, and the company is not obliged to avoid all ventures which involve an element of risk, but the company owes a duty to its creditors to keep its property inviolate and available for the repayment of its debts. The conscience of the company, as well as its management, is confided to its directors. A duty is owed by the directors to the company and to the creditors of the company to ensure that the affairs of the company are properly adminis-tered and that its property is not dissipated or exploited for the benefit of the directors themselves to the prejudice of the creditors.

The new duty to promote the success of the company for the benefit of its members, incorpo-rated in CA 2006 s 172(1), is made subject to 'any enactment or rule of law requiring directors, in certain circumstances, to consider or act in the interests of creditors of the company' (s 172(3)). In this context, see IA 1986 s 214, below, p 671.

Directors' 'duties' to employees

CA 1985 s 309(1) (the predecessor of CA 2006 s 172(1)(b)[15]) provided that 'the matters to which the directors of a company are to have regard in the performance of their functions include the interests of the company's employees in general, as well as the interests of its members'. Much of the interest in this provision centred on the question of enforcement. It is plain from the wording that the directors are not merely *permitted* to consider the employees' interest but *bound* to do so; but the border line between 'may' and 'must' in this context is probably meaningless, for there is no requirement that the interests of the employ-ees should be *preferred* to those of the members. Additionally, there will be many cases in which a decision adverse to the employees will be justifiable by reference to the benefits of long term profitability and thus the interests of the members. However, this is an argument that can cut both ways: a decision that is unpopular with the members or shareholders or adverse to their interest may also be defended because in reaching it the directors took account of its effect on the company's employees. In *Re Welfab Engineers Ltd* [1990] BCLC 833, the company's liquidator alleged that the company's directors, faced with insolvency, had improperly sold the company's business for less than its full value. But Hoffmann J held them not liable because the purchaser was prepared to take on the company's workforce and work in progress, whereas another, higher, offer which they might have been able to accept was for the company's freehold premises alone, and would have led to all the employees being made redundant.

➤ **Questions**

1. What difference does an enactment such as CA 1985 s 309(1) or CA 2006 s 172(1)(b) make in theory or in practice to company law?

2. The CLR described CA 1985 s 309 as 'ambiguous and unsatisfactory', but its repeal as 'nei-ther desirable nor politically sustainable'. Has CA 2006 s 172(1)(b) resolved the issues?

---

[15] See Lord Wedderburn, 'Employees, Partnership and Company Law' (2002) 31 ILJ 99.

3. In so far as directors may be said to be under a duty to have regard to the interests of creditors, do shareholders have a similar duty? (See *Re Halt Garage (1964) Ltd* **[5.04]**, and contrast the *Kuwait Asia Bank* case **[6.31]**.)

Scope and nature of directors' general duties: CA 2006 s 170

The next sections of this chapter examine, in turn, each of the general duties imposed by CA 2006, Part 10, ss 170ff.[16] The provisions themselves are not generally repeated in the text. It is essential, therefore, to have a copy of the Act close at hand.

Section 170 restates the fundamental principle that directors' duties are owed to the company (see above). This means that only the company can bring actions for a breach of these duties. Such actions may be initiated on behalf of the company by the board of directors, a liquidator, etc, or by means of a derivative action (see below, pp 535 ff).

Section 250 defines 'director' as including 'any person occupying the position of director, by whatever name called'. This means these general duties apply equally to *de facto* directors. The position with *shadow directors* (see below, pp 359 ff)is less clear. Section 170(5) says shadow directors are subject to the duties to the same extent that, before the Act, they were subject to the corresponding common law rules and equitable principles. The difficult decision is thus left to the courts. For example, the mere fact that a person is a shadow director, and exercises indirect influence, is not enough to impose fiduciary duties: the facts must go further and suggest that there is a fiduciary relationship (*Ultraframe (UK) Ltd v Fielding* [2005] EWHC 1638).

In addition, the duties in ss 175 (conflicts of interest) and 176 (benefits from third parties) *may* continue after a person has ceased to be a director, but they apply only 'to the extent stated' in s 710(2), and 'subject to any necessary adaptation', indicating that the courts may be flexible. Existing case law is likely to remain relevant, but this provision offers some clarification: see *Industrial Development Consultants Ltd v Cooley*, below, p 325; *CMS Dolphin Ltd v Simonet* **[6.19]**.

Importantly, s 170(3) explains that these general statutory duties replace the common law rules and equitable principles from which they are derived. Actions against directors will have to be based on breach of some statutory provision, not breach of related common law rules and equitable principles. But s 170(4) then provides a new way of interpreting and applying the statute. It requires the court to have regard to the existing interpretation and the continuing development of the common law rules and equitable principles on which the statutory statement is based. This is not normally allowed. In Grand Committee Lord Goldsmith explained the Government's intention:

> Although the duties in relation to directors have developed in a distinctive way, they are often manifestations of more general principles. Subsection (4) is intended to enable the courts to continue to have regard to developments in the common law rules and equitable principles applying to these other types of fiduciary relationship. The advantage of that is that it will enable the statutory duties to develop in line with relevant developments in the law as it applies elsewhere. (HL GC Day 3, Hansard HL 678 6/2/06 Cols 243–245)

The practical effect of this is that reference will have to be made to the statutory statement of duties, but in order to understand and apply these duties the surrounding case law must also

---

[16] These parts draw on contributions made earlier to *Palmer's Company Law Annotated Guide to the Companies Act 2006* (2007).

be read. Practitioners and judges will therefore continue to be required to refer back to the cases.

Duty to act within powers: CA 2006 s 171

Section 171 requires directors to (a) act in accordance with the company's constitution (as defined in s 257, which is wider than s 17); and (b) only exercise powers for the purposes for which they are conferred.

Section 171(b) codifies the *proper purposes doctrine* as it applies to directors, thus putting to rest earlier debates about whether such a duty exists. The precursor equitable duty to 'act *bona fide* in what they [ie the directors] consider—not what a court may consider—is in the interests of the company, and not for any collateral purpose' (*Re Smith and Fawcett Ltd* **[9.09]**) was variously urged as imposing either one duty or two. CA 2006 separates the two limbs, with the proper purposes aspect appearing here in s 171, and the 'interests of the company', reformulated as the 'duty to promote the success of the company', appearing in s 172. The separation, and in particular the objective test embraced by the proper purposes doctrine, allows for greater judicial intervention in corporate decision-making than might otherwise be the case.

The positive formulation of the proper purposes obligation in s 171(b) (a director 'must . . . exercise powers for . . . [proper] purposes') as opposed to the negative version in *Smith and Fawcett* (must not act for any collateral purpose) also aligns the duty more closely with the common law version that is familiar in public and administrative law (*Associated Provincial Picture Houses Ltd v Wednesbury Corporation* [1948] 1 KB 223, Lord Greene MR).

Nominee directors in particular are at risk of breaching this duty: they may be tempted to use their powers improperly to advance the interests of their nominator, not the interests of the company itself (see *Scottish Cooperative Wholesale society Ltd v Meyer* **[11.19]**; *Kuwait Asia Bank EC v National Mutual Life Nominees Ltd* **[6.31]**).

Failure to act in accordance with the company's 'constitution'

See the cases in Chapter 3, pp 96 ff. The next case is a little harder to classify.

[6.06] Bishopsgate Investment Management Ltd (in liq) v Maxwell (No 2) [1994] 1 All ER 261, [1993] BCLC 814 (Court of Appeal)

Ian Maxwell, a director of BIM, had signed a number of share transfers whereby shares held by that company as trustee of various pension schemes were transferred for no consideration to Maxwell Group plc, a company controlling his father Robert Maxwell's private interests. The transfers had not been authorised by the board of directors and he had signed them without inquiry because his brother (a co-director) had done so. He was held accountable to the company for the value of the shares: not on the basis of any finding of negligence, but simply because he had misapplied these assets of the company.

HOFFMANN LJ: Mr Maxwell's evidence was that he knew that the company's business consisted principally, if not exclusively, of managing the assets of the pension funds. He knew that he was a director. Nevertheless, he took no interest whatever in the management of the company. He attended few meetings and paid little attention to business when he did. He said he trusted and relied upon the other directors.

The judge did not decide whether Mr Maxwell's failure to acquaint himself with the company's business was a breach of duty. In the older cases the duty of a director to participate in the management of a company is stated in very undemanding terms. The law may be evolving in response to changes in public attitudes to corporate governance, as shown by the enactment of the provisions consolidated in the Company Directors Disqualification Act 1986. Even so, the existence of a duty to participate must depend upon how the particular company's business is organised and the part which the director could reasonably have been expected to play . . . Mr Ian Maxwell was in breach of his fiduciary duty because he gave away the company's assets for no consideration . . . In the case of breach of the fiduciary duty, it seems to me that the cause of action is constituted not by failure to make inquiries but simply by the improper transfer of the shares . . .

RALPH GIBSON LJ delivered a concurring judgment.

LEGGATT LJ concurred.

> ➤ Question

Is this an example of 'failure to act in accordance with the constitution'? Or is it better classified as breach of some other duty or rule or requirement? Does the remedy depend upon the classification of the breach?

Failure to act for proper purposes

See *Re Smith & Fawcett Ltd* **[9.09]**: '[Directors] must exercise their discretion *bona fide* in what they consider—not what a court may consider—is in the interests of the company, and not for any collateral purpose.' This puts together the two elements (good faith and proper purposes) that are separated by ss 171 and 172.

Compare this case with the cases next cited. These cases reflect a slow working out by the courts of the nature of these duties, and, in particular, the recognition of a separate duty to act for proper purposes (so that directors might act in complete good faith, but nevertheless find themselves in breach of the requirement to act for proper purposes).[17]

[6.07] Punt v Symons & Co Ltd [1903] 2 Ch 506 (Chancery Division)

[For the facts and another part of the decision, see **[4.22]**.] In order to secure the passing of a special resolution, the directors had issued new shares to five additional members. This was held to be an abuse of their powers.

BYRNE J: I now come to the last and most important point. It is argued on the evidence that but for the issue by the directors of the shares under their powers as directors, and, therefore, in their fiduciary character under the general power to issue shares, it would have been impossible to pass the resolution proposed; and that the shares were not issued bona fide, but with the sole object and intention of creating voting power to carry out the proposed alteration in the articles. On the evidence I am quite clear that these shares were not issued bona fide for the general advantage of the company, but that they were issued with the immediate object of controlling the holders of the greater number of shares in the company, and of obtaining the necessary statutory majority for passing a special resolution while, at the same time, not conferring upon the minority the power to demand a poll. I need not go through the affidavits. I am quite satisfied that the meaning, object and intention of the issue of these shares was to enable the shareholders holding the smaller amount of shares to control the holders of a very considerable majority. A power of the kind exercised by the

---

[17] See LS Sealy, '"Bona fides" and "Proper Purposes" in Corporate Decisions' (1989) 15 Mon UL Rev 265; S Worthington, 'Corporate Governance: Remedying and Ratifying Directors' Breaches' (2000) 116 LQR 638.

directors in this case, is one which must be exercised for the benefit of the company: primarily it is given them for the purpose of enabling them to raise capital when required for the purposes of the company. There may be occasions when the directors may fairly and properly issue shares in the case of a company constituted like the present for other reasons. For instance, it would not be at all an unreasonable thing to create a sufficient number of shareholders to enable statutory powers to be exercised; but when I find a limited issue of shares to persons who are obviously meant and intended to secure the necessary statutory majority in a particular interest, I do not think that it is fair and bona fide exercise of the power . . .

If I find as I do that shares have been issued under the general fiduciary power of the directors for the express purpose of acquiring an unfair majority for the purpose of altering the rights of parties under the articles, I think I ought to interfere. I propose to grant an injunction . . .

[6.08] Hogg v Cramphorn Ltd [1967] Ch 254 (Chancery Division)

The directors of the defendant company, acting in good faith, had issued 5,707 shares with special voting rights to the trustees of a scheme set up for the benefit of the company's employees, in an attempt (which proved successful) to forestall a take-over bid by one Baxter. This was held to be an improper use of the directors' power to issue shares, but to be capable of ratification by the shareholders in general meeting.

BUCKLEY J: I am satisfied that Mr Baxter's offer, when it became known to the company's staff, had an unsettling effect upon them. I am also satisfied that the directors and the trustees of the trust deed genuinely considered that to give the staff through the trustees a sizeable, though indirect, voice in the affairs of the company would benefit both the staff and the company. I am sure that Colonel Cramphorn and also probably his fellow directors firmly believed that to keep the management of the company's affairs in the hands of the existing board would be more advantageous to the shareholders, the company's staff and its customers than if it were committed to a board selected by Mr Baxter. The steps which the board took were intended not only to ensure that if Mr Baxter succeeded in obtaining a shareholding which, as matters stood, would have been a controlling shareholding, he should not secure control of the company, but also, and perhaps primarily, to discourage Mr Baxter from proceeding with his bid at all . . .

Accepting as I do that the board acted in good faith and that they believed that the establishment of a trust would benefit the company, and that avoidance of the acquisition of control by Mr Baxter would also benefit the company, I must still remember that an essential element of the scheme, and indeed its primary purpose, was to ensure control of the company by the directors and those whom they could confidently regard as their supporters. Was such a manipulation of the voting position a legitimate act on the part of the directors?

[His Lordship referred to *Punt v Symons & Co Ltd* **[6.07]** and *Piercy v S Mills & Co Ltd*,[18] and continued:] Unless a majority in a company is acting oppressively towards the minority, this court should not and will not itself interfere with the exercise by the majority of its constitutional rights or embark upon an inquiry into the respective merits of the views held or policies favoured by the majority and the minority. Nor will this court permit directors to exercise powers, which have been delegated to them by the company in circumstances which put the directors in a fiduciary position when exercising those powers, in such a way as to interfere with the exercise by the majority of its constitutional rights; and in a case of this kind also, in my judgment, the court should not investigate the rival merits of the views or polices of the parties . . . It is not, in my judgment, open to the directors in such a case to say, 'We genuinely believe that what we seek to prevent the majority from

---

[18] [1920] 1 Ch 77.

doing will harm the company and therefore our act in arming ourselves or our party with sufficient shares to outvote the majority is a conscientious exercise of our powers under the articles, which should not be interfered with'.

Such a belief, even if well founded, would be irrelevant. A majority of shareholders in general meeting is entitled to pursue what course it chooses within the company's powers, however wrong-headed it may appear to others, providing the majority do not unfairly oppress other members of the company. These considerations lead me to the conclusion that the issue of the 5,707 shares, with the special voting rights which the directors purported to attach to them, could not be justified by the view that the directors genuinely believed that it would benefit the company if they could command a majority of the votes in general meetings . . . The power to issue shares was a fiduciary power and if, as I think, it was exercised for an improper motive, the issue of these shares is liable to be set aside.

Mr Goulding, however, contends that the present case is distinguishable from those I have cited in an important respect. In both *Punt v Symons & Co Ltd* and *Piercy v S Mills & Co Ltd* the majority and the minority were already arrayed for battle on a specific issue when the latter attempted to create reinforcements by issuing additional shares. If the question whether that issue should be allowed to stand had been referred to a general meeting at which the newly issued shares were excluded from voting, the resulting answer would in each case have been a negative one. Such a meeting would have served no useful purpose. In the present case, on the other hand, no battle had been joined when the 5,707 shares were issued; the directors were merely fearful that Mr Baxter would acquire control and that in any ensuing battle they would find themselves outnumbered. In the event, as I said, Mr Baxter's offer lapsed. One cannot say what the result would have been if the directors had sought the approval of a general meeting before making the issue, and it is very possible that if the issue of the shares were now submitted to the company for approval it would be approved.

Mr Instone says, no doubt rightly, that the company in general meeting could not by ordinary resolution control the directors in the exercise of the powers under article 10. He goes on to say, with less justification, that what they could not ordain a majority could not ratify. There, is however, a great difference between controlling the directors' exercise of a power vested in them and approving a proposed exercise of such a power, especially where the proposed exercise of the power is of a kind which might be assailed if it had not the manifest approval of the majority. Had the majority of the company in general meeting approved the issue of the 5,707 shares before it was made, even with the proposed special voting rights attached (assuming that such rights could have been so attached conformably with the articles), I do not think that any member could have complained of the issue being made; for in these circumstances, the criticism that the directors were by the issue of the shares attempting to deprive the majority of their constitutional rights would have ceased to have any force. It follows that a majority in a general meeting of the company at which no votes were cast in respect of the 5,707 shares could ratify the issue of those shares. Before setting the allotment and issue of the 5,707 shares aside, therefore, I propose to allow the company an opportunity to decide in general meeting whether it approves or disapproves of the issue of these shares to the trustees. Mr Goulding will undertake on behalf of the trustees not to vote at such a meeting in respect of the 5,707 shares. . . .

[The action of the directors was ratified by the members at the subsequent meeting. Compare *Bamford v Bamford* [4.33].]

[6.09] Howard Smith Ltd v Ampol Petroleum Ltd [1974] AC 821 (Privy Council)

Rival take-over offers for all the issued shares in RW Miller (Holdings) Ltd had been made by Howard Smith Ltd and Ampol Ltd. Since Ampol, with an associated company ('Bulkships'), already owned 55 per cent of Millers' shares, there was no prospect that Howard Smith's offer would succeed; but a majority of Millers' directors favoured this offer, both because its terms were more generous and because of fears as to the future of Millers if it were to pass into Ampol's control. Millers' directors resolved to issue some $10m worth of new shares to Howard Smith. This served the dual purposes of providing Millers with much needed capital to finance the completion of two tankers, and of converting the Ampol-Bulkships holding into a minority one, so that the Howard Smith offer was likely to succeed. In these proceedings, Ampol challenged the validity of the share issue. At first instance, Street J found that, while Millers' directors were not motivated by any consideration of self-interest or desire to retain control, their primary purpose was not to satisfy Millers' admitted need for capital but to destroy the majority holding of Ampol and Bulkships. He rejected as 'unreal and unconvincing' the directors' own statements to the contrary in the witness-box, and set aside the allotment. The Privy Council upheld his decision.

The opinion of their Lordships was delivered by LORD WILBERFORCE: The directors, in deciding to issue shares, forming part of Millers' unissued capital, to Howard Smith, acted under clause 8 of the company's articles of association. This provides, subject to certain qualifications which have not been invoked, that the shares shall be under the control of the directors, who may allot or otherwise dispose of the same to such persons on such terms and conditions and either at a premium or otherwise and at such time as the directors may think fit. Thus, and this is not disputed, the issue was clearly intra vires the directors. But, intra vires though the issue may have been, the directors' power under this article is a fiduciary power: and it remains the case that an exercise of such a power, though formally valid, may be attacked on the ground that it was not exercised for the purpose for which it was granted. It is at this point that the contentions of the parties diverge. The extreme argument on one side is that, for validity, what is required is bona fide exercise of the power in the interests of the company; that once it is found that the directors were not motivated by self-interest—ie by a desire to retain their control of the company or their positions on the board—the matter is concluded in their favour and that the court will not inquire into the validity of their reasons for making the issue. All decided cases, it was submitted, where an exercise of such a power as this has been found invalid, are cases where directors are found to have acted through self-interest of this kind.

On the other side, the main argument is that the purpose for which the power is conferred is to enable capital to be raised for the company, and that once it is found that the issue was not made for that purpose, invalidity follows.

It is fair to say that under the pressure of argument intermediate positions were taken by both sides, but in the main the arguments followed the polarisation which has been stated.

In their Lordships' opinion neither of the extreme positions can be maintained. It can be accepted, as one would only expect, that the majority of cases in which issues of shares are challenged in the courts are cases in which the vitiating element is the self-interest of the directors, or at least the purpose of the directors to preserve their own control of the management . . .

Further it is correct to say that where the self-interest of the directors is involved, they will not be permitted to assert that their action was bona fide thought to be, or was, in the interest of the company; pleas to this effect have invariably been rejected . . .

But it does not follow from this, as the appellants assert, that the absence of any element of self-interest is enough to make an issue valid. Self-interest is only one, though no doubt the commonest, instance of improper motive: and, before one can say that a fiduciary power has been exercised for the purpose for which it was conferred, a wider investigation may have to be made . . . On the other hand, taking the respondents' contention, it is, in their Lordships' opinion, too narrow an approach to say that the only valid purpose for which shares may be issued is to raise capital for the company. The discretion is not in terms limited in this way: the law should not impose such a limitation on directors' powers. To define in advance exact limits beyond which directors must not pass is, in their Lordships' view, impossible. This clearly cannot be done by enumeration, since the variety of situations facing directors of different types of company in different situations cannot be anticipated. No more, in their Lordships' view, can this be done by the use of a phrase—such as 'bona fide in the interest of the company as a whole', or 'for some corporate purpose'. Such phrases, if they do anything more than restate the general principle applicable to fiduciary powers, at best serve, negatively, to exclude from the area of validity cases where the directors are acting sectionally, or partially: ie improperly favouring one section of the shareholders against another . . .

In their Lordships' opinion it is necessary to start with a consideration of the power whose exercise is in question, in this case a power to issue shares. Having ascertained, on a fair view, the nature of this power, and having defined as can best be done in the light of modern conditions the, or some, limits within which it may be exercised, it is then necessary for the court, if a particular exercise of it is challenged, to examine the substantial purpose for which it was exercised, and to reach a conclusion whether that purpose was proper or not. In doing so it will necessarily give credit to the bona fide opinion of the directors, if such is found to exist, and will respect their judgment as to matters of management; having done this, the ultimate conclusion has to be as to the side of a fairly broad line on which the case falls.

The main stream of authority, in their Lordships' opinion, supports this approach. In *Punt v Symons & Co Ltd* **[6.07]** Byrne J expressly accepts that there may be reasons other than to raise capital for which shares may be issued. In the High Court case of *Harlowe's Nominees Pty Ltd v Woodside (Lakes Entrance) Oil Co NL*,[19] an issue of shares was made to a large oil company in order, as was found, to secure the financial stability of the company. This was upheld as being within the power although it had the effect of defeating the attempt of the plaintiff to secure control by buying up the company's shares . . .

Their Lordships were referred to the recent judgment of Berger J in the Supreme Court of British Columbia, in *Teck Corpn Ltd v Miller*.[20] This was concerned with the affairs of Afton Mines Ltd in which Teck Corporation Ltd, a resource conglomerate, had acquired a majority shareholding. Teck was indicating an intention to replace the board of directors of Afton with its own nominees with a view to causing Afton to enter into an agreement (called an 'ultimate deal') with itself for the exploitation by Teck of valuable mineral rights owned by Afton. Before this could be done, and in order to prevent it, the directors of Afton concluded an exploitation agreement with another company 'Canex'. One of its provisions, as is apparently common in this type of agreement in Canada, provided for the issue to Canex of a large number of shares in Afton, thus displacing Teck's majority. Berger J found: 'their [*sc* the directors'] purpose was to obtain the best agreement they could while . . . still in control. Their purpose was in that sense to defeat Teck. But, not to defeat Teck's attempt to obtain control, rather it was to foreclose Teck's opportunity of obtaining for itself the ultimate deal. That was . . . no improper purpose.' His decision upholding the agreement with Canex on this basis appears to be in line with the English and Australian authorities to which reference has been made . . .

By contrast to the cases of *Harlowe* and *Teck*, the present case, on the evidence, does not, on the findings of the trial judge, involve any considerations of management, within the proper sphere of the directors. The purpose found by the judge is simply and solely to dilute the majority voting power held by Ampol and Bulkships so as to enable a then minority of shareholders to sell their shares more advantageously. So far as authority goes, an issue of shares purely for the purpose of creating voting power has repeatedly been condemned . . . And, though the reported decisions, naturally enough, are expressed in terms of their own facts, there are clear considerations of principle which support the trend they establish. The constitution of a limited company normally provides for directors, with powers of management, and shareholders, with defined voting powers having power to appoint the directors, and to take, in general meeting, by majority vote, decisions

---

[19]   (1968) 121 CLR 483, Aust HCt.
[20]   (1972) 33 DLR (3d) 288.

on matters not reserved for management. Just as it is established that directors, within their management powers, may take decisions against the wishes of the majority of shareholders, and indeed that the majority of shareholders cannot control them in the exercise of these powers while they remain in office (*Automatic Self-Cleansing Filter Syndicate Co Ltd v Cuninghame* **[4.05]**), so it must be unconstitutional for directors to use their fiduciary powers over the shares in the company purely for the purpose of destroying an existing majority, or creating a new majority which did not previously exist. To do so is to interfere with that element of the company's constitution which is separate from and set against their powers. If there is added, moreover, to this immediate purpose, an ulterior purpose to enable an offer for shares to proceed which the existing majority was in a position to block, the departure from the legitimate use of the fiduciary power becomes not less, but all the greater . . . Directors are of course entitled to offer advice, and bound to supply information, relevant to the making of such a decision, but to use their fiduciary power solely for the purpose of shifting the power to decide to whom and at what price shares are to be sold cannot be related to any purpose for which the power over the share capital was conferred upon them. That this is the position in law was in effect recognised by the majority directors themselves when they attempted to justify the issue as made primarily in order to obtain much needed capital for the company. And once this primary purpose was rejected, as it was by Street J, there is nothing legitimate left as a basis for their action, except honest behaviour. That is not, itself, enough.

Their Lordships therefore agree entirely with the conclusion of Street J that the power to issue and allot shares was improperly exercised by the issue of shares to Howard Smith . . .

[6.10] Mills v Mills (1938) 60 CLR 150 (High Court of Australia)

The plaintiff, Ainslie Mills, and his uncle, Neilson Mills (the defendant) were two of the directors and the largest shareholders of a family company. Neilson Mills (who was managing director) held mostly ordinary shares, and Ainslie Mills mostly preference shares. A resolution was passed by a majority of the directors, including Neilson Mills, by which accumulated profits were capitalised and distributed to the ordinary shareholders in the form of fully paid bonus shares. Such profits would have gone to the ordinary shareholders had the same sums been paid as dividends rather than bonus shares. This resolution greatly strengthened the voting power of the ordinary shareholders (and in particular of Neilson Mills) and diminished the rights of the preference shareholders to share in assets in a winding up. However, it did not encroach upon the rights to dividends of either preference or ordinary shareholders. Lowe J found that the majority of directors had acted honestly in what they believed to be the best interests of the company, and he held that the fact that Neilson Mills stood to gain from their decision did not invalidate it. This view was upheld by the High Court.

LATHAM CJ: . . . It is urged that the rule laid down by the cases is that directors must act always and solely in the interests of the company and never in their own interest . . .

It must, however, be recognised that as a general rule, though not invariably . . . directors have an interest as shareholders in the company of which they are directors. Most sets of articles of association actually require the directors to have such an interest, and it is generally desired by shareholders that directors should have a substantial interest in the company so that their interests may be identified with those of the shareholders of the company. Ordinarily, therefore, in promoting the interests of the company, a director will also promote his own interests. I do not read the general phrases which are to be found in the authorities with reference to the obligations of directors to act solely in the interests of the company as meaning that they are prohibited from acting in any matter where their own interests are affected by what they do in their capacity as directors. Very many actions of directors who are shareholders, perhaps all of them, have a direct or indirect relation to their own interests. It would be ignoring realities and creating impossibilities in the administration of companies to require that directors should not advert to or consider in any way the effect of a particular decision upon their own interests as shareholders. A rule which laid down such a principle would paralyse the management of companies in many directions. Accordingly, the judicial observations which suggest that directors should consider only the interests of the company and never their own interests should not be pressed to a limit which would create a quite impossible position.

Directors are required to act not only in matters which affect the relations of the company to persons who are not members of the company but also in relation to matters which affect the rights of shareholders inter se. Where there are preference and ordinary shares a particular decision may be of such a character that it must necessarily affect adversely the interests of one class of share-holders and benefit the interests of another class. In such a case it is difficult to apply the test of act-ing in the interests of the company. The question which arises is sometimes not a question of the interests of the company at all, but a question of what is fair as between different classes of share-holders. Where such a case arises some other test than that of 'the interests of the company' must be applied, and the test must be applied with knowledge of the fact already mentioned that the law permits directors, and by virtue of provisions in articles of association often requires them, to hold shares, ordinary or preference, as the case may be. A director who holds one or both classes of such shares is not, in my opinion, required by the law to live in an unreal region of detached altruism and to act in a vague mood of ideal abstraction from obvious facts which must be presented to the mind of any honest and intelligent man when he exercises his powers as a director. It would be setting up an impossible standard to hold that, if an action of a director were affected in any degree by the fact that he was a preference or ordinary shareholder, his action was invalid and should be set aside . . .

DIXON J: When the law makes the object, view or purpose of a man, or of a body of men, the test of validity of their acts, it necessarily opens up the possibility of an almost infinite analysis of the fears and desires, proximate and remote, which, in truth, form the compound motives usually animating human conduct. But logically possible as such an analysis may seem, it would be imprac-ticable to adopt it as a means of determining the validity of the resolutions arrived at by a body of directors, resolutions which otherwise are ostensibly within their powers. The application of the general equitable principle to the acts of directors managing the affairs of a company cannot be as nice as it is in the case of a trustee exercising a special power of appointment. It must, as it seems to me, take the substantial object, the accomplishment of which formed the real ground of the board's action. If this is within the scope of the power, then the power has been validly exercised. But if, except for some ulterior and illegitimate object, the power would not have been exercised, that which has been attempted as an ostensible exercise of the power will be void,[21] notwithstand-ing that the directors may incidentally bring about a result which is within the purpose of the power and which they consider desirable . . .

RICH and STARKE JJ delivered concurring judgments.

EVATT J concurred.

➤ Questions

1. How are the 'proper purposes' for the exercise of any given power determined? Can dir-ectors be confident they are acting for 'proper purposes'?

2. Is *Mills v Mills* a 'proper purposes' case or a '*bona fide* / good faith in the interests of the company' case? Does it matter?

3. Was the judge in *Re Halt Garage (1964) Ltd* [5.04] applying a 'proper purposes' test when he examined the 'genuineness' of the payment of the directors' remuneration? If so, why did he not think that a similar payment made out of undistributed profits was wrong? If not, was he applying merely a '*bona fides*' test?

---

[21] [More accurately, voidable: see *Bamford v Bamford* [4.33].]

4. Do these takeover cases miss the real issue by focusing on the scope of the power exercised by the directors on the particular occasion? Would it be more satisfactory to build on the basis of such cases as *John Shaw & Sons (Salford) Ltd v Shaw* **[4.07]**, where the separate roles of the different constitutional organs are recognised, and to say that the real issue is which organ should have control of this decision? If it were seen to be the members, then the sanction of a members' vote would be required in all such cases, not simply under the guise of ratifying an ill-purposed act of the directors, but because the decision involved a matter which was not within the directors' sphere of action. This point was recognised, but was not made the *ratio decidendi*, in the speech of Lord Wilberforce in *Howard Smith*, above. It is also in keeping with CA 2006 s 551(1), which allows directors to allot shares only where authorised under the company's articles or by resolution of the company (see below, p 377).

5. When, if ever, might it be proper for the directors to use their powers to ensure that they retain control? Could it ever be their *duty* to do so?

6. A quite different approach to the problem is mooted in *Criterion Properties plc v Stratford Properties llc* **[3.10]**. The former managing director of the claimant company had caused it to enter into a contract which left it with a 'poison pill' in the form of a right by an outsider to demand a potentially crippling payment if control of the company should change hands or if the managing director or chairman should leave office. Lord Scott pointed out that the payment would have to be made even if the directors resigned voluntarily or there was a wholly beneficial takeover, and questioned whether the managing director had *authority* (real or apparent) to make the contract (see above, pp 120 ff). On this approach, what remedies are available to the various affected parties, and how do these differ from the remedies available on an approach that relies on proper purposes? Is this approach defensible?

7. Where the directors are motivated by more than one purpose, the decision in *Howard Smith* indicates that regard is to be held to their *primary* purpose in deciding whether the court will intervene. However, in *Whitehouse v Carlton Hotel Pty Ltd* (1987) 162 CLR 285, the High Court of Australia appeared to favour a narrower interpretation. The majority (Mason, Deane and Dawson JJ) in a joint judgment said (at 721):

> In this court, the preponderant view has tended to be that the allotment will be invalidated only if the impermissible purpose or a combination of impermissible purposes can be seen to have been dominant— 'the substantial object' (per Williams ACJ, Fullagar and Kitto JJ, *Ngurli Ltd v McCann*[22] quoting Dixon J in *Mills v Mills* **[6.10]** and see *Harlowe's Nominees*); 'the moving cause' (per Latham CJ, *Mills v Mills*). The cases in which that view has been indicated have not, however, required a determination of the question whether the impermissible purpose must be *the* substantial object or moving cause or whether it may suffice to invalidate the allotment that it be one of a number of such objects or causes. As a matter of logic and principle, the preferable view would seem to be that, regardless of whether the impermissible purpose was the dominant one or but one of a number of significantly contributing causes, the allotment will be invalidated if the impermissible purpose was causative in the sense that, but for its presence, 'the power would not have been exercised' per Dixon J, *Mills v Mills*.

What difference, if any, would the different tests make in the above cases?

8. There does not, as yet, seem to be a parallel concept of 'proper purposes', as a test separate from that of *bona fides*, in members' decision-making, although cases such as *Re Halt Garage (1964) Ltd* **[5.04]**, in which decisions have been struck down as not 'genuine', come very close.[23]

---

[22] (1953) 90 CLR 425, Aust HCt, at 445.
[23] But see P Finn, *Fiduciary Obligations* (1977) p 73, who contends that members' decisions should be subject to a similar test to those of the directors; also S Worthington, who advocates a proper purposes test (but not fiduciary duties) for all members' decisions: 'Corporate Governance: Remedying and Ratifying Directors' Breaches' (2000) 116 *Law Quarterly Review* 638.

In Australia, by contrast, the High Court has declared a 'proper purpose' test to be preferred over one based on *bona fides* for the review of some, and perhaps all, members' resolutions: see *Gambotto v WPC Ltd* (1995) 182 CLR 432, Aust HCt. For an example from Canada, see *Western Mines Ltd v Shield Development Co Ltd* [1976] 2 WWR 300. Is such a test emerging in the UK? Revisit the cases on alteration of the company's constitution (above, pp 204 ff), variations of class rights (below, pp 443 ff), and ratification of directors' wrongdoing (above, pp 221 ff, and below, pp 310, 347 ff). In the context of ratification, note especially CA 2006 s 239(3) and (4).

Duty to promote the success of the company: CA 2006 s 172

This section is one of the more important and controversial provisions in the Act, and took up much of the discussion through the various stages of the Bill. Its approach purports to end the debate over the meaning of 'the company', and 'in the interests of the company' (see above, p 275). Section 172 specifies that the director's duty is to promote the success of the company for the benefit of its members as a whole (not for the benefit of other stakeholders or constituencies). This rejects the 'pluralist approach' and adopts the 'enlightened shareholder value' recommendations of the Law Commissions and CLR.[24] One important reason for this choice is that the pluralist view risks leaving directors accountable to no one, since there is no clear yardstick for judging their performance.[25] The section also explicitly favours a long-term, rather than short-term, outlook in corporate decision-making (see s 172(1)(a)).

The crucial elements of s 172

Section 172(1) enshrines a number of important elements:

(i) 'The success of the company for the benefit of its members as a whole'

This statement relates the success of the company to the interests of its members as a whole. This approach was advocated by the CLR (CLR, *Modern Company Law for a Competitive Economy: Developing the Framework* (URN 00/656), para 3.51):

> We believe there is value in inserting a reference to the success of the company, since what is in view is not the individual interests of members, but their interests as members of an association with the purposes and the mutual arrangements embodied in the constitution; the objective is to be achieved by the directors successfully managing the complex of relationships and resources which comprise the company's undertaking.

The primacy of the company is significant. If the interests of the company as a separate entity are in conflict with the interests of the members as a whole, or at least some of them, it would appear that the interests of the company should be preferred (*Mutual Life Assurance Co of New York v Rank Organisation Ltd* [1985] BCLC 11, 21 (Goulding J); *Re BSB Holdings Ltd (No 2)* [1996] 1 BCLC 155, 251 (Arden J)).

(ii) Directors and members to decide what 'success' means

Directors' good faith business judgements must be calculated to promote the success of the company. 'Success' is to be determined on a company-by-company basis. It is for the directors to interpret the company's objectives and make practical decisions about how best to achieve

---

[24] See Company Law Reform Bill—White Paper 2005, para 3.3; CLR, *Modern Company Law for a Competitive Economy: A Strategic Framework*, at para 5.

[25] Committee on Corporate Governance, *Final Report*, para 1.17.

them. At its simplest, success may often mean the long-term increase in financial value of the company, but even this has its difficulties. It is not clear, eg, whether the directors should favour increased dividend rates, increased market price for the shares, or some other manifestation of the long-term growth and stability of the company.

(iii) Success for the members as a whole

The directors must make decisions that are calculated to be for the long-term benefit of the members as a whole. It follows that promoting sectional interests would be a breach of the duty to promote the success of the company (see *Mills v Mills* **[6.10]**).

(iv) Directors to make decisions—subjective test

The essential principle is that it is for *directors* to make decisions, in good faith, as to how to promote the success of the company for the benefit of the members as a whole. This test repeats the common law rule from which it is derived (*Re Smith and Fawcett Ltd* **[9.09]**, and above, p 284). A court will not inquire whether, objectively, the decision was actually the best decision for the company (*Howard Smith Ltd v Ampol Petroleum Ltd* **[6.09]**; *Regentcrest plc v Cohen* [2001] 2 BCLC 80, 105), nor whether the director's honestly held belief was a reasonable one (*Smith v Fawcett*; *Regentcrest plc v Cohen*).

(v) Regard to the specified factors

Section 172(1), especially when read with s 170, makes it clear that the duty imposed on directors is to consider the interests of persons other than the company (eg employees, suppliers, customers, the community) but that directors do not owe a duty directly to those persons. A director's duties are owed to the company alone (s 170).

(vi) Conflicting factors

Where consideration of different 'factors' suggests conflicting courses of action, it seems directors must simply take their own 'good faith business decisions' to promote the success of the company (HC Comm D 11/7/06 Cols 591–593, Margaret Hodge).

(vii) Failure to have regard to the specified matters

If a director acts *without* adopting the form of consideration required by subs (1), how will a court respond? If there is no basis on which a director could reasonably have concluded that the action was likely to promote the success of the company, a court is likely to find the director in breach of this duty (see *Item Software (UK) Ltd v Fassihi* **[6.11]**). But if a reasonable director, giving due consideration, might well have concluded that the action was likely to promote the success of the company, the court's reaction is not so clear. Assuming the director acted *bona fide*, perhaps a court will find there has been no breach of duty (see *Charterbridge Corporation Ltd v Lloyds Bank Ltd* **[3.06]**), or at least that the breach has caused no harm (also see Attorney-General, Lord Goldsmith, Hansard HL, 9/05/06, col 846).

But on a strict legal interpretation it is also possible that the decision may be subjected to review, and deemed voidable because it has been made without taking into account all material considerations (see the discussion in relation to s 171, above). Subs (1), in effect, specifies some (not all) of the matters deemed to be relevant to decisions made by directors. Setting out such a list may expand the grounds for judicial review of directors' decision-making, whether under s 172 or s 171.

(viii) No need for a paper trail

Concerns were expressed during the legislative process that s 172 would require directors to keep a 'paper trail' of all business judgements made, and that the section would lead to an increase in litigation. The concerns are linked insofar as an increase in litigation would require directors to undertake more defensive practices and procedures, and, conversely, the lower the threat of litigation the less the requirement for paper trails. The Government strongly denied that the section introduced a 'tick-box culture' whereby directors would be required to consider each factor one by one. The list of factors is non-exclusive and is intended to illustrate elements of the wider principle that directors are required to make good faith business judgements to promote the success of the company for the long-term benefit of its members as a whole. As such directors should not be liable for a 'process failure'. (On the other hand, see s 417 (contents of directors' report: business review), especially s 417(2).)

(ix) No risk of increased litigation

The second fear expressed was that a failure to take into account specific factors may lead to increased litigation. This fear was said to be over-exaggerated (see HC Comm D 11/7/06 Cols 568–575). The only duty at stake is the duty to promote the success of the company, and so long as directors have made good faith business judgements with reasonable care, skill and diligence they are unlikely to be in breach of this duty (see HL Rep, Hansard HL 681 9/5/06 Cols 845–846). In Committee Stage in the House of Commons, David Howarth made the important additional observation that the class of potential litigants is limited, and that it will also often be difficult to identify any loss. For these reasons, the risk of litigation is minimal. The class of potential litigants is limited to the board, a majority of members, a minority of members under Part 11, and liquidators acting on behalf of an insolvent company. It is only during a takeover that a board or a majority of members is likely to bring an action against a director; in most cases there are far better remedies available against directors, eg removal of the director. Further, a derivative action under Part 11 is extremely difficult to advance against the wishes of the majority of members. In reality, it is only during takeovers and liquidation proceedings that the section is likely to be utilised. Moreover, an action will only be useful where there is a loss to the company; a breach of the duty to promote the success of the company is unlikely, alone, to give rise to significant calculable financial loss.

(x) A defence rather than duty?

Although the 'enlightened shareholder value' approach was designed to avoid the problems of director accountability inherent in the 'pluralist approach', it is not clear that this ambition is fully achieved. Subs (1) sets out proper considerations for director decision-making, but these considerations will allow directors to justify almost any bona fide approach to delivering the success of the company. Where directors have made a good faith business judgment to favour employees' interests[26] over short-term financial gain, for example, in order to promote the success of the company for the benefits of its members as a whole, then this legitimate decision cannot be challenged (see Re Welfab Engineers Ltd (1990) BCLC 833). Similarly, directors are not compelled to make decisions according to the wider interests of community and the environment, and they are protected from reproach if they choose to do so.

(xi) Duty to disclose misconduct?

The controversial finding in Item Software (UK) Ltd v Fassihi [6.11] at [44], may be embraced by the terms of s 172. Fassihi suggests that a director who acts in breach of his fiduciary duty is under a further duty to disclose the breach to the company if disclosure is required by the general equitable duty to act bona fide in what the director considers to be the interests of the company. The analogy with the statutory duty in s 172(1) is obvious. It is difficult to see when it would not be in the company's interest to know of a breach of duty, and on that basis any breach of duty will always involve a further breach in failing to disclose. The further breach may result in loss of employment benefits (eg termination rights, share options, pension benefits), and may provide justification for summary dismissal (Tesco Stores Ltd v Pook [2003]

---

[26] In the context of s 172(1)(b), also see the power to make provision for employees on cessation or transfer of business (s 247): s 247(2) states that this latter power 'is exercisable notwithstanding the general duty imposed by s 172'.

EWHC 823 (Ch); *Fulham Football Club (1987) Ltd v Tigana* [2004] EWHC 2585 (QB)). On the other hand, this aspect of the *Fassihi* decision represents a radical extension of the traditional equitable duties owed by directors, and the approach to these statutory rules advocated in s 170 may argue against its acceptance.

Less controversially, a director also has an equitable duty to disclose breaches of duty committed by fellow directors if this is what the director, acting *bona fide*, considers to be in the best interests of the company (*British Midland Tool Ltd v Midland International Tooling Ltd* [2003] EWHC 466 (Ch), [2003] 2 BCLC 523). Again, the analogy with the statutory duty in s 172(1) is apparent.

The duty to act in good faith for the success of the company

Re-read the cases at **[6.01]–[6.09]**.

The duty to act bona fide in the interests of the company includes the duty to disclose misconduct by the director to the company.

[6.11] Item Software (UK) Ltd v Fassihi [2004] EWCA Civ 1244, [2005] 2 BCLC 91 (Court of Appeal)

Fassihi was both a director and employee of Item Software (IS), a distributor of products for Isograph. In November 1998, the company tried to renegotiate its distribution agreement with Isograph on more favourable terms. During negotiations, Fassihi approached Isograph with the idea of establishing a new company to take over the distribution agreement. On the other hand, he also encouraged IS to take an aggressive stance with respect to the negotiations with Isograph. Negotiations between IS and Isograph broke down because Isograph refused to accept IS's terms. Isograph terminated the distribution agreement with IS and entered into a new agreement with Fassihi's own company. IS dismissed Fassihi when it learned of this and commenced proceedings against Fassihi, alleging that his actions amounted to a breach of his duty as both a director and an employee to act *bona fide* in the interests of the company (ie IS). It was also alleged that this duty was breached by Fassihi's failure to disclose his misconduct to the company.

> ARDEN LJ: . . . it seems to me that the logical place to start in relation to the disclosure issue is to consider the position of Mr Fassihi as a director since the duties of a director are in general higher than those imposed by law on an employee. This is because a director is not simply a senior manager of company. He is a fiduciary and with his fellow directors he is responsible for the success of the company's business. Merely to call a person a fiduciary is only the beginning of the analysis. It is necessary to identify the respects in which he is a fiduciary and the duties which follow . . .
>
> For my part, I do not consider that it is correct to infer from the cases to which I have referred that a fiduciary owes a separate and independent duty to disclose his own misconduct to his principal or more generally information of relevance and concern to it. So to hold would lead to a proliferation of duties and arguments about their breadth. I prefer to base my conclusion in this case on the fundamental duty to which a director is subject, that is the duty to act in what he in good faith considers to be the best interests of his company. This duty of loyalty is the 'time-honoured' rule: per Goulding J in *Mutual Life Insurance Co of New York v Rank Organisation Ltd* [1985] BCLC 11, 21. The duty is expressed in these very general terms, but that is one of its strengths: it focuses on principle not on the particular words which judges or the legislature have used in any particular case or context. It is dynamic and capable of application in cases where it has not previously been applied but the principle or rationale of the rule applies. It reflects the flexible quality of the doctrines of equity . . .
>
> The only reason that I can see that it could be said that the duty of loyalty does not require a fiduciary to disclose his own misconduct is that it has never been applied to this situation before. As I have explained, that is not a good objection to the application of the fiduciary principle . . .

Furthermore, on the facts of this case, there is no basis on which Mr Fassihi could reasonably have come to the conclusion that it was not in the interests of Item to know of his breach of duty. In my judgment, he could not fulfil his duty of loyalty in this case except by telling Item about his setting up of RAMS, and his plan to acquire the Isograph contract for himself . . .

Both counsel have addressed the court on the policy reasons for holding that Mr Fassihi was in breach of his duty of loyalty in this case. These are relevant questions. If the approach of the law were overly intrusive, legitimate entrepreneurial activity would be discouraged and this would not be a beneficial outcome. But that is not in my judgment the result of holding that a duty of loyalty applies in the present case. This is because, on well established principles of law, Mr Fassihi's setting up of a new company to which the business of Item would be diverted was not a legitimate entrepreneurial activity. In addition, the effect of my decision in this case (if the majority of the court is of the same opinion) is not to make any substantive extension of the duties of directors, such as would be involved for example if the courts held that a director of one company could not accept a directorship of another company . . .

A conclusion that a director owes no obligation to disclose his improper actions would be also inefficient in economic terms. It would mean that the company has to expend resources in investigating his conduct and that the enforcement of a liability to compensate the company for misconduct depends on the happenchance of the company finding out about the impropriety. To this it may be said that the law ought not to hold that the duty of loyalty involves a positive duty to disclose because it is unlikely that the consciously misbehaving director will comply with it: this indeed is the rationale for the fraud exception (in *Re Hampshire Land Co*[27]) referred to above.

My answer to that is two wrongs do not make a right: the fact that a director is unlikely to comply with a duty is not a logically sustainable reason for not imposing it if it is otherwise appropriate. As the facts of this case demonstrate, the consequence of non-disclosure may be that the company makes erroneous business decisions because it lacks essential information. A legal rule which condones this, in my judgment, condones inefficient outcomes. Moreover, there is a constant dilemma in company law as to the manner in which the shareholders of a company can monitor those who manage its business on their behalf. The duty upheld above helps to ameliorate these problems (often called agency problems) by encouraging the provision of information on which proper decision-making can take place. In many companies, an agency problem exists not only between shareholders and directors but between the board and executive or managing directors. There is an oversight duty owed by the board in respect of executives by virtue of their duty of care. (The precise extent of the duty depends on the facts of the case: *Re Barings plc (No.5)* **[5.12]**.) The duty of loyalty as applied by me above supports the board in the performance of this duty and is thus efficient for that reason also. Accordingly, in so far as my conclusion on this issue involves a new application of the duty of loyalty, it is supported for policy reasons. For all these reasons, in my judgment, the appeal against the judge's judgment on the disclosure issue must be dismissed.

HOLMAN J delivered a concurring judgment.

MUMMERY LJ concurred.

[Also see *Industrial Development Consultants Ltd v Cooley*, below, p 320.]

➤ Questions

1. Is there any indication in the cases of how the necessary balancing of different interests of stakeholders or constituencies is to be carried out?

2. Perhaps the real issue in *Fassihi* **[6.11]** is one of remedies. A director's contract may provide that he or she is to be dismissed for any breach of duty, and may add further options in favour of the company. This is not in issue. But in *Fassihi* the company was not seeking the

---

[27] [1896] 2 Ch 743.

traditional remedy of an account of profits from Fassihi for the profits he had made from his own new company (under the conflicts of interest rule, see below, pp 308 ff). It was seeking compensation for the losses it had suffered in losing its own contract. Were these losses caused by a failure to 'act in good faith in the interests of the company'? If so, what does a 'failure to disclose' add? What losses are caused by a failure to disclose?

Duty to exercise independent judgement: CA 2006 s 173

Directors must exercise independent judgement (traditionally expressed as 'directors must not fetter their discretion'). This duty is not breached if the director merely takes advice, or acts in accordance with an agreement duly entered into by the company that restricts the *future* exercise of discretion by its directors, or in a way permitted by the company's constitution. The duty does not confer a power on the directors to delegate, but nor does it prevent a director from exercising a power to delegate conferred by the company's constitution (provided the exercise is in accordance with the company's constitution).

The duty applies equally to nominee directors, who cannot blindly follow the judgement of those who appointed them, although they may rely on their advice provided they make the judgement their own: *Scottish Co-operative Wholesale Society Ltd v Meyer* [11.19]; *Kuwait Asia Bank EC v National Mutual Life Nominees Ltd* [6.31].

Directors may not fetter their discretion by contracts with outsiders.

[6.12] Kregor v Hollins (1913) 109 LT 225 (King's Bench Division and Court of Appeal)

Hollins had invested £5,000 in a company, and he agreed to pay Kregor £200 to act as a director of the company on his nomination. Kregor sued to recover this remuneration and succeeded, the jury finding that the agreement did not contemplate that he should put Hollins' interests above those of the company.

AVORY J, addressing the jury, said:
If he was to look after the interests of the defendant in the sense that he was to prefer them to the interests of the whole body of shareholders—that is to say, if they came into conflict that he was to promote the defendant's interests rather than the interests of the whole body of shareholders which were in conflict—then in my opinion it was an unlawful agreement.

[The Court of Appeal (HAMILTON LJ and BRAY J, VAUGHAN WILLIAMS LJ dissenting) held that the bargain was in any event not corrupt in that the company had assented to and approved it; the majority did not refer to these remarks of AVORY J, but they were approved by VAUGHAN WILLIAMS LJ.]

➤ Notes

1. *Fulham Football Club Ltd v Cabra Estates plc* [1994] 1 BCLC 363, CA shows that in certain circumstances directors may legitimately bind themselves to act in a certain way in the future without being in breach of this rule. Here the club and its directors, in return for a substantial payment, had contracted with the landlords of the football ground which they held on lease that they would not oppose any future application to the planning authorities which the

landlords might make for the development of the ground. The directors later wished to go back on this undertaking, and pleaded that it was an unlawful fetter on their ability to act in the best interests of the company at any relevant time in the future. The Court of Appeal rejected this argument: if the directors had properly, in the exercise of their discretion, entered into contractual arrangements which conferred substantial benefits on the company in exchange for undertakings that they would act in a certain way in the future, they were bound to honour those undertakings. Neill LJ quoted the following passage from the judgment of Kitto J in the Australian case *Thorby v Goldberg* (1964) 112 CLR 597 (Aust HCt) at 605–606:

> The argument for illegality postulates that since the discretionary powers of directors are fiduciary, in the sense that every exercise of them is required to be in good faith for the benefit of the company as a whole, an agreement is contrary to the policy of the law and void if thereby the directors of a company purport to fetter their discretion in advance . . . There may be more answers than one to the argument, but I content myself with one. There are many kinds of transactions in which the proper time for the exercise of the directors' discretion is the time of the negotiation of a contract, and not the time at which the contract is to be performed. A sale of land is a familiar example. Where all the members of a company desire to enter as a group into a transaction such as that in the present case, the transaction being one which requires action by the board of directors for its effectuation, it seems to me that the proper time for the directors to decide whether their proposed action will be in the interests of the company as a whole is the time when the transaction is being entered into, and not the time when their action under it is required. If at the former time they are bona fide of opinion that it is in the interests of the company that the transaction should be entered into and carried into effect, I see no reason in law why they should not bind themselves to do whatever under the transaction is to be done by the board. In my opinion the defendants' contention that the agreement is void for illegality should be rejected.

2. Also see *Scottish Co-operative Wholesale Society Ltd v Meyer* **[11.19]**, in which the special position of a 'nominee director' is discussed.[28] That case confirms the view that a nominated director must not put the principal's interest above those of the company (or, to be more accurate, that members of the company may be able to invoke CA 1985 s 459 (now CA 2006 s 994) if this happens).

But in Australia and New Zealand there are cases which suggest that this may be too narrow a view. The whole object of having a director appointed to represent a special interest may have been the furtherance of some ulterior corporate good, and in such circumstances it may be justifiable to put that interest first. Thus in *Levin v Clark* [1962] NSWR 686, directors nominated to the board to represent the interests of a secured creditor were held not to be in breach of any fiduciary duties to the company when they acted to enforce the security: the company, by accepting the credit on the terms in question, had waived its right to have the unqualified loyalty of those directors.

Again, in *Berlei Hestia (NZ) Ltd v Fernyhough* [1980] 2 NZLR 150 at 165–166, Mahon J (without deciding the point) adverted to the possibility that the normal fiduciary duties might be modified where a company had been set up as a joint venture between two or more participants on the understanding that each of them would be separately represented on its board by nominee directors. However, for a recent case where the joint venture nature of a company was held not to abrogate the duties a director owed to it, see *Gwembe Valley Development Co Ltd v Koshy (No. 3)* **[6.22]**.

---

[28] On nominee directors, see E Boros, 'The Duties of Nominee and Multiple Directors' (1989) 10 Co Law 211, (1990) 11 Co Law 6; and P Crutchfield, 'Nominee Directors: the Law and Commercial Reality' (1991) 12 Co Law 136.

> ➤ **Questions**

1. If a company's constitution provides for the election of employee representatives to the board, is there a case for adopting the reasoning in *Levin v Clark*?

2. Directors sometimes confer upon a 'management company' all their powers of management, pursuant to a 'management agreement'. (eg *Lee Panavision Ltd v Lee Lighting Ltd* [1992] BCLC 22, CA.) Does such an arrangement infringe the principle of *Kregor v Hollins*? To be effective, must such an arrangement have the shareholders' approval?

3. If such an arrangement is put in place, what, if any, duties would the directors continue to owe to the company?

Duty to exercise reasonable care, skill and diligence: CA 2006 s 174

Traditionally, the courts did not require directors to exhibit a greater degree of skill than may reasonably be expected from a person with their knowledge and experience (a subjective test). This test allowed inherently poor directors to escape liability for company losses, even when most reasonable people would have regarded their decisions as negligent. More recently, the courts have said that the common law standard was not so low, but mirrored the tests laid down in IA 1986 s 214, which includes an objective assessment of a director's conduct. CA 2006 s 174 is modelled on the IA 1986 section. It provides that a director owes a duty to the company to exercise the same standard of care, skill and diligence that would be exercised by a reasonably diligent person with:

(i) the general knowledge, skill and experience that may reasonably be expected of a person carrying out the same functions as the director in relation to that company (*an objective test*); and

(ii) the general knowledge, skill and experience that the director actually has (*a subjective test*).

The CA 2006 provision thus codifies the still somewhat controversial approach found in more recent case law, and marks an end to the subjective test enunciated in *Re City Equitable Fire Insurance Co Ltd* [**6.13**]. The approach adopts as the minimum standard that objectively expected of person in the directors' position; that standard may be raised by the subjective element of the test if the particular director has any special knowledge, skill and experience.

The Act does not indicate whether this duty is a common law or equitable duty, but it is not fiduciary (see CA 2006 s 178). The duty is owed to the company (s 170), not to the members. Members have no right, for example, to expect a reasonable standard of general management from the company's managing director: management quality is one of the normal risks of investing (*Re Elgindata Ltd* [1991] BCLC 959).

As well as liability to the company, breach of this duty may show unfitness to be concerned in the management of the company and so lead to disqualification under the CDDA 1986, s 6 (see above, pp 264 ff).

The old subjective test

[6.13] Re City Equitable Fire Insurance Co Ltd [1925] Ch 407 (Chancery Division)

The company had lost £1,200,000 (a fantastic amount at the time), owing partly to the failure of certain investments but mainly to the frauds of the chairman of directors, Bevan, 'a daring and unprincipled scoundrel'. In this action the liquidator sought to make the other directors liable for the losses on the ground of negligence.[29] The action failed because of a provision in the articles which exempted the directors from liability apart from losses caused by 'their own wilful neglect or default'.[30] The decision of Romer J remains important as a summary of the old 'subjective-only' duties of care and skill. It also indicates some of the potential problems in applying an objective test, and defining the outlook of a 'reasonable director'.

ROMER J: It has sometimes been said that directors are trustees. If this means no more than that directors in the performance of their duties stand in a fiduciary relationship to the company, the statement is true enough. But if the statement is meant to be an indication by way of analogy of what those duties are, it appears to me to be wholly misleading. I can see but little resemblance between the duties of a director and the duties of a trustee of a will or of a marriage settlement. It is indeed impossible to describe the duty of directors in general terms, whether by way of analogy or otherwise. The position of a director of a company carrying on a small retail business is very different from that of a director of a railway company. The duties of a bank director may differ widely from those of an insurance director, and the duties of a director of one insurance company may differ from those of a director of another. In one company, for instance, matters may normally be attended to by the manager or other members of the staff that in another company are attended to by the directors themselves. The larger the business carried on by the company the more numerous, and the more important, the matters that must of necessity be left to the managers, the accountants and the rest of the staff. The manner in which the work of the company is to be distributed between the board of directors and the staff is in truth a business matter to be decided on business lines . . .

In order, therefore, to ascertain the duties that a person appointed to the board of an established company undertakes to perform, it is necessary to consider not only the nature of the company's business, but also the manner in which the work of the company is in fact distributed between the directors and the other officials of the company, provided always that this distribution is a reasonable one in the circumstances, and is not inconsistent with any express provisions of the articles of association. In discharging the duties of his position thus ascertained a director must, of course, act honestly; but he must also exercise some degree of both skill and diligence. To the question of what is the particular degree of skill and diligence required of him, the authorities do not, I think, give any very clear answer. It has been laid down that so long as a director acts honestly he cannot be made responsible in damages unless guilty of gross or culpable negligence in a business sense. But as pointed out by Neville J in *Re Brazilian Rubber Plantations and Estates Ltd*,[31] one cannot say whether a man has been guilty of negligence, gross or otherwise, unless one can determine what is the extent of the duty which he is alleged to have neglected. For myself, I confess to feeling some difficulty in understanding the difference between negligence and gross negligence, except in so far as the expressions are used for the purpose of drawing a distinction between the duty that is

---

[29] The action also sought to make the auditors liable, and on these issues went to the Court of Appeal; but the auditors too were held, having acted honestly, to be exonerated by the special provision in the company's articles.

[30] Such articles are now invalidated by statute: see CA 2006 ss 232 and 532, although auditors can limit their liability (ss 534–536).

[31] [1911] 1 Ch 425.

owed in one case and the duty that is owed in another . . . If, therefore, a director is only liable for gross or culpable negligence, this means that he does not owe a duty to his company, to take all possible care. It is some degree of care less than that. The care that he is bound to take has been described by Neville J in the case referred to above as 'reasonable care' to be measured by the care an ordinary man might be expected to take in the circumstances on his own behalf . . .

There are, in addition, one or two other general propositions that seem to be warranted by the reported cases: (1) A director need not exhibit in the performance of his duties a greater degree of skill than may reasonably be expected from a person of his knowledge and experience. A director of a life insurance company, for instance, does not guarantee that he has the skill of an actuary or of a physician. In the words of Lindley MR: 'If directors act within their powers, if they act with such care as is reasonably to be expected from them, having regard to their knowledge and experience, and if they act honestly for the benefit of the company they represent, they discharge both their equitable as well as their legal duty to the company': see *Lagunas Nitrate Co v Lagunas Syndicate*.[32] It is perhaps only another way of stating the same proposition to say that directors are not liable for mere errors of judgment. (2) A director is not bound to give continuous attention to the affairs of his company. His duties are of an intermittent nature to be performed at periodical board meetings, and at meetings of any committee of the board upon which he happens to be placed. He is not, however, bound to attend all such meetings, though he ought to attend whenever, in the circumstances, he is reasonably able to do so. (3) In respect of all duties that, having regard to the exigencies of business, and the articles of association, may properly be left to some other official, a director is, in the absence of grounds for suspicion, justified in trusting that official to perform such duties honestly. In the judgment of the Court of Appeal in *Re National Bank of Wales Ltd*,[33] the following passage occurs in relation to a director who had been deceived by the manager, and managing director, as to matters within their own particular sphere of activity: 'Was it his duty to test the accuracy or completeness of what he was told by the general manager, and the managing director? This is a question on which opinions may differ, but we are not prepared to say that he failed in his legal duty. Business cannot be carried on upon principles of distrust. Men in responsible positions must be trusted by those above them, as well as those below them, until there is reason to distrust them. We agree that care and prudence do not involve distrust; but for a director acting honestly himself to be held legally liable for negligence, in trusting the officers under him not to conceal from him what they ought to report to him, appears to us to be laying too heavy a burden on honest businessmen.' . . .

These are the general principles that I shall endeavour to apply in considering the question whether the directors of this company have been guilty of negligence . . .

[His Lordship then considered a number of specific allegations and made various observations about points of detail. These must, of course, be understood to be applicable primarily to the facts before him, and to companies the size and nature of the City Equitable Co; but they are of value if only as illustrations of the extent of a director's duty in a typical case. Some of these observations follow.]

. . . [A] director who signs a cheque that appears to be drawn for a legitimate purpose is not responsible for seeing that the money is in fact required for that purpose or that it is subsequently applied for that purpose, assuming, of course, that the cheque comes before him for signature in the regular way having regard to the usual practice of the company. If this were not so, the business of a large company could not be carried on. In the case of an insurance company, for instance, the cheques to be signed at the board meeting would often include cheques in payment of insurance claims. If a claim appears to have been examined into and passed by the manager or other proper official for the purpose, a director who signs the necessary cheque in payment of the claim (the cheque being brought before him in the customary way) cannot be expected to investigate the whole matter over again, for the purpose of satisfying himself that the claim is well founded. A director must of necessity trust the officials of the company to perform properly and honestly the duties allocated to those officials . . .

---

[32] [1899] 2 Ch 392 at 435, CA.
[33] [1899] 2 Ch 629 at 673, and on appeal, *Dovey v Cory* [1901] AC 477, HL.

It is the duty of each director to see that the company's moneys are from time to time in a proper state of investment, except in so far as the company's articles of association may justify him in delegating that duty to others. So far as the respondent directors, other than Mr Haig Thomas and Mr Grenside, are concerned, they were justified in delegating this general duty to the finance committee, and thought that they had done so. The position of Mr Thomas and Mr Grenside was, however, very different. They knew that neither the board nor the finance committee were attending to the temporary investments and were content to leave the duty of doing so to Mr Bevan and Mr Mansell. In this they were wrong. Thinking, as they did, that the duty had not been delegated to the finance committee, they should have regarded it as being still reposed in the board as a whole. That Bevan and Mansell were persons enjoying the highest reputation is beside the mark. If the shareholders had desired to leave hundreds of thousands of pounds of the company's money under the sole control of Bevan, they would have done so. But the shareholders had preferred to have associated with Bevan a board of six or seven other directors, and it was not for these other directors to leave Bevan to discharge one of the most important of the duties that had been entrusted by the shareholders to the board as a whole, however reasonable and however safe it might have seemed to the directors to do so. Still less would it be permissible to leave the control of the company's temporary investments to the general manager. It is not any part of the functions of a manger of an insurance company to decide upon the method of investment of the company's cash resources. His advice and assistance will no doubt be sought. But the responsibility for the ultimate decision as to investment must rest with the directors or, when the articles permit, with a committee of the directors, and none the less that the investment is only a temporary one. In my judgment, Mr Haig Thomas and Mr Grenside were guilty of a breach of their duty in failing to control and safeguard the moneys of the company that were not in a state of permanent investment.

The Official Receiver . . . seeks to charge the respondent directors . . . upon the ground that it was a breach of their duty to allow securities of the company to be retained by their brokers. Had any one of the respondent directors been aware of the fact that securities were left in the hands of Ellis & Co for safe custody he would have been guilty of breach of duty if he had not insisted on the practice being summarily stopped. But in fact they were all ignorant that this was being done. The Official Receiver contends, however, that this ignorance does not protect them, as they ought to have initiated some system of safeguarding the company's securities under which it would have been impossible for Ellis & Co to obtain possession of them. This object could, no doubt, have been attained if the directors had taken the securities to the bank in person or had personally supervised the locking up of the securities in a safe, retaining sole control of the key. But it is not the duty of a director of such a company as the City Equitable to see in person to the safe custody of securities. That is one of the matters which the directors must almost of necessity leave to some official who is at the office daily, such as the manager, accountant or secretary. When an investment is made through the brokers, it would be quite impracticable for the directors to receive actual delivery of the securities. So too when investments are sold, delay and great inconvenience would result if the delivery of the securities to the brokers had to await a meeting of the board or of a committee of directors. The respondent directors would therefore be justified in trusting to Mr Mansell, their general manger, or Mr Lock, their accountant, to perform the duty of putting into safe custody the securities of the company. And this is what in fact the respondent directors appear to have done . . .

➤ Questions

1. *Does* Romer J apply a subjective test in this case, or an objective one? The orthodox view is that it is the former, but see A Hicks, 'Directors' Liability for Management Errors' (1994) 110 LQR 390; and A Walters, 'Directors' Duties: The Impact of CDDA 1986' (2000) 21 Co Law 110.

2. Would a subjective duty alone work satisfactorily? See C Riley, 'The Case for an Onerous but Subjective Duty of Care.' (1999) 63 MLR 697.

The subjective/objective test

[6.14] Re D'Jan of London Ltd [1994] 1 BCLC 561 (Chancery Division)

[The facts appear from the judgment.]

HOFFMANN LJ (sitting as a judge of the Chancery Division): This is a summons under s 212 of the Insolvency Act 1986 by a liquidator against a former officer of the company. This is a summary procedure which used to be called a misfeasance summons but has been extended to include breaches of any duty including the duty of care. The liquidator alleges that the respondent Mr D'Jan was negligent in completing and signing a proposal form for fire insurance with Guardian Royal Exchange Assurance plc. As a result, the insurers repudiated liability for a fire at the company's premises in Cornwall which had destroyed stock said to be worth some £174,000. The company is insolvent, having a deficiency as regards unsecured creditors of about £500,000. The liquidator therefore brings these proceedings for the benefit of the unsecured creditors.

Mr D'Jan signed the insurance proposal on 18 September 1986. It was headed 'Business Insurances Proposal'. Mr D'Jan signed on the front page, under the words:

I declare that to the best of my knowledge and belief all the statements and particulars made with regard to this proposal are true and I agree that this proposal shall be the basis of a contract of insurance to be expressed in the usual terms of the policy issued by Guardian Royal Exchange Assurance plc.

On the same page the form required certain information to be filled in and also asked three specific questions, including:

7. Have you or any director or partner . . . been director of any company which went into liquidation . . . ?

The question was answered 'No'. Mr D'Jan admits that this was wrong. In the previous year, a company called Harleyshield Ltd, of which Mr D'Jan was a director, had gone into insolvent liquidation. And there had been a couple of other insolvencies about five years earlier . . .

Mr D'Jan says he realises—perhaps more clearly now than he did at the time—the importance of giving correct answers on insurance proposals. But he says that he did not fill in the form himself or read it before he signed. It was filled in by his insurance broker, one Tarik Shenyuz, who had been handling his personal and corporate insurance affairs for about five years. Mr D'Jan says that Mr Shenyuz had demonstrated his competence by obtaining good rates and recommending him to loss adjusters who had obtained satisfactory settlements on his claims. So he trusted Mr Shenyuz to fill in the form correctly . . .

Nevertheless I think that in failing even to read the form, Mr D'Jan was negligent. Mr Russen [counsel for D'Jan] said that the standard of care which directors owe to their companies is not very exacting and signing forms without reading them is something a busy director might reasonably do. I accept that in real life, this often happens. But that does not mean that it is not negligent. People often take risks in circumstances in which it was not necessary or reasonable to do so. If the risk materialises, they may have to pay a penalty. I do not say that a director must always read the whole of every document which he signs. If he signs an agreement running to 60 pages of turgid legal prose on the assurance of his solicitor that it accurately reflects the board's instructions, he may well be excused from reading it all himself. But this was an extremely simple document asking a few questions which Mr D'Jan was the best person to answer. By signing the form, he accepted that he was the person who should take responsibility for its contents. In my view, the duty of care owed by a director at common law is accurately stated in s 214(4) of the Insolvency Act 1986. It is the conduct of—

a reasonably diligent person having both—(a) the general knowledge, skill and experience that may reasonably be expected of a person carrying out the same functions as are carried out by that director in relation to the company, and (b) the general knowledge, skill and experience that that director has.

Both on the objective test and, having seen Mr D'Jan, on the subjective test, I think that he did not show reasonable diligence when he signed the form. He was therefore in breach of his duty to the company.

Mr Russen said that nevertheless the company could not complain of the breach of duty because it is a principle of company law that an act authorised by all the shareholders is in law the act of the company: see *Multinational Gas and Petrochemical Co v Multinational Gas and Petrochemical Services Ltd* **[6.25]**. Mr D'Jan held 99 of the 100 issued ordinary shares and Mrs D'Jan held the other. Mr D'Jan must be taken to have authorised the wrong answer in the proposal because he signed it himself. As for Mrs D'Jan, she had never been known to object to anything which her husband did in the management of the company. If she had known about the way he signed the form and it was too late to put the matter right the chances are that she would also have approved. She could hardly have brought a derivative action to sue her husband for negligence because he could have procured the passing of a resolution absolving himself from liability.

The difficulty is that unlike the *Multinational* case, in which the action alleged to be negligent was specifically mandated by the shareholders, neither Mr nor Mrs D'Jan gave any thought to the way in which the proposal had been filled in. Mr D'Jan did not realise that he had given a wrong answer until the insurance company repudiated. By that time the company was in liquidation. In my judgment the *Multinational* principle requires that the shareholders should have, whether formally or informally, mandated or ratified the act in question. It is not enough that they probably would have ratified if they had known or thought about it before the liquidation removed their power to do so.

It follows that Mr D'Jan is in principle liable to compensate the company for his breach of duty. But s 727 of the Companies Act 1985 [equivalent to CA 2006 s 1157] gives the court a discretionary power to relieve a director wholly or in part from liability for breaches of duty, including negligence, if the court considers that he acted honestly and reasonably and ought fairly to be excused. It may seem odd that a person found to have been guilty of negligence, which involves failing to take reasonable care, can ever satisfy a court that he acted reasonably. Nevertheless, the section clearly contemplates that he may do so and it follows that conduct may be reasonable for the purposes of s 727 despite amounting to lack of reasonable care at common law.

In my judgment, although Mr D'Jan's 99% holding of shares is not sufficient to sustain a *Multinational* defence, it is relevant to the exercise of the discretion under s 727. It may be reasonable to take a risk in relation to your own money which would be unreasonable in relation to someone else's. And although for the purposes of the law of negligence the company is a separate entity [to] which Mr D'Jan owes a duty of care which cannot vary according to the number of shares he owns, I think that the economic realities of the case can be taken into account in exercising the discretion under s 727. His breach of duty in failing to read the form before signing was not gross. It was the kind of thing which could happen to any busy man, although, as I have said, this is not enough to excuse it. But I think it is also relevant that in 1986, with the company solvent and indeed prosperous, the only persons whose interests he was foreseeably putting at risk by not reading the form were himself and his wife. Mr D'Jan certainly acted honestly. For the purposes of s 727 I think he acted reasonably and I think he ought fairly to be excused for some, though not all, of the liability which he would otherwise have incurred.

[His Lordship accordingly gave judgment against D'Jan for an amount limited to the sum which he remained entitled to claim as an unsecured creditor of the company.]

➤ Questions

1. Why was this case not brought under IA 1986 s 214? (Look closely at the conditions that must be met for the liquidator to bring such a claim.)

2. *Could* the company have authorised the breach before the event (however unlikely that scenario)? *Could* the shareholders have ratified the breach afterwards? See *Kinsela v Russell Kinsela Pty Ltd* [6.04]. Also see CA 2006 ss 180 and 239 for the current provisions.

3. Was the application of CA 1985 s 727 [CA 2006 s 1157] sensible in the circumstances?

4. How do the courts decide on the qualities of a 'reasonable director'? The problem here is that companies range from the very large to the very small, and that even within the same company the roles of different directors may vary considerably: some may be highly qualified and bring wide commercial experience to their post, and work for the company full-time for a substantial salary; while others may serve as non-executive directors and be required only to attend monthly or quarterly board meetings. Yet others may be appointed to bring expertise of a technical nature—as engineers or scientists, for instance—without any background in business. And, of course, the law allows those who form a small family company or a one-person company to appoint themselves directors regardless of their abilities and circumstances. The subjective standards brought to the role will certainly be different, but so too are the objective standards of a 'reasonable director' in the circumstances. So it is not altogether surprising that the search for an objective standard has proven, and likely will continue to prove, elusive.

➤ Notes

1. Directors cannot escape liability for negligence by avoiding activities in their director's role. In *Dorchester Finance Co Ltd v Stebbing* (1977), reported [1989] BCLC 498, a money-lending company had three directors, Stebbing, Parsons and Hamilton. Stebbing worked full time for the company; the other two paid very little attention to it and visited its premises only rarely. They signed blank cheque forms at Stebbing's request, and he used these to make loans that were illegal and accordingly irrecoverable. No board meetings were held. All three directors were held liable to make good the company's losses. Foster J laid some stress on the fact that the two non-executive directors were experienced in accountancy; but it appears that this was not crucial to his decision. He said:

> For a chartered accountant and an experienced accountant to put forward the proposition that a non-executive director has no duties to perform I find quite alarming. It would be an argument which, if put forward by a director with no accountancy experience, would involve total disregard of many sections of the Companies Act 1948 . . . The signing of blank cheques by Hamilton and Parsons was in my judgment negligent, as it allowed Stebbing to do as he pleased. Apart from that, they not only failed to exhibit the necessary skill and care in the performance of their duties as directors, but also failed to perform any duty at all as directors of Dorchester. In the Companies Act 1948 the duties of a director whether executive or not are the same.

2. For the extent to which directors can, without being negligent, rely on other officials and employees, see: *Dovey v Cory* [1901] AC 477 (the CA decision noted in *City Equitable* [6.13]) and *Re Barings plc (No 5)* [5.12] (a disqualification case).

3. For the suggestion that directors have a duty to take positive action and keep themselves informed, see *Re Barings plc (No 5)* [5.12] (a disqualification case), and its references to *Re Westmid Packing Services Ltd* [1998] 2 All ER 124.

Problems in bringing successful claims based on care, skill and diligence

The problems of proof of breach have already been mentioned. These cases are also hampered by problems in proving a causative loss. Typically, the facts are similar to those of *City Equitable*: [6.13] a rogue, reasonably trusted by all, at the centre of the action, his frauds deceiving even the auditors; and a board of directors, many of them non-executive, meeting only at intervals and justifiably delegating many functions to committees or subordinate officers. On such facts, it is virtually impossible to hold that the acts (or, more likely, the omissions) of those directors who were not directly involved in the wrongdoing were the *cause* of the company's loss.

This difficulty probably explains why the law on directors' negligence is now being driven not by these breach of duty cases, but primarily by the cases on director disqualification (with some input also from cases under CA 2006 s 994 and its predecessors (unfairly prejudicial conduct) and IA 1986 s 214 (wrongful trading)).

Already, reported cases provide examples of individuals who have accepted the office of director but not appreciated the responsibility that goes with it (commonly because the company is run by a dominant individual), and have had disqualification orders made against them. Subjective factors such as their youth or lack of business experience have been held to be no excuse. Thus, in *Cohen v Selby* [2001] 1 BCLC 176, CA a father-and-son company was in fact run by the father (who was a *de facto* director only, not formally appointed). His son, a student, was a director, but took no part in the company's affairs. The father took jewellery, worth £395,000, which the company had bought but not paid for on a trip without insuring it and it was stolen on the ferry. The father was held fully liable for the loss. The son escaped personal liability based on negligence because it was not considered unreasonable for him to have trusted his father, an experienced businessman, and also for lack of a sufficient causal link between his conduct and the company's loss. But he was nevertheless disqualified (in separate proceedings) for three years.

The most significant of these disqualification cases, however, is *Re Barings plc (No 5)* **[5.12]**. This case was concerned with a company at the opposite end of the spectrum and its most senior, highly paid, directors. Disqualification orders were made against the respondents on the ground that they had failed to ensure that proper management and supervision systems and processes were in place, and had, accordingly, fallen short of the objective standards appropriate to directors of their status and experience. It could well have been far more difficult to establish liability for the losses suffered by the company had the case been brought for compensation at common law.

A similar development has taken place in Australia. In *Daniels v Anderson* (1995) 16 ACSR 607, NSWCA (commonly know as the *AWA* case), the court signalled a new approach with a number of emphatic statements: that it is no longer appropriate to judge directors' conduct by the subjective tests applied in the older cases; that (by analogy with cases under the Australian insolvent trading legislation) ignorance should not be regarded as a defence to proceedings brought against directors; and that more is required of directors than supine indifference.[34] It was alleged (by the auditors) that the chief executive and several non-executive directors of AWA were liable in negligence for their failure to prevent the massive foreign exchange trading losses caused by one of their employees. In the event, only the chief executive was held to have acted negligently. The same duty of care was owed by both types of director but, in the circumstances, the non-executive directors were entitled to assume (contrary to the fact) that they had been given a comprehensive account of the company's problems, especially given their publicly expressed concerns and frequent requests for detailed information and considered action. AWA's chief executive, on the other hand, was deemed to have acted negligently: knowing nothing himself about foreign exchange trading, he had delegated the function to someone relatively inexperienced and had allowed this person to operate without ensuring that appropriate management controls were in place; the

---

[34] The controversial opinion of the majority of the court in this case, that directors' liability could be founded in the tort of negligence rather than as a breach of purely equitable obligations, is now academic in the UK, given the introduction of a statutory rule in s 174. The controversy persists in other forms, however: see the note to *Medforth v Blake* [14.06].

obvious problems this was likely to cause were compounded because this was a novel venture for AWA and so its managers lacked experience in the area; moreover, when the problems eventually came to light, the chief executive failed to obtain all the information necessary to take remedial action, failed to delegate the rescue operation to someone sufficiently experienced, and failed to give the entire matter the degree of personal attention, energy and detailed supervision that its obvious seriousness demanded in order to achieve a successful resolution. One practical consequence of application of an objective test is that directors are increasingly focused on ensuring that management systems, processes and procedures are adequately developed, documented and applied—and that their application is assured by systematic measurement, reporting and audit processes.

Duty to avoid conflicts of interest: CA 2006 s 175

This section is the first of three general sections, appearing in succession, that address the true fiduciary duties of loyalty owed by directors to their companies (also see chapter 4 on specific transactions between directors and the company and Part 14 on political donations and expenditure).[35] This section replaces the equitable *no-conflict rule*, although *only* as it applies to conflicts of interest arising from third party dealings by a director (s 175(3)).

Statutory changes to the equitable rules

The general rule set out in s 175(1) is a reformulation of the statement of the equitable rule in *Aberdeen Railway Co v Blaikie Bros* [6.21]. It comprehends actual and potential conflicts. The codification does, however, effect a number of important changes to the law:

(i)   The exclusion of conflicts of interest arising in relation to transactions or arrangements *with* the company (s 175(3)), noted above, is perhaps statutory acknowledgement that companies' articles routinely permit their directors to have interests in company transactions, provided they are declared. Instead, these transactions will merely have to be declared to the other directors (see s 176 and chapter 3), unless the transaction is a substantial transaction requiring the approval of members (as defined in chapter 4).

(ii)   The statutory duty to avoid conflicts of interest replaces the equitable *no-conflict* and *no-profit* rules by a single rule[36] (although also see s 176 below). To the extent (if any) that the no-conflict rule fails to cover the no-profit rule, the new statutory regime deviates from existing equitable rules.

(iii)   The statutory duty substantially modifies the equitable rules with regard to *authorisation of conflicts of interest* (see subss (4)(b), (5) and (6)).

(iv)   The statutory duty covers both conflicts of interest and duty and conflicts of duties (see subs (7)). The precise implications and remedial consequences of this bundling may need further working out.

---

[35] Also see R Nolan, 'Directors' Self-Interested Dealings: Liabilities and Remedies' [1999] CfiLR 235; J Lowry and R Edmunds, 'The Corporate Opportunity Doctrine: The Shifting Boundaries of the Duties and its Remedies' (1998) 61 MLR 515; D Kershaw, 'Lost in Translation: Corporate Opportunities in Comparative Perspective' (2005) 25 OJLS 603.

[36] This approach, where the no-profit rule is regarded as part of the no-conflict rule, is evident in *Bray v Ford* [1896] AC 44, 51–2, and *Boardman v Phipps* [1967] 2 AC 46, 123. But other cases have regarded the two rules as distinct, although overlapping, so that a breach of the no-profit rule cannot always be readily analysed as a conflict of duty and interest (see eg *Regal (Hastings) Ltd v Gulliver* [6.16]).

(v)   Section 170(2) makes it clear that a person who ceases to be a director will continue to be subject to the duty to avoid conflicts of interest as regards the exploitation of any property, information or opportunity of which he became aware at a time when he was a director.

Conflicts of interest and corporate opportunities

The general rule set out in s 175(1) bars unauthorised conflicts of the director's personal interest with the *interests* of the company, not with *duties* to the company (as in the formulation in *Bray v Ford* [1896] AC 44, 51–2). The wider formulation may make it easier, especially in relation to corporate opportunities, to argue that pursuit of the opportunity involves a conflict. Earlier cases on the equitable rule vary in their approach, some taking a narrow view of which opportunities are caught (*Balston Ltd v Headline Filters Ltd* [1990] FSR 385, 412; *Industrial Development Consultants Ltd v Cooley*, below, p 320), and some a wider view (*Bhullar v Bhullar* **[6.17]**).

Section 175(2) repeats the equitable rule that it is immaterial whether the company could take advantage of the property, information or opportunity exploited by the defaulting director. This must also indicate that this element is immaterial in deciding whether a situation can reasonably be regarded as likely to give rise to a conflict of interest (subs (4)(a)). This accords with the equitable rule (see *Keech v Sandford* (1726) Sel Cas Ch 61; *Regal (Hastings) Ltd v Gulliver* **[6.16]**).

Section 175(4)(a) indicates the duty is not infringed if the situation cannot reasonably be regarded as likely to give rise to a conflict of interest. On this basis, it may now be the case that if a company considers a new venture and concludes, on a properly informed and *bona fide* basis, that it will not pursue the venture, then the company's directors will be free to pursue the venture on their own account (see the controversial Canadian decision to this effect, *Peso Silver Mines Ltd (NPL) v Cropper* **[6.20]**).

The company's articles may include exemption clauses preventing a conflict of interest arising in the first place. Whether such a restriction on the liability of directors will be valid is left to the common law: see s 232 (provisions protecting directors from liability).

Prior authorisation by the directors will excuse a potential breach

Section 175(4)(b) states that the duty is not infringed if the matter has been authorised by the directors, and subs (5) describes how and when such authorisation may be given by the directors. Subs (5) distinguishes between private and public companies. Authorisation may be given by the directors of a private company so long as the constitution does not contain any provision to the contrary; whereas authorisation may only be given by the directors of a public company if the constitution contains a provision enabling the directors to authorise the matter and they do so in accordance with this provision.

Section 175(6) states the minimum procedural requirements for an authorisation to be effective. It appears to override any more lenient approaches to disapplying the conflicts rules that might be set out in a company's articles (so, eg, the approach in *Boulting v Association of Cinematograph, Television and Allied Technicians* [1963] 2 QB 606, 636 is not longer relevant). However, in Grand Committee, Lord Goldsmith explained that this kept in place any constitutional rules or rules of the common law:

[A]ny requirements under the common law for what is necessary for a valid authorisation remain in force. I draw the Committee's attention to [s 175](6), which says: "The authorisation is effective only if". It then sets out certain specific requirements. It deliberately does not say that if those requirements are met the authorisation is effective. There might be other conditions in relation to the authorisation that would be required—for example, the company's constitution may have some specific provision with which it would be necessary to comply. Those formalities and those conditions need to be complied with as well. (HL GC Day 4, Hansard HL 678 9/2/06 Col 326)

For example, the common law indicates that any authorisation must be 'informed authorisation' in order to be effective.

Ratification of breaches of duty

Note that a breach of the duty to avoid conflicts may be ratified by a majority of members in general meeting, although the statutory rules on this (see s 180(4)(a) (consent, approval and authorisation by members)) effect several important changes when compared with the common law (eg *North-West Transportation Co Ltd v Beatty* **[4.34]**). Ratification may be useful where the board has either failed or refused to authorise a conflict of interest.

Conflicts of duty and duty

Section 175(7) makes it clear that a conflict of interest includes conflicts of interest and duty and conflicts of duties. The general equitable rule prohibits a fiduciary from entering into a position which gives rise to conflicting fiduciary duties to another person, without the informed consent of both principals (*Clark Boyce v Mouat* [1994] 1 AC 428). The statutory formulation adopts this equitable rule (see *In Plus Group Ltd v Pyke* **[6.18]**), and discards the controversial approach found in *London and Mashonaland Exploration Co Ltd v New Mashonaland Exploration Co Ltd* [1891] WN 165, *Bell v Lever Bros Ltd* [1932] AC 161, 195; and *Item Software (UK) Ltd v Fassihi* **[6.11]** (Arden LJ, *obiter*). These latter cases suggested that a director of one company may be a director of competing companies unless prohibited by contract. This is inconsistent with the equitable rule on conflict of duties.

Since conflicting multiple directorships are now caught by the duty to avoid conflicts of interest, these appointments will need to be authorised according to the process outlined in subs (5) and (6).

Illustrations of the rules

This area of directors' duties has probably generated more case law than any of the others. What follows is an illustrative selection. The cases that pre-date CA 2006 not only apply the equitable concepts of the no-conflict and no-profit duties; they also apply the equitable rules on authorisation and ratification. These have been profoundly affected by CA 2006, so care is needed in using the cases as persuasive authorities. On the other hand, since s 178 preserves the common law and equitable rules as to remedies, these cases remain applicable.

Taking corporate opportunities for personal benefit—constructive trust remedies.

[6.15] Cook v Deeks [1916] 1 AC 554 (Privy Council)

Three of the four directors of the Toronto Construction Company (Deeks, Deeks and Hinds—the three defendants) resolved to break their business relations with the fourth director, Cook (the plaintiff). The company had built up considerable goodwill with the Canadian Pacific Railway Company as a result of the satisfactory performance of a series of construction contracts, each of which had been negotiated with the railway company's representative by one of the defendants. The last of these contracts, the Shore Line contract, was negotiated in the same way, but when the arrangements were completed, the defendants took the contract in their own names and not that of the company. Cook claimed that the company was entitled to the benefit of the contract, and that a shareholders' resolution (which the defendants had carried by their own votes) purporting to confirm (ie ratify) that the company claimed no interest in the contract was ineffective. The Privy Council upheld both contentions, reversing the decisions of the courts in Ontario in favour of the defendants.

The opinion of their Lordships was delivered by LORD BUCKMASTER, who stated the facts, and continued: Two questions of law arise out of this long history of fact. The first is whether, apart altogether from the subsequent resolutions, the company would have been at liberty to claim from the three defendants the benefit of the contract which they had obtained from the Canadian Pacific Railway Company; and the second, which only arises if the first be answered in the affirmative, whether in such event the majority of the shareholders of the company constituted by the three defendants could ratify and approve of what was done and thereby release all claim against the directors.

It is the latter question to which the Appellate Division of the Supreme Court of Ontario have given most consideration, but the former needs to be carefully examined in order to ascertain the circumstances upon which the latter question depends.

It cannot be properly answered by considering the abstract relationship of directors and companies; the real matter for determination is what, in the special circumstances of this case, was the relationship that existed between Messrs Deeks and Hinds and the company that they controlled. Now it appears plain that the entire management of the company, so far as obtaining and executing contracts in the east was concerned, was in their hands, and indeed, it was in part this fact which was one of the causes of their disagreement with the plaintiff. The way they used this position is perfectly plain. They accelerated the work on the expiring contract of the company in order to stand well with the Canadian Pacific Railway when the next contract should be offered, and although Mr McLean [Manager of the Toronto Construction Co] was told that the acceleration was to enable the company to get the new contract, yet they never allowed the company to have any chances whatever of acquiring the benefit, and avoided letting their co-director have any knowledge of the matter. Their Lordships think that the statement of the trial judge upon this point is well founded when he said that 'it is hard to resist the inference that Mr Hinds was careful to avoid anything which would waken Mr Cook from his fancied security', and again, that 'the sole and only object on the part of the defendants was to get rid of a business associate whom they deemed, and I think rightly deemed, unsatisfactory from a business standpoint'. In other words, they intentionally concealed all circumstances relating to their negotiations until a point had been reached when the whole arrangement had been concluded in their own favour and there was no longer any real chance that there could be any interference with their plans. This means that while entrusted with the conduct of the affairs of the company they deliberately designed to exclude, and used their influence and position to exclude, the company whose interest it was their first duty to protect . . .

It is quite right to point out the importance of avoiding the establishment of rules as to directors' duties which would impose upon them burdens so heavy and responsibilities so great that men of good position would hesitate to accept the office. But, on the other hand, men who assume the complete control of a company's business must remember that they are not at liberty to sacrifice the interests which they are bound to protect, and, while ostensibly acting for the company, divert in their own favour business which should properly belong to the company they represent.

Their Lordships think that, in the circumstances, the defendants TR Hinds and GS and GM Deeks were guilty of a distinct breach of duty in the course they took to secure the contract, and that they cannot retain the benefit of such contract for themselves, but must be regarded as holding it on behalf of the company.

There remains the more difficult consideration of whether this position can be made regular by resolutions of the company controlled by the votes of these three defendants. The Supreme Court have given this matter the most careful consideration, but their Lordships are unable to agree with the conclusion which they reached.

In their Lordships' opinion the Supreme Court has insufficiently recognised the distinction between two classes of case and has applied the principles applicable to the case of a director selling to his company property which was in equity as well as at law his own, and which he could dispose of as he thought fit,[37] to the case of the director dealing with property which, though his own at law, in equity belonged to his company. The cases of *North-West Transportation Co v Beatty* **[4.34]** and *Burland v Earle* **[11.10]** both belonged to the former class. In each, directors had sold to the company property in which the company had no interest at law or in equity. If the company claimed any interest by reason of the transaction, it could only be by affirming the sale, in which case such sale, though initially voidable, would be validated by subsequent ratification. If the company refused to affirm the sale the transaction would be set aside and the parties restored to their former position, the directors getting the property and the company receiving back the purchase price. There would be no middle course. The company could not insist on retaining the property while paying less than the price agreed. This would be for the court to make a new contract between the parties.[38] It would be quite another thing if the director had originally acquired the property which he sold to his company under circumstances which made it in equity the property of the company. The distinction to which their Lordships have drawn attention is expressly recognised by Lord Davey in *Burland v Earle* and is the foundation of the judgment in *North-West Transportation Co v Beatty*, and is clearly explained in the case of *Jacobus Marler Estates Ltd v Marler*[39] . . .

If, as their Lordships find on the facts, the contract in question was entered into under such circumstances that the directors could not retain the benefit of it for themselves, then it belonged in equity to the company and ought to have been dealt with as an asset of the company. Even supposing it be not ultra vires of a company to make a present to its directors, it appears quite certain that directors holding a majority of votes would not be permitted to make a present to themselves. This would be to allow a majority to oppress the minority. To such circumstances the cases of *North-West Transportation Co v Beatty* **[4.34]** and *Burland v Earle* **[11.10]** have no application. In the same way, if directors have acquired for themselves property or rights which they must be regarded as holding on behalf of the company, a resolution that the rights of the company should be disregarded in the matter would amount to forfeiting the interest and property of the minority of shareholders in favour of the majority, and that by the votes of those who are interested in securing the property for themselves. Such use of voting power has never been sanctioned by the court, and, indeed, was expressly disapproved in the case of *Menier v Hooper's Telegraph Works* **[11.11]**.

If their Lordships took the view that, in the circumstances of this case, the directors had exercised a discretion or decided on a matter of policy (the view which appears to have been entertained by the Supreme Court) different results would ensue, but this is not a conclusion which their Lordships are able to accept. It follows that the defendants must account to the Toronto Company for the profits which they have made out of the transaction . . .

[Also see *Fassihi* **[6.11]**.]

➤ Note

The ratification rules set out in cases such as *North-West Transportation Co Ltd v Beatty* (which allowed the interested director to vote in shareholder meetings to approve or ratify the offending transaction, even if the vote was only carried by the director's shares) have been abrogated by statute: CA 2006 s 239. There is now no difference between the procedures that must be followed to ratify the various different directors' duties. Note that s 239(7) does not

---

[37] [These cases are now dealt with by CA 2006 s 177, requiring only notification to the directors *before* the transaction takes place, but where there *is* a breach, it seems the statutory ratification rules in s 239 apply equally; the equitable difference has been abolished.]

[38] [Cf the discussion on promoters, above, p 79.]

[39] (1913) 85 LJPC 167n.

affect any other rules of law imposing additional requirements or rendering acts incapable of being ratified by the company.

➤ Questions

1. Would the position have been any different if the defendants had told Cook beforehand of their plans? Or if the matter had been put to a members' meeting in advance, and the defendants had used their majority votes to carry a resolution giving them a 'clearance' to proceed independently of the company? Now see s 175(4)-(6), and above, pp 308 ff.

2. Can you suggest circumstances in which the directors might be said to have 'exercised a discretion or decided on a matter of policy', with the result that the defendants could have had the benefit of the Shore Line contract for themselves?

3. Did the Privy Council regard this breach as 'unratifiable'? Should it be, or has CA 2006 s 239 adopted appropriate safeguards?

Taking corporate opportunities for personal benefit—personal restitutionary remedies.

[6.16] Regal (Hastings) Ltd v Gulliver [1942] 1 All ER 378, [1967] 2 AC 134n (House of Lords)

The appellant company ('Regal') owned a cinema in Hastings, and the directors decided to acquire two others in the same area and sell all three to an outsider as a going concern. For this purpose, they formed a subsidiary company, Hastings Amalgamated Cinemas Ltd ('Amalgamated') to lease the other two cinemas. The landlord of the cinemas insisted on either a personal guarantee of the rent from the directors or that the paid-up capital of Amalgamated be increased to £5,000. Regal was unable to pay for more than 2,000 £1 shares in Amalgamated from its own resources, and so the directors, not wishing to give the requested guarantees, agreed to take up the other 3,000 shares between themselves. In the event, four directors took 500 shares each personally, the chairman Gulliver found outside subscribers for 500, and the remaining 500 were offered by the board to Garton, the company's solicitor. Some three weeks later, the proposal for a sale of the actual cinemas was abandoned, and was replaced by an agreement to sell to the purchasers all the shares in the two companies. As a result, the directors and others who had subscribed for the 3,000 shares in Amalgamated made a profit of £2 16s 1d [£2.80] per share. Regal, now under the control of the purchasers, then issued a writ claiming reimbursement of this profit from the four directors and Gulliver and Garton. The action was based alternatively in negligence, misfeasance, and money had and received. Before the House of Lords, only the last of these claims was argued, and the four directors (but not Gulliver or Garton) were held severally liable to account.

LORD RUSSELL OF KILLOWEN: The case has, I think, been complicated and obscured by the presentation of it before the trial judge. If a case of wilful misconduct or fraud on the part of the respondents had been made out, liability to make good to Regal any damage which it had thereby suffered could, no doubt, have been established; and efforts were apparently made at the trial, by cross-examination and otherwise, to found such a case. It is, however, due to the respondents to make it clear at the outset that this attempt failed. The case was not so presented to us here. We have to consider the question of the respondents' liability on the footing that, in taking up these shares in Amalgamated, they acted with bona fides, intending to act in the interest of Regal.

Nevertheless, they may be liable to account for the profits which they have made, if, while standing in a fiduciary relationship to Regal, they have by reason and in course of that fiduciary relationship made a profit. This aspect of the case was undoubtedly raised before the trial judge, but, in so far as he deals with it in his judgment, he deals with it on a wrong basis. Having stated at the outset quite truly that what he calls 'this stroke of fortune' only came the way of the respondents because they were the directors and solicitors of Regal, he continues thus: 'But in order to succeed the plaintiff company must show the defendants both ought to have caused and could have caused the plaintiff company to subscribe for these shares, and that the neglect to do so caused a loss to the plaintiff company. Short of this, if the plaintiffs can establish that, though no loss was made by the company, yet a profit was corruptly made by the directors and the solicitor, then the company can claim to have that profit handed over to the company, framing the action in such a case for money had and received by the defendants for the plaintiffs' use.' Other passages in his judgment indicate that, in addition to this 'corrupt' action by the directors, or, perhaps, alternatively, the plaintiffs in order to succeed must prove that the defendants acted mala fide, and not bona fide in the interests of the company, or that there was a plot or arrangement between them to divert from the company to themselves a valuable investment. However relevant such considerations may be in regard to a claim for damages resulting from misconduct, they are irrelevant to a claim against a person occupying a fiduciary relationship towards the plaintiff for an account of the profits made by that person by reason and in course of that relationship.

In the Court of Appeal, upon this claim to profits, the view was taken that in order to succeed the plaintiff had to establish that there was a duty on the Regal directors to obtain the shares for Regal. Two extracts from the judgment of Lord Greene MR show this. After mentioning the claim for damages, he says: 'The case is put on an alternative ground. It is said that, in the circumstances of the case, the directors must be taken to have been acting in the matter of their office when they took those shares; and that accordingly they are accountable for the profits which they have made . . . There is one matter which is common to both these claims which, unless it is established, appears to me to be fatal. It must be shown that in the circumstances of the case it was the duty of the directors to obtain these shares for their company.' Later in his judgment he uses this language: 'But it is said that the profit realised by the directors on the sale of the shares must be accounted for by them. That proposition involves that on 2 October, when it was decided to acquire these shares, and at the moment when they were acquired by the directors, the directors were taking to themselves something which properly belonged to the company.' Other portions of the judgment appear to indicate that upon this claim to profits, it is a good defence to show bona fides or absence of fraud on the part of the directors in the action which they took or that their action was beneficial to the company, and the judgment ends thus: 'That being so, the only way in which these directors could secure that benefit for their company was by putting up the money themselves. Once that decision is held to be a bona fide one, and fraud drops out of the case, it seems to me there is only one conclusion, namely, that the appeal must be dismissed with costs.'

My Lords, with all respect I think there is a misapprehension here. The rule of equity which insists on those, who by use of a fiduciary position make a profit, being liable to account for that profit, in no way depends on fraud, or absence of bona fides; or upon such questions or considerations as whether the profit would or should otherwise have gone to the plaintiff, or whether the profiteer was under a duty to obtain the source of the profit for the plaintiff, or whether he took a risk or acted as he did for the benefit of the plaintiff, or whether the plaintiff has in fact been damaged or benefited by his action. The liability arises from the mere fact of a profit having, in the stated circumstances, been made. The profiteer, however honest and well-intentioned, cannot escape the risk of being called upon to account.

The leading case of *Keech v Sandford*[40] is an illustration of the strictness of this rule of equity in this regard, and of how far the rule is independent of these outside considerations. A lease of the profits of a market had been devised to a trustee for the benefit of an infant. A renewal on behalf of the infant was refused. It was absolutely unobtainable. The trustee, finding that it was impossible

---

[40] (1726) Sel Cas Ch 61.

to get a renewal for the benefit of the infant, took a lease for his own benefit. Though his duty to obtain it for the infant was incapable of performance, nevertheless he was ordered to assign the lease to the infant, upon the bare ground that, if a trustee on the refusal to renew might have a lease for himself, few renewals would be made for the benefit of cestuis que trust. Lord King LC said, at p 62: 'This may seem hard, that the trustee is the only person of all mankind who might not have the lease: but it is very proper that the rule should be strictly pursued, and not in the least relaxed . . . 'One other case in equity may be referred to in this connection, viz *Ex p James*,[41] decided by Lord Eldon LC. This was a case of a purchase of a bankrupt's estate by the solicitor to the commission, and Lord Eldon LC refers to the doctrine thus, at p 345: 'This doctrine as to purchases by trustees, assignees, and persons having a confidential character, stands much more upon general principles than upon the circumstances of any individual case. It rests upon this: that the purchase is not permitted in any case however honest the circumstances; the general interests of justice requiring it to be destroyed in every instance; as no court is equal to the examination and ascertainment of the truth in much the greater number of cases.'

Let me now consider whether the essential matters, which the plaintiff must prove, have been established in the present case. As to the profit being in fact made there can be no doubt. The shares were acquired at par and were sold three weeks later at a profit of £2 16s 1d [£2.80] per share. Did such of the first five respondents as acquired these very profitable shares acquire them by reason and in course of their office of directors of Regal? In my opinion, when the facts are examined and appreciated, the answer can only be that they did . . .

It now remains to consider whether in acting as directors of Regal they stood in a fiduciary relationship to that company. Directors of a limited company are the creatures of statute and occupy a position peculiar to themselves. In some respects they resemble trustees, in others they do not. In some respects they resemble agents, in others they do not. In some respects they resemble managing partners, in others they do not. [His Lordship considered a number of the authorities and continued:]

In the result, I am of the opinion that the directors standing in a fiduciary relationship to Regal in regard to the exercise of their powers as directors, and having obtained these shares by reason and only by reason of the fact that they were directors of Regal and in the course of the execution of that office, are accountable for the profits which they have made out of them. The equitable rule laid down in *Keech v Sandford* and *Ex p James* and similar authorities applies to them in full force. It was contended that these cases were distinguishable by reason of the fact that it was impossible for Regal to get the shares owing to lack of funds, and that the directors in taking the shares were really acting as members of the public. I cannot accept this argument. It was impossible for the cestui que trust in *Keech v Sandford* to obtain the lease, nevertheless the trustee was accountable. The suggestion that the directors were applying simply as members of the public is a travesty of the facts. They could, had they wished, have protected themselves by a resolution (either antecedent or subsequent) of the Regal shareholders in general meeting. In default of such approval, the liability to account must remain. The result is that, in my opinion, each of the respondents Bobby, Griffiths, Bassett and Bentley is liable to account for the profit which he made on the sale of his 500 shares in Amalgamated.

The case of the respondent Gulliver, however, requires some further consideration, for he has raised a separate and distinct answer to the claim. He says: 'I never promised to subscribe for shares in Amalgamated. I never did so subscribe. I only promised to find others who would be willing to subscribe. I only found others who did subscribe. The shares were theirs. They were never mine. They received the profit. I received none of it.' If these are the true facts, his answer seems complete. The xevidence in my opinion establishes his contention . . . As regards Gulliver, this appeal should, in my opinion be dismissed . . .

---

[41] (1803) 8 Ves 337.

There remains to consider the case of Garton. He stands on a different footing from the other respondents in that he was not a director of Regal. He was Regal's legal adviser; but, in my opinion, he has a short but effective answer to the plaintiffs' claim. He was requested by the Regal directors to apply for 500 shares. They arranged that they themselves should each be responsible for £500 of the Amalgamated capital, and they appealed, by their chairman, to Garton to subscribe the balance of £500 which was required to make up the £3,000. In law his action, which has resulted in a profit, was taken at the request of Regal, and I know of no principle or authority which would justify a decision that a solicitor must account for profit resulting from a transaction which he has entered into on his own behalf, not merely with the consent, but at the request of his client.

My Lords, in my opinion the right way in which to deal with this appeal is (i) to dismiss the appeal as against the respondents Gulliver and Garton with costs, (ii) to allow it with costs as against the other four respondents, and (iii) to enter judgment as against each of these four respondents for a sum of £1,402 1s 8d [£1402.08] with interest at 4% . . .

LORD PORTER: My Lords, I am conscious of certain possibilities which are involved in the conclusion which all your Lordships have reached. The action is brought by the Regal company. Technically, of course, the fact that an unlooked for advantage may be gained by the shareholders of that company is immaterial to the question at issue. The company and its shareholders are separate entities. One cannot help remembering, however, that in fact the shares have been purchased by a financial group who were willing to acquire those of Regal and Amalgamated at a certain price. As a result of your Lordships' decision that group will, I think, receive in one hand part of the sum which has been paid by the other. For the shares in Amalgamated they paid £3 16s 1d [£3.80] per share, yet part of that sum may be returned to the group, though not necessarily to the individual shareholders, by reason of the enhancement in value of the shares in Regal—an enhancement brought about as a result of the receipt by the company of the profit made by some of its former directors on the sale of Amalgamated shares. This, it seems, may be an unexpected windfall, but whether it be so or not, the principle that a person occupying a fiduciary relationship shall not make a profit by reason thereof is of such vital importance that the possible consequence in the present case is in fact as it is in law an immaterial consideration.

VISCOUNT SANKEY and LORDS MACMILLAN and WRIGHT delivered concurring opinions.

➤ Notes

1. In an editorial note to the All ER report of this case, it is stated: 'As their Lordships point out, no question as to the right to retain this profit could have arisen if the respondents had taken the precaution of obtaining the approval of the appellant company in general meeting, and this would have been a mere matter of form, since they doubtless controlled the voting.' In contrast, in *Prudential Assurance Co Ltd v Newman Industries (No 2)* **[11.13]**, Vinelott J at first instance said [1980] 2 All ER 841 at 862: 'I can see nothing in the report which indicates that the defendant directors controlled the voting and, as I understand this passage in the speech of Lord Russell of Killowen, he contemplated that the defendant directors might have protected themselves by a resolution in general meeting precisely because they had no control of the majority of the votes.' Unfortunately for Vinelott J, the researches of Richard Nolan show that the directors did control a majority of the votes and, as this fact is stated in the judgments of the courts below, Lord Russell was no doubt aware of the position. Now see s 175(4)–(6).

2. Although there is superficially a close resemblance between this case and *Cook v Deeks* **[6.15]**, it is most difficult to attempt to reconcile them on points of detail, and especially to deal satisfactorily with this question of ratification. The nature of the claim brought in *Regal* may be of relevance: we should note that the defendants were held *severally* liable in *money had and received* proceedings, ie accountable in each case as *debtor* for what he had received. On this basis, the observation that that transaction could have been authorised or ratified by the company in general meeting was consistent with some earlier authorities, such as *Lister*

& *Co v Stubbs* (1890) 45 Ch D 1 (although this case is now discredited in view of the ruling in *A-G for Hong Kong v Reid* [1994] 1 AC 324, PC). Had the claim in negligence succeeded, *all five* of the directors would have been *jointly* and *severally* liable for the loss suffered by the company, but the company, might, it seems, still have ratified (see the *Multinational Gas* case [6.25]; but *Daniels v Daniels*, below, p 348, may suggest the contrary); while had the court been prepared to hold, analogously with *Cook v Deeks*, that the business opportunity which the defendants exploited 'belonged' in equity to the company, all *six* defendants could have been held jointly and severally liable as constructive trustees for the value of the 'property' improperly paid away, and the members could not have ratified. But the distinction between the two cases is perhaps impossible to pin down: the task is not made easier by the absence of any reference to *Cook v Deeks*, or to the constructive trust remedy, in the judgments. It is plain that Lord Russell of Killowen would have taken a different view of the matter had he thought that the profit had been 'corruptly' made, or that there had been a 'plot or arrange-ment to divert from the company to themselves a valuable investment' (above, p 314); but even on this view he was contemplating a remedy by way of 'damages for misconduct', which is not what was awarded in *Cook v Deeks*. To say that in *Cook v Deeks* the directors were under a 'duty' to give their company the benefit of the opportunity, but that there was no correspon-ding duty in *Regal*, is not merely to beg the question, but also to ignore the result reached in the latter case: there was plainly a 'duty' in both cases, albeit perhaps different 'duties' with different sanctions. It seems also to beg the question to say that the opportunity in *Cook v Deeks* 'belonged in equity' to the company: this too readily assumes that our jurisprudence has accepted the concept of an 'opportunity' as property: and it also does not explain why the opportunity in *Regal* was not so regarded. Unless, therefore, it is thought that the finding of *bona fides* was crucial, it is difficult to say why the impropriety in *Regal* was assumed to be capable of ratification (whether or not by the directors' own votes as members), while that in *Cook v Deeks* was held not to be.

➤ Questions

1. Would it have mattered whether the directors of *Regal* had voted as shareholders on a resolution to ratify their acts?

2. Now see CA 2006 s 175(4)–(6). Applying these statutory rules, the matter could not have been authorised by the board of directors prior to the transaction. How might the directors have protected themselves, prior to the deal, in these circumstances?

Conflicts arise even when the company is not pursuing the opportunities in question, and they are presented to the directors in their private capacity

[6.17] Bhullar v Bhullar [2003] 2 BCLC 241 (Court of Appeal)

Two brothers, M and S, founded and equally controlled a family company (BBL), later divid-ing their respective shareholdings among their wives and sons. By May 1998, family relations had broken down to the point where negotiations to split the company's assets and business between the M family and the S family had taken place but were not successful. Around this time, M and one of his sons told S and his sons, I and J (the appellants), at a board meeting that they did not wish any more properties to be purchased by the company, which S and his sons accepted in principle. In June 1999, I and J learned that the property next door to one of the company's existing properties was for sale, and they purchased it in the name of Silvercrest, a company controlled by them. The M family issued a petition under CA 1985 s 459 (now see CA 2006 s 994, the 'unfair prejudice' provision) seeking relief on this basis or on the basis of breach of fiduciary duty. The judge held that I and J had committed a breach of their fiduciary duty by purchasing the property for their own benefit. As a consequence, he held that Silvercrest held the property on trust for the company and ordered the appellants to compel Silvercrest to transfer the property to the company at cost, and to account for any other profits. I and J appealed, arguing that a director was under no duty to offer to the company business opportunities which came to him privately, notwithstanding that the company might be in a position to exploit such opportunities. The Court of Appeal upheld the judgment of the lower court, with Jonathan Parker LJ delivering the leading judgment. This case also provides a useful summary of older precedents.

JONATHAN PARKER LJ: . . . the [lower court] judge addressed the allegation of breach of fiduciary . . . as follows: . . .

'Mr Corbett QC drew to my attention to passages from the speech of Lord Upjohn in *Boardman v Phipps* [1966] 3 All ER 721 at 756, [1967] 2 AC 46 at 123–124 including the following:

"Rules of equity have to be applied to such a great diversity of circumstances that they can be stated only in the most general terms and applied with particular attention to the exact circumstances of each case. The relevant rule for the decision of this case is the fundamental rule of equity that a person in a fiduciary capacity must not make a profit out of his trust, which is part of the wider rule that a trustee must not place himself in a position where his duty and his interest may conflict. I believe that the rule is best stated in *Bray v Ford* by Lord Herschell, who plainly recognised its limitations ([1895–99] All ER Rep 1009 at 1011, [1896] AC 44 at 51):

'It is an inflexible rule of the court of equity that a person in a fiduciary position, such as the plaintiff's, is not, unless otherwise expressly provided, entitled to make a profit; he is not allowed to put himself in a position where his interest and duty conflict. It does not appear to me that this rule is, as has been said, founded upon principles of morality. I regard it rather as based on the consideration that, human nature being what it is, there is danger, in such circumstances, of the person holding a fiduciary position being swayed by interest rather than by duty, and thus prejudicing those whom he was bound to protect. It has, therefore, been deemed expedient to lay down this positive rule. But I am satisfied that it might be departed from in many cases, without any breach of morality, without any wrong being inflicted, and without any consciousness of wrong-doing. Indeed, it is obvious that it might sometimes be to the advantage of the beneficiaries that their trustee should act for them professionally rather than a stranger, even though the trustee were paid for his services.'

It is perhaps stated most highly against trustees or directors in the celebrated speech of Lord Cranworth LC, in *Aberdeen Rly Co v Blaikie Bros* **[6.21]**, ((1854) 1 Macq 461 at 471, [1843–60] All ER Rep 249 at 252) where he said:

'. . . and it is a rule of universal application that no one having such duties to discharge shall be allowed to enter into engagements in which he has or can have a personal interest conflicting or which possibly may conflict with the interests of those whom he is bound to protect.' The phrase 'possibly may conflict' requires consideration. In my view it means that the reasonable man looking at the relevant facts and circumstances of the particular case would think that there was a real sensible possibility of conflict; not that you could imagine some situation arising which might, in some conceivable possibility in events not contemplated as real sensible possibilities by any reasonable person, result in a conflict."

Mr Corbett QC accordingly submits that when one looks at the undisputed facts surrounding the acquisition of Whitehall Mill there was a clear conflict of interest between the interests of Inderjit and Jatinderjit, and the interests of BBL. Accordingly he submits that there was a breach of fiduciary duty by Inderjit and Jatinderjit in making the acquisition without making full disclosure to BBL. I have to confess that I have not found the resolution of this part of the case easy. Indeed it was for that reason that I invited the parties to make detailed oral submissions on the point notwithstanding the very full final submission I had received. I agree with Mr Berragan that it cannot be said that the acquisition of Whitehall Mill was a "maturing business opportunity" within the meaning ascribed to it in the authorities to which I have referred. BBL were not in any sense negotiating for Whitehall Mill at the time of its acquisition. On the other hand I agree with Mr Corbett QC that the question of whether this was a maturing business opportunity is not conclusive. The question I have to ask is the wider question posed in the passages in Lord Upjohn's speech to which I have referred. In my view when one considers the undisputed facts of the case, in particular the facts relied on by Mr Corbett QC set out above, this was a case where the interests of BBL and those of Inderjit and Jatinderjit conflicted in the sense explained by Lord Upjohn. That is to say reasonable men looking at the facts would think there was a real sensible possibility of conflict.' . . .

In a case such as the present, where a fiduciary has exploited a commercial opportunity for his own benefit, the relevant question, in my judgment, is not whether the party to whom the duty is owed (the company, in the instant case) had some kind of beneficial interest in the opportunity: in my judgment that would be too formalistic and restrictive an approach. Rather, the question is simply whether the fiduciary's exploitation of the opportunity is such as to attract the application of the rule. As Lord Upjohn made clear in *Boardman v Phipps* [1966] 3 All ER 721 at 756, [1967] 2 AC 46 at 123, flexibility of application is of the essence of the rule. Thus, he said:

> 'Rules of equity have to be applied to such a great diversity of circumstances that they can be stated only in the most general terms and applied with particular attention to the exact circumstances of each case.'

Later in his speech Lord Upjohn gave this warning against attempting to reformulate the rule by reference to the facts of particular cases ([1966] 3 All ER 721 at 757, [1967] 2 AC 46 at 125):

> 'The whole of the law is laid down in the fundamental principle exemplified in Lord Cranworth's statement [in *Aberdeen Rly Co v Blaikie Bros*] . . . But it is applicable, like so many equitable principles which may affect a conscience, however innocent, to such a diversity of different cases that the observations of judges and even in your lordships' House in cases where this great principle is being applied must be regarded as applicable only to the particular facts of the particular case in question and not regarded as a new and slightly different formulation of the legal principle so well settled.'

To my mind that warning is particularly apt in the instant case, given that the joint bundle of authorities which has been placed before us contains no less than 23 authorities, including Australian and American authorities. As it seems to me, the rule is essentially a simple one, albeit that it may in some cases be difficult to apply. The only qualification which is required to Lord Cranworth's formulation of it is that which was supplied by Lord Upjohn in *Boardman v Phipps* [1966] 3 All ER 721 at 756, [1967] 2 AC 46 at 124, where he said:

> 'The phrase "possibly may conflict" requires consideration. In my view it means that the reasonable man looking at the relevant facts and circumstances of the particular case would think that there was a real sensible possibility of conflict; not that you could imagine some situation arising which might, in some conceivable possibility in events not contemplated as real sensible possibilities by any reasonable person, result in conflict.'

The strictness of the rule, and the flexibility of its application, was stressed by Lord Wilberforce in the Privy Council decision in *New Zealand Netherlands Society 'Oranje' Inc v Kuys* [1973] 2 All ER 1222 at 1225, [1973] 1 WLR 1126 at 1129, where he said:

> 'The obligation not to profit from a position of trust, or, as it sometimes relevant to put it, not to allow a conflict to arise between duty and interest, is one of strictness. The strength, and indeed the severity, of the rule has recently been emphasised by the House of Lords in *Boardman v Phipps* . . . It retains its vigour in all jurisdictions where the principles of equity are

applied. Naturally it has different applications in different contexts. It applies, in principle, whether the case is one of a trust, express or implied, of partnership, of directorship of a limited company, of principal and agent, or master and servant, but the precise scope of it must be moulded according to the nature of the relationship.' . . .

In so far as reference to authority is of assistance in applying the rule to the facts of any particular case, the authority which (of those cited to us) is nearest on its facts to those of the instant case is the decision of Roskill J in *Industrial Development Consultants Ltd v Cooley* [1972] 2 All ER 162, [1972] 1 WLR 443 [see below, p 325]. In that case, a commercial opportunity was offered to the defendant, who was at the time the managing director of the plaintiff company, in his private capacity. The defendant subsequently obtained his release by the company in order to exploit that opportunity for his own benefit. Had the company known that he had been offered that opportunity, it would not have agreed to release him. He was held accountable for the benefits he had received by exploiting the opportunity. The opportunity was not one which the company could itself have exploited.

Roskill J, after quoting extensively from Lord Upjohn's speech in *Boardman v Phipps*, observed (plainly correctly, if I may respectfully say so) that although Lord Upjohn dissented (with Viscount Dilhorne) in the result, there was no difference between any of their Lordships as to the applicable principles, but only as to the application of those principles to the facts of the case. Turning to the facts, Roskill J said this ([1972] 2 All ER 162 at 173–174, [1972] 1 WLR 443 at 451):

'The first matter that has to be considered is whether or not the defendant was in a fiduciary relationship with his principals, the plaintiffs. Counsel for the defendant argued that he was not because he received this information which was communicated to him privately. With respect, I think that argument is wrong. The defendant had one capacity and one capacity only in which he was carrying on business at that time. That capacity was as managing director of the plaintiffs. Information which came to him while he was managing director and which was of concern to the plaintiffs and was relevant for the plaintiffs to know, was information which it was his duty to pass on to the plaintiffs because between himself and the plaintiffs a fiduciary relationship existed . . .' . . .

He went on to stress the rigidity with which the rule had since been applied. As confirmation of this, he cited the following well-known passage from the judgment of James LJ in *Parker v McKenna* (1874) 10 Ch App 96 at 124–125:

'I do not think it is necessary, but it appears to me very important, that we should concur in laying down again and again the general principle that in this Court no agent in the course of his agency, in the matter of his agency, can be allowed to make any profit without the knowledge and consent of his principal; that that rule is an inflexible rule, and must be applied inexorably by this Court, which is not entitled, in my judgment, to receive evidence, or suggestion, or argument as to whether the principal did or did not suffer any injury in fact by reason of the dealing of the agent; for the safety of mankind requires that no agent shall be able to put his principal to the danger of such an inquiry as that.'

I turn, then, to the facts of the instant case. Like the defendant in *Industrial Development Consultants Ltd v Cooley*, the appellants in the instant case had, at the material time, one capacity and one capacity only in which they were carrying on business, namely as directors of the company. In that capacity, they were in a fiduciary relationship with the company. At the material time, the company was still trading, albeit that negotiations (ultimately unsuccessful) for a division of its assets and business were on foot. As Inderjit accepted in cross-examination, it would have been 'worthwhile' for the company to have acquired the property. Although the reasons why it would have been 'worthwhile' were not explored in evidence, it seems obvious that the opportunity to acquire the property would have been commercially attractive to the company, given its proximity to Springbank Works. Whether the company could or would have taken that opportunity, had it been made aware of it, is not to the point: the existence of the opportunity was information which it was relevant for the company to know, and it follows that the appellants were under a duty to communicate it to the company. The anxiety which the appellants plainly felt as to the propriety of purchasing the property through Silvercrest without first disclosing their intentions to their co-directors—anxiety which led Inderjit to seek legal advice from the company's solicitor—is, in my view, eloquent of the existence of a possible conflict of duty and interest. I therefore agree with the judge when he said . . . that 'reasonable men looking at the facts would think there was a real sensible possibility of conflict'.

[This case is noted, Prentice and Payne (2004) 120 LQR 198.]

Conflicts of duty and duty: competing directorships.

Section 175(7) makes it clear that conflicts of duty and duty (ie conflicting duties of loyalty owed to two different principals) are within the remit of s 175.

The controversial House of Lords authority in this area is *Bell v Lever Bros Ltd* [1932] AC 161. It treats directors more leniently than employees are treated by employment law; it holds that directors are not under an obligation to refrain from competing with their companies or from becoming directors of rival companies, although this conclusion assumes that the first company has no concern in the contracts of the second, and that in earning the profit on those contracts the director has not made use of either the property or the confidential information belonging to the first company (see the opinion of Lord Blanesburgh).

The next case is unusual, but airs some of the concerns in this area.

[6.18] In Plus Group Ltd v Pyke [2002] BCLC 201

The company, In Plus Group Ltd, was controlled by two men, Pyke and Plank, its only directors and members. When the business relationship between Pyke and Plank deteriorated, Pyke was entirely excluded from the management of the company. He was refused access to financial records, no longer received his monthly payments from the company and his office was relocated without consultation or notice. With neither job nor income, Pyke established a new company and started doing business with Constructive, one of the company's major clients. The claimants argued that this competition with the company amounted to a breach of Pyke's fiduciary duties to it, and they sought an account of Pyke's profits.

BROOKE LJ: . . . There is no completely rigid rule that a director may not be involved in the business of a company which is in competition with another company of which he was a director. A rather startling illustration of this proposition can be seen in the case of *London and Mashonaland Exploration Co Ltd v New Mashonaland Exploration Co Ltd* [1891] WN 165. Lord Mayo was a director and chairman of the board of directors of the first company which was incorporated for the purpose which its name suggests. He never in fact acted as a director, or attended a board meeting, or agreed, either expressly or in the articles of association, not to become a director of any similar company. Four months later the second company was formed for the same purpose. The first company had had some success with a share prospectus advertising Lord Mayo's name as director and chairman, and it took umbrage when it saw its rival's prospectus with Lord Mayo's name at the head of its list of directors.

After summarising the facts, and adding that there was no contract, express or implied, obliging Lord Mayo to give his personal services to the plaintiff company and not to another company, Chitty J dismissed the plaintiffs' application for an injunction. He said that no case had been made out that

Lord Mayo was about to disclose to the defendants any information that he had obtained confidentially in his character of chairman, and that an analogy sought to be drawn between the present case and partnership was incomplete.

This decision was applied with approval by Lord Blanesburgh in *Bell v Lever Bros Ltd* [above], at pp 193–196. He distinguished between contracts in which the director's own company was concerned and contracts by which the director was bound to some outside party. In relation to the latter class of contract he said that the company had no concern in the director's profit, and could not make him accountable for it unless it appeared—and this was the essential qualification—that in earning that profit he had made use either of the company's property or of some confidential information which had come to him as director of the company.

I have read in draft the judgment of Sedley LJ, and I need not repeat his description of the unease with which some modern text book writers have viewed the Mashonaland case. It is unnecessary on the present occasion to resolve this controversy, because the facts of the present case are so unusual. . . .

In the present case Mr Pyke, who was a sick man following his stroke, had been effectively expelled from the companies of which he was a director more than six months before any of the events occurred of which the claimants now make complaint. Although he had invested a very large sum of money in the first and second claimants on interest free loan accounts, he was not being permitted to withdraw any of it. At the same time he was being denied any remuneration from the companies. When he entered into business with Constructive in the autumn of 1997 he was not using any of the claimants' property for the purpose of that business. Nor was he making use of any confidential information which had come to him as a director of any of the companies.

In these circumstances I consider that the judge was right when he held that Mr Pyke committed no breach of fiduciary duty in trading with Constructive. . . .

SEDLEY LJ: *London & Mashonaland Exploration Co Ltd v New Mashonaland Exploration Co Ltd*, in its solitary briefly reported form [1891] WN 165, establishes that there is nothing inherently objectionable in the position of a company director (and chairman) who, without breaching any express restrictive agreement or disclosing any confidential information, becomes engaged, whether personally or as a director of another company, in the same line of business. The extempore judgment of Chitty J on what appears to have been an interlocutory motion for injunctive relief, was given the imprimatur of the House of Lords by Lord Blanesburgh in *Bell v Lever Bros* [above], at p 195. The case had not, according to the report, been referred to by counsel on either side in argument; but Lord Blanesburgh, with whom Lord Atkin and Lord Thankerton agreed, explicitly endorsed the principle set out by Chitty J. This, therefore, is the law which binds us. That it can produce outcomes of debatable morality is evident from the speeches in *Bell v Lever Bros* itself. Lord Blanesburgh remarked in conclusion (at p 200):

'Nor is it to my mind unjust that, their profit accounted for, the appellants should be left in possession by way of return for their services of sums which, while they may seem bountiful to minds disciplined in a school of progressive austerity, would doubtless, by those engaged in great business, he regarded as no more than adequate to the occasion.'

Lord Atkin on the other hand, though concurring in the result, said (at p 229):

'The result is that in the present case servants unfaithful in some of their work retain large compensation which some will think they do not deserve. Nevertheless it is of greater importance that well established principles of contract should be maintained than that a particular hardship should be redressed; . . .'

The problem is obvious if one thinks of how shareholders in X Ltd or X plc, or for that matter its creditors, would regard a director who used his boardroom vote, perhaps crucially, in a way which helped a competitor, when the competitor was the director himself or another company of which he was also a director. Whatever the perceived commercial morality of such a situation, I do not consider that it is sanctioned by law. The fiduciary duty of a director to his company is uniform and universal. What vary infinitely are the elements of fact and degree which determine whether the duty has been breached. If Mr Pyke's solicitors' view of the law is as widely held as it seems to be, it needs to be revised. They wrote this:

'The authorities are quite clear that it is no breach of any fiduciary duty to be involved with a business either of the same kind or in competition with the company of which he is a director.'

Counsel have put before us what three of the leading modern textbooks say about this received view of the law. The authors' and editors' views range from the dubious to the sceptical. [He then cited from *Gore-Browne on Companies* (Jordans), para 27.17; *Palmer's Company Law* (Sweet & Maxwell), para 8.534, and continued:]

Gower's Principles of Modern Company Law (Davies, Sweet & Maxwell), 6th ed., says at p 622:

'Competing with the company. One of the most obvious examples of a situation which might be expected to give rise to a conflict between a director's interests and his duties is where he carries on or is associated with a business competing with that of the company. Certainly a fiduciary without the consent of his beneficiaries is normally strictly precluded from competing with them and this is specifically stated in the analogous field of partnership law. Yet, strangely, it is by no means clear on the existing case law that a similar rule applies to directors of a company. Indeed, it is generally stated that it does not, and there appears to be a definite, if inadequately reported, decision that a director cannot be restrained from acting as a director of a rival company. And it has been said that "What he could do for a rival company he could, of course, do for himself." This view is becoming increasingly difficult to support. It has been held that the duty of fidelity flowing from the relationship of master and servant may preclude the servant from engaging, even in his spare time, in work for a competitor, notwithstanding that the servant's duty of fidelity imposes lesser obligations than the full duty of good faith owed by a director or other fiduciary agent. How, then, can it be that a director can compete whereas a subordinate employee cannot? Moreover it has been recognised that one who is a director of two rival concerns is walking a tight-rope and at risk if he fails to deal fairly with both.

In arguing that a director who carries on a business which competes with that of his company inevitably places himself in a position where his personal interest will conflict with his duty to the company, it is not being contended that he will necessarily have breached his fiduciary duty; he will not if the company has consented so long as he observes his subjective duty to the company by subordinating his interests to those of the company. Nor is it being suggested that there is anything objectionable in his holding other directorships so long as all the companies have consented if their businesses compete. But in both cases consent is unlikely if he is a full-time executive director or if the extent of the competition is substantial. And even if the consent is given the director is likely to be faced with constant difficulties in avoiding breaches of his subjective duty of good faith to the company or companies concerned. He may be able to subordinate his personal interests to those of a single company but it is less easy to reconcile conflicting duties to more than one company. Nor would a reformed rule be inconsistent with the modern emphasis on a more important role for non-executive directors, who are often executive directors of other companies. Even if executive directors are regarded as a good source of non-executive talent for other companies (which some would question), a reformed rule would simply require executive directors not to become non-executive or competing companies, which they are, in fact, rarely asked to become.'

If one bears in mind the high standard of probity which equity demands of fiduciaries, and the reliance which shareholders and creditors are entitled to place upon it, the *Mashonaland* principle is a very limited one. If, for example, the two Mashonaland Exploration companies had been preparing to tender for the same contract, I doubt whether Lord Mayo's position would have been tenable, at least in the absence of special arrangements to insulate either company from the conflict of his interests and duties, for I see no reason why the law should assume that any directorship is merely cosmetic. A directorship brings with it not only voting rights and emoluments but responsibilities of stewardship and honesty, and those who cannot discharge them should not become or remain directors.

All the foregoing concerns breach of fiduciary duty. From such a breach, appropriate remedies will follow. But both common sense and equity indicate that it is not necessary to wait for a breach giving rise to a remedy before the possibility of intervention arises. . . .

That the law will take notice of a situation of impending or potential breach, as well as of an actual one, is clear . . . [he cited various decisions, and continued:] Without the need of any proven breach, the court will set aside a transaction entered into in the shadow of such a conflict. It will also in an appropriate case restrain entry into such a transaction or restrain the director from involving himself in it. The distinction . . . between a director's putting himself into a position of conflict and his being in breach of fiduciary duty is of course legally correct and is relevant to remedies; but it does not mean that a director can cheerfully go to the brink so long as he does not fall over the edge. It means that if he finds himself in a position of conflict he must resolve it openly or extract himself from it. . . .

In this situation the room in the present case for absolving Mr Pyke was very limited indeed. . . .

. . . Quite exceptionally, the defendant's duty to the claimants had been reduced to vanishing point by the acts (explicable and even justifiable though they may have been) of his sole fellow director and fellow shareholder Mr Plank. Accepting as I do that the claimants' relationship with Constructive was consistent with successful poaching on Mr Pyke's part, the critical fact is that it was done in a situation in which the dual role which is the necessary predicate of Mr Yell's case is absent. The defendant's role as a director of the claimants was throughout the relevant period entirely nominal, not in the sense in which a non-executive director's position might (probably wrongly) be called nominal but in the concrete sense that he was entirely excluded from all decision-making and all participation in the claimant company's affairs. For all the influence he had, he might as well have resigned.

For the rest, I agree with the judgments of my Lords. . . .

JONATHAN PARKER LJ: I agree with the order proposed by Brooke LJ, for the reasons which he has given.

I further agree with him that this is not an appropriate case in which to examine the scope and application of what Sedley LJ refers to as the Mashonaland principle. . . .

➤ Question

By bundling up conflicts of interest and duty and conflicts of duty and duty in the same provision (s 175), is CA 2006 likely to encourage a hardening of the courts' approach to the latter types of conflicts?

Resigning to take up a corporate opportunity.

Section 170(2) indicates that s 175 is to apply to a limited extent to directors who are no longer in office (see above, p 309). The following cases are illustrative of the equitable rules. Note that the statute may now lead to different conclusions on the same facts.

In *Canadian Aero Service Ltd v O'Malley* (1973) 40 DLR (3d) 371, the president and the executive vice-president of the plaintiff company ('Canaero') had been engaged on behalf of Canaero in negotiating for a large aerial surveying and mapping contract with the government of Guyana, to be financed by the external aid programme of the Canadian government. Instead of securing the contract for Canaero, they resigned their managerial posts and formed their own company ('Terra'), to which they successfully diverted the contract. The Supreme Court of Canada held that their fiduciary duty had survived their resignation and that that duty was enforceable against Terra as well as the individual defendants. The remedy took the form of an award of damages for breach of duty, rather than an account of profits. Key factors in this case were that: (1) the defendants had diverted for their own benefit a 'maturing business opportunity' which their company was actively pursuing; (2) they were participants in the negotiations on behalf of the company; (3) their resignation had been 'prompted or influenced' by a wish to acquire the opportunity for themselves; and (4) it was their position with the company rather than a 'fresh initiative' which led them to the opportunity which they later required.

These elements were all present in *Industrial Development Consultants Ltd v Cooley* [1972] 1 WLR 443, where Cooley, an architect, was managing director of the plaintiff company, which was in business as building and development consultants. As the company's representative, he took part in negotiations with officers of the Eastern Gas Board, endeavouring to secure contracts for the company to build four large depots; but these negotiations were unsuccessful because the Board would not engage a firm of consultants (as distinct from a private architect). Shortly afterwards, the work was offered to Cooley in his private capacity. Cooley obtained a release from his employment (by falsely representing that he was in ill health), and was later given the contract by the Gas Board. Roskill J held that he was accountable to the company for the whole of his benefits under the contract or, alternatively, liable in damages for breach of his service contract. The amount awardable under the second head would, however, have been relatively small—it was put by the judge at 'a 10% chance'—because the likelihood that the company might itself have secured the contract was so remote.

Note that in these two cases the issue was relatively straightforward because the officers in question had an express mandate from the board to negotiate for the acquisition of the particular contract on behalf of their company; and there was also no question of ratification.

In contrast with *Canaero* and *Cooley*, Umunna the director in *Island Export Finance Ltd v Umunna* [1986] BCLC 460 was allowed to keep the profit which he had derived from contracts that he had obtained for himself after he had resigned as the managing director of his company, IEF. These contracts to supply postal boxes to the Cameroons postal authorities were of the same kind, and made with the same party, as an earlier contract which he had secured for the IEF while working as its managing director. But Hutchinson J accepted evidence that IEF was not actively seeking further orders either when Umunna resigned or when he later obtained the contracts; that the resignation was for unrelated reasons; and that Umuna had not made improper use of any confidential information.

So which opportunities are caught? In *Balston Ltd v Headline Filters Ltd* [1990] FSR 385, Head, an employee and director of Balston who had worked for it for 17 years, gave notice terminating his employment and resigned his directorship. He had already agreed to lease premises where he intended to set up his own business, but he said in evidence that he had not then decided what that business was to be. Shortly afterwards one of Balston's customers telephoned Head after being notified by Balston that it would continue to supply him with a particular kind of filter tubes for only a limited further period. As a result of this call, Head commenced business making the filter tubes and supplied them to the customer. Falconer J held that it was not a breach of fiduciary duty for a director to form an intention to set up business in competition with his company after his directorship had ceased, and that there was no maturing business opportunity in which the company had a 'specific interest' which Head had improperly diverted to himself.

More recently, in *Quarter Master UK Ltd v Pyke* [2004] EWHC 1815 (Ch), Paul Morgan QC indicated:

It is not absolutely clear whether liability only attaches in a case of a maturing business opportunity where the former director resigns with the motive of taking advantage of the maturing business opportunity for himself or for another company controlled by him. Possibly such a motive is required where the director did not, before the resignation, act in breach of duty (eg by preferring his own interests to those of the company before the resignation as in *Industrial Development Consultants*

Ltd v Cooley [1972] 2 All ER 86, [1972] 1 WLR 443) and does not, after the resignation, use pre-existing property of the company which remains impressed with a fiduciary obligation to the company.

And in *Coleman Taymar Ltd v Oakes* [2001] 2 BCLC 749, Robert Reid QC stated that:

> the general fiduciary duties of a director or an employee do not prevent a person from forming the intention, whilst still a director, to set up in competition after his directorship or employment has ceased. Nor do they prevent the taking of any preliminary steps to investigate or forward that intention so long as there is no actual competitive activity whilst the directorship or employment continues (see *Balston Ltd v Headline Filters Ltd* [1990] FSR 385). The question will frequently be whether the activities during the course of the employment or directorship went beyond the taking of preliminary steps.

[Also see *Bhullar v Bhullar* **[6.17]** and *CMS Dolphin Ltd v Simonet* **[6.19]**.]

➤ Questions

1. Of the four 'key factors' identified in *Canaero* (above), which were missing in *Island Exports Finance Ltd v Umunna* and in *Balston Ltd v Headline Filters Ltd* (above)? Do the more modern cases adopt the same set of 'key factors'?

2. Jane is a director of three unrelated investment companies. She is approached in confidence by two young scientists whose company needs a major injection of finance to develop a newly discovered drug. After investigating the project, she forms the view that it is likely to be a highly profitable venture for one of the three companies. What advice should Jane be given?

3. Do these cases represent the current state of the law, applying CA 2006 ss 170(2), 175, and 239?

Resigning directors, maturing business opportunities, and remedies.

[6.19] CMS Dolphin Ltd v Simonet [2001] 2 BCLC 704

[The facts appear from the judgment.]

LAWRENCE COLLINS J: . . . In my judgment the underlying basis of the liability of a director who exploits after his resignation a maturing business opportunity of the company is that the opportunity is to be treated as if it were property of the company in relation to which the director had fiduciary duties. By seeking to exploit the opportunity after resignation he is appropriating for himself that property. He is just as accountable as a trustee who retires without properly accounting for trust property. In the case of the director he becomes a constructive trustee of the fruits of his abuse of the company's property, which he has acquired in circumstances where he knowingly had a conflict of interest, and exploited it by resigning from the company . . . .

In many cases, an account of profits will be a more advantageous remedy than equitable compensation, since the actual profits obtained by the director may be higher than the damages for the loss of opportunity suffered by the company, particularly where (as in *Industrial Development Consultants Ltd v Cooley* and *Canadian Aero Service Ltd v O'Malley*) the company had little or no prospect of obtaining the benefit of the opportunity. The fiduciary is liable for the whole of the profit. There are no firm rules for determining which is the relevant profit: see *Hospital Products Ltd v United States Surgical Corp* [1985] LRC (Comm) 411 at 464, (1984) 156 CLR 41 at 110 per Mason J. Where, as here, the business (to use a neutral term, not distinguishing between Mr Simonet and Blue) is not restricted exclusively to the performance of contracts which were obtained from CMSD, the fiduciary should be accountable for the profits properly attributable to the breach of fiduciary duty, taking into account the expenses connected with those profits and a reasonable allowance for overheads (but not necessarily salary for the wrongdoer), together with a sum to take account of other benefits derived from those contracts. For example, other contracts might not have been won, or profits made on them, without (for example) the opportunity or cash-flow benefit which flowed from contracts unlawfully obtained. There must, however, be some reasonable connection between the breach of duty and the profits for which the fiduciary is accountable . . .

Does it make a difference to the remedy for an account of profits whether the director exploits the opportunity personally, or through a partnership, or through a company controlled by him? In particular, is there a remedy against the director where the profits are made by a company against which there is no effective remedy, because for reasons unconnected with the relevant contracts it is hopelessly insolvent? The question is one of practical importance because the case of an individual trading as such (as distinct from through a corporate vehicle) is rare in purely commercial transactions. In this case the trading was done through the Millennium partnership for about two weeks, and then through Blue. Where the director puts the contract into a partnership, he is fully accountable even if his partners are entitled to part of the profit and are ignorant of his breach of fiduciary duty. In *Imperial Mercantile Credit Association v Coleman* (1873) LR 6 HL 189 Mr Coleman, a director, was accountable for a profit on a contract with the company in which he had not disclosed an interest. The profit was made on a contract with a firm of stockbrokers, Messrs Knight & Coleman, for the placing of debentures on commission. It was argued that even if Mr Coleman was liable to the company, it was only his share of the profits which he was bound to restore, and not those attributable to Mr Knight's share. That argument was rejected by the House of Lords. Lord Chelmsford said (LR 6 HL 189 at 202):

' . . . the liability of partners who are implicated in a breach of trust (and this is an analogous case) has been held to be joint and several. It would be a strange conclusion that Mr. Coleman, who was the active agent in diverting the money, which belonged to the association, to the partnership funds, should not be answerable for the whole, whether his co-partner, Mr. Knight, was liable or not for any part of it.'

Lord Cairns said (LR 6 HL 189 at 208):

'The profit on the transaction was obtained by Mr. Coleman, and . . . was obtained by him as a director of the association. Whether he desired or whether he determined to reserve it all to himself or to share it with his firm appears to be perfectly immaterial. The source from which the profit is derived is Mr. Coleman. It is only through him that his firm can claim. He is liable for the whole of the profits which were obtained; and it is not the course for a Court of Equity to enter into the consideration of what afterwards would have become of these profits.'

Where the business is put into a company which is established by the directors who have wrongfully taken advantage of the corporate opportunity, it was held in *Cook v Deeks* [1916] 1 AC 554, [1916–17] All ER Rep 285 (PC) that both the directors and the company are liable to account for profits . . .

Is the position different where (as here) the corporate vehicle genuinely carries on business, and has real premises and a staff? Even in such a case it is possible that the piercing the corporate veil approach may be justified if the company was incorporated to perpetrate what must be regarded as wrongdoing close to fraud: cf *Re H* (restraint order: realisable property) [1996] 2 BCLC 500. But I do not think that it is necessary to resort to piercing or lifting the corporate veil, since *Cook v Deeks* shows clearly (as does *Canadian Aero Service Ltd v O'Malley*) that the directors are equally liable with the corporate vehicle formed by them to take unlawful advantage of the business opportunities. The reason is that they have jointly participated in the breach of trust. Nor in my judgment does it make a difference whether the business is taken up by the corporate vehicle directly, or is first taken up by the directors and then transferred to a company . . .

Consequently I do not consider that Mr Simonet can derive any assistance from one aspect of *Regal (Hastings) Ltd v Gulliver* on which Mr Croxford relied. As I have indicated, in *Regal (Hastings) Ltd v Gulliver* the chairman, Mr Gulliver, who had instigated the whole scheme, was held not to be liable. In particular it was held that he had not profited from the scheme notwithstanding that he held minority interests in two companies which had subscribed for shares in Amalgamated. There was no finding at trial that the shares in Amalgamated belonged to him, and there was no evidence that he had made a profit from his shares in the two companies. This is not authority for the proposition that where a director puts the profit into a company in which he has an interest he is not accountable for profits. First, one of the striking features of *Regal (Hastings) Ltd v Gulliver* is that the directors were held to have acted in good faith. Second, Mr Gulliver did not establish the companies to take the benefit of the shares in Amalgamated. Third, there was no evidence that the companies in which Mr Gulliver had an interest knew of the matters which made the actions of the directors a breach of fiduciary duty. Fourth, Mr Gulliver had only a minority interest, and there was an express finding that he had made no profit from the companies . . .

Mr Simonet put the benefit of the contracts or business opportunities in the partnership Millennium, and then he and Mr Patterson transferred the business without any consideration (other than perhaps the issue of shares) to Blue. Mr Simonet cannot escape the consequences of his own breach of fiduciary duty by transferring the fruits of that breach to a company. He remains the person principally liable. In this case Millennium was a partnership and the facts are directly comparable to the position in *Imperial Mercantile Credit Association v Coleman*, and the transfer of the benefit of the contracts and the business opportunities to a company owned and controlled by Mr Simonet and Mr Patterson is precisely what happened in *Cook v Deeks* and cannot relieve them of liability. Mr Simonet is responsible for breach of fiduciary duty, and is accountable for profits emanating from the property which he put into the partnership and then transferred to Blue. I would have come to the same conclusion if he had diverted the contracts and business opportunities directly to Blue.

Situations that 'cannot reasonably be regarded as likely to give rise to a conflict'

Board authorisation can be given where there *is* a conflict of interest (s 175(4)–(6)). But, in addition, s 175(4)(a) provides that the duty is not infringed if the situation cannot reasonably be regarded as likely to give rise to a conflict of interest. Some situations will fall very clearly into this category. But the next case is controversial: it deals with the difficult question of whether an opportunity, once declined by the company, may then be taken up by one of the directors on his own account, without any notification to or approval by the other directors or the shareholders. There are no UK cases adopting this approach.

[6.20] Peso Silver Mines Ltd v Cropper (1966) 58 DLR (2d) 1 (Supreme Court of Canada)

The board of directors of the appellant company Peso was approached by an outsider named Dickson, who wished to sell to it 126 prospecting claims near to the company's own mining territories. The proposal was rejected by the company after *bona fide* consideration by the board. Later, a syndicate was formed by Dr Aho, the company's geologist, to purchase Dickson's claims. The syndicate included Cropper a director of Peso. A company called Cross Bow Mines Ltd was incorporated by the syndicate for the purpose. Cropper had taken part in the earlier decision of Peso's. board to reject Dickson's proposal. Control of Peso later passed to a company referred to as 'Charter', who caused this action to be brought, claiming that Cropper was accountable to the company for the Cross Bow shares which he had thus obtained. The Supreme Court of Canada decided that he held them on his own behalf and was not bound to account.[42]

---

[42] See S Beck, 'The Saga of *Peso Silver Mines*: Corporate Opportunity Reconsidered' (1971) 49 Can B Rev 80; and, by the same author, 'The Quickening of the Fiduciary Obligation' (1975) 53 Can B Rev 771.

The judgment of the court (CARTWRIGHT, MARTLAND, JUDSON, RITCHIE and HALL JJ) was delivered by CARTWRIGHT J: On the facts of the case at bar I find it impossible to say that the respondent obtained the interests he holds in Cross Bow and Mayo by reason of the fact that he was a director of the appellant and in the course of the execution of that office.

When Dickson, at Dr Aho's suggestion, offered his claims to the appellant it was the duty of the respondent as director to take part in the decision of the board as to whether that offer should be accepted or rejected. At that point he stood in a fiduciary relationship to the appellant. There are affirmative findings of fact that he and his co-directors acted in good faith, solely in the interests of the appellant and with sound business reasons in rejecting the offer. There is no suggestion in the evidence that the offer to the appellant was accompanied by any confidential information unavailable to any prospective purchaser or that the respondent as director had access to any such information by reason of his office. When, later, Dr Aho approached the appellant it was not in his capacity as a director of the appellant, but as an individual member of the public whom Dr Aho was seeking to interest as a co-adventurer.

The judgments in the *Regal* case **[6.16]** in the Court of Appeal are not reported but counsel were good enough to furnish us with copies. In the course of his reasons Lord Greene MR said: 'To say that the company was entitled to claim the benefit of those shares would involve this proposition: Where a board of directors considers an investment which is offered to the company and bona fide comes to the conclusion that it is not an investment which their company ought to make, any director, after that resolution is come to and bona fide come to, who chooses to put up the money for that investment himself must be treated as having done it on behalf of the company, so that the company can claim any profit that results to him from it. That is a proposition for which no particle of authority was cited; and goes, as it seems to me, far beyond anything that has ever been suggested as to the duty of directors, agents, or persons in a position of that kind.'

In the House of Lords, Lord Russell of Killowen concluded his reasons with the following paragraph: 'One final observation I desire to make. In his judgment Lord Greene MR stated that a decision adverse to the directors in the present case involved the proposition that, if directors bona fide decide not to invest their company's funds in some proposed investment, a director who thereafter embarks his own money therein is accountable for any profits which he may derive therefrom. As to this, I can only say that to my mind the facts of this hypothetical case bear but little resemblance to the story with which we have had to deal.'

I agree with Bull JA[43] when after quoting the two above passages he says: 'As Greene MR was found to be in error in his decision, I would think that the above comment by Lord Russell on the hypothetical case would be superfluous unless it was intended to be a reservation that he had no quarrel with the proposition enunciated by the Master of the Rolls, but only that the facts of the case before him did not fall within it.'

As Bull JA goes on to point out, the same view appears to have been entertained by Lord Denning MR in *Phipps v Boardman*.[44]

If the members of the House of Lords in *Regal* had been of the view that in the hypothetical case stated by Lord Greene the director would have been liable to account to the company, the elaborate examination of the facts contained in the speech of Lord Russell of Killowen would have been unnecessary.

The facts of the case at bar appear to me in all material respects identical with those in the hypothetical case stated by Lord Greene and I share the view which he expressed that in such circumstances the director is under no liability. I agree with the conclusion of the learned trial judge and of the majority in the Court of Appeal that the action fails . . .

---

[43] [Bull JA was one of the majority judges in the court below (British Columbia Court of Appeal (1965) 56 DLR (2d) 117.)]

[44] [1965] Ch 992, affd by the House of Lords [1967] 2 AC 46: see the Note below.

> ➤ Note

Boardman v Phipps [1967] 2 AC 46, HL, referred to above, was not a company law case, but is of interest as an application of the principle of *Regal (Hastings) Ltd v Gulliver* **[6.16]**. B, a solicitor, and P, acting together as agents for the trustees of an estate, attended the annual general meeting of a company in which the estate had a minority holding of shares. Later, they obtained information about share prices from that company. They formed the opinion that the company could be made more profitable and, acting honestly and without concealment (but not having first obtained the 'informed consent' of all the trustees), used their own money to bid for and eventually to acquire a controlling interest in it. The estate itself could not have made the bid without the trustees committing a breach of trust, and in any case it had no funds available for the purpose. Ultimately, they succeeded in making considerable profits for both themselves and the estate from capital distributions on their respective holdings of shares. By a majority of three to two, the House of Lords held that they must account to the trust for the profit which they had made from their own investment: the profit had been made by reason of their fiduciary position as agents and by reason of the opportunity and the knowledge which had come to them while acting in that capacity. However, the House of Lords did think it proper to decree that the defendants should be paid 'on a liberal scale' for their work and skill.

> ➤ Questions

1. Can the decision in the *Peso Silver Mines* case be reconciled with *Boardman v Phipps* (above), *Aberdeen Rly Co v Blaikie Bros* **[6.21]** and the passage from *Keech v Sandford* quoted in *Regal (Hastings) Ltd v Gulliver* **[6.16]**, above, p 315?

2. Is *Peso Silver Mines* likely to be embraced in the UK, even with the introduction of s175(4)(a)?

Duty not to accept benefits from third parties: CA 2006 s 176

For directors, this provision reformulates and replaces the equitable principle that fiduciaries must not accept bribes or secret commissions (*Attorney-General for Hong Kong v Reid* [1994] 1 AC 324 (PC)).

Several points are worth noting:

(i) The statutory duty does not embrace the entire ambit of the broader equitable 'no-profit' rule, which is subsumed in s 175 above. On the other hand, this duty is clearly related to the no conflicts duty in s 175, since this duty, too, is not infringed if acceptance of the benefit cannot reasonably be regarded as likely to give rise to a conflict of interest (s 176(4)).

(ii) 'Benefits' are not defined in CA 2006. During parliamentary debates on the Bill, the Solicitor-General said: 'In using the word "benefit", we intend the ordinary dictionary meaning of the word. The *Oxford English Dictionary* defines it as 'a favourable or helpful factor, circumstance, advantage or profit' (HC Comm D, 11/7/06 Cols 621–622). A benefit may be financial or non-financial, of any shape or size, although s 176(4) ensures that trivial benefits are not caught by the provision, and s 176(3) covers payment of normal salary and benefits.

(iii) The most significant difference between s 175 (no conflicts) and this section (s 176, no benefits from third parties) is that there is no provision for authorisation by the board of directors. Of course, the company's articles could (although it is most unlikely) contain specific provisions concerning benefits from third parties (see s 180(4)(b) and s 232(4): provisions protecting directors from liability). Alternatively, s 180(4)(a) (Consent, approval and authorisation by members) may apply, but see Questions, below. Finally, the members may ratify the receipt under s 239 (Ratification of acts of directors): again, see the Questions below.

> ➤ Questions

1. What 'benefits' received by directors will be assessed under this section rather than under s 175? Section 175 catches a director's capture of corporate opportunities (benefits?) from third parties for personal benefit rather than for the company's benefit. Is the difference that the 'benefits' contemplated under s 175 could have been pursued *legitimately* by the company itself (and the section makes the likelihood of success in that pursuit irrelevant: s 175(2)), whereas the benefits contemplated under s 176 are benefits that the company could not (or not legitimately) have requested or accepted for itself, such as bribes and secret commissions? This approach would add much to these sections that is certainly not apparent from their terms. Indeed, the qualification in s 175(2), above, is worded sufficiently widely to cover situations where the company could not *legally* take the advantage, so discrimination in this way is not compelled by the terms of section itself. Does the answer to this question matter?

2. Section 176 does not provide for board authorisation as a 'whitewashing' procedure. If the board *did* consent (in the manner fully set out in s 175(5)–(6)), could anyone obtain a remedy against the director for breach of duty?

3. The authorisation and ratification procedures for members (ss 180 and 239) expressly import any general law restrictions on granting pre-transaction approval or post-event ratification (see ss 180(4)(a) and 239(7)). Does the general law prevent members approving or ratifying a director's receipt of benefits from third parties? Are there any s 175 conflicts that could not be authorised or ratified?

Duty to declare an interest in a proposed or existing transaction or arrangement: CA 2006 ss 177 and 182

Section 177 is the third of the general provisions designed to reformulate and codify the fiduciary duties owed by directors. It deals with conflicts of interest in *proposed* transactions or arrangements *with* the company. Directors with direct or indirect[45] interests in transactions proposed by the company must declare to the other directors the nature and extent of those interests, unless it is an interest, or involves a transaction, of which the director is unaware.

Section 180 then makes it clear that, *subject to the company's constitution*, if directors comply with s 177, the transaction is not liable to be set aside by virtue of the usual equitable rule requiring the consent of the company's members. This is the significant reform introduced by this provision.

Failure to comply with s 177 constitutes a breach of duty, for which the purely civil remedies in s 178 apply. If the company then enters into the impugned transaction, the director is under a new and continuing duty to disclose, expressed in substantially similar terms in s 182 (declaration of interest in existing transaction or arrangement). Breach of s 182 is an offence

---

[45] Note that this means that the director need not necessarily be a party to the deal for the transaction or arrangement to be subject to this section.

(s 183).[46] Why the two regimes need to be separated at all, or by three intervening provisions, is not clear. (On s 182, see below, pp 353 ff.)

Under various subsections in s 177, directors are treated as being aware of matters of which they ought to be aware; declarations must be updated if necessary; the form of disclosure is not prescibed, but may be made at a meeting of directors, by notice in writing, or by general notice. The articles may impose further requirements. Certain exceptions exist; all are reflected in existing common law rules. These apply where there is no reasonable likelihood of a conflict (*Cowan de Groot Properties Ltd v Eagle Trust plc* [1991] BCLC 1045); where the other directors are already aware or ought reasonably to be aware of the interest; and where the interest concerns service contracts which have been, or are to be, considered by a meeting of directors or by a remuneration committee (*Runciman v Walter Runciman plc* [1992] BCLC 1084). A fourth exception, not included in the section but recognised in s 186, is that the director of a company with only one director is not required to make a declaration to himself, although the terms of these arrangements must be set out in writing or recorded in the minutes (s 231).

If a director enters into a transaction or arrangement with the company in breach of s 177 (ie without making the appropriate declaration to the directors), then the transaction is voidable.[47] For the ramifications of this, see the Note following **[6.21]**. The more general issues relating to remedies are discussed below at pp 334 ff.

For the impact of possible authorisation or ratification by the members, see pp 347 ff.

[6.21] Aberdeen Rly Co v Blaikie Bros (1854) 1 Macq 461 (House of Lords)

The respondents, Blaikie Bros, had agreed to manufacture iron chairs for the railway company at £8.50 per ton, and sued to enforce the contract. The railway company pleaded that it was not bound by the contract because, at the time when it was made, the chairman of its board of directors was also managing partner of the respondents. This plea was upheld by the House of Lords.

LORD CRANWORTH LC: This, therefore, brings us to the general question, whether a director of a railway company is or is not precluded from dealing on behalf of the company with himself, or with a firm in which he is a partner.

The directors are a body to whom is delegated the duty of managing the general affairs of the company.

A corporate body can only act by agents, and it is of course the duty of those agents so to act as best to promote the interests of the corporation whose affairs they are conducting. Such agents have duties to discharge of a fiduciary nature towards their principal.[48] And it is a rule of universal application that no one, having such duties to discharge, shall be allowed to enter into engagements in which he has, or can have, a personal interest conflicting, or which possibly may conflict, with the interests of those whom he is bound to protect.

So strictly is this principle adhered to that no question is allowed to be raised as to the fairness or unfairness of a contract so entered into.

It obviously is, or may be, impossible to demonstrate how far in any particular case the terms of such a contract have been the best for the interest of the cestui que trust, which it was possible to obtain.

---

[46] So, in practice, retaining the criminal sanctions imposed by the predecessor provision, CA 1985 s 317.

[47] That, at least, is clear from the separation of ss 177 and 182, which eliminates many of the early debates that surrounded CA 1985, s 317. These debates were finally resolved by recognising as quite separate the different requirements of s 317 and the equitable conflict rules: failure to comply with the disclosure obligations in s 317 constituted an offence; failure to make the disclosures required by the equitable rules (ie to the shareholders), as amended by the articles (often substituting the directors for the shareholders), rendered the offending contract voidable, not void: see *Hely-Hutchinson v Brayhead Ltd* [1968] 1 QB 549, CA **[3.09]**; and *Guinness plc v Saunders*, HL **[5.02]**.

[48] *York and North Midland Rly Co v Hudson* (1853) 16 Beav 485.

It may sometimes happen that the terms on which a trustee has dealt or attempted to deal with the estate or interest of those for whom he is a trustee, have been as good as could have been obtained from any other person—they may even at the time have been better.

But still so inflexible is the rule that no inquiry on that subject is permitted. The English authorities on this head are numerous and uniform.

The principle was acted on by Lord King in *Keech v Sandford*,[49] and by Lord Hardwicke in *Whelpdale v Cookson*,[50] and the whole subject was considered by Lord Eldon on a great variety of occasions . . .

It is true that the questions have generally arisen on agreements for purchases or leases of land, and not, as here, on a contract of a mercantile character. But this can make no difference in principle. The inability to contract depends not on the subject-matter of the agreement, but on the fiduciary character of the contracting party, and I cannot entertain a doubt of its being applicable to the case of a party who is acting as manager of a mercantile or trading business for the benefit of others, no less than to that of an agent or trustee employed in selling or letting land.

Was then Mr Blaikie so acting in the case now before us?—If he was, did he while so acting contract on behalf of those for whom he was acting with himself?

Both these questions must obviously be answered in the affirmative. Mr Blaikie was not only a director, but (if that was necessary) the chairman of the directors. In that character it was his bounden duty to make the best bargains he could for the benefit of the company.

While he filled that character, namely, on 6 February 1846, he entered into a contract on behalf of the company with his own firm, for the purchase of a large quantity of iron chairs at a certain stipulated price. His duty to the company imposed on him the obligation of obtaining these chairs at the lowest possible price.

His personal interest would lead him to an entirely opposite direction, would induce him to fix the price as high as possible. This is the very evil against which the rule in question is directed, and here I see nothing whatever to prevent its application.

I observe that Lord Fullerton seemed to doubt whether the rule would apply where the party whose act or contract is called in question is only one of a body of directors, not a sole trustee or manager.

But, with all deference, this appears to me to make no difference. It was Mr Blaikie's duty to give to his co-directors, and through them to the company, the full benefit of all the knowledge and skill which he could bring to bear on the subject. He was bound to assist them in getting the articles contracted for at the cheapest possible rate. As far as related to the advice he should give them, he put his interest in conflict with his duty, and whether he was the sole director or only one of many, can make no difference in principle.

The same observation applies to the fact that he was not the sole person contracting with the company; he was one of the firm of Blaikie Brothers, with whom the contract was made, and so interested in driving as hard a bargain with the company as he could induce them to make . . .

LORD BROUGHAM delivered a concurring opinion.

➤ Questions

1. Given the reasons for the strict rule set out in this case, is the approach adopted in CA 2006 s 177 warranted? Will the company get 'the full benefit of all the knowledge and skill which [the director] could bring to bear on the subject'?

2. The traditional equitable rule was that disclosure must be to the members; disclosure to a disinterested quorum of directors was insufficient (unless the articles provided otherwise, which they usually did). This is now amended by s 177. But was the equitable rule itself open to question? Directors owe their fiduciary duties to the company, so the *company* must

---

[49] (1726) Sel Cas Ch 61.
[50] (1747) 1 Ves Sen 9.

consent to any potential conflicts. So do cases such as *John Shaw & Sons (Salford) Ltd v Shaw* **[4.07]** suggest that where there is a board of directors capable of acting, it and it alone is competent to make business decisions for the company?

> ➤ Note

In these cases where the director's breach involves a contract *with* the company, the contract is voidable at the option of the company. It follows that the company will lose its right to rescind, on general contractual principles, if it has affirmed the transaction, or cannot make proper restitution (*restitutio in integrum*), or the rights of a third party would be adversely affected.

On orthodox principles, rescission is the *only* remedy (unless the director has also infringed some other rule that will deliver an alternative), and if rescission is no longer possible for any of these reasons, then the court will not intervene. The cases dealing with promoters, eg *Erlanger v New Sombrero Phosphate Co* **[2.24]** and *Re Cape Breton Co* (above, p 86), confirm this. Even though impugned contracts between the director and the company are an illustration of the 'no conflicts' duty, for which directors are typically required to disgorge the profits they have made (holding them on constructive trust for the company, see below, p 335), the courts in these cases say that the director's profit is 'unquantifiable' since that would involve the courts fixing a new contract price for the parties. Given all the other situations in which courts are content to make commercial assessments of value, this seems precious.

And if the courts will not give a 'profits' remedy for breach of the fiduciary duty, few options remain. The company cannot sue the director for breach of the contract, because by definition the contract is either affirmed (not breached) or rescinded (so rendered totally ineffective from the outset). The only option is to avoid (rescind) the contract and seek a personal (monetary) restitutionary remedy; this practice seems to be becoming increasingly acceptable.[51]

Remedies for breach of general duties: CA 2006 s 178

The remedies for breach of directors' duties have not been codified, despite the recommendations of the Law Commissions. CA 2006 s 178 preserves the existing civil consequences of breach (or threatened breach) of any of the general duties. If the statutory duty departs from its equitable equivalent, the court will have to identify the equivalent rule and apply the same consequences and remedies. For the avoidance of doubt, s 179 makes the obvious point that more than one of the general duties may apply in any given case.

The consequences of breach may include:

(i)   injunctions and declarations (generally only when the breach is still threatened);

(ii) common law damages or equitable compensation where the company has suffered loss;[52]

(iii) restoration of the company's property, following a declaration that the property is held by the director on constructive trust for the company;

(iv) an account of profits made by the director; or

(v)   rescission of a contract where the director failed to disclose an interest.

---

[51] See J Poole and A Keyser, 'Justifying Partial Rescission in English Law' (2005) 121 LQR 273.

[52] CA 2006 does not spell out whether the remedies for breach of s 174 (duty to exercise reasonable care, skill and diligence) should be assessed on common law or equitable principles. Arguably it is the former, given the exclusion of s 174 in s 178(2). This would lay to rest the debates in that area (*Henderson v Merrett Syndicates Ltd* [1995] 2 AC 145; *Bristol & West Building Society v Mothew* [1998] Ch 1).

Also see s 1157 (Power of court to grant relief in certain circumstances) that replaces CA 1985, s 727.

General issues

The next two case extracts are unusually long. However, they repay careful reading. They help explain and illustrate many of the more significant problems in this area.[53] Note, in particular, the irrelevance of the fact that the company could not have made the profit now being claimed from the director or that the company would have given consent if requested; note also the deterrence function, the objective to strip profits, and the problems in identifying the relevant profits.

[6.22] Gwembe Valley Development Co Ltd v Koshy (No 3)
[2004] 1 BCLC 131 (Court of Appeal)

[The facts appear from the judgment.]

MUMMERY LJ for the Court (MUMMERY, HALE and CARNWATH LJJ):
  Despite the thickets of company law, contract, fiduciary law, limitation of actions and equitable remedies, which have grown around this case, the central questions for decision can be stated quite concisely: between 1986 and 1988 did the managing director of a joint venture company deliberately and dishonestly fail to disclose his personal interest in transactions with the company and, if so, is he liable to account to the company for all, or for only part of, the unauthorised profits made by him; alternatively, did that failure to disclose his interest render him liable to compensate the company for its losses in the joint venture? [A large part of the appeal concerned related limitation issues, not extracted here.] . . .
  In 1986 a joint venture was formed in Zambia. Its aim was to develop a cotton and wheat farm of 2,500 hectares at Sinazongwe on the shores of Lake Kariba. A group of investors funded the project. Each investor was allowed representation on the board of Gwembe Valley Development Company Limited (GVDC), a Zambian company incorporated in November 1985 as the corporate vehicle for the project. Representation on the board was proportionate to the size of the investment. There were no outside "independent" directors.
  The venture faltered. The investors fell out. GVDC became insolvent. The project collapsed. Litigation broke out. In September 1993 GVDC was put into administrative receivership by one of the investors (DEG). As late as 14 December 2000 the Court of Appeal appointed a receiver. His receivership was confined to the causes of action vested in GVDC. . . .
  The relief claimed in the GVDC action included an account of profits made by its managing director, Mr Thomas Koshy. He is an accountant. Alternative claims were made against him for equitable compensation for breaches of fiduciary duty and for damages for deceit and conspiracy. A declaration was also sought that Mr Koshy and a company controlled by him (Lasco) were liable as constructive trustees of all GVDC's money received by them. [This is not pursued here.] [He then described the course of the litigation, and continued:]
  . . . Rimer J found that, dishonestly and in breach of fiduciary duty, Mr Koshy had procured GVDC to enter into loan transactions with Lasco without making proper disclosure to the other directors of GVDC, or to its shareholders, of the existence and extent of his personal interest and that of his company, Lasco, in the transactions and the size of the profit which they would make out of them. His grounds of appeal are that there was no evidence to support Rimer J's finding of dishonesty; that the judge wrongly held that he was liable to account to GVDC; that he ought to have held that,

[53] Also see M Conaglen, 'Equitable Compensation for Breach of Fiduciary Dealing Rules' (2003) 119 LQR 246; M Conaglen, 'The Nature and Function of Fiduciary Loyalty' (2005) 121 LQR 452.

in any event, the claim for an account of profits was statute-barred under the provisions of the Limitation Act 1980 . . .

GVDC appealed on the ground that Rimer J was wrong to limit the scope of the account of profits against Mr Koshy. The judge limited the account to the value of property, belonging in equity to GVDC, that Mr Koshy had received. He refused a more general account of profits. GVDC contended that the judge should have ordered an account of *all* the unauthorised profits made by Mr Koshy, in whatever form, as a result of his dishonest breaches of fiduciary duty. . . . Alternatively, Rimer J wrongly refused to award, or to direct an inquiry to assess the amount of, equitable compensation payable by Mr Koshy to GVDC for loss resulting from his dishonest breach of fiduciary duty. GVDC was entitled to be restored to the position that it was in prior to the loan transactions procured by Mr Koshy's dishonest breaches of fiduciary duty. . . .

. . . The essential point in all the claims against Mr Koshy is that he was at the same time both the managing director of GVDC, in which the majority interest was held by Lasco, and a director and the controlling shareholder of Lasco. . . .

Basis of liability

Rimer J concluded that Mr Koshy was liable to account to GVDC for profits made by him from the pipeline loan transactions (see paragraph 258). Mr Koshy's liability arose in two ways:

(1) Under the "no profit rule" i.e. the rule of equity that a company director may not make an unauthorised (secret) profit from his fiduciary position (see paragraphs 249 and 291–294 of the judgment). The rule stems from the general principle that a director, like the trustee of a trust, must avoid conflicts of duty and interest when discharging the fiduciary duties undertaken by him in the management of property beneficially belonging to the company (GVDC in this case) and in pursuing his personal interests. Liability to account could arise under this rule, even if Mr Koshy did not commit any breach of fiduciary duty, dishonest or otherwise, or misapply any of GVDC's assets, or cause GVDC any loss.

(2) Dishonest breaches of fiduciary duty i.e. dishonestly using his position as managing director of GVDC to procure, in his own interests rather than in the interests of the company, GVDC to enter into the pipeline loan transactions, while deliberately not disclosing to the other directors and to the shareholders of GVDC his controlling interest in Lasco and the scale of Lasco's, and his, intended profit from the transactions . . . . The judge found that the non-disclosure was deliberate, that it was part of Mr Koshy's dishonest scheme to benefit himself and that it involved the misapplication of GVDC's assets.

The no profit rule

The relevant principle was forcefully expressed and elegantly explained in the joint judgment of Rich, Dixon and Evatt JJ in the High Court of Australia in *Furs Ltd v. Tomkies* (1936) 54 CLR 583 at 592 as:

" . . . the inflexible rule that, except under the authority of a provision in the articles of association, no director shall obtain for himself a profit by means of a transaction in which he is concerned on behalf of the company unless all the material facts are disclosed to the shareholders and by resolution a general meeting approves of his doing so or all the shareholders acquiesce. An undisclosed profit which a director so derives from the execution of his fiduciary duties belongs in equity to the company. It is no answer to the application of the rule that the profit is of a kind which the company itself could not have obtained, or that no loss is caused to the company by the gain of the director. It is a principle resting upon the impossibility of allowing the conflict of duty and interest which is involved in the pursuit of private advantage in the course of dealing in a fiduciary capacity with the affairs of the company. If, when it is his duty to safeguard and further the interests of the company, he uses the occasion as a means of profit to himself, he raises an opposition between the duty he has undertaken and his own self interest, beyond which it is neither wise nor practicable for the law to look for a criterion of liability. The consequences of such a conflict are not discoverable. Both justice and policy are against their investigation."

That is the same equitable doctrine of accountability for unauthorised profits as was applied by the House of Lords in *Regal (Hastings) Ltd v Gulliver* **[6.16]** . . . [He cited from this case, and continued:]

. . . It was submitted that (a) Mr Koshy was expressly exempted by Article 89 of the Articles of Association of GVDC from the strict duty to account to the company for the profits made from the pipeline loan transactions, even if he had made no disclosure to the board of his personal interest in the transactions or of his profits; and that (b) the disclosure in fact made by him was sufficient for that purpose and under the general law.

. . . We are unable to accept this submission. It is necessary to read Article 89 in its proper context and, in particular, in conjunction with Article 88, which requires a formal declaration of interest to be made by a director at a meeting of the board of the company. The profits intended to be made by the investing *shareholders* are beside the point. This case concerns unauthorised profits made by a director of GVDC. Further, the relaxation in Article 89 of the strict doctrines of equity against unauthorised self-dealing and secret profits, applicable to directors as fiduciaries, is made on the basis of compliance with the director's duty of disclosure under Article 88, even though not expressed to be conditional on it. . . .

The trustee-like nature of directors' duties has always been recognised as very relevant to the statutory limitation periods for actions by beneficiaries against express trustees for breach of trust and for the recovery of trust property, whether those periods are applied directly or by analogy: . . . [He considered a wealth of authorities, and continued:]

The most recent of the Court of Appeal cases is *JJ Harrison v Harrison* [2002] BCLC 162 in which a company director, who had failed to make sufficient disclosure of his interest on the purchase of a property from the company some 11 years before proceedings were commenced, was held liable to account to the company for the profits made by him from the transaction. Chadwick LJ, with whose judgment the other two members of the court agreed, helpfully stated four propositions which were beyond argument (paragraph 25):

" . . . (i) that a company incorporated under the Companies Acts is not trustee of its own property; it is both legal and beneficial owner of that property; (ii) that the property of a company so incorporated cannot lawfully be disposed of other than in accordance with the provisions of its memorandum and articles of association; (iii) that the powers to dispose of the company's property, conferred upon the directors by the articles of association, must be exercised by the directors for the purposes, and in the interests of, the company; and (iv) that, in that sense, the directors owe fiduciary duties to the company in relation to those powers and a breach of those duties is treated as a breach of trust."

Chadwick LJ continued:

"26. It follows from the principle that directors who dispose of the company's property in breach of their fiduciary duties are treated as having committed a breach of trust that a person who receives the property with knowledge of breach of duty is treated as holding it upon trust for the company. He is said to be a constructive trustee of the property. . . .

27. It follows, also, from the principle that directors who dispose of the company's property in breach of their fiduciary duties are treated as having committed a breach of trust that a director who is himself the recipient of the property holds it upon a trust for the company . . ." . . .

Scope of the account

In our judgment, Rimer J was wrong in limiting the scope of the account as he did. . . .

The point is not, as Mr Page contended, whether the loan transactions are void or voidable, or whether they were rescinded or not, or whether the property in the sums repaid passed out of the beneficial ownership of GVDC and became the property of Lasco, or even whether Lasco received the sums as trust property. The point is that Mr Koshy was not, as a fiduciary vis a vis GVDC, entitled to retain for his personal benefit any of the unauthorised profits dishonestly made from transactions between him and the company. If he received those profits directly in the form of payments to him or indirectly by, for example, the consequent increase in the value of his shareholding in Lasco, he cannot be heard to say, as against the beneficiary company, that he was entitled to retain any of the profits for himself. . . .

Equitable Compensation

. . . A company director may be held personally liable to pay equitable compensation to a company where, as a result of a breach of fiduciary duty on his part, the company has suffered loss. The paradigm case is the application of the company's property, without authority, for a purpose which is in the interests of the directors, but is not in the interests of the company. In such cases the measure of compensation is the value of the company's property which has been misapplied. The director may be held liable for the company's loss, even though he has not himself received any of the misapplied property. (In cases in which he has actually received property of the company, as a result of a breach of fiduciary duty on his part, the company is more likely to seek to establish liability as a constructive trustee).

In view of the judge's findings of a deliberate and dishonest concealment by Mr Koshy of his interest in the pipeline loan transactions it is unnecessary to enter into the debate whether the mere failure by a director to disclose his interest in a transaction with the company is a breach of the fiduciary-dealing rules for which the remedy of equitable compensation, as distinct from the remedies of rescission and account of profits, is available. There are arguments, both on authority and in principle, for holding that the remedy of equitable compensation is available in such a case: they are deployed in a recent article, which discusses the relevant case law (including the decision of this court in *Swindle v Harrison* [1997] 4 All ER 704 and academic writings on the topic)—"Equitable Compensation for Breach of Fiduciary Dealing Rules" by Matthew DJ Conaglen Vol 119 LQR 246. The judicial resolution of that question must await a case in which it arises for decision.

It is, however, necessary to consider the question concerning the place of causation in claims for relief for breach of the fiduciary-dealing rules. We agree that causation has no part to play in determining whether there has been non-compliance by the director with the fiduciary-dealing rules. Non-disclosure is non-compliance. If there has been non-compliance, the company is entitled to seek rescission of the transaction and an account of profits made by the director. In order to establish breach of the rules the company does not have to prove that it would not have entered into the transaction, if there had been compliance by the director with the fiduciary-dealing rules and he had made disclosure of his interest in the transaction. . . .

The strictness of the rule of equity that a fiduciary should not profit from the trust and confidence placed in him in respect of the management of the property and affairs of another is such that the transaction should not be allowed to stand, if it is still possible to rescind it, and that the director, who has failed to disclose his interest in the transaction, should not be allowed to retain the unauthorised gains that he has made from the transaction. In considering whether the transaction should be rescinded for non-disclosure or whether the director should account for unauthorised profits, what would have happened, if the required disclosure had been made, is irrelevant.

As with a claim for damages for a common law wrong, such as a tort or a breach of contract, the company, in a claim for compensation for non-disclosure of material facts, must first establish that a wrong has been committed. The wrong in this case was a dishonest and deliberate decision by Mr Koshy not to disclose his interest in the pipeline loan transactions entered into by GVDC with Lasco. As already explained, it is not relevant, when determining whether the non-disclosure was actionable as a civil wrong, to consider what would have happened if Mr Koshy had complied with the fiduciary-dealing rules by making the required disclosure.

However, when determining whether any compensation, and, if so, how much compensation, should be paid for loss claimed to have been caused by actionable non-disclosure, the court is not precluded by authority or by principle from considering what would have happened if the material facts had been disclosed. If the commission of the wrong has not caused loss to the company, why should the company be entitled to elect to recover compensation, as distinct from rescinding the transaction and stripping the director of the unauthorised profits made by him? There is no sufficient causal link between the non-disclosure of an interest by Mr Koshy and the loss suffered by GVDC, if it is probable that, even if he had made the required disclosure of his interest in the transaction, GVDC would nevertheless have entered into it. In our judgment, a director is not legally responsible for loss, which the company would probably have suffered, even if the director had complied with the fiduciary-dealing rules on disclosure of interests. . . .

Conclusion

In our judgment, Rimer J was entitled to refuse to order equitable compensation on the factual basis that he was not satisfied that loss had been caused to GVDC as a result of the breaches of duty by Mr Koshy. The crux of Mr Koshy's wrongdoing was non-disclosure of his personal interest in the pipeline loan transactions and the unauthorised profit made by him from the transactions. The appropriate remedy for non-disclosure is to make him account to GVDC for that profit. It is not appropriate, if GVDC so elected, to require him to compensate GVDC for loss suffered in the venture when the probabilities are, as the judge, on the evidence, found them to be, that disclosure by Mr Koshy of his interest would have made no difference to what GVDC would have done.

We accordingly dismiss GVDC's appeal on the equitable compensation point. . . .

➤ Questions

1. Why, if at all, was it material that Koshy's behaviour was fraudulent?

2. Why was the claimant pursuing both an account of profits and equitable compensation? Could *both* be recovered? Is one generally preferable to the other?

[6.23] Murad v Al-Saraj [2005] EWCA Civ 959 (Court of Appeal)

[The facts appear from the judgment.]

ARDEN LJ: . . . The claimants in this action, who are the respondents to this appeal, are two sisters, Aysha and Layla Mohammed Murad [the Murads]. . . . they sought . . . wide-ranging relief including rescission, declarations, damages and an account of profits and other benefits. The respondents are Westwood Business Inc and Mr Hashim Ibrahim Khahil Al-Saraj, whom I will call respectively Westwood and Mr Al-Saraj. Westwood is a company owned by Mr Al-Saraj.

In about September 1997, Mr Al-Saraj proposed to the Murads that they should together buy a hotel, called the Parkside Hotel in Clapham, London, for £4.1 million, of which £1 million was to be paid by the Murads, and £ 500,000 by Mr Al-Saraj. The balance was to be raised by way of bank loan. It was orally agreed between the parties that Mr Al-Saraj and the Murads would share the revenue profits from the hotel as to one third each. If the hotel was sold, the capital profit would be shared 50:50 between Mr Al-Saraj on the one hand and the Murads on the other hand. The purchase of the hotel was effected . . . and the consideration stated in the transfer was £3.6 million. . . .

In the action the Murads contended that prior to the purchase of the hotel Mr Al-Saraj represented to them that the purchase price for the hotel would be £4.1 million and that he would make his contribution of £500,000 to the purchase price in cash. In the event, this contribution had been made by offsetting unenforceable obligations of the same nominal aggregate amount due from the vendor, a Mr Al Arbash, to Mr Al-Saraj against part of the price. The obligations included a sum of £369,000, which represented Mr Al-Saraj's commission for introducing the purchasers to

Mr Al Arbash. Mr Al-Saraj argued that it was not necessary for him to contribute the £500,000 in cash. However, the judge found against Mr Al-Saraj. He held that Mr Al-Saraj had fraudulently represented that the total price for the hotel would be £4.1 million and that his contribution of £500,000 would be in cash. He also accepted the Murads' case that the actual price of the hotel was £3.6 million not £4.1 million. However, the judge found in favour of Mr Al-Saraj that, although the £500,000 set off could not be described as part of the purchase price for the hotel, the seller would not have sold the hotel for anything less than £4.1 million in total. The judge further held that there was a fiduciary relationship between the Murads and Mr Al-Saraj in relation to the joint venture to acquire the hotel. . . . The judge further held that Mr Al-Saraj was in deliberate breach of his fiduciary duty in not disclosing to the Murads that he was making his contribution by way of set off. . . .

The argument which Mr Cogley [counsel] makes is a powerful one. His case is that, where a fiduciary is made to account, there has to be a link between the profit and his wrongful act. . . .

. . . It is (he submits) wrong in principle that the Murads should receive the benefit of any profits which, if there had been full disclosure, they would have been content for Mr Al-Saraj to have. They all along anticipated being co-venturers with him and so expected him to have a share of the profits . . .

To test Mr Cogley's argument on the extent of the liability to account, in my judgment it is necessary to go back to first principle. It has long been the law that equitable remedies for the wrongful conduct of a fiduciary differ from those available at common law . . . Equity recognises that there are legal wrongs for which damages are not the appropriate remedy. In some situations therefore, as in this case, a court of equity instead awards an account of profits. . . . the purpose of the account is to strip a defaulting fiduciary of his profit. . . .

I would highlight two well-established points about the reach of the equitable remedies:

(1) the liability of a fiduciary to account does not depend on whether the person to whom the fiduciary duty was owed could himself have made the profit.

(2) when awarding equitable compensation, the court does not apply the common law principles of causation.

Proposition (1) is established by numerous authorities. It is sufficient for me to cite the well-known passage from the speech of Lord Russell of Killowen in the *Regal* case **[6.16]** at pages 144G-145A:
. . . .

The position is no different in Australia: see *Warman International Ltd v Dwyer*,[54] where the High Court specifically rejected the notion of unjust enrichment:

"It has been suggested that the liability of the fiduciary to account for a profit made in breach of the fiduciary duty should be determined by reference to the concept of unjust enrichment, namely, whether the profit is made at the expense of the person to whom the fiduciary duty is owed, and to the honesty and bona fides of the fiduciary (23). But the authorities in Australia and England deny that the liability of a fiduciary to account depends upon detriment to the plaintiff or the dishonesty and lack of bona fides of the fiduciary." (page 557)

The High Court went on to say that (in a context such as this) the fiduciary will be liable to account (only) "for a profit or benefit if it was obtained . . . by reason of his taking advantage of [an] opportunity or knowledge derived from his fiduciary position" (page 557).

It must of course be the case that no fiduciary is liable for all the profits he ever made from any source. However, it is clear that the High Court contemplated that the relevant profits would be ascertained through the process of the account. The court held: "Ordinarily a fiduciary will be ordered to render an account of the profits made within the scope and ambit of his duty." (page 559)

The High Court considered the allowances appropriate in that case. It concluded that a distinction should be drawn between the profits made from the use of a specific asset and those generated by

[54] (1995) 182 CLR 544, Aust HCt.

a business which the defaulting fiduciary had diverted to himself. In the latter case, an allowance for skill, experience and expenses might have to be made. . . .

The High Court made it clear that the power to make an allowance for skill and efforts (or some other reason):

"is not to say that the liability of a fiduciary to account should be governed by the doctrine of unjust enrichment, though that doctrine may well have a useful part to play; it is simply to say that the stringent rule requiring a fiduciary to account for profits can be carried to extremes and that in cases outside the realm of specific assets, the liability of the fiduciary should not be transformed into a vehicle for the unjust enrichment of the plaintiff." (page 561)

. . . The fact that the fiduciary can show that that party would not have made a loss is, on the authority of the *Regal* case, an irrelevant consideration so far as an account of profits is concerned. Likewise, it follows in my judgment from the *Regal* case that it is no defence for a fiduciary to say that he would have made the profit even if there had been no breach of fiduciary duty.

In the present case, the conduct of Mr Al-Saraj was held to be fraudulent. This was not the position of the directors in the *Regal* case. The principle, however, established by the *Regal* case applies even where the fiduciary acts in the mistaken belief that he is acting in accordance with his fiduciary duty. As Lord Russell made clear [in *Regal*], liability does not depend on fraud or lack of good faith. The existence of a fraudulent intent will, however, be relevant to the question of the allowances to be made on the taking of the account (which subject I consider below).

. . . The next issue is that of authorisation or consent to the breach of duty. There was no consent in fact in this case. What is said is that the Murads would have consented to the set off arrangement and reduction in the purchase price for the hotel, if they had been asked. The House of Lords in the *Regal* case recognised that there would have been no liability to account in that case if the directors had been authorised by their company to take the opportunity which they had appropriated for themselves. . . .

In my judgment it is not enough for the wrongdoer to show that, if he had not been fraudulent, he could have got the consent of the party to whom he owed the fiduciary duty to allow him to retain the profit. The point is that the profit here was in fact wholly unauthorised at the time it was made and has so remained. To obtain a valid consent, there would have to have been full and frank disclosure by Mr Al-Saraj to the Murads of all relevant matters. It is only actual consent which obviates the liability to account.

Proposition (2) . . . above is also established by many authorities. Most recently, in *Target Holdings Ltd v Redferns* [1996] 1AC 421, 436, Lord Browne-Wilkinson held:

"[But] the basic equitable principle applicable to breach of trust is that the beneficiary is entitled to be compensated for any loss that he would not have suffered but for the breach."

This principle is not applicable simply to fraudulent breaches of trust. . . .

As Lord Eldon LC said in *Caffrey v Darby* (1801) 6 Ves 488; 31ER 1159 [then followed a long quotation, which included the critical assertion that " . . . if they [ie fiduciaries] have been already guilty of negligence, they must be responsible for any loss in any way to that property: for whatever may be the immediate cause, the property would not have been in a situation to sustain that loss, if it had not been for their negligence."] . . .

It may be asked why equity imposes stringent liability of this nature. The passage just cited from the judgment of Lord Eldon LC makes it clear that equity imposes stringent liability on a fiduciary as a deterrent—*pour encourager les autres*. Trust law recognises what in company law is now sometimes called the 'agency' problem. There is a separation of beneficial ownership and control and the shareholders (who may be numerous and only have small numbers of shares) or beneficial owners cannot easily monitor the actions of those who manage their business or property on a day to day basis. Therefore, in the interests of efficiency and to provide an incentive to fiduciaries to resist the temptation to misconduct themselves, the law imposes exacting standards on fiduciaries and an extensive liability to account. . . .

I accept that any rule that makes a wrongdoer liable for all the consequences of his wrongful conduct or for actions which did not cause the injured party any loss needs to be justified by some special policy. But the authorities just cited show that in the field of fiduciaries there are policy reasons which have for a long time been accepted by the courts.

For policy reasons, the courts decline to investigate hypothetical situations as to what would have happened if the fiduciary had performed his duty. . . .

Again, for the policy reasons, on the taking of an account, the court lays the burden on the defaulting fiduciary to show that the profit is not one for which he should account . . . This shifting of the onus of proof is consistent with the deterrent nature of the fiduciary's liability. The liability of the fiduciary becomes the default rule.

This principle was applied by the High Court of Australia in the *Warman* case:

> "It is for the defendant to establish that it is inequitable to order an account of the entire profits. If the defendant does not establish that that would be so, then the defendant must bear the consequences of mingling the profits attributable to those earned by the defendant's efforts and investment, in the same way that a trustee of a mixed fund bears the onus of distinguishing what is his own."

In the *Warman* case, the defaulting fiduciary was able to show that some of the profit was not attributable to his wrongful act, but to his own skill and effort. The Court limited the account accordingly. . . .

. . . cases can be found where the fiduciary or trustee acted in all good faith believing that he was acting in the interests of his beneficiary but yet has been made to account for the profits obtained as a result of the breach of trust without limitation. Now, in a case like the *Regal* case, if the rule of equity under which the defendants were held liable to account for secret profits were not inflexible, the crucial issue of fact would be: what the company would have done if the opportunity to subscribe for shares in its subsidiary had been offered to it? In the passage just cited, as I have said, Lord Wright makes the point that it is very difficult to investigate that issue. However, while that may have been so in the past in the days of Lord Eldon and Lord King, that would not be the case today. The court has very extensive powers under the Civil Procedure Rules for instance to require information to be given as to a party's case. If the witness cannot attend the hearing, it may be possible for his evidence to be given by way of a witness statement or it may be possible for him to give evidence by video-link. The reasons for the rule of equity are many and complex (for a recent discussion, see Conaglen, The Nature and Function of Fiduciary Loyalty ([2005] LQR 452). There have been calls for its re-examination (see, for example, the articles cited at [2005] LQR 452,478 at footnote 151). It may be that the time has come when the court should revisit the operation of the inflexible rule of equity in harsh circumstances, as where the trustee has acted in perfect good faith and without any deception or concealment, and in the belief that he was acting in the best interests of the beneficiary. I need only say this: it would not be in the least impossible for a court in a future case, to determine as a question of fact whether the beneficiary would not have wanted to exploit the profit himself, or would have wanted the trustee to have acted other than in the way that the trustee in fact did act. Moreover, it would not be impossible for a modern court to conclude as a matter of policy that, without losing the deterrent effect of the rule, the harshness of it should be tempered in some circumstances. In addition, in such cases, the courts can provide a significant measure of protection for the beneficiaries by imposing on the defaulting trustee the affirmative burden of showing that those circumstances prevailed. Certainly the Canadian courts have modified the effect of equity's inflexible rule (see *Peso Silver Mines Ltd v Cropper* **[6.20]**; see also the decision of the Privy Council on appeal from Australia in *Queensland Mines v Hudson* [below, p 352]), though I express no view as to the circumstances in which there should be any relaxation of the rule in this jurisdiction. That sort of question must be left to another court.

In short, it may be appropriate for a higher court one day to revisit the rule on secret profits and to make it less inflexible in appropriate circumstances, where the unqualified operation of the rule operates particularly harshly and where the result is not compatible with the desire of modern courts to ensure that remedies are proportionate to the justice of the case where this does not conflict with some other overriding policy objective of the rule in question . . . .

However that is not this case. Mr Al-Saraj was found to have made a fraudulent misrepresentation to the Murads who had placed their trust in him. I do not consider that, even if we were free to revisit the *Regal* case, this would be an appropriate case in which to do so. The appropriate remedy is that he should disgorge all the profits, whether of a revenue or capital nature, that he made from inducing the Murads by his fraudulent representations from entering into the Parkside Hotel venture, subject to any allowances permitted by the court on the taking of the account.

The imposition of liability to account for secret profits and the placing of the burden of proof on the defaulting trustee are not, however, quite the end of the matter. The kind of account ordered in this case is an account of profits, that is a procedure to ensure the restitution of profits which ought to have been made for the beneficiary and not a procedure for the forfeiture of profits to which the defaulting trustee was always entitled for his own account. That is Mr. Cogley's case and I agree with him on this point. Even when the fiduciary is not fraudulent, the profit obtained from the breach of trust has to be defined. It may indeed be derivative, as where a trustee misappropriates trust property and then sells it and make a profit out of something else. But equity does not take the view that simply because a profit was made as part of the same transaction the fiduciary must account for it. . . . In the present case, any recognisable contribution made by Mr. Al-Saraj was to the business of the joint venture. . . .

JONATHAN PARKER LJ: I agree that the appeal should be dismissed and the cross-appeal allowed, essentially for the reasons given by Arden LJ. However, since Clarke LJ (whose judgment I have had the benefit of reading in draft) takes a different view from Arden LJ on question of the extent of Mr Al-Saraj's liability to account for the profits which he has made from the joint venture, I will give my reasons for agreeing with Arden LJ's conclusion on that issue in my own words. . . . [He then proceeded to discuss the various authorities, and continued:]

It is thus clear on authority, in my judgment, that the 'no conflict' rule is neither compensatory nor restitutionary: rather, it is designed to strip the fiduciary of the unauthorised profits he has made whilst he is in a position of conflict. As Lord Keith observed in *Attorney-General v Guardian Newspapers Ltd (No 2)* [1990] 1 AC 109, at 262E-F, the remedy of an account of profits:

" . . . is, in my opinion, more satisfactorily to be attributed to the principle that no one should be permitted to gain from his own wrongdoing".

. . . By contrast, however, in addressing a claim for equitable compensation for breach of trust the court may have regard to what would have happened but for the breach (see the passage from the judgment of Millett LJ in *Bristol & West Building Society v Mothew* [1998] Ch 1 at 17H . . .

I therefore conclude, on the basis of long-standing authority, that Mr Al-Saraj's liability to account extends to the entirety of the profits which he made from the joint venture. As the judge put it (at the hearing on 12 July 2004):

" . . . the general principle is that a fiduciary is obliged by the strict rule of equity to disgorge all the profits that he has made from the transaction, which has involved his breach of duty, . . . it does not matter whether or not the transaction would have been entered into by the beneficiary instead of the fiduciary in its entirety or as to part."

. . . All that said, there can be little doubt that the inflexibility of the 'no conflict' rule may, depending on the facts of any given case, work harshly so far as the fiduciary is concerned. It may be said with force that that is the inevitable and intended consequence of the deterrent nature of the rule. On the other hand, it may be said that commercial conduct which in 1874 was thought to imperil the safety of mankind may not necessarily be regarded nowadays with the same depth of concern. [He continued that some relaxation may be warranted, but not in the Court of Appeal, and not on these facts.]

CLARKE LJ: With one important exception, I agree with the conclusions reached by Arden LJ. That exception relates to the principles applicable to the taking of an account in a case of this kind. I have reached the conclusion that the principles applicable to the correct approach to the amount of the profits in respect of which an account should be ordered are more flexible than Arden LJ suggests. . . .

There is, in my opinion, considerable force in those submissions and, if the matter were free from authority I would hold that a person who makes a profit in the course of a fiduciary relationship must account for the profits he makes, that prima facie he must account for all the profits but that it should be open to him to show that it was always intended that he would make a profit from the transaction and to persuade the court if he can that, in the exercise of its equitable jurisdiction to order an account, in the circumstances of the particular case, he should not be ordered to account for the whole of the profits. Thus I would hold that, while the question what the claimant would have done if told the true facts, is irrelevant to the question whether the fiduciary should be ordered to account, it is or may be relevant to the extent of the account.

. . . The correct approach can to my mind be seen from the next two paragraphs of the judgment in *Warman* at pages 561–562:

"It is for the defendant to establish that it is inequitable to order an account of the entire profits. If the defendant does not establish that that would be so, then the defendant must bear the consequences of mingling the profits attributable to the defendant's breach of fiduciary duty and the profits attributable to those earned by the defendant's efforts and investment, in the same way that a trustee of a mixed fund bears the onus of distinguishing what is his own.

Whether it is appropriate to allow an errant fiduciary a proportion of profits or to make an allowance in respect of skill, expertise and other expenses is a matter of judgment which will depend on the facts of the given case. However, as a general rule, in conformity with the principle that a fiduciary must not profit from a breach of fiduciary duty, a court will not apportion profits in the absence on an antecedent arrangement for profit-sharing but will make an allowance for skill, expertise and other expenses."

. . . In all these circumstances I have reached a different conclusion from Arden LJ. I would hold that the finding that the Murads would have entered into this joint venture in any event is relevant to the scope of the account which should be ordered. . . .

. . . in reaching the above conclusion, I do not intend to accept the proposition set out in the grounds of appeal . . . that, in the light of the judge's finding that the Murads would have agreed to share some of the profits with Mr Al-Saraj if they had had full knowledge of the facts, it was wrong in principle to order Mr Al-Saraj to account for the whole of the profit but must be limited as there set out. My conclusion is simply that the judge's finding is relevant to the question whether Mr Al-Saraj has shown that it would be inequitable to order him to account for the whole of the profits. . . .[Accordingly, he would allow the appeal to this extent, and otherwise agreed with Arden LJ.]

➤ Questions

1. When is an account of profits awarded? When is equitable compensation awarded? How is each quantified?

2. How did Arden and Jonathan Parker LJJ distinguish the approach to quantifying (and cutting back) the recoverable profits in *Warman* (above) from the approach they felt obliged to take on the facts before them? Is their approach more satisfactory than that of Clarke LJ?

3. Do the rules on account of profits need to be relaxed? (See Arden LJ, above.)

Profits held on constructive trust.

[6.24] JJ Harrison (Properties) Ltd v Harrison [2001] EWCA Civ 1467, [2002] 1 BCLC 162 (Court of Appeal)

H, a director of HP, acquired land from HP without making the necessary disclosures. He then argued that the claim against him was statute-barred. The Court of Appeal held that P's claim fell within s 21(1)(b) of the Limitations Act 1980—ie an action 'to recover trust property or the proceeds of trust property previously received by the trustee and converted to his use'—and therefore was not statute barred. It also ordered an account of profits on the value of the land (now resold).

CHADWICK LJ:

The constructive trust issue

25 I start with four propositions which may be regarded as beyond argument: (i) that a company incorporated under the Companies Acts is not trustee of its own property; it is both legal and beneficial owner of that property; (ii) that the property of a company so incorporated cannot lawfully be disposed of other than in accordance with the provisions of its memorandum and articles of association; (iii) that the powers to dispose of the company's property, conferred upon the directors by the articles of association, must be exercised by the directors for the purposes, and in the interests, of the company; and (iv) that, in that sense, the directors owe fiduciary duties to the company in relation to those powers and a breach of those duties is treated as a breach of trust. . . .

26 It follows from the principle that directors who dispose of the company's property in breach of their fiduciary duties are treated as having committed a breach of trust that a person who receives that property with knowledge of the breach of duty is treated as holding it upon trust for the company. He is said to be a constructive trustee of the property. . . .

27 It follows, also, from the principle that directors who dispose of the company's property in breach of their fiduciary duties are treated as having committed a breach of trust that, a director who is, himself, the recipient of the property holds it upon a trust for the company. He, also, is described as a constructive trustee. But, as Millett LJ explained in *Paragon Finance plc v Thakerar & Co* [1999] 1 All ER 400, at pp 408g–409g, his trusteeship is different in character from that of the stranger. He falls into the category of persons who, in the words of Millett LJ (at [1999] 1 All ER 400, 408j) . . . ' though not strictly trustees, were in an analogous position and who abused the trust and confidence reposed in them to obtain their principal's property for themselves.'

28 Millett LJ referred to persons within that category—that is to say, persons who had abused their powers so as to obtain their principal's property for themselves—as 'persons [who] are properly described as constructive trustees'. He went on to say this:

'Regrettably, however, the expressions "constructive trust" and "constructive trustee" have been used by equity lawyers to describe two entirely different situations. The first covers those cases already mentioned, where the defendant, though not expressly appointed a trustee, has assumed the duties of a trustee by a lawful transaction which was independent of and preceded the breach of trust and is not impeached by the plaintiff. The second covers those cases where the trust obligation arises as a direct consequence of the unlawful transaction which is impeached by the plaintiff.

A constructive trust arises by operation of law whenever the circumstances are such that it would be unconscionable for the owner of property (usually but not necessarily the legal estate) to assert his own beneficial interest in the property and deny the beneficial interest of another. In the first class of case, however, the constructive trustee really is a trustee. He does not receive the trust property in his own right but by a transaction by which both parties intend to create a trust from the outset and which is not impugned by the plaintiff. His possession of the property is coloured from the first by the trust and confidence by means of which he obtained it, and his subsequent appropriation of the property to his own use is a breach of that trust . . .

The second class of case is different. It arises when the defendant is implicated in a fraud. Equity has always given relief against fraud by making any person sufficiently implicated in the fraud accountable in equity. In such a case he is traditionally though I think unfortunately described as a constructive trustee and said to be "liable to account as a constructive trustee". Such a person is not in fact a trustee at all, even though he may be liable to account as if he were . . .'

29 There is no doubt that Millett LJ regarded it as beyond dispute that a director who obtained the company's property for himself by misuse of the powers with which he had been entrusted as a director was a constructive trustee within the first category. . . . The reason is that a director, on appointment to that office, assumes the duties of a trustee in relation to the company's property. If, thereafter, he takes possession of that property, his possession 'is coloured from the first by the trust and confidence by means of which he obtained it'. His obligations as a trustee in relation to that property do not arise out of the transaction by which he obtained it for himself. The true analysis is that his obligations as a trustee in relation to that property predate the transaction by which it was conveyed to him. The conveyance of the property to himself by the exercise of his powers in breach of trust does not release him from those obligations. He is trustee of the property because it has become vested in him; but his obligations to deal with the property as a trustee arise out of his pre-existing duties as a director; not out of the circumstances in which the property was conveyed.

30 In the present case the deputy judge found that . . . Mr Harrison acted in breach of his fiduciary duties as a director in failing to ensure that the land was sold at its full value . . . Not only did Mr Harrison fail to make a proper disclosure of his interest; his existing duties as a director required him to ensure that the development land was not conveyed at all until the company had received and considered advice as to its value in the light of the change in planning potential. In those circumstances it seems to me impossible to reach a conclusion that Mr Harrison did not hold the development land as a constructive trustee, in the sense described by Millett LJ in the first of the two categories identified [above]. . . .

49 On the basis that Mr Harrison held the development land as trustee for the company, the remedy sought by the cross-appeal is an order that he account for the value of the land as at 23 December 1988—that being the date of the sale of the barn.

50 It seems to me right that Mr Harrison should account for the £110,300 which he received on that sale. He should be entitled to bring to the credit of that account a proportionate part of the £8,400 which he paid for the development land and the cost of any works which led to an enhancement in the value of that part of the land. It is pertinent to have in mind that the costs of pursuing planning applications has already been borne by the company.

51 I am not persuaded, however, that it would be right to require Mr Harrison to account for the value of the remainder of the development land—that is to say, the site of the replica Elizabethan manor house—at its 1988 value [which was a higher value than at the time of its sale, later on.]. . . .

52 In the absence of any evidence that the value of the development land as a whole was diminished by the sale of part in December 1988, it seems to me that the appropriate order is to require the value of the manor house site to be brought in at the price (£122,500) obtained on the further sale in April 1992. Again Mr Harrison can bring to the credit of that account the balance of the £8,400 and the cost of any works which led to an enhancement in the value of that part of the land. Subject to the proviso that he is not to take credit for expenditure which did not preserve or lead to an enhancement in the value of the land, the question what costs and allowances can be set off against the proceeds of sale will be determined on the taking of the account . . .

LAWS LJ and SIR ANTHONY EVANS concurred.

[Also see *Cook v Deeks* [6.15]; *Regal (Hastings) Ltd v Gulliver* [6.16]; *In Plus Group Ltd v Pyke* [6.18]; *Ultraframe (UK) Ltd v Fielding* [6.30], paras [1511]–[1576]]

Further issues on remedies

Extent of liability for profits

See *Regal (Hastings) Ltd v Gulliver* [6.16]; *Ultraframe (UK) Ltd v Fielding* [6.30] (director only liable for profits made personally, not for profits made by others, unless the claim can be brought under some other head of liability, eg knowing receipt, dishonest assistance, partnership law, etc).

Equitable allowance granted to the director

For cases taking a restrictive approach, see: *Murad v Al-Saraj* [6.23]; *Quarter Master UK Ltd v Pyke* (above, p 325); *Guinness plc v Saunders* [5.02]; for a more lenient approach, see: *Warman International Ltd v Dwyer* (cited extensively in *Murad*, [6.23]); *Boardman v Phipps* (see above, p 330).

Rescission

See above, Note at p 334.

Equitable compensation

The orthodox view is that equitable compensation is not available for breach of the equitable no-conflict and no-profit rules, except to compensate for losses caused by breach of the equitable duty of care (if this duty exists distinct from the common law duty) and the equitable duties to exercise powers independently, *bona fide* and for proper purposes (ie the equitable equivalents of ss 171–174). Note that misuse of the company's property may involve a conflict of duty and interest (for which profits are recoverable) *and* a breach of the duty to act *bona fide* and for proper purposes (for which equitable compensation is recoverable, even if the director has not made a profit from the misuse (*Gwembe Valley Development Co Ltd v Koshy (No 3)* [6.22], in which Mummery LJ raises but does not answer the question whether compensation is available if the *only* breach is of the no-conflict or no-profit rules).

If equitable compensation is available, the loss is measured at the time of the trial and must be causally related to the breach (*Target Holdings Ltd v Redferns* [1996] 1 AC 421, a case concerning fiduciary obligations of solicitors, not directors).

Limitation periods

The normal limitation period for breach of equitable fiduciary duties is 6 years, unless the Limitation Act 1980, s 21(1) applies, in which case there is no limitation (eg *JJ Harrison (Properties) Ltd v Harrison* [6.24]; *Gwembe Valley Development Co Ltd v Koshy (No 3)* [6.22]).

Consent, approval or authorisation by members: CA 2006 s 180

Section 180 deals with the ways in which directors can avoid liability for breaches of their general statutory duties by making the appropriate declaration or obtaining the appropriate consent, approval or authorisation from either the directors or the members.

Recall that a director may already have exemptions from liability because he or she has board of directors' authorisation for dealings with outsiders (s 175) or has made a declaration to the directors about dealings with the company (s 177). Section 180(1) indicates that these mechanisms replace the equitable rule which requires the members, not the directors, to authorise these types of breaches of duty. This is subject to any contrary enactment (eg chapter 4), or any provision in the company's constitution imposing additional demands.

Section 180(4) is the crucial subsection. It retains the equitable and common law rules which allow *companies* to authorise (in *advance*—note the wording of 180(4)(a)) what would otherwise be a breach of duty by the directors, and to make provision in their articles for dealing with conflicts of interest in specific ways.

Equitable rules for authorisation by the company

The equitable rules indicate that authorisation must be given by the members, not the directors (*Furs Ltd v Tomkies* (1936) 54 CLR 583, 590, 599), unless perhaps the members and directors are the same persons (*Queensland Mines Ltd v Hudson* (1978) 18 ALR 1, PC, see below, p 352).

Consent is effective only if it is proper and fully informed (*Kaye v Croydon Tramways Co* [1898] 1 Ch 358; *Knight v Frost* [1999] 1 BCLC 364). This means that the decision of the members must not be a fraud on the creditors (*Re Halt Garage (1964) Ltd* **[5.04]**) or (it seems) a fraud on the minority or an abuse of power (*North West Transportation Co Ltd v Beatty* **[4.34]**. This last aspect is controversial (*Burland v Earle* **[11.10]**; *Cook v Deeks* **[6.15]**; *Prudential Assurance Co Ltd v Newman Industries Ltd (No 2)* **[11.13]**; *Smith v Croft (No 2)* **[11.14]**). It is sometimes alleged that authorisation or ratification of negligence is more controversial, but arguably the same rules apply—companies, like other individuals, can waive the duty of care and forgive past acts of negligence. However, see *Pavlides v Jensen* [1956] Ch 565; *Daniels v Daniels* [1978] Ch 406 (for both these cases, see below, p 520); *Re Horsley and Weight Ltd* **[3.05]**; *Multinational Gas and Petrochemical Co v Multinational Gas and Petrochemical Services Ltd* **[6.25]**).

Ratification of acts of directors: CA 2006 s 239

This important provision settles new minimum requirements for effective ratification. The provision draws on existing equitable rules, but imposes more stringent demands. In addition, to the extent (if any) that the statutory version may still be more lenient than the equitable rules, the latter rules—and rules in any other enactment—remain effective to supplement or enhance the statutory requirements (s 239((7)).

Section 239(1) makes it clear that the provision is designed to afford a mechanism for the company, via its members, to forgive a defaulting director for conduct amounting to negligence, default, breach of duty or breach of trust in relation to the company (ie the provision includes all the wrongs which are the subject of Part 10, including negligence, and not simply fiduciary wrongs).

Section 239(2) insists that the ratification must be by resolution of the members of the company. This minimum requirement will apply regardless of any more lenient alternative provided by company's articles, or by existing general law. And s 239(3) and (4) indicate that ratification is effective only if the resolution is passed *without* votes in favour of the resolution by the defaulting director (if a member of the company) and any member connected with him.

This changes the law as expressed in *North West Transportation Co Ltd v Beatty* **[4.34]**; *Burland v Earle* **[11.10]**; and *Pavlides v Jensen* [1956] Ch 565 (see below, p 520). Instead, it adopts the approach advocated in *Atwool v Merryweather* **[11.09]**; *Cook v Deeks* **[6.15]**; *Hogg v Cramphorn* **[6.08]**; *Bamford v Bamford* **[4.33]**; *Howard Smith Ltd v Ampol Petroleum Ltd* **[6.09]**; *Daniels v Daniels* [1978] Ch 406 (see below, p 520); *Prudential Assurance Co Ltd v Newman Industries Ltd (No 2)* **[11.13]**; and *Smith v Croft (No 2)* **[11.14]**.

➤ **Notes and Questions**

1. Does CA 2006 s 239 create difficulties for smaller companies? If the majority of shares in a company are held by directors (which is the norm for smaller family-type companies), then their votes will be disregarded for ratification purposes, giving much more power to small shareholders (or, in an insolvency, to a liquidator), who will then have leverage over the owners, which will not necessarily serve the best interests of the company. What if the minority shareholders own say only 1% of the company? Should they still have a veto over ratification? What if there are no independent shareholders? On the other hand, it is difficult to see why wrongdoers should be able to vote to forgive themselves.

2. Section 239(6) makes clear that nothing in this clause changes the law on unanimous consent, so the restrictions imposed by this clause as to who may vote on a ratification resolution will not apply when every members votes (informally or otherwise) in favour of the resolution. On unanimous consent, see: *Re Duomatic Ltd* [1969] 2 Ch 365, 373 (need the agreement of every member entitled to vote) (above, p 192); *Re D'Jan of London Ltd* **[6.14]** (confirming that all members must actually apply their minds to the question and decide in favour of the proposal)

3. Section 239(6) also makes clear that nothing in the section removes any power of the directors to 'agree not to sue, or to settle or release a claim made by them on behalf of the company'. Does this abrogate the entire section, allowing the directors to override the tough members' ratification rule, and agree themselves to ratify (ie forgive, and agree not to sue) any wrongdoing director?

Approval or ratification by the shareholders.

[6.25] Multinational Gas and Petrochemical Co Ltd v Multinational Gas and Petrochemical Services Ltd [1983] Ch 258, [1983] 2 All ER 563 (Court of Appeal)

Three international oil companies established a joint venture to deal in liquified gas. They set up the plaintiff company to carry on the business, and the defendant company 'Services' to manage it and to provide advisory services. The three oil companies were the sole shareholders in both companies and appointed their directors. The plaintiff company went into liquidation owing approximately £114m, and its liquidator sued its directors and also the defendant company, alleging that they had all been negligent. The Court of Appeal held that the action was not founded on any tort committed within the jurisdiction and so refused leave to serve the proceedings on those defendants who were abroad. But Lawton and Dillon LJJ also accepted an argument that there could be no complaint about commercial decisions, alleged to be negligent, which had been made by the directors with the approval of the three oil companies as shareholders.

LAWTON LJ: No allegation had been made that the plaintiff's directors had acted ultra vires or in bad faith. What was alleged was that when making the decisions which were alleged to have caused the plaintiff loss and giving instructions to Services to put them into effect they had acted in accordance with the directions and behest of the three oil companies. These oil companies were the only shareholders. All the acts complained of became the plaintiff's acts. The plaintiff, although it had a separate existence from its oil company shareholders, existed for the benefit of those shareholders, who, provided they acted intra vires and in good faith, could manage the plaintiff's affairs as they wished. If they wanted to take business risks through the plaintiff which no prudent businessman would take they could lawfully do so. Just as an individual can act like a fool provided he keeps within the law so could the plaintiff, but in its case it was for the shareholders to decide whether the plaintiff should act foolishly. As shareholders they owed no duty to those with whom the plaintiff did business. It was for such persons to assess the hazards of doing business with them. It follows, so it was submitted, that the plaintiff, as a matter of law, cannot now complain about what they did at their shareholders' behest.

This submission was based on . . . a long line of cases starting with *Salomon v A Salomon & Co Ltd* **[2.01]** and ending with the decision of this court in *Re Horsley & Weight Ltd* **[3.05]**. In my judgment these cases establish the following relevant principles of law: first, that the plaintiff was at law a different legal person from the subscribing oil company shareholders and was not their agent (see *Salomon v A Salomon & Co Ltd*). Secondly, that the oil companies as shareholders were not liable to anyone except to the extent and the manner provided by the Companies Act 1948 (see *Salomon v A Salomon & Co Ltd*). Thirdly, that when the oil companies acting together required the plaintiff's directors to make decisions or approve what had already been done, what they did or approved became the plaintiff's acts and were binding on it: see by way of examples *A-G for Canada v Standard Trust Co of New York*,[55] *Re Express Engineering Works Ltd*[56] and *Re Horsley & Weight Ltd*. When approving whatever their nominee directors had done, the oil companies were not, as the plaintiff submitted, relinquishing any causes of action which the plaintiff may have had against its directors. When the oil companies, as shareholders, approved what the plaintiff's directors had done there was no cause of action because at that time there was no damage. What the oil companies were doing was adopting the directors' acts and as shareholders, in agreement with each other, making those acts the plaintiff's acts.

It follows that the plaintiff cannot now complain about what in law were its own acts. Further, I can see no grounds for adjudging that the oil companies as shareholders were under any duty of care to the plaintiff.

DILLON LJ: It is not alleged that the joint venturers or the directors of the plaintiff acted fraudulently or in bad faith in any way or were guilty of fraudulent trading. What is alleged is that they all acted negligently in that they made five speculative decisions in relation to the ships, when they knew or ought to have known that they did not have sufficient information to make sensible business decisions. The decisions which they took in good faith went, it is said, outside the range of reasonable commercial judgment.

The heart of the matter is therefore that certain commercial decisions which were not ultra vires the plaintiff were made honestly, not merely by the directors but by all the shareholders of the plaintiff at a time when the plaintiff was solvent. I do not see how there can be any complaint of that.

An individual trader who is solvent is free to make stupid, but honest, commercial decisions in the conduct of his own business. He owes no duty of care to future creditors. The same applies to a partnership of individuals.

A company, as it seems to me, likewise owes no duty of care to future creditors. The directors indeed stand in a fiduciary relationship to the company, as they are appointed to manage the affairs of the company and they owe fiduciary duties to the company though not to the creditors, present or future,[57] or to individual shareholders. The duties owed by a director include a duty of care, as was recognised by Romer J in *Re City Equitable Fire Insurance Co Ltd* **[6.13]**, though as he pointed out the nature and extent of the duty may depend on the nature of the business of the company and on the particular knowledge and experience of the individual director.

The shareholders, however, owe no duty to the company. Indeed, so long as the company is solvent the shareholders are in substance the company . . .

---

55   [1911] AC 498.
56   [1920] 1 Ch 46, CA.
57   [Dillon LJ qualified this in *West Mercia Safetywear Ltd v Dodd* (1988) 4 BCLC 30, by saying that these remarks only apply to a company which is solvent at the time.]

The well known passage in the speech of Lord Davey in *Salomon v A Salomon & Co Ltd* that the company is bound in a matter intra vires by the unanimous agreement of its members is, in my judgment, apt to cover the present case whether or not Lord Davey had circumstances such as the present case in mind.

If the company is bound by what was done when it was a going concern, then the liquidator is in no better position. He cannot sue the members because they owed no duty to the company as a separate entity and he cannot sue the directors because the decision which he seeks to impugn were made by, and with the full assent of, the members.

MAY LJ (dissenting): It is well established by such authorities as *Salomon v A Salomon & Co Ltd* and the many authorities to like effect to which we were referred that a company is bound, in a matter which is intra vires and not fraudulent, by the unanimous agreement of its members or by an ordinary resolution of a majority of its members. However, I do not think that this line of authority establishes anything more than that a company is bound by the legal results of a transaction so entered into: that is to say, for instance, by the terms of contract which is so approved; or that neither it nor for that matter its liquidator can challenge the legal consequences, such as a transfer of title, of a transaction to which its members have agreed to the extent that I have mentioned.

This, however, is very different from saying that where all the acts of the directors of a company, for instance, Services, have been carried out by them as nominees for, at the behest and with the knowledge of all the members of the company, namely the joint venturers, then forever the company as a separate legal entity is precluded from complaining of the quality of those acts in the absence of fraud or unless they were ultra vires. If we assume for the purposes of this argument that the directors of the plaintiff did commit breaches of the duty of care that they owed that company, as a result of which it suffered damage, then I agree with the submission made by counsel for the plaintiff that the company thereby acquired a cause of action against those directors in negligence. The fact that all the members of the company knew of the acts constituting such breaches, and indeed knew that those acts were in breach of that duty, does not of itself in my opinion prevent them from constituting the tort of negligence against the company or by itself release the directors from liability for it. Of course, in the circumstances of the present case, whilst the joint venturers retained effective control of the company they would be extremely unlikely to complain of the negligence of their nominees. But such restraint on their part could not and did not in my opinion amount to any release by the company of the cause of action which ex hypothesi had become vested in it against its directors. *Salomon*'s case and the subsequent authorities make it clear that a limited company is a person separate and distinct from its members, even though a majority of the latter have the power to control its activities so long as it is not put into liquidation and whilst they remain members and a majority. Once, however, the joint venturers ceased to be able to call the tune, either because the company went into liquidation or indeed, though it is not this case, because others took over their interest as members of the company, then I can see no legal reason why the liquidator or the company itself could not sue in respect of the cause of action still vested in it. I agree with counsel's submission that that cause of action was an asset of the company which could not be gratuitously released . . .

➤ Notes

1. All three members of the Court of Appeal in this case referred to the doubts expressed *obiter dicta* by Templeman and Cumming-Bruce LJJ in *Re Horsley & Weight Ltd* **[3.05]** whether directors holding a majority of shares were competent to ratify their own making of a corporate gift. This is now outlawed by s 239(3) and (4). CA 2006 therefore abrogates the rule in *North-West Transportation Co Ltd v Beatty* (1887) 12 App Cas 589, PC, which held that a contract between the director and his company, which was voidable because of the director's undisclosed interest in it, could be ratified by the company in general meeting; and that the interested director could vote as a member in such a meeting, even though he held the majority of votes.

2. In *Queensland Mines Ltd v Hudson* (1978) 18 ALR 1, 52 ALJR 399, PC, the plaintiff company was set up as a joint venture by A Ltd, a company controlled by Hudson, and F Ltd, a company controlled by Korman. Hudson, as managing director of Queensland Mines, was involved in negotiations with the Tasmanian government for licences to mine iron ore. Just before the licences were issued, Korman and his company F Ltd ran into financial difficulties and Korman told Hudson that he had not the financial resources to proceed with the venture. Hudson took the licence in his own name. He later resigned as managing director of Queensland Mines and formed his own new company, which, at considerable risk and expense, exploited the licences and earned profits. The Privy Council held (i) that the opportunity to make the profits had come to Hudson through his position as managing director of Queensland Mines, but (ii) that since the board of that company had known of Hudson's interest at all times (and had resolved a year after the issues of the licences that Queensland Mines 'should not pursue the matter [ie the licences] any further'), Hudson was not accountable for his profit.

> Questions

1. What were the members in the *Multinational Gas* case purporting to do: exercise management decision-making power themselves; or authorise the directors in advance of the directors' action in order to enable the directors to pursue activities that would otherwise be in breach of duty; or ratify, after the event, thereby indicating that the company would not sue the defaulting directors for their breaches?

2. If the members were ratifying the wrongdoing (see above, p 342), would their decision bind a liquidator who was subsequently appointed to the company and inclined to sue the wrongdoers?

3. If the alleged acts of negligence were committed by the directors with the *prior authorisation* of the members, do you consider the reasoning of Lawton LJ or that of May LJ more appropriate?

4. If the alleged acts of negligence were committed by the directors on their own initiative and later approved by the members, do you consider the reasoning of Lawton LJ or that of May LJ more appropriate?

5. In *Queensland Mines*, how could a decision of the board have this effect? Was the board the legitimate organ of the company to make arrangements with Hudson in advance of any breach? Or was the board of directors really also the 'general meeting' in all but name, representing all the corporate joint venturer members, and so able to count in effect as a 'members' vote at a members' meeting?

Relief from liability granted by the court: CA 2006 s 1157

The court has a discretion to grant relief to directors and other officers from liability for breach of duty, similar to that which exists in relation to trustees, if they have 'acted honestly and reasonably and . . . ought fairly to be excused': CA 2006 s 1157 (replacing CA 1985 s 727).

The court in *Coleman Taymar Ltd v Oakes* [2001] 2 BCLC 749 held that the section could apply to a liability to account for profits, as well as to a liability to pay damages to the company. The discretion was exercised in *Re D'Jan of London Ltd* **[6.14]**, but refused, in a number of well-known cases, eg *Dorchester Finance Co Ltd v Stebbing* (above, p 306), *Guinness plc v Saunders* **[5.02]**, and *Clark v Cutland* [2003] EWCA Civ 810, CA. (Note that in *Re Produce Marketing Consortium Ltd* [1989] 1 WLR 745, Knox J ruled that, as a matter of principle, relief under CA 1985 s 727 could not be granted in favour of a director who is held liable to pay compensation for wrongful trading under IA 1986 s 214: see below, p 671).

Contracting out of liability: CA 2006 ss 232–238

Under CA 2006 s 232, '[a]ny provision that purports to exempt a director of a company (to any extent) from any liability that would otherwise attach to him in connection with any negligence, default, breach of duty or breach of trust in relation to the company is void.' The rule covers provisions in the articles and in separate contracts (s 232(3)). The early predecessors to this section were introduced as a knee-jerk reaction to the decision in *Re City Equitable Fire Insurance Co Ltd* **[6.13]**.

Specific exceptions are allowed by way of providing the director with insurance, qualifying third party indemnity provisions or qualifying pension scheme indemnity provisions (s 232(2)). A further exception is provided in s 205 (exception for expenditure on defending proceedings etc).

Section 232 retains the unresolved difficulty of its predecessors, however, since s 232(4) provides: 'nothing in the section is to be taken as preventing the company's articles from making such provision as had previously been lawful for dealing with conflicts of interest.' Such provisions in the articles are common, permitting certain activities by directors that would otherwise constitute breaches of the no conflict rule. How these provisions could be regarded as legitimate in the face of the predecessor to s 232 (CA 1985 s 309A-C) was troubling.

In *Movitex Ltd v Bulfield* [1988] BCLC 104, Vinelott J attempted to resolve the issue by holding that the rule against self-dealing by a trustee or a director is properly seen as a *disability* or restriction on the conduct of a fiduciary and not a *duty*: articles which exclude or modify the application of this rule did not, therefore, infringe CA 1985 ss 309A-310. It did not help matters much, and the analysis was described in *Gwembe Valley Development Co Ltd v Koshy (No 3)* **[6.22]** as a 'needless complication'. In any event, all this rather unsatisfying mental gymnastics is no longer possible now that the codified rules expressly regard all the rules as 'duties'.

Special rules on notice requirements and members' approval for certain transaction: CA 2006 ss 182–231

Declarations of interest in existing transactions or arrangements: ss 182–187

Section 182 provides that if a director enters into a transaction or arrangement with the company without declaring his interest under s 177 (duty to declare interest in proposed transaction or arrangement), he will be under an immediate obligation to declare that interest and failure to do so will constitute a criminal offence (see s183 (offence of failure to declare interest)). Even in these circumstances, however, it seems that the director is given a reasonable amount of time in which to comply with the duty in s 182 (see subs. (4)). (This provision replaces CA 1985 s 317 with regard to existing transactions and arrangements.)

Unlike s 177, s 182 (2) makes it clear that directors must use one of the three prescribed methods of declaration. Sections 184–187 elaborate on these, and in particular provide rules for sole directors of companies that ought to have two or more directors, and for shadow directors. Presumably a failure to make a declaration in the prescribed manner will render the declaration either a nullity or incomplete, and a further declaration will be required (s 182(3)); how this requirement will be reconciled with s 182(6)(b), indicating that the duty does not apply if the other directors are already aware of the interest, or ought to be aware of the interest, is unclear.

As with s 177, certain interests do not have to be declared.

Unlike the duty to declare an interest in a *proposed* transaction or arrangement (s 177), it is a criminal offence not to comply with the duty to declare an interest in an *existing* transaction or arrangement. The Attorney-General, Lord Goldsmith, in Grand Committee explained the rationale behind this:

> ... because one is here concerned with an existing transaction or arrangement, the failure to declare cannot affect the validity of the transaction or give rise to any other civil consequences. That is to be contrasted with the position where there is a failure to disclose an interest in relation to a proposed transaction where the law can say that as a result of the failure to disclose that interest— and the company then enters into the transaction in ignorance of that—consequences follow. The transaction may be voidable, to be set aside. The company may wish to claim financial redress in one form or another as a result of what has taken place. But, as I say, that is different from a failure to declare an interest in an existing transaction where those considerations probably cannot arise. That is why a criminal offence is created." (HL GC Day 4, Hansard HL 678 9/2/06 Col 338)

This does not appear to be an accurate description of the differences between these two provisions. If a director *complies* with s 177, then the company can decide on a fully informed basis whether to proceed with the proposed transaction or arrangement. Section 180 indicates that this declaration replaces the need for the approval of the company's members under the equitable rules, although any additional requirements imposed by the articles will still have to be met. Assuming these additional requirements (if any) have also been met, the transaction cannot be impugned for breach of s 177 or for breach of the no-conflict and no-profit rules in relation to transactions with the company. However, note that the deal might nevertheless be a breach of some other general statutory duty, and give rise to an action for a remedy under some other head. The availability of the relevant remedies in those particular circumstances will then need to be assessed in the usual way.

On the other hand, if s 177 is *not* complied with, and the company nevertheless enters into the proposed transaction or arrangement, then the director will be in breach of s 177 and, if the breach continues, will also be in breach of s 182. The equitable remedies for breach of the general statutory duty can be pursued against the defaulting director (and, again, an assessment will have to be made about the availability of various remedies—eg rescission will not be available against a *bona fide* third party purchaser, but will be available against other parties not protected by this equitable rule, including the director). In addition, the director will also be liable for the criminal offence described in s 183. Put this way, there is no logical divide between the remedies available for breach of ss 177 and 182; indeed, if s 177 is breached, and the proposed arrangement is pursued, s 182 will also be breached so long as the director fails to declare the interest. Section 177 is therefore not a provision designed to *impose* liability on directors, but a provision designed to afford protection to those who comply with it.

In this sense, there is the same relationship between ss 183 and 178 (as influenced by s 180) as there is between CA 1985 s 317 and the equitable consequences of breach of the no-conflict and no-profit rules (as influenced by any relevant consents given by the members or given in the way allowed by the articles). See *Guinness plc v Saunders* [1990] 2 AC 663, 697 (Lord Goff) **[5.02]**; *Coleman Taymar Ltd v Oakes* [2001] 2 BCLC 749.

Transactions with directors requiring the approval of members

Certain transactions between the company and its directors are deemed sufficiently 'risky' to require members' approval for their validity, rather than the simpler procedure of board approval set out in s 177. The details of the statutory provisions are not addressed here, but the sections repay careful reading. Several categories of transactions are affected, namely:

(i) Directors' long term service contracts: ss 188–189:

See above, pp 249 ff.

(ii) Substantial property transactions: ss 190–196

Section 190 replaces CA 1985 s 320(1), and makes certain changes. Substantial property transactions (defined in s 191) are permitted, provided they are approved by the members. Failure to obtain the necessary authorisation will not result in any liability for the company (s 190(3)).

An 'arrangement' includes an agreement or understanding that does not have contractual effect (*Re Duckwari plc* **[6.26]**). Note the exceptions in ss 192–194. The civil consequences are described in s 195. These sections apply equally to shadow directors: s 223(1)(b).

The remedies provided by s 195 enlarge both the types of recovery (including recovery of losses, and not just profits) and the persons against whom recovery is available, when compared with the remedies available in equity for breach of fiduciary duty in entering into transactions involving a conflict of interest. These remedies are not available if the members approve the transaction within a reasonable time (s 196). Also see s 1157 (Power of court to grant relief in certain circumstances) (replacing CA 1985 s 727).

See below, *Re Duckwari plc* **[6.26]** (general remedies issues) and *Re Ciro Citterio Menswear plc* **[6.27]** (no constructive trust before rescission).

(iii) Loans, quasi-loans and credit transactions: ss 197–214

Sections 197–214 are derived from CA 1985 ss 330ff. The significant change is that loans to directors and connected persons are no longer generally prohibited but are subject to the requirement of member approval, and sometimes also approval of the members of its holding company. The sections apply equally to shadow directors (s 223(1)(c)).

The provisions relating to loans apply to all UK-registered companies (with the exception of wholly-owned subsidiaries (s 197(5)). The provisions for quasi-loans and credit transactions apply only to public companies and associated companies (ss 198, 201). See other related restrictions (ss 198–203).

The requirement for members' approval is subject to the exceptions in ss 204–209 inclusive: the exceptions extend to expenditure on company business; expenditure on defending proceedings etc, in connection with regulatory action or investigation; expenditure for minor and business transactions; expenditure for intra-group transactions and expenditure for money-lending companies). Of these, the most general is s 207, which sets the minimum threshold value for transactions requiring the approval of members (£10,000 for loans, etc; £15,000 for credit transactions).

The remedies are set out in s 213, and there is, again, a provision for subsequent affirmation (s 214).

(iv) Payments for loss of office: ss 215–222

See above, pp 258 ff.

(v) Directors' service contracts—definition and inspection rights of members: ss 227–230

See above, pp 249 ff.

(vi) Contracts not in the ordinary course of business with sole member who is also a director: s 231

Outside the range of Part 10, directors are subject to a raft of statutory provisions imposing liability for:

(i)   losses of capital, eg through issuing shares without complying with the statutory rules about payment; or for making an improper repurchase of shares out of capital (see below, pp 399 ff);

(ii)   'insider dealing': see below, pp 594 ff;

(iii) directors are liable to reimburse the company if political donations are made without shareholder authorisation: CA 2006 s 366ff and see above, pp 146 ff.

Remedies—indemnities

It is crucial to read the relevant statutory provisions if you want to understand this area.

Statutory remedies for breach of duty may include losses not caused by the breach itself

[6.26] Re Duckwari plc [1999] Ch 253, [1998] 2 BCLC 315 (Court of Appeal)

Mr Cooper was a director of Offerventure Ltd and also of Duckwari plc. Offerventure had contracted to buy a property in High Wycombe for development for £495,000 (a fair price). Cooper offered to pass on the property to Duckwari at cost, on terms that he would receive a 50% share of any profits resulting from the development. This offer was accepted by the board of Duckwari, but not approved by its members. After Duckwari had bought the property, there was a fall in the market and the property was eventually sold for £177,970. The Court of Appeal held that Cooper, Duckwari's other directors and Offerventure (as an associated company) were liable under CA 1985 ss 320–322 [now CA 2006 s 190ff] to indemnify Duckwari for the whole of its loss, including that due to the fall in market values, and not simply for the difference between the price paid for the property and its value at the time of the transaction (which would have been nil).

NOURSE LJ: It is convenient to start with the judge's comparison of the purchase with an unauthorised investment by a trustee. The assets of a company being vested in the company, the directors are not accurately described as trustees of those assets. Nevertheless, they have always been treated as trustees of assets which are in their hands or under their control. The principle is best stated by Lindley LJ in *Re Lands Allotment Co*:[58]

Although directors are not properly speaking trustees, yet they have always been considered and treated as trustees of money which comes to their hands or which is actually under their control; and ever since joint stock companies were invented directors have been liable to make good moneys which they have misapplied upon the same footing as if they were trustees . . .

As to what is meant by a misapplication in this context, I adopt as correct the statement in *Gore-Browne on Companies*, 44th edn (1986), p 27/010, para 27.6:

any disposition of the company's property which by virtue of any provision of the company's constitution or *any statutory provision* or any rule of general law the company or the board is forbidden or incompetent or unauthorised to make, or which is carried out by the directors otherwise than in accordance with their duty to act bona fide in the interests of the company and for the proper purposes. (Emphasis added.)

[58]   [1894] 1 Ch 616, CA.

A statutory provision well known in this context was section 54 of the Companies Act 1948 (now re-enacted, though with substantial amendments, by sections 151 to 158 of the Act of 1985), which prohibited a company from giving financial assistance for the acquisition of its own shares. It has been held that directors who cause the company's funds to be applied in breach of that prohibition are to be treated as trustees of those funds: see, for example, *Belmont Finance Corpn Ltd v Williams Furniture Ltd (No 2)* **[8.10]**. Similarly, by virtue of section 320(1)(b) Duckwari was prohibited from entering into the arrangement with Offerventure pursuant to which it purchased the property unless the arrangement was first approved by a resolution of Duckwari in general meeting. Such approval not having been obtained, the payment of £495,000, together with the other costs of the acquisition, was a misapplication of Duckwari's funds which, had section 320 stood alone, the directors responsible would have been liable to make good as if they were trustees.

The basis on which trustees would have been liable to make good the misapplication is well settled. If a trustee applies trust moneys in the acquisition of an unauthorised investment, he is liable to restore to the trust the amount of the loss incurred on its realisation: see *Knott v Cottee* (1852) 16 Beav 77. He is also liable for interest. Where more than one trustee is responsible for the acquisition their liability is joint and several.

If these rules were to apply to the present case, the directors responsible would prima facie appear to be jointly and severally liable to restore to Duckwari the difference between the gross acquisition cost, £505,923, and the £177,970 which has since been realised on the sale of the property, plus interest, credit being given for the amount of any rents and profits received before completion of the sale.

That would have been the position if section 320 had stood alone, which it does not. A company's remedies for a contravention of that section are spelled out in section 322, in this case in section 322(3)(b). So the question is what loss or damage is comprehended by that provision. The persons who are rendered liable to indemnify Duckwari are not only Mr Cooper and the other directors responsible but also Offerventure, as a person connected with Mr Cooper.

[His Lordship outlined the arguments of counsel and continued:] In considering these rival submissions I return once more to the wording of section 322(3)(b), which provides for an indemnity 'for any loss or damage resulting from the arrangement or transaction.' Plainly those words, if read in isolation, are capable of including a loss incurred by Duckwari on a realisation of the property for less than the cost of its acquisition. Such a loss can fairly be said to result from the purchase, on the ground that if the purchase had not been made the loss would not have been incurred. But the loss can also fairly be said to result from the fall in value of the property. So it is necessary to look at the other provisions of sections 320 and 322 and the general law in order to see whether a loss of the former kind was intended to be included.

I agree with Mr Richards [counsel for the company] that the judge was wrong both in thinking that the general distinction between the decision-making powers of directors and trustees had some relevance to the question and in restricting the mischief addressed by the provisions to acquisitions at an inflated value or disposals at an undervalue. It is obvious that there will be many other circumstances in which it is appropriate for the approval of shareholders to be obtained. In the present case, for example, the shareholders might well have declined to approve the purchase either because it was a new kind of venture or, more pertinently, because Offerventure or Mr Cooper was to take 50 per cent of any profits arising from the development of the property but was not to bear a share of any loss. A one-sided arrangement thus favourable to the director would seem to be an exemplar of the kind of arrangement which was intended to be within the scope of section 320.

Bearing in mind the evident purpose of sections 320 and 322 to give shareholders specific protection in respect of arrangements and transactions which will or may benefit directors to the detriment of the company, I am unable to construe section 322(3)(b) as denying the company a remedy which appears to flow naturally from a combination of section 320(1)(b) and the general law. No doubt it is possible to cite instances where Parliament has been held to take away with one hand what it appears to give with the other. But I cannot conceive that one would be found where the result was to give a narrow effect to provisions plainly intended to afford a protection and equally amenable to being given some wider effect.

This broad approach to section 322(3)(b) is entirely consistent with the provisions of section 322(2)(a) and (3)(a) . . .

It is well recognised that the basis on which a trustee is liable to make good a misapplication of trust moneys is strict and sometimes harsh, especially where, as here, there has been a huge depreciation in the value of the asset acquired. I can understand what I believe to have been the reluctance of the judge to visit Mr Cooper (with whom I include Offerventure) with the consequences of the loss. But the loss has to fall somewhere and, if a proposal to purchase the property had been put to and rejected by the shareholders, it would have lain with Mr Cooper. The approval of the shareholders not having been obtained, it is not unfair that the loss should continue to lie with Mr Cooper rather than Duckwari . . .

PILL and THORPE LJJ concurred.

Not every case in which a director receives a loan (or a quasi-loan) results in a constructive trusteeship.

[6.27] Ciro Citterio Menswear Plc v Thakrar [2002] EWHC 662, [2002] 1 WLR 2217

ANTHONY MANN QC: The principal question in this part of this case is whether an unlawful loan gives rise to constructive trusteeship at any stage. I take as a starting point that a loan to a director is not of itself the sort of transaction that is inevitably a misapplication of company moneys. There is nothing inherently wrong with such a transaction in the abstract. It may or may not be a misapplication on any particular set of facts, but it is not, as such, a breach by a director of his trusteeship of company assets. Statute did not intervene until the Companies Act 1929, when the predecessor of section 330 made its first appearance. The bar was repeated in the Companies Act 1948, but without the civil consequences of the bar being spelt out. It was not until 1985 that statute specified civil consequences.

The civil consequences are specified as being that the loan is voidable. That is of obvious significance to this part of the case. If a loan is voidable, it stands until avoided. That means that property in the money paid under the loan passes to the borrower. In my view that concept is inimical to the existence of a constructive trusteeship, or any form of tracing claim, at least in the absence of special circumstances. That view is supported by the speech of Lord Goff of Chieveley in *Guinness plc v Saunders* **[5.02]**, 698. Lord Goff was considering a breach by a Guinness director of the disclosure rules in section 317 of the companies Act 1985 [CA 2006, s 177]. The consequences of that breach were that the contract in question, under which the director took considerable financial benefits, was voidable, not void. The Court of Appeal had held that the director, therefore, became a constructive trustee of the moneys he had received under that contract and had to pay them back. Lord Goff, with whom Lord Griffiths agreed, held that this part of the analysis could not be sustained. A voidable contract stood until avoided. He considered, at p 698, an argument by counsel for Guinness to the effect that the director

"having received the money as constructive trustee, must pay it back. This appears to have formed, in part at least, the basis of the decision of the Court of Appeal. But the insuperable difficulty in the way of this proposition is again that the money was on this approach paid not under a void, but under a voidable, contract. Under such a contract, the property in the money would have vested in Mr Ward (who, I repeat, was ex hypothesi acting in good faith); and Guinness cannot short circuit an unrescinded contract simply by alleging a constructive trust."

In my view, that reasoning applies in this case. Until any avoidance by the company the loan stood, and there was no constructive trust. In the case of section 330 that conclusion is reinforced by the terms of section 341 [Now see CA 2006 s 213]. That sets out the civil consequences, and it seems to me that in the absence of special facts making the loan a breach of fiduciary duty they leave no room for constructive trusteeship. Section 341(2)(a) [CA 2006 s 213(3)(a)] seems to presuppose the absence of constructive trusteeship, because it expressly provides for what would otherwise be one of the consequences of constructive trusteeship, namely an obligation to account for gains made."

[Also see *Currencies Direct Ltd v Ellis* [2002] 2 BCLC 821, CA, which addresses the issue of whether payments received by a director from his company should be characterised as loans or remuneration.]

Shadow directors and 'connected persons': CA 2006 ss 251–253

Many of the provisions discussed above apply to 'shadow directors' (CA 2006 s 251), and affect 'connected persons' (CA 2006 s 252).

'Shadow directors': s 251

A 'shadow director' is defined as 'a person in accordance with whose directions or instructions the directors of a company are accustomed to act'. The court in *Ultraframe (UK) Ltd v Fielding* **[6.30]** interpreted this as meaning that at least a consistent majority of the directors must be accustomed to act in that way. If only a minority of the company's directors are accustomed so to act is not enough to make the person a shadow director (*Lord v Sinai Securities Ltd* [2004] EWHC 1764 (Ch)).

Section 251(2), however, excludes a professional person on whose advice the directors act. The definition of a 'shadow director' appears to preclude persons from being both a shadow director and a *de jure* director (*Re Hydrodam (Corby) Ltd* [1994] 2 BCLC 180), but this is not explicit in the section.

[6.28] Re Hydrodam (Corby) Ltd [1994] 2 BCLC 180

MILLETT J: I would interpose at this point by observing that in my judgment an allegation that a defendant acted as de facto or shadow director, without distinguishing between the two, is embarrassing. It suggests—and counsel's submissions to me support the inference—that the liquidator takes the view that de facto or shadow directors are very similar, that their roles overlap, and that it may not be possible to determine in any given case whether a particular person was a de facto or a shadow director. I do not accept that at all. The terms do not overlap. They are alternatives, and in most and perhaps all cases are mutually exclusive.

A de facto director is a person who assumes to act as a director. He is held out as a director by the company, and claims and purports to be a director, although never actually or validly appointed as such. To establish that a person was a de facto director of a company it is necessary to plead and prove that he undertook functions in relation to the company which could properly be discharged only by a director. It is not sufficient to show that he was concerned in the management of the company's affairs or undertook tasks in relation to its business which can properly be performed by a manager below board level.

A de facto director, I repeat, is one who claims to act and purports to act as a director, although not validly appointed as such. A shadow director, by contrast, does not claim or purport to act as a director. On the contrary, he claims not to be a director. He lurks in the shadows, sheltering behind others who, he claims, are the only directors of the company to the exclusion of himself. He is not held out as a director by the company. To establish that a defendant is a shadow director of a company it is necessary to allege and prove: (1) who are the directors of the company, whether de facto or de jure; (2) that the defendant directed those directors how to act in relation to the company or that he was one of the persons who did so; (3) that those directors acted in accordance with such directions; and (4) that they were accustomed so to act. What is needed is, first, a board of directors claiming and purporting to act as such; and, secondly, a pattern of behaviour in which the board did not exercise any discretion or judgment of its own, but acted in accordance with the directions of others.

➤ Notes

1. In appropriate cases, a holding company (and possibly also its directors), a consultant called into assist in a corporate rescue, and a company's bank could be held to be 'shadow directors': see eg *Re Hydrodam (Corby) Ltd* **[6.28]**. But for this to be the case, the whole board has to act in accordance with the shadow director's instructions or directions.

2. In *Ultraframe (UK) Ltd v Fielding* **[6.30]** it was held that, the fact that the directors of a company are obliged to conduct it in accordance with requirements laid down by a major lender or customer for the protection of that person's interests does not necessarily make that person a shadow director.

3. The leading judicial analysis of the concept of shadow director is to be found in the judgment of Morritt LJ in *Secretary of State for Trade and Industry v Deverell* [2000] 2 BCLC 133, [2001] Ch 300, CA. In particular, Morritt LJ stressed that its interpretation may depend on the statutory context (eg a stricter construction may be more appropriate in a criminal or quasi-criminal provision); that the purpose of the legislation is to identify those with 'real influence' in the corporate affairs of the company, or part of them; that advice (other than professional advice) is capable of coming within the phrase 'directions or instructions'; and that it is not necessary that the board should be reduced to a subservient role or surrender its discretion.

'Persons connected with a director': s 252

A person is 'connected with' a director for the purposes, at least, of Part 10 of the Act and much of the insolvency legislation, in the circumstances laid down by s 252. The people connected with a director are (defined exclusively): members of the director's family, other companies with which the director is 'connected' (ie in which he has, with his 'connected persons', at least a 20% stake), any trustee of a family trust, and any partners.

It is important to bear in mind that statutory rules may affect these people as well as the directors. The statutory provisions do not, of course, affect matters at common law (but then the common law has some healthy rules of its own to cope with problems of this sort: see eg *Gilford Motor Co Ltd v Horne* **[2.17]** and *Selangor United Rubber Estates Ltd v Cradock* **[8.11]**).

Secondary liability (liability of third parties associated with directors' wrongs)

When directors act in breach of their fiduciary duties to the company, third parties may sometimes also be liable to the company for their role in the wrongdoing. The company may be keen to pursue such claims, especially if the defaulting director has absconded or is insolvent.

The favoured third parties to sue are 'deep pockets', such as banks and law firms. Third parties may be:

(i)   Personally liable as *'knowing recipients'* ie people who 'knowingly' receive the company's property as a result of the director's breach of duty. Since liability is personal, not proprietary, it is irrelevant whether these people still have the property or its proceeds in their possession when the claim is brought. The necessary degree of knowledge to make these people liable remains unsettled (see the unconscionability test, below). These people are liable to the extent of the personal benefit received.

(ii)   Personally liable as *'dishonest accessories'* ie people who dishonestly assist or procure the director's breach of duty. These people are liable with the defaulting director, as accessories.[59]

(iii)   Subject to a proprietary claim, having received the company's property without being able to assert the protection of *bona fide* purchaser for value without knowledge of the company's interests; ie people who are donees of gifts of the company's property, or who purchase it without the necessary *bona fides*. These people hold the property on trust for the company.

The cases extracted below illustrate the types of claims.

Required knowledge for secondary liability

In *Baden Delvaux & Lecuit v Société Général pour Favoriser le Développement du Commerce et de l'Industrie en France SA* [1983] BCLC 325 at 407, [1993] 1 WLR 509n at 575, Peter Gibson J identified five different kinds of mental state which might be relevant in assessing the knowledge required for the secondary liability, as follows:

(i)   actual knowledge;

(ii)   wilfully shutting one's eyes to the obvious;

(iii)   wilfully and recklessly failing to make such inquiries as an honest and responsible man would make;

(iv)   knowledge of circumstances which would indicate the facts to an honest and reasonable man;

(v)   knowledge of circumstances which would have put an honest and reasonable man on inquiry.

However, in *Bank of Credit and Commerce International (Overseas) Ltd v Chief Akindele* [2000] BCLC 968, the Court of Appeal ruled that it was time to make a clean break, and that there should be a single test of knowledge for *knowing receipt*, namely: was the recipient's state of knowledge such as to make it unconscionable for him to retain the benefit of the receipt? Although the five-fold classification had often been found 'helpful', the new test would 'better enable the courts to give common-sense decisions in the commercial context in which claims in knowing receipt are now frequently made'.

With *'knowing assistance'*, there has also been radical change. In the *Royal Brunei Airlines* case (also sometimes referred to simply as *Tan*) **[6.29]** it was held that what is relevant is the state of mind of the person who, as an accessory, procures or assists in the breach of trust or other fiduciary obligation. For this purpose it must be shown that the accessory was dishonest.

The test of dishonesty applied by Lord Nicholls in *Tan* was widely assumed to be an objective test: would a reasonable person in the same circumstances have thought the transaction or arrangements dishonest? But in *Twinsectra Ltd v Yardley* [2002] UKHL 12, [2002] 2 AC 164 the majority of the House adopted a double objective/subjective test of dishonesty. Not only

---

[59]   See S Elliott and C Mitchell, 'Remedies for Dishonest Assistance' (2004) 67 MLR 16.

must the transaction be dishonest according to reasonable standards of honesty, but the defendant must also appreciate that fact. Lord Hutton gave the leading speech, purporting to apply the *Royal Brunei Airlines* principles of accessory liability, and Lord Hoffman added that these required 'more than knowledge of the facts which make the conduct wrongful. They require a dishonest state of mind, that is to say, consciousness that one is transgressing ordinary standards of honest behaviour' (at paragraph 20). Lord Hoffman went on to clarify: 'I do not suggest that one cannot be dishonest without a full appreciation of the legal analysis of the transaction. A person may dishonestly assist in the commission of a breach of trust without any idea of what a trust means. The necessary dishonest state of mind may be found to exist simply on the fact that he knew perfectly well that he was helping to pay away money to which the recipient was not entitled' (at paragraph 24). Lord Millett gave a powerful dissent, suggesting the subjective element was inappropriate in civil cases, and wrongly borrowed from the criminal law.

Lord Millett's (and Lord Nicholls') views now seem to have prevailed. In *Barlow Clowes v Eurotrust International* [2005] UKPC 37, [2006] 1 WLR 1476, Lord Hoffmann delivered the opinion of the Privy Council (which included Lord Nicholls), and explicitly adopted the objective test of honesty: would a reasonable person, knowing what the defendant knew, regard the transaction or arrangement as dishonest?

'Dishonest assistance'—meaning of dishonesty.

[6.29] Royal Brunei Airlines Sdn Bhd v Tan Kok Ming [1995] 2 AC 378, [1995] 3 All ER 97 (Privy Council)

Royal Brunei Airlines appointed Borneo Leisure Travel as its agent to sell passenger and cargo transportation, on written terms which provided that moneys collected by BLT for the sale of such services should be held by it on trust for RBA. BLT became insolvent owing over $335,000 to RBA. The question was whether Tan Kok Ming, who was BLT's managing director and principal shareholder, was accountable to RBA for this sum as a constructive trustee. In holding that he was, the Privy Council formulated revised rules of liability.

The opinion of the Judicial Committee was delivered by LORD NICHOLLS OF BIRKENHEAD: The proper role of equity in commercial transactions is a topical question. Increasingly plaintiffs have recourse to equity for an effective remedy when the person in default, typically a company, is insolvent. Plaintiffs seek to obtain relief from others who were involved in the transactions, such as directors of the company, or its bankers, or its legal or other advisers. They seek to fasten fiduciary obligations directly onto the company's officers or agents or advisers, or to have them held personally liable for assisting the company in breaches of trust or fiduciary obligations.

This is such a case. An insolvent travel agent company owed money to an airline. The airline seeks a remedy against the travel agent's principal director and shareholder. Its claim is based on the much-quoted dictum of Lord Selborne LC, sitting in the Court of Appeal in Chancery, in *Barnes v Addy*.[60]

[His Lordship quoted from the judgment in this case and continued:] In the conventional shorthand, the first of these two circumstances in which third parties (non-trustees) may become liable to account in equity is 'knowing receipt', as distinct from the second, where liability arises from 'knowing assistance'. Stated even more shortly, the first limb of Lord Selborne LC's formulation is concerned with the liability of a person as a *recipient* of trust property or its traceable proceeds. The second limb is concerned with what, for want of a better compendious description, can be called the liability of an *accessory* to a trustee's breach of trust. Liability as an accessory is not dependent

---

[60]   (1874) 9 Ch App 244.

upon receipt of trust property. It arises even though no trust property has reached the hands of the accessory. It is a form of secondary liability in the sense that it only arises where there has been a breach of trust. In the present case the plaintiff airline relies on the accessory limb. The particular point in issue arises from the expression 'a dishonest and fraudulent design on the part of the trustees' . . .

In short, the issue on this appeal is whether the breach of trust which is a prerequisite to accessory liability must itself be a dishonest and fraudulent breach of trust by the trustee.

The honest trustee and the dishonest third party

. . . Take the simple example of an honest trustee and a dishonest third party. Take a case where a dishonest solicitor persuades a trustee to apply trust property in a way the trustee honestly believes is permissible but which the solicitor knows full well is a clear breach of trust. The solicitor deliberately conceals this from the trustee. In consequence, the beneficiaries suffer a substantial loss. It cannot be right that in such a case the accessory liability principle would be inapplicable because of the innocence of the trustee. In ordinary parlance, the beneficiaries have been defrauded by the solicitor. If there is to be an accessory liability principle at all, whereby in appropriate circumstances beneficiaries may have direct recourse against a third party, the principle must surely be applicable in such a case, just as much as in a case where both the trustee and the third party have been dishonest. Indeed, if anything, the case for liability of the dishonest third party seems stronger where the trustee is innocent, because in such a case the third party alone was dishonest and that was the cause of the subsequent misapplication of the trust property.

The position would be the same if, instead of *procuring* the breach, the third party dishonestly *assisted* in the breach. Change the facts slightly. A trustee is proposing to make a payment out of the trust fund to a particular person. He honestly believes he is authorised to do so by the terms of the trust deed. He asks a solicitor to carry through the transaction. The solicitor well knows that the proposed payment would be a plain breach of trust. He also well knows that the trustee mistakenly believes otherwise. Dishonestly he leaves the trustee under his misapprehension and prepares the necessary documentation. Again, if the accessory principle is not to be artificially constricted, it ought to be applicable in such a case.

These examples suggest that what matters is the state of mind of the third party sought to be made liable, not the state of mind of the trustee. The trustee will be liable in any event for the breach of the trust, even if he acted innocently, unless excused by an exemption clause in the trust instrument or relieved by the court. But *his* state of mind is essentially irrelevant to the question whether the *third party* should be made liable to the beneficiaries for the breach of trust. If the liability of the third party is fault-based, what matters is the nature of his fault, not that of the trustee. In this regard dishonesty on the part of the third party would seem to be a sufficient basis for his liability, irrespective of the state of mind of the trustee who is in breach of trust. It is difficult to see why, if the third party dishonestly assisted in a breach, there should be a further prerequisite to his liability, namely that the trustee also must have been acting dishonestly. The alternative view would mean that the dishonest third party is liable if the trustee is dishonest, but if the trustee did not act dishonestly that of itself would excuse a dishonest third party from liability. That would make no sense.

[His Lordship discussed the authorities further, and continued:]

Drawing the threads together, their Lordships' overall conclusion is that dishonesty is a necessary ingredient of accessory liability. It is also a sufficient ingredient. A liability in equity to make good resulting loss attaches to a person who dishonestly procures or assists in a breach of trust or fiduciary obligation. It is not necessary that, in addition, the trustee or fiduciary was acting dishonestly, although this will usually be so where the third party who is assisting him is acting dishonestly.

[It was held, accordingly that, even on the assumption that dishonesty could not be imputed to BLT, Tan Kok Ming's own dishonesty rendered him liable. But it was also held that BLT's breach of trust was itself dishonest.]

Remedies associated with secondary liability.

[6.30] Ultraframe (UK) Ltd v Fielding [2005] EWHC 1638 (Chancery Division)

[The facts, so far as necessary, appear from the judgment.]

LEWISON J:

1 This is (for the moment) the culmination of a long war of attrition . . . The trial alone, on liability only, occupied 95 days of court time. Both Ultraframe and Burnden are competitors in the market for the manufacture and supply of conservatories, and conservatory roofs in particular . . . . The war has been bitterly fought. There have been accusations and counter-accusations of forgery, theft, false accounting, blackmail and arson, not to mention the widespread allegations that many of the principal witnesses are lying. At the heart of the litigation is a dispute about the ownership of businesses in the field of conservatory roof design and manufacture originally developed by Mr Howard Davies. . . .

[Lewison J's judgment is extremely long and thorough: at para [1476]ff he describes the two types of secondary liability and how they arise; at paras [1511]-[1576] he surveys the law on remedies for fiduciary breaches; and at various places, extracted below, he addresses the issue of remedies against third parties.]. . . .

1483 . . .

Personal or proprietary liability?

1484 It is important to keep distinct the two forms of secondary liability; because they have different consequences in terms of remedy.

Knowing receipt

1485 In *Twinsectra* Lord Millett said:

> "Liability for "knowing receipt" is receipt-based. It does not depend on fault. The cause of action is restitutionary and is available only where the defendant received or applied the money in breach of trust for his own use and benefit . . ."

1486 Although a claim in knowing receipt is receipt-based, it is not dependent on the recipient having retained the trust property. If he has retained it, or if he has retained property which is an identifiable substitute for the original trust property, then the claimant is entitled simply to assert his proprietary rights in that property. He does this by invoking the principles of following and tracing. If the original recipient has passed on the property or its substitute to another person then, subject to any defence which that other may be entitled to raise, the principles of following or tracing continue to apply to the property or its substitute in the hands of that other. If the recipient has not retained the trust property, and its proceeds are no longer identifiable, then the claimant has a personal remedy against the recipient.

What counts as trust property for the purposes of knowing receipt?

. . . 1488 Plainly, property which is vested in the company, both legally and beneficially, before any disposition in breach of fiduciary duty, will count as trust property. This was the case in *JJ Harrison (Properties) Ltd v Harrison* **[6.24]** where a director who had bought land belonging to the company, without disclosing its development potential, was held to have acquired the property as constructive trustee.

1489 But property will also count as the company's property if it is property which the fiduciary has acquired for his own benefit but which, consistently with his fiduciary duties, he ought to have acquired on behalf of the company. . . . [He cited *A-G of Hong Kong v Reid* [1994] 1 AC 324 and *Keech v Sandford* (1726) Sel Cas Ch 61, and continued:]

Dishonest assistance

1495 In *Tan* Lord Nicholls said (p 387):

"Within defined limits, proprietary rights, whether legal or equitable, endure against third parties who were unaware of their existence. But accessory liability is concerned with the liability of a person who has not received any property. His liability is not property-based. His only
sin is that he interfered with the due performance by the trustee of the fiduciary obligations
undertaken by the trustee. These are personal obligations. They are, in this respect, analogous
to the personal obligations undertaken by the parties to a contract."

1496 In similar vein Lord Millett said in *Twinsectra* (p 194, dissenting, although not on this
point):

"The accessory's liability for having assisted in a breach of trust is quite different. It is fault-
based, not receipt-based. The defendant is not charged with having received trust moneys for
his own benefit, but with having acted as an accessory to a breach of trust. The action is not
restitutionary; the claimant seeks compensation for wrongdoing. The cause of action is concerned with attributing liability for misdirected funds. Liability is not restricted to the person
whose breach of trust or fiduciary duty caused their original diversion. His liability is strict. Nor
is it limited to those who assist him in the original breach. It extends to everyone who consciously assists in the continuing diversion of the money. Most of the cases have been concerned, not with assisting in the original breach, but in covering it up afterwards by helping to
launder the money." . . .

What counts as dishonest assistance?

1509 It is clear that the passive receipt of trust property does not count as assistance: *Brown v
Bennett* [1999] BCLC 525 , 533. As Morritt LJ said:

" . . . if there is no causative effect and therefore no assistance given by the person . . . on
whom it is sought to establish the liability as constructive trustee, for my part I cannot see that
the requirements of conscience require any remedy at all."

1510 Likewise in *Brink's Ltd v Abu-Saleh* Rimer J held that Mrs Elcombe's presence in the car
accompanying her husband abroad on money laundering trips did not amount to assistance "of a
nature sufficient to make her an accessory". She was in the car merely in her capacity as
Mr Elcombe's wife . . . .

Remedies against the knowing recipient

1577 In addition to the proprietary remedy (if it is still available) the claimant has a personal remedy
for an account against the knowing recipient. Obviously, the personal remedy depends on establishing knowing receipt, but it does not depend on retention. Indeed it is needed precisely where the
recipient has not retained the property. In addition, the personal remedy requires the knowing recipient to account for any benefit he has received or acquired as a result of the knowing receipt.
However, a knowing recipient is not, in my judgment, liable to account for a benefit received by
someone else. [He then went on to explain that the remedy must be fashioned to ensure that there
is no double recovery, and continued:]

Fashioning the account

1579 The ordering of an account is an equitable remedy. It is not discretionary in the true sense. It
is granted or withheld on the basis of equitable principles. But one of those principles is that of pro-
portionality. In *Satnam Investments Ltd v Dunlop Heywood* [1999] 3 All ER 652 property agents had
acquired confidential information about a potential development site in the course of acting for a
client. In breach of duty they disclosed that information to a rival (Morbaine). The question arose

whether Morbaine (which had since purchased the site) could be made liable to account for profits. Nourse LJ said:

"What the judge found was that some at least of the information was confidential at the time that it was disclosed, in that its disclosure to a rival developer would or might be detrimental to Satnam. However, even assuming that but for the disclosure Morbaine would not have acquired the Brewery Street site, it does not follow that it would be a proportionate response to hold it liable for an account of profits. All the circumstances must be considered. The information, though confidential, was not of the same degree of confidentiality as the information in the *Spycatcher* case and in *Schering Chemicals Ltd v Falkman Ltd* . All of it was either already available to Morbaine or would have been available to it on reasonable inquiry once, as was inevitable, the news of Satnam's receivership became known. There being no other basis of recovery available, it would in our view be inequitable and contrary to commercial good sense to allow Satnam to recover simply on the basis that there was a degree of confidentiality in the information at the time that it was disclosed to Morbaine."

[He then considered various cases, including *Warman v Dwyer* (above, p 340), and *CMS Dolphin v Simonet* **[6.19]**, and continued:]

1588 . . . The governing principles are, in my judgment, these:

i)   The fundamental rule is that a fiduciary must not make an unauthorised profit out of his fiduciary position;

ii)   The fashioning of an account should not be allowed to operate as the unjust enrichment of the claimant;

iii)   The profits for which an account is ordered must bear a reasonable relationship to the breach of duty proved;

iv)   It is important to establish exactly what has been acquired;

v)   Subject to that, the fashioning of the account depends on the facts. In some cases it will be appropriate to order an account limited in time; or limited to profits derived from particular assets or particular customers; or to order an account of all the profits of a business subject to all just allowances for the fiduciary's skill, labour and assumption of business risk. In some cases it may be appropriate to order the making of a payment representing the capital value of the advantage in question, either in place of or in addition to an account of profits.

Remedies against a dishonest assistant

1600 I can see that it makes sense for a dishonest assistant to be jointly and severally liable for any *loss* which the beneficiary suffers as a result of a breach of trust. I can see also that it makes sense for a dishonest assistant to be liable to disgorge any profit which he *himself* has made as a result of assisting in the breach. However, I cannot take the next step to the conclusion that a dishonest assistant is also liable to pay to the beneficiary an amount equal to a profit which he did not make and which has produced no corresponding loss to the beneficiary. . . . .

[Applying these various principles to the complicated facts, he then settled detailed orders between the parties, with some matters reserved for later.]

Finally, in the context of making third parties liable for breaches of directors' duties, it should be noted that a substantial shareholder in a company who appoints a nominee director to its board owes no duty to anybody for the way in which the nominee performs his duties as a director. It makes no difference that the director is an employee of the shareholder who nominates him.

[6.31] Kuwait Asia Bank EC v National Mutual Life Nominees Ltd [1991] 1 AC 187, [1990] 3 All ER 404 (Privy Council)

The Kuwait Asia bank owned 40% of the shares in AICS, a New Zealand company which had taken money on deposit from the public. The plaintiff company, NMLN, had acted as trustee for the depositors pursuant to requirements of the New Zealand securities legislation. House and August, employees of the bank, were appointed by the bank to be two of the five directors of AICS; the remaining three were nominees of another large shareholder, Kumutoto. When AICS went into liquidation, NMLN settled claims brought by the depositors for breach of its duties as their trustee, and in these proceedings NMLN sought contribution from, *inter alia* (i) House and August and (ii) the bank, contending that it (NMLN) had relied on certificates of AICS's financial position which were inaccurate and for which the directors bore collective responsibility. The Judicial Committee held that while a *prima facie* case existed against House and August, no claim lay against the bank. The bank was not vicariously liable for any breach of duty which might be proved against the two directors whom it had nominated, and this was so even though they were also its employees; and it did not *qua* shareholder owe duties to anybody.

The opinion of the Judicial Committee was delivered by LORD LOWRY: . . . Their Lordships now proceed to consider the causes of action pleaded by the plaintiff against the bank. Two general principles may first be stated. (1) A director does not by reason only of his position as director owe any duty to creditors or to trustees for creditors of the company. (2) A shareholder does not by reason only of his position as shareholder owe any duty to anybody . . .

But although directors are not liable *as such* to creditors of the company, a director may by agreement or representation assume a special duty to a creditor of the company. A director may accept or assume a duty of care in supplying information to a creditor analogous to the duty described by the House of Lords in *Hedley Byrne & Co Ltd v Heller & Partners Ltd* [[1964] AC 465, HL].

[His Lordship held that there was an arguable case against House and August personally on this ground, and continued:]

As against the bank, the statement of claim pleaded that the bank was liable to contribute to the loss suffered by the plaintiff in settling the claims of the depositors against the plaintiff for all or any of the following reasons: (1) House and August were appointed to the board of directors of AICS by the bank, were employed by the bank and carried out their duties as directors in the course of their employment by the bank. (2) House and August were, as directors of AICS, the agents of the bank which was the principal. (3) As a substantial shareholder . . . the bank owed a duty of care to the plaintiff and to the depositors to ensure that the business of AICS was not conducted negligently or recklessly or in such a manner as to materially disadvantage the interests of those unsecured depositors. (4) House and August were persons occupying a position of directors of AICS who were accustomed to act in accordance with the bank's directions, and therefore the bank was a director of AICS within the meaning of section 2 of the Companies Act 1955.

As to (1) the power of appointing a director of a company may be exercised by a shareholder or a person who is not a shareholder by virtue of the articles of association of the company, or by virtue of the control of the majority of the voting shares of the company, or by virtue of the agreement or acquiescence of other shareholders. In the present case, the bank and Kumutoto, who together controlled AICS, decided that the bank should nominate two directors. In the absence of fraud or bad faith (which are not alleged here), a shareholder or other person who controls the appointment of a director owes no duty to creditors of the company to take reasonable care to see that directors so appointed discharge their duties as directors with due diligence and competence . . .

The liability of a shareholder would be unlimited if he were accountable to a creditor for the exercise of his power to appoint a director and for the conduct of the director so appointed. It is in the interests of a shareholder to see that directors are wise and that the actions of the company are not foolish; but this concern of the shareholder stems from self-interest, and not from duty . . . It does not make any difference if the directors appointed by a shareholder are employed by the shareholder and are allowed to carry out their duties as directors while in the shareholder's employment. House and August owed three separate duties. They owed in the first place to AICS the duty to perform their duties as directors without gross negligence; 9 the liability of a director to his company is set forth in the judgment of Romer J in *Re City Equitable Fire Insurance Co Ltd* **[6.13]**. They owed a duty to the plaintiff to use reasonable care to see that the certificates complied with the requirements of the trust deed. Finally, they owed a duty to their employer, the bank, to exercise reasonable diligence and skill in the performance of their duties as directors of AICS.

If House and August did not exercise reasonable care to see that the quarterly certificates were accurate, they committed a breach of the duty they owed to the plaintiff and may have committed a breach of the duty they owed to the plaintiff and may have committed a breach of the duty they owed to the bank to exercise reasonable diligence and skill. But these duties were separate and distinct and different in scope and nature. The bank was not responsible for a breach of the duties owed by House and August to AICS or to the plaintiff any more than AICS or the plaintiff were responsible for a breach of duty by House and August. If House and August committed a breach of the duty which was imposed on them and other directors of AICS and was owed to the plaintiff under and by virtue of the trust deed they did so as individuals and as directors of AICS and not as employees of the bank; House and August were not parties to the trust deed, nor was the bank. House and August were allowed by the bank to perform their duties to AICS in the bank's time and at the bank's expense. It was in the interest of the bank that House and August should discharge with diligence and skill the duties which they owed to AICS, but these facts do not render the bank liable for breach by House and August of the duty imposed on them by the trust deed. In the performance of their duties as directors and in the performance of their duties imposed by the trust deed, House and August were bound to ignore the interests and wishes of their employer, the bank. They could not plead any instruction from the bank as an excuse for breach of their duties to AICS and the plaintiff. Of course, if the bank exploited its position as employers of House and August to obtain an improper advantage for the bank or to cause harm to the plaintiff then the bank would be liable for its own misconduct. But there is no suggestion that the bank behaved with impropriety . . .

(2) Then it is said that House and August were the agents of the bank. But, as directors of AICS, they were the agents of AICS and not of the bank. As directors of AICS, House and August were agents of AICS for the purposes of the trust deed and, by the express terms of the trust deed, responsibility for the accuracy of the quarterly certificates was assumed by the directors of AICS. House and August accepted responsibility for the quarterly certificates as directors of AICS and not as agents or employees of the bank.

(3) Next it was said that the bank owed a personal duty of care to the plaintiff. For the protection of the depositors the plaintiff stipulated for and obtained by the trust deed a duty of care in the preparation of the quarterly certificates by the directors of AICS. The plaintiff may or may not have known that two of the directors of AICS were employed by the bank and that the bank would allow those two directors to carry out their duties as directors while in the employment of the bank. Any of these circumstances, even if known, could change at any time. The plaintiff may or may not have known that the bank was beneficially interested in 40 per cent of the shares of AICS. That circumstance also could change at any time. The plaintiff did not rely on any of these circumstances . . . An

employer who is also a shareholder who nominates a director owes no duty to the company unless the employer interferes with the affairs of the company. A duty does not arise because the employee may be dismissed from his employment by the employer or from his directorship by the shareholder or because the employer does not provide sufficient time or facilities to enable the director to carry out his duties. It will be in the interests of the employer to see that the director discharges his duty to the company but this again stems from self-interest and not from duty on the part of the employer.

[His Lordship ruled, finally, that the bank was not in the position of a 'shadow director'. The proceedings against the bank were accordingly struck out as disclosing no valid cause of action.]

7

THE RAISING OF CAPITAL

Company 'capital' and its importance

'Capital' is a word that can have many meanings. In company law, however, *legal capital* (or simply '*capital*') may be used in a restricted technical sense. Broadly speaking, it is cash (or, less often, the value of the assets) received by the company from investors who subscribe for the company's shares.[1] The company's capital, in this technical sense, is measured in terms of 'value received' into the company, rather than the current value of the assets themselves, since that will change with the business activities of the company. If the company receives cash in exchange for its shares, for example, the company will use that cash to promote and expand the company's business. If the business is successful, the value of the business will increase; if not, it will decrease.

The value of the company's legal capital is likely to be far less than the total value of the company's assets. Even before the company begins to trade, and certainly once it is up and running, the company is likely to borrow money from banks and from other lending sources. It is also likely to rely on other sources of credit, such as debt funding from suppliers who supply the company with goods and services on deferred payment terms or 'on credit'. None of this large and small scale '*debt funding*' is part of the company's legal capital. Important distinctions exist between the treatment of debt, and the *creditors* who provide those funds,[2] and the treatment of '*equity funding*' (as fundraising by share issues is known) and the *shareholders* who provide those funds. Both sources of funds will be deployed in the company's business, however, and, if the business is successful, will generate additional company assets by way of retained business profits. These profits do not form part of the company's legal capital either. Of course, if the business is unsuccessful and losses are incurred, the total value of the company's assets, and hence its *capital*, may fall below the company's legal capital.

Why is such a sharp distinction drawn between legal capital (or contributions from shareholders) and other assets held by the company? The distinction reflects the special protection provided to creditors by the company's legal capital. This is seen most dramatically when the company is in financial difficulty. Take a simple example. Suppose a company is set up with £100,000 in 'equity funding' contributed by shareholders, and £200,000 in 'debt funding' provided over time by the bank and other creditors. If the business fails, and the company is put into insolvency, then whatever remains of the company's assets will be used to repay the company's creditors, in full if possible, before any of the shareholders are repaid any part of their contribution to funding the company. In other words, the two types of financiers of the company's operation do not share the losses equally. In the example given, suppose the company's remaining assets amount to £150,000. The creditors clearly cannot be repaid in

---

[1] This is a simplification: as is explained below (see p 373), the total sum received by the company in exchange for the share may include both a 'capital' sum and a 'premium' sum. Both of these sums are subject to substantially similar restrictions on the possible uses the company may make of them, but the 'company's capital', in the strictest sense, includes only the former sums.

[2] See Chapters 11 and 14 below.

full, but they will share *all* of this sum (obtaining 75 pence in the pound), and the shareholders will receive nothing. Of course, in practice the situation is usually more complicated. There are invariably different types of creditors (some with security provided by mortgages and charges, others unsecured, and still others given special privileges and priorities by statute), and there may be different classes of shareholders (perhaps with different rights when the company goes into insolvency). And some part of the company's assets will need to be spent simply in the mechanics of sale and distribution to those entitled (the expenses of liquidation and receivership). All of this detail is covered later.[3]

The outlook for the shareholder is not all gloomy, of course. If the company is successful, then the shareholders, not the creditors, will share in the company's profits. The shareholders will receive dividends (distributions based on company profits),[4] and the value of their shares is likely to increase by the value of retained profits and enhanced expectations about future profits (so that if they sell their investment to a third party, they will reap a capital gain). The creditors, on the other hand, are restricted to the scale of return defined by their contract with the company (eg a loan with specified rate of interest, or a sale of goods with a built in profit margin).

Finally, by way of concluding introductory comment, note that contributions to a company's capital are made only by shareholders purchasing shares *from the company*. When these shareholders then sell their shares to third parties (who will become the new shareholders), they may sell at a price far greater, or far less, than the price initially paid to the company for the share. But this sale price is received *by the shareholders*, and, although it will reflect their personal profit or loss on the investment, it will not alter the company's legal capital.

Many shareholders are motivated by the possibility of realising an increase in total shareholder value comprising capital gain on their share investment and dividends (ie income from the investment), rather than by the attraction of being an 'owner' of a small business (ie by the benefits of management or voting control). Markets, such as the London Stock Exchange, were originally set up and regulated precisely to provide for this possibility. Their importance in attracting investors is well recognised by the increasing efforts put into appropriate regulation.[5]

Attracting and protecting shareholders and creditors

The interplay between the rights of shareholders and the rights of creditors is critical to the success of companies as business entities. A company is a separate legal person. It follows that the claims of the company's creditors must be met from the company's assets.[6] The shareholders' capital contributions mitigate the risks to which creditors are exposed. The returns for shareholders are proportionately greater if the company is a success, and proportionately worse if the company is a failure. That is why the cost of equity funding (in terms of *expected* total shareholder return) is generally higher than for debt funding (an *expected* interest entitlement). In addition, if shareholders are to be attracted to this form of investment, then there must be appropriate protections of their rights and appropriate limitations on their obligations. And, unless shareholders are attracted, creditors are unlikely to be forthcoming.

[3] See Chapter 14.
[4] See Chapter 8.
[5] See Chapter 12.
[6] It is not the same with partnerships, where the partners are personally liable for the debts of the partnership (with limitations on that liability only if the partnership is a Limited Liability Partnership): see above, pp 22 ff. Of course, if the company's directors have caused an unwarranted diminution in the company's assets, then the *company*, not the creditors, can sue the directors, and the recoveries will augment the company's assets, and be available for the benefit of the company's creditors (and its shareholders, if the company is solvent): see below, pp 498 ff. If the company is being wound up, different rules determine who may sue, and who may be sued: see below, pp 628 ff.

For shareholders, these protections include:

(i) limitations on the issue of new shares, so that shareholders' interests in the company are not unacceptably diluted (*pre-emption rights* and *limitations on the directors' powers of allotment*) (see below, p 377);

(ii) protection against misleading inducements to purchase shares (see below, pp 378 ff);

(iii) protection of the financial rights attached to shares (including protection of 'class rights') (see Chapter 9);

(iv) protection of shareholders' established and agreed relationships with the company (via shareholder control over changes to the company's constitution (see Chapter 2), or by personal claims by shareholders against the company or its managers, as permitted by common law (under CA 2006 s 33) or by statute (eg CA 2006 s 994) (see Chapter 10);

(v) protection of shareholders' influence over the potential success of the company (via control over the management, and, sometimes, control over the pursuit of claims on behalf of the company) (see Chapters 4, 5 and 10).

Only the first two of these are directly associated with the process of raising capital for the company, and are dealt with in this chapter.

What of the protection provided for company lenders and other creditors? Normal rules of contract law and security law (see Chapters 11 and 14) provide much assistance. Here, however, we are concerned with the special protections associated with the acquisition and treatment of company capital. These protective rules include:

(i) rules requiring the company to have a certain minimum level of capital before it begins trading ('*minimum capital requirements*') (see below, p 376);

(ii) rules designed to ensure that the amount of legal capital shown in the company records is in fact received in full by the company (rules relating to *payment for shares*) (see below, p 382);

(iii) rules designed to ensure the maintenance of stated levels of legal capital by restricting the freedom of companies to return assets to its shareholders ('*capital maintenance rules*' and '*dividend distribution rules*') (see Chapter 8).

Terminology associated with legal capital

Various terms are commonly used, and need to be understood. These include 'allotment' and 'issue' of shares, and 'authorised' or 'nominal' capital (the terms are interchangeable, and are of less concern now that CA 2006 has abolished the requirement to state this value, although of course it appears in older cases), 'nominal value' or 'par value' (again used interchangeably), 'issued capital', and 'share premiums'.

Formally a share is not *issued* to a shareholder until the investor's name is registered in the company's register of members (CA 2006 s 113). This is when the shareholder acquires the legal title to the share. Until this has been done the person entitled to the shares is neither a member nor their legal owner. Of course, there is an earlier stage, where the company enters into a binding contract with the investor to sell a share in return for payment of the price, and the investor acquires an unconditional right to be included in the company's register of members in respect of the shares: a share is then said to be *allotted* to the investor (CA 2006 s 558).

All companies with shares used to be incorporated with a '*nominal*' or '*authorised*' capital, the total amount of which had to be stated in the memorandum (ie the document which, with the articles, provided the company's constitution). This figure had very little practical significance. It merely fixed a ceiling upon the amount of capital the company could raise by the issue of shares without further formalities. For example, a company might be incorporated with an authorised capital of £1million, indicating that it was entitled to sell £1million worth of shares to shareholders; in fact it might only issue £500,000 worth of shares, or even only £100,000 worth of shares.[7] Indeed, companies typically plucked large figures out of the air for authorised capital, since the only significance was to set this notional cap on issues, a cap which could in any event be increased by ordinary resolution of the shareholders.

The specified authorised capital was required to be divided into shares of a fixed unit value. In other words, a monetary value had (and still has: CA 2006 s 542[8]) to be attached to the shares. As a consequence, it is common to describe a company's capital as divided into a certain number of '£1' shares, or '10p' shares. We would then say that the '*nominal value*' or '*par value*' of the shares was £1 or 10p respectively.

When the company *allots* or, later on, *issues* some of these shares, it is possible to speak of 'allotted' or 'issued' capital (CA 2006 s 546). The '*issued capital*' (or, in the case of the first shareholders, the '*subscribed capital*') is the sum equivalent to the nominal value or par value of all the shares that have been issued, and the '*paid-up capital*' is so much of the issued capital as is represented by money which the shareholders have in fact paid: there may be an unpaid balance on each share which is not due for payment until a call is made (although this is rarely the case now; shares are usually issued fully-paid, so the issued capital and paid-up capital are identical). CA 2006 s 547 also defines 'called-up share capital', which is the aggregate of paid up capital plus capital that has been called-up (whether or not paid) plus any defined commitments to pay share capital at a future date, but which has not yet been called-up or paid.

So, in *Salomon*'s case **[2.01]**, the authorised or nominal capital was £40,000 comprising 40,000 shares of £1 each; the subscribed capital was £7, the total issued capital was £20,007, which was fully paid up, and the debt capital (a loan secured by the debenture) was a further £10,000.

Note that the 'issued capital' is *not* simply the consideration received by the company for the sale of its shares. The calculation is more convoluted. The advantage of this, if there is one, is that it enables a creditor to calculate that if a company has issued 100,000 shares with a nominal value of £1, for example, then the company's issued capital is £100,000, and this sum is subject to all the capital maintenance and other creditor protection rules supplied by company law. In other words, the creditor has an easy basis on which to assess the company's legal capital.

In fact, this easy calculation underestimates the extent to which a creditor is protected. It is perhaps obvious, given the way the nominal value is determined, that it bears no necessary relationship to the price at which the shares may be sold. When the company issues shares, it may well sell its '£1' shares at a *premium* of £0.50 to the nominal value, ie for £1.50, if that is what the market will bear.[9] The 'legal capital' rules insist that the company cannot sell its shares for *less* than the nominal value (see below, p 382). But if it sells its shares for *more* than the nominal value, as in the above case, then the £1 (representing the nominal value) received by the company must be allocated to the company's '*capital account*', and the £0.50 'premium' to the '*share premium account*'. The creditor is then super-protected, because the

---

[7] And indeed, as indicated below, a sale of '£100,000 worth of shares' might well net the company more than £100,000.

[8] And note the permission in s 542(3), subject to s 765, to have share capital denominated in different currencies.

[9] And (although this has nothing to do with legal capital) when existing shareholders sell their shares to willing purchasers, whether privately or on a recognised market, they will again sell at whatever price the market will bear. This may be more or less than the nominal value of the shares, depending upon the success of the company and the estimated value of an interest in it.

restrictions on the use of both accounts are reasonably similar, although not identical (see below, p 385); in other words, the company does not receive a 'premium' which it is free to use at will, and the creditor receives buffering protection beyond the company's strict legal capital.[10]

CA 2006 specifies the acceptable uses of the share premium account: in line with the recommendations of the CLR, the section imposes restrictions on the application of the share premium account that go beyond the CA 1985 rules. Companies are no longer able to use the account to write off preliminary expenses (that is, expenses incurred in connection with the company's formation). Apart from two 'exceptions', and two forms of 'relief', the account can only be used as if it was a share capital account. The two exceptions are that the account may be used to write off any expenses incurred, or commission paid, in connection with the particular issue of shares, and also to pay up new shares to be allotted to existing members as fully paid bonus shares (CA 2006 s 610). The two forms of relief are related to mergers and reconstructions, and ensure that undistributed profits are not reallocated to share premium accounts, thus making them undistributable (CA 2006 ss 611 and 612).

As noted earlier, a company no longer needs to register its authorised capital when it is incorporated. Instead, the company must provide the registrar with a statement of capital and initial shareholdings. This statement must contain the following information:

(i) the total number of shares of the company to be taken on formation by the subscribers to the memorandum;

(ii) the aggregate nominal value of those shares;

(iii) for each class of shares: prescribed particulars of the rights attached to those shares, the total number of shares of that class and the aggregate nominal value of shares of that class; and

(iv) the amount to be paid up and the amount (if any) to be unpaid on each share (whether on account of the nominal value of the shares or by way of premium).

One historical point is worth making. It was very common practice in the early days for companies to issue shares on terms that only a small part of the capital—perhaps only 5% or 10% of the nominal value—was to be paid up, and so a very large sum of uncalled capital was left in reserve as a kind of 'guarantee fund' for creditors. Such shares were called *partly-paid shares*; and the balance of unpaid capital could generally be *called up* by the company (or its liquidators) upon demand. This could have horrendous consequences for investors in the event of a liquidation (or, worse still, a spate of liquidations, as might occur in a recession) when the shareholder was obliged to pay up the balance of unpaid capital when there was no possibility of recovering any value via increased share value or future dividend. It also coloured much of the thinking in company law matters generally. Nowadays, the whole of the issue price of shares is normally payable on or soon after allotment, and so partly-paid shares are not at all common. In some jurisdictions, they have been banned altogether, primarily for the sake of simplifying the law, but perhaps also out of a desire that investors should not be over-committed with potential liabilities.

➤ Questions

1. When shares in British Telecom plc were sold to the public in 1984, the company was permitted to issue a simplified prospectus, for the benefit of the 'wider' public. This prospectus omitted to state that the nominal value of the shares was 25p. Why might it have been thought appropriate to withhold this information?

---

[10] Note that the shareholder does not receive similar benefits: different shareholders may have purchased the same class of shares for different prices (ie paying different premia for shares of the same par value); if the company goes into solvent liquidation (ie there are assets to be returned to shareholders), then all shareholders will receive a return of their capital (ie the nominal capital associated with the share) and share equally in the division of any surplus profits.

2. The issue price of a 25p British Telecom share was £1.30. Were the shares expensive at that price?

3. If a dividend of 10p is paid on a share of nominal value 25p, does this mean that the investor has done well?

4. What protection is provided to creditors by having shares with a nominal value, and capital and share premium accounts, that could not be equally well provided by eliminating the concept of nominal value and simply having a capital account for all the consideration received by a company for issue of its shares? (See CLR, *Completing the Structure* URN 00/1335, November 2000, para 7.3; also see below, p 382, on the inability of companies to issue shares at a discount.)

5. Are the exceptions and reliefs that apply in relation to use of the share premium account in accord with a philosophy that is actually designed to treat in the same way all the consideration received by a company for issue of its shares?

The legal nature of shares

Before investigating the detailed rules relating to legal capital, it is worth giving some attention to the legal nature of a share: what does a shareholder receive in return for providing the company with legal capital?

A share in a partnership reflects the partner's proprietary interest in the partnership assets: the assets are jointly owned by the partners. In the case of a company, it is not the shareholders but the company that owns the corporate assets, and the concept of a share serves somewhat different functions. In the first place, it is a fraction of the capital, denoting the holder's proportionate *financial stake* in the company and defining his or her liability to contribute to its equity funding. Second, it is a measure of the holder's interest in the company as *an association of members or shareholders* and the basis of his or her right to become a member and to enjoy the rights of voting, etc, so conferred. And, third, it is a *species of property*, in its own right, a rather complex form of chose in action, which the holder can buy, sell, charge, etc, and in which there can be both legal and beneficial interests.[11] None of this is quite revealed in the definition in CA 2006 s 540.

The terms '*shareholder*' and '*member*' are commonly regarded as interchangeable, but this is not always the case. A company limited by guarantee has members, but it cannot have shareholders, for it has no shares. On the other hand, the holders of bearer shares ('share warrants', CA 2006 s 779—in practice these are rare) do not become members, since entry in the register of members is necessary for this purpose (s 112). The most common form of company is a company limited by shares, however, and in these companies the members are the shareholders.

Finally, a company can issue classes shares with different rights attaching to each class (ie shares with different '*class rights*', see chapter 9). For example, shares may have different voting rights (recall the weighted voting rights in *Bushell v Faith* [5.05]), different rights to dividends, or different rights to capital on a return of capital or on winding up (all these rights are explained in chapters 8 and 9). '*Preference shares*' have a preferred right (as defined in the articles or in the share issue itself) to a specified dividend (if any dividend is declared), and

---

[11] Where conflict of laws rules must be applied to decide which national law is appropriate to determine questions of title, etc in relation to the shares, the accepted rule is that where ownership of the shares is recorded in a register, the appropriate law is that of the place where the register is kept, which is normally (but not always) the country of incorporation; but where the shares are in bearer form the certificates or warrants are regarded as negotiable instruments and the relevant law is that of the place where the documents happen to be (*Re Harvard Securities Ltd* [1997] 2 BCLC 369).

perhaps to a return of capital while the company is operating or on winding up. *'Ordinary shares'* are defined in CA 2006 s 560 as shares *other than* shares that carry a right to participate only up to a specified amount in a distribution of dividends or capital (ie other than preference shares). And *'equity securities'*, also defined in CA 2006 s 560, are ordinary shares *and* rights to subscribe for, or convert securities into, ordinary shares. These definitions are important later, because certain rights, such as pre-emption rights, are given only to equity securities (see below, p 377).

[7.01] Borland's Trustee v Steel Bros & Co Ltd [1901] 1 Ch 279 (Chancery Division)

The company's articles provided that the shares of a member should in certain events, including bankruptcy, be transferable compulsorily to designated persons at a fair price not exceeding the par value.[12] On the bankruptcy of Borland, who held 73 £100 shares, the company gave notice to his trustee in bankruptcy requiring him to transfer the shares in accordance with the articles. The trustee objected that this provision in the articles was void, either on the ground that it was repugnant to absolute ownership, or as tending to perpetuity. The court rejected both contentions.

> FARWELL J: It is said, first of all, that such provisions are repugnant to absolute ownership. It is said, further, that they tend to perpetuity. They are likened to the case of a settlor or testator who settles or gives a sum of money subject to executory limitations which are to arise in the future, interpreting the articles as if they provided that if at any time hereafter, during centuries to come, the company should desire the shares of a particular person . . . he must sell them. To my mind that is applying to the company law a principle which is wholly inapplicable thereto. It is the first time that any such suggestion has been made, and it rests, I think, on a misconception of what a share in a company really is. A share, according to the plaintiff's argument, is a sum of money which is dealt with in a particular manner by what are called for the purpose of argument executory limitations. To my mind it is nothing of the sort. A share is the interest of a shareholder in the company measured by a sum of money, for the purpose of liability in the first place, and of interest in the second, but also consisting of a series of mutual covenants entered into by all the shareholders inter se in accordance with s 16 of the Companies Act 1862 [CA 2006, s 33]. The contract contained in the articles of association is one of the original incidents of the share. A share is not a sum of money settled in the way suggested, but is an interest measured by a sum of money and made up of various rights contained in the contract, including the right to a sum of money of a more or less amount . . . [His Lordship then held that the rule against perpetuities had no application to personal contracts such as this, and ruled that the article was valid and enforceable.]

Minimum capital requirements for company formation

A *public company* must have a nominal value of allotted share capital which is not less than the statutory 'authorised minimum' amount fixed by CA 2006 s 761. At present, the prescribed authorised minimum is £50,000, or the prescribed euro equivalent (s 763), denominated in sterling or euros, but not both (s 765). At least a quarter of this must be paid up (s 586).

The protection that this minimum delivers to creditors is dubious: the sum is relatively trivial, and is measured at the time the company commences trading, paying little account to what business risks or mishaps may happen as business continues. CA 2006 s 656 requires

---

[12] See above, p 372, for the meaning of 'par value'.

directors of public companies to call a general meeting to consider what to do if the company's assets fall to half or less than its called up share capital. The equivalent CA 1985 predecessor to this seemed unimportant in practice: well before that stage some sort of rescue or insolvency procedure was likely to be in place (see chapter 14).

There is no minimum capital requirement for *private* companies.

Limiting access to shares: directors' allotment rights and shareholders' pre-emption rights

Allotment

There is a risk that directors may use their power of allotment of shares to influence the composition of the company's membership, and in particular to ensure that the majority of members supports them and will keep them in office (see pp 285 ff above, on directors' use of power for improper purposes).

CA 2006 ss 549–551 limits this possibility of abuse by providing as a general rule that it is an offence for directors to allot shares (or grant options to subscribe for shares or issue securities convertible into shares) without the authority of the members given either in the articles or by ordinary resolution. This authority must be renewed every five years.

The exceptions relate to: (i) issues of shares to the original subscribers, to an employees' share scheme, or to existing holders of rights to acquire or convert their shares (CA 2006 s 549); and (ii) in the case of a private company, issues of shares where the company has only one class of share (CA 2006 s 550), although such a company may restricts its directors' allotment powers by inserting a provision to that effect in the company's articles (s 550(b)).

Since there is now no 'authorised capital' limit, a company's changes to issued capital must be notified to the Registrar at Companies House each time a new allotment is made (CA 2006 s 555).

Pre-emption rights

A *pre-emption right* is a right of first refusal given to the shareholders of a company to subscribe for any new shares that the company issues in proportion to their existing shareholdings. In this way, the balance of control between the respective shareholders can be maintained. A pre-emption right may also prevent the 'watering' or dilution in value of existing shares, which will happen if the new shares are issued at a price which is below their true value.

Prior to 1980, shareholders were legally entitled to pre-emption rights only if this was expressly provided for in the company's articles; although it was a requirement under the London Stock Exchange's Listing Rules that equity shares of listed companies should be offered in the first instance on a pro rata basis to existing equity shareholders. Since 1980, UK legislation implementing the Second EC Directive (and extending its provisions to private companies), has provided a statutory pre-emption right. The relevant provisions are in CA 2006 ss 560–577. The statutory right is given to ordinary shareholders (excluding the company itself as holder of treasury shares), and applies only to new issues of 'equity securities' (s 560).

The right is subject to certain *exceptions* (issues of bonus shares or shares as part of an employee share scheme, and issues for non-cash consideration); *exclusions* (by the articles of private companies); *disapplications* (by the articles for private companies with only one class of shares, or generally by special resolution, or by statute for the sale of treasury shares); and *savings* (for other rules and for certain older pre-emption procedures) (see ss 564–577). The wide ambit of these exceptions means that in practice the statutory provisions do not impose a serious restriction on companies that wish not to be bound by them.

Breach of these provisions does not invalidate the new issue, but generally exposes the company and every officer who knowingly authorised or permitted the contravention to compensation claims in favour of those to whom offers should have been made (CA 2006 s 653).

Offers to purchase shares and remedies for misleading offers

When shares are offered to the public, a prospectus must be published and, additionally, when an application is made for listing on a stock exchange either a prospectus or listing particulars must be published. There are special rules about liability for errors or omissions in those documents (see below, pp 588 ff). In practice, however, the professionalisation of the investment industry and the high standards set both by Stock Exchanges and by investment practitioners themselves mean that the chances of a misleading document getting into circulation in consequence of sharp or sloppy practice have been virtually eliminated.

Here the special rules under FSMA 2000 are ignored, and what is described is the general law applicable to those who have been induced by misrepresentation to subscribe for shares in a company. These rules, although of general application, are usually invoked only when the special rules on public offers are inapplicable.

The different remedies available may be summarised as follows:

(i)   As against the company, rescission of the contract and consequent rectification of the share register (for material misrepresentation of *any* kind).

(ii)   Damages for deceit (for *fraudulent* misrepresentation).[13]

(iii)   Damages under the Misrepresentation Act 1967 s 2(2) (in lieu of rescission) and also possibly under s 2(1) (for so-called 'negligent' misrepresentation).

(iv)   As against the company, a possible claim in damages for breach of contract, on the basis that the statements in the prospectus or offer have been incorporated as terms of the contract.

Note that no civil remedy lies against the *company* at common law for the *omission* of information required to be included in the listing particulars or prospectus: *Re South of England Natural Gas and Petroleum Co Ltd* [1911] 1 Ch 573.

Misrepresentation

If a person is induced to enter into a contract by false statements of fact made by the other party, then there is a misrepresentation, and the innocent party is entitled to rescind the contract. A number of issues may prevent an allottee of shares from obtaining an appropriate remedy, however. The misrepresentation must have been made by the other party to the contract (ie by the company), be one of fact, and have induced the contract.

---

[13] The measure of damages is normally the difference between the price that was paid for the shares and their true value at the time of the transaction, together with any consequential loss. Exceptionally (eg where the defendant's fraud has created a false market or was such as to have prevented the victim from realising the shares at that time), a different value may be substituted: *Smith New Court Securities Ltd v Citibank NA* [1997] AC 254, HL.

The misrepresentation must have been made by the company.

[7.02] Lynde v Anglo-Italian Hemp Spinning Company [1896] 1 Ch 178

ROMER J: The first question I desire to deal with is this—Assuming that Mr. Waithman [a promoter] made material misrepresentations to the plaintiff which induced him to apply for the shares, could the plaintiff, on that ground, hold the company liable, and have the contract set aside? It appears to me that, speaking generally, to make a company liable for misrepresentations inducing a contract to take shares from it the shareholder must bring his case within one or other of the following heads: — (1.) Where the misrepresentations are made by the directors or other the general agents of the company entitled to act and acting on its behalf—as, for example, by a prospectus issued by the authority or sanction of the directors of a company inviting subscriptions for shares; (2.) Where the misrepresentations are made by a special agent of the company while acting within the scope of his authority—as, for example, by an agent specially authorized to obtain, on behalf of the company, subscriptions for shares. This head of course includes the case of a person constituted agent by subsequent adoption of his acts; (3.) Where the company can be held affected, before the contract is complete, with the knowledge that it is induced by misrepresentations—as, for example, when the directors, on allotting shares, know, in fact, that the application for them has been induced by misrepresentations, even though made without any authority; (4.) Where the contract is made on the basis of certain representations, whether the particulars of those representations were known to the company or not, and it turns out that some of those representations were material and untrue—as, for example, if the directors of a company know when allotting that an application for shares is based on the statements contained in a prospectus, even though that prospectus was issued without authority or even before the company was formed, and even if its contents are not known to the directors.[14]

. . . Now, it appears to me that the plaintiff does not bring his case within any of these heads. Such misrepresentations, if any, as were made to the plaintiff were made by Mr Waithman, one of the two promoters of the company. But the company at the time had two directors entitled to act for it, and Mr Waithman was not a director or general agent of the company. No doubt the promoters had a great deal to do with the company at the time, and their wishes and views may have been highly regarded by the directors. But I see nothing to justify me in coming to the conclusion that the promoters are to be regarded as really constituting the company, or that the directors left everything in their hands, or were what may be called dummies, or left it to the promoters to do whatever they pleased in the affairs of the company. Nor was Mr Waithman, when he made the representations he did make to the plaintiff, authorized to act on behalf of the company in procuring shares or authorized to make any representations on behalf of the company to the plaintiff or others to induce him or them to apply for shares. The fact that Mr Waithman was a promoter of the company did not in itself authorize him to procure shares for the company, or to make representations to the plaintiff on the company's behalf. . . . And although the company knew that Waithman was applying to his friends to get them to subscribe for shares, that did not, in my opinion, make him the company's agent, or put the company to inquire as to whether he had made any, and, if any, what, representations to those friends to induce them to subscribe. In most cases directors must be aware that subscriptions for shares are obtained through the intermediary of persons interested in the company, and it would lead to the most astonishing results if that was held sufficient to affect the directors with knowledge of, or to put them upon inquiry as to, the representations, if any, made by those persons to the people applying for the shares. The fact that in the case of this company some applications, including that of the plaintiff, were made on printed forms prepared by the company's solicitor does not, in my opinion, make any real difference. Mr Waithman got his forms by applying to the company's solicitor, because he wanted his friends to make proper applications for shares. No authority was given by the directors to the solicitor to supply Mr Waithman with forms,

---

[14] [This has now been modified by *Collins v Associated Greyhound Racecourses Ltd* [1930] 1 Ch 1, to require that, to the knowledge of the company or its agents, the contract was made on the basis of particular representations that later turned out to be untrue.]

nor can the directors, by seeing these forms used, be held thereby to have adopted Mr Waithman as their agent in obtaining applications for shares. The directors did not issue any prospectus them-selves or try to get applications for shares, and, no doubt, because they thought Waithman and Thomson would get a sufficient number of their friends to take up the necessary number of shares. But this did not, in my opinion, make Waithman and Thomson the special agents of the company to procure subscriptions on its behalf, or authorize them to make any representations on behalf of the company with a view of inducing their friends to subscribe.

And, lastly, this is not a case . . . coming at all within the fourth head. The application for shares made by the plaintiff was not one made conditional upon, or to the knowledge of the directors based upon, any special or other representations made by Waithman. The application was not even, to the knowledge of the directors, induced by representations by Waithman, though, even if it had been, whether that would in itself have been sufficient to bring the case within my fourth head or have entitled the plaintiff to rescind I need not now inquire.

On this ground, therefore, I hold that the action must fail, for in my judgment the plaintiff has not shewn any ground upon which I can rescind this contract by reason of misrepresentations, if any, made to him which induced him to apply for these shares.

[And, further, on the questions of fact, Romer J also held that the alleged misrepresentations were not made out, nor the fact that they had induced the contract.]

Loss of the remedy of rescission

The allottee will lose the right to rescission if the parties cannot be returned to their pre-contractual positions (ie if *restitutio in integrum* is no longer possible; see below), if the contract has been affirmed, if third party rights have intervened, or if the allottee has delayed for too long after discovering the misrepresentation.

[7.03] Oakes v Turquand and Harding (1867) LR 2 HL 325 (House of Lords)

Overend, Gurney & Co Ltd was incorporated in July 1865 to take over the long-established banking business of Overend, Gurney & Co. The prospectus issued to the public concealed the fact that the business was insolvent and had been carried on at a loss for some years. Within a year after the incorporation of the company it stopped payment and went into liquidation. In order to meet the claims of its creditors, large calls were made on the numerous members of the public who had become shareholders. Many of them combined to form a defence asso-ciation, which appointed Oakes (an original allottee of shares) and Peek (who had bought shares in the market) as representatives to conduct test cases on behalf of all the shareholders. In this case they claimed that their names should be taken off the list of contributories on the ground that their contracts to take and to purchase shares, respectively, had been induced by fraud, but it was held that they had lost the right to rescind.

(In later proceedings (*Peek v Gurney* (1873) LR 6 HL 377) Peek was again unsuccessful, this time in a claim against the directors. Among the score or so of other reported cases arising out of the same liquidation, the best-known is *Overend, Gurney & Co v Gibb and Gibb* (1872) LR 5 HL 480, in which the liquidators failed in a claim against the directors, alleging that they had been negligent in allowing the company to purchase the business.)

LORD CHELMSFORD LC: It is said that everything which is stated in the prospectus is literally true, and so it is. But the objection to it is, not that it does not state the truth as far as it goes, but that it conceals most material facts with which the public ought to have been made acquainted, the very concealment of which gives to the truth which is told the character of falsehood. If the real circum-stances of the firm of Overend, Gurney & Co had been disclosed it is not very probable that any company founded upon it would have been formed. Indeed, it was admitted in the course of the argument that if the true position of the affairs of Overend, Gurney & Co had been published it would have entailed the ruin of the old firm, and would have been utterly prohibitory of the formation of the new. To which the only answer which fairly suggests itself is, 'Then no company ought ever to have been attempted, because it was only possible to entice persons to become shareholders by improper concealment of facts' . . .

It is quite clear, therefore, that Oakes might originally have disaffirmed that contract, and divested himself of his shares, and that he never did any act to affirm it, nor was aware of the true state of the firm of Overend, Gurney & Co at the time of the formation of the new company, nor until after the failure . . .

Such was the position of Oakes when the order for winding up the company was made on 22 June 1866. His name being upon the register of shareholders, was placed (as a matter of course) by the liquidators upon the list of contributories . . .

On the part of the creditors, it is said that every person whose name is found upon the register at the time when the order for winding up is made is a shareholder, and liable to contribute towards the payments of the debts of the company to the extent of the sums due upon his shares, unless he can prove that his name was put upon the register without his consent.

Did the appellant then agree to become a member? His counsel answer this question in the negative; because they say that a person who is induced by fraud to enter into an agreement cannot be said to have agreed; the word 'agreed' meaning having entered into a binding agreement. But this is a fallacy. The consent which binds the will and constitutes the agreement is totally different from the motive and inducement which led to the consent. An agreement induced by fraud is certainly, in one sense, not a binding agreement, as it is entirely at the option of the person defrauded whether he will be bound by it or not. In the present case, if the company formed on the basis of the partnership of Overend, Gurney & Co had realised the expectations held out by the prospectus, the appellant would probably have retained his shares, as he would have had an undoubted right to do. But when the order for winding up came, and found him with the shares in his possession, and his name upon the register, the agreement was a subsisting one. How could it then be said that he was not a person who had agreed to become a member? To hold otherwise would be to disregard the long and well-established distinction between void and voidable contracts . . .

[His Lordship then held that the supervening rights of the creditors in a winding up barred the right of a member to avoid the contract on the ground of fraud. He concluded:] It only remains to observe that all that has been said with respect to Oakes applies with greater force to Peek, even if his situation as a purchaser of shares in the market did not preclude him from most of the objections which have been raised in Oakes' case.

LORD CRANWORTH and LORD COLONSAY delivered concurring opinions.

Availability of the remedy of damages

Damages are available instead of rescission, or in addition to rescission for consequential losses: (i) at common law if the misrepresentation was fraudulent (*Derry v Peek* (1889) 14 App Cas 337): see the important and detailed analysis of Lord Steyn in *Smith New Court Securities Ltd Citibank NA* [1997] AC 254; (ii) at common law for negligent misstatement;[15] and (iii) under the Misrepresentation Act 1967, but only between parties to an induced contract, for any form of misrepresentation, unless the misrepresentor can prove that he or she had reasonable grounds to believe, and did believe, up to the time the contract was made, that the facts represented were true (s 2(1)).[16]

---

[15] See *Hedley Byrne and Co ltd v Heller and Partners Ltd* [1964] AC 465; *Caparo Industries plc v Dickman* [1990] 2 AC 605, but so far no cases seem to have been brought for misstatements in offers.

[16] Under the statute, damages are said to be measured in the in the same way as for fraud, regardless of the type of misrepresentation: *Royscot Trust Ltd v Rogerson* [1991] 2 QB 297, strongly criticised in R Hooley, 'Damages and the Misrepresentation Act 1967' (1991) 107 LQR 547.

➤ Notes

1. For over 100 years, the rule laid down in *Houldsworth v City of Glasgow Bank* (1880) 5 App Cas 317, HL prevented a person who had been induced by fraud to take shares in a company from claiming damages against the company while he or she remained a member. The same principle was applied where damages for breach of contract were sought, based on the contract of shareholding: *Re Addlestone Linoleum Co* (1887) 37 Ch D 191, CA. The juridical basis of this rule was never satisfactorily explained, but it has now been reversed by statute: CA 2006 s 655. There is one statutory exception: CA 2006 s 735 expressly excludes the possibility of a claim in damages when a company has broken an obligation to redeem or repurchase shares (but without prejudice to other remedies, which may include an action for specific performance or an application for relief under s 994 (unfairly prejudicial conduct) (see below, pp 552 ff) or for winding up on the 'just and equitable' ground (see below, pp 653 ff)).

2. In *Peek v Gurney* (1873) LR 6 HL 377, the House of Lords held that a prospectus should be regarded as addressed only to those who might become allottees of shares directly from the company, and that it could not be relied on by someone who had bought shares from another source. FSMA 2000 now imposes civil liability for breach of the listing particulars and prospectus requirements in favour of any person who has acquired securities, and this term is defined in terms sufficiently wide to include both original allottees and persons who have purchased shares on the market (see below, pp 592 ff). In *Possfund Custodian Trustee Ltd v Diamond* [1996] 2 BCLC 665 Lightman J held that, in the light of changes in market practice, a person who had bought shares on the market might nowadays be regarded as someone to whom a prospectus was addressed, particularly if the prospectus made reference to future dealing on that market. (This judgment also contains an excellent summary of the various remedies available to a person deceived by misstatements in a prospectus, and their historical development.)

Collecting in the company's capital: payment for shares

Issue of shares at a discount

A company is, in general, forbidden to issue shares[17] at a discount: see CA 2006 s 552 and the cases cited below. But the professional people and institutions who handle new issues must, of course, be remunerated for their services, or compensated for taking the risk of an issue not being fully subscribed for by the public (ie for 'underwriting' the issue). Accordingly, CA 2006 s 553 authorises the payment of commissions and discounts up to a statutory limit (currently 10%), subject to certain safeguards.

A company may not issue shares at a discount.

[7.04] Ooregum Gold Mining Co of India Ltd v Roper [1892] AC 125 (House of Lords)

This action was brought by a holder of ordinary shares to test the validity of an issue of preference shares which had been made by the directors, in accordance with resolutions duly passed by the members, on the basis that each new share of £1 nominal value should be automatically credited with 75p paid, leaving an actual liability of only 25p per share. The transaction

---

[17] But not debentures: see below, p 384.

was *bona fide* thought to be the best way of raising further funds for the company, especially since the ordinary shares stood at a great discount. The House of Lords held, however, that it was beyond the power of the company to issue the shares at a discount, and that in consequence the holders were liable for the full nominal amount of the shares.

LORD HALSBURY LC: My Lords, the question in this case has been more or less in debate since 1883, when Chitty J decided that a company limited by shares was not prohibited by law from issuing its shares at a discount. That decision was overruled, though in a different case, by the Court of Appeal in 1888, and it has now come to your Lordships for final determination.

My Lords, the whole structure of a limited company owes its existence to the Act of Parliament, and it is to the Act of Parliament one must refer to see what are its powers, and within what limits it is free to act. Now, confining myself for the moment to the Act of 1862, it makes one of the conditions of the limitation of liability that the memorandum of association shall contain the amount of capital with which the company proposes to be registered, divided into shares of a certain fixed amount. It seems to me that the system thus created by which the shareholder's liability is to be limited by the amount unpaid upon his shares, renders it impossible for the company to depart from that requirement, and by any expedient to arrange with their shareholders that they shall not be liable for the amount unpaid on the shares, although the amount of those shares has been, in accordance with the Act of Parliament, fixed at a certain sum of money. It is manifest that if the company could do so the provision in question would operate nothing.

I observe in the argument it has been sought to draw a distinction between the nominal capital and the capital which is assumed to be the real capital. I can find no authority for such a distinction. The capital is fixed and certain, and every creditor of the company is entitled to look to that capital as his security.

It may be that such limitations on the power of a company to manage its own affairs may occasionally be inconvenient, and prevent its obtaining money for the purposes of its trading on terms so favourable as it could do if it were more free to act. But, speaking for myself, I recognise the wisdom of enforcing on a company the disclosure of what its real capital is, and not permitting a statement of its affairs to be such as may mislead and deceive those who are either about to become its shareholders or about to give it credit.

I think . . . that the question which your Lordships have to solve is one which may be answered by reference to an inquiry: What is the nature of an agreement to take a share in a limited company? and that that question may be answered by saying, that it is an agreement to become liable to pay to the company the amount for which the share has been created. That agreement is one which the company itself has no authority to alter or qualify, and I am therefore of opinion that, treating the question as unaffected by the Act of 1867, the company were prohibited by law, upon the principle laid down in *Ashbury Co v Riche* **[3.02]**, from doing that which is compendiously described as issuing shares at a discount.

LORDS WATSON, HERSCHELL, MACNAGHTEN and MORRIS delivered concurring opinions.

➤ Notes and Questions

1. The position in which this company found itself is not at all uncommon: unprofitable trading had led to a depressed market price for the shares, and the company was seeking an injection of new funds to 'keep head above water' while the directors endeavoured to surmount the immediate financial difficulties and find a way back to profitability.[18] The classical solution of an earlier generation was to issue preference shares, so that those who provided the new capital ranked ahead of the existing shareholders as regards both income and capital rights (see below, pp 427 ff). The other possible solution—to issue new shares

---

[18] As in fact happened in *Ooregum*: soon afterwards, the company struck gold and its ordinary shares rose in value from 12½p to £2.

ranking *pari passu* with the existing shares but at a discounted price—is, on the authority of the above case, unlawful in England. Does the rule protect the company's creditors? Does it protect the existing shareholders?

2. One way of making such a course of action possible would be for the law to authorise companies to create and issue *no par value* shares—something which is permitted in many jurisdictions and, indeed, compulsory in some. There is, after all, something unreal and simplistic about the concept of a par or nominal value. If the share in question was originally issued at a premium, or in exchange for a non-cash consideration, it may never have been worth its face value; and certainly after the date of its issue its market value is never again likely to bear any relation to the historic figure which was once ascribed to it. If it were lawful for companies to issue shares of no par value, many of the misunderstandings associated with the concept of a nominal value would disappear, and in addition it would be possible for a company to issue shares, ranking *pari passu*, at a price of £1 in January, £1.05 in February, and £0.90 in March (depending on what the market would stand), without any implication that there was a par value which was being enhanced by a premium or reduced by a discount. Recommendations have been made at different times for such an innovation to be made in the UK—eg by the Gedge Committee (1954, Cmd 9112), the Jenkins Committee (1962, Cmnd 1749, paras 32–34) and the Wilson Committee (1980, Cmnd 7937, para 735), as well as by professional bodies—but the response from successive governments has been nil. The CLR also considered the possibility of allowing (or even requiring) private companies to issue no-par shares. (This would not be possible for public companies unless the Second EC Directive were to be amended.) In the end, no change was proposed.

3. In more modern company law codes where shares of no par value are permitted, the 'maintenance of capital' rules do not apply (see Chapter 8); but the payment of dividends and other distributions to shareholders, and analogous transactions such as the repurchase by a company of its issued shares, are permitted only if the company is able to satisfy a statutory 'solvency test' at the relevant time. In consequence, attention is focused on the company's current financial position rather than on what may be quite misleading historic costs as shown in the accounts—indeed, the whole business of accounting is made much more straightforward and meaningful.

Issue of debentures at a discount

There is ordinarily no prohibition on the issue of debentures at a discount, because the 'maintenance of capital' principle does not apply to debt capital. A company may find it attractive to create debentures on terms which give the holders the option at some later date of converting the debentures into shares at a predetermined rate of exchange. Such *convertible* debentures may not be issued, at a discount on terms that they may be immediately exchanged for shares of an equivalent nominal value, for this would be only an indirect way of achieving an issue of shares at a discount (*Mosely v Koffyfontein Mines Ltd* [1904] 2 Ch 108). The rate at which the exchange of securities is to take place must, to be above challenge, represent a realistic assessment of future trends in the value of money and the market prices in securities.

➤ Questions

1. What might be the attractions of an issue of convertible debentures, rather than a straightforward issue of shares, for (a) the company, (b) the investor?

2. The basis of conversion set out in the terms of issue of convertible debentures commonly prescribes a declining tariff, eg 75 shares for every £100 of debentures converted after three years, 70 shares per £100 converted after four years, 65 shares per £100 after five years. Why?

Issue of shares at a premium

The rule that shares may not be issued at a discount means that a company which allots a share of nominal value £1 must get £1 and nothing less for it; but there is no corresponding rule which says that the company must get £1 and nothing more for it. If investors can be found who are willing to pay the company £1.20 or £2 or £5 for a share of nominal value £1, the company is free to charge that sum. (Indeed, it may give the company's existing shareholders cause for complaint if a new issue of shares is made at par, for that would reduce (or 'water down') the value of their shareholdings.[19])

The excess received by the company over the nominal value of the shares is called a *premium*, and, as noted earlier, the CA 2006 requires such sums to be shown in the company's accounts under a separate head, as the 'share premium account'. This ensures that these are treated for almost all purposes as capital in the company's hands and not in any sense as income or profit: see above, pp 373 ff.

Shareholders who have paid a premium for their shares have no right to the return of their premium in a winding up: at least in the absence of specific provision in the terms of issue, any surplus remaining after the return of the nominal amount of the shares is distributable on a rateable basis (*Re Driffield Gas Light Co* [1898] 1 Ch 451).

A company is not bound to issue its shares at a premium even though a price above par could be obtained.

[7.05] Hilder v Dexter [1902] AC 474 (House of Lords)

Immediately after its incorporation, the company issued one-sixth of its shares to selected private persons in order to obtain working capital. These shares were issued at par on the terms that the allottees should later have the option to take up further shares at par on a one for one basis. Hilder exercised his option at a time when the shares were worth £2 17s 6d [£2.87] per £1 share. Dexter, another shareholder, sought and obtained an injunction restraining Hilder and the company from carrying out the agreement on the ground that such an arrangement was forbidden by s 8(2) of the Act of 1900 [CA 2006 s 582]. The House of Lords reversed this decision and discharged the injunction.

LORD DAVEY: The advantage which the appellant will derive from the exercise of his option is certainly not a 'discount or allowance', because he will have to pay 20s [100p] in the pound for every share. Nor is it, in my opinion, a commission paid by the company, for the company will not part with any portion of its capital which is received by it intact, or indeed with any moneys belonging to it. But the words relied on are, 'either directly or indirectly', and the argument seems to be that the company, by engaging to allot shares at par to the shareholder at a future date, is applying or using its shares in such a manner as to give him a possible benefit at the expense of the company in this sense, that it foregoes the chance of issuing them at a premium. With regard to the latter point, it may or may not be at the expense of the company. I am not aware of any law which obliges a company to issue its shares above par because they are saleable at a premium in the market. It depends on the circumstances of each case whether it will be prudent or even possible to do so, and it is a question for the directors to decide. But the point which, in my opinion, is alone material for the present purpose is that the benefit to the shareholder from being able to sell his shares at a premium is not obtained by him at the expense of the company's capital. . . .

---

[19] The directors would not breach any legal duty to the company (see below, [7.07]), but the existing shareholders might complain of unfairly prejudicial treatment (CA 2006 s 994). The statutory pre-emption rights are designed to help, but do not always apply or meet the problem: see above p 377.

The EARL OF HALSBURY LC and LORD BRAMPTON delivered concurring opinions.
LORD ROBERTSON concurred.

Shares may be issued at a premium even though not issued for cash.

[7.06] Henry Head & Co Ltd v Ropner Holdings Ltd [1952] Ch 124 (Chancery Division)

The defendant company was formed to acquire by way of amalgamation the shares of two shipping companies, and did so by exchanging the shares in these companies for shares in itself of equivalent nominal value. In this way it acquired assets worth some £7m in exchange for shares of a nominal value of £1,175,000. The court held that the difference of just over £5m had rightly been shown in the company's balance sheet as carried to a share premium account.

HARMAN J: The directors have been advised that they are bound to show their accounts in that way, and not only they but the plaintiffs, who are large shareholders, regard that as a very undesirable thing, because it fixes an unfortunate kind of rigidity on the structure of the company, having regard to the fact that an account kept under that name, namely, the Share Premium Account, can only have anything paid out of it by means of a transaction analogous to a reduction of capital. It is, in effect, as if the company had originally been capitalised at approximately £7,000,000 instead of £1,750,000.

The question which I have to determine is whether the defendants were obliged to keep their accounts in that way. That depends purely on s 56 of the Companies Act 1948 [CA 2006, s 610], which is a new departure in legislation and was, it is said, intended to make compulsory that which had long seemed to be desirable, namely, the practice of putting aside as a reserve and treating in the ordinary way as capital cash premiums received on the issue of shares at a premium . . .

Counsel for the plaintiff company asks who would suppose that a common type of transaction of the sort now under consideration was the issue of shares at a premium and says that nobody in the city or in the commercial world would dream of so describing it. It is with a sense of shock at first that one hears that this transaction was the issue of shares at a premium. Everybody, I suppose, who hears those words thinks of a company which, being in a strong trading position, wants further capital and puts forward its shares for the subscription of the public at such a price as the market in those shares justifies, whatever it may be, [£1.50] a £1 share, £5 a £1 share, or any price obtainable; and the [50p] or £4 above the nominal value of a share which it acquires as a result of that transaction is no doubt a premium. That is what is ordinarily meant by the issue of shares at a premium. The first words of sub-s (1) are: 'Where a company issues shares at a premium'. If the words had stopped there, one might have said that the subsection merely refers to cash transactions of that sort, but it goes on to say 'whether for cash or otherwise'.

What 'otherwise' can there be? It must be a consideration other than cash, namely, goods or assets of some physical sort.

➤ Note

The general principle expressed in this case remains valid, but CA 2006 (and its predecessors) contain relief against the application of the share premium restrictions in the case of certain mergers and reconstructions (ss 611–613), and the Secretary of State has power to make further regulations, either amplifying or restricting the relief so provided (s 614).

Issue of shares in exchange for property

It is not necessary that shares be allotted for cash. It is very common instead for the issue price to be satisfied by the transfer to the company of property, such as a business, previously owned by the allottee: this is what Mr Salomon [2.01] did. Or the new shares may be exchanged for shares in another company: see, for example, *Henry Head* [7.06].

Two problems may arise here. If the property taken by the company as consideration is worth *more than* the nominal value of the new shares, then the shares will have been issued at a premium, and this will bring into play the burdensome and restrictive accounting provisions of CA 2006 ss 610ff discussed above. If, on the other hand, the property is worth *less than* the nominal value of the shares (as may well have been true in Mr Salomon's case), then in practical terms the shares will have been issued at a discount, contrary to law. Creditors who assume that the shares have been paid for in full may then suffer loss, or at least be exposed to risk, and existing shareholders also may be prejudiced through the 'watering down' of their own investment.

The common law leaves this problem to be settled by the business judgment and integrity of the directors, and courts will normally accept the valuation made at the time of the allotment unless it is shown to have been made dishonestly or falsely or the contract for allotment is itself set aside for fraud (*Re Wragg* [7.07]). This means that the rule against issuing shares at a discount can be circumvented fairly easily, for challenges to the board's decisions are rarely mounted, and those that are face the formidable procedural obstacles of *Foss v Harbottle* [11.01]: compare the analogous cases of *Pavlides v Jensen* [1956] Ch 565 (sale of assets at alleged undervalue) and *Prudential Assurance Co Ltd v Newman Industries Ltd (No 2)* [11.13] (purchase of assets at alleged overvalue). The case for some form of statutory control has always seemed a strong one.

Such a step has been taken in regard to *public* companies, as a result of the Second EC Directive (which was implemented in 1980). The relevant provisions are now in CA 2006 ss 584–587 and 593–609. Some forms of consideration for the allotment of shares are banned altogether, eg an undertaking to do work for the company in the future (s 585(1)) and an undertaking of a long-term nature (other than a promise to pay cash) which may take five years or more to perform (s 587(1)). Other forms of 'non-cash' consideration have to be valued by an expert (ss 593–4, 603), and sometimes a second expert has to certify that the first one is competent (s 1150(2))! Rules of even greater severity are laid down for subscribers to the memorandum (ss 584, 598–599). In all, it is a very elaborate (and costly) procedure that the Act spells out, in the most finicky detail: a pretty large sledgehammer to crack a fairly small nut.

It is not so important, here, to explain all the finer points of the statutory procedure. But something must be said about the code of sanctions for a failure to comply—even with these finer points; and these are formidable. The allottee is obliged to pay to the company the nominal value of the shares and any premium, with interest, regardless of any benefit that the company may already have had (so that he or she may in effect have to pay for the shares twice over); and, in addition, a subsequent holder of the shares is jointly and severally liable with the allottee to pay the same amounts, unless the holder is (or has derived title through) a *bona fide* purchaser for value without (actual) notice: see ss 588, 605. The only relief that those who are caught by these provisions have against what may be potentially a double liability to pay for their shares is that they have a right to make application to the court and ask for exemption from some or all of the statutory liability (ss 589, 606: see *Re Bradford Investments plc (No 2)*, below). In addition to these civil consequences, criminal penalties are imposed upon the company and its officers; and the transactions which infringe the statutory rules, though enforceable by the company against the allottee, are (by implication, and in the case of a contract with a subscriber to the memorandum, expressly) unenforceable or 'void' as against the company.

There is an exception from the valuation requirement in the case of a take-over in which all or part of the consideration for the shares allotted is the exchange of shares in the offeree company (s 594(1)-(3)); and it also does not apply in a merger (s 595).

One last point is worth emphasising: all of these rules apply only to issues by public companies for non-cash consideration; if the consideration is cash, the rules are not relevant. 'Cash' is defined in CA 2006 s 583(3): it includes undertakings to pay in the future, or to release a liability of the company (the latter is useful in debt for equity swaps).

It should be remembered that the rules stated above govern public companies only; private companies continue to be subject to the common law, as declared in the case next cited **[7.07]**.

➤ Questions

1. Fred comes to an arrangement with the directors of XYZ plc that he will subscribe for 200,000 £1 ordinary shares in the company at their par value. He also agrees to sell to XYZ plc a leasehold shop property for a price of £200,000. On 1 April the shares are allotted to him in exchange for his cheque, payable to the company, for £200,000, and on the same day, the leasehold interest in the shop is transferred to the company in return for the company's cheque, payable to Fred, for £200,000. What legal issues arise?

2. What do you consider is the policy reasoning behind CA 2006 ss 598-599? Suppose that X and Y are the promoters of a public company and intend within a few days of its incorporation to transfer a business to it: is there any need to have regard to ss 598-599 if they take the precaution of ensuring that the memorandum is subscribed only by two clerks in their solicitor's office?

3. Why do you think that the legislation requires a copy of the valuation to be sent to the proposed allottee (s 593(1)(c))? If the valuer's report advises the company that the transferor's property would be a snip at twice the price, can the allottee withdraw from the transaction and negotiate for more? If the valuer negligently overvalues the property, could the allottee sue the valuer in tort?

4. Where there has been an infringement of s 593, could the company and the allottee effectively agree that the latter should be released from liability under s 593(3) without going to court under s 606?

Private company issues for non-cash consideration.

[7.07] Re Wragg Ltd [1897] 1 Ch 796 (Court of Appeal)

This case indicates that a *private* company may buy property at any price it thinks fit, and pay for it in fully paid shares. Unless the transaction itself is impeached (eg on the ground of fraud), the actual value of the consideration received by the company for its shares cannot be inquired into. Wragg and Martin had sold to the company on its incorporation their omnibus and livery-stable business for £46,300, which was paid partly in cash and debentures and partly by the allotment to them of the whole of the company's original capital of £20,000 in fully paid shares. The liquidator of the company later sought to show that the value of the business had been overstated by some £18,000; and he claimed either to be entitled to treat shares representing this amount as unpaid, or alternatively to charge Martin and Wragg as directors with misfeasance in connection with the purchase. Both claims failed.

LINDLEY LJ: . . . That shares cannot be issued at a discount was finally settled in the case of the *Ooregum Gold Mining Co of India v Roper* **[7.04]**, the judgments in which are strongly relied upon by the appellant in this case. It has, however, never yet been decided that a limited company cannot buy property or pay for services at any price it thinks proper, and pay for them in fully paid-up shares. Provided a limited company does so honestly and not colourably, and provided that it has not been so imposed upon as to be entitled to be relieved from its bargain, it appears to be settled by *Pell's* case,[20] and the others to which I have referred, of which *Anderson's* case[21] is the most striking, that agreements by limited companies to pay for property or services in paid-up shares are valid and binding on the companies and their creditors . . .

[If] a company owes a person £100, the company cannot by paying him £200 in shares of that nominal amount discharge him . . . from his obligation as a shareholder to pay up the other £100 in respect of those shares. That would be issuing shares at a discount. The difference between such a transaction and paying for property or services in shares at a price put upon them by a vendor and agreed to by the company may not always be very apparent in practice. But the two transactions are essentially different, and whilst the one is ultra vires the other is intra vires. It is not law that persons cannot sell property to a limited company for fully paid-up shares and make a profit by the transaction. We must not allow ourselves to be misled by talking of value. The value paid to the company is measured by the price at which the company agrees to buy what it thinks it worth its while to acquire. Whilst the transaction is unimpeached, this is the only value to be considered . . .

A L SMITH and RIGBY LJJ delivered concurring judgments.

➤ Note

This common law ruling may be contrasted with *Re Bradford Investments plc (No 2)* [1991] BCLC 688, which illustrates the operation of the statutory rules governing the issue of shares by public companies for a non-cash consideration. Here the four members of a partnership had converted a dormant private company into a public company and transferred the business of the partnership to it in consideration of the allotment to them of 1,059,000 fully paid £1 ordinary shares. No valuation of the business was obtained, as required by CA 1985 s 103 [CA 2006 s 593]. Two-and-a-half years later, the company, now under independent management, claimed £1,059,000 from the original partners as the issue price of the shares. The partners applied to the court under s 113 [CA 2006 s 606] to be relieved from liability to pay this sum. In this they were unsuccessful, for s 113 places the onus of proving that value was given on the applicants, and they were unable to satisfy the court that the partnership business had any net value at the time when it was transferred to the company.

[20] (1869) 5 Ch App 11.
[21] (1877) 7 Ch D 75.

8

DISTRIBUTIONS AND CAPITAL MAINTENANCE

Controls over a company's distribution of capital

The previous chapter illustrated the concern of the law to see that those who take shares in a company do, in fact, contribute the value of their shares in money or money's worth. This fund of such contributions, being the company's legal capital, is intended by law to provide creditor protection, in some senses at the expense of the company's members. The law does not restrict every disposal of the company's assets—companies are free to run more or less successful businesses. However, the ambition of creditor protection would be defeated if, once the funds had been received, the company were completely free to return them to the members, thereby adversely affecting the creditors' overall position *vis à vis* the company.

This chapter examines the rules that are designed to ensure that a company's legal capital is, as far as possible, maintained in the company's hands consistently with all the risks associated with any business venture. In particular, these rules ensure that a company's legal capital is not returned to the members themselves, directly or indirectly, except through some statutory procedure, such as a reduction of capital (CA 2006 ss 641ff) or a redemption or a repurchase of shares (ss 684ff), which provides proper safeguards for creditors and others who might be prejudiced by the diminution of the company's assets. In this way, the law does its best for the company's creditors who are, generally, denied any direct recourse against the members, or against the directors, whilst at the same time allowing corporate entrepreneurial activity to continue without too much state intervention.

There is, of course, only so much protection that any formal rules of law can give. In addition to the normal business risks mentioned above, the historic figure representing the issued capital may be eroded in real terms by the effects of inflation. But these are risks which creditors necessarily accept; and UK company law does provide a further measure of protection through the publicity given to company accounts and through the remedial regime provided by the insolvency legislation.

The rules providing for 'maintenance of capital' were formulated in the first place by the courts in the latter part of the 19th century. But the Second EC Directive (No 77/9/EEC) required the UK to make specific legislative provision for many matters relating to the use of capital and the payment of dividends. The required rules to some extent overlapped with the existing judge-made law, and in other respects went much further. English statutory provisions are now more extensive than the directive required, in that some of the provisions apply not just to public companies (as the directive stipulated) but to private companies as well.

English statute law later introduced still further changes, in the form of rules allowing a company to repurchase its own shares.[1] This had been declared unlawful in *Trevor v Whitworth* **[8.06]**, and the common law ban is, indeed, still confirmed as a general rule in CA 2006 s 658. It also made changes to the rules related to the giving by a company of financial assistance towards the purchase of its shares. Much of the earlier case law was superseded as

---

[1] A limited statutory exception allowing companies to issue redeemable *preference* shares had existed since 1929. Now redeemable shares can be of any class.

a result. It need hardly be said that the greatest caution is needed when referring to decisions of the courts prior to 1980. It is not possible here to describe the detail of all the statutory rules—still less to try to explain their byzantine obfuscations; all that can be attempted is to summarise them, and to cite some of the relevant judicial pronouncements.

This chapter deals, in turn, with:[2]

(i)   permitted returns of capital implemented by a *reduction of capital* (see below, pp 391 ff);

(ii) permitted returns of capital implemented by a *repurchase or redemption of shares* (see below, pp 399 ff);

(iii) prohibitions on a company giving *financial assistance* to others for the purchase of its shares (see below, pp 403 ff);

(iv) rules requiring *dividend distributions* to be made out of profits, not capital (see below, pp 415 ff); and

(v) impermissible *'disguised' returns of capital* (see below, pp 422 ff).

Permitted reductions of capital

Once a company has raised a particular level of legal capital, can it adjust the amount downwards? If this could happen at will, the rules on legal capital would become meaningless. On the other hand, there may be good reason for adjustments.

If the company has excess capital that it cannot, or prefers not to, use profitably in pursuing its objectives, it may wish to return this to the members rather than expand or diversify the company's business. This involves no risk to the creditors, provided they are satisfied first.

By contrast, if the company has traded unsuccessfully, the value of its existing assets may fall well short of the legal capital. Potential new equity investors may want the value of the company's existing shares to be reduced to reflect the actual value of the company's assets before new investments are made. This is desired so that, if the business is resuscitated, its profits can be paid out to members (including the new members) rather than going to meet the shortfall in undistributable legal capital. Although this type of revaluation does not involve paying any of the company's cash to its shareholders, it does have a detrimental impact on creditors: the value of the protective 'creditor buffer' is reduced, and the risk to creditors therefore increases.

CA 2006 imposes restraints on a company wishing to reduce its capital. In summary, it can only do so by: (i) special resolution confirmed by the court (CA 2006 ss 641(1)(b), 645–651); or (ii) for private companies, by special resolution supported by a solvency statement by the directors, filed with the registrar, and so long as at least one shareholder remains (CA 2006 ss 641(1)(a), 642–644).[3] This is a major relaxation for private companies, introduced by CA 2006. Under (i), the court must not confirm a reduction unless it is satisfied that affected creditors have consented, been paid, or had their debts secured (s 648), and then the court order and the new statement of capital must be registered at Companies House. Creditors may object to the proposed reduction if it involves either a diminution of shareholder liability in respect of unpaid capital, or the payment to any shareholder of paid up capital (s 646), unless

---

[2] Also see: J Armour, 'Share Capital and Creditor Protection: Efficient Rules for a Modern Economy' (2000) 63 MLR 355; J Rickford et al, 'Reforming Capital' (2004) *European Business Law Review* 919; J Armour, 'Legal Capital: An Outdated Concept?' (2006) 7 *European Business Organization Law Review* 5; E Ferran, 'Creditors' Interests and "Core" Company Law' (1999) *Company Lawyer* 314; E Ferran, 'Financial Assistance: Changing Policy Perceptions but Static Law' [2004] CLJ 225.

[3] If the company contains a prohibition in its articles on reductions of capital, then the company's articles will first have to be altered before this procedure can be followed: see CA 2006 s 641(6) and p 392, below.

the court thinks that creditors should not be able to object, or should be able to object in an even wider range of circumstances (s 645). Subject to this, a company may reduce its capital in any way, and s 641(4) provides illustrations.

Court approval, in (i), is designed to ensure that the prescribed formalities have been strictly observed (including creditor approval), and that the reduction treats the company's shareholders fairly (see the cases cited below).

In practice, the procedure is little used by private companies, now that they can repurchase their own shares out of capital (see below, p 399), and so use this approach to buy out retiring or deceased members. Public companies may still find the procedure useful on occasion, but note the requirement in s 656 for directors of public companies to call a general meeting if the company's assets fall below half or less of the company's called up capital (see above, pp 376–377).

Finally, where the rights of a *class* of shareholders are affected by a reduction, it may be necessary to have regard also to the provisions of CA 2006 s 630 (especially since s 630(6) indicates that references to 'variation' of class rights is taken to include references to 'abrogation'), but the approach of the courts to this topic gives less scope to that section than its draftsman probably appreciated: see below, **[8.04]** and pp 394 ff).

A company may not bind itself not to exercise the power conferred on it by statute to alter its capital, but an agreement by members that they will not support a resolution to alter capital is binding.

[8.01] Russell v Northern Bank Development Corpn Ltd [1992] 1 WLR 588 (House of Lords)

A company (referred to in the report as TBL) was set up in 1979 as the parent company in a group of brick-making companies based in Northern Ireland. It had five shareholders: the respondent bank, which held 120 shares, and four executives (including Russell), who each held 20 shares. Soon after the incorporation of TBL, an agreement was entered into between the five shareholders and the company which provided (*inter alia*) that no further share capital would be created or issued without the consent of each of the parties. In 1988 the board of directors proposed to make an increase of capital to £4 million by a rights issue. Russell objected to this and was successful in obtaining a declaration that the agreement was binding on his fellow-shareholders (although not on the company itself).

LORD JAUNCEY OF TULLICHETTLE: . . . The issue between the parties in this House was whether art 3 of the agreement constituted an unlawful and invalid fetter on the statutory power of TBL to increase its share capital or whether it was no more than an agreement between the shareholders as to their manner of voting in a given situation. Both parties accepted the long-established principle that 'a company cannot forgo its right to alter its articles' (*Southern Foundries (1926) Ltd v Shirlaw* **[5.07]**, per Lord Porter), a principle that was earlier stated in *Allen v Gold Reefs of West Africa Ltd* **[4.23]** per Lindley MR:

. . . the company is empowered by the statute to alter the regulations contained in its articles from time to time by special resolutions . . ., and any regulation or article purporting to deprive the company of this power is invalid on the ground that it is contrary to the statute . . .

Murray J and MacDermott LJ [judges in the courts below] both considered that this principle applied also to the right of a company to alter its memorandum and I agree that this must be the case. Mr McCartney QC for the appellant advanced a number of arguments to the effect that the agreement in no way contravened the above principle inasmuch as it was merely an agreement between shareholders outside the scope of company legislation which in no way fettered the statutory power of TBL to alter its memorandum and articles. Mr Girvan QC, on the other hand, submitted that the agreement was not only a voting arrangement between shareholders inter se but was tantamount to an article of association which constituted a restriction on the power of TBL to alter its share capital.

My Lords, while a provision in a company's articles which restricts its statutory power to alter those articles is invalid an agreement dehors the articles between shareholders as to how they shall exercise their voting rights on a resolution to alter the articles is not necessarily so. In *Welton v Saffery*,[4] which concerned an ultra vires provision in the articles of association authorising the company to issue shares at a discount, Lord Davey said:

Of course, individual shareholders may deal with their own interests by contract in such way as they may think fit. But such contracts, whether made by all or some only of the shareholders, would create personal obligations, or an exceptio personalis against themselves only, and would not become a regulation of the company, or be binding on the transferees of the parties to it, or upon new or non-assenting shareholders. . . .

I understand Lord Davey there to be accepting that shareholders may lawfully agree inter se to exercise their voting rights in a manner which, if it were dictated by the articles, and were thereby binding on the company, would be unlawful.

[His Lordship examined parts of the agreement and referred to *Bushell v Faith* **[5.05]**. He continued:] Turning back to cl 3 of the agreement it appears to me that its purpose was twofold. The shareholders agreed only to exercise their voting powers in relation to the creation or issue of shares in TBL if they and TBL agreed in writing. This agreement is purely personal to the shareholders who executed it and as I have already remarked does not purport to bind future shareholders. It is, in my view, just such a private agreement as was envisaged by Lord Davey in *Welton v Saffery*. TBL on the other hand agreed that its capital would not be increased without the consent of each of the shareholders. This was a clear undertaking by TBL in a formal agreement not to exercise its statutory powers for a period which could, certainly on one view of construction, last for as long as any one of the parties to the agreement remained a shareholder and long after the control of TBL had passed to shareholders who were not party to the agreement. As such an undertaking it is, in my view, as obnoxious as if it had been contained in the articles of association and therefore is unenforceable as being contrary to the provisions of art 131 of the Companies (Northern Ireland) Order 1986 [CA 2006 s 617]. TBL's undertaking is, however, independent of and severable from that of the shareholders and there is no reason why the latter should not be enforceable by the shareholders inter se as a personal agreement which in no way fetters TBL in the exercise of its statutory powers. I would therefore allow the appeal. . . .

LORDS GRIFFITHS, LOWRY, MUSTILL and SLYNN OF HADLEY concurred.

➤ Question

Can the first ruling in this case (that a company cannot agree that it will not exercise its statutory power to alter its capital) be readily circumvented by the second (that members may agree by contract, either with each other or with a third party, that they will not vote for a change in the company's capital structure)? If so, is the reasoning flawed?

The court's discretion in confirming a reduction of capital.

[8.02] Scottish Insurance Corpn Ltd v Wilsons and Clyde Coal Co Ltd [1949] AC 462 (House of Lords)

The company's business had been nationalised, so that it could no longer earn profits. Its proposal to pay off the preference capital[5] in anticipation of liquidation was opposed, partly

---

[4] [1897] AC 299, 331.
[5] See below, pp 427 ff.

because it was believed that this would rob the preference shareholders of a right to participate in 'surplus assets' in a liquidation. The House of Lords rejected this construction of the
preference shareholders' rights (see **[9.04]**) and held that the reduction was in any case fair.

LORD SIMONDS: The Companies Act 1929, no more than its predecessors, prescribes what is to
guide the court in the exercise of its discretionary jurisdiction to confirm or to refuse to confirm a
reduction in capital. But I agree with the learned Lord President [in the court below] that, important
though its task is to see that the procedure, by which a reduction is carried through, is formally correct and that creditors are not prejudiced, it has the further duty of satisfying itself that the scheme
is fair and equitable between the different classes of shareholders: see eg *British and American
Trustee and Finance Corpn Ltd v Couper*.[6] But what is fair and equitable must depend upon the circumstances of each case and I propose . . . to consider the elements on which the appellants rely
for saying that this reduction is not fair to them.

In the formal case which they have presented to the House the element of unfairness on which
the appellants insist is that the reduction deprives them of their right to participate in the surplus
assets of the company on liquidation and leaves the ordinary stockholders in sole possession of
those assets. But in their argument both in the Court of Session and before your Lordships they
have further relied on the fact that they have been deprived of a favourable 7% investment which
they cannot hope to replace and might have expected to continue to enjoy. They further contend
that the deprivation of these rights, which would in any case have been unmerited hardship, is rendered more unfair because it is likely to be followed at an early date by liquidation of the company
or, as it is less accurately expressed, because it is itself only a step in the liquidation of the company.

The first plea makes an assumption, viz that the articles give the preference stockholders the
right in a winding up to share in surplus assets, which I for the moment accept but will later examine. Making that assumption, I yet see no validity in the plea. The company has at a stroke been
deprived of the enterprise and undertaking which it has built up over many years: it is irrelevant for
this purpose that the stroke is delivered by an Act of Parliament which at the same time provides
some compensation. Nor can it affect the rights of the parties that the only reason why there is
money available for repayment of capital is that the company has no longer an undertaking to carry
on. Year by year the 7% preference dividend has been paid; of the balance of the profits some part
has been distributed to the ordinary stockholders, the rest has been conserved in the business. If I
ask whether year by year the directors were content to recommend, the company in general meeting to vote, a dividend which has left a margin of resources, in order that the preference stockholders might in addition to repayment of the capital share also in surplus assets, I think that directors
and company alike would give an emphatic negative. Anyway they would, I think, add that they have
always had it in their power, and have it still, by making use of articles 139 or 141, to see that what
they had saved for themselves they do not share with others[7] . . . Reading these articles as a
whole with such familiarity with the topic as the years have brought, I would not hesitate to say,
first, that the last thing a preference stockholder would expect to get (I do not speak here of the
legal rights) would be a share of surplus assets, and that such a share would be a windfall beyond
his reasonable expectations and, secondly, that he had at all times the knowledge, enforced in this
case by the unusual reference in article 139 to the payment off of the preference capital, that at
least he ran the risk, if the company's circumstances admitted, of such a reduction as is now proposed being submitted for confirmation by the court. Whether a man lends money to a company at
7% or subscribes for its shares carrying a cumulative preferential dividend at that rate, I do not think
that he can complain of unfairness if the company, being in a position lawfully to do so, proposes to
pay him off. No doubt, if the company is content not to do so, he may get something that he can
never have expected but, so long as the company can lawfully repay him, whether it be months or

---

[6] [1894] AC 399.

[7] [These articles dealt respectively with the paying off of the preference capital out of a reserve fund, and the distribution of capitalised profits, in the form of bonus shares, to the ordinary shareholders.]

years before a contemplated liquidation, I see no ground for the court refusing its confirmation. [His Lordship later held that the preference shareholders had in any case no right to participate in 'surplus assets' in a liquidation: see **[9.04]**.]

VISCOUNT MAUGHAM and LORD NORMAND delivered concurring opinions.

LORD MORTON OF HENRYTON dissented.

In a reduction of capital, the prima facie rule is that money is to be repaid and losses are to be borne in the order in which the different classes of shares would rank, as regards repayment or loss of capital respectively, in a winding up.

[8.03] Re Chatterley-Whitfield Collieries Ltd [1948] 2 All ER 593 (Court of Appeal)

The company's principal business had been nationalised. It proposed to continue operations on a much smaller scale, for which it would need far less capital. It therefore proposed to reduce its capital by paying off its preference shareholders, leaving the ordinary shareholders unaffected. This was confirmed by the court as fair, since it was in accordance with the respective rights of the two classes in a winding up.

LORD GREENE MR: . . . [T]he company is faced with the following situation. Its principal business has gone and it is proposing to embark on certain new activities which may or may not turn out to be successful. So long as it was possessed of its colliery it clearly required to keep all its issued capital in the business—there was no question of its having capital surplus to its business requirements. The reduced form of its activities is, however, such that it has a great deal more capital than it requires . . .

What is a company in that situation to do? The business answer to this question does not admit of doubt, particularly where a substantial part of its capital consists of preference shares bearing a higher rate of dividend than the company is reasonably likely to earn in the future. It will do what this company seeks to do, ie reduce its capital by paying off as much of its preference capital as it is able to pay off out of its surplus. A company which satisfies its capital requirements by issuing preference shares only does so where it is satisfied that the new capital will earn at least the promised rate of dividend. A company which has issued preference shares carrying a high rate of dividend and finds its business so curtailed that it has capital surplus to its requirements and sees the likelihood, or at any rate the possibility, that its preference capital will not, if I may use the expression, 'earn its keep', would be guilty of financial ineptitude if it did not take steps to reduce its capital by paying off preference capital so far as the law allowed it to do so. That is mere commonplace in company finance.

There has been a tendency, indeed more than a tendency, to represent a company confronted by this sort of practical question as though it were nothing but an uneasy and warring combination of hostile classes of shareholders. In a sense, no doubt, it is. But it is more than this. The position of the company itself as an economic entity must be considered, and nothing can be more destructive of a company's financial equilibrium than to have to carry the burden of capital which it does not need, bearing a high rate of dividend which it cannot earn. In a company so situated, the ordinary shareholders will be unfairly treated vis-à-vis the preference shareholders, and the company may well fall into the situation when its preference dividends will begin to fall into irretrievable arrears. It is a fallacy to suppose that because ordinary shareholders will benefit, the transaction ought to be vetoed as being unfair to the preference shareholders.

It is a clearly recognised principle that the court, in confirming a reduction by the payment off of capital surplus to a company's needs, will allow, or rather require, that the reduction shall be effected in the first instance by payment off of capital which is entitled to priority in a winding up. Apart from special cases where by agreement between classes the incidence of reduction is arranged in a different manner, this is and has for years been the normal recognised practice of the courts, accepted by the courts and by businessmen as the fair and equitable method of carrying out a reduction by payment off of surplus capital. I know of no case where this method has, apart from agreement, been departed from . . .

In the result, I am of opinion that the present appeal should be allowed and the proposed reduction confirmed, the application being otherwise in order.

ASQUITH LJ delivered a concurring judgment.

EVERSHED LJ dissented.

[This decision was affirmed by the House of Lords: *Prudential Assurance Co Ltd v Chatterley-Whitfield Collieries Ltd* [1949] AC 512.]

No separate class meetings are necessary to approve a reduction of capital if priority is given to the different classes in accordance with the terms on which they were issued.

[8.04] Re Saltdean Estate Co Ltd [1968] 1 WLR 1844 (Chancery Division)

The company's preferred shareholders were entitled to participate in the 'balance of profits' in each year after a 10% preferred dividend and an equivalent sum in dividends on the ordinary shares had been paid; but in a winding up they had no right to participate in surplus capital. The ordinary shareholders controlled the voting. The court was asked to confirm a reduction of capital which was to be effected by paying off the preferred shares at 75p per 50p share. The reduction was approved by the court, which ruled that there was no 'variation' of the preferred shareholders' rights which would call for approval by a separate class meeting.

BUCKLEY J: [It] is said that the proposed cancellation of the preferred shares will constitute an abrogation of all the rights attached to those shares which cannot validly be effected without an extraordinary resolution of a class meeting of preferred shareholders under article 8 of the company's articles. In my judgment, that article has no application to a cancellation of shares on a reduction of capital which is in accord with the rights attached to the shares of the company. Unless this reduction can be shown to be unfair to the preferred shareholders on other grounds, it is in accordance with the right and liability to prior repayment of capital attached to their shares. The liability to prior repayment on a reduction of capital, corresponding to their right to prior return of capital in a winding up is a liability of a kind of which Lord Greene MR [in the *Chatterley-Whitfield* case **[8.03]**] said that anyone has only himself to blame if he does not know it. It is part of the bargain between the shareholders and forms an integral part of the definition or delimitation of the bundle of rights which make up a preferred share. Giving effect to it does not involve the variation or abrogation of any right attached to such a share. Nor, in my judgment, has s 72 of the Companies Act 1948 [CA 2006 s 633], upon which the opponents place some reliance, any application to this case. That section relates to variation of rights attached to shares, not to cancellation of shares . . .

The fact is that every holder of preferred shares of the company has always been at risk that his hope of participating in undrawn or future profits of the company might be frustrated at any time by a liquidation of the company or a reduction of its capital properly resolved upon by a sufficient majority of his fellow members. This vulnerability is, and always has been, a characteristic of the preferred shares. Now that the event has occurred, none of the preferred shareholders can, in my judgment, assert that the resulting state of affairs is unfair to him.

For these reasons the opposition to this petition, in my judgment, fails.

> Notes

1. In *House of Fraser plc v ACGE Investments Ltd* [1987] AC 387, [1987] BCLC 478, HL, the House of Lords endorsed the above decision, and approved the following passage from one of the judgments in the court below (1987 SLT 273 at 278):

> In our opinion the proposed cancellation of the preference shares would involve fulfilment or satisfaction of the contractual rights of the shareholders, and would not involve any variation of their rights. Variation of a right presupposes the existence of the right, the variation of the right, and the subsequent continued existence of the right as varied. A different situation obtains where a right is fulfilled and satisfied and thereafter ceases to exist.

2. The above rulings do not apply where the company's articles of association expressly provide that the rights attached to a class of shares shall be deemed to be varied by a reduction of the capital paid up on the shares. A separate class meeting must then be held: *Re Northern Engineering Industries plc* [1994] 2 BCLC 704, CA.

> Questions

1. How do these decisions relate to the statutory provision in CA 2006 s 630, especially s 630(6) which indicates that references to a 'variation' of class rights is taken to include references to 'abrogation'? (See Chapter 9, pp 433 ff.)

2. If the company has a *shortfall* of capital, how should a capital reduction be implemented as between the company's ordinary shareholders (class A), preference shareholders with a preferential right to both a dividend and a return of capital on a winding up (class B), and preference shareholders with only a preferential right to a dividend (class C)?

3. If the company has a *surplus* of capital, how should a capital reduction be implemented as between the company's ordinary shareholders (class A), preference shareholders with a preferential right to both a dividend and a return of capital on a winding up (class B), and preference shareholders with only a preferential right to a dividend (class C)?

A shareholder voting at a class meeting held in connection with a reduction of capital must have regard to the interests of the class of shareholders as a whole.

[8.05] Re Holders Investment Trust Ltd [1971] 1 WLR 583 (Chancery Division)

The company petitioned for confirmation of a reduction of capital, under which it was proposed to cancel its redeemable preference shares and to allot to the holders an equivalent amount of unsecured loan stock.[8] The reduction was approved by both a special resolution of the company and an extraordinary resolution of a separate class meeting of the preference shareholders. At the latter meeting, some 90% of the votes cast were held by certain trustees (referred to in the judgment as 'the supporting trustees') who also held about 52% of the ordinary stocks and shares, and in that respect stood to gain substantially from the reduction. Megarry J held that the vote at the class meeting was ineffectual, because the majority preference shareholders had considered their own interests, without regard to what was best for the preference shareholders as a class.

MEGARRY J: Unopposed petitions by a company for the confirmation of a reduction of capital are a commonplace of the Companies' Court; but an opposed petition such as the one I have before me is a comparative rarity . . .

---

[8] A company, in reducing its capital, is not bound to pay off its shareholders in cash: see *Ex p Westburn Sugar Refineries Ltd* [1951] AC 625, HL.

Put briefly, Mr Drake's opposition to the confirmation of the reduction is twofold. First, he contends that the extraordinary resolution of the preference shareholders was not valid and effectual because the supporting trustees did not exercise their votes in the way that they ought to have done, namely, in the interests of the preference shareholders as a whole. Instead, being owners of much ordinary stock and many shares as well, they voted in such a way as to benefit the totality of the stocks and shares that they held. Secondly, Mr Drake contends that even if the extraordinary resolution was valid, the terms on which the reduction of capital is to be effected are not fair, in particular in that the increase in the rate of interest from 5% to 6% is not an adequate recompense for having the right of repayment or redemption postponed from 31 July 1971, until at earliest 31 October 1985, and at latest some unspecified date in 1990. I may say at the outset that it is common ground that the proposed reduction is not in accordance with the class rights of the preference shareholders . . .

[His Lordship referred to *Carruth v ICI Ltd*,[9] *British America Nickel Corpn Ltd v M J O'Brien Ltd* **[9.06]** and *Shuttleworth v Cox Bros & Co (Maidenhead) Ltd* **[5.09]** and continued:]

In the *British America* case, Viscount Haldane, in speaking for a strong Board of the Judicial Committee, referred to 'a general principle, which is applicable to all authorities conferred on majorities of classes enabling them to bind minorities; namely, that the power given must be exercised for the purpose of benefiting the class as a whole, and not merely individual members only . . .' The matter may, I think, be put in the way in which Scrutton LJ put it in the *Shuttleworth* case, where the question was the benefit of the company rather than of a particular class of members. Adapting his language . . . I have to see whether the majority was honestly endeavouring to decide and act for the benefit of the class as a whole, rather than with a view to the interests of some of the class and against that of others . . .

I pause here to point the obvious. Without guidance from those skilled in these matters, many members of a class may fail to realise what they should bear in mind when deciding how to vote at a class meeting. The beneficial owner of shares may well concentrate on his own personal interests: even though he regards the proposal per se as one to be rejected, collateral matters affecting other interests of his may lead him to vote in favour of the resolution. Trustees, too, are under a fiduciary duty to do the best they properly can for their beneficiaries. A proposal which, in isolation, is contrary to the interests of those owning the shares affected may nevertheless be beneficial to the beneficiaries by reason of the improved prospects that the proposal will confer on other shares in the company which the trustees hold on the same trusts: and that, in essence, is what is in issue here . . .

[His Lordship referred to correspondence between the 'supporting trustees' and their professional advisers, and continued:] That exchange of letters seems to me to make it perfectly clear that the advice sought, the advice given, and the advice acted upon, was all on the basis of what was for the benefit of the trusts as a whole, having regard to their large holdings of the equity capital. From the point of view of equity, and disregarding company law, this is a perfectly proper basis; but that is not the question before me. I have to determine whether the supporting trustees voted for the reduction in the bona fide belief that they were acting in the interests of the general body of members of that class. From first to last I can see no evidence that the trustees ever applied their minds to what under company law was the right question, or that they ever had the bona fide belief that is requisite for an effectual sanction of the reduction. Accordingly, in my judgment there has been no effectual sanction for the modification of class rights . . .

[His Lordship considered the evidence, and ruled that the reduction had not been shown to be fair to the preference shareholders. Accordingly, he refused to confirm the reduction.]

➤ Notes

1. This case was decided at common law, before the enactment of the statutory provisions on class rights which are now to be found in CA 2006 ss 630ff.

[9] [1937] AC 707.

2. In this case, Megarry J appears to have expected from the majority preference shareholders a 'detached altruism' which the court in such cases as *Mills v Mills* **[6.10]** dismissed as
unrealistic. See LS Sealy, 'Equitable and other fetters on the shareholder's freedom to vote,' in
NE Eastham and B Krivy (eds) *The Cambridge Lectures 1981*, attacking the rule as wrong.

Analogous transactions

The principle of *Trevor v Whitworth* **[8.06]** applies where the 'return' of capital to the shareholders is effected indirectly. For instance, if B holds redeemable preference shares in company A and by a tripartite arrangement (i) company A undertakes to redeem B's shares on a
certain date, (ii) C agrees that if A fails to do so it will buy the shares from B at the redemption price, and (iii) A promises C that it will redeem B's shares or in default of doing so pay C
damages equivalent to the redemption price, this will be treated as a return of B's capital and
the promise to pay damages as unlawful: *Barclays Bank plc v British and Commonwealth
Holdings plc* [1996] 1 BCLC 1 (on appeal, [1996] 1 BCLC 1 at 26, CA, but not on this issue)
(see below, p 425). For another illustration, see *Aveling Barford Ltd v Perion Ltd* **[8.14]**.

Redemptions and repurchases of shares

The general rule in CA 2006 s 658 is that a company is not permitted to acquire its own shares,
except in accordance with the Act. Any contravention is an offence committed by the company and by every officer in default, and the purported acquisition of shares is void. This provision confirms the rule established at common law by *Trevor v Whitworth* **[8.06]**, which
recognised the issue was not a domestic matter concerned with compliance with the articles,
or even a question of *vires* dependent upon the powers set out in the memorandum, but a
matter of legality under the Companies Act itself.

   In fact, both law and practice in this area have moved well away from the restrictive attitudes
embodied in the general rule. This is because the general prohibition is subject to a number
of substantial statutory exceptions, the most significant being the various rules permitting
companies to *redeem* and to *repurchase* their own shares in defined circumstances. It is
now quite common to see listed public companies advertise billion pound on-market and off-
market share buy-backs, usually at a discount to the market price. The exercise demonstrates
the company's commitment to capital discipline, and the terms maximise the economic value
for the remaining shareholders, who benefit from the enhanced value of their shares through
increased value and returns attributable to each share. The repurchase is, in effect, a judgement by the company that its shares are undervalued and represent a better investment than
any available alternative acquisition of assets or investment in a business opportunity it owns
or to which it has access. Any redemption or repurchase effected otherwise than in full compliance with the statutory rules will not displace the general prohibition, however, so the purported transaction will be void. This makes it important to address the technical details of the
Act very carefully. The repurchased shares are either cancelled or held by the company as so
called 'treasury shares' until cancelled or other permitted disposal (see p 402 below)

General rule: it is illegal for a company to acquire its own shares, except as provided in CA 2006.

[8.06] Trevor v Whitworth (1887) 12 App Cas 409, House of Lords

LORD WATSON: . . . One of the main objects contemplated by the legislature, in restricting the power
of limited companies to reduce the amount of their capital as set forth in the memorandum, is to

protect the interests of the outside public who may become their creditors. In my opinion the effect of these statutory restrictions is to prohibit every transaction between a company and a shareholder, by means of which the money already paid to the company in respect of his shares is returned to him, unless the court has sanctioned the transaction. Paid-up capital may be diminished or lost in the course of the company's trading; that is a result which no legislation can prevent; but persons who deal with, and give credit to a limited company, naturally rely upon the fact that the company is trading with a certain amount of capital already paid, as well as upon the responsibility of its members for the capital remaining at call; and they are entitled to assume that no part of the capital which has been paid into the coffers of the company has been subsequently paid out, except in the legitimate course of its business.

When a share is forfeited or surrendered, the amount which has been paid upon it remains with the company, the shareholder being relieved of liability for future calls, whilst the share itself reverts to the company, bears no dividend, and may be re-issued. When shares are purchased at par, and transferred to the company, the result is very different. The amount paid up on the shares is returned to the shareholder; and in the event of the company continuing to hold the shares (as in the present case) is permanently withdrawn from its trading capital. It appears to me that . . . it is inconsistent with the essential nature of a company that it should become a member of itself. It cannot be registered as a shareholder to the effect of becoming debtor to itself for calls, or of being placed on the list of contributories in its own liquidation . . .

General exceptions to the prohibition in CA 2006 s 658

CA 2006 s 659 provides particular exceptions to the general prohibition in s 658.

These include instances where the company's *fully paid* shares are acquired for no consideration, so there is no detriment to creditors because the company's legal capital is unaffected.

It also includes instances where a court has ordered or approved the acquisition (eg by way of formal reduction of capital (see above), or by court order following complaints of unfair prejudice (see below, pp 552 ff)), or where the company has acquired its shares by forfeiture or surrender for non-payment of calls.[10]

Shares so acquired by a *public* company or by a nominee on its behalf must normally be cancelled within a maximum period of three years (one year in the case of shares which have been purchased by third parties with direct or indirect financial assistance from the company (see below, pp 403 ff)), and the company's share capital reduced accordingly, and pending cancellation or disposal no voting rights may be exercised in respect of those shares (s 662). If this were permitted, the directors of the company would have a voting power disproportionate to their personal stake as shareholders. (We may quite reasonably ask why these rules, including the prohibition on voting, are restricted to public companies.)

Redeemable shares

CA 2006 s 684 permits a company to issue redeemable shares if authorised by its articles (public companies) or if not prohibited by its articles (private companies), and so long as the company also has issued shares that are not redeemable.

CA 2006 ss 685–689 provide rules for the issue and redemption of such shares. Note that:

(i)   the terms on which redeemable shares are issued is determined by the directors, provided they are authorised by the articles or by an ordinary resolution (even if this ordinary resolution effects a change to the articles) (s 685);

(ii)   shares cannot be redeemed unless they are fully paid (s 686);

---

[10] There is no return of capital to the member in such cases: the company keeps whatever payments have already been made on the shares, and under the terms of the company's articles the forfeited shares may normally be re-issued to another holder.

(iii) the shares must be paid for in full on redemption, unless the agreement between the company and holder allows for deferred payment (s 686);

(iv) private companies can redeem shares out of capital (although only subject to the onerous condition in ss 709–723, including a requirement for a directors' statement and an auditor's report, and a right for members and creditors to apply to court for the cancellation of the resolution); public companies must redeem out of distributable profits (see below, pp 416 ff) or from the proceeds of a new share issue made for the purpose (s 687);

(v) redeemed shares must then be cancelled, and the company must reduce its issued share capital by the nominal value of the cancelled shares (s 688);

(vi) to the extent that the redemption is made out of profits, the company must also transfer an amount equivalent to the nominal value of the redeemed shares to a new capital account called the 'capital redemption reserve', which can only be reduced by transfer to the share capital account to pay up fully paid bonus shares, or otherwise as if it were part of the paid up share capital (s 733). In effect, this means that the company must have available a surplus equivalent to double the funds needed to effect the repurchase, and one half has to be set aside and treated as capital thereafter.

(vii) there are extensive disclosure provisions.

Repurchase of shares

The essential difference between a *repurchase* and a *redemption* is as follows: in the former, the buyer and seller need to agree to the terms and conditions of repurchase at the time of the repurchase; whereas with the latter, the shares will have been issued as redeemable shares, so that the terms and conditions of the re-acquisition will be known from the outset. Subject to that essential difference, however, the two transactions are treated by the CA 2006 in broadly similar ways.

A company's power to repurchase its own shares is broad: subject to any constraints or prohibitions in the company's articles, a company may repurchase its shares in accordance with the rules set out in CA 2006 ss 690ff.

Again, it is necessary to pay strict attention to the detailed wording of the Act itself, although with the warning that these sections are long-winded and not easy to follow. Note that different rules apply to:

(i) a purchase by a company of its own shares *off the market*: a special resolution is necessary, and for public companies this authority cannot be granted for longer than 18 months (ss 694, 697, 700); the shareholders whose shares are to be repurchased cannot be counted in the vote (ss 695, 698);

(ii) a purchase by a (public) company of its own shares *on the market*: an ordinary resolution is required (s 701); the authority granted may be general or specific, and unconditional or conditional, but this authority cannot be granted for longer than 18 months.

Note, too, that:

(i) the company's right to repurchase its shares cannot be assigned (s 704);

(ii) shares cannot be repurchased unless fully paid (s 691);

(iii) the shares must be paid for in full at the time of repurchase (s 691);

(iv) the permitted sources of the purchase funds for repurchases by private and public companies are the same as for redemptions (see above) (ss 692, 705), and when a private company uses capital to fund the purchase a declaration of solvency is needed;

(v) the rules on creation of a capital redemption reserve are the same as for redemptions (see above) (s 733);

(vi) the repurchased shares must be cancelled, and the company must reduce its issued share capital by the nominal value of the cancelled shares, *unless* the shares can be held and dealt with as '*treasury shares*'[11] in accordance with ss 724ff (s 706), and no more than 10% or the nominal value of the issued share capital of the relevant class can be held in this way (s 725);

(vii) there are extensive disclosure provisions.

Protection of shareholders

The rules discussed in this section are primarily aimed at protecting creditors while allowing companies to use their resources in an efficient and financially sensible manner. But the rules have built in protections for both exiting and remaining shareholders that are worth noting:

(i) Share redemptions: these work largely on the 'buyer beware' principle, since the exiting shareholder is aware of the exit terms before the shares are purchased, and the ordinary shareholders are assumed to know that the company may issue such shares (either as a general power (private companies), or as expressly permitted in the articles (public companies)).

(ii) Share repurchases: agreement to the terms of the repurchase is a matter of choice for the exiting shareholder, who cannot be forced to exit; and the non-exiting ordinary shareholders are protected, either by majority vote plus normal on-market purchase rules, or by the protective requirement for a special resolution for off-market repurchases; and in both cases the intending exiting shareholders cannot vote in these general meetings. This is a rare formal protection in the context of shareholder voting.

➤ Notes

1. A statutory rule which has some links with these principles is that contained in CA 2006 s 136. This states that a company cannot itself be a member of a company which is its holding company, either directly or through a nominee (s 144).[12] The weakness of this provision, however, is that it is confined in its operation to 'holding companies' and their subsidiaries as these terms are defined by ss 1159ff. There is nothing in these definitions which stops company A from owning 40% of the shares in company B, which itself has 40% of the shares in company A. If a majority of the board of each of the two companies consists of the same persons, they can usually, in practice, wield unrestricted control of both companies, regardless of the size of their own individual shareholdings.

2. In *Acatos & Hutcheson plc v Watson* [1995] BCLC 446 it was held not to be unlawful for a company, A & H plc, to acquire all of the shares in another company, A Ltd, whose only asset was a 29.4% shareholding in A & H plc itself, even though it would not have been legitimate for it to have bought these latter shares directly.

3. Analogous to the acquisition of its own shares by a company is the taking of security over them. This, too, is forbidden by the Act in the case of *public* companies: see s 670, although there are exceptions when (a) the charge is to secure calls on partly-paid shares, or (b) it is an ordinary business dealing by a money-lending company.

➤ Questions

1. In the example given above, in which A Ltd and B Ltd have cross-shareholdings of 40 per cent in each other, why is it that the board will usually have *de facto* control?

2. Is there any infringement of the principle of maintenance of capital in such a case?

---

[11] Treasury shares cannot vote or receive dividends (other than by way of bonus shares); they can be sold (or used to fund a bonus issue or employee share scheme), or may be cancelled (ss 726–731).

[12] There are exceptions for subsidiaries acting as personal representatives or trustees, or as authorised dealers in securities.

Financial assistance by a company for the acquisition of its own shares

Another statutory rule that has links with the maintenance of capital principle is that contained in CA 2006 s 678, which imposes a prohibition against a *public* company or any of its subsidiaries[13] giving financial assistance to a person directly or indirectly for the purpose of an acquisition of its own shares.[14] Contravention of the prohibition constitutes an offence committed by every officer who is in default, and, more surprisingly, also by the company whose protection the section is intended to promote.

Before the introduction of the 2006 Act, the prohibition applied to all companies, although private companies had their own special 'whitewash' procedures which enabled them to avoid the application of the rule in certain circumstances. The exclusion of private companies from the prohibition means that there is no inhibition, at least from this source,[15] for private company 'management buy-outs' and other 'hiving-down' arrangements, under which a business or part of it is sold off to the existing managers or to similar entrepreneurial figures who wish to become owner-executives of the business but cannot finance the purchase except through the direct or indirect use of the company's own assets as security.

The general prohibition on the giving of financial assistance by a public company is required by the Second Company Law Directive (77/91/EEC). The prohibition in the UK Act extends to post-acquisition assistance (see s 678(3)), although only if the company in which the shares were acquired is a public company at the time that the assistance is given.[16]

'Financial assistance' is defined in s 677, and includes any provision by the public company (or its subsidiaries) of assistance by way of gifts, loans, security arrangements, guarantees, and indeed any arrangements where the company fulfils its side of deal but those of the other party remain unfulfilled. There is also a catch all provision that includes 'any other financial assistance given by the company' where the company has no net assets, or where the net assets of the company are reduced to a material extent.

Examples of the kind of transaction in question are where the public company (or its subsidiary):

(i)   lends money to A to put A in funds so that he can buy shares from an existing member;

(ii)   guarantees B's bank overdraft, and on the security of this the bank advances money to B so that he can buy shares in the company;

(iii)   lends money to C so that C can repay a loan provided earlier by C's bank which C has already used to buy shares in the company;

(iv)   buys an asset from D, on terms that materially reduce the net assets of the company, so that D can use the purchase money she receives to pay for shares in the company that she has agreed to buy.

---

[13] But not a subsidiary which is a foreign company: CA 2006 s 1(1), as applied to s 678, and giving effect to *Arab Bank plc v Mercantile Holdings Ltd* [1994] Ch 71 (Millett J).

[14] There is also a prohibition on the provision of financial assistance by a *public* company subsidiary for the acquisition of shares in its *private* holding company (s 689).

[15] Although of course there are other control mechanisms: eg, directors' duties (pp 273 ff), 'wrongful trading' provisions (pp 671 ff), and other CA 2006 and IA 1986 rules.

[16] It follows that where a company has re-registered as a private company since the shares were acquired and is a private company at the time the post-acquisition assistance is given, the prohibition will not apply. On the other hand, if at the time the shares were acquired the company was a private company, but at the time the post-acquisition assistance is given it has re-registered as a public company, the prohibition will apply.

The same kind of assistance can readily occur in a take-over: the person who seeks to buy all the shares, or a controlling block of shares, in a company may wish to use some of the company's own funds or assets to pay for the shares or provide security for their price.

If, in examples (i) to (iii) above, the purchaser of the shares repays the money he or she has borrowed, then no harm may be done. However, the risk is that the loan may never be repaid or that the bank may enforce the guarantee against the company after the customer has defaulted so that the company will have lost money which was part of its capital. Indeed, it may have been lost in favour of one of its shareholders so that the 'maintenance of capital' rule is infringed. Similar consequences necessarily follow in (iv) if the asset is not worth what the company has paid D for it. So it is not surprising that a statutory prohibition similar to s 678 has been in the Companies Acts since 1929.

Earlier versions of this provision (before 1981) were both much wider in their terms and notorious for the uncertainty of their language, which seemed to catch many quite innocent transactions. Responsible lending institutions and professional advisers were unwilling to be associated with schemes which might offend against the vague wording of the statute, and so companies were often prevented from taking a course of action which made good business sense and was not morally objectionable. At the same time, the relatively low penalty imposed for the offence was no real deterrent to the unscrupulous.

In 1981, amendments were made which were intended to define more precisely the conduct to be prohibited and introduce general and specific exemptions. These changes are all substantially carried forward in CA 2006 ss 677ff (apart from the provisions relating to private companies).

There is a *general exemption* from the prohibition on the giving of financial assistance: such assistance is not prohibited if (i) the principal purpose of the assistance is not for an acquisition of shares, *or* (ii) the assistance is incidental to some other larger purpose of the company, *and* (in either case) the assistance is given in good faith in the interests of the company (ss 678(2) and (4), 679(2) and (4)). There are also a number of types of financial assistance (eg the payment of lawful dividends) that are specifically allowed (s 681), and a number of transactions that are exempted subject to specified conditions (s 682).

The principal cases on the meaning of 'financial assistance' and the application of the general exemptions are all somewhat controversial. The words of the Act must remain the primary source of guidance. The cases below that deal with the civil consequences of an infringement of the statute arose under older versions of the statutory provisions, but may still be regarded as authoritative on the issues cited (although not on the application of the prohibition itself).

The meaning of 'financial assistance'

The test of financial assistance is one of commercial substance and reality.

[8.07] Chaston v SWP Group Ltd [2002] EWCA Civ 1999, [2003] 1 BCLC 675

This case was decided under the CA 1985 provisions. CA 2006 s 678 would not apply, since the target company was a private company, but the Court of Appeal's discussion of the meaning of 'financial assistance' remains relevant.

The company allegedly providing financial assistance was the subsidiary, DRC Polymer Products Ltd (DRC) and its parent was Dunstable Rubber Company Holdings Ltd (DRCH). Chaston (C) was a director and majority shareholder in DRC. SWP wished to acquire the DRC Group by acquiring the shares of the holding company, DRCH, and needed a due diligence report on the Group for its members. Work for this report was done by the accountants,

Deloitte and Touche (D&T). C agreed that D&T should invoice DRC for their fees for that work. It was not entirely clear whether DRC committed itself to pay the fees before the invoices were rendered, nor was it clear when the fees were paid by DRC.

The Court of Appeal held that the payment of D&T's fees by the subsidiary, DRC, was within the definition of unacceptable 'financial assistance' in CA 1985 s 152 [now CA 2006 s 677].

ARDEN LJ: . . . It is clear from the way in which s 151 and s 152 [CA 2006 ss 678 and 677] are drafted that it covers financial assistance in many forms apart from loans (see for example the wide wording of s 152(3)). The general mischief, however, remains the same, namely that the resources of the target company and its subsidiaries should not be used directly or indirectly to assist the purchaser financially to make the acquisition. This may prejudice the interests of the creditors of the target or its group, and the interests of any shareholders who do not accept the offer to acquire their shares or to whom the offer is not made.

Thus although s 152 proscribes a number of forms of financial assistance, it does not define the words 'financial assistance'. It is clear from the authorities that what matters is the commercial substance of the transaction: 'The words ["financial assistance"] have no technical meaning and their frame of reference is the language of ordinary commerce' (per Hoffmann J in *Charterhouse v Tempest Diesels* [see below], approved by the Court of Appeal in *Barclays Bank plc v British & Commonwealth Holdings plc* [1996] 1 BCLC 1 at 40).

. . . It is thus apparent that ss 151 to 153 distinguish between various categories of transactions. First, there are the categories of financial assistance listed in s 152(1)(a)(i) to (iii) [CA 2006 s 677(1)(a)-(c)] which are prohibited whether or not there is any diminution in net assets, unless s 153 applies [ie certain exemption provisions noted below]. Second, there is financial assistance of a kind not specifically mentioned in s 152(1)(a)(i) to (iii). This does not contravene s 151 [CA 2006 s 678] provided the company has positive net assets and the reduction in actual net assets is immaterial [CA 2006 s 677(1)(d)]. (Again, I leave to one side the case of companies with no net assets). Third, there are those which although carried out for the purpose of an acquisition of shares and have financial implications do not constitute financial assistance for the purposes of s 151. This category includes lawful dividends: see s 153(3) [CA 2006 s 681]. Fourth, there are transactions which although they constitute financial assistance within s 152(1)(a) are taken outside the prohibition in s 151 by the principal purpose defences in s 153(1) and (2) [CA 2006 s 678(2) and (4)]. Fifth, there are the transactions exempted by s 153(4), such as the lending of money by a money-lending company in the ordinary course of its business [CA 2006 s 682].

. . . Here as a commercial matter assistance was clearly given. D&T received payment for their services and both the purchaser and the vendors were relieved of any obligation to pay for this service themselves. Mr Cunningham submits that s 151 should be restricted to assistance given to purchasers, alternatively to assistance given to vendors and purchasers. However, in so far as that point matters in this case there is no mandate in my judgment for reading any such limitation in that section. There is no reason why assistance which is paid to a subsidiary or associated company or other person nominated by one of the parties to the transaction should not be assistance contrary to the section.

. . . Mr Cunningham made a further submission that there was a distinction to be drawn between financial assistance given in advance of a transaction and financial assistance given in the course of a transaction. As to the former, this was not prohibited. On this, he relied on the four cases referred to above. In my judgment, this distinction is not justified by s 151. It prohibits financial assistance given 'directly or indirectly' and those words are sufficiently wide to cover 'pre-transactional' financial assistance. Moreover, s 151(1) provides that a transaction can offend the section even though a person is only 'proposing' to acquire shares.

➤ Note

In this case it was irrelevant to the finding of financial assistance that:

(i)   The value of the fees (about £20,000) was trivial in comparison with the total consideration for the acquisition (about £2.55m).

(ii)   The assistance was not provided to the purchaser of the shares. The reality was that the instructions to D&T were given at least in part to enable SWP to conclude a due diligence exercise which was SWP's responsibility and for SWP's benefit and which should therefore have been paid by SWP. By paying for part of that exercise DRC had given financial assistance to SWP.

(iii)   There had been no financial detriment to the company being acquired, the financial assistance was not given in advance of nor in the course of the takeover, and the payment of the fees had no impact on the share price.

Further guidance on the meaning of 'financial assistance'

The cases noted below were all decided under the predecessors to CA 2006 ss 677 and 678, but to the extent that they discuss the meaning of 'financial assistance' they remain relevant to the interpretation of the 2006 Act.[17]

On its terms, *Chaston* [8.07] adopts a market-friendly test of financial assistance, looking to the 'commercial substance and reality' of the transaction; but in its application to the facts, the Court of Appeal's approach might lead to the conclusion that many transactions will fall foul of the provisions and will find no relief in the 'principal purpose' test.

Earlier and later cases have adopted a more 'commercial' approach, often finding as a matter of commercial reality that *no* financial assistance has been given. *Chaston* [8.07] may well come to be regarded as a high water mark, much like *Brady* [8.08] on the 'principal purpose'/ 'main purpose' exceptions. See:

(i)   *Charterhouse Investment Trust Ltd v Tempest Diesels Ltd* [1986] BCLC 1: This case was decided under the repealed CA 1948 s 54, and concerned a 'management buy-out' transaction under which Charterhouse hived off a subsidiary company, Tempest, by selling its entire shareholding to one of its managers, Allam. Hoffmann J was asked to decide whether a surrender of tax losses by Tempest to Charterhouse, as part of the transaction, constituted financial assistance. In ruling that it did not, he said:

> . . . There is no definition of giving financial assistance in the section, although some examples are given. The words have no technical meaning and their frame of reference is in my judgment the language of ordinary commerce. One must examine the commercial realities of the transaction and decide whether it can properly be described as the giving of financial assistance by the company, bearing in mind that the section is a penal one and should not be strained to cover transactions which are not fairly within it.
>
> The *Belmont* case [8.10] indicates that the sale of an asset by the company at a fair value can properly be described as giving financial assistance if the effect is to provide the purchaser of its shares with the cash needed to pay for them. It does not matter that the company's balance sheet is undisturbed in the sense that the cash paid out is replaced by an asset of equivalent value. In the case of a loan by a company to a creditworthy purchaser of its shares, the balance sheet is equally undisturbed but the loan plainly constitutes giving financial assistance. It follows that if the only or main purpose of such a transaction is to enable the purchaser to buy the shares, the section is contravened. But the *Belmont* case is of limited assistance in deciding whether or not an altogether different transaction amounts to giving financial assistance.

---

[17] In applying those findings to cases concerning acquisitions of shares in *private* companies, however, they have been superseded by CA 2006 s 678.

The need to look at the commercial realities means that one cannot consider the surrender letter [relating to the tax losses] in isolation. Although it constituted a collateral contract, it was in truth part of a composite transaction under which Tempest both received benefits and assumed burdens. It is necessary to look at this transaction as a whole and decide whether it constituted the giving of financial assistance by Tempest. This must involve a determination of where the net balance of financial advantage lay. I see no contradiction between this view and anything which was said in the *Belmont* case. In *Belmont* the company made cash available to the purchaser. This amounted to giving financial assistance and no less so because it was done without any net transfer of value by the company. On the facts of this case there is no question of cash being provided and the only way in which it can even plausibly be suggested that Tempest gave financial assistance is if it made a net transfer of value which reduced the price Mr Allam would have had to pay for the shares if the transaction as a whole had not taken place.

(ii) *M T Realisations Ltd v Digital Equipment Co Ltd* [2003] EWCA Civ 494, [2003] 2 BCLC 117: the Court of Appeal held that there was no financial assistance in breach of CA 1985 s 151, since the chosen method of arranging the share purchase reflected the commercial realities of the deal, not some disguised form of financial assistance. The claimant, MTR, was a subsidiary in the Digital group of companies, which were suppliers of computer equipment. MTR was loss-making and insolvent. It owed £8m to another company in the group, repayable on demand. MTI bought all the shares in MTR from Digital for £1, and also bought the £8m loan for £6.5m, payable in instalments. The facts are complicated, but the fundamental claim was that when money due to MTR was paid to MTI and then used by MTI to pay the loan instalments to Digital, financial assistance was given for the purchase of MTR's shares. The Court of Appeal rejected the argument on the basis that: (i) it was never claimed that the shares were worth more than £1, or that MTI could not afford £1, so no assistance was needed; (ii) the liability to make the loan repayments was not incurred for the purpose of acquiring the shares; and (iii) when MTR made payments to MTI under the loan agreement, it was only paying a debt which it already owed before any of the acquisition dealings were commenced.

(iii) *Dyment v Boyden* [2004] EWCA Civ 1586, [2005] 1 WLR 792, CA: the applicant and the two respondents entered into partnership to run a residential care home. The real property was owned by the partners in equal shares. The business was operated through a company, and the partners were each directors of the company. The company's registration under the Registered Homes Act 1984 was cancelled by the local authority when one of the respondents was charged with assault. The partnership was then dissolved by an agreement under which the respondents transferred their shares in the company to the applicant who in turn transferred her interest in the property to the respondents, who then granted a 21-year lease of the property to the company at a rental well above the market rate. The applicant contended that payment of the additional rent above the market rate was 'financial assistance' because it had the effect of reducing the company's net assets to a material extent, and since that assistance had been given in relation to a transaction involving the acquisition by the applicant of the respondents' shares it had therefore been given either directly or indirectly for the purposes of that acquisition, contrary to s 151(1). The Court of Appeal affirmed the finding of the trial judge that the rent insisted on by the respondents was simply not linked to the acquisition of the shares, and not agreed 'for the purpose of' acquiring the shares.

Exceptions to the statutory prohibition

Recall the statutory exceptions noted above, p 404. Here the focus is on the 'purpose' exceptions.

Proof by the company that the 'principal purpose' is not the acquisition of shares, or that the acquisition is merely 'an incidental part of a larger purpose' requires proof of something more than an alternative reason why the transaction was entered into.

[8.08] Brady v Brady [1989] AC 755, [1988] 2 All ER 617 (House of Lords)

A group of companies run by the Brady brothers, Bob and Jack, had a haulage and drinks business in Barrow-in-Furness. Following differences between the two brothers, it was agreed that they should divide the business in two, Jack taking the haulage side and Bob the drinks side. A complex scheme of reconstruction was drawn up under which drinks business assets were transferred from the principal company ('Brady') to a new company controlled by Bob. Jack, (through his company Motoreal) acquired his brother's shares in Brady. This transfer, it was conceded, involved the giving of financial assistance by Brady towards discharging the liability of its holding company ('Motoreal') for the price of shares which Motoreal had purchased in Brady, and so there was a *prima facie* infringement of CA 1985 s 151 [CA 2006 s 678]. Accordingly, when Jack brought proceedings for specific performance of the agreement, Bob (who had had second thoughts) argued that the transaction was illegal.[18] However, Jack contended that the financial assistance was an incidental part of a larger purpose of the company, namely the resolution of the conflict and deadlock between the brothers which was paralysing its business and threatening to lead to its liquidation, so that the exception set out in s 153(2)(a) [CA 2006 s 678(2)] applied. The House of Lords rejected this argument: the alleged 'larger purpose' was nothing more than the reason why the transaction was entered into. However, it ruled that an order for specific performance should be made because Brady was a solvent private company and could lawfully give financial assistance by following the procedure prescribed by ss 155–158 [abolished by CA 2006, since s 678 no longer applies to private companies].

LORD OLIVER OF AYLMERTON: Where I part company both from the trial judge and from the Court of Appeal is on the question of whether para (a) [of CA 1985 s 153(2), now CA 2006 s 678(2)] can, on any reasonable construction of the subsection, be said to have been satisfied. As O'Connor LJ observed, the section is not altogether easy to construe. It first appeared as part of s 42 of the Companies Act 1981 and it seems likely that it was introduced for the purpose of dispelling any doubts resulting from the query raised in *Belmont Finance Corpn Ltd v Williams Furniture Ltd (No 2)* [8.10] whether a transaction entered into partly with a genuine view to the commercial interests of the company and partly with a view to putting a purchaser of shares in the company in funds to complete his purchase was in breach of s 54 of the Companies Act 1948. The ambit of the operation of the section is, however, far from easy to discern, for the word 'purpose' is capable of several different shades of meaning. This much is clear, that para (a) is contemplating two alternative situations. The first envisages a principal and, by implication, a subsidiary purpose [CA 2006 s 678(2)(a)]. The inquiry here is whether the assistance given was principally in order to relieve the purchaser of shares in the company of his indebtedness resulting from the acquisition or whether it was principally for some other purpose—for instance, the acquisition from the purchaser of some asset which the company requires for its business. That is the situation envisaged by Buckley LJ in the course of his judgment in the *Belmont Finance* case as giving rise to doubts. That is not this case, for the purpose of the assistance here was simply and solely to reduce the indebtedness incurred by Motoreal . . . . The alternative situation is where it is not suggested that the financial assistance was intended to achieve any other object than the reduction or discharge of the indebtedness but where that result (ie the reduction or discharge) is merely incidental to some larger purpose of the company [CA 2006 s 678(2)(b)]. Those last three words are important. What has to be sought is

---

[18] It was also claimed that the transfer by Brady of its assets was *ultra vires*. In the Court of Appeal, Nourse LJ accepted this contention; but the House of Lords held that the transfer was within the company's objects.

some larger overall corporate purpose in which the resultant reduction or discharge is merely incidental. The trial judge found Brady's larger purpose to be that of freeing itself from the deadlock and enabling it to function independently and this was echoed in the judgment of O'Connor LJ where he observed that the answer 'embraces avoiding liquidation, preserving its goodwill and the advantages of an established business'. Croom-Johnson LJ found the larger purpose in the reorganisation of the whole group. My Lords, I confess that I have not found the concept of a 'larger purpose' easy to grasp, but if the paragraph is to be given any meaning that does not in effect provide a blank cheque for avoiding the effective application of s 151 in every case, the concept must be narrower than that for which the appellants contend.

The matter can, perhaps, most easily be tested by reference to s 153(1)(a) where the same formula is used. Here the words are 'or the giving of the assistance for that purpose' (ie the acquisition of shares) 'is but an incidental part of some larger purpose of the company'. The words 'larger purpose' must here have the same meaning as the same words in sub-s (2)(a). In applying sub-s (1)(a) one has, therefore, to look for some larger purpose in the giving of financial assistance than the mere purpose of the acquisition of the shares and to ask whether the giving of assistance is a mere incident of that purpose. My Lords, 'purpose' is, in some contexts, a word of wide content but in construing it in the context of the fasciculus of sections regulating the provision of finance by a company in connection with the purchase of its own shares there has always to be borne in mind the mischief against which s 151 is aimed. In particular, if the section is not, effectively, to be deprived of any useful application, it is important to distinguish between a purpose and the reason why a purpose is formed. The ultimate reason for forming the purpose of financing an acquisition may, and in most cases probably will, be more important to those making the decision than the immediate transaction itself. But 'larger' is not the same thing as 'more important' nor is 'reason' the same as 'purpose'. If one postulates the case of a bidder for control of a public company financing his bid from the company's own funds—the obvious mischief at which the section is aimed—the immediate purpose which it is sought to achieve is that of completing the purchase and vesting control of the company in the bidder. The reasons why that course is considered desirable may be many and varied. The company may have fallen on hard times so that a change of management is considered necessary to avert disaster. It may merely be thought, and no doubt would be thought by the purchaser and the directors whom he nominates once he has control, that the business of the company will be more profitable under his management than it was heretofore. These may be excellent reasons but they cannot, in my judgment, constitute a 'larger purpose' of which the provision of assistance is merely an incident. The purpose and the only purpose of the financial assistance is and remains that of enabling the shares to be acquired and the financial or commercial advantages flowing from the acquisition, whilst they may form the reason for forming the purpose of providing assistance, are a by-product of it rather than an independent purpose of which the assistance can properly be considered to be an incident. Now of course in the instant case the reason why the reorganisation was conceived in the first place was the damage being occasioned to the company and its shareholders by reason of the management deadlock, and the deadlock was the reason for the decision that the business should be split in two, so that the two branches could be conducted independently. What prompted the particular method adopted for carrying out the split was the commercial desirability of keeping Brady in being as a corporate entity. That involved, in effect, Jack buying out Bob's interest in Brady and it was, presumably, the fact that he did not have free funds to do this from his own resources that dictated that Brady's own assets should be used for the purpose. No doubt the acquisition of control by Jack was considered, at any rate by Jack and Robert [Jack's nephew], who were and are Brady's directors, to be beneficial to Brady. Indeed your Lordships have been told that the business has thrived under independent management. But this is merely the result, and no doubt the intended result, of Jack's assumption of control and however one analyses the transaction the only purpose that can be discerned in the redemption of loan stock is the payment in tangible form of the price payable to enable the Brady shares to be acquired and ultimately vested in Jack or a company controlled by him. The scheme of reorganisation was framed and designed to give Jack and Robert control of Brady for the best of reasons, but to say that the 'larger purpose' of Brady's financial assistance is to be found in the scheme of reorganisation itself is to say only that the larger purpose was the acquisition of the Brady shares on their behalf. For my part, I do not think that a larger purpose can be found in the benefits considered to be likely to flow or the disadvantages considered to be likely to be avoided by the acquisition which it was the purpose of the assistance to facilitate. The acquisition was not a mere incident of the scheme devised to break the deadlock. It was the essence of the scheme itself and the object which the scheme set out to achieve. In my judgment therefore, sub-s (2)(a) of s 153 is not satisfied and if the matter rested there the appeal ought to fail on that ground.

[His Lordship went on to hold that, since the transaction involved a private company, an order for specific performance could be made, the parties being directed to follow the 'whitewash' procedure in CA 1985 ss 155–158.[19]]

LORDS KEITH OF KINKEL, HAVERS, TEMPLEMAN and GRIFFITHS concurred.

➤ Note

This was regarded a very restrictive interpretation of statutory provisions which, it had been widely believed, were intended not only to clarify the former law but also to make it possible for many routine business transactions—some of them of long-standing—to go ahead without the fear that they might be illegal because they incidentally involved a breach of the financial assistance rule. This uncertainty is very costly—it has been estimated that well over £20m a year is spent on obtaining legal advice in an endeavour to ensure that proposed transactions do not fall foul of 'financial assistance' prohibitions. In consequence, there has been a demand ever since *Brady* for further reform of the law. That has been given, at least to some extent, by CA 2006. *Brady*, being concerned with a private company, would now not be caught by the prohibition at all. But the uncertainty in interpreting the 'purpose' exceptions, as illustrated by *Brady*, unfortunately remains in full. The reason given is that, at least for public companies, the UK must keep in place a provision sufficiently strong to meet the requirements of the Second EC Directive.

Consequences when a transaction breaches the prohibition

The only statutory sanction for breaching the financial assistance prohibition is that an offence is committed by the company and by every officer of the company who is in default (being an offence that can lead to a prison term): CA 2006 s 680. Note that criminal liability is imposed on the company itself, even though the provisions are allegedly designed to *protect* the company against disposal of its assets.

In practice the civil consequences are usually even more important, but for a time they seemed more troubling. The difficulty arose from the wording of the section (which has not changed in successive re-enactments): instead of making it illegal for the purchaser to *accept* financial assistance, CA 2006 s 678 makes it illegal *for the company* (or its subsidiary) to *give* financial assistance. This suggested to some judges that the object was not to protect the company, but to punish it, and for a while the consequences of illegality were analysed in that rather counter-intuitive way.[20]

[19] Given the detailed legal examination that this problem must have been subjected to, it seems remarkable that no one had thought of this option well before the case was concluded in the House of Lords.
[20] See especially the much criticised case of *Victor Battery Co Ltd v Curry's Ltd* [1946] Ch 242. This case has now been disapproved or not followed in a series of subsequent cases, and is accepted as wrong.

A transaction which infringes CA 2006 s 678 is illegal and unenforceable by either party.

[8.09] Re Hill and Tyler Ltd (in administration) [2004] EWHC 1261, [2005] 1 BCLC 41

[The facts are immaterial.]

RICHARD SHELDON QC: The argument can be broken down into three questions: (1) Is a contract involving the provision of financial assistance in contravention of s 151 [CA 2006, s 678], even where the whitewash procedure is available but not properly complied with, void and unenforceable as a matter of statutory interpretation of s 151? (2) If not, under the common law, is such a contract illegal as to its formation? (3) If not, is such a contract illegal as to its performance?

I consider first whether every contract which constitutes financial assistance within s 151 is rendered void and unenforceable as a matter of statutory interpretation. In Chitty on Contracts (29th edn) paras 16–141 to 16–146 the following is stated (citations omitted):

> 'Unenforceability by statute . . . arises where a statute itself on its true construction deprives one or both of the parties of their civil remedies under the contract in addition to, or instead of, imposing a penalty upon them. If the statute does so, it is irrelevant whether the parties meant to break the law or not . . .' (para 16–141) 'where the statute is silent as to the civil rights of the parties but penalises the making or performance of the contract, the courts consider whether the Act, on its true construction, is intended to avoid contracts of the class to which the particular contract belongs or whether it merely prohibits the doing of some particular act . . . it is important to note that where a contract or its performance is implicated with breach of statute this does not entail that the contract is avoided. Where the Act does not expressly deprive the plaintiff of his civil remedies under the contract the appropriate question to ask is whether, having regard to the Act and the evils against which it was intended to guard and the circumstances in which the contract was made and to be performed, it would in fact be against public policy to enforce it.' (para 16–145)
>
> 'If, on the true construction of the statute, "the contract be rendered illegal, it can make no difference, in point of law, whether the statute which makes it so has in mind the protection of the revenue or any other object. The sole question is whether the statute means to prohibit the contract". If, on the other hand, the object of the statute is the protection of the public from possible injury or fraud, or is the promotion of some object of public policy, the inference is that contracts made in contravention of its provisions are prohibited.' (para 16–146)

Applying these principles, and having regard to the mischief to which s 151 is directed, I consider that contracts which are entered into in breach of s 151 are rendered illegal by that section. The section provides that it is 'not lawful' for a company to give financial assistance directly or indirectly for the purpose of the acquisition of its own shares. It seems to me to follow that contracts which are entered into in contravention of that section are illegal. In consequence, such contracts are void and unenforceable. Although the consequences on an innocent party may be harsh, it is well recognised that the courts will not lend their assistance to transactions which are rendered unlawful by statute.

Although a company which is a party to a transaction which infringes CA 2006 s 678 cannot enforce the illegal contract, it is not prevented by law from suing others who have participated in the wrongdoing, eg in an action for damages for conspiracy.

[8.10] Belmont Finance Corpn Ltd v Williams Furniture Ltd [1979] Ch 250 (Court of Appeal)

It was alleged that four of the defendants, with the connivance of two of the three directors of the plaintiff company, had sold its property worth £60,000 for a price of £500,000 and that the four had then used the money to purchase all the issued shares in the plaintiff. The company claimed damages for conspiracy against the defendants. It was held that the company could sue, despite the fact that it had been itself a party to the transaction which infringed the statute.

BUCKLEY LJ: In the course of the argument in this court counsel for the first and second defendants conceded that the plaintiff company is entitled in this appeal to succeed on the conspiracy point, unless it is debarred from doing so on the ground that it was a party to the conspiracy, which was the ground that was relied upon by the judge.

The plaintiff company points out that the agreement was resolved on by a board of which the seventh and eighth defendants constituted the majority, and that they were the two directors who countersigned the plaintiff company's seal on the agreement, and that they are sued as two of the conspirators. It is conceded by Mr Miller [counsel] for the plaintiff company that a company may be held to be a participant in a criminal conspiracy, and that the illegality attending a conspiracy cannot relieve the company on the ground that such an agreement may be ultra vires; but he says that to establish a conspiracy to which the company was a party, having as its object the doing of an illegal act, it must be shown that the company must be treated as knowing all the facts relevant to the illegality; he relies on *R v Churchill*[21] . . . But I feel impelled to ask: can the plaintiff company sensibly be regarded as a party to the conspiracy, and in law ought it to be regarded as a party to the conspiracy?

Section 54 of CA 1948 [CA 2006 s 678] is designed for the protection of the relevant company whose shares are dealt with in breach of the section; that was so held in *Wallersteiner v Moir*.[22]

In the present case the object of the alleged conspiracy was to deprive the plaintiff company of over £400,000-worth of its assets, assuming always, of course, that it succeeds in establishing that allegation. The plaintiff company was the party at which the conspiracy was aimed. It seems to me that it would be very strange that it should also be one of the conspirators. The majority of the board which committed the company to carry out the project consisted of two of the alleged conspirators.

The judge said that the plaintiff company was a vital party to the agreement, and it could not be said that the other parties were conspirators but not the plaintiff company. With deference to the judge, who I think probably had very much less reference to authority in the course of the argument before him than we have had in this court, that view seems to me to be too simplistic a view, and not to probe far enough into the true circumstances of the case.

On the footing that the directors of the plaintiff company who were present at the board meeting on 11 October 1963 knew that the sale was at an inflated value, and that such value was inflated for the purpose of enabling the third, fourth, fifth and sixth defendants to buy the share capital of the plaintiff company, those directors must be taken to have known that the transaction was illegal under s 54.

It may emerge at a trial that the facts are not as alleged in the statement of claim, but if the allegations in the statement of claim are made good, the directors of the plaintiff company must then have known that the transaction was an illegal transaction.

---

[21] [1967] 2 AC 224 (sub nom *Churchill v Walton*).
[22] [1974] 1 WLR 991.

But in my view such knowledge should not be imputed to the company, for the essence of the arrangement was to deprive the company improperly of a larger part of its assets. As I have said, the company was a victim of the conspiracy. I think it would be irrational to treat the directors, who were allegedly parties to the conspiracy, notionally as having transmitted this knowledge to the company; and indeed it is a well-recognised exception from the general rule that a principal is affected by notice received by his agent that, if the agent is acting in fraud of his principal and the matter of which he has notice is relevant to the fraud, that knowledge is not to be imputed to the principal.

So in my opinion the plaintiff company should not be regarded as a party to the conspiracy, on the ground of lack of the necessary guilty knowledge.

GOFF LJ: [In] support of what Buckley LJ has said, I would wish to cite two short passages from *Wallersteiner v Moir*, the first passage is in the judgment of Lord Denning MR where he said:

In *Essex Aero Ltd v Cross*,[23] Harman LJ said: 'the section was not enacted for the company's protection, but for that of its creditors; . . . the company . . . cannot enforce it.' I do not agree. I think the section was passed so as to protect the company from having its assets misused. If it is broken, there is a civil remedy by way of an action for damages.

Scarman LJ spoke to the same effect and said:

There was, on these facts, a breach of duty by Dr Wallersteiner as a director. The companies were, also, in breach of the section. But the maxim 'potior est conditio defendentis' is of no avail to Dr Wallersteiner, for the section must have been enacted to protect company funds and the interests of shareholders as well as creditors. I do not agree with the dictum of Harman LJ in *Essex Aero Ltd v Cross* . . . to the effect that the section was enacted not for the company's protection but for that of its creditors.

ORR LJ delivered a concurring opinion.

A company which has been a party to a transaction which infringes CA 2006 s 678 may bring an action against its directors and other persons implicated for recovery of its property misapplied, on the grounds of breach of trust or constructive trust.

[8.11] Selangor United Rubber Estates Ltd v Cradock (No 3) [1968] 1 WLR 1555 (Chancery Division)

[The facts are immaterial to this part of the judgment.]

UNGOED-THOMAS J: Does [this] principle, however, prevent an action succeeding for breach of trust in doing what is illegal?

In *Steen v Law*[24] directors of a company, incorporated in New South Wales, lent the company's funds which the directors had to give financial assistance to purchase the company's shares. The liquidator of the company claimed that there had thus been a breach of a New South Wales section, which, so far as material, was in the terms of s 54 [CA 2006 s 678]; and that the directors had thereby committed a breach of their fiduciary duty to the company and should reimburse the company the sums so illegally applied. It was not contended that the directors were absolved from accounting by reason of the illegality of the loan by the company. Such illegality was clearly before the Privy Council and, if available against such a claim, provided a complete answer to it. Yet the point was neither taken by the defendants nor by the Privy Council; and it seems to me for the very good reason that the company was not relying for its claim on the unlawful loan and the relationship

[23] [1961] CA Transcript 388.
[24] [1964] AC 287.

of creditor and debtor thereby created, but upon the misapplication by the directors of the company's moneys by way of the unlawful loan. That is the position with regard to the plaintiff company's claim in our case. It was founding its claim, as in our case, not on a wrong done by it as a party to the unlawful loan, but as a wrong done to it by parties owing a fiduciary duty to it. The courts were being invited, as in our case, not to aid illegality but to condemn it. If this were not so, the courts would give redress to companies against directors for misapplication and breach of fiduciary duty which did not involve the company in illegality, but no redress if they were so serious as to involve the company in illegality.

I appreciate that, in the ordinary case of a claim by a beneficiary against a trustee for an illegal breach of trust, the beneficiary is not a party to the illegality; but that, when directors act for a company in an illegal transaction with a stranger, the company is itself a party to that transaction and therefore to the illegality.[25] The company, therefore, could not rely on that transaction as 'the source of civil rights' and, therefore, for example, it could not successfully sue the stranger with regard to rights which it was claimed that the transaction conferred . . . [But in] a claim based on an illegal breach of trust the claimant does not rely on a right conferred or created by that breach. On the contrary, he relies on a right breached by the breach, as the very words 'breach of trust' indicate. It is only on the footing that there is a breach of trust that the defence of illegality becomes relevant. So it is assumed, for present purposes, that there is a breach of trust against the plaintiff company by those who are directors and by those who are claimed to be constructive trustees. The constructive trustees are, it is true, parties with the plaintiff company itself to the transaction which is illegal. The plaintiff company's claim, however, for breach of trust is not made by it as a party to that transaction, or in reliance on any right which that transaction is alleged to confer, but against the directors and constructive trustees for perpetrating that transaction and making the plaintiff company party to it in breach of trust owing to the plaintiff company. The breach of trust includes the making of the plaintiff a party to the illegal transaction. So it seems to me clear on analysis that the plaintiff company is not precluded from relying on breach of trust by a party to an illegal transaction, to which the plaintiff itself is a party, when the breach includes the making of the plaintiff a party to that very transaction. Those who proved to be constructive trustees, sharing the responsibility with the directors for the breach of trust, share the liability too.

The result is that the plaintiff company in this case would not, by reason of illegality, be prevented from being reimbursed money paid by it unlawfully under a transaction to which it is a party. But this does not mean that this would nullify the ordinary operation of illegality with regard to companies and parties outside the company, and not being or treated as being a trustee to it. But it would prevent such operation shielding those whose position or conduct makes them responsible as owing a fiduciary duty or as constructive trustee . . .

➤ Questions

1. In the light of the reasoning in *Belmont* **[8.10]**, will a company ever have the *mens rea* necessary for it to be convicted under CA 2006 ss 678, 680?

2. Tortuous plc lends £5,000 to Smith for the purpose of a purchase by Smith of Tortuous shares. Can it recover £5,000 or any sum from Smith: (i) as repayment of the loan when due; (ii) as damages on the basis of *Belmont*; or (iii) on the ground that Smith is liable to it as a constructive trustee, following *Selangor*?

3. In *Armour Hick Northern Ltd v Armour Trust Ltd* [1980] 1 WLR 1520, A Ltd was a subsidiary of B Ltd. B owed £93,000 to X, the owner of 7,000 shares in B. Y and Z wished to buy these shares, but X was unwilling to sell them unless the debt was first repaid. A accordingly paid off the debt out of its own funds. Y and Z then used their own money to buy the shares. Would there in your opinion be an infringement of CA 1985 s 151 on these facts (the 1985 Act being, for relevant purposes, in the same form as CA 2006, but applying also to private companies)?

---

25 [See, however, the ruling in the *Belmont* case **[8.10]**, above,]

Dividend distributions

Permitted distributions

Pre-1980 position

Before 1980, there were no general rules in the Companies Acts regulating the distribution of dividends to the members of a company, although there were specific bans on using the share premium account and the capital redemption reserve for this purpose. The only legal constraint was a broad prohibition established by the cases that dividends should not be paid out of 'capital'. Most of these cases were decided in the late Victorian period, and reflected concepts of bookkeeping which were regarded as odd even then by some contemporary critics. In fact, for the greater part of the past century the standards of propriety in relation to distributions have been set by the accountancy profession and not by the law at all; and these standards have increased progressively over time. This continues to be so, even though we now have formal statutory rules about the payment of dividends in CA 2006 s 829ff (repeating for the most part the CA 1985 provisions). These rules implement in part the Second EC Directive and also incorporate some recommendations made by the Jenkins Committee in 1962 and the CLR more recently.

The current Act, CA 2006, makes separate rules for private companies, public companies and investment companies (defined in s 833).

The first and primary rule, applicable to all companies, is that a company may not make a '*distribution*' to any of its members except out of profits which are available for that purpose (s 830(1)). 'Distribution' is defined exceptionally widely in s 829, to mean 'every description of distribution of a company's assets to its members, whether in cash or otherwise, subject to [specified] exceptions', being issues of bonus shares, reductions of capital, share redemptions or repurchases, and distributions on winding up.

This rule may be thought to correspond in its effect to the common law principle laid down in *Re Exchange Banking Co, Flitcroft's Case* [8.13], that dividends could not be paid from 'capital'; but when taken with other sections of the Act its consequences are altogether different from the position at common law. This may be illustrated by the following older common law cases:

(i)   *Lee v Neuchatel Asphalte Co* (1889) 41 Ch D 1: a company could pay dividends out of its current trading profits without making provision for the depreciation of its fixed assets;

(ii)   *Verner v General and Commercial Investment Trust* [1894] 2 Ch 239: a dividend could be paid from current trading profits without making good earlier losses in fixed capital;

(iii)   *Ammonia Soda Co Ltd v Chamberlain* [1918] 1 Ch 266: a company could pay dividends out of current trading profits without making good past revenue losses;

(iv)   *Dimbula Valley (Ceylon) Tea Co Ltd v Laurie* [1961] Ch 353: a surplus resulting from the increase in the overall book value of a company's assets could be treated as a distributable profit even though it had not been realised by sale.[26]

In short, at common law, the current year's profit and loss account only was looked at, and the profits for that particular year reckoned by taking it in isolation; money lost in earlier years of trading, and *a fortiori* capital losses, did not have to be brought into account. And it was not necessary for profits to be realised profits before they were regarded as distributable— although of course, as a practical matter, the company had to have available or be able to raise the cash necessary to pay the dividend when declared.

---

[26]   This was never the law in Scotland: *Westburn Sugar Refineries Ltd v IRC* [1960] TR 105.

Current position

As noted above, the primary rule is that a company may not make a distribution to any of its members except out of profits which are available for the purpose (CA 2006 s 830(1)). Under Part 23 of CA 2006 (re-enacting changes made from 1980), however, 'profits' available for distribution by a company are to be 'its accumulated, realised, profits, so far as not previously utilised by distribution or capitalisation, less its accumulated, realised losses, so far as not previously written off in a reduction or reorganisation of capital duly made' (s 830(2)).

The two major changes introduced by this formulation are:

(i)   it is now necessary to look not at the current year's trading figures in isolation, but at the net overall position of the company, taking into account its *accumulated* surpluses and losses over the years up to date; and

(ii)   the figures used in the calculation of profits must be those for the company's *realised*[27] profits and losses: mere 'revaluation surpluses'—the 'paper profits' relied on in the *Dimbula Valley* case (above)—cannot be brought into account in reckoning profits.

As a result, the current approach involves a change to what is sometimes called the 'balance sheet surplus' approach: the company's cumulative position, involving past years as well as the current year, has to be considered, and dividends can be paid only if justified by the picture as a whole.

Special rules apply to *public* companies and to *investment* companies:

(i)   A *public company* must ensure that its net assets (aggregate assets less aggregate liabilities) after the distribution does not fall below the value of its share capital and undistributable reserves,[28] and its 'undistributable reserves' are defined so as to require public companies to allow for any excess of *unrealised* losses over unrealised profits on the capital account—ie provision must be made for any unrealised revaluation deficit (s 831).

(ii)   An *investment company* (defined in s 833) must draw a distinction between its revenue (trading) profits and its capital profits, and it may make a distribution only out of the accumulated, realised revenue profits (ie not including even realised capital profits, and taking into account realised revenue profits and both realised and unrealised revenue losses), and it may make such a distribution provided that its assets are not thereby reduced to less than one-and-a-half times its aggregate liabilities to creditors (s 832).

Requirement to pay dividends

There is no rule that all profits must be distributed (until, of course, the company is wound up), and there has been no English case in which a shareholder has succeeded in an action brought to compel a company to pay a dividend. Indeed, in *Burland v Earle* [11.10] the Privy Council made it clear that this was a matter where the court would not interfere. By contrast, in the well-known US case *Dodge v Ford Motor Co* 170 NW 668 (1919), Ford was ordered to pay a substantial dividend to its shareholders when the directors would have preferred to expend the company's trading surplus on increasing the wages and improving the work conditions of its employees, reducing prices to its customers and similar altruistic objects.

However, in *Re a Company* (1988) 4 BCLC 506 Harman J did not rule out the possibility that failure to pay a dividend might, in a particular case, be a ground for ordering the winding up of a company on the just and equitable ground (below, pp 653 ff) if it had pursued a restrictive

---

[27] The term 'realised' is not defined in the Act (although see s 841), but formal guidance is given by accountancy practice. It is, however, acknowledged that the concepts of realised profits and losses will change over time, reflecting changes in the financial environment, and accountancy guidelines change accordingly.

[28] Given the general rule on available profits in s 830, this requirement seems to add nothing, but it is specifically included in s 831(1) for public companies.

dividend policy and denied the shareholders a return on their investment which they were reasonably entitled to expect. In *Re Sam Weller & Sons Ltd* [1990] Ch 682, Peter Gibson J held that such a policy might also justify relief on the ground of 'unfairly prejudicial conduct' (then CA 1985 s 459, now CA 2006 s 994). This section has since been amended so as to put it beyond doubt that the view of Peter Gibson J could be followed where this was justified on the facts (see below, pp 562 ff).

Payment of a dividend

No dividend is payable on a company's shares, even on the preference shares, until the company has 'declared' (or decided to pay) a dividend. Authority to make the decision is usually determined in the articles and the entitlements, as between shareholders, are determined by the class rights attached to the shares. In *Precision Dippings Ltd v Precision Dippings Marketing Ltd* [1986] Ch 447, CA, it was held that the statutory procedure prescribed for the declaration of a dividend (involving, *inter alia*, an auditors' report on the accounts) was mandatory and that a departure from it could not be rectified by a subsequent resolution of the shareholders.

Once the dividend is payable, it is a debt owed by the company to the member, and is subject to all the usual rules on debts (limitation periods, etc). Unless the articles provide otherwise, distributions must be in cash (*Wood v Odessa Waterworks Co* (1889) 42 Ch D 636).

Distributions in kind

If a distribution in kind is made, then the valuation rules in CA 2006 ss 845–846 apply.

➤ Notes

1. *Clydebank Football Club Ltd v Steedman* 2002 SLT 109: a transaction which is genuinely conceived of and effected as an exchange for value is not a distribution despite being for less than the amount of a professional valuation.

2. *Aveling Barford Ltd v Perion Ltd* [8.14]: a sale at an undervalue of assets of Aveling Barford Ltd to another company controlled by the sole beneficial shareholder of Aveling Barford was held to be a distribution to him. Now see below.

3. Particularly in the case of a small company whose affairs are conducted with little formality, it may at times be necessary for the court to distinguish between a payment which can be justified as directors' remuneration and a distribution of assets made in breach of this Part of the Act which is unlawful, either because there were not realised profits available or because the statutory procedure has not been followed. See, for instance, *Re Halt Garage (1964) Ltd* [5.04]. See below, pp 422 ff.

The new CA 2006 s 845 is intended to remove the doubts that arose after *Aveling Barford* [8.14]. In particular, that case left it unclear whether intra-group transfers of assets could be conducted by reference to the asset's book value rather than its market value (which will frequently be higher than the book value, and which would require expensive formal valuation). A transfer at book value may have an element of undervalue, and would therefore constitute a distribution requiring the company to have distributable profits sufficient to cover the difference in value. As a result, companies often abandoned their plans or structured them in more complex ways. CA 2006, s 845 does not disturb the position in the *Aveling Barford* case if the company does not have distributable profits: then the transaction will be an unlawful distribution; it does, however, clarify the position where a company has an appropriate level of available distributable profits, and it then permits asset transfers at book value.

Consequences of an unauthorised distribution

There are no criminal consequences. The statutory civil consequences are set out in CA 2006 s 847, which provides that a member who 'knows or has reasonable grounds for believing' that the distribution contravenes the statutory requirements is obliged to repay the sum (or the value of the asset) received in contravention. This remedy is without prejudice to general remedies available at law. Nevertheless, its usefulness may be rather limited. Except in relation to small private companies, it is unlikely that members will have the necessary knowledge that any distributions are unauthorised. The common law equivalent is similar (see below, **[8.12]**), although earlier cases suggest the added advantage of a better remedy by way of constructive trust of the distribution (although that now seems doubtful[29]): *Precision Dippings Ltd v Precision Dippings Marketing Ltd* [1986] Ch 447; *Allied Carpets plc v Nethercott* [2001] BCLC 81.

Statutory and general law remedies against the members.

[8.12] It's a Wrap (UK) Ltd (in liq) v Gula [2006] EWCA Civ 544, [2006] BCLC 634 (Court of Appeal)

This case concerned the statutory liability under CA 1985 s 277(1) [CA 2006 s 847] of an insolvent company's directors and shareholders to repay certain dividends that had been paid out in contravention of CA 1985 Pt VIII [CA 2006 ss 630ff].

ARDEN LJ:

1 This appeal raises a short point of law. [CA 1985 s 277(1)] provides a statutory remedy against a shareholder for recovery of an unlawful distribution paid to him if he knew or had reasonable grounds to believe that it was made in contravention of the Act. I will call the first kind of knowledge actual knowledge, and the second kind of knowledge constructive knowledge [but see CHADWICK LJ below]. The question that we have to decide is this: if a company brings a claim against a shareholder under this section, is the actual or constructive knowledge that the section requires actual or constructive knowledge of:

(i)   the relevant facts constituting the contravention, or

(ii) those facts and in addition the fact that the Act was contravened?

2 The deputy judge held . . . that the second of these alternatives was correct. In my judgment, the deputy judge was wrong on this question of law. I reach my conclusions by the following steps:

(A) s 277(1) has to be interpreted in conformity with Art.16 of the second EC directive on company law . . . which it is designed to implement;

(B) Art.16 has to be read in the context of the rules on distributions in Art.15 of the second directive and the general principles of Community law;

(C) the provisions of ss 263–276 of the Act [CA 2006 s 830ff] are designed to implement Art.15 of the second directive;

(D) on its true interpretation, Art.16 means that a shareholder is liable to return a distribution if he knows or could not have been unaware that it was paid in circumstances which amount to a contravention of the restrictions on distributions in the second directive, whether or not he knew of those restrictions;

---

[29] These proprietary remedies may now be excluded by the analysis adopted in *Westdeutsche Landesbank Girozentrale v Islington London Borough Council* [1996] AC 669, HL.

(E) accordingly s 277 must be interpreted as meaning that the shareholder cannot claim that he is not liable to return a distribution because he did not know of the restrictions in the Act on the making of distributions. He will be liable if he knew or ought reasonably to have known of the facts which mean that the distribution contravened the requirements of the Act.

. . . As to remedies against shareholders who receive dividends not lawfully made, the general law of the United Kingdom was, arguably at least, not to exactly the same effect as Art.16 . . . .Liability under the general law attaches where the shareholder knew or ought to have known that the distribution was unlawful. . . .

The following are some of the differences between the two types of liability, that is, liability under s 277(1) and liability under the general law. First, s 277(1) only applies where the distribution contravenes the Act, and thus it does not apply where the distribution for instance violates a provision of the general law or the company's constitution. Secondly, there is no defence in s 277(1) for the member who acts on advice. The member is instead left to sue the person who gave him inaccurate advice (if he can). By contrast, under the general law a shareholder may be able to claim that he did not have the requisite knowledge where he acted on advice. As a constructive trustee he would be able to claim that he was entitled in appropriate circumstances to relief under s 61 of the Trustee Act 1925 (see the definition of "trustee" in s 68(7) of that Act). (I would add, however, that there is no inquiry under the general law into the question whether the shareholder was aware of the law's requirements regarding the payment of dividends.) In sum, the remedy under Art.16 is more absolute and stringent than that available under the general law. That is no doubt because it has been tailor made to facilitate the recovery of unlawful distributions whereas the remedy under the general law is an adaptation of the law of constructive trusteeship. However, the need for some form of actual or constructive knowledge on the part of the shareholder is common to both forms of remedy.

. . . The underlying rationale for this rule [on distributions] is that capital constitutes the security for creditors. A distribution that is not paid out of profits available for distribution is paid out of the reserves that must remain available for the payment of debts. The claims of shareholders rank behind those of creditors. It is a factor to be borne in mind that any defence given to shareholders who receive a distribution paid in contravention of this Act detracts from the protection available to creditors. One of the objects of the second directive was to give protection to creditors by harmonising restrictions on the profits which may be used for the payment of distributions. . . .

SEDLEY LJ delivered a concurring judgment.

CHADWICK LJ delivered a concurring judgment, but differed from ARDEN LJ on one point (which was not material on the facts):

. . . I take the view that it is unnecessary, on the facts of this case, to decide what meaning should be given to the words "has reasonable grounds for believing that". Those words, plainly, do enable the second (or knowledge) condition in s 277(1) to be established without proof of actual knowledge. But, to my mind, it is by no means self-evident that they are to be equated with "constructive knowledge" if by that expression is meant knowledge which a person would have but for his negligence. I do not think that the composite phrase "knows or has reasonable grounds for believing" has the same meaning as "knows or ought to know".

General law remedies against the directors

Directors who pay dividends improperly are liable to compensate the company personally for the money so paid away (regardless of whether it was paid to the director).

[8.13] Re Exchange Banking Co, Flitcroft's Case (1882) 21 Ch D 519 (Court of Appeal)

At common law, dividends could not be paid from capital. The directors had for several years made it appear that the company had made profits, when in fact it had not, by laying before the shareholders reports and balance sheets in which debts known to be bad were entered as assets. On the faith of these reports, the shareholders had passed resolutions declaring dividends, which the directors had paid. In the winding up of the company the liquidator successfully applied to have the directors who had been responsible on each occasion made accountable to the company for the sums wrongly paid away.

JESSEL MR: A limited company by its memorandum of association declares that its capital is to be applied for the purposes of the business. It cannot reduce its capital except in the manner and with the safeguards provided by statute, and looking at the Act . . . it clearly is against the intention of the legislature that any portion of the capital should be returned to the shareholders without the statutory conditions being complied with. A limited company cannot in any other way make a return of capital, the sanction of a general meeting can give no validity to such a proceeding, and even the sanction of every shareholder cannot bring within the powers of the company an act which is not within its powers. If, therefore, the shareholders had all been present at the meetings, and had all known the facts, and had all concurred in declaring the dividends, the payment of the dividends would not be actually sanctioned. One reason is this—there is a statement that the capital shall be applied for the purposes of the business, and on the faith of that statement, which is sometimes said to be an implied contract with creditors, people dealing with the company give it credit. The creditor has no debtor but that impalpable thing the corporation, which has no property except the assets of the business. The creditor, therefore, I may say, gives credit to that capital, gives credit to the company on faith of the representation that the capital shall be applied only for the purposes of the business, and he has therefore a right to say that the corporation shall keep its capital and not return it to the shareholders, though it may be a right which he cannot enforce otherwise than by a winding-up order. It follows then that if directors who are quasi trustees for the company improperly pay away the assets to the shareholders, they are liable to replace them. It is no answer to say that the shareholders could not compel them to do so. I am of opinion that the company could in its corporate capacity compel them to do so, even if there were no winding up . . .

COTTON LJ: It was contended that though the directors might be ordered to repay what they had themselves retained, they ought not to be ordered to refund what they had paid to the other shareholders. But directors are in the position of trustees, and are liable not only for what they put into their own pockets, but for what they in breach of trust pay to others . . .

BRETT LJ delivered a concurring judgment.

This liability is in addition to the liability imposed on directors who pay dividends improperly *to themselves*: they will hold these receipts on constructive trust for the company, according to normal fiduciary principles (see above, pp 345 ff).

> Notes

1. This obligation to repay illegal dividends is imposed on the directors who authorised the excessive payment regardless of whether the company is solvent or insolvent when it claims repayment. See *Bairstow v Queens Moat Houses plc* [2001] EWCA Civ 712, [2002] BCLC 91.

2. In *Allied Carpets Group plc v Nethercott* [2001] BCLC 81 it was held that the object of the remedy is restitution of what was wrongfully paid out by the company, not compensation for the loss the company has suffered. Therefore where the dividend was unlawful because the accounts were erroneous, it is irrelevant that the dividends might have been lawful if the accounts had been drawn up correctly.

3. In *Re Marini Ltd* [2003] EWHC 334, [2004] BCLC 172, the court did not accept that, because the dividend had been paid on the advice of the company's accountant, the directors should qualify for relief under CA 1985 s 727 [CA 2006 s 1157]. Although they agreed that the

directors had acted reasonably and honestly on their accountant's advice, the honesty of their actions did not allow them to enjoy a benefit at the expense of the company's creditors.

➤ Questions

1. According to *Re Exchange Banking Co, Flitcroft's Case* **[8.13]**, the fact that the illegal distribution was approved by the shareholders does not cure the defect, nor does it ratify the directors' acts so as to resolve them from liability. *Could* a shareholder resolution fail to achieve the former goal but succeed on the latter? See above, pp 407 ff.

2. What knowledge does a *shareholder* need to have, and of what, to be fixed with liability to repay unauthorised distributions?

3. What knowledge does a *director* need to have, and of what, to be fixed with liability to repay unauthorised distributions?

4. Can a director be excused from liability? See *Dovey v Corey* [1901] AC 477 and CA 2006 s 1157. Can a shareholder be excused from liability?

5. Can an auditor be made liable for unauthorised distributions?

Capitalisations and bonus shares

A profitable company that does not distribute all its profits as dividends will accumulate reserves (retained earnings). The shares will in consequence have a market value which is greater than their nominal value. There will be a similar situation when a company's fixed assets appreciate in value as a result of inflation or of a movement in their market value. Suppose, for example, that a company with a nominal capital of 10,000 £1 shares, all issued and fully paid, has accumulated profits of £90,000. Instead of paying out this surplus to its shareholders as dividends it may resolve to 'capitalise' these reserves by issuing a further 90,000 shares, so that nine new shares are allotted to the holder of each existing share, and treating the new shares as fully paid because the £90,000 is appropriated to meet the issue price. No cash changes hands at all. The formal result will be that the reserve has become capital and ceases to be available for distribution as dividend, the company's issued share capital has risen from £10,000 to £100,000, each shareholder now has ten times as many shares as before, and the market value of each share will have fallen back from something like £10 to £1.[30] (Of course, other factors influence the market price of shares, apart from their 'asset backing', but this in simplified terms will be what happens.)

A capitalisation issue is not a 'distribution' of profits or assets for the purposes of the statutory restrictions in CA 2006 ss 829ff (see s 829(2)(a)). It follows that profits which are not distributable (eg because they are unrealised profits) may be capitalised and issued to members as bonus shares provided the articles are so worded as to permit this.[31] Note, however, that in *EIC Services Ltd v Phipps* [2004] EWCA Civ 1069, [2005] 1 WLR 1377, an issue of bonus shares was declared void for mistake because the underlying ordinary shares were totally unpaid and no resolution allowing the issue was ever passed.

➤ Questions

1. What might be the advantages to (i) the company, (ii) its shareholders, of making an issue of bonus shares?

2. Are the shareholders better off in any real sense as a result? Is the expression 'bonus shares' misleading?

---

[30] Bonus issues may also be financed out of the share premium account and capital redemption reserve.

[31] This confirms the position at common law declared by Buckley J in *Dimbula Valley (Ceylon) Co Ltd v Laurie* [1961] Ch 353, but the judge's reasoning (based on the view that such profits were distributable) has not survived the statutory changes of 1980.

Disguised returns of capital

The above rules provide various mechanisms for controlling what are seen as unacceptable disposals of the company's property. However, they do not seem to touch the ability of small companies to pay away its assets to its members in the form of directors' fees or employees' salaries, or, in corporate groups, for subsidiaries to pay large fees to holding companies for 'group services' or other notional (or real) benefits. There is no rule that directors' fees (see above [5.04]), still less employees' wages or business expenses, must be paid out of profits.

But it is also true, as we saw earlier, that directors cannot make gifts out of the company's assets unless (i) in furtherance of the company's objects, or (ii) out of distributable profits (and even then subject to certain limitations): see above, pp 146 ff. This rule provides a further avenue for restraining unacceptable distributions of the company's assets, although it catches only the most blatant of abuses.

The possibility of recovery of the company's assets from *third party recipients* is limited. The abolition of the doctrine of *ultra vires* by CA 1989 deprived the courts of the most potent of their traditional weapons when dealing with allegations that corporate property has been misapplied. Of course, vastly expanded objects clauses and changes in judicial analyses of their impact meant that the occasions on which the doctrine could be successfully invoked were always destined to become rather fewer—particularly after the Court of Appeal's ruling in the *Rolled Steel* case [3.07/3.17]; but the doctrine did serve to deal with the most blatant cases of misappropriation such as *International Sales and Agencies Ltd v Marcus* [1982] 3 All ER 551, [1982] 2 CMLR 46 (QBD).

With the demise of the *ultra vires* doctrine, the courts needed to have recourse to other rules and remedies in such cases. As *Rolled Steel* itself shows, it may be possible to show that *directors* have behaved unconstitutionally, exceeded their authority, abused their powers or acted in breach of their fiduciary duties, with the consequence that they may be liable to make compensation to the company, and in addition (or alternatively) the relevant transaction may be declared void or voidable and both they and any third person who has received corporate assets with knowledge of the circumstances will be liable to reimburse the company (*Selangor United Rubber Estates Ltd v Cradock (No 3)* [8.11]). If the third party has dealt in good faith, for value and without notice of the irregularity, the company's remedy against that person will, of course, be lost; but very often the person will be an 'insider' or party to the wrong-doing and not able to plead this defence. There is also the possibility that a formal or informal ratification of the irregular act will be alleged to have occurred. But some breaches of directors' duty are not capable of ratification (*Cook v Deeks* [6.15], *Kinsela v Russell Kinsela Pty Ltd* [6.04]); and where the act involves breach of statutory prohibitions (eg a prohibited distribution (s 830) or a breach of the 'financial assistance' prohibition (s 678)), it will not be capable of ratification at all. So the courts are still relatively well equipped to deal with cases of wrongful depletion of corporate assets.

The cases cited below illustrate a possible approach to these issues, perhaps linked as a matter of underlying principle with the 'maintenance of capital' doctrine. So, in *Re Halt Garage (1964) Ltd* [5.04], Oliver J struck down a payment of remuneration to an inactive director as 'not genuine' and a 'dressed-up return of capital' to her. While the basis of this reasoning is open to question (not least because as a shareholder she held only one £1 share), it has since been adopted and applied by Hoffmann J in *Aveling Barford Ltd v Perion Ltd* [8.14], where again the 'dressed-up return of capital' argument was somewhat shaky because the beneficiary of the asset-stripping, although totally lacking in merit, was not strictly a shareholder.

Matters are simpler when the company is insolvent or approaching insolvency. There is now an abundance of statutory provisions which may be invoked when corporate assets have been plundered or imperilled in the run-up to liquidation. These include preferences (IA 1986 s 239), transactions at an undervalue (IA 1986 ss 238, 423), floating charges subject to avoidance (IA 1986 s 245), fraudulent and wrongful trading (IA 1986 ss 231, 214) and misfeasance proceedings (IA 1986 s 212).[32] In the light of these statutory developments in the UK, it is unlikely that a new common-law remedy will develop based on a duty owed by directors to creditors (see above, p 280).

A sale at an undervalue made by a company to one of its shareholders (or to another company controlled by him) may be open to challenge on the ground that it is not a genuine sale but a disguised return of capital.

[8.14] Aveling Barford Ltd v Perion Ltd [1989] BCLC 626 (Chancery Division)

Aveling Barford and Perion were both owned and controlled by Lee. Aveling Barford, which was not at the material time insolvent but was not in a position to make any distribution to its shareholders, owned a sports ground which had planning permission for residential development. In October 1986 its directors resolved to sell this property to Perion for £350,000 when they knew that it had recently been valued at £650,000, but no binding contract was entered into at that stage. A later valuation put it at £1.15m and Perion was subsequently offered £1.4m. There was some evidence of an agreement reached in January 1987 that a further payment of £400,000 was to be paid to Aveling Barford by Perion if it resold the property within a year for more than £800,000. The property was conveyed to Perion for £350,000 in February 1987 and resold by it for £1.52m the following August. Aveling Barford was subsequently put into liquidation and successfully sued in this action to have Perion declared a constructive trustee of the proceeds of the sale.

HOFFMANN J: Counsel for the defendants said that even if the 10 January contract was a rewriting of history in the summer of 1987, when it was plain that Perion would be reselling for more than £800,000, it was reasonable for the parties retrospectively to affirm the sale at £750,000, which would have been a proper sum to fix as the value in February 1987. I do not agree. If the February sale was, as I think, a breach of duty and liable to be set aside at the time, Dr Lee or Mr Chapman [solicitor to all the parties] on his behalf had no right to confirm it retrospectively as a sale at £750,000 at a time when they knew the value to be over £1,400,000. It was the duty of the directors to set aside the February sale and obtain the full value of the land for Aveling Barford. On any view, therefore, the sale was a breach of fiduciary duty by Dr Lee. Perion, through Dr Lee and Mr Chapman, knew all the facts which made it a breach of duty and was therefore accountable as a constructive trustee.

In the alternative, counsel for the defendant submitted that whether or not the sale to Perion was a breach of fiduciary duty by Dr Lee, it cannot be challenged by the company because it was unanimously approved by the shareholders. This approval was both informal and formal. Informal approval was given at the time of sale by virtue of the fact that Dr Lee owned or controlled the entire issued share capital. Formally, a sale at £750,000 was approved when the 1987 accounts were adopted at the company's annual general meeting. For the purposes of this motion I shall assume that shareholder consent was given in both these ways.

The general rule is that any act which falls within the express or implied powers of a company conferred by its memorandum of association, whether or not a breach of duty on the part of the directors, will be binding on the company if it is approved or subsequently ratified by the shareholders: see *Rolled Steel Products (Holdings) Ltd v British Steel Corpn* **[3.07/3.17]**. But this rule is

---

[32] See below, pp 662 ff.

subject to exceptions created by the general law and one such exception is that a company cannot without the leave of the court or the adoption of a special procedure return its capital to its shareholders. It follows that a transaction which amounts to an unauthorised return of capital is ultra vires and cannot be validated by shareholder ratification or approval. Whether or not the transaction is a distribution to shareholders does not depend exclusively on what the parties choose to call it. The court looks at the substance rather than the outward appearance. [His Lordship referred to *Re Halt Garage (1964) Ltd* **[5.04]** and an earlier case, *Ridge Securities Ltd v IRC* [1964] 1 All ER 275, [1964] 1 WLR 479, and continued:]

So it seems to me in this case that looking at the matter objectively, the sale to Perion was not a genuine exercise of the company's power under its memorandum to sell its assets. It was a sale at a gross undervalue for the purpose of enabling a profit to be realised by an entity controlled and put forward by its sole beneficial shareholder. This was as much a dressed-up distribution as the payment of excessive interest in *Ridge Securities* or excessive remuneration in *Halt Garage*. The company had at the time no distributable reserves and the sale was therefore ultra vires and incapable of validation by the approval or ratification of the shareholder. The fact that the distribution was to Perion rather than to Dr Lee or his other entities which actually held the shares in Aveling Barford is in my judgment irrelevant . . .

Counsel for the defendants says that this was an act within the terms of the memorandum. It may have been a sale at an undervalue, but it was certainly a sale: a conveyance in exchange for a payment in money. It was not a sham. The terms of the transaction were in no way different from those appearing on the face of the documents. The purpose for which it was done was therefore irrelevant. Counsel submits that the test for the genuineness of the transaction proposed by Oliver J in *Re Halt Garage* admits by the back door all the questions about the motives, state of mind and knowledge of the company's directors which the Court of Appeal appeared to have expelled by the front door in the *Rolled Steel* case.

It is clear however that Slade LJ [in *Rolled Steel*] excepted from his general principle cases which he described as involving a 'fraud on creditors'. As an example of such a case, he cited *Re Halt Garage*. Counsel for the defendants said that frauds on creditors meant transactions entered into when the company was insolvent. In this case Aveling Barford was not at the relevant time insolvent. But I do not think that the phrase was intended to have such a narrow meaning. The rule that capital may not be returned to shareholders is a rule for the protection of creditors and the evasion of the rule falls within what I think Slade LJ had in mind when he spoke of a fraud on creditors. There is certainly nothing in his judgment to suggest that he disapproved of the actual decisions in *Re Halt Garage* or *Ridge Securities*. As for the transaction not being a sham, I accept that it was in law a sale. The false dressing it wore was that of a sale at arms' length or at market value. It was the fact that it was known and intended to be a sale at an undervalue which made it an unlawful distribution.

It follows that in my judgment even on the view of the facts most favourable to Perion, it has no arguable defence . . .

➤ Question

In *Re Halt Garage (1964) Ltd* **[5.04]**, referred to above, the issued capital of the company was two £1 shares, of which Mrs Charlesworth held one. Was the judge right to describe the overpayment of £20 per week as a disguised 'return of capital' to her?

➤ Notes

1. Although in *Aveling Barford* Hoffmann J several times described the transaction as *ultra vires* (and accordingly unratifiable), his remarks will continue to be valid and relevant despite the abolition of the *ultra vires* doctrine because of his ruling that the transaction was illegal as an unauthorised return of capital.

2. In declining to make a distinction between Lee and his company Perion, Hoffmann J was 'lifting the veil', in circumstances somewhat similar to cases like *Jones v Lipman* (above, p 63).

3. This case was cited with approval by Harman J in *Barclays Bank plc v British and Commonwealth Holdings plc* [1996] 1 BCLC 1. Here B & C plc had issued redeemable preference shares to C and had undertaken to redeem them on a certain date. If B & C plc failed to do so (which would be unavoidable if it had no distributable profits or was insolvent), T Ltd promised to buy the shares from C, and B & C plc promised to indemnify T against the cost of doing so. The arrangement was held to be unlawful. Harman J said (at 17): 'as it seems to me it must . . . be unlawful to make an agreement expressed to impose a liability to make a gratuitous payment, that is, one not for the advancement of a company's business nor made out of distributable profits, at a future date when in the event the company has no distributable profits.'

4. However defensible the *Aveling Barford* decision may be on the merits, it caused concern in commercial circles because it created uncertainty as to when payments by a company to its members in other circumstances may infringe s 830 of the Act. CA 2006 has clarified the legislation to make it clear that the rules apply only to distributions to members in their capacity as members: see above, p 416. Alternative protection is provided by other provisions of company law and insolvency law that apply on similar facts.

➤ Questions

1. What are the principal objectives of the capital maintenance rules—creditor protection against removal of a preferential capital 'buffer', or company/shareholder protection against asset stripping?

2. Do the current rules provide effective protection, either for creditors or for shareholders?

3. What are the advantages and disadvantages in adopting 'solvency declarations' as a simple hurdle to these types of transactions?

4. The Second EC Directive (No 77/9/EEC) is apparently being reviewed as part of the EU Company Law Action Plan announced in May 2003, but until then many of the identified problems will necessarily remain on the statute books. What are the principal problems for which solutions might be found?

9

SHARES

The nature and classification of shares

Recall the description of a share given earlier, at p 375, *Borland's Trustee v Steel Bros & Co Ltd* [7.01]. It indicated that shares are a means of denoting three things: first, the shareholders' *financial stake* in the company (including the shareholders' liability to contribute funds to the company, and rights to capital and income receipts from the company); second, their *interest in the company as an association* (including rights as members, especially voting rights and rights conferred by statute and the company's constitution); and third, their rights as owners of a species of *property* (which is able to be bought, sold, charged, etc, and in which there can be both legal and equitable interest).

This chapter is about the nature of the asset held by shareholders, and the rights that accrue as a result of that ownership.[1] It does not consider the *uses* that shareholders may make of their voting power in the company or their rights to influence and control the management of the company in other ways. That is discussed at various stages in this book, especially in Chapters 5, 6 and 11. It does, however, look at the initial allocation of financial and voting rights to different classes of shares and the variation of those rights, the rights to transfer shares and the protections associated with that and, finally, the valuation of shares.

In total, these combined privileges and limitations on voting and financial rights raise the question of what it means when we say that the shareholders 'own' the company. The answer is material in differentiating the rights of shareholders from those of creditors, employees and other outsiders, as highlighted in the corporate governance debates associated with this: recall the 'shareholder' and 'stakeholder' views of a company and their impact on corporate governance issues (see above, pp 275 ff).

Classes of shares and class rights

'Classes of shares' and 'class rights' are not defined in CA 2006, other than in s 629. Nevertheless, the shares in a company may be divided into different classes, either by the company's constitution, or by the terms of the share issue itself. The differing rights usually relate to entitlements to vote, entitlements to dividends, and entitlements to a return of capital when the company is wound up. Some classes of shares may fall into a well-known category such as 'preference shares', but even so there is no fixed formula defining such shares: it is a matter of construction of the terms of issue in each case what the rights of the particular class are. In broad terms, however, we may describe some well-known types of shares as follows.

---

[1] See RR Pennington, 'Can Shares in Companies Be Defined?' (1989) 10 Co Law 140; S Worthington, 'Shares and Shareholders: Property, Power and Entitlement—Parts I and II' (2001) 22 *Company Lawyer* 258 and 307.

Ordinary shares. This is the basic or residual category. If all the company's shares are issued without differentiation, they will be ordinary shares. If the shares are divided into classes, and the special rights of such classes are set out, the remaining shares will be ordinary shares. Where the class or classes of shares are preference shares, then the ordinary shares are commonly called 'equity' shares; but in the Companies Act this term has a more elaborate definition (see CA 2006 s 548).

Preference shares. These shares will usually be entitled to have dividends paid, at a pre-determined rate (eg at a rate of 10% on their nominal value) in priority to any dividend on the ordinary shares. Of course, it is first necessary for the company to have distributable profits, and for a dividend to be declared. However, if these conditions are met, the first claim on the corporate profits in any year will be that of the preference shareholders. The right to a preference dividend may be *cumulative* (in which case arrears of preference dividends not declared in earlier years must be paid, as well as that for the current year, before any dividend is paid to the ordinary shareholders) or *non-cumulative* (when only the current year's preference dividend is payable). Where the preference shares are *participating*, they will be entitled to a further distribution after the ordinary shareholders have received a dividend equivalent to their own 10% (or whatever the rate is). A company may have more than one class of preference shares, ranking one behind the other.

Preference shareholders commonly also have a right to priority over the ordinary shareholders when capital is returned to the members in a winding up. It is quite usual for preference shareholders to have no voting rights at shareholders' meetings, or alternatively to have a vote only if the preference dividend is in arrear.

Deferred shares. These are sometimes called 'founders' shares' reflecting the founders' offer to defer their own entitlements to those of other investors from whom additional capital is sought. They are not common today except as part of tax-saving schemes. As the name implies, deferred shares normally enjoy rights to distributable profit or to return of capital ranking *after* the claims of the preference shareholders (if any) and the ordinary shareholders.

Redeemable shares. These are created on terms that they shall be (or, at the option of the company or of the member, may be) bought back by the company at a future date. The rules governing such shares and their redemption are set out in CA 2006 ss 684ff. Prior to 1981, only preference shares could be issued as redeemable. Although that rule fell away, it is now clear that a company must always have *some* non-redeemable shares (s 684(4)). The rules on the issue of redeemable shares and their redemption were discussed above, pp 399 ff.

Non-voting shares. These may be issued where it is sought to restrict control of the company to the holders of the remaining shares. This is quite commonly desired when a family-controlled company looks to outside investors for additional capital (although it may, of course, find that the latter are not prepared to invest on those terms). A capital structure which includes non-voting shares may also be imposed on a company by an outside body, eg as a condition of obtaining a broadcasting licence (see *Heron International Ltd v Lord Grade* **[6.03]**). The Stock Exchange does not encourage listed companies to create non-voting shares, although it does not ban them altogether; they must, however, be clearly designated.

Shares with limited voting rights or enhanced voting rights. These may also be created, even to the extent of giving one shareholder a right of veto in specified circumstances. We have seen examples in *Quin & Axtens Ltd v Salmon* **[4.06]** and *Bushell v Faith* **[5.05]**.[2]

Employees' shares. Many companies issue shares to their employees, commonly under an 'employees' share scheme' (defined in CA 2006 s 1166), which carries certain tax advantages. Employees' shares are not usually designated as a separate class of shares by the memorandum or articles of association, but are issued simply as ordinary shares (or, as the case may

---

[2] In *Investment Trust Corpn Ltd v Singapore Traction Co Ltd* [1935] Ch 615, one 'management share' could outvote the remaining 399,999! A device of this kind (normally termed a 'golden share') is sometimes employed to retain government control when a nationalised industry is privatised.

be, preference shares, etc) ranking *pari passu* with the other shares of this class. Normally, however, they are subject to special restrictions (eg as to the holder's right of disposal) and would undoubtedly be regarded as a separate class of shares for some legal purposes. Various sections of the Companies Act make special provision for employees' shares: eg CA 2006 s 566 excludes shares that are to be held under an employees' share scheme from the restrictions (but not the benefits) of the usual pre-emptive rights rules.

In addition, of course, classes of shares may be created for other reasons. Thus a 'quasi-partnership' company with three founding shareholders might well have a capital of £300 divided into £100 in 'A' shares, £100 in 'B' shares and £100 in 'C' shares, the shares to rank equally in all respects except that each class should have the right to appoint one of the directors to the board. In this way, the right of each founder to participate in management could be entrenched.

Some common law rules about classes of shares and about the construction of the terms of issue of shares are illustrated by the cases which follow. The question of variation of class rights is discussed in the next section.

A company may alter its articles so as to take power to issue shares ranking in preference to its existing shares. There is no implied condition in a company's articles that all the shares in a company shall be equal.

[9.01] Andrews v Gas Meter Co [1897] 1 Ch 361 (Court of Appeal)

[The facts appear from the judgment.]

The judgment of the court (LINDLEY, AL SMITH AND RIGBY LJJ) was delivered LINDLEY LJ: The question raised by this appeal is whether certain preference shares issued by a limited company as long ago as 1865 were validly issued or not . . . The company's original capital as stated in its memorandum of association was '£60,000, divided into 600 shares of £100 each, every share being sub-divisible into fifths, with power to increase the capital as provided by the articles of association'. By the articles of association which accompanied the memorandum of association, and were registered with it, power was given to the company to increase the capital (article 27), and it was provided that any new capital should be considered as part of the original capital (article 28). The issue of preference shares was not contemplated or authorised. In 1865 the company desired to acquire additional works, and passed a special resolution . . . altering the articles and authorising the issue of 100 shares of £100 each, fully paid, and bearing a preferential dividend of £5 per cent per annum. Those shares were accordingly issued to the vendors of the works referred to, and are the shares the validity of which is now in question . . . The learned judge has held that the creation of the preference shares was ultra vires, and that their holders never became and are not now shareholders in the company, and that they have none of the rights of shareholders, whether preference or ordinary . . . The judgment against the validity of the preference shares is based upon the well-known case of *Hutton v Scarborough Cliff Hotel Co Ltd*,[3] which came twice before Kindersley V-C in 1865, and which Kekewich J [the trial judge] very naturally held to be binding on him. Kindersley V-C's first decision was that a limited company which had not issued the whole of its original capital could not issue the unallotted shares as preference shares unless authorised so to do by its memorandum of association or by its articles of association. This decision was affirmed on appeal, and was obviously correct; and would have been correct even if the whole of the original capital had been issued and the preference shares had been new and additional capital. The company, however, afterwards passed a special resolution altering the articles and authorising an issue of preference shares. This raised an entirely different question, and led to the second decision. The Vice-Chancellor granted an

[3] (1865) 2 Drew & Sm 514, 521.

injunction restraining the issue of the preference shares, and he held distinctly that the resolution altering the articles was ultra vires. He did so upon the ground, as we understand his judgment, that there was in the memorandum of association a condition that all the shareholders should stand on an equal footing as to the receipt of dividends, and that this condition was one which could not be got rid of by a special resolution altering the articles of association under the powers conferred by ss 50 and 51 of the Act [CA 2006 ss 21 and 283 (changed)]. The judgment of the Vice-Chancellor is a little obscure, because he treats the condition as a condition of the constitution of the company, and he may have meant by that expression either the constitution as fixed by the memorandum of association or the constitution as fixed by the memorandum of association and the original articles. But unless he had meant the constitution of the company as fixed by the memorandum of association his decision is unintelligible; for, so far as the constitution depended on the articles, it clearly could be altered by special resolution under the powers conferred by ss 50 and 51 of the Act . . .

[His Lordship examined a number of cases, and continued:] These decisions turned upon the principle that although by s 8 of the Act [CA 2006 changes these rules; see above, Chapter 1] the memorandum is to state the amount of the original capital and the number of shares into which it is to be divided, yet in other respects the rights of the shareholders in respect of their shares and the terms on which additional capital may be raised are matters to be regulated by the articles of association rather than by the memorandum, and are, therefore, matters which . . . may be determined by the company from time to time by special resolution pursuant to s 50 of the Act. This view, however, clearly negatives the doctrine that there is a condition in the memorandum of association that all shareholders are to be on an equality unless the memorandum itself shows the contrary. That proposition is, in our opinion, unsound . . .

➤ Note

Although this case established that there is no implied condition in the constitution of a company that all its shares should rank equally, there is nevertheless a presumption (as is shown by the cases which follow) that all shares do enjoy equal rights unless the terms of issue make some express provision to the contrary.

In many jurisdictions of the United States, the principle of equality as between shares was developed much further by the courts, so that shareholders commonly have pre-emptive rights as regards any new shares issued. This has been achieved in the UK only by legislation; see above, p 377.

Where the terms of issue make no express distinction between the rights of different categories of share in respect of (a) dividend, (b) the return of capital (and participation in surplus assets in a winding up), or (c) voting, the rule of construction in each case is that, prima facie, all shareholders rank equally. The fact that a preference in respect of any one of these matters is conferred does not imply any right to preference in some other respect: the presumption of equality is undisturbed.

[9.02] Birch v Cropper (1889) 14 App Cas 525 (House of Lords)

The articles of the Bridgewater Navigation Co Ltd provided that dividends should be paid in proportion to the amounts paid up on the shares. There was no express provision governing the distribution of assets in a winding up. The company had issued 5% preference shares at £10 each which were paid up in full, and ordinary shares of £10 on which £3.50 had been paid. The House of Lords, reversing the Court of Appeal and varying the order of North J, held that in distributing the surplus assets available in the company's liquidation after the return of capital, the paid-up and partly paid shares were to be treated alike; and that the preference shareholders were to participate rateably with the ordinary shareholders in proportion to the nominal amounts of the shares held.

LORD MACNAGHTEN: . . . Every person who becomes a member of a company limited by shares of equal amount becomes entitled to a proportionate part in the capital of the company, and, unless it be otherwise provided by the regulations of the company, entitled, as a necessary consequence, to the same proportionate part in all the property of the company, including its uncalled capital. He is liable in respect of all moneys unpaid on his shares to pay up every call that is duly made upon him. But he does not by such payment acquire any further or other interest in the capital of the company. His share in the capital is just what it was before. His liability to the company is diminished by the amount paid. His contribution is merged in the common fund. And that is all.

When the company is wound up, new rights and liabilities arise. The power of the directors to make calls is at an end; but every present member, so far as his shares are unpaid, is liable to contribute to the assets of the company to an amount sufficient for the payment of its debts and liabilities, the costs of winding up, and such sums as may be required for the adjustment of the rights of the contributories[4] amongst themselves . . .

Amongst the rights to be adjusted, the most important are those which arise when there is a difference between shareholders in the amount of calls paid in respect of their shares. Before winding up no such rights exist; whatever has been paid by the shareholders of one issue in excess of the contributions of their fellow shareholders of a different issue, must have been paid in pursuance of calls duly made or in accordance with the conditions under which the shares were held. While the company is a going concern no capital can be returned to the shareholders, except under the statutory provisions in that behalf. There is therefore during that period no ground for complaint; no room for equities arising out of unequal contributions. In the case of winding up everything is changed. The assets have to be distributed. The rights arising from unequal contributions on shares of equal amounts must be adjusted, and the property of the company, including its uncalled capital not required to satisfy prior claims, must be applied for that purpose. But when those rights are adjusted, when the capital is equalised, what equity founded on inequality of contribution can possibly remain? The rights and interests of the contributories in the company must then be simply in proportion to their shares . . .

It now only remains to deal with the various claims put forward in the course of the argument.

The ordinary shareholders say that the preference shareholders are entitled to a return of their capital, with 5% interest up to the day of payment, and to nothing more. That is treating them as if they were debentureholders, liable to be paid off at a moment's notice. Then they say that at the utmost the preference shareholders are only entitled to the capital value of a perpetual annuity of 5% upon the amounts paid up by them. That is treating them as if they were holders of irredeemable debentures. But they are not debenture holders at all. For some reason or other the company invited them to come in as shareholders, and they must be treated as having all the rights of shareholders, except so far as they renounced those rights on their admission to the company. There was an express bargain made as to their rights in respect of profits arising from the business of the company. But there was no bargain—no provision of any sort—affecting their rights as shareholders in the capital of the company.

Then the preference shareholders say to the ordinary shareholders, 'We have paid up the whole of the amount due on our shares; you have paid but a fraction on yours. The prosperity of a company results from its paid-up capital; distribution must be in proportion to contribution. The surplus assets must be divided in proportion to the amounts paid up on the shares.' That seems to me to be ignoring altogether the elementary principles applicable to joint-stock companies of this description. I think it rather leads to confusion to speak of the assets which are the subject of this application as

---

4 [The term 'contributory' is used in a winding up to refer to members and some former members: see IA 1986 s 79.]

'surplus assets' as if they were an accretion or addition to the capital of the company capable of being distinguished from it and open to different considerations. They are part and parcel of the property of the company—part and parcel of the joint stock or common fund—which at the date of the winding up represented the capital of the company. It is through their shares in the capital, and through their shares alone, that members of a company limited by shares become entitled to participate in the property of the company. The shares in this company were all of the same amount. Every contributory who held a preference share at the date of the winding up must have taken that share and must have held it on the terms of paying up all calls duly made upon him in respect thereof. In paying up his share in full he has done no more than he contracted to do; why should he have more than he bargained for? Every contributory who was the holder of an ordinary share at the date of the winding up took his share and held it on similar terms. He has done all he contracted to do; why should he have less than his bargain? When the preference shareholders and the ordinary shareholders are once placed on exactly the same footing in regard to the amounts paid up upon their shares, what is there to alter rights which were the subject of express contract? . . .

Then it is said on behalf of the preference shareholders that the provision for payment of dividends in proportion to the amounts paid up on the shares leads to an inference that the distribution of surplus assets was to be made in the same proportion. I do not think that it leads to any inference of the kind. It is a very common provision nowadays, though it is not what you find in Table A, and it is a very reasonable provision, because during the continuance of the company, and while it is a going concern, it prevents any sense of dissatisfaction on the part of those who have paid more on their shares than their fellow shareholders of a different issue. But when it has come to an end I cannot see how it can be used to regulate or disturb rights with which it had nothing to do even while it was in force . . .

LORDS HERSCHELL and FITZGERALD delivered concurring opinions.

Where the terms of issue do make express provision as to the rights of a class of shares in respect of (a) dividend, (b) the return of capital (and participation in surplus assets), or (c) voting, then that provision is presumed to be an exhaustive statement of the rights of the class in that particular respect.

[9.03] Re National Telephone Co [1914] 1 Ch 755 (Chancery Division)

SARGANT J: [It] appears to me that the weight of authority is in favour of the view that, either with regard to dividend or with regard to the rights in a winding up, the express gift or attachment of preferential rights to preference shares, on their creation, is, prima facie, a definition of the whole of their rights in that respect, and negatives any further or other right to which, but for the specified rights, they would have been entitled . . .

[9.04] Scottish Insurance Corpn Ltd v Wilsons and Clyde Coal Co Ltd [1949] AC 462 (House of Lords)

[For the facts and another part of the decision, see above, [8.02].]

The rights of the preference shareholders were, so far as is material, defined by articles 159 and 160 of the articles of association as follows:

159. In the event of the company being wound up, the preference shares (first issue) shall rank before the other shares of the company on the property of the company, to the extent of repayment of the amounts called up and paid thereon.

160. In the event of the company being wound up, the preference shares (second issue) shall rank before the ordinary shares but after the said preference shares (first issue) on the property of the company to the extent of repayment of the amounts called up and paid thereon.

LORD SIMONDS: It is clear from the authorities, and would be clear without them, that, subject to any relevant provision of the general law, the rights inter se of preference and ordinary shareholders must depend on the terms of the instrument which contains the bargain that they have made with the company and each other. This means that there is a question of construction to be determined, and undesirable though it may be that fine distinctions should be drawn in commercial documents such as articles of association of a company, your Lordships cannot decide that the articles here under review have a particular meaning, because to somewhat similar articles in such cases as *Re William Metcalfe & Sons Ltd* [5] that meaning has been judicially attributed. Reading the relevant articles, as a whole, I come to the conclusion that articles 159 and 160 are exhaustive of the rights of the preference stockholders in a winding up. The whole tenor of the articles, as I have already pointed out, is to leave the ordinary stockholders masters of the situation. If there are 'surplus assets' it is because the ordinary stockholders have contrived that it should be so, and, though this is not decisive, in determining what the parties meant by their bargain, it is of some weight that it should be in the power of one class so to act that there will or will not be surplus assets . . .

But, apart from those more general considerations, the words of the specifically relevant articles, 'rank before the other shares . . . on the property of the company to the extent of repayment of the amounts called up and paid thereon', appears to me apt to define exhaustively the rights of the preference stockholders in a winding up. Similar words, in *Will v United Lankat Plantations Co Ltd* [6] 'rank, both as regards capital and dividend, in priority to the other shares', were held to define exhaustively the rights of preference shareholders to dividend, and I do not find in the speeches of Viscount Haldane LC or Earl Loreburn in that case any suggestion that a different result would have followed if the dispute had been in regard to capital. I do not ignore that in the same case in the Court of Appeal [7] the distinction between dividend and capital was expressly made by both Cozens-Hardy MR and Farwell LJ, and that in *Re William Metcalfe & Sons Ltd*, Romer LJ reasserted it. But I share the difficulty, which Lord Keith has expressed in this case, in reconciling the reasoning that lies behind the judgments in *Will*'s case and *Re William Melcalfe & Sons Ltd* respectively. [His Lordship accordingly held that the latter decision should be overruled.]

VISCOUNT MAUGHAM and LORD NORMAND delivered concurring opinions.

LORD MORTON OF HENRYTON dissented.

➤ Note

The conclusion reached in the *Scottish Insurance* case naturally made preference shares a less secure form of investment. It was also thought at the time to be harsh on the holders of such shares, for the overruling of *Metcalfe*'s case inevitably depressed the value of shares carrying a high rate of return. To offset the effect of the *Scottish Insurance* decision, many listed companies have since adopted the 'Spens formula', under which the sum to be repaid to preference shareholders on a reduction of capital is geared to the recent market price of the shares. For an example, see below, Appendix, p 710.

[5] [1933] Ch 142.
[6] [1914] AC 11 at 13.
[7] [1912] 2 Ch 571.

Variation of class rights

Statutory requirements

If the share capital of a company has been divided into classes,[8] statutory provisions come into play, defining the ability of the company to alter the rights attached to a class of shares. CA 2006 ss 630 provides that class rights may only be varied:

(i) in accordance with the relevant provisions in the company's articles; or

(ii) if no provision is made in the articles, if three-quarters in value of the shares of that class consent in writing, or a special resolution is passed at a separate meeting of the holders of such shares (also see ss 283, 334).[9]

The company's articles may specify either more *or* less onerous provisions for variation of class rights than the default provisions in the Act.[10] However, if the company *entrenches* the class rights in its articles (ie sets conditions for change that are more demanding than the special resolution procedure) then that protection cannot be circumvented by changing the rights attached to the class of shares under s 630: see CA 2006 ss 630(3) and 22.

Additional common law requirements

These statutory provisions are reinforced by a rule of common law established in the *British American Nickel* case **[9.06]**. This case establishes the rule that members voting at a class meeting must act 'in the interest of the class as a whole'. This obviously has some links with the principle of *Allen v Gold Reefs of West Africa Ltd* **[4.23]**, that members must vote 'bona fide for the benefit of the company as a whole'. That principle has been extended in some later cases (eg *Re Holders Investment Trust Ltd* **[8.05]**). If taken literally, the rule as so interpreted would not allow a class to subordinate its own interests to those of the company as a whole, and class rights could never be varied except to the holders' advantage. This surely cannot have been intended.

Meaning of 'class right'

These statutory provisions apply only if the shareholders have a 'class rights',[11] and only if those rights have been 'varied'. Both requirements have caused more debate than might be imagined. Indeed, some textbooks devote considerable attention to the meaning and scope of the term 'class right'. If the preference shareholders have a right under the articles to a 10% preference dividend, that is obviously a 'class right', but if the articles say nothing about the dividend rights of ordinary shareholders in the same company, is their dividend right a 'class

---

[8] Note that the new CA 2006 provisions on variation of class rights extend the rules to companies without share capital, eg companies limited by guarantee with different classes of members having different voting rights. CA 2006 ss 631, 335 and 635 provide appropriate rules in the same terms as those discussed above.

[9] This effects a change to CA 1985, which only allowed the company to impose conditions that were *more* onerous than the statute. The company could do this by inserting the conditions into the memorandum, the articles, or the terms of the share issue itself: see CA 1985 s 125.

[10] And any provisions inserted in a company's memorandum before CA 2006 will be treated as contained in the company's articles: CA 2006 s 28.

[11] Interestingly, the term is used in the heading to s 630, but not in the section itself, which refers to 'variation of the rights attached to a class of shares'. The 2006 Act then specifies that 'shares are of one class if the rights attached to them are in all respects uniform' (s 629(1)). Another way of putting the question posed in the paragraph above is to ask whether shares are of a *different* class, for the purpose of s 630, if some of the rights attached to them are different, even if the right being varied is the same for all of them. The assumed answer is no, and the analysis is invariably one that approaches the issue from a 'class rights' perspective, as above. CA 1985 s 125 was in the same terms in this respect (although not in others), and this was the conclusion.

right' too? And if nothing is said about voting in regard to either class of shares in their terms of issue, are their voting rights 'class rights'? In the example on p 428 above, where the only expressed right is that of appointing a director, are the dividend rights of each class 'class rights'?

The only light thrown on this issue by the Act itself is in ss 630(5) and 630(6). Section 630(5) states that amendment or insertion of a 'variation of rights' provision in the articles is itself a variation of rights. Section 630(6) deals with the extinction of rights but not the extinction of the share itself: *Re Saltdean Estate Co Ltd* [8.04].

In the *Cumbrian Newspapers* case [9.05], Scott J was called on to give the first judicial consideration to the meaning of the terms 'class of shares' and 'class rights'. His conclusion was that they might extend to include cases where rights are enjoyed by a particular member or category of members but no specific shares are designated to which those rights are referable.[12] This is a surprisingly wide interpretation, but has the merit of ensuring that the protection conferred by s 630 will be applied fairly comprehensively.

Defining a 'variation' of class rights

Paradoxically, the judges have not shown themselves anything like so solicitous for the interests of class members in the cases concerned with the interpretation of the term 'variation'. In many cases it may be possible to make class rights less effective without effecting any technical 'variation' of the rights themselves: this is illustrated by *White v Bristol Aeroplane Co* [9.07] and *Greenhalgh v Arderne Cinemas Ltd* [9.08].

Right of dissenting member to object to court

CA 2006 s 633 gives dissenting members of a class, who hold at least 15% of the shares of that class, the right to challenge the variation in court within 21 days. They are thus given access to the court free from the hazards of *Foss v Harbottle* [11.01], but the requirements of 15% and the need to act within 21 days may lead to difficulties, especially in a large company.

Rights enjoyed by a member may be class rights although they are not referable to particular shares.

[9.05] Cumbrian Newspapers Group Ltd v Cumberland and Westmorland Herald Newspaper and Printing Co Ltd [1987] Ch 1 (Chancery Division)

The plaintiff had acquired 10.67% of the ordinary shares in the defendant company ('Cumberland') in 1968 as part of an arrangement designed to concentrate the local newspaper publishing business under one title and to make it difficult for an outsider to acquire control of this paper. The articles of Cumberland were altered so that the plaintiff had (i) rights of pre-emption over the company's other ordinary shares (arts 7 and 9), (ii) rights in respect of un-issued shares (art 5), and (iii) the right to appoint a director, so long as it held at least 10% of the shares (art 12). Scott J held that these were class rights enjoyed by the plaintiff which could only be altered pursuant to CA 1985 s 125 [CA 2006 s 630].

SCOTT J: I turn to the critical question: are the plaintiff's rights under articles 5, 7, 9 and 12, rights attached to a class of shares?

Rights or benefits which may be contained in articles can be divided into three different categories. First, there are rights or benefits which are annexed to particular shares. Classic examples

---

[12] This is not covered by the new CA 2006 s 631, which concerns companies without share capital.

of rights of this character are dividend rights and rights to participate in surplus assets on a winding up. If articles provide that particular shares carry particular rights not enjoyed by the holders of other shares, it is easy to conclude that the rights are attached to a class of shares, for the purpose both of s 125 of the Act of 1985 and of article 4 of Table A [1948]. It is common ground that rights falling into this category are rights attached to a class of shares for those purposes. Mr Howarth submitted at first that this category should be restricted to rights that were capable of being enjoyed by the holders for the time being of the shares in question. Such a restriction would exclude rights expressly attached to particular shares issued to some named individual, but expressed to determine upon transfer of the shares by the named individual. *Palmer's Company Precedents*, 17th edn (1956), Pt I, p 818, contains a form for the creation of a life governor's share in a company. Mr Howarth accepted that the rights attached to a share in accordance with this precedent would be rights attached to a class of shares. He accepted, rightly in my judgment, that a provision for defeasance of rights on alienation of the share to which the rights were attached, would not of itself prevent the rights, pre-alienation, from being properly described as rights attached to a class of shares. The plaintiff's rights under articles 5, 7, 9 and 12 cannot, however, be brought within this first category. The rights were not attached to any particular shares. In articles 5, 7 and 9, there is no reference to any current shareholding held by the plaintiff. The rights conferred on the plaintiff under article 12 are dependent on the plaintiff holding at least 10% of the issued ordinary shares in the defendant. But the rights are not attached to any particular shares. Any ordinary shares in the defendant, if sufficient in number and held by the plaintiff, would entitle the plaintiff to exercise the rights.

A second category of rights or benefits which may be contained in articles (although it may be that neither 'rights' nor 'benefits' is an apt description), would cover rights or benefits conferred on individuals not in the capacity of members or shareholders of the company but, for ulterior reasons, connected with the administration of the company's affairs or the conduct of its business. *Eley v Positive Government Security Life Assurance Co Ltd* **[4.36]** was a case where the articles of the defendant company had included a provision that the plaintiff should be the company solicitor. The plaintiff sought to enforce that provision as a contract between himself and the company. He failed. The reasons why he failed are not here relevant, and I cite the case only to draw attention to an article which, on its terms, conferred a benefit on an individual but not in the capacity of member or shareholder of the company. It is, perhaps, obvious that rights or benefits in this category cannot be class rights. They cannot be described as rights attached to a class of shares. The plaintiff in *Eley v Positive Government Security Life Assurance Co Ltd* was not a shareholder at the time the articles were adopted. He became a shareholder some time thereafter. It is easy, therefore, to conclude that the article in question did not confer on him any right or benefit in his capacity as a member of the company. In a case where the individual had been issued with shares in the company at the same time and as part of the same broad arrangement under which the article in question had been adopted, the conclusion might not be so easy. But if, in all the circumstances, the right conclusion was still that the rights or benefits conferred by the article were not conferred on the beneficiary in the capacity of member or shareholder of the company, then the rights could not, in my view, be regarded as class rights. They would not be rights attached to any class of shares . . .

In my judgment, the plaintiff's rights under those articles do not fall within this second category.

That leaves the third category. This category would cover rights or benefits that, although not attached to any particular shares, were nonetheless conferred on the beneficiary in the capacity of member or shareholder of the company. The rights of the plaintiff under articles 5, 7, 9 and 12 fall, in my judgment, into this category. Other examples can be found in reported cases.

In *Bushell v Faith* **[5.05]**, articles of association included a provision that on a resolution at a general meeting for the removal of any director from office, any shares held by that director should carry the right to three votes. The purpose of this provision was to prevent directors being removed from office by a simple majority of the members of the company. The validity of the article was upheld by the Court of Appeal and by the House of Lords; the reasons do not, for present purposes, matter. But the rights conferred by the article in question fall, in my view, firmly in this third category. They were not attached to any particular shares. On the other hand, they were conferred on the director/beneficiaries in their capacity as shareholders. The article created, in effect, two classes of shareholders—namely, shareholders who were for the time being directors, on the one hand, and shareholders who were not for the time being directors, on the other hand.

The present case is, and *Bushell v Faith* was, concerned with rights conferred by articles. The other side of the coin is demonstrated by *Rayfield v Hands* **[4.38]**. That case was concerned with obligations imposed on members by the articles. The articles of the company included an article entitling every member to sell his shares to the directors of the company at a fair valuation. In effect, the members enjoyed 'put' options exercisable against the directors. Vaisey J held that the obligations imposed by the article on the directors for the time being were enforceable against them. He held that the obligations were imposed on the directors in their capacity as members of the company. It follows from his judgment that, as in *Bushell v Faith*, there were in effect two classes of shareholders in the company. There were shareholders who were not for the time being directors, and shareholders who were for the time being directors: the former had rights against the latter which the latter did not enjoy against the former. The two classes were identifiable not by reference to their respective ownership of particular shares, but by reference to the office held by the latter. But the rights of the former, and the obligations of the latter, required their respective ownership of shares in the company. Accordingly, as a matter of classification, the rights in question fall, in my view, into the third category.

In the present case, the rights conferred on the plaintiff under articles 5, 7, 9 and 12 were, as I have held, conferred on the plaintiff as a member or shareholder of the defendant. The rights would not be enforceable by the plaintiff otherwise than as the owner of ordinary shares in the defendants. If the plaintiff were to divest itself of all its ordinary shares in the defendant, it would not then, in my view, be in a position to enforce the rights in the articles. But the rights were not attached to any particular share or shares. Enforcement by the plaintiff of the rights granted under articles 5, 7 and 9, would require no more than ownership by the plaintiff of at least some shares in the defendant. Enforcement by the plaintiff of the rights granted under article 12 require the plaintiff to hold at least 10% of the issued shares in the defendant. But any shares would do. It follows, in my judgment, that the plaintiff's rights under the articles in question fall squarely within this third category.

The question for decision is whether rights in this third category are within the meaning of the phrase in s 125 of the Companies Act 1985 and in article 4 of Table A, rights attached to a class of shares. [His Lordship examined the language and the background of the section and concluded that this was the case.]

➤ Question

The implications of this case are potentially far-reaching. In the *Bushell v Faith* case, for example, the director's right to deploy super-voting powers on a motion for his dismissal could only be changed by the class rights procedure (s 630, requiring his agreement, as the only member of the relevant class). If the director's right had been classified differently, it could have been changed by the statutory procedure for changing the articles (s 21, requiring a special majority of *all* the shareholders). Which is the preferable outcome? Which outcome was likely to have been contemplated at the time the right was created?

A vote on a resolution to modify class rights must be exercised for the purpose, or dominant purpose, of benefiting the class as a whole.

[9.06] British America Nickel Corpn Ltd v O'Brien [1927] AC 369 (Privy Council)

The company had issued mortgage bonds, secured by a trust deed, which provided (*inter alia*) that a majority of the bondholders, representing not less than three-fourths in value, might sanction any modification of the rights of the bondholders. A scheme for the reconstruction of the company, which involved a modification of the bondholders' rights, was approved by the requisite majority. However, it was objected that one of the bondholders, without whose vote the proposal would not have been carried, had been induced to give his support by a promise of a large block of ordinary stock. The Privy Council, affirming the decision of the Ontario courts, held that the vote was invalid.

The opinion of their Lordships was delivered by VISCOUNT HALDANE: To give a power to modify the terms on which debentures in a company are secured is not uncommon in practice. The business interests of the company may render such a power expedient, even in the interests of the class of debentureholders as a whole. The provision is usually made in the form of a power, conferred by the instrument constituting the debenture security, upon the majority of the class of holders. It often enables them to modify, by resolution properly passed, the security itself. The provision of such a power to a majority bears some analogy to such a power as that . . . which enables a majority of the shareholders by special resolution to alter the articles of association. There is, however, a restriction of such powers, when conferred on a majority of a special class in order to enable that majority to bind a minority. They must be exercised subject to a general principle, which is applicable to all authorities conferred on majorities of classes enabling them to bind minorities; namely, that the power given must be exercised for the purpose of benefiting the class as a whole, and not merely individual members only. Subject to this, the power may be unrestricted. It may be free from the general principle in question when the power arises not in connection with a class, but only under a general title which confers the vote as a right of property attaching to a share. The distinction does not arise in this case, and it is not necessary to express an opinion as to its ground. What does arise is the question whether there is such a restriction on the right to vote of a creditor or member of an analogous class on whom is conferred a power to vote for the alteration of the title of a minority of the class to which he himself belongs . . .

[T]heir Lordships do not think that there is any real difficulty in combining the principle that while usually a holder of shares or debentures may vote as his interest directs, he is subject to the further principle that where his vote is conferred on him as a member of a class he must conform to the interest of the class itself when seeking to exercise the power conferred on him in his capacity of being a member. The second principle is a negative one, one which puts a restriction on the completeness of freedom under the first, without excluding such freedom wholly.

The distinction, which may prove a fine one, is well illustrated in the carefully worded judgment of Parker J in *Goodfellow v Nelson Line*.[13] It was there held that while the power conferred by a trust deed on a majority of debentureholders to bind a minority must be exercised bona fide, and while the court has power to prevent some sorts at least of unfairness or oppression, a debentureholder may, subject to this, vote in accordance with his individual interests, though these may be peculiar to himself and not shared by the other members of the class. It was true that a secret bargain to secure his vote by special treatment might be treated as bribery, but where the scheme to be voted upon itself provides, as it did in that case, openly for special treatment of a debentureholder with a special interest, he may vote, inasmuch as the other members of the class had themselves known from the first of the scheme. Their Lordships think that Parker J accurately applied in his judgment the law on this point . . .

Their Lordships are of opinion that judgment was rightly given for the respondents in this appeal . . . [It] is plain, even from his own letters, that before Mr JR Booth would agree to the scheme of 1921 his vote had to be secured by the promise of $2,000,000 ordinary stock of the Nickel Corporation. No doubt he was entitled in giving his vote to consider his own interests. But as that vote had come to him as a member of a class he was bound to exercise it with the interests of the class itself kept in view as dominant. It may be that, as Ferguson JA thought, he and those with

[13] [1912] 2 Ch 324.

whom he was negotiating considered the scheme the best way out of the difficulties with which the corporation was beset. But they had something else to consider in the first place. Their duty was to look to the difficulties of the bondholders as a class, and not to give any one of these bondholders a special personal advantage, not forming part of the scheme to be voted for, in order to induce him to assent . . .

➤ Questions

1. You are asked to advise a preference shareholder about a class meeting which is to be held to consider a scheme to replace the preference shares with debentures. There is evidence suggesting that this will be to the disadvantage of the preference shareholders as a class, but that the scheme as a whole will benefit the company. Should the preference shareholder have regard to the interests of the class, or of the company, in deciding how to cast her vote; or is she free to weigh the relative merits of each? (See *Re Holders Investment Trust Ltd* [8.05] and *Re Hellenic and General Trust Ltd* [13.04], and contrast *Re Chatterley Whitfield Collieries Ltd* [8.03].)

2. If all the members of a class are to take account of the same considerations when voting, will a resolution invariably be carried (or lost) by 100% to nil?

The rights of a class of shareholders are not altered, or even 'affected', by a change in the company's structure (or in the rights attached to other shares) if this change affects merely the enjoyment of such rights.

[9.07] White v Bristol Aeroplane Co [1953] Ch 65 (Court of Appeal)

Article 68 of the defendant company's articles provided that the rights attached to any class of shares might be 'affected, modified, varied, dealt with, or abrogated in any manner' with the sanction of an extraordinary resolution passed at a separate meeting of the members of that class. The plaintiff, on behalf of the preference shareholders, claimed that a proposal to increase the capital of the company by a bonus issue of new shares to the existing shareholders (to both preference and ordinary shareholders) 'affected' the voting rights attached to their shares, and therefore came within the terms of the article cited. The company's view, which was upheld by the Court of Appeal, was that the rights themselves (as distinct from the enjoyment or the effectiveness of those rights) were not 'affected' by the proposal, so that no class meeting was required.

ROMER LJ: The rights attaching to the preference stockholders are those which are conferred by articles 62 and 83; and the only relevant article for present purposes is article 83. Under that article it is provided . . . that on a poll every member present in person or by proxy shall have one vote for every share held by him, or in the case of the preference stock, one vote for every £1 of preference stock held by him. It is suggested that, as a result of the proposed increase of capital, that right of the preference stockholders will in some way be 'affected'; but I cannot see that it will be affected in any way whatever. The position then will be precisely the same as now—namely, that the holder of preference stock will have on a poll one vote for every £1 of preference stock held by him. It is quite true that the block vote, if one may so describe the total voting power of the class, will, or may, have less force behind it, because it will pro tanto be watered down by reason of the increased total voting power of the members of the company; but no particular weight is attached to the vote, by the constitution of the company, as distinct from the right to exercise the vote, and certainly no right is conferred on the preference stockholders to preserve anything in the nature of an equilibrium between their class and the ordinary stockholders or any other class.

During the course of the discussion I asked Mr Gray [counsel] whether it would not be true to say that the logical result of his argument would be that the rights of ordinary shareholders would be affected by the issue of new ordinary capital on the ground that every one of the considerations on which he was relying would be present in such a case. The votes of the existing shareholders would be diminished in power; and they would have other people with whom to share the profits, and, on a winding up, to share the capital assets. In answer to that he was constrained, I think rightly, to say that was so. But in my opinion it cannot be said that the rights of ordinary shareholders would be affected by the issue of further ordinary capital; their rights would remain just as they were before, and the only result would be that the class of persons entitled to exercise those rights would be enlarged; and for my part I cannot help thinking that a certain amount of confusion has crept into this case between rights on the one hand, and the result of exercising those rights on the other hand. The rights, as such, are conferred by resolution or by the articles, and they cannot be affected except with the sanction of the members on whom those rights are conferred; but the results of exercising those rights are not the subject of any assurance or guarantee under the constitution of the company, and are not protected in any way. It is the rights and those alone, which are protected, and . . . the rights of the preference stockholders will not, in my judgment, be affected by the proposed resolutions . . .

EVERSHED MR delivered a concurring judgment.

DENNING LJ concurred.

[9.08] Greenhalgh v Arderne Cinemas Ltd [1946] 1 All ER 512 (Court of Appeal)

For later litigation between the same parties, see [4.27] above. The company had issued ordinary shares of 10s [50p] each and other ordinary shares of 2s [10p] each (created in 1941), ranking *pari passu* for all purposes. On a poll, every member had one vote for each share held by him, which meant that Greenhalgh, who held the bulk of the 2s shares, could control about 40% of the votes and so block a special resolution. The holders of the 10s shares procured the passing of an ordinary resolution subdividing the 10s shares into five 2s shares, each ranking *pari passu* with the 1941 2s shares. Greenhalgh objected unsuccessfully that the rights attaching to his 2s shares were 'varied' by this manoeuvre.

LORD GREENE MR: Looking at the position of the original 2s ordinary shares, one asks oneself: What are the rights in respect of voting attached to that class within the meaning of article 3 of Table A [of the 1929 Act; there is no equivalent in later model articles] which are to be unalterable save with the necessary consents of the holders? The only right of voting which is attached in terms to the shares of that class is the right to have one vote per share pari passu with the other ordinary shares of the company for the time being issued. That right has not been taken away. Of course, if it had been attempted to reduce that voting right, eg by providing or attempting to provide that there should be one vote for every five of such shares, that would have been an interference with the voting rights attached to that class of shares. But nothing of the kind has been done; the right to have one vote per share is left undisturbed . . . I agree, the effect of this resolution is, of course, to alter the position of the 1941 2s shareholders. Instead of Greenhalgh finding himself in a position of control, he finds himself in a position where the control has gone, and to that extent the rights of the 1941 2s shareholders are affected, as a matter of business. As a matter of law, I am quite unable to hold that, as a result of the transaction, the rights are varied; they remain what they always were—a right to have one vote per share pari passu with the ordinary shares for the time being issued which include the new 2s ordinary shares resulting from the subdivision.

In the result, the appeal must be dismissed with costs.

MORTON LJ delivered a concurring judgment.

SOMERVELL LJ concurred.

➤ Notes

1. See also *Re Saltdean Estate Co Ltd* **[8.04]** and *House of Fraser plc v ACGE Investments Ltd* (above, p 397), where it was held that no variation of rights was involved in the *cancellation* of a class of shares on a reduction of capital, this being consistent with the terms of issue of the shares in question.

Reference may also be made to *Re Hellenic and General Trust Ltd* **[13.04]**, where Templeman J ruled that, for the purposes of a scheme of arrangement under CA 1985 ss 425–427A [CA 2006 ss 895ff], ordinary shares owned by the intending purchaser's subsidiary constituted a different 'class' from ordinary shares owned by outsiders, although the terms of issue of all these shares were identical. This approach, taking account (as it does) of matters peculiar to the holder rather than to the shares themselves, is in strong contrast with that in the two cases last cited. However, it may be justified by reference to the wording of s 425, which refers to classes *of members* rather than classes *of shares* [CA 2006 s 895 is the same].

2. These cases deal with the *rights* of the different classes of shareholder as a matter of formal law. But an act which is within the rights of the controlling shareholders in this sense may nevertheless sometimes justify the grant of relief to minority members under CA 2006 s 994 ('unfairly prejudicial' conduct: see below, pp 552 ff) or IA 1986 s 122(1)(g) (winding up on the 'just and equitable' ground: see below, pp 653 ff).

Transfer of shares

This section examines the transfer of shares, but most of the remarks apply also to dealings in other company securities, such as loan stock or debenture stock. A number of general points can be made.

Shares in a company are in principle freely transferable, subject to any restrictions imposed by the company's articles of association (CA 2006 s 544). However, the articles of nearly all (if not all) private companies restrict their members' rights to transfer their shares. This is done to ensure control over the management and direction of the company.

Although a share is a chose in action, the transfer of shares is not governed solely by the ordinary rules of assignment of choses in action. The *legal* title to shares is transferred only by registration of the new holder's name in the company's register of members.[14] Oddly, it is not possible to find any categorical statement to this effect in the Companies Act, although it is perhaps implicit from a reading of ss 540ff. The rule goes back to the days when shares normally had a substantial element of unpaid liability, and the act of registration established beyond argument the contractual bond of the new member to the company, so that his or her liability for calls could be enforced. (There was also probably some analogy with the transfer of government stock, where the requirement of registration is statutory.)

CA 2006 s 770 provides that a transfer of shares (or of company debentures[15]) cannot be registered (unless the transfer occurs by operation of law) unless: (i) a proper instrument of transfer has been delivered to the company; (ii) it is an exempt transfer within the Stock Transfer Act 1982; or (iii) it is a transfer undertaken in accordance with CA 2006, Part 21, Ch 2, dealing with uncertificated transfers.

---

[14] Bearer shares ('share warrants', CA 2006 s 779—these are rare in practice) are an exception: these are transferable by delivery. In Canada, the transfer of shares is governed by a modern code which comes close to making all share certificates negotiable instruments.

[15] See below, Chapter 10.

On ordinary contract law principles, specific performance will be ordered of contracts for the sale of company shares unless there is a ready market for the purchase of substitute shares using a damages award (*Re Schwabacher* (1907) 98 LT 127).

Share certificates, uncertificated shares and dematerialised securities

The primary record of the ownership of company shares is the register of members (CA 2006 s 112). Companies also provide their shareholders with share certificates, which provide evidence of ownership. Until 1996, every sale of shares had to be accompanied by the relevant share certificate. Since 1996, the London Stock Exchange has developed a centralised securities depository, called CREST,[16] which is a computer-based system that records title to shares and enables title to be transferred. When the title to a share is recorded in CREST, no share certificate is issued, and the share is said to be '*uncertificated*' or '*dematerialised*'. At present, only listed companies need to have uncertificated shares. In all other companies, shares are certificated.

Transfer of certificated securities

The holder of fully paid certificated shares transfers them by completing and signing a share-transfer form which indicates the name of the company, the details of the shares being transferred (number, nominal value, class), the consideration for the transfer (nil if by way of gift), and the name and address of both the transferor and the transferee.[17]

In the simplest case of a sale of all the shares represented on one share certificate, the transferor sends the completed transfer form, plus the share certificate,[18] to the transferee, who pays the price and the relevant stamp duty, and requests the company to register the transfer. The transfer is recorded by the company in the register of members and a new certificate, made out in the transferee's name, is issued to him. This procedure (prescribed by the Stock Transfer Act) may be used for all fully paid securities even though the company's articles provide otherwise. Further practical steps are added if the transferor wants to sell only part of a holding denominated on one share certificate, or if the transferee wants the shares to be converted to uncertificated securities.

If a share transfer is made as a result of fraudulently forged share certificates, then anyone who suffers loss as a result can sue the fraudster in deceit (see below, p 444). The same measure of remedy (ie as in deceit) is available against a company that makes a negligent false certification (CA 2006, s 775(3), and the certification is taken to have been made by the company if it was issued and signed by the person authorised to issue certifications (s 775(4)(b)) (see below, p 446).

Transfer of uncertificated shares

The rules above apply in the main to shares (or other securities) not traded on a public market. Although the rules could apply in a wider context, most purchasers of publicly traded shares use a different process. For shares traded on a public market, the Listing Rules do not permit any restrictions on transferability; the buyers and sellers deal through the Exchange, via a broker, not face-to-face; and the transfer is effected in uncertificated form, through

---

[16] A great deal of information about CRESTCo is given on its website: www.crestco.co.uk

[17] 'Blank' transfer forms, sometimes used by shareholders to provide security to lenders, are these transfer forms completed in all the details other than the name of the transferee.

[18] A share certificate is *prima facie* evidence of title: CA 2006 s 768.

CREST, on the basis of real time delivery against payment. This electronic system of transfer reduces costs and risks.

As mentioned above, CREST is a computer-based securities transfer settlement system which enables securities to be transferred electronically without a written instrument, and title to be evidenced without a certificate. CREST came into operation in July 1996. It is operated by a company called CRESTCo Ltd, authorised for the purpose by the Financial Services Authority under powers delegated by the Treasury. Securities held on CREST are recorded in electronic form and are transferred by means of electronic instructions received from participating members (primarily brokers), subject to elaborate provisions for security. Participation in the CREST scheme is optional, in the sense that a company may choose to have some or all of its securities to be held in uncertificated form, and there is also an option for any individual holder of the securities to hold his or her securities in one form or the other.

Until 2001, CREST did not itself maintain any register of holders, but merely provided a settlement system, and an instruction to the company to amend its share register accordingly. An entry in the company's register remained evidence of title in the same way as if the entry related to certificated securities. Since 2001, CRESTCo has maintained an Operator register (separate from the company's own register), and registers the transfers immediately they occur. The Operator register is *prima facie* evidence of the title to uncertificated shares (just as the company's register is for certificated shares).

Restrictions on transfer: directors' approval and pre-emption rights

Listed companies are not permitted to impose restrictions on transfer. Private companies typically do, however. The two provisions most commonly found are: (i) an article giving the directors a discretion to refuse to register any transfer; and (ii) some form of pre-emptive right for existing members. A transfer of certificated shares is not complete until the transfer is registered in the company's register of members. After paying for the shares and before registration, the transferee only has an equitable interest in the shares.

If the directors are given absolute discretion to refuse to transfer the shares, they must, as directors, exercise this power *bona fide* and for proper purposes: see above, pp 284 ff, and below, *Re Smith and Fawcett Ltd* [9.09]. CA 2006 s 771(1) requires the directors to consider the matter and either register the transfer or give the transferee notice of and reasons for refusal as soon as practicable and, in any event, within two months. The reasons for refusal must be such as may reasonably be requested, but need not extend to the minutes of board meetings at which the matter was considered.

If transfers are subject to pre-emption rights (requiring the shares to be offered first to the existing shareholders), then directors must refuse to register transfers to outsiders until this is done. Absent this, the existing shareholders' equitable interest in the shares takes priority over the transferee's equitable interest under the sale: *Tett v Phoenix Property and Investments Co Ltd* [1984] BCLC 599.

Where the articles confer on the directors a discretion to refuse to register a transfer of shares, they must exercise their power bona fide and for proper purposes; but, subject to this qualification, they may be given an absolute discretion.

[9.09] Re Smith and Fawcett Ltd [1942] Ch 304 (Court of Appeal)

Article 10 of the company's articles provided that the directors might in their absolute and uncontrolled discretion refuse to register any transfer of shares. There were only two directors and shareholders, Smith and Fawcett, who held 4,001 shares each. After Fawcett's death, Smith and a co-opted director refused to register a transfer of his shares into the names of his executors, or one of them; but Smith offered instead to register 2,001 shares and to buy the remaining 2,000 shares at a price fixed by himself. The court refused to intervene in the exercise of this discretion without evidence of *mala fides*.

LORD GREENE MR: The principles to be applied in cases where the articles of a company confer a discretion on directors with regard to the acceptance of transfer of shares are, for the present purposes, free from doubt. They must exercise their discretion bona fide in what they consider—not what a court may consider—is in the interests of the company, and not for any collateral purpose. They must have regard to those considerations, and those considerations only, which the articles on their true construction permit them to take into consideration, and in construing the relevant provisions in the articles it is to be borne in mind that one of the normal rights of a shareholder is the right to deal freely with his property and to transfer it to whomsoever he pleases. When it is said, as it has been said more than once, that regard must be had to this last consideration, it means, I apprehend, nothing more than that the shareholder has such a prima facie right, and that right is not to be cut down by uncertain language or doubtful implications. The right, if it is to be cut down, must be cut down with satisfactory clarity. It certainly does not mean that articles, if appropriately framed, cannot be allowed to cut down the right of transfer to any extent which the articles on their true construction permit. Another consideration which must be borne in mind is that this type of article is one which is for the most part confined to private companies. Private companies are in law separate entities just as much as are public companies, but from the business and personal point of view they are much more analogous to partnerships than to public corporations. Accordingly, it is to be expected that in the articles of such a company the control of the directors over the membership may be very strict indeed. There are, or may be, very good business reasons why those who bring such companies into existence should give them a constitution which confers on the directors powers of the widest description.

The language of the article in the present case does not point out any particular matter as being the only matter to which the directors are to pay attention in deciding whether or not they will allow the transfer to be registered. The article does not, for instance, say, as is to be found in some articles, that they may refuse to register any transfer of shares to a person not already a member of the company or to a transferee of whom they do not approve. Where articles are framed with some such limitation on the discretionary power of refusal as I have mentioned in those two examples, it follows on plain principle that if the directors go outside the matters which the articles say are to be the matters and the only matters to which they are to have regard, the directors will have exceeded their powers.

Mr Spens [counsel], in his argument for the plaintiff, maintained that whatever language was used in the articles, the power of the directors to refuse to register a transfer must always be limited to matters personal to the transferee and that there can be no personal objection to the plaintiff becoming a member of the company because the directors are prepared to accept him as the holder of [2001] of the shares which have come to him as legal personal representative of his father. Mr Spens relies for his proposition on the observations in several authorities, but on examination of those cases it becomes clear that the form of article then before the court by its express language confined the directors to the consideration of the desirability of admitting the proposed transferee to membership on grounds personal to him . . .

There is nothing, in my opinion, in principle or in authority to make it impossible to draft such a wide and comprehensive power to directors to refuse to transfer as to enable them to take into account any matter which they conceive to be in the interests of the company, and thereby to admit or not to admit a particular person and to allow or not to allow a particular transfer for reasons not personal to the transferee but bearing on the general interests of the company as a whole—such matters, for instance, as whether by their passing a particular transfer the transferee would obtain too great a weight in the councils of the company or might even perhaps obtain control. The question, therefore, simply is whether on the true construction of the particular article the directors are limited by anything except their bona fide view as to the interests of the company. In the present case the article is drafted in the widest possible terms, and I decline to write into that clear language any limitation other than a limitation, which is implicit by law, that a fiduciary power of this kind must be exercised bona fide in the interests of the company. Subject to that qualification, an article in this form appears to me to give the directors what it says, namely, an absolute and uncontrolled discretion . . .

LUXMOORE LJ and ASQUITH J concurred.

> ➤ Notes

1. *Re Smith and Fawcett Ltd* is also a leading case on the general subject of directors' powers and duties: see above, pp 273 ff.

2. In *Re Swaledale Cleaners Ltd* [1968] 1 WLR 1710 it was held that the discretionary power of directors to refuse registration of a transfer must be affirmatively exercised. The directors must consider the matter and make a decision not to register within a reasonable time after the transfer has been submitted, failing which the transferee is entitled to registration. In the light of CA 2006 s 771(1), a reasonable time for this purpose is *prima facie* two months. However, in *Popely v Planarrive Ltd* [1997] 1 BCLC 8 it was held that, so long as the directors had reached a decision not to register a transfer within two months, it was not fatal to the effectiveness of their decision that the applicant had not been informed of it within that period. In *Re New Cedos Engineering Co Ltd* [1994] 1 BCLC 797 the company had no directors during the whole of the two months following the receipt by it of an application to have a transfer of shares registered. It was held, following *Swaledale Cleaners*, that the transferee was entitled to registration.

Forged and fraudulent transfers

A share certificate is prima facie evidence of a person's title. The company is estopped from denying, as against a bona fide purchaser of the shares, that the person named is entitled to the shares referred to.

[9.10] Re Bahia and San Francisco Rly Co (1868) LR 3 QB 584
(Court of Queen's Bench)

Five shares in the company were owned by Miss Amelia Trittin. Without her knowledge Stocken and Goldner procured a forged transfer of the shares to themselves, and lodged the transfer and Miss Trittin's share certificate with the company for registration. The secretary in due course entered their names on the share register in place of Miss Trittin's, and issued a new share certificate in their names. Relying on this certificate, Burton and Mrs Goodburn, acting in good faith, bought the five shares on the stock exchange. After they had been registered as holders of the shares and issued with share certificates, the company was obliged to restore Miss Trittin's name to the share register. This action was brought by Burton and Mrs Goodburn, who claimed to be entitled to equivalent shares in the company, or damages. The court awarded them damages, holding the company estopped by the share certificate from denying the title of Stocken and Goldner.

COCKBURN CJ: I am of opinion that our judgment must be for the claimants. If the facts are rightly understood, the case falls within the principle of *Pickard v Sears*[19] and *Freeman v Cooke.*[20] The company are

[19]   (1837) 6 Ad & El 469.
[20]   (1848) 2 Exch 654.

[sic] bound to keep a register of shareholders, and have power to issue certificates certifying that each individual shareholder named therein is a registered shareholder of the particular shares specified. This power of granting certificates is to give the shareholders the opportunity of more easily dealing with their shares in the market, and to afford facilities to them of selling their shares by at once showing a marketable title, and the effect of this facility is to make the shares of greater value. The power of giving certificates is, therefore, for the benefit of the company in general; and it is a declaration by the company to all the world that the person in whose name the certificate is made out, and to whom it is given, is a shareholder in the company, and it is given by the company with the intention that it shall be so used by the person to whom it is given, and acted upon in the sale and transfer of shares. It is stated in this case that the claimants acted bona fide, and did all that is required of purchasers of shares; they paid the value of the shares in money on having a transfer of the shares executed to them, and on the production of the certificates which were handed to them. It turned out that the transferors had in fact no shares, and that the company ought not to have registered them as shareholders or given them certificates, the transfer to them being a forgery. That brings the case within the principle of the decision in *Pickard v Sears*, as explained by the case of *Freeman v Cooke*, that, if you make a representation with the intention that it shall be acted upon by another, and he does so, you are estopped from denying the truth of what you represent to be the fact.

The only remaining question is, what is the redress to which the claimants are entitled. In whatever form of action they might shape their claim, and there can be no doubt that an action is maintainable, the measure of damages would be the same. They are entitled to be placed in the same position as if the shares, which they purchased owing to the company's representation, had in fact been good shares, and had been transferred to them, and the company had refused to put them on the register, and the measure of damages would be the market price of the shares at that time; if no market price at that time, then a jury would have to say what was a reasonable compensation for the loss of the shares.

BLACKBURN, MELLOR and LUSH JJ delivered concurring judgments.

➤ Notes

1. A similar estoppel operates as regards the amount stated in the certificate to be paid up on the shares: see *Burkinshaw v Nicolls* (1878) 3 App Cas 1004.

2. At the time this case was decided it was particularly important to establish liability on the basis of an estoppel, since there is no privity as between the company and the transferee which would give a remedy in contract, and the notion of a duty of care which would allow a claim to be based in negligence was then a century away. But now that liability in negligence for misrepresentations is well established (*Hedley Byrne & Co Ltd v Heller & Partners Ltd* [1964] AC 465, and, perhaps most pertinently, *Ministry of Housing and Local Government v Sharp* [1970] 2 QB 223), a transferee might well have a remedy on this ground, although of course it would be necessary to be able to prove negligence.

3. Although in *Re Bahia and San Francisco Rly Co* [9.10] the final purchaser could recover damages from the company, the company would have been able to recover damages from the vendor who had presented the company with the forged transfer initially. This would be true even if the presenter of those documents had been unaware of the fraud or forgery (see below, and *Royal Bank of Scotland plc v Sandstone Properties Ltd* [1998] 2 BCLC 429).

➤ Questions

1. Is the protection given by CA 2006 s 588 to transferees of shares which are not fully paid more, or less, extensive than that which they would get under *Burkinshaw v Nicolls* (above)?

2. Note the ambit of CA 2006 s 775. Would this have affected the outcome in this case?

In an appropriate case, the certificate holder may rely on an estoppel.

[9.11] Balkis Consolidated Co v Tomkinson [1893] AC 396 (House of Lords)

Tomkinson, who held a share certificate stating that he was the owner of 1,000 shares in the company, sold the shares on the market to various purchasers. The company refused to register the transfers, on the ground that Powter, who had transferred the shares to Tomkinson, had had no title at the time, and that Powter had procured the issue of Tomkinson's certificate by fraud. Tomkinson bought shares on the market to honour the contracts with his transferees, and sued the company in damages to recoup this expenditure. The House of Lords, affirming the courts below, upheld Tomkinson's claim.

LORD HERSCHELL LC: After carefully considering the able arguments at the Bar, I have no hesitation in expressing my concurrence in the law laid down by the Court of Queen's Bench in *Re Bahia and San Francisco Rly Co* **[9.10]** . . . The appellants argued, however, and correctly, that the present case is distinguishable from that in the Queen's Bench, inasmuch as it is not the purchasers who are seeking to render the company liable by way of estoppel, but the vendor of the shares, who himself received the certificate from the company. Does that, in the circumstances which your Lordships have to consider, make any difference? If the company must have known, as was said in the *Bahia and San Francisco Rly* case, that persons wanting to purchase shares might act upon the statement of fact contained in the certificate, it must equally have been within the contemplation of the company that a person receiving the certificate from them might on the faith of it enter into a contract to sell the shares. The plaintiff did enter into such a contract, and thereby altered his position by rendering himself liable to the persons with whom he contracted to sell the shares. All the elements necessary to create an estoppel would appear, therefore, to be present . . .

LORDS MACNAGHTEN and FIELD delivered concurring opinions.

➤ Notes

1. There is one exception to the principle illustrated by the above cases. Where a certificate is issued which is based on the registration of a forged transfer, no estoppel against the company arises in favour of the person who submitted the transfer for registration. The law takes the view that since this person has at least equally good means as the company of knowing whether the transfer is genuine, it should not be deemed to have made any representation to him: *Simm v Anglo-American Telegraph Co* (1879) 5 QBD 188, CA.

2. Later cases show that the company's position in such a case is even stronger. A person who presents a transfer to a company for registration, whether it is in favour of himself or someone else (eg a broker presenting a transfer on behalf of his or her client) impliedly warrants that it is genuine and, if it is not, may be liable to indemnify the company if it suffers loss by acting on it: *Sheffield Corpn v Barclay* [1905] AC 392, HL; *Yeung Kai Yung v Hong Kong and Shanghai Banking Corpn* [1981] AC 787, PC; *Royal Bank of Scotland plc v Sandstone Properties Ltd* [1998] 2 BCLC 429.

3. These exceptions require qualification in the case of reliance upon an erroneous statement in a share certificate issued by the company. Ordinarily, a person who presents a share transfer for registration is required to indemnify the company against any liability it incurs to other persons as a result of registering the transfer. However, where the person presenting a share certificate for registration relied upon an erroneous statement of ownership on a share certificate, the estoppel raised against the company overrides the company's right to an indemnity (see above, and also *Cadbury Schweppes plc v Halifax Share Dealing Ltd* [2006] EWHC 1184, Ch).

A forged share certificate is a nullity and does not bind the company.[21]

[9.12] Ruben v Great Fingall Consolidated [1906] AC 439 (House of Lords)

The plaintiffs Ruben and Ladenburg, who were stockbrokers, had procured a loan for one Rowe (the secretary of the defendant company) on the security of a share certificate for 5,000 shares in the defendant company, to which Rowe had affixed his own signature and the company's seal and had forged the signatures of two directors. The plaintiffs, having reimbursed the mortgagees, claimed damages from the company for failure to register them as owners of the shares. It was held that the company was not estopped by the certificate.

LORD MACNAGHTEN: My Lords, this case was argued at some length and with much ingenuity by the learned counsel for the appellants. In my opinion there is nothing in it.

Ruben and Ladenburg are the victims of a wicked fraud. No fault has been found with their conduct. But their claim against the respondent company is, I think, simply absurd.

The thing put forward as the foundation of their claim is a piece of paper which purports to be a certificate of shares in the company. This paper is false and fraudulent from beginning to end. The representation of the company's seal which appears upon it, though made by the impression of the real seal of the company, is counterfeit, and no better than a forgery. The signatures of the two directors which purport to authenticate the sealing are forgeries pure and simple. Every statement in the document is a lie. The only thing real about it is the signature of the secretary of the company, who was the sole author and perpetrator of the fraud. No one would suggest that this fraudulent certificate could of itself give rise to any right or bind or affect the company in any way. It is not the company's deed, and there is nothing to prevent the company from saying so.

Then how can the company be bound or affected by it? The directors have never said or done anything to represent or lead to the belief that this thing was the company's deed. Without such a representation there can be no estoppel.

The fact that this fraudulent certificate was concocted in the company's office and was uttered and sent forth by its author from the place of its origin cannot give it an efficacy which it does not intrinsically possess. The secretary of the company, who is a mere servant, may be the proper hand to deliver out certificates which the company issues in due course, but he can have no authority to guarantee the genuineness or validity of a document which is not the deed of the company.

I could have understood a claim on the part of the appellants if it were incumbent on the company to lock up their seal and guard it as a dangerous beast and if it were culpable carelessness on the part of the directors to commit the care of the seal to their secretary or any other official. That is a view which once commended itself to a jury, but it his been disposed of for good and all by the case of *Bank of Ireland v Evans' Charities Trustees*[22] in this House . . .

LORD LOREBURN LC and LORDS DAVEY and JAMES OF HEREFORD delivered concurring opinions. LORDS ROBERTSON and ATKINSON concurred.

➤ Notes

1. *Ruben*'s case is defensible upon only the narrowest possible *ratio decidendi*, as set out at the head of this extract. As has already been observed (above, p 446), the company ought to be bound in such circumstances if a person who may be assumed to have authority to do so has put forward the share certificate as genuine. Now that it is recognised that the secretary of a company is not a 'mere servant', but a responsible officer having an important role in administrative matters (see the *Panorama* case [3.13]), it could not be seriously argued that he or she does not have usual authority to guarantee the genuineness of a document such as a share certificate.

---

[21] But see the Notes following this case extract.
[22] (1855) 5 HL Cas 389.

2. Even less supportable nowadays is the decision in *South Greyhound Racecourses Ltd v Wake* [1931] 1 Ch 496, where the share certificate which was issued to Wake bore genuine signatures and a true impression of the company's seal, and the only irregularity was that the latter had been affixed without authority. Clauson J considered himself bound by the decision in *Ruben's* case to hold that the certificate was a 'forgery', upon which Wake could not base any claim.

3. A similar issue has arisen in a number of cases concerning the 'certification' of share transfers. Where part only of the shares to which a share certificate relates are transferred, it is customary for the transferor to lodge the certificate either with the company itself or with the stock exchange, instead of handing it to the purchaser. A 'certification' is then endorsed on the transfer form by the secretary of the company (or by an official of the stock exchange), confirming that the share certificate has been lodged. When the transfer is later presented to the company for registration, separate share certificates are issued which 'split' the original holding between those now entitled as separate owners. On the ordinary principles of vicarious liability, as recognised ever since *Lloyd v Grace Smith & Co* [1912] AC 716, the secretary's certification ought to be binding on the company (and that of the official binding on the stock exchange), even if the secretary has acted fraudulently.

However, in two decisions of the House of Lords, *George Whitechurch Ltd v Cavanagh* [1902] AC 117 and *Kleinwort, Sons & Co v Associated Automatic Machine Corpn Ltd* (1934) 50 TLR 244, it was ruled that a secretary had no apparent authority to act for a company in the matter of the certification of transfers, so that where no certificate had in fact been lodged, the certification of a dishonest secretary was not binding on the company in favour of an innocent purchaser of the shares.

These cases are seen by most commentators as an anomalous exception to the principle of *Lloyd v Grace Smith & Co*; but in the light of the new status accorded to the company secretary by the *Panorama* case **[3.13]**, there is really no ground upon which they can be supported.

It is, of course, now open to the House of Lords to disown its earlier rulings, in view of the relaxation of the strict doctrine of precedent. It is also possible that CA 2006 s 775 modifies the effect of these cases, but the repeated use of the word 'authorised' in s 755(4) leaves room for doubt, since a court might well hold that this means 'having *actual* authority' as opposed to having *either* actual or ostensible authority.

4. If the transfer takes place within CREST, then different rules apply. SI 2001/3755 provides that the court may make an order against the CREST Operator, although several limitations apply to such orders. The most significant is that if the perpetrator of the forgery is identified, then no compensation order can be made against CREST even where the loss cannot be recovered from the perpetrator. See SI 2001/3755, reg 36.

➤ Question

CA 2006 s 44(5) reads as follows:

(5) In favour of a purchaser a document shall be deemed to have been duly executed by a company if it purports to be signed in accordance with subsection (2).

A "purchaser" means a purchaser in good faith for valuable consideration and includes a lessee, mortgagee or other person who for valuable consideration acquires an interest in property.

And subsection (2) reads:

(2) A document is validly executed by a company if it is signed on behalf of the company—

(a) by two authorised signatories, or

(b) by a director of the company in the presence of a witness who attests the signature.

Would *Ruben's* case **[9.12]** or *South London Greyhound Racecourses Ltd v Wake* (above) be decided differently today in the light of this provision?

Competing claims to shares

A legal title to shares will prevail over an earlier equitable title; but a transfer of the legal title is not perfected until registration of the transferee as holder of the shares.[23]

[9.13] Shropshire Union Railways and Canal Co v R (1875) LR 7 HL 496 (House of Lords)

Mrs Robson sought a writ of mandamus to compel the directors of the company to register a transfer of stock to her from George Holyoake, in whose name it stood. (Holyoake had given the transfer as security for a loan made by Mrs Robson's late husband.) She failed because Holyoake had only a bare legal title (the beneficial interest being in the defendants themselves) and nothing which had happened had displaced the defendants' earlier equity.

LORD CAIRNS LC: [Undoubtedly] the position of matters was, that the defendants had the whole beneficial interest in the stock . . . Theirs was the equitable title. Holyoake was a person who held merely the legal title and the right to transfer the stock. He was able, if not interfered with, to transfer the stock to any other person, and to give a valid receipt for the purchase-money to any person who had not notice of the beneficial interest of the defendants. On the other hand, any person with whom Holyoake might deal by virtue of his title upon the register, had, or ought to have had, these considerations present to his mind. He ought to have known that although Holyoake's name appeared upon the register as the owner of these shares, and although Holyoake could present to him the certificates of this ownership, still it was perfectly possible either that these shares were the beneficial property of Holyoake himself, or that they were the property of some other person. If he dealt merely by equitable transfer, or equitable assignment with Holyoake, and if it turned out that the beneficial ownership of Holyoake was co-incident and co-extensive with his legal title, well and good; his right would be accordingly, so far as Holyoake was concerned, complete. But, if, on the other hand, it should turn out that Holyoake's beneficial interest was either nil, or was not coextensive with the whole of his apparent legal title, then I say any person dealing with Holyoake, by way of equitable bargain or contract, should have known that he could only obtain a title which was imperfect, and would not bind the real beneficial owner. And, my Lords, he also might have known, and should have known, this, that if he desired to perfect his title, and make it entirely secure, he had the most simple means open to him—he had only to take Holyoake at his word. If Holyoake represented that he was the real owner of these shares, the proposed transferee had only to go with Holyoake, or to go with the authority of Holyoake in his possession, to the company, and to require a transfer of those shares from the name of Holyoake into his own name. If he had obtained that transfer, and the company had made it, no question could have arisen, and no litigation could subsequently have taken place . . .

LORDS HATHERLEY and O'HAGAN delivered concurring opinions.

---

[23] The requirement of registration had some justification in an earlier period when it was common for shares to be only partly paid up, but it makes less sense in the case of the fully-paid, listed security, of the present day, where the responsibilities of a shareholder are negligible, the directors have no discretion to refuse registration, and the mechanics of transfer are a matter of pure routine. It is not obvious, for example, why the law should continue to refuse to recognise the possibility of a transfer of the legal title to such shares by (say) a deed of gift.

Where the equities as between successive transferees of shares are equal, the first in time prevails.

[9.14] Peat v Clayton [1906] 1 Ch 659 (Chancery Division)

Clayton assigned all his property, including the blocks of shares in question, to trustees for the benefit of his creditors, but failed to hand over the share certificates when requested to do so. The trustees then gave notice of the assignment to the company, but took no further steps. (It should be appreciated that the company was not bound to receive this notice: see s 360 of the Act [CA 2006 s 126].) Clayton later sold the shares through Cohen & Co, brokers, on the stock exchange, handing over the certificates and transfers duly executed. When the company refused registration, Cohen & Co provided their purchaser with other shares in the company, and then in these proceedings sought to resist a claim brought by the trustees, as plaintiffs, for a declaration that they were entitled to the shares. It was held, however, that the trustees' interest prevailed, being prior in time.

> JOYCE J: As I understand the law, where there are several claimants to shares registered in the name of a third person, the equitable title which is prior in time prevails, unless the claimant under a subsequent equitable title proves that, as between him and the company, he had acquired an absolute and unconditional right to be registered as the owner of the shares before the company received notice of the other claim.[24] In my opinion, therefore, the plaintiffs appear to be entitled to these forty shares in the Randfontein company. But Messrs Cohen claim a lien upon them. If they have any lien, however, it is only equitable, and can only be upon Clayton's interest, which is subject to the right of the plaintiffs under the deed of assignment. Then it was said that the plaintiffs had disentitled themselves by negligence. I see no negligence on the part of the plaintiffs, unless it be, as Messrs Cohen allege, in not adopting the procedure now substituted by Ord 46, r 4, for the old procedure by distringas.[25] I cannot accede to the contention that by reason of the omission to adopt this course the plaintiffs must be postponed. If they had proceeded by distringas the result would have been just the same. It would only have prevented the company from registering the transfer to the purchaser, which in fact they did refuse to do by reason of the notice given to them on 8 November on behalf of the plaintiffs . . .
>
> The result is that the plaintiffs are entitled to a declaration in their favour, and to an order . . . to register them as the holders of the shares.

[Also see *Hawks v McArthur* [9.16].]

Although a company is not ordinarily bound by notice of a trust or other equitable interest affecting its shares, this rule does not apply when the company itself asserts an interest in the shares in competition with the person who gave notice.

[9.15] Mackereth v Wigan Coal and Iron Co Ltd [1916] 2 Ch 293 (Chancery Division)

Shares in the defendant company which had formerly belonged to James Hodgson, deceased, were registered in the name of the trustees of his estate, one of whom was the son of the deceased, James Hodgson, junior. The company had notice that the registered shareholders held only as trustees. Later James Hodgson, junior, became indebted to the company and the

---

[24] [In spite of assertions to this effect both here and in other cases, it is generally accepted that nothing short of the registration of the subsequent transferee as legal owner will defeat the prior equity.]

[25] [This is a 'stop notice': see below, p 451.]

company, purporting to exercise a lien conferred upon it by the articles, impounded certain dividends due on the shares and subsequently sold the shares to reduce the amount of the debt. It was held that this was an infringement of the rights of the beneficiaries of the estate, and that neither s 27 of CA 1908 [CA 2006 s 126] nor an article in similar terms applied in a case such as this, where the company was itself involved in the transaction.

> PETERSON J: For the company it was argued that under s 27 of the Act of 1908, and the articles of association, no notice of any equitable interest or trust can affect the company in any way, and that, as the notice of the trust in the present case, which the company in fact received, must be treated as non-existent, or at least ineffectual, the lien which is conferred by the articles is operative. The argument leads far; for it would follow that, if a trustee of shares in a company informed the company that he held the shares for the benefit of other persons, and that he had not as against his cestui que trust any power of mortgaging them for his own benefit, he could yet effectually charge them to the company as security for money lent to him by the company . . . In several cases it has been stated in broad terms that a company 'need not take notice in any way of trusts': per Brett MR in *Société Générale de Paris v Tramways Union Co*;[26] or that any notice is absolutely inoperative to affect a company with any notice: per Lord Selborne in the same case in the House of Lords—*Société Générale de Paris v Walker*.[27] These observations had, however, reference to the obligation of the company to register transfers of shares. If the passages in the judgments to which I have referred were intended to be of universal application, they are not in accordance with the judgments of the House of Lords in *Bradford Banking Co Ltd v Briggs, Son & Co Ltd*.[28] The effect of this decision is briefly stated by Stirling LJ in *Rainford v Keith and Blackman Co Ltd*,[29] in these words: 'Where the company in which the shares are held sees fit to deal with the shares for its own benefit, then that company is liable to be affected with notice of the interest of a third party.'
>
> I am therefore of opinion that s 27 of the Act of 1908 and article 9 of the articles of association do not protect a company which, in the face of notice that the shareholder is not the beneficial owner of the shares, makes advances or gives credit to the shareholder . . . The result is that the company in the present case was wrong in asserting a lien against the beneficiaries, and must account for the proceeds of sale of the shares, and for the dividends which it has applied towards the satisfaction of the indebtedness of James Hodgson, junior.

➤ Note

Although CA 2006 s 126 provides that no notice of any trust affecting shares shall be 'entered on the register of members . . . or be receivable by the registrar',[30] it is possible by using the procedures described as 'stop orders' or a 'stop notices' (Charging Orders Act 1979, s 5(2)(a) and (b) respectively, and Civil Procedure Rules 1998, rr 73.11–73.15 and 73.16–73.21 respectively) to prohibit a company from registering any transfer of the shares in question or paying any dividend on them, or, alternatively, to require a company to refrain from doing these things without first sending a notice to the person serving the stop notice and giving him or her a specified time to take action.

---

[26] (1884) 14 QBD 424 at 439.
[27] (1885) 11 App Cas 20 at 30.
[28] (1886) 12 App Cas 29.
[29] [1905] 2 Ch 147 at 161.
[30] This wording is probably not quite what might be expected of a provision having the effect described in **[9.15]** above.

➤ Question

To what extent does a stop notice give a person with an equitable interest in shares effective protection?

A transfer of shares for valuable consideration, even if it is irregular under the company's articles, is effective to transfer an equitable interest to the purchaser which will prevail over another equitable right accruing at a later date, eg a charging order.

[9.16] Hawks v McArthur [1951] 1 All ER 22 (Chancery Division)

[The facts appear from the judgment.]

VAISEY J: The plaintiff is the holder of a charging order affecting five hundred ordinary shares of £1 each in a private company called W Lucas & Sons Ltd, which stand in the name of, and were originally the property of, the first defendant, Mr Theodore Hunter McArthur, who has not entered an appearance in these proceedings. He claims that that charging order operates on Mr McArthur's interest in those shares, which, he says, is a complete interest, both legal and equitable. The second and third defendants, Mr Roberts and Mr Fraser, claim that the beneficial interest in the shares in question has passed to them as a result of transfers executed in their favour by Mr McArthur in pursuance of certain agreements entered into between themselves and Mr McArthur prior to the execution of those transfers, and they allege that Mr McArthur had no interest in the shares at the date of the charging order on which the charge could operate . . .

There is, undoubtedly, a basic principle that a charging order only operates to charge the beneficial interest of the person against whom the order is made, and that it is not possible, for instance, to obtain an effective charging order over shares where the person against whom the order is made holds them as a bare trustee. The charging order affects only such interest, and so much of the property affected, as the person whose property is purported to be affected could himself validly charge . . . [His Lordship then observed that the transfers of the shares had been made in total disregard of the requirements of the articles of association, which obliged an intending transferor to give notice to the company so that the other members could exercise rights of pre-emption. He continued:]

The real question in this case, I think, is whether the alleged agreements . . . operated so as to amount in equity to a transfer of the shares held by Mr McArthur, as to 200 of them to Mr Roberts, and as to 300 of them to Mr Fraser, or whether the failure or neglect to follow the code laid down by articles 11, 12 and 13 completely vitiates the whole transaction, so that the transfers are worthless and there has been a total failure of consideration for the moneys which were admittedly paid over by Mr Roberts and Mr Fraser to Mr McArthur. It is suggested on behalf of Mr Roberts and Mr Fraser that, notwithstanding the complete failure to comply with the articles, the transfers and the antecedent agreements which must have been made—for one does not execute a transfer without a previous intention to do so—did, in fact, operate as a sale by Mr McArthur to Mr Roberts and Mr Fraser of, at any rate, the beneficial interest in the shares—otherwise the result would be that Mr Roberts and Mr Fraser paid their money and got nothing for it . . .

Admittedly, Mr McArthur is still the legal owner of the shares. Admittedly, the plaintiff's rights under this charging order are in the nature of equitable rights. And admittedly, the rights of Mr Roberts and Mr Fraser, if they have any rights, are also equitable rights. As I have come to the conclusion that Mr Roberts and Mr Fraser have some rights and that what they did was not a complete nullity, the question is whose rights should prevail. A not irrelevant circumstance is that the equitable rights of Mr Roberts and Mr Fraser precede the equities or quasi-equitable rights under the charging order. In my opinion, the rights of Mr Roberts and Mr Fraser had already accrued at the time the charging order was obtained, and I think, as between the merits (not moral merits, but legal merits) of the plaintiff and the defendants, the rights of the second and third defendants, Mr Roberts and Mr Fraser, must prevail over the claims of the plaintiff . . .

> ➤ Note

A gratuitous transfer of shares may sometimes also be effective to transfer an equitable title to the shares. In two cases, each coincidentally named *Re Rose*, reported in [1949] Ch 78 and [1952] Ch 499, it has been held that where a donor of shares has done everything in his power to divest himself in favour of the donee (eg by delivering to the donee, or to the company, an executed transfer and the relevant share certificate), the gift is complete in equity despite the absence of registration. This rule applies even where the directors have a discretion to refuse registration of the transfer. These decisions make all the more anomalous the old ruling in *Milroy v Lord* (1862) 4 De GF & J 264 that a gift of shares by deed is ineffective: equity seems willing to assist some volunteers, but not others.

Disclosure of substantial interests in shares

It is often material to know who has controlling interests in a company. For public companies, there are requirements relating to disclosure of substantial interests in shares: see below, pp 586 ff.

Valuation of shares

In the valuation of shares,[31] *the valuer is entitled to consider the realities of the company's situation, and may, eg, decline to value the company's assets as a going concern if there is no expectation that the business will make profits.*

[9.17] Dean v Prince [1954] Ch 409 (Court of Appeal)

Dean (now deceased), Prince and Cowen had formed a private company in 1938, taking respectively 140, 30 and 30 shares. All three were 'working directors'. The company's articles provided that on the death of a director his shares should be bought by the surviving directors at a price to be certified as fair by the auditor. On Dean's death in 1951, his holding was valued for the purpose of this article at £7 per share. His widow challenged the valuation in these proceedings, but the Court of Appeal, reversing Harman J, held that the correct principles had been followed by the auditor and upheld his valuation.

DENNING LJ: In this case Harman J has upset the valuation on the ground that the auditor failed to take into account some factors and proceeded on wrong principles. I will take the points in order:

1. *The right to control the company.* Harman J said that the auditor should have taken into account the fact that the 140 shares were a majority holding and would give a purchaser the right to control the company. I do not think that the auditor was bound to take that factor into account.

---

[31] See generally N Easterway, H Booth and K Eamer, *Practical Share Valuation*, 4th edn (1998); A Gregory and A Hicks, 'Valuation of Shares: A Legal and Accounting Conundrum' [1995] JBL 56.

Test it this way: suppose it had been Prince who had died, leaving only 30 shares. Those 30 shares, being a minority holding, would fetch nothing in the open market. But does that mean that the other directors would be entitled to take his shares for nothing? Surely not. No matter which director it was who happened to die, his widow should be entitled to the same price per share, irrespective of whether her husband's holding was large or small. It seems to me that the fair thing to do would be to take the whole 200 shares of the company and see what they were worth, and then pay the widow a sum appropriate to her husband's holding. At any rate if the auditor was of opinion that that was a fair method, no one can say that he was wrong. The right way to see what the whole 200 shares were worth, would be to see what the business itself was worth: and that is what the auditor proceeded to do.

2. *Valuation of the business 'as a going concern'.* Harman J seems to have thought that the auditor should have valued the business as a going concern. I do not think that the auditor was bound to do any such thing. The business was a losing concern which had no goodwill: and it is fairly obvious that, as soon as Mrs Dean had sold the 140 shares to the other two directors—as she was bound to do—she would in all probability call in the moneys owing to herself and to her husband amounting to over £2,000. The judge said that she was not likely to press for the moneys because that would be 'killing the goose that laid the eggs', but he was wrong about this; because as soon as she sold the shares, she would have got rid of the goose and there was no reason why she should not press for the moneys. She was an executrix and the company's position was none too good. It had only £1,200 in the bank to meet a demand for £2,200. In these circumstances the auditor was of opinion that there was a strong probability of the company having to be wound up: and he rejected the going-concern basis. For myself, I should have thought he was clearly right, but at any rate no one can say that his opinion was wrong.

3. *Valuation of the assets of the business.* Once the going-concern basis is rejected, the only possible way of valuing the business is to find out the value of the tangible assets. Harman J thought that the assets should have been valued as a whole in situ. It was quite likely, he said, that 'some one could have been found who would make a bid for the whole thing, lock, stock and barrel'. But the judge seems to have forgotten that no one would buy the assets in situ in this way unless he could also buy the premises; and the company had no saleable interest in the premises. In respect of part of the premises the company had only a monthly tenancy; in respect of the rest the company had only a contract for the purchase of the premises on paying £200 a year for twenty-five years. It had no right to assign this contract; and its interest was liable to be forfeited if it went into liquidation, either compulsory or voluntary; and the probability was, of course, that, if it sold all the assets, it would go into liquidation, and hence lose the premises. The company could, therefore, only sell the assets without the premises. That is how the auditor valued them and no one can say that he was wrong in so doing.

4. *Valuation on a 'break-up' basis.* The auditor instructed the valuer, Colonel Riddle, to value the plant and machinery at the break-up value as loose chattels on a sale by auction. Harman J thought that that was a wrong basis because it was equivalent to a forced sale. I would have agreed with the judge if the business had been a profitable concern. The value of the tangible assets would then have been somewhere in the region of £4,000 or £5,000, being either the balance sheet figure of £4,070 or Pressley's figure of £4,835. But the business was not a profitable concern. It was a losing concern: and it is a well-known fact that a losing concern cannot realise the book value of its assets. There is an element to be taken into account which is sometimes spoken of as 'negative goodwill'. It comes about in this way: if a business is making a loss, that shows that its assets, regarded as an entity, are not a good investment. A purchaser will decline, therefore, to buy on that basis. He will only buy on a piecemeal basis, according to what the various assets taken individually are worth: and it is obvious that on a sale of assets piecemeal, the vendor will suffer heavy losses as compared with the book figures. The auditor was therefore quite justified in asking the valuer to value the

assets as loose chattels sold at an auction. At any rate, if he honestly formed that opinion, no one can say that he was wrong.

5. *The special purchaser.* Harman J thought that someone could have been found to buy the 140 shares who would use his majority holding to turn out the two directors, and reorganise the factory and put in his own business. In other words, that the shares would have a special attraction for some person (namely, the next-door neighbour) who wanted to put his own business into these premises. I am prepared to concede that the shares might realise an enhanced value on that account: but I do not think that it would be a fair price to ask the directors to pay. They were buying these shares—under a compulsory sale and purchase—on the assumption that they would con-tinue in the business as working directors. It would be unfair to make them pay a price based on the assumption that they would be turned out. If the auditor never took that possibility into account, he cannot be blamed; for he was only asked to certify the fair value of the shares. The only fair value would be to take a hypothetical purchaser who was prepared to carry on the business if it was worth while so to do, or otherwise to put it into liquidation. At any rate if that was the auditor's opinion, no one can say that he was wrong.

I have covered, I think, all the grounds on which Harman J upset the valuation. I do not think they were good grounds. I would, therefore, allow the appeal and uphold the valuation.

EVERSHED MR and WYNN-PARRY J delivered concurring judgments.

> Notes

1. In holding that it was proper for the auditor not to take into account the fact that the block of shares carried with it control of the company, Denning LJ was no doubt correct on the particular facts of this case; but his remarks should not be accepted as laying down a general rule. In the court below, Harman J had held that the control factor was of paramount import-ance. In the Court of Appeal, Evershed MR said that he 'should not himself quarrel' with a rateable apportionment of an assets valuation among all the shares, but his judgment turned essentially on other points; while Wynn-Parry J held that no extra value should be placed on the controlling shares because (a) the article in question referred to the current worth of *the company's* shares, not the deceased director's shares, and (b) whereas the seller might be parting with control, none of the surviving directors was necessarily *buying* it, since they were more than one in number.

2. It was established by *Short v Treasury Comrs* [1948] AC 534 that where one purchaser is buying control but none of the vendors is itself selling a controlling interest, the extra value should be disregarded. But there are *dicta* in that case which strongly support the view that where a majority shareholding is sold by a single seller to a single buyer, it is proper to value the holding more highly. The same point is made *obiter dicta* in *Re Grierson, Oldham & Adams Ltd* [13.10] and *Gold Coast Selection Trust Ltd v Humphrey* [1948] AC 459 at 473.

3. An indication of the value of 'control' in practice can be gained from the following relative figures put by an expert on the value of different holdings in a small private company.[32]

Value of 100% shareholding:	£100,000
" 51% "	48,000
" 50% "	35,000
" 20% "	5,000
" 10% "	1,000

[32] R M Walters [1977] Brit Tax Rev 34, 44.

4. There are other alternatives to assets-based formulae for ascertaining the value of a share. For example, in *Re Macro (Ipswich) Ltd* **[11.22]** Arden J preferred to use a valuation reckoned by grossing up the average dividend yield. This would be appropriate in a case where the company is making steady profits but its assets are difficult to value or are undervalued in its accounts.

5. Special considerations arise when the price of a minority holding of shares has to be fixed when the court orders it to be bought by the majority shareholders pursuant to an order under the 'unfairly prejudicial conduct' section (CA 2006 s 994): see below, pp 552 ff.

10

BORROWING, DEBENTURES AND CHARGES

General issues

Most companies do not operate using only equity funding from shareholders. Borrowing from lenders, and use of credit such as deferred payment for goods and services, provide additional and important methods of financing corporate activity.

The rights of lenders (bank lenders, creditors, debentureholders, etc: see below) depend on the precise terms of their contract with the company. As a general rule, creditors are entitled to an agreed rate of interest (fixed or variable) regardless of the commercial success of the company. Their loan agreements may be secured or unsecured providing different protection to different creditors should the company become insolvent. However, all creditors are paid out, in full if possible, before the shareholders are entitled to any return (see chapter 14). Shareholders, on the other hand, generally expect to receive a higher total return (dividend plus capital growth of share value) on their equity funding than providers of debt funding. The level of dividend depends on the commercial success of the company and on the discretion of the directors. The rate of share value growth depends upon the company's overall actual and projected success. Debt is a commonly considered a cheaper (ie its cost in terms of interest, versus dividend plus share value appreciation) but less flexible form of corporate funding than equity funding.

In this chapter, the focus is on *secured* debt, looking at options that are used by small and large companies alike. But some general comments are warranted first. Like any other legal person, a company may borrow money, subject to any restrictions in its constitution.[1] There are, however, a number of special features of corporate borrowing that are worth noting.

(i) To raise very large sums of money, a company may wish to attract funds on the investment market, ie to borrow from very many lenders at once, or in sequence, all on the same terms. The mechanics of such a procedure are not greatly different from those involved in making an issue of shares, and indeed such issues may (but need not be) be traded on the Stock Exchange subject to the same rules as equivalent dealings in equity securities (see below, pp 459 ff). The investors will become a class of *creditors* of the company rather than *members* of the company; and the *debentures* (or more often *bonds*, in Europe and the US, and increasingly here) held by each creditor will be *marketable securities*. The theoretical differences between being a creditor and a member are considerable, from a legal point of view, but (at least in the case of a solvent and prosperous company) the practical consequences (including, often, the total returns, i.e. interest plus capital appreciation) for investors, apart sometimes from tax considerations, may be very similar.

(ii) Where numerous investors advance money to a company in this way, it is usual for their rights to be regulated by a debenture trust deed, under which trustees are appointed to represent the investors as a class *vis-à-vis* the company. In the trust deed, provision is made for the

---

[1] A lender may, however, be protected from the effect of such restrictions by the internal management rules (above pp 135 ff), by CA 2006 ss 39–40, or by a provision in the articles.

collective views of investors to be ascertained by votes taken at meetings, with the usual appara-
tus of proxies, etc. Two basic arrangements are common. In the first, each investor lends to the
company directly, and simultaneously agrees to be bound by the terms of the trust deed in his
dealings with the company. In the second (which is the more usual form in modern practice),
all the loans are consolidated into one fund and the aggregate sum is advanced to the company
by the trustees, who alone stand in a contractual relationship with the company: each investor
then subscribes for so much 'debenture stock' or 'loan stock' out of the fund. Creditors can
realise their investments strictly according to the terms of the debenture, or, if the debentures
are marketable securities, by trading on the market. The ability to trade has advantages for
creditors (increased liquidity and potentially higher total returns), and for the company (the
loan repayment dates are certain, and not affected by creditors wanting early repayment).

(iii) A company can give security for its obligations, just like any other legal person. Where
a company *charges* its property to secure an obligation to a creditor (not necessarily, of course,
a borrowing obligation), CA 2006 may require that particulars of the charge to be *registered*
under the provisions of Pt 25 (s 860ff), failing which the security will be for many (but not all)
purposes void: see below, pp 464 ff.

(iv) A company has the ability, not enjoyed by an individual in English law,[2] to create a
'*floating charge*' over assets such as stock-in-trade and book debts,[3] which may fluctuate from
time to time, on terms that the company remains free to deal with them in the ordinary course
of business: see below, pp 467 ff.

(v) When a company makes default in any of its obligations under the document creating
a charge, or when the security it has created is in jeopardy, the company's obligation is normally enforced by the appointment by the creditors (or the trustee for such creditors in the
case of a debenture trust deed that creates a change) of a *receiver* to look after the creditors'
interests: see below, pp 637 ff. Note, however, that changes to the statutory regime, especially
as it applies to floating charges, are ensuring that *administration*, rather than administrative
receivership, is increasingly the norm (see below, pp 631 ff).

(vi) Borrowing transactions, and especially those secured by a floating charge, may raise
special questions in a *winding up*: see above, pp 407 ff, indicating the relative disadvantages
of floating charges over other forms of security in providing protection to the security holder.

➤ Notes

1. It is apparent from the above commentary that an investment in debentures or debenture
stock is very similar to an investment in shares: both are 'securities' in the corporate sector of
the economy offering different kinds of risk and different kinds of return. Many companies
have their debentures or debenture stock listed for dealing on the Stock Exchange. These
securities are transferred in the same way as shares, with companies maintaining registers of
debenture holders alongside their registers of members.

2. The form of the prospectus required for debt securities is prescribed in Regulation (EC) No
809/2004. This distinguishes between the retail market (intended for the general public) and

---

[2] To do so would infringe the Bills of Sale Acts of 1878 and 1882 (which do not apply to companies), and in any event
it would be impossible to specifically describe the goods affected where these are to include assets acquired in the future.
The Cork Committee recommended that it should be made possible for an individual to create a floating charge for business purposes: see Cmnd 8558 (1982), para 1569.

[3] The term 'book debts' is well established in English law, although its exact scope is unclear. Broadly speaking, in
the present context it is used to describe the sums due to a company for goods sold or services rendered which have
been, or are due to be, invoiced but have not yet been paid. There is growing support for the American expression
'receivables', which is more or less equivalent.

the wholesale market (intended for professional investors). The distinguishing criterion is the nominal value of the securities: those with a nominal value of less than EUR 50,000, are regarded as intended for the retail market. And by Directive 2003/71/EC (art 3(2)(c)), no prospectus is required for a public offer of wholesale debt securities (traded on the Professional Securities Market).

3. Under CA 2006 s 616, companies are no longer be able to use their share premium account to write off any expenses incurred, commission paid or discount allowed in respect of an issue of debentures or in providing for the premium payable on a redemption of debentures.

4. Major companies may also raise money by the issue of 'bonds', commonly referred to as 'Eurobonds' or 'international bonds' (a form of bearer security), which are usually denominated in a currency other than sterling and, because they are for large amounts, will be bought and dealt in by banks and other institutional investors rather than the general public. There are various international markets and securities exchanges for dealings in such bonds.

➤ Questions

1. List some of the points of similarity and difference between shareholders and debenture holders which follow from the fact that a shareholder is a *member*, while a debenture holder is a *creditor*, of the company. Think of:
   (a) the right to income;
   (b) application of the 'maintenance of capital' rules;
   (c) the right to return of capital during the lifetime of the company;
   (d) the right to return of capital in a liquidation;
   (e) taxation;
   (f) voting.

2. Some of these points may be varied by the terms of issue of the share or debenture, eg a share *may* carry no vote, a debenture holder *may* be given a vote in some circumstances. Which of the points listed above may be varied in this way?

Debentures

Definition

CA 2006 s 738

738 In the Companies Acts 'debenture' includes debenture stock, bonds and any other securities of a company, whether or not constituting a charge on the assets of the company.

[10.01] Levy v Abercorris Slate and Slab Co (1887) 37 Ch D 260 (Chancery Division)

[The facts are immaterial.]

CHITTY J: In my opinion a debenture means a document which either creates a debt or acknowledges it, and any document which fulfils either of these conditions is a 'debenture'. I cannot find any precise legal definition of the term, it is not either in law or commerce a strictly technical term, or what is called a term of art.

An instrument may be a debenture although it is not under seal and gives no security to creditors for the company's obligation.

[10.02] British India Steam Navigation Co v IRC (1881) 7 QBD 165 (Queen's Bench Division)

The company had issued instruments described on their face as 'debentures', by which the company undertook to pay the holder £100 on 30 November 1882, and to pay interest half-yearly at 5% per annum. It was argued unsuccessfully that the instruments, not being under seal, came within the definition of a promissory note and so did not attract the higher rate of stamp duty ordinarily payable on debentures.

> LINDLEY LJ: Now, what the correct meaning of 'debenture' is I do not know. I do not find anywhere any precise definition of it. We know that there are various kinds of instruments commonly called debentures. You may have mortgage debentures, which are charges of some kind on property. You may have debentures which are bonds; and, if this instrument were under seal, it would be a debenture of that kind. You may have a debenture which is nothing more than an acknowledgment of indebtedness. And you may have a thing like this, which is something more; it is a statement by two directors that the company will pay a certain sum of money on a given day, and will also pay interest half-yearly at certain times and at a certain place, upon production of certain coupons by the holder of the instrument. I think any of these things which I have referred to may be debentures within the Act.
>
> [His Lordship accordingly held that the instrument was a debenture and liable to be stamped as such.]

➤ Note

It is established that the term 'debenture' is capable in law of having a very wide meaning—simply a document evidencing a debt of any kind. But both in commercial usage and in the layman's understanding, it is commonly understood that the expression refers to a document evidencing some *secured* obligation, and so the Listing Rules require that any issue of unsecured debentures be denominated 'unsecured', and indeed it is more common for the word to be avoided altogether in this situation and a term such as 'loan stock' or 'loan notes' used instead.

Debentures and debenture stock may be issued in bearer form (ie not requiring registration for legal effect), and may also be created on terms which make them negotiable instruments: *Bechuanaland Exploration Co v London Trading Bank* [1898] 2 QB 658. As regards convertible debentures, see above, p 384.

Secured debt: mortgages, fixed and floating charges

Many companies will need to provide security for the repayment of their funding obligations, and not only obligations by way of loan. Only the largest companies, invariably trading on the London Stock Exchange or some other national equivalent, can avoid this. Since the issue is so common, and so important, the rest of this Chapter is devoted to examining the rules relating to corporate security, especially fixed and floating charges. First, though, some definitions of the types of interests used to provide security.

Mortgages

A mortgage is a security interest created by transfer of legal title in the secured asset from the borrower/mortgagor to the lender/mortgagee. The borrower has an *'equity of redemption'*, allowing recovery of legal title once the secured obligation is fulfilled (eg the loan, interest, etc repaid) and, in the meantime, the lender has the right to take possession and foreclose if the borrower defaults.

Historically, purchases of real property were secured by mortgages of this type over the land being bought. Now, however, the legal title to the land is *not* transferred to the lending bank (or other mortgagee), and the bank merely takes a legal *charge* over the property. (Nevertheless, we continue to speak of mortgages over land, and describe buyers as mortgagors and banks as mortgagees.) This charge over land is anomalous only in the sense that it is a *legal* charge, created by statute (Law of Property Act 1925, ss 85–87), whereas the charges discussed in this Chapter are all necessarily *equitable*, not legal.

Charges

A *charge* is a security interest created in or over an asset or assets by their owner (the '*chargor*') in favour of a creditor (the '*chargee*'), by which it is agreed[4] that that property shall be appropriated to the discharge of a debt or other obligation. There is no transfer of title. The chargee's rights are proprietary, but created by contract, and only for real consideration (since this is in equity, a deed will not do: see *Re Earl of Lucan* (1890) 45 Ch D 470). The chargee's right may be enforced by the sale of the property, if necessary by court order; but in practice most security documents expressly empower the chargee to sell the property for this purpose without recourse to the court (See Slade J in *Re Bond Worth Ltd* [1980] Ch 228, 250.). Legal charges are possible over some forms of property, such as land (see above), but not over personalty. The charges discussed in this section are all equitable charges.

Fixed charges

All charges are either fixed or floating. A fixed charge (or 'specific' charge) is a charge created over identified property which restricts the debtor's power to dispose of or otherwise deal with the property without the creditor's consent. It is not necessary that the property should be presently owned by the chargor: future property may be the subject of an agreement to charge, provided that it is sufficiently described to be identifiable when acquired. The effect of such an agreement, if for value consideration, is that a charge is deemed to come into existence as soon as the property is acquired by the chargor (*Holroyd v Marshall* (1862) 10 HL Cas 191).

Floating charges

A floating charge also requires the property affected to be identified, in the same sense, but it is of the essence of a floating charge that it contemplates that the chargor will be free to deal with the charged property in the ordinary course of business without reference to the chargee (sometimes called the 'trading power'). The floating charge thus allows a company to give security over assets which are continually turned over or used up and replaced as a matter of routine trading. This is an enormously valuable invention, devised by equity draftsmen in the latter part of the nineteenth century, founded upon the agreement of the parties and owing nothing to legislation—rather like the device of hire-purchase which evolved at about the same time.[5] What successive Companies Acts and Insolvency Acts have done since its creation is adopt a variety of rules designed to restrict the full power of its impact, which is

---

[4] The charges described in this chapter are all created by agreement between the parties. Charges may also sometimes be created by operation of law (and then are referred to as *equitable liens*, although note that, despite the name, the rights associated with them mirror the non-statutory rights associated with equitable charges, and not the rights associated with contractual liens, which are quite different), but these equitable liens are not relevant for present purposes.

[5] A voluminous literature exists on floating charges, covering both practical and theoretical aspects. The latest collection is contained in J Getzler and J Payne (eds), *Company Charges: Spectrum and Beyond* (OUP, 2006), and that provides reference to much of the earlier literature.

potentially to sweep up *all* the company's resources (by securing '*the undertaking*' or '*all the assets and undertaking*' of the company) and dedicate them to securing the debt of *one* of the company's creditors,[6] leaving all the others unprotected, unable even to share *pari passu* in the company's resources on a winding up.

The significance of the floating charge lies in the fact that, for many businesses, fluctuating assets such as stock-in-trade, raw materials and book debts may form a significant part of the property of the concern, and may be the only worthwhile security available for an advance. Indeed, the proprietors of an unincorporated business which is in need of finance may find themselves compelled to form a company if they are to raise the loans they are seeking: hence the ability to grant a floating charge can be an important consideration in deciding whether or not to trade in the corporate form. Banks, in particular, have wide experience of the floating charge and encourage its use by their clients.

[10.03] National Provincial Bank v Charnley [1924] 1 KB 431 (Court of Appeal)

[The facts are immaterial.]

ATKIN LJ: It is not necessary to give a formal definition of a charge, but I think there can be no doubt that where in a transaction for value both parties evince an intention that property, existing or future, shall be made available as security for the payment of a debt, and that the creditor shall have a present right to have it made available, there is a charge, even though the present legal right which is contemplated can only be enforced at some future date, and though the creditor gets no legal right of property, either absolute or special, or any legal right to possession, but only gets a right to have the security made available by an order of the Court. If those conditions exist I think there is a charge. If, on the other hand, the parties do not intend that there should be a present right to have the security made available, but only that there should be a right in the future by agreement, such as a licence, to seize the goods, there will be no charge . . .

Debenture holders' remedies and the protection afforded by charges

We have not yet examined the approach the courts adopt in determining whether the security the parties have created is effective, and if so whether it is fixed or floating in form. However, in large measure the reason for the efforts in that direction are because a valid security delivers particular protections to the security holder. It is helpful to be aware of what those are before descending into the detail of the analysis required to establish the security itself.

A creditor whose debt is unsatisfied may, of course, sue to recover payment, and may also seek to have the company wound up if it fails to meet a statutory demand for payment (IA 1986 ss 122(1)(f), 123(1)(a): see below pp 651 ff). But a secured creditor will naturally wish to have recourse to his security. Where the charge affects specific property, powers of sale and of entry into possession may be exercised by the creditor of a company in the same way as against an individual, but (especially in the case of a floating charge) the remedy usually invoked will be to appoint a *receiver*. This may always be done by obtaining a court order; but almost invariably the need to go to court will be obviated by the inclusion in the instrument

---

[6] *Re Panama, New Zealand and Australian Royal Mail Co* (1870) 5 Ch App 318, CA, provided early confirmation that this is possible.

creating the charge of a clause empowering the creditor itself (or the trustees, where there is a trust deed) to appoint a receiver in the event of default. Note, however, that if the charge is a floating charge secured over the whole or substantially the whole of the company's property, then the holder may no longer appoint an administrative receiver (IA 2006 s 72A), subject to certain limited exceptions in IA 2006 ss 72B—72EA.

The subject of receivers, including administrative receivers, is discussed further below, at pp 637 ff.

If the borrowing company is insolvent (ie unable to pay all its debts in full), then security affords secured creditors priority in repayment of their debts. Basically, the secured assets are used first to fund repayment of the secured debt, and any remaining assets are then used to repay all the debts owed to unsecured creditors. If a company owes £100,000 to a secured creditor and £100,000 to its unsecured creditors, for example, and its assets are only worth £100,000, then those assets (assuming these are the assets over which security has been taken) will go entirely to repaying the secured debt, and the unsecured creditors will get nothing. In practice, the statutory rules are more sophisticated and more complicated, but this gross generalisation is fundamentally true. The statutory rules are considered in detail below, in Chapter 14.

For the moment it is sufficient to note that the advantages afforded to holders of fixed charges are substantially greater than those afforded to holders of floating charges.

Different protections afforded to fixed and floating charge holders

The distinction between fixed and floating charges has important consequences. These charges are treated differently during the term of the security, during receivership and on the insolvency of the debtor. For example, with floating charges (but not with fixed charges):

(i)   the chargor can legitimately deal with floating charge assets in the ordinary course of business (until an event of default that causes the charge to *crystallise*—see below, p 476), so the value of the security may be depleted before the chargee calls on it;

(ii)   all floating charges need to be registered, but not all fixed charges (see CA 2006 s 860 and below, p 464);

(iii)   a floating charge is subordinated to the costs and expenses of administration and liquidation (see IA 1986, Sch B1, paras 70 and 99, and IA 1986, s 176ZA; and below, pp 631 ff and pp 647 ff);

(iv)   an administrator can dispose of assets subject a floating charge without first obtaining court approval (IA 1986, Sch B1, paras 70–71, and below, p 634);

(v)   preferential creditors rank ahead of the floating charge holder in their call on assets subject to the floating charge (IA 1986 ss 40, 175(2)(b), Sch B1, para 65(2), and Sch 6 paras 8–12; see below, pp 646 ff);

(vi)   on insolvency, a statutory proportion of floating charge realisations must be set aside for the unsecured creditors (see IA 1986 s 176A, and below, p 647);

(vii)   a floating charge created for no new value in the period immediately leading up to insolvency may be set aside (IA 1986 s 245, and see below, p 664). No equivalent exists for fixed charges, which can only be set aside if they involve a preference (IA 1986 s 239, and see below, p 664).

Requirement to register charges

Statutory requirements

Part 25 of CA 2006 imposes on companies a statutory obligation to register particulars of charges which they have created over their property. This requirement was first imposed by CA 1900. It is not every category of charge which is affected—charges over shares and those over negotiable instruments, for instance, escape the net; but the list, as set out in the Act (s 860), is a fairly comprehensive one. In particular, all floating charges are caught by the legislation. But it should be noted that it is only charges *created by the company* which come within Pt 25: a charge created by operation of law, such as an unpaid vendor's lien over land which is the subject of a contract of sale, is outside the scope of the Act.

For every charge that is within the categories set out in the statutory list, CA 2006 s 860 requires companies to deliver to the registrar for registration the 'prescribed particulars' of the charge, together with a copy of the instrument of charge (if any), and to do so within the period allowed for this (basically 21 days, but see s 870). The charge-holder may also see to the registration, and would be well advised to do so if there is any risk that the company will default: s 860(2).

If a company acquires property which is already subject to a charge, particulars of the charge must similarly be delivered for registration (s 862). Where the charge (eg a charge over land or a ship) requires registration under other legislation, both that legislation and CA 2006 must be complied with.

Certificate of registration

The registrar's staff checks the accuracy of the particulars before they are entered on the register. On registration, a certificate is issued which is conclusive evidence that the requirements of the Act have been complied with (s 869(6)). This is so even where the certificate is inaccurate (*Re Mechanisations (Eaglescliffe) Ltd* [1966] Ch 20), or the facts on which the certificate is based are untrue (eg where the charge instrument is falsely dated: *Re CL Nye Ltd* [1971] Ch 442), or the charge was registered by mistake (*Ali v Top Marques Car Rental Ltd* [2006] EWHC 109).

The effect is that notwithstanding that the details on the register will be incorrect, and people inspecting the register will be misled, the certificate will be conclusive proof that the statutory requirements have been met. As a consequence, the *actual* charge as created by the company will be deemed to be duly registered, and it will have to be observed by the company's creditors and its liquidator or administrator. Because the certificate is conclusive evidence that the requirements have been met, it is impossible to have proceedings for judicial review of the registrar's decision.

Despite all this, the conclusiveness of the certificate was seen as a crucial benefit of the registration system, and a proposed downgrading of it was in large measure the reason for the unpopularity of proposed 1989 reforms (see below).

Effect of failure to register

If particulars are not registered within 21 days of the creation of the charge (s 870), CA 2006 s 874 declares that the *security* is void against the liquidator, administrator and any creditor of the company.[7] There are also criminal penalties for non-compliance (s 860).

---

[7] But see *Smith v Bridgend County Borough Council* [2001] UKHL 58, [2002] AC 336 (the appeal of *Cosslett* [10.08], below), Lord Hoffmann: 'When a winding-up order is made and a liquidator appointed, there is no divesting of the company's assets. The liquidator acquires no interest, whether beneficially or as trustee. The assets continue to belong to the company but the liquidator is able to exercise the company's right to collect them for the purposes of the liquidation . . . It must in my opinion follow that when [CA 1985] s 395 [now CA 2006 s 874] says that the charge shall be 'void

The nature of this sanction of 'partial voidness' is curious. First, it should be noted that it is the *security* that is avoided, and not the obligation, which remains good as an unsecured debt. Indeed, s 874(3) strengthens the position of the creditor by providing that the money secured by a charge which is rendered void becomes immediately payable. Second, the charge is void only as against the persons mentioned and not, for instance, *inter partes*, nor against an execution creditor. And the chargee may dispose of the property in exercise of a power of sale and give a good title to the purchaser, even though the charge is 'void'.

Extension of the registration period and rectification of the register

CA 2006 s 873 enables applications to court to extend the 21 day registration period or to make other corrections to the register. The court may make whatever orders it sees as just and expedient provided certain pre-conditions are satisfied (s 873(1)), including that it is just and equitable to grant relief. (See *Barclays Bank plc v Stuart Landon Ltd* [2001] EWCA Civ 140, CA for a discussion of the factors to be considered by the court when dealing with an application for late registration of a charge created by a company which is close to liquidation.)

Registration, priority and constructive notice of registered charges

Registration does not of itself confer priority or give any protection to a charge-holder, although of course non-registration brings all but fatal consequences for his security. Priority as between different charges over the same property is determined by the ordinary rules of law. Thus, for example, a legal charge will normally have priority over an equitable charge, a fixed charge over a floating charge, and, as between two equitable charges, the earlier in time will prevail. So, if a company were to create a charge in favour of A on the first of the month, and then give an identical charge over the same property to B on the 10th, registering particulars on the 15th, B (who had searched the register on the 10th and found it clear) could in all innocence believe that he has a first charge, only to discover later than A has a charge which ranks ahead of his own, so long as it has been registered within the statutory 21 days. B is deemed to have notice of the earlier charge provided A files for registration within the statutory 21 day period. (This is referred to in the CLR as 'the 21-day invisibility problem'. It could be eliminated if 'notice filing' were introduced, although even then there could be a gap between the time when a document is delivered to Companies House and the time when it is recorded on the register.)

The doctrine of constructive notice has not been abolished in regard to particulars of charges held by the registrar, and so everyone dealing with a company is deemed to have notice of those particulars which are required by statute to be registered. These are defined by s 869(4), and include the date of creation of the charge, the amount secured, short particulars of the property charged, and the persons entitled to the charge.

However, a practice has developed of including additional information, and in particular, details of any 'negative pledge' clause contained in the charge instrument, ie a provision by which the company undertakes not to create other charges ranking in priority to or *pari passu* with the charge. It was held in *Siebe Gorman & Co Ltd v Barclays Bank Ltd* [1979] 2 Lloyd's Rep 142 (Ch) (overruled in *Spectrum* **[10.20]**, but not on this issue) that the constructive notice doctrine does not extend to such additional information, but only to those matters which the Act prescribes, and so a searcher will be taken to know of such a clause only if he has *actual* notice of it. The point remains controversial, and there is little persuasive authority or argument.[8]

---

against the liquidator', it means void against a company acting by its liquidator, that is to say, a company in liquidation.' The same analysis applies to administration.

[8] See *Wilson v Kelland* [1910] 2 Ch 306. Also see J de Lacy, 'Constructive notice and company charge registration' [2001] Conv 122.

Section 872 contains provision for entering on the register a 'memorandum' that the debt secured by a charge has been satisfied or some or all of the property charged has been released from the security. But there is no *obligation* to register this information under the existing law.

Company's own register of charges

The *company itself* is also required to keep a register of charges, together with a copy of every instrument creating or evidencing a registrable charge over its property, and to make these available for inspection, without cost to any creditor or member of the company, and for cost to anyone else (ss 875–877).

Since the register covers every kind of charge, and not only those of which particulars must be filed with the registrar, its obligations are potentially very burdensome indeed. But neither the validity of the charge nor any question relating to priority is affected by a failure to observe the requirement of this section, and in practice the criminal sanctions prescribed are never invoked.

Reform of the registration system

The need for some sort of registration system is accepted, but the present system, which has changed little for over a century, has long been thought to be deficient. Indeed, changes were made in CA 1989 that were intended to sweep away the old law and replace it with a completely new regime, containing provisions which would reduce the burden on Companies House but at the same time give rather less protection to persons who relied on the registration system. Those proposed reforms met with such opposition from business and professional circles that the government was dissuaded from bringing the regime into operation. Instead, a consultation process was begun which envisaged retaining the earlier CA 1985 provisions, but introducing some modifications. That idea was in turn overtaken by the decision to set up the CLR, which published its own consultation document seeking views on possible ways forward. Following that, the Law Commission was asked to examine the whole of the law on the registration, perfection and priority of company charges, and to consider the case for a new registration system. It was also asked to consider whether such a system should be extended to quasi-securities (retention of title agreements, etc), and to securities created by individuals as well as companies.

The Law Commission, looking to have changes included in CA 2006, made various recommendations, including adoption of a notice filing system (see below) for company charges (see *Company Security Interests*, Law Com No 296, Cm 6654, 2005). The government then issued a further consultation document (*The Registration of Companies' Security Interests (Company Charges): The Economic Impact of the Law Commissions' Proposals*, 2005). This received a rather negative response, and so all these issues now remain subject to still further discussions and deliberations before any decision will be taken on what ought to be done.

This rocky road to reform might be seen as both surprising and disappointing. Both the Crowther Committee (which was concerned with reform of the law on consumer credit: Cmnd 4596, 1971) and Professor Diamond in his report (*A Review of Security Interests in Property* (HMSO, 1989)) categorically recommended that this country should follow the lead of the United States and Canadian jurisdictions in setting up an entirely new system of registration for all personal property security interests, whether created by individuals or companies, on the model of Art 9 of the American Uniform Commercial Code. This would make a separate regime for company charges unnecessary. The same conclusion was reached independently by reform bodies in other Commonwealth jurisdictions, such as Australia and

New Zealand—each of which has taken active steps to implement this major change. But, sadly, there seems to be little enthusiasm for any such reform here.

Article 9 is at the same time a more comprehensive system and yet a simpler and more flexible one: it governs all transactions which *in effect* create a security, whatever their form (including eg hire-purchase agreements and sales on retention of title (*Romalpa* [10.21]) terms), and works on the principle of 'notice filing'. Priority as between competing registered securities is governed simply by the time of filing of the notice of such security: the security filed first has priority over all that follow. It gives better protection—first, for security holders, in that registration confers priority over others who may claim interests in the same property; secondly, for those intending to take security who, by filing a notice, can cover their position provisionally until the security is completed or the charge attaches; and thirdly, for those seeking to rely on searches of the register, who can take the record at its face value.

Fixed and floating charges: definitions

Now that the structure of the regime for company securities has been examined, it is time to look at the nature of the securities themselves. Recall that charges may be over present or future property and can be either fixed or floating. A *fixed* (or 'specific') charge is one which restricts the debtor's power to dispose of or otherwise deal with the specific property charged, without first obtaining the creditor's consent. A *floating* charge, on the other hand, permits the debtor the freedom to deal with the charged property in the ordinary course of business without recourse to the creditor for approval. This liberty to deal with the charged assets continues until the floating charge *crystallises* into a fixed charge. The parties can nominate in the charge document the conditions, or time, at which this will happen. Additionally, the charge will crystallise by operation of law if the debtor company ceases to carry on business for any reason (see below, pp 476 ff).

The distinction between fixed and floating charges is completely irrelevant in assessing the rights, as between the company (chargor) and the lender (chargee) arising under the charge; these are determined by the charge document. The distinction is critical solely because various statutory rules relating to validity and priority are worded to apply to one form of security but not the other: see above, p 463.

Categorisation of a charge as fixed or floating is based on the *substance* of the arrangement between the parties, not on the label they attach to their arrangement.[9] The cases extracted below (pp 468 ff) indicate the process adopted by the courts in making this determination.

---

[9] Eg *Re Armagh Shoes Ltd* [1984] BCLC 405 *per* Hutton J, holding that the charge was floating even though stated to be fixed. Although there was no provision for crystallisation, this did not matter: the charge would crystallise on the winding up of the company or the appointment of a receiver (pp 408–11, 419). Also see *Re Brightlife Ltd* [1987] Ch 200, 209 *per* Hoffmann J (see [10.12] below). There is a vast body of precedent, going back to the earliest Bills of Sale Acts last century, concerned with the question of whether a composite transaction such as a sale and lease-back is what it purports to be or is in reality a concealed form of charge. For contrasting modern illustrations, see *Welsh Development Agency v Export Finance Co Ltd* [1992] BCLC 148, CA (agency with power to sell held genuine) and *Re Curtain Dream plc* [1990] BCLC 925 (purported sale and repurchase held to be a disguised form of security).

[10.04] Agnew v Commissioner of Inland Revenue (Re Brumark Investments Ltd) [2001] UKPC 28, [2002] 2 AC 710 (Privy Council)

[The facts and a longer extract appear at [10.19].]

LORD MILLETT: The most celebrated, and certainly the most often cited, description of a floating charge is that given by Romer LJ in *In re Yorkshire Woolcombers Association Ltd* [1903] 2 Ch 284, 295:

> I certainly do not intend to attempt to give an exact definition of the term 'floating charge', nor am I prepared to say that there will not be a floating charge within the meaning of the Act, which does not contain all the three characteristics that I am about to mention, but I certainly think that if a charge has the three characteristics that I am about to mention it is a floating charge. (1) If it is a charge on a class of assets of a company present and future; (2) if that class is one which, in the ordinary course of the business of the company, would be changing from time to time; and (3) if you find that by the charge it is contemplated that, until some future step is taken by or on behalf of those interested in the charge, the company may carry on its business in the ordinary way as far as concerns the particular class of assets I am dealing with.

This was offered as a description and not a definition. The first two characteristics are typical of a floating charge but they are not distinctive of it, since they are not necessarily inconsistent with a fixed charge. It is the third characteristic which is the hallmark of a floating charge and serves to distinguish it from a fixed charge. Since the existence of a fixed charge would make it impossible for the company to carry on business in the ordinary way without the consent of the charge holder, it follows that its ability to so without such consent is inconsistent with the fixed nature of the charge.

[Also see the *Spectrum* decision, [10.20] below.]

[10.05] Illingworth v Houldsworth [1904] AC 355 (House of Lords)

[This is the appeal to the House of Lords of the decision in *Re Yorkshire Woolcombers Association*, cited by Lord Millett at [10.04] above.]

EARL OF HALSBURY LC: In the first place you have that which in a sense I suppose must be an element in the definition of a floating security, that it is something which is to float, not to be put into immediate operation, but such that the company is to be allowed to carry on its business. It contemplates not only that it [the security] should carry with it the book debts [the charged assets] which were then existing, but it contemplates also the possibility of those book debts being extinguished by a payment to the company, and that other book debts should come in and take the place of those that had disappeared. That . . . seems to me to be an essential characteristic of what is properly called a floating security . . .

LORD MACNAGHTEN: I should have thought there was not much difficulty in defining what a floating charge is in contrast to what is called a specific charge. A specific charge, I think, is one that without more fastens on ascertained and definite property or property capable of being ascertained and defined; a floating charge, on the other hand, is ambulatory and shifting in its nature, hovering over and so to speak floating with the property which it is intended to affect until some event occurs or some act is done which causes it to settle and fasten on the subject of the charge within its reach and grasp . . .

[10.06] Evans v British Granite Quarries Ltd [1910] 2 KB 979 (Court of Appeal)

[The facts are immaterial.]

BUCKLEY LJ: A floating charge is not a future security; it is a present security which presently affects all the assets of the company expressed to be included in it. . . . A floating security is not a specific mortgage of the assets plus a licence to the mortgagor to dispose of them in the course of his business, but it is a floating mortgage applying to every item comprised in the security, but not specifically affecting any item until some act or event occurs or some act on the part of the mortgagee is done which causes it to crystallise into a fixed security. . . .

[10.07] Re Bond Worth [1980] 1 Ch 228

[The case concerned an unsuccessful attempt to give a supplier of goods the benefit of a retention of title clause (discussed below, p 495).]

SLADE J: There is, however, one type of charge (and I think one type only) which, by its very nature, leaves a company at liberty to deal with the assets charged in the ordinary course of its business, without regard to the charge, until stopped by a winding up or by the appointment of a receiver or the happening of some other agreed event. I refer to what is commonly known as a "floating charge" . . . Such a charge remains unattached to any particular property and leaves the company with a licence to deal with, and even sell, the assets falling within its ambit in the ordinary course of business, as if the charge had not been given, until it is stopped by one or other of the events to which I have referred, when it is said to "crystallise"; it then becomes effectively fixed to the assets within its scope.

. . . This description of a floating charge shows that it need not extend to all the assets of the company. It may cover assets merely of a specified category or categories . . .

. . . The critical distinction in my judgment is that between a specific charge on the one hand and a floating charge on the other. Vaughan Williams L.J. pointed out in the *Woolcombers* case [1903] 2 Ch. 284 that it is quite inconsistent with the nature of a specific charge, though not of a floating charge, that the mortgagor is at liberty to deal with the relevant property as he pleases. He said, at p 294:

> I do not think that for a 'specific security' you need have a security of a subject matter which is then in existence. I mean by 'then' at the time of the execution of the security; but what you do require to make a specific security is that the security whenever it has once come into existence, and been identified or appropriated as a security, shall never thereafter at the will of the mortgagor cease to be a security. If at the will of the mortgagor he can dispose of it and prevent its being any longer a security, although something else may be substituted more or less for it, that is not a 'specific security'.

Floating charges: creation and effect

Creation of floating charges and impact of failure to register

It is possible for a floating charge to arise even though the parties never contemplated that this might be the result of their actions.[10]

[10.08] Re Cosslett (Contractors) Ltd [1998] Ch 495 (Court of Appeal)

[This case went on appeal to the House of Lords, but not on this issue: [2002] AC 336.] Cosslett had contracted with the Mid-Glamorgan County Council to carry out land reclamation work which involved the washing of large amounts of coal-bearing shale, and for this purpose it brought two coal-washing plants onto the site. A clause in the contract empowered the Council, if the company abandoned the work, (a) to use the plants to complete the job, or (b) to sell the plants and use the proceeds towards the satisfaction of any sums due to it from Cosslett. Before the work was completed, the company abandoned the site, leaving the plants behind. The company then went into administration. The Council applied to the court for an order requiring the administrator to deliver the plants to it; the company contended that the clause in the contract created a charge which was a floating charge and void because it had not been registered. At first instance, Jonathan Parker J held that there was a charge, but that it was a fixed charge. On appeal, it was held that although no charge was created by paragraph (a) of the clause in question, a floating charge was created by paragraph (b); but that non-registration of (b) did not stand in the way of the Council's right to enforce (a).

MILLETT LJ: . . . There are only four kinds of consensual security known to English law: (i) pledge; (ii) contractual lien; (iii) equitable charge and (iv) mortgage. A pledge and a contractual lien both depend on the delivery of possession to the creditor. The difference between them is that in the case of a pledge the owner delivers possession to the creditor as security, whereas in the case of a lien the creditor retains possession of goods previously delivered to him for some other purpose. Neither a mortgage nor a charge depends on the delivery of possession. The difference between them is that a mortgage involves a transfer of legal or equitable ownership to the creditor, whereas an equitable charge does not.

In the present case the council's rights in relation to the plant and materials are exclusively contractual, and are not attributable to any delivery of possession by the company. When the company brings plant and materials onto the site they remain in the possession of the company to enable it to use them in the completion of the works. There is no question of the company delivering possession at that stage, either by way of security (i.e. as a pledge) or otherwise (i.e. by way of lien). The council comes into possession of the plant and materials when it expels the company from the site leaving the plant and materials behind. But this does not amount to a voluntary delivery of possession by the company to the council. It is rather the exercise by the council of a contractual right to take possession of the plant and materials against the will of the company.

In my judgment, therefore, the council's rights are derived from contract not possession and, in so far as they are conferred by way of security, constitute an equitable charge . . .

Is the charge a fixed or floating charge?

In my judgment the three characteristics of a floating charge which were identified by Romer L.J. in *In re Yorkshire Woolcombers Association Ltd.; Houldsworth v. Yorkshire Woolcombers Association Ltd.* [1903] 2 Ch. 284, 295 are all present. There is no difficulty in regard to the first two

---

[10] Unsurprisingly, then, these charges are not registered as required by CA 2006 s 874 [or its predecessor, CA 1985 s 395] and so are ineffective to give priority on the chargor's insolvency: see above, p 464.

characteristics. Plant and materials become subject to the charge as they are brought onto the site and cease to be subject to it as they are removed from the site. Accordingly the charge is a charge on present and future assets of the company which, in the ordinary course of the business of the company, would be changing from time to time. The dispute has centred on the third characteristic. The administrator submits that, until the council takes steps under clause 63(1) to enter upon the site and expel the company therefrom, the company is free to carry on its business in the ordinary way with the plant and materials on the site. The judge accepted the council's submission that this was not so, because of the council's absolute right under clause 53(6) to refuse to permit the company to remove from the site plant and materials immediately required to complete the works, and its qualified right to refuse permission for the removal of plant and materials not immediately required for this purpose provided only that it acts reasonably. I am unable to agree with him.

The judge held that it is of the essence of a floating charge that until the charge crystallises the chargor should retain an unfettered freedom to carry on his business in the ordinary way. He relied for this purpose on two passages, one in the judgment of Vaughan Williams L.J. in the *Yorkshire Woolcombers* case, at p 294, and the other in the judgment of Slade J. in *In re Bond Worth Ltd.* **[10.07]** [1980] Ch. 228, 266. The first passage reads as follows:

"If *at the will of the mortgagor* he can dispose of [the asset] and prevent its being any longer a security, although something else may be substituted more or less for it, that is not a 'specific security.' " (My emphasis.)

The second passage reads:

"It is in my judgment quite incompatible with the existence of an effective trust by way of specific charge in equity over specific assets that *the alleged trustee* should be free to use them as he pleases for his own business in the course of his own business." (My emphasis.)

But with respect the converse does not follow. The chargor's unfettered freedom to deal with the assets in the ordinary course of his business free from the charge is obviously inconsistent with the nature of a fixed charge; but it does not follow that his unfettered freedom to deal with the charged assets is essential to the existence of a floating charge. It plainly is not, for any well drawn floating charge prohibits the chargor from creating further charges having priority to the floating charge; and a prohibition against factoring debts is not sufficient to convert what would otherwise be a floating charge on book debts into a fixed charge: see in *In re Brightlife Ltd.* **[10.12]** [1987] Ch. 200, 209, per Hoffmann J.

The essence of a floating charge is that it is a charge, not on any particular asset, but on a fluctuating body of assets which remain under the management and control of the chargor, and which the chargor has the right to withdraw from the security despite the existence of the charge. The essence of a fixed charge is that the charge is on a particular asset or class of assets which the chargor cannot deal with free from the charge without the consent of the chargee. The question is not whether the chargor has complete freedom to carry on his business as he chooses, but whether the chargee is in control of the charged assets.

The business of the company was to carry out works of civil engineering. In the ordinary course of that business it entered into the contract with the council. In bringing plant and materials onto the site and carrying out the works for the council it was carrying on the ordinary course of its business. It is not to be supposed that its business was confined to the performance of its contract with the council; and if it wished to remove plant or materials from the site and deploy them elsewhere this too would be in the ordinary course of its business. In forbidding the company from removing from the site plant or materials required, whether immediately or not, for the completion of the works, the council was, therefore, placing a restriction on the way in which the company carried on business.

Thus far I agree with the judge. Where I part company from him is that I do not regard this restriction as having any relation to the council's security. The council's purpose in imposing the restriction was not to protect its security but to ensure that the company would give proper priority to the completion of the works. A similar restriction would have been appropriate even if the council had not taken any security interest.

In a case where the plant or materials are not immediately required, the engineer's consent is not to be unreasonably withheld. As Evans L.J. pointed out in argument, the fact that the decision is left to the engineer shows that it is to be made on operational grounds. If completion of the works will not be prejudiced or delayed by the removal of an item of plant or materials, then consent to its removal must be given; consent cannot be withheld on the ground that the remaining plant and materials would be insufficient security if the company were in default.

In the course of argument it was pointed out that the council must give seven days' notice before expelling the company from the site, and it was suggested that once such notice has been given and while it has not yet expired the engineer may properly refuse his consent on the ground that the remaining security is insufficient. I do not agree with this; but even if I did it would make no difference. If the council's right to prevent removal on security and non-operational grounds arises only upon notice of expulsion, then in my judgment the effect of giving such notice is to crystallise the charge.

Accordingly, and in disagreement with the judge, I hold the charge to be a floating charge.

What are the consequences of the want of registration?

Of all the contractual rights which the council enjoys only one, the power of sale, constitutes a charge of a kind which is registrable under section 395 of the Companies Act 1985 [CA 2006 s 860]. The section provides that the failure to register a charge makes the charge (that is to say the registrable charge) void as a security against a liquidator or administrator of the company [now see CA 2006 s 874]. The effect of this is to entitle the liquidator or administrator to deal with the company's assets free from the security created by the charge in question.

In my judgment, therefore, the failure to register the charge renders the security created by the power of sale void as against the administrator, but does not affect any other right of the council which is not a security and which does not require registration. In particular, it does not invalidate the council's contractual right to retain possession of plant and materials and use them to complete the works. But after the completion of the works the council's right to continue in possession [and certainly to sell] is referable to a security which is void against the administrator and cannot prevail against him . . .

Limitations on the assets which may be made subject to a floating charge

If a company has a proprietary interest in an asset, then it usually assumed that the asset can be charged by the company as security for an obligation.

The possible limits to this assumption were tested in the House of Lords. The issue arose from a practice adopted by banks in attempting to enlarge the security they take from borrowing customers. Banks typically take fixed and floating charges over all a customer's fixed assets and stock-in-trade. But what of any sums of money the customer might have on deposit with the bank? Put in contractual terms, these are sums of money that the bank owes to the customer. The customer 'owns' a debt owed to it by the bank. Can the bank take a charge over this asset to secure a loan it might make to its customer? The issue has now been resolved in favour of this form of security, as illustrated by the extract below.

[10.09] Re Bank of Credit and Commerce International SA (No 8)
[1998] AC 214 (House of Lords)

[The facts are immaterial.]

LORD HOFFMANN: The doctrine of conceptual impossibility was first propounded by Millett J in *In re Charge Card Services Ltd.* [1987] Ch 150, 175–176 and affirmed, after more extensive discussion, by the Court of Appeal in this case. It has excited a good deal of heat and controversy in banking circles; the Legal Risk Review Committee, set up in 1991 by the Bank of England to identify areas of obscurity and uncertainty in the law affecting financial markets and propose solutions, said that a very large number of submissions from interested parties expressed disquiet about this ruling. It seems clear that documents purporting to create such charges have been used by banks for many years. The point does not previously appear to have been expressly addressed by any court in this country. Supporters of the doctrine rely on the judgments of Buckley L.J. (in the Court of Appeal) and Viscount Dilhorne and Lord Cross of Chelsea (in the House of Lords) in *Halesowen Presswork Assemblies Ltd. v.Westminster Bank Ltd.* [1971] 1 Q.B. 1; [1972] A.C. 785. The passages in question certainly say that it is a misuse of language to speak of a bank having a lien over its own indebtedness to a customer. But I think that these observations were directed to the use of the word "lien", which is a right to retain possession, rather than to the question of whether the bank could have any kind of proprietary interest. Opponents of the doctrine rely upon some 19th century cases, of which it can at least be said that the possibility of a charge over a debt owed by the chargee caused no judicial surprise.

The reason given by the Court of Appeal [1996] Ch. 245, 258 was that "a man cannot have a proprietary interest in a debt or other obligation which he owes another." In order to test this proposition, I think one needs to identify the normal characteristics of an equitable charge and then ask to what extent they would be inconsistent with a situation in which the property charged consisted of a debt owed by the beneficiary of the charge. [Lord Hoffmann then considered the general attributes of charges, and continued:]

The depositor's right to claim payment of his deposit is a chose in action which the law has always recognised as property. There is no dispute that a charge over such a chose in action can validly be granted to a third party. In which respects would the fact that the beneficiary of the charge was the debtor himself be inconsistent with the transaction having some or all of the various features which I have enumerated? The method by which the property would be realised would differ slightly: instead of the beneficiary of the charge having to claim payment from the debtor, the realisation would take the form of a book entry. In no other respect, as it seems to me, would the transaction have any consequences different from those which would attach to a charge given to a third party. It would be a proprietary interest in the sense that, subject to questions of registration and purchaser for value without notice, it would be binding upon assignees and a liquidator or trustee in bankruptcy. The depositor would retain an equity of redemption and all the rights which that implies. There would be no merger of interests because the depositor would retain title to the deposit subject only to the bank's charge. The creation of the charge would be consensual and not require any formal assignment or vesting of title in the bank. If all these features can exist despite the fact that the beneficiary of the charge is the debtor, I cannot see why it cannot properly be said that the debtor has a proprietary interest by way of charge over the debt.

The Court of Appeal said that the bank could obtain effective security in other ways. . . . All this is true. It may well be that the security provided in these ways will in most cases be just as good as that provided by a proprietary interest. But that seems to me no reason for preventing banks and their customers from creating charges over deposits if, for reasons of their own, they want to do so. The submissions to the Legal Risk Review Committee made it clear that they do. . . .

Since the decision in *In re Charge Card Services Ltd.* [1987] Ch. 150 statutes have been passed in several offshore banking jurisdictions to reverse its effect. . . . The striking feature about all these provisions is that none of them amend or repeal any rule of common law which would be inconsistent with the existence of a charge over a debt owed by the chargee. They simply say that such a charge can be granted. If the trick can be done as easily as this, it is hard to see where the conceptual impossibility is to be found.

In a case in which there is no threat to the consistency of the law or objection of public policy, I think that the courts should be very slow to declare a practice of the commercial community to be conceptually impossible. Rules of law must obviously be consistent and not self-contradictory; thus in *Rye v. Rye* [1962] A.C. 496, 505, Viscount Simonds demonstrated that the notion of a person granting a lease to himself was inconsistent with every feature of a lease, both as a contract and as an estate in land. But the law is fashioned to suit the practicalities of life and legal concepts like "proprietary interest" and "charge" are no more than labels given to clusters of related and selfconsistent rules of law. Such concepts do not have a life of their own from which the rules are inexorably derived. It follows that in my view the letter was effective to do what it purported to do, namely to create a charge over the deposit in favour of B.C.C.I . . .

➤ Questions

1. Is the analysis persuasive?

2. Is such a charge registrable? Lord Hoffmann, in **[10.09]**, suggested the asset was not a 'book debt', but does it fall under some other subsection in CA 2006 s 860(7)?

Dealings with assets subject to a floating charge

A vital feature of the floating charge is that, until the company defaults in its obligations, the charge authorises the company to deal with the charged assets in the ordinary course of business. It follows that the company may not only use, sell and buy such property during the currency of a floating charge, but may also create mortgages and fixed charges, ranking in priority to the floating charge itself.

Even where, by what is commonly termed a 'negative pledge clause' or 'restrictive clause', the creation of later charges is forbidden by the terms of the original charge, the claim of a subsequent debenture holder will prevail if he took the charge without notice of the restrictive clause.

In practice, however, floating charges generally provide for automatic crystallisation into a fixed charge in the event that the chargor attempts in any way to create a mortgage or fixed charge over any of the company's assets or undertaking the subject of the floating charge. (See **[10.12]** below)

A floating charge is also vulnerable to set-offs and other claims arising in favour of unsecured creditors while the company's power to trade continues.

This freedom to deal with the assets continues until the floating charge 'crystallises'. (We must ignore the mixed metaphor, which has been hallowed by a century's use.) On crystallisation, the charge becomes a fixed charge attaching to the company's assets at that point of time, and the company's freedom to trade and to incur cross-claims ceases; but until then, the security is subject to all the risks to which the assets may be exposed in the ordinary course of business.

A fixed charge (and other subsequent interests) may be created having priority over an earlier floating charge.

[10.10] Re Castell and Brown Ltd [1898] 1 Ch 315 (Chancery Division)

In 1885, the company issued a series of debentures secured by a floating charge over all of its assets. The title deeds of various properties, which had been left in the possession of the company, were later deposited with the company's bank to secure an overdraft. The bank's charge was held to have priority over the earlier floating charge debentures.[11]

---

[11] The debentures contained a provision that the company was not at liberty to create any mortgage or charge having priority to the floating charge, but the bank had no knowledge or notice of this 'negative pledge' provision, and so was held not to have been affected by it.

ROMER J: In the first place, I cannot hold that there was any negligence on the part of the bank. When making its advances to Castell & Brown Ltd (which I will hereafter call the company), it found the company in possession of the deeds in question, and apparently able, as unincumbered owner, to charge the property.

The company purported as such unincumbered owner to give a charge to the bank, and I think the bank was, under the circumstances, entitled to rely upon obtaining a charge free from incumbrance. It is suggested on behalf of the debentureholders that the bank ought to have made some special inquiries of the company. But it is not suggested that the bank wilfully abstained from making inquiries, and as the bank had no reason to suppose that the company was not fully able to give a valid first charge, and found the company in possession of the deeds, which showed no incumbrance, I think the bank was not bound to make any special enquiry . . .

And I now look to see how it was that the company retained possession of the deeds notwithstanding the issue of the debentures. The reason appears to me obvious. The debentures were only intended to give what is called a floating charge, that is to say, it was intended, notwithstanding the debentures, that the company should have power, so long as it was a going concern, to deal with its property as absolute owner. And I infer it was on this account that the company was allowed to, and did, retain possession of the deeds. In other words, the debentureholders, notwithstanding their charge, and indeed by its very terms, authorised their mortgagor, the company, to deal with its property as if it had not been incumbered, and left with their mortgagor the deeds in order to enable the company to act as owner.

➤ Notes

1. This decision gives rise to the following related questions:

(i)   Can a company which has given a floating charge over its assets to A later give a fixed charge to B over part of those assets, having priority? Answer—yes: *Re Castell and Brown Ltd* **[10.10]**. It is immaterial whether B's charge is legal or equitable, or whether B has notice of A's charge.[12]

(ii)   Can a company which has given a floating charge over its assets to A later give a fixed charge to B over all of those assets, having priority? Answer (it seems) yes; but if the class of assets affected is extensive the second transaction may not be 'in the ordinary course of business' and may therefore be outside the terms of the express or implied trading power. What impact will this have on third parties? Is knowledge relevant?

(iii)   Can a company which has given a floating charge over its assets to A later give a *floating* charge to B over the *same* assets, having priority? Held—no, in *Re Benjamin Cope & Sons Ltd* [1914] 1 Ch 800: the equities being equal, the first in time prevails.

(iv)   Can a company which has given a floating charge over its assets to A later give a floating charge to B over part of those assets, having priority? Held—yes, in *Re Automatic Bottle Makers Ltd* [1926] Ch 412, CA, where the first charge expressly empowered the company to do so. Where no such power is reserved, commentators generally agree that the first charge, being first in time, should have priority.

2. Where a company has created more than one charge over the same property, it is open to the charge holders to agree to vary the order of priority which would otherwise apply, and it is not necessary to obtain the company's consent: *Cheah Theam Swee v Equiticorp Finance Group Ltd* [1992] 1 AC 472, PC.

---

[12]   If B has *actual* notice that A's charge prohibits the creation of a later charge having priority, A's charge will prevail: see *Siebe Gorman & Co Ltd v Barclays Bank Ltd* [1979] 2 Lloyd's Rep 142, Ch, overruled by *Spectrum* **[10.20]**, but not on this point.

A floating charge does not operate as an assignment to the debenture holder of the company's book debts and other choses in action. Until the charge has crystallised, the company's unsecured creditors may set off debts due by the company against sums which they owe to it.

[10.11] Biggerstaff v Rowatt's Wharf Ltd [1896] 2 Ch 93 (Court of Appeal)

[For another part of the decision in this case, see [3.11].]

The respondent company had, to the knowledge of Harvey Brand & Co, issued debentures secured by a floating charge. A receiver was appointed, who took possession on 30 October 1894. On this date Harvey Brand & Co owed the respondent a liquidated sum for rent, while Harvey Brand & Co had a cross-claim against it for the price of 4,000 barrels at 3s 6d [17½ p] each. Harvey Brand & Co was held entitled to set off its claim, on the ground that there had been no assignment of the respondent company's property to the debenture holders prior to the appointment of the receiver, so that Harvey Brand & Co had the earlier equity.

LOPES LJ: In the present case I think that Harvey, Brand & Co could sue for money had and received . . . There is a total failure of consideration as regards the barrels not delivered, and the demand is a liquidated demand which can be set off against the rent.

But it is said that there is no right of set-off against an assignee of a chose in action where the person claiming the set-off had notice of the assignment when the debt due to him was contracted. That is quite true in ordinary cases; but a debenture differs from an ordinary assignment. If this doctrine were applied to debentures, no creditor of a company could ever get the benefit of a set-off where debentures had been issued. Now, it is the essence of a floating security that it allows the company to carry on business in its ordinary way until a receiver is appointed; and it would paralyse the business of companies to give to the issuing of debentures the effect now contended for. I am of opinion, therefore, that the set-off must be allowed . . .

KAY LJ: It is true that as against an assignee there can be no set-off of a debt accrued after the person claiming set-off has notice of the assignment. But does that apply to debentures such as these? Counsel hesitated to go so far as that, but said that there was no right of set-off, as no action had been brought in which it could have been asserted before 30 October 1894. I think that is not so. I think that if at the time of the assignment there was an inchoate right to set-off it can be asserted after the assignment, for the assignment is subject to the rights then in existence. The question is whether the assignment took place at the issue of the debentures or at the appointment of a receiver. The debentures contain provisions the effect of which is that the company is at liberty to go on with its business as if the debentures did not exist, until possession is taken under them. From that time the company cannot deal with its assets as against the title of the debentureholders; up to that time it can deal with them in every legitimate way of business. Therefore the date to be regarded is the time of taking possession. A conclusion that set-off could not arise during the period before taking possession would be injurious to debentureholders, for it would hamper the company in carrying on its business, and so injure the debentureholders, whose interest is that the company should carry on a prosperous business. There was an inchoate right of set-off at the time when the receiver was appointed; and that, and not the time of issuing the debentures, is the time to be looked to. The debentures must be regarded as incomplete assignments which do not become complete until the time when the receiver is appointed . . .

LINDLEY LJ delivered a concurring judgment.

Crystallisation of floating charges

A floating charge will crystallise, and become a fixed charge attaching to the assets of the company at that time: (i) when a receiver is appointed; (ii) when the company goes into liquidation (since the licence to deal with the assets in the ordinary course of business will then necessarily terminate); (iii) when the company ceases to carry on business (see [10.13] below) or sells its business (*Re Real Meat Co Ltd* [1996] BCLC 254); (iv) in the case where the debenture empowers the charge-holder to convert the floating charge into a fixed charge by giving the company 'notice of conversion', and such a notice is given (see **[10.13]** below); and (v) where an event occurs which under the terms of the debenture causes 'automatic' crystallisation.[13]

This last ground (automatic crystallisation) depends upon there being a provision in the document creating the charge which states that the charge will crystallise on the happening of some particular event—eg if a creditor of the company should levy execution against its property, or if the company should give security over assets covered by the charge to a third party without the charge-holder's consent.

Historically, these automatic crystallisation clauses generated considerable controversy, both as to their legality and as to whether, as a matter of policy, their use should be prohibited or subjected to restrictions by law.[14] However, they are now generally accepted as part of the architecture of floating charges (see *Re Brightlife Ltd* **[10.12]** below).

A floating charge crystallises according to the terms of any automatic crystallisation clause.

[10.12] Re Brightlife Ltd [1987] Ch 200

HOFFMANN J: . . . [Counsel] said that public policy required restrictions upon what the parties could stipulate as crystallising events. A winding up or the appointment of a receiver [should this happen to the company during its lifetime] would have to be noted on the register. But a notice [of conversion of a floating charge to a fixed charge] need not be registered and a provision for automatic crystallisation might take effect without the knowledge of either the company or the debentureholder. The result might be prejudicial to third parties who gave credit to the company. Considerations of this kind impressed Berger J in the Canadian case of *R v Consolidated Churchill Copper Corpn Ltd*[15] where the concept of 'self-generating crystallisation' was rejected.

I do not think that it is open to the courts to restrict the contractual freedom of parties to a floating charge on such grounds. The floating charge was invented by Victorian lawyers to enable manufacturing and trading companies to raise loan capital on debentures. It could offer the security of a charge over the whole of the company's undertaking without inhibiting its ability to trade. But the mirror image of these advantages was the potential prejudice to the general body of creditors, who might know nothing of the floating charge but find that all the company's assets, including the very goods which they had just delivered on credit, had been swept up by the debentureholder. The public interest requires a balancing of the advantages to the economy of facilitating the borrowing of money against the possibility of injustice to unsecured creditors. These arguments for and against the floating charge are matters for Parliament rather than the courts and have been the subject of public debate in and out of Parliament for more than a century.

Parliament has responded, first, by restricting the rights of the holder of a floating charge and secondly, by requiring public notice of the existence and enforcement of the charge. For example, priority was given to preferential debts . . . [Hoffmann J continued with other examples of the restrictions imposed by statute on floating charge holders] . . .

---

[13] A majority of the court in *Fire Nymph Products Ltd v Heating Centre Pty Ltd* (1992) 7 ACSR 365 (NSWCA) held that a floating charge also crystallises when the charged assets are dealt with otherwise than in the ordinary course of business. This might well be the case where the assets concerned comprised all or a substantial part of the company's property, or the whole of the assets affected by the charge, but it is doubtful that the *dictum* would apply to the disposal of individual items.

[14] The Cork Committee (1982, Cmnd 8558, paras 1578–79) considered that automatic crystallisation was 'not merely inconvenient', but that there was 'no place for it in a modern insolvency law'. The Committee recommended that the circumstances in which a floating charge crystallised should be defined by statute, and that all other ways (including automatic crystallisation) should be banned.

[15] [1978] 5 WWR 652.

These limited and pragmatic interventions by the legislature make it in my judgment wholly inappropriate for the courts to impose additional restrictive rules on grounds of public policy. It is certainly not for a judge of first instance to proclaim a new head of public policy which no appellate court has even hinted at before. . . .

A floating charge crystallises when the company ceases to carry on business.

[10.13] Re Woodroffes (Musical Instruments) Ltd [1986] Ch 366 (Chancery Division)

The company had given a first floating charge to its bank and a second floating charge to Mrs Woodroffe. A provision in the latter instrument empowered Mrs Woodroffe by giving notice to the company to convert the charge into a fixed charge, and this she did on 27 August 1982. The bank appointed receivers on 1 September 1982. In this action, which was brought to establish the priorities as between the two debenture holders and the company's other creditors, Nourse J held that Mrs Woodroffe's notice did not have the effect of crystallising the bank's charge, as well as her own, on 27 August. He also ruled that the bank's charge would have crystallised if the company had ceased to carry on business at any time between 27 August and 1 September, but that there was no sufficient evidence that this had happened.

NOURSE J: On what date did the bank's floating charge crystallise? Mr Jarvis, for the bank, supported by Mr Marks, for Mrs Woodroffe, arguing in favour of 27 August, submit in the first instance that the effect of Mrs Woodroffe's notice of conversion was to crystallise not only her own charge, but also the bank's. They say that the notice, by determining Mrs Woodroffe's licence to the company to employ the assets subject to the charge in the ordinary course of its business, rendered any further use of those assets unlawful and impracticable, with the result that the company's business must be taken to have ceased at that time. Consequently, they submit that there was a crystallisation of both charges.

I find myself quite unable to accept that submission, which appears to me to run contrary to fundamental principles of the law of contract. I do not see how the determination of Mrs Woodroffe's licence can in some way work a determination of the bank's, or produce the effect that the bank has had its charge crystallised over its head and possibly contrary to its own wishes. The relationship between the company and the bank was governed by the [bank's] debenture, which, although it contained a prohibition against creating any subsequent charge without consent—see clause 5— did not provide for the bank's floating charge to crystallise either on the creation or crystallisation of a subsequent charge.

On analysis it appears to me that the arguments of Mr Jarvis on this point are founded, and can only be founded, on an implied term in the [bank's] debenture . . . It does not seem to me to be at all clear that a term to the effect contended for by Mr Jarvis must be implied. Why should it be assumed that the bank and the company, in particular the bank, intended that the crystallisation of a subsequent charge should in all circumstances cause a crystallisation of the bank's? No doubt it might suit the bank's interests in the great majority of circumstances, but that does not mean that it can be assumed in all. For example, the bank might have taken the view that it was in its own interests that the business of the company should continue. Unless Mrs Woodroffe had either appointed her own receiver, or had applied for an injunction restraining it from dealing with its assets in contravention of her own fixed charge, I can see no reason why the company could not have continued to carry on its business. True it could only have done so in breach of its contract with Mrs Woodroffe, but the bank might have been prepared to indemnify it against that liability or even to pay off Mrs Woodroffe. I can see no ground for any species of implication to the effect contended for . . .

The question whether the cessation of the company's business causes an automatic crystallisation of a floating charge is one of general importance upon which there appears to be no decision directly in point. Such authorities as there are disclose a uniform assumption in favour of crystallisa-tion. There is a valuable discussion of them in *Picarda on The Law Relating to Receivers and Managers*, pp 16–18. One of the questions there raised is whether there is any distinction for this purpose between a company ceasing to carry on business on the one hand and ceasing to be a going concern on the other. My own impression is that these phrases are used interchangeably in the authorities . . . but whether that be right or wrong, I think it clear that the material event is a ces-sation of business and not, if that is something different, ceasing to be a going concern.

[His Lordship referred to a number of authorities, and continued:] It is unnecessary for me to examine any of those cases in detail, or to quote extracts from the judgments of the many judges who decided them. They all, to a greater or lesser extent, assume that crystallisation takes place on a cessation of business . . .

[His Lordship then held that the evidence did not support the view that the company had ceased business before 1 September.]

Relevant assets received by the company after the floating charge crystallises automatically become subject to the (now fixed) charge over the company's property.

[10.14] N W Robbie & Co Ltd v Witney Warehouse Co Ltd
[1963] 1 WLR 1324 (Court of Appeal)

The plaintiff company had given a debenture, secured by a floating charge, to the Bank of Ireland. The bank put in a receiver, who continued to carry on the company's business. The company sold goods to the defendants worth in all £1,346, and in this action the receiver claimed payment of the price. The defendants had meantime taken an assignment of a debt of £852 due by the company to English Spinners Ltd, and claimed to be entitled to set off this sum against the £1,346 sued for. It was held that the claim failed, because the debenture holder's equity had priority. In particular, each debt accruing due to a company after a float-ing charge which affects its future property has crystallised becomes immediately fixed with an equity in favour of the debenture holder. No debt arising, or first coming into the hands of a creditor, after crystallisation may be set off by that creditor so as to give him priority over the debenture holder.[16]

RUSSELL LJ: The first question for consideration is whether on the true construction of the deben-ture the debt owed by the defendants as it arose became a chose in action of the company subject to an equitable charge in favour of the debentureholders.

I consider that it did.

The relevant clauses and conditions of the debenture have already been referred to . . . There is under clause 3 a charge on all future assets of the company without restriction: that amounts to an agreement for valuable consideration to charge all such future assets, which agreement enables equity to fasten a charge on those future assets when they arise: and every such equitable charge as it arises operates as an equitable assignment to the debentureholders of that asset . . . The fact that [the floating charge has crystallised and is now fixed] . . . in no way justifies the conclusion that the field of the charge is in any way restricted: it only means that after this particular quality disap-pears equity will fasten the charge directly upon all assets thereafter coming into existence as soon as they do so . . .

If that be a correct view of the construction of the debenture, then the choses in action consist-ing of the debts now sued upon became as they arise subject to an equitable charge—an equitable assignment—to the debentureholders . . .

---

[16] Exceptionally, such a debt may be set off if it arises out of the same contract as that which gives rise to the assigned debt, or is closely connected with that contract: *Business Computers Ltd v Anglo-African Leasing Ltd* [1977] 2 All ER 741 at 748, per Templeman J.

Thus far, in my judgment, by force of the debenture charge an equitable charge attached in favour of the debentureholders not only on the £95 debt existing at the date of the appointment of the receiver and manager, but also upon the other debts constituting the total of £1,346 as they came into existence on delivery of goods to the defendants after such appointment. These choses in action belonging to the company became thus assigned in equity to the debentureholders, at times when the defendants had no cross-claim of any kind against the company and consequently no right of set-off. Before the defendants acquired by assignment this cross-claim the defendants must be fixed with knowledge of this equitable assignment to the debentureholders (by way of charge) of the debt owed by the defendants to the company. A debtor cannot set off his claim against X against a claim by X against him which the debtor knows has been assigned by X to Y before the debtor's claims arose. Just as an assignee of a chose in action takes subject to an already existing right of set-off, so a debtor with no existing right of set-off cannot assert set-off of a cross-claim which he first acquires after he has notice of the assignment of the claim against him: here, for instance, no part of the £852 could have been set off against the £95.

Applying these considerations to the present case, at the time when the defendants first acquired the claim for £852, the choses in action sought to be enforced against the defendants had been assigned to the debentureholders by way of charge, but the £852 claim in no way involved the debentureholders . . .

SELLERS LJ delivered a concurring judgment.

DONOVAN LJ dissented.

➤ Question

Contrast this case with the *Biggerstaff* case **[10.11]** above, and also see *Rother Iron Works Ltd v Canterbury Precision Engineers Ltd* [1974] QB 1, CA. What is the essential difference that explains the contrasting outcomes?

Priorities as between the floating charge, even after crystallisation, and other interests are determined by the usual rules.

[10.15] George Barker Ltd v Eynon [1974] 1 WLR 462 (Court of Appeal)

The case concerned a priority dispute between the holder of a contractual lien and the holder of a floating charge. The claimants had a contractual lien over the goods of a meat importing company whose indebtedness to a bank was secured by a mortgage debenture creating a floating charge. The debenture holder's rights crystallised on the appointment of a receiver, but the Court of Appeal held that the lien took priority because the contractual rights arose even earlier, before the appointment of the receiver and so before crystallisation of the charge. This was notwithstanding that the claimants did not acquire actual possession of the goods until three days after the receiver's appointment.

STAMP LJ: . . . Shorn of the arguments supporting it, the receiver's contention before this court was that this is a case of priorities. The lien was a possessory lien which did not come into existence until the carriers were in possession of the goods. Before the carriers came into possession of the goods the charge in favour of the debenture holder crystallised by the effect of the appointment of the receiver. The goods had become the subject of an equitable assignment to the debenture holder and the lien could not come into existence as against the debenture holder.

These submissions are not, in my judgment, well founded. What is in law described under the convenient label of a "lien" is in relation to a carrier . . . the contractual right to hold the goods which have been carried in respect of the debt for the carriage and in respect of the debts of the same character previously contracted. The duty of the carriers here was to carry the goods and deliver them, or they might say after they had carried them, "We will hold these goods in exercise of the right to do so conferred by the contract of carriage until we have been paid," and they might say, "Moreover, we will, unless we are paid within a reasonable time, in exercise of our right under the contract, sell the goods and pay ourselves out of the proceeds. These are the terms upon which we carried the goods." In my judgment, these rights did not arise or come into existence at the time the carriers took possession of the goods. . . . The rights were rights created by the contract which became exercisable at the moment of time when the goods had been carried. The rights which were conferred on the carriers by condition 13 of the contract are conveniently and accurately described as a "lien," but you do not by so describing them alter their character. They are conveniently described as "a possessory lien," because it is only if the carriers have possession that they can be exercised. But to say that a lien, because it is so described, does not come into existence until possession is assumed is to reason falsely. Contractual rights come into existence at the time of the contract creating them notwithstanding that they may not be exercisable except upon the happening of a future event. . . .

There was nothing remarkable about the contract. It was simply a contract for the carriage of goods incorporating the Conditions of Carriage of the Road Haulage Association. It was, in my judgment, clearly a contract into which, so long as the charge created by the debenture was a floating charge, the company could, consistently with the terms of the debenture, properly enter into. It was, as I have indicated, a contract which was not determined by the effect of the appointment of the receiver. The receiver might, so I will assume, have repudiated it before the carriers started the journey, so preventing the carriers obtaining possession of the goods and carrying out their obligations under it. He did not do so. How then could the receiver or the debenture holder as assignee of the goods and of the rights of the company under the contract be in any better position than would the company have been to insist at the end of the journey that the goods be handed over without making the payments for which condition 13 provided? In my judgment, Mr. Tugendhat was right in his contention that the assignment to the debenture holder brought about by the appointment of the receiver was subject to the rights already given by the company to other persons under ordinary trading contracts. As against the company, the carriers on arriving at the door of the consignees at Gravesend could have withheld the goods against payment, and in my judgment, the debenture holder as assignee from the company can be in no better position. The debenture holder as assignee of the company's rights under the contract can be in no better position than any other assignee of the company's rights under the contract . . .

Treatment of floating charges on the company's liquidation

The point has already been made that floating charges can be a vulnerable form of security. Certain statutory provisions cut down the effectiveness of the floating charges on liquidation of administration, by giving priority to other debts (eg the costs of liquidation and administration, preferred debts, and unsecured debts (at least to the extent of a statutory proportion of the floating charge assets)): the statutory provisions are noted above, at p 463, and their effect is considered in more detail below, in Chapter 14.

In addition, IA 1986 s 245 avoids certain floating charges not given for 'new consideration' in the run up to liquidation or administration. The intention is to prevent unsecured creditors from securing existing debts when the company is in difficulty, and thus obtaining an advantage over other unsecured creditors. IA 1986, s 245 provides that, subject to certain qualifications, a *floating* charge (not a *fixed* charge) that is created within twelve months of a liquidation or an administration shall be invalid except to the extent that the charge-holder advances 'new money' or supplies goods or services to the company. This rule does not apply, at least in the normal case, if it is shown that the company immediately after the creation of the charge was solvent. But stricter conditions are applicable where the floating charge is given in favour of a person who is 'connected' with the company (see IA 1986 s 435, including eg a director or major shareholder, or a close relative of either, or an associated company). In this case the twelve-month period is extended to two years, and the exemption on the ground of solvency is not available.

A floating charge which has already been redeemed cannot be attacked under IA 1986 s 245, but the payment of the debt may be open to challenge as a preference.

[10.16] Re Parkes Garage (Swadlincote) Ltd [1929] 1 Ch 139 (Chancery Divisional Court)

On 15 June, the (insolvent) company executed a floating charge to secure debts owed to a group of its creditors. On 27 July, the company received a sum of money from the purchaser of part of its business, and used this sum to pay off the group of creditors, who endorsed a memorandum of discharge on the debenture. On 14 September a winding-up order was made on the petition of another creditor. It was held that the then equivalent of IA 1986 s 245 could not be invoked to compel repayment of the moneys once the debenture had been redeemed, but the court indicated that it was open to the liquidator to challenge the transaction as a fraudulent preference.[17]

EVE J: Having regard to the facts which I have stated, about which there is no dispute, it is quite obviously that the learned county court judge had no option but to declare the charge to be invalid, and he so did. That part of his judgment, however, was not of much practical importance, because the charge had been satisfied by the payments which had been made, and it was then argued that the declaration of invalidity involved the further question: whether the debenture was still subsisting for any purpose, and if so were the simple contract debts, to secure which it had been issued, merged in the covenant contained in the debenture. An argument on those lines was addressed to the learned judge, at the conclusion of which he held that the simple contract debts were merged, and forgetting for the moment the limited extent to which he had declared the debenture invalid, he referred to the whole debenture as invalid, and held that the simple contract debts having been merged, and the debenture being invalid, the creditors were not entitled to retain the money paid to them through their trustee on 27 July.

At the first hearing the learned judge had not declared, nor could he declare, the debenture invalid; all he could declare invalid was the charge therein contained. The rest of the document, the covenants to pay principal and interest, survived and was valid, for nothing in s 212 [IA 1986 s 245] affects them. The position therefore was that the simple contract creditors, by their trustee, who was the covenantee, were entitled to the benefit of the covenants to pay principal and interest, and on 27 July, when the company was in sufficient funds to pay the principal and interest, they had no alternative but to pay the same, and the trustee cannot on this summons be ordered to repay. But having regard to what has been disclosed in these proceedings, that the company was hopelessly insolvent from the beginning of March down to the date of the winding-up order, and that the effect of the payments to these half-dozen creditors on 27 July was to apply the whole available assets of the company to the payment of their debts in full and to leave other creditors whose debts largely exceeded the aggregate amount paid to the half-dozen unprovided for, raises a doubt whether the whole transaction, which culminated in the payments on 27 July, was not in the nature of a fraudulent preference. We desire therefore to give the liquidator an opportunity of considering the position from this standpoint, and in allowing this appeal to state that the order is without prejudice to any application to set aside the payments or to question the validity of the debenture on the ground of

[17] The statute did not then provide remedies against non-fraudulent preferences. Now see IA 1986 ss 238–241, and *Re M C Bacon Ltd* [14.16], below))

its being a fraudulent preference or on any other grounds which the liquidator may think fit to advance . . .

MAUGHAM J concurred.

➤ Note

Re Parkes Garage was followed in *Mace Builders (Glasgow) Ltd v Lunn* [1987] Ch 191, [1987] BCLC 55, where the debenture holder had put in a receiver to enforce the charge and the receiver had sold the charged assets before the commencement of the winding up. Although the charge had been created within twelve months of the liquidation, and at a time when the company was insolvent, it was held that the provision corresponding to IA 1986 s 245 (CA 1948 s 322) was inapplicable: transactions completed before the liquidation were not affected by the section.

The phrase 'money[18] paid to the company' in IA 1986 245 includes cheques met by a bank on the company's behalf.

[10.17] Re Yeovil Glove Co Ltd [1965] Ch 148 (Court of Appeal)

The company had gone into liquidation having unsecured debts totalling £94,000 and an over-draft with the National Provincial Bank Ltd amounting to £67,000. This overdraft was secured by a floating charge given less than twelve months previously. During the currency of the charge the bank had met cheques drawn by the company amounting to £110,000, and received some £111,000 for payment into the company's account. (There were in fact four accounts, but this is not important.) The unsecured creditors attacked the security under CA 1948 s 322 (broadly comparable with IA 1986 s 245), alleging that no 'cash' had been 'paid to the company' by the bank within the meaning of that section; but the court treated the bank's acts in meeting the company's cheques as equivalent. It followed that, by virtue of the rule in *Clayton*'s case,[19] the bank could claim that the whole of the £67,000 was cash advanced subsequently to the creation of the charge, so that the security was valid for this sum.

HARMAN LJ: [The] only question which arises is whether there was cash paid to the company at the time of or subsequently to the creation of, and in consideration for, the charge. It was admittedly created within twelve months of the winding up at a time when the company was insolvent. It is further agreed that so far as the overdraft was incurred before the date of the floating charge, the charge would not be a valid security for it. The liquidator's claim is a simple one, namely, that as neither cash nor a covenant to pay cash was made at the time of the execution of the document, there was no consideration for it in the legal sense of that term except the bank's immediate forbearance. This seemed to me, I confess, an attractive argument . . .

It was argued that consideration in law is a well-known term and ought to receive its ordinary meaning, and that subsequent payments provided by the bank to defray the company's day-to-day outgoings or wages or salaries or indebtedness to its suppliers by cheque would not be consideration in law for the execution of a charge bearing an earlier date unless those payments were made in pursuance of a promise contained in, or made at or before the date of, the charge itself. It was, however, pointed out that such subsequent payments would in fact not be made in consideration for the charge, but in consideration for the promise.

---

[18] Prior to IA 1986, the legislation used the phrase 'cash paid to the company': but it would appear that the decision in *Re Yeovil Glove Co Ltd* is not affected by the change in wording.

[19] (1816) 1 Mer 572, under which the earliest payments into an account are set off against the earliest payments out, and vice versa.

Now it is apparent on the fact of the section that cash subsequently paid to the company may be within the exception if so paid in consideration for the anterior charge, and the argument is that the words 'in consideration for' in this section cannot, therefore, be used in the technical sense, but mean 'by reason of' or 'having regard to the existence of' the charge. Oddly enough, there is no reported decision on these words, nor are they discussed in any of the well-known textbooks. There has, however, come to light a decision of Lord Romer, when a judge of first instance, in *Re Thomas Mortimer Ltd*,[20] in 1925, a decision on the corresponding section of the Companies (Consolidation) Act 1908, which was in the same terms as the present section except that the period was three instead of twelve months. A transcript of this judgment was before us. The facts of that case were, I think, indistinguishable from those of the present, and Romer J held that payments by the bank after the date of the charge were made in consideration for the charge . . .

That decision, if right, is enough to cover the present question, and Plowman J [at first instance] so held . . .

In the instant case some £111,000, representing its trading receipts, was paid into the no 1 account by the company between the date of the charge and the appointment of the receiver, and the bank paid out during the same period about £110,000. Those payments were either made directly to or to the order of the company, or were transfers to the no 3 and no 4 accounts against advances previously made to the company to defray wages or salaries. All the company's accounts were at all times overdrawn, so that every payment was a provision of new money by means of which, on the figures, it is overwhelmingly probable that all the creditors existing at the date of the charge were in fact paid off.

There arises at this point the consideration which has given me most trouble in this case, namely, that as the no 1 account was carried on after as well as before the charge in precisely the same way, the bank would be entitled in accordance with the rule in *Clayton*'s case, to treat payments in as being in satisfaction of the earliest advances made. The result is startling, for thus the bank pays itself out of moneys received subsequent to the charge for the whole of the company's indebtedness to it prior to the charge, and which was admittedly not covered by it. The result is that the whole of the pre-charge indebtedness is treated as paid off, and the bank is left bound to set off against its post-charge advances only the excess received after satisfying the company's pre-charge indebtedness. This would seem largely to nullify the effect of the section in the case of a company having at the date of the charge a largely overdrawn account with its bank, and which continues to trade subsequently. Of course, if at the date of the charge a line were drawn in the bank's books and a new account opened, then the company could successfully argue that payments out by the bank subsequent to the charge were, within a few hundred pounds, wholly repaid by the company from its trading receipts, with the result that no substantial sum would be due on the charge. It was, however, held by Romer J in *Re Thomas Mortimer Ltd* that *Clayton*'s case be applied with the result stated, and I can see no escape from it, nor in spite of frequent pressing by the court did the appellant's counsel put forward any alternative . . . [It] follows, if the decision in *Re Thomas Mortimer Ltd* be right, that there is admittedly nothing left for the unsecured creditors. In my judgment Romer J's decision was right, and was rightly followed by Plowman J in the present case.

The fallacy in the appellant's argument lies, in my opinion, in the theory that, because the company's payments into the bank after the date of the charge were more or less equal to the payments out by the bank during the same period, no 'new money' was provided by the bank. This is not the fact. Every such payment was in fact new money having regard to the state of the company's accounts, and it was in fact used to pay the company's creditors. That the indebtedness remained approximately at the same level was due to the fact that this was the limit set by the bank to the company's overdraft. I can find no reason to compel the bank to treat all payments in after the charge as devoted to post-charge indebtedness. The law is in fact the other way . . .

WILLMER and RUSSELL LJJ delivered concurring judgments.

---

[20] (1925), reported [1965] Ch 186n.

➤ Note

The exception to IA 1986 s 245 discussed in the *Yeovil Glove* case applies only where the money in question is paid, or the goods or services supplied, to the company 'at the same time as, or after, the creation of the charge' (s 245(2)). There has recently been some debate in the cases about the meaning of this phrase: how nearly contemporaneous must the payment and the execution of the charge document be? In the past, this question was treated rather loosely, a delay of even two months or so being thought unimportant if the payment was made in anticipation of and in reliance on the creation of the charge. But in *Power v Sharp Investments Ltd* [1994] 1 BCLC 111, CA (also known as *Re Shoe Lace Ltd*) the Court of Appeal, agreeing with Hoffmann J in the court below, held that, while the question was one of fact and degree, a delay of any substantial length—although not, perhaps, the time taken to have a coffee-break—would be fatal to the application of the exception.

➤ Questions

1. What do you think are the policy reasons behind the enactment of IA 1986 s 245?

2. What do you think are the policy reasons behind the enactment of IA 1986 s 40 (see below, p 647)?

Distinguishing between fixed and floating charges

The previous sections indicate the need to distinguish between fixed and floating charges, and the substantial attractions to the charge holder in having a charge classified as fixed rather than floating. Lenders therefore devote considerable energy to drafting charges that will be construed as fixed rather than floating. Before considering the case extracts, several general points can be made.

(i) Prior to 1986, it was possible for the holder of a floating charge to evade the disadvantageous statutory rules simply by showing that the charge had crystallised (and thereby become a *fixed* charge) before the commencement of the liquidation or other relevant statutory date.[21] This loophole was quickly eliminated by IA 1986 s 251, which provides that 'floating charge' means 'a charge which, *as created*, was a floating charge'. Despite this setback, lenders have not been discouraged from seeking to achieve the same end-result with ever more astutely worded documents.

(ii) In *Agnew v Commissioner of Inland Revenue (Re Brumark)*, **[10.19]** below (one of the leading cases in this area), the Privy Council held that, in analysing a charge agreement to determine whether it creates a fixed or a floating charge, the court's task is not to discover whether the parties *intended* to create a fixed or floating charge and then give effect to their intention. The court's task is to discover what *rights* the parties intended to create, and then to decided whether, as a matter of law, those rights constitute a fixed or a floating charge. See Lord Millett, below, at p 490.

(iii) In the Irish case *Re Armagh Shoes Ltd* [1984] BCLC 405, Hutton J held that the fact that a document by its express words purports to create a fixed or specific charge does not prevent the court from construing the charge as a floating one. The judge in that case was also

---

[21] This was the case in *Re Brightlife Ltd* **[10.12]**, where the debenture holder had given the company a notice converting the floating charge into a fixed charge a week before a resolution for voluntary winding up was passed. The court held that the preferential creditors no longer had any right to be paid in priority to the charge.

prepared to infer from the terms of the charge as a whole that the company had a licence to deal with the assets charged in the ordinary course of its business, even though this was not stated.

(iv) In *Re Brightlife Ltd* [10.12], in considering the scope of the freedom to deal with the charged assets, Hoffmann J held that a charge over book debts which was expressed to be a fixed charge, and imposed some restrictions on the use of the charged assets, was in reality a floating charge. He said, at 209:

> Although clause 3(A)(ii)(a) speaks of a 'first specific charge' over the book debts and other debts, the rights over the debts created by the debenture were in my judgment such as to be categorised in law as a floating charge . . .
>
> It is true that clause 5(ii) does not allow Brightlife to sell, factor or discount debts without the written consent of Norandex [the debenture-holder]. But a floating charge is consistent with some restriction upon the company's freedom to deal with its assets. For example, floating charges commonly contain a prohibition upon the creation of other charges ranking prior to or pari passu with the floating charge. Such dealings would otherwise be open to a company in the ordinary course of its business. In this debenture, the significant feature is that Brightlife was free to collect its debts and pay the proceeds into its bank account. Once in the account, they would be outside the charge over debts and at the free disposal of the company. In my judgment a right to deal in this way with the charged assets for its own account is a badge of a floating charge and is inconsistent with a fixed charge.

(v) Despite this, freedom to deal with the charged assets is clearly a relative rather than an absolute concept, and some degree of freedom is not incompatible with a charge being a fixed charge. In *Re Cimex Tissues Ltd* [1994] BCLC 626 a charge over plant and machinery was held to be a fixed charge even though it was contemplated that some of the items of plant might be replaced from time to time as they wore out.

(vi) Nevertheless, it is precisely this issue of control over the use of the charged assets which plagues analysis (along with the related issue of control over their proceeds, as, eg, with a charge over book debts, where it is relevant to look at the related control over their proceeds). Suppose the charge holder is a bank with a charge over a company's book debts: if use of the proceeds of the book debts is not controlled at all, then the charge is floating (*Re Brightlife Ltd* [10.12], although in this case the chargee was not itself a bank); and if use of the proceeds is completely restricted, then the charge is fixed (*Re Keenan Bros Ltd* [1986] BCLC 242, where the chargee bank stipulated that the account could not be drawn against without the counter-signature of one of its officers). But if neither the freedom nor the control is absolute, then a judgement is required. In *Siebe Gorman & Co Ltd v Barclays Bank Ltd* [1979] 2 Lloyd's Rep 142, for example, the company was forbidden to deal with the book debts *before collection* in certain specified ways but not in every conceivable way; there was also a right to obtain absolute control by giving notice, but this right was never exercised. The charge was held by Slade J to be a fixed charge, but his decision was overruled 25 years later by the House of Lords in *Spectrum*, [10.20] below.

(vii) Clearly there are limits to what can be achieved by drafting alone. In *Royal Trust Bank v National Westminster Bank plc* [1996] 2 BCLC 699, CA, an instrument creating a charge over book debts gave the chargee bank the *right* to demand that the company should open a dedicated account and pay all moneys received on the collection of the debts into that account, but the bank never exercised this right, and in practice moneys collected went into the company's ordinary trading account. The charge was held by Millett LJ to be floating. (All three members of the court concurred in the result; Nourse LJ on other grounds, and Swinford Thomas LJ without giving reasons.)

(viii) Similarly, in *Re Double S Printers Ltd* [1999] 1 BCLC 220 the chargee, as a director of the company, had *de facto* control over the proceeds of the charged book debts since he had actual control of the bank account, but this was not backed by any contractual restraint on their disposal in the instrument itself. As in the *Royal Trust Bank* case, it was held that the company's freedom (at least in law) to deal led to the conclusion that the charge was floating.

(ix) More imaginative structures have been adopted. Perhaps the most notorious is that which was successfully proposed in *Re New Bullas Trading Ltd* **[10.18]** (although subsequently held to be wrong by the Privy Council in *Brumark* **[10.19]**, and now overruled by the House of Lords in *Spectrum*, **[10.20]** below). In *New Bullas*, the company granted a charge over book debts which was expressed to be a fixed charge over the uncollected book debts and a floating charge over their proceeds. The Court of Appeal, overruling Knox J, held that this was possible. The decision caused a good deal of controversy. It was followed in Australia (*Whitton v CAN 003 266 886 Pty Ltd* (1997) 42 NSWLR 123) but disowned by the New Zealand Court of Appeal (*Re Brumark Investments Ltd, Commissioner of Inland Revenue v Agnew* [2000] 1 BCLC 353, [2000] 1 NZLR 223). The Privy Council subsequently upheld the *Brumark* ruling, and held that *New Bullas* was wrongly decided: see **[10.19]**.

(x) It is apparent from all of this that, of the three attributes of the floating charge identified by Romer LJ in *Re Yorkshire Woolcombers Ltd* (above, p 468), it is the third—the trading power—which is normally regarded as crucial. The other two features, while characteristic of most floating charges, are less essential: in *Bond Worth* **[10.07]** two of the classes of assets affected were not 'present and future' but exclusively present (the goods) and exclusively future (the proceeds) respectively. And in *Welch v Bowmaker (Ireland) Ltd* [1980] IR 251 the second of the criteria—the expectation that the class of assets would be turned over in the course of business—was lacking: a charge over a parcel of land presently owned by the company was ruled to be a floating charge.

(xi) This makes it rather extraordinary that in *Re Atlantic Computer Systems plc* [1992] Ch 505, CA (followed on similar facts in *Re Atlantic Medical Ltd* [1993] BCLC 386) the Court of Appeal appears to have been influenced almost entirely by the fact that the property affected by the charge was specific (rental moneys payable to the company under existing, identified computer-leasing agreements) in holding that the charge was a fixed charge. The fact that this property was not 'ambulatory and shifting in nature' seems to have been regarded as conclusive in itself, even though the rental moneys when received by the company were used by it in the ordinary course of business and the instrument did not prohibit this. Since this is a ruling of the Court of Appeal, it must be accorded due weight; but after the decisions of the Privy Council in *Brumark* **[10.19]** and the House of Lords in *Spectrum* **[10.20]** (neither of which referred to these cases), their authority must now be regarded as questionable.

A fixed charge may be created over book debts, including future book debts, but will be treated as a floating charge if the chargor is free to realise or collect the debts for his own account.

[10.18] Re New Bullas Trading Ltd [1994] 1 BCLC 485 (Court of Appeal)

This case, now overruled, is not extracted here, but given its notoriety and the continued reference to it in subsequent cases, it seems sensible to give it some attention. The case was decided on the basis of the contractual freedom of the parties to do what they proposed, in the absence of contrary arguments based on public policy. Reaction to the Court of Appeal decision was probably the impetus for the subsequent radical overhaul and a more tightly reasoned judicial approach to this area.

The company had executed a security document in favour of 3i plc which purported to create a fixed charge over book debts, so long as they remained uncollected, but when the proceeds of the debts had been collected and paid into a designated bank account, (unless written instructions to the contrary were given by 3i) the moneys so received were released from the fixed charge and became subject to a floating charge. At first instance Knox J held that the charge was a floating charge throughout and that in consequence the company's preferential creditors were entitled in a receivership to priority under IA 1986 s 40 as regards the uncollected debts. The Court of Appeal reversed this decision, holding that there were commercial advantages for both parties in these arrangements (having a fixed charge over the uncollected debts and a floating charge over the proceeds when collected); that the parties were free to agree to such terms; and that the wording of the debenture did have the effect of making the security over the uncollected book debts a fixed charge.

➤ Note

The ruling in this case was strongly criticised by Professor Goode ('Charges over Book Debts: a Missed Opportunity' (1994) 110 LQR 592). In his view, it is not possible to create separate security interests over a debt and its proceeds: all that is possible to have is a single, continuous security interest which moves from debts to proceeds. If the chargee does not retain sufficient control over the proceeds when collected, the charge, '*as created*', must be regarded as a floating charge. This is because 'the distinctive feature of debts as an object of security is that they are realised by payment, upon which they cease to exist'.

Goode's view later received support from Millett LJ in *Royal Trust Bank v National Westminster Bank plc* [1996] 2 BCLC 682, where he said (at 704): ' . . . while it is obviously possible to distinguish between a capital asset and its income, I do not see how it can be possible to separate a debt or other receivable from the proceeds of its realisation'.

New Bullas drew comment from other academic commentators. Griffin (1995) 46 NILQ 163, in reply to Professor Goode, condemned the notion that a charge over book debts and their proceeds must always be of an indivisible nature as 'misconceived'. A similar view was taken by McLauchlan in (2000) 116 LQR 211. Worthington, in contrast (1997) 113 LQR 563, while not supporting the view that a book debt and its proceeds constitute an indivisible asset, considered that the wrong conclusion had been reached in *New Bullas* because the security arrangement had left the chargor free to remove the charged assets from the ambit of the security without recourse to the chargee.

In the event, it is this last view which has been upheld. The Privy Council, in an appeal from New Zealand in the case next cited, has categorically stated that *New Bullas* was wrongly decided and so it must be taken as having been to all intents and purposes overruled.

[10.19] Agnew v Commissioner of Inland Revenue (Re Brumark Investments Ltd) [2001] UKPC 28, [2001] 2 AC 710 (Privy Council)

[See the shorter extract at **[10.04]** above.]

Brumark had given security over its book debts to its bank (Westpac) in terms which were indistinguishable from those in *New Bullas* **[10.18]**—ie which purported to make the debts subject to a fixed charge so long as they were uncollected but a floating charge over the proceeds once they had been collected and received by the company. The company was free to collect the debts for its own account and to use the proceeds in its business. Brumark went into receivership and the receivers collected the outstanding debts. Fisher J at first instance held that, as uncollected debts, they were subject to a fixed charge (as the parties had agreed) and, as such, not subject to the claims of the company's preferential creditors. The New

Zealand Court of Appeal, declining to follow *New Bullas*, held that the fact that the company was free to collect the debts for its own account (and so remove them from the bank's security) was inconsistent with the charge being a fixed charge. It was accordingly a floating charge and the preferential creditors had a prior claim to the proceeds. This ruling was affirmed by the Privy Council.

The opinion of the Judicial Committee was delivered by LORD MILLETT: . . . The question in this appeal is whether a charge over uncollected book debts of a company which leaves the company free to collect them and use the proceeds in the ordinary course of its business is a fixed charge or a floating charge.

[His Lordship set out the facts and the terms of the debenture and continued:] The question is whether the company's right to collect the debts and deal with their proceeds free from the security means that the charge on the uncollected debts, though described in the debenture as fixed, was nevertheless a floating charge until it crystallised by the appointment of the receivers. This is a question of characterisation. To answer it their Lordships must examine the nature of a floating charge and ascertain the features which distinguish it from a floating charge. . . . [His Lordship traced the history of the floating charge, referring to cases from *Re Panama, New Zealand and Australian Royal Mail Co*[22] to *Re Cosslett (Contractors) Ltd* **[10.08]**, emphasising in particular the following passage from the judgment of Vaughan Williams LJ in *Re Yorkshire Woolcombers Association Ltd* (above, p 471):

' . . . but what you do require to make a specific security is that the security whenever it has once come into existence, and been identified and appropriated as a security, *shall never thereafter at the will of the mortgagor cease to be a security. If at the will of the mortgagor he can dispose of it and prevent its being any longer a security, although something else may be substituted more or less for it, that is not a "specific security"* ' (emphasis added).]

[His Lordship referred to the wording of the debentures in this case and in *New Bullas* and continued:] The intended effect of the debenture was the same in each case. Until the charge holder intervened the company could continue to collect the debts, though not to assign or factor them, and the debts once collected would cease to exist. The proceeds which took their place would be a different asset which had never been subject to the fixed charge and would from the outset be subject to the floating charge.

The question in *New Bullas*, as in the present case, was whether the book debts which were uncollected when the receivers were appointed were subject to a fixed charge or a floating charge. . . .

The principal theme of the judgment [in *New Bullas*] . . . was that the parties were free to make whatever agreement they liked. The question was therefore simply one of construction; unless unlawful the intention of the parties, to be gathered from the terms of the debenture, must prevail. It was clear from the descriptions which the parties attached to the charges that they had intended to create a fixed charge over the book debts while they were uncollected and a floating charge over the proceeds. It was open to the parties to do so, and freedom of contract prevailed.

Their Lordships consider this approach to be fundamentally mistaken. The question is not merely one of construction. In deciding whether a charge is a fixed charge or a floating charge, the court is engaged in a two-stage process. At the first stage it must construe the instrument of charge and seek to gather the intentions of the parties from the language they have used. But the object at this stage of the process is not to discover whether the parties intended to create a fixed or a floating charge. It is to ascertain the nature of the rights and obligations which the parties intended to grant each other in respect of the charged assets. Once these have been ascertained, the court can then embark on the second stage of the process, which is one of categorisation. This is a matter of law. It does not depend on the intention of the parties. If their intention, properly gathered from the

[22] (1870) 5 Ch App 318, CA.

language of the instrument, is to grant the company rights in respect of the charged assets which are inconsistent with the nature of a fixed charge, then the charge cannot be a fixed charge however they may have chosen to describe it. . . . In construing a debenture to see whether it creates a fixed or a floating charge, the only intention which is relevant is the intention that the company should be free to deal with the charged assets and withdraw them from the security without the consent of the holder of the charge; or, to put the question another way, whether the charged assets were intended to be under the control of the company or of the charge holder.

[His Lordship considered and rejected an argument which had been upheld by the Court of Appeal in *New Bullas*: that the book debts did not cease to be subject to the charge at the will of the company but that they ceased to be subject to the charge because that was what the parties had agreed in advance when they entered into the debenture. He also rejected as irrelevant a distinction which Fisher J had drawn between a power on the part of the company to *dispose of* the debts (eg by factoring them) and a power to *consume* them (by realising them). He continued:] Their Lordships turn finally to the questions which have exercised academic commentators: whether a debt or other receivable can be separated from its proceeds; whether they represent a single security interest or two; and whether a charge on book debts necessarily takes effect as a single indivisible charge on the debts and their proceeds irrespective of the way in which it may be drafted.

Property and its proceeds are clearly different assets. On a sale of goods the seller exchanges one asset for another. Both assets continue to exist, the goods in the hands of the buyer and proceeds of sale in the hands of the seller. If a book debt is assigned, the debt is transferred to the assignee in exchange for money paid to the assignor. The seller's former property right in the subject matter of the sale gives him an equivalent property right in its exchange product. The only difference between realising a debt by assignment and collection is that, on collection, the debt is wholly extinguished. As in the case of alienation, it is replaced in the hands of the creditor by a different asset, viz its proceeds.

The Court of Appeal saw no reason to examine the conceptual problems further. They held that, even if a debt and its proceeds are two different assets, the company was free to realise the uncollected debts, and accordingly the charge on those assets (being the assets whose destination was in dispute) could not be a fixed charge. There was simply no need to look at the proceeds at all. . . .

If the company is free to collect the debts, the nature of the charge on the uncollected debts cannot differ according to whether the proceeds are subject to a floating charge or are not subject to any charge. In each case the commercial effect is the same: the charge holder cannot prevent the company from collecting the debts and having the free use of the proceeds. But it does not follow that the nature of the charge on the uncollected book debts may not differ according to whether the proceeds are subject to a fixed charge or a floating charge; for in the one case the charge holder can prevent the company from having the use of the proceeds and in the other it cannot The question is not whether the company is free to collect the debts, but whether it is free to do so for its own benefit. . . .

To constitute a charge on book debts a fixed charge, it is sufficient to prohibit the company from realising the debts itself, whether by assignment or collection. But . . . it is not inconsistent with the fixed nature of a charge on book debts for the holder of the charge to appoint the company its agent to collect the debts for its account and on its behalf. *Siebe Gorman*[23] and *Re Keenan* [above, p 486] merely introduced an alternative mechanism for appropriating the proceeds to the security. The proceeds of the debts collected by the company were no longer to be trust moneys but they were required to be paid into a blocked account with the charge holder. The commercial effect was the same: the proceeds were not at the company's disposal. Such an arrangement is inconsistent with the charge being a floating charge, since the debts are not available to the company as a source of its cash flow. But their Lordships would wish to make it clear that it is not enough to provide in the debenture that the account is a blocked account if it is not operated as one in fact. . . .

Their Lordships consider that *New Bullas* was wrongly decided.

---

[23] [1979] 2 Lloyd's Rep 142.

[10.20] Re Spectrum Plus Ltd [2005] UKHL 41, [2005] 2 AC 680
(House of Lords)

The company granted a charge over its book debts to the bank, expressed to be 'by way of specific charge', prohibiting disposal of the book debts and requiring the proceeds to be paid into an account with chargee bank. The bank permitted the company to draw on these proceeds for use in the ordinary course of business, subject to certain restrictions. In its terms, the charge was in the same form as that which had been accepted by Slade J as a fixed charge in *Siebe Gorman*.[24] If it was a floating charge, the preferential creditors would be entitled to have their debts paid out of the proceeds of the book debts in priority to the bank (IA 1986 s 175); if not, the bank would be entitled to the whole of the proceeds. The amount at stake was relatively trivial (approximately £16,000). But the case was run as a test case, with several hundred liquidations held up pending the resolution of the issue. The debenture was in a form used by many banks and other commercial lenders. Indeed, the company had gone into liquidation and took no part in the proceedings; the case was argued between the bank (as the secured creditor) and the Crown (as preferential creditor in the liquidation (see below, p 647)).

LORD HOPE: . . . it is competent for anyone to whom book debts may accrue in the future to create for good consideration an equitable charge upon those book debts which will attach to them as soon as they come into existence. But if this is to be effective as a fixed security everything depends on the way the security agreement ensures that the charge over the book debts is fixed. It is not easy to reconcile the company's need to continue to collect and use these sums for its own business purposes with the lender's wish to escape from the priority which section 175(2)(b) of the 1986 Act gives to preferential debts . . .

There are, as Professor Sarah Worthington has pointed out, a limited number of ways to ensure that a charge over book debts is fixed: "An 'Unsatisfactory Area of the Law'—Fixed and Floating Charges Yet Again" (2004) 1 International Corporate Rescue 175, 182. One is to prevent all dealings with the book debts so that they are preserved for the benefit of the chargee's security. . . . One can, of course, be confident where this method is used that the book debts will be permanently appropriated to the security which is given to the chargee. But a company that wishes to continue to trade will usually find the commercial consequences of such an arrangement unacceptable. Another is to prevent all dealings with the book debts other than their collection, and to require the proceeds when collected to be paid to the chargee in reduction of the chargor's outstanding debt. But this method too is likely to be unacceptable to a company which wishes to carry on its business as normally as possible by maintaining its cash flow and its working capital. A third is to prevent all dealings with the debts other than their collection, and to require the collected proceeds to be paid into an account with the chargee bank. That account must then be blocked so as to preserve the proceeds for the benefit of the chargee's security. A fourth is to prevent all dealings with the debts other than their collection and to require the collected proceeds to be paid into a separate account with a third party bank. The chargee then takes a fixed charge over that account so as to preserve the sums paid into it for the benefit of its security.

The method that was selected in this case comes closest to the third of these. It was selected, no doubt, because it enabled the company to continue to trade as normally as possible while restricting it, at the same time, to some degree as to what it could do with the book debts. The critical question is whether the restrictions that it imposed went far enough. There is no doubt that their effect was to prevent the company from entering into transactions with any third party in relation to

---

[24] *Ibid.*

the book debts prior to their collection. The uncollected book debts were to be held exclusively for the benefit of the bank. But everything then depended on the nature of the account with the bank into which the proceeds were to paid under the arrangement described in clause 5 of the debenture. As McCarthy J said in *In re Keenan Bros Ltd* [1986] BCLC 242, 247, one must look, not at the declared intention of the parties alone, but to the effect of the instruments whereby they purported to carry out that intention. Was the account one which allowed the company to continue to use the proceeds of the book debts as a source of its cash flow or was it one which, on the contrary, preserved the proceeds intact for the benefit of the bank's security? Was it, putting the point shortly, a blocked account?

I do not see how this question can be answered without examining the contractual relationship in regard to that account between the bank and its customer. An account from which the customer is entitled to withdraw funds whenever it wishes within the agreed limits of any overdraft is not a blocked account. In *Agnew v Comr of Inland Revenue* [2001] 1 AC 710, 722, para 22 Lord Millett said that the critical feature which led the Irish Supreme Court in In *re Keenan Bros Ltd* [1986] BCLC 242 to characterise the charge on book debts as a fixed charge was that their proceeds were to be segregated in a blocked account where they would be frozen and unusable by the company without the bank's written consent. I respectfully agree. . . . [He then considered the arrangements in *Siebe Gorman* and in this case, and decided that neither were effective to block the account in the way required. He then continued:]

Should Siebe Gorman be overruled?

Lord Phillips of Worth Matravers MR [in this case in the CA] said that, even if Slade J's construction of the debenture in *Siebe Gorman & Co Ltd v Barclays Bank Ltd* [1979] 2 Lloyd's Rep 142 had appeared to him to be erroneous, he would have been inclined to hold that the form of the debenture had, by custom and usage, acquired the meaning and effect that he had attributed to it: [2004] Ch 337, 383, para 97. This was because the form had been used for 25 years under the understanding that this was its meaning and effect. Banks had relied upon this understanding, and individuals had guaranteed the liabilities of companies to banks on the understanding that the banks would be entitled to look first to their charges on book debts unaffected by the claims of preferred creditors. The respondents say that this is the course that ought now to be followed in the interests of commercial certainty.

. . . It is hard to think of an area of the law where the need for certainty is more important than that with which your Lordships are concerned in this case. The commercial life of this country depends to a large extent on the reliability of the security arrangements that are entered into between debtors and their creditors. The law provides the context in which these arrangements are entered into, and it lays down the rules that have to be applied when the arrangements break down. Mistakes as to the law can make all the difference between success and failure when the creditor seeks to realise his security. So a heavy responsibility lies on judges to provide the lending market with guidance that is accurate and reliable. This is so that mistakes can be avoided and transactions entered into with confidence that they will achieve what is expected of them.

These are powerful considerations, but I am in no doubt that the proper course is for the *Siebe Gorman* decision to be overruled. . . . This is not one of those cases where there are respectable arguments either way. With regret, the conclusion has to be that it is not possible to defend the decision on any rational basis. It is not enough to say that it has stood for more than 25 years. The fact is that, like any other first instance decision, it was always open to correction if the country's highest appellate court was persuaded that there was something wrong with it. Those who relied upon it must be taken to have been aware of this. . . .

[He therefore held *Siebe Gorman* was wrong and should be overruled, and allowed the appeal.]

LORD SCOTT: . . . The question for decision, therefore, is whether a charge over present and future book debts, where the chargor cannot dispose of or charge the uncollected book debts but can deal with its debtors and collect the debts and where the chargor is obliged to place the payments made to it by its debtors in a designated account with the chargee bank but can freely draw on the account for its business purposes provided the overdraft limit is not exceeded, is capable in law of being a fixed charge. . . . [He then went on to consider the rival lines of authority, and then continued:]

What is a floating charge?

[He explored the history and commercial need for floating charges, and the relevant precedents, then continued:]

. . . Indeed if a security has Romer LJ's third characteristic I am inclined to think that it qualifies as a floating charge, and cannot be a fixed charge, whatever may be its other characteristics. Suppose, for example, a case where an express assignment of a specific debt by way of security were accompanied by a provision that reserved to the assignor the right, terminable by written notice from the assignee, to collect the debt and to use the proceeds for its (the assignor's) business purposes, ie, a right, terminable on notice, for the assignor to withdraw the proceeds of the debt from the security. This security would, in my opinion, be a floating security notwithstanding the express assignment. The assigned debt would be specific and ascertained but its status as a security would not. Unless and until the right of the assignor to collect and deal with the proceeds were terminated, the security would retain its floating characteristic. Or suppose a case in which the charge were expressed to come into existence on the future occurrence of some event and then to be a fixed charge over whatever assets of a specified description the chargor might own at that time. The contractual rights thereby granted would, in my opinion, be properly categorised as a floating security. There can, in my opinion, be no difference in categorisation between the grant of a fixed charge expressed to come into existence on a future event in relation to a specified class of assets owned by the chargor at that time and the grant of a floating charge over the specified class of assets with cystallisation taking place on the occurrence of that event. . . . Nor, in principle, can there be any difference in categorisation between those grants and the grant of a charge over the specified assets expressed to be a fixed charge but where the chargor is permitted until the occurrence of the specified event to remove the charged assets from the security. In all these cases, and in any other case in which the chargor remains free to remove the charged assets from the security, the charge should, in principle, be categorised as a floating charge. The assets would have the circulating, ambulatory character distinctive of a floating charge. . . .

In my opinion, the essential characteristic of a floating charge, the characteristic that distinguishes it from a fixed charge, is that the asset subject to the charge is not finally appropriated as a security for the payment of the debt until the occurrence of some future event. In the meantime the chargor is left free to use the charged asset and to remove it from the security. On this point I am in respectful agreement with Lord Millett. Moreover, recognition that this is the essential characteristic of a floating charge reflects the mischief that the statutory intervention to which I have referred was intended to meet and should ensure that preferential creditors continue to enjoy the priority that section 175 of the 1986 Act and its statutory predecessors intended them to have. . . .

[He therefore held *Siebe Gorman* was wrong and should be overruled, and allowed the appeal.]

LORD WALKER:

The essential difference

This passage brings us close to the issue of legal principle, that is the essential difference between a fixed charge and a floating charge. Under a fixed charge the assets charged as security are permanently appropriated to the payment of the sum charged, in such a way as to give the chargee a proprietary interest in the assets. So long as the charge remains unredeemed, the assets can be released from the charge only with the active concurrence of the chargee. The chargee may have good commercial reasons for agreeing to a partial release. If for instance a bank has a fixed charge over a large area of land which is being developed in phases as a housing estate (another example of a fixed charge on what might be regarded as trading stock) it might be short-sighted of the bank not to agree to take only a fraction of the proceeds of sale of houses in the first phase, so enabling the remainder of the development to be funded. But under a fixed charge that will be a matter for the chargee to decide for itself.

Under a floating charge, by contrast, the chargee does not have the same power to control the security for its own benefit. The chargee has a proprietary interest, but its interest is in a fund of circulating capital, and unless and until the chargee intervenes (on crystallisation of the charge) it is for the trader, and not the bank, to decide how to run its business. . . .

[He therefore held *Siebe Gorman* was wrong and should be overruled, and allowed the appeal.]

BARONESS HALE and LORDS NICHOLLS, STEYN and BROWN all delivered concurring opinions.

➤ Notes

1. *Spectrum* **[10.20]** and *Brumark* **[10.19]** are worth reading in full for a proper appreciation of the area. The *Spectrum* case also addresses the issue of 'prospective overruling' by the House of Lords (pursuant to the argument put by the bank that even if *Siebe Gorman* were overruled, the overruling should only have an impact on charges created after the date of the decision). The Law Lords unanimously agreed the power existed, but refused to exercise it in the circumstances.

2. *Re SSSL Realisations Ltd* [2004] EWHC 1760, confirmed, if that were necessary, that it is possible to create a charge only on the proceeds of collection of debts without charging the debts themselves at all.

3. In *Arthur D Little Ltd v Ableco Finance LLC* [2002] EWHC 701, it was reaffirmed that a chargor may enjoy the 'fruits' of the property that has been subjected to a *fixed* charge, without thereby converting the charge to a floating charge. Mr Roger Kaye QC said:

As Nichols LJ put it in *Re Atlantic Computer Systems Plc* [1992] Ch 505 at 534G: "A mortgage of land does not become a floating charge by reason of a mortgagor being permitted to remain in possession and enjoy the fruits of the property charged from time to time." The receipt of dividends and other rights arising by virtue of the shares seem to me to be examples of exploitation of the principal subject matter of the charge, i.e. the shares. As Lord Millett again expressed in the *Brumark* case[25] at page 727, paragraph 37: "The judge drew a distinction between a power of disposition and a power of consumption. There is nothing he suggested inconsistent with a fixed charge in prohibiting the Company from disposing of the charged asset to others, but allowing it to exploit the characteristics inherent in the nature of the asset itself. Their Lordships agree with this."

➤ Question

Does it follow from these decisions that the commercial objectives which *New Bullas* sought to meet are now impossible to achieve? Draftsman will clearly need to make sure that collections made by the company are held for the chargee's account (eg by being paid into a blocked bank account) and only after that released by an act of the chargee into the chargor's general funds. Can this be done in a way that is commercially attractive?

---

[25] [2001] 2 AC 710.

Avoiding the statutory regime for company securities

There are various practical mechanisms that can be adopted by way of 'quasi-security' in order to gain some of the benefits of being a secured creditor without the effort and expense (and possible disadvantages) of the fixed and floating charge regime just described. To this end, creditors use conditional sales, hire-purchase arrangements, trusts (eg, building retention trusts, *Quistclose* trusts,[26] etc), and other such devices.

Retention of title agreements are considered here, simply by way of illustration.

Retention of title agreements

Most trading companies use bank overdrafts to meet their short-term financial needs, and commonly also rely on bank loans for longer-term credit. Almost invariably, such advances will be secured by floating charges over all the company's assets, and possibly by an array of fixed charges as well. In the event of insolvency, the bank and those creditors who are entitled to a statutory preference (see below, pp 646–647) are likely between them to claim all that the company has, leaving ordinary trade creditors with nothing.

Many commentators have considered this situation to be unfair—see, for example, the Cork Committee's report (1982, Cmnd 8558, para 1950) and the remarks of Templeman J in *Business Computers v Anglo-African Leasing Ltd* [1977] 1 WLR 578 at 580. Admittedly, some of these criticisms centred on the statutory provisions that accorded to the Crown status as a preferred creditor for many of the debts (including taxes) owed to the Crown. This preference was abolished by the Enterprise Act 2002 (see below, p 647).

Nevertheless, even as regards the normal operation of floating charges, there is particular unfairness in relation to those who supply the company with goods on credit—perhaps the raw materials needed for its manufacturing processes. The goods delivered become subject immediately to the floating charge (if, as is usual, it affects future property), even though it is the seller and not the bank who is providing this particular asset by way of credit. So suppliers have endeavoured to protect themselves by 'retention of title' clauses. There is nothing novel about this: the familiar hire-purchase agreement serves the same purpose. A Dutch supplier succeeded in defeating the claims of a receiver in this way in the celebrated *Romalpa* case [**10.21**] in 1976.

[10.21] Aluminium Industrie Vaassen BV v Romalpa Aluminium Ltd
[1976] 1 WLR 676 (Chancery Division and Court of Appeal)

Aluminium foil was supplied by the plaintiffs, a Dutch company, to the defendants for processing in their factory. It was stipulated in the contract of sale that ownership of the foil should not be transferred to the buyers (the defendant purchasing company) until the price had been paid in full; that products made from the foil should be kept by the buyers as bailees (the contract, which was a translation from a Dutch draft, used the un-English expression 'fiduciary owners') separately from other stock, on the supplier's behalf, as 'surety' for the outstanding price; but that the buyers should have power to sell the manufactured articles in the ordinary course of business, such sales to be made by them as the suppliers' agents. Mocatta J, whose judgment was affirmed by the Court of Appeal, held that the retention of title clause was effective to retain legal title to the aluminium in the hands of the supplier; in addition, the suppliers could trace the price due to them into the proceeds of

---

[26] Named after the seminal case, *Barclays Bank Ltd v Quistclose Investments Ltd* [1970] AC 567, HL.

sales of the finished goods made by the buyers, ahead of the latter's secured and unsecured creditors.[27]

> MOCATTA J: The preservation of ownership clause contains unusual and fairly elaborate provisions departing substantially from the debtor/creditor relationship and shows, in my view, the intention to create a fiduciary relationship to which the [tracing] principle stated in *Re Hallett's Estate*[28] applies. A further point made by Mr Pickering was that if the plaintiffs were to succeed in their tracing claim this would, in effect, be a method available against a liquidator to a creditor of avoiding the provisions establishing the need to register charges on book debts: see s 95(1), (2)(e) of the Companies Act 1948 [CA 2006, s 860(7)(g)]. He used this only as an argument against the effect of clause 13 contended for by Mr Lincoln. As to this, I think Mr Lincoln's answer was well founded, namely, that if property in the foil never passed to the defendants with the result that the proceeds of sub-sales belonged in equity to the plaintiffs, s 95(1) had no application.
>
> The plaintiffs accordingly succeeded and are entitled to the reliefs sought.
>
> [The decision of Mocatta J was affirmed by the Court of Appeal.]

➤ Notes

1. Since this decision, draftsmen of suppliers' contracts have endeavoured to adopt and improve upon 'Romalpa clauses' with varying success. In those cases where the goods sold are still in the hands of the company and identifiable, the supplier has usually been successful. But in other cases the danger is that the court will hold that a charge has been created, which may be void in a subsequent insolvency for non-registration under CA 2006 ss 860ff and will, in any event, probably rank after the bank.

2. *Re Bond Worth Ltd* **[10.07]** established that an attempt to reserve a mere equitable title (at least in a case where the buyer was free to resell) created a charge in the nature of a floating charge, which was void unless registered; and later cases have held that the same result follows where the manufacturing process is such as to destroy the identity of the raw material which was originally supplied: *Borden (UK) Ltd v Scottish Timber Products Ltd* [1981] Ch 25 (resin used in making chipboard); *Re Peachdart Ltd* [1984] Ch 131 (leather used for handbags).

3. In regard to claims against the proceeds of sale, suppliers have not been successful unless the clause has created a duty to keep the moneys separate from other funds: *Hendy Lennox (Industrial Engines) Ltd v Grahame Puttick Ltd* [1984] 1 WLR 485. Even then, the natural inference is that a charge has been created, since almost invariably the amount of the price owing to the supplier will be part only of the proceeds of resale: *E Pfeiffer Weinkellerei-Weineinkauf GmbH & Co v Arbuthnot Factors Ltd* [1988] 1 WLR 150, [1987] BCLC 522; *Compaq Computers Ltd v Abercorn Group Ltd* [1993] BCLC 602.

4. There have been pleas for reform of the law so as to make all contracts containing retention of title clauses (and presumably also hire-purchase and leasing contracts) registrable as charges. The Diamond Report (HMSO, 1989), paras 17.8ff, 23.6.10, proposed that a distinction should be drawn between 'simple' clauses, which do no more than retain title to the actual goods sold, or their proceeds if resold, but only in regard to a claim for the original price, and more complex clauses, such as those which purport to assert title to a manufactured product. Professor Diamond recommended that the law should be clarified by a statutory provision which declares the latter category to be registrable as charges and the former to be exempt. These recommendations have not been taken up by the legislature, and the

---

[27] This second aspect of the decision is now regarded as justifiable, if at all, on the special terms of the contract. But the analysis in relation to basic retention of title clauses stands firm, and is much used in commercial practice.

[28] (1880) 13 Ch D 696.

question has been left in limbo during the decade or so while various groups have been debating possible reforms to the charges registration system (see above, p 466).

5. The Insolvency Act 1986 s 15 empowers an administrator, with the leave of the court, to sell property affected by such contracts free from the supplier's interest on terms that the net proceeds are paid in discharge of the debt due to the supplier.

11

REMEDIES FOR MALADMINISTRATION OF THE COMPANY

General issues

The earlier chapters illustrate that either the directors or the members in general meeting (but generally the directors) have responsibility for the affairs of the company. This chapter looks both at who can seek remedies if the company is poorly run and at what matters are the legitimate subject of complaint. In particular, it examines whether complaints be made only about 'legal wrongs'—negligence, breach of statutory duty, etc—or also about more general issues of perceived 'maladministration', including management approaches that are simply not in accordance with expectations. It also considers some of the problems that arise because the company is an 'association' of members, run by a 'board' of directors, so issues of majority rule have to be addressed (see below, pp 500 ff). Finally, it looks at the problems of potential double recovery where both the company and its individual members seem to be entitled to remedies for particular wrongs (see below, pp 540 ff).

Pursuing claims for maladministration

In pursuing claims for maladministration, the usual problem, of course, is that the people causing harm to the company (whether the directors or the majority shareholders) are usually also the people in control of the company. They are unlikely to pursue litigation against themselves. The relevant company law rules must address this difficult issue, while at the same time avoiding the problem of allowing every vexatious or litigious member to complain about activity that is to all intents and purposes acceptable to the company's various participants and interest groups.

The types of action examined in this chapter fall into slightly overlapping categories (the overlaps caused in large measure by statutory interventions).

Actionable wrongs against the company

If an actionable wrong has been done to the company, then the company has a cause of action which it may pursue in legal proceedings, just like any other legal person. Again, like any other legal person, it is not *obliged* to pursue every possible claim it has. Where the company's claim is against its own directors, however, it is clearly unsafe to leave the decision about whether the company should sue in the hands of those same directors. Accordingly, one special rule that allows members to pursue these company claims in very tightly defined circumstances has been added to the general rules in an attempt to address this problem. In sum, and including the special rule, the company may pursue its own legal claims (in its own name in all but (iv) below) by means of a decision to do so taken by:

(i) The company's directors, acting within their normal powers of management of the company (if, as is usual, this is what the articles provide by way of power sharing within the company). Pragmatically, if the action is against one or more of the company's own directors, then such a decision to sue is only likely if the majority of directors is not aligned with the wrongdoers (even though the wrongdoers remain in post), or if a new board has taken over the management of the company and the old directors have been ousted. See eg *John Shaw and Sons (Salford) Ltd v Shaw* [**4.07**] and *Regal (Hastings) Ltd v Gulliver* [**6.16**].

(ii) The company's administrator or liquidator (in an administration or a winding up), since neither is likely to be diverted by personal allegiances to past directors.

(iii) The general meeting, in those rare cases where it seems that the general meeting has either primary or residual control over the company's power to litigate (but see below *Breckland Group Holdings Ltd v London & Suffolk Properties Ltd* [**11.07**]).

(iv) Individual members, using the statutory procedure that allows them to take a '*derivative action*': CA 2006 ss 260ff. A derivative action is taken in the name of the member, but in pursuit of a claim that belongs to the company, and for a remedy that will accrue to the company and not to the member as an individual. The company is brought before the court compulsorily (and so as a *defendant*, rather than a claimant), so as to ensure that it is subject to the jurisdiction and orders of the court in circumstances where those with actual power to cause the company to pursue its own claims are resisting this option.[1]

(v) The Secretary of State, under powers set out in CA 1985 s 438 (see below, pp 595 ff; note, these few CA 1985 provisions remain operative).

Actionable wrongs against individual members

If a wrong has been done to the member personally (rather than to the company), then the member may pursue his or her claim against the company, or against the other (ie majority) members in the company, by way of:

(i) A *personal action* (or a *representative action*[2]) based on the contract the member has with the company as set out in the company's constitution (CA 2006 s 33) (see above, pp 230 ff).

(ii) A *personal action* (or a *representative action*) based on other contracts the member may have with the company or with the body of members (see above, p 229).

(iii) A *statutory action* permitted by certain specific provisions in CA 2006 (see eg the provisions applying to reductions of capital or variation of class rights, see above pp 391 ff and pp 433 ff).

(iv) A statutory action to remedy '*unfair prejudice*' (CA 2006 s 994) (see below, pp 552 ff).

It is not necessary to examine all of these options in detail in this chapter. However, it is necessary to be alert to the range of different procedures that are available for remedying different forms of maladministration. Where the normal process for pursuing well recognised legal claims is adopted (as where the *company* sues its directors for *negligence*), then nothing more needs to be added to the earlier discussion of how a company acts (see above, pp 273 ff) and what constitutes directors' negligence (see above, pp 300 ff). Similarly, where the company or an individual pursues claims that are based on special statutory rights, it is not necessary to re-examine those special rights described earlier (eg individual member's rights of action based on the statutory contract with the company, or the statutory right to complain about reductions of capital or variation of class rights, see above pp 230 ff, 391 ff and 433 ff). This chapter therefore focuses only on the availability of special rights of access to the court (see company claims (iii) and (iv) above), and special grounds of complaint (see members' claims, (iv) above) in relation to maladministration.

---

[1] Also see below, p 535.

[2] A 'representative action' is a court procedure allowing one or more individuals to appear as claimants or defendants on behalf of a larger number of people having an identical interest in the proceedings, and so obtain a remedy (or provide a defence) for the entire class of them, as individuals, without each appearing individually before the court. See the Civil Procedure Rules 1998, r 19.6; also see below, p 541, fn 55.

Some of the issues addressed need to be seen in the context of historical practices, now replaced by provisions in CA 2006 that are imported from CA 1985 amendments or entirely new provisions in CA 2006. There is, therefore, a little more history in this chapter than elsewhere in this book.

Majority rule: principles and problems

Sometimes complaints about maladministration do not concern the particular action taken by the directors or the members, but rather *how* the (majority) decision to take that action was reached. Because the general rule *is* majority rule, whether by directors or by members (sometimes, in the latter case, with the added protection of supermajorities, or segregated classes of interest groups), there is the likelihood of disaffected dissenting minorities. 'Majority rule' applies not only to decisions to pursue business activities, but also to decisions *not* to pursue corporate wrongdoers (especially directors). The practice of proper majority rule is therefore especially important in this chapter.

We have already seen that the law normally allows members to treat their rights to vote as an incident of property which they may *prima facie* exercise for their own advantage (*Peter's American Delicacy Co Ltd v Heath* [4.26]). Further, it is established that even the strict fiduciary duties of directors do not go so far as to prohibit them altogether from acting in matters where their own personal interests are affected by what they do as directors (*Mills v Mills* [6.10]), still less from voting as they like in their capacity as members (*North-West Transportation Co Ltd v Beatty* [4.34]). The three cases just referred to, and many others, also illustrate the traditional unwillingness of the courts to review matters of commercial judgement or policy, or of internal administration. 'This Court,' said Lord Eldon, 'is not to be required on every Occasion to take the Management of every Playhouse and Brewhouse in the Kingdom'.[3]

The time-honoured and democratic principle of majority rule, backed by these other factors, necessarily means that quite substantial power is placed in the hands of those who control more than half of the votes on the board or at a members' meeting. Indeed, where shares are widely dispersed among a large number of members, comparable power can be wielded with command of a good deal less than 51 per cent of the votes.[4] Minority members must, in principle, accept the decisions of the majority and must also acknowledge that the power lawfully enjoyed by their more numerous brethren is a fact of business life. In theory it is, of course, open to them to seek to bring about change by the normal democratic processes of persuasion, lobbying, publicity and so on; and it may sometimes be appropriate to argue that a member who does not agree with the policy of those in control should sell his shares and invest his money elsewhere. In reality, however, neither of these courses may offer him a practical solution. He may not have the resources and will often lack access to the necessary information to mount a successful campaign against those in the seat of power. And in a smaller company there will almost always be no market for his shares: the only available buyers (assuming that they are interested) will probably be the very majority members with whom he is in disagreement, and they are likely to offer him only a derisory price.

---

[3] *Carlen v Drury* (1812) 1 Ves & B 154 at 158.

[4] This is because the controllers can usually count on a high degree of apathy and inertia on the part of the small 'armchair' investor. In addition, various devices such as 'pyramid', circular and cross-holdings of shares between companies can be used to concentrate power: see the classic analysis of Berle and Means *The Modern Corporation and Private Property* (New York, 1932) and MA Pickering, 'Shareholders' Voting Rights and Company Control' (1965) 81 LQR 248. More generally, see JE Parkinson, *Corporate Power and Responsibility* (OUP, 1993) pp 241–259.

In such circumstances, a frustrated minority member may turn to the law for help. Clearly, the law must provide some remedies to meet those cases in which majority power has been abused. There cannot be power—including the power of control over other people's investments—without corresponding responsibility. But the law has to strike a delicate balance. If it too readily supports the majority and is prepared to condone unfair and wrongful acts and decisions on their part, the minority will be prejudiced and, in a small company, 'locked in' with an unrealisable investment which the majority can exploit to their own advantage. If, on the other hand, too great indulgence is shown to complaining minorities, they will be able to obstruct the company's legitimate business with tiresome requisitions and objections, and exploit their nuisance value.

Both the legislature and the judiciary have made attempts to reconcile the opposing needs and interests of controllers and minorities.

Statutory protection is given to minorities by formalities of various kinds, eg:

(i)   requiring a special resolution rather than a simple majority vote in important matters, such as constitutional alterations;

(ii)   requiring the court's sanction, in matters like a reduction of capital or scheme of arrangement;

(iii)   giving dissentients a right to apply to the court to have a resolution cancelled, eg in a variation of class rights, and sometimes empowering the court to order, alternatively, that they be bought out.

To balance this, some checks are imposed on the use of these measures by safeguards such as a requirement that dissentients applying to the court must have at least 15% support from their fellows.

Other statutory provisions give members direct access to the courts. Foremost among these are the right to petition to have a company compulsorily wound up (IA 1986 s 124) (see below, pp 648 ff) and the right to seek relief for 'unfairly prejudicial' conduct (CA 2006 s 994) (see below, pp 552 ff).

The judges for their part have also developed rules which are aimed at curbing the abuse of power by those with control. The directors, for example, are restrained by their fiduciary duties and by the 'bona fide' and 'proper purposes' principles. Majority members, at least in the context of an alteration of articles and a variation of class rights, are also constrained to act *bona fide* in the common interest. But apart from these well-recognised (though not necessarily well-defined) limitations, the courts have by and large allowed *laissez-faire* principles to reign and majority rule to operate unchecked. They have thus avoided putting themselves into the position which so alarmed Lord Eldon. Later in this chapter the issue of what counts as a 'proper' decision of the general meeting emerges with renewed force as a problem in this area of remedying maladministration (see especially *Prudential* [11.13] and *Smith v Croft (No 2)* [11.14]).

But the main judicial instrument by which this policy of non-intervention has been maintained is a rule not of substance but of procedure, which all company lawyers know as the rule in *Foss v Harbottle* [11.01]. Minority members who complain of a wrong or irregularity may well find this a formidable, and perhaps an insurmountable, barrier to their quest for justice, even where they have a real and well-founded grievance. The rule has attracted criticism from across the Atlantic both because of its complexity[5] and because it is considered unjust to recognise a substantive right but deny a remedy on procedural grounds.[6] But it has

---

[5] Dickerson, Howard and Getz, in *Proposals for a New Business Corporation Law for Canada* (Ottawa, 1971), §482, called it an 'infamous doctrine' which they recommended should be 'relegated to legal limbo without compunction'.

[6] Hornstein [1967] JBL 282.

been defended with enthusiasm by the Court of Appeal in the *Prudential* case **[11.13]**, which itself was cited with approval in the recent House of Lords decision in *Johnson v Gore Wood and Co* **[11.17]**. The rule is linked with problems of 'proper' expressions of authority by the general meeting, and has now been substantially reformed by CA 2006 (see below, pp 535 ff). Whether the latter changes have adequately addressed the various criticisms is not yet clear.

➤ Questions

1. Reconsider the cases on *directors'* decision-making (see Chapter 6, above) and assess the extent to which a *company* can complain that its directors have not acted *bona fide*, or not acted for proper purposes, and so impugn a decision on those grounds without having to prove that a particular *commercial* decision is inappropriate and in itself constitutes maladministration. Do the CA 2006 provisions on directors' duties strengthen the law in this regard?

2. Once you have read this entire chapter, assess the extent to which a *member* can complain about the sorts of directors' activities just described. If action *is* possible, is the remedy one for the company or one for the shareholders personally?

3. Reconsider the cases on *members'* decision-making (eg see above, pp 230 ff, 391 ff, and 433 ff) and assess the extent to which a *company* can complain that its members have not acted *bona fide*, or not acted for proper purposes. Can *members* use this as a ground for complaint, in seeking a remedy for the company *or* a remedy for themselves personally?

Restricting litigation: the rule in *Foss v Harbottle*

The general rule in *Foss v Harbottle*

The general rule, known as 'the rule in *Foss v Harbottle*',[7] is that, *subject to certain limited exceptions* (see below, p 514):

(i)   the proper claimant in an action for a wrong alleged to have been done to the company is the company itself (the '*proper claimant principle*'); and

(ii)   if the alleged wrong is a matter which it is competent for the company to settle itself (the '*internal management principle*') or, in the case of an irregularity to ratify or condone by its own internal procedure (the '*irregularity principle*'), then no individual member may bring action.

Notice that the rule has an impact on potential court actions in pursuit of wrongs done to a company *and* wrongs done personally to the members of the company. In both cases the rule restricts litigation by individual members unless they can bring themselves within the exceptions to the rule.

---

[7] (1843) 2 Hare 461 **[11.01]**. For further reading, see AJ Boyle, 'The Minority Shareholder in the Nineteenth Century' (1965) 28 MLR 317; Lord Wedderburn, 'Shareholders' Rights and the Rule in *Foss v Harbottle*' [1957] CLJ 194; [1958] CLJ 93; SM Beck, 'An Analysis of *Foss v Harbottle*', in JS Ziegel (ed), *Studies in Canadian Company Law* (1967); C Baxter, 'The True Spirit of *Foss v Harbottle*' (1987) 38 NILQ 6 and 'Shareholders' Derivative Action' (1974) 52 Can B Rev 159; LS Sealy, 'Problems of Standing, Pleading and Proof in Corporate Litigation' in *Company Law in Change* (1987), p 1; Hirt, 'The Company's Decision to Litigate Against its Directors' [2005] JBL 159.

Reforms to the rule in *Foss v Harbottle* introduced by CA 2006

The issue of minority member action in pursuit of company claims (along with the broader issues of member remedies discussed later in this Chapter) has been the subject of intensive study by the Law Commissions and the CLR. Both recommended the introduction of a new statutory derivative procedure, now provided by CA 2006 s 260ff, and made various other suggestions, most of which have now been adopted.[8]

The reforms introduced by CA 2006 do not touch the rule in *Foss v Harbottle* as it relates to personal claims: these remain subject to the full force of any limitations that emerge from the rule in *Foss v Harbottle*.

Instead, the CA 2006 reforms are directed at the permitted pursuit of the *company's* claims by individual members, ie at the *exceptions* to the rule in *Foss v Harbottle* as they apply to company claims. CA 2006 ss 260ff provides for a *statutory derivative action*[9] that may be used by members in their pursuit of these claims. The statutory procedure is exclusive, so the common law exceptions to the rule in *Foss v Harbottle* are replaced by these statutory conditions under which such claims may be pursued. It might have seemed possible, therefore, to omit any examination of the complicated common law rules relating to *Foss v Harbottle* for the future, but many of the conditions imposed by statute have links to conditions previously imposed by the common law, so the learning remains relevant, although no longer decisive.

The extracts below should be read with these qualifications in mind. Depending upon the issue in dispute, the cases may remain fully authoritative, or may simply provide illustrations of issues the courts must consider in exercising their statutory discretion (see below, pp 538 ff).

Operation of the rule in Foss v Harbottle

Statement of the general rule.

[11.01] *Foss v Harbottle* (1843) 2 Hare 461 (Court of Chancery (Vice-Chancellor))

This case was brought by two shareholders in the Victoria Park Co (incorporated by statute) against the company's five directors and others, alleging that the property of the company had been misapplied and wasted and certain mortgages improperly given over the company's property. It asked that the defendants should be held accountable to the company, and also sought the appointment of a receiver. The Vice-Chancellor ruled, however, that it was incompetent for the plaintiffs to bring such proceedings, the sole right to do so being that of the company in its corporate character.

WIGRAM V-C: The Victoria Park Company is an incorporated body, and the conduct with which the defendants are charged in this suit is an injury not to the plaintiffs exclusively; it is an injury to the whole corporation by individuals whom the corporation entrusted with powers to be exercised only for the good of the corporation. And from the case of *A-G v Wilson*[10] (without going further) it may

---

[8] See Law Commission, *Shareholder Remedies*, Law Com No 246, 1997, especially Part 6. The earlier Consultation Paper, *Shareholder Remedies-A Consultation Paper* (Law Commission Consultation Paper No 142, 1996) provides a good analysis of the rule in *Foss v Harbottle*, and other existing law. The Company Law Review, *Final Report*, 2001, largely endorsed the Law Commissions' proposals, but also proposed restrictions on interested members voting on ratification resolutions (see above, p 348) and enhancement of the power of disinterested members of both the board and the general meeting to provide input that could block derivative actions (see below, p 539): see CLR, *Developing the Framework* (2000) paras 4.112–4.139. These proposals were adopted in CA 2006.

[9] See above, pp 498 ff, and below, p 535.

[10] (1840) Cr & Ph 1.

be stated as undoubted law that a bill or information by a corporation will lie to be relieved in respect of injuries which the corporation has suffered at the hands of persons standing in the situation of the directors upon this record. This bill, however, differs from that in *A-G v Wilson* in this—that, instead of the corporation being formally represented as plaintiffs, the bill in this case is brought by two individual corporators, professedly on behalf of themselves and all the other members of the corporation, except those who committed the injuries complained of—the plaintiffs assuming to themselves the right and power in that manner to sue on behalf of and represent the corporation itself.

It was not, nor could it successfully be, argued that it was a matter of course for any individual members of a corporation thus to assume to themselves the right of suing in the name of the corporation. In law the corporation and the aggregate members of the corporation are not the same thing for purposes like this; and the only question can be whether the facts alleged in this case justify a departure from the rule which, prima facie, would require that the corporation should sue in its own name and in its corporate character or in the name of someone whom the law has appointed to be its representative . . .

The first objection taken in the argument for the defendants was that the individual members of the corporation cannot in any case sue in the form in which this bill is framed. During the argument I intimated an opinion, to which, upon further consideration, I fully adhere, that the rule was much too broadly stated on the part of the defendants. I think there are cases in which a suit might properly be so framed. Corporations like this, of a private nature, are in truth little more than private partnerships; and in cases which may easily be suggested it would be too much to hold that a society of private persons associated together in undertakings, which, though certainly beneficial to the public, are nevertheless matters of private property, are to be deprived of their civil rights, inter se, because, in order to make their common objects more attainable, the Crown or the legislature may have conferred upon them the benefit of a corporate character. If a case should arise of injury to a corporation by some of its members, for which no adequate remedy remained, except that of a suit by individual corporators in their private characters, and asking in such character the protection of those rights to which in their corporate character they were entitled, I cannot but think that . . . the claims of justice would be found superior to any difficulties arising out of technical rules respecting the mode in which corporations are required to sue.

But, on the other hand, it must not be without reasons of a very urgent character that established rules of law and practice are to be departed from, rules which, though in a sense technical, are founded on general principles of justice and convenience; and the question is whether a case is stated in this bill entitling the plaintiffs to sue in their private characters . . .

Now, that my opinion upon this case may be clearly understood, I will consider separately the two principal grounds of complaint to which I have adverted, with reference to a very marked distinction between them. The first ground of complaint is one which, though it might prima facie entitle the corporation to rescind the transactions complained of, does not absolutely and of necessity fall under the description of a void transaction. The corporation might elect to adopt those transactions, and hold the directors bound by them. In other words, the transactions admit of confirmation at the option of the corporation. The second ground of complaint may stand in a different position; I allude to the mortgaging in a manner not authorised by the powers of the Act. This, being beyond the powers of the corporation, may admit of no confirmation whilst any one dissenting voice is raised against it.[11] . . .

On the first point it is only necessary to refer to the clauses of the Act to show that, whilst the supreme governing body, the proprietors at a special general meeting assembled, retain the power of exercising the functions conferred upon them by the Act of Incorporation, it cannot be competent to individual corporators to sue in the manner proposed by the plaintiffs on the present record. This in effect purports to be a suit by cestui que trusts complaining of a fraud committed or alleged

---

11 [It had not at this time been settled that an *ultra vires* transaction was incapable of ratification.]

to have been committed by persons in a fiduciary character. The complaint is that those trustees have sold lands to themselves, ostensibly for the benefit of the cestui que trusts. The proposition I have advanced is that, although the act should prove to be voidable, the cestui que trusts may elect to confirm it. Now, who are the cestui que trusts in this case? The corporation, in a sense, is undoubtedly the cestui que trust; but the majority of the proprietors at a special general meeting assembled, independently of any general rules of law upon the subject, by the very terms of the incorporation in the present case, has power to bind the whole body, and every individual corporator must be taken to have come into the corporation upon the terms of being liable to be so bound. How then can this court act in a suit constituted as this is, if it is to be assumed, for the purposes of the argument, that the powers of the body of the proprietors are still in existence, and may lawfully be exercised for a purpose like that I have suggested? Whilst the court may be declaring the acts complained of to be void at the suit of the present plaintiffs, who in fact may be the only proprietors who disapprove of them, the governing body of proprietors may defeat the decree by lawfully resolving upon the confirmation of the very acts which are the subject of the suit. The very fact that the governing body of proprietors assembled at the special general meeting may so bind even a reluctant minority is decisive to show that the frame of this suit cannot be sustained whilst that body retains its functions . . .

The second point which relates to the charges and incumbrances alleged to have been illegally made on the property of the company is open to the reasoning which I have applied to the first point, upon the question whether, in the present case, individual members are at liberty to complain in the form adopted by this bill; for why should this anomalous form of suit be resorted to, if the powers of the corporation may be called into exercise? But this part of the case is of greater difficulty upon the merits. I follow, with entire assent, the opinion expressed by the Vice-Chancellor in *Preston v Grand Collier Dock Co*,[12] that if a transaction be void, and not merely voidable, the corporation cannot confirm it, so as to bind a dissenting minority of its members. But that will not dispose of this question. The case made with regard to these mortgages or incumbrances is, that they were executed in violation of the provisions of the Act. The mortgagees are not defendants to the bill, nor does the bill seek to avoid the security itself, if it could be avoided, on which I give no opinion. The bill prays inquiries with a view to proceedings being taken aliunde to set aside these transactions against the mortgagees. The object of this bill against the defendants is to make them individually and personally responsible to the extent of the injury alleged to have been received by the corporation from the making of the mortgages. Whatever the case might be, if the object of the suit was to rescind these transactions, and the allegations in the bill showed that justice could not be done to the shareholders without allowing two to sue on behalf of themselves and others, very different considerations arise in a case like the present, in which the consequences only of the alleged illegal acts are sought to be visited personally upon the directors. The money forming the consideration for the mortgages was received, and was expended in, or partly in, the transactions which are the subject of the first ground of complaint. Upon this, one question appears to me to be, whether the company could confirm the former transactions, take the benefit of the money that has been raised, and yet, as against the directors personally, complain of the acts which they have done, by means whereof the company obtains that benefit which I suppose to have been admitted and adopted by such confirmation. I think it would not be open to the company to do this; and my opinion already expressed on the first point is that the transactions which constitute the first ground of complaint may possibly be beneficial to the company, and may be so regarded by the proprietors, and admit of confirmation. I am of opinion that this question—the question of confirmation or avoidance—cannot properly be litigated upon this record, regard being had to the existing state and powers of the corporation, and that therefore that part of the bill which seeks to visit the directors personally with the consequences of the impeached mortgages and charges, the benefit of which the company enjoys, is in the same predicament as that which relates to the other subjects of complaint. Both

[12] (1840) 11 Sim 327.

questions stand on the same ground, and, for the reasons which I stated in considering the former point, these demurrers must be allowed.

The proper plaintiff principle: deciding whether a wrong has been done to the company or to the members personally.

[11.02] Mozley v Alston (1847) 1 Ph 790 (Court of Chancery (Lord Chancellor))

[The facts appear from the judgment.]

LORD COTTENHAM LC: This is a case in which two persons, not alleging distinctly that they are shareholders in a railway company, but so describing themselves, file a bill in which they allege that, owing to circumstances which I do not particularly enter into, twelve persons, who were originally appointed directors, ought, at a day now past, to have balloted out four of their number in order that four others might be elected in their stead; that they omitted to do so, and that, consequently, there is not now a body of directors constituted according to the Act; and, therefore, praying an injunction to the effect that these twelve persons may be restrained from voting or acting as directors of the company . . .

Now, it is not my intention to give any opinion upon the construction of the Act, because I see quite enough to make it my duty to allow these demurrers, without going into that question; and, indeed, one of the grounds on which I have come to this conclusion is, that it is not within the jurisdiction of this court to entertain that question at all, and I therefore abstain from expressing any opinion upon it.

The bill, as I stated, is a bill by two shareholders in their individual characters only, praying relief, in which all the other shareholders are interested. It is quite clear that some years ago no one would have entertained any doubt that such a bill was demurrable. It is true that the rule which requires all persons interested to be parties has been relaxed to meet the exigencies of modern times, it being found that too strict an adherence to it would operate in many cases as a denial of justice, and leave parties who had a real grievance without a remedy. And, therefore, where the grievance complained of is common to a body of persons too numerous to be all made parties, the court has permitted one or more of them to sue on behalf of all, subject, however, to this restriction, that the relief which is prayed must be one in which the parties whom the plaintiff professes to represent, have all of them an interest identical with his own . . .

The complaint against the defendants is, that they are illegally exercising the powers of directors, and illegally retaining the seal and property of the company. That, if it be an injury at all, it is an injury not to the plaintiffs personally, but to the corporation of which they are members—a usurpation of the office of directors, and, therefore, an invasion of the rights of the corporation; and yet no reason is assigned by the bill why the corporation does not put itself in motion to seek a remedy.

A case occurred some time ago before Vice-Chancellor Wigram, which is identical in principle with the present, I mean the case of *Foss v Harbottle* [11.01]. An attempt, indeed, was made to distinguish them, but it entirely failed. In one respect, that was a stronger case for the interposition of this court than the present, for the bill stated a case of malversation in the corporate officers which was properly a subject of equitable relief. The plaintiffs sued, not as here in their individual characters only, but on behalf of themselves and all the other shareholders, except a few who were made defendants; but the Vice-Chancellor, after examining all the authorities, decided that such a bill could not be supported; and, as one of the reasons for coming to that conclusion, he said that, for anything that appeared to the contrary, there existed in the company the means of rectifying what was complained of, by a suit in the name of the corporation. And the same observation applies with still greater force to the present case, for not only does it not appear that the plaintiffs have not the means of putting the corporation in motion, but the bill expressly alleges that a large majority of the shareholders are of the same opinion with them; and, if that be so, there is obviously nothing to prevent the company from filing a bill in its corporate character to remedy the evil complained of. Such a bill would be free from the objections to which I have referred as existing in this case, for it would be a bill by a body legally authorised to represent the interests of the shareholders generally; but to allow, under such circumstances, a bill to be filed by some shareholders on behalf of themselves and others, would be to admit a form of pleading which was originally introduced on the ground of necessity alone, to a case in which it is obvious that no such necessity exists . . .

➤ **Note**

Lord Cottenham's references to the novel form of pleading, modifying 'the rule which requires all persons interested to be parties . . . a form of pleading which was originally introduced on the ground of necessity alone' are an allusion to the representative action (above, p 499), which had been devised not long before.

➤ **Question**

Was the Lord Chancellor right in saying that the acts complained of were not 'an injury to the plaintiffs personally'? (Cf *Pulbrook v Richmond Consolidated Mining Co* **[5.01]**.)

The 'internal management principle'.

[11.03] Bamford v Bamford [1970] Ch 212 (Court of Appeal)

[For the facts and another part of the decision, see **[4.33]**.]

RUSSELL LJ: It is true that the point before us is not an objection to the proceedings on *Foss v Harbottle* **[11.01]** grounds. But it seems to me to march in step with the principles that underlie the rule in that case. None of the factors that admit exceptions to that rule appear to exist here. The harm done by the assumed improperly motivated allotment is a harm done to the company, of which only the company can complain. It would be for the company by ordinary resolution to decide whether or not to proceed against the directors for compensation for misfeasance. Equally, assuming that the allottee could not rely upon *Royal British Bank v Turquand* **[3.15]** it would be for the company to decide whether to institute proceedings to avoid the voidable allotment: and again this decision would be one for the company in general meeting to decide by ordinary resolution. To litigate or not to litigate, apart from very special circumstances, is for decision by such a resolution. If, as I consider, the company could validly decide by ordinary resolution not to institute proceedings to avoid the voidable allotment—a resolution which could not possibly be said to contradict or alter the articles—it seems to me to support entirely the view that an ordinary resolution in the terms posed in the point of law[13] would be effective, having as it would in substance the same purpose and effect as a resolution not to bring proceedings to avoid the allotment . . .

HARMAN LJ delivered a concurring judgment.

KARMINSKI LJ concurred.

➤ **Notes**

1. In *Re a Company* [1987] BCLC 82 at 84 Hoffmann J said:

Although the alleged breach of fiduciary duty by the board is in theory a breach of its duty to the company, the wrong to the company is not the substance of the complaint. The company is not

---

13   [Ie a resolution to ratify the allotment made irregularly by the directors.]

particularly concerned with who its shareholders are. The true basis of the action is an alleged infringement of the petitioner's individual rights as a shareholder. The allotment is alleged to be an improper and unlawful exercise of the powers granted to the board by the articles of association, which constitute a contract between the company and its members. These are fiduciary powers, not to be exercised for an improper purpose, and it is generally speaking improper 'for the directors to use their fiduciary powers over the shares in the company purely for the purpose of destroying an existing majority, or creating a new majority which did not previously exist'. (See *Howard Smith Ltd v Ampol Petroleum Ltd* **[6.09]**.) An abuse of these powers is an infringement of a member's contractual rights under the articles.

2. Similarly, in *Residues Treatment and Trading Co Ltd v Southern Resources Ltd (No 4)* (1988) 14 ACLR 569, the Supreme Court of South Australia held that an action to challenge an allotment of shares on the ground that the directors had acted for an improper purpose came within the 'personal rights' exception to the rule in *Foss v Harbottle* **[11.01]** (as well as being a breach of duty to the company for which the company itself could have sued), since such an allotment brought about an impermissible dilution of the plaintiff member's voting rights. King CJ said, at p 575:

A member's voting rights and the rights of participation which they provide in the decision-making of the company are a fundamental attribute of membership and are rights which the member should be able to protect by legal action against improper diminution.

(He also expressed doubts whether *Bamford v Bamford* **[11.03]** was correct in treating such an act on the part of the directors as ratifiable by the members, but it is submitted that *Bamford v Bamford* may be defended on this point.)

➤ Questions

1. Given the comments in the Note above, was Russell LJ right to say that the harm done by an improperly motivated allotment was a harm to the company of which only the company could complain? Are these various views reconcilable?

2. Is it of any concern to a company who has control of it?

The 'irregularity principle'.

[11.04] MacDougall v Gardiner (1875) 1 Ch D 13 (Court of Appeal)

[For other proceedings between the same parties, see **[11.05]**.]

Gardiner, the chairman of the Emma Silver Mining Co, had adjourned a general meeting of the company without acceding to the request of a shareholder, MacDougall, and others, that a poll be held on the question of the adjournment. MacDougall now claimed a declaration that the chairman's action was improper, and an injunction restraining the directors from taking further action. The Court of Appeal held that this was a matter of internal management in which it should not interfere.

MELLISH LJ: In my opinion, if the thing complained of is a thing which in substance the majority of the company are entitled to do, or if something has been done irregularly which the majority of the company are entitled to do regularly, or if something has been done illegally which the majority of the company are entitled to do legally, there can be no use in having a litigation about it, the ultimate end of which is only that a meeting has to be called, and then ultimately the majority gets its wishes. Is it not better that the rule should be adhered to that if it is a thing which the majority are the masters of, the majority in substance shall be entitled to have their will followed? If it is a matter of that nature, it only comes to this, that the majority are the only persons who can complain that a thing which they are entitled to do has been done irregularly; and that, as I understand it, is what has been decided by the cases of *Mozley v Alston* **[11.02]** and *Foss v Harbottle* **[11.01]**. In my opinion that is the rule that is to be maintained. Of course if the majority are abusing their powers, and are depriving the minority of their rights, that is an entirely different thing, and there the minority are entitled to come before this court to maintain their rights; but if what is complained of is simply that something which the majority are entitled to do has been done or undone irregularly, then I think it is quite right that nobody should have a right to set that aside, or to institute a suit in Chancery about it, except the company itself.

➤ Note

For a comment on this case, and a suggested reconciliation with the apparently contrary ruling in *Pender v Lushington* **[11.15]**, see C Baxter, 'Irregular Company Meetings' [1976] JBL 323, and the same author's 'The Role of the Judge in Enforcing Shareholder Rights' [1983] CLJ 96. His view is that 'the court will not interfere in the affairs of a company unless it is necessary to do so and that interference is always unnecessary when it has no practical consequence'. In the context of irregularities in company meetings, references to *Foss v Harbottle* are often gratuitous and irrelevant.

➤ Questions

1. The company's articles of association gave any five or more members the right to demand a poll, and MacDougall had the necessary support. Was there not a wrong done here to MacDougall, a denial of his rights as a member? If so, how do you think he might have enforced them?

2. Is the *ratio decidendi* of this case the same as that of the court in *Foss v Harbottle*?

Ensuring the company is acting legitimately in litigating in its own name

Modern company constitutions are likely to give the board of directors exclusive competence to decide to litigate. No problem arises, therefore, if an action is brought in the company's name on the instruction of the board of directors (or other appropriate organ).

If other people begin an action in the name of the company, however, they do so at their peril, for the defendant may challenge their right to use the company's name, and if they cannot show that they have proper authorisation, the case will be struck out and both they and their solicitors will be personally liable to pay the costs.

In circumstances where it is not clear that proper authority exists for use of the company name, it seems the court will not intervene in the company's affairs to *order* a meeting of members to determine the matter where those who are constitutionally empowered to summon or requisition a meeting *bona fide* decline to do so (see below, *MacDougall v Gardiner* **[11.05]**). On the other hand, it also seems that the court will adjourn proceedings to enable a general meeting (or other competent organ) to provide the necessary ratification of what would otherwise be an unauthorised exercise of power in bringing the claim in the company's name. Then the problem becomes one of determining whether the irregularity can be cured by such a process (see below, *Danish Mercantile v Co Ltd v Beaumont* **[11.06]** and the associated Note).

[11.05] MacDougall v Gardiner (1875) 10 Ch App 606
(Court of Appeal in Chancery)

The plaintiff in a representative action sought a declaration that certain resolutions had been validly passed at a general meeting, or alternatively an order that a meeting of members be summoned for the purpose of putting the resolutions to it afresh. Malins V-C ordered a meeting to be held, but on appeal it was held that the court had no power to do so.

[For other proceedings between the same parties, see [11.04].]

JAMES LJ: [The] court has no jurisdiction whatever to do that which it is for the company itself to do according to the provisions of the articles. If a general meeting is wanted for any purpose, then the directors, if they think it for the interests of the company, have power to call a general meeting; but I do not think that the court has any jurisdiction to compel the directors to call the meeting, when they may honestly think it not for the interests of the company to do so. Then if the directors do not call the meeting, it is left to the shareholders to call it, with these restrictions, that before the company can be called together, and before they can be put to any such inconvenience, one-fifth[14] of the shareholders must give in a requisition to the directors, and if one-fifth do not join in it, then there is no power to call the meeting.

Now, what power have we to say that a general meeting is to be called, if the directors do not think it right, and if one-fifth of the shareholders will not sign a requisition for the purpose? We have no authority, and there is, as it appears to me, no reason why we could interfere to do that which the shareholders have a right to do for themselves. The great principle laid down in the two cases of *Mozley v Alston* [11.02] and *Foss v Harbottle* [11.01] was, that whatever should be done by the company itself through its own internal organisation, ought to be left to the company, and ought not to be interfered with by this court . . .

MELLISH LJ delivered a concurring judgment.

> ➤ Note

This was not a case involving a dispute about the right to use the company's name in litigation: all that the judge was doing was enunciating the principle of majority rule, and drawing attention to the good sense that lies behind the normal constitutional provisions which allow a meeting to be requisitioned only when a significant percentage of supporters can be mustered.

[11.06] Danish Mercantile Co Ltd v Beaumont [1951] Ch 680
(Court of Appeal)

The defendants applied in interlocutory proceedings to strike out the name of the plaintiff company on the ground that the action had been commenced by the plaintiff's managing director without authority. Roxburgh J held that whether this was so or not, the action had since been ratified by the company (or rather by its liquidator, it being now in liquidation). The Court of Appeal affirmed his decision.

JENKINS LJ: I would refer to the passage in *Buckley on the Companies Acts* (12th edn), p 169, where the relevant law is, in my view, correctly summarised. The passage occurs in the course of a discussion on the circumstances in which a company's name can be used as plaintiff in an action and the

---

[14] Now generally 10%: see CA 2006 s 303.

exceptions to the general rule that a company is the only proper plaintiff in respect of a wrong done to the company, a discussion, in short, of the aspect of company law related to what is commonly called the rule in *Foss v Harbottle* **[11.01]**.

The relevant passage (in *Buckley*) for the present purpose is in these terms: '(6) If the case be one in which the company ought to be plaintiff, the fact that the seal is in the possession of the adverse party will not necessarily preclude the intending plaintiffs from using the company's name. Neither will it be necessary to obtain the resolution of a general meeting in favour of the action before the writ is issued. In many cases the delay might amount to a denial of justice. In a case of urgency, the intending plaintiffs may use the company's name at their peril, and subject to their being able to show that they have the support of the majority. In an action so constituted, the court may give interlocutory relief, taking care that a meeting be called at the earliest possible date to determine whether the action really has the support of the majority or not.'

That passage, where it refers to the calling of a meeting, accords with the well-settled practice of the court in cases in which, in proceedings brought by a company, a dispute arises as to the authority with which the company's name has been used as plaintiff. It is common practice in such cases to adjourn any motion brought to strike out the company's name, with a view to a meeting being called to see whether the company desires the action to be brought or not . . .

I think that the true position is simply that a solicitor who starts proceedings in the name of a company without verifying whether he has proper authority so to do, or under an erroneous assumption as to the authority, does so at his own peril, and that, so long as the matter rests there, the action is not properly constituted. [It] can be stayed at any time, provided that the aggrieved defendant does not unduly delay his application; but it is open at any time to the purported plaintiff to ratify the act of the solicitor who started the action to adopt the proceedings, to approve all that has been done in the past, and to instruct the solicitor to continue the action. When that has been done, then, in accordance with the ordinary law of principal and agent and in accordance with the ordinary doctrine of ratification, in my view the defect in the proceedings as originally constituted is cured; and it is no longer open to the defendant to object on the ground that the proceedings thus ratified and adopted were, in the first instance, brought without proper authority.

For these reasons I am of the opinion that Roxburgh J came to a right conclusion, and that this appeal fails . . .

HODSON LJ delivered a concurring judgment.

➤ Note

See the similar decision of the House of Lords in *Alexander Ward & Co Ltd v Samyang Navigation Co Ltd* [1975] 1 WLR 673, where ratification by a liquidator of proceedings instituted without authority was held to operate retrospectively, so as to validate every step taken in the proceedings, including the arrest of a ship, which had occurred before the liquidator's appointment.

[11.07] Breckland Group Holdings Ltd v London & Suffolk Properties Ltd [1989] BCLC 100 (Chancery Division)

An action against A and others had been commenced in the name of L Ltd. The solicitors had acted on the instructions of H. H and A indirectly controlled respectively 51% and 49% of the votes at a general meeting of L Ltd, but under the terms of a shareholder agreement no decision on various matters, including the institution of legal proceedings, could be taken by the board of L Ltd without the affirmative support of two directors, each representing one of the major shareholders. Harman J held that this procedure could not be by-passed: without such a decision the action would not be properly constituted, and a general meeting (at which, of course, H's votes would carry the day) had no competence to interfere in the matter. The learned judge's ruling was based in part on the terms of the shareholder agreement and in part on the wording of an article which gave power to the directors to manage the business of the company.

HARMAN J: . . . [Mr Tuckey, counsel for the defendants] conceded that the action at the date of issue of the writ and today was and is unauthorised. . . .

There has been convened a board meeting . . . at which . . . a resolution is likely to be proposed adopting and ratifying [the action] which will, following *Danish Mercantile Co Ltd & Ors v Beaumont & Anor* [1951] Ch 680, amount to complete ratification and the adoption from the beginning of the action. The action will become completely valid from square one if the board so decide. . . .

. . . One can plainly say that if and when a validly convened general meeting is held one can be sure of what the outcome will be. It would be an affirmative vote in favour of the wishes of [the defendant]. Thus, says Mr. Tuckey, it does not really matter whether the board meeting will or will not come to a conclusion in favour of ratifying and adopting [the action] because it can be foreseen now that that action will be ratified and adopted at a general meeting when one is properly convened, if necessary, and since one can forecast with certainty the outcome the court is not in the business of making people jump through unnecessary hoops and therefore will not wait for the outcome of a pre-ordained meeting.

I believe that is sound argument so far as it goes. It omits the difficult point of law with which I am faced at 4.20 on a Friday evening; can a general meeting in circumstances of this sort pass a resolution to adopt "material legal proceedings" when by the provisions of art. 80 of the articles of association which govern this company such a matter is within the remit of the board. It is not only placed within the remit of the board by the articles because of some drafting process. The shareholders' agreement points to the shareholders thinking it was a matter that the board ought to control and consider. What is more the shareholders' agreement points to it being accepted by both parties that consent of both parties to the institution of legal proceedings at a board meeting was a requirement for such valid institution.

The question whether articles of association in the form of art. 80, which applies to this company, are such as to allow a general meeting to give directions to directors about the conduct of the business of a company has long been known to be a vexed subject. The decision of Sir George Jessel M.R., one of the greatest of all equity judges, in *Pender v. Lushington* **[11.15]**, is, as always with that great judge, trenchant, clear and to the point. He firmly holds that in that case he ought not, there being an action started without any proper authorisation on behalf of the company, to strike out the name of the company on the ground that the action was unauthorised, but he ought to stand the matter over to let a general meeting be called to decide whether the company's name is to be used or not. However, that matter does not appear to have turned on the terms of the articles of association there, and I cannot find in the citation of facts in the report of that case any reference to an article in terms anything like art. 80 in this case.

[He then examined other relevant precedents, and continued:]

[Farwell LJ in *Salmon v Quin and Axtens Ltd* **[4.06]**] goes on to say that the case is entirely governed if not by the decision, at any rate by the reasoning of the Lords Justices in *Automatic Self Cleansing* **[4.05]**, and he cites Buckley LJ in *Gramophone and Typewriter Ltd v Stanley* [1908] 2 KB 89 **[2.05]**, at p 105:

" . . . even a resolution of a numerical majority at a general meeting of the company cannot impose its will upon the directors when the articles have confided to them the control of the company's affairs. The directors are not servants to obey directions given by the shareholders as individuals; they are not agents appointed by and bound to serve the shareholders as their principals. They are persons who may by the regulations be entrusted with the control of the business, and if so entrusted they can be dispossessed from that control only by the statutory majority which can alter the articles."

Farwell LJ went on to say:

"Any other construction might, I think, be disastrous, because it might lead to an interference by a bare majority very inimical to the interests of the minority who had come into a company on the footing that the business should be managed by the board of directors."

[Harman J then considered other authorities, including *John Shaw & Sons* **[4.07]**, and continued:]

Thus, as it seems to me, there is little doubt that the law is that where matters are confided by articles such as art. 80 to the conduct of the business by the directors, it is not a matter where the general meeting can intervene. Mr. Tuckey sought to distinguish the cases by saying that in the cases which we have referred to the directors had come to one decision and the general meeting sought to overrule them and come to an opposite decision. In my belief that factor or distinction which undoubtedly exists is not a distinction which in law affects the principles which I have to try and apply. The principle, as I see it, is that art. 80 confides the management of the business to the directors and in such a case it is not for the general meeting to interfere. It is a fortiori when the shareholders coming together have specifically resolved some matters be required to have their joint consent and have confided that matter particularly to the directors. That seems to me to reinforce the general proposition which I derive from the authorities cited.

Thus, as it seems to me, the action was, as is admitted, wrongly brought; it cannot at present be known whether the board will adopt it or ratify it on 3 August. If the board do not adopt it, a general meeting would have no power whatever to override that decision of the board and to adopt it for itself. Thus at the moment there can be no certainty whatever as to what would happen. It seems to me that in those circumstances I ought to restrain further steps in this action pending a decision as to whether the company will by its proper organ, that is the board, adopt it. It may do so. If so it will be valid and ratified and adopted from its initiation. . . .

➤ Questions

1. Does it follow from the approach in *Breckland* **[11.07]** that the practice referred to in *Danish Mercantile Co Ltd v Beaumont* **[11.06]** is out of line with modern views on the division of powers between a company's two principal organs, and that where there is a board capable of acting (and *a fortiori* where the articles or the terms of a shareholder agreement require some special procedure), a reference to the general meeting would be wrong?

2. Does the *Breckland* judgment display a confusion between authority to *instigate* litigation, and authority to *ratify* an unauthorised instigation? Could it ever be the case that although the board has sole authority to instigate litigation, the general meeting has authority to ratify an unauthorised instigation?

3. Are the legal requirements for a proper decision to instigate litigation (by the board or any other appropriate organ) different from the legal requirements for a proper decision to ratify an unauthorised action (see above, pp 509 ff and 348 ff)?

4. Is *Danish Mercantile* **[11.06]** in conflict with *MacDougall v Gardiner* **[11.04]**, in that in the former case it seems to be assumed that a meeting to ratify will be held at the court's suggestion, even though the self-appointed initiator of the litigation probably could not have requisitioned a meeting on his own and nobody else may wish to call one? It is doubtful whether for this purpose the court could invoke its powers under CA 2006 s 306, since s 306 applies only where it is 'impracticable' to call a meeting in the ordinary way.

Exceptions to the general rule in *Foss v Harbottle*

The true exceptions[15] to the rule in *Foss v Harbottle* are those anomalous instances recognised by the common law where members, acting alone or together, are permitted to pursue a cause of action that is vested in the company. If successful, the members will obtain a remedy that accrues to the company, not to the members who have taken the action.

This type of claim by members in pursuit of a remedy for the company is called a *derivative claim*, indicating that the rights being pursued are not the personal rights of the litigating members, but rights *derived from* the company.

Until CA 2006, the circumstances in which these claims were possible were defined by the common law 'exceptions to the rule in *Foss v Harbottle*', and the 'derivative claim' procedure then followed by the members was set out in the Civil Procedure Rules.[16] CA 2006 ss 260ff has changed this fundamentally. The Act provides a new derivative procedure (to be supplemented by amended Civil Procedure Rules[17]). It sets out what sorts of company claims can be pursued, and when. It provides that derivative claims may *only* be brought under the provisions of the CA 2006 (s 260ff) or in pursuance of a court order in 'unfair prejudice' proceedings under CA 2006 s 994 (see below, pp 552 ff): CA 2006, s 260(2) (see below, pp 535 ff). These new rules make reference to ideas that are fundamental to the common law exceptions to the rule in *Foss v Harbottle*, so some of those cases are retained in this chapter, and appear below.

The common law exceptions to the rule in *Foss v Harbottle* are usually grouped under four heads. The general rule (restricting claims to the court) is said to have no application where:[18]

(i)   the act complained of is *ultra vires* or illegal;

(ii)   the matter is one which could validly be done or sanctioned only by some special majority of members;

---

[15] As will be apparent later, some of the recognised 'exceptions' to the rule in *Foss v Harbottle* are nothing of the sort. They are instances where it is recognised that shareholders can pursue *personal* claims (against the company or against other shareholders) for a remedy that accrues to them personally. Once it is recognised that the wrong in question has been done to the *shareholder*, there is nothing exceptional about this outcome (although the rule in *Foss v Harbottle* limits even these claims by means of the 'irregularity principle', see above, p 508).

[16] See *Barrett v Duckett* [1995] 1 BCLC 243, below, p 534. Also see Civil Procedure Rules 1998, r 19.9 (Derivative Claims):

(1) This rule applies where a company, other incorporated body or trade union is alleged to be entitled to claim a remedy and a claim is made by one or more members of the company, body or trade union for it to be given that remedy (a 'derivative claim').

(2) The company, body or trade union for whose benefit a remedy is sought must be a defendant to the claim.

(3) After the claim form has been issued the claimant must apply to the court for permission to continue the claim and may not take any other step in the proceedings except—
    (a) as provided by paragraph (5);
    (b) where the court gives permission.

(4) An application in accordance with paragraph (3) must be supported by written evidence.

(5) The—
    (a) claim form;
    (b) application notice; and
    (c) written evidence in support of the application, must be served on the defendant within the period within which the claim form must be served and, in any event, at least 14 days before the court is to deal with the application.

(6) If the court gives the claimant permission to continue the claim, the time within which the defence must be filed is 14 days after the date on which the permission is given or such period as the court may specify.

(7) The court may order the company, body or trade union to indemnify the claimant against any liability in respect of costs incurred in the claim.

[17] See *Explanatory Notes*, para 493.

[18] These are the heads used as a basis for discussion by Wedderburn, 'Shareholders' Rights and the Rule in *Foss v Harbottle*' [1957] CLJ 194 at 203, to whom grateful acknowledgement is made. The same exceptions are listed (in a different order) by Jenkins LJ in *Edwards v Halliwell* [11.08].

(iii) the personal and individual rights of the claimant as a member have been invaded; or

(iv) what has been done amounts to a 'fraud on the minority'[19] and the wrongdoers are themselves in control of the company.

Whether these are properly regarded as exceptions depends upon the form in which the rule is stated. If the rule is expressed simply—that the only proper claimant in the case of a wrong affecting a company is the company itself—then all four may be seen as exceptions, for in each case an individual member is allowed to sue. But if we think of acts which are strictly (and exclusively) wrongs to the company as a corporate body, then only the fourth is a true exception.

Of course, not all wrongs that a member complains of will be exclusively one thing or the other: an unconstitutional act by those in control may violate *both* shareholder's individual membership rights *and* those of the company, as has been recognised on many occasions: see, eg *Pulbrook v Richmond Consolidated Mining Co* **[5.01]** and *Pender v Lushington* **[11.15]**. It ought to be possible in such a case for an action to be brought in the name of either the member or the company (for different remedies), but unfortunately the courts have not always appreciated this. We find them giving an individual complainant short shrift and showing him the door of the court on the basis of a somewhat peremptory ruling that the wrong person has been named as plaintiff. For an example, see *Lee v Chou Wen Hsien* (below, p 543); and contrast the views of Hoffmann J in *Re a Company* (above, p 507) with those expressed in *Bamford v Bamford* **[11.03]**. If there really is a *de facto* policy to discourage minority members from engaging in litigation, it could hardly be better illustrated! And, added to that, there is the modern debate on '*reflective loss*', which aims to ensure that if both forms of action are possible, there is no chance of double recovery for the same loss (see below, pp 543 ff).

Exception 1: the act complained of is ultra vires or illegal

This exception now needs to be restated in consequence of the abolition of the *ultra vires* doctrine (by CA 2006 s 39), and the protections afforded to third parties dealing with the company in good faith where directors have acted beyond their constitutional powers (s 40). These provisions do not affect the normal rights of members (whatever they are) to bring proceedings to restrain the doing of an act by the directors which is beyond their constitutional powers to bind the company (except an act to be done in fulfilment of an existing legal obligation): CA 2006 s 40(4).

Exception 1 also applies to acts which are illegal: eg the support of an unlawful strike *(Taylor v National Union of Mineworkers (Derbyshire Area)* (below, p 533), or a transaction which violates the capital maintenance or financial assistance provisions of the Companies Acts *(Smith v Croft (No 2)* **[11.14]**). These two cases tend to confirm the view that, in regard to illegal acts, the rules worked out with reference to *ultra vires* transactions will apply. That is, an individual member has a right to sue to restrain a *threatened* unlawful act *(Simpson v Westminster Palace Hotel Co* (1860) 8 HL Cas 712, HL) and to bring a derivative action to have an unlawful act set aside—which may involve restitutionary relief against a third party *(Russell v Wakefield Waterworks Co* (1875) LR 20 Eq 474); however, a claim to have directors and possibly others made personally liable for loss suffered by the company as a result of such a transaction will be treated in the same way as a fraud on the minority (below, pp 517 ff), and may not proceed without the support of a majority of disinterested shareholders. And, of course, illegal acts, like those under the former *ultra vires* doctrine, will continue to be unratifiable.

---

[19] More properly described in most cases as a fraud on the *company*: see the discussion below, pp 524 ff.

Exception 2: the matter is one which could validly be done or sanctioned only by some special majority of members

The rule in *Foss v Harbottle* has no application where the articles require a special majority or procedure and the proceedings are brought to challenge a decision which has disregarded such a requirement.

[11.08] Edwards v Halliwell [1950] 2 All ER 1064 (Court of Appeal)

The plaintiffs as members of a trade union sued the union and the members of its executive committee claiming a declaration that a decision to increase the union dues payable by members was invalid on the ground that the union's rules, requiring a two-thirds majority vote on a ballot of members, had not been observed. Vaisey J granted the declaration, and his decision was affirmed by the Court of Appeal.

JENKINS LJ: The rule in *Foss v Harbottle* **[11.01]**, as I understand it, comes to no more than this. First, the proper plaintiff in an action in respect of a wrong alleged to be done to a company or association of persons is prima facie the company or the association of persons itself. Secondly, where the alleged wrong is a transaction which might be made binding on the company or association and on all its members by a simple majority of the members, no individual member of the company is allowed to maintain an action in respect of that matter for the simple reason that, if a mere majority of the members of the company or association is in favour of what has been done, then cadit quaestio. No wrong has been done to the company or association and there is nothing in respect of which anyone can sue. If, on the other hand, a simple majority of members of the company or association is against what has been done, then there is no valid reason why the company or association itself should not sue. In my judgment, it is implicit in the rule that the matter relied on as constituting the cause of action should be a cause of action properly belonging to the general body of corporators or members of the company or association as opposed to a cause of action which some individual member can assert in his own right.

The cases falling within the general ambit of the rule are subject to certain exceptions. It has been noted in the course of argument that in cases where the act complained of is wholly ultra vires the company or association the rule has no application because there is no question of the transaction being confirmed by any majority. It has been further pointed out that where what has been done amounts to what is generally called in these cases a fraud on the minority and the wrongdoers are themselves in control of the company, the rule is relaxed in favour of the aggrieved minority who are allowed to bring what is known as a minority shareholders' action on behalf of themselves and all others. The reason for this is that, if they were denied that right, their grievance could never reach the court because the wrongdoers themselves, being in control, would not allow the company to sue. Those exceptions are not directly in point in this case, but they show, especially the last one, that the rule is not an inflexible rule and it will be relaxed where necessary in the interests of justice.

There is a further exception which seems to me to touch this case directly. That is the exception noted by Romer J in *Cotter v National Union of Seamen*.[20] He pointed out that the rule did not prevent an individual member from suing if the matter in respect of which he was suing was one which could validly be done or sanctioned, not by a simple majority of the members of the company or association, but only by some special majority, as, for instance, in the case of a limited company under the Companies Act, a special resolution duly passed as such. As Romer J pointed out, the reason for that exception is clear, because otherwise, if the rule were applied in its full rigour, a company which, by its directors, had broken its own regulations by doing something without a special resolution which could only be done validly by a special resolution could assert that it alone was the proper plaintiff in any consequent action and the effect would be to allow a company acting in

[20] [1929] 2 Ch 58.

breach of its articles to do de facto by ordinary resolution that which according to its own regulations could only be done by special resolution. That exception exactly fits the present case inasmuch as here the act complained of is something which could only have been validly done, not by a simple majority, but by a two-thirds majority obtained on a ballot vote. In my judgment, therefore, the reliance on the rule in *Foss v Harbottle* in the present case may be regarded as misconceived on that ground alone.

I would go further. In my judgment, this is a case of a kind which is not even within the general ambit of the rule. It is not a case where what is complained of is a wrong done to the union, a matter in respect of which the cause of action would primarily and properly belong to the union. It is a case in which certain members of a trade union complain that the union, acting through the delegate meeting and the executive council in breach of the rules by which the union and every member of the union are bound, has invaded the individual rights of the complainant members, who are entitled to maintain themselves in full membership with all the rights and privileges appertaining to that status so long as they pay contributions in accordance with the tables of contributions as they stood before the purported alterations of 1943, unless and until the scale of contributions is validly altered by the prescribed majority obtained on a ballot vote. Those rights, these members claim, have been invaded. The gist of the case is that the personal and individual rights of membership of each of them have been invaded by a purported, but invalid, alteration of the tables of contributions. In those circumstances, it seems to me the rule in *Foss v Harbottle* has no application at all, for the individual members who are suing sue, not in the right of the union, but in their own right to protect from invasion their own individual rights as members . . .

EVERSHED MR and ASQUITH LJ delivered concurring judgments.

Exception 3: the personal and individual rights of the claimant as a member have been invaded

This is a false 'exception', in that members are simply being allowed to pursue their own claims. *Edwards v Halliwell* **[11.08]**, above, is an example. *Personal claims* by members to remedy maladministration are considered below, at pp 540 ff.

Exception 4: what has been done amounts to a 'fraud on the minority' and the wrongdoers are themselves in control of the company

This is the most important common law exception to the rule in *Foss v Harbottle*, and perhaps the only true exception. Aspects of the cases extracted below will remain relevant to successful pursuit of the new statutory derivative action (CA 2006 ss 260ff).

Fraud by the directors; voting of newly acquired shares prohibited.

[11.09] Atwool v Merryweather (1867) LR 5 Eq 464n
(Court of Chancery (Vice-Chancellor))

Atwool brought this action on behalf of himself and all the other shareholders in the East Pant Du Lead Mining Co Ltd against Merryweather, Whitworth and the company, claiming rescission of a contract for the sale of certain mines by Merryweather and Whitworth to the company, and the return of money paid and shares allotted to them as consideration for the sale, on the ground that they had made a concealed profit. An earlier action, in which Atwool had filed a bill in the name of the *company* as claimant/plaintiff, had been declared incompetent because a majority of the shareholders, including Merryweather and Whitworth, had opposed it. Page Wood V-C held that the plaintiff was entitled to bring an action in the present form (ie a derivative action) since, disregarding the votes of the alleged wrongdoers, a majority of the shareholders supported the plaintiff.

PAGE WOOD V-C: I think that, upon principle, a contract of this kind cannot stand, and that there is not such a defect in the constitution of the suit as would be fatal according to the authority of *Foss v Harbottle* **[11.01]**.

Looking at the facts as they come out, I am clearly of opinion that this arrangement, by which Merryweather was to have £4,000 and Whitworth £3,000, was concealed from everybody, and that Merryweather assisted in that concealment by allowing his name to appear as the sole vendor, and taking the purchase-money.

Upon such a transaction the court will hold that the whole contract is a complete fraud . . .

With regard to the frame of the suit, a question of some nicety arises how far such relief can be given at the instance of a shareholder on behalf of himself and other shareholders on the ground that the transaction might be confirmed by the whole body if they thought fit, and that the case would fall within *Foss v Harbottle*, according to which the suit must be by the whole company. On the previous occasion, when it was desired to take proceedings to set aside this transaction, a gentleman took upon himself to file a bill in the name of the company. A motion was made to take that bill off the file, as the person filing the bill was not the solicitor of the company, and was not authorised to file the bill, and I ordered the bill to be taken off the file. There was a majority against setting aside this transaction. The number of votes for rescinding the transaction was 324, and 344 the other way. But Merryweather, in respect of the shares obtained by this sale, which I have held cannot stand, had 78 votes, and Whitworth 28, making altogether 106 out of the 344. If I were to hold that no bill could be filed by shareholders to get rid of the transaction on the ground of the doctrine of *Foss v Harbottle*, it would be simply impossible to set aside a fraud committed by a director under such circumstances, as the director obtaining so many shares by fraud would always be able to outvote everybody else. I held on a former occasion, and I adhere to that decision, that the court must first be satisfied that the plaintiffs were authorised to call themselves the company, the solicitor who put the bill upon the file having no retainer under the corporate seal.

This bill being filed by the plaintiff on behalf of himself and the other shareholders, it is suggested that the proper course would be to file a bill on behalf of himself and the other shareholders for leave to use the name of the company, in order to set aside that contract. I do not think that circuitous course is necessary under any circumstances. It is quite clear that it is not necessary here, because in this case the purchase of the mines is the only thing for which this company was incorporated. It appears to me that it would not be competent for a majority of the shareholders against a minority to say that they insist upon a matter of that kind where the whole inception of the company is simply a motion by a fraudulent agent, qua director, to confirm a purchase as made for £7,000, which was made for £4,000. The whole thing was obtained by fraud, and the persons who may possibly form a majority of the shareholders, could not in any way sanction a transaction of that kind.

I think in this particular case it is hardly necessary to rely upon that, because, having it plainly before me that I have a majority of the shareholders, independent of those implicated in the fraud, supporting the bill, it would be idle to go through the circuitous course of saying that leave must be obtained to file a bill for the company, and pro forma have a totally different litigation. The only course now to take is to set aside the contract for sale and purchase of the mines, and cancel the agreement for such sale . . .

Self-interested transactions between directors and the company they control; directors allowed to vote their shares.

[11.10] Burland v Earle [1902] AC 83 (Privy Council)

The respondents, as shareholders, sued (*inter alia*) to compel the directors to declare a dividend, and to obtain an account from Burland, a director, of a profit made by him out of the purchase and resale to the company of certain plant and materials. The Privy Council rejected both claims. The question here discussed concerns the right of minority shareholders to sue when the alleged wrongdoers are in control.

The opinion of their Lordships was delivered by LORD DAVEY: It is an elementary principle of the law relating to joint stock companies that the court will not interfere with the internal management of companies acting within their powers, and in fact has no jurisdiction to do so. Again, it is clear law that in order to redress a wrong done to the company or to recover moneys or damages alleged to be due to the company, the action should prima facie be brought by the company itself. These cardinal principles are laid down in the well-known cases of *Foss v Harbottle* **[11.01]**, and *Mozley v Alston* **[11.02]**, and in numerous later cases which it is unnecessary to cite. But an exception is made to the second rule, where the persons against whom the relief is sought themselves hold and control the majority of the shares in the company, and will not permit an action to be brought in the name of the company. In that case the courts allow the shareholders complaining to bring an action in their own names. This, however, is a mere matter of procedure in order to give a remedy for a wrong which would otherwise escape redress, and it is obvious that in such an action the plaintiffs cannot have a larger right to relief than the company itself would have if it were plaintiff, and cannot complain of acts which are valid if done with the approval of the majority of the shareholders, or are capable of being confirmed by the majority. The cases in which the minority can maintain such an action are, therefore, confined to those in which the acts complained of are of a fraudulent character or beyond the powers of the company. A familiar example is where the majority are endeavouring directly or indirectly to appropriate to themselves money, property or advantages which belong to the company, or in which the other shareholders are entitled to participate, as was alleged in the case of *Menier v Hooper's Telegraph Works* **[11.11]**. It should be added that no mere informality or irregularity which can be remedied by the majority will entitle the minority to sue, if the act when done regularly would be within the powers of the company and the intention of the majority of the shareholders is clear. This may be illustrated by the judgment of Mellish LJ in *MacDougall v Gardiner* **[11.04]**.

There is yet a third principle which is important for the decision of this case. Unless otherwise provided by the regulations of the company, a shareholder is not debarred from voting or using his voting power to carry a resolution by the circumstance of his having a particular interest in the subject-matter of the vote. This is shown by the case before this Board of the *North-West Transportation Co Ltd v Beatty* **[4.34]**.[21] In that case the resolution of a general meeting to purchase a vessel at the vendor's price was held to be valid, notwithstanding that the vendor himself held the majority of the shares in the company, and the resolution was carried by his votes against the minority who complained . . .

➤ Questions

1. Is the *ratio decidendi* of this case the same as that of Page Wood V-C in *Atwool v Merryweather* **[11.09]**?

2. In *Atwool v Merryweather*, did the Vice-Chancellor rule that the votes of Merryweather and Whitworth should not be counted because their right to the shares was in dispute, or because they were the alleged wrongdoers? (Note that, if the former is the case, much of the succeeding case law is based on a misapprehension.)

---

[21] [But note that even in that case the view was expressed that the minority ought to be allowed to sue, in order to try to establish that there *had* been impropriety.]

➤ Notes

1. In *Cook v Deeks* [6.15], at p 564, Lord Buckmaster took the view that if:

> ... the contract in question was entered into under such circumstances that the directors could not retain the benefit of it for themselves, then it belonged in equity to the company and ought to have been dealt with as an asset of the company. Even supposing it be not *ultra vires* of a company to make a present to its directors, it appears quite certain that directors holding a majority of votes would not be permitted to make a present to themselves. This would be to allow a majority to oppress the minority. To such circumstances the cases of *North-West Transportation v Beatty* [4.34] and *Burland v Earle* [11.10] have no application.

2. In *Daniels v Daniels* [1978] Ch 406, three minority shareholders brought an action against Mr and Mrs Daniels, the two directors and majority shareholders of the company, alleging *negligence* (rather than breach of the conflicts rules), in that they had negligently caused the company to sell land to Mrs Daniels at a fraction of its true value. In preliminary proceedings, Templeman J held that the plaintiffs had standing to sue, notwithstanding *Foss v Harbottle*. He said:

> The authorities which deal with simple fraud on the one hand and gross negligence on the other do not cover the situation which arises where, without fraud, the directors and majority shareholders are guilty of a breach of duty which they owe to the company, and that breach of duty not only harms the company but benefits the directors. In that case it seems to me that different considerations apply. If minority shareholders can sue if there is fraud, I see no reason why they cannot sue where the action of the majority and the directors, though without fraud, confers some benefit on those directors and majority shareholders themselves. . . . To put up with foolish directors is one thing; to put up with directors who are so foolish that they make a profit of £115,000 odd at the expense of the company is something entirely different. The principle which may be gleaned from *Alexander v Automatic Telephone Co*[22] (directors benefiting themselves), from *Cook v Deeks* [6.15] (directors diverting business in their own favour) and from dicta in *Pavlides v Jensen*[23] (directors appropriating assets of the company) is that a minority shareholder who has no other remedy may sue where directors use their powers, intentionally or unintentionally, fraudulently or negligently, in a manner which benefits themselves at the expense of the company.

3. *Daniels v Daniels* is always contrasted with *Pavlides v Jensen*,[24] where a minority shareholder unsuccessfully attempted to bring an action against the directors alleging negligence in the sale of an asbestos mine to an associated company at a gross undervalue. The directors objected that the shareholder had no right to sue, and the court agreed, there being no evidence of fraud or personal benefit.[25] Is the case legitimately distinguishable on this basis?

Self-interested transactions between a majority member and the company.

[11.11] Menier v Hooper's Telegraph Works (1874) 9 Ch App 350 (Court of Appeal in Chancery)

Hooper's company was a substantial shareholder in the European Telegraph Co, and had contracted with it to make and lay a cable to South America under certain concessions granted to the European company by the foreign governments concerned. Menier, a minority

---

[22] [1900] 2 Ch 56, CA.
[23] [1956] Ch 565.
[24] [1956] Ch 565.
[25] This distinction between different forms of negligence is eliminated in CA 2006 ss 260ff, where, *prima facie*, all claims based on negligence can be pursued, although the relevance of proper confirmation by the general meeting remains: see below, p 538.

shareholder in the European company, claimed that Hooper's company had used its votes to procure the diversion of this business to a third company, to cause the abandonment of proceedings brought by the European company to assert its right to the concessions, and to have the European company wound up. The court, affirming Bacon V-C, held that a minority shareholder's action was properly brought in these circumstances.

JAMES LJ: The defendants, who have a majority of shares in the company, have made an arrangement by which they have dealt with matters affecting the whole company, the interest in which belongs to the minority as well as to the majority. They have dealt with them in consideration of their obtaining for themselves certain advantages. Hooper's company have obtained certain advantages by dealing with something which was the property of the whole company. The minority of the shareholders say in effect that the majority has divided the assets of the company, more or less, between themselves, to the exclusion of the minority. I think it would be a shocking thing if that could be done, because if so the majority might divide the whole assets of the company, and pass a resolution that everything must be given to them, and that the minority should having nothing to do with it. Assuming the case to be as alleged by the bill, then the majority have put something into their pockets at the expense of the minority. If so, it appears to me that the minority have a right to have their share of the benefits ascertained for them in the best way in which the court can do it, and given to them.

It is said, however, that this is not the right form of suit, because, according to the principles laid down in *Foss v Harbottle* **[11.01]**, and other similar cases, the court ought to be very slow indeed in allowing a shareholder to file a bill, where the company is the proper plaintiff. This particular case seems to me precisely one of the exceptions referred to by Vice-Chancellor Wood in *Atwool v Merryweather* **[11.09]**, a case in which the majority were the defendants, the wrongdoers, who were alleged to have put the minority's property into their pockets. In this case it is right and proper for a bill to be filed by one shareholder on behalf of himself and all the other shareholders.

Therefore the demurrer ought to be overruled.

MELLISH LJ: I am entirely of the same opinion.

It so happens that Hooper's company are the majority in this company, and a suit by this company was pending which might or might not turn out advantageous to this company. The plaintiff says that Hooper's company being the majority, have procured that suit to be settled upon terms favourable to themselves, they getting a consideration for settling it in the shape of a profitable bargain for the laying of a cable. I am of opinion that although it may be quite true that the shareholders of a company may vote as they please, and for the purpose of their own interests, yet that the majority of shareholders cannot sell the assets of the company and keep the consideration, but must allow the minority to have their share of any consideration which may come to them. I also entirely agree that, under the circumstances, the suit is properly brought in the name of the plaintiff on behalf of himself and all the other shareholders.

The appeal will be dismissed with costs.

➤ Question

Was it important to the reasoning in this case that a winding up was imminent? Should this fact have made any difference?

Stultification of the purposes for which the company was formed, against the wishes of the minority, may constitute 'fraud on the minority'.

[11.12] Estmanco (Kilner House) Ltd v Greater London Council [1982] 1 WLR 2 (Chancery Division)

The Council, when under Conservative control, had formed the Estmanco company to regulate the management of a block of sixty flats which it had rehabilitated and had begun to sell off to owner-occupiers. As each flat was sold, one of the sixty shares in the company was transferred by the Council to the buyer, but the right to vote in respect of each share was retained by the Council until all sixty flats had been sold. The Council had entered into an agreement with the company by which it covenanted to use its best endeavours to sell all the flats. After 12 flats had been sold, there were local elections and control of the Council changed. The new Council members resolved upon a new housing policy and decided to break the terms of the agreement and use the unsold flats to accommodate the needy. A shareholder, one of the flatowners, sought leave to pursue a derivative action against the Council to enforce the covenant, in the face of opposition from the Council itself as the sole voting shareholder. Megarry V-C held that a derivative action would lie.

MEGARRY V-C: If the rule in *Foss v Harbottle* **[11.01]** had remained unqualified, the way would have been open for the majority to stultify any proceedings which were for the benefit of the minority and to the disadvantage of the majority. Accordingly a number of exceptions from the rule have been established; and it is here that the difficulties begin. For convenience, I use the word 'exceptions' to embrace cases which are outside the true scope of the rule. It is far from clear just what the exceptions are, or what is the ambit of some of them. I do not think that it can simply be said that there is an exception from the rule whenever the justice of the case requires it. There are some dicta which support such a view (see, eg *Edwards v Halliwell* **[11.08]**), and this seems to have been part of the ratio [of Vinelott J] in *Prudential Assurance Co Ltd v Newman Industries Ltd (No 2)* **[11.13]**. But in the Court of Appeal in the latter case, the court . . . observed that this was 'not a practical test'; and I would respectfully concur. If it were the test, I feel no doubt that in this case the applicant would succeed.

Although the concept of injustice is not the test, I think that it is nevertheless a reason, and an important reason, for making exceptions from the rule; yet the reasons for an exception must not be confused with the exception itself. If the test were simply justice or injustice, this would mean different things to different men; and the courts have in fact proceeded by way of formulating, not always with great clarity, a number of individual exceptions. The subject has, indeed, been gradually developing; and unless the remedy introduced by s 75 of the Companies Act 1980 [CA 2006 s 994] inhibits that development, no doubt one day the courts will distil from the exceptions some guiding principle that is wide enough to comprehend them all and yet narrow enough to be practicable and workable. It may be that the test may come to be whether an ordinary resolution of the shareholders could validly carry out or ratify the act in question; but I do not think that a motion in the Long Vacation is the time or place for a judge to attempt any far-reaching analysis of the exceptions, or any distillation of a guiding principle to be found in them . . .

Plainly there must be some limit to the power of the majority to pass resolutions which they believe to be in the best interests of the company and yet remain immune from interference by the court. It may be in the best interests of the company to deprive the minority of some of their rights or some of their property, yet I do not think that this gives the majority an unrestricted right to do this, however unjust it may be, and however much it may harm shareholders whose rights as a class differ from those of the majority. If a case falls within one of the exceptions from *Foss v Harbottle*, I cannot see why the right of the minority to sue under that exception should be taken away from them merely because the majority of the company reasonably believe it to be in the best interests of the company that this should be done. This is particularly so if the exception from the rule falls under the rubric of 'fraud on a minority'.

It was on the firmly established exception of 'fraud on a minority' that Mr Steinfeld mainly relied. It does not seem to have yet become very clear exactly what the word 'fraud' means in this context; but I think it is plainly wider than fraud at common law, in the sense of *Derry v Peek*.[26] On a valuable survey of the authorities, Templeman J recently came to the conclusion that this head permitted the minority to sue even though there had not been even an allegation of fraud: *Daniels v Daniels*[27] . . . The principle which he derived from the cases was that

> . . . a minority shareholder who has no other remedy may sue where directors use their powers, intentionally or unintentionally, fraudulently or negligently, in a manner which benefits themselves at the expense of the company.

Apart from the benefits to themselves at the company's expense, the essence of the matter seems to be an abuse or misuse of power. 'Fraud' in the phrase 'fraud on a minority' seems to be being used as comprising not only fraud at common law but also fraud in the wider equitable sense of that term, as in the equitable concept of a fraud on a power.

Now of course *Daniels v Daniels* was a case on acts by directors as such, rather than by shareholders, and I do not forget this. At the same time it seems to me to be useful as preventing 'fraud' from being read too narrowly. Suppose, too, the decision to sell the land had been made not by the husband and wife qua directors, but by a resolution of the company carried by their votes: could it then be said that the minority could not sue? Is this exception from the rule in *Foss v Harbottle* open to easy evasion by directors who hold the majority of votes in general meeting if they take care to reach their decisions not by voting as directors but by voting as shareholders? I think not.

In considering whether there is a fraud on a minority in this case in the sense which this phrase has acquired . . . certain matters seem plain enough. First, I do not think that it can reasonably be said to have been established that it is, or could reasonably be thought to be, for the benefit of the company that [this] action should be discontinued. This is not a case of a trading company, seeking to make a profit. The company is a non-profit-making company, and so the test cannot be the financial benefit of the company. The company was formed for a particular purpose, namely to manage the block of flats under the control of the purchasers of the flats; and the covenant by the council with the company was part of the mechanism for securing this result. On the face of it I do not think that it can readily be said to be for the benefit of a company to stultify a substantial part of the purpose for which it was formed . . .

Second, it is very far from clear that the council, or any properly authorised organ of the council, ever adequately considered and decided what was for the company's benefit before voting at the extraordinary general meeting . . .

Third, the council does not appear to have considered the effect of its vote on the rights of purchasers qua shareholders. Mr Brodie emphasised more than once that the applicant's real complaint was not as a shareholder but as a purchaser of a flat. Instead of having as her neighbours the occupants of 59 other flats which had all been purchased on long leases, she would have only 11 flats occupied thus, and 48 occupied by tenants who would not have the stake in the block of flats which the purchase of long leases would have bought. That, of course, is so; but it is not all. What she bought, inter alia, was a share which had no voting rights, but would have voting rights at a future point of time, namely, when all the other flats had been sold . . . Furthermore, when she obtained her voting rights, she and all the other purchasers of flats would be in control of the company, which would not only manage the block of flats as they collectively wished, but would also, as landlord, be able to enforce the terms of the leases against all the purchasers. The council's conclusion that it is in the best interests of the company that clause 3(1) of the agreement should not

---

[26] (1889) 14 App Cas 337.
[27] [1978] Ch 406. [See above, p 520.]

be enforced is a conclusion that it is in the best interests of the company (including the applicant as one of the corporators) that this state of affairs, so plainly intended by the documents, should never be reached; and there is not a shred of evidence to suggest that this was ever considered by the council . . .

As I have indicated, I do not consider that this is a suitable occasion on which to probe the intricacies of the rule in *Foss v Harbottle* and its exceptions, or to attempt to discover and expound the principles to be found in the exceptions. All that I need say is that in my judgment the exception usually known as 'fraud on a minority' is wide enough to cover the present case, and that if it is not, it should now be made wide enough. There can be no doubt about the 12 voteless purchasers being a minority; there can be no doubt about the advantage to the council of having the action discontinued; there can be no doubt about the injury to the applicant and the rest of the minority, both as shareholders and as purchasers, of that discontinuance; and I feel little doubt that the council has used its voting power not in order to promote the best interests of the company but in order to bring advantage to itself and disadvantage to the minority. Furthermore, that disadvantage is no trivial matter, but represents a radical alteration in the basis on which the council sold the flats to the minority. It seems to me that the sum total represents a fraud on the minority in the sense in which 'fraud' is used in that phrase, or alternatively represents such an abuse of power as to have the same effect.

I appreciate, of course, that there is a difference between the applicant's rights as a shareholder and her rights as a purchaser of a flat; but I think, first, that the injury to her rights as a shareholder suffices in itself, and, second, that her rights as a shareholder form such an integral part of the scheme as a whole as to make it unreal to consider those rights independently of her rights as a purchaser. No right of a shareholder to vote in his own selfish interests or to ignore the interests of the company entitle him with impunity to injure his voteless fellow shareholders by depriving the company of a cause of action and stultifying the purpose for which the company was formed . . .

➤ Note

The cases of *Atwool v Merryweather* **[11.09]** and *Menier v Hooper's Telegraph Works* **[11.11]** are classic instances of the exception to the rule in *Foss v Harbottle* which is commonly known as 'fraud on the minority' It is in this situation that a derivative action is allowed to be brought by a member even though the wrong that is being complained of is a corporate wrong and not one to him as an individual. 'Fraud on the minority' is plainly a misnomer in these cases, since the primary victim is the company itself, and a good deal of confusion would be avoided if the concept were renamed 'fraud on the company'. It is true that the minority members suffer loss indirectly, since their investment is damaged or destroyed, but it would be wrong to attach much weight to this fact, since the Court of Appeal in the *Prudential* case **[11.13]** and the House of Lords subsequently in *Johnson v Gore Wood* **[11.17]** have ruled that such an indirect loss may not be relied on by a member suing in his own right.

There are other cases in which a minority member is allowed to sue to complain that he has been discriminated against or disadvantaged by the action of the *majority members* (eg *Estmanco (Kilner House) Ltd v GLC* **[11.12]**), and these may perhaps be termed 'fraud on the minority' in a true sense. The scope of the concept is not clearly settled: there is a difference of opinion, for instance, as to whether this exception includes the cases in which an alteration of articles has been challenged (see above, pp 204 ff).

Meaning of 'fraud on the minority' and 'wrongdoer control'

Undoubtedly the most significant decision on *Foss v Harbottle* and the 'fraud on the minority' exception is *Prudential Assurance Co Ltd v Newman Industries Ltd (No 2)* [1982] Ch 204 **[11.13]**. It is, however, difficult to say precisely what this case has decided.

At first instance Vinelott J examined with some care the concepts of 'fraud' and 'control' which lie at the heart of a member's right to bring a derivative suit. The extracts from his judgment which are cited below must, however, be read with the caveat that it is by no means certain that the Court of Appeal would have endorsed them if the issue had been argued on appeal.

[11.13] Prudential Assurance Co Ltd v Newman Industries Ltd (No 2)
[1981] Ch 257; [1982] Ch 204 (Chancery Division and Court of Appeal)

[For another part of the litigation between these parties, see below at [11.16].]

The plaintiff, a large institutional investor, held 3% of the shares in Newman. It brought an action against Bartlett and Laughton, two directors of Newman who, the plaintiff alleged, had defrauded Newman of over £400,000. These directors did not have a majority of the shares in Newman and so did not formally have 'control' of it. The transaction by which Newman had been allegedly defrauded had been approved by the shareholders in general meeting, but it was claimed that the shareholders had been misled into doing so. The plaintiff sought declaratory relief and damages on three grounds: (1) its own personal cause of action against the defendants; (2) its derivative claim against the defendants on behalf of Newman; and (3) its representative claim on behalf of Newman shareholders. Vinelott J, after hearing all the evidence, found the case proved and held that there had been a 'fraud' by those in 'control' (in the sense that the wrongdoers had *de facto* control). The Court of Appeal allowed the appeal in part, and expressed the view that the plaintiff should not have been allowed to bring a derivative suit.

VINELOTT J: . . .

Fraud

[The] authorities show that the exception [to the rule in *Foss v Harbottle* **[11.01]**] applies not only where the allegation is that directors who control a company have improperly appropriated to themselves money, property or advantages which belong to the company or, in breach of their duty to the company, have diverted business to themselves which ought to have been given to the company, but more generally where it is alleged that directors though acting 'in the belief that they were doing nothing wrong' (per Lindley MR in *Alexander v Automatic Telephone Co*[28]) are guilty of a breach of duty to the company, including their duty to exercise proper care, and as a result of that breach obtain some benefit. In the latter case it must be unnecessary to allege and prove that the directors in breaking their duty to the company acted with a view to benefiting themselves at the expense of the company; for such an allegation would be an allegation of misappropriation of the company's property. On the other hand, the exception does not apply if all that is alleged is that directors who control a company are liable to the company for damages for negligence, it not being shown that the transaction was one in which they were interested or that they have in fact obtained any benefit from it.[29] It is not easy to see precisely where the line between these cases is to be drawn. For instance, is an action to be allowed to proceed if the allegation is that the controlling director is liable to the company for damages for negligence and that as a result of his negligence a benefit has been obtained by his wife or a friend or by a company in which he has a substantial shareholding? In *Pavlides v Jensen*[30] would it have been enough if, in addition to the allegation of negligence, it had been alleged that Portland Tunnel had a substantial shareholding in the Cyprus company and therefore benefited indirectly? It is also not easy to see what principle underlies the

---

[28] [1900] 2 Ch 56.
[29] This is now changed by CA 2006 s 260; see below, pp 535 ff.
[30] [1956] Ch 565.

distinction. Whether the claim is for property improperly withheld or for damages for negligence or breach of fiduciary duty and, in the latter case, whether those controlling the company have or have not obtained some benefit the reason for the exception is the same, namely that the claim is brought against persons whose interests conflict with the interest of the company. It may be said, in a perfectly intelligible sense, to be a fraud on the minority that those against whom the claim would be brought are in a position to procure, and, if the derivative claim is not brought, will procure, that the company's claim, however strong it may appear to be, will not be enforced. Mr Scott, very frankly, admitted that he could not put forward any valid ground of distinction between a case where the claim by the company is of a proprietary nature and one where it is for damages only, nor between a claim for damages for negligence where the loss to the company is matched by a benefit to those in control and a claim for damages for negligence where the loss to the company is either not matched by any benefit to anybody or is not matched by a benefit to those in control. However, Mr Scott also conceded that the claim by Prudential is a claim founded on acts of a 'fraudulent character', whatever meaning is attributed to those words. . . .

Control

The central issue in this case is whether a derivative action can be brought against defendants who do not have voting control of the company on whose behalf the derivative claim is brought and, if it can, in precisely what circumstances such a claim will be allowed to proceed.

At an early stage in these proceedings . . . Mr Scott . . . indicated that it would be his submission that the court has no jurisdiction to entertain a derivative action at the suit of a minority shareholder unless the persons against whom relief is sought on behalf of the company are able to control a majority of votes capable of being cast in general meeting.

The rule and the exception have sometimes been expressed in terms of jurisdiction. In *Heyting v Dupont*[31] Plowman J, of his own motion, raised and decided the question whether the court could entertain the action. In the Canadian case of *Burrows v Becker*,[32] Norris JA said: ' . . . once the rule is applied, any judgment or order that the learned trial judge may purport to give must be void and of no effect', and he cited with approval an observation of Taschereau J in *Re Sproule*,[33] that proceedings brought in breach of the rule were 'a complete nullity, a nullity of non esse'. However, it became clear as Mr Scott's argument later developed that his initial simple and rigid formulation of the rule and of the exception to it is inconsistent with early authorities, in particular *Atwool v Merryweather* **[11.09]**. [His Lordship discussed the facts and judgment in that case, and continued:]

The second ground of the decision in *Atwool v Merryweather* is inconsistent with the proposition that the exception to the rule in *Foss v Harbottle* is limited to cases where the persons against whom relief is sought control a majority of the votes in general meeting. It is also inconsistent, as I see it, with the proposition that the rule, and the exception to it, are founded upon any limitation in the court's jurisdiction, if by that is meant jurisdiction in the strict sense of the power of the court to enter upon and determine a dispute . . . *Atwool v Merryweather* shows that the court has jurisdiction to entertain a claim by a minority shareholder and to make an order in favour of the defendant company even where the other defendants, alone or together with the plaintiff, do not have a majority of votes in general meeting and where the other shareholders are not parties. If that is so, then as I see it, the exception can only be founded on a general jurisdiction of the court to make an order for recovery of property or damages in favour of a defendant company against co-defendants where the jurisdiction is invoked by a minority shareholder. The question is then whether, in any given case, the jurisdiction is properly invoked. But that is a question not of jurisdiction but of the circumstances in which the court will allow the action to proceed and will make an order for the recovery of property or damages by the company . . .

---

[31] [1963] 1 WLR 1192.
[32] (1967) 63 DLR (2d) 100 at 121.
[33] (1886) 12 SCR 140 at 242.

Burrows v Becker shows that the exception applies—at least in Canada—where the persons alleged to have wronged the company do not control the company in general meeting, and are not a majority of the board of directors, and where it is not shown, as in *Atwool v Merryweather*, that a resolution has been passed by the use of the votes of the wrongdoers that no proceedings should be brought by the company but where it is otherwise shown that it would be 'futile' to call a general meeting because of the influence exercised by the wrongdoers over the board of directors, and directly or indirectly, through the use of proxy votes, over the votes capable of being cast in general meeting.

If the rule and the exception cannot be confined within the rigid formulation expressed in terms of voting control by the persons against whom relief is sought on behalf of the company, then the question whether a given case falls within the exception can only be answered by reference to the principle which underlies the rule and the exception to it. Mr Scott submitted, I think rightly, that the principle which underlies the rule is that it would be wrong to allow a minority shareholder to bring proceedings joining the company as defendant and claiming against other defendants relief on behalf of the company for a wrong alleged to have been done to it if the majority of the members of the company take the view that it is not in the interests of the company that the proceedings should be pursued. Indeed, it would be so plainly wrong that it might be said that, in a broad sense, the court would have no jurisdiction to allow the wishes of the minority to override the wishes of the majority in that way. The principle which underlies the exception to the rule is that in ascertaining the view of the majority whether it is in the interests of the company that the claim be pursued, the court will disregard votes cast or capable of being cast by shareholders who have an interest which directly conflicts with the interest of the company. Those are general principles of substantive law and are not mere rules of procedure. But in any derivative action the plaintiff must allege in his statement of claim some ground which, if established at the trial, would bring the case within the exception and justify an order that the company recover damages or property from the other defendants: see *Birch v Sullivan*.[34] Thus the question whether an action falls within the exception will normally be tested at an early stage. So, if the defendants against whom relief is sought on behalf of the company control the majority of votes, the action will be allowed to proceed whether a resolution that no action should be brought by the company has been passed or not; so also, if the persons against whom relief is sought do not control a majority of the votes but it is shown that a resolution has been passed and passed only by the use of their votes . . .

But there are an infinite variety of possible circumstances . . . If shareholders having a majority of votes in general meeting are nominees, the court will look behind the register to the beneficial owners to see whether they are the persons against whom relief is sought: see *Pavlides v Jensen*. There seems no good reason why the court should not have regard to any other circumstances which show that the majority cannot be relied upon to determine in a disinterested way whether it is truly in the interests of the company that proceedings should be brought. For instance, some shareholders able to exercise decisive votes may have been offered an inducement to vote in favour of the wrongdoers . . . Moreover, today it would be uncommon for any large number of shareholders to attend and vote in person at a general meeting of a large public company, and—an instance suggested by Mr Scott—directors alleged to be liable to the company might be able to determine the outcome of a resolution in general meeting in their own favour by the use of proxy votes. Similarly, most modern articles confide to the directors, the management of the business of the company (see eg, article [70] of Table A) and it is possible that an article in these terms vests in the directors a discretion whether proceedings should be commenced by the company which cannot be overridden by resolution in general meeting; see *Buckley on the Companies Acts*, 13th edn (1957), p 860 and *John Shaw & Sons (Salford) Ltd v Shaw* **[4.07]**. If directors who have an interest direct or indirect in the question whether proceedings should be commenced refuse to submit that question to the shareholders in general meeting, the majority could in theory remove the directors,

---

[34] [1957] 1 WLR 1247.

but might only be able to ensure that the question whether proceedings should be commenced is properly considered by a disinterested board by taking that extreme step, which, in turn, they might consider would involve damage to the company greater than any benefits to be derived from the action against the directors. Mr Scott at the end of his very clear and helpful argument summarised the principle that underlies the exception to the rule in these terms: it applies wherever the persons against whom the action is sought to be brought on behalf of the company are shown to be able 'by any means of manipulation of their position in the company' to ensure that the action is not brought by the company. That broad formulation I accept, provided that the means of manipulation of the defendant's position in the company are not too narrowly defined . . .

[The judgment of the Court of Appeal (Cumming-Bruce, Templeman and Brightman LJJ) included the following passages:]

It is commonly said that an exception to the rule in *Foss v Harbottle* arises if the corporation is 'controlled' by persons implicated in the fraud complained of, who will not permit the name of the company to be used as plaintiffs in the suit . . . But this proposition leaves two questions at large, first, what is meant by 'control', which embraces a broad spectrum extending from an overall absolute majority of votes at one end, to a majority of votes at the other end made up of those likely to be cast by the delinquent himself plus those voting with him as a result of influence or apathy. Secondly, what course is to be taken by the court if, as happened in *Foss v Harbottle*, in the *East Pant Du* case[35] and in the instant case, but did not happen in *Atwool v Merryweather* **[11.09]**, the court is confronted by a motion on the part of the delinquent or by the company, seeking to strike out the action? For at the time of the application the existence of the fraud is unproved. It is at this point that a dilemma emerges. If, upon such an application, the plaintiff can require the court to assume as a fact every allegation in the statement of claim, as in a true demurrer, the plaintiff will frequently be able to outmanoeuvre the primary purpose of the rule in *Foss v Harbottle* by alleging fraud and 'control' by the fraudster. If on the other hand the plaintiff has to prove fraud and 'control' before he can establish his title to prosecute his action, then the action may need to be fought to a conclusion before the court can decide whether or not the plaintiff should be permitted to prosecute it. In the latter case the purpose of the rule in *Foss v Harbottle* disappears. Either the fraud has not been proved, so cadit quaestio; or the fraud has been proved and the delinquent is accountable unless there is a valid decision of the board or a valid decision of the company in general meeting, reached without impropriety or unfairness, to condone the fraud.

We think that this brief look at the authorities is sufficient for present purposes. For it so happens that this court cannot properly on this appeal decide the scope of the exception to the rule in *Foss v Harbottle*. The reason is this . . .

Newman by its counsel, acting (as we must assume) upon due authority conferred by the company, stated before us that if the finding of fraud stood it would accept the benefit of the order made in its favour. That is the end of *Foss v Harbottle* so far as this appeal is concerned.

It was in the light of these considerations that we declined to hear any argument from Mr Caplan and Mr Curry on the topic of *Foss v Harbottle*. However desirable it might be in the public interest that we should express our conclusions on Vinelott J's analysis of the rule in *Foss v Harbottle* and what he saw as the exception to it, it was necessary for us to bear in mind that the rule had ceased to be of the slightest relevance to the case. It would have been a grave injustice to all parties to increase the already horrendous costs of this litigation by allowing time for argument on an interesting but irrelevant point. Such consideration of the law as appears in this judgment is, apart from a few submissions made by Mr Bartlett, merely a reflection of our own thoughts without the benefit of sustained argument.

---

[35] (1864) 2 Hem & M 254.

In the result it would be improper for us to express any concluded view on the proper scope of the exception or exceptions to the rule in *Foss v Harbottle*. We desire, however, to say two things. First, as we have already said, we have no doubt whatever that Vinelott J erred in dismissing the summons of May 10 1979. He ought to have determined as a preliminary issue whether the plaintiffs were entitled to sue on behalf of Newman by bringing a derivative action. It cannot have been right to have subjected the company to a 30-day action (as it was then estimated to be) in order to enable him to decide whether the plaintiffs were entitled in law to subject the company to a 30-day action. Such an approach defeats the whole purpose of the rule in *Foss v Harbottle* and sanctions the very mischief that the rule is designed to prevent. By the time a derivative action is concluded, the rule in *Foss v Harbottle* can have little, if any, role to play. Either the wrong is proved, thereby establishing conclusively the rights of the company; or the wrong is not proved, so cadit quaestio. In the present case a board, of which all the directors save one were disinterested, . . . had reached the conclusion before the start of the action that the prosecution of the action was likely to do more harm than good. That might prove a sound or unsound assessment, but it was the commercial assessment of an apparently independent board. Obviously the board would not have expected at that stage to be as well informed about the affairs of the company as it might be after 36 days of evidence in court and an intense examination of some 60 files of documents. But the board clearly doubted whether there were sufficient reasons for supposing that the company would at the end of the day be in a position to count its blessings; and clearly feared, as counsel said, that it might be killed by kindness. Whether in the events which have happened Newman (more exactly the disinterested body of shareholders) will feel that it has all been well worth while, or must lick its wounds and render no thanks to those who have interfered in its affairs, is not a question which we can answer. But we think it is within the bounds of possibility that if the preliminary issue had been argued, a judge might have reached the considered view that the prosecution of this great action should be left to the decision of the board or of a specially convened meeting of the shareholders, albeit less well informed than a judge after a 72-day action.

So much for the summons of May 10. The second observation which we wish to make is merely a comment on Vinelott J's decision that there is an exception to the rule in *Foss v Harbottle* whenever the justice of the case so requires. We are not convinced that this is a practical test, particularly if it involves a full-dress trial before the test is applied. On the other hand we do not think that the right to bring a derivative action should be decided as a preliminary issue upon the hypothesis that all the allegations in the statement of claim of 'fraud' and 'control' are facts, as they would be on the trial of a preliminary point of law. In our view, whatever may be the properly defined boundaries of the exception to the rule, the plaintiff ought at least to be required before proceeding with his action to establish a prima facie case (i) that the company is entitled to the relief claimed, and (ii) that the action falls within the proper boundaries of the exception to the rule in *Foss v Harbottle*. On the latter issue it may well be right for the judge trying the preliminary issue to grant a sufficient adjournment to enable a meeting of shareholders to be convened by the board, so that he can reach a conclusion in the light of the conduct of, and proceedings at, that meeting . . .

The rule in *Foss v Harbottle* is founded on principle but it also operates fairly by preserving the rights of the majority. We were invited to give judicial approval to the public spirit of the plaintiffs who, it was said, are pioneering a method of controlling companies in the public interest without involving regulation by a statutory body. In our view the voluntary regulation of companies is a matter for the City. The compulsory regulation of companies is a matter for Parliament. We decline to draw general conclusions from the exceptional circumstances of the present case. But the results of the present action give food for thought. Vinelott J thought it possible that Newman had suffered damage amounting to £445,000 by the fraud of Mr Bartlett and Mr Laughton. Counsel for Newman submitted in the court below that damage to Newman by the prosecution of the action exceeded the benefits liable to be derived from the action. The costs of the proceedings at the end of the trial were said in newspaper reports to be in the region of £750,000 . . .

If this appeal succeeds the burden of the costs on the plaintiffs will be enormous. The innocent shareholders of Newman . . . and [of] the plaintiffs may well wonder, whether this appeal succeeds or not, if there is not something to be said after all for the old-fashioned rule in *Foss v Harbottle*.

[The Court of Appeal allowed the appeal in part, reducing the damages payable to £45,000.]

➤ Note

The importance of this case lies mainly in the fact that the Court of Appeal firmly declined to give any encouragement to the notion that the rule in *Foss v Harbottle* might be due for some relaxation in the broad interests of justice.

The circumstances of the case were unusual. At first instance, Vinelott J had deferred a ruling on the question of the plaintiff's standing to sue (under *Foss v Harbottle*), because he considered himself bound to hear all the evidence in any event for the purpose of a claim in conspiracy which the plaintiff had brought on the same facts; and when, at the end of an exceptionally long hearing, he found fraud proved, it seemed plain in the interests of justice that the procedural obstacle of *Foss v Harbottle* should not be allowed to stand in the plaintiff's way. But when the case came before the Court of Appeal, it was not faced with the issue of *Foss v Harbottle* because the company itself (in whose favour the judgment of the lower court had been entered) had 'adopted' the plaintiff's case and the benefit of his victory. A very large sum had been run up in costs on all sides, and the Court of Appeal declined to increase the expense further by hearing argument on the question of the plaintiff's standing, which was by then academic. Even so, the Court of Appeal did offer some observations on the subject of *Foss v Harbottle* generally. Among these we may note:

(i) A shareholder cannot bring a *personal* claim against a wrongdoer, even in a claim based on fraud or deceit, when the loss which he claims that he has suffered is the diminution in the value of his investment in the company as a consequence of the effect of the fraud on the company. The company alone can sue for such a wrong.[36]

(ii) A judge must always give his ruling on an application to strike out an action because of the plaintiff's want of standing *before* proceeding to hear the substantive case.[37]

(iii) There is no broad exception to *Foss v Harbottle* based on 'the interests of justice'.[38]

---

[36] See below, on 'reflective loss', pp 543 ff.

[37] In Australia, this ruling has been rejected as too inflexible: *Hurley v BGH Nominees Pty Ltd* (1982) 6 ACLR 791. It appears to be totally at odds with the reasoning of the House of Lords in the well-known 'judicial review' case in administrative law, *IRC v National Federation of Self-Employed and Small Businesses Ltd* [1982] AC 617, decided just a few months before *Prudential*.

[38] Again, this view has been disowned in Australia: see *Biala Pty Ltd v Mallina Holdings Ltd* (1993) 11 ACSR 785, where Ipp J said (at 846, 848) that 'the courts should not shrink from determining whether the justice of the case should allow a shareholder to proceed with a derivative action . . . Equity is concerned with substance and not form, and it seems to me contrary to principle to require wronged minority shareholders to bring themselves within the boundaries of the well recognised exceptions and to deny jurisdiction to a court of equity even where an unjust or unconscionable result may otherwise ensue'.

'Control': impact of an independent dissenting majority

A minority member who has standing to sue on behalf of the company, under an established exception to the rule in Foss v Harbottle, may be debarred from proceeding if a majority of the members, who are independent of the defendants, are opposed to the litigation.

[11.14] Smith v Croft (No 2) [1988] Ch 114 (Chancery Division)

The plaintiffs were minority shareholders claiming (*inter alia*) to recover, on behalf of their company, sums which had been paid away in transactions which were both *ultra vires* and in breach of the statutory prohibition on financial assistance (above, pp 403 ff). With their supporters, the plaintiffs had 14% of the voting rights in the company and the defendants 63%; and there were other shareholders commanding 21% of the votes who did not wish the litigation to proceed. Knox J held that: (i) a *prima facie* case of *ultra vires* and illegality had been made out, for which the company was entitled to relief; (ii) the plaintiffs accordingly had standing to bring a derivative action; but that (iii) the plaintiffs nevertheless had no right to sue if a majority of the shareholders who were independent of the defendants did not want the action to continue.

KNOX J: The questions of law can be formulated as follows.

(1) Is a minority shareholder always entitled as of right to bring and prosecute an action for the company to recover money paid away in the course of a transaction which was ultra vires the company[39] or is the prosecution of such an action susceptible of coming within the rule in *Foss v Harbottle* so that there can be circumstances in which the court will not allow it to continue?

(2) If the latter view is the correct one in relation to those categories of claims based on ultra vires transactions, and also in all cases of minority shareholders' actions to recover money for the company in respect of acts which constitute a fraud on the minority, will the court pay regard to the views of the majority of shareholders who are independent of the defendants to the action on the question whether the action should proceed? . . .

Another way of putting the question is to ask whether if a minority has been the victim of a fraud entitling the company in which they are shareholders to financial redress, the majority within that minority can prevent the minority within that minority from prosecuting the action for redress. The usual reason in practice for wanting to abandon such an action is that there is far more to lose financially by prosecuting the right to redress than by abandoning or not pursuing it, and that view will be reinforced in the minds of those who wish to abandon the claim if their opinion is that it is a bad claim anyway.

The third question which arises is whether in this case Wren Trust [a minority shareholder alleged to be connected with the defendants] should be treated as independent, if the views of an independent majority are relevant? That is a question of fact . . .

Upon the first question of law which arises, in my judgment the solution is to be found by a correct analysis of the rights which the minority shareholder is seeking to exercise or enforce in relation to the result of an ultra vires transaction. There was no dispute before me but that any individual shareholder, be he in a minority or not, has a personal right to apply to the court to restrain a threatened action which if carried out would be ultra vires. Neither the right to object to such an action nor the shareholder's locus standi to bring proceedings admits of any doubt. The rule in *Foss v Harbottle* poses no obstacle, because neither of the two bases for the rule is applicable, that is to say the matter is not, by definition, a mere question of internal management nor is the transaction capable of ratification by or on behalf of the company . . .

---

[39] [These transactions were illegal as well as ultra vires the company. See the comment above, p 515.]

The difficulty arises in this case when one considers not the restraint of an illegal or ultra vires transaction but the recovery on behalf of the company of money or property which the company is entitled to claim as the result of the ultra vires transaction . . .

Treating the matter as a question of principle for the moment, when a minority shareholder seeks to enforce a right of the company to claim compensation for a past ultra vires transaction there are two quite separate rights involved. First, there is the minority shareholder's right to bring proceedings at all and secondly, there is the right of recovery which belongs to the company but is permitted to be asserted on its behalf by the minority shareholder.

But as Lord Davey said in *Burland v Earle* **[11.10]** the plaintiffs cannot have a larger right to relief than the company itself would have if it were plaintiff. And from that it follows in my judgment that if there is a valid reason why the company should not sue it will equally prevent the minority shareholder from suing on its behalf. He is therefore liable to be defeated on two points, first by any ground preventing him from exercising his procedural remedy, and secondly by any ground preventing the company from exercising its substantive right . . .

Where ultra vires transactions are involved the number of grounds upon which the company can be debarred from suing is limited. In particular it was not argued that ratification of the ultra vires transaction, by however large a majority of shareholders, could prevent the company from suing. There is, however, a clear difference in principle between ratifying what has been invalidly done in the past and abandoning, compromising or not pursuing rights of action arising out of a past ultra vires transaction, and I see no reason in principle why in appropriate circumstances the latter should not intervene to prevent the prosecution of a suit on behalf of the company in relation to such rights of action . . .

I turn now to the question whether it is right for the court to have regard to the views of the majority inside a minority which is, I assume for this purpose, in a position to bring an action to recover on behalf of the company in respect of breaches of duty by persons with overall control.

The . . . defendants claim that it is, the plaintiffs claim that it is not. On their view of the matter all that the court is concerned with, in cases where the exception to the rule in *Foss v Harbottle* based on frauds on the minority applies, is the single question whether the defendants have control . . .

Mr Potts submitted that no reported authority held that in a case falling within the fraud on a minority exception to the rule in *Foss v Harbottle* the court should go beyond seeing whether the wrongdoers are in control and count heads to see what the other shareholders, ie those other than the plaintiff and the wrongdoers, think should be done. I accept that in many reported cases the court has not gone on to the second stage.

[His Lordship examined the authorities and continued:] In my judgment the word 'control' was deliberately placed in inverted commas by the Court of Appeal in *Prudential Assurance Co Ltd v Newman Industries Ltd (No 2)* **[11.13]** because it was recognised that voting control by the defendants was not necessarily the sole subject of investigation. Ultimately the question which has to be answered in order to determine whether the rule in *Foss v Harbottle* applies to prevent a minority shareholder seeking relief as plaintiff for the benefit of the company is 'Is the plaintiff being improperly prevented from bringing these proceedings on behalf of the company?' If it is an expression of the corporate will of the company by an appropriate independent organ that is preventing the plaintiff from prosecuting the action he is not improperly but properly prevented and so the answer to the question is 'No'. The appropriate independent organ will vary according to the constitution of the company concerned and the identity of the defendants who will in most cases be disqualified from participating by voting in expressing the corporate will.

Finally on this aspect of the matter I remain unconvinced that a just result is achieved by a single minority shareholder having the right to involve a company in an action for recovery of compensation for the company if all the other minority shareholders are for disinterested reasons satisfied that the proceedings will be productive of more harm than good. If Mr Potts' argument is well founded once control by the defendants is established the views of the rest of the minority as to the advisability of the prosecution of the suit are necessarily irrelevant. I find that hard to square with the concept of a form of pleading originally introduced on the ground of necessity alone in order to prevent a wrong going without redress.

I therefore conclude that it is proper to have regard to the views of independent shareholders. In this case it is common ground that there would be no useful purpose served by adjourning to enable a general meeting to be called. For all practical purposes it is quite clear how the votes would be cast . . .

[His Lordship then held that a majority of shareholders, excluding the defendants but including the Wren Trust (which he ruled was 'independent'[40]) were opposed to continuing the action, and ordered that it should be struck out.]

➤ Notes

1. The Vice-Chancellor's suggestion in *Estmanco* **[11.12]** that the test for making exceptions to the rule 'may come to be whether an ordinary resolution of the shareholders could validly carry out or ratify the act in question' echoes the theme of the important article by Lord Wedderburn, 'Shareholders' Rights and the Rule in *Foss v Harbottle*' [1957] CLJ 194, [1958] CLJ 93. But, as the case above shows, it is plainly an over-simplification to run together all the questions of authorisation, ratification or affirmation of a transaction that is otherwise voidable, or the release and condoning of wrongdoers and wrongdoing, etc, and to try to match them up with the issue of a plaintiff's right to sue.[41]

2. Also see *Taylor v National Union of Mineworkers (Derbyshire Area)* [1985] BCLC 237, where Vinelott J held that individual members of a trade union were entitled to sue for orders restraining its officers from making *ultra vires* payments, but that an action to make the officers personally liable to make restitution of moneys wrongly paid away might be barred if the members voted by a majority not to pursue the claim: this shows how mistaken it may be to try to bring everything within one formula. Can the 'ratifiability' test be squared with decided cases such as: *Alexander v Automatic Telephone Co*,[42] *Hogg v Cramphorn Ltd* **[6.08]** and *Devlin v Slough Estates Ltd* (below, p 543), for example?

3. Other cases establishing further restrictions on the availability of the exceptions to the rule in *Foss v Harbottle* may be mentioned. In *Birch v Sullivan* [1957] 1 WLR 1247, Harman J held that when an individual plaintiff institutes a derivative action to enforce a right belonging to the company, he must specifically allege in his pleadings, and be prepared to prove, that those in control of the company would prevent the company from suing in its own name.

4. In *Heyting v Dupont* [1963] 1 WLR 1192 (affd [1964] 1 WLR 843), Plowman J declared that the issue of standing under the rule in *Foss v Harbottle* was a matter going to jurisdiction, which the court could, and should, raise on its own initiative and which the parties had no power to waive.[43]

5. In *Wallersteiner v Moir (No 2)* [1975] QB 373, the Court of Appeal considered the question of the plaintiff member's costs. The court ruled that it was proper in a minority member's action to order that the company should indemnify the plaintiff against the costs of the action. This was so even if the action should fail, provided that it was brought on reasonable grounds

---

[40] His test of independence was: 'In my judgment in this case votes should be disregarded if, but only if, the court is satisfied either that the vote or its equivalent is actually cast with a view to supporting the defendants rather than securing benefit to the company . . . The court should not substitute its own opinion but can, and in my view should, assess whether the decision making process is vitiated by being or being likely to be directed to an improper purpose' (at 186D-F).

[41] On this question, see RJC Partridge, 'Ratification and the Release of Directors from Personal Liability' [1987] CLJ 122; S Worthington, 'Corporate Governance: Remedying and Ratifying Directors' Breaches' (2000) 116 *LQR* 638.

[42] [1900] 2 Ch 56.

[43] Vinelott J in the *Prudential* case **[11.13]** expressed doubts whether this view was consistent with *Atwool v Merryweather* **[11.09]**.

and provided that a plaintiff might apply *ex parte* to the Master at an early stage in the proceedings for an order approving their continuance, at the company's eventual expense, until close of pleadings or until after discovery, or until trial.[44]

6. In *Nurcombe v Nurcombe* [1985] 1 WLR 370, the Court of Appeal declared that a plaintiff member seeking to bring a derivative suit must 'come with clean hands'. A defendant was entitled to raise against the plaintiff any defence which could have been raised against him in an action that had been brought by him personally. (But the mere fact of acquiescence by the member in the defendant's wrongdoing will not necessarily be fatal to his right to bring a derivative claim: in *Knight v Frost* [1999] 1 BCLC 364 Hart J ruled that the court had to consider all the circumstances with a view to seeing whether it was fair and equitable that, having given his concurrence, he should afterwards be allowed to 'turn round and sue'.) Do these various limitations accord with the primary principles and policies behind the rule in *Foss v Harbottle*?

7. In *Barrett v Duckett* [1995] 1 BCLC 243, CA, the Court of Appeal appears to have added two further hurdles for a would-be plaintiff to surmount: first, the proceedings must be brought for a proper purpose and, second, the plaintiff will be allowed to bring a derivative suit only if he or she has no other remedy available. The minority member in this case was the widow of the company's founder. Control had passed into the hands of her estranged son-in-law Christopher and his second wife, to the exclusion of members of the founder's family and in particular his daughter Carol (Christopher's ex-wife), who was not herself a shareholder. The widow was denied standing to sue in a derivative action because her primary motive was not to see the company's wrongs righted but to secure something of the family inheritance for Carol. There were also suggestions that she ought to have tried some other form of procedure, although it is fairly clear on the facts that she had no realistic alternative course of action available.

8. Similarly, in *Portfolios of Distinction Ltd v Laird* [2004] EWHR 207 (Ch); [2004] 2 BCLC 741, in deciding whether to permit a derivative action to continue, the court considered it relevant to ask whether the claimant's pursuit of the claim was in the best interests of the company, and whether alternative remedies were available. Launcelot Henderson QC (sitting as a Deputy High Court Judge), at paras 57–58, said:

> In *Barrett v Duckett*,[45] Peter Gibson LJ (with whom Russell LJ agreed) helpfully set out the general principles governing derivative actions in respect of wrongs done to a company in the following terms:
>
> "The general principles governing actions in respect of wrongs done to a company or irregularities in the conduct of its affairs are not in dispute:
>
> (1) The proper plaintiff is prima facie the company.
>
> (2) Where the wrong or irregularity might be made binding on the company by a simple majority of its members, no individual shareholder is allowed to maintain an action in respect of that matter.

---

[44] The *Wallersteiner* order has since had a rather chequered career: see DD Prentice, 'Wallersteiner v Moir: a Decade Later' [1987] Conv 167. In *Smith v Croft* [1986] BCLC 207, [1986] 1 WLR 580 Walton J formulated a number of qualifications calculated to restrict the availability of the procedure. In particular, he ruled that an order should not be made where the plaintiff had sufficient resources to finance the action out of his own pocket. In the later case of *McDonald v Horn* [1995] 1 All ER 961, CA further restrictions were suggested: in particular, that the court should not normally authorise the funding of proceedings until there had been an investigation of the plaintiff's complaints made by an independent party. (Note that the Civil Procedure Rules 1998, r 19.9(7) (above, p 514 fn 16) contemplates that a *Wallersteiner* order may be made at the same time as an order giving permission for a derivative claim to be continued.) What difference, if any, does CA 2006 make to this option?

[45] [1995] BCLC 362.

(3) There are however recognised exceptions, one of which is where the wrongdoer has control which is or would be exercised to prevent a proper action being brought against the wrongdoer: in such a case the shareholder may bring a derivative action (his rights being derived from the company) on behalf of the company.

(4) When a challenge is made to the right claimed by a shareholder to bring a derivative action on behalf of the company, it is the duty of the court to decide as a preliminary issue the question whether or not the plaintiff should be allowed to sue in that capacity.

(5) In taking that decision it is not enough for the court to say that there is no plain and obvious case for striking out; it is for the shareholder to establish to the satisfaction of the court that he should be allowed to sue on behalf of the company.

(6) The shareholder will be allowed to sue on behalf of the company if he is bringing the action bona fide for the benefit of the company for wrongs to the company for which no other remedy is available. Conversely if the action is brought for an ulterior purpose or if another adequate remedy is available, the court will not allow the derivative action to proceed."

This guidance predated the introduction of the CPR, but *Barrett v Duckett* is cited in the notes to r 19.9 in the White Book and I see no reason to doubt that those principles remain valid today and should inform the exercise by the court of its discretion whether or not to permit a claimant to continue a derivative claim under that rule. I emphasise in particular Peter Gibson LJ's propositions 5 and 6, which make it clear that the shareholder must establish a positive case for being allowed to sue on behalf of the company, and that the shareholder will be allowed to do so only if two conditions are satisfied, namely that he is bringing the action bona fide for the benefit of the company, and that no other adequate remedy is available.

9. Finally, it was held in *Fargo Ltd v Godfroy* [1986] 1 WLR 1134, that a minority member may not bring a derivative claim when a company has gone into liquidation: only the liquidator is competent to represent the company in a winding up.

The statutory derivative action: CA 2006 ss 260ff

This statutory procedure is now the exclusive method for pursuing derivative claims, replacing the common law rules associated with the rule in *Foss v Harbottle* **[11.01]** (so far as they apply to derivative claims): see CA 2006 s 260(2).[46]

The statutory rules

The provisions of CA 2006, Part 11 deserve close reading.

CA 2006 s 260: Derivative claims

(1) This Chapter applies to proceedings in England and Wales or Northern Ireland by a member of a company—
  (a) in respect of a cause of action vested in the company, and
  (b) seeking relief on behalf of the company.

---

[46] Although note that the *Explanatory Notes* to the 2006 Act specifically states at para 491 that 'The sections in this Part do *not* formulate a substantive rule to replace the rule in *Foss v Harbottle*, but instead reflect the recommendations of the Law Commission that there should be a "new derivative procedure with more modern, flexible and accessible criteria for determining whether a shareholder can pursue an action" (*Shareholder Remedies*, paragraph 6.15).' [emphasis added] Also see above, p 503, for references to earlier reform proposals.

This is referred to in this Chapter as a 'derivative claim'.

(2) A derivative claim may only be brought—

  (a) under this Chapter, or

  (b) in pursuance of an order of the court in proceedings under section 994 (proceedings for protection of members against unfair prejudice).

(3) A derivative claim under this Chapter may be brought only in respect of a cause of action arising from an actual or proposed act or omission involving negligence, default, breach of duty or breach of trust by a director of the company.

  The cause of action may be against the director or another person (or both).

(4) It is immaterial whether the cause of action arose before or after the person seeking to bring or continue the derivative claim became a member of the company.

(5) For the purposes of this Chapter—

  (a) 'director' includes a former director;

  (b) a shadow director is treated as a director; and

  (c) references to a member of a company include a person who is not a member but to whom shares in the company have been transferred or transmitted by operation of law.

CA 2006 s 261: Application for permission to continue derivative claim

(1) A member of a company who brings a derivative claim under this Chapter must apply to the court for permission (in Northern Ireland, leave) to continue it.

(2) If it appears to the court that the application and the evidence filed by the applicant in support of it do not disclose a prima facie case for giving permission (or leave), the court—

  (a) must dismiss the application, and

  (b) may make any consequential order it considers appropriate.

(3) If the application is not dismissed under subsection (2), the court—

  (a) may give directions as to the evidence to be provided by the company, and

  (b) may adjourn the proceedings to enable the evidence to be obtained.

(4) On hearing the application, the court may—

  (a) give permission (or leave) to continue the claim on such terms as it thinks fit,

  (b) refuse permission (or leave) and dismiss the claim, or

  (c) adjourn the proceedings on the application and give such directions as it thinks fit.

[s 262 defines the exclusive circumstances in which a member can take over, by way of derivative claim, an action commenced by the company.]

CA 2006 s 263: Whether permission to be given

(1) The following provisions have effect where a member of a company applies for permission (in Northern Ireland, leave) under section 261 or 262.

(2) Permission (or leave) must be refused if the court is satisfied—

  (a) that a person acting in accordance with section 172 (duty to promote the success of the company) would not seek to continue the claim, or

  (b) where the cause of action arises from an act or omission that is yet to occur, that the act or omission has been authorised by the company, or

  (c) where the cause of action arises from an act or omission that has already occurred, that the act or omission—

    (i) was authorised by the company before it occurred, or

    (ii) has been ratified by the company since it occurred.

(3) In considering whether to give permission (or leave) the court must take into account, in particular—

(a) whether the member is acting in good faith in seeking to continue the claim;

(b) the importance that a person acting in accordance with section 172 (duty to promote the success of the company) would attach to continuing it;

(c) where the cause of action results from an act or omission that is yet to occur, whether the act or omission could be, and in the circumstances would be likely to be—

(i) authorised by the company before it occurs, or

(ii) ratified by the company after it occurs;

(d) where the cause of action arises from an act or omission that has already occurred, whether the act or omission could be, and in the circumstances would be likely to be, ratified by the company;

(e) whether the company has decided not to pursue the claim;

(f) whether the act or omission in respect of which the claim is brought gives rise to a cause of action that the member could pursue in his own right rather than on behalf of the company.

(4) In considering whether to give permission (or leave) the court shall have particular regard to any evidence before it as to the views of members of the company who have no personal interest, direct or indirect, in the matter.

(5) The Secretary of State may by regulations—

(a) amend subsection (2) so as to alter or add to the circumstances in which permission (or leave) is to be refused;

(b) amend subsection (3) so as to alter or add to the matters that the court is required to take into account in considering whether to give permission (or leave).

(6) Before making any such regulations the Secretary of State shall consult such persons as he considers appropriate.

(7) Regulations under this section are subject to affirmative resolution procedure.

[s 264 defines the conditions under which the court will grant permission to a member to continue a derivative claim brought by another member.]

Grounds for bringing a derivative claim

CA 2006 broadens (but also makes exclusive) the grounds upon which a derivative claim (as defined in s 260(1)) is available to members.[47] Under s 260(3), a cause of action arising from an actual or proposed act or omission *by a director* involving negligence, default, breach of duty or breach of trust are recognised as the only basis upon which to commence such a claim. Perhaps not all the wrongs which a director could conceivably commit against the company are included in the section, but breach of duty includes the newly codified directors' duties examined in Chapter 6, and 'director' for these purposes includes both former directors and shadow directors. Breach of duty presumably also includes other breaches under the Act (beyond the directors' general duties), and breaches of common law duties not within the Act at all.

Provided the cause of action is in respect of a relevant breach by a director, third parties may also be made defendants in the derivative claim, either in lieu of or in addition to the wrongdoing director (s 260(3)). The general rules on third party liability in respect of breaches of duty by the directors are not set out in the Act, but rely on the common law rules on dishonest assistance and knowing receipt (above, pp 360 ff).

It does not matter whether the cause of action arose before or after the person seeking to bring the derivative claim became a member (s 260(4)).

[47] A 'member' is defined in CA 2006 s 112, and is not restricted to a shareholder.

➤ Question

The *Eastmanco* litigation, above **[11.12]**, could not be pursued in derivative form by the members under the new CA 2006 rules since the wrong in question was not committed by the directors. How will remedies now be provided in this type of case?

Court permission to continue a derivative claim

General issues

The new statutory provisions oblige a member seeking to bring a derivative claim to apply to the court for permission to continue it (s 261). There are also provisions, which, in specific circumstances, allow a member to continue: (i) as a derivative claim, a proceeding which might appropriately be pursued as such but was initially brought by the company (s 262); or (ii) a derivative claim brought by another member (s 264).

Section 263 lies at the heart of the new procedure. This section sets out the criteria the courts must use in granting permission to members to pursue derivative claims.

Compulsory refusal of permission

Section 263(2) sets out the only three matters that are complete bars to pursuit of a derivative claim. Other considerations will, at most, play into the court's exercise of its discretion under s 260(3). The court *must* refuse permission to continue a derivative claim where:

(i)   a person acting in accordance with s 172 (ie the duty to promote the success of the company) would not seek to continue the claim (s 263(2)(a)); or

(ii) the proposed conduct constituting the wrongdoing has been authorised by the company (s 263(2)(b)); or

(iii) the wrongdoing has occurred, but was previously authorised or subsequently ratified by the company (s 263(2)(c)).

The action is not designed to promote the success of the company

Section 260(2)(a) reflects the fundamental philosophy of the derivative claim (and, it might be hoped, of the rule in *Foss v Harbottle*): a member ought to be permitted to pursue a derivative claim *because* this is for the benefit of the company, not because this is for the benefit of the member personally.[48] But the test that must be applied by the court is not quite as tough as this. The court does not have to decide whether a hypothetical director (subject to the duty in s 172) *would* think the claim worth pursuing (although that is relevant under s 263(3)(b)); the court merely has to refuse permission if it considers (on the balance of probabilities, presumably) that such a director would *not* seek to continue the claim. It remains to be seen whether the courts will use this power simply to order refusal in cases that are patently not in the company's interest, or whether it will engage in more 'commercial' deliberations, and order refusal cases that it considers, on a more finely tuned balance, are not in the company's interests.

Proper authorisation or ratification

Sections 263(2)(b) and (c) follow logically from the fundamental philosophy outlined above: if an act has been *properly* authorised or ratified, then it no longer constitutes a wrong to the company, and the company cannot pursue a claim in relation to it, either through a derivative claim or otherwise.

---

[48] The possibility of personal benefit should be addressed via personal claims, either at common law or under the statutory 'unfair prejudice' provisions in CA 2006 s 994.

The issue of proper authorisation and ratification is thus brought centre stage. This is a difficult and controversial area of law.[49] CA 2006 makes some specific provisions (see especially ss 175 and 180 on authorisation and s 239 on ratification), and, crucially, both ss 175 and 239 indicate that the votes of the 'wrongdoers' are not to count in determining the outcome in the decision-making body (the board of directors and the general meeting, respectively). This provides welcome clarification in an area where there has been great uncertainty.[50] These sections impose further requirements. Beyond that, however, the common law rules are preserved (see ss 180(4) and 239(7)), with all their complications and uncertainties. In particular, the question of whether the particular actions by the directors *can* be authorised[51] or ratified[52] remains a live issue.

Discretionary refusal of permission

If the court does not refuse permission to continue the derivative action under s 263(2), then it must exercise its discretion in deciding whether to grant permission to the member to continue with the derivative claim. In exercising this discretion, the court *must* take into account, 'in particular' the non-exclusive list of matters provided in s 263(3) (see above, p 537).

In addition, s 263(4) requires the court to have 'particular regard' to any evidence of the views of members of the company who have no direct or indirect personal interest in the matter. This effectively adopts the *Smith v Croft (No 2)* [11.14] test.

> **Questions**

1. Is the order of the list in s 263(3) significant? In particular, is it significant that the views of the 'hypothetical director' are not given greater prominence?

2. Does segregation of s 263(4) from the list of issues provided in s 263(3) indicate that the views of disinterested members should have *more* or *less* influence that the other matters on the court's decision?

3. Is an agreed hierarchy of discretionary considerations essential? What is a court likely to do if, for example, the member is *not* acting in good faith, but a 'hypothetical director' *would* think the claim likely to promote the success of the company?

4. Do any of the cases considered earlier (above, pp 533 ff) suggest how the courts might regard these various factors? Do the cases suggest additional factors that might be relevant to exercise of the court's discretion? What has happened to the idea of 'control' of the company by the wrongdoers?

The consequences of the new statutory derivative action are difficult to predict. Much will depend on how willing the courts will be to intervene into a company's decision-making processes. On the one hand, the traditional reluctance of the courts to intervene, and experience of codification of derivative actions from other jurisdictions, suggest that a wild proliferation in the number of derivative claims allowed to proceed is unlikely. On the other hand, the expanded breadth of grounds upon which a derivative claim may be based, combined with new statutory expressions of directors' duties, are likely to make it easier for activist or aggrieved members to initiate a derivative claim. In any event, the new statutory derivative claim underscores a theme that runs through the CA 2006: namely, the strengthening of legal measures to counteract wrongdoing on the part of directors.

---

[49] See above, Chapter 6, and the cases and articles cited.
[50] See the cases cited in Chapter 6, especially *Smith v Croft (No 2)* **[11.14]**.
[51] See the law on authorisation by the board or the general meeting, above, Chapter 6.
[52] See the law on 'non-ratifiable wrongs', above, Chapter 6.

Personal claims by members

The rights of individual members are derived from various statutory and non-statutory sources. It follows that members have various avenues of complaint in pursuing personal remedies for any wrongs done to them. Much of the relevant substantive law has been addressed in earlier Chapters. The one omission is an enormously significant one. Members have a statutory right to complain to court that the company's affairs are being conducted in a manner that is unfairly prejudicial to the member's interests (CA 2006 s 994). This provision is commonly known as the 'unfair prejudice' section. The court has wide powers to make orders as it sees fit if a claim of unfair prejudice is made out (s 996). The relevant rules are discussed in detail below, at pp 552 ff, but first it is necessary to consider some of the more general issues that are relevant to pursuit of personal claims by members.

The sources of members' personal rights

Members' claims for a personal remedy are generally based on wrongs committed in relation to:

(i) The contractual rights derived from the *company's constitution* (CA 2006 s 33):[53] see above, pp 230 ff. Recall the difficult learning on the nature of the statutory contract, including the distinction between 'insider' and 'outsider' rights. In addition, these claims are subject to the 'internal irregularity principle' imposed by *Foss v Harbottle*: see *Macdougall v Gardiner* **[11.04]** and *Pender v Lushington* **[11.15]**. These rights are relevant in the pursuit of claims concerning amendments to the constitution, variations of class rights, capital reductions, etc, at least to the extent that the shareholder is not simply relying on specific statutory rights given to dissenting minorities to complain.

(ii) The contractual rights derived from outside contracts, especially *shareholder agreements*:[54] see above, pp 229 ff. See especially *Southern Foundries (1926) Ltd v Shirlaw* **[5.07]**; *Read v Astoria Garage (Streatham) Ltd* **[5.08]**; and *Russell v Northern Bank Ltd* **[8.01]**.

(iii) The *duties owed by directors* to members individually, in those rare cases where this can be asserted successfully: see above, pp 276 ff. See especially *Percival v Wright* **[6.01]**; *Peskin v Anderson* [2001] BCLC 874, CA; *Coleman v Myers* [1977] 2 NZLR 225 and also see p 594.

(iv) The entitlements inherent in the 'unfair prejudice' section (CA 2006 s 994): see below, pp 552 ff. This section provides a procedural mechanism for a member to raise a wide variety of complaints, including those noted in (i)–(iii) above, although the court cannot give a remedy unless the 'unfair prejudice' basis is established. But this section also permits shareholders to complain of, and obtain legal remedies for, acts and omissions that do not of themselves constitute legal wrongs.

The procedural form of members' personal claims

Two types of proceedings may be brought by shareholders to enforce personal rights. These need to be distinguished from the derivative claim discussed earlier (see above, p 535):

(i) A member may sue alone to enforce some personal or individual right: for instance, in *Pender v Lushington* **[11.15]** the right to have a vote recorded or a proxy recognised. *Rayfield v Hands* **[4.38]** shows that the company is not a necessary party to such proceedings—unless, of course, it is claimed that the company is a party to the wrongdoing.

---

[53] See CLR *Completing the Framework*, paras 5.64–5.74; Drury, 'The Relative Nature of a Shareholder's Right to Enforce the Company Contract' [1986] CLJ 219.

[54] See Ferran [1994] CLJ 343.

(ii) A member may sue alone, or with others, but in a *representative* capacity, claiming that a right has been infringed which, although affecting him as an individual member, also affects in a similar way either all or a number of the other members. Cases where a member has succeeded in a claim to have the directors observe the requirements of the Act or the constitution of the company itself are examples of this kind of action. This is a *representative action.*[55]

Problems of litigating both derivative and personal actions together

Establishing that personal and corporate claims co-exist

An individual member or shareholder whose personal rights have been infringed may pursue a personal claim even when the conduct complained of also constitutes a wrong to the company itself.

[11.15] Pender v Lushington (1877) 6 Ch D 70 (Court of Chancery (Master of the Rolls))

Pender had split his shareholding among nominees in order to defeat a provision in the articles that fixed the maximum number of votes to which any one shareholder was entitled. The chairman refused to accept the nominees' votes and accordingly declared lost a resolution proposed by Pender, which would otherwise have been carried. The Master of the Rolls granted Pender (who brought a representative action on behalf of himself and the other shareholders, and also an action in the name of the company) an injunction restraining the directors from acting on the basis that the nominees' votes had been bad. He also held that Pender had a right to sue in the company's name, at least until a general meeting resolved otherwise,[56] and a further right to sue in his own name.

JESSEL MR: But there is another ground [other than the claim in the company's name] on which the action may be maintained. This is an action by Mr Pender for himself. He is a member of the company, and whether he votes with the majority or the minority he is entitled to have his vote recorded—an individual right in respect of which he has a right to sue. That has nothing to do with the question like that raised in *Foss v Harbottle* and that line of cases. He has a right to say, 'Whether I vote in the majority or minority, you shall record my vote, as that is a right of property belonging to my interest in this company, and if you refuse to record my vote I will institute legal

---

[55] This procedure allows one or more individuals to appear as claimants or defendants on behalf of a number of persons having an identical interest in the proceedings. It was developed by the courts of Chancery in the early nineteenth century especially to deal with the problems of large unincorporated associations. Now the procedural rules are found in the Civil Procedure Rules 1998, 19.6 (*Representation of parties with the same interest*):

(1) Where more than one person has the same interest in a claim—
    (a) the claim may be begun; or
    (b) the court may order that the claim be continued,
    by or against one or more of the persons who have the same interest as representatives of any other persons who have that interest.

(2) The court may direct that a person may not act as a representative.

(3) Any party may apply to the court for an order under paragraph (2).

(4) Unless the court otherwise directs any judgment or order given in a claim in which a party is acting as a representative under this rule—
    (a) is binding on all persons represented in the claim; but
    (b) may only be enforced by or against a person who is not a party to the claim with the permission of the court . . .
It should be obvious that a *derivative* claim can be pursued by a shareholder acting in a *representative* capacity, so the two types of procedures may be in use at the same time.

[56] The analysis is not persuasive, however, and in the light of the comments above, at p 533, seems of doubtful authority.

proceedings against you to compel you'. What is the answer to such an action? It seems to me it can be maintained as a matter of substance, and that there is no technical difficulty in maintaining it . . .

➤ Notes

1. The real problem in these cases is to determine whether a member *does* have a personal right, and one that can be pursued despite the 'irregularity principle' in *Foss v Harbottle*: see *Macdougall v Gardiner* [11.04] above, which is difficult to reconcile with *Pender v Lushington*.

2. Personal rights do arise under some basic constitutional provisions, such as the right to vote or to exercise a pre-emptive power over a retiring member's share, and *Edwards v Halliwell* [11.08] illustrates the right in operation in a trade union context, protecting a member against having his dues raised without proper procedure and from unjustifiable expulsion. But all these 'constitutional' rights have an element of property linked with them, so it is easier to understand the readiness of the courts to come to the aid of a victimised member.

3. Where the complaint is about a mere matter of procedure, the courts seem much less willing to recognise a 'right to have the company observe the terms of its own constitution' which an individual member might invoke to claim standing to sue. One difficulty about such a supposed right is that it is balanced by an obligation to abide by majority decisions (see above, p 531). Another is that there are some constitutional irregularities which members may waive by a majority vote, or even, on the reasoning of *MacDougall v Gardiner* [11.05], to acquiesce in. Certainly, *obiter dicta* in cases such as *Re HR Harmer Ltd* [1959] 1 WLR 62, CA (see below, p 555), to the effect that members have a right to have their company conduct its affairs in accordance with its articles cannot be understood to apply without some such qualification.

4. Another difficulty concerns rights purportedly conferred on members by the company's articles, but not in their character as members. Cases like *Eley v Positive Life Assurance Co* [4.36] are accepted as laying down a rule that 'outsider rights' are not enforceable on a contractual basis by the member against the company. Nor can this rule be avoided simply by bringing an action as a 'member' to compel the company to comply with its 'constitutional obligations' to recognise the right. But the distinction between 'insider' and 'outsider' rights is not always clear. In *Pulbrook v Richmond Consolidated Mining Co* [5.01], a director who had been excluded from board meetings was held to have suffered an individual wrong, and held able to sue in his own name; also see *Quin and Axtens Ltd v Salmon* [4.06].

5. Of course, if the member *waives* the personal right, then there can be no complaint later on, even if it becomes apparent that the waiver was unwise. For example, in *Euro Brokers Holdings Ltd v Monecor (London) Ltd* [2003] EWCA Civ 105, special decision making procedures were set out in a shareholders' agreement specifically to protect the interests of certain members. All the members nevertheless took a decision, unanimously, without following the special procedures. The decision was held valid. The key point in this case, however, was that the decision attracted the support of all members at the time, and the court therefore held that it should not be subsequently reviewable on the basis of non-compliance with some specified procedure. In *Edwards v Halliwell* [11.8] type situations, it is precisely the lack of agreement to waive the special procedural requirements on the part of those protected by such requirements which gives rise to the arguments about personal rights and exceptions to the rule in *Foss v Harbottle*.

➤ Questions

1. In *Pender v Lushington* [11.15], if a general meeting had been called and had voted against continuing the action, what would have happened to Pender's personal and derivative claims?

2. In *Devlin v Slough Estates Ltd* [1983] BCLC 497 a member sought a declaration that the directors had acted in breach of duty. He alleged that they had prepared accounts which failed to conform with the requirements of the Companies Acts, and also that they had failed to distribute accounts properly prepared in accordance with the Acts to the members in advance of the annual general meeting as required by the company's articles. Dillon J held that Devlin did not have standing to bring either a derivative action on the company's behalf or an action in his own right complaining that his personal rights as a member had been infringed. How, if at all, can Dillon J's decision be reconciled with *Edwards v Halliwell, Pender v Lushington* and the Note above?

3. In *Lee v Chou Wen Hsien* [1984] 1 WLR 1202, [1985] BCLC 45, the plaintiff sued in his own name complaining that he had been improperly removed as a director by his fellow directors, who had purportedly acted under a power conferred by the articles. The Privy Council took the view that if a wrong had been done, it was done to the *company*, and that the rule in *Foss v Harbottle* precluded any action by the director in his own name. Do you agree?

The 'no reflective loss' principle

The 'no reflective loss' principle ensures that a defendant can be sued only once for the same loss, *and*, in doing that, prioritises the company's claim as a matter of principle. Regardless of the type of claim (common law or equity), or the form of remedy (compensation or restitution), or the status of the member (majority or minority), the principle prevents a person other than the company suing for the loss even when the person has a cause of action against the defendant, and even if the cause of action is different from the company's.

A member has no right to sue in a personal capacity where the loss merely reflects the loss suffered by the company (the 'no reflective loss' principle).

[11.16] Prudential Assurance Co Ltd v Newman Industries Ltd (No 2)
[1982] Ch 204 (Chancery Division and Court of Appeal)

[For the facts and details of other issues arising between the parties, see **[11.13]** above.]

The Court of Appeal allowed the appeal in part, but expressed the view that the plaintiff's claim in its own right was 'misconceived'. The judgment of the Court of Appeal (Cumming-Bruce, Templeman and Brightman LJJ) included the following:

In our judgment the personal claim is misconceived. It is of course correct, as the judge found and Mr. Bartlett did not dispute, that he and Mr. Laughton . . . owed the shareholders a duty to give . . . advice in good faith and not fraudulently. It is also correct that if directors convene a meeting on the basis of a fraudulent circular, a shareholder will have a right of action to recover any loss which he has been personally caused in consequence of the fraudulent circular; this might include the expense of attending the meeting. But what he cannot do is to recover damages merely because the company in which he is interested has suffered damage. He cannot recover a sum equal to the diminution in the market value of his shares, or equal to the likely diminution in dividend, because such a "loss" is merely a reflection of the loss suffered by the company. The shareholder does not suffer any personal loss. His only "loss" is through the company, in the diminution in the value of the net assets of the company, in which he has (say) a 3 per cent. shareholding. The plaintiff's shares are merely a right of participation in the company on the terms of the articles of association . . .

Counsel for the plaintiffs sought to answer this objection by agreeing that there cannot be double recovery from the defendants, but suggesting that the personal action will lie if the company's remedy is for some reason not pursued. But how can the failure of the company to pursue its remedy against the robber entitle the shareholder to recover for himself? What happens if the robbery takes place in year 1, the shareholder sues in year 2, and the company makes up its mind in year 3 to pursue its remedy? Is the shareholder's action stayed, if still on foot? Supposing judgment has already been recovered by the shareholder and satisfied, what then?

A personal action could have the most unexpected consequences . . .

The plaintiffs in this action were never concerned to recover in the personal action. The plaintiffs were only interested in the personal action as a means of circumventing the rule in *Foss v. Harbottle*. The plaintiffs succeeded. A personal action would subvert the rule in *Foss v. Harbottle* and that rule is not merely a tiresome procedural obstacle placed in the path of a shareholder by a legalistic judiciary. The rule is the consequence of the fact that a corporation is a separate legal entity. Other consequences are limited liability and limited rights. The company is liable for its contracts and torts; the shareholder has no such liability. The company acquires causes of action for breaches of contract and for torts which damage the company. No cause of action vests in the shareholder. When the shareholder acquires a share he accepts the fact that the value of his investment follows the fortunes of the company and that he can only exercise his influence over the fortunes of the company by the exercise of his voting rights in general meeting. The law confers on him the right to ensure that the company observes the limitations of its memorandum of association and the right to ensure that other shareholders observe the rule, imposed upon them by the articles of association. If it is right that the law has conferred or should in certain restricted circumstances confer further rights on a shareholder the scope and consequences of such further rights require careful consideration. In this case it is neither necessary nor desirable to draw any general conclusions. . . .

[11.17] Johnson v Gore Wood and Co [2002] 2 AC 1 (House of Lords)

A company, WWH, commenced proceedings against a firm of solicitors, GW, for professional negligence related to the exercise of an option to purchase land. That claim was eventually settled. Subsequently, Johnson, a majority member in the company, commenced proceedings against the same firm for personal losses sustained which arose out of the same circumstances. It was argued by the firm that Johnson could not recover his own personal losses as these were essentially the same as the losses sustained by the company. The House of Lords explained the relevant legal rules.

LORD BINGHAM:

The recoverability of the damages claimed by Mr Johnson

. . . GW's first argument before the House, applicable to all save two of the pleaded heads of damage, was in principle very simple. It was that this damage, if suffered at all, had been suffered by WWH, and Mr Johnson, being for this purpose no more than a shareholder in the company, could not sue to recover its loss. As the Court of Appeal pointed out in *Prudential Assurance Co Ltd v Newman Industries Ltd* (No 2) [1982] Ch 204, 210:

> "A derivative action is an exception to the elementary principle that A cannot, as a general rule, bring an action against B to recover damages or secure other relief on behalf of C for an injury done by B to C. C is the proper plaintiff because C is the party injured, and, therefore, the person in whom the cause of action is vested."

Here, it was argued, Mr Johnson was seeking to recover damage which had been suffered by WWH.

Mr Johnson's response was equally simple. It was accepted, for purposes of the application to strike out the damages claim, that GW owed a duty to him personally and was in breach of that duty. Therefore, subject to showing that the damage complained of was caused by GW's breach of duty and was not too remote, which depended on the facts established at trial and could not be determined on the pleadings, he was entitled in principle to recover any damage which he had himself suffered as a personal loss separate and distinct from any loss suffered by the company.

On this issue we were referred to a number of authorities which . . . support the following propositions.

(1) Where a company suffers loss caused by a breach of duty owed to it, only the company may sue in respect of that loss. No action lies at the suit of a shareholder suing in that capacity and no other[57] to make good a diminution in the value of the shareholder's shareholding where that merely reflects the loss suffered by the company. A claim will not lie by a shareholder to make good a loss which would be made good if the company's assets were replenished through action against the party responsible for the loss, even if the company, acting through its constitutional organs, has declined or failed to make good that loss. So much is clear from *Prudential Assurance Co Ltd v Newman Industries (No 2)* **[11.13/11.16]** . . . .

(2) Where a company suffers loss but has no cause of action to sue to recover that loss, the shareholder in the company may sue in respect of it (if the shareholder has a cause of action to do so), even though the loss is a diminution in the value of the shareholding. . . .

(3) Where a company suffers loss caused by a breach of duty to it, and a shareholder suffers a loss separate and distinct from that suffered by the company caused by breach of a duty independently owed to the shareholder, each may sue to recover the loss caused to it by breach of the duty owed to it but neither may recover loss caused to the other by breach of the duty owed to that other. . . .

These principles do not resolve the crucial decision which a court must make on a strike-out application, whether on the facts pleaded a shareholder's claim is sustainable in principle, nor the decision which the trial court must make, whether on the facts proved the shareholder's claim should be upheld. On the one hand the court must respect the principle of company autonomy, ensure that the company's creditors are not prejudiced by the action of individual shareholders and ensure that a party does not recover compensation for a loss which another party has suffered. On the other, the court must be astute to ensure that the party who has in fact suffered loss is not arbitrarily denied fair compensation. The problem can be resolved only by close scrutiny of the pleadings at the strike-out stage and all the proven facts at the trial stage: the object is to ascertain whether the loss claimed appears to be or is one which would be made good if the company had enforced its full rights against the party responsible, and whether (to use the language of *Prudential Assurance Co Ltd v Newman Industries (No 2)* . . . the loss claimed is "merely a reflection of the loss suffered by the company". In some cases the answer will be clear, as where the shareholder claims the loss of dividend or a diminution in the value of a shareholding attributable solely to depletion of the company's assets, or a loss unrelated to the business of the company. In other cases, inevitably, a finer judgment will be called for. At the strike-out stage any reasonable doubt must be resolved in favour of the claimant.

I turn to consider the heads of claim now pleaded by Mr Johnson. (1) . . . The claim is for sums which Mr Johnson, acting on GW's advice, invested in . . . companies and lost. This claim is unobjectionable in principle, . . . (2) Cost of personal borrowings: loan capital and interest. The claim is for sums which Mr Johnson claims he was obliged to borrow at punitive rates of interest to fund his personal outgoings and those of his businesses. Both the ingredients and the quantum of this claim will call for close examination, among other things to be sure that it is not a disguised claim for loss of dividend, but it cannot at this stage be struck out as bad on its face. The same is true of Mr Johnson's claims for bank interest and charges and mortgage charges and interest (which will raise obvious questions of remoteness). (3) Diminution in value of Mr Johnson's pension and majority shareholding in WWH. In part this claim relates to payments which the company would have made into a pension fund for Mr Johnson: I think it plain that this claim is merely a reflection of the company's loss and I would strike it out. In part the claim relates to enhancement of the value of Mr Johnson's pension if the payments had been duly made. I do not regard this part of the claim as

---

[57] [Ie suing personally or in a representative capacity, but not pursuing a derivative claim.]

objectionable in principle. An alternative claim, based on the supposition that the company would not have made the pension payments, that its assets would thereby have been increased and that the value of Mr Johnson's shareholding would thereby have been enhanced, is also a reflection of the company's loss and I would strike it out. (4) Loss of 12.5% of Mr Johnson's shareholding in WWH. Mr Johnson claims that he transferred these shares to a lender as security for a loan and that because of his lack of funds, caused by GW's breach of duty, he was unable to buy them back. This claim is not in my view objectionable in principle. (5) Additional tax liability. If proved, this is a personal loss and I would not strike it out . . .

LORD MILLETT:

. . . A company is a legal entity separate and distinct from its shareholders. It has its own assets and liabilities and its own creditors. The company's property belongs to the company and not to its shareholders . . . If the company has a cause of action, this represents a legal chose in action which represents part of its assets. Accordingly, where a company suffers loss as a result of an actionable wrong owed to it, the cause of action is vested in the company and the company alone can sue. No action lies at the suit of a shareholder suing as such, though exceptionally he may be permitted to bring a derivative action in right of the company and recover damages on its behalf: see *Prudential Assurance Co Ltd v Newman Industries Ltd (No 2)*. Correspondingly, of course, a company's shares are the property of the shareholder and not the company, and if he suffers loss as a result of an actionable wrong done to him, then prima facie he alone can sue and the company cannot. On the other hand, although a share is an identifiable piece of property which belongs to the shareholder and has an ascertainable value, it also represents a proportionate part of the company's met assets, and if these are depleted the diminution in its assets will be reflected in the diminution in the value of the shares. The correspondence may not be exact, especially in the case of a company whose shares are publicly traded, since their value depends on market sentiment. But in the case of a small private company like this company, the correspondence is exact.

This causes no difficulty where the company has a cause of action and the shareholder has none; or where the shareholder has a cause of action and the company has none . . . . Where the company suffers loss as a result of a wrong to the shareholder but has no cause of action in respect of its loss, the shareholder can sue and recover damages for his own loss, whether of a capital or income nature, measured by the diminution in the value of his shareholding. He must, of course show that he has an independent cause of action of his own and that he has suffered personal loss caused by the defendant's actionable wrong. Since the company itself has no cause of action in respect of its loss, its assets are not depleted by the recovery of damages by the shareholder.

The position is, however, different where the company suffers loss caused by the breach of a duty owed both to the company and to the shareholder. In such a case the shareholder's loss, in so far as this is measured by the diminution in value of his shareholding or the loss of dividends, merely reflects the loss suffered by the company in respect of which the company has its own cause of action. If the shareholder is allowed to recover in respect of such loss, then either there will be double recovery at the expense of the defendant or the shareholder will recover at the expense of the company and its creditors and other shareholders. Neither course can be permitted. This is a matter of principle; there is no discretion involved. Justice to the defendant requires the exclusion of one claim or the other; protection of the interests of the company's creditors requires that it is the company which is allowed to recover to the exclusion of the shareholder. These principles have been established in a number of cases, though they have not always been faithfully observed . . .

[After discussing two cases he regarded as incorrectly decided, he continued:] I cannot accept this reasoning as representing the position in English law. It is of course correct that the diminution in the value of the plaintiff's shares was by definition a personal loss and not the company's loss, but that is not the point. The point is that it merely reflected the diminution of the company's assets. The test is not whether the company could have made a claim in respect of the loss in question; the question is whether, treating the company and the shareholder as one for this purpose, the shareholder's loss is franked by that of the company. If so, such reflected loss is recoverable by the company and not by the shareholders.

[One of the judges in the cases criticised] acknowledged that double recovery could not be permitted, but thought that the problem did not arise where the company had settled its claim. He considered that it would be sufficient to make an allowance for the amount paid to the liquidator. With respect, I cannot accept this either. As Hobhouse LJ observed in *Gerber Garment Technology Inc v Lectra Systems Ltd* [1997] RPC 443, 471, if the company chooses not to exercise its remedy, the loss to the shareholder is caused by the company's decision not to pursue its remedy and not by the defendant's wrongdoing. By a parity of reasoning, the same applies if the company settles for less than it might have done. Shareholders (and creditors) who are aggrieved by the liquidator's proposals are not without remedy; they can have recourse to the Companies Court, or sue the liquidator for negligence.

But there is more to it than causation. The disallowance of the shareholder's claim in respect of reflective loss is driven by policy considerations. In my opinion, these preclude the shareholder from going behind the settlement of the company's claim. If he were allowed to do so then, if the company's action were brought by its directors, they would be placed in a position where their interest conflicted with their duty; while if it were brought by the liquidator, it would make it difficult for him to settle the action and would effectively take the conduct of the litigation out of his hands. The present case is a fortiori; Mr Johnson cannot be permitted to challenge in one capacity the adequacy of the terms he agreed in another . . .

For the reasons given by Lord Bingham, I too would strike out Mr Johnson's claims to damages for mental distress and anxiety and aggravated damages. Accordingly, I would dismiss the cross-appeal while varying the order of the Court of Appeal in the manner proposed . . .

Despite the 'no reflective loss' principle, if a company is unable to pursue its own cause of action precisely because of the actions of the wrongdoer, a member may be able to recover all the personal losses arising out of the same wrongdoing.

[11.18] Giles v Rhind [2002] EWCA Civ 1428, [2003] Ch 618 (Court of Appeal)

G and R had been members in a company which became insolvent following the diversion by R of a contract to a third party, in contravention of a shareholders' agreement. The company discontinued its proceedings against R as a consequence of its insolvency, but G sought to pursue in his own right damages against R. G contended that his claims were not merely reflective of the company's loss. Accepting this argument, the Court of Appeal held G had a cause of action against R separate from that of the company. In any case, with regard to G's losses which reflected those of the company, G was entitled to proceed with his personal claim, as the company had been prevented from pursuing its own action as a result of R's wrongdoing. Hence, this case can be distinguished from *Johnson v Gore Wood*, where additional claims by a member in relation to reflective losses were barred where the company was in fact able to pursue its own action (and had pursued it to settlement).

WALLER LJ: . . . There are certain facts which distinguish our present case from *Johnson v Gore Wood & Co* [11.17]. First, *Johnson v Gore Wood & Co* was a case as emphasised by Lord Bingham and Lord Millett where Mr Johnson carried on his business through a small private company. His position was practically indistinguishable from that of his company. It was a case where the depletion in the value of the assets reflected in the diminution in the value of the shares was likely to correspond exactly (in the words of Lord Millett at 121B). Second, W Ltd had brought an action and compromised the same; indeed Johnson was the directing mind of the company when it agreed to the compromise. There is no reason to think that the company would not have recovered if it had chosen to do so precisely that value which would have reflected the diminution in value of the shares which Johnson was claiming. There was no question of W Ltd having been disabled from bringing the claim by the very wrongdoing which by contract the defendant had promised the plaintiff he would not carry out. Third, the action was tried on the assumption that the solicitors owed an independent duty to Johnson, but the nature of the case was such that it was not easy to assume such a totally independent duty. Fourth, it could not be argued ultimately that the loss of value was other than reflective of the company's loss despite the way the claim was pleaded. But, so far as the damage in relation to investment in shares in this case is concerned, Mr Giles' losses are not as it seems to me "merely reflective". The shares became valueless on his case because the company's business as a whole was destroyed. Obviously the value of his shares reflect to some extent the value of the assets of the company but in his case they also reflect what Lord Millett described as market sentiment or what would have been considered their value because of the potential which the business had. Fifth, it certainly is not in my view in reality a case where Mr Giles is seeking to recover as damages, damages which the company could have recovered. The company's claim for damages for breach of contract would have been of a quite different nature based on an assessment of profits lost by virtue of the confidential information being used to take the Netto contract. Mr Giles' loss relates to the fact that the business as a whole was totally destroyed. Indeed even if the company had recovered damages the Netto contract would never have been restored, the business would never have been the same and Mr Giles' share would inevitably have been devalued by Mr Rhind's activities. The value of the shares when Mr Rhind obtained £300,000 for them in 1993 reflected not only the assets of the company but the good prospects of the company into the future and that loss of value could not be recovered by SHF in any action that it might have brought. . . .

Thus neither Lord Bingham nor Lord Millett would I think argue with the following propositions. First that the principle which *Johnson v Gore Wood & Co* establishes will not in the words of Sir Christopher Slade in *Walker v Stones* [2000] 4 All ER 412 at 438:

> "operate to deprive a claimant of an otherwise good cause of action in a case where (a) the claimant can establish that the defendant's conduct has constituted a breach of some legal duty owed to him personally (whether under the law of contract, torts, trusts or any other branch of the law) *and* (b) on its assessment of the facts, the court is satisfied that such breach of duty has caused him personal loss, separate and distinct from any loss that may have been occasioned to any corporate body in which he may be financially interested."

Second (as they both recognised) if shareholders have a cause of action in relation to damage suffered by the company in which they hold the shares where that company does not have a cause of action, the shareholders may bring a claim even if in reality they are claiming damages reflective of the loss suffered by the company. The logic of that second exception ought to be based on the injustice of a wrongdoer being able to defeat a claim by suggesting that the loss being suffered was suffered by the company and is thus irrecoverable by the shareholder although the company does not or may not have a cause of action. But it is right to say that Lord Millett justifies that exception on the basis that "since the company itself has no cause of action in respect of its loss, its assets are not depleted by the recovery of damages by the shareholder". Thus Lord Millett appears to have in mind the concept that the cause of action which a company has (if it has) is one which enables the company to bring about full recovery . . .

In my view there are two aspects of the case which Mr Giles seeks to bring which point to Mr Giles being entitled to pursue his claim for the loss of his investment. First, as it seems to me, part of that loss is not reflective at all. It is a personal loss which would have been suffered at least in some measure even if the company had pursued its claim for damages. Second, even in relation to that part of the claim for diminution which could be said to be reflective of the company's loss, since, if the company had no cause of action to recover that loss the shareholder could bring a claim, the same should be true of a situation in which the wrongdoer has disabled the company from pursuing that cause of action. I accept that on the language of Lord Millett's speech there are difficulties with this second proposition, but I am doubtful whether he intended to go so far as his literal words would take him. Furthermore it seems to me that on Lord Bingham's speech supported by the others, it would not be right to conclude that the second proposition is unarguable . . .

In my judgment Mr Giles should be entitled to pursue his head of damage relating to his case that his shares became valueless as a result of the activities of Mr Rhind.

As regards his other heads of loss, again on the basis that Mr Rhind disabled the company from pursuing any claim for damages, I would suggest that Mr Giles should not be precluded from proceeding with those claims. In any event I do not see that the other heads are pure "reflective loss". If Mr Giles had not been a shareholder but simply an employee or a lender with an enforceable covenant in his favour, those losses surely would have been recoverable. The fact that he is also a shareholder should not deny him his claims under those other heads. There will of course have to be detailed consideration given to the quantification of those claims. It may be relatively straightforward to demonstrate that the shares should have had the value of £330,000 as at April 1994 and that he would also have recovered his loan plus arrears of remuneration if the breach of contract had not taken place when it did. But what might have happened if the Netto contract had not been taken wrongfully as it was, is far more speculative. Would Mr Giles have continued with the company? What would the company's fortunes have been? Certainly he would not be entitled as it seems to me to have the value of his shares as at April 1994 and future remuneration because the sale of the shares would presumably have meant resignation from the company. In any event all those matters need proper enquiry and investigation at assessment. All it is necessary for us to decide is whether the heads of claim should be struck out as at this stage and I would be in favour of allowing them to go forward. I would thus allow the appeal . . .

CHADWICK LJ:

. . . Subject to two reservations, I do not quarrel with the propositions which the judge derived from the speeches in *Johnson v Gore Wood*. They are, I think, consistent, with the analysis of those speeches in the judgments in this Court in *Day v Cook*. As Lady Justice Arden put it, where the loss suffered by the shareholder is merely a reflection of the loss suffered by the company, "the company's claim, if it exists, will always trump that of the shareholder". [He then introduced his two reservations, and continued:]

The first issue: is this a case in which the no reflective loss principle should be applied?

The paradigm case in which, by reason of the wrong done to it, the company is unable, in practice, to pursue its claim against the wrongdoer is one in which the company is obliged to abandon its claim because the wrong has deprived it of the funds needed for that purpose. *Johnson v Gore Wood* was not such a case. The company (WWH) had pursued its claim against Gore Wood & Co to trial. It had compromised that claim, in the sixth week of that trial, upon payment of a substantial sum. Although the company was in financial difficulties at the time of the compromise, those difficulties were caused by other factors . . .

. . . To put the point more starkly, the effect of the judge's decision [Lord Bingham in *Johnson v Gore Wood*]—as he himself recognised—is that a wrongdoer who, in breach of his contract with the company and its shareholders, "steals" the whole of the company's business, with the intention that the company should be so denuded of funds that it cannot pursue its remedy against him, and who gives effect to that intention by an application for security for costs which his own breach of contract has made it impossible for the company to provide, is entitled to defeat a claim by the shareholders on the grounds that their claim is "trumped" by the claim which his own conduct was calculated to prevent, and has in fact prevented, the company from pursuing.. If that were, indeed, the law following the decision in *Johnson v Gore Wood*, I would not find it easy to reconcile the result with Lord Bingham's observation, at [2002] 2 AC 1, 36C-D, that "the court must be astute to ensure that the party who has in fact suffered loss is not arbitrarily denied fair compensation".

In my view the reasoning in *Johnson v Gore Wood* does not compel the conclusion that the law requires that result . . .

I confess that I have found it difficult to reconcile the point which Lord Millett appears to be making in the sentence "The test is not whether the company could have made a claim in respect of the loss in question; the question is whether, treating the company and the shareholder as one for this purpose, the shareholder's loss is franked by that of the company" with the second of Lord Bingham's propositions [see above, **[11.17]**] or with the decision in *Gerber*,[58] which Lord Millett did not criticise. In a case where the company never had a cause of action in respect of the wrong which has caused it loss, the shareholder may sue on his own cause of action (if he has one) even though the loss is a diminution in the value of the shareholding—see [2002] 2 AC 1, 35H, 43B. I do not think that Lord Millett could have intended it to be understood, from that sentence, that the question whether the company ever had a cause of action in respect of the wrong which has caused its loss is irrelevant. And, in the light of his approval (in the following paragraph) of Lord Justice Hobhouse's reasoning in *Gerber*, he could not have intended it to be understood that the circumstances in which the company fails to pursue its remedy are necessarily irrelevant.

It is clear, however, that Lord Millett did not think that the inability of the shareholder to establish causation was the sole reason for the no reflective loss principle. In the paragraph which immediately follows that which I have just set out Lord Millett said this (*ibid* at page 66F-G),:

> "*But there is more to it than causation. The disallowance of the shareholder's claim in respect of reflective loss is driven by policy considerations.* In my opinion, these preclude the shareholder from going behind the settlement of the company's claim. If he were allowed to do so then, if the company's action were brought by its directors, they would be placed in a position where their interest conflicted with their duty; while if it were brought by the liquidator, it would make it difficult for him to settle the action and would effectively take the conduct of the liquidation out of his hands." [emphasis added]

The policy consideration to which, as it seems to me, Lord Millett is referring in that passage is the need to avoid a situation in which the wrongdoer cannot safely compromise the company's claim without fear that he may be met with a further claim by the shareholder in respect of the company's loss. That, I think, is what he had in mind when he referred to the difficulty which a liquidator would have in settling the action if a shareholder, or creditor, were able to go behind the settlement. He had recognised, in the previous paragraph, that an aggrieved shareholder or creditor could sue the liquidator; his concern was to limit their remedy to a claim against the liquidator. Similar considerations apply where the company's claim is settled by the directors. But, in such a case, there is the further consideration that directors who are also shareholders (or creditors) should not be in a position where settlement of the company's claim at less than its true value (or abandonment of that claim) leaves them with a claim which they can pursue against the wrongdoer in their own interest. If that is a correct analysis of that passage, then the passage presents no difficulty in the case where the company has not settled its claim, but has been forced to abandon it by reason of impecuniosity attributable to the wrong which has been done to it. In such a case the policy considerations to which Lord Millett referred are not engaged. And it is difficult to see any other consideration of policy which should lead to the conclusion that a shareholder or creditor who has suffered loss by reason of a wrong which, itself, has prevented the company from pursuing its remedy should be denied any remedy at all . . .

For those reasons, I am satisfied that the decision in *Johnson v Gore Wood* does not compel the conclusion which the judge reached on the preliminary issue which he had to decide. In my view, on the particular facts alleged in this case, it cannot be held—on what is, in effect, an application to strike out the claim to damages without a trial—that the no reflective loss principle is applicable. The question whether or not the wrong done to the company by Mr Rhind was a direct cause of the receiver's decision to discontinue the claim made by the company in proceedings 1994 S 755 cannot be determined without a trial in the present proceedings. If and so far as that question is not

---

[58] *Gerber Garment Technology Inc v Lectra Systems Ltd* [1997] RPC 443.

raised squarely on the pleadings, I would think it right (in the circumstances in which the question arose) to give permission to amend. I would allow the appeal on that ground.

The second issue: is the loss of future benefits properly to be regarded as reflective of the company's loss?

The question turns on whether the loss which Mr Giles has suffered as a result of the termination of his employment by the receivers is reflective of loss suffered by the company by reason of the wrong done to it by Mr Rhind. In my view the judge was wrong to hold that it was. I think that he fell into error by confusing the loss claimed under this head with the circumstances which had given rise to that loss. There is a distinction to be drawn between the claim for accrued remuneration under the first head and the claim for loss of future benefits under the second head. In the first case, the loss suffered by Mr Giles as an employee is reflective of the company's own loss; if the company had been able to enforce its rights against Mr Rhind, it would have the funds needed to pay its debts. In the second case, the loss suffered by Mr Giles is not reflective of any loss suffered by the company; it flows from the termination of his employment following the destruction of the company's business. If the company had been able to enforce its rights against Mr Rhind, following the destruction of its business, the damages which the company might recover would not compensate Mr Giles for the loss which flows from the termination of his employment. I would allow the appeal, in relation to the second head of loss, on this ground also . . .

➤ Notes

1. In *Humberclyde Finance Group Ltd v Hicks* 2001 WL 1346978, the court held that the 'no reflective loss' principle from *Johnson v Gore Wood* did not infringe the European Convention on Human Rights, as embodied in the UK's Human Rights Act 1998.

2. Both *Johnson v Gore Wood* [11.17] and *Giles v Rhind* [11.18] were considered in *Gardner v Parker* [2004] EWCA Civ 781, [2004] 2 BCLC 554. G, the assignee of the rights of action of B, a company, sought recovery for an alleged breach of fiduciary duty by P (the sole director of B) and S, a second company in which B held a minority of shares. G claimed that P had sold an asset of S at an undervalue, forcing S into administrative receivership. G argued that the 'no reflective loss' principle should not apply where: (1) the shareholder's claim concerned a breach of fiduciary duty; (2) P's actions had prevented S from commencing legal proceedings to recover its losses from P; and (3) the shareholder's claim was in the capacity of creditor. Dismissing the case, the Court of Appeal held that: (1) the 'no reflective loss' principle was applicable where breaches of fiduciary duty were concerned, as the principle governed recovery for particular kinds of loss and thus the cause of action and relief sought in any particular case was irrelevant; (2) a lack of evidence prevented the conclusion being drawn that P's actions precluded S from seeking recovery; and (3) applying *Johnson v Gore Wood*, no reason existed to disapply the 'no reflective loss' principle where the shareholder's claim as creditor was based on his position as an employee. All these cases do, however, emphasise the need for careful assessment of the facts to determine accurately whether the loss being pursued is indeed a 'reflected' loss.

3. In *Perry v Day* [2004] EWHC 3372; [2005] 2 BCLC 405, P and D were both shareholders in a private company. P sought damages from D for breach of a shareholders' agreement which bound the shareholders, *inter alia*, to use their 'best endeavours to promote the interests and prospects of the company'. D had sold a parcel of land to the company, but as the consequence of a mistake, an important strip of land had been excluded from the conveyance. The mistake only became evident when the company tried to sell the land to a third party, and then D would only agree to transfer the excluded strip of land on payment of further consideration. The court upheld P's claim on the basis that: (1) D's demand for more money was a clear breach of his obligations under the shareholders' agreement; (2) it was only D's demand

for more money in exchange for the transfer of the strip that caused the relevant loss, as the loss caused by the defective sale itself could be repaired by D's agreement to transfer the strip; and (3) though P's loss was reflective of the company's loss, and the company could have successfully brought a claim for rectification of the title, the company was precluded from doing this because of D's wrongdoing. By demanding the company surrender its claim on terms generous to D, D had breached his obligations, and this constituted a wrongdoing sufficient to bring the situation within the parameters of the *Giles v Rhind* exception to the no reflective loss principle upheld in *Johnson v Gore Wood*.

Unfairly prejudicial conduct of the company's affairs

So far in this Chapter the focus has been on maladministration that constitutes a legal wrong, either to the company itself or to its members. CA 2006 s 994ff gives the court, on the application of a member, a wide-ranging power to remedy conduct of a company's affairs that is 'unfairly prejudicial to the interests of members generally or to some part of its members'.[59] The most common complaint is that a controlling majority has acted in a manner that is 'unfairly prejudicial' (the meaning of this term is explored below). The most common remedy sought is an order that the majority purchase the minority's shares at a price that reflects their proportion of the company's value. This is despite s 996(1), which gives the court the power to make 'such order as it thinks fit', with s 996(2) merely providing examples of possible orders, including compulsory share purchases. Most of the cases concern 'quasi-partnerships', although the provision has general application.

The scope of CA 2006 s 994

CA 2006 s 994 repeats CA 1985 s 459, so the doctrinal and practical learning on the earlier provision remains relevant. Indeed, some of the cases on the initial provision (CA 1948 s 210), which provided remedies for 'oppression' rather than unfair prejudice, are still considered influential.

CA 1985 s 459 was a popular provision, not least because the courts adopted a purposive approach and interpreted the section liberally where necessary in order not to stultify its development. Moreover, by its very terms the section clearly aimed to address management problems ranging well beyond traditional legal wrongs done to a company or its shareholders. But this popularity created problems of its own. The courts were required to handle large numbers of cases, each often demanding the hearing of a great deal of evidence and examination of the conduct of the parties, sometimes going back over many years. This caused costs to escalate, even though most cases concerned relatively small companies, where costs of full High Court hearings are discouraging, if not entirely prohibitive.[60]

---

[59] See the parallel provision applying to the acts and omissions of the administrator, which can be invoked by creditors as well as shareholders: IA 1986, Sch B1, para 74. This substitutes the word 'harm' for 'prejudice' (it is not clear whether this was intended to have substantive implications) and specifically allows for complaints that the administrator is not performing his functions 'as quickly or as efficiently as is reasonably practicable'.

[60] One unreported case *(Re Freudiana Music Co Ltd* (1993)) lasted for 165 full court days, with the respondent awarded *costs* of £2m. In *Re Elgindata Ltd* **[11.21]**, costs totalling £320,000 were run up in a dispute over shares worth less than £25,000: see [1993] BCLC 119. The judgment of Arden J in *Re Macro (Ipswich) Ltd* **[11.22]** reviews the history of the company over a period of nearly 50 years and extends to 56 pages. In *Re Unisoft Group Ltd (No 3)* [1994] 1 BCLC 609 at 611, Harman J said: 'Petitions under s 459 have become notorious to judges of this court—and also to the Bar—for their length, their unpredictability of management, and the enormous and appalling costs which are incurred upon them.'

In the light of these factors, there were frequent calls for reform (not least from the judges themselves). Both the Law Commissions and the CLR examined CA 1985 s 459 and proposed possible reforms.[61] The Law Commissions recommended that the excessive length and cost of many s 459 proceedings should be dealt with primarily by active case management by the courts. This is happening. They also recommended encouraging the use of alternative dispute resolution procedures. Their other recommendations (not so far adopted) included:

(i)   making legislative provision for a statutory buy-out remedy (at a price reckoned on a *pro rata* and not a discounted basis) where a member of a private company with a shareholding of at least 10% has been excluded from participation in management, coupled with a presumption in such cases that the expulsion was unfairly prejudicial. Since research shows that the most common s 459 application is made in this kind of case, and that a buy-out is invariably ordered if the claimant is successful, it seems likely that a rule along these lines would lead to many cases being settled out of court.

(ii)   providing a time limit for bringing s 459 claims, to stop so much past history being put before the court.

(iii)   adding a winding up remedy to the remedies available under s 459 (but also providing that an application to seek this remedy should require the leave of the court).[62]

(iv)   prohibiting advertisement (ie publicity) of s 459 proceedings, unless the court orders otherwise.

(v)   encouraging the use of 'shareholder's exit' articles in the constitutions of private companies (ie articles which settle in advance the terms on which members will leave the company in the event of future disputes), and providing such an article in the Model Articles for private companies.

The CLR gave these suggestions a cool reception, and expressly opposed recommendations (i) and (iii). It did, however, put forward one suggestion which features in the law of some other countries, but would be a novelty here: ie that s 459 should apply not only to the abuse of power by a majority, but also to cases where a *minority* exercises its powers to block company decisions—eg where it improperly prevents the passing of a special resolution which is demonstrably in the best interests of the company. As matters have emerged, CA 2006 has not taken up any of these suggestions, and CA 2006 s 994 adopts precisely the same form as CA 1985 s 459.

Although an enormous number of decisions are reported every year, not many repay prolonged study. Since the remedy is at the court's discretion, and depends upon the facts, there is often a lengthy account of all the evidence given in the case, but little chance of finding statements of principle of any significance. Included here are extracts from the few leading cases, and from a further selection of illustrative cases.   ·

[11.19] Scottish Co-operative Wholesale Society Ltd v Meyer
[1959] AC 324 (House of Lords)

(This case was decided under the old CA 1948 s 210 'oppression' section, but is still regarded as influential. Despite the differences in the wording of CA 2006 s 994 and s 210, there can be little doubt that the same conclusion would be reached today.)

---

[61] See Law Commission, *Shareholder Remedies* (Law Com Consultation Document No 142, 1996) pp 55–102; and *Shareholder Remedies* (Law Com 246, 1997), Parts 2–4 (for reform proposals); CLR, *Developing the Framework*, paras. 4.100–4.111; *Completing the Structure*, paras 5.75–5.81, and *Final Report I*, paras 7.41–7.45. Also see C Riley, 'Contracting Out of Company Law: Section 459 of the Companies Act 1985 and the Role of the Courts' (1992) 55 MLR 782.

[62] Since CA 2006 s 996 gives the court the widest possible discretion (as did CA 1985 s 461), this might seem unnecessary, but precedents suggested that courts could not make such an order, given that it would profoundly affect parties not before the court, without providing all the protections delivered by the IA 1986 procedures.

Scottish Textile & Manufacturing Co Ltd was a private company formed in 1946 by the appellant society and the respondents, Meyer and Lucas, to manufacture rayon cloth at a time when this product was subject to a system of state licensing. The society held the majority of the issued shares and had appointed three of its own directors to the board; the respondents, who held the rest of the shares, were joint managing directors and as such filled the remaining seats on the board. The society had formed this subsidiary because it could not have secured a licence to produce rayon cloth without experienced managers, and the respondents had the necessary experience. After licensing ceased in 1952, the society, by transferring the company's business to another branch of its organisation and cutting off the supply of raw materials on which the company was dependent, caused its activities to come to a standstill, with the result that it made no profits and the value of its shares fell greatly. The respondents petitioned for relief under s 210, and the House of Lords, confirming the decision of the Court of Session, ordered the society to purchase their shares at a fair price.

LORD DENNING discussed the facts, and continued: Such being 'the matters complained of' by Dr Meyer and Mr Lucas, it is said: 'Those are all complaints about the conduct of the co-operative society. How do they touch the real issue—the manner in which the affairs of the textile company were being conducted?' The answer is, I think, by their impact on the nominee directors. It must be remembered that we are here concerned with the manner in which the affairs of the textile company were being conducted. That is, with the conduct of those in control of its affairs. They may be some of the directors themselves, or, behind them, a group of shareholders who nominated those directors or whose interests those directors serve. If those persons—the nominee directors or the shareholders behind them—conduct the affairs of the company in a manner oppressive to the other shareholders, the court can intervene to bring an end to the oppression.

What, then, is the position of the nominee directors here? Under the articles of association of the textile company the co-operative society was entitled to nominate three out of the five directors, and it did so. It nominated three of its own directors and they held office, as the articles said, 'as nominees' of the co-operative society. These three were therefore at one and the same time directors of the co-operative society—being three out of twelve of that company—and also directors of the textile company—three out of five there. So long as the interests of all concerned were in harmony, there was no difficulty. The nominee directors could do their duty by both companies without embarrassment. But, so soon as the interests of the two companies were in conflict, the nominee directors were placed in an impossible position. It is plain that, in the circumstances, these three gentlemen could not do their duty by both companies, and they did not do so. They put their duty to the co-operative society above their duty to the textile company in this sense, at least, that they did nothing to defend the interests of the textile company against the conduct of the co-operative society. They probably thought that 'as nominees' of the co-operative society their first duty was to the co-operative society. In this they were wrong. By subordinating the interests of the textile company to those of the co-operative society, they conducted the affairs of the textile company in a manner oppressive to the other shareholders.

It is said that these three directors were at most only guilty of inaction—of doing nothing to protect the textile company. But the affairs of a company can, in my opinion, be conducted oppressively by the directors doing nothing to defend its interests when they ought to do something—just as they can conduct its affairs oppressively by doing something injurious to its interests when they ought not to do it . . .

Your Lordships were referred to *Bell v Lever Bros Ltd,*[63] where Lord Blanesburgh said that a director of one company was at liberty to become a director also of a rival company. That may have

[63] [1932] AC 161, HL.

been so at that time. But it is at the risk now of an application under s 210 if he subordinates the interests of the one company to those of the other.

So I would hold that the affairs of the textile company were being conducted in a manner oppressive to Dr Meyer and Mr Lucas . . .

One of the most useful orders mentioned in the section—which will enable the court to do justice to the injured shareholders—is to order the oppressor to buy their shares at a fair price: and a fair price would be, I think, the value which the shares would have had at the date of the petition, if there had been no oppression . . .

VISCOUNT SIMONS and LORDS MORTON OF HENRYTON and KEITH OF AVONHOLM delivered concurring opinions.

➤ Note

The 'most useful' remedy of compulsory buy-out at a fair price, recognised above, has become almost the only remedy called upon in these cases. *Re HR Harmer Ltd* [1959] 1 WLR 62, CA, remains notable for a more imaginative approach. The trial judge found that an autocratic father, in his role as 'governing director', was behaving 'oppressively'. He granted the sons relief, ordering, *inter alia*, 'that the company should contract for the services of the father as philatelic consultant at a named salary, that the father should not interfere in the affairs of the company otherwise than in accordance with the valid decision of the board of directors, and that he should be appointed president of the company for life, but that this office should not impose any duties or rights or powers'. The order was upheld by the Court of Appeal.

[11.20] Re City Branch Group Ltd [2005] 1 WLR 3505 (Court of Appeal)

This case was decided under CA 1985 s 459, and provides a modern example of what may constitute 'unfairly prejudicial' conduct. R and G each held 50% of the shares in a company, C. C had three wholly owned subsidiaries. All the business of C, which involved investment property portfolios, was carried out through its subsidiaries. C's business was effectively a quasi partnership between R and G, which broke down following differences between them. R had applied for C to be wound up on the 'just and equitable' ground (see below, pp 653 ff), and G had sought an order under CA 1985 s 459 on the ground that C's affairs had been conducted in a manner unfairly prejudicial to the interests of C, citing breaches of fiduciary duty and misappropriation of funds by R in respect of two of C's subsidiaries. On appeal, R argued that his alleged conduct related solely to C's subsidiaries and not to C itself, and therefore the petition could not succeed in relation to C. The Court of Appeal, dismissing the appeal, held that the 'the affairs of the company' (in s 459) had a broad application and could include the affairs of a subsidiary, particularly as in the instant case where the directors of the holding company and the subsidiary were substantially the same.

SIR MARTIN NOURSE: . . .

Broadly stated, the main question arising on this appeal is whether an order may be made under [CA 1985, s 459] in relation to a holding company where, first, it is the affairs of its wholly-owned subsidiary that are being or have been conducted in an unfairly prejudicial manner and, secondly, the directors of the holding company are also directors of the subsidiary.

The question arises on an application by the holders of 50% of the shares in a company called Citybranch Group Ltd ("the company") to strike out a petition presented under section 459 by the holders of the remaining 50% of the shares. . . .

The petition claims an order regulating the future management of the affairs of the company and the subsidiaries, an order that the Rackind family, alternatively Mr Rackind alone, should sell their or his shares to Mr Gross and ancillary relief. Mr Oliver, for the Rackind family, has submitted that the relief sought is very unusual and in that he may be right. However, he has been unable to persuade me that that is a relevant consideration for today's purposes. . . .

. . . the allegedly unfairly prejudicial conduct is summarised in five sub-paragraphs. . . . First, it is said that Mr Rackind caused, or substantially caused, an irrevocable breakdown in the relationship of trust and confidence between himself and Mr Gross and/or Mr Gerald Gross which formed the basis of their quasi-partnership association through the company and the other companies in the group. Secondly, it is said that Mr Rackind threatened a winding up of the company by the court in order to put pressure on Mr Gross and the other Gross family shareholders to agree to Mr Rackind's demands for control or a purchase of the Gross family's shares, despite the fact that there was (and remains) no basis for the company being wound up on the petition of Mr Rackind. Thirdly, it is said that Mr Rackind breached his fiduciary duties owed to the company and/or to Blaneland [one of the subsidiaries] by refusing to agree to and/or obstructing attempts to finance a payment by Blaneland of corporation tax due from it, in order to put pressure on Mr Gross and the other Gross family share-holders to agree to Mr Rackind's demands for control or a purchase of the Gross family's shares. . . . The fourth allegation made in para 59 is that Mr Rackind continued to use Citybranch's office . . . and continued to draw a consultancy fee, or a full consultancy fee, in each case despite not working full-time for the group. . . . The fifth allegation is that Mr Rackind dishonestly or improp-erly appropriated the funds of Citybranch and attempted to hide that fact. That is the most serious allegation against Mr Rackind. . . . In essence it is an allegation of a conspiracy between Mr Rackind and a firm of surveyors acting for Citybranch to render false invoices to that company resulting in the unlawful extraction by Mr Rackind of £8,320 plus VAT of Citybranch's moneys. It was the dis-covery by Mr Gross of that matter in May and June 2003 which finally led to the irrevocable break-down in the relationship of trust and confidence. Again, that allegation is capable of being an allega-tion of unfairly prejudicial conduct of the affairs of Citybranch.

The principal submission of Mr Oliver and Miss Nicholson, [counsel] for the Rackind family, is that none of the five allegations is capable in law of constituting an allegation as to the conduct of the affairs of the company, as opposed to the affairs of one or more of its subsidiaries. Accordingly, they say that section 459 cannot be invoked in relation to the company. They rely on what they claim is the plain wording of the section, on what they say is the principle of the thing and also on the prin-ciple of *Salomon v Salomon & Co Ltd* [2.01].

In regard to the first and second allegations . . . [counsel for R] submit that the matters com-plained of, causing an irrevocable breakdown in the relationship of trust and confidence and threat-ening the winding up of the company in order to put pressure on the Gross family, were not conduct of the affairs of the company, or indeed of any company, but conduct of the affairs of the sharehold-ers. Here I am entirely content to adopt the approach of Judge Weeks QC. As to the first allegation he said:

"It seems to me at least arguable that causing an irrevocable breakdown in the relationship of trust and confidence is capable of being considered conduct of the company's affairs against the background of a quasi-partnership and an agreement that both should cooperate in the con-duct of the affairs."

In dealing with the second allegation, which he described as more questionable, the judge said:

"The threat of a winding up of the company by the court is, I think, a threat made by Mr Rackind-if indeed it was made-in his capacity as shareholder or contributory, and only by a very wide stretch of the imagination could it be said to be conduct of the company's affairs. . . ."

. . . Before turning to their principal submission, I will deal with some subsidiary submissions made by Mr Oliver and Miss Nicholson. They submit that, even if the conduct complained of in the third, fourth and fifth allegations did constitute conduct of the company's affairs, such conduct was incapable of prejudicing the Gross family's interests in their capacity as members of the company. The short answer to that submission is that the conduct complained of is certainly capable of prejudicing the interests of the subsidiary concerned, on which footing there will be a risk of a diminution in value of the company's investment in the subsidiary, which in turn will mean actual or potential prejudice to the interests of the shareholders in the company.

The Rackind family further submit that in relation to the fifth allegation, Mr Rackind's false invoicing in Citybranch, his conduct was "dehors" that company, an expression used by Harman J in one of the authorities cited. They also raise a new point, or at any rate one not dealt with by the judge, to the effect that in relation to the Citybranch allegations, allegations (4) and (5), the Gross family themselves, by virtue of their majority on the board of that company, have it in their power to remedy the consequences of the acts complained of by means other than a petition under section 459. The factual premise of that second submission is questioned by Mr Potts and Mr Thompson [counsel for G] in their skeleton argument on behalf of the Gross family. Each of these two submissions appears to be one raising an issue which can only be satisfactorily determined at a trial.

I now come to the main question. Does the court have power to make an order under section 459 in relation to a holding company where, first, it is the affairs of its wholly-owned subsidiary that are being or have been conducted in an unfairly prejudicial manner and, secondly, the directors of the holding company are also directors of the subsidiary? I emphasise that here Mr Gross and Mr Rackind are the only directors of the company and of Blaneland and are also directors of Citybranch, of which Mr Gerald Gross is an additional director.

There is no English authority which directly answers this question. . . . [He then examined various potentially relevant authorities, and continued:] [These observations] demonstrate that the expression "the affairs of the company" is one of the widest import which can include the affairs of a subsidiary. Equally, I would hold that the affairs of a subsidiary can also be the affairs of its holding company, especially where, as here, the directors of the holding company, which necessarily controls the affairs of the subsidiary, also represent a majority of the directors of the subsidiary. (In the case of Blaneland they are identical). . . . [He then examined various Australian authorities, and continued:]

. . . The decision in *In re Norvabron (No 2)*[64] was followed and applied by Powell J, sitting in the Equity Division of the Supreme Court of New South Wales, in *In re Dernacourt Investments Pty Ltd* (1990) 2 ACSR 553 . . . It was held that the conduct of the affairs of the holding company towards a subsidiary may constitute the conduct of the affairs of the subsidiary and vice versa. Powell J said, at p 556:

"8. The words 'affairs of the company' are extremely wide and should be construed liberally: (a) in determining the ambit of the 'affairs' of a parent company for the purposes of section 320 [the equivalent of CA 1985 s 459], the court looks at the business realities of a situation and does not confine them to a narrow legalistic view; (b) 'affairs' of a company encompass all matters which may come before its board for consideration; (c) conduct of the 'affairs' of a parent company includes refraining from procuring a subsidiary to do something or condoning by inaction an act of a subsidiary, particularly when the directors of the parent and the subsidiary are the same." (Reference was there made to three authorities including *In re Norvabron (No 2)*.)

Powell J said, at p 561:

"although the relevant plaintiff must demonstrate that it is the relevant company's affairs which are being so conducted, I am prepared to proceed upon the bases, first, that, in an appropriate case, the conduct of a holding company, or of such of its directors who happen to be directors of the relevant subsidiary, towards a subsidiary, may constitute conduct in the affairs of that subsidiary (*Scottish Cooperative Wholesale Society Ltd v Meyer* [11.19]), and, secondly, that, in an appropriate case, the conduct of a subsidiary, or of some or all of its directors who happen

[64] (1986) 11 ACLR 279.

as well to be directors of the holding company, may be regarded as part of the conduct of the affairs of the holding company: *In re Norvabron Pty Ltd (No 2)* 11 ACLR 279."

In my view the second basis identified by Powell J, following and applying the decision in *In re Norvabron (No 2)*, is of great value in the decision of the present case. I accept that decisions of courts in other Commonwealth countries are of persuasive value only. But those two decisions certainly persuade me that the view taken by Judge Weeks QC, without their assistance, was correct. . . . Those were considered judgments of judges of the Supreme Courts of Queensland and New South Wales respectively and they are directly in point. I would follow them accordingly.

For these reasons, I would decide the main question, like the subsidiary questions, in favour of the Gross family. In conclusion I refer to the decisive passage in Judge Weeks QC's judgment:

"In my judgment, there is no authority which forces me to hold that conduct of a subsidiary's affairs can never also be conduct of the parent company's affairs, and in the circumstances of the present case I think it not beyond the bounds of possibility that the court may reach the conclusion that the acts complained of were also acts in the conduct of the parent company's affairs. This is a strikeout application, and I should not strike out the petition if it has any realistic prospect of success. In my judgment, those paragraphs do have a realistic prospect of success."

That was an entirely correct approach to the main question. . . .
I would dismiss this appeal.
KEENE and JACOB LJJ concurred.

Basic principles

A very large number of cases have been reported under CA 1985 s 459 (the predecessor to CA 2006 s 994). However, (no doubt out of a concern to save costs) many of them are rulings on preliminary points of law or on applications to strike out the proceedings, dealing with isolated issues, so that it is possible to identify the principles which are emerging only after fairly wide reading of the reports. But certain points as summarised below are now regarded as reasonably well settled. These principles can be assumed also to apply in full to CA 2006, s 994, since the wording is identical.

Who may apply

CA 2006 s 994 allows applications to court from:

(i)   a member (s 994(1), as defined in CA 2006 s 112), or members, including nominee shareholders,[65] not necessarily constituting a numerical minority,[66] but not holding a voting majority;[67]

(ii)   a person to whom shares have been 'transmitted by operation of law' (s 994(2)), such as a trustee in bankruptcy or the personal representative of a deceased member: these people can apply even though they are not registered as members; but 'transmitted by operation of law' does not include persons holding by way of constructive trust (*Re a Company (No 007828 of 1985)* (1985) 2 BCC 98,951);

(iii)   a person to whom shares have been 'transferred' (s 994(2)): these people can apply even though they are not registered as members, but the cases have drawn a line indicating that mere agreement to transfer will not suffice; there must be a proper instrument of

---

[65]   *Atlasview Ltd v Brightview Ltd* [2004] EWHC 1056 (Ch), [2004] 2 BCLC 191.
[66]   Eg in *Re HR Harmer Ltd* (above, p 555) the petitioners were majority shareholders but did not have voting control.
[67]   A petition may not be brought by persons having voting control, since they may have recourse to domestic remedies (such as changing the directors) to remedy the conduct which is the source of complaint: *Re Legal Costs Negotiators Ltd* [1999] 2 BCLC 171, CA.

transfer executed and delivered to either the transferee or the company (*Re Quickdome Ltd* [1988] BCLC 370; *Re McCarthy Surfacing Ltd* [2006] EWHC 832); or

(iv) the Secretary of State (s 995).

But a former member has no standing to apply, even if the conduct complained of occurred while he or she was a member *(Re a Company* [1986] 2 All ER 253). On the other hand, members (and presumably others) *with* standing can rely on conduct that pre-dates their registration as shareholders (*Lloyd v Casey* [2002] 1 BCLC 454).

Petitioners seeking relief need not 'come with clean hands', although their conduct may be relevant in deciding whether relief should be granted and what the nature of such relief should be: *Re London School of Electronics Ltd* [1986] Ch 211.

Although most s 459 petitions have been brought by shareholders in private companies, the jurisdiction does not exclude public companies from its scope. The same trend is likely with CA 2006 s 994 petitions.

Respondents

Normally, the respondents are the controlling members and/or directors. If the company is made a party, this is usually on a nominal basis. Several cases have held that it is improper for the controllers to use the company's funds to fight their case (see eg *Re a Company, ex p Johnson* [1992] BCLC 701).

Orders can, however, be sought against more remote respondents. In *Re Little Olympian Each-Ways Ltd (No 3)* [1995] 1 BCLC 636, the company's assets had been sold at an under-value by those in *de facto* control to another company which was also controlled by them. It was held that an order could be made against the *second* company requiring it to buy out the petitioner's shares at a price which reflected their value before the wrongful sale.

And in *Re a Company* [1986] 1 WLR 281, Hoffmann J ruled that an order could be made against a former member, so ensuring that a potential respondent cannot escape liability by transferring his shares away before proceedings are commenced.

Procedure

Since the introduction of the Civil Procedure Rules 1998, courts have started to take a much more vigorous and proactive stance (see eg *Re Rotadata Ltd* [2000] 1 BCLC 122). The Rules require the court to take the initiative from the outset and manage cases actively. The court registrar is required to consult the parties with a view to narrowing the issues, to consider bringing in outside experts and/or conciliators, etc, so as to minimise the length of any court hearing and cut down costs. The litigants are reminded that it is their duty to co-operate and to agree as much as possible on the issues in a constructive and sensible way.

In this area, combined claims can cause special problems. In particular, it is possible for a complaint under s 994 and an application for winding up[68] to be combined in the same petition. Since there are several reported cases in which a member has failed on the former ground but succeeded on the latter, judges could hardly complain when this became more or less standard practice. But since the presentation of a petition for winding up is likely to attract unfavourable publicity (and lead almost invariably to the freezing of the company's bank account), so putting considerable pressure on the controllers, this may give a minority shareholder an unfair bargaining advantage. In an attempt to counter this, *Practice Direction* [1999] BCC 741, para 9, requires petitioners to seek a winding-up order only where this is genuinely considered appropriate and, where they do, to consent to a standard-form interim order which enables the company to continue to trade and use its bank account pending the hearing of the case.

---

[68] On the 'just and equitable' ground (IA 1986 s 122(1)(g)), see below, pp 653 ff.

Grounds

CA 2006 s 994 requires the petitioner to show that 'the *company's affairs* are being or have been conducted in a manner that is *unfairly prejudicial* to the *interests of members* generally or of some part of its members . . .' (s 994(1)(a)); or that 'an actual or proposed act or omission of the company . . . is or would be so prejudicial' (s 994(1)(b)). Each of the highlighted requirements has proved troublesome.

Meaning of 'the company's affairs'

The complaint must be about the conduct of the company's affairs, not the conduct of the affairs a member or director in a private capacity. So, in *Re Unisoft Group Ltd (No 3)* [1994] 1 BCLC 609, and again in *Re Leeds United Holdings plc* [1996] 2 BCLC 545, relief under s 459 was refused where the respondent was alleged not to have honoured a shareholders' agreement relating to the transfer of shares. But the leading case of *Scottish Wholesale Co-operative Society Ltd v Meyer* **[11.19]** shows that a broad view may also be taken of this requirement. And in *Re City Branch Group Ltd* **[11.20]**, it was held that 'the affairs of the company' could be interpreted widely, and could extend to the affairs of a subsidiary company, especially where, as in that case, the directors of the holding company and the subsidiary were almost identical.

Meaning of 'unfairly prejudicial'

The conduct complained of must be both unfair *and* prejudicial, not merely unfair (*Re Saul D Harrison & Sons plc* **[11.23]**; *Rock Nominees Ltd v RCO* [2004] 1 BCLC 439), nor merely prejudicial (*Re London School of Electronics Ltd* [1986] Ch 211; *Nicholas v Soundcraft Electronics Ltd* (below, pp 568 ff)).

The courts also stress that unfairly prejudicial conduct and wrongful or illegal conduct are separate concepts, each leading to its own remedies (*Re Charnley Davies Ltd* ([1990] BCLC 760).

The test is objective, so the emphasis is not so much on the motive or intention of the controllers, as on the effect that the conduct has had on the complaining member (*Re Sam Weller & Sons Ltd* [1990] Ch 682). In *Re Guidezone Ltd* [2000] 2 BCLC 321, at 355, Jonathan Parker J said that *O'Neill v Phillips* **[11.24]** established that:

> . . . 'unfairness' for the purposes of s 459 is not to be judged by reference to subjective notions of fairness, but rather by testing whether, applying established equitable principles, the majority has acted, or is proposing to act, in a manner which equity would regard as contrary to good faith.

Examples of 'unfairly prejudicial' conduct are given below, pp 568 ff.

Meaning of 'interests of members'

The conduct must be unfairly prejudicial to the 'interests' of all or some part of the members. Whether the affected interests must be those of members, in their capacity as members, is considered below. But certainly the term 'interests' is wider than 'rights', and the cases show that regard can be had to 'legitimate expectations'[69] (particularly in a small company) that the member will be employed by the company, or have a say in its management, or receive some return in the form of dividends.

But the judge 'does not sit under a palm tree':[70] although the court may have regard to 'wider' equitable considerations beyond the parties' strict constitutional and statutory rights,

---

[69] Lord Hoffmann in *O'Neill v Phillips* **[11.24]** expressed reservations about the use of this expression (borrowed from administrative law) in the s 456 [CA 2006 s 994] context, but it is fairly well established—and no one has yet suggested a better alternative.

[70] The expression used by Warner J in *Re J E Cade & Sons Ltd* [1992] BCLC 213 at 227.

it cannot simply add still further rights and obligations arising from its own concept of fairness (*Re J E Cade & Son Ltd* [1992] BCLC 213 at 227; *O'Neill v Phillips* **[11.24]**).

It follows that the more clearly and fully the parties have spelt out their arrangements, the less scope there will be for the court to find that there were other, unrecorded, 'legitimate expectations'. And if the company is a public company (more particularly if it has made a public issue of its shares) the court is most unlikely to take notice of any alleged arrangement that is not recorded in the company's published documents, for to do so would fly in the face of the principle that all material information must be disclosed to potential investors. Thus, in *Re Blue Arrow plc* [1987] BCLC 585 the court refused to grant any relief to a petitioner who alleged an agreement that she should remain in office as chairman; and in *Re Tottenham Hotspur plc* [1994] 1 BCLC 655 it declined to give effect to an alleged understanding that Terry Venables, the club's team manager, would continue to have a say in the company's management even after he had ceased to be a 50% shareholder.

Members in their capacity as members

A petitioner must show unfair prejudice in his or her character as a member and not, for example, as a director or creditor. *Re J E Cade & Son Ltd* [1992] BCLC 213 provides an illustration: the petitioner was a shareholder in a family farming company and was also the owner of land which the company held on an agricultural tenancy. The court found that his real object in bringing s 459 proceedings was not to obtain any relief in his capacity as a member but to obtain possession of the land, as landlord, and dismissed his claim.

But the rule is now applied more flexibly, following a lead given by the House of Lords in *Ebrahimi v Westbourne Galleries Ltd* **[14.14]**. In *Ebrahimi* the petitioner had been removed from office as a salaried director and so deprived of both his employment and any say in the management of the company, contrary to the basic assumptions on which this two-man company had been set up. In what is now the leading decision on the winding up of small companies, the House of Lords held that it was proper to have regard to 'wider' equitable considerations and not just the parties' strict legal rights in circumstances such as these, and granted him a winding-up order. But he failed on an alternative claim under CA 1948, s 210 (the forerunner of the present s 994) because, as that section was then construed, it was necessary for him to show that he had suffered oppression *as a member* rather than as a director or salaried employee. Soon after, s 210 was replaced and it was made clear that there would be a new departure: the same 'wider' equitable considerations would be applied in interpreting s 459 as the House of Lords had considered appropriate in the winding-up context in *Ebrahimi*.

For example, in *Re a Company* [1986] BCLC 376, Hoffmann J said (at 379):

> In the case of a small private company in which two or three members have invested their capital by subscribing for shares on the footing that dividends are unlikely but that each will earn his living by working for the company as a director . . . [the] member's interests as a member who has ventured his capital in the company's business may include a legitimate expectation that he will continue to be employed as a director and his dismissal from that office and exclusion from the management of the company may therefore be unfairly prejudicial to his interests as a member.

For a more recent case where this reasoning resulted in the court issuing a buy-out order, see *Re Eurofinance Group Ltd* [2001] BCC 551.

Use of CA 2006 s 994 to protect non-member interests

[11.21] Gamlestaden Fastigheter AB v Baltic Partners Ltd [2007] UKPC 26 (Privy Council)

Gamlestaden was both a member and a creditor of Baltic. It sued under the Jersey equivalent of CA 2006 s 994, alleging unfair prejudice occasioned by the mismanagement of Baltic by its directors. It sought, by way of remedy, an order of the court that the directors pay damages to Baltic for their mismanagement. If successful, this claim would: (i) avoid possible limitation problems that existed in Baltic suing its own directors for their breach of duty; and (ii) put Baltic in funds which might be used to repay its creditors, including Gamlestaden, although not in sufficient funds to allow for any distribution to Baltic's members. The issue for the Board was whether the unfair prejudice provisions could deliver these ends.

The decision of the Board was delivered by LORD SCOTT OF FOSCOTE: . . . Baltic is insolvent and the main issue for decision is whether it is open to a member of a company to make an unfair prejudice application for relief in circumstances where, as here, the company in question is insolvent, will remain insolvent whatever order is made on the application and where the relief sought will confer no financial benefit on the applicant *qua* member. The main relief now sought by Gamlestaden on its Article 141 application [the Jersey equivalent of CA 2006 s 994] is an order under Article 143(1) ordering the directors to pay damages to Baltic for breaches of the duty they owed to Baltic as directors. But it is accepted that the damages, assuming the claim succeeds, will not restore Baltic to solvency. It will, however, if it does succeed, produce a considerable sum which will be available to Baltic's creditors. Gamlestaden, either itself or as representing its parent company Gamlestaden AB, is a substantial creditor. The indebtedness in question was a major part of Gamlestaden's investment in Baltic's business ventures. So, it is said, Gamlestaden has a legitimate interest, in the particular circumstances of this case, justifying the making of the Article 141 application.

The directors, however, applied to have the application struck out on the ground that it was bound in law to fail. They contended before the Bailiff of the Royal Court and before the Court of Appeal, and have repeated the contention before the Board, that the alleged improprieties in the management of Baltic of which Gamlestaden complain cannot be shown to have caused Gamlestaden any financial loss in its capacity as shareholder. Its loss, if any, is suffered as a creditor. An application under Article 141 (or under section 459 of the 1985 Act) is, it is argued, a shareholder's remedy, not a creditor's remedy. Once it becomes clear that the only benefit to be derived from the relief sought in an unfair prejudice application would be a benefit to the company's creditors, and that no benefit would be obtained by the company's shareholders, it becomes clear that the application is an abuse of process, cannot succeed and should be struck out. The learned Bailiff agreed and struck out the application. The Court of Appeal dismissed Gamlestaden's appeal. The point is now before the Board for a final decision. It must be emphasised that, since this appeal arises out of a strike out of the Article 141 application, the facts pleaded in support of the application must be taken as true (save for any that can be shown by incontrovertible evidence to be untrue). The Bailiff and the Court of Appeal approached the case on that footing and so must their Lordships.

The point at issue (identified in para.3 above) depends, first, upon the scope of the power of the court under Articles 141 and 143, properly construed, in dealing with the unfair prejudice application and, secondly, upon the particular circumstances that are relied on for bringing this application within that scope. . . .

Various other acts of mismanagement by the directors of Baltic are complained of but it is the allegedly damaging effect of the withdrawal of DM112.5 million from SPK [a limited partnership that was Baltic's only asset] and the conversion of SPK into SPG [a limited liability company] that seems to their Lordships to be the essential complaint. It is alleged by Gamlestaden that the effect of these two things was to transform Baltic's investment in German property from an investment in a vehicle with solid cash assets (SPK without the withdrawals) into an investment in a vehicle (SPG) without cash assets . . .

The scope of Articles 141 and 143

In order to qualify for relief under Article 143 Gamlestaden must be a member of Baltic (which it is) and must satisfy the court that the company's affairs "have been conducted in a manner unfairly prejudicial" to itself. If the facts alleged in Gamlestaden's Representation, and, in particular, the facts giving rise to the two matters of complaint that their Lordships have identified, are true there can, in their Lordships' opinion, be no doubt that the court would be so satisfied. Mr Gabriel Moss QC, counsel for the directors, has not suggested otherwise. The focus then shifts to Article 143.

Article 143(1) empowers the court, if satisfied that an Article 141 application is well founded, to "make such order as it thinks fit in respect of the matters complained of." . . .

The first question to be addressed, therefore, is whether an order for payment of damages to the company whose affairs have allegedly been conducted in an unfairly prejudicial manner can be sought and made in an unfair prejudice application. Another way of putting the question is whether a cause of action allegedly vested in the company can be prosecuted to judgment in an unfair prejudice application. It would, of course, always be essential for the parties allegedly liable on the cause of action to be respondents to the proceedings. But that is not a problem in the present case.

There is nothing in the wide language of Article 143(1) to suggest a limitation that would exclude the seeking or making of such an order: the court "may make such order as it thinks fit for giving relief in respect of the matters complained of." The point was raised and considered by the Hong Kong Court of Final Appeal (the CFA) in *re Chime Corp. Ltd* (2004) 7 HKCFAR 546. An unfair prejudice application had been made in respect of Chime and one of the issues was whether the court had power on such an application to make an order for the payment of damages or compensation to the company. The CFA held that the court did have power to make such an order (see the judgment given by Lord Scott of Foscote at paragraphs 39 to 49, concurred in by the other members of the court, and the cases there cited). No reason has been advanced to their Lordships on this appeal why the decision in *Chime* should not be followed. Accordingly, no objection to Gamlestaden's prayer in its Article 141 application for an order that the directors pay damages to Baltic for breach of duty can be taken at this strike-out stage.

That leaves the important issue regarding Baltic's insolvency. Here, too, it is appropriate to start by noting the breadth of the Article 143(1) discretion conferred on the court. The court "may make such order as it thinks fit for giving relief in respect of the matters complained of . . . " . . . .

Bar the relatively trivial sum that Gamlestaden must have paid in subscribing for its 1100 shares in Baltic, Gamlestaden's investment took the form of the provision of loans to Baltic to enable Baltic to fund SPK. Baltic was the corporate vehicle through which the joint venture enterprise of Gamlestaden and Mr Karlsten of investment in German commercial property was to be pursued. If mismanagement by the directors of that corporate vehicle has led to loss it seems to their Lordships somewhat artificial to insist that the qualifying loss, for Article 141 (or section 459) purposes, must be loss which has reduced the value of the investor's equity capital and that it is not sufficient to show that it has reduced the recoverability of the investor's loan capital. This artificiality was pointed out by Robert Walker J (as he then was) in *R&H Electric Ltd v Haden Bill Electricial Ltd* [1995] 2 BCLC 280. This was a case where the applicant for section 459 relief was, of course, a shareholder in the company but, via another company that he controlled, had also provided working capital to the company. He was removed by the majority shareholders from any management role and accordingly applied under section 459 for an order requiring the majority shareholders to purchase his shares and, alternatively, petitioned for the company to be wound up on the just and equitable ground. One of the grounds relied on by the majority shareholders for resisting any section 459 relief was that the applicant's "only real involvement was as an agent for [the other company] which was a loan creditor, not a shareholder . . . ; therefore . . . there was no prejudice to [the applicant] in his capacity as a shareholder." As to this point Robert Walker J said this:

"If [the applicant] himself had been [the company's] loan creditor, under arrangements made between him and the majority shareholders when the company was first being planned, I should have had little hesitation in coming to the conclusion that the arrangements were a reflection of, and sufficiently closely connected with, [the applicant's] membership of [the company] as to be within the scope of s.459."

Robert Walker J then addressed the question whether the fact that the loan creditor was not the shareholder applicant, but was the other company that he controlled, mattered. He concluded that it did not:

"On the whole I have come to the conclusion that I should not treat the separateness of [the applicant] and [the other company] as excluding him from seeking relief under s.459 on the basis that [the other company's] loans to [the company] were procured by [the applicant] and formed part (and an essential part) of the arrangements entered into for the venture to be carried on by that company."

In the outcome the judge made an order for relief under section 459. He ordered that the applicant's shares be purchased by the majority shareholders at a fair value and that the loans from the applicant's other company be repaid as soon as reasonably possible.

Robert Walker J's approach in the *R&H Electric Ltd* case commends itself to their Lordships. Mr Moss QC has pointed out, rightly, that the company in question in the case was not insolvent and that the order for purchase of the applicant's shares was plainly a benefit to him as a member. These he represented as being essential differences between that case and this. His submission comes to this, that it is a fatal and insurmountable bar in any and every application for Article 141 (or section 459) relief if the relief sought cannot be shown to be of some benefit to the applicant shareholder in his capacity as shareholder.

Mr Moss supported his submission by reference, in particular, to the well established rule that a shareholder cannot petition for a winding-up order to be made in respect of a company that is insolvent. The reason is that the petitioning shareholder cannot obtain any benefit from the winding-up. The company's assets will be realised; dividends may be paid to creditors but nothing, if the company is insolvent, will go to the members. The rule that Mr Moss prays in aid is a long established one and one on which their Lordships cast no doubt. But there is a significant difference between a creditor's winding-up petition and an Article 141 (or section 459) application. The former is seeking an order to put the company into an insolvent liquidation that will affect the interests of all creditors as well as of all members. It will involve the administration of the liquidation either by the Viscount (or, in England, the Official Receiver) and his officials or by a professional liquidator who, in carrying out his duties, will be an officer of the court. The liquidation, although from a financial point of view carried out for the benefit of creditors, is a public act or process in which the public has an interest. It seems to their Lordships quite right that a member with no financial interest in the process or its outcome should be denied *locus standi* to initiate the process.

Where relief is sought via an unfair prejudice application, on the other hand, the position is quite different. There is no public involvement or interest in the proceedings, other than the natural interest that may attend any proceedings heard in open court. The purpose of Article 141, or of section 459, or of their counterpart in Hong Kong, is to provide a means of relief to persons unfairly prejudiced by the management of the company in which they hold shares. If the company is a joint venture company and the joint venturers have arranged that one, or more, or all of them, shall provide working capital to the company by means of loans, it would, in their Lordships' opinion, be inconsistent with the purpose of these statutory provisions to limit the availability of the remedies they offer to cases where the value of the share or shares held by the applicant member would be enhanced by the grant of the relief sought. If the relief sought would, if granted, be of real, as opposed to merely nominal, value to an applicant joint venturer, such as Gamlestaden, in facilitating recovery of some part of its investment in the joint venture company, that should, in their Lordships' opinion, suffice to provide the requisite locus standi for the application to be made.

Mr Moss placed reliance on *Re J.E.Cade & Son Ltd* [1992] BCLC 213 where Warner J refused section 459 relief because the applicant was "pursuing his interests as a freeholder of the farm and not his interests as a member of the company" (p 229). But there was no counterpart in that case with the feature in this case that the loans made by Gamlestaden were made pursuant to and for the purposes of the joint venture to be carried on by Gamlestaden and Mr Karlsten via Baltic.

There are several cases in which judicial approval is given to affording a wide scope to section 459. Some of these were referred to by Robert Walker J in *R&H Electric Ltd*. Thus, in *re a Company (No.08477 of 1986)* BCLC 376 at 378, Hoffmann J as he then was, commenting on the proposition that section 459 should be limited to conduct unfairly prejudicial to the interests of members as members and could not extend to conduct prejudicial to other interests of members, said that

" . . . the application [of the proposition] must take into account that the interests of a member are not necessarily limited to his strict legal rights under the constitution of the company. The use of the word 'unfairly' in s.459, like the use of the words 'just' and 'equitable' in s.517(1)(g) enables the court to have regard to wider considerations."

In *re Macro (Ipswich) Ltd* [1994] 2 BCLC 354, Arden J (as she then was) said that

" . . . the jurisdiction under s.459 has an elastic quality which enables the courts to mould the concepts of unfair prejudice according to the circumstances of the case".

In *re Little Olympian Each-Ways Ltd* [1994] 2 BCLC 420 at 429 Lindsay J said that

" . . . in point of jurisdiction the wide language of ss.459 and 461 is not to be cut down."

And in *O'Neill v Phillips* [1999] 1 WLR 1092 at 1105 Lord Hoffmann said that

"As cases such as *R&H Electric Ltd v Haden Bill Electrical Ltd* [1995] 2 BCLC 280 show, the requirement that prejudice must be suffered as a member should not be too narrowly or technically construed."

In their Lordships' opinion Articles 141 and 143 properly construed do not ipso facto rule out the grant of relief simply on the ground that the relief sought will not benefit the applicant in his capacity as member. In many cases such a feature might justifiably lead to the refusal of relief. Miss Newman suggested in her submissions on behalf of Gamlestaden that Gamlestaden's desire as a member to restore to the company the loss which the directors' allegedly negligent management of its affairs has caused was by itself sufficient to justify the grant of the relief sought, regardless of any financial benefit that might accrue to Gamlestaden. She suggested, as their Lordships understood it, that Gamlestaden, as a member, had some sort of obligation to the creditor banks to take steps to pursue the directors for their allegedly negligent breach of their duties to Baltic and had an interest in preserving its reputation with the banks that would thereby be served. Their Lordships are unimpressed by that submission. The justification for Gamlestaden seeking Article 141 and Article 143 relief must be based on a real financial benefit that Gamlestaden as an investor via Baltic in SPK might achieve if the relief sought were to be granted. Their Lordships do not accept that the benefit must be a benefit to Gamlestaden in its capacity as a shareholder but they do accept that there must, where the only purpose of the application is to obtain payment of a sum of money to Baltic, be some real financial benefit to be derived therefrom by Gamlestaden.

In particular, in a case where an investor in a joint venture company has, in pursuance of the joint venture agreement, invested not only in subscribing for shares but also in advancing loan capital, the investor ought not, in their Lordships' opinion, be precluded from the grant of relief under Article 143(1) (or section 461(1)) on the ground that the relief would benefit the investor only as loan creditor and not as member.

In the present case the provision of loan capital to Baltic seems to have been mainly, if not wholly, made by Gamlestaden AB, rather than by Gamlestaden, although procured by Gamlestaden pursuant to its obligation to do so under its joint venture agreement with Mr Karlsten. But their Lordships, in agreement with the view expressed by Robert Walker J in relation to similar arrangements made by the applicant for section 459 relief in the *R&H Electric Ltd* case (see the second of the citations in para.30 above), conclude that that feature should not bar Gamlestaden from relief under Article 141.

Their Lordships take the view that the learned Bailiff and the Court of Appeal construed Article 143(1) too narrowly and that this appeal against the strike-out of Gamlestaden's Article 141 application ought to be allowed. . . .

➤ Question

This case is likely to prove controversial. Is the legal analysis defensible? What practical consequences are likely to flow from this approach to the unfair prejudice provisions? Are these consequences either practically or commercially desirable?

Remedies

Section 996(1) gives the court the power to make 'such order as it thinks fit', and s 996(2) provides examples of possible orders, including the commonly used compulsory share buy-back.

In particular, as indicated in s 996(2), the order may:

(i)   regulate the conduct of the company's affairs in the future (*Re H R Harmer Ltd*, above, p 555);

(ii)   require the company to do or not to do some specified act (eg in *McGuinness, Petitioners* (1988) 4 BCC 161, the directors were ordered to comply promptly with a shareholders' requisition for the calling of a general meeting);

(iii)   authorise civil proceedings to be brought in the name of the company (this is a possible way around the restrictions of *Foss v Harbottle* [11.01]; see, eg, *Bhullar v Bhullar* [6.17];

(iv)   prohibit the alteration of all or a specified part of the company's constitution without the leave of the court; or

(v)   provide for the purchase of the shares of any members of the company by other members or by the company itself (see below).

Buy-out orders

In almost all successful cases brought under s 459, the court has ordered one faction of shareholders to buy out the others. Section 994 is unlikely to prove different. Usually, the majority is required to buy out the minority, although the reverse was ordered (on certain conditions) in *Re a Company, ex p Shooter* [1990] BCLC 384, where the controlling shareholder had shown himself unfit to continue to manage the business, and also in *Re Brenfield Squash Racquets Club Ltd* [1996] 2 BCLC 184.

Three questions arise. First, at what date should the valuation be made? Secondly, on what basis should the shares be valued and, in particular, should the holding be discounted to reflect the fact that it is a minority holding? Thirdly, should the conduct of the parties be taken into account in making the valuation?

As will be seen below, pp 576 ff, the courts have reserved to themselves a discretion as regards the first two questions, and have also held that the parties' conduct, and in particular their relative blameworthiness in the events leading to the breakdown in good relations between them, is a factor to be taken into account.

Although this may have some justification in logic, the consequences have been most unfortunate, for parties have felt obliged to make a s 459 hearing the occasion to review the whole of the company's history from its very beginnings and to reopen many old battles, thus greatly adding to the length and cost of the case and, at times, attracting unfavourable comment from the judges concerned.

Finally, the prevalence of the courts' exercise of its discretion to order a buy-out once unfair prejudice has been proved appears, by weight of precedent, to be becoming a *right* accruing to the petitioner once the unfair prejudice grounds are established: see *Grace v Biagioli* [2005] EWCA Civ 1222, [2006] BCC 85, CA. There the Court of Appeal held that the trial judge had erred when he declined to issue a buy-out order in circumstances where unfairly prejudicial conduct (in this case, non-payment of a dividend) had been established. The trial judge had considered the request, but refused to make a buy-out order, and instead ordered payment of a sum representing the dividend plus interest. The Court of Appeal affirmed the broad discretion in CA 1985 s 461 [CA 2006 s 996], but nevertheless ordered a buy-out, holding that these orders were the usual remedy under s 459 for addressing disputes within small companies, and for good reason, since it was normally only this order that could achieve the full purpose behind the court's power to intervene.

Relevance of alternative remedies

In *Re Baltic Real Estate Ltd (No 2)* [1993] BCLC 503 and *Re Legal Costs Negotiators Ltd* [1999] 2 BCLC 171 the court refused relief to a petitioner who was complaining about a situation which he could remedy by using his own votes. In *Re a Company, ex p Schwarcz (No 2)* [1989] BCLC 427 Peter Gibson J said:

> The developing jurisprudence on s 459 petitions has established that the court, even on a striking-out application, will consider whether the relief sought by a petitioner is inappropriate and whether it is unreasonable to pursue a petition when, for example, it is clear that the petitioner must leave the company and a fair offer has been made for the petitioner's shares (see, for example, *Re a Company (No 003843 of 1986)*[71] [or] when a petitioner seeking an order for the sale of his shares might have achieved that result by invoking the transfer machinery available in the articles but failed to do so (see *Re a Company (No 007623 of 1984)*[72] and *Re a Company (No 004377 of 1986)*[73]). If the court is of the view that the relief sought is wholly inappropriate and the petitioner is acting unreasonably in pursuing the petition, it may stay or strike out the petition as being an abuse of the process.

A parallel may perhaps be drawn between these remarks and the approach of the courts in giving rulings under IA 1986 s 125(2), where a petitioner has sought the winding up of a company and it is contended that he ought to have pursued some other remedy: see below, p 657.

An alternative remedy may be provided by the articles; then the general approach of the courts is to leave the parties to their constitutional rights, unless there are special circumstances. For example, where the majority shareholders had followed a procedure laid down by the company's articles to deal with a breakdown in relations, Hoffmann J in *Re a Company* [1987] 1 WLR 102, [1987] BCLC 94 held that this was not unfairly prejudicial conduct. The procedure in this case provided for the remaining shareholders to purchase the minority member's shares at a price fixed by the company's auditors. In similar circumstances, in *Re a Company (No 00836 of 1995)* [1996] 2 BCLC 192, the court took the view that what was on offer under the articles would give the minority shareholder all the relief which he could realistically expect to obtain under s 459. But in several other cases it has been thought not unreasonable for a minority shareholder to persist in his desire to have his shares bought out on terms fixed by the court rather than at a price determined by the company's auditors, since he might have reason to fear that the auditors would not be wholly independent and objective. (See, eg the longish list of cases (all reported as *Re a Company*) cited in the last-mentioned case, and compare the Court of Appeal's ruling in *Virdi v Abbey Leisure Ltd* (below, p 658), a winding-up case.)

Examples of 'unfairly prejudicial' conduct

The cases provide guidance. But note that many of the rulings are not given on the basis of real evidence, but on presumed facts on an application to strike out the proceedings as disclosing no cause of action, or on a preliminary point of law. Then the decision is no more than

---

[71] [1987] BCLC 562.
[72] [1986] BCLC 362.
[73] [1987] 1 WLR 102.

a ruling that the conduct in question is (or is not), in theory, *capable* of being unfairly prejudicial within CA 1985 s 459 (or CA 2006 s 994). This can at best provide only a rough guide.

Examples of conduct that has been held to be (or held capable of being) unfairly prejudicial, include:

(i)   exclusion from management (in a company formed as a quasi-partnership[74]): *Re R A Noble & Sons (Clothing) Ltd* [1983] BCLC 273 (below, p 657); *Re OC (Transport) Services Ltd* [1984] BCLC 251;

(ii)   taking excessive remuneration: *Re Cumana Ltd* [1986] BCLC 430;

(iii)   diversion of a corporate asset or business opportunity: *Re London School of Electronics Ltd* [1986] Ch 211;

(iv)   not paying dividends: *Re a Company, ex p Glossop* [1988] 1 WLR 1068; *Re Sam Weller & Sons Ltd* [1990] Ch 682;

(v)   making or proposing a rights issue which the minority cannot afford to take up: *Re Cumana Ltd* (above); cf *Pennell Securities Ltd v Venida Investments Ltd* (25 July 1974, noted by Barridge (1981) 44 MLR 40);

(vi)   stacking the board with directors having interests adverse to the company: *Whyte, Petitioner* (1984) 1 BCLC 99,044;

(vii)   failure on the part of the directors to advise the shareholders impartially on the merits of rival take-over bids (in one of which the directors were personally interested): *Re a Company* [1986] BCLC 382;

(viii)   misuse of fiduciary powers: *Re Bovey Hotel Ventures Ltd* (unreported, 31 July 1981);

(ix)   mismanagement, but only if 'serious': *Re Macro (Ipswich) Ltd* [11.23]; contrast *Re Elgindata Ltd* [11.22];

(x)   failing to allow minority shareholders independent representation on the board when all control is in the hands of the majority faction which has potentially conflicting interests: *Re Macro (Ipswich) Ltd* [11.23].

Examples of conduct which has been held *not* to be (or not to be capable of being) unfairly prejudicial include:

(i)   declining to implement a scheme to make it possible for petitioners, 'locked in' to a private company, to realise their shares: *Re a Company* [1983] Ch 178 (below, p 657);

(ii)   mere breakdown of confidence between the parties: *Re RA Noble & Sons (Clothing) Ltd* (below, p 657);

(iii)   a situation which the petitioner could remedy by using his own votes: *Re Baltic Real Estate Ltd (No 2)* [1993] BCLC 503; *Re Legal Costs Negotiators Ltd* [1999] 2 BCLC 171;

(iv)   the non-payment by a parent company of debts owing to a subsidiary when this course was considered to be in the interests of the group as a whole: *Nicholas v Soundcraft Electronics Ltd* [1993] BCLC 360; contrast *Scottish Co-operative Wholesale Society Ltd v Meyer* [11.19];

(v)   continuing to run a loss-making business when the minority shareholders stood to receive a substantial capital distribution if the company were wound up: *Re Saul D Harrison plc* [11.23].

---

[74] Note that it is not necessary that the members of a 'quasi-partnership' should have equal shares in the venture: a junior partner in *Quinlan v Essex Hinge Co Ltd* [1996] 2 BCLC 417 successfully petitioned following his exclusion from management by a dominant senior partner.

(vi)   the dismissal of a member director of a quasi-partnership company as a result of his own misconduct, which jeopardised the company's ongoing survival: *Woolwich v Milne* [2003] EWHC 414;

(vii)   certain valuation offers: eg, the valuation procedure at a discounted rate which underpinned the original offer made to Larvin in *Phoenix Office Supplies Ltd v Larvin*, **[11.27]**;

(viii)   the company's decision to achieve, by legitimate means, a result which avoids the need for a special resolution, even though this disempowers the minority from opposing the intended result: *CAS (Nominees) Ltd v Nottingham Forest plc* [2002] BCC 145.

Legitimate expectations and equitable considerations

As a general rule, managerial decisions are unlikely to amount to unfairly prejudicial conduct.

[11.22] Re Elgindata Ltd [1991] BCLC 959 (Chancery Division)

Rowland, the petitioner, had invested in a company controlled by Mr and Mrs Purslow, taking a minority shareholding. The company had been in existence for over four years. The remarks of Warner J quoted here relate to the question whether mismanagement is capable of constituting unfairly prejudicial conduct.

[Warner J referred to *Re Five Minute Car Wash Service Ltd* [1966] 1 WLR 745, a case under CA 1948 s 210 in which it had been held that mere mismanagement, however damaging, did not amount to 'oppression' for the purposes of that section, and continued:]

I was referred, on this point also, to the judgment of Peter Gibson J in *Re Sam Weller & Sons Ltd*[75] at the end of which he said that he had no doubt that the court would ordinarily be very reluctant to accept that managerial decisions could amount to unfairly prejudicial conduct. . . .

I do not doubt that in an appropriate case it is open to the court to find that serious mismanagement of a company's business constitutes conduct that is unfairly prejudicial to the interests of minority shareholders. But I share Peter Gibson J's view that the court will normally be very reluctant to accept that managerial decisions can amount to unfairly prejudicial conduct.

Two considerations seem to me to be relevant. First, there will be cases where there is disagreement between petitioners and respondents as to whether a particular managerial decision was, as a matter of commercial judgment, the right one to make, or as to whether a particular proposal relating to the conduct of the company's business is commercially sound. . . . In my view, it is not for the court to resolve such disagreements on a petition under s 459. Not only is a judge ill-qualified to do so, but there can be no unfairness to the petitioners in those in control of the company's affairs taking a different view from theirs on such matters.

Secondly, as was persuasively argued by Mr Chivers, a shareholder acquires shares in a company knowing that their value will depend in some measure on the competence of the management. He takes the risk that that management may prove not to be of the highest quality. Short of a breach by a director of his duty of skill and care (and no such breach on the part of either Mr Purslow or Mrs Purslow was alleged) there is prima facie no unfairness to a shareholder in the quality of the management turning out to be poor. It occurred to me during the argument that one example of a case where the court might none the less find that there was unfair prejudice to minority shareholders would be one where the majority shareholders, for reasons of their own, persisted in retaining in charge of the management of the company's business a member of their family who

---

75   [1990] Ch 682.

was demonstrably incompetent. That of course would be a very different case from this. Mr Rowland deliberately invested in a company controlled and managed by Mr Purslow, whom he had known for five years or so. Indeed, he did so, despite Mr Purslow's reluctance to have him as a shareholder in his company. Mr Nourse submitted that Mr Rowland had a right to expect a reasonable standard of general management from Mr Purslow. In my view, he had no such right. He took the risk that Mr Purslow's management of the company might not be up to the standard that he, Mr Rowland, had hoped and expected. . . .

However, exceptionally, significant and serious mismanagement may justify relief.

[11.23] Re Macro (Ipswich) Ltd [1994] 2 BCLC 354 (Chancery Division)

The applicants claimed that the two property-owning companies in which they were minority shareholders had suffered losses because a firm referred to as 'Thompsons' (the companies' property-managing agents) had committed various improprieties which Mr Thompson (an elderly, autocratic person who was the founder of Thompsons and the companies' sole director) had connived at or inadequately supervised. Arden J held that this was unfairly prejudicial conduct and ordered that the applicants' shares be bought out.

ARDEN J: . . . The question whether any action was or would be 'unfairly prejudicial' to the interests of the members has to be judged on an objective basis. Accordingly it has to be determined, on an objective basis, first whether the action of which complaint is made is prejudicial to members' interests and secondly whether it is unfairly so. Based on the findings of fact that I have made, I am satisfied that the companies suffered prejudice in consequence of failure to have a planned maintenance programme, the failure to supervise repairs, the failure to inspect properties regularly, the failure to let on protected shorthold tenancies, the taking of commissions from builders doing work for the companies by employees of Thompsons, the charging of excessive management charges and secretarial salary and the mismanagement of litigation. The absence of an effective system to prevent excessive amounts being retained on Thompsons' client account instead of paying it over to the companies is also in my judgment likely to cause loss to the companies in the future. All of these matters are within the responsibility of Thompsons as the companies' managing agent but they are attributable to the lack of effective supervision by Mr Thompson on behalf of the companies. It is this conduct of the companies' affairs by Mr Thompson which, in my judgment, is prejudicial in the respects I have mentioned. As the conduct is prejudicial in a financial sense to the companies, it must also be prejudicial to the interests of the plaintiffs as holders of its shares. . . .

[This] is not a case where what happened was merely that quality of management turned out to be poor (cf Re Elgindata Ltd [11.22]). This is a case where there were specific acts of mismanagement by Thompsons, which Mr Thompson failed to prevent or rectify. Moreover, several of the acts of mismanagement which the plaintiffs have identified were repeated over many years, as for example in relation to the failure to inspect repairs. In my judgment, viewed overall, those acts (and Mr Thompson's failures to prevent or rectify them) are sufficiently significant and serious to justify intervention by the court under s 461. . . .

➤ Note

Although there is no finding in the judgment that Mr Thompson was guilty of anything other than mismanagement, it is pertinent to note that, like the negligence of the directors in *Daniels v Daniels*,[76] there was a self-serving aspect to this mismanagement, since it was Mr Thompson's own firm which stood to gain from (*inter alia*) the excessive management charges.

---

[76] [1978] Ch 406, above, p 520.

> **Question**

In *Re Macro (Ipswich) Ltd* **[11.23]**, Arden J also said:

> Given the presence of minority interests, the absence of an independent director would in my judgment be prejudicial to the position of the plaintiffs as shareholders in the companies. If support were needed for such proposition, it can be found in the recent report of the Committee on the Financial Aspects of Corporate Governance (the Cadbury Committee) published in December 1992. This report, which has been accepted by, inter alia, the Stock Exchange, emphasises that no one individual within a company should have unfettered powers of decision and that, where the chairman is also chief executive, there should be a strong and independent element on the board. While that report is directed to listed companies, the desirability of having a truly independent board is applicable to all cases where there are minority shareholders. In my judgment neither Mr Thompson nor Mr Farley [Mr Thompson's proposed nominee] would be able to act independently of Mr Thompson's position as majority shareholder and sole proprietor of Thompsons. That situation would in my judgment not only be prejudicial to the interests of the minority shareholders, but unfairly so.

Does the modern law on private companies adopt this approach, or even suggest that it is best practice?

'Legitimate expectations'.

[11.24] Re Saul D Harrison & Sons plc [1995] 1 BCLC 14 (Court of Appeal)

The petitioner held 'C' class shares in a company that made industrial cleaning cloths. The business had been founded by her great-grandfather in 1891. The 'C' class shares carried rights to dividends and to capital distributions in a liquidation, but no entitlement to vote. The company had substantial assets but had recently been run at a loss. The petitioner complained that the directors (her cousins) had unreasonably continued to run the business (and to pay themselves salaries, although the court ruled that these were not excessive), instead of closing the business down and distributing the assets to the shareholders. Vinelott J and the Court of Appeal held that the petitioner had no 'legitimate expectations' over and above an expectation that the board would manage the company in accordance with their fiduciary obligations and the terms of the articles of association and the Companies Act, and that no breach of these obligations had been shown.

> HOFFMANN LJ: Mr Purle, who appeared for the petitioner, said that the only test of unfairness was whether a reasonable bystander would think that the conduct in question was unfair. This is correct, so far as it goes, and has some support in the cases. Its merit is to emphasise that the court is applying an objective standard of fairness. But I do not think that it is the most illuminating way of putting the matter. For one thing, the standard of fairness must necessarily be laid down by the court. In explaining how the court sets about deciding what is fair in the context of company management, I do not think that it helps a great deal to add the reasonable company watcher to the already substantial cast of imaginary characters which the law uses to personify its standards of justice in different situations. An appeal to the views of an imaginary third party makes the concept seem more vague than it really is. It is more useful to examine the factors which the law actually takes into account in setting the standard.
>
> In deciding what is fair or unfair for the purposes of s 459, it is important to have in mind that fairness is being used in the context of a commercial relationship.[77] The articles of association are just

---

[77] [Note, however, that in *O'Neill v Phillips* **[11.24]** Lord Hoffmann states that 'conduct which is perfectly fair between competing businessmen may not be fair between members of a family', a consideration which weighed with the judge in giving a petitioner relief in *Brownlow v GH Marshall Ltd* [2000] 2 BCLC 655.]

what their name implies: the contractual terms which govern the relationships of the shareholders with the company and each other. They determine the powers of the board and the company in general meeting and everyone who becomes a member of a company is taken to have agreed to them. Since keeping promises and honouring agreements is probably the most important element of commercial fairness, the starting point in any case under s 459 will be to ask whether the conduct of which the shareholder complains was in accordance with the articles of association. . . .

Although one begins with the articles and the powers of the board, a finding that conduct was not in accordance with the articles does not necessarily mean that it was unfair, still less that the court will exercise its discretion to grant relief. . . .

Not only may conduct be technically unlawful without being unfair: it can also be unfair without being unlawful. In a commercial context, this may at first seem surprising. How can it be unfair to act in accordance with what the parties have agreed? As a general rule, it is not. But there are cases in which the letter of the articles does not fully reflect the understandings upon which the shareholders are associated.

[His Lordship referred to *Ebrahimi v Westbourne Galleries Ltd* **[14.14]**, and continued:]

Thus the personal relationship between a shareholder and those who control the company may entitle him to say that it would in certain circumstances be unfair for them to exercise a power conferred by the articles upon the board or the company in general meeting. I have in the past ventured to borrow from public law the term 'legitimate expectation' to describe the correlative 'right' in the shareholder to which such a relationship may give rise. It often arises out of a fundamental understanding between the shareholders which formed the basis of their association but was not put into contractual form, such as an assumption that each of the parties who has ventured his capital will also participate in the management of the company and receive the return on his investment in the form of salary rather than dividend. . . .

Although the petition speaks of the petitioner having various 'legitimate expectations', no grounds are alleged for saying that her rights are not 'adequately and exhaustively' laid down by the articles. And in substance the alleged 'legitimate expectations' amount to no more than an expectation that the board would manage the company in accordance with their fiduciary obligations and the terms of the articles and the Companies Act. . . .

[11.25] O'Neill v Phillips [1999] 1 WLR 1092 (House of Lords)

In 1985 Phillips, who had owned all the shares in the company, gave a 25% share to O'Neill, its foreman and principal employee, and appointed him as a director. He told O'Neill that he hoped O'Neill would be able to take over the whole day-to-day management of the business, and on that basis he would be allowed to draw 50% of the profits. This in due course occurred and, indeed, Phillips retired from the board, leaving O'Neill as sole director. The company prospered for the next five years, during which time there were discussions about increasing O'Neill's shareholding to 50%. But then the construction industry went into recession and the company's fortunes declined. Phillips took back control of the business and reduced O'Neill's status to that of a branch manager, and also withdrew his share of the profits. O'Neill took steps to leave the company, and also issued a s 459 petition. Lord Hoffmann, with the support of all the other members of the House, held that there was no basis for a court to hold that Phillips had acted unfairly.

LORD HOFFMANN: . . .

'Unfairly prejudicial'

In s 459 Parliament has chosen fairness as the criterion by which the court must decide whether it has jurisdiction to grant relief. It is clear from the legislative history (which I discussed in *Re Saul D Harrison & Sons plc* **[11.23]**) that it chose this concept to free the court from technical considerations of legal right and to confer a wide power to do what appeared just and equitable. But this does not mean that the court can do whatever the individual judge happens to think fair. The concept of fairness must be applied judicially and the content which it is given by the courts must be based upon rational principles. As Warner J said in *Re J E Cade & Sons Ltd* [1992] BCLC 213 at 227: 'The court . . . has a very wide discretion, but it does not sit under a palm tree.'

Although fairness is a notion which can be applied to all kinds of activities, its content will depend upon the context in which it is being used. Conduct which is perfectly fair between competing businessmen may not be fair between members of a family. In some sports it may require, at best, observance of the rules, in others ('it's not cricket') it may be unfair in some circumstances to take advantage of them. All is said to be fair in love and war. So the context and background are very important.

In the case of s 459, the background has the following two features. First, a company is an association of persons for an economic purpose, usually entered into with legal advice and some degree of formality. The terms of the association are contained in the articles of association and sometimes in collateral agreements between the shareholders. Thus the manner in which the affairs of the company may be conducted is closely regulated by rules to which the shareholders have agreed. Secondly, company law has developed seamlessly from the law of partnership, which was treated by equity, like the Roman *societas*, as a contract of good faith. One of the traditional roles of equity, as a separate jurisdiction, was to restrain the exercise of strict legal rights in certain relationships in which it considered that this would be contrary to good faith. These principles have, with appropriate modification, been carried over into company law.

The first of these two features leads to the conclusion that a member of a company will not ordinarily be entitled to complain of unfairness unless there has been some breach of the terms on which he agreed that the affairs of the company should be conducted. But the second leads to the conclusion that there will be cases in which equitable considerations make it unfair for those conducting the affairs of the company to rely upon their strict legal powers. Thus unfairness may consist in a breach of the rules or in using the rules in a manner which equity would regard as contrary to good faith.

This approach to the concept of unfairness in s 459 runs parallel to that which your Lordships' House, in *Ebrahimi v Westbourne Galleries Ltd* **[14.14]**, adopted in giving content to the concept of 'just and equitable' as a ground for winding up.

[His Lordship cited extracts from that case, and continued:]

I would apply the same reasoning to the concept of unfairness in s 459. The Law Commission, in its report on Shareholder Remedies (Law Com No 246) (1997) para 4.11, p 43 expresses some concern that defining the content of the unfairness concept in the way I have suggested might unduly limit its scope and that 'conduct which would appear to be deserving of a remedy may be left unremedied'. In my view, a balance has to be struck between the breadth of the discretion given to the court and the principle of legal certainty. Petitions under s 459 are often lengthy and expensive. It is highly desirable that lawyers should be able to advise their clients whether or not a petition is likely to succeed. Lord Wilberforce, after the passage which I have quoted, said that it would be impossible 'and wholly undesirable' to define the circumstances in which the application of equitable principles might make it unjust, or inequitable (or unfair) for a party to insist on legal rights or to exercise them in particular way. This of course is right. But that does not mean that there are no principles by which those circumstances may be identified. The way in which such equitable principles operate is tolerably well settled and in my view it would be wrong to abandon them in favour of some wholly indefinite notion of fairness. . . .

I agree with Jonathan Parker J when he said in *Re Astec (BSR) plc* [1998] 2 BCLC 556 at 588:

. . . in order to give rise to an equitable constraint based on 'legitimate expectation' what is required is a personal relationship or personal dealings of some kind between the party seeking to exercise the legal right and the party seeking to restrain such exercise, such as will affect the conscience of the former.

This is putting the matter in very traditional language, reflecting in the word 'conscience' the ecclesi-astical origins of the long-departed Court of Chancery. . . . I have no difficulty with this formulation. But I think that one useful cross-check in a case like this is to ask whether the exercise of the power in question would be contrary to what the parties, by words or conduct, have actually agreed. Would it conflict with the promises which they appear to have exchanged? . . . In a quasi-partnership com-pany, they will usually be found in the understandings between the members at the time they entered into association. But there may be later promises, by words or conduct, which it would be unfair to allow a member to ignore. Nor is it necessary that such promises should be independently enforceable as a matter of contract. A promise may be binding as a matter of justice and equity although for one reason or another (for example, because in favour of a third party) it would be enforceable in law. . . .

I do not suggest that exercising rights in breach of some promise or undertaking is the only form of conduct which will be regarded as unfair for the purposes of s 459. For example, there may be some event which puts an end to the basis upon which the parties entered into association with each other, making it unfair that one shareholder should insist upon the continuance of the associ-ation. The analogy of contractual frustration suggests itself. The unfairness may arise not from what the parties have positively agreed but from a majority using its legal powers to maintain the associ-ation in circumstances to which the minority can reasonably say it did not agree: non haec in foed-era veni.

Legitimate expectations

In *Re Saul D Harrison & Sons plc* I used the term 'legitimate expectation', borrowed from public law, as a label for the 'correlative right' to which a relationship between company members may give rise in a case when, on equitable principles, it would be regarded as unfair for a majority to exercise a power conferred upon them by the articles to the prejudice of another member. I gave as an example the standard case in which shareholders have entered into association upon the under-standing that each of them who has ventured his capital will also participate in the management of the company. In such a case it will usually be considered unjust, inequitable or unfair for a majority to use their voting power to exclude a member from participation in the management without giving him the opportunity to remove his capital upon reasonable terms. The aggrieved member could be said to have had a 'legitimate expectation' that he would be able to participate in the management or withdraw from the company.

It was probably a mistake to use this term, as it usually is when one introduces a new label to describe a concept which is already sufficiently defined in other terms. In saying that it was 'correla-tive' to the equitable restraint, I meant that it could exist only when equitable principles of the kind I have been describing would make it unfair for a party to exercise rights under the articles. It is a consequence, not a cause, of the equitable restraint. The concept of a legitimate expectation should not be allowed to lead a life of its own, capable of giving rise to equitable restraints in circumstances to which the traditional equitable principles have no application. That is what seems to have hap-pened in this case.

Was Mr Phillips unfair?

The Court of Appeal found that by 1991 the company had the characteristics identified by Lord Wilberforce in *Ebrahimi v Westbourne Galleries Ltd* as commonly giving rise to equitable restraints upon the exercise of powers under the articles. They were (1) an association formed or continued on the basis of a personal relationship involving mutual confidence, (2) an understanding that all, or some, of the shareholders shall participate in the conduct of the business and (3) restrictions on the transfer of shares, so that a member cannot take out his stake and go elsewhere. I agree. It follows that it would have been unfair of Mr Phillips to use his voting powers under the articles to remove Mr O'Neill from participation in the conduct of the business without giving him the opportunity to sell his interest in the company at a fair price. Although it does not matter, I should say that I do not think that this was the position when Mr O'Neill first acquired his shares in 1985. He received them as a gift and an incentive and I do not think that in making that gift Mr Phillips could be taken to have surrendered his right to dismiss Mr O'Neill from the management without making him an offer for the shares. Mr O'Neill was simply an employee who happened to have been given some shares. But over the following years the relationship changed. Mr O'Neill invested his own profits in the company by leaving some on loan account and agreeing to part being capitalised as shares. He worked to build up the company's business. He guaranteed its bank account and mortgaged his house in support. . . .

The difficulty for Mr O'Neill is that Mr Phillips did not remove him from participation in the management of the business. After the meeting on 4 November 1991 he remained a director and continued to earn his salary as manager of the business in Germany. The Court of Appeal held that he had been constructively removed by the behaviour of Mr Phillips in the matter of equality of profits and shareholdings. So the question then becomes whether Mr Phillips acted unfairly in respect of these matters.

To take the shareholdings first, the Court of Appeal said that Mr O'Neill had a legitimate expectation of being allotted more shares when the targets were met. No doubt he did have such an expectation before 4 November and no doubt it was legitimate, or reasonable, in the sense that it reasonably appeared likely to happen. Mr Phillips had agreed in principle, subject to the execution of a suitable document. But this is where I think that the Court of Appeal may have been misled by the expression 'legitimate expectation'. The real question is whether in fairness or equity Mr O'Neill had a right to the shares. On this point, one runs up against what seems to me the insuperable obstacle of the judge's finding that Mr Phillips never agreed to give them. He made no promise on the point. From which it seems to me to follow that there is no basis, consistent with established principles of equity, for a court to hold that Mr Phillips was behaving unfairly in withdrawing from the negotiation. This would not be restraining the exercise of legal rights. It would be imposing upon Mr Phillips an obligation to which he never agreed. Where, as here, parties enter into negotiations with a view to a transfer of shares on professional advice and subject to a condition that they are not to be bound until a formal document has been executed, I do not think it is possible to say that an obligation has arisen in fairness or equity at an earlier stage.

The same reasoning applies to the sharing of profits. The judge found as a fact that Mr Phillips made no unconditional promise about the sharing of profits. He had said informally that he would share the profits equally while Mr O'Neill managed the company and he himself did not have to be involved in day-to-day business. He deliberately retained control of the company and with it, as the judge said, the right to redraw Mr O'Neill's responsibilities. This he did without objection in August 1991. The consequence was that he came back to running the business and Mr O'Neill was no longer managing director. He had made no promise to share the profits equally in such circumstances and it was therefore not inequitable or unfair for him to refuse to carry on doing so. . . .

LORDS JAUNCEY OF TULLICHETTLE, CLYDE, HUTTON and HOBHOUSE OF WOODBOROUGH concurred.

➤ Note

O'Neill v Phillips [11.25] is the first (and, to date, the only) House of Lords case on the 'unfair prejudice' provisions (rather than the earlier CA 1948, s 210 'oppression' provisions). The case has generated a good deal of debate as to whether Lord Hoffmann (both in this case and in his earlier judgment in *Re Saul D Harrison & Sons plc* [11.24]) has given a restrictive interpretation to s 459 (and in particular to the concept of 'legitimate expectations'), so that the remedy is likely to be less readily available (as the Law Commissions seem to think), or whether the law remains substantially unchanged (as the CLR believes).

Valuing shares in buy-out orders

Relevance of parties' conduct to the valuation of shares.

[11.26] Bird Precision Bellows Ltd [1984] Ch 419 (Nourse J), affd [1986] Ch 658 (Court of Appeal)

The only issue before the court was the issue of valuing shares when (in this case pursuant to an order made by consent) the petitioner's shares were to be purchased by the majority under CA 1980 s 75 [now CA 2006 s 994]. Nourse J, at first instance, held that the conduct of the parties could be relevant in determining whether the shares of the respective parties in the company were to be valued *pro rata* or whether the minority's interest should be discounted.

NOURSE J: Broadly speaking, shares in a small private company are acquired either by allotment on its incorporation or by transfer or devolution at some later date. In the first category it is a matter of common occurrence for a company to be incorporated in order to acquire an existing business or to start a new one, and in either event for it to be a vehicle for the conduct of a business carried on by two or more shareholders which they could, had they wished, have carried on in partnership together. Although it has been pointed out . . . that the description may be confusing, it is often convenient and it is certainly usual to describe that kind of company as a quasi-partnership. In the second category, irrespective of the nature of the company, it is a matter of common occurrence for a shareholder to acquire shares from another at a price which is discounted because they represent a minority holding. It seems to me that some general observations can usefully be made in regard to each of these examples . . .

I would expect that in a majority of cases where purchase orders are made under s 75 in relation to quasi-partnerships the vendor is unwilling in the sense that the sale has been forced upon him. Usually he will be a minority shareholder whose interests have been unfairly prejudiced by the manner in which the affairs of the company have been conducted by the majority. On the assumption that the unfair prejudice has made it no longer tolerable for him to retain his interest in the company, a sale of his shares will invariably be his only practical way out short of a winding up. In that kind of case it seems to me that it would not merely not be fair, but most unfair, that he should be bought out on the fictional basis applicable to a free election to sell his shares in accordance with the company's articles of association, or indeed on any other basis which involved a discounted price. In my judgment the correct course would be to fix the price pro rata according to the value of the shares as a whole and without any discount, as being the only fair method of compensating an unwilling vendor of the equivalent of a partnership share. Equally, if the order provided . . . for the purchase of the shares of the delinquent majority, it would not merely not be fair, but most unfair, that they should receive a price which involved an element of premium.

Of the other, I would expect more rare, cases in which the court might make a purchase order in relation to a quasi-partnership, the arguments of Mr Jacob require me to mention one. Suppose the case of a minority shareholder whose interests had been unfairly prejudiced by the conduct of the majority, but who had nevertheless so acted as to deserve his exclusion from the company. It is difficult to see how such a case could arise in practice, because one would expect acts and deserts of that kind to be inconsistent with the existence of the supposed conduct of the majority. Be that as it may the consideration of that possibility has been forced upon me by the agreement for the price to be determined by the court without any admission of unfairly prejudicial conduct on the part of the respondents. As will appear, Mr Jacob submitted that the petitioners did act in such a way as to deserve their exclusion from the company. He further submitted that it would therefore be fair for them to be bought out on the basis which would have been applicable if they had made a free election to sell their shares pursuant to the articles, ie at a discount. Assuming, at present, that the respondents can establish the necessary factual basis, I think that Mr Jacob's further submission is correct. A shareholder who deserves his exclusion has, if you like, made a constructive election to sever his connection with the company and thus to sell his shares.

On appeal, the Court of Appeal declined to interfere with the judge's approach, which was a matter for his discretion.

➤ Note

In *Re OC (Transport) Services Ltd* [1984] BCLC 251, Mervyn Davies J held that it was proper to backdate a valuation to the commencement of the 'unfairly prejudicial' conduct, so that the value of the shares would not be affected by the changes which that conduct had brought about. In this, he was following the approach of the House of Lords under the old s 210 in the *Scottish Co-operative* case [11.19].

Even in quasi-partnerships, purchase at an undiscounted price is not inevitable.

[11.27] Re Phoenix Office Supplies Ltd [2003] 1 BCLC 76 (Court of Appeal)

P appealed against a decision ordering its two remaining directors to purchase the shares of a departing director, L, at their full undiscounted value. L had decided to leave his employment with P for personal reasons but had remained a director whilst seeking to sell his shareholding without a discount to reflect his minority holding. The remaining directors had refused L's request to pay one third of the company's net asset value for the shares and had further rejected his requests for copies of management accounts. The Court of Appeal, allowing the appeal, held that a director leaving his position of his own volition was not entitled to have his shares bought out at their full undiscounted value: not every quasi-partnership entitles directors to a 'no fault divorce', and L could not 'put' his shares on the company.

AULD LJ: Section 459 has two roles, as explained by Lord Hoffmann in *O'Neill v Phillips* [11.25] at pp 1098G-1099A. First, it protects shareholders against the breach of terms on which they have agreed the affairs of the company should be conducted, through the articles of association or, say, some collateral agreement. Secondly, it protects them against some inequity that makes it unfair for those conducting the company's affairs to rely upon their strict legal power, for example, a resolution by majority shareholders to remove a minority director under s 303 of the 1985 Act [see CA 2006 s 168]. As Lord Wilberforce had earlier explained in *Re Westbourne Galleries Ltd* [14.14], the latter protection is the source of the notion of a relationship of quasi-partnership between shareholders . . .

[He then referred to various authorities, including *O'Neill v Phillips* [11.25], citing some of the passages above on 'legitimate expectations' and whether exclusion might be in breach of such expectations. He then continued:]

Given the breadth of such propositions, it is important to keep in mind that s 459 is designed for the protection of the members of companies. It is in that capacity that they seek its protection, not as directors or employees, an important reminder where the provision is prayed in aid by a departing member who may also be a director or employee. And, as Lord Hoffmann indicated in *O'Neill v Phillips* at p 614B; 1107B-C, where the member is departing because he has been excluded by other members from his involvement as a director and/or employee, the provision is aimed not at unfairness in such exclusion for its own sake, but at unfairness in his exclusion without a reasonable offer for his shares . . .

How then is the principle to be applied in a quasi-partnership company where the departing minority shareholder, not the majority shareholders, seeks to put an end to the association for personal reasons and take his investment in it with him, and where, as the judge found, there was no agreement for such a 'no-fault divorce'? I have already indicated the answer in my summary of Lord Hoffmann's propositions, but here is the place to put it in his own words, at pp 611G–612D; 1104D–1105B:

> 'Mr Hollington's submission comes to saying that, in a "quasi-partnership" company, one partner ought to be entitled at will to require the other partner or partners to buy his shares at a fair value. All he need do is to declare that trust and confidence has broken down . . .
>
> I do not think that there is any support in the authorities for such a stark right of unilateral withdrawal. There are cases, such as *Re a Company No 006834 of 1988* (1989) 5 BCC 218, in which it has been said that if a breakdown in relations has caused the majority to remove a shareholder from participation in the management, it is usually a waste of time to try to investigate who caused the breakdown. Such breakdowns often occur . . . without either side having done anything seriously wrong or unfair. It is not fair to the excluded member, who will usually have lost his employment, to keep his assets locked in the company. But that does not mean that a member who has not been dismissed or excluded can demand that his shares be purchased simply because he feels that he has lost trust and confidence in the others. I rather doubt whether even in partnership law a dissolution would be granted on this ground in a case in which it was still possible under the articles for the business of the partnership to be continued. And as Lord Wilberforce observed in *Re Westbourne Galleries Ltd* . . . [at] p 380B, one should not press the quasi-partnership analogy too far: "A company, however small, however domestic, is a company not a partnership or even a quasi-partnership . . ."
>
> The Law Commission, in the report to which I have already referred, *Shareholder Remedies* . . . considered whether to recommend the introduction of a statutory remedy "in situations where there is no fault", so that members of a quasi-partnership could exit at will. They said, in para 3.66:
>
> "In our view there are strong economic arguments against allowing shareholders to exit at will. Also, as a matter of principle, such a right would fundamentally contravene the sanctity of the contract binding the members and the company which we considered should guide our approach to shareholder remedies."
>
> The Law Commission plainly did not consider that s 459 already provided a right to exit at will and I do not think so either.'

The [trial] judge . . . ruled that a consequence of the quasi-partnership here was that Mr Larvin was entitled to the full undiscounted value of his shares. In so ruling, he appears to have proceeded as if it had been Messrs Parish and Ogden who had taken the initiative to server the association rather than, as was the case, Mr Larvin. True it was that they refused to recognise him as a director or to give him access to certain company information, but that was only after he had made plain that he wanted to sever all relationship with the company and them and to take the value of his shareholding with him. In my judgment, this is not the sort of case that Lord Hoffmann had in mind when formulating his propositions applicable to excluded members. The judge did not expressly refer to such propositions, but he appears to have had them in mind in the passages that I have emphasised . . .

Lord Hoffmann's different treatment of those cases where there is a withdrawal because of a sense of loss of trust and confidence applies *a fortiori* to a shareholder who, even without such a sense, but for other personal reasons, simply wishes to leave and take his investment in the company with him. Where, as here, the company is small and with only a few shareholders each holding a significant proportion of the company's issued capital, a sudden demand from one of them, for essentially personal reasons, to seek to withdraw his investment could be very damaging, even potentially ruinous, to them and the company.

As to the judge's reliance on the 'lock-in' effect of art. 6 of the company's articles of association, I do not consider that the 'absolute discretion' it purported to give to the directors to decline to register any transfer of any share pointed to an intention that if any one of them wanted to move elsewhere, for whatever reason, he could be sure of realising the full value of his shareholding. Such an entitlement could, for the reasons I have just given, be ruinous to the company and its members. The company's directors have a fiduciary duty as such to act in the interests of the company. The power of veto on a transfer, despite its terms, is not absolute. It is subject to the equitable jurisdiction of the court to intervene by winding up the company on the just and equitable ground or to the provisions of s 459 itself. . . .

As Mr Crawford submitted, not every quasi-partnership company relationship gives rise to an entitlement to a 'no-fault divorce'; there must be something more. . . .

Accordingly, it does not follow from the fact that the company was a quasi-partnership that Mr Larvin was entitled to insist on leaving with an undiscounted value of his minority shareholding. . . .

Depending on the issues as they developed between the parties, there might have been a claim for an appropriately discounted value of his holding. Or Mr Larvin could have continued with his substantial minority holding, with a view eventually to agreeing a price with the others or for its transfer to a third party. Failing such agreement, he might have been able to seek such relief as might then be appropriate under s 459 or for the company to be wound up on the just and equitable ground. But that was not the basis of his petition. . . .

[He then went on to allow the appeal.]

CLARKE LJ concurred.

JONATHAN PARKER LJ delivered a concurring judgment.

➤ Note

By contrast, in *Strahan v Wilcock* [2006] EWCA Civ 13, [2006] BCC 320, CA, purchase at the undiscounted price was ordered. The company was held to be a quasi-partnership. This despite the facts that S had not participated in the business from the outset; had commenced the relationship as a consultant; had only later became a shareholder and manager; and had held only a minority of the shares. Given the quasi-partnership nature of the relationship at the time the shares were acquired, however, there were equitable considerations which bound W to purchase S's shares on a non-discounted basis once S had been dismissed by the company. S's departure from the company was involuntary. He did not take a unilateral decision to leave and nor was he guilty of misconduct. Fairness demanded that he should be entitled to claim back not simply the cost of acquiring the shares, but their value at the date of the buy-out order.

Date of valuation.

[11.28] Profinance Trust SA v Gladstone [2002] 1 WLR 1024 (Court of Appeal)

[The facts are immaterial.]

ROBERT WALKER LJ for the Court (SCHIEMANN and ROBERT WALKER LJ and LLOYD J): In our judgment the deputy judge was right in his view that an order for the equivalent of interest [ie a sum paid in addition to the settled price of the shares to be bought out, where the valuation has been carried out early] is not beyond the powers of the court under section 461(1) of the Companies Act 1985 [re-enacted in CA 2006 s 996]. The court has repeatedly emphasised the width of the discretion conferred by that subsection, which is not limited to the particular powers enumerated in subsection (2). The House of Lords has (in relation to the court's closely comparable powers under section 210 of the Companies Act 1948) approved the making of adjustments in the valuation process which mean that the court is actually valuing shares, not as they are, but as they would have been if events had followed a different course; and that practice is regularly followed by the court in orders under section 461(1). In these circumstances a denial of the court's power to award the equivalent of interest would come close to straining at a gnat.

It is however a power which should be exercised with great caution. Miss Newman [counsel] has rightly drawn attention to the need for lawyers to be able to advise their clients as to the likely range of outcomes of section 459 proceedings, in order to encourage compromise in an area in which litigation can be cripplingly expensive. If a petitioner seeking an order for the purchase of his shares contends (either as his only claim or in the alternative) that they should be valued at a relatively early date but then augmented by the equivalent of interest, he must put forward that claim clearly and persuade the court by evidence that it is the only way, or the best way, to a fair result. It should not be a last-minute afterthought (as it may have been, to some extent, in *In re Bird Precision Bellows Ltd* [1984] Ch 419 and *Elliott v Planet Organic Ltd* [2000] BCC 610). Unless a petitioner is asking for no more than simple interest at a normal rate he should also put before the court evidence on which the court can decide what amount (if any) to allow. The exercise which the deputy judge undertook, as described in the last paragraph of his judgment, does not appear to have had a solid evidential basis. . . .

[and on the more general issue of valuation of shares:]

The starting point should in our view be the general proposition stated by Nourse J in *In re London School of Electronics Ltd* [1986] Ch 211, 224: "Prima facie an interest in a going concern ought to be valued at the date on which it is ordered to be purchased." That is, as Nourse J said, subject to the overriding requirement that the valuation should be fair on the facts of the particular case.

The general trend of authority over the last 15 years appears to us to support that as the starting point, while recognising that there are many cases in which fairness (to one side or the other) requires the court to take another date. It would be wrong to try to enumerate all those cases but some of them can be illustrated by the authorities already referred to.

(i) Where a company has been deprived of its business, an early valuation date (and compensating adjustments) may be required in fairness to the claimant: see *Scottish Co-operative Wholesale Society Ltd v Meyer* **[11.19]**.

(ii)   Where a company has been reconstructed or its business has changed significantly, so that it has a new economic identity, an early valuation date may be required in fairness to one or both parties: see *In re OC (Transport) Services Ltd* [1984] BCLC 251, and to a lesser degree *In re London School of Electronics Ltd* [1986] Ch 211. But an improper alteration in the issued share capital, unaccompanied by any change in the business, will not necessarily have that outcome: see *In re DR Chemicals Ltd* (1988) 5 BCC 39.

(iii)   Where a minority shareholder has a petition on foot and there is a general fall in the market, the court may in fairness to the claimant have the shares valued at an early date, especially if it strongly disapproves of the majority shareholder's prejudicial conduct: see *In re Cumana Ltd* [1986] BCLC 430.

(iv)   But a claimant is not entitled to what the deputy judge called a one-way bet, and the court will not direct an early valuation date simply to give the claimant the most advantageous exit from the company, especially where severe prejudice has not been made out: see *In re Elgindata Ltd* [1991] BCLC 959 **[11.22]**.

(v)   All these points may be heavily influenced by the parties' conduct in making and accepting or rejecting offers either before or during the course of the proceedings: see *In re A Company (No 00709 of 1992)* [1999] 1 WLR 1092.

In our judgment the fairest course in this case would be to take the agreed value as at the time of the first instance hearing, that is £215,000. We allow this appeal and substitute an order that Mr Gladstone should purchase Profinance's 40% holding in the company for £86,000.

Unfair prejudice and other remedies

Before leaving this discussion of CA 2006 s 994, it is worth noting that this avenue for complaint by members might fruitfully be used to remedy a wide variety of wrongs that have been considered elsewhere in this book. Many of the cases traditionally located in some other part of the company law syllabus, such as those relating to the alteration of a company's articles, might well be decided differently today if proceedings were brought under this section. For example, consider the saga which culminated in the case of *Greenhalgh v Arderne Cinemas Ltd* [4.27/19.08]. Mr Greenhalgh might well have claimed (possibly with success) that he had been the victim of unfairly prejudicial conduct. It is also possible that minority shareholders who were in fact successful in some older cases might now choose to seek a remedy under CA 2006 s 994 rather than whatever was then available to them: for instance, the petitioners in *Loch v John Blackwood Ltd* [14.12] might well have preferred a buy-out rather than having the company compulsorily wound up.

On the other hand, where CA 2006 s 994 seems less than satisfactory, members might resort to petitioning the court for a winding-up order on the 'just and equitable' ground: see below, pp 653 ff. There is also, at least in theory, the possibility of invoking the powers of the Department of Trade and Industry under CA 1985, Part XIV (not re-enacted in CA 2006), to have the affairs of the company investigated (see below, pp 595 ff). In practice, the Department's powers are most commonly invoked in cases of insolvency, fraudulent trading and financial scandal—that is, in matters of interest to the investing public and to creditors—while minority shareholders who seek aid are sent away empty-handed. Mr Moir (see *Wallersteiner v Moir (No 2)* above, p 533) is reported to have made 15 unsuccessful requests to the Department (*Economist*, 8 February 1975).

12

PUBLIC DISCLOSURE, MARKET REGULATION AND PUBLIC INVESTIGATIONS OF COMPANIES

Public disclosure and the disclosure philosophy

It has long been recognised that the 'price' that companies must pay for the privileges of incorporation (separate personality) and limited liability is a fair degree of openness and publicity about their affairs. The Companies Acts have been largely based on this philosophy. Even the obligatory term 'Limited' is intended to achieve this purpose, warning those dealing with a company that its resources are finite.

In the ordinary course of business of a company disclosure under the Act is secured by: (i) delivery of information to the registrar of companies; (ii) publication in the *Gazette*; (iii) information made available at the company's registered office; and (iv) notifications in various business documents. The Stock Exchange imposes additional obligations on listed companies. And, quite outside any legal regime, the market, and the financial press, may publicly disclose information considered significant.

Companies are also subject to special disclosure rules designed to give interested parties information on substantial share ownership in the company and to provide appropriate information to investors when new shares are issued to the public. Finally, there are rules restricting the use of non-public information by those acquiring shares in the market.

General disclosure obligations

The Registrar of Companies

A company's obligation to make public disclosure is generally fulfilled by delivering the required information to the Registrar of Companies. Section 1061 of CA 2006 confirms the role of the Registrar, whose duties and functions date back to 1844.

There are three separate registrars, for England and Wales (situated in Cardiff), for Scotland, and for Northern Ireland. The registrar maintains a file for every company and adds to it all the documents relating to that company as they are lodged for registration over the years. Files are open to public search, either electronically or using a microfiche system. Certain information delivered after 1 January 2007 must be filed electronically (CA 2006 s 1078); otherwise the filing mechanism is discretionary (CA 2006 s 1080).

All the company's most important documents relating to its constitution and its history subsequent to its incorporation, together with information about its membership, finances and management must be notified to the registrar with, as history shows, each successive Act stepping up the reporting obligations.

A person searching the records of a company at the registry will find the following documents available: the memorandum and articles of association, notices giving the situation of its registered office and details of its directors and secretary, particulars of charges over its property and trust deeds covering issues of debentures, copies of any prospectus or listing particulars that may have been issued, returns of allotments and lists of current members. In addition, there must be filed once a year an annual return giving all the information specified by regulations (ss 854–856, and see s 858 for the consequences of non-compliance), and various accounts and reports depending upon the size of the company (s 441), but generally including copies of the company's annual accounts (ss 394, 399), together with the directors' report (s 415), the auditors' report (ss 475, 495–497, unless the company is exempt under ss 477 or 480, although s 476, gives the members the power to require an audit in any event), and, for quoted companies, a directors' remuneration report (s 420). Other events in the life of a company, both major ones such as alterations of its constitution (s 21) or the appointment of a receiver (s 871), and more minor ones where shares in public companies are issued for a non-cash consideration (ss 593, 597), or where public companies agree to certain transfers of non-cash assets (ss 598, 602), may trigger filing obligations. Today, company secretaries (or their equivalent for companies without secretaries) need the aid of very extensive checklists.

The registration system is first and foremost an information service: not many legal consequences turn on the fact that a document has or has not been filed. Of these, the most important for the student are (i) what remains of the constructive notice doctrine (above, pp 141 ff), (ii) the sanction of partial voidness which follows from the non-registration of charges (above, pp 464 ff), and (iii) official notification (see below).

Although the information provided by the registration system was initially seen as a means of helping creditors to assess the risks of dealing with a limited company (the 'forewarned is forearmed' principle), the disclosure regime is now seen as increasingly essential in reducing the risks of managerial self-interest and incompetence, and facilitating the efficient operation of the capital markets.

Publication in the Gazette

The registrar is obliged to give publicity in the *Gazette* to a company's incorporation (CA 2006 s 1064) and to various events affecting a company's administration or status—an alteration of its constitution or change in its directorate, for instance, or the appointment of a liquidator or redemption of shares out of capital. Most 'official notifications' in the *Gazette* are made under CA 2006 s 1077 in compliance with the First Company Law Directive (68/151/EEC).

These s 1077 notifications are really only token publicity, for very few copies of the special Companies Supplement to the Gazette (which is available only on microfiche) are sold. The CLR suggested electronic publication might be more effective (Final Report, para 11.48). Accordingly, CA 2006 s 1116 provides a power for the Secretary of State to specify alternative means which the registrar may then approve for use. To ensure that any such change in current practice is itself publicised, s 1116(5) requires it to be announced first in the Gazette.

In contrast to the registers maintained at Companies House, legal consequences do flow from failures to secure the necessary official notification of specified events. These include the making of winding-up orders or appointments of liquidators in voluntary liquidations, alteration of the company's articles, changes in the company's directors, or changes in the company's registered office (at least for service of documents on the company). Third parties dealing with the company are protected by CA 2006 s 1079: it provides that the company cannot rely, as against a third party, on the happening of the specified events if, at the material time, the event had not been officially notified, unless the company can prove that the third party knew of the event at the material time.

On the other hand, notification in the *Gazette* is intended to protect third parties, not the company, so notification does not operate as constructive notice to third parties that the event has occurred: *Official Custodian for Charities v Parway Estates Developments Ltd* [1985] Ch 151 **[3.18]**.

Publicity at the company's own registered office

Many of the statutory provisions requiring registration of matters at the Companies Registry are duplicated or supplemented by obligations to maintain copies of documents and other information at the company's own office, and to have facilities there for searching these records. Normally, this means public search, but sometimes the right is restricted to members of the company or to members and creditors. In practice, little use is made of these search facilities: people generally prefer the anonymity of the registrar's public office, even if it means getting less up-to-date or less detailed information. Despite this, companies are required to keep registers of directors (s 162), directors' residential addresses (s 165—not open for inspection—see Part 10, Chapter 8), directors' service contracts (ss 228, 229), secretaries (s 275—public companies only), members (ss 114, 116), members' substantial shareholdings (ss 808, 809; also see below, p 586), debenture holders (s 743), and company charges (ss 876, 877). CA 2006 no longer requires companies to keep a register of directors' interests in shares and debentures.

Specific provision of information to members

Most of the material which the Act requires a company to send to its members is linked to the annual general meeting. Copies of the accounts for the past year, the auditors' report and directors' report are required to be sent to members along with the notice summoning the meeting (ss 423, 424). The confidentiality which one might associate with these essentially domestic reports is, however, destroyed by the statutory requirement that they also be filed with the registrar and made available at Companies House for public inspection. The directors' report, in particular, has in recent times become a vehicle for giving publicity to matters of general interest, such as the company's policy on employment or the environment. CA 2006, s 416 lists those items currently required to be covered, and allows the Secretary of State to make regulations as to other matters that must be disclosed. Unless the company is subject to the small companies' regime (s 381), the directors' report must also contain a business review (s 417), as required by the EU Accounts Modernisation Directive (2003/51/EEC), which is intended to inform members or members and help them assess how the directors have performed in their duty to promote the success of the company (s 172).

There are other scattered sections of the Act which make it obligatory to provide information to members, or to keep documents available for them to inspect, eg directors' service contracts (ss 228, 229) and contracts relating to share repurchase (s 702).

Publicity on business documents

The Act may require a company to display its name outside its offices and places of business, and to state its name and registration details on its business letters and certain other business documents (CA 2006 s 82, authorising the Secretary of State to make appropriate regulations). In addition, if the company wishes to mention its share capital or directors names on its business stationery, the Act may provide for the appropriate form. Finally, investment companies, charitable companies and insolvent companies must reveal that status on their business stationery.

Enforcement of the disclosure regime

CA 2006 seeks to secure compliance with these various disclosure obligations by a vast array of criminal sanctions (see the various penalties set out in Act in relation to the individual sections noted above), which—depending upon the wording of the particular provision—may be imposed upon the company or its officers, or both. In practice, at least so far as the predecessor provisions in CA 1985 were concerned, virtually no attempt was made to police or enforce any of these provisions except the requirements to file accounts (now CA 2006 ss 441, 451–453) and annual returns (now CA 2006 ss 854, 858). Note the range of sanctions for failure to file accounts: the directors commit an offence and may be subjected to a fine (s 451); the company is automatically liable to a 'civil penalty' (which is a fine in all but name) (s 453); and the court may order immediate compliance with the statutory provision on pain of punishment for contempt of court (s 452).

Whether it makes best sense to use the criminal law to sanction compliance with a purely commercial regime—particularly if it is not enforced in practice—is a matter of debate. Some overseas systems largely manage without. The CLR reviewed the scheme, but saw advantages in retaining criminal sanctions: even though the number of prosecutions is relatively small, a high degree of compliance with the statutory filing obligations is achieved by the practice of sending pre-prosecution warning letters (threatening 'worse to come'). The CLR did, however, recommend that most of the criminal sanctions imposed on companies should be removed, and only the individual officers concerned should be made liable. CA 2006 has largely adopted this suggestion.

Listed companies and the Stock Exchange

Those companies whose shares are listed for dealing on the Stock Exchange (including the Alternative Investment Market) are required, by the Listing Rules, as one of the conditions for the admission of their securities to listing, to undertake to make more frequent periodic disclosures about their financial and other affairs[1] to the Quotations Department and to the investing public (see below, pp 588). In addition, such companies are subject to a '*continuing disclosure*' obligation which requires them to ensure prompt publicity of any matters which are likely to have, when made public, a substantial effect on the price of the company's shares.

These enhanced disclosure requirements are motivated primarily by a desire to ensure accurate pricing by the market of the securities traded on it, so promoting investor confidence.

Public regulation of securities markets

Most of the world's developed countries have a Securities Regulation Act of some kind. Uniquely, the control of securities dealing in the United Kingdom was traditionally not a matter for the law at all. Until relatively recently, it was largely left in the hands of 'self-regulatory' agencies such as the London Stock Exchange, with some informal backing from institutions like the Bank of England. For the enforcement of their rules, these bodies relied almost entirely on extra-legal sanctions, such as the disciplinary powers which they could exercise over their own members (eg stockbrokers) who acted as intermediaries in securities dealings, and the power to suspend or withdraw the listing of a particular company's securities. These sanctions were, on the whole, remarkably effective, but only because the self-regulatory bodies had virtual monopoly control of access to the securities markets. Supplementing this informal regime was a modest array of legislation, such as the Prevention of Fraud (Investments) Act

---

[1] Eg the Listing Rules require companies to state in their annual reports the extent to which they have complied with the Combined Code (see above, p 242).

1958, which imposed limitations on the distribution of circulars and other inducements to invest.

Since then we have moved, in several steps, to the point where the conduct of financial investment businesses is now subject to an all-embracing, statute based regime in the form of the Financial Services and Markets Act 2000 (FSMA 2000). This Act was in gestation from the earliest days of the Blair administration. The essence of the new scheme is the creation of a single regulator for financial businesses of every description—not just investment businesses, but fund managers, banking and insurance firms, clearing houses, building societies, friendly societies, and so on. The Financial Services Authority (FSA) is the supreme regulator, and under the 2000 Act it has full statutory authority and corresponding accountability.

Such radical reform was inspired by a combination of factors. First, the proliferation of regulatory and self-regulatory bodies meant that there were some areas of overlap, some areas not covered, and many inconsistencies; moreover, the fragmentation of management effort between these bodies was both inefficient and expensive. Secondly, many of the leading firms in the City were multi-functional, and under the earlier regime were required to seek multiple authorisations. Thirdly, there was a growing belief that self-regulation was no longer working well: there were well-publicised scandals to do with pensions mis-selling, Lloyd's insurance, and the collapse of banks such as BCCI and Barings, and doubts whether foreign-based businesses could ever be effectively policed by a voluntary regime.

Under FSMA 2000 there is one 'super' regulator, one authorisation procedure, one rule book, and one monitoring and disciplinary procedure. Overall responsibility lies with the Treasury, and little now remains of the City's long-standing self-regulatory tradition.

Transparency obligations: investigation and notification of major voting shareholdings in certain public companies

The Transparency Directive

The register of members of a company does not necessarily reveal the true identity of its shareholders: nominees often hold shares for unnamed beneficial owners. The Transparency Directive (2004/109/EC) replaces earlier Directives (and corresponding provisions in CA 1985) and makes detailed provision for disclosure of substantial interests in the shares of public companies that are traded on regulated markets (ie not all public companies—see below, pp 588). The object of these measures is to enable both the company and the market to know who has a controlling interest, or who may be in a position to acquire such an interest in the company. More particularly, they enable a close eye to be kept on those who might otherwise obtain control without adhering to the principles laid down in the City Code on Takeovers (see below, pp 616 ff).

The Directive also makes provision for the periodic financial disclosures that must be made by issuers admitted to trading on a regulated market.

Substantial holdings

The new Transparency Directive was implemented in the UK on 20 January 2007, and responsibility for major shareholding disclosures moved from the Department of Trade and Industry (DTI) to the FSA. According to the Directive, a notification requirement is triggered when the size of a shareholder's voting holdings reaches, exceeds or moves below certain thresholds stated in the Directive (5%, 10%, 15%, 20%, 25%, 30%, 50% and 75%). The shareholder is required to inform the issuer, and the issuer must then inform the market.

In preparation for this implementation, CA 2006 s 1266 inserts seven new sections into the Financial Services and Markets Act 2000 (FSMA 2000 ss 89A–89G). These new sections enable new rules to be made by the FSA to implement the Directive. The UK's new rules, the Disclosure and Transparency Rules (DTR), Chapter 5, go beyond those required by the Directive, in that the notification thresholds are tighter (3% then +/– every 1%), the range of issuers subjected to the disclosure obligations is more extensive (including both regulated markets and prescribed markets (such as AIM and PLUS)), and the time limitations for notification are stricter. These tighter rules substantially repeat the rules previously contained in CA 1985.

The thresholds and resulting notification requirements are subject to some practical exemptions and modifications:

(i)   clearing and settling—shares acquired for the sole purpose of clearing and settlement within the usual short settlement cycle will be exempt from the requirement to notify.

(ii)   custodians—shares held by custodians in their custodian capacity will not be required to notify, provided that they can only exercise the voting rights attached to such shares under instructions given in writing or electronically.

(iii)   market makers—market makers are exempt from the 5% threshold when acting in the capacity of market maker. This is provided that they are authorised under the Market in Financial Instruments Directive and do not intervene in the management of the issuer or exert any influence on the issuer to buy back shares or back the share price.

(iv)   Investment Management Companies—the parent undertakings of management companies, as defined by the Transparency Directive, are not required to aggregate their holdings with those of their controlled undertakings. This is provided that the controlled undertaking exercises the voting rights independently from the parent.

Since the sections are concerned with questions of control, it is only voting shares that are affected, but in assessing this both options and rights convertible into shares are also covered (see s 1266, inserting s 89F into FSMA 2000).

Consequences of infringement of transparency obligations

If the FSA discovers that an issuer of securities admitted to trading on a regulated market (but not, it seems, other markets) has failed to comply with the various transparency rules, it may publicly censure the issuer (after a warning notice) and/or suspend or prohibit trading in the securities (s 1268, inserting ss 89K and 89L into FSMA 2000).

Liability for false or misleading statements concerning the transparency rules

The primary liability of issuers and directors for the accuracy of the required disclosures lies in criminal and administrative penalties under CA 2006 Part 15 and FSMA 2000 Part VI. In addition, restitution can be ordered by the court on the application of the FSA or the Secretary of State under FSMA 2000 s 382, or directly by the FSA under FSMA 2000 s 384.

CA 2006, through FSMA 2000, now also establishes a regime for civil liability to third parties in respect of disclosures that are made public in response to the transparency rules (including periodic financial disclosures) by issuers admitted to trading on regulated markets (CA 2006 s 1270 inserts ss 90A and 90B into FSMA 2000). The aim of this provision is to reduce the legal uncertainty as to whether any actionable duty is owed by issuers and their directors to investors. The section is intended to ensure that the potential scope of any civil liability is reasonable, and that the duties owed to investors are not extended unnecessarily, so that there is some protection for company members, employees and creditors. Clearly, however, there is some doubt about the potential impact of the new section, and FSMA 2000 s 90B enables the provision on liability to be amended if a wider or narrower civil liability regime is deemed appropriate.

This new civil liability regime leaves undisturbed any other liability owed by directors to the issuer and to members of the company under UK and any other national law, and any liability under other FSA rules. It also leaves undisturbed any liability of the issuer in respect of any loss or damage arising other than as a result of acquiring securities in reliance on the relevant statement or report.

Company investigations into share ownership and the disclosure register

Although the disclosure obligations just noted are limited to issuers on regulated and prescribed markets, it is possible for every public company to obtain information about the voting control over its shares. Under CA 2006 s 793, a public company is empowered to require a person to inform it whether he or she has, or has had at any time within the past three years, an interest in its voting shares and, if so, to supply information about that interest. The information so obtained must be recorded on the company's register of interests in shares (s 808). These powers apply against anyone, not just to members. And members who themselves hold 10% or more of the voting shares may requisition the exercise of these powers by the company (s 803). For example, the members may want to act if they suspect that the directors are building up a holding behind the shelter of nominees.

These sections serve a different purpose from the automatic disclosure obligations discussed above. They enable a company to discover the identity of those with direct or indirect voting rights that fall below the threshold for automatic disclosure, and to ascertain the underlying beneficial ownership of shares. To this end, the definition of an interest in shares is exceptionally wide (s 820): it includes the right to acquire or subscribe for shares (ss 824, 821), and provides for indirect and family interests to be attributed to the same person (s 823).

If a person fails to give the company the information it requests, or gives false information, the person is not only subject to a penalty (ss 795), but the company may apply to the court for an order directing that the shares be subject to restrictions (s 794) which may in effect freeze the right to transfer the shares and to receive dividends, vote and take advantage of rights offers (ss 797–802), and may even permit the sale of the shares with court approval (s 801). The restriction order can be a particularly effective sanction in the case where holdings of shares are being built up secretly through nominees based overseas, who are not easily made amenable to the local jurisdiction and who may be able to shelter behind laws in their own country which protect the confidentiality of nominee arrangements. The weakness of the sections is, however, that the company must know which of its shares are being affected by the scheme which it supposes to exist.

Disclosure and public offerings of shares

Companies wishing to raise capital may offer their shares for sale to the general public. To do this legally, the company must be a public company. The shares in public companies are often widely held, and individual members are usually more interested in capital and income returns than in close involvement in the management of the company. In order to make a company's shares more attractive to such investors, it is necessary to assure them that the initial sale is conducted on the basis of full and proper information, and that the new shares can easily be sold in the market to liquidate the investment, switch to a new investment, or realise the capital gains.

These activities, and others, are regulated by the FSMA 2000. This Act replaces the Financial Services Act 1986 and other legislation under which different aspects of the financial services industry were separately regulated by a mixture of public bodies, trade associations and professional institutes. Now there is a single regulator, the Financial Services Authority (FSA), with members of its board appointed by the Treasury. The FSA has to meet four regulatory objectives (FSMA 2000 ss 1-6):

(i)   maintaining confidence in the financial system;

(ii)   promoting public awareness of the financial system;

(iii) securing the appropriate degree of protection for consumers; and

(iv) reducing the extent to which the financial system can be used to support financial crime.

History

During the nineteenth century (and, indeed, for a considerable period before that), the formation of almost all companies was followed immediately by an appeal to the public to participate in the new venture by joining as members and subscribing for 'shares' in the 'joint stock'. The main reason for 'going public' in this way was to raise funds in the large amounts necessary for the enterprises of the period—often massive operations which built a large proportion of the world's railways, laid submarine cables, opened up trade and investment in distant parts and provided the banking, insurance and other services to support such activities. The promoters of the company would publish a 'prospectus', giving information about the undertaking and inviting subscriptions. This process is often referred to as a 'flotation' of the company or, more accurately, of its securities. Today, big business still has need of funding on a large scale, and this can be sought by the same process of appealing to the public to become investors in the enterprise. But it would be very unlikely nowadays that this would be attempted by the promoters of a new company immediately after its incorporation. The reason for this is that people will usually be prepared to become investors in shares or other securities only if they can be readily sold and turned back into cash, more or less at will. To meet this need there must be a 'market', available to all comers, where shares can be bought and sold and prices can fluctuate in response to supply and demand. Access to the sharemarket is virtually indispensable if investors are to be attracted in any large numbers. And rules have been developed by the London Stock Exchange—the body which has for many years controlled the only markets of any significance in the country—which will not normally allow a company's securities to be accepted for dealing on the market unless it has an established business record. For a 'full' or 'official' listing on the Main market this record must go back for at least three years. The requirements are less demanding, though still quite strict, if the listing is to be on the Alternative Investment Market (AIM). Responsibility for the formulation of the Listing Rules was an 'in-house' matter for the Stock Exchange until October 1999 (originally, as a matter of self-regulation but later with the blessing of legislation). With the introduction of FSMA, this function has now been taken over by the FSA.

Securities markets

Securities markets make it easier for investors to buy and sell securities. These markets are regulated in the interests of investors, since attracting these people will maximise the amount of capital available to the issuers of the securities traded on the market. But this form of regulation imposes costs on the issuers, who must provide information and subject themselves to public scrutiny. The greater the regulation, the greater the cost. Regulators have therefore adopted a variety of regimes, so that the securities of larger, better-known and more stable companies can be traded on highly regulated exchanges, while the securities of smaller, less well-known and riskier companies can be traded elsewhere.

FSMA 2000 s 285 allows investment exchanges to become *recognised investment exchanges* (RIEs). To become recognised in this way, and exchange must have sufficient financial resources, be a 'fit and proper person', and ensure its business is conducted in an orderly manner so as to afford proper protection to investors (including deciding which investments should be 'admitted to trading' and what information should be made available to investors).

Exchanges that are not RIEs must obtain permission under FSMA 2000, Part IV to carry on regulated activities, and are then subject to lesser regulation than RIEs. These exchanges are now normally classed as *alternative trading systems* (ATSs) by the FSA, but will soon be called *multilateral trading facilities* when Directive 2004/39/EC (the Markets in Financial Instruments Directive) is transposed into UK law (expected to be in November 2007).

A RIE (or, theoretically, an ATS[2]) can operate a *'regulated market'* as defined in the Investment Services Directive Article 16 (Council Directive 93/22/EEC). RIEs and ATSs can also operate *'exchange-regulated markets'* that are regulated by the exchange itself. For example, the London Stock Exchange is an RIE, and it operates a number of markets subject to different regulatory regimes. The most significant are the Main Market, the Alternative Investment Market (AIM), and the Professional Securities Market (PSM). The Main Market is a 'regulated market'; AIM is an 'exchange-regulated market'.

The regulations operate at three levels: (i) at EU level for all securities admitted to trading on regulated markets (*'traded companies'*); (ii) at EU level for any security which is the subject of a public offer; and (iii) at national level (subject to EU minimum requirements) for listed securities on a domestic exchange (*'listed companies'*). In addition, *'quoted companies'* (CA 2006 s 385) are companies officially listed on various specified UK and other exchanges.

The London Stock Exchange's Main Market provides the most expensive and extensive form of regulation for listed securities. A company whose equity share capital is admitted to trading on this market is simultaneously listed, traded and quoted. A company whose shares are admitted to trading on AIM is not usually listed, traded or quoted.

Official listing

Official listing is an optional additional regulatory regime for securities markets. There are minimum EU standards for official listing (2001/34/EC), but the UK domestic rules (set out in the FSA's Listing Rules (LR)) are particularly extensive, and are said to contribute to the sound financial reputation of the London Stock Exchange's Main Market.

EU rules require an issuer to have a demonstrable track record, a certain financial size, and a wide enough spread in public shareholdings to create a realistic market. In addition, the rules oblige publication of half-yearly reports. The LR impose additional obligations, requiring adherence to the Listing Principles, continuing obligations requiring extra information in annual accounts and reports, preliminary statements of annual results, compliance with the Model Code which restricts dealings in securities by company managers and others, and — compliance with the Combined Code on corporate governance (or an explanation of non-compliance).

The FSA may permanently discontinue or temporarily suspend a listing, without notice, if it suspects irregularities that preclude normal dealings in the securities (FSMA 2000 s 77). It may also impose public censure or financial penalties, or launch a public investigation (FSMA 2000 ss 91, 97).

---

[2] The UK list of 'regulated markets' are all operated by RIEs. 'Regulated market' is also sometimes used to refer to markets which are protected from insider trading by the Criminal Justice Act 1993, Part V (see below, pp 593 ff).

Prospectuses

As it applies in the UK, the Prospectus Directive (2003/71/EC), implemented by FSMA 2000, Part VI, provides that, with defined exceptions, whenever there is a public offer of securities or a request for admission of securities to trading on a regulated market, a prospectus approved by the FSA must be published (FSMA 2000 s 85). The prospectus must contain all the information required by investors to make an informed assessment of the securities. A person who contravenes the requirement for a prospectus commits an offence, and is liable to be sued for breach of statutory duty by anyone who suffers loss as a result of the contravention (FSMA 2000 s 85(3) and (4)).

When the FSA acts as the competent UK authority for these purposes, it sometimes uses the name United Kingdom Listing Authority (UKLA), and its rules on prospectuses are to be found in the Prospectus Rules Sourcebook (PR) in the FSA Handbook.

Restrictions on public offers by private companies

A private limited company is not permitted to offer its unlisted shares to the public (CA 2006 s 755, and s 756 for the meaning of 'offer to the public'), although an allotment following such an offer is not invalid (s 760).

Exceptions from the prohibition exist where the company acts in good faith in pursuance of arrangements to re-register as a public company before the shares are allotted, or as part of the terms of the offer it undertakes to and does in fact re-register as a public company (s 755).

The court may make an order restraining the company from contravening the prohibition, order the company to re-register as a public company, order it to be wound up, or make a remedial order intended to put a person affected by the contravention in the position he or she would have been in had the contravention not occurred (ss 757–759).

Content of prospectuses

The prospectus must contain all the information required by investors to make an informed assessment of the securities, the rights attaching to them, and the status of the issuer (assets and liabilities, financial position, profits and losses, and prospects). This must be presented in a form that is easy to analyse and comprehend, and must contain a brief summary in non-technical language (FSMA 2000 s 87A). Once approved in the issuer's home state, the prospectus is valid throughout the EU. This is to facilitate the development of a single European capital market in which an issue of shares can be offered to the public and traded throughout the EU.

If a significant new factor arises, or a material mistake or inaccuracy is noted, between the time of approval of the prospectus and the final closing of the offer of securities to the public or the beginning of trading on a regulated market, then a *supplementary prospectus* must be issued by way of correction (FSMA 2000 s 87G).

Exemptions from the prospectus requirements

An approved prospectus need not be published:

(i)   if the offer of securities is addressed solely to qualified investors (FSMA 2000 ss 86(1)(a) and 86(7));

(ii)   if the offer of securities is addressed to fewer than 100 persons, other than qualified investors (FSMA 2000 s 86(1)(b));

(iii)   if the total consideration for the offer is less than 2.5 million euro, with the exemption applying only once during a 12 month period, and applying on an EU-wide basis (FSMA 2000 ss 85(5)(a), 87, and Sch 11A para 9);

(iv)   if the minimum consideration payable by each investor is 50,000 euro (or its equivalent in another currency), or the nominal value of each security is 50,000 euro (or its equivalent in another currency)[3] (FSMA 2000 s 86(1)(c) and (d));

(v)   if the additional shares being offered for trading (and not offered to the public, unless to existing or former directors or employees) are of the same class as existing shares and number less than 10% of those already admitted, with the 10% limit available once every 12 months (FSMA 2000 s 85(6)(b) and (5)(b));

(vi)   if the offer of securities is in exchange for shares of the same class already issued or admitted to trading, provided there is no increase in issued capital, or if the shares result from conversion or exchange other transferable securities or from rights associated with such securities (FSMA 2000 s 85(5)(b) and (6)(b));

(vii)   if the offer of securities is in connection with a takeover or merger, provided there is another document which the UKLA considers contains equivalent information (FSMA 2000 s 85(5)(b) and (6)(b));

(viii)   if the offer of securities is by way of bonus shares or shares issued in lieu of a dividend, provided there is a document explaining the offer (FSMA 2000 s 85(5)(b) and (6)(b)); or

(ix)   the shares have been admitted to trading on one EU regulated market for more than 18 months, and the proposal is to admit them on another regulated market (FSMA 2000 ss 85(6)(b)).

In cases (i)–(iv) above, although the particular offer is exempt, it may still be necessary to publish a prospectus if the issuer wishes to obtain admission of the securities to trading on a regulated market (and exemptions (v)–(ix) do not apply).

FSA sanctions

The FSA has extensive powers to:

(i)   suspend or prevent a public offer of securities, or an application for admission to trading on a regulated market (FSMA 2000 ss 87K and 87L);

(ii)   publicly censure or impose a financial penalty (FSMA 2000 ss 87M and 91); or

(iii)   instigate an investigation (FSMA 2000 s 97).

Liability for misleading statements and omissions in prospectuses

The primary object of the prospectus legislation (like the listing rules) is to ensure that potential investors in companies whose shares are offered to the public or traded on the market are provided with sufficient information to enable them to make informed decisions. Disclosure is the key. But the current legislation sets high standards; it imposes a *general* duty to ensure that the prospectus contains all such information as investors would reasonably require and reasonably expect to find there for the purpose of making an informed assessment of the financial position of the issuing company and the rights attaching to the securities.

If investors suffer a loss as a result of an untrue or misleading statement in, or omission from, a prospectus or supplementary prospectus, then, in addition to the various remedies available under the general rules described above at p 378, various remedies are available:

(i)   statutory compensation remedies under FSMA 2000 s 90(1) for losses caused by reliance on any untrue or misleading statements in the prospectus or supplement, or any omissions of matters required to be included by FSMA 2000 ss 87A or 87G; or

---

[3] This exemption applies in practice to debt securities and convertibles intended for the wholesale market (professional investors) rather than the retail market (general public).

(ii)   statutory remedies under FSMA 2000 s 90(4) for losses suffered in respect of failures to issue necessary supplementary prospectuses as required by FSMA 2000 s 87G.

'Compensation', under FSMA 2000 s 90(1) and (4), is likely to be assessed in the same way as damages for the tort of deceit (see *Clark v Urquhart* [1930] AC 28 in relation to predecessor provisions).

Under the FSMA provisions, compensation is payable by any person 'responsible for' the misleading prospectus (FSMA 2000 s 90(1)). This includes the company, every director at the time the prospectus was published (unless published without the director's knowledge or consent, and on becoming aware of it the director gave public notice to that effect as soon as practicable); every person named as being or having agreed to become a director (provided this statement was made with the person's consent); every person named as accepting responsibility for the prospectus (or the relevant specific parts of it); and every person who authorised the contents of the prospectus (or the relevant specific parts of it), although giving professional advice does not make a person responsible.

Certain defences are available to these potential defendants, including their own reasonable belief in the accuracy of the information, reasonable reliance on experts, reasonable efforts to effect corrections, or, alternatively, proof of the claimant's knowledge that the relevant statements were false or misleading or that there was a relevant omission (FSMA 2000, Sch 10).

It appears arguable that anyone who has 'acquired' shares, whether as the original allottee or on the market, is able to sue for compensation (FSMA 2000 s 90(1) and (4)). According to the common law, only the original allottees could sue, on the basis that a prospectus was intended for subscribers, not for subsequent purchasers (*Peek v Gurney* (1873) LR 6 HL 377). But Lightman J, in *obiter dicta*, suggested a different and broader approach to the FSMA provisions, on the basis that prospectuses are now intended to encourage subsequent trading in shares: *Possfund Custodian Trustee Ltd v Diamond* [1996] 1 WLR 1351. The decision is controversial.

Under-subscription for the new issue

CA 2006 ss 578–579, a company must not allot any shares unless the issue is fully subscribed or the offer makes it clear that some other conditions are to apply. If the issue is not fully subscribed (or other specified conditions are not met) within 40 days, then the subscribed funds must be returned to the investors forthwith, but without interest. Interest is payable after 48 days, with the directors becoming jointly and severally liable. Any attempt to contract out of this provision is void. If an allotment is made in contravention of this section, then the allottee may rescind the allotment within one month even if the company is in the course of being wound up.

Both the company and any allottee can recover any loss or damage sustained as a result of the contravention from any director who knowingly committed, permitted or authorised the contravention.

Market abuse: insider dealing and market manipulation

Controlling market abuse

Market confidence exists only if traders believe that market prices reflect the true value of what is bought and sold. Correct pricing is more likely if both buyers and sellers have all the relevant information to hand. Public confidence in the market is easily damaged if people close to the company use 'inside information' about the company to revalue the shares ahead of the market, and trade on that privileged basis (this is known as *'insider dealing'*). Public confidence is also damaged if false information about the value of shares is spread, creating a false market (this is known as *'market manipulation'*).

Control of these forms of market abuse on regulated markets is required by the Market Abuse Directive (2003/6/EC), and is implemented in FSMA 2000, Part VIII (which extends to all markets operated by RIEs) by:

(i)   penalising insider dealing and market manipulation;

(ii) requiring insiders to declare their trading; and

(iii) requiring companies to disclose price sensitive information promptly to the market.

If the FSA discovers that a person has engaged in market abuse (on the balance of probabilities), it may request the court to issue an injunction restraining the activity, or order restitution or some form of mitigation, or issue a freezing injunction preventing the person dealing with his or her assets (FSMA 2000 ss 381, 383–4). Alternatively, the FSA itself may impose a financial penalty or publicly censure the individual (FSMA 2000 s 123). The imposition of a penalty does not make the transaction void or unenforceable (FSMA 2000 s 131).

Insider dealing

There has been much interest in the past few decades in the topic of *'insider dealing'* or *'insider trading'*. These terms are used to describe the use (or, rather, the misuse) of confidential information by people who, as company officers or employees or as civil servants, avail themselves of knowledge which they acquire in the course of their work, or by reason of their office, to deal to their own profit in a company's securities. Most people regard this practice as unfair in itself and damaging to the confidence of investors in the integrity of the share market.

Insider dealing: common law protection

Until 1980, the only constraints available to deal with insider trading were those imposed extra-legally by the self-regulatory agencies of the City, and in particular by the Takeover Panel, and the possibility that there might be civil liability in at least some cases. It seemed that decisions like *Regal (Hastings) Ltd v Gulliver* **[6.16]** and *Boardman v Phipps* [1967] 2 AC 46 (see pp 330 ff above) might be used as authority for making directors, and others similarly placed, liable to account to their company for any profit that they made, and indeed that is very much what happened in *Regal*. There was also the possibility of some form of liability for breach of confidence as an equitable remedy in its own right (*Seager v Copydex Ltd* [1967] 2 All ER 415, [1967] 1 WLR 923). But all these possible claims are open to the criticism that in most insider dealing cases the company is not the real loser, and may have no incentive to pursue the wrongdoer. *Percival v Wright* **[6.01]** seems to bar the development of a claim based on breach of duty between the director (or other 'insider') and the person to whom he or she has sold or from whom he or she has bought the shares. However, there have been hints in cases such as *Coleman v Myers* ([1977] 2 NZLR 225) that a civil remedy for victims of insider trading could be developed, similar to that which has evolved in the United States through such cases as *SEC v Texas Gulf Sulphur Co* 401 F 2d 833 (1968) and *Diamond v Oreamuno* 24 NY 2d 494 (1969) (though the authority of the latter is questionable, since it was not followed in the company's home State, Florida: see *Schein v Chasen* 313 So 2d 739 (1975)).

All these questions centred on possible civil liability for insider dealing remain live issues, but they have had less of the limelight since 1980, when successive legislative provisions established both criminal and civil penalties for those guilty of the offences of insider dealing as there defined. Nevertheless, they remain important in cases where the statutory provisions do not apply (eg, in cases of dealings in shares of private companies).

Insider dealing: statutory civil protection (FSMA 2000 s 118)

FSMA 2000 Part VIII protects prescribed markets, being all regulated markets and markets operated by RIEs (and, under legacy provisions operating until 2008, all markets operated by UK RIEs and OFEX) (FSMA 2000 s 130A). Within these markets, it protects against three forms of insider dealing (FSMA 2000 s 118): dealing by an insider (s 118B) on the basis of inside information (s 118C) relating to the investment in question (*insider dealing*); improper disclosure by an insider otherwise than in the proper course of his or her duties (*improper disclosure* or *tipping*); and (only until 2008, under the legacy provisions) use by anyone of information not generally available (*misuse of information*).

Insider dealing: criminal protection (Criminal Justice Act 1993, Part V)

The definitions of regulated market, inside information and insider dealing are all slightly different under the 1993 Act from the rules adopted in FSMA 2000. Within these definitions, and subject to limited exceptions, insiders cannot deal in the relevant securities, encourage others to deal, or disclose inside information to others. On indictment for an offence, the penalty can be imprisonment for up to seven years, and/or a fine for which there is no limit (Criminal Justice Act 1993, s 61(1)). Criminal proceedings may only be instituted by the FSA (FSMA 2000 s 402), or by, or with the consent of, either the Secretary of State or the Director of Public Prosecutions (Criminal Justice Act 1993, s 61(2)). A transaction entered into in contravention of the Criminal Justice Act 1993 is neither void nor voidable (s 63(2)), although, being illegal, it is unlikely to be enforced by any court.

Market abuse

FSMA 2000 s 118 identifies six forms of market manipulation as market abuse, all of which have the capacity to distort the market price of the relevant securities. The FSA provides some safe harbours for practices regarded as proper (eg company share buy-backs, or a public authority's pursuit of monetary or exchange rate policies, etc).

The civil penalties for such conduct were outlined earlier (see pp 587 above). In addition, FSMA 2000 s 397 makes creating a false market a criminal offence, subject to certain statutory defences (s 397(3) and (5)).

Public investigation of companies

The past fifty years have seen a continuing increase in the involvement of government in the affairs of companies. This reflects a long-held recognition that abuse of corporate power is unlikely to be adequately constrained by leaving all regulation and litigation to the company's members. It is further evidence of the loss of privacy that comes with limited liability. That said, the United Kingdom is one of the few jurisdictions to go further and provide for more controversial inspectorship provisions, allowing investigation of companies' affairs by the Companies Investigations Branch (CIB) of the DTI, and providing for extensive powers to collect evidence and pass it on to regulatory or prosecuting authorities.

These powers of the Secretary of State to appoint inspectors to investigate the affairs of companies under CA 1985, Part XIV (not transported to CA 2006, although CA 2006 ss 1035–1039 introduced certain amendments) may seem of little significance in comparison with the various forms of regulation ensuring control of fair practices, unfair competition, mergers and monopolies, takeovers (and mergers effected by takeover), and so on. Nevertheless, the possibility of such public investigation of companies sets them apart from individuals and partnerships. Investigations may be launched into the affairs of companies (CA 1985 ss 431, 432) or into the membership and control of companies (CA 1985 s 442).

Powers of investigation

CA 1985 confers powers of investigation of two different kinds. The first is more formal. The Secretary of State may appoint inspectors 'to investigate the affairs of a company and to report on them in such manner as he may direct' (CA 1985 s 431(1)). The appointment may be initiated by the Secretary of State (see below). It may also be initiated on the application of the company itself, or by a requisition having the support of at least 200 members or members holding not less than one-tenth of the issued shares (CA 1985 s 432(2)), but then the applicants must show that they have good reason and be prepared to pay the costs. Not surprisingly, there are few occasions when this has been done. Alternatively, an investigation of this type may be ordered by the court (CA 1985 s 432(1)).

The mere announcement of an inspection is likely to have a substantial and detrimental impact on the company's standing and profit. The powers are therefore used sparingly, and only in the most serious of cases, often after public outcry and extensive media coverage. In the past decade, only five or six investigations have been launched, often with long and expensive consequences. For example, the Mirror Group Newspapers trials lasted nine years and cost £9.5 million.[4]

Inspections are most commonly initiated by the Secretary of State. This may be done if the Secretary of State considers there is fraud or other improper conduct, or that the company's members have not been given all the information that they might reasonably expect (CA 1985 s 432(2)); or it is necessary to ascertain where the true ownership of shares or debentures or control of the company actually lies (CA 1985 s 442); or there has been insider dealing (FSMA 2000 s 168(3), also allowing the FSA to initiate such investigations).

In a straightforward case the inspectors may be officers in the Secretary of State's own department, but, for the more serious cases, it is usual to appoint a QC and a leading accountant. The report may be published, and usually is if the matter is one that has attracted public interest.

The second form of power held by the Secretary of State is lower key, allowing for an informal, unpublicised inquiry, requiring a company to produce specified documents for inspection by his officers or some other competent person, or, if they are not in its possession, to state where it believes they are (CA 1985 s 447). Failure to comply may be punished as contempt of court. This latter power (which avoids much expense and publicity) can be used alone, but is often used as a first step, before a decision is taken whether to set up a full-scale investigation under CA 1985 s 432(2). Use of this power is controversial. Many complain that the exercise is as detrimental, probing and traumatic as a formal inspection, yet often reveals no cause for follow-up. In 2005/2006, 3,702 companies were named in requests, but formal investigations were started in only 148 cases (ie in approximately 4% of cases). The investigations rarely concern the accountability of management to members, but almost always focus on fraudulent trading, theft, breach of disqualification orders and undertakings, and such like.

An investigation may lead to a number of consequences. If criminal conduct is revealed, or suspected, the inspectors' findings may be followed by a prosecution. The Secretary of State

---

[4] Although the CLR found the length of investigations to be often necessary and certainly difficult to control, CA 2006, Part 32 nevertheless indicates a legislative desire to control proceedings more closely and terminate them when necessary (see the new CA 1985 ss 446A and 446B inserted by CA 2006 s 1035).

may apply for disqualification orders against directors and other persons involved in the management of the company (CDDA 1986 s 8), or for the winding-up of the company (IA 1986 s 124A), or for a remedy under CA 2006 s 995. The Secretary of State may also institute proceedings for a civil remedy in the name of the company (CA 1985 s 438). Documents and information obtained during the investigation may be disclosed to regulatory authorities; comparable powers may also be used to assist certain overseas law enforcement and regulatory authorities (CA 1989 s 82ff). If satisfactory information about the ownership or control of a company is not forthcoming, this may lead to the imposition of a 'freezing' order on the shares in question (CA 1985 s 445; see above, p 588).

Conduct of the investigation

The cases that follow illustrate aspects of the working of the investigatory powers in practice.

In reaching a decision whether to appoint inspectors to investigate the affairs of a company, the Secretary of State is not bound by the rules of natural justice.

[12.01] Norwest Holst Ltd v Secretary of State for Trade
[1978] Ch 201, [1978] 3 All ER 280 (Court of Appeal)

[The facts appear from the judgment.]

LORD DENNING MR: Ever since 1948 there has been a valuable provision of the Companies Act by which the Board of Trade can appoint inspectors to investigate the affairs of a company. Many investigations have been held by inspectors, usually one of Queen's Counsel, and the other an accountant. In a case we had fairly recently, *Re Pergamon Press Ltd* **[12.02]**, we had to consider the position of the inspectors under such an inquiry. It was held by this court that the inspectors were under a duty to act fairly in the conduct of their inquiry.

Now we have to consider a different point. It is said that the minister himself has done wrong. His conduct is challenged. It is said that the minister has acted beyond his powers in appointing inspectors. He ought, it is said, to have warned the company beforehand and given them a chance of being heard. Furthermore, it is said that the minister exercised his discretion erroneously. He ought to have had sufficient reasons, and he had none in this case. It is said further that he is acting on the information of informers, which is inadmissible as being against the public interest.

On these grounds the company has brought an action to try to stop the inspectors proceeding with the inquiry. The minister applied to strike it out. Foster J struck it out. The company appeal to this court . . .

On 11 March 1977, the Secretary of State ordered the inquiry now in question. He did it under s 165(b)(ii) of the Companies Act 1948 [CA 1985 s 432(2)]. On 25 March 1977, the secretary of the group wrote:

I am authorised to say that it does not appear to my board that there are any circumstances which would justify the exercise of your discretionary power under the section to appoint inspectors.

He asked: What were the circumstances? Would they be disclosed? The Secretary of State declined to give that information . . .

As the minister gave no information, the company started this action. They delivered a statement of claim, which they afterwards amended. The burden of the statement of claim is that the company know of no wrongdoing which has been done by them or any of their people; and therefore it is wrong that the minister should appoint inspectors without, as they say, any proper justification. They put it in these words in their final amended pleadings:

> . . . It is implicit in the provisions of s 165(b)(ii) of the said Act that the discretionary power to appoint inspectors is to be exercised fairly and/or in accordance with the principles of natural justice.

They ask for a declaration that the appointment or purported appointment was ultra vires and invalid.

It is important to know the background of the legislation. It sometimes happens that public companies are conducted in a way which is beyond the control of the ordinary shareholders. The majority of the shares are in the hands of two or three individuals. These have control of the company's affairs. The other shareholders know little and are told little. They receive the glossy annual reports. Most of them throw them into the wastepaper basket. There is an annual general meeting but few of the shareholders attend. The whole management and control is in the hands of the directors. They are a self-perpetuating oligarchy: and are virtually unaccountable. Seeing that the directors are the guardians of the company, the question is asked: Quis custodiet ipsos custodes—Who will guard the guards themselves?

It is because companies are beyond the reach of ordinary individuals that this legislation has been passed so as to enable the Department of Trade to appoint inspectors to investigate the affairs of a company. Mr Brodie, who appears for Norwest Holst Ltd, drew our attention to the practice of the Board of Trade from 1948 to 1962. It was given in evidence to Lord Jenkins' Company Law Committee (1962) (Cmnd 1749). The Board of Trade said (at p 79) that it was very necessary to hear both sides before deciding whether or not an inspector should be appointed. By so doing it is often possible in cases where no fraud is alleged to bring the parties together or for them to reach a mutually satisfactory arrangement so that an investigation is not necessary.

That was the practice before 1962. Mr Brodie submitted that that practice was required by the common law. He said that the principles of natural justice are to be applied; and, accordingly, both sides should be heard before an inspector is appointed.

That may have been the practice of the Board of Trade in those years; but I do not think that this was required by the common law. There are many cases where an inquiry is held—not as a judicial or quasi-judicial inquiry—but simply as a matter of good administration. In these circumstances there is no need to give preliminary notice of any charge, or anything of that sort. Take the case where a police officer is suspected of misconduct. The practice is to suspend him pending inquiries. He is not given notice of any charge at that stage, nor any opportunity of being heard. The rules of natural justice do not apply unless and until it is decided to take proceedings. Other instances can be given in other fields. For instance, the Stock Exchange may suspend dealings in a company's shares. They go by what they know, without warning the company beforehand.

Equally, so far as s 109 [CA 1985 s 447] is concerned, when the officers of the Department of Trade are appointed to examine the books, there is no need for the rules of natural justice to be applied. If the company was forewarned and told that the officers were coming, what is to happen to the books? In a wicked world, it is not unknown for books or papers to be destroyed or lost.

So also with the appointment of inspectors, under s 165(b)(ii). The inspectors are not to decide rights or wrongs. They are to investigate and report. This inquiry is a good administrative arrangement for the good conduct of companies and their affairs. It is not a case to which the rules of natural justice apply. There is no need for them to be given notice of a charge, or a fair opportunity of meeting it. I would say that, so long as the minister acts in good faith, it is not incumbent upon him to disclose the material he has before him, or the reasons for the inquiry.

ORMROD and GEOFFREY LANE LJJ delivered concurring judgments.

Inspectors appointed by the Secretary of State must act fairly, but their function is not judicial or quasi-judicial.

[12.02] Re Pergamon Press Ltd3 [1971] Ch 388,
[1970] 3 All ER 535 (Court of Appeal)

Maxwell and others, the directors of a company which was the subject of an investigation ordered under s 165(b) of the Act of 1948 [CA 1985 s 432(2)] had declined to answer questions unless they were first given assurances that, in effect, the proceeding would be conducted as if it were a judicial inquiry. The inspectors, acting under CA 1948 s 167(3) [CA 1985 s 436(2),(3)] referred this refusal to the court. The Court of Appeal, affirming Plowman J, held that the directors were not entitled to the assurances.

LORD DENNING MR: [Counsel for the directors] claimed that they had a right to see the transcripts of the evidence of the witnesses adverse to them . . . [and] to cross-examine the witnesses [and] that they ought to see any proposed finding against them before it was included finally in the report. In short, the directors claimed that the inspectors should conduct the inquiry much as if it were a judicial inquiry in a court of law in which Mr Maxwell and his colleagues were being charged with an offence.

It seems to me that this claim on their part went too far. This inquiry was not a court of law. It was an investigation in the public interest, in which all should surely co-operate, as they promised to do. But if the directors went too far on their side, I am afraid that Mr Fay, for the inspectors, went too far on the other. He did it very tactfully, but he did suggest that in point of law the inspectors were not bound by the rules of natural justice. He said that in all the cases where natural justice had been applied hitherto, the tribunal was under a duty to come to a determination or decision of some kind or other. He submitted that when there was no determination or decision but only an investigation or inquiry, the rules of natural justice did not apply . . .

I cannot accept Mr Fay's submission. It is true, of course, that the inspectors are not a court of law. Their proceedings are not judicial proceedings . . . They are not even quasi-judicial, for they decide nothing; they determine nothing. They only investigate and report. They sit in private and are not entitled to admit the public to their meetings . . . They do not even decide whether there is a prima facie case . . .

But this should not lead us to minimise the significance of their task. They have to make a report which may have wide repercussions. They may, if they think fit, make findings of fact which are very damaging to those whom they name. They may accuse some; they may condemn others; they may ruin reputations or careers. Their report may lead to judicial proceedings. It may expose persons to criminal prosecutions or to civil actions. It may bring about the winding up of the company, and be used itself as material for the winding up . . . When they do make their report, the Board are bound to send a copy of it to the company; and the Board may, in their discretion, publish it, if they think fit, to the public at large. Seeing that their work and their report may lead to such consequences, I am clearly of the opinion that the inspectors must act fairly. This is a duty which rests on them, as on many other bodies, even though they are not judicial, nor quasi-judicial, but only administrative: see *R v Gaming Board for Great Britain, ex p Benaim and Khaida*.[5] The inspectors can obtain information in any way they think best, but before they condemn or criticise a man, they must give him a fair opportunity for correcting or contradicting what is said against him. They need not quote chapter and verse. An outline of the charge will usually suffice.

That is what the inspectors here propose to do, but the directors of the company want more. They want to see the transcripts of the witnesses who speak adversely of them, and to see any documents which may be used against them. They, or some of them, even claim to cross-examine the witnesses.

---

[5] [1970] 2 QB 417, [1970] 2 All ER 528.

In all this the directors go too far. This investigation is ordered in the public interest. It should not be impeded by measures of this kind. Witnesses should be encouraged to come forward and not hold back. Remember, this not being a judicial proceeding, the witnesses are not protected by an absolute privilege, but only by a qualified privilege . . . It is easy to imagine a situation in which, if the name of a witness were disclosed, he might have an action brought against him, and this might deter him from telling all he knew. No one likes to have an action brought against him, however unfounded. Every witness must, therefore, be protected. He must be encouraged to be frank. This is done by giving every witness an assurance that his evidence will be regarded as confidential and will not be used except for the purpose of the report. This assurance must be honoured. It does not mean that his name and his evidence will never be disclosed to anyone. It will often have to be used for the purpose of the report, not only in the report itself, but also by putting it in general terms to other witnesses for their comments. But it does mean that the inspectors will exercise a wise discretion in the use of it so as to safeguard the witness himself and any others affected by it. His evidence may sometimes, though rarely, be so confidential that it cannot be put to those affected by it, even in general terms. If so, it should be ignored so far as they are concerned. For I take it to be axiomatic that the inspectors must not use the evidence of a witness so as to make it the basis on an adverse finding unless they give the party affected sufficient information to enable him to deal with it.

It was suggested before us that whenever the inspectors thought of deciding a conflict of evidence or of making adverse criticism of someone, they should draft the proposed passage of their report and put it before the party for his comments before including it. But I think this also is going too far. This sort of thing should be left to the discretion of the inspectors. They must be masters of their own procedure. They should be subject to no rules save this: they must be fair. This being done, they should make their report with courage and frankness, keeping nothing back. The public interest demands it. They need have no fear because their report, so far as I can judge, is protected by an absolute privilege. . . .

SACHS AND BUCKLEY LJJ delivered concurring judgments.

> ➤ Notes

1. In later proceedings (reported as *Maxwell v Department of Trade and Industry* [1974] QB 523, [1974] 2 All ER 122), Robert Maxwell claimed that the inspectors had not acted fairly in that, before making their report, they had not first formulated their criticisms of him in tentative form and given him an opportunity of meeting them. The Court of Appeal, affirming Wien J, held that this procedure was unnecessary: it was sufficient that, in the course of the inquiry, all the matters which appeared to call for an explanation or an answer by a witness should have been put to him; and in substance this had been done.

2. In *R v Secretary for Trade, ex p Perestrello* [1981] QB 19, [1980] 3 All ER 28, Woolf J held that there was a similar obligation to act fairly, but, again, no requirement to observe the rules of natural justice, in exercising the power to demand production of a company's books and papers under CA 1967 s 109 [CA 1985 s 447].

[12.03] Re an Inquiry into Mirror Group Newspapers plc
[2000] Ch 194, [1999] 2 All ER 694 (Chancery Division)

Nearly 30 years after **[12.02]** above, and after Robert Maxwell's death and the collapse of his business empire, his son Kevin was the subject of a DTI investigation. The Secretary of State had appointed inspectors to look into the affairs of the company (MGN) of which Kevin Maxwell had been a director. Their investigation was put on hold until criminal proceedings against him (in which he was acquitted) had been concluded. Meanwhile, he had been cross-examined at the trial and questioned under other statutory procedures for a total of 61 days. The inspectors required Maxwell to sign an undertaking that he would not disclose information put to him in the course of their questioning, which he was unwilling to do. He also objected that the course which the inspectors proposed to take was unfair and unreasonable (especially since he had no legal representation), and in particular that they intended to question him at length on matters which had already been covered in the previous interrogations. Scott V-C ruled that his objections were largely justified.

SIR RICHARD SCOTT V-C: . . .

The issues

There are two issues in this case. First, there is the issue of confidentiality. Are inspectors who have been appointed under Part XIV of the Companies Act 1985 entitled to demand of a person who is placed under a statutory obligation to attend before them and answer their questions that the person enter into an undertaking of confidentiality on the lines of that which Mr Maxwell was asked to sign or, indeed, any confidentiality undertaking at all?

This issue is one of general importance. As I have said, it appears to be the general practice of inspectors to insist on being given confidentiality undertakings. Are those who appear before them obliged to comply?

Second, there is an issue as to what, if any, limits there are on the right of inspectors to require officers and agents of a company under investigation to attend before them and assist them in their investigation. Is there a point at which the demands made by the inspectors become so onerous that a witness's refusal to co-operate becomes excusable? If there is such a point, has it been reached in the present case? . . .

The confidentiality issue

. . . I do not accept that the inspectors have any legal obligation to those from whom they obtain information or documents to insist on confidentiality undertakings being given by others before whom, for the purposes of their inquiry, they wish to put the information or documents. If they wish to preserve and protect the confidentiality of the information and documents, they need do no more than make sure that every person to whom the information is communicated, or before whom the documents are put, is on notice of their confidential character. Such a person would not be inhibited by being given such notice from making use of the information and documents for the purpose of answering the inspectors' questions. He could take advice from lawyers and others. He could con-sult others who had been involved, in order to check his recollection or remedy his lack of recollec-tion. In doing so he would not, in my judgement, be in breach of any duty owed either to those from whom the information and documents had originated or to the inspectors. If, on the other hand, the new witness were to disclose the contents of the documents or information for a purpose not con-nected with the purposes for which they had been supplied to him, he would, in my view, prima facie commit a breach of duty to those from whom the information or documents had been obtained . . .

Unfairness and oppression

The starting point is the statutory obligation of persons such as Mr Maxwell to answer relevant questions put to them by Companies Act inspectors . . . None the less, the assistance that those on whom the statutory obligation is placed must give is not unlimited. They must give the assistance that they are 'reasonably able to give'. The word 'reasonably' limits the extent of their obligation. To put the point another way, the inspectors cannot place demands on them that are unreasonable, whether as to the time they must expend or the expense they must incur in preparation for the questions or in any other respect. . . .

In my opinion, the inspectors should do their best to avoid questioning Mr Maxwell on topics on which he has been questioned before. They should, so far as possible, rely on the answers he has given in previous interrogations . . .

All the circumstances must, in my judgment, be taken into account in deciding whether or not assistance which a person is, in an absolute sense, able to give is also assistance which he is reasonably able to give. But, if, in all the circumstances, the demands made on the person go beyond what he is reasonably able to give, his failure to comply with the demands will not be a breach of his statutory duty and should not be treated as a contempt of court. . . .

[His Lordship accordingly declined to rule that Maxwell had been in contempt.]

➤ Note

In *Re A-G's Reference (No 3 of 1998)* [2000] QB 401, CA the court was asked to rule on the meaning of the phrase 'to provide an explanation' of documents which had been produced to inspectors under CA 1985 s 447. It was held that this was not limited to giving an exposition of the text of the document, but covered 'not only the contents, but also the date of creation, the authorship, provenance, accuracy, completeness, intended purpose, destination and significance of the document or its contents, and of the use to which it was in fact put', and also (subject to a test of reasonableness) to explain discrepancies between the documents and other evidence.

Inspections and the privilege against self-incrimination

A person who is being interviewed by inspectors has no privilege against self-incrimination. In *Re London United Investments plc* [1992] Ch 578, [1992] 2 All ER 842 it was held that this common-law privilege had been impliedly abrogated by CA 1985, Pt XIV. This means that the person is compellable to answer questions put to him, on pain of punishment for contempt of court if he refuses. There is similarly no privilege where a person is being examined (eg as to the causes of a company's insolvency) under the provisions of IA 1986, s 236: *Bishopsgate Investment Management Ltd v Maxwell* [1993] Ch 1, [1992] 2 All ER 856, CA.

Indeed, in *Re an Inquiry under the Company Securities (Insider Dealing) Act 1985* [1988] AC 660, [1988] 1 All ER 203, HL, a journalist, Jeremy Warner, declined to answer questions put to him by inspectors because he felt obliged as a journalist to protect sources of information which had been given to him in confidence. The House of Lords held that this fact did not of itself provide a reasonable excuse, and that he was liable to punishment for contempt.

Inspections and subsequent fair trials—criminal and civil cases

Prior to 1994, courts had ruled in a number of cases that evidence given by a person during an investigation could be used against him in a subsequent criminal trial, or in proceedings brought to have a disqualification order made against him. This was so notwithstanding the fact that he was compellable to give the evidence, even if it was incriminating, on pain of punishment for contempt of court. Evidence obtained under compulsion in other statutory procedures (eg IA 1986 s 236) was the subject of similar rulings.

However, in 1994 the European Court of Human Rights ruled in the *Saunders* case (*Saunders v United Kingdom* (1996) 23 EHRR 313) that the use of such evidence in a *criminal* prosecution violated the individual's right to a fair trial under Art 6 of the European Convention on Human Rights. Following this decision, the Crown changed its practice and ceased to use evidence so obtained in subsequent criminal trials. Now the law itself has been changed to reflect this: see CA 1985 s 434(5A) and (5B). (Note that notwithstanding the ruling by the Strasbourg court, Saunders' conviction was upheld by the Court of Appeal: *R v Saunders* [1996] 1 Cr App Rep 463, CA.)

The protection is not absolute, however. For example, both the European Court and UK courts have ruled that disqualification proceedings are not criminal proceedings, but civil proceedings 'of a regulatory nature', in which the use of such evidence involves no infringement of Art 6.[6]

Although *Saunders* prompted legislative change, there is a lack of clarity in the case as to whether the right to silence and the right not to incriminate oneself are absolute rights. Two recent decisions, *Brown v Stott* [2001] 2 All ER 97 and *R v Kearns* [2002] 1 WLR 2815 CA suggest that Article 6 may be limited if national authorities have a clear and proper public objective.

---

[6] See *DC, HS and AD v United Kingdom* [2000] BCC 710, ECHR; and *Re Westminster Property Management Ltd* [2000] 2 BCLC 396, CA.

13

RECONSTRUCTIONS, MERGERS AND TAKEOVERS

Overview

Companies can generally undertake the full gamut of normal business activities using no more than basic company and common law rules, assisted by market forces: they can expand and contract, change business focus, undergo shifts in corporate control, and make various advantageous contractual arrangements with members and creditors and the like. But when companies want to act rapidly and decisively, or enter into arrangements with large numbers of members or creditors, or effect mergers with other corporate entities, or de-mergers of their own conglomerate business, then some more efficient way of proceeding is essential.

Modern company law provides three formal mechanisms to facilitate major corporate reconstructions:

(i)   arrangements or reconstructions under IA 1986 ss 110–111 (see below, pp 606 ff);

(ii) arrangements, reconstructions, mergers or divisions under CA 2006, Parts 26 and 27 (see below, pp 609 ff);

(iii) takeovers under CA 2006, Part 28 (see below, pp 616 ff).

Companies make use of these provisions for a variety of reasons. They may want to restructure the mutual rights and obligations of the company and its members or creditors. Economic motivations may prompt them to expand the company's business, whether by diversification, vertical integration (with companies performing other functions in the production process chain) or horizontal integration (with companies at the same stage in the production process). Alternatively, financial or fiscal considerations may prompt changes that will reduce liability to tax or improve the balance sheet.

Meaning of the terms

The terms employed in this chapter are commonly used without any great precision, but some generalisations are possible.

A '*reconstruction*' is usually the transfer of the undertaking and business of a company (or, sometimes, several companies) to a new company specially formed for the purpose. The old company is put into liquidation and its members, instead of being repaid their capital by the liquidator in cash, agree to take equivalent shares in the new company. In the result, the same members carry on the same, or some part of, the enterprise through the medium of a new company. The simpler set of statutory provisions governing this procedure is contained in IA 1986 ss 110–111 (below, pp 606 ff).[1] The sanction of the court is not required, but a dissentient member may always require that he or she be paid out in cash rather than take the new shares. Creditors who do not agree to look to the new company for payment of their debts may prove in the liquidation of the old company.

This procedure is popular with private and family companies, and with investment trust companies undergoing restructuring. The process can enable the creation of a new company

---

[1] The other set is in CA 2006, Parts 26 and 27, see below, pp 609 ff.

with wider or different objects, or a change in the rights of classes of members, or a necessary reorganization prior to a de-merger which splits the company's businesses into more discrete units.

A '*merger*' or '*amalgamation*' takes place when the assets and undertakings of more than one company are brought under the ownership and control of a single company, which may be one of the companies involved or a new one. The result is that the shareholders who were members of the several amalgamating companies now together own and control the same enterprises as one aggregated venture. In a straightforward case, the procedure laid down by IA 1986 s110 may be used. In more complicated cases, the other procedures are used.

Much the same consequences of merger and amalgamation may follow from a '*takeover*', which is a general term used to describe the acquisition by one company (or by one or more individuals, or by a group of companies) of the share capital (all or part) and control of another, usually by buying all or a majority of its shares (below pp 616 ff). In the ordinary case, the company taken over is the smaller; in a '*reverse takeover*', a smaller company gains control of a larger one.[2] An offer addressed to all the shareholders of a company to buy the shares of each member at a stated price is known as a 'take-over bid'. It is usually expressed to be conditional upon a designated percentage of shares being accepted by a given date. This is commonly set at 51%, which is a sufficient majority for the bidder to replace the board of directors. Alternatively, it may be as high as 90%, because CA 2006, s 979 permits a company that has acquired 90% or more of a company's shares by a take-over bid to buy the remaining shares compulsorily, and conversely s 983 empowers the minority shareholders in such a situation to insist on being bought out.

Where the company making a take-over bid offers to exchange its own shares for those in the company being acquired, rather than make a bid for cash, the result is to all intents and purposes an amalgamation of the two companies as described above.

A '*scheme of arrangement*' or a '*reconstruction*' under CA 2006, Part 26 and Part 27 (additional requirements for public companies) enables a company to effect mergers and amalgamations, and also to alter the rights of its members *or its creditors*, with the sanction of the court. The provisions are sufficiently wide to accommodate schemes having a considerable diversity of objectives and range of complexity, which may involve more than one company. The more elaborate kinds of merger will usually need to be dealt with under these sections, as will any scheme of reconstruction which is intended to affect creditors (and especially debenture holders) as well as shareholders. Unless the court orders otherwise, the members or creditors who dissent are nevertheless bound to accept the terms of the scheme. In contrast with IA 1986 s 110, there is no liquidation of the company or companies involved.

Corporate businesses may, of course, be split up as well as aggregated. The most common procedure by which part of a company's assets and undertaking is sold off is usually referred to as '*hiving down*'. The company forms a subsidiary and vests the assets in question in its name, or transfers the assets to an existing subsidiary, and sells the shareholding in that subsidiary to new owners. These may include the managers of that part of the business who have hitherto been employees of the vendor (a '*management buy-out*'). Alternatively, there may be a simple sale of the assets, either for cash or in consideration of the allotment of shares in the purchasing company to the vendor, or to the shareholders of the vendor if it is a company. This last type of transaction, which is not common in this country, is known as a '*division*',[3] '*demerger*' or '*scission*'.

A merger or division that involves a public company and is achieved by a transfer of *assets and undertaking* in consideration of the allotment of shares in the transferee company to the former shareholders of the transferor must observe the requirements of CA 2006, Part 27 (which modifies or excludes some of the provisions in Part 26). These provisions implement

---

[2] Paradoxically, however, if this is done by the bidding company exchanging its own shares for the shares of the target company, the former shareholders in the target will end up controlling the bidder.

[3] See CA 2006, Part 27.

the Third and Sixth EC Company Law Directives, although the independence requirements for experts and valuers in CA 2006 ss 936 and 937 are new, and correspond with the independence requirements for a statutory auditor (s 1214). The provisions have less impact than might be supposed, however, since the standard procedures for takeover and hiving down usually involve the purchase and sale of *shares* and not of assets.

Finally, the *economic* consequences of a merger may be such as to create a monopoly or other situation or one which distorts competition. Both the EU and successive governments in the United Kingdom have enacted measures which have as their object the control of mergers, as part of the wider legislation designed to promote competition and regulate restrictive and anti-competitive practices. These statutes and the associated regulations often impose additional restrictions, especially on large-scale mergers.

Schemes of reconstruction under IA 1986 ss 110–111

Under this type of reorganisation, the company resolves, first, to go into voluntary liquidation (members' or creditors'), and, secondly, to authorise by special resolution the transfer by the liquidator of the whole or part of the company's business or assets to another company (or limited liability partnership (LLP)) in consideration of shares in that company (or membership of the LLP).

The procedure provides a relatively simple method for reconstructing a single company or effecting a simple merger or takeover. Its advantage is that court approval is not generally required.[4] But its use is limited. The liquidator must ensure that the creditors' proved claims are met, and cannot rely on any indemnity given by the acquiring company.[5] And in a members' voluntary liquidation, dissenting members have a right to veto the scheme, or to be bought out at a price determined by agreement or arbitration (an appraisal right).[6]

A company cannot by a provision in its constitution authorise a scheme of reconstruction which disregards the rights of dissentients under IA 1986 s 111.

[13.01] Bisgood v Henderson's Transvaal Estates Ltd
[1908] 1 Ch 743 (Court of Appeal)

The company in general meeting resolved to carry out a scheme whereby each fully paid £1 share was to be exchanged for one £1 share in a new company, to be credited as paid up to an amount of 87½ p. Under the scheme, the 'new' shares of those who dissented were to be sold *en bloc* for what they would fetch, and the proceeds distributed *pro rata* amongst them. The company's memorandum and articles purported to authorise such a transaction; but it was held to be unlawful.

The judgment of the court (COZENS-HARDY MR and FLETCHER MOULTON and BUCKLEY LJJ) was delivered by BUCKLEY LJ: The question involved is whether by clauses even in the memorandum of association of a company limited by shares the limit upon the shareholder's liability can be raised—whether the constitution of the company can provide that the majority may impose upon the minority a scheme under which the member must either come under an increased liability or accept such compensation as the scheme offers him. Section 161 of the Companies Act 1862 [IA 1986 s 111] protects the dissentient member by securing him the value of his interest to be determined by arbitration or agreement. The purpose of schemes such as that here in question is to evade or escape the provisions of that section. Their object is to impose upon

---

[4] It is required if the creditors' liquidation committee does not give approval: IA 1986, s 110(3)(b).
[5] *Pulsford v Devenish* [1903] 2 Ch 625.
[6] IA 1986 s 111.

the shareholders what is generally called an assessment—to require that in a limited company after the shares are fully paid the shareholder must either come under liability to make further contributions to capital or submit to take, not the value of his interest to be determined by arbitration or agreement, but such satisfaction as the scheme offers him. That satisfaction commonly means, and in substance means in this case, the surrender of his interest in the company . . .

The question is whether the reorganisation scheme contained in the agreement and resolutions is intra vires. The argument is that it is because it is justified by clauses in the memorandum of association . . .

The purpose of the memorandum and articles . . . is not confined to defining and limiting the purposes of the corporation; it extends also within proper limits to defining and ascertaining the rights of the corporators. I have no doubt that within proper limits the memorandum and articles may provide how, as between the corporators, the corporate assets shall be dealt with after liquidation. But in this, as in many matters, there are limits imposed by the statutes. There are matters in respect of which the constitution of the company cannot provide that the corporator shall not enjoy rights and immunities which the statute gives him. For instance, s 82 of the Companies Act 1862 [IA 1986 s 124] empowers a contributory to present a winding-up petition. His right in that respect cannot be excluded by the articles: *Re Peveril Gold Mines* **[14.07]** . . . Upon a like principle the articles cannot exclude a shareholder from his right of dissent under s161 of the Companies Act 1862 . . . It is, therefore, not necessarily true that, because there are found in the memorandum and articles clauses such as those upon which the question here arises, the corporators as individuals are contractually bound by them. The question is not whether each individual corporator can bind himself in respect of his distributive share in the assets. The question is whether, consistently with the statutes, the constitution of the corporation can be such that every corporator shall in the matter of distribution—or a fortiori of distribution and further liability—be bound by the vote of the majority . . .

In the matter of liability upon his shares the statute provides in plain terms by s 38(4) [IA 1986 s 74(2)(d)], that in the case of a company limited by shares no contribution shall be required from any member exceeding the amount unpaid on his shares. In my opinion, any attempt so to define the constitution of the company as that the member shall in any event be liable for a larger sum is in breach of the statute and is ultra vires. Any clauses which can be used to maintain a scheme which imposes upon the member the alternative of accepting liability for a larger sum or of being dispossessed of his status as shareholder upon terms which he is not bound to accept are, I think, ultra vires . . .

The company, it is true, have issued the allotment letters in such form as that the shareholder could sell his right to an allotment and put forward the name of a purchaser if he found one. And the old company could within the language of the agreement sell the shares which are not applied for, and under the fifth resolution the proceeds would be distributable among the non-assenting members. Shortly stated, the scheme is one under which the shareholder is told that he may take the share in the new company with its liability or sell the share in the new company with its liability, but he shall have nothing but the share in the new company or its proceeds; that he must be assessed or find some one who will take the new share with the assessment or take his chance that the liquidator may find someone who will do so, but that he shall have nothing else. In my opinion this is ultra vires. The plaintiff is, in my judgment, entitled to an injunction to restrain the defendants from carrying out the reorganisation scheme.

In a reconstruction under IA 1986 ss 110–111, the general meeting has no power to decide that the consideration received shall be distributed among the members otherwise than in accordance with their rights in a winding up.

[13.02] Griffith v Paget (1877) 5 Ch D 894 (Chancery Division)

The capital of the Argentine Tramways Co Ltd was divided into preferred shares and deferred shares each of a nominal value of £10, the former being entitled to a cumulative 12% preferential dividend. There was no provision as to the relative rights of the classes in a winding up. The preferred dividend had not been paid in full for many years. A scheme of reconstruction was proposed under which the shares in the existing company should be exchanged for shares, all of one class, in a new company, on a basis which gave the preferred shareholders approximately the par value of their existing holdings, but the deferred shareholders only about 15% of such value. The plaintiff, a preferred shareholder, who considered that this scheme gave the deferred shareholders more than the market value of their shares, objected that the general meeting had no power to fix the mode of distribution of the new shares; and the court upheld his view.

JESSEL MR: The question which is now raised, as far as I know for the first time, is this, whether in the case of a limited liability company, when there are two or more classes of shareholders having different rights inter se, and the powers conferred by the Companies Act 1862, s 161 [IA 1986 s 110], are exercised, the company can do more than decide on the nature of the consideration to be accepted, or whether it can, at the same time, by the statutory majority, decide as to the mode of distribution of the consideration so accepted between the two classes of shareholders. In my opinion it cannot do the latter at all.

I think the meaning of s 161, stated broadly, was this, that instead of disposing of the assets of the company, wound up under a voluntary winding up, for money, you may dispose of them for shares in any other company, or policies, or any like interest, or future profits or other benefit from the purchasing company, but that whatever the benefit was, in whatever shape it was taken, it was to be given, or paid, or handed over to the liquidators for the benefit of the contributories, if I may call them so, of the company wound up—of course subject to the payment of their debts; and that there was no authority conferred by the Act of Parliament on the general meeting, or rather the statutory majority, to direct a distribution as between those contributories otherwise than according to their rights inter se. I think that is tolerably plain from the nature of the case.

First, what is to become of the assets of the company when wound up voluntarily in the ordinary way? In that case we find, by s 133 [IA 1986 s 107], the property, after being applied in satisfaction of the liabilities, is to 'be distributed among the members according to their rights and interests in the company'. Therefore, if the liquidator sells the assets for money, there is no power given to a general meeting to alter the rights of the contributories inter se. They are to share according to their rights and interests . . .

➤ Note

There is an obvious advantage to a company in proceeding under CA 2006, Parts 26 and 27 (see below, p 609) rather than IA 1986 s 110, in that dissentient shareholders can be forced to accept a scheme under the former section, rather than being allowed to insist on their right under IA 1986 s 111 to be paid out in cash. In the next case cited, an attempt was made to formulate rules governing the freedom of a company to choose between the two forms of procedure.

[13.03] Re Anglo-Continental Supply Co Ltd [1922] 2 Ch 723 (Chancery Division)

[The facts are immaterial.]

ASTBURY J: As a result of his researches, Mr Maugham [counsel for the company] has formulated three propositions which, when expressed as follows, are in my judgment sound: (1) When a so-called scheme is really and truly a sale, etc under s 192 [IA 1986 s 110] simpliciter, that section must be complied with and cannot be evaded by calling it a scheme of arrangement under s 120

[CA 2006, Part 26]: see per Warrington LJ in *Re Guardian Assurance Co.*[7] (2) Where a scheme of arrangement cannot be carried through under s 192, though it involves (inter alia) a sale to a company within that section for 'shares, policies and other like interests', and for liquidation and distribution of the proceeds, the court can sanction it under s 120 if it is fair and reasonable in accordance with the principles upon which the court acts in these cases, and it may, but only if it thinks fit, insist as a term of its sanction on the dissentient shareholders being protected in manner similar to that provided for in s 192. (3) Where a scheme of arrangement is one outside s 192 entirely, the court can also and a fortiori act as in proposition (2), subject to the conditions therein mentioned . . .

Arrangements and reconstructions under CA 2006 ss 895–901

The procedures in CA 2006 Parts 26 (ss 895–901) and 27 (applying to specific types of mergers and divisions of public companies only[8]) can be used to effect compromises or arrangements of one company with its members or its creditors,[9] but can also be used to amalgamate two or more companies, or to achieve the equivalent of a takeover.[10] The procedure requires:

(i)   a court order convening meetings of the appropriate classes of members or creditors who will be affected by the scheme;

(ii)   class meetings, seeking the approval of a majority in number *and* representing 75% in value of the groups affected by the proposal (ie members or classes of members, and creditors or classes of creditors); and

(iii)   sanction by the court of the approved scheme (CA 2006 s 899): the court must form its own judgement of the merits of the scheme, not simply confirm the view of the majority voters.

The procedure has the advantage that, with court sanction, the proposed scheme is binding with only 75% approval, whereas a takeover leading to a compulsory buy-out requires 90% acceptance by the members being made the offer. The difference may be justified on the basis that the scheme procedure also requires court approval before the dissentients are bound. On the other hand, because the scheme is not binding until the vote and court approval, competing proposals can be organised to defeat the objectives. By contrast, takeover bidders can solicit irrevocable commitments even before the formal takeover offer is made.

Defining the classes for member or creditor meetings

The classic definition of a class is that of Bowen LJ in *Sovereign Life Assurance Co v Dodd*: a class consists of 'those persons whose rights are not so dissimilar as to make it impossible for them to consult together with a view to their common interest.'[11]

---

[7] [1917] 1 Ch 431.
[8] See above, pp 604 ff.
[9] Moratoria on debts and compromises with creditors (even, occasionally, including compromises that provide for different entitlements than those obtaining on winding up: *Anglo American Insurance Ltd* [2001] 1 BCLC 755) can be agreed under these provisions. However, a new, quicker and simpler alternative may be provided by company voluntary arrangements (CVAs) (see IA 1986, Part I and Sch AI: see below, pp 630 ff).
[10] Such a scheme is also subject to the Takeover Code: see below, pp 616 ff.
[11] [1892] 2 QB 573, 583. This was endorsed in *Re Hawk Insurance Co Ltd* [**13.06**].

[13.04] Re Hellenic & General Trust Ltd [1976] 1 WLR 123, [1975] 3 All ER 382 (Chancery Division)

Hambros Ltd, through a wholly owned subsidiary (referred to in the judgment as 'MIT') held 53% of the ordinary shares of the company, Hellenic & General Trust Ltd. A scheme of arrangement was proposed under which Hambros would acquire all the ordinary shares for a cash consideration of 48p per share. At a meeting of ordinary members, over 80% approved the scheme: MIT voted in support, but the National Bank of Greece, a minority shareholder holding some 14% of the shares, opposed the scheme because it would be liable to pay heavy taxes under Greek law. Templeman J refused to sanction the scheme, first, because he ruled that there should have been a separate 'class' meeting of those ordinary members who were not already a wholly owned subsidiary of Hambros, and secondly because, although the scheme was objectively fair, it was as a matter of discretion, not fairness, to allow the use of CA 1948 s 206 (CA 2006 ss 895ff) to achieve the compulsory purchase of shares which could not be acquired by the use of the takeover procedure now contained in CA 2006 ss 974ff.

TEMPLEMAN J: The first objection put forward is that the necessary agreement by the appropriate class of members has not been obtained. The shareholders who were summoned to the meeting consisted, it is submitted, of two classes. First there were the outside shareholders, that is to say the shareholders other than MIT; and secondly MIT, a subsidiary of Hambros. MIT were a separate class and should have been excluded from the meeting of outside shareholders. Although s 206 [CA 2006 s 896] provides that the court may order meetings, it is the responsibility of the petitioners to see that the class meetings are properly constituted, and if they fail then the necessary agreement is not obtained and the court has no jurisdiction to sanction the arrangement . . .

The question therefore is whether MIT, a wholly owned subsidiary of Hambros, formed part of the same class as the other ordinary shareholders.[12] What is an appropriate class must depend upon the circumstances but some general principles are to be found in the authorities. In *Sovereign Life Assurance Co v Dodd*,[13] the Court of Appeal held that for the purposes of an arrangement affecting the policyholders of an assurance company the holders of policies which had matured were creditors and were a different class from policyholders whose policies had not matured. Bowen LJ said: 'It seems plain that we must give such a meaning to the term "class" as will prevent the section being so worked as to result in confiscation and injustice, and that it must be confined to those persons whose rights are not so dissimilar as to make it impossible for them to consult together with a view to their common interest.' Vendors consulting together with a view to their common interest in an offer made by a purchaser would look askance at the presence among them of a wholly owned subsidiary of the purchaser . . . Mr Heyman, on behalf of the petitioners, submitted that since the parent and subsidiary were separate corporations with separate directors, and since MIT were ordinary shareholders in the company, it followed that MIT had the same interests as the other shareholders. The directors of MIT were under a duty to consider whether the arrangement was beneficial to the whole class of ordinary shareholders, and they were capable of forming an independent and unbiased judgment, irrespective of the interests of the parent company. This seems to me to be unreal. Hambros are purchasers making an offer. When the vendors meet to discuss and vote whether or not to accept the offer, it is incongruous that the loudest voice in theory and the most significant voice in practice should come from the wholly owned subsidiary of the purchaser. No one can be both a vendor and a purchaser and in my judgment, for the purpose of the class meetings in the present case, MIT were in the camp of the purchaser. Of course this

---

[12] [Note that this is not the same question as that arising under CA 2006 s 630, which speaks of rights 'attached to' a class of shares. Section 896 contemplates that creditors, as well as members, may fall into different classes.]

[13] [1892] 2 QB 573.

does not mean that MIT should not have considered at a separate class meeting whether to accept the arrangement. But their consideration will be different from the considerations given to the matter by the other shareholders. Only MIT could say, within limits, that what was good for Hambros must be good for MIT . . .

Accordingly I uphold the first objection, which is fatal to the arrangement. But in view of the careful arguments put forward by both sides I will consider the other objections which are raised by Mr Wright and which are material if the class meeting in the present case, contrary to my view, was properly constituted.

The second objection is founded on the analysis of the arrangement as an offer by Hambros to acquire the ordinary shares for 48p. Section 209 [CA 2006 ss 974ff] provides safeguards for minority shareholders in the event of a takeover bid and in a proper case provides machinery for a small minority of shareholders to be obliged to accept a takeover against their wishes . . . If the present arrangement had been carried out under s 209, MIT as a subsidiary of Hambros would have been expressly forbidden to join in any approval for the purposes of s 209,[14] and in any event the objectors could not have been obliged to sell because they hold 10% of the ordinary shares of the company.

[It] seems to me that it is unfair to deprive the objectors of shares which they were entitled to assume were safe from compulsory purchase and with the effect of putting on the objectors a simply and quite properly by refusing to join in approving the scheme under that section.

Accordingly in the result, both as a matter of jurisdiction and as a matter of discretion, I am not prepared to make any order approving this scheme.

[13.05] Re BTR plc [1999] 2 BCLC 675

A proposed scheme of arrangement, designed to effect a merger between BTR and another company, Siebe plc, had been carried by a 97% majority of BTR's ordinary shareholders at a single class meeting. Some dissentient shareholders contended that there should have been a separate class meeting for those BTR shareholders who already held shares in Siebe.

In rejecting this argument, Jonathan Parker J said of *Re Hellenic & General Trust Ltd* **[13.04]** (at 682):

For myself, I find it difficult to understand the concept of an interest arising out of a right as being something separate from the right itself. Nor do I think that such a process of analysis is necessary in relation to the *Hellenic* case where the majority of shares in the company the subject of the scheme were already held by a subsidiary of the intended purchaser. Templeman J effectively discounted the views of the registered holder of those shares and he did so, as I read the judgment, on the basis that in substance the scheme affected only the remainder of the shares. That is, in my judgment, the ratio of Templeman J's decision in so far as it addressed the question of separate classes . . .

It does not, as I see it, involve any analysis of interests and rights, nor is it inconsistent with the submission made by Mr Sykes (which I accept) that the relevant test is that of differing rights rather than differing interests. Nor do I agree with Mr Northcote that 'interest' in this connection is synonymous with right. Shareholders with the same rights in respect of the shares which they hold may be subject to an infinite number of different interests and may therefore, assessing their own personal interests (as they are perfectly entitled to do), vote their shares in the light of those interests. But that in itself, in my judgment, is simply a fact of life: it does not lead to the conclusion that shareholders who propose to vote differently are in some way a separate class of shareholders entitled to a separate class meeting. Indeed a journey down that road would in my judgment lead to impracticability and unworkability. In the course of his submissions Mr Northcote accepted that in

---

[14] [See now the more detailed provisions contained in CA 2006 ss 977(2) and 988.]

the instant case it may well be that (if he is right) a very large number of separate class meetings would be required in order properly to reflect the differing interests of shareholders. The question then arises how the company could possibly reach an informed decision as to the division of shareholders into separate classes without first requiring a considerable amount of personal information from individual shareholders; a wholly unworkable, and highly undesirable, situation.

In my judgment, therefore, there was no warrant in this case for the convening of more than one meeting of the holders of the scheme shares, and I reject the submission that there are separate classes of holders of scheme shares for the purposes of this scheme . . .

[13.06] Re Hawk Insurance Co Ltd [2001] 2 BCLC 675; [2002] BCC 300 (Court of Appeal)

This was an appeal against a decision of the lower court refusing to sanction an unopposed scheme of arrangement under CA 1985 s 425 [CA 2006, s 895] on the ground that the court had no jurisdiction to do so because it was not satisfied that the creditors who had (without dissent) approved the scheme at a single meeting did in fact constitute a single class. The court allowed the appeal.

CHADWICK LJ:

The decision whether to summon more than one meeting

13 The decision whether to summon more than one meeting—and, if so, who should be summoned to which meeting—has to be made at the first stage [at the hearing for a court order summoning the meetings]. If the matter were free from authority, I would have regarded the basis upon which that decision has to be taken as self-evident. The relevant question is: between whom is the proposed compromise or arrangement to be made? There are, as it seems to me, three possible answers to that question. Which answer is correct in any particular case will depend upon the circumstances peculiar to that case.

14 First, there will be cases where it is plain that the compromise or arrangement proposed is between the company and all its creditors. In such a case [the Act] provides for the court to order a single meeting of all the creditors.

15 Secondly, there will be cases where it is plain that the compromise or arrangement proposed is between the company and one distinct class of creditors; for example, unsecured trade creditors whose debts accrued before (or after) a given date. Or it may be plain that there are two (or more) separate compromises or arrangements with two (or more) distinct classes of creditors; for example, one compromise with unsecured trade creditors whose debts accrued before a given date and a separate compromise (on different terms) with unsecured trade creditors whose debts accrued after that date. In such a case, the section provides for the court to order a meeting of each class of creditors with whom the compromise or arrangement is to be made. . . .

16 Cases which fall into the two categories which I have described above are likely to be recognised without difficulty. More difficult to recognise are cases in a third category. Those are cases where what appears at first sight to be a single compromise or arrangement between the company and all its creditors (or all creditors of a particular description, say, unsecured creditors) can be seen, on a true analysis, to be two or more linked compromises or arrangements with creditors whose rights put them in several and distinct classes. The compromises or arrangements are linked in the sense that each is conditional upon the other or others taking effect. In such a case, . . . [there should be] separate meetings of each of the distinct classes of creditors.

17 If the correct decision is not made at the first stage [ordering the meetings], the court may find, at the third stage [sanctioning the scheme], that it is without jurisdiction. . . . . . That is what the judge [in the lower court] found to be the position in the present case.

18 It might be thought that the structure of the statutory provisions required the court to consider, at the first stage . . . whether the scheme proposed was a single compromise or arrangement . . . or was (on a true analysis) two or more linked compromises or arrangements. . . . That has not been the practice in the Companies Court. [He then described, and criticised, the 65 year old Practice Note, at [1934] WN 142, which set the approach taken. See below for the current revisions.]. . . .

21 In my view an applicant is entitled to feel aggrieved if, in the absence of opposition from any creditor, the court holds, at the third stage and on its own motion, that the order which it made at the first stage was pointless. It is, to my mind, no answer to say that that is a risk which the applicant must accept. It may be inevitable that an applicant must accept the risk that a dissentient creditor will persuade the court at the third stage that the order which it made at the first stage (without hearing that creditor) was the wrong order. But that is not to say that the applicant must be required to accept that, when exercising what is plainly a judicial discretion at the first stage, the court will not address the question whether the order which it makes serves any useful purpose; or that, if it has addressed that question at the first stage, it will change its mind, of its own motion, at the third stage. . . .

How is it to be determined whether separate class meetings are required?

23 As I have indicated, I would have regarded it as self-evident, in the absence of authority, that the relevant question at the outset is: between whom is it proposed that a compromise or arrangement is to be made? Are the rights of those who are to be affected by the scheme proposed such that the scheme can be seen as a single arrangement; or ought the scheme to be regarded, on a true analysis, as a number of linked arrangements? The question may be easy to state; but, as the cases show, it is not always easy to answer. Nor can it be said that, hitherto, the courts have posed the question in quite those terms.

24 The starting point, and (so far as I am aware) the only decision of this court on the point, is *Sovereign Life Assurance Co v Dodd* [1892] 2 QB 573. [He then discussed this case at some length and concluded that Bowen LJ's answer to his question was that . . .] [t]he scheme proposed may be regarded as a single arrangement with those creditors whom it is intended to bind if, but only if, the rights of those creditors are not so dissimilar as to make it impossible for them to consult together with a view to their common interest. If the rights of those creditors whom the scheme is intended to bind are such as to make it impossible for them to consult together with a view to their common interest, then the scheme must be regarded as a number of linked arrangements. In the latter case it will be necessary to have a separate meeting of each class of creditors; a class being identified by the test that the rights of those creditors within it are not so dissimilar as to make it impossible for them to consult together with a view to their common interest. . . .

29 I have thought it right to examine the judgments in *Sovereign Life Assurance Co v Dodd* [1892] 2 QB 573 at some length, not only because the decision in that appeal is the only authority binding upon this court, but because the decision has been relied upon from time to time in later cases for the proposition that creditors whose rights have vested must, necessarily, be regarded as a different class from creditors whose rights are contingent. . . . [and] that 'in the case of a life assurance company holders of matured policies are a different class from holders of current policies': . . . . In my view, the *Sovereign Life* case is authority for neither of those propositions. . . .

30 . . . it will not necessarily follow, in every case, that the treatment under the scheme of vested and contingent rights, or the rights under matured and current policies, will be so dissimilar that the holders of those rights must be regarded as persons in different classes in the context of the question 'with whom is the compromise or arrangement made'. In each case the answer to that question will depend upon analysis (i) of the rights which are to be released or varied under the scheme and (ii) of the new rights (if any) which the scheme gives, by way of compromise or arrangement, to those whose rights are to be released or varied. It is in the light of that analysis that the test formulated by Bowen LJ in order to determine which creditors fall into a separate class-that is to say,

that a class 'must be confined to those persons whose rights are not so dissimilar as to make it impossible for them to consult together with a view to their common interest'—has to be applied. . . . .

33 When applying Bowen LJ's test to the question 'are the rights of those who are to be affected by the scheme proposed such that the scheme can be seen as a single arrangement; or ought it to be regarded, on a true analysis, as a number of linked arrangements?' it is necessary to ensure not only that those whose rights really are so dissimilar that they cannot consult together with a view to a common interest should be treated as parties to distinct arrangements—so that they should have their own separate meetings—but also that those whose rights are sufficiently similar to the rights of others that they can properly consult together should be required to do; lest by ordering separate meetings the court gives a veto to a minority group. The safeguard against majority oppression . . . is that the court is not bound by the decision of the meeting. It is important Bowen LJ's test should not be applied in such a way that it becomes an instrument of oppression by a minority.

[He then continued his analysis and concluded that separate class meetings were not required in the present case, and therefore allowed the appeal.]

PILL LJ gave a concurring judgment and WRIGHT LJ concurred with both.

> Notes

1. The risk that the classes have not been correctly identified so that, at the later stages, the court will not sanction the scheme has been reduced by a change in practice: see Practice Statement [2002] 3 All ER 96. This requires greater attention to the issues at the convening hearing, where application is made to the court for an order convening the necessary meetings. In addition, courts have adopted the approach of Chadwick LJ above that they should find, on their own motion and without the intervention of dissentient voices, that the initial selection of classes was inappropriate.

2. By analogy with creditors' meetings in insolvency law, it is possible for the court to direct at stage 1 that split voting is possible at the creditors' meetings, particularly by nominee or trustee creditors, so that they might vote both for and against the scheme in relation to different parts of the value of that creditor's claim (*Re Equitable Life Assurance Society* [2002] BCC 319).

The function of the courts in considering whether to sanction a scheme.

[13.07] Re Alabama, New Orleans, Texas and Pacific Junction Rly Co [1891] 1 Ch 213 (Court of Appeal)

[The facts are immaterial.]

LINDLEY LJ: [What] the court has to do is to see, first of all, that the provisions of that statute have been complied with; and, secondly, that the majority has been acting bona fide. The court also has to see that the minority is not being overridden by a majority having interests of its own clashing with those of the minority whom they seek to coerce. Further than that, the court has to look at the scheme and see whether it is one as to which persons acting honestly, and viewing the scheme laid before them in the interests of those whom they represent, take a view which can be reasonably taken by businessmen . . .

> Notes

1. Also see *Re Hellenic & General Trust Ltd* [**13.04**] above, and the observations of Maugham J in *Re Dorman Long & Co* [**4.11**].]

2. In *Re National Farmers' Union Development Trust Ltd* [1973] 1 All ER 135, [1972] 1 WLR 1548 a non-profit-making company wished to write down its capital and reduce the number of its members from 94,000 to 7 in order to reduce its administrative expenses. The proposal had the support of an 85% majority vote. But Brightman J held that he had no power to sanction the scheme under what is now CA 2006 s 899, since the statutory terms 'compromise' and 'arrangement' implied some element of accommodation on each side and were not appropriate to describe a scheme under which some members surrendered their rights altogether.

3. The court has extensive powers under CA 2006 s 900 to make such ancillary orders as are necessary to facilitate implementation of any sanctioned scheme.

Compulsory binding of dissentient minorities and the HRA 1998.

[13.08] Re Equitable Life Assurance Society [2002] BCC 319

Arguably the strength of Part 26 lies in the ability to bind dissenting minorities. Lloyd J rejects the suggestion that compelling dissenting individuals to accept a scheme that alters their rights may be contrary to Article 1, First Protocol, ECHR, as implemented by the Human Rights Act 1998:

> [T]his type of rule, essential in a liberal society, cannot in principle be considered contrary to art. 1 of the First Protocol, provided that the law does not create such inequality that one person could be arbitrarily and unjustly deprived of property in favour of another. It seems to me plain that, given the terms of section 425 [s 899] and the case law that has been established concerning its application, there is no possible argument for saying that the approval of a scheme under s 425, so as to bind dissentients among the relevant classes, breaches the rights afforded by art 1 of the First Protocol. . . . [In order to be sanctioned by the court] the scheme does both in law and in fact [have to] involve exchange of rights and thus consideration. No arrangement capable of being approved under s 425 could, in my view, amount to a confiscation such that art. 1 would be infringed.

> ➤ Question

You are consulted in advance of the meeting by the National Bank of Greece (in *Re Hellenic & General Trust Ltd* **[13.04]**, above), and asked to advise it whether it would be proper for the Bank to consider its tax position in deciding how to cast its vote at the class meeting. What would your advice be? (See *Re Holders Investment Trust Ltd* **[8.05]**.)

Proposals for reform of the law

1. The Cork Committee on Insolvency made the following observations about the procedure under ss 425–427A [now CA 2006, Part 26] and its utility in corporate insolvencies (1982, Cmnd 8558, paras 406ff):

> Because of the long and involved procedure, it is virtually impossible to shorten the period of time between initial formulation of a scheme of arrangement and its becoming effective by Court Order below eight weeks. During those eight weeks each individual creditor can exercise all the rights and remedies available to him against the company debtor . . .

> The insolvent company's inability—particularly if it is a trading company—to hold the position (that is to prevent winding up or the random seizure of assets by individual creditors) during the period necessary for the devising and processing of a scheme, makes it extremely difficult for even the most uncomplicated scheme of arrangement to be launched. A straightforward moratorium on the payment of debts to unsecured creditors for a limited period, or such a moratorium coupled with

a composition, say the reduction of all debts by 25%, may be the plainest good sense for all concerned, but it often cannot be done . . .

The Court is heavily involved in the procedure under section [425]. There are two distinct phases. First, the convening of the necessary meetings of creditors and contributories and, secondly, the petition to the Court for the sanctioning of the scheme as approved by the appropriate majorities at the meetings . . .

[We] believe that the Court procedure could be substantially streamlined and greatly improved. We cannot believe that there is the need for quite so many applications to, or attendances on, the Court. We doubt whether painstaking perusal of documents by Court officials with little or no experience of commerce or finance provides any real protection for creditors or contributories.

2. The report of the Insolvency Service's Review Group on Company Rescue and Business Reconstruction Mechanisms (May 2000) proposed that consideration be given to augmenting what is now CA 2006, Part 26 by introducing the option of a moratorium while a scheme for a composition between a company and its creditors is being put together. This would bring UK law in this regard into line with that of Canada and South Africa.

3. The CLR queried whether there was any real point in preserving the distinction between the IA 1986 s 110 and the CA 2006, Part 26[15] procedures, and suggested there might be a case for combining the two, giving the company the option of choosing between providing cash appraisal rights for dissenting members or seeking the sanction of the court.

4. The CLR doubted whether the IA 1986 s 111 system of cash appraisal which provides for compulsory arbitration without recourse to a court is compatible with the Human Rights Act.[16]

5. The CLR considered that there may be a case for introducing a statutory procedure (as is available in New Zealand) which would allow wholly owned companies within the same group to merge with each other or with their holding company without the need for court approval and with little more formality than the approval of all the directors, a declaration of solvency and appropriate notification to creditors.

There is no reform embedded in the new CA 2006, Part 26 itself to meet these various criticisms. However, certain procedures introduced into the Insolvency Act 1986 over the years do meet some of the needs identified above. These measures include the statutory procedures for company voluntary arrangements (CVAs), with and without moratorium periods (IA 1986, Pt I and Sch A1), and also administration orders (IA 1986, Pt II): see below, pp 628 ff.

Takeovers

Where a company acquires control over another by buying all or a majority holding of its shares, this is termed a 'takeover'.[17] A general offer to buy addressed to all the members of a company is called a 'takeover bid'. This is by far the commonest method used in this country for merging one corporate business with another. The two companies are usually referred to respectively as the 'offeror' company or 'bidder' and the 'target' or 'offeree' company.

---

[15] Or, more accurately, its predecessor in CA 1985 s 425, which is in substantially the same form.

[16] IA 1986 s 111 invokes the arbitration provisions of the Companies Clauses Consolidation Act 1845, and does not specify the basis of valuation.

[17] For further reading, see Sir A Johnson, *The City Take-over Code* (Oxford, 1980); L Rabinowitz (ed), *Weinberg and Blank on Take-overs and Mergers* (5th edn, 1989); RR Pennington, 'Take-over Bids in the United Kingdom' [1969] Am J Comp L 159; DD Prentice, 'Take-over Bids—the City Code on Take-overs and Mergers' (1972) 18 McGill LJ 385; Lord Alexander of Weedon, 'Take-overs: the Regulatory Scene' [1990] JBL 203; D Calcutt, 'The Work of the Take-over Panel' (1990) 11 Co Law 203; N Boardman, 'What the Takeover Directive Means for the UK' (2006) 25(7) IFL Review 174; M Mejucq, 'The European Regime on Takeovers' (2006) 3(2) ECFR 222.

If the target is a private company, control can usually only be exercised by a group holding more than 50% of the voting shares. Moreover, the target will probably have a provision in its articles authorising the directors to refuse to register a transfer of shares. It follows that a takeover of a private company usually requires the agreement of the directors.

On the other hand, if the target is a listed company, control can often be exercised by the holder of fewer than 50% of the voting shares because the other shareholders are either apathetic or lack co-ordination. But the bidder is unlikely to be able to acquire the necessary shareholding simply by purchases on the Stock Exchange. It is usually necessary to send a circular (a takeover bid) to the target's members offering to buy their shares.

For many years, economists have argued about whether takeovers and mergers are beneficial for the economy. The argument in favour is essentially that assets should be owned and/or managed in the most productive way possible: less productive or efficient ownership and/or management should be replaced by a more efficient one, via a takeover. Takeovers thus form part of the market for corporate ownership and control of assets.[18] On the other hand, empirical evidence suggests that underperforming management is not a primary inducement to a takeover, so the bids do not have a disciplining effect. And even where there is such an effect, the mechanism has been described as a costly, disruptive, and counterproductive in motivating long-term good corporate governance.[19]

Regulation of takeovers

CA 2006, Part 28 deals with the regulation of takeovers. Apart from Chapter 3,[20] its provisions are new.[21] It implements the European Directive on Takeover Bids (2004/25/EC) (the Takeovers Directive), takes account of criticisms and comments from the CLR and the DTI,[22] and applies some of the rules beyond the sphere of operation required by the Directive.

The Takeovers Directive lays down, for the first time, minimum EU rules concerning the regulation of takeovers of companies whose shares are traded on a regulated market. It aims to strengthen the Single Market in financial services by facilitating cross-border restructuring and enhancing minority shareholder protection. It contains:

(i)   general principles that apply to the conduct of takeover bids;

(ii)   a regulatory framework for bodies that supervise takeover bids (in the UK, the Panel on Takeovers and Mergers ('Panel'));

(iii)   basic rules about takeover bids (eg when a bid must be made, the price that must be paid to members, the contents of offer documents prepared by the bidder, requirements to inform employees and the time period a bid will be open for);

(iv)   provisions restricting barriers to takeovers (eg action that might be taken to prevent a takeover by a company or its board of directors);

(v)   disclosure requirements for companies whose shares are traded on a regulated market; and

(vi)   provisions dealing with the problems of, and for, residual minority members following a successful takeover bid (ie 'squeeze-out' and 'sell-out' provisions).

---

[18] See K Hopt and E Wymeersch (eds), *European Takeovers: Law and Practice* (1992), especially the chapters by R Romano, 'A Guide to Takeovers: Theory, Evidence and Regulation' and R Cranston, 'The Rise and Rise of the Hostile Takeover'.

[19] Moerland, 'Alternative Disciplinary Mechanisms in Different Corporate Systems' (1995) 26 J of Economic Behaviour and Organisation 17.

[20] This restates and amends CA 1985, Part XIIIA.

[21] See DTI, 'Implementation of the EU Directive on Takeover Bids—Guidance on changes to the rules on company takeovers' February 2007, URN 07/659.

[22] DTI, 'Company Law-Implementation of the European Directive on Takeover Bids', January 2005.

The Panel on Takeovers and Mergers (the 'Panel')

The Takeovers Directive requires certain significant structural changes to UK practices.

Since 1968, takeover regulation in the UK has been overseen by the Panel. The Panel's function is to ensure that shareholders are treated fairly and placed in a position to decide on the merits of a takeover, and that shareholders of the same class are afforded equivalent treatment by an offeror. The Panel administers rules contained in the City Code on Takeovers and Mergers ('the Takeovers Code'), which historically had no legal force.[23] The Takeovers Code was prepared and first issued in 1968 by representatives of various City bodies, including the Bank of England, The Stock Exchange, and the Issuing Houses Association, as a statement of the principles of commercial morality which those taking part in a takeover were expected to follow. The Takeover Code is not concerned with the financial or commercial advantages of a takeover. These are matters for the company and its shareholders. Wider questions of public interest are dealt with by the Competition Commission, the Office of Fair Trading, the Department of Trade and Industry or the European Commission.

There are six General Principles governing the Takeovers Code:

(i) All holders of the securities of an offeree company of the same class must be afforded equivalent treatment; moreover, if a person acquires control of a company, the other holders of securities must be protected.

(ii) The holders of the securities of an offeree company must have sufficient time and information to enable them to reach a properly informed decision on the bid; where it advises the holders of securities, the board of the offeree company must give its views on the effects of implementation of the bid on employment, conditions of employment and the locations of the company's places of business.

(iii) The board of an offeree company must act in the interests of the company as a whole and must not deny the holders of securities the opportunity to decide on the merits of the bid.

(iv) False markets must not be created in the securities of the offeree company, of the offeror company or of any other company concerned by the bid in such a way that the rise or fall of the prices of the securities becomes artificial and the normal functioning of the markets is distorted.

(v) An offeror must announce a bid only after ensuring that he/she can fulfil in full any cash consideration, if such is offered, and after taking all reasonable measures to secure the implementation of any other type of consideration.

(vi) An offeree company must not be hindered in the conduct of its affairs for longer than is reasonable by a bid for its securities.

The Takeovers Directive requires certain regulatory activities of the Panel to be placed within a legal framework. CA 2006, Part 28 seeks to do this in a way that retains the considerable strengths of the previous system of takeover regulation overseen by the Panel, including:

(i) flexibility, speed and certainty in decision-making;

(ii) independence and regulatory autonomy;

(iii) principles-based regulation;

(iv) involvement of key City and business participants in developing takeover rules and the regulatory framework;

---

[23] Further information about the Panel and copies of the City Code on Takeovers and Mergers are available on the Panel's website (http://www.thetakeoverpanel.org.uk/new/).

(v)   professional expertise in regulatory activities, notably through Panel membership and secondments; and

(vi)   consensual approach to regulation amongst those involved in the markets.

Part 28 therefore provides a statutory underpinning to the regulatory activities of the Panel, but leaves the Panel with considerable scope to decide its internal structures and operational framework. The Panel remains an unincorporated body. As such, it has rights and obligations under common law, supplemented by the relevant legislative provisions. It has power to make rules in relation to takeover regulation, and will continue to make rulings on the interpretation, application and effect of the Takeovers Code and to give directions (CA 2006 ss 943–946).

Decisions of the Panel are in principle subject to judicial review. However, the court will not normally intervene while the Panel is actively dealing with a matter, but will only grant relief of a declaratory nature after the event.

[13.09] R v Panel on Take-overs and Mergers, ex p Datafin plc [1987] QB 815, [1987] 1 All ER 564 (Court of Appeal)[24]

[The facts are immaterial, although some of the descriptions of the Panel are now out of date, given the changes implemented by CA 2006, Part 28.]

SIR JOHN DONALDSON MR: The Panel on Take-overs and Mergers is a truly remarkable body. Perched on the 20th floor of the Stock Exchange building in the City of London, both literally and metaphorically it oversees and regulates a very important part of the United Kingdom financial market. Yet it performs this function without visible means of legal support.

The panel is an unincorporated association without legal personality . . . It has no statutory, prerogative or common law powers and it is not in contractual relationship with the financial market or with those who deal in that market.

[His Lordship read extracts from the City Code, and continued:] 'Self-regulation' is an emotive term. It is also ambiguous. An individual who voluntarily regulates his life in accordance with stated principles, because he believes that this is morally right and also, perhaps, in his own long-term interests, or a group of individuals who do so, are practising self-regulation. But it can mean something quite different. It can connote a system whereby a group of people, acting in concert, use their collective power to force themselves and others to comply with a code of conduct of their own devising. This is not necessarily morally wrong or contrary to the public interest, unlawful or even undesirable. But it is very different.

The panel is a self-regulating body in the latter sense. Lacking any authority de jure, it exercises immense power de facto by devising, promulgating, amending and interpreting the City Code on Take-overs and Mergers, by waiving or modifying the application of the code in particular circumstances, by investigating and reporting upon alleged breaches of the code and by the application or threat of sanctions. These sanctions are no less effective because they are applied indirectly and lack a legally enforceable base.

The principal issue in this appeal, and only issue which may matter in the longer term, is whether this remarkable body is above the law. Its respectability is beyond question. So is its bona fides. I do not doubt for one moment that it is intended to, and does, operate in the public interest and that the enormously wide discretion which it arrogates to itself is necessary if it is to function efficiently and effectively. Whilst not wishing to become involved in the political controversy on the relative merits of self-regulation and governmental or statutory regulation, I am content to assume for the purposes of this appeal that self-regulation is preferable in the public interest. But that said, what is to

---

[24]   See Lord Alexander of Weedon, 'Judicial Review and City Regulators' (1989) 52 MLR 640.

happen if the panel goes off the rails? Suppose, perish the thought, that it were to use its powers in a way which was manifestly unfair. What then? . . .

[His Lordship outlined the facts of the case and continued:] It will be seen that there are three principal issues, viz: (a) Are the decisions of the panel susceptible to judicial review? This is the 'jurisdictional' issue. (b) If so, how in principle is that jurisdiction to be exercised given the nature of the panel's activities and the fact that it is an essential part of the machinery of a market in which time is money in a very real sense? This might be described as the 'practical' issue. (c) If the jurisdictional issue is answered favourably to the applicants, is this a case in which relief should be granted and, if so, in what form? . . .

The jurisdictional issue

As I have said, the panel is a truly remarkable body, performing its function without visible means of legal support. But the operative word is 'visible', although perhaps I should have used the word 'direct'. Invisible or indirect support there is in abundance. Not only is a breach of the code, so found by the panel, ipso facto an act of misconduct by a member of the Stock Exchange, and the same may be true of other bodies represented on the panel, but the admission of shares to the Official List may be withheld in the event of such a breach. This is interesting and significant for listing of securities is a statutory function performed by the Stock Exchange in pursuance of . . . [and he went on to name various regulations and rules now incorporated in FSA 1986].

. . . The picture which emerges is clear. As an act of government it was decided that, in relation to take-overs, there should be a central self-regulatory body which would be supported and sustained by a periphery of statutory powers and penalties wherever non-statutory powers and penalties were insufficient or non-existent or where EEC requirements called for statutory provisions . . .

The issue is thus whether the historic supervisory jurisdiction of the Queen's courts extends to such a body discharging such functions, including some which are quasi-judicial in their nature, as part of such a system. Mr Alexander, for the panel, submits that it does not. He says that this jurisdiction only extends to bodies whose power is derived from legislation or the exercise of the prerogative. Mr Lever, for the applicants, submits that this is too narrow a view and that regard has to be had not only to the source of the body's power, but also to whether it operates as an integral part of a system which has a public law character, is supported by public law in that public law sanctions are applied if its edicts are ignored and performs what might be described as public law functions.

[His Lordship referred to the analogous position of the Criminal Injuries Compensation Board, which had been considered by the Divisional Court in *R v Criminal Injuries Compensation Board, ex p Lain*,[25] and continued:] In fact, given its novelty, the panel fits surprisingly well into the format which this court had in mind in the *Criminal Injuries Compensation Board* case. It is without doubt performing a public duty and an important one. This is clear from the expressed willingness of the Secretary of State for Trade and Industry to limit legislation in the field of take-overs and mergers and to use the panel as the centrepiece of his regulation of that market. The rights of citizens are indirectly affected by its decisions . . . At least in its determination of whether there has been a breach of the code, it has a duty to act judicially and it asserts that its raison d'être is to do equity between one shareholder and another. Its source of power is only partly based upon moral persuasion and the assent of institutions and their members, the bottom line being the statutory powers exercised by the Department of Trade and Industry and the Bank of England. In this context I should be very disappointed if the courts could not recognise the realities of executive power and allowed their vision to be clouded by the subtlety and sometimes complexity of the way in which it can be exerted . . .

In reaching my conclusion that the court has jurisdiction to entertain applications for the judicial review of decisions of the panel, I have said nothing about the substantial arguments of

[25] [1967] 2 QB 864, [1967] 2 All ER 770.

Mr Alexander based upon the practical problems which are involved. These, in my judgment, go not to the existence of the jurisdiction, but to how it should be exercised and to that I now turn.

The practical issue

. . . In many cases of judicial review where the time scale is far more extended than in the financial markets, the decision-maker who learns that someone is seeking leave to challenge his decision may well seek to preserve the status quo meanwhile and, in particular, may not seek to enforce his decision pending a consideration of the matter by the court. If leave is granted, the court has the necessary authority to make orders designed to achieve this result, but usually the decision-maker will give undertakings in lieu. All this is but good administrative practice. However, against the background of the time scales of the financial market, the courts would not expect the panel or those who should comply with its decisions to act similarly. In that context the panel and those affected should treat its decisions as valid and binding, unless and until they are set aside. Above all they should ignore any application for leave to apply of which they become aware, since to do otherwise would enable such applications to be used as a mere ploy in take-over battles which would be a serious abuse of the process of the court and could not be adequately penalised by awards of costs.

[His Lordship referred to the various functions of the panel and expressed the opinion that it was unlikely that the courts would often have occasion to intervene. He continued:] Nothing that I have said can fetter or is intended to or should be construed as fettering the discretion of any court to which application is made for leave to apply for judicial review of a decision of the panel or which, leave having been granted, is charged with the duty of considering such an application. Nevertheless, I wish to make it clear beyond a peradventure that in the light of the special nature of the panel, its functions, the market in which it is operating, the time scales which are inherent in that market and the need to safeguard the position of third parties, who may be numbered in thousands, all of whom are entitled to continue to trade upon an assumption of the validity of the panel's rules and decisions, unless and until they are quashed by the court, I should expect the relationship between the panel and the court to be historic rather than contemporaneous. I should expect the court to allow contemporary decisions to take their course, considering the complaint and intervening, if at all, later and in retrospect by declaratory orders which would enable the panel not to repeat any error and would relieve individuals of the disciplinary consequences of any erroneous finding of breach of the rules. This would provide a workable and valuable partnership between the courts and the panel in the public interest and would avoid all of the perils to which Mr Alexander alluded.

[His Lordship then ruled that a case for intervention in the present instance had not been made out.]

LLOYD and NICHOLLS LJJ delivered concurring judgments.

➤ Notes

1. On two occasions since *Datafin* the Court of Appeal has declined to intervene by way of judicial review in decisions of the Panel. See *R v Panel on Take-overs and Mergers, ex p Guinness plc* [1990] 1 QB 146, [1989] 1 All ER 509, CA and *R v Panel on Take-overs and Mergers, ex p Fayed* [1992] BCLC 938, CA. However, in the *Guinness* case the Panel did not escape criticism, some of its decisions being condemned as 'insensitive and unwise'.

2. It should be borne in mind that not all take-overs are contested: many are settled by agreement between the respective boards and accepted by the members without opposition. Also (more particularly in the case of smaller companies), a change of control is commonly effected by a simple share sale and purchase agreement concluded between the outgoing and incoming members. (Although 'simple' may not be a particularly apt word to use here: the documents in these transactions often run to hundreds of pages!) For reference, see G Stedman and J Jones, *Shareholders' Agreements* (3rd edn, 1998).

Restricting barriers to takeovers

The Takeovers Directive seeks to override certain steps that may be taken by companies both prior to and during a takeover bid which have the aim of frustrating a bid, including:

(i)   Pre-bid defences (Takeovers Directive, Art 11): this provides 'breakthrough provisions' that will defeat strategies including differential share structures under which minority share-holders exercise disproportionate voting rights; limitations on share ownership; and restrictions on transfer of shares set out in the company's articles or in contractual agreements. Companies with voting shares traded on a regulated market may opt in to these breakthrough provisions should they wish to do so (CA 2006, ss 966–972); the Directive rules are not compulsory.

(ii)   Post-bid defences (Takeovers Directive, Art 9): the management of a target company cannot take action to frustrate a bid (eg by sale of the company's key assets) without the approval of the members at the time of the bid. The rules banning this type of defensive action are contained in the Takeover Code.

New disclosure requirements

CA 2006, Part 28, Chapter 4 (s 992) amends the 1985 Act in relation to the content of annual reports of companies traded on a regulated market, compelling disclosure of matters such as the share and control structures of companies.

Mandatory offer rules

The Takeovers Code recognises that a public company may be controlled by holders of less than 50% of its voting rights. It therefore requires that a person who gains 30% of the voting rights in a public company must make a takeover bid for all the voting shares (Rule 9.1). The price that has to be offered is the highest price at which the offeror (or persons acting in concert with it) has dealt in the offeree's shares in the 12 months preceding the announcement of the mandatory offer. This rule is designed to prevent an offeror obtaining a controlling interest at a premium price from a few large members and then buying out the remaining small members cheaply.

Position of minority members following a takeover

The concepts of 'squeeze out' and 'sell out'[26] are designed to address the problems of, and for, residual minority members following a successful takeover bid. Squeeze out rights (CA 2006, s 979) enable a successful bidder to purchase compulsorily the shares of remaining minority members who have not accepted the bid. Sell out rights (CA 2006 s 983) enable minority members to require the majority member to purchase their shares. Because these procedures involve compulsory purchase or acquisition of shares against the will of the holder or the acquirer, higher thresholds apply to the exercise of such rights, there are protective rules on the price that must be paid for the shares, and the procedure can be challenged in the court (CA 2006 s 986).

CA 2006, Part 28, Chapter 3 makes some changes to the 1985 Act to ensure compliance with the Takeovers Directive and to implement certain recommendations from the CLR. Chapter 3 applies to all companies and all bids within the ambit of Part 28, whether or not the Takeovers Directive requires this.

---

[26] Previously contained in CA 1985, Part XIIIA.

Grounds on which the court will interfere in a squeeze out

CA 2006 s 986, like its predecessors, does not specify the grounds on which a court will interfere. Given the similar wording of the provisions, the earlier cases on this issue remain relevant.

[13.10] Re Grierson Oldham and Adams Ltd [1968] Ch 17, [1967] 1 All ER 192 (Chancery Division)

The company, which dealt in wines and spirits, had been the subject of a successful take-over bid by John Holt & Co (Liverpool) Ltd. The offer made by Holts of 6s [30p] per 2s [10p] ordinary share had been accepted by 99.9% of the shareholders, and notice had been given of Holt's intention to acquire the remaining shares compulsorily at the same price pursuant to CA 1948 s 209 [CA 2006 ss 979 and 986]. The applicants, who had paid between 6s 7½ d [33p] and 6s 9d [34p] per share for their holdings, objected on the ground that the price offered was unfair to them; but the court declined to intervene.

PLOWMAN J: The contentions which are put forward by the applicants fall under two main heads. In the first place it is said that the price of 6s a share is unfair, taking into account the assets and future prospects of the company and the advantages which will accrue to Holts by the take-over; and secondly, that it is unfair to the applicants that they should be compelled to sell their shares at a loss. Before considering those contentions in more detail, there are two or three general observations which I should make and which I think are justified by the authorities on this section to which I have been referred.

The first general observation is that the onus of proof here is fairly and squarely on the applicants, and indeed they accepted that that is so. The onus of proof is on them to establish, if they can, that the offer was unfair . . .

The second general observation which seems to me to be relevant is this: that since this is not a case of a purchase of assets, but of a purchase of shares, the market price on the stock exchange of those shares is cogent evidence of their true value; not conclusive evidence, of course, but cogent evidence . . . And in this case it is a formidable onus that the applicants have set out to discharge, bearing in mind that not only was the offer price above the stock exchange price, but that over 99% of the ordinary shareholders accepted the offer.

The third general observation which arises out of the arguments that have been put forward concerns the question whether the test of the fairness of the offer is fairness to the individual shareholder or fairness to the body of shareholders as a whole. In my judgment, the test of fairness is whether the offer is fair to the offerees as a body and not whether it is fair to a particular shareholder in the peculiar circumstances of his own case . . . It would quite obviously be impossible, at any rate in most cases, for the offeror to know the circumstances of every individual shareholder and, therefore, to frame an offer which would necessarily be fair to every individual shareholder in the peculiar circumstances of his case.

The other general observation, which arises from the *Sussex Brick* case,[27] is that the fact that the applicants may be able to demonstrate that the scheme is open to criticism, or is capable of improvement, is not enough to discharge the onus of proof which lies upon them. Vaisey J said:

I agree that certain criticisms set out in the applicant's affidavit show that a good case could be made out for the formulation of a better scheme, of a fairer scheme, of one which would be more attractive to the shareholders if they could have understood the implications of the criticisms. I have no doubt at all that a better scheme could have been evolved, but is that enough? . . .

A scheme must be obviously unfair, patently unfair, unfair to the meanest intelligence. It cannot be said that no scheme can be effective to bind a dissenting shareholder unless it complies to the extent of 100 per cent with the highest possible standards of fairness, equity and reason . . .

---

27 *Re Sussex Brick Co Ltd* [1961] Ch 289n, [1960] 1 All ER 772n.

It must be affirmatively established that, notwithstanding the view of the majority, the scheme is unfair, and that is a different thing from saying that it must be established that the scheme is not a very fair one or not a fair one: a scheme has to be shown affirmatively, patently, obviously and convincingly to be unfair.

With those general observations, let me refer in a little more detail to some of the points which have been put forward on the part of the applicants. They have complained that the market price was substantially higher than 6s a share for a number of years [His Lordship cited prices ranging up to 9s 9d [49p]]; equally, as Mr Gurney-Champion said, in each of those years the lowest price for the shares was under 6s. But however that may be, it seems to me that the real point is, was 6s a fair price at the time when the offer was made, namely, in September 1965?

Then Mr Gurney-Champion submitted that it was unfair that he should be compelled to sell these shares at a loss, particularly having regard to the fact that the loss would be one which was not available for capital gains tax purposes, for the reason that he had bought the shares before 6 April 1965, and on that day the price of the shares was less than the purchase price. If I am right in thinking that the question of unfairness has to be judged without reference to the particular circumstances of the applicant, then it seems to me that this argument is irrelevant, and I am bound to reject it because I have already indicated the view that the particular circumstances of the applicant is not a matter with which the court is concerned. What the court is concerned with is the fairness of the offer as a whole . . .

Squeeze out provisions in s 979 may not be used by majority shareholders to expropriate a minority.

[13.11] Re Bugle Press Ltd [1961] Ch 270, [1960] 3 All ER 791 (Court of Appeal)

The £10,000 issued share capital of Bugle Press Ltd was held as to 4,500 £1 shares each by Shaw and Jackson ('the majority shareholders') and as to the remaining 1,000 shares by Treby. The majority shareholders formed a £100 company, Jackson & Shaw (Holdings) Ltd, which they caused to make an offer, addressed to the shareholders in Bugle Press Ltd, to purchase their holdings at £10 per share. After Shaw and Jackson had accepted this offer, and Treby had refused it on the ground that the price was too low, the offeror company gave Treby notice of its intention to purchase his holding compulsorily under CA 1948 s 209 [CA 2006 ss 979 and 986]. The Court of Appeal, affirming Buckley J, exercising the discretion conferred by the section, declared that the scheme was not binding on Treby.

LORD EVERSHED MR: Mr Instone [Counsel for the offeror company] freely accepts that the mechanism of the section has here been invoked by means of the incorporation of this holding company, Jackson & Shaw (Holdings) Ltd, especially for the purpose, and in order to enable the two persons, Shaw and Jackson, to expropriate the shares of their minority colleague, Treby. He says that although that is undoubtedly true, nevertheless, in the result, the case does fall within the strict language of the section and falling within it the consequences must follow. If that argument is right, it would enable by a device of this kind the 90% majority of the shareholders always to get rid of a minority shareholder whom they did not happen to like. And that, as a matter of principle, would appear to be contrary to a fundamental principle of our law that prima facie, if a man has a legal right which is an absolute right, then he can do with it or not do with it what he will . . .

[It] is, I think, relevant . . . to note that by the terms of the section itself one must have regard to what lies behind the invocation of the section . . . . [It] seems to me plain that what the section is directed to is a case where there is a scheme or contract for the acquisition of a company, its amalgamation, reorganisation or the like, and where the offeror is independent of the shareholders in the transferor company or at least independent of that part of fraction of them from which the 90% is to be derived. Even, therefore, though the present case does fall strictly within the terms of s 209, the fact that the offeror, the transferee company, is for all practical purposes entirely equivalent to the nine-tenths of the shareholders who have accepted the offer, makes it in my judgment a case in which, for the purposes of exercising the court's discretion, the circumstances are special . . . It is no doubt true to say that it is still for the minority shareholder to establish that the discretion should be exercised in the way he seeks. That, I think . . . follows from the language of the section which uses the formula which I have already more than once read 'unless on an application made by the dissenting shareholder the court thinks fit to order otherwise'. But if the minority shareholder does show, as he shows here, that the offeror and the 90% of the transferor company's sharehold-ers are the same, then as it seems to me he has, prima facie, shown that the court ought otherwise to order, since if it should not so do the result would be . . . that the section has been used not for the purpose of any scheme or contract properly so called or contemplated by the section but for the quite different purpose of enabling majority shareholders to expropriate or evict the minority; and that, as it seems to me, is something for the purposes of which, prima facie, the court ought not to allow the section to be invoked—unless at any rate it were shown that there was some good rea-son in the interests of the company for so doing, for example, that the minority shareholder was in some way acting in a manner destructive or highly damaging to the interests of the company from some motives entirely of his own . . .

HARMAN LJ delivered a concurring judgment.

DONOVAN LJ concurred.

> Notes

1. In most cases of substantial identity of interest, the accepting members will be 'associates' of the offeror (CA 2006, s 988), so their shares will not count in the calculation of the 90 per cent acceptance limit.

2. Another special circumstance (beyond substantial identity of interest, as illustrated in *Re Bugle Press Ltd*, above) is where insufficient information has been given to the members to enable them to evaluate the offer properly: *Fiske Nominees Ltd v Dwyka Diamond Ltd* [2002] EWHC 770 (Ch), [2002] 2 BCLC 123. Note that the court may take into account the extent to which the bidder has made the disclosure required by the Takeover Code and otherwise com-plied with it, even where the company is a private company and so not subject to the Code.

3. Technical failures can derail a squeeze out. In *Chez Nico (Restaurants) Ltd* [1992] BCLC 192, the squeeze out letters invited the remaining members to *offer* their shares for purchase, and were accordingly only invitations to treat. The court held that CA 1985 ss 428ff [CA 2006 ss 979 and 986] did not apply, since the 'bidders' had not made an offer.

Directors' role in a takeover

The duties imposed on directors apply with equal force during a takeover. The position of directors of the target company has been the subject of judicial consideration in a variety of contexts:

(i) It is well established that directors may not use their powers (eg to issue further shares[28]) for improper purposes, and this may include their use as a defensive tactic to thwart a take-over bid (see *Hogg v Cramphorn Ltd* [6.08] and the other cases cited above, pp 286 ff.[29] The use of *any* defensive tactics by directors without members' approval is forbidden by the Takeover Code, Rule 21.

(ii) In addition, the directors owe fiduciary duties to the company and cannot use their powers to further their own personal interests (see conflicts of duty and interest rules).

[28] Although the pre-emption rights in CA 2006 s 561 have reduced the incidence of such cases.

[29] Note that there is no legal principle suggesting that it is inevitably improper for directors to take action designed to defeat a takeover bid: *Cayne v Global Natural Resources plc* (12 August 1982, unreported); *Darvall v North Sydney Brick and Tile Co Ltd* (1989) 16 NSWLR 260, 235. But also see *Re a Company (No 008699 of 1985)* [13.12], and *Dawson International plc v Coats Patons plc* [13.13]).

(iii) On the other hand, the ruling in *Heron International Ltd v Lord Grade* [6.03] that the directors in that case owed fiduciary duties towards the company's *members* (as distinct from the company) cannot be taken to be of general application, since it turned upon the special article which gave the board control over the transfer of the voting shares.

(iv) In addition, in giving information relevant to the bid to their members—as they are required to do by the Takeover Code, for example—the directors must act in an honest way and not seek to mislead the members (*Gething v Kilner* [1972] 1 All ER 1166, [1972] 1 WLR 337).

(v) The directors must not exercise their powers in such a way as to prevent the members obtaining the best price for the shares (*Heron International Ltd v Lord Grade* [6.03]; *Re a Company (No 008699 of 1985)* [13.12]) although they are not under a positive duty to recommend and facilitate implementation of the highest offer (*Re a Company (No 008699 of 1985)* [13.12]; *Dawson International plc v Coats Patons plc* [13.13]).

The extracts which follow throw some light on the question, but each must be read in the light of the facts of the particular case.

[13.12] Re a Company (No 008699 of 1985) [1986] BCLC 383 (Chancery Division)

Rival take-over bids had been made for the shares in a private company, one (referred to in the judgment as 'the N bid') by a company controlled by the target company's own directors and another, higher, bid by a trade competitor. The chairman had sent a circular to the members urging them to accept the N bid and explaining, with reasons, why the higher bid could not succeed. In these proceedings it was claimed that the directors had been in breach of duty in not recommending the higher offer and in not taking steps to facilitate the chances of that offer being successful, and that these breaches of duty had been unfairly prejudicial to the company's shareholders so as to justify relief under CA 1985 s 459 [CA 2006 s 994].

> HOFFMANN J: I cannot accept the proposition that the board must inevitably be under a positive duty to recommend and take all steps within their power to facilitate whichever is the highest offer. In a case such as the present, where the directors propose to exercise their undoubted right as shareholders to accept the lower offer in respect of their own shares and, for understandable and fully disclosed reasons, hope in their personal capacities that a majority of other shareholders will accept it as well, it seems to me that it would be artificial to say that they were under a positive duty to advise shareholders to accept the highest offer. The fact that they would get more money by taking the higher offer is hardly something which needs to be pointed out. I do not think that fairness can require more of the directors than to give the shareholders sufficient information and advice to enable them to reach a properly informed decision and to refrain from giving misleading advice or exercising their fiduciary powers in a way which would prevent or inhibit shareholders from choosing to take the better price. Thus I doubt whether it would have been unfair if the directors, on receipt of the rival bid, had issued a statement saying something along the following lines:
>
> > Shareholders will have received both bids. We think that they contain sufficient information to enable shareholders to reach a properly informed decision and there is nothing which the board wish to add. As individual shareholders, your directors propose to accept the N bid and hope that other shareholders who have no contrary fiduciary duties will have sufficient family loyalty to do so also.

[His Lordship held, however, that the circular which the directors had in fact sent to the members was arguably misleading and that accordingly the petition should be allowed to proceed.]

[13.13] Dawson International plc v Coats Patons plc (1988) 4 BCC 305 (Court of Session (Outer House))

[The facts are immaterial.]

LORD CULLEN: At the outset I do not accept as a general proposition that a company can have no interest in the change of identity of its shareholders upon a take-over. It appears to me that there will be cases in which its agents, the directors, will see the take-over of its shares by a particular bidder as beneficial to the company. For example, it may provide the opportunity for integrating operations or obtaining additional resources. In other cases the directors will see a particular bid as not in the best interests of the company . . .

I next consider the proposition that in regard to the disposal of their shares on a take-over the directors were under a fiduciary duty to the shareholders and accordingly obliged to act in such a way as to further their best interests. It is well recognised that directors owe fiduciary duties to the company. Thus the directors have the duty of fiduciaries with respect to the property and funds of the company . . .

In contrast I see no good reason why it should be supposed that directors are, in general, under a fiduciary duty to shareholders, and in particular current shareholders with respect to the disposal of their shares in the most advantageous way. The directors are not normally the agents of the current shareholders. The cases and other authorities to which I was referred do not seem to me to establish any such fiduciary duty. It is contrary to statements in the standard textbooks . . . The absence of such a duty is demonstrated by the remarkable case of *Percival v Wright* [6.01]. I think it is important to emphasise that what I am being asked to consider is the alleged fiduciary duty of directors to current shareholders as sellers of their shares. This must not be confused with their duty to consider the interests of shareholders in the discharge of their duty to the company. What is in the interests of current shareholders as sellers of their shares may not necessarily coincide with what is in the interests of the company. The creation of parallel duties could lead to conflict. Directors have but one master, the company. Further it does not seem to me to be relevant to the present question to build an argument upon the rights, some of them very important rights, which shareholders have to take steps with a view to seeing that directors act in accordance with the constitution of the company and that their own interests are not unfairly prejudiced.

If on the other hand directors take it upon themselves to give advice to current shareholders, the cases cited to me show clearly that they have a duty to advise in good faith and not fraudulently, and not to mislead whether deliberately or carelessly. If they fail to do so the affected shareholders may have a remedy, including the recovery of what is truly the personal loss sustained by them as a result. However, these cases do not, in my view, demonstrate a pre-existing fiduciary duty to the shareholders but a potential liability arising out of their words or actions which can be based on ordinary principles of law. This, I may say, appears to be a more satisfactory way of expressing the position of directors in this context than by talking of a so-called secondary fiduciary duty to the shareholders.

Enforcement

The Panel is responsible for enforcing the rules contained in the Takeover Code. The Panel has power to order compensation in circumstances where a rule requiring the payment of money has been breached and to apply to the court to enforce its rulings and directions (CA 2006 ss 954 and 955). The Panel can also impose a range of sanctions upon persons who breach its rules, including reporting conduct to other regulatory authorities, such as the Financial Services Authority.

The DTI is responsible for enforcement of other provisions in the Act, including the new criminal offences created in connection with unlawful disclosure of information subject to secrecy provisions, bid documentation which fails to meet the standards required by the Takeovers Directive and where a company fails to notify relevant takeover authorities of its decision to opt-in or out of the breakthrough provisions.

14

RESCUE AND INSOLVENCY PROCEDURES

Introduction

When a company is in financial difficulty, various procedures exist to effect either the timely rescue of viable commercial enterprises or the orderly and competent management of the company's affairs before the company's existence is brought to an end (by a process of *liquidation* or *winding up*: the terms are used interchangeably).

That said, it is worth noting that there is no necessary connection between *insolvency* and *winding up*: a very large number of companies are wound up whose balance sheets are in healthy surplus. A solvent company may be wound up because the business opportunity the company was formed to exploit has come to an end, or the members may wish to retire or reinvest their capital in other ventures, or there may be internal disputes. In this chapter, however, we concentrate on liquidations occasioned by insolvency.

With companies in difficulty, the important procedures include:

(i) voluntary arrangements (see below, pp 630 ff);

(ii) administration (see below, pp 631 ff);

(iii) administrative receiverships (see below, pp 637 ff); and

(iv) liquidations (including voluntary liquidations by the members[1] or creditors, and court-ordered liquidations) (see below, pp 647 ff).

Each is considered in this chapter. In each case, the governance of the company is assumed by a qualified insolvency practitioner or (in compulsory liquidations, at least at the outset) an official receiver.[2] The role of the directors is, at least temporarily, displaced.

If the rescue procedure envisaged by the voluntary arrangement or administration is successful, or if the company survives receivership, then the company will continue in business. If not, then the company is likely to be put into liquidation. This is a process by which the company's business is wound up, its contracts completed, transferred or brought to an end, and its assets and undertaking realised for the benefit of its creditors and (if there is a surplus of assets over liabilities) its members.[3] Finally, the company must be removed from the register of companies and dissolved.[4]

---

[1] This procedure is only available to solvent companies.

[2] The official receiver attached to the court automatically becomes the company's liquidator in a court-ordered (compulsory) liquidation (see below p 647), but the creditors, the Secretary of State or the official receiver himself can seek his replacement by an insolvency practitioner (IA 1986 ss 136 and 137).

[3] Unless the articles provide otherwise, as with charitable companies.

[4] There is statutory provision for restoration of companies to the register, if dissolution is later found to have been premature: see below, p 680.

Insolvency and rescue

There are many ways of defining insolvency. For present purposes it is sufficient to note three. These serve to illustrate that when a company is in financial difficulty a judgement needs to be made about the likelihood of successful rescue, or alternatively the advisability of efficient liquidation.

'Commercial' insolvency

A company may be described as insolvent if it is unable to pay its debts as they fall due. In other words, even though its overall asset position may not be in deficit, it has cash-flow problems which prevent it from paying its way. This is the most common reason for the making of a compulsory winding-up order (IA 1986 s 122(1)(f)). There is a statutory definition of this type of insolvency (and also certain rules and presumptions relating to proof) in IA 1986 s 123(1).

'Balance-sheet' insolvency

A company may also be said to be insolvent if the value of its assets is less than the amount of its liabilities. While the company is a going concern, an assessment of insolvency in this sense will depend upon the business judgment of those concerned. For this purpose it is proper to take account of the company's contingent and prospective liabilities (see IA 1986 s 123(2)), although the value of these will necessarily be difficult to estimate. A company which is insolvent in balance-sheet terms will not necessarily be commercially insolvent: it may, for instance, have a heavy potential liability in tort and yet for the time being have a perfectly satisfactory cash flow. And, of course, it may happen that if its assets are realised there is in fact a surplus at the end of the day.

'Ultimate' insolvency

This definition of insolvency is based on the final position when the company's assets are sold up, eg by a liquidator, and there is not sufficient realised to pay the creditors in full. This unhappy result may occur even though the company has previously seemed solvent under definitions (1) and (2), for assets which are quite reasonably valued highly on a historic cost or going concern basis may fetch very little in a forced sale.

Statutory framework

The principal statute governing the procedures discussed in this chapter is the Insolvency Act 1986 (IA 1986). This Act is a consolidation of IA 1985 and those parts of CA 1985 which dealt with receivership and winding up. The insolvency legislation of 1985 introduced comprehensive reforms to both the law of corporate insolvency and that of individual bankruptcy—the first major overhaul of either subject for over a hundred years—based largely on the report of the Cork Committee (*Report of the Review Committee on Insolvency Law and Practice* (Cmnd 8558, 1982)). IA 1986 is supplemented by the Insolvency Rules 1986 (SI 1986/1925 as amended), which specify the relevant procedural rules and requirements.

The IA 1986 has been amended on various occasions, most significantly by:

(i) Insolvency Act 2000 (IA 2000), which introduced new rules on company voluntary arrangements, allowing for a moratorium;

(ii) Enterprise Act 2002 (EA 2002), which provided a new regime for administration, restricted the right to appoint administrative receivers, and substantially changed the rules for distribution of company assets on liquidation.

Company voluntary arrangements (CVAs)

One of the most useful rescue mechanisms for a distressed company is the ability to make binding compromises or arrangements with all its creditors. The IA 1986 now provides two mechanisms for this.[5] The first is an older, informal and relatively private procedure, open to all companies, introduced by IA 1986, Part I, ss 1–7, under which a company may seek to achieve an accommodation with its creditors under the supervision of a 'nominee', being a qualified insolvency practitioner. The arrangement is proposed by the company's directors (or its liquidator or administrator), reported to the court (but court approval is not necessary), and, if then approved by the requisite majority (over 75%) of unsecured creditors and members at separate single meetings, is binding on the dissenting minorities.

Some protection of minorities is provided by IA 1986 s 6, which allows the majority approvals to be challenged in court by anyone entitled to vote in the meetings, or by the nominee or the liquidator or administrator, on the ground that the scheme is unfairly prejudicial or that there is some material process irregularity affecting either of the meetings.

Although this procedure was a progressive one, enabling companies to continue trading while ensuring creditors received at least part of their debt, it got off to a slow start: only 21 arrangements were recorded in the first year of its operation and, although the number gradually increased, it has never reached more than a few hundred per annum, in contrast with the voluntary arrangement procedure for individuals, which is used in nearly a quarter of all personal insolvency cases. There are two main reasons for this: first, that a CVA cannot be made binding on secured or preferential creditors[6] without their consent; and, secondly, that (contrary to the Cork Committee's recommendation) the Act originally contained no provision for a moratorium to be put in place while the quite lengthy formalities are gone through: thus one impatient creditor can thwart the whole scheme.

A way round this second difficulty was, eventually, found, and a second option was introduced allowing for CVAs with a moratorium (IA 1986, Sch A1). But this was achieved only at the cost of making the whole procedure more elaborate, public and expensive. In addition, the option is only available to 'eligible companies' (primarily small private companies). The procedure allows for an automatic 28-day moratorium to come into force as soon as the documents containing a proposal for a CVA are filed in court. During this period (which may be extended for up to a further two months), the company may not be wound up and no steps may be taken, at least without the leave of the court, to enforce security over the company's property[7] or to take proceedings against it. The success of the much sought-after provision remains unclear, however. The advantages of the moratorium may be outweighed by the relative complexity (and cost) in terms of the companies which are eligible, the role of the nominee, the restrictions on directors during the moratorium, and the possible liabilities of directors and the nominee for actions taken during the moratorium. In addition, even the advantages of the procedure pale in significance now that the Enterprise Act 2002 permits the appointment of administrators out of court (with their own associated moratorium provisions) (see below, pp 631ff).

On the other hand, the major attraction of CVAs, in either form, is that the directors remain in post, they retain control over the choice of the nominee, and the nominee is not required to make a report of unfitness to the Insolvency Service under the CDDA 1986.

---

[5] Theoretically a scheme of arrangement, under CA 2006 s 895 provides a further alternative, but the process is generally considered too complex, time-consuming and expensive: see p 609 above.

[6] See IA 1986 s 175 and Sch 6. See below at p 647.

[7] And it is not possible for a floating charge holder to specify that obtaining or preparing for a moratorium crystallises the floating charge: IA 1986, Sch A1, para 43.

The under-use of these CVA procedures must be a source of disappointment, particularly since much of the thrust of the reforms proposed by the Cork Committee was the fostering and promotion of a 'rescue culture' for failed (or failing) businesses: whereas the liquidation of a company frequently involves the break up of its assets, the destruction of its goodwill and business connections, and the displacement of its employees, less drastic (and less costly) solutions can often be found if steps are taken in time to bring the affairs of the company under control with a view to ensuring the survival, if not of the entire concern, at least of the viable parts of it.

Administration

A statutory administration procedure has been in operation since the IA 1986 was introduced, but the EA 2002 made substantial amendments, and the new rules are now found in IA 1986 s 8 and Sch B1.[8] The amendments introduced fundamental changes in the purpose, appointment and powers of administrators, although the procedure remains open only to companies that are, or are likely to become, insolvent.

Purpose of administration

Administration, after EA 2002, is explicitly designed to rescue an insolvent company, saving it from liquidation if at all possible. The amended IA 1986, Sch B1, para 3(1), specifies a hierarchy of purposes: the administrator must perform his[9] functions with the objective of:

(i) rescuing the company as a going concern;

(ii) achieving a better result for the company's creditors as a whole than would be likely if the company were wound up; or

(iii) realising property in order to make a distribution to one or more secured or preferential creditors.

The administrator must pursue (i) rather than (ii) unless it is not reasonably practicable to pursue (i), or unless (ii) would achieve a better result for the company's creditors as a whole. Moreover, the administrator may only pursue (iii) if it is not reasonably practicable to achieve the other two objectives *and* the goal is pursued in such a way that it will not unnecessarily harm the interests of the creditors of the company as a whole. In addition, the administrator must act in the interests of the creditors as a whole (IA 1986, Sch B1, para 3(2)), and as quickly and efficiently as reasonably practicable (para 4).

Administration orders reflect the philosophical premise, held since the findings of the Cork Committee, that appointing a receiver and manager to a company (as is commonly done by floating charge holders) offered outstanding benefits to the commercial community and public as a whole, advancing the possibility of restoring an ailing enterprise to profitability, or disposing of a business as a going concern.[10] The administration procedure attempts to mirror this, allowing an ailing company an alternative to liquidation where there is a chance that it may be rehabilitated. In the Light of the EA 2002 changes, administration has now largely replaced receiverships, at least for floating change holders, and has the merit of being

---

[8] The 'old' provisions on administration contained in the IA 1986, Part II are retained and apply to special categories of companies (water companies, railway companies, air traffic services companies, public-private partnership companies and building societies). They are not discussed here.

[9] 'He', 'his', 'him', etc are used throughout this chapter for brevity of expression, notwithstanding that the insolvency practitioners occupying the formal roles discussed here may, of course, be women rather than men.

[10] Report of Review Committee on Insolvency Law and Practice (1982, Cmnd 8558, para 495).

conducted in the interest of all concerned rather than only the secured creditor. The process is associated with a moratorium (Sch B1, para 43), so it also provides the company with breathing space, free from creditors' claims, where the administrator can determine the future of the company even where liquidation is inevitable, so that its assets can be realised to better advantage—ideally, by selling the business as a going concern.

Appointment of the administrator

An administrator may be appointed by the court (in response to or application by the company itself, or its directors, or a creditor) or out of court, by the holder of a floating charge relating to the whole or substantially the whole of the company's property, by the company itself or by the company's directors. An out of court appointment must be reported to the court. In each case, the company must be unable to pay its debts,[11] or likely to become unable to do so.

Pre-conditions for a court order for administration: 'likely' and 'reasonably likely'

For an administration order to be made by the court, the court must be satisfied that the company 'is or is likely to become' unable to pay its debts (Sch B1, para 11(a)), and that the administration order 'is reasonably likely' to achieve the purpose of the administration (Sch B1, para 11(b)). The next case predates EA 2002, and the previous test was that the order be 'likely to achieve' the set purpose. The courts interpreted this as a requirement that there be 'a real prospect' (see below). It is not clear whether this remains the test, or whether there should be some lower threshold in recognition of Parliament's intention that administration be more readily available, especially as the administrator who cannot achieve the set purpose may always convert the administration into a creditors' voluntary winding up.

Even if this threshold is met, the court has a discretion as to whether to make the order, and will not do so where, weighing all the circumstances, this seems inappropriate (see below).

[14.01] Re Harris Simons Construction Ltd [1989] 1 WLR 368, [1989] BCLC 202 (Chancery Division)

[The facts appear from the judgment.]

HOFFMANN J: The company carries on business as builders. Over the past four years there has been a spectacular increase in turnover, from £830,000 in the year to April 1985 to £17m in the year to April 1987 and £27m in the year to April 1988. Almost all of this increased turnover has come from one client, a property developer called Berkley House plc, with which the directors had a close relationship. Recently the relationship has turned sour. There are disputes over a number of contracts and Berkley House has purported to dismiss the company and require its employees to leave their sites. It is also withholding sums running into several million pounds which the company says are due and in respect of which Berkley House says it has cross-claims. The effect on the company's cash flow has been that it is unable to pay its debts as they fall due and several writs and a statutory demand have been served. If no administration order is made, the company cannot carry on trading. There is no debentureholder who can be invited to appoint a receiver. The company will have to go into liquidation more or less immediately. The workforce will have to be dismissed and the contracts and work in progress will become a tangle of disputes and probably litigation. The report of the proposed administrator says that in those circumstances it would be extremely difficult to sell any part of the business.

---

[11] For appointments by a floating charge holder, the floating charge must simply be enforceable.

If an administration order is made, the company will have what is usually called a breathing space but unless some source of funding can be found, will continue to have serious respiratory problems with its cash flow. It has however been able to negotiate at least an armistice with Berkley House by which the latter will, conditionally upon an administration order being made, provide sufficient funding to enable the company to complete four current contracts on condition that it quietly removes itself from the other sites in dispute. It is hoped that the four remaining contracts will produce a profit and that it may thereby be possible to stabilise and preserve a business which can either survive or be sold to a third party. In the meanwhile, it may be possible to arrive at a negotiated settlement of the underlying dispute with Berkley House. The administration order is therefore proposed to achieve two of the purposes specified in section 8(3) of the Act [IA 1986, but prior to the EA 2002 amendments]: '(a) the survival of the company, and the whole or any part of its undertaking, as a going concern;' and '(d) a more advantageous realisation of the company's assets than would be effected on a winding up' . . .

Section 8(1) gives the court jurisdiction to make an administration order if it '(a) is satisfied that a company is or is likely to become unable to pay its debts' and it '(b) considers that the making of an order . . . would be likely to achieve' one or more of the purposes specified in section 8(3). I am satisfied on the evidence that the company is unable to pay its debts. Whether the order would be likely to achieve one of the specified objects is not so easy to answer. When the statute says that I must consider it likely, what degree of probability does this involve? In *Re Consumer and Industrial Press Ltd*,[12] Peter Gibson J said:

> As I read section 8 the court must be satisfied on the evidence put before it that at least one of the purposes in section 8(3) is likely to be achieved if it is to make an administration order. That does not mean that it is merely possible that such purpose will be achieved; the evidence must go further than that to enable the court to hold that the purpose in question will more probably than not be achieved.

He therefore required that on a scale of probability of 0 (impossibility) to 1 (absolute certainty) the likelihood of success should be more than 0.5. I naturally hesitate to disagree with Peter Gibson J, particularly since he had the benefit of adversarial argument. But this is a new statute on which the judges of the Companies Court are still feeling their way to a settled practice and I therefore think I should say that in my view he set the standard of probability too high. My reasons are as follows. First, 'likely' connotes probability but the particular degree of probability intended must be gathered from qualifying words (very likely, quite likely, more likely than not) or context. It cannot be a misuse of language to say that something is likely without intending to suggest that the probability of its happening exceeds 0.5, as in 'I think that the favourite, Golden Spurs at 5–1, is likely to win the Derby'. Secondly, the section requires the court to be 'satisfied' of the company's actual or likely insolvency but only to 'consider' that the order would be likely to achieve one of the stated purposes. There must have been a reason for this change of language and I think it was to indicate that a lower threshold of persuasion was needed in the latter case than the former. . . . Thirdly, some of the stated purposes are mutually exclusive and the probability of any one of them being achieved may be less than 0.5 but the probability of one or other of them being achieved may be more than 0.5. I doubt whether Parliament intended the courts to embark on such calculations of cumulative probabilities. Fourthly, as Peter Gibson J said, section 8(1) only sets out the conditions to be satisfied before the court has jurisdiction. It still retains a discretion as to whether or not to make the order. It is therefore not unlikely that the legislature intended to set a modest threshold of probability to found jurisdiction and to rely on the court's discretion not to make orders in cases in which, weighing all the circumstances, it seemed inappropriate to do so. Fifthly, the Report of the Review Committee on Insolvency Law and Practice (1982), (Cmnd 8558), para 508, which recommended the introduction of administratorship, said that the new procedure was likely to be beneficial only in

[12] [1988] BCLC 177, 178.

cases where there is a business of sufficient substance to justify the expense of an administration, and where there is a real prospect of returning profitability or selling as a going concern.

Elsewhere the report speaks of an order being made if there is a 'reasonable possibility' of a scheme of reconstruction. I think that this kind of phraseology was intended to be reflected in the statutory phrase 'considers that [it] would be likely' in section 8(1)(b).

For my part, therefore, I would hold that the requirements of section 8(1)(b) are satisfied if the court considers that there is a real prospect that one or more of the stated purposes may be achieved. It may be said that phrases like 'real prospect' lack precision compared with 0.5 on the scale of probability. But the courts are used to dealing in other contexts with such indications of the degrees of persuasion they must feel. 'Prima facie case' and 'good arguable case' are well known examples. Such phrases are like tempo markings in music; although there is inevitably a degree of subjectivity in the way they are interpreted, they are nevertheless meaningful and useful.

On the facts as they appear from the evidence before me, I think there is a real prospect that an administration order, coupled with the agreement with Berkley House, will enable the whole or part of the company's undertaking to survive or at least enable the administrator to effect a more advantageous realisation of the assets than would be effected in a winding up. Certainly the prospects for the company, its employees and creditors look bleak if no administration order is made and there has to be a winding up. Consequently, although I cannot say that it is more probable than not that one of the specified purposes will be achieved, I accept the opinion of the prospective administrator that 'the making of an administration order offers the best prospect for preserving the company's future and maximising the realisation of the company's assets for the benefit of its creditors.' I therefore make the order.

➤ **Note**

Other judges, including Peter Gibson J, have since followed the views expressed in this case. In *Re AA Mutual International Insurance Co Ltd* [2004] EWHC 2430, Ch, [2005] 2 BCLC 8, Lewison J held that the test under the reformed provisions, IA 1986, Sch B1, para 11 (a) was 'more probable than not', while for para 11(b) it was a 'real prospect' (as in [14.01]).

Powers and duties of the administrator

The first task of the administrator is to formulate a set of proposals for the company which must, within eight weeks, be submitted to the registrar and to the company's unsecured creditors, for approval within ten weeks by a simple majority in value of creditors present and voting in person or by proxy. If the creditors approve the proposals, the administrator must act accordingly. If they fail to approve them, the court may make any order it thinks fit, including terminating the administrator's appointment (Sch B1, para 55).

In the period between the appointment of the administrator and submission of proposals to the creditors' meeting, the administrator may exercise all of the exceptionally wide powers conferred by Sch B1 para 59 and Sch 1 (conferred by Sch B1, para 60). These include the power to sell the company's property (including the power to sell property subject to a floating charge, and, with court approval, property subject to any other charge[13]). Para 59(1) provides that the administrator '. . . may do anything necessary or expedient for the management of the affairs, business and property of the company'. The administrator can act without the approval of the creditors, or the court, if he considers this is in the best interests of the creditors: *Re Transbus International Ltd* [2004] EWHC 932, Ch, [2004] 2 All ER 911; *Re Osmosis Group Ltd* [1999] 2 BCLC 329. The administrator is deemed to be an agent of the company (para 69).

---

[13] Sch B1, paras 70 and 71, although the proceeds must be deployed according to the statutory priorities accorded to such chargees.

The administrator also has the benefit of the statutory moratorium (Sch B1, para 43). This prevents a winding up,[14] and prevents anyone taking action against the company, or any creditors from enforcing security, putting in execution, distraining on the company's goods, repossessing goods sold under hire-purchase, conditional sales, chattel-leasing or retention of title agreements, except, in every case, with the consent of the administrator or the permission of the court. The Court of Appeal has given guidance on exercising security rights against companies in administration: re *Atlantic Computer Systems plc (No 1)* [1992] Ch 505, 541–4.

Duties owed by the administrator to the company

[14.02] Re Charnley Davies Ltd (No 2) [1990] BCLC 760 (Chancery Division)

[The facts are immaterial.]

MILLETT J: It was common ground that an administrator owes a duty to a company over which he is appointed to take reasonable steps to obtain a proper price for its assets. That is an obligation which the law imposes on anyone with a power, whether contractual or statutory, to sell property which does not belong to him. A mortgagee is bound to have regard to the interests of the mortgagor, but he is entitled to give priority to his own interests, and may insist on an immediate sale whether or not that is calculated to realise the best price; he must 'take reasonable care to obtain the true value of the property at the moment he chooses to sell it': see *Cuckmere Brick Co Ltd v Mutual Finance Ltd*.[15] An administrator, by contrast, like a liquidator, has no interest of his own to which he may give priority, and must take reasonable care in choosing the time at which to sell the property. His duty is 'to take reasonable care to obtain the best price that the circumstances permit': see *Standard Chartered Bank Ltd v Walker*.[16]

It is to be observed that it is not an absolute duty to obtain the best price that circumstances permit, but only to take reasonable care to do so; and in my judgment that means the best price that circumstances *as he reasonably perceives them to be* permit. He is not to be made liable because his perception is wrong, unless it is unreasonable.

An administrator must be a professional insolvency practitioner. A complaint that he has failed to take reasonable care in the sale of the company's assets is, therefore, a complaint of professional negligence and in my judgment the established principles applicable to cases of professional negligence are equally applicable in such a case. It follows that the administrator is to be judged, not by the standards of the most meticulous and conscientious member of his profession, but by those of an ordinary, skilled practitioner. In order to succeed the claimant must establish that the administrator has made an error which a reasonably skilled and careful insolvency practitioner would not have made . . .

No duty owed by the administrator to creditors.

[14.03] Kyrris v. Oldham [2004] BCC 111 (Court of Appeal)

[The facts are immaterial.]

JONATHAN PARKER LJ: 141 In my judgment it matters not whether one adopts the approach of the House of Lords in *Caparo Industries plc v Dickman* [[1990] 2 AC 605, HL], or the 'assumption of responsibility' approach which it adopted in *Henderson v Merrett Syndicates* [[1995] 2 AC 145, HL]:

---

14 Except on a public interest petition by the Secretary of Sate or the FSA (Sch B1, para 42).
15 [1971] Ch 949, [1971] 2 All ER 633. [See, however, below, pp 641ff.]
16 [1982] 3 All ER 938, [1982] 1 WLR 1410.

on either approach the result is the same, namely that, absent some special relationship, an administrator appointed under the 1986 Act owes no general common law duty of care to unsecured creditors in relation to his conduct of the administration.

142 In paras 31–34 of his judgment in *Peskin v Anderson* [[2001] BCC 87C, CA], Mummery LJ said this:

'31 . . . [Counsel for the directors] accepted that the fiduciary duties owed by the directors to the company do not necessarily preclude, in special circumstances, the coexistence of additional duties owed by the directors to the shareholders. In such cases individual shareholders may bring a direct action, as distinct from a derivative action, against the directors for breach of fiduciary duty.

32. A duality of duties may exist. In *Stein v Blake* [1998] BCC 316 at pp 318 and 320 Millett LJ recognised that there may be special circumstances in which a fiduciary duty is owed by a director to a shareholder personally and in which breach of such a duty has caused loss to him directly (eg by being induced by a director to part with his shares in the company at an undervalue), as distinct from loss sustained by him by a diminution in the value of his shares (eg by reason of the misappropriation by a director of the company's assets), for which he (as distinct from the company) would not have a cause of action against the director personally.

33. The fiduciary duties owed to the company arise from the legal relationship between the directors and the company directed and controlled by them. The fiduciary duties owed to the shareholders do not arise from that legal relationship. They are dependent on establishing a special factual relationship between the directors and the shareholders in the particular case. Events may take place which bring the directors of the company into direct and close contact with the shareholders in a manner capable of generating fiduciary obligations, such as a duty of disclosure of material facts to the shareholders, or an obligation to use confidential information and valuable commercial and financial opportunities, which have been acquired by the directors in that office, for the benefit of the shareholders, and not to prefer and promote their own interests at the expense of the shareholders.

34. These duties may arise in special circumstances which replicate the salient features of well established categories of fiduciary relationships. Fiduciary relationships, such as agency, involve duties of trust, confidence and loyalty. Those duties are, in general, attracted by and attached to a person who undertakes, or who, depending on all the circumstances, is treated as having assumed, responsibility to act on behalf of, or for the benefit of, another person. That other person may have entrusted or, depending on all the circumstances, may be treated as having entrusted, the care of his property, affairs, transactions or interests to him. There are, for example, instances of the directors of a company making direct approaches to, and dealing with, the shareholders in relation to a specific transaction and holding themselves out as agents for them in connection with the acquisition or disposal of shares; or making material representations to them; or failing to make material disclosure to them of insider information in the context of negotiations for a take-over of the company's business; or supplying to them specific information and advice on which they have relied. These events are capable of constituting special circumstances and of generating fiduciary obligations, especially in those cases in which the directors, for their own benefit, seek to use their position and special inside knowledge acquired by them to take improper or unfair advantage of the shareholders.'

143 It has not been suggested (nor could it be, in my judgment) that there is any relevant distinction for present purposes between a fiduciary duty and a common law duty of care. Further, I accept Miss Hilliard's submission that the position of an administrator appointed under the 1986 Act vis-à-vis creditors is directly analogous to that of a director vis-a-vis shareholders.

144 Section 8(2) of the 1986 Act defines an administration order as: '. . . an order directing that, during the period for which the order is in force, the affairs, business and property of the company shall be managed by a person ("the administrator") appointed for the purpose by the court.'

145 Section 14(1) of the 1986 Act confers on an administrator a number of specific powers of management set out in Sch 1, including (in para 14) a power to carry on the business of the company, together with a general power: '. . . to do all such things as may be necessary for the management of the affairs, business and property of the company'.

146 Given the nature and scope of an administrator's powers and duties, I can for my part see no basis for concluding that an administrator owes a duty of care to creditors in circumstances where a director would not owe such a duty to shareholders. In each case the relevant duties are, absent special circumstances, owed exclusively to the company.

147 It is also material, in my judgment, to consider the nature of the remedy provided by s 212 of the 1986 Act. Section 212(3) provides that on an application under the section the court may compel an administrator (among others):

(a) to repay, restore or account for the money or property or any part of it, with interest at such rate as the court thinks just, or

(b) to contribute such sum to the company's assets by way of compensation in respect of the misfeasance or breach of fiduciary or other duty as the court thinks just.'

148 To my mind, this is a further indication that, absent some special relationship of the kind described by Mummery LJ in *Peskin v Anderson*, an administrator owes no general duty to creditors.

Effect of appointment on directors

The appointment of an administrator leaves the directors with very limited authority (though they retain their statuory responsibilities). IA 1986, Sch B1, para 64 provides that any power of the company or its officers that could be exercised in such a way as to interfere with the exercise by the administrator of his powers is not exercisable except with the consent of the administrator.

Termination of administration

Administration ends automatically after one year, unless the term is extended by consent of the creditors or order of the court (Sch B1, para 76). Otherwise it can be terminated by the administrator (unilaterally or under directions from a creditors' meeting), or by a creditor on application to the court (Sch B1, paras 79–83).

Priority of expenses of administration

The expenses of an administration have priority over a debt secured by a floating charge (Sch B1, para 99). But debts or liabilities arising out of contracts entered into by the administrator (including contracts of employment adopted by the administrator so far as they relate to post-adoption work) have priority over the administrator's own remuneration and expenses ('super-priority') (Sch B1, para 99(3) and (4)).

Receivership and administrative receivership

Receivership generally

Any secured creditor may enforce his security by the appointment of a receiver. So, for example, if a company has given a creditor a fixed charge over its book-debts, the appointment of a receiver will enable the debts to be collected and applied in satisfaction of the company's obligation. This may always be done by order of the court; but in practice the instrument by which the security is created will invariably confer on the holder of the security a power to appoint a receiver without recourse to the court. Receiverships (and administrative receiverships, to the extent that they still exist) are thus insolvency procedures operating largely without the involvement of the courts.

Until the reforming insolvency legislation of 1985–86, the subject of receivership was largely a matter for the common law. There are now a number of provisions in IA 1986, Pt III which apply generally to receiverships: for example, there is a prohibition on the appointment of a body corporate or an undischarged bankrupt (ss 30–31); there must be notification on the company's stationery of the appointment of a receiver (s 39); and it is declared that normally a receiver is personally liable on any contracts he makes, but subject to a right of indemnity out of the assets under his control (ss 37(1), 44).

A receiver appointed by the court is an officer of the court and accountable to it, and is not subject to direction or to dictation by the creditor in whose interests he has been appointed. A receiver appointed independently may in theory be the agent either of the company or of the creditor who appointed him: in practice, he is always expressly made the former (and this is now a statutory rule in the case of an *administrative receiver* (see below)). This agency (whether contractual or statutory) enables the receiver to enter into contracts in the company's name, employ staff and so on, but it ceases if the company goes into liquidation. From then on he continues to be competent to realise the company's assets for the purpose of discharging the secured debt, and to take any necessary steps to protect and preserve those assets, but he cannot any longer incur credit in the company's name or cause it to incur executory obligations.

The primary duty of a receiver is to get in and, as necessary, realise sufficient of the company's assets and undertaking to satisfy the outstanding debt of the creditor on whose behalf he has been appointed. He does not owe duties of a fiduciary nature (in the fullest sense) to the company or the other creditors, although he may be liable to them if he uses his powers for an improper purpose *(Downsview Nominees Ltd v First City Corpn Ltd* **[14.05]**). He is under an obligation to keep and produce to the company proper accounts *(Smiths Ltd v Middleton* [1979] 3 All ER 842). In these respects his position may be contrasted with that of an administrator or a liquidator. A receiver's duties are owed first and foremost to the security-holder who has appointed him, and the interests of the company, its trade creditors and any other person concerned can legitimately be subordinated to those of the security-holder. An administrator or liquidator, however, is required to deal with the company's assets for the benefit of *all* the interested parties.

It is very common for an appointment to be made, not simply of a receiver, but of a *receiver and manager*—a twin office under which the appointee is empowered to manage the business and not just get in and sell off its assets. This is done in the hope either that the company may be able to trade its way back into profitability or, at the very least, that its business can be sold as a going concern rather than on a break-up basis and in that way fetch more. Of course, a power to manage 'the business' of a company can be given to a receiver only if the charge is over the whole of the company's undertaking—which means that it must be a floating charge.

The appointment of a receiver and manager puts an end to the directors' powers to manage the business, though they will revert once he has discharged his functions, so long as the business or part of it has survived. But the directors do retain their *office*, and their other powers and functions: in *Newhart Developments v Co-operative Commercial Bank* [1978] QB 814, [1978] 2 All ER 896 it was held that they had power to issue a writ claiming damages for breach of contract against the very creditor who had appointed the receiver.[17] Likewise, the directors have the power to take proceedings to challenge the validity of the receiver's

---

[17] In *Tudor Grange Holdings Ltd v Citibank NA* [1992] Ch 53, [1991] 4 All ER 1 Browne-Wilkinson V-C expressed doubts whether the *Newhart* case was rightly decided. He ruled that in any event the directors could not sue on a cause of action which it was competent for the receiver to bring, and later cases have made it plain that any action brought by the directors must be funded from sources other than the assets under the receiver's control.

appointment, to oppose a petition to wind up the company, or to cause the company to sue the receiver for breach of duty.

A company which is in receivership may be put into liquidation. The liquidator has then, in principle, to allow the receiver to continue to act until the claims of his debenture holders or chargee are met out of the security. Conversely, a receiver may be appointed after a company has gone into liquidation; and, as we have seen, the fact of liquidation is itself effective to crystallise a floating charge.

Where a receiver is appointed to enforce a floating charge, the claims of certain preferential creditors (eg employees for certain claims) must be paid ahead of the debenture holder: IA 1986 s 40. In addition, a certain proportion must be set aside for the unsecured creditors: IA 1986 s 176A.

Administrative receivership

The main innovation made by the insolvency legislation of 1985–86 was the introduction of a separate category of receiver, the *administrative receiver*. Although this was a major innovation at the time, the reforms of the Enterprise Act 2002 signal the end for most administrative receiverships (see below).

An administrative receiver is defined by IA 1986 s 29(2): essentially, he is a receiver and manager of the whole, or substantially the whole, of the property of a company appointed by or on behalf of the holders of a debenture of the company secured by a floating charge.[18] IA 1986 stipulates that an administrative receiver must be a qualified insolvency practitioner (ss 45(2), 388–389), and confers on him a number of statutory powers (ss 42–43, and Sch 1). It also declares that he is deemed to be the company's agent, unless the company is in liquidation (s 44); this confirms as a rule of law what was already the standard practice under the usual terms of floating charge debentures before the Act.[19] The Act requires the directors to provide an administrative receiver with information about the company by submitting to him a statement of affairs (s 47), but in turn requires the administrative receiver to keep the company's unsecured creditors informed about the progress of the receivership (s 48). This report must also be sent to secured creditors and to the registrar at Companies House.

Enterprise Act 2002 reforms—limited scope for administrative receiverships

After the reforms of EA 2000, it is not now possible to appoint an administrative receiver under a floating charge created on or after 15 September 2003 (IA 1986 s 72A; SI 2003/2095), except in special cases specified in IA 1986 ss 72B-72H.[20] Instead, the chargee has the right to appoint an administrator (IA 1986, Sch B1, para 14). Recall that an administrator is an officer of the court (Sch B1, para 5) who performs his functions in the interests of the company's creditors as a whole (Sch B1, para 3(2)).

Chargees with floating charges created before 15 September 2003 retain the right to appoint an administrative receiver, but also have the option to appoint an administrator. A chargee whose floating charge does not cover the whole or substantially the whole of the company's assets can still appoint a receiver, who will by definition not be an administrative receiver, but cannot appoint an administrator.[21] An administrator, administrative receiver or receiver cannot be appointed unless the charge is enforceable.

---

[18] Or a person who would be such a receiver but for the fact that there is someone else already in office as the receiver of part of the company's property under a prior-ranking charge.

[19] The practice was adopted to avoid the receiver being the agent of the chargee, and thus exposing the chargee to the onerous duties of a mortgagee in possession.

[20] The exceptions relate to large-scale marketable loans, projects with step-in rights, financial market charges, registered social landlords, and some utility companies.

[21] But note *Re Croftbell Ltd* [1990] BCLC 844, where a receiver appointed under a charge over 'the whole of [the company's] undertaking and all its property and assets' was held to be an administrative receiver notwithstanding that, at the time of appointment, the company's only asset (other than a small debt owed by the parent company) would not come into the receiver's control because it was separately charged to a third party.

These EA 2002 reforms, largely doing away with administrative receivership, were intended to favour the rescue culture. An administrative receiver is entitled to put the secured creditor's interests first, and a suspicion prevailed that the interests of unsecured creditors and the company itself were not always best served; by contrast, an administrator must manage the company's affairs for the benefit of everybody concerned.

Powers of management—company contracts

An administrative receiver may cause the company to repudiate any contracts entered into before he was appointed. The only remedy the injured party will have is a claim against the company for breach of contract. If the claim sounds in damages only, then the company is unlikely to be able to pay once the claims of the secured creditor are met (*Airlines Airspares Ltd v Handley Page Ltd* [1970] Ch 193). If, on the other hand, the contract is one for which the court will award specific performance or an injunction, then the injured party is protected (*Freevale Ltd v Metrostores (Holdings) Ltd* [1984] Ch 199).

An administrative receiver is personally liable on any new contract entered into in the performance of his functions, except insofar as the contract otherwise provides (IA 1986 s 44(1)(b)). So far as personal liability is assumed, the administrative receiver is entitled to an indemnity out of the assets of the company (IA 1986 s 44(1)(c)). In practice, he will also have an indemnity from the chargee. In the majority of cases, however, his aim will be to expressly or impliedly exclude all personal liability.

Employment contracts are a special class. Since the administrative receiver is the company's agent, the appointment does not automatically terminate these contracts. If the administrative receiver finds that the employees cannot be retained, he may dismiss them, and this will almost certainly not be unfair dismissal. On the other hand, if he wants to retain employees, he may either adopt their existing contracts or negotiate new ones on behalf of the company. An administrative receiver who adopts existing contracts is, by statute, and with no ability to contract out, personally liable in respect of services rendered wholly or partly after the adoption (IA 1986 s 44(1)(b) and (2A)–(2D)). He can, however, opt out of personal liability for newly negotiated contracts (s 44(1)9b)). Nothing the administrative receiver does in the first 14 days after appointment is taken as indicating adoption of existing contracts (s 44(2)), but if he continues to employ people and pay them according to their existing contracts after that time, he is taken to have impliedly adopted the contracts: *Powdrill v Watson* [1995] 2 AC 394.

The role of an administrative receiver and his relationship to the company and its property.

[14.04] Re Atlantic Computer Systems plc [1992] Ch 505, [1992] 1 All ER 476 (Court of Appeal)

[The facts are immaterial.]

NICHOLLS LJ: . . . Typically, when lending money to a company, a bank will take as security a charge over all or most of the assets of the company, present and future, the charge being a fixed charge on land and certain other assets, and a floating charge over the remaining assets. The deed authorises the bank to appoint a receiver and manager of the company's undertaking, with power to carry on the company's business. Such a receiver is referred to in the Act of 1986 as an 'administrative receiver'.

Normally the deed creating the floating charge and authorising his appointment provides that an administrative receiver shall be the agent of the company. Now the Act of 1986, in s 44(1)(a), provides that this shall always be so, unless and until the company goes into liquidation. For many years the position regarding a receiver appointed as agent of the company was that in general he was not personally liable for contracts entered into by him for and on behalf of the company. He was no more personally liable than was a director who entered into a contract for and on behalf of his company. . . . The position now, with regard to administrative receivers, is set out in s 44(1) and (2) of the Act of 1986.[22] Under that section an administrative receiver is personally liable on (a) any contract entered into by him in the carrying out of his functions, except in so far as the contract otherwise provides, and (b) on any contract of employment 'adopted' by him in the carrying out of those functions. In the latter regard the administrative receiver has, in effect, a period of 14 days' grace after his appointment. . . . In cases where he is personally liable an administrative receiver is entitled to an indemnity out of the assets of the company: s 44(1)(c). But even today an administrative receiver is not, in general, personally liable, and hence the statutory indemnity out of the assets of the company does not arise, in respect of contracts adopted by him in the course of managing the company's business, other than contracts of employment. With that one special exception, personal liability is confined, in general, to new contracts made by him. Thus he is not personally liable for the rent payable under an existing lease, or for the hire charges payable under an existing hire-purchase agreement. This is not a surprising conclusion. It does not offend against basic conceptions of justice or fairness. The rent and hire charges were a liability undertaken by the company at the inception of the lease or hire-purchase agreement. The land or goods are being used by the company even when an administrative receiver is in office. It is to the company that, along with other creditors, the lessor and the owner of the goods must look for payment.

Nor is a lessor or owner of goods in such a case entitled to be paid his rent or hire instalments as an 'expense' of the administrative receivership, even though the administrative receiver has retained and used the land or goods for the purpose of the receivership. The reason is not far to seek. The appointment of an administrative receiver does not trigger a statutory prohibition on the lessor or owner of goods such as that found in s 130 in the case of a winding-up order. If the rent or hire is not paid by the administrative receiver the lessor or owner of the goods is at liberty, as much after the appointment of the administrative receiver as before, to exercise the rights and remedies available to him under his lease or hire-purchase agreement. Faced with the prospect of proceedings, an administrative receiver may choose to pay the rent or hire charges in order to retain the land or goods. But if he decides not to do so, the lessor or owner of goods has his remedies. There is no occasion, assuming that there is jurisdiction, for the court to intervene and order the administrative receiver to pay these outgoings . . .

> ➤ Note

IA 1986 s 44 has been amended since Nicholls LJ delivered his judgment in the *Atlantic Computer Systems* case, to meet the difficulties revealed in *Powdrill v Waston* and *Talbot v Cadge* [1995] 2 AC 394, [1995] 2 All ER 65, HL (and more particularly in the rulings of the lower courts in these cases). The effect of this amendment (effected by IA 1994 s 2) is to make it clear that the receiver's personal liability is restricted to payments due to the employee in respect of services actually rendered during the receivership.

Duties of administrative receivers

This area of law remains troublesome. Clearly the way in which an administrative receiver carries out his duties can have a profound and practical impact on the financial well-being of the security holder, the debtor company, any subsequent security holders with interests in the same assets, and any third parties who have guaranteed the secured debt. What duties, if any, does the administrative receiver owe to these parties?

---

[22] [Section 44 has since been amended: see the Note following.]

[14.05] Downsview Nominees Ltd v First City Corpn Ltd [1993] AC 295, [1993] 3 All ER 626 (Privy Council)

The company, which carried on a motor dealing and garage business in New Zealand, had given a first debenture to the Westpac bank and a second debenture to FCC, each secured by a floating charge over all of its assets. It had defaulted under the second debenture and FCC had appointed receivers who formed the view that the company's business was unprofitable and that it should be closed down. The company's managing director appealed to Russell (the second defendant) for help. His response was (i) to procure Downsview (a company which he controlled) to take an assignment of W bank's first debenture and (ii) to have Downsview appoint himself as a receiver under that debenture. FCC's receivers were thus ousted from any but a residual role. FCC at once offered to pay Downsview all the moneys owing under the first debenture, so that it would be redeemed and FCC's receivers could again take charge. But this offer was declined, and Russell continued to carry on the company's business, incurring further losses of over $500,000. The Privy Council held that (i) Russell had used his powers not for the proper purpose of realising Downsview's security but in order to meet the managing director's wish that the company should continue trading; (ii) Downsview ought to have accepted FCC's offer to redeem; and (iii) each of them should compensate FCC for its losses. But it rejected the view of the trial judge and the New Zealand Court of Appeal that any liability lay in negligence.

The opinion of the Judicial Committee was delivered by LORD TEMPLEMAN: . . . The first submission made on behalf of the first and second defendants is that they owed no duty to the first plaintiff because the first plaintiff was only a debenture holder and not a mortgagee. This submission is untenable.

A mortgage, whether legal or equitable, is security for repayment of a debt. The security may be constituted by a conveyance, assignment or demise or by a charge on any interest in real or personal property. . . . A security issued by a company is called a debenture but for present purposes there is no material difference between a mortgage, a charge and a debenture. Each creates a security for the repayment of a debt.

The second argument put forward on behalf of the first and second defendants is that though a mortgagee owes certain duties to the mortgagor, he owes no duty to any subsequent encumbrancer, so the first and second defendants owed no duty to the first plaintiff. This argument also is untenable. The owner of property entering into a mortgage does not by entering into that mortgage cease to be the owner of that property any further than is necessary to give effect to the security he has created. The mortgagor can mortgage the property again and again. A second or subsequent mortgage is a complete security on the mortgagor's interests subject only to the rights of prior encumbrancers. If a first mortgagee commits a breach of his duties to the mortgagor, the damage inflicted by that breach of duty will be suffered by the second mortgagee, subsequent encumbrancers and the mortgagor, depending on the extent of the damage and the amount of each security. Thus if a first mortgagee in breach of duty sells property worth £500,000 for £300,000, he is liable at the suit of any subsequent encumbrancer or the mortgagor. Damages of £200,000 will be ordered to be taken into the accounts of the first mortgagee or paid into court or to the second mortgagee who, after satisfying, as far as he can, the amount of any debt outstanding under his mortgage, will pay over any balance remaining to the next encumbrancer or to the mortgagor if there is no subsequent encumbrancer. . . .

The next submission on behalf of the first and second defendants is that, even if a mortgagee owes certain duties to subsequent encumbrancers, a receiver and manager appointed by a mortgagee is not under any such duty where, as in the present case, the receiver and manager is deemed to act as agent for the mortgagor. The fallacy in the argument is the failure to appreciate that, when a receiver and manager exercises the powers of sale and management conferred on him by the mortgage, he is dealing with the security; he is not merely selling or dealing with the interests of the mortgagor. He is exercising the power of selling and dealing with the mortgaged property for the purpose of securing repayment of the debt owing to his mortgagee and must exercise his powers in good faith and for the purpose of obtaining repayment of the debt owing to his mortgagee. The receiver and manager owes these duties to the mortgagor and to all subsequent encumbrancers in whose favour the mortgaged property has been charged.

The next question is the nature and extent of the duties owed by a mortgagee and a receiver and manager respectively to subsequent encumbrancers and the mortgagor.

Several centuries ago equity evolved principles for the enforcement of mortgages and the protection of borrowers. The most basic principles were, first, that a mortgage is security for the repayment of a debt and, secondly, that a security for repayment of a debt is only a mortgage. From these principles flowed two rules, first, that powers conferred on a mortgagee must be exercised in good faith for the purpose of obtaining repayment and secondly that, subject to the first rule, powers conferred on a mortgagee may be exercised although the consequences may be disadvantageous to the borrower. These principles and rules apply also to a receiver and manager appointed by the mortgagee.

It does not follow that a receiver and manager must immediately upon appointment seize all the cash in the coffers of the company and sell all the company's assets or so much of the assets as he chooses and considers sufficient to complete the redemption of the mortgage. He is entitled, but not bound, to allow the company's business to be continued by himself or by the existing or other executives. The decisions of the receiver and manager whether to continue the business or close down the business and sell assets chosen by him cannot be impeached if those decisions are taken in good faith while protecting the interests of the debentureholder in recovering the moneys due under the debenture, even though the decisions of the receiver and manager may be disadvantageous for the company. . . . But since a mortgage is only security for a debt, a receiver and manager commits a breach of his duty if he abuses his powers by exercising them otherwise than 'for the special purpose of enabling the assets comprised in the debenture holders' security to be preserved and realised'[23] for the benefit of the debenture holder. In the present case the evidence of the second defendant himself and the clear emphatic findings of Gault J show that the second defendant accepted appointment and acted as receiver and manager not for the purpose of enforcing the security under the Westpac debenture but for the purpose of preventing the enforcement by the plaintiffs of the [FCC] debenture.

This and other findings to similar effect establish that, ab initio and throughout his receivership, the second defendant did not exercise his powers for proper purposes. He was at all times in breach of the duty, which was pleaded against him, to exercise his powers in good faith for proper purposes.

Gault J rested his judgment not on breach of a duty to act in good faith for proper purposes but on negligence. He said:

on an application of negligence principles, a receiver owes a duty to the debenture holders to take reasonable care in dealing with the assets of the company . . . [The first defendant's] position is merely a specific example of the duty a mortgagee has to subsequent chargeholders to exercise its powers with reasonable care . . .

Richardson J, delivering the judgment of the Court of Appeal, agreed that duties of care in negligence as defined by Gault J were owed by the second defendant as receiver and manager and by the first defendant as first debentureholder to the plaintiffs as second debenture holders. Richardson J agreed that the second defendant was in breach of his duty but, differing from Gault J, held that the first defendant had committed no breach.

---

[23] [The quotation is from the judgment of Jenkins LJ in *Re B Johnson & Co (Builders) Ltd* [1955] Ch 634 at 662–663.]

The general duty of care said to be owed by a mortgagee to subsequent encumbrancers and the mortgagor in negligence is inconsistent with the right of the mortgagee and the duties which the courts applying equitable principles have imposed on the mortgagee. If a mortgagee enters into possession he is liable to account for rent on the basis of wilful default; he must keep mortgage premises in repair; he is liable for waste. Those duties were imposed to ensure that a mortgagee is diligent in discharging his mortgage and returning the property to the mortgagor. If a mortgagee exercises his power of sale in good faith for the purpose of protecting his security, he is not liable to the mortgagor even though he might have obtained a higher price and even though the terms might be regarded as disadvantageous to the mortgagor. *Cuckmere Brick Co Ltd v Mutual Finance Ltd*[24] is Court of Appeal authority for the proposition that, if the mortgagee decides to sell, he must take reasonable care to obtain a proper price but is no authority for any wider proposition. A receiver exercising his power of sale also owes the same specific duties as the mortgagee. But that apart, the general duty of a receiver and manager appointed by a debenture holder . . . leaves no room for the imposition of a general duty to use reasonable care in dealing with the assets of the company. The duties imposed by equity on a mortgagee and on a receiver and manager would be quite unnecessary if there existed a general duty in negligence to take reasonable care in the exercise of powers and to take reasonable care in dealing with the assets of the mortgagor company. . . .

A mortgagee owes a general duty to subsequent encumbrancers and to the mortgagor to use his powers for the sole purpose of securing repayments of the moneys owing under his mortgage and a duty to act in good faith. He also owes the specific duties which equity has imposed on him in the exercise of his powers to go into possession and his powers of sale. It may well be that a mortgagee who appoints a receiver and manager, knowing that the receiver and manager intends to exercise his powers for the purpose of frustrating the activities of the second mortgagee or for some other improper purpose or who fails to revoke the appointment of a receiver and manager when the mortgagee knows that the receiver and manager is abusing his powers, may himself be guilty of bad faith but in the present case this possibility need not be explored.

The liability of the second defendant in the present case is firmly based not on negligence but on the breach of duty. There was overwhelming evidence that the receivership of the second defendant was inspired by him for improper purposes and carried on in bad faith, ultimately verging on fraud. The liability of the first defendant does not arise under negligence but as a result of the first defendant's breach of duty in failing to transfer the Westpac debenture to the first plaintiff at the end of March 1987. It is well settled that the mortgagor and all persons having any interest in the property subject to the mortgage or liable to pay the mortgage debt can redeem. It is now conceded that the first plaintiff was entitled to require the first defendant to assign the Westpac debenture to the first plaintiff on payment of all moneys due to the first defendant under the Westpac debenture. . . .

The first defendant was from the end of March 1987 in breach of its duty to assign the Westpac debenture to the first plaintiff. If that debenture had been assigned, the second defendant would have ceased to be the receiver and manager and none of the avoidable losses caused by the second defendant would have been sustained. . . .

A receiver who is appointed to manage the business of the chargor has a duty to do so with due diligence.

[14.06] Medforth v Blake [2000] Ch 86, [1999] 3 All ER 97 (Court of Appeal)

Medforth was a pig-farmer on a very large scale: his annual turnover was over £2 million. He ran into financial difficulties and his bank appointed receivers, who ran the business for four and a half years, until Medforth was able to find a new source of finance and repay the bank. Although Medforth repeatedly told the receivers that they could claim large discounts

---

[24] [1971] Ch 949.

from the suppliers of feedstuffs, amounting to some £1,000 a week, they failed to do so. The court held that the receivers owed a duty (subject to their primary duty to the bank) to manage the business with due diligence, and that for breach of this duty they were liable to Medforth.

SIR RICHARD SCOTT, V-C: . . . As a Privy Council case, the *Downsview Nominees* case **[14.05]** is not binding but, as Mr. Smith submitted, is a persuasive authority of great weight. But what did it decide as to the duties owed by a receiver/manager to a mortgagor? It decided that the duty lies in equity, not in tort. It decided that there is no general duty of care in negligence. It held that the receiver/manager owes the same specific duties when exercising the power of sale as are owed by a mortgagee when exercising the power of sale. Lord Templeman cited with approval the *Cuckmere Brick* case [1971] Ch 949 test, namely, that the mortgagee must take reasonable care to obtain a proper price. . . .

The *Cuckmere Brick* case test can impose liability on a mortgagee notwithstanding the absence of fraud or mala fides. It follows from the *Downsview Nominees* case and *Yorkshire Bank plc v Hall* [1999] 1 WLR 1713 that a receiver/manager who sells but fails to take reasonable care to obtain a proper price may incur liability notwithstanding the absence of fraud or mala fides. Why should the approach be any different if what is under review is not the conduct of a sale but conduct in carrying on a business? If a receiver exercises this power, why does not a specific duty, corresponding to the duty to take reasonable steps to obtain a proper price, arise? If the business is being carried on by a mortgagee, the mortgagee will be liable, as a mortgagee in possession, for loss caused by his failure to do so with due diligence. Why should not the receiver/manager, who, as Lord Templeman held, owes the same specific duties as the mortgagee when selling, owe comparable specific duties when conducting the mortgaged business? It may be that the particularly onerous duties constructed by courts of equity for mortgages in possession would not be appropriate to apply to a receiver. But, no duties at all save a duty of good faith? That does not seem to me to make commercial sense nor, more importantly, to correspond with the principles expressed in the bulk of the authorities. . . .

I do not accept that there is any difference between the answer that would be given by the common law to the question what duties are owed by a receiver managing a mortgaged property to those interested in the equity of redemption and the answer that would be given by equity to that question. I do not, for my part, think it matters one jot whether the duty is expressed as a common law duty or as a duty in equity. The result is the same. The origin of the receiver's duty, like the mortgagee's duty, lies, however, in equity and we might as well continue to refer to it as a duty in equity.

In my judgment, in principle and on the authorities, the following propositions can be stated. (1) A receiver managing mortgaged property owes duties to the mortgagor and anyone else with an interest in the equity of redemption. (2) The duties include, but are not necessarily confined to, a duty of good faith. (3) The extent and scope of any duty additional to that of good faith will depend on the facts and circumstances of the particular case. (4) In exercising his powers of management the primary duty of the receiver is to try and bring about a situation in which interest on the secured debt can be paid and the debt itself repaid. (5) Subject to that primary duty, the receiver owes a duty to manage the property with due diligence. (6) Due diligence does not oblige the receiver to continue to carry on a business on the mortgaged premises previously carried on by the mortgagor. (7) If the receiver does carry on a business on the mortgaged premises, due diligence requires reasonable steps to be taken in order to try to do so profitably. . . .

[His Lordship accordingly ruled that the trial judge had rightly held the receivers liable for breach of duty.]

SWINTON THOMAS and TUCKEY LJJ concurred.

➤ Questions

1. Does the duty described in *Downsview* **[14.05]** meet commercial needs and expectations? Does it contribute to a 'rescue culture'? See Lightman, 'The Challenges Ahead: Address to the Insolvency Lawyers' Association' [1996] JBL 113, 119–120; contrast Rajak, 'Can a Receiver be Negligent?' in Rider (ed), *The Corporate Dimension* (1998).

2. Does it matter whether the receiver's duty is an equitable duty or a common law duty?[25]

3. What difference does it make to say that the receiver owes a duty of good faith, rather than a duty of care, to the company and to subsequent encumbrancers or guarantors?[26]

4. What duty does the *chargee* owe in deciding *when* or *whether* to appoint a receiver? See *Shamji v Johnson Matthey Bankers Ltd* [1986] BCLC 278, ChD, affd [1991] BCLC 36, CA. If an offer is made to redeem the secured debt (thereby extinguishing the charge), must the debentureholder accept it?

5. What duty does the *receiver* owe in deciding *whether* to exercise the power of sale or continue the business, and in deciding *when* to sell? See *Cuckmere Brick Co Ltd v Mutual Finance Ltd* [1971] Ch 949, CA.

6. Is the duty owed by the receiver when exercising the power of sale or the power to carry on the business one of good faith, due diligence, or reasonable care? See Sealy, 'Mortgagees and Receivers—A Duty of Care Resurrected and Extended' [2000] CLJ 31; Frisby, 'Making a Silk Purse out of a Pig's Ear—*Medforth v Blake*' (2000) 63 MLR 413.

Distribution of assets subject to the receivership

If there is more than one charge over the secured assets, then priority as between chargees depends upon rules discussed earlier (see pp 465 ff above). IA 1986 s 43 provides for sale of the secured assets by a receiver other than one appointed by the chargee with first claim on the proceeds.

If the charge over the secured assets is floating, then various claims rank ahead of the secured creditor's claim to have the secured debt repaid. This is one of the disadvantages of floating charges. The order of payment out of the realisations is as follows:

(i) The *expenses of winding up* (including the remuneration of the liquidator),[27] *if* the company goes into liquidation at any time while the administrative receiver has in his possession undistributed realisations from the charged assets—see CA 2006 s 1282, inserting a new provision in the IA 1986 s 176ZA,[28] providing that property subject to a floating charge may, where necessary, be used to fund the general expenses of winding up in priority to the floating charge holder and to any preferential creditors entitled to be paid out of the property, but not providing for payment of these expenses out of the statutory share of assets for the

---

[25] See the earlier case of *Standard Chartered Bank Ltd v Walker* [1982] 1 WLR 1410, CA, discussing the duty as if it were a common law duty; contrast *Downsview* **[14.05]**.

[26] Contrast *Standard Chartered Bank Ltd v Walker* [1982] 1 WLR 1410, CA, and *Downsview* **[14.05]**; the conclusion in the former case must now be regarded as wrong, given the decision in *Downsview*.

[27] IA 1986 s 115 (and s 156 for compulsory liquidations), and IR 1986, r 4.218, defining both what counts as a liquidation expense (according to *Re Toshoku Finance UK plc, Kahn v IRC* [2002] UKHL 6, [2002] 1 WLR 671, HL), and setting out the order of priority in which they are to be paid.

[28] So reversing the controversial decision in *Re Leyland Daf Ltd, Buchler v Talbot* [2004] UKHL 9, [2004] 2 AC 298, which denied priority to liquidation expenses (and which had itself overruled the long-standing CA authority allowing such priority: *Re Barleycorn Enterprises Ltd* [1970] Ch 465).

unsecured creditors (see (iii) below). IA 1986 s 176ZA also provides for the power to make rules requiring the authorisation or approval of the floating charge holder, or the preferential creditors, or the court, to the expenditures in certain circumstances.

(ii)   The *expenses of receivership*: these are payable in priority to the other preferred claims, on the basis that the person who has produced a fund for distribution should have the costs of doing so paid in priority. But the receiver has a duty not to incur expenses if this would lessen the amount available for the preferred creditors (see (iv) below): *Woods v Winskill* [1913] 2 Ch 303.

(iii)   The *statutory share of assets for unsecured creditors*: a prescribed percentage of floating charge asset realisations must be set aside to pay the company's unsecured creditors—see IA 1986, s 176A, and SI 2003/2097, art 3. The prescribed percentage is: (a) 50% of the first £10,000; and (b) 20% or the remainder, up to a maximum grand total of £600,000.[29] The rule does not apply if the company's net assets are worth less than £10,000 (s 176A(3)(a)), or if the costs of distribution to unsecured creditors would be disproportionate to the benefits (s 176A(5)).

(iv)   The *'preferential debts'*[30] (now primarily owed to employees, since EA 2002 abolished Crown priority), being debts that Parliament has decided should be paid in priority to all other debts, other than the expenses of winding up—see IA 1986 ss 40 and 175(2)(b). Any payment of preferential debts may be recouped out of the assets of the company available for the payment of unsecured creditors (if there are any such assets remaining in the company's insolvency) (IA 1986 s 40(3)).

(v)   Finally, the *debt owed to the charge holder*.

By contrast, if the charge over the secured assets is fixed, rather than floating, then the property cannot be used to pay off the debts in (i), (iii) and (iv) above. This is so even if the charge secures the same debt to the same charge holder as a floating charge in the creditor's favour expressed to be over all the company's assets and undertakings. This distinction between treatment of fixed and floating charge realisations is one reason why creditors expend such efforts in drafting charges that are classified as fixed rather than floating (see pp 485 ff above). It also explains why creditors adopt the practice of taking a fixed charge over as many assets as possible and an equally ranking floating charge over whatever assets remain. The same receiver can then be appointed over both classes of assets, but the distributions will follow quite different rules.

Liquidation or winding up

Both solvent and insolvent companies may be wound up. In the *winding up* or *liquidation* (the terms are synonymous), the company gives up its business, sells off its assets, pays its debts (or, if it is insolvent, does so to the extent that its funds allow) and distributes whatever surplus remains amongst its members or otherwise as its constitution may provide. The event must be notified in the *Gazette* (see above p 583).

The conduct of the winding up is placed by law in the hands of a *liquidator*; and on his appointment the directors' power to manage the business of the company ceases.[31]

---

[29] It is possible to vary this rule by means of a CVA: IA 1986 s 176A(4).

[30] Defined in IA 1986 s 386 and Sch 6, although the Crown preference was abolished by EA 2002 reforms.

[31] By statute in voluntary liquidations (IA 1986 s 90(2)), and by common law in compulsory liquidations (*Re Farrow's Bank Ltd* [1921] 2 Ch 164).

The company continues in being throughout the process of winding up: there is still a corporate personality and all corporate acts in the course of the liquidation, such as the transfer of property and the institution of legal proceedings, are done in its name rather than by the liquidator in his own name. The company ceases to exist only by the formal act of *dissolution* (IA 1986 ss 201ff) after the winding up procedure has been completed (see below at p 679).

A company may be wound up *compulsorily*, ie by court order, or *voluntarily*, as a consequence of an extraordinary resolution passed by the members.

Voluntary winding up

In a voluntary winding up, following an extraordinary resolution passed by the members (IA 1986 s 84, also indicating limited exceptions), the liquidator is appointed by the members if the directors are able to declare that the company will be able to meet its debts in full (a '*members' voluntary winding up*') (IA 1986 ss 89, 91 setting out the detailed requirements); if not, the company's creditors have the power of appointment and exercise general control over the conduct of the liquidation (a '*creditors' voluntary winding up*') (IA 1986 ss 90, 96).

The court need not be involved in a voluntary winding up, although court confirmation gives the winding up recognition throughout the EU, which is important if the company has assets in other EU states (IR 1986, r 7.62).

Compulsory winding up

In a compulsory (or court ordered) winding up the Official Receiver[32] automatically becomes the liquidator and is in law regarded as an officer of the court acting under its direction and control. Various people are entitled to petition the court for the compulsory liquidation of a company (IA 1986 s 124, and note the conditions specified), including company creditors (who bring almost all petitions), the company itself and the company's directors. The Secretary of State may petition for winding up, in the public interest, generally in cases of notoriety, most often following an investigation of the company's affairs under CA 1985, Part XIV or FSMA 2000 (see above, pp 595 ff) (IA 1986 ss 124(4), 124A). By way of additional protection, these people may also petition for the appointment of a *provisional liquidator*, as an interim measure designed to maintain the status quo and prevent prejudice to any party pending the court's decision on the petition itself (IA 1986 s 135).

A company may be wound up by the court only if it is shown that one of the circumstances listed in IA 1986 s 122(1) exists. In practice, companies are usually wound up because the company is unable to pay its debts (s 122(1)(f)), or because the court is of the opinion that it is 'just and equitable' to do so (s 122(1)(g)).[33] IA 1986 s 123 describes circumstances that a court will take as sufficient evidence of a company's inability to pay its debts.

---

[32] The Official Receiver is a public officer who is appointed by the Secretary of State to act in the administration of bankruptcies and company liquidations. There are in fact many Official Receivers, each attached to a particular court. Since the coming into force of IA 1986, many more bankruptcies and liquidations have been placed in the hands of private insolvency practitioners than was the case under the former law, so enabling the Official Receiver to devote his attention to the larger or more complex insolvencies, and in particular those in which fraud or other wrongdoing is suspected.

[33] The 'just and equitable' ground is less common now that CA 2006 s 994 provides better and more tailored remedies.

Permitted petitioners for a compulsory winding up

Every contributory has a statutory right[34] *to petition for a winding up, which cannot be excluded or limited by any provision in the articles*

[14.07] Re Peveril Gold Mines Ltd [1898] 1 Ch 122 (Court of Appeal)

The company's articles provided that no member should petition for the winding up of the company unless (a) two directors had consented in writing, or (b) a general meeting had so resolved, or (c) the petitioner held at least 20% of the issued capital. A member presented a petition without satisfying any of these conditions. It was held that the articles were ineffective to prevent him from doing so.

LINDLEY MR: Anyone who is familiar with the Companies Act knows perfectly well that these registered limited companies are incorporated on certain conditions; they continue to exist on certain conditions; and they are liable to be dissolved on certain conditions. The important sections of the Act of 1862, with regard to dissolution, are ss 79 and 82 [IA 1986 ss 122, 124]. Section 79 states the circumstances under which such a company may be dissolved by the court, and s 82 states the persons who may petition for a dissolution. Any article contrary to these sections—any article which says that the company is formed on the condition that its life shall not be terminated when any of the circumstances mentioned in s 79 exist, or which limits the right of a contributory under s 82 to petition for a winding up, would be an attempt to enforce on all the shareholders that which is at variance with the statutory conditions, and is invalid. It is no answer to say that the right to petition may be waived by any contributory personally. I do not intend to decide whether a valid contract may or may not be made between the company and an individual shareholder that he shall not petition for the winding up of the company. That point does not arise now. But to say that a company is formed on the condition that its existence shall not be terminated under the circumstances, or on the application of the persons, mentioned in the Act is to say that it is formed contrary to the provisions of the Act, and upon conditions which the court is bound to ignore. The view taken by Byrne J was right, and the appeal must be dismissed.

CHITTY LJ delivered a concurring judgment.

VAUGHAN WILLIAMS LJ concurred.

➤ Questions

1. Lindley MR left open the question whether a contract outside the articles between the company and a member that he would not petition for a winding-up order was enforceable. Is it?

2. Would a contractual promise by a company that it would not petition for its own winding up be binding? Consider *Russell v Northern Development Corpn Ltd* [8.01].

3. Would an agreement between a shareholder and an outsider, or between several or all of the shareholders *inter se*, containing a promise that none of the parties would petition for a winding-up order, be upheld?

---

[34] Although note the conditions in IA 1986 s 124(2) and (3).

A member cannot petition for a winding-up unless there are assets available for distribution to members.

[14.08] Re Rica Gold Washing Co (1879) 11 Ch D 36 (Court of Appeal)

[The facts appear from the judgment.]

JESSEL MR: This is an appeal from the decision of Vice-Chancellor Hall dismissing a petition to wind up the company, on the ground that it was not a bona fide petition, and that the petitioner, as I read the judgment, had not sufficient interest to support it . . .

Now I will say a word or two on the law as regards the position of a petitioner holding fully paid-up shares. He is not liable to contribute anything towards the assets of the company, and if he has any interest at all, it must be that after full payment of all the debts and liabilities of the company there will remain a surplus divisible among the shareholders of sufficient value to authorise him to present a petition. That being his position, and the rule being that the petitioner must succeed upon allegations which are proved, of course the petitioner must show the court by sufficient allegation that he has a sufficient interest to entitle him to ask for the winding up of the company. I say 'a sufficient interest', for the mere allegation of a surplus or of a probable surplus will not be sufficient. He must show what I may call a tangible interest. I am not going to lay down any rule as to what that must be, but if he showed only that there was such a surplus as, on being fairly divided, irrespective of the costs of the winding up, would give him £5, I should say that would not be sufficient to induce the court to interfere in his behalf . . .

I cannot believe that a shareholder who has 75 £1 paid-up shares can imagine that he has sufficient interest to make it worth his while to present a winding-up petition . . . I have no doubt that, as the Vice-Chancellor says, this is not a bona fide petition, but a petition presented with a very different object than that of obtaining for the petitioner, the £75, or any part of it. In my opinion it is either presented for the purpose of obtaining costs, or for the purpose of annoyance to some other person or persons; and I entirely agree with the Vice-Chancellor that it is not a bona fide petition. Therefore I think we must dismiss this appeal.

BRETT LJ delivered a concurring judgment.

BRAMWELL LJ concurred.

➤ Questions

1. What is the *ratio decidendi* of this case?

2. If a petition for winding up is presented by a holder of a small parcel of fully-paid shares on facts similar to *Re German Date Coffee Co* (1882) 20 Ch 169, CA or *Re Thomas Edward Brinsmead & Sons* **[14.10]** should the court apply the *Rica Gold* rule?

3. The Jenkins Committee (1962, Cmnd 1749, para 503(h)) recommended the reversal of this rule by statute. In *Re Chesterfield Catering Co Ltd* [1977] Ch 373, the decision was affirmed as being still good law, notwithstanding an argument by counsel that in the light of *Ebrahimi v Westbourne Galleries Ltd* **[14.14]** the principle of *Rica Gold* should be regarded not as a strict rule, but merely as one of the considerations for the court to take into account in assessing whether it was just and equitable to order a winding up. Is this logic persuasive?

4. Given the imposition of filing fees to lodge a winding-up petition, plus legal fees (a hefty sum for a contested case), plus the chance that a petition which is not well founded may be dismissed with an order against that the petitioner pay the company's costs, or may be struck out as vexatious (see *Charles Forte Investments Ltd v Amanda* below, p 662), does the law need the rule in *Rica Gold*?

➤ Notes

1. Note the other restrictions on the circumstances in which a contributory can bring a petition: IA 1986 s 124(2)–(4A).

2. The petitioner is not required to prove a tangible interest if the petition is based on, or alleges, company defaults that themselves make it impossible to determine whether there is a surplus for contributories: *Re Wessex Computer Stationers Ltd* [1992] BCLC 366.

3. By contrast, and subject to the wishes of the class of creditors, an unpaid creditor of an insolvent company will not be refused an order on the ground that there are no assets, unless it is shown that making the order would be pointless: *Re Crigglestone Coal Co Ltd* [1906] 2 Ch 327, [1906] 2 Ch 327 at 336; IA 1986 ss 195, 125(1).

➤ Question

In *Bell Group Finance (Pty) Ltd v Bell Group (UK) Holdings Ltd* [1996] 1 BCLC 304, Chadwick J granted a winding-up order to a petitioning creditor where the company had no assets, so that the liquidator could investigate whether there had been impropriety in the conduct of the company's affairs. Is there any reason in principle for having one rule for a creditor (see above) and an opposite rule for a member **[14.08]**?

Grounds for compulsory winding up—company unable to pay its debts

A winding up order will not be made on the basis of a debt which is bona fide disputed.

[14.09] Stonegate Securities Ltd v Gregory [1980] Ch 576 (Court of Appeal)

Prior to the presentation of a petition to wind up the plaintiff company, the defendant, in accordance with CA 1948 s 223 (a) [IA 1986 s 123], served a notice on the company demanding the payment of a debt within 21 days. The company, while accepting that there was a contingent or prospective liability to the defendant, denied that the debt was presently due. It issued a writ and sought interlocutory relief restraining the defendant from presenting a petition. The trial judge found that there was a *bona fide* dispute whether the defendant was a creditor for a sum presently due and granted an injunction restraining the defendant from presenting a petition in respect of the alleged debt provided that, within three weeks, the directors of the plaintiff company made a declaration of solvency of the company. The company successfully appealed.

BUCKLEY LJ: . . . The relevant statutory provisions are contained in sections 222, 223 and 224 of the Companies Act 1948 [IA 1986 ss 122, 123, and 124]. Section 222, as is very familiar, provides that a company may be wound up by the court if "(e) the company is unable to pay its debts." Section 223 provides that a company shall be deemed to be unable to pay its debts if, among other things, a creditor to whom the company is indebted in a sum exceeding £50 [now £750] then due—and I emphasise those last two words—has served a statutory demand upon the company and the company has failed for three weeks to comply with it. That provision has no application to a case in which the creditor is a creditor in respect of a sum which is not presently due. . . .

. . . in my opinion, the expression "contingent creditor" means a creditor in respect of a debt which will only become due in an event which may or may not occur; and a "prospective creditor" is a creditor in respect of a debt which will certainly become due in the future, either on some date which has been already determined or on some date determinable by reference to future events.

Where a creditor petitions for the winding up of a company, the proceedings will take one of two courses, depending upon whether the petitioner is a creditor whose debt is presently due, or one whose debt is contingent or prospective . . . If the creditor petitions in respect of a debt which he claims to be presently due, and that claim is undisputed, the petition proceeds to hearing and adjudication in the normal way; but if the company in good faith and on substantial grounds disputes any liability in respect of the alleged debt, the petition will be dismissed or, if the matter is brought before a court before the petition is issued, its presentation will in normal circumstances be restrained. That is because a winding up petition is not a legitimate means of seeking to enforce payment of a debt which is bona fide disputed.

Ungoed-Thomas J. put the matter thus in *Mann v Goldstein* [1968] 1 WLR 1091, 1098–1099:

"For my part, I would prefer to rest the jurisdiction directly on the comparatively simple propositions that a creditor's petition can only be presented by a creditor, that the winding up jurisdiction is not for the purpose of deciding a disputed debt (that is, disputed on substantial and not insubstantial grounds), since, until a creditor is established as a creditor he is not entitled to present the petition and has no locus standi in the Companies Court; and that, therefore, to invoke the winding up jurisdiction when the debt is disputed (that is, on substantial grounds) or after it has become clear that it is so disputed is an abuse of the process of the court."

I gratefully adopt the whole of that statement, although I think it could equally well have ended at the reference to want of locus standi. In my opinion a petition founded on a debt which is disputed in good faith and on substantial grounds is demurrable for the reason that the petitioner is not a creditor of the company within the meaning of section 224 (1) at all, and the question whether he is or is not a creditor of the company is not appropriate for adjudication in winding up proceedings.

The circumstances may, however, be such that the company adopts an intermediate position, denying that the debt is presently due but not denying that it will or may become due in the future—in other words, accepting it as a contingent or prospective debt. The present case is of the last-mentioned kind and the present appeal involves consideration of what is proper in such a case.

. . . The company now admits that the defendant is a contingent creditor at any rate in a sum of £33,000, but not that any part of that sum is immediately due. . . . and the defendant now accepts that there is a bona fide dispute as to whether any part of the £33,000 is now due, and he further admits that in so far as the debt is contingent, the relevant contingency may never happen. So the situation is such that the defendant cannot petition to wind the company up on the basis that he is a debtor for a sum which is presently due [ie via the statutory demand that had been issued], because that position is disputed in good faith and on substantial grounds; but he is competent to petition as a contingent creditor. . . .

If the only established footing upon which the defendant can petition to wind up the company is as a contingent or prospective creditor, the burden rests on him to show prima facie that there is a case for winding up the company . . . If the ground for seeking a winding up order is that the company is unable to pay its debts—and no other ground is suggested here—it would be incumbent on the defendant to establish a prima facie case that this was so. The condition [imposed in the trial judge's injunction, requiring the directors to make a declaration of solvency] seems to me to reverse this burden of proof, for if the condition is not complied with it would be open to the defendant as a petitioner to rely upon that fact as some evidence of the company's inability to pay its debts; and moreover, having regard to the nature of the declaration of solvency . . . the condition imposes upon the company, through its directors, a heavier burden of proof than the burden of establishing merely that the company is not commercially solvent; it imposes the burden of proof of establishing that the company will ultimately be solvent on the basis of a prospective liquidation within 12 months. It seems to me that such a condition cannot be supported in principle. . . .

The whole of the doctrine of this part of the law is based upon the view that winding up proceedings are not suitable proceedings in which to determine a genuine dispute about whether the company does or does not owe the sum in question; and equally I think it must be true that winding up proceedings are not suitable proceedings in which to determine whether that liability is an immediate liability or only a prospective or contingent liability. . . .

GOFF LJ and SIR DAVID CAIRNS delivered concurring judgments.

Grounds for compulsory winding up—'just and equitable' ground

Members are entitled, as 'contributories', to petition for the compulsory winding up of the company (IA 1986 s 124). They are not restricted to using the 'just and equitable' ground[35] (and nor is this ground restricted to members), but this is the one most commonly used by members who find themselves unable to proceed on the basis of a special resolution for the voluntary winding up of the company (IA 1986 s 84(1)(b)).

A company formed for a fraudulent purpose may be wound up on the 'just and equitable' ground.

[14.10] Re Thomas Edward Brinsmead & Sons [1897] 1 Ch 406 (Court of Appeal)

Three men named Brinsmead, former employees of John Brinsmead & Sons, the well-known piano makers, formed the present company to make pianos which were to be passed off as the product of the older-established firm. An injunction had been obtained, restraining the company from this action; but meantime shares in the company worth many thousands of pounds had been subscribed for by the public in a promotion fraud instigated by the Consolidated Contract Corporation. On this evidence, it was held to be just and equitable to grant a winding-up order.

The judgment of the court (LINDLEY, AL SMITH and RIGBY LJJ) was read by AL SMITH LJ: In our judgment it has been proved that this company—ie Thomas Edward Brinsmead & Sons Limited—was initiated to carry out a fraud, and that, until restrained by injunction, it continued therein; and that a strong prima facie case has been made out that the Consolidated Contract Corporation are at the present moment dishonestly keeping the shareholders' money to which the shareholders, and not they, are entitled, and are resisting the petition to wind up in order to continue to do so. If the sums which they have improperly obtained from the company can be recovered from them, there will probably be something to distribute among the shareholders and, although the petitioner is a fully paid-up shareholder, he cannot be said to have no locus standi. The company is hopelessly embarrassed by the actions already brought against it, and there will, no doubt, be many more of the same sort if this petition is dismissed; and if it is not wound up the £35,000 obtained from it by its promoters will remain in their hands.

Although the words 'just and equitable' have had a narrow construction put upon them,[36] they have never been construed so narrowly as to exclude such a case as this. If ever there was a case in which it was just and equitable that a company should be wound up by the court, we cannot doubt that the case is this case. For the reasons above, we dismiss this appeal with costs.

➤ Note

The entire scheme for the company must be fraudulent in order to justify liquidation under this principle. Usually if the company itself has been defrauded, or if subscribers for shares have been misled or defrauded, these parties must simply apply for a remedy against the wrongdoer; the company will not be wound up.

[35] On the 'just and equitable' ground generally, see BH McPherson, 'Winding up on the Just and Equitable Ground' (1964) 27 MLR 282, suggesting that the decided cases fall into three broad categories: (i) where it initially is, or later becomes, impossible to achieve the objects for which the company was formed; (ii) where it has become impossible for the company to carry on its business; and (iii) where there has been serious fraud, misconduct or oppression in regard to the affairs of the company.

[36] [This narrow construction was later rejected: see the *Ebrahimi* case [14.14].]

*It is just and equitable to wind up a company when its 'substratum' or principal object
has failed.*

[14.11] Re Kitson & Co Ltd [1946] 1 All ER 435 (Court of Appeal)

The company was incorporated in 1899. The first two sub-clauses of the objects clause in its
memorandum read as follows:

(1) To acquire and take over as a going concern the business now carried on at Airedale
Foundry, Hunslet, in the city of Leeds, under the style or firm of 'Kitson & Co', and all or any
of the assets and liabilities . . .

(2) To carry on the business of locomotive engine manufacturers, iron-founders, mechanical
engineers and manufacturers of agricultural implements and other machinery, tool makers,
brass founders, metal workers, boiler makers . . .

In July 1945, the company agreed to sell the goodwill and assets of the engineering business
which was carried on at the Airedale foundry, and acquire the assets of a subsidiary
('Balmforth') and to continue an engineering business. It was held that the substratum had
not gone.

LORD GREENE MR: [The] form of the memorandum is the common form where a business is being
acquired. It sets out in the usual way the acquisition of the business as the first step which the company is going to undertake. We are not considering now whether failure in 1899 to acquire the business of Kitson & Co would have destroyed the substratum of the company. It might possibly have
been thought that unless it got this business it was not really starting its career in the way in which
the shareholders bargained it should be started; but the question we have to decide is whether, that
business having been acquired, forty-six years ago, the disposal of it last year amounted to a
destruction of the substratum. In my opinion, the main and paramount object of this company was
to carry on an engineering business of a general kind. It was such a business that was carried on by
Kitson & Co, and I cannot bring myself to construe this memorandum as limiting the paramount
object and restricting the contemplated adventure of the shareholders to the carrying on of what
could be called the business of Kitson & Co. The impossibility of applying such a construction
seems to me to be manifest when one remembers that a business is a thing which changes. It
grows or it contracts. It changes; it disposes of the whole of its plant; it moves its factory; it entirely
changes its range of products, and so forth. It is more like an organic thing. Counsel for the respondents quoted to us a number of very well-known authorities on which it has been held that on particular facts the substratum of particular companies had gone. I do not propose to examine those
authorities because they do not assist me in construing this particular memorandum. It must be
remembered in these substratum cases that there is every difference between a company which
on the true construction of its memorandum is formed for the paramount purpose of dealing with
some specific subject-matter and a company which is formed with wider and more comprehensive
objects. I will explain what I mean. With regard to a company which is formed to acquire and exploit
a mine, when you come to construe its memorandum of association you must construe the language used in reference to the subject-matter, namely, a mine, and, accordingly, if the mine cannot
be acquired or if the mine turns out to be no mine at all, the object of the company is frustrated,
because the subject-matter which the company was formed to exploit has ceased to exist. It is
exactly the same way with a patent, as in the well-known German Date Coffee case.[37] A patent is
a defined subject-matter, and, if the main object of a company is to acquire and work a patent and it
fails to acquire that patent, to compel the shareholders to remain bound together in order to work
some other patent or make some unpatented article is to force them into a different adventure to
that which they contracted to engage in together; but, when you come to subject-matter of a totally
different kind like the carrying on of a type of business, then, so long as the company can carry on

---

[37]   *Re German Date Coffee Co* (1882) 20 Ch D 169, CA.

that type of business, it seems to me that prima facie at any rate it is impossible to say that its substratum has gone. So far as this stage of the argument is concerned, it is to my mind quite impossible upon the true construction of this memorandum of association to limit the paramount object of this company to the specific business of Kitson & Co, so as to lead to the result that as soon as Kitson & Co's business was sold the substratum of the company had gone . . .

MORTON and TUCKER LJJ delivered concurring judgments.

> Note

In *Re Tivoli Freeholds Ltd* [1972] VR 445 (SC Vic) a winding-up petition was granted on the just and equitable ground. The main objects of the company had been to own and build theatres and to carry on theatrical and similar entertainment businesses. An outside group acquired control of the company and, having realised nearly all of its assets, used the funds so raised to mount corporate raids on other firms. (These activities were quite profitable and dividends were regularly paid on the strength of the profits, so an alternative petition based on alleged oppression of the minority members (see above, pp 552 ff) was rejected by the judge.) Although it was not contended that the company could not, if it chose, have continued to pursue its original objects, the court accepted that the evidence showed that the business for which the company was formed had been conclusively abandoned, and granted relief on a basis analogous to a failure of substratum.

It is just and equitable to wind up a company when there is a complete deadlock in the management.

What is meant by 'deadlock' is not completely clear from the cases. Deadlock requires at least an impasse in the corporate decision-making process. But in most cases the courts will hold that there is no deadlock if a legal means exists to get decisions made, using some procedure under either the company's constitution or the general law. On the other hand, in quasi-partnerships, it may be unjust or inequitable to leave one faction to exercise its legal rights over the other (see the *Ebrahimi* case [14.14]).

It is just and equitable to wind up a company where there is such a justifiable (and, it seems, insoluble) lack of confidence in the management of the company's affairs that it is unjust and inequitable to require the petitioner to remain a member.

[14.12] Loch v John Blackwood Ltd [1924] AC 783 (Privy Council)

The engineering business of John Blackwood had, after his death, been formed into a company and run by one of his trustees, McLaren, for the benefit of the three beneficiaries in his estate: McLaren's wife (who was to take one half), Mrs Loch (one-quarter) and Rodger (since deceased, one quarter). The business had been run very profitably by McLaren, but (as is described in the judgment) he had run it in a manner which was oppressive to the beneficiaries other than his wife. They accordingly petitioned for the winding up of the company on the ground that it was just and equitable to do so. The Chief Justice of Barbados made an order, which was reversed by the West Indian Court of Appeal but restored by the Privy Council. [The remaining facts appear from the judgment.]

The opinion of the Privy Council was delivered by LORD SHAW OF DUNFERMLINE: The board of directors now consists of Mr McLaren, his wife Mrs McLaren, who was appointed in 1913, and Mr Yearwood. Under this directorate the business of the company appears to have been energetically managed and to have amassed considerable profits.

The arrangement of the capital was this: the total amount was 40,000 in £1 shares; 20,000 of these were allotted to Mrs McLaren; of the remaining 20,000, 10,000 should have gone to Mrs Loch and 10,000 to Mr Rodger. Mrs Loch, however, was allotted 9,999; Mr Rodger, 9,998; and the three shares left over were allotted one to Mr McLaren and one each to Mr Yearwood and Mr King (Mrs McLaren's nominees; the first being Mr McLaren's clerk and the second his solicitor). This was quite a natural and proper arrangement; but, of course, in the event of a division of opinion in the family between what may be called the McLaren interest on the one hand, and the interest of the nephew and niece on the other, the preponderance of voting power lay with the former. It is thus seen that although taking the form of a public company the concern was practically a domestic and family concern. This consideration is important,[38] as also is the preponderance of voting power just alluded to.

In the petition for winding up eight different reasons are assigned therefor. The first is: that the statutory conditions as to general meetings have not been observed; the second that balance-sheets, profit and loss accounts and reports have not been submitted in terms of the articles of the company; and the third is that the conditions under the statute and articles as to audit have not been complied with. All these allegations are true, and it seems naturally to follow from the preponderance already alluded to, that there is at least considerable force in the fifth reason that it is impossible for the petitioners to obtain any relief by calling a general meeting of the company. There are further submissions—namely, that the company and the managing director, Mr McLaren, have refused to submit the value of the shares to arbitration, and that without winding up it is impossible for the petitioners to realise the true value of their shares. But the principal ground of the petitioner is that in the circumstances to be laid before the court it is just and equitable that the company should be ordered to be wound up. This last ground was affirmed by the Court of Common Pleas.

With regard to the first three submissions made in the petition, it was strenuously argued on behalf of the company, which practically means the directorate or the McLaren interest, that however true it might be that owing to the informal way in which the books of the company had been kept it appeared as if both the statute and the articles of association had been violated in various particulars and that no general meetings of the company had been held, and no auditors properly appointed, and it was certain that no balance-sheets, profit and loss accounts and reports had been submitted for the critical years 1919 and 1920, still these were no grounds for winding up. Other applications, it was said, might competently be made to the court to compel the statute and articles to be properly complied with. It may be doubtful whether such a course of conduct lasting in several particulars since its inception until now, would be insufficient as a ground for winding the company up. But their Lordships think it unnecessary to give any separate decision upon such a point.

In their opinion, however, elements of that character in the history of the company, together with the fact that a calling of a meeting of shareholders would lead admittedly to failure and be unavailable as a remedy, cannot be excluded from the point of view of the court in a consideration of the justice and equity of pronouncing an order for winding up. Such a consideration, in their Lordships' view, ought to proceed upon a sound induction of all the facts of the case, and should not exclude, but should include circumstances which bear upon the problem of continuing or stopping courses of conduct which substantially impair those rights and protections to which shareholders, both under statute and contract, are entitled. It is undoubtedly true that at the foundation of applications for winding up, on the 'just and equitable' rule, there must lie a justifiable lack of confidence in the conduct and management of the company's affairs. But this lack of confidence must be grounded on conduct of the directors, not in regard to their private life or affairs, but in regard to the company's business.[39] Furthermore the lack of confidence must spring not from dissatisfaction at being

---

[38] [Although an important factor, it is probably not vital. In some jurisdictions overseas it has been held that the principle is not confined to domestic companies: see Re Wondoflex Textiles Pty Ltd [1951] VLR 458; Re R J Jowsey Mining Co Ltd [1969] 2 OR 549.]

[39] [Later cases, particularly those in which there has been a breakdown of personal relationships between the parties (eg a husband and wife who have divorced), seem to adopt a less restrictive approach: see eg Belman v Belman (1995) 26 OR (3d) 56, and cf the remarks of Lord Wilberforce in the Ebrahimi case [14.14], ' . . . any circumstances of justice or equity which affect him in his relations . . . with the other shareholders'.]

outvoted on the business affairs or on what is called the domestic policy of the company. On the other hand, wherever the lack of confidence is rested on a lack of probity in the conduct of the company's affairs, then the former is justified by the latter, and it is under the statute just and equitable that the company be wound up. . . .

Mr McLaren, for reasons not unnatural, had come to be of opinion that the business owed much of its value and prosperity to himself. But he appears to have proceeded to the further stage of feeling that in these circumstances he could manage the business as if it were his own. Had Mrs Loch and Mr Rodger, or after his death Mr Rodger's executor, obtained a dividend which year by year represented in any reasonable measure a just declaration out of the undoubted profits of the concern, they might no doubt have been content to allow this state of matters to go on; but although on one or two occasions, Mr McLaren paid trifling and fragmentary sums to Mrs Loch, neither she nor the Rodger family have ever obtained any dividend at all. And it is not to be wondered at that in the transaction now about to be mentioned they completely lost confidence in Mr McLaren, and had only too great justification for doing so . . .

[His Lordship then referred to a decision of the directors to pay McLaren an increased salary and to transfer to him £12,500 War Loan stock, and continued:] No notice was given to the respondents, as shareholders, of this piece of business being contemplated, and no notice was given of what had been done. Four days after this extraordinary transaction, Mr McLaren wrote to Mrs Loch's husband a letter dated 5 May 1920 proposing to her that £10,000 should be given by him as the cumulative value of Mrs Loch's shares and Mr JB Rodger's executor's shares. These shares in all amounted to one-half of the capital of the company—namely, £20,000—and, as already mentioned, it is evident that the true value of assets much exceeded this amount. The proposal was to buy Mrs Loch and the Rodger family out for £10,000. But a further suggestion, which in some ways seems to have been mixed up with the umbrage felt by Mr McLaren in regard to the contents of Mr Rodger's will, was made, and that was that Mrs Loch should be a participant in a scheme whereby the £10,000 to be paid should be distributed—£8,000 to herself and only £2,000 to the Rodgers family.

Their Lordships do not desire to characterise these suggestions in the language which perhaps they fully deserve. The Rodger family, entitled to one-fourth of the holding in the company, nominally £10,000, but in reality of a much higher value, were to be bought off for £2,000, and Mrs Loch was to be the agent in this scheme. No confidence in the directorate could survive such a proposal. To crown all this, as was afterwards discovered, the £10,000 could be comfortably paid by Mr McLaren out of the £12,500 which, four days before, he and his wife and clerk had voted to himself out of the funds of the company. Their Lordships express no surprise at the instant repudiation of Mr McLaren's proposals by Mrs Loch—a repudiation which is creditable to her—and at the application for a winding up of the company being made. Upon the principles already set forth in this judgment that application must succeed. The broad ground is that confidence in its management was, and is, and that most justifiably, at an end . . .

➤ Notes

1. In *Re R A Noble & Sons (Clothing) Ltd* [1983] BCLC 273, Nourse J held that, so long as the conduct of those in control has been 'the substantial cause' of the destruction of the mutual confidence between the parties, it is unnecessary to show either that that conduct has been in some way underhand or that the petitioner's own conduct has been above reproach. The Privy Council took a similar view in *Vujnovich v Vujnovich* [1990] BCLC 227.

2. But note that the court has a discretion under IA 1986 s 125(2) to refuse an order on the 'just and equitable' ground if the petitioner is acting unreasonably in seeking to have the company wound up instead of pursuing some other remedy. In *Re a Company* [1983] 2 All ER 854, [1983] 1 WLR 927, Vinelott J held that a petitioner had acted unreasonably in refusing an offer made by the majority members to buy his shares, following a breakdown of confidence,

and refused him a winding-up order. That case may be contrasted with *Virdi v Abbey Leisure Ltd* [1990] BCLC 342, CA, where the court exercised its discretion in the petitioner's favour on a similar issue.

It is just and equitable to wind up a company which is a quasi-partnership when there has been a sufficiently serious breach of mutual understandings.

[14.13] Re Yenidje Tobacco Co Ltd [1916] 2 Ch 426 (Court of Appeal)

The company was formed by two tobacco manufacturers, Rothman and Weinberg, in order to amalgamate their businesses. They were the only members, with equal voting rights, and the only directors. The parties had been for some time in a state of continuous quarrel. Rothman had brought an action against Weinberg alleging fraud; they had spent over £1,000 [a substantial sum at the time] in litigation over the validity of the dismissal of a factory manager; they had argued over the terms of employment of a traveller; and they had been communicating with each other only through the secretary of the company. In this situation (despite the fact that the company was making larger profits than ever before), the court granted a winding-up order on Weinberg's petition.

LORD COZENS-HARDY MR: In those circumstances, supposing it had been a private partnership, an ordinary partnership between two people having equal shares, and there being no other provision to terminate it, what would have been the position? I think it is quite clear under the law of partnership, as has been asserted in this court for many years and is now laid down by the Partnership Act, that that state of things might be a ground for dissolution of the partnership for the reasons which are stated by Lord Lindley in his book on Partnership at p 657 in the passage which I will read, and, which, I think, is quite justified by the authorities to which he refers:

'Refusal to meet on matters of business, continued quarrelling, and such a state of animosity as precludes all reasonable hope of reconciliation and friendly co-operation have been held sufficient to justify dissolution. It is not necessary, in order to induce the Court to interfere, to show personal rudeness on the part of one partner to the other, or even any gross misconduct as a partner. All that is necessary is to satisfy the Court that it is impossible for the partners to place that confidence in each other which each has a right to expect, and that such impossibility has not been caused by the person seeking to take advantage of it' . . .

I ask myself the question: When one of the two partners has commenced, and has not discontinued, an action charging his co-partner with fraud in the inception of the partnership, is it likely, is it reasonable, is it common sense, to suppose those two partners can work together in the manner in which they ought to work in the conduct of the partnership business?

[His Lordship referred to other aspects of the dispute and continued:] Is it possible to say that it is not just and equitable that that state of things should not be allowed to continue, and that the court should not intervene and say this is not what the parties contemplated by the arrangement into which they entered? They assumed, and it is the foundation of the whole of the agreement that was made, that the two would act as reasonable men with reasonable courtesy and reasonable conduct in every way towards each other, and arbitration was only to be resorted to with regard to some particular dispute between the directors which could not be determined in any other way. Certainly, having regard to the fact that the only two directors will not speak to each other, and no business which deserves the name of business in the affairs of the company can be carried on, I think the company should not be allowed to continue. I have treated it as a partnership, and under the Partnership Act of course the application for a dissolution would take the form of an action; but this is not a partnership strictly, it is not a case in which it can be dissolved by action. But ought not precisely the same principles to apply to a case like this where in substance it is a partnership in the form of the guise of a private company? It is a private company, and there is no way to put an end to the state of things which now exists except by means of a compulsory order. It has been urged upon us that, although it is admitted that the 'just and equitable' clause is not to be limited to cases ejusdem generis, it has nevertheless been held, according to the authorities, not to apply except where the substratum of the company has gone or where there is a complete deadlock. Those are the two instances which are given, but I should be very sorry, so far as my individual opinion goes, to hold that they are strictly the limits of the 'just and equitable' clause as found in the Companies Act. I think that in a case like this we are bound to say that circumstances which would justify the winding up of a partnership between these two by action are circumstances which should induce the court to exercise its jurisdiction under the just and equitable clause and to wind up the company . . . [His Lordship then ruled it irrelevant that the company was making large profits.]

WARRINGTON LJ delivered a concurring judgment.

PICKFORD LJ concurred.

[14.14] Ebrahimi v Westbourne Galleries Ltd [1973] AC 360 (House of Lords)

This is probably the most cited case in this area. The company was formed in 1958 to take over a business which Nazar and Ebrahimi had run in partnership for over a decade. At first, the two were equal shareholders and the only directors, but soon afterwards Nazar's son joined the company as a director and shareholder, so that Ebrahimi found himself in a minority position both on the board of directors and at a general meeting. In 1969, after some disagreement between the parties, an ordinary resolution was passed under s 184 of the Act of 1948 [CA 2006 s 168], removing Ebrahimi as director. Ebrahimi sought relief under s 210, or, alternatively, s 222(f) of the 1948 Act [respectively CA 2006 s 994 and IA 1986 s 122(1)(g)]. Plowman J declined to make an order under s 210 because (*inter alia*) Ebrahimi's complaint was in his capacity as director rather than as member (see above, pp 230 ff); but he did make a winding-up order. The Court of Appeal reversed the latter ruling, holding that the exercise by a majority of its constitutional and statutory rights, unless shown to be *mala fide*, was not a ground for 'just and equitable' relief under s 222(f). The House of Lords restored the decision of the trial judge.

LORD WILBERFORCE: My Lords, the petition was brought under s 222(f) of the Companies Act 1948 [IA 1986, s 122(1)(g)], which enables a winding-up order to be made if 'the court is of the opinion that it is just and equitable that the company should be wound up'. This power has existed in our company law in unaltered form since the first major Act, the Companies Act 1862. For some fifty years, following a pronouncement by Lord Cottenham LC in 1849, the words 'just and equitable' were interpreted so as only to include matters ejusdem generis as the preceding clauses of the section, but there is now ample authority for discarding this limitation. There are two other restrictive interpretations which I mention to reject. First, there has been a tendency to create categories or headings under which cases must be brought if the clause is to apply. This is wrong. Illustrations may be used, but general words should remain general and not be reduced to the sum of particular instances. Secondly, it has been suggested, and urged upon us, that (assuming the petitioner is a shareholder and not a creditor) the words must be confined to such circumstances as affect him in his capacity as shareholder. I see no warrant for this either. No doubt, in order to present a petition, he must qualify as a shareholder, but I see no reason for preventing him from relying upon any circumstances of justice or equity which affect him in his relations with the company, or, in a case such as the present, with the other shareholders.

One other signpost is significant. The same words 'just and equitable' appear in the Partnership Act 1890, s 35, as a ground for dissolution of a partnership and no doubt the considerations which they reflect formed part of the common law of partnership before its codification. The importance of this is to provide a bridge between cases under s 222(f) of the Act of 1948 and the principles of equity developed in relation to partnerships.

The winding-up order was made following a doctrine which has developed in the courts since the beginning of this century. As presented by the appellant, and in substance accepted by the learned judge, this was that in a case such as this the members of the company are in substance partners, or quasi-partners, and that a winding up may be ordered if such facts are shown as could justify a dissolution of partnership between them. The common use of the words 'just and equitable' in the company and partnership law supports this approach. Your Lordships were invited by the respondents' counsel to restate the principle on which this provision ought to be used; it has not previously been considered by this House. The main line of his submission was to suggest that too great a use of the partnership analogy had been made; that a limited company, however small, essentially differs from a partnership; that in the case of a company, the rights of its members are governed by the articles of association which have contractual force; that the court has no power or at least ought not to dispense parties from observing their contracts; that, in particular, when one member has been excluded from the directorate, or management, under powers expressly conferred by the Companies Act and the articles, an order for winding up, whether on the partnership analogy or under the just and equitable provision, should not be made. Alternatively, it was argued that before the making of such an order could be considered the petitioner must show and prove that the exclusion was not made bona fide in the interests of the company.

[His Lordship discussed a number of earlier cases and continued:]

My Lords, in my opinion these authorities represent a sound and rational development of the law which should be endorsed. The foundation of it all lies in the words 'just and equitable' and, if there is any respect in which some of the cases may be open to criticism, it is that the courts may sometimes have been too timorous in giving them full force. The words are a recognition of the fact that a limited company is more than a mere legal entity, with a personality in law of its own: that there is room in company law for recognition of the fact that behind it, or amongst it, there are individuals, with rights, expectations and obligations inter se which are not necessarily submerged in the company structure. That structure is defined by the Companies Act and by the articles of association by which shareholders agree to be bound. In most companies and in most contexts, this definition is sufficient and exhaustive, equally so whether the company is large or small. The 'just and equitable' provision does not, as the respondents suggest, entitle one party to disregard the obligation he assumed by entering a company, nor the court to dispense him from it. It does, as equity always does, enable the court to subject the exercise of legal rights to equitable considerations, considerations, that is, of a personal character arising between one individual and another, which may make it unjust, or inequitable, to insist on legal rights, or to exercise them in a particular way.

It would be impossible, and wholly undesirable, to define the circumstances in which these considerations may arise. Certainly the fact that a company is a small one, or a private company, is not enough. There are very many of these where the association is a purely commercial one, of which it can safely be said that the basis of association is adequately and exhaustively laid down in the articles. The superimposition of equitable considerations requires something more, which typically may include one, or probably more, of the following elements: (i) an association formed or continued on the basis of a personal relationship, involving mutual confidence—this element will often be found where a pre-existing partnership has been converted into a limited company; (ii) an agreement, or understanding, that all, or some (for there may be 'sleeping' members), of the shareholders shall participate in the conduct of the business; (iii) restriction upon the transfer of the members' interest in the company—so that if confidence is lost, or one member is removed from management, he cannot take out his stake and go elsewhere.

It is these, and analogous, factors which may bring into play the just and equitable clause, and they do so directly, through the force of the words themselves. To refer, as so many of the cases do, to 'quasi-partnerships' or 'in substance partnerships' may be convenient but may also be confusing. It may be convenient because it is the law of partnership which has developed the conceptions of probity, good faith and mutual confidence, and the remedies where these are absent, which become relevant once such factors as I have mentioned are found to exist: the words 'just and equitable' sum these up in the law of partnership itself. And in many, but not necessarily all, cases there has been a pre-existing partnership the obligations of which it is reasonable to suppose continue to underlie the new company structure. But the expressions may be confusing if they obscure, or deny, the fact that the parties (possibly former partners) are now co-members in a company, who have accepted, in law, new obligations. A company, however small, however domestic, is a company, not a partnership or even a quasi-partnership and it is through the just and equitable clause that obligations, common to partnership relations, may come in.

My Lords, this is an expulsion case, and I must briefly justify the application in such cases of the just and equitable clause. The question is, as always, whether it is equitable to allow one (or two) to make use of his legal rights to the prejudice of his associate(s). The law of companies recognises the right, in many ways, to remove a director from the board. Section 184 of the Companies Act 1948 [CA 2006, s 168] confers this right upon the company in general meeting whatever the articles may say. Some articles may prescribe other methods: for example, a governing director may have the power to remove (compare *Re Wondoflex Textiles Pty Ltd*).[40] And quite apart from removal powers, there are normally provisions for retirement of directors by rotation so that their re-election can be opposed and defeated by a majority, or even by a casting vote. In all these ways a particular director-member may find himself no longer a director, through removal, or non-re-election: this situation he must normally accept, unless he undertakes the burden of proving fraud or mala fides. The just and equitable provision nevertheless comes to his assistance if he can point to, and prove, some special underlying obligation of his fellow member(s) in good faith, or confidence, that so long as the business continues he shall be entitled to management participation, an obligation so basic that, if broken, the conclusion must be that the association must be dissolved . . .

I come to the facts of this case. It is apparent enough that a potential basis for a winding-up order under the just and equitable clause existed. The appellant after a long association in partnership, during which he had an equal share in the management, joined in the formation of the company. The inference must be indisputable that he, and Mr Nazar, did so on the basis that the character of the association would, as a matter of personal relation and good faith, remain the same. He was removed from his directorship under a power valid in law. Did he establish a case which, if he had remained in a partnership with a term providing for expulsion, would have justified an order for dissolution? This was the essential question for the judge. Plowman J dealt with the issue in a brief paragraph in which he said: 'while no doubt the petitioner was lawfully removed, in the sense that he ceased in law to be a director, it does not follow that in removing him the respondents did not do him a wrong. In my judgment, they did do him a wrong, in the sense that it was an abuse of power and a breach of the good faith which partners owe to each other to exclude one of them from all participation in the business upon which they have embarked on the basis that all should participate in its management. The main justification put forward for removing him was that he was perpetually complaining, but the faults were not all on one side and, in my judgment, this is not sufficient justification. For these reasons, in my judgment, the petitioner, therefore, has made out a case for a winding-up order.' Reading this in the context of the judgment as a whole, which had dealt with the specific complaints of one side against the other, I take it as a finding that the respondents were not entitled, in justice and equity, to make use of their legal powers of expulsion and that . . . the only just and equitable course was to dissolve the association . . .

LORD CROSS OF CHELSEA delivered a concurring opinion.

VISCOUNT DILHORNE, LORD PEARSON and LORD SALMON concurred.

➤ Notes

1. The *Ebrahimi* case **[14.14]** makes it clear that it may be just and equitable to wind up a company even though the controllers have acted within their strict legal rights.

---

[40] [1951] VLR 458.

2. The *Ebrahimi* case **[14.14]** also makes it clear that it may be just and equitable to wind up a company when the complaint relates to behaviour that is contrary to the settled and accepted course of conduct between the parties, whether or not reinforced by contract of by the articles.

3. Many of the above cases, especially the earlier ones, in which a winding-up order was made on the 'just and equitable' ground, might now be more appropriately made the subject of proceedings under CA 2006 s 994 (discussed above, pp 552 ff). On the other hand, there are modern quasi-partnership cases where the courts refuse to find prejudicial conduct (under CA 1985 s 459, the predecessor of CA 2006 s 994), but will order a just and equitable winding up: eg *Re RA Noble (Clothing) Ltd* [1983] BCLC 273.

The court's discretion to order a compulsory winding up

Once the petitioner has established the right to bring a petition, and proved the grounds alleged, the court has to decide whether or not to make the order to wind up the company. Normally their decision will follow from proof of the elements of the claim, but it is worth noting that:

(i)   On a member's or contributor's petition, the court has a statutory discretion to refuse the petition if some other remedy is available to the petitioners *and* it seems that the petitioners are acting unreasonably in seeking to have the company wound up rather than relying on that other remedy (IA 1986 s 125(2)). The court is frequently asked to exercise this discretion where minority shareholders seek an order on the grounds of 'unfair prejudice' (CA 2006 s 994, see pp 552 ff) and, alternatively, a winding up on the 'just and equitable' ground.

(ii)   The court has an inherent jurisdiction to refuse a winding up order brought for extraneous or improper purposes. In *Re Surrey Garden Village Trust Ltd* [1995] 1 WLR 974, ChD, Plowman J said '. . . I go further and say that in my judgment it is oppressive and an abuse of the process of the court for shareholders to make use of a winding-up petition for the purpose of seeking to facilitate the achievement of a purely sectional and extraneous object which . . . has no relevance to the interests of the members as such . . . '. Similarly, in *Re J E Cade & Sons Ltd* [1992] BCLC 213, a minority member owned the freehold of a farm which had been occupied under licence by the company for some years. He sought a winding-up order on the 'just and equitable' ground or, alternatively, relief under CA 1985 s 459 [CA 2006 s 994]; but the court struck out his petition because his real object in bringing the proceedings was not to protect his interests as a member but to secure possession of the farm.

(iii)   Finally, the court has an inherent jurisdiction to strike out a petition for winding up which is bound to fail, as an abuse of the process of the court, and it may grant an injunction to restrain the presentation of such a petition (see *Charles Forte Investments Ltd v Amanda* [1964] Ch 240, CA, where Amanda was attempting to use the winding-up procedure as a means of putting pressure on the directors to register certain share transfers).

By invoking these statutory and inherent jurisdictions to have petitions dismissed, a company may avoid the unfavourable publicity that a winding-up petition inevitably attracts.

The functions, powers and duties of the liquidator

The basic duty of the liquidator is to wind up the company's affairs, collect in and realise the company's assets and undertaking, and make the appropriate distributions to the creditors and, if there is a surplus, to the shareholders.

The rules governing the functions, powers and duties of a liquidator are partly set out in the Insolvency Act 1986 and Insolvency Rules 1986, and partly established by the case-law. The Act now makes it obligatory for a liquidator to be a qualified insolvency practitioner (s 230(3)). In a compulsory liquidation, the liquidator is also an officer of the court.

A liquidator acts in the name of the company (which continues to have a separate corporate personality) and not in his own name (except where he is exercising certain special statutory powers), although sometimes, exceptionally, an order of the court is sought vesting all or part of the company's property in the liquidator's name (IA 1986 s 145). This might be necessary, for example, to deal with the local assets of a foreign company which had already been dissolved in its home jurisdiction. Although a liquidator acts in the company's name and not in his own name, he can sometimes incur personal liability, eg where he institutes proceedings and the costs exceed the amount of the company's assets: *Re Wilson Lovatt & Sons Ltd* [1977] 1 All ER 274.

A liquidator owes his duties to the company, not to individual creditors or contributories (*Knowles v Scott* [1891] 1 Ch 717). He may be personally liable for breach of duty, and sued in misfeasance proceedings under IA 1986 s 212, if he:

(i)   fails to comply with the strict statutory terms of his office (eg in wrongly admitting a claim by an alleged creditor: *Re Home and Colonial Insurance Co Ltd* [1930] 1 Ch 102; or in distributing the company's assets properly among the persons entitled: *Pulsford v Devenish* [1903] 2 Ch 625);

(ii)   performs his functions negligently (*Re Windsor Steam Coal Co (1901) Ltd* [1928] Ch 609); or

(iii) breaches his fiduciary duties to the company by taking secret profits or placing himself in positions of conflict.

Certain statutory powers of a liquidator are conferred by IA 1986 ss 165ff and Sch 4. These, or rather the circumstances in which they may be exercised, vary slightly depending on the type of winding up. Other powers (eg to make calls upon the contributories) are given by the Act in the first place to the court but are then delegated to the liquidator by the rules, pursuant to s 160.

The conduct of the liquidation

The way in which a liquidation is conducted can be described in general terms, but there are differences in detail between compulsory and voluntary liquidations, and between a members' and a creditors' voluntary winding up, which can be discovered only from a study of the 1986 Act and the Insolvency Rules.

The Act confers a wide range of powers on a liquidator. There is an extensive list of specific powers set out in Sch 4, eg the power to bring and defend proceedings, to carry on the company's business, to borrow and to charge the company's property as security. By ss 178ff a liquidator is empowered to 'disclaim' what are described as 'unprofitable contracts' and 'onerous property'—in other words, to wash his hands of any responsibility under the contract or any interest in the property. A common example is a lease of property which is let at a rental higher than the current market rate. Anyone who suffers loss as a result of a disclaimer can prove for it as a debt in the winding up, but will usually be an unsecured creditor with all the disadvantages that entails. Other powers (which are also given to an administrator) include the power to examine directors and other persons on oath in order to gain information about the company's affairs (s 236, see below at pp 678 ff): recall that the person being examined cannot refuse to give answers even where they are incriminating (see p 602 above).

'Commencement' of winding up

For many statutory purposes,[41] a winding up takes effect from its 'commencement', which may involve some back-dating. Section 86 of IA 1986 provides that a voluntary winding up is

---

[41] But not all: for example, the value of a debt is reckoned for the purpose of proof at the date when the company goes into liquidation: *Re Lines Bros Ltd* [1983] Ch 1, [1982] 2 All ER 183, CA; and the periods of time prescribed by the Limitation Act 1980 cease to run against the company's creditors (other than the petitioning creditor himself) on the making of the winding-up order: *Re Cases of Taff's Well Ltd* [1992] Ch 179, [1992] BCLC 11.

deemed to commence at the time of the passing of the resolution for winding up. In the case of a compulsory winding up, the liquidation is deemed to commence at the time of the presentation of the petition (and not the making of the order itself), but if the company is already in voluntary liquidation when the petition is presented, the relevant time is when the winding-up resolution was passed (s 129).

These provisions have important consequences because from the date of commencement:

(i)   dispositions of property by the company (in a compulsory winding up) are avoided, unless the court otherwise orders (s 127);

(ii)   attachments, distress and execution (in a compulsory winding up) which have not been completed are void (s 128);[42]

(iii) transfers of shares are avoided (ss 88, 127);

(iv) some categories of creditor are given preferential rights in regard to debts incurred within prescribed periods before that date, eg up to four months' salaries and wages (ss 175, 386 and Sch 6) (see below, pp 676 ff);

(v)   transactions entered into within prescribed periods before that date may be invalidated as having been 'at an undervalue' or 'preferences' (ss 238–241: see *Re M C Bacon Ltd* [14.16]);

(vi) a floating charge created within twelve months (or, in some cases, two years) of that date may be invalidated (s 245; see *Re Parkes Garage* [10.16], and *Re Yeovil Glove* [10.17]).

It is not easy to reconcile these 'back-dating' provisions with those of CA 2006 s 1079, which aims to protect third parties without actual notice until 15 days after the 'official notification' in the *Gazette* of the making of a winding-up order or, in a voluntary liquidation, of the appointment of a liquidator (see above, pp 583 ff). It is plain that the full implications of this statutory misfit (which are the result of implementing the First EC Directive) have not been fully thought through by the legislators.

The liquidator's ability to 'claw back' property—unwinding transactions

The effect of the statutory provisions referred to above, in paras (i), (ii), (v) and (vi), is to allow the liquidator to 'claw back' property which has been transferred away by the company, and to avoid some transactions which it has entered into in the period immediately preceding the winding up, thus increasing the assets available for distribution to the creditors generally.

The Insolvency Act 1986 dramatically extended the scope of these provisions by comparison with the previous law. The existing provisions do not depend upon proof of fraud and dishonesty, but simply require that there be '*transactions at an undervalue*' (s 238), and '*preferences*' (s 239). The rules also operate more strictly where the other party to the transaction is a person 'connected with' the company (eg a director or a substantial shareholder, or a close relative of such a person, or another company in the same group: for the full definition, see ss 249, 435). Where a connected person is involved, the time limits may be extended (ss 240(1)(a), 245(3)(a)), the onus of proof may be reversed (ss 239(6), 249(2)), or a possible defence disallowed (s 245(4)). It goes without saying that a very careful reading of the Act is necessary to discover exactly which rules are applicable in a particular case.

The liquidator's ability to require wrongdoers to make personal contributions to the assets of the company

The Insolvency Act 1986 (in addition to imposing criminal liability for various forms of misconduct which may be revealed in the course of a winding up) contains a number of provisions under which the directors of a company in liquidation, and in some cases others,

---

[42] In any case, the rights of creditors in levying execution, etc, are restricted by ss 183–184 in every type of winding up.

may be made liable to account, pay compensation or contribute to the assets of the company in the hands of the liquidator:

(i)   IA 1986 s 212 (commonly called the 'misfeasance' section) provides a summary remedy[43] for establishing accountability or assessing damages against delinquent officers (excluding administrators[44]). This is a purely procedural provision, which creates no new liabilities but provides a simpler mechanism for the recovery of property or compensation in a winding up. It does, however, give the court a discretion to require such compensation to be paid in full or in part, 'as the court thinks just', and does not specify conditions for the exercise of this discretion (s 212(3)).[45]

(ii)   If, in the course of a winding up, it is found that any business of the company has been carried on with intent to defraud creditors or for any other fraudulent purpose ('*fraudulent trading*'), the court may order those who were knowingly parties to this misconduct to contribute to the company's assets (s 213). For the purposes of this provision, actual dishonesty must be proved (*Re Patrick and Lyon Ltd* [1933] Ch 786). The sum to be contributed is now to be assessed on a compensatory basis only, with no punitive element: *Morphitis v Bernasconi* [2002] EWCA Civ 289, [2003] Ch 552, CA.[46]

(iii)   A director, former director or 'shadow director' of a company in liquidation may be ordered to contribute personally to the assets in the hands of the liquidator if there have been circumstances constituting '*wrongful trading*' (a phrase used in the side-note, but not the text, of the Act): s 214. The complex provisions of this section need careful study.

Prerequisites for liability are that (i) the person has been a director (or 'shadow director') and (ii) the company has gone into insolvent liquidation. The person must have known, or should have concluded, that there was no reasonable prospect that the company would avoid going into insolvent liquidation. However, he can avoid liability if the court is satisfied that he 'took every step with a view to minimising the potential loss to the company's creditors' that he ought to have taken. Only the liquidator has standing to bring proceedings.

Although described as 'wrongful trading', as noted above, the possible scope of this section is very wide indeed. It can cover passive inactivity just as much as positive wrongdoing; there need be no actual 'trading', but conduct such as allowing the payment of unjustified remuneration or dividends could be caught; and as s 214(4) makes clear, and, as the *Produce Marketing* case **[14.17]** confirms, the director's behaviour is to be judged by objective as well as subjective standards.

It has also been held, as a matter of law, that CA 2006 s 1157 (which empowers a court to relieve a director from liability for breach of duty where he has acted honestly and reasonably and ought fairly to be excused) is not available to a director in s 214 proceedings, although the logic of that analysis appears questionable.[47] On the other hand, s 214(1) itself allows the court to declare that the person is 'liable to make such contribution (if any) to the company's assets as the court thinks proper', so the court can exercise a discretion in any event.

Although the statutory charge of *fraudulent* trading (s 213) remains on the books, the introduction in 1986 of the concept of 'wrongful' trading, which can lead to the same consequences with a much lighter burden of proof, means that s 213 is only rarely invoked. It is invoked, however, if the objective is to attach liability to defendants who are not subject to s 214, which has a much narrower remit than s 213 (eg over the past decade, the liquidators of BCCI have made significant use of s 213).

---

[43]   Note that the liquidator, too, may be sued under this provision, and may be sued by a creditor or any contributory.
[44]   They are dealt with in IA 1986, Sch B1, para 75.
[45]   Contrast CA 2006 s 1157.
[46]   Also note the fraudulent trading provision in CA 2006 s 993, where *criminal* liability is imposed in circumstances not limited to winding up. This is the provision where penal remedies are appropriate.
[47]   *Re Produce Marketing Consortium Ltd (Halls v David)* [1989] 1 WLR 745, (1989) 5 BCC 399, **[14.17]**.

Money that is ordered to be paid under ss 213 and 214 (and, similarly, ss 238, 239) goes into the general assets of the company in the hands of the liquidator. It is not awardable directly to those affected by the fraudulent or wrongful trading. This avoids the danger that a particular creditor might bring pressure on the directors of a company that was close to insolvency in order to induce them to pay him off out of their own pockets and so gain an advantage over the other creditors. On the other hand, sums recovered under s 212 are the product of a chose in action vested in the company prior to liquidation. Accordingly they are 'assets of the company', which are capable of being caught by the provisions of an appropriately drafted charge (*Re Anglo-Austrian Printing & Publishing Union* [1895] 2 Ch 891), or of being assigned by the company or its liquidator (*Re Oasis Merchandising Services Ltd* [1998] Ch 170).

Finally, the CDDA 1986 authorises the court to make a disqualification order (above, pp 264 ff) against anyone held liable for fraudulent or wrongful trading.

Re-use of company names and the 'Phoenix Syndrome'

The Cork Committee, on whose recommendation the concept of wrongful trading was introduced, were concerned also with another situation, popularly referred to as 'the phoenix syndrome'. This occurs where a person who had been trading through the medium of a company allows it to go into insolvent liquidation and then forms a new company, sometimes with a similar name, and carries on trading much as before. He might even use assets in the new business which he had bought at a knock-down price in the liquidation of the old company, so that the old company's creditors subsidise his fresh start. The Committee (1982, Cmnd 8558, para 1827) recommended that such a person should be personally liable for the second company's debts if it went into insolvent liquidation within three years.

However, instead of this targeted liability, the Insolvency Act simply focuses on the re-use of the name of a defunct company by a person who was one of its directors. Criminal and civil liability follow: the behaviour is made a criminal offence (s 216) which, in *R v Cole* [1998] 2 BCLC 234, CA was held to be one of strict liability.[48] In addition, the director, without the need of any court order, is made personally liable, without limitation, for the debts of the new business, whether or not it becomes insolvent (s 217). The conditions for liability are stringently drawn, the criminal and civil consequences are severe, and liability is automatic: the court has no discretion to absolve the defendant (*Ricketts v Ad Valorem Factors Ltd* [2003] EWCA Civ 1706, [2004] BCC 164). The provisions seem to be used increasingly frequently.

Insolvency and corporate groups

Another problem discussed by the Cork Committee was that of 'group trading'—the 'runt of the litter' situation criticised by Templeman LJ in *Re Southard & Co Ltd* (above, p 69). Is it in keeping with commercial morality that a parent company can allow one of its subsidiaries to decline into insolvency while the rest of the group prospers? *A fortiori*, for the debts owed by the subsidiary to other members of the group to rank equally with those of outside creditors— or even, if secured, ahead of them? The Committee recommended (para 1963) that the law should be changed so that inter-company indebtedness could in some circumstances be postponed to the claim of outside creditors. But, it hesitated to follow the bolder reforms made in New Zealand and Ireland, which empower the court to order one company in a group to pay the debt of another in the insolvent winding up of the latter.

The Insolvency Act contains no special provisions relating to insolvent groups, although it may have met these problems in part by its 'wrongful trading' provisions (which might extend to a parent company as a 'shadow director') and by its measures to extend the circumstances in which floating charges given to 'connected persons' can be invalidated (companies within the same group are 'connected persons').

---

[48] Unless leave of the court has been obtained permitting such activity: s 216(3).

The cases which follow illustrate the operation in practice of some of the provisions of IA 1986 that are discussed above.

Avoidance of property dispositions: IA 1986 s 127.

[14.15] Re Gray's Inn Construction Co Ltd [1980] 1 WLR 711 (Court of Appeal)

The company, which carried on a building business, was ordered to be wound up by the court. Between the time when the petition was presented and the date of the order its bank had allowed it to continue to operate its account. During this period it had traded unprofitably. The Court of Appeal held that both the amounts credited to the company's account and those debited to it constituted 'dispositions' of the company's property (although now see the Note following) and, in the exercise of its discretion under IA 1986 s 127, declined to validate most of these banking transactions. In the course of his judgment, Buckley LJ enunciated some principles for the guidance of courts in relation to the jurisdiction under s 127.

BUCKLEY LJ: It is a basic concept of our law governing the liquidation of insolvent estates, whether in bankruptcy or under the Companies Acts, that the free assets of the insolvent at the commencement of the liquidation shall be distributed rateably amongst the insolvent's unsecured creditors as at that date. . . . In a company's compulsory winding up [this] is achieved by section 227 [of CA 1948, equivalent to IA 1986, s 127]. There may be occasions, however, when it would be beneficial, not only for the company but also for its unsecured creditors, that the company should be enabled to dispose of some of its property during the period after the petition has been presented but before a winding-up order has been made. An obvious example is if the company has an opportunity by acting speedily to dispose of some piece of property at an exceptionally good price. Many applications for validation under the section relate to specific transactions of this kind or analogous kinds. It may sometimes be beneficial to the company and its creditors that the company should be enabled to complete a particular contract or project, or to continue to carry on its business generally in its ordinary course with a view to a sale of the business as a going concern. In any such case the court has power under section 227 of the Companies Act 1948 to validate the particular transaction, or the completion of the particular contract or project, or the continuance of the company's business in its ordinary course, as the case may be. In considering whether to make a validating order the court must always, in my opinion, do its best to ensure that the interests of the unsecured creditors will not be prejudiced. Where the application relates to a specific transaction this may be susceptible of positive proof. In a case of completion of a contract or project the proof may perhaps be less positive but nevertheless be cogent enough to satisfy the court that in the interests of the creditors the company should be enabled to proceed, or at any rate that proceeding in the manner proposed would not prejudice them in any respect. The desirability of the company being enabled to carry on its business generally is likely to be more speculative and will be likely to depend on whether a sale of the business as a going concern will probably be more beneficial than a break-up realisation of the company's assets. In each case, I think, the court must necessarily carry out a balancing exercise . . . Each case must depend upon its own particular facts.

Since the policy of the law is to procure so far as practicable rateable payments of the unsecured creditors' claims, it is, in my opinion, clear that the court should not validate any transaction or series of transactions which might result in one or more pre-liquidation creditors being paid in full at the expense of other creditors, who will only receive a dividend, in the absence of special circumstances making such a course desirable in the interests of the unsecured creditors as a body. If, for example, it were in the interests of the creditors generally that the company's business should be carried on, and this could only be achieved by paying for goods already supplied to the company when the petition is presented but not yet paid for, the court might think fit in the exercise of its discretion to validate payment for those goods. . . .

It may not always be feasible, or desirable, that a validating order should be sought before the transaction in question is carried out. The parties may be unaware at the time when the transaction is entered into that a petition has been presented; or the need for speedy action may be such as to preclude an anticipatory application; or the beneficial character of the transaction may be so obvious that there is no real prospect of a liquidator seeking to set it aside, so that an application to the court would waste time, money and effort. But in any case in which the transaction is carried out without an anticipatory validating order the disponee is at risk of the court declining to validate the transaction. It follows, in my view, that the parties when entering into the transaction, if they are aware that it is liable to be invalidated by the section, should have in mind the sort of considerations which would influence the court's decision.

A disposition carried out in good faith in the ordinary course of business at a time when the parties are unaware that a petition has been presented may, it seems, normally be validated by the court . . . unless there is any ground for thinking that the transaction may involve an attempt to prefer the disponee, in which case the transaction would probably not be validated. In a number of cases reference has been made to the relevance of the policy of ensuring rateable distribution of the assets . . .

But although that policy might disincline the court to ratify any transaction which involved preferring a pre-liquidation creditor, it has no relevance to a transaction which is entirely post-liquidation, as for instance a sale of an asset at its full market value after presentation of a petition. Such a transaction involves no dissipation of the company's assets, for it does not reduce the value of those assets. It cannot harm the creditors and there would seem to be no reason why the court should not in the exercise of its discretion validate it. A fortiori, the court would be inclined to validate a transaction which would increase, or has increased, the value of the company's assets, or which would preserve, or has preserved, the value of the company's assets from harm which would result from the company's business being paralysed . . .

GOFF LJ and SIR DAVID CAIRNS concurred.

➤ Note

The transactions which were challenged in this case were payments into and out of the company's bank account, and the court held, or accepted concessions made by counsel, that all such payments were 'dispositions' by the company within s 127. But later cases have shown that this is not always true. In *Re Barn Crown Ltd* [1994] 2 BCLC 186 it was held that there was no 'disposition', but only an adjustment of entries in the statement recording the accounts between the customer and the banker, when cheques belonging to the company were paid into an account which was already in credit. (However, Professor Goode, *Principles of Corporate Insolvency Law* (3rd edn, 2005), paras 11.128ff, disagrees: if the bank were to become insolvent, the money would be lost, and accordingly there must have been a 'disposition'.) More recently, in *Hollicourt (Contracts) Ltd v Bank of Ireland* [2001] Ch 555, CA, it has been held that where a bank meets a cheque drawn by its customer (whether the account is in credit or overdrawn), it does so merely as the customer's agent. As a result, while there is clearly a disposition by the customer in favour of the payee, there is no disposition to the bank itself—as had been assumed in the *Gray's Inn* case. *Hollicourt* no doubt provides considerable comfort to the banking community, since it reduces concern about this type of restitutionary liability.

Preferences and transactions at an undervalue: IA 1986 ss 239 and 238.

[14.16] Re MC Bacon Ltd [1990] BCLC 324 (Chancery Division)

The company, which carried on business as a bacon importer and wholesaler, had been profitable until it lost its principal customer. It continued trading on a reduced scale for a time, but eventually had to go into liquidation. This action was brought to challenge a debenture which had been given to its bank during this latter period, at a time when it was actually or virtually insolvent and could not have continued without the bank's support. Millett J held that the debenture was not liable to be struck down either (a) as a preference under IA 1986 s 239, since the directors in granting it had not been motivated by a desire to prefer the bank but only by a desire to avoid the calling in of the overdraft and their wish to continue trading, or (b) as a transaction at an undervalue under s 238 because the giving of the security had neither depleted the company's assets nor diminished their value.

MILLETT J: . . .

Voidable preference

So far as I am aware, this is the first case under the section [s 239] and its meaning has been the subject of some debate before me. I shall therefore attempt to provide some guidance.

The section replaces s 44(1) of the Bankruptcy Act 1914, which in certain circumstances deemed fraudulent and avoided payments made and other transactions entered into in favour of a creditor 'with a view of giving such creditor . . . a preference over the other creditors'. Section 44(1) and its predecessors had been construed by the courts as requiring the person seeking to avoid the payment or other transaction to establish that it had been made 'with the dominant intention to prefer' the creditor.

Section 44(1) has been replaced and its language has been entirely recast. Every single word of significance, whether in the form of statutory definition or in its judicial exposition, has been jettisoned. 'View', 'dominant', 'intention' and even 'to prefer' have all been discarded. These are replaced by 'influenced', 'desire', and 'to produce in relation to that person the effect mentioned in sub-s (4)(b)'.

I therefore emphatically protest against the citation of cases decided under the old law. They cannot be of any assistance when the language of the statute has been so completely and deliberately changed. It may be that many of the cases which will come before the courts in future will be decided in the same way that they would have been decided under the old law. That may be so, but the grounds of decision will be different. What the court has to do is to interpret the language of the statute and apply it. It will no longer inquire whether there was 'a dominant intention to prefer' the creditor, but whether the company's decision was 'influenced by a desire to produce the effect mentioned in sub-s (4)(b)'.

This is a completely different test. It involves at least two radical departures from the old law. It is no longer necessary to establish a dominant intention to prefer. It is sufficient that the decision was influenced by the requisite desire. That is the first change. The second is that it is no longer sufficient to establish an intention to prefer. There must be a desire to produce the effect mentioned in the subsection.

This second change is made necessary by the first, for without it it would be virtually impossible to uphold the validity of a security taken in exchange for the injection of fresh funds into a company in financial difficulties. A man is taken to intend the necessary consequences of his actions, so that an intention to grant a security to a creditor necessarily involves an intention to prefer that creditor in the event of insolvency. The need to establish that such intention was dominant was essential under the old law to prevent perfectly proper transactions from being struck down. With the abolition of that requirement intention could not remain the relevant test. Desire has been substituted. That is a very different matter. Intention is objective, desire is subjective. A man can choose the lesser of two evils without desiring either.

It is not, however, sufficient to establish a desire to make the payment or grant the security which it is sought to avoid. There must have been a desire to produce the effect mentioned in the subsection, that is to say, to improve the creditor's position in the event of an insolvent liquidation. A man is not to be taken as desiring all the necessary consequences of his actions. Some consequences may be of advantage to him and be desired by him; others may not affect him and be matters of indifference to him; while still others may be positively disadvantageous to him and not be desired by him, but be regarded by him as the unavoidable price of obtaining the desired advantages. It will still be possible to provide assistance to a company in financial difficulties provided that the company is actuated only by proper commercial considerations. Under the new regime a transaction will not be set aside as a voidable preference unless the company positively wished to improve the creditor's position in the event of its own insolvent liquidation.

There is, of course, no need for there to be direct evidence of the requisite desire. Its existence may be inferred from the circumstances of the case just as the dominant intention could be inferred under the old law. But the mere presence of the requisite desire will not be sufficient by itself. It must have influenced the decision to enter into the transaction. It was submitted on behalf of the bank that it must have been the factor which 'tipped the scales'. I disagree. That is not what sub-s (5) says; it requires only that the desire should have influenced the decision. That requirement is satisfied if it was one of the factors which operated on the minds of those who made the decision. It need not have been the only factor or even the decisive one. In my judgment, it is not necessary to prove that, if the requisite desire had not been present, the company would not have entered into the transaction. That would be too high a test.

It was also submitted that the relevant time was the time when the debenture was created. That cannot be right. The relevant time was the time when the decision to grant it was made. In the present case that is not known with certainty. . . . But it does not matter. If the requisite desire was operating at all, it was operating throughout.

[His Lordship ruled that the directors had been motivated by the desire to continue trading and not by a desire to give the bank a preference in the event of a liquidation. He continued:]

Transactions at an undervalue

Section 238 of the 1986 Act is concerned with the depletion of a company's assets by transactions at an undervalue. [His Lordship read s 238(4) and continued:]

The granting of the debenture was not a gift, nor was it without consideration. The consideration consisted of the bank's forbearance from calling in the overdraft and its honouring of cheques and making of fresh advances to the company during the continuance of the facility. The applicant relies therefore on para (b).

To come within that paragraph the transaction must be (i) entered into by the company; (ii) for a consideration; (iii) the value of which measured in money or money's worth; (iv) is significantly less than the value; (v) also measured in money or money's worth; (vi) of the consideration provided by the company. It requires a comparison to be made between the value obtained by the company for the transaction and the value of consideration provided by the company. Both values must be measurable in money or money's worth and both must be considered from the company's point of view.

In my judgment, the applicant's claim to characterise the granting of the bank's debenture as a transaction at an undervalue is misconceived. The mere creation of a security over a company's assets does not deplete them and does not come within the paragraph. By charging its assets the company appropriates them to meet the liabilities due to the secured creditor and adversely affects the rights of other creditors in the event of insolvency. But it does not deplete its assets or diminish their value. It retains the right to redeem and the right to sell or remortgage the charged assets. All it loses is the ability to apply the proceeds otherwise than in satisfaction of the secured debt. That is not something capable of valuation in monetary terms and is not customarily disposed of for value.

In the present case the company did not suffer that loss by reason of the grant of the debenture. Once the bank had demanded a debenture the company could not have sold or charged its assets without applying the proceeds in reduction of the overdraft; had it attempted to do so, the bank would at once have called in the overdraft. By granting the debenture the company parted with nothing of value, and the value of the consideration which it received in return was incapable of being measured in money or money's worth.

Counsel for the applicant (Mr Vos) submitted that the consideration which the company received was, with hindsight, of no value. It merely gained time and with it the opportunity to lose more money. But he could not and did not claim that the company ought to have received a fee or other capital sum in return for the debenture. That gives the game away. The applicant's real complaint is not that the company entered into the transaction at an undervalue but that it entered into it at all.

In my judgment, the transaction does not fall within sub-s (4) . . .

> Notes

1. *Phillips v Brewin Dolphin Bell Lawrie Ltd* [2001] 1 WLR 143, HL, establishes that the consideration for a transaction may be provided by various parties, and that it may be appropriate to consider the details of a complex series of linked transactions to assess any 'undervalue'. Here, even doing that, the transaction was held to be one at an undervalue.

2. IA 1986 s 238(5) provides that the court shall not make an order in respect of a transaction at an undervalue if it is satisfied that the company entered into the transaction in good faith and for the purpose of carrying on its business, and that at the time it did so there were reasonable grounds for thinking that the a transaction would benefit the company. This is clearly a difficult test to apply.

'Wrongful trading': IA 1986 s 214.

[14.17] Re Produce Marketing Consortium Ltd (No 2) [1989] BCLC 520 (Chancery Division)

This was the first reported case decided under IA 1986 s 214 ('wrongful trading'). The two directors, David and Murphy, had continued to run the company's fruit importing business when they ought to have known that there was no prospect of avoiding insolvent liquidation. Knox J, in holding them liable for wrongful trading, emphasised that their conduct was to be judged, in part, by the objective standards laid down by s 214—that is, by more exacting criteria than those of the traditional common law, although CA 2006 s 174 now adopts this same s 214 standard (see above, pp 664 ff).

[KNOX J read IA 1986 s 214, and continued:] The first question is whether it appears that sub-s (2) applies to Mr David and Mr Murphy. There is no question but that they were directors at all material times and that PMC [the company] has gone into insolvent liquidation. The issue is whether at some time after 27 April 1986 and before 2 October 1987, when it went into insolvent liquidation, they knew or ought to have concluded that there was no reasonable prospect that PMC would avoid going into insolvent liquidation. It was inevitably conceded by counsel for the first respondent that this question has to be answered by the standards postulated by sub-s (4), so that the facts which Mr David and Mr Murphy ought to have known or ascertained and the conclusions that they ought to have reached are not limited to those which they themselves showing reasonable diligence and having the general knowledge, skill and experience which they respectively had, would have known, ascertained or reached but also those that a person with the general knowledge, skill and experience of someone carrying out their functions would have known, ascertained or reached. . . .

The 1986 Act now has two separate provisions; s 213 dealing with fraudulent trading, . . . and s 214 which deals with what the sidenote calls 'wrongful trading'. It is evident that Parliament intended to widen the scope of the legislation under which directors who trade on when the company is insolvent may, in appropriate circumstances, be required to make a contribution to the assets of the company which, in practical terms, means its creditors.

Two steps in particular were taken in the legislative enlargement of the court's jurisdiction. First, the requirement for an intent to defraud and fraudulent purpose was not retained as an essential, and with it goes what Maugham J[49] called 'the need for actual dishonesty involving real moral blame'.

I pause here to observe that at no stage before me has it been suggested that either Mr David or Mr Murphy fell into this category.

The second enlargement is that the test to be applied by the court has become one under which the director in question is to be judged by the standards of what can reasonably be expected of a person fulfilling his functions, and showing reasonable diligence in doing so. I accept the submission of counsel for the first respondent in this connection, that the requirement to have regard to the functions to be carried out by the director in question, in relation to the company in question, involves having regard to the particular company and its business. It follows that the general knowledge, skill and experience postulated will be much less extensive in a small company in a modest way of business, with simple accounting procedures and equipment, than it will be in a large company with sophisticated procedures.

Nevertheless, certain minimum standards are to be assumed to be attained. Notably there is an obligation laid on companies to cause accounting records to be kept which are such as to disclose with reasonable accuracy at any time the financial position of the company at that time: see the Companies Act 1985, s 221(1) and (2)(a) [CA 2006 s 386]. In addition directors are required to prepare a profit and loss account for each financial year and a balance sheet as at the end of it: Companies Act 1985, s 227(1) and (3) [CA 2006 ss 394, 399]. Directors are also required, in respect of each financial year, to lay before the company in general meeting copies of the accounts of the company for that year and to deliver to the registrar of companies a copy of those accounts, in the case of a private company, within 10 months after the end of the relevant accounting reference period (see the Companies Act 1985, ss 241 (1) and (3) and 242(1) and (2)) [CA 2006 ss 437, 441, providing different rules].

As I have already mentioned, the liquidator gave evidence that the accounting records of PMC were adequate for the purposes of its business. The preparation of accounts was woefully late, more especially in relation to those dealing with the year ending 30 September 1985 which should have been laid and delivered by the end of July 1986.

The knowledge to be imputed in testing whether or not directors knew or ought to have concluded that there was no reasonable prospect of the company avoiding insolvent liquidation is not limited to the documentary material actually available at the given time. This appears from s 214(4) which includes a reference to facts which a director of a company ought not only to know but those which he ought to ascertain, a word which does not appear in sub-s (2)(b). In my judgment this indicates that there is to be included by way of factual information not only what was actually there but what, given reasonable diligence and an appropriate level of general knowledge, skill and experience, was ascertainable. This leads me to the conclusion in this case that I should assume, for the purposes of applying the test in s 214(2), that the financial results for the year ending 30 September 1985 were known at the end of July 1986 at least to the extent of the size of the deficiency of assets over liabilities.

Mr David and Mr Murphy, although they did not have the accounts in their hands until January 1987, did, I find, know that the previous trading year had been a very bad one. They had a close and intimate knowledge of the business and they had a shrewd idea whether the turnover was up or down. In fact it was badly down in that year to £526,459 and although I have no doubt that they did not know in July 1986 that it was that precise figure, I have no doubt that they had a good rough idea

49 [In *Re Patrick and Lyon Ltd* [1933] Ch 786 at 790.]

of what it was and in particular that it was well down on the previous year. A major drop in turnover meant almost as night follows day that there was a substantial loss incurred, as indeed there was. That in turn meant again, as surely as night follows day, a substantial increase in the deficit of assets over liabilities.

That deals with their actual knowledge but in addition I have to have regard to what they have to be treated as having known or ascertained and that includes the actual deficit of assets over liabilities of £132,870. . . . It was a deficit that, for an indefinite period in the future could not be made good even if the optimistic prognostications of level of turnover entertained by Mr David and Mr Murphy were achieved. . . .

Counsel for the first respondent was not able to advance any particular calculation as constituting a basis for concluding that there was a prospect of insolvent liquidation being avoided. He is not to be criticised for that for in my judgment there was none available. Once the loss in the year ending 30 September 1985 was incurred PMC was in irreversible decline, assuming (as I must) that the respondents had no plans for altering the company's business and proposed to go on drawing the level of reasonable remuneration that they were currently receiving. . . .

The next question which arises is whether there is a case under s 214(3) for saying that after the end of July 1986 the respondents took every step with a view to minimising the potential loss to the creditors of PMC as, assuming them to have known that there was no reasonable prospect of PMC avoiding insolvent liquidation, they ought to have taken. This clearly has to be answered No, since they went on trading for another year. . . .

I am therefore driven to the conclusion that the court's discretion arises under s 214(1). . . .

In my judgment the jurisdiction under s 214 is primarily compensatory rather than penal. Prima facie the appropriate amount that a director is declared to be liable to contribute is the amount by which the company's assets can be discerned to have been depleted by the director's conduct which caused the discretion under sub-s (1) to arise. But Parliament has indeed chosen very wide words of discretion and it would be undesirable to seek to spell out limits on that discretion, more especially since this is, so far as counsel were aware, the first case to come to judgment under this section. . . .

I take into account the following factors in addition to those set out above, which give rise to the existence of the court's discretion under s 214(1).

This was a case of failure to appreciate what should have been clear rather than a deliberate course of wrongdoing.

There were occasions when positive untruths were stated which cannot just be treated as unwarranted optimism. . . .

The most solemn warning given by the auditor in early February 1987 was effectively ignored.

The affairs of PMC were conducted during the last seven months of trading in a way which reduced the indebtedness to the bank, to which Mr David had given a guarantee, at the expense of trade creditors . . . . The bank is, if not fully, at least substantially secured. If this jurisdiction is to be exercised, as in my judgment it should be in this case, it needs to be exercised in a way which will benefit unsecured creditors . . . .

Taking all these circumstances into account I propose to declare that Mr David and Mr Murphy are liable to make a contribution to the assets of PMC of £75,000. . . .

➤ Notes

1. Recall that the 'fruits' of litigation instituted under s 214 are not at any time assets or property of the company, but the outcome of a power vested in the liquidator which only he can exercise. It follows that a charge over the company's assets—even if expressed to include its future assets—does not extend to sums ordered to be paid under s 214. The same reasoning applies to the various other 'clawback' provisions which vest similar powers in a liquidator, eg transactions at an undervalue (s 238) and preferences (s 239): *Re Yagerphone Ltd* [1935] Ch 392.

2. In contrast, it has been held that moneys recovered under the 'misfeasance' provision (s 212) are the fruits of a right of action which was vested in the company before it went into liquidation, and therefore an asset of the company capable of being caught by a suitably worded charge: *Re Anglo-Austrian Printing and Publishing Union* [1895] 2 Ch 891.

3. It is also possible for a charge to extend to money or property which was disposed of by the company between the presentation of a winding-up petition and the making of a winding-up order but, as a result of the disposition being declared void under IA 1986 s 127, comes back into its hands (*Mond v Hammond Suddards* [1996] 2 BCLC 470).

4. The 'charge' issue is only one aspect of the more general question raised by the meaning of the term 'assets (or property) of the company'. Schedules 1 and 4 of IA 1986 confer on an administrator and a liquidator respectively a statutory power to sell or otherwise dispose of 'the property of the company', and 'property' in this context plainly includes the right to bring proceedings to enforce any chose in action vested in the company (eg a right to sue a third party in tort: *Norglen Ltd v Reeds Rains Prudential Ltd* [1999] 2 AC 1, [1998] 2 All ER 218, HL). In *Re Oasis Merchandising Services Ltd* [1998] Ch 170, [1997] 1 All ER 1009, CA, however, it was held that this power did not extend to an assignment by a liquidator of the 'fruits' of a s 214 action, since the right to bring such proceedings does not belong to the company but is conferred exclusively on the liquidator by the statute. It followed that there was no statutory authority justifying the assignment, and so it was liable to be held void at common law on the ground that it was champertous and against public policy. (Paradoxically, given the ruling in *Mond v Hammond Suddards* (above), it has been held that the right to have dispositions of the company declared void under s 127 is also an incident of the office of liquidator which he cannot assign: *Re Ayala Holdings Ltd (No 2)* [1996] 1 BCLC 467.)

5. In *Re DKG Contractors Ltd* [1990] BCC 903 the respondent was held liable to the company under IA 1986 s 212 (misfeasance), s 214 (wrongful trading) and s 239 (preference). The court ordered that these liabilities should not all be cumulative but that payments made under ss 212 and 239 should go towards satisfying the liability under s 214. The judge in *Re Brian D Pierson (Contractors) Ltd* [1999] BCC 26 was similarly considerate: not only did she rule that the respondents' liability for wrongful trading should not be increased by sums recoverable from them as preferences and on the ground of misfeasance, but she held also that the company's losses were in part due to extraneous factors, such as bad weather conditions, and reduced the contribution for wrongful trading by 30 per cent. However, it is clear from other decisions that the jurisdiction is entirely discretionary, and that there is nothing to stop an order being made in an appropriate case which makes such liabilities cumulative (eg *Re Purpoint Ltd* [1991] BCLC 491).

6. A transaction at an undervalue may also be challenged under IA 1986, s 423 ('*transactions defrauding creditors*'), which replaces earlier legislation that can be traced back at least as far as 1571. Under this provision there are no time limits and the company need not be in liquidation or even insolvent. However, it must be shown that the transaction was entered into *for the purpose* of putting assets beyond the reach of a creditor or potential creditor or of prejudicing the interests of such a person. For an example, see *Arbuthnot Leasing International Ltd v Havelet Leasing Ltd (No 2)* [1990] BCC 636, where a company's business and assets had been transferred on legal advice to an off-the-shelf company shortly before it went into receivership, and the court ordered the reversal of the transaction.

➤ Questions

1. What difference might the insolvency legislation of 1986 have made to the outcome of the following cases:

    (a) *Salomon v Salomon & Co Ltd* **[2.01]**;

  (b) *the Multinational Gas case* **[6.25]**;

  (c) *Re Horsley & Weight Ltd* **[3.05]**;

  (d) *Re Halt Garage (1964) Ltd* **[5.04]**.

2. Would any of the persons concerned in the cases (a) to (d) above have been liable to disqualification or compensation orders, as directors or shadow directors?

Assets available for distribution by the liquidator

The assets available to the liquidator in a winding up will include the following (or their proceeds after realisation):

(i)   all property beneficially owned by the company at the commencement of the winding up, apart from any property that the liquidator elects to disclaim under IA 1986 ss 178ff;

(ii)   calls recovered from contributories;

(iii) moneys paid out of capital within the preceding 12 months for the repurchase of shares and recovered from past members and directors (s 76);

(iv) money or property recouped as a result of a court order nullifying a 'transaction at an undervalue' entered into within the preceding two years (ss 238, 240);

(v)   property and money paid away by the company within the preceding six months (or, if the recipient is a 'connected person', two years) and recovered by the liquidator as a preference (ss 239, 240);

(vi) property disposed of after the commencement of the liquidation under transactions which are invalidated by s 127, unless the court orders otherwise;

(vii) property not fully seized in execution or distress (s 183), or attached after the commencement of the winding up (s 128);

(viii) property recovered and compensation ordered to be paid by court order made against directors and others on the grounds of misfeasance (s 212), fraudulent trading (s 213) and wrongful trading (s 214).

The liquidator will take the assets—with one important qualification—subject to any security validly created in favour of a debentureholder or other creditor prior to the commencement of the winding up unless it is:

(i)   void against the liquidator for non-registration under CA 2006 s 874;

(ii) void as a preference under IA 1986 s 239;

(iii) a *floating* charge created within the preceding 12 months (or, if the chargee is a 'connected person', two years), except to the extent that it is valid under s 245.

The one qualification is that such security can be created only over *the property of the company* (present or future), and some of the categories of assets listed above are regarded as falling outside this description—eg money recovered by the liquidator as a preference: see Note 1 above, p 673. These sums are therefore freely available for distribution among the company's unsecured creditors.

    Property in the hands of the company will also be taken by the liquidator subject to any equities and set-offs enforceable against the company before it went into liquidation.

Application of assets by the liquidator

The claims of a secured creditor to the secured assets rank in principle ahead of any claim in the winding up—including even the costs of the liquidation. But recall that a *floating* charge-holder must meet: (i) the claims of the unsecured creditors to a statutory share of the assets (IA 1986 s 176A, and SI 2003/2097, art 3); (ii) the claims of the preferential creditors under s 175; and (iii) somewhat anomalously, the expenses of the winding up (including the liquidator's remuneration): see IA 1986 ss 175(2)(a) and 197ZA (see above, p 646).

Assets will be applied, after the claims of secured creditors (other than holders of floating charges) have been satisfied, in the following order of priority:

(i)   the expenses of the liquidation (including the liquidator's remuneration, post-liquidation debts, and certain pre-liquidation debts) (s 115 (voluntary liquidations) and s 156 (compulsory liquidation)). What amounts to an expense of winding up has been the subject of major litigation: *Re Toshoku Finance UK plc, Kahn v IRC* [2002] UKHL 6, [2002] 1 WLR 671, HL, concluding that IR 1986, r 4.218 is a definitive statement of what counts as a liquidation expense[50] and of the priorities as between expenses;

(ii)   the debts declared to be preferential debts by s 386 and Sch 6;

(iii)   floating charge-holders (but see above, p 647, for the precise working out of this, including the statutory share to unsecured creditors, if the assets are not sufficient to meet (i)–(iii) in total);

(iv)   unsecured creditors—but note that some debts owed by the company to shareholders, such as moneys paid in advance of calls and sums due by way of dividends, are postponed to outside creditors (s 74(2)(f));

(v)   interest on all debts proved in the winding up (s 189);

(vi)   money due to a member under a contract to redeem or repurchase shares which has not been completed prior to the winding up (CA 2006, s 735);

(vii)   the debts due to members mentioned in (iv) above;

(viii) repayment of capital to preference members; and

(ix)   repayment of capital to ordinary members.

Any 'surplus assets' then go to whoever is entitled under the Constitution; normally, this will be the ordinary members.

A DTI review, now rather dated, suggested that average recovery rates in formal insolvency procedures were: 77% for the bank; 27% for preferential creditors; and virtually nil or unsecured creditors.[51]

A contract under which creditors agree to vary the statutory rules governing the distribution of a company's assets in a liquidation is contrary to public policy and void.

[14.18] British Eagle International Air Lines Ltd v Cie Nationale Air France [1975] 1 WLR 758, [1975] 2 All ER 390 (House of Lords)

Many airlines set up a 'clearing house' scheme under which their mutual debits and credits were not set off one against another but were pooled with a third party, IATA. Under the agreement, participants could not claim against each other but only against IATA for any net balance due to the particular airline under the scheme. British Eagle went into liquidation at

---

[50] And this rule has also been amended to cover litigation expenses under IA 1986 ss 213, 214, 238, 239, 242, 243, and 423, all of which are claims to recover assets or seek contributions to the company's assets, but where the *claims* are not 'assets of the company' (see above, p 673), and so litigation expenses relating to them were not previously allowed: *Re MC Bacon Ltd* [1990] BCLC 607; *Re Floor Fourteen Ltd, Lewis v IRC* [2001] 2 BCLC 392, CA.

[51] Insolvency Service, *A Review of Company Rescue and Business Reconstruction Mechanisms, Report by the Review Group* (2000), para 57.

a time when it was a net debtor to the scheme in respect of its aggregated claims but, as between itself and Air France, it was a net creditor. The liquidator successfully challenged the legality of the clearing house arrangement.

> LORD CROSS OF CHELSEA: [What] the respondents are saying here is that the parties to the 'clearing house' arrangements by agreeing that simple contract debts are to be satisfied in a particular way have succeeded in 'contracting out' of the provisions contained in [CA 1948 s 302] [IA 1986, s 107] for the payment of unsecured debts 'pari passu'. In such a context it is to my mind irrelevant that the parties to the 'clearing house' arrangements had good business reasons for entering into them and did not direct their minds to the question how the arrangements might be affected by the insolvency of one or more of the parties. Such a 'contracting out' must, to my mind, be contrary to public policy. The question is, in essence, whether what was called in argument the 'mini liquidation' flowing from the clearing house arrangements is to yield to or to prevail over the general liquidation. I cannot doubt that on principle the rules of the general liquidation should prevail . . .
>
>   LORDS DIPLOCK and EDMUND-DAVIES concurred.
>
>   LORDS MORRIS OF BORTH-Y-GEST and SIMON OF GLAISDALE dissented.

> ➤ **Notes**

1. There may be strong public policy arguments for allowing creditors to vary the statutory priorities by arrangement among themselves. One such situation is when the existing creditors of a company in difficulties are willing to let a new creditor advance money in an attempt to save the company from liquidation, on the understanding that if the attempt is unsuccessful the claim of the 'rescuer' should not rank equally with their own, but have priority. Following *British Eagle*, there was for a time considerable uncertainty whether such an arrangement—at least if effected by contract between the parties—would be lawful. There was pressure for legislation to be passed which would expressly permit subordination agreements. However, in two decisions of Vinelott J, *Re British & Commonwealth Holdings plc (No 3)* [1992] BCLC 322 and *Re Maxwell Communications Corpn plc (No 2)* [1994] 1 BCLC 1 (where the agreements took the forms respectively of a trust and a contract), it was held that no violation of the *pari passu* principle is involved, where all that the subordinating creditor agrees to is that his rights in and insolvency shall be *less than* what would obtain under the statutory scheme.

2. Special legislative provision has been made by Pt VII of CA 1989 [not moved to CA 2006] and the Financial Markets and Insolvency (Settlement Finality) Regulations 1999 (SI 1999/2979) to allow 'netting' arrangements of the type rejected in the *British Eagle* case to be used by investment exchanges, clearing houses and money market institutions and in banking and securities settlement arrangements.

3. It is also sometimes possible to avoid the application of the *British Eagle* ruling by establishing a *trust*, so that the sum which would ordinarily be payable as a debt to a particular creditor is held by the company as a trustee on his behalf: see *Re Kayford Ltd* [1975] 1 WLR 279; *Carreras Rothmans Ltd v Freeman Mathews Treasure Ltd* [1985] Ch 207. The courts have, on occasion, been prepared to *infer* the existence of a trust in such circumstances: eg *Barclays Bank Ltd v Quistclose Investments Ltd* [1970] AC 567, HL.

4. The statutory rules as to set-off, like the *pari passu* distribution rule, are also regarded as mandatory and cannot be excluded by agreement between the parties: *National Westminster Bank Ltd v Halesowen Presswork and Assemblies Ltd* [1972] AC 785, HL, or under any discretionary power of the court (*Re Bank of Credit and Commerce International SA (No 10)* [1997] Ch 213.

5. In *Barclays Bank plc v British & Commonwealth Holdings plc* [1996] 1 BCLC 1 (on appeal, but not on this issue, [1996] 1 BCLC 1 at 26) Harman J held as unlawful a tripartite arrangement

between a company, one of its members and a third party which breached, by an indirect route, the principle that a company may not return capital to its members except by a procedure authorised by statute (see above, p 418). It was also a consequence of the arrangement that a sum of money which would have been repayable to the shareholder *qua* shareholder in a liquidation was replaced by an equivalent amount payable to the third party as a debt. In effect, this altered the statutory order of priorities in a liquidation (since creditors rank before shareholders) and was a further ground justifying the finding of illegality.

6. In the United States, the courts have developed an equitable jurisdiction under which they have a discretion to subordinate the claims of some creditors to others—eg to postpone the claims of creditors who are members of the same corporate group. It would require legislation to bring about any reform along these lines in this country.

Investigating and reporting the affairs of the company

In any of the insolvency or rescue procedures just noted, an insolvency practitioner must take charge of the affairs of the company and put himself in a position to take action quickly. The IA 1986, therefore, makes special provision for acquisition of information by the office-holder. In addition, an insolvency office-holder is required to investigate potential wrongdoing in relation to the company's affairs, in particular for the purpose of action under the CDDA 1986.

Investigations

The office-holder has available the following rights against specified persons involved in the management of the company:

(i)   The right to require a 'statement of affairs' from persons connected with the company (IA 1986 ss 47, 131, 99 and IR 1986 r 1.5).

(ii)   Other than under CVAs, the right to require reasonable co-operation from persons connected with the company (IA 1986 ss 234(1) and 235). See *Bishopsgate Investment Management Ltd v Maxwell* [1993] Ch 1, at 57, for 'reasonableness'. Failure to comply without reasonable excuse is an offence (s 235).

(iii)   Other than under CVAs, the right to require production of the company's books, papers and records (IA 1986 ss 234, 246).

(iv)   Other than under CVAs, the right to apply to court for an order requiring a 'private examination' (ie appearance for oral examination but with limited attendance); submission of an affidavit; or production of books, papers or other documents (IA 1986 ss 234, 236, 237). An examinee is not entitled to privilege against self-incrimination (*Bishopsgate Investment Management Ltd v Maxwell* [1993] Ch 1), so the statutory protection that followed from *Saunders v United Kingdom* (1996) 23 EHRR 313 applies (see above p 602). On the discretion to order a private examination, see *British and Commonwealth Holdings plc v Spicer and Oppenheim* [1993] AC 426; and on the conduct of private examinations, see *Re Richbell Strategic Holdings Ltd (No 2)* [2000] 2 BCLC 794.

(v)   In compulsory (court-ordered) liquidations, the right of the official receiver (himself, or pursuant to a request by specified majorities of the company's creditors or contributories) to apply for a public examination of parties concerned in the promotion, formation or management of the company (IA 1986 s 133). Again, there is no privilege against self-incrimination (*Bishopsgate Investment Management Ltd v Maxwell* [1993] Ch 1). If the company is in voluntary liquidation, it seems a public examination may still be ordered (IA

1986, ss 122(1) and 133: see *Bishopsgate Investment Management Ltd v Maxwell* [1993] Ch 1, at 24, 46).

Reporting

When a company is subject to any of the insolvency or liquidation procedures other than a CVA, the relevant office-holder must submit a report to the Secretary of State on the conduct of any director whom the office-holder believes should be disqualified under the CDDA 1986 s 6 (CDDA 1986 s 7(3)), and must, in any event, within six months of appointment, submit a return listing every director and stating whether a report has been made and, if not, why not (SI 1986/2134, r 4).

In compulsory liquidations, the official receiver has a duty to investigate the affairs of the company, and may make a report to the court (IA 1986 s 132(1)).

In any type of liquidation, the liquidator must report any criminal offences apparently committed in relation to the company by any past or present officers or members (IA 1986 s 118). This may lead to a public investigation of the company (see above, p 595).

Dissolution of the company

The corporate entity created under the Companies Act ceases to exist by the formal act of *dissolution*, effected by removing the name of the company from the register at Companies House. Dissolution ends the company's separate personality, terminates any legal relationships,[52] and dissolves the relationship between the company and its members.

Dissolution may take place in a variety of ways (most requiring some form of publication in the *Gazette* at an appropriate stage in the process), including:

(i)   On completion of liquidation, automatically, three months after the registrar has been notified of the completion of the winding-up procedure (IA 1986 ss 94, 106, 172(8), 201, 205). The processes vary slightly for voluntary and compulsory liquidations.

(ii)   By the registrar, where the registrar has reasonable cause to believe that no liquidator is acting or the affairs of the company have been fully wound up, and yet the required returns (see (i) above) have not been made for a period of 6 months (CA 2006 s 1001).

(iii)   On application by the official receiver, automatically, three months after requesting early dissolution (unless some interested person intervenes meantime), if it appears that the realisable assets of the company are insufficient to cover the expenses of liquidation and that the affairs of the company do not require further investigation (IA 1986 s 202).

(iv)   On completion of administration, three months after notification by the administrator that there is nothing to distribute to the creditors (IA 1986, Sch B1, para 84).

(v)   By order of the court, in conjunction with compromises, arrangements and reconstructions (CA 2006 s 900).

(vi)   On application by the company itself, three months after publication of the application in the *Gazette* (CA 2006, s 1003). This option for voluntary striking off is subject to a wide variety of restrictions and conditions (CA 2006 ss 1004–1010), but it does enable the expense of a formal liquidation to be avoided.

(vii)   By the registrar, exercising an administrative power to strike off (CA 2006 s 1000). In practice, the largest number of companies are dissolved by the simple administrative procedure of 'striking off the register'. CA 2006 s 1000 empowers the registrar to do this, after

---

[52] So eg the company's property passes as *bona vacantia* to the Crown: CA 2006 s 1012.

advertisement, if his inquiries show or suggest that the company has ceased to carry on business. This is a useful sanction in the case of a company which has failed to file accounts or annual returns.

Restoration to the register

Restoration of dissolved companies to the register may be necessary if, for example, further assets are discovered, or someone wishes to bring a damages claim for which the former company was insured.

There are two procedures available for restoring companies to the register:

(i) an administrative procedure, available when companies have been incorrectly struck off as defunct under CA 2006 ss 1000 or 1001 (see (ii) and (vii) above), requiring application to the registrar by the company's former directors or former members within six years of the date of dissolution (CA 2006 s 1024); and

(ii) a judicial procedure, requiring application to court (CA 2006 s 1029), in all other cases. The application may be made by a wide class of people (s 1029(2)), and must generally be made within six years of the dissolution of the company, although there are various exceptions. For example, there is no time limit where the application is for the purpose of bringing proceedings against the company for damages for personal injury (s 1030(1)). The court has wide powers to make restoration, including any case in which the court thinks it just to do so (s 1031(1)(c)).

CA 2006 ss 1024–1034 provide details rules on the pre-conditions and consequences of the procedures, including special supplementary rules dealing with company names and with restoration of property that had vested in the Crown.

Appendix

The forms and tables which follow are reproduced by permission of the persons and bodies mentioned on p vii to whom acknowledgment is again made.

These documents are intended to be used solely by students and their teachers for the purposes of instruction. They should not be used as precedents or relied on in any other way. The companies and firms concerned and the author and publishers do not accept liability to any person should they be so used or relied upon.

A. Forms

1. Certificate of incorporation
2. Prospectus
3. Directors' annual report and accounts
4. Notice of Annual General Meeting
5. Share certificate (preference shares)

B. Tables

1. Summary of changes in the number of companies on the register, 2005–2006
2. Public and private companies incorporated and on the GB register, 2005–2006
3. New incorporations of companies with share capital: analysed by amount of nominal capital, 2005–2006
4. Liquidations and receiverships notified, 2005–2006
5. Searches of company records at Companies House, 2005–2006
6. Disqualification orders notified to the Secretary of State, 2005–2006

A. Forms

1. Certificate of incorporation

No 561235

[Royal Arms]
Certificate of Incorporation
I Hereby Certify, That
VARSITY PUBLICATIONS LIMITED
is this day Incorporated under the Companies Act 1948, and that the Company is Limited.

Given under my hand at London this *Tenth* day of *February* One Thousand Nine Hundred and Fifty *six*.

WB Langford
Registrar of Companies

2. Prospectus

[This prospectus has been much abbreviated: the original is a substantial booklet containing 124 A4 pages.

An asterisk following a heading or other entry indicates that details (or, as appropriate, further details) have been omitted, in the interests of saving space.

This prospectus was issued in 1994. There have been a few changes in City practice since that date (for instance, the formal title of the Stock Exchange is no longer 'The International Stock Exchange of the United Kingdom and the Republic of Ireland Limited'), and of course the entire legislative background has changed following the enactment of the Financial Services and Markets Act 2000; but in all respects that matter this may be taken as typical of any well-drawn prospectus which would be issued today. Students may find it interesting to compare the facts and figures given in this document with those in the company's Annual Report for 2006 (below, p 691). The prospectus is prefaced by the following introductory statements:]

A copy of this Prospectus, which comprises listing particulars relating to 3i Group plc in accordance with the listing rules made under section 142 of the Financial Services Act 1986, has been delivered to the Registrar of Companies for registration as required by section 149 of that Act.

Application has been made to the London Stock Exchange for the Shares to be admitted to the Official List. It is expected that such admission will become effective and that dealings in the Shares will begin on 18 July 1994. The Directors . . . accept responsibility for the information contained in this document. To the best of the knowledge and belief of the Directors (who have taken all reasonable care to ensure that such is the case) the information contained in this document is in accordance with the facts and does not omit anything likely to affect the import of such information.

The procedure for application and an Application Form for use in connection with the Offer are set out at the end of this document.

Persons receiving this document should note that, in connection with the Offer, Baring Brothers & Co, Limited is acting for the Company and the Bank Shareholders and will not be responsible to anyone other than the Company and the Bank Shareholders for providing the protections afforded to customers of Baring Brothers & Co, Limited nor for providing advice in relation to the Offer.

The Shares have not been, and will not be, registered under the United States Securities Act of 1933. The Shares may not be offered, sold or delivered within the United States or to US Residents (as defined herein) in connection with the Offer. As further provided herein, it is prohibited to use any means of United States interstate commerce (including mail, telecopy and telephone) to offer, sell or deliver the Shares after sale, in connection with the Offer. . . .

3i Group plc

(Incorporated and Registered in England and Wales. Registered No 1142830)

Offer
By
Baring Brothers & Co, Limited

as agent, of 261,587,221 Shares of 50p each at 272p per Share
payable in full on application

INDEBTEDNESS

At the close of business on 20 May 1994 the Group had outstanding borrowings or indebtedness in the nature of borrowings of £1,600 million. . . . The Group also had contingent liabilities of £181 million, comprising guarantees of £29 million and an unprovided deferred taxation liability of £152 million.

Save as disclosed above, and apart from intra-group liabilities, at the close of business on 20 May 1994 neither the Company nor any of its subsidiaries had any material loan capital (whether outstanding or created but unissued) or term loans, or any other material borrowings or indebtedness in the nature of borrowings, including bank overdrafts and liabilities under acceptances or acceptance credits, hire purchase commitments and obligations under finance leases, or any material guarantees or other material contingent liabilities.

At the close of business on 20 May 1994, the Group had cash balances of £289 million.

SHARE CAPITAL IMMEDIATELY FOLLOWING THE OFFER

Authorised			Issued and fully paid	
Number	*Amount*		*Number*	*Amount*
700,000,000	£350,000,000	Shares of 50p each	581,304,932	£290,652,466

The Offer Shares will rank *pari passu* in all respects with the other Shares of the Company, except that they will not confer the right to receive the final dividend to be paid in respect of the year ended 31 March 1994 nor the special dividend to be paid upon Listing becoming effective in described further in Part 7 of this document. . . .

PART 1 KEY INFORMATION

The information in this section is derived from, and should be read in conjunction with, the full text of this document.

Offer Price	272p
Number of Shares in issue after the Offer	581,304,932
Market capitalisation at the Offer Price	£1,581.1m
Gross value of the Offer	£711.5m

Net Asset Value per Share (fully diluted)[1]   314.4p
Offer Price discount to fully diluted Net Asset Value per Share   13.5%
Gross dividend yield at the Offer Price[2]   3.0%

3i and its objectives

3i is the leading specialist provider of investment capital to unquoted businesses in the UK. Its objectives are to achieve long term growth in the value of its net assets and to distribute an increasing dividend to its shareholders.

Operations

3i has a network of 18 offices in the UK and 6 offices in France, Germany, Italy and Spain. The Directors believe that this network enhances 3i's ability to identify and access potentially attractive investment opportunities.

Investment approach

3i has a long term approach to making investments. It has a general policy of not predetermining the timing or strategy for realisation of its unquoted equity investments. 3i does not generally participate directly in the management of investment businesses.

The Directors believe that 3i's long term investment approach is attractive to businesses seeking capital and provides a competitive advantage in obtaining new investment business.

Market position

Since its formation in 1945, 3i has invested more than £6 billion in over 11,000 businesses including more than 1,300 management buy-outs and 300 management buy-ins. In the year ended 31 December 1993, based on information provided to the BVCA[3] by its members, 3i accounted for 41 per cent by number of the companies that received capital from BVCA members and 17 per cent by value of all financings reported to the BVCA. In each of the five years to 31 December 1993, 3i has arranged the largest number of management buy-outs and management buy-ins in the UK. In addition, 3i has a growing portfolio in continental Europe and is already a substantial provider of investment capital to unquoted businesses in France and Germany.

Investment portfolio

3i's investment activities include providing start-up, early stage and development capital, providing capital for management buy-outs and management buy-ins and acquiring existing holdings in businesses. An initial investment by 3i in a business will usually take the form of a mix of equity capital, fixed income shares and loan capital.

At 31 March 1994, the value of 3i's portfolio was £2,980 million consisting of investments in over 3,400 businesses in a wide range of industries. . . .

Valuation of the portfolio and realisations*[4]

Restructuring

In recent years, the Group has taken action to concentrate on its investment business in the UK and continental Europe, reduce overheads and improve operational efficiencies. As a result of these actions, 3i has reduced costs from £80 million in the year ended 31 March 1990 to £67 million in the year ended 31 March 1994.

---

[1] Based on net assets and share capital as at 31 March 1994 as described in notes 15 and 34 to the accountants' report in Part 7 of this document.

[2] The gross dividend yield calculation is based on the dividends paid and recommended for the year ended 31 March 1994 plus the associated tax credit.

[3] [British Venture Capital Association.]

[4] [An asterisk following a heading indicates that details have been omitted.]

Financial highlights

The summary financial information for the three years ended 31 March 1994 set out below is extracted from the accountants' report in Part 7 of this document.

	Years ended 31 March		
	1992	*1993*	*1994*
	£m	£m	£m
Profit on ordinary activities before tax	40	53	65
Dividends	26	27	38
Shareholders' funds	1,268	1,330	1,851

. . .

Comparative performance

Over the ten years to 31 March 1994, 3i's compound average annual total return (assuming the re-investment of dividends net of basic rate tax) to shareholders was 16.1 per cent. . . . .

Investment trust status

The Directors intend to manage the affairs of the Company so that it will satisfy the conditions for approval by the Inland Revenue as an investment trust under section 842 of the Income and Corporation Taxes Act 1988 ('section 842'). Approval as an investment trust is granted retrospectively for each accounting period. As an approved investment trust, the Company would be exempt from UK corporation tax on chargeable gains for each accounting period in respect of which approval is granted As is the case with all applications for approval as an investment trust, there can be no guarantee in advance of any accounting period that retro-spective approval for that period will be given.

Based on the advice that the Directors have received as to the requirements of section 842, they consider that the steps which the Company has already taken and those which it pro-poses to take will together enable the Company, under current legislation, to satisfy the requirements of that section for the short accounting period ending on 31 March 1995. Thereafter, the Directors intend to monitor the position carefully so as to ensure that the requirements continue to be satisfied.

Dividend policy

The objectives of 3i will continue to be the achievement of long term growth in the value of its net assets and the distribution of an increasing dividend to its Shareholders. The Company has increased its dividend in each of the last nine years and the Directors intend that it will continue to do so, provided an increase is justified by the trend in 3i's revenue earnings.

Future prospects

3i's strategy is to concentrate on its investment business in the UK and continental Europe. The Directors have confidence in the long term prospects of the Group, based on the size and diversity of its investment portfolio, its leading market position and the scope for expansion of demand for investment capital within its markets.

The Offer

A total of 261,587,221 Shares are being offered under the Offer, which has been fully under-written by Barings at the Offer Price. Immediately following the Offer, the interests of the Bank Shareholders will be reduced to an aggregate of approximately 301.6 million Shares, representing approximately 51.9 per cent of the issued share capital of the Company.

PART 2 DIRECTORS, SECRETARY AND ADVISERS*

PART 3 THE BUSINESS

*History**

Description

3i invests in small and medium sized businesses that do not have ready access to the capital markets. 3i's investment activities include providing start-up, early stage and development capital, providing capital for management buyouts and management buy-ins and acquiring existing holdings in businesses. Its objectives are to achieve long term growth in the value of its net assets and to distribute an increasing dividend to its shareholders.

3i's target market is unquoted businesses with annual turnover of between £1 million and £100 million but 3i will provide capital to businesses outside this range provided their growth potential is believed to be sufficiently attractive. 3i operates primarily in the UK and continental Europe and employed 566 staff at 31 March 1994.

[There follow further details relating to the company, under the headings Operations, Market position, Investment approach, Investment process, Support activities, Restructuring, Funding policy, Board and management structure, Committee structure, Directors, Company secretary, Senior executives, Pension schemes, Employee incentive schemes.]

PART 4 THE PORTFOLIO AND VALUATION POLICY*

PART 5 FINANCIAL INFORMATION AND PROSPECTS

Statement of total recognised gains and losses

Set out below is a summary of the total recognised gains and losses of the Group for the three years to 31 March 1994, which has been derived from the accountants' report in Part 7 of this document:

	Years ended 31 March		
	1992	*1993*	*1994*
	£m	£m	£m
Revenue profit for the year	32	34	50
Profits on property in use by the Group realised in the year	–	3	1
Profits on investments, less provisions and tax, realised in the year	12	(16)	85
Unrealised appreciation after tax of the year	77	142	352
	121	163	488
Release of deferred tax on unrealised appreciation on intended change of status	–	–	204
Write back of deferred tax on provisions on intended change of status	–	–	(52)
Profits recognised in unrealised appreciation in prior years	(55)	(77)	(83)
Currency translation adjustment	3	2	(2)
Total recognised gains and losses relating to the year	69	88	555

The statement of total recognised gains and losses summarises the three major components of the Group's overall return: revenue profits (accounted for in the consolidated revenue statement), realised capital profits (accounted for in investments realisation profits) and the unrealised net growth in the value of investments (accounted for in unrealised appreciation). Each of these components has shown considerable improvement over the period, particularly in the last year. . . .

Financial record

Set out below is a summary of the revenue, investment realisation profits and unrealised appreciation statements of the Group for the three years ended 31 March 1994 which have been derived from the accountants' report in Part 7 of this document.

[There follow similar details derived from the company's balance sheets and cash flow statements and an analysis of realised equity investments for the three years to 31 March 1994. Other information is given relating to the Comparative performance of 3i relative to investment trusts and smaller quoted companies, and to Current business conditions, Investment trust status, Dividend policy, and Future prospects.]

PART 6 THE OFFER

Offer structure

A total of 261,587,221 Shares are being offered under the Offer. Barings has undertaken to use its reasonable endeavours, through the Company's brokers, to place all of the Offer Shares with institutional and other investors at the Offer Price and to make the Public Offer. Shares equivalent to 25 per cent of the Offer Shares are to be placed subject to a right of recall to satisfy valid applications from the public under the Public Offer. The Offer has been fully underwritten by Barings at the Offer Price.

The Company has, conditional on Listing, declared a special dividend of £288.7 million in aggregate, and will issue 106,132,392 Shares by way of rights at a price per Share equal to the Offer Price to its existing Shareholders to raise the entire amount of this special dividend. The Offer Shares comprise a mixture of existing Shares held by the Bank Shareholders and Shares provisionally allotted to the Shareholders by way of rights, which are to be made available to successful applicants in the Public Offer or to placees in the Placing. The Company will, after payment of the special dividend, retain no net proceeds from the Placing and Offer.

Up to 6,539,681 Shares, representing 10 per cent of the Shares comprised in the Public Offer, have been reserved for Preferential Applicants. Individuals who apply on a preferential basis may also apply for Shares under the Public Offer. To the extent that total applications received from Preferential Applicants are in excess of the 10 per cent limit, applications may be scaled down on a basis determined by Barings, in its absolute discretion, after consultation with the Company. Any excess Shares applied for will be treated as having been made on the Public Application Form. If Preferential Applicants apply for fewer Shares than those reserved for them, the excess will be made available to applicants under the Public Offer. . . .

Further details about the Offer are set out in Part 8 of this document.

Reasons for flotation

The Directors believe that it is now appropriate to seek a listing of the Company's share capital on the London Stock Exchange. A listing is one of the conditions which must be fulfilled for the Company to qualify as an investment trust. The flotation will provide the Bank Shareholders with an opportunity to reduce their shareholdings in the Company.

Relationship with Bank Shareholders

Immediately following the Offer, the interests of the Bank Shareholders will be reduced to an aggregate of approximately 301.6 million Shares, representing approximately 51.9 per cent of the issued share capital of the Company.

The Bank Shareholders have held investments in the business since its establishment in 1945 but 3i has, for many years, operated as an independent business.

. . .

The Bank Shareholders have agreed that they will not, before the publication of 3i's results for the period ending 31 March 1995, sell any further Shares without the prior agreement of Barings.

PART 7 ACCOUNTANTS' REPORT

ERNST & YOUNG

Chartered Accountants
Becket House
1 Lambeth Palace Road
London SE1 7EU

The Directors   22 June 1994
3i Group plc
91 Waterloo Road
London
SE1 8XP

The Directors
Baring Brothers & Co Limited
8 Bishopsgate
London
EC2N 4AE

Dear Sirs

We report in connection with the application for listing ('the Listing') of the issued share capital of 3i Group plc ('the Company') on the Official List of The International Stock Exchange of the United Kingdom and the Republic of Ireland Limited referred to in the listing particulars dated 22 June 1994.

We have examined the audited accounts of the Group for the three years ended 31 March, from 1992 to 1994 inclusive. Audited accounts have not been prepared in respect of the Group for any period subsequent to 31 March 1994. We have acted as auditors for the Group throughout the period covered by this report, and our audit reports were unqualified. Our examination has been carried out in accordance with the Auditing Guideline 'Prospectuses and the reporting accountant'.

The financial information set out below is based on the audited accounts of the Group after making such adjustments as we consider necessary. The information set out in this report is presented to comply with the layout required by the amended Schedule 9 to the Companies Act 1985 which first applied to the Group for the financial year ended 31 March 1994. The financial information in the previously published audited accounts for the two years ended 31 March 1992 and 1993 has been re-presented accordingly.

In our opinion the financial information gives, for the purpose of the listing particulars dated 22 June 1994, a true and fair view of the profits, cash flow and total recognised gains and losses of the Group for the three years ended 31 March 1994 and of the state of affairs of the Group at the end of each of those years.

Accounting policies

The principal accounting policies which have been consistently applied in arriving at the financial information set out in this report are: [details omitted].

[The report then sets out the company's financial statements for each of the three years ending 31 March 1994, with accompanying Notes.]

Yours faithfully,

Ernst & Young

3. Directors' annual report and accounts*⁵

3i Group plc

Report and Accounts 2006

CHAIRMAN'S STATEMENT

3i entered the financial year with strong momentum and buoyant market conditions, which continued throughout the period. Our market position enabled the Group to take advantage of these factors and to deliver a return of £831 million for the year to 31 March 2006. This was substantially up from £501 million last year and represented a return of 22.5% on opening shareholders' funds.

Having invested in and developed companies of strategic value to others, 3i was well placed to sell into receptive markets. Realisations totalled £2.2 billion and were made at a profit of 35% over opening value.

The Board is recommending a final ordinary dividend of 9.7p, making a total ordinary dividend for the year of 15.2p, up 4.1% on last year. Meanwhile, the £500 million return of capital approved by shareholders at our Extraordinary General Meeting last year has essentially been completed. The Board intends to return a further £700 million to shareholders by way of a bonus issue of listed B shares, which is currently expected to take place in July. Resolutions relating to the return of capital proposals will be put to shareholders at an EGM.

High quality new investment is a key driver of future value. Despite remaining highly selective, we were able to increase investment by 47% to £1.1 billion, drawing on our in-depth sector knowledge and local relationships in a range of different markets. The international proportion of our investment rose in the year to 63% and our widening international reach is illustrated by the fact that over half of our assets are now outside the UK.

In Asia we established teams in Shanghai and Mumbai during the year, and made groundbreaking investments in both China and India. 3i's Growth Capital business has also recently entered the US market and, in addition, our Infrastructure team is now in place and has made a number of investments. . . .

Underpinning this year's performance is a high level of staff engagement. A survey of our staff during the year, conducted by Ipsos MORI, showed high commitment, and that 3i's level of staff engagement exceeded that of many other leading companies.

This commitment also characterises our approach to corporate responsibility. For a company like 3i, our direct impact on the community and the environment will be much less significant than that of the companies in which we invest. We nevertheless are refining measurement of our own impact, while continuing to review our standards for these issues in portfolio selection and management.

I would like to thank all our staff for their skill, effort and teamwork in achieving these good results and also pay tribute to the management teams and the advisers of our portfolio companies.

---

⁵ An asterisk following a heading indicates that details have been omitted. In this report. 3i Group plc is referred to as 'the Company' and, with its subsidiaries, as 'the Group'. 3i plc is one of the subsidiaries.

So, in summary, this has been a good year for 3i shareholders, with the Group taking advantage of favourable market conditions, delivering a high level of return on shareholders' funds, growing investment levels and improving the strategic position of the business. In developing our strategy we will continue to combine ambition with rigour in pursuit of value for our investors.

[The Chairman's statement is not a legal requirement, but is a customary introduction to the annual report and accounts. There follow similar statements by the Chief Executive; and (again, unofficial) summarised details under the headings Our vision, Business review, Corporate responsibility and Board of Directors and management Committee.]

Director's report

This is the Directors' report of 3i Group plc for the year to 31 March 2006 ('the year').

Principal activity 3i Group plc is a world leader in private equity and venture capital. The principal activity of the Company and its subsidiaries ('the Group') is investment. It invests in a wide range of growing independent businesses. Its objective is to maximise shareholder value through growth in total return.

Tax and investment company status The Company is an investment company as defined by section 266 of the Companies Act 1985 and carries on business as an investment trust.

HM Revenue & Customs has approved the Company as an investment trust under section 842 of the Income and Corporation Taxes Act 1988 for the financial period to 31 March 2005. Since that date the Company has directed its affairs to enable it to continue to be so approved.

Regulation The Company was authorised and regulated by the Financial Services Authority ('FSA') until 27 May 2005, when it relinquished its deposit taking status. 3i Investments plc, a wholly owned subsidiary of the Company, is authorised and regulated by the FSA under the Financial Services and Markets Act 2000. Where applicable, certain Group subsidiaries' businesses outside the United Kingdom are regulated locally by relevant authorities.

Results and dividends The financial statements of the Company and the Group for the year to 31 March 2006 appear [below].

Total recognised income and expense for the year was £831 million (2005: £501 million, as restated for IFRS). As part of the arrangements approved by shareholders to return value to shareholders, a special dividend of 40.7p per share was paid on 22 July 2005 in respect of the year to 31 March 2006. A further interim dividend of 5.5p per share in respect of that year was paid on 4 January 2006. The Directors recommend a final dividend of 9.7p per share be paid in respect of the year to 31 March 2006 to shareholders on the register at the close of business on 23 June 2006.

. . .

Operations The Group operates through a network of offices in Europe, Asia and the US. The Group also manages a number of funds established with major institutions and pension funds to make equity and equity-related investments in unquoted businesses in Europe and Asia.

Management arrangements*

Business review The Chairman's statement [above], the Chief Executive's statement [above], the 'Our vision' section [below] and the Business review [below][6] report on the Group's development during the year to 31 March 2006, its position at that date and the Groups likely future development.

---

6 [The 'Our vision' section and the Business Review occupy a total of 28 pages of the Report.]

Share capital

Pre-consolidation share capital movements The issued share capital of the Company as at 1 April 2005 was 614,409,167 ordinary shares of 50p each. This increased by 268,792 shares to 614,677,959 ordinary shares of 50p each in the period from 1 April 2005 to 10 July 2005 on the issue of shares to the trustee of The 3i Group Share Incentive Plan and on the exercise of options under the Group's executive share option plans and The 3i Group Sharesave Scheme.

Consolidation of share capital Pursuant to resolutions passed at an Extraordinary General Meeting ('EGM') of the Company, on 11 July 2005 the issued share capital of the Company, of 614,677,959 ordinary shares of 50p each, was consolidated into 578,520,432 ordinary shares of 53⅛p each.

Post-consolidation share capital movements At the EGM in July 2005, the Directors were authorised to repurchase up to 57,800,000 shares of 53⅛p each in the Company (representing approximately 10% of the Company's issued share capital as at 10 May 2005) until the Company's Annual General Meeting in 2006 or 5 October 2006, if earlier. The Board indicated that it would only use this authority to repurchase Company shares with an aggregate value of approximately £250 million. In the year to 31 March 2006, the Company cancelled 30,186,896 ordinary shares of 53⅛p each which had been purchased pursuant to this authority.

In the period from 11 July 2005 to 31 March 2006, a total of 2,222,966 ordinary shares of 53⅛p were issued (to the trustee of The 3i Group Share Incentive Plan and on the exercise of options under the Group's executive share option plans and The 3i Group Sharesave Scheme).

Accordingly, between 11 July 2005 and 31 March 2006, the consolidated share capital of the Company decreased by 27,963,930 ordinary shares to 550,556,502 ordinary shares of 53⅛p each.

Major interests in shares As at 3 May 2006, the Company had been notified of the following interests in the Company's shares in accordance with sections 198 to 208 of the Companies Act 1985.

	%	Number of shares
Prudential plc and subsidiary companies	6.14	34,716,123
FMR Corporation and Fidelity International Limited and their subsidiary companies	4.95	27,255,702
Legal & General Group	3.85	21,844,391

Directors' interests Details of the Directors' interests in the Company's shares are shown in Note 39 to the financial statements [below] Save as shown in Note 39, no Director had any disclosable interest in the shares, debentures or loan stock of the Company or in the shares, debentures or loan stock of its subsidiaries during the period and there have been no changes in the above interests between 1 April 2006 and 3 May 2006.

Corporate governance Throughout the year, the Company complied with the provisions of section 1 of the Combined Code on corporate governance published by the Financial Reporting Council in July 2003.

The Company's approach to corporate governance The Company has a policy of seeking to comply with established best practice in the field of corporate governance. The Board has adopted core values and Group standards which set out the behaviour expected of staff in their dealings with shareholders, customers, colleagues, suppliers and other stakeholders of the Company. One of the core values communicated within the Group is a belief that the highest standard of integrity is essential in business.

The Board's responsibilities and processes The Board is responsible to shareholders for the overall management of the Group. It determines matters including financial strategy and planning and takes major business decisions. The Board has put in place an organisational structure. This is further described under the heading 'internal control'. The Board has approved a formal schedule of matters reserved to it and its duly authorised Committees for decision. These include:

–approval of the Group's overall strategy, strategic plan and annual operating budget;

–approval of the Company's interim and annual financial statements and changes in the Group's accounting policies or practices;

–changes relating to the capital structure of the Company or its regulated status;

–major capital projects;

–major changes in the nature of business operations;

–investments and divestments in the ordinary course of business above certain limits set by the Board from time to time;

–adequacy of internal control systems;

–appointments to the Board and Management Committee;

–principal terms and conditions of employment of members of Management Committee; and

–changes in employee share schemes and other long-term incentive schemes.

Matters delegated to management include implementation of the Board approved strategy, day-to-day operation of the business, the appointment of all executives below Management Committee and the formulation and execution of risk management policies and practices.

A Group succession and contingency plan is prepared by management and reviewed periodically by the Board. The purpose of this plan is to identify suitable candidates for succession to key senior management positions, agree their training and development needs, and ensure the necessary human resources are in place for the Company to meet its objectives.

During the year, the principal matters considered by the Board included:

–the Group strategic plan, budget and financial resources;

–the Group's capital structure, balance sheet efficiency and the return of capital to shareholders;

–regular reports from the Chief Executive;

–the recommendations of the Valuations Committee on valuations of investments;

–the Company's share price performance and findings from a shareholder perception study;

–organisational capability, succession planning and findings from a staff survey;

–the establishment of a European Commercial Paper programme;

–establishing a further European Buyout Fund;

–risk management;

–requirements for operating and financial reviews and Key performance indicators;

–independence of non-executive Directors; and

–funding of the 3i Group Pension Plan.

Information Reports and papers are circulated to the Directors in a timely manner in preparation for Board and Committee meetings. These papers are supplemented by information specifically requested by the Directors from time to time.

During the year, there were six meetings of the Board of Directors. The Directors who served throughout the year attended all six meetings save for [one director] who attended five meetings. . . .

Performance evaluation During the year, the Board conducted its annual review of performance of the Board as a whole and of individual contributions. . . .

The roles of the Chairman and the Chief Executive The division of responsibilities between the Chairman of the Board and the Chief Executive is clearly defined and has been approved by the Board.

The Chairman The Chairman leads the Board in the determination of its strategy and in the achievement of its objectives. The Chairman is responsible for organising the business of the Board, ensuring its effectiveness and setting its agenda. The Chairman has no involvement in the day-to-day business of the Group. The Chairman facilitates the effective contribution of non-executive Directors and constructive relations between executive and non-executive Directors. The Chairman ensures that regular reports from the Company's brokers are circulated to the non-executive Directors to enable non-executive Directors to remain aware of shareholders' views. The Chairman ensures effective communication with the Company's shareholders.

The Chief Executive The Chief Executive has direct charge of the Group on a day-to-day basis and is accountable to the Board for the financial and operational performance of the Group. The Chief Executive has formed a committee called Management Committee to enable him to carry out the responsibilities delegated to him by the Board. . . . The Committee meets on a regular basis to consider operational matters and the implementation of the Group's strategy.

Senior Independent Director The Board has appointed [. . .] as Senior Independent Director, to whom, in accordance with the Combined Code, concerns can be conveyed.

Directors The Board comprises the Chairman, . . . six other independent non-executive Directors and three executive Directors. Biographical details for each of the Directors are set out [below].

In addition to fulfilling their legal responsibilities as Directors, non-executive Directors are expected to bring an independent judgment to bear on issues of strategy, performance, resources and standards of conduct, and to help the Board provide the Company with effective leadership. They are also expected to ensure high standards of financial probity on the part of the Company and to monitor the effectiveness of the executive Directors.

The Board's discussions, and its approval of the Group's strategic plan and annual budget, provide the non-executive Directors with the opportunity to contribute to and validate management's plans and assist in the development of strategy. The non-executive Directors receive regular management accounts, reports and information which enable them to scrutinise the Company's and management's performance against agreed objectives.

Directors' independence All the non-executive Directors, including the Chairman, are considered by the Board to be independent for the purposes of the Combined Code. The Board assesses and reviews the independence of each of the non-executive Directors at least annually having regard to the potential relevance and materiality of a Director's interests and relationships rather than applying rigid criteria in a mechanistic manner. . . .

No Director was materially interested in any contract or arrangement subsisting during or at the end of the financial period that was significant in relation to the business of the Company.

Directors' service contracts Details of Directors' employment contracts are set out in the Directors' remuneration report [below].

Training and development The Company has developed a training policy which provides a framework within which training for Directors is planned with the objective of ensuring Directors understand the duties and responsibilities of being a Director of a listed company. All Directors are required to update their skills and maintain their familiarity with the Company and its business continually . . .

During the year the Directors received training on Directors' responsibilities for the operating and financial review, the new Listing Rules, the Market Abuse Regime and the Company Law Reform Bill. . . .

The Company has procedures for Directors to take independent legal or other professional advice about the performance of their duties.

Re-election Subject to the Company's Articles of Association, the Companies Acts and satisfactory performance evaluation, non-executive Directors are appointed for an initial period of three years. Before the third and sixth anniversaries of an non-executive Director's first appointment, the Director discusses with the Board whether it is appropriate for a further three year term to be served. The reappointment of non-executive Directors who have served for more than nine years is subject to annual review.

The Company's Articles of Association provide for:

a) Directors to retire at the first Annual General Meeting ('AGM') after their appointment by the Board and for the number nearest to, but not exceeding, one-third of the remaining Directors to retire by rotation at each AGM;
b) all Directors to retire at least every three years; and
c) any Director aged 70 or over at the date of the AGM to retire.

Subject to the Articles of Association, retiring Directors are eligible for reappointment. . . .

Directors' indemnities The Company's Articles of Association provide that, subject to the provisions of the Companies Acts, the Directors shall be indemnified against liabilities incurred by them as Directors in defending any proceedings in which judgment is given in their favour, or where they have been acquitted or been granted relief by the court. Pursuant to the Companies (Audit, Investigations and Community Enterprise) Act 2004 and the Company's Articles of Association, during the year the Company put in place Qualifying Third Party Indemnity Provisions (as defined under section 309B of the Companies Act 1985) for the benefit of the Company's Directors and the Company Secretary. These provisions remain in force.

Under the rules of the 3i Group Pension Plan ('the plan'), the Company has granted an indemnity to the directors of Gardens Pension Trustees Limited (a corporate trustee of the Plan and a wholly owned subsidiary of the Company) against liabilities incurred as directors of that corporate trustee.

The Board's committees The Board is assisted by various standing committees of the Board which report regularly to the Board. The membership of these committees is regularly reviewed by the Board. When considering committee membership and chairmanship, the Board aims to ensure that undue reliance is not placed on particular Directors.

These committees all have clearly defined terms of reference which are available at www.3igroup.com. The terms of reference of the Audit and Compliance Committee, the Remuneration Committee and the Nominations Committee provide that no one other than the particular Committee chairman and members may attend a meeting unless invited to attend by the Committee.

Audit and Compliance Committee The Audit and Compliance Committee comprises [. . .], all of whom served throughout the period. All the members of the Committee are independent non-executive Directors.

During the year, the Committee:

–reviewed the effectiveness of the internal control environment of the Group and the Group's compliance with its regulatory requirements and received reports on bank covenants, third party liabilities and off-balance sheet liabilities;

–reviewed and recommended to the Board the accounting disclosures comprised in the interim and annual financial statements of the Company and reviewed the scope of the annual audit plan and the audit findings;

–reviewed matters relating to the Group's key performance indicators, the introduction of International Financial Reporting Standards and proposals for operating and financial reviews and enhanced business reviews;

–received regular reports from the internal audit function, monitored its activities and effectiveness, and agreed the annual internal audit plan;

–received regular reports from the regulatory compliance function and Risk Committee, and monitored their activities and effectiveness;

–oversaw the Company's relations with its external auditors including assessing auditor performance and independence, recommending the auditors' reappointment and approving the auditors' fees;

–*met with the external auditors and the heads of the internal audit and compliance functions* individually, all in the absence of management;

–reviewed the Company's 'whistle blowing' policy to ensure that arrangements were in place for staff to raise, in confidence, matters of concern; and

–considered whether matters existed which could give rise to conflicts of interests between Directors and the Company.

Remuneration Committee The Remuneration Committee comprises [. . .] all of whom served throughout the period. All the members of the Committee are independent non-executive Directors. . . .

Details of the work of the Remuneration Committee are set out in the Directors' remuneration report.

Nominations Committee The Nominations Committee comprises [. . .], all of whom served throughout the period. The terms of reference of the Nominations Committee provide that the Chairman of the Board shall not chair the Committee when dealing with the appointment of the Chairman's successor.

During the year, the Nominations Committee, together with the Board, reviewed the composition of the Board to ensure that the balance of its membership, as between executive and non-executive Directors, and that its profile, in terms of size and length of service and experience of individual Directors, remained appropriate.

A formal, rigorous and transparent process for the appointment of Directors has been established with the objective of identifying the skills and experience profile required of new Directors and identifying suitable candidates. The procedure includes the appraisal and selection of potential candidates, including (in the case of non-executive Directors) whether they have sufficient time to fulfil their roles. Specialist recruitment consultants assist the Committee to identify suitable candidates for appointment. The Committee's recommendations for appointment are put to the full Board for approval.

The Company's major shareholders are offered the opportunity to meet newly-appointed non-executive Directors.

Valuations Committee The Valuations Committee comprises [. . .]

During the year, the Valuations Committee considered and made recommendations to the Board on valuations of the Group's investments to be included in the interim and annual financial statements of the Group and reviewed the valuations policy and methodology.

The Company Secretary All Directors have access to the advice and services of the Company Secretary. The Company Secretary is responsible for advising the Board, through the Chairman, on governance matters. The Company's Articles of Association and the schedule of matters reserved to the Board or its duly authorised Committees for decision provide that the appointment and removal of the Company Secretary is a matter for the full Board.

Relations with shareholders The Board recognises the importance of maintaining a purposeful relationship with all its shareholders. The Chief Executive and the Finance Director, together with the Group Communications Director, meet with the Company's principal institutional shareholders to discuss relevant issues as they arise. The Chairman maintains a dialogue with shareholders on strategy, corporate governance and Directors' remuneration as required.

The Board receives reports from the Company's brokers on shareholder issues and non-executive Directors are invited to attend the Company's presentation to analysts and are offered the opportunity to meet shareholders.

The Company also uses its AGM as an opportunity to communicate with its shareholders.

Portfolio management and voting policy In relation to unquoted investments, the Group's approach is to seek to add value to the businesses in which the Group invests through the Group's extensive experience, resources and contacts. In relation to quoted investments, the Group's policy is to exercise voting rights on matters affecting the interests of the Group.

Internal control The Board is responsible for the Group's system of internal control and reviews its effectiveness at least annually. Such a system is designed to manage rather than eliminate the risk of failure to achieve business objectives and can provide only reasonable and not absolute assurance against material misstatement or loss. [There follows a detailed account of the activities and policies of the Board and its Risk Committee and the Group's reporting and control systems.]

Employment The Group's policy is one of equal opportunity in the selection, training, career development and promotion of employees, regardless of gender, orientation, ethnic origin, religion and whether disabled or otherwise.

The Group treats applicants and employees with disabilities equally and fairly and provides facilities, equipment and training to assist disabled employees to do their jobs. . . .

The Group's principal means of keeping in touch with the views of its employees are through employee appraisals, informal consultations, team briefings, and staff conferences and surveys. Managers throughout the Group have a continuing responsibility to keep their staff fully informed of developments and to communicate financial results and other matters of interest. This is achieved by structured communication including regular meetings of employees.

The Group has clear grievance and disciplinary procedures in place, which include comprehensive procedures on discrimination and the Group's equal opportunities policy. . . .

There are clearly defined staff policies for pay and working conditions. The Group's employment policies are designed to provide a competitive reward package which will attract and retain high quality staff, whilst ensuring that the cost element of these rewards remains at an appropriate level. . . .

Charitable and political donations Charitable donations made by the Group in the year to 31 March 2006 amounted to £390,570. Excluding the Company's matching of Give As You Earn contributions by staff, charitable donations amounted to £290,028, of which approximately

58% were to causes which aim to relieve poverty or benefit the community, or both, approximately 23% were to charities which advance education, and approximately 6% were to medical charities. Further details of charitable donations are set out in the Corporate responsibility section [below].

In line with Group policy, no donations were made to political parties during the year. . . .

Policy for paying creditors The Group's policy is to pay creditors in accordance with the CBI Prompt Payers Code of Good Practice . . . The Company had no trade creditors during the year. 3i plc had trade creditors outstanding at the year end representing on average 15 days purchases.

Statement of Directors' responsibilities The Directors are required by UK company law to prepare financial statements which give a true and fair view of the state of affairs of the Company and the Group as at the end of the period and of the profit for the period. The Directors have responsibility for ensuring that proper accounting records are kept which disclose with reasonable accuracy the financial position of the Group and enable them to ensure that the financial statements comply with the Companies Act 1985. They have a general responsibility for taking such steps as are reasonably open to them to safeguard the assets of the Group and to prevent and detect fraud and other irregularities. Suitable accounting policies, which follow generally accepted accounting practice and are explained in the notes to the financial statements, have been applied consistently and applicable accounting standards have been followed. In addition, these financial statements comply with International Financial Reporting Standards as adopted by the European Union and reasonable and prudent judgments and estimates have been used in their preparation.

Going concern The Directors are satisfied that the Company and the Group have adequate resources to continue to operate for the foreseeable future. For this reason, they continue to adopt the 'going concern' basis for preparing the financial statements.

Auditors' independence and objectivity Subject to annual appointment by shareholders, auditor performance is monitored on an ongoing basis and formally reviewed every five years, the next review being scheduled for 2008. The Audit and Compliance Committee reviewed auditor performance during the year and concluded that Ernst & Young LLP's appointment as the Company's auditors should be continued. . . .

Details of the fees paid to the auditors are disclosed in note 6 to the financial statements [below].

Audit information Pursuant to section 234ZA (2) of the Companies Act 1985, each of the Directors confirms that: (a) so far as they are aware, there is no relevant audit information of which the Company's auditors are unaware; and (b) they have taken all steps they ought to have taken to make themselves aware of any relevant audit information and to establish that the Company's auditors are aware of such information.

Appointment of auditors In accordance with section 384 of the Companies Act 1985, a resolution proposing the reappointment of Ernst & Young LLP as the Company's auditors will be put to members at the forthcoming Annual General Meeting.

By order of the Board

[Signed]
Secretary

10 May 2006

Registered Office
16 Palace Street
London SW1E 5JD

INDEPENDENT AUDITORS' REPORT TO THE MEMBERS OF 3I GROUP PLC

We have audited the Group and Parent Company financial statements (the 'financial statements') of 3i Group plc for the year ended 31 March 2006 which comprise the Consolidated income statement, the Group and Parent Company Statement of recognised income and expense, the Group and Parent Company Reconciliation of movements in equity, the Group and Parent Company Balance sheets, the Group and Parent Company Cash flow statements, Significant accounting policies and the related notes . . . These financial statements have been prepared under the accounting policies set out therein. We have also audited the information in the Directors' remuneration report that is described as having been audited.

This report is made solely to the Company's members, as a body, in accordance with section 235 of the Companies Act 1985. Our audit work has been undertaken so that we might state to the Company's members those matters we are required to state to them in an auditors' report and for no other purpose. To the fullest extent permitted by law, we do not accept or assume responsibility to anyone other than the Company and the Company's members as a body, for our audit work, for this report, or for the opinions we have formed.

Respective responsibilities of Directors and auditors The Directors are responsible for preparing the Annual Report, the Directors' remuneration report and the financial statements in accordance with applicable United Kingdom law and International Financial Reporting Standards (IFRSs) as adopted by the European Union as set out in the Statement of Directors' responsibilities.

Our responsibility is to audit the financial statements and the part of the Directors' remuneration report to be audited in accordance with relevant legal and regulatory requirements and International Standards on Auditing (UK and Ireland).

We report to you our opinion as to whether the financial statements give a true and fair view, the financial statements and the part of the Directors' remuneration report to be audited have been properly prepared in accordance with the Companies Act 1985 and Article 4 of the IAS Regulation and the information given in the Directors' report is consistent with the financial statements.

We also report to you if, in our opinion, the Company has not kept proper accounting records, if we have not received all the information and explanations we require for our audit, or if information specified by law regarding Directors' remuneration and other transactions are not disclosed.

We review whether the Corporate Governance statement reflects the Company's compliance with the nine provisions of the 2003 FRC Combined Code specified for our review by the Listing Rules of the Financial Services Authority, and we report if it does not. We are not required to consider whether the Board's statements on internal control cover all risks and controls, or form an opinion on the effectiveness of the Group's corporate governance procedures or its risk and control procedures.

We read other information contained in the Annual Report and consider whether it is consistent with the audited financial statements . . . We consider the implications for our report if we become aware of any apparent misstatements or material inconsistencies with the financial statements. Our responsibilities do not extend to any other information.

Basis of audit opinion We conducted our audit in accordance with International Standards on Auditing (UK and Ireland) issued by the Auditing Practices Board. An audit includes examination, on a test basis, of evidence relevant to the amounts and disclosures in the financial statements and the part of the Directors' remuneration report to be audited. It also includes an assessment of the significant estimates and judgments made by the Directors in the preparation of the financial statements, and of whether the accounting policies are appropriate to the Group's and Company's circumstances, consistently applied and adequately disclosed.

We planned and performed our audit so as to obtain all the information and explanations which we considered necessary in order to provide us with sufficient evidence to give reasonable assurance that the financial statements and the part of the Directors' remuneration report to be audited are free from material misstatement, whether caused by fraud or other irregularity or error. In forming our opinion we also evaluated the overall adequacy of the presentation of information in the financial statements and the part of the Directors' remuneration report to be audited.

Opinion

In our opinion:

–the Group financial statements give a true and fair view, in accordance with IFRSs as adopted by the European Union, of the state of the Group's affairs as at 31 March 2006 and of its profit for the year then ended;

–the Parent Company financial statements give a true and fair view, in accordance with IFRSs as adopted by the European Union as applied in accordance with the provisions of the Companies Act 1985, of the state of the Parent Company's affairs as at 31 March 2006;

–the financial statements and the part of the Directors' remuneration report to be audited have been properly prepared in accordance with the Companies Act 1985 and Article 4 of the IAS Regulation; and

–the information given in the Directors' report is consistent with the financial statements.

Ernst & Young LLP
Registered auditor
London
10 May 2006

Consolidated income statement

for the year to 31 March 2006[7]

	2006 £m
Realised profits over value on the disposal of investments	576
Unrealised profits on the revaluation of investments	245
	821
Portfolio income	
Dividends	75
Income from loans and receivables	133
Fees receivable	24
Gross portfolio return	1,053
Carried interest	
Carried interest receivable from managed funds	79
Carried interest payable to executives	(64)
Fund management fees	24
Operating expenses	(211)
Net portfolio return	881
Treasury interest receivable	55
Interest payable	(72)
Movements in the fair value of derivatives	(78)
Exchange movements	47
Other income	22
Profit before tax	855
Income taxes	(3)
Profit after tax and profit for the year	852
Earnings per share	
Basic (pence)	152.0
Diluted (pence)	147.3

[7] [Comparative numbers for the year to 31 March 2005 are also given. A Statement of Significant Accounting Policies, and Notes to the Financial Statements, together extending over 24 pages, are not reproduced.]

Statement of recognised income and expense

for the year to 31 March 2006

	Group 2006 £m	Company 2006 £m
Profit for the year	852	643
Revaluation of property	–	–
Exchange differences on translation of foreign operations	(5)	–
Actuarial losses	(16)	–
Total recognised income and expense for the year	831	643
Analysed in reserves as:		
Revenue	117	87
Capital	719	556
Translation reserve	(5)	–
	831	643

Reconciliation of movements in equity

for the year to 31 March 2006

	Group 2006 £m	Company 2006 £m
Opening total equity	3,699	3,626
Total recognised income and expense for the year	831	643
Share-based payments	8	–
Ordinary dividends	(86)	(86)
Special dividends	(245)	(245)
Issues of shares	13	13
Share buy-backs	(222)	(222)
Own shares	8	–
Closing total equity	4,006	3,729

Balance sheet

as at 31 March 2006

Assets	Group 2006 £m	Company 2006 £m
Non-current assets		
Investments		
Quoted equity investments	259	173
Unquoted equity investments	2,514	1,349
Loans and receivables	1,366	735
Investments portfolio	4,139	2,257
Carried interest receivable	77	77
Interests in joint ventures	–	–
Interests in Group entities	–	1,483
Property, plant and equipment	31	9
Investment property	–	–
Total non-current assets	4,247	3,826
Current assets		
Other current assets	149	193
Derivative financial instruments	19	19
Deposits	1,108	1,052
Cash and cash equivalents	847	776
Total current assets	2,123	2,040
Total assets	6,370	5,866
Liabilities		
Non-current liabilities		
Carried interest payable	(83)	(83)
Loans and borrowings	(1,243)	(968)
Convertible Bonds	(365)	(365)
Subordinated liabilities	(24)	–
Retirement benefit obligation	(17)	–
Deferred income tax	(1)	–
Provisions	(5)	–
Total non-current liabilities	(1,738)	(1,416)

Current liabilities

Trade and other payables	(160)	(271)
Carried interest payable	(60)	(60)
Loans and borrowings	(231)	(230)
Derivative financial instruments	(168)	(160)
Current income tax	(2)	–
Provisions	(5)	–
Total current liabilities	(626)	(721)
Total liabilities	(2,364)	(2,137)
Net assets	4,006	3,729

Equity

Issued capital	292	292
Share premium	376	376
Capital redemption reserve	17	17
Share–based payment reserve	17	–
Translation reserve	–	–
Capital reserve	3,110	2,767
Revenue reserve	263	277
Own shares	(69)	–
Total equity	4,006	3,729

Cash flow statement
for the year to 31 March 2006

	Group 2006 £m	Company 2006 £m
Cash flow from operating activities		
Purchase of investments	(1,068)	(873)
Proceeds from investments	2,213	1,949
Interest received	67	42
Dividends received	76	70
Fees received from investment and fund management activities	46	13
Carried interest received	9	9
Carried interest paid	(30)	–
Operating expenses	(216)	(182)
Income tax paid	(8)	(5)
Net cash inflow from operations	1,089	1,023
Cash flow from financing activities		
Proceeds from issues of share capital	13	13
Purchase of own shares	(222)	(222)
Dividend paid	(331)	(331)
Interest received	50	46
Interest paid	(60)	(38)
Payment of finance lease liabilities	–	–
Proceeds from long-term borrowings	69	92
Repayment of long-term borrowings	(54)	–
Net cash flow from short-term borrowings	188	156
Net cash flow from deposits	(223)	(261)
Net cash flow from financing activities	(570)	(545)
Cash flow from investing activities		
Purchases of property, plant and equipment	(15)	–
Sales of property, plant and equipment	24	17
Divestment from joint venture	2	2
Net cash flow from investing activities	11	19
Change in cash and cash equivalents	530	497
Opening cash and cash equivalents	314	279
Effect of exchange rate fluctuations	3	–
Closing cash and cash equivalents	847	776

4. Notice of Annual General Meeting

Notice of Annual General Meeting

Notice is hereby given that the thirty-third Annual General Meeting of 3i Group plc ('the Company') will be held at The Institution of Engineering and Technology (formerly The Institution of Electrical Engineers), Savoy Place, London WC2R OBL on Wednesday 12 July 2006 at 10.30 am to transact the business set out below.

In accordance with the Listing Rules of the UK Listing Authority, Resolution 2 (Remuneration report), Resolutions 9 and 10 (Renewal of 'Donations' and 'EU political expenditure' authority), Resolution 11 (Directors' participation in co-investment arrangements), Resolution 12 (Increase in limit on shares held in the Employee Trust) and Resolution 15 (Purchase of own shares) are special business.

The remaining resolutions are ordinary business.

To consider and, if thought fit, pass the following as ordinary resolutions:

1   To receive and consider the Company's Accounts for the year to 31 March 2006, the Directors' report and the Auditors' report on those Accounts and on the auditable part of the Directors' remuneration report.

2   To approve the Directors' remuneration report for the year to 31 March 2006.

3   To declare a final dividend of 9.7p per share, payable to those shareholders whose names appear on the Register of Members at close of business on 23 June 2006.

4–6   To reappoint [three named persons] as a Director of the Company.

7   To reappoint Ernst & Young LLP as Auditors of the Company to hold office until the conclusion of the next General Meeting at which Accounts are laid before the Members.

8   To authorise the Board to fix the Auditors' remuneration.

9   THAT, in accordance with section 347C of the Companies Act 1985 ('the 1985 Act'), the Company be and it is hereby authorised to make Donations to EU political organisations not exceeding £12,000 in total and incur EU political expenditure not exceeding £12,000 in total . . . .

10   THAT, in accordance with section 347C of the Companies Act 1985 ('the 1985 Act'), 3i plc, a wholly owned subsidiary of the Company, be and it is hereby authorised to make [similar] Donations.

11   THAT executive Directors be and they are hereby authorised to participate in the co-investment arrangements described in the notes relating to this Resolution 11 set out in the Notice of Annual General Meeting dated 10 May 2006.

12   THAT for the purposes of clause 7.2 of the Deed dated 25 May 1994 establishing The 3i Group Employee Trust, the trustees of that Trust be and they are hereby authorised to acquire or agree to acquire shares in the capital of the Company as though the limit set out in that clause referred to 5% rather than 2.5% of the number of shares in issue.

13   THAT, in substitution for all subsisting authorities to the extent unused, the Directors be and they are hereby generally and unconditionally authorised to exercise all powers of the Company to allot relevant securities (within the meaning of section 80 of the Companies Act 1985) up to an aggregate nominal amount of £97,497,000 PROVIDED THAT this authority shall expire at the conclusion of the Annual General Meeting of the Company to be held in 2007 or, if earlier, 11 October 2007, save that the Company may before such expiry make an offer or agreement which would or might require relevant securities to be allotted after such expiry and the Directors may allot relevant securities in pursuance of such an offer or agreement as if the authority conferred hereby had not expired.

To consider and, if thought fit, pass the following as special resolutions:

14 THAT, subject to the passing of Resolution 13 above and in substitution for all subsisting authorities to the extent unused, the Directors be and they are hereby empowered pursuant to section 95 of the Companies Act 1985 to allot equity securities (within the meaning of section 94 of the said Act) for cash pursuant to the authority conferred by Resolution 13 above, and/or to allot equity securities where such allotment constitutes an allotment of equity securities by virtue of section 94(3A) of the said Act, as if sub-section (1) of section 89 of the said Act did not apply to any such allotment, PROVIDED THAT this power shall be limited to the allotment of equity securities:

(a) in connection with an offer of such securities by way of rights, or other pre-emptive offer, to holders of ordinary shares in proportion to their respective holdings of such shares, excluding any holder holding shares as treasury shares, but subject to such exclusions or other arrangements as the Directors may deem necessary or expedient in relation to fractional entitlements or legal or practical problems under the laws of, or the requirements of any regulatory body or any stock exchange in, any territory or otherwise howsoever; and

(b) (otherwise than pursuant to sub-paragraph (a) above) up to an aggregate nominal value of £14,624,000. . . .

15 THAT the Company be generally and unconditionally authorised, in accordance with Article 7 of the Company's Articles of Association, to make market purchases (as defined in section 163(3) of the Companies Act 1985) of its ordinary shares PROVIDED THAT:

(a) the Company does not purchase under this authority more than 55,057,000 ordinary shares;

(b) the Company does not pay for each such ordinary share less than the nominal amount of such ordinary share at the time of purchase; and

(c) the Company does not pay for each such ordinary share more than 105% of the average of the closing mid-market prices of the ordinary shares for the five business days immediately preceding the date on which the Company agrees to buy the share concerned, based on the share prices published in the Daily Official List of the London Stock Exchange. . . .

By order of the Board

[Signed]
Secretary

10 May 2006

[The Notice of AGM is accompanied by Notes, which set out the members' rights to vote in person and by proxy, and explain the purpose of the various resolutions.]

5. Share certificate (preference shares)

Security Code   Number of Shares . . .
  0–28654–3
    No. 0000

5½% Cumulative Preference

The Preference Shares confer the dividend and capital rights specified
on the reverse of this certificate

THE DUNLOP COMPANY LIMITED
Incorporated under the Companies Acts

This is to Certify that . . . .

is/are registered proprietor(s) of . . . .

FIVE AND A HALF PER CENT CUMULATIVE PREFERENCE SHARES OF £1 EACH. *fully paid, in* THE DUNLOP COMPANY LIMITED, *subject to the Memorandum and Articles of Association of the Company.*

GIVEN under the Common Seal of the Company,
this . . . day of . . . 19 . . .

No transfer of any of the Shares represented by this Certificate will be registered without this Certificate being surrendered to the Company's Registrars: Midland Bank Limited, Registrar's Department, Beaufort House, Gravel Lane, London, El.

[The terms set out on the reverse of the certificate incorporate the 'Spens formula' (see above, p 432):]

The 5½ per cent Cumulative Preference Shares confer the right to receive in priority to all other shares out of the profits of the Company which it shall be determined to distribute a cumulative preferential dividend at the rate of 5½ per cent per annum on the capital paid up thereon and the prior right on a return of assets on liquidation or otherwise to payment of the prescribed sum in respect of every such Preference Share together with payment of all arrears and accruals of the preferential dividend down to the date of repayment of capital (whether earned or declared or not) but do not confer any further right to participate in profits or assets.

The prescribed sum shall be the greater of (a)[£1.10] or (b) the nominal amount paid up on such share together with a sum equal to the amount by which the average of the respective means of the daily nominal quotation of the said Preference Shares on The Stock Exchange, London, during the six months preceding the date of the notice of the meeting at which the Resolution for such liquidation or return of capital is passed exceeds the nominal amount paid up on such share (such average to be calculated and certified by the Auditors of the Company).

B. Tables[8]

1. **Summary of changes in the number of companies on the register, 2005–2006**

	(000)
On register at start of period	2,044.4
New companies incorporated	354.4
Dissolved	202.8
Restored to the register	1.3
On register at end of period	2,198.9
Change on previous year	7.6%
Of which: in liquidation	63.9
in course of removal	118.0
Effective numbers on register	
at end of period	2,017.0
Change on previous year	7.6%

2. **Public and private companies incorporated and on the GB register, 2005–2006[9]**

	(000)
Public companies	
New incorporations	1.0
Conversions from private	3.8
Dissolved	0.6
In liquidation/course of removal	1.4
Effective number on register at end of period	11.5
Public companies as percentage of effective register	0.5%
Private companies	
New incorporations	370.8
Conversions from public	5.5
Dissolved	211.5
In liquidation/course of removal	191.6
Effective number on register at end of period	2,118.7
Of which: Unlimited	5.3
GB total of effective numbers of public and private companies	2,130.2

8 [Numbers relate to England and Wales, except as stated.]
9 [Including Scotland.]

3. New incorporations of companies with share capital: analysed by amount of nominal capital, 2005–2006

	(000)
Up to £100	127.7
Over £100 & under £1,000	4.9
£1,000 & under £5,000	173.8
£5,000 & under £10,000	1.6
£10,000 & under £20,000	14.1
£20,000 & under £50,000	1.4
£50,000 & under £100,000	2.5
£100,000 & under £200,000	10.5
£200,000 & under £500,000	1.0
£500,000 & under £1m	1.2
£1m & over	6.2
Companies with share capital	346.0
Companies without share capital	8.4

4. Liquidations and receiverships notified,[10]

	(000)
Compulsory liquidations	1,672
Creditors' voluntary liquidations	2,193
Administration orders converted to creditors' voluntary liquidations	212
Total insolvencies	4,077
Members' voluntary liquidations	829
Total liquidations	4,906
Receiverships notified	180
Administrator appointments[11]	755
Company voluntary arrangements	124

---

10 [In addition 113,400 companies were struck off the register and dissolved under CA 1985 s 652 during the period.]
11 [Including these filed under the Enterprise Act 2000.]

5. Searches of company records at Companies House, 2005–2006[12]

	(000)
Public Searches:	
London	0.2
Cardiff	2.3
Postal Searches:	
Cardiff[13]	
Image Searches:	965
Searches per live company	0.5
Total	967

6. Disqualification orders notified to the Secretary of State, 2005–2006

Company Directors Disqualification Act 1986	
Disqualification of directors by undertaking	900
ss 2–5 Disqualification on conviction of indictable offence, for persistent breaches of companies legislation, for fraud in winding-up and on summary conviction	135
s 6 Disqualification of unfit directors of insolvent companies	136
s 8 Disqualification following investigation of companies	26
s 10 Disqualification for wrongful trading	0
Total	1197

---

[12] Note: Search volumes are for microfiche based products and exclude computer and rollfilm products.
[13] [Fewer than 50.]

Index